PRACTICAL
BoatOwn

SMALL
CRAFT
ALMANAC
2004

EDITORS
Neville Featherstone & Lucinda Roch

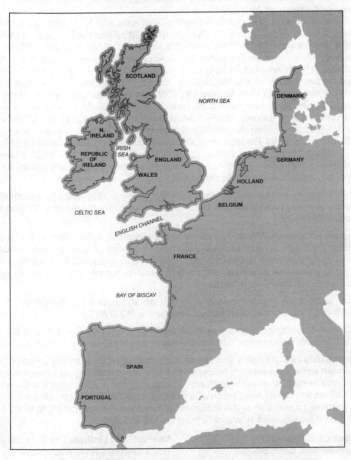

THE UNITED KINGDOM & IRELAND
AND DENMARK TO GIBRALTAR

PRACTICAL
BOATOWNER®
SMALL
CRAFT
ALMANAC
2004

Editors: Neville Featherstone & Lucinda Roch

The Editors would like to thank the many official bodies who have kindly provided essential information in the preparation of this Almanac. They include the UK Hydrographic Office, Trinity House, Northern Lighthouse Board, Irish Lights, HM Nautical Almanac Office, HM Stationery Office, HM Customs, Meteorological Office and the Maritime and Coastguard Agency.

Information from the Admiralty List of Lights, Admiralty Tide Tables and the Admiralty List of Radio Signals is reproduced with the permission of the UK Hydrographic Office and the Controller of HMSO. Extracts from the following are published by permission of the Controller of HM Stationery Office: International Code of Signals, 1969; Meteorological Office Weather Services for Shipping. Phases of the Moon and Sun/ Moon rising and setting times are derived from the current editions of the Channel and Eastern Almanacs, and are included by permission of HM Nautical Almanac Office. UK and Foreign tidal predictions are supplied by the UK Hydrographic Office, Taunton TA1 2DN. Acknowledgment is also made to the following authorities for permission to use tidal predictions stated: Royal Danish Administration of Navigation and Hydrography, Farvandsvæsnet: Esbjerg. SHOM, France: Dunkerque, Dieppe, Le Havre, Cherbourg, St Malo, Brest, Pointe de Grave, Authorisation (No. 146/02). Rijkswaterstaat, The Netherlands: Vlissingen, and Hoek van Holland. BSH, Hamburg and Rostock: Helgoland, Wilhelmshaven and Cuxhaven (BSH 8095·02/99- Z1102). Marina Institute Hidrográfico, Portugal: Lisboa, Authorisation (No. 4/02). **Warning:** The UK Hydrographic Office has not verified the reproduced data and does not accept any liability for the accuracy of reproduction or any modifications made thereafter.

Corrections Any necessary corrections will be published on a monthly basis by *Practical Boat Owner* Magazine and on the web site www.ybw.com. Data in this almanac is corrected up to Edition 41/2003 of the *Admiralty Notices to Mariners*.

Important note This Almanac is intended as an aid to navigation only. The information contained within should not solely be relied on for navigational use, rather it should be used in conjunction with official hydrographic data. Whilst every care has been taken in compiling the information contained in this Almanac, the publishers, editors and their agents accept no responsibility for any errors or omissions, or for any accidents or mishaps which may arise from its use.

Correspondence Letters on nautical matters should be addressed to: The Editor, PBO Almanac, The Book Barn, White Chimney Row, Westbourne, Hampshire, PO10 8RS.

Practical Boat Owner is published monthly by IPC Magazines Ltd, Kings Reach Tower, Stamford Street, London SE1 9LS. For subscription enquiries and overseas orders call 0845 676 7778 (fax: 01444 445599).

Production control: Chris Stevens
Cartography & production: Scott Stacey, Chris Stevens
Cover design: Nautical Data
Cover photography: Matthew Stevens

Nautical Data Limited, The Book Barn
White Chimney Row, Westbourne
Hampshire, PO10 8RS, UK
Tel: +44 (0)1243 389352 Fax: +44 (0)1243 379136
www.nauticaldata.com

FOREWORD

Good things come in small packages, and the *PBO Small Craft Almanac* crams a wealth of vital information into a handy-sized book that's easy to carry, stow and use. Combined with the appropriate charts and pilot books, it gives you all the data you need for cruising in Britain, the Channel Islands, up to Denmark and down to Gibraltar. And at a budget price well below that of other almanacs.

There's much more to the book than tide tables, although these can often be among the most used pages by yachtsmen. How to obtain weather forecasts, VHF channels for marinas, conversion tables, radar beacons and first aid are just some of the other items contained in this concise *PBO* almanac.

The latest edition has recently undergone a significant overhaul so that the material is more logically sequenced with a clearer presentation style. New for 2004 is tidal gate data for many of Britain's major headlands including Land's End, the Lizard, Start Point, Portland Bill, the Needles Channel and Dungeness. As we exposed in an article in *PBO* magazine, insurance claims for accidental groundings have increased by over 50 per cent, so all the more reason to refer to our large, easy to use tidal curves. And now that the SOLAS regulations require us to have passage planning information at our fingertips, keeping a copy of the *PBO Small Craft Almanac* on board is becoming ever more important.

Finally, our aim each year is to make the almanac even better, so please let us know if there are any further changes or additions which you would like to see included in the 2005 edition.

Wishing you happy boating in 2004.

Sarah Norbury

Sarah Norbury
Editor
Practical Boat Owner
Britain's biggest selling boating magazine

CONTENTS

CHAPTER 1 - NAVIGATION

Contents 5
Conversion tables 6
Area planners with waypoints, lights etc .... 7 to 47
Marinas .... 48 to 53
Sunrise/set, moonrise/set .... 54 to 57
Radar beacons .... 58 to 60
Speed, time & distance table 61
Distance from dipping light table 62

CHAPTER 2 - WEATHER

Contents 63
UK shipping forecast areas 64
Shipping forecast record 65
Beaufort scale & Met terminology 66
Weather sources in the UK .... 67 to 77
Weather sources abroad .... 78 to 89
Weather terms language glossary .... 89 to 90

CHAPTER 3 - COMMUNICATIONS

Contents 91
Radio operation .... 92 to 93
Radio data .... 94 to 95
Port radio .... 96 to 104
VTS charts .... 105 to 108
Coast radio .... 109 to 111
Signals by sounds & shapes 112

CHAPTER 4 - SAFETY

Contents 113
Think about safety 114
Mayday .... 115 to 116
First aid .... 117 to 120
Coastguard services .... 121 to 128
Emergency VHF Direction Finding Service .... 129 to 131
Military exercise areas .... 132 to 135
GMDSS .... 136 to 137
Common terms in five languages .... 138 to 140

CHAPTER 5 - TIDES

Contents 141
Dover tidal ranges 142
Brest tidal coefficients 143
Tidal calculations .... 144 to 149
Secondary ports & tidal differences .... 150 to 168
Tidal gates .... 169 to 177
Tidal stream charts .... 178 to 215
Tidal curves, Christchurch to Selsey .... 240 to 241
Tidal curves & prediction tables .... 216 to 413

Abbreviations 414
Index .... 415 to 416

CHAPTER 1 - NAVIGATION

CONTENTS

Conversion tables 6

Area planners 7
  Key 7
  Area planner 1 - SW England 8
  Area planner 2 - S Central England 10
  Area planner 3 - SE England 12
  Area planner 4 - E England 14
  Area planner 5 - E Scotland 16
  Area planner 6 - NW Scotland 18
  Area planner 7 - SW Scotland 20
  Area planner 8 - NW England, Wales & E Ireland 22
  Area planner 9 - SW England, S Wales & S Ireland 24
  Area planner 10 - Ireland 26
  Area planner 11 - Denmark & NW Germany 28
  Area planner 12 - Germany & N Holland 30
  Area planner 13 - Holland & Belgium 32
  Area planner 14 - N France 34
  Area planner 15- N Central France & Channel Is 36
  Area planner 16 - NW France & Biscay 38
  Area planner 17 - W France & NE Spain 40
  Area planner 18 - NW Spain 42
  Area planner 19 - Portugal 44
  Area planner 20 - S Portugal & SW Spain 46

Marina charts with telephone, VHF and access times 48
  England - South East 48
  Scotland & East England 49
  Ireland & West UK 50
  Germany, Netherlands & Belgium 51
  France 52
  Spain, Portugal & Gibraltar 53

Sun and Moon tables - rising, setting & twilight 54

Radar beacons 58

Speed, time and distance table 61

Distance from dipping light table 62

Conversion Tables

Sq inches to sq millimetres *multiply by* **645.20**	**Sq millimetres to sq inches** *multiply by* **0.0016**
Inches to millimetres *multiply by* **25.40**	**Millimetres to inches** *multiply by* **0.0394**
Sq feet to square metres *multiply by* **0.093**	**Sq metres to sq feet** *multiply by* **10.7640**
Inches to centimetres *multiply by* **2.54**	**Centimetres to inches** *multiply by* **0.3937**
Feet to metres *multiply by* **0.305**	**Metres to feet** *multiply by* **3.2810**
Nautical miles to kilometres *multiply by* **1.852**	**Kilometres to nautical miles** *multiply by* **0.5400**
Statute miles to kilometres *multiply by* **1.609**	**Kilometres to statute miles** *multiply by* **0.6214**
Statute miles to nautical miles *multiply by* **0.8684**	**Nautical miles to statute miles** *multiply by* **1.1515**
HP to metric HP *multiply by* **1.014**	**Metric HP to HP** *multiply by* **0.9862**
Pounds per sq inch to kg per sq centimetre *multiply by* **0.0703**	**Kg per sq centimetre to pounds per sq inch** *multiply by* **14.2200**
HP to kilowatts *multiply by* **0.746**	**Kilowatts to HP** *multiply by* **1.341**
Cu inches to cu centimetres *multiply by* **16.39**	**Cu centimetres to cu inches** *multiply by* **0.0610**
Imperial gallons to litres *multiply by* **4.540**	**Litres to imperial gallons** *multiply by* **0.2200**
Pints to litres *multiply by* **0.5680**	**Litres to pints** *multiply by* **1.7600**
Pounds to kilogrammes *multiply by* **0.4536**	**Kilogrammes to pounds** *multiply by* **2.2050**

AREA PLANNERS

England, Scotland, Wales, Ireland, Denmark, Germany,

Holland, Belgium, France, Spain & Portugal

Ports, waypoints, principal lights, courses and distance tables

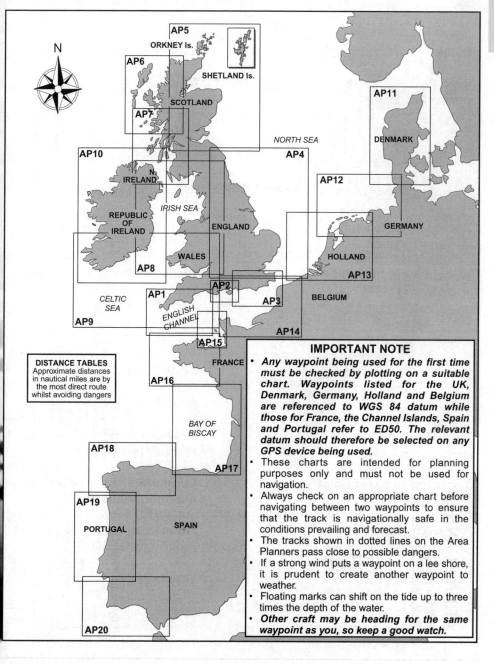

IMPORTANT NOTE

- *Any waypoint being used for the first time must be checked by plotting on a suitable chart. Waypoints listed for the UK, Denmark, Germany, Holland and Belgium are referenced to WGS 84 datum while those for France, the Channel Islands, Spain and Portugal refer to ED50. The relevant datum should therefore be selected on any GPS device being used.*
- These charts are intended for planning purposes only and must not be used for navigation.
- Always check on an appropriate chart before navigating between two waypoints to ensure that the track is navigationally safe in the conditions prevailing and forecast.
- The tracks shown in dotted lines on the Area Planners pass close to possible dangers.
- If a strong wind puts a waypoint on a lee shore, it is prudent to create another waypoint to weather.
- Floating marks can shift on the tide up to three times the depth of the water.
- *Other craft may be heading for the same waypoint as you, so keep a good watch.*

DISTANCE TABLES
Approximate distances in nautical miles are by the most direct route whilst avoiding dangers

7

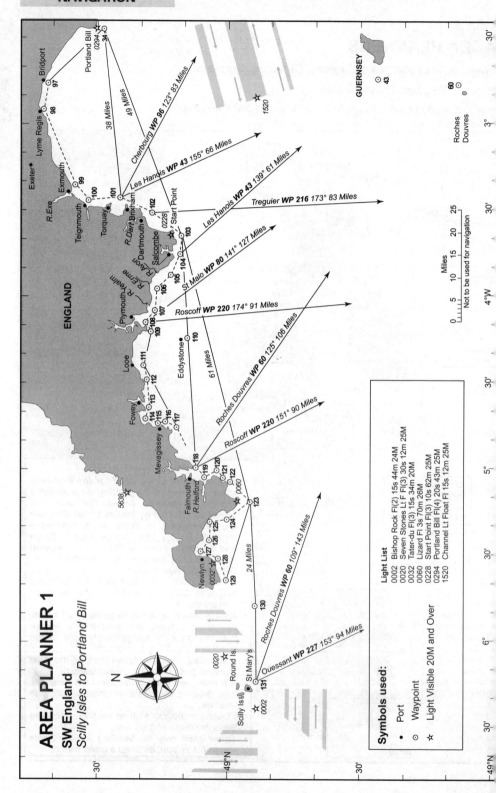

AREA PLANNER 1
SW England
Scilly Isles to Portland Bill

Symbols used:
- ● Port
- ⊙ Waypoint
- ☆ Light Visible 20M and Over

Light List
0002 Bishop Rock Fl(2) 15s 44m 24M
0020 Seven Stones Lt F Fl(3) 30s 12m 25M
0032 Tater-du Fl(3) 15s 34m 20M
0060 Lizard Fl 3s 70m 26M
0228 Start Point Fl(3) 10s 62m 25M
0294 Portland Bill Fl(4) 20s 43m 25M
1520 Channel Lt Float Fl 15s 12m 25M

Not to be used for navigation

Miles
0 5 10 15 20 25

AREA PLANNER 1

UK waypoints are referenced to WGS84 datum
French waypoints to ED50

WAYPOINTS

South West England - *Scilly Isles to Portland Bill*

92 Portland Bill - *5M S of* .... 50°25'·85N 02°27'·38W
93 Guernsey SW - *1·8M W of Les Hanois* .... 49°26'·10N 02°45'·08W
94 Roches Douvres light - *2·5M NE of* .... 49°08'·18N 02°46'·70W
95 St Malo - *1·3M NW of Grande Jardin light Bn* .... 48°41'·04N 02°06'·48W
96 Cherbourg - *0·5M N of W entrance* .... 49°40'·95N 01°39'·35W
97 Bridport - *1M S of entrance* .... 50°41'·53N 02°45'·79W
98 Lyme Regis - *1M SSE on Ldg Lts* .... 50°42'·83N 02°54'·89W
99 River Exe - *0·3M S of E Exe ECM* .... 50°35'·70N 03°22'·37W
100 Teignmouth - *1M E of Bar* ... 50°32'·33N 03°27'·87W
101 Torbay - *1·7M NE of Berry Head* ...... 50°25'·13N 03°27'·01W
102 Dartmouth - *2M 150° from entrance* ...... 50°18'·28N 03°31'·67W
103 Start Point - *2M S of* .... 50°11'·30N 03°38'·54W
104 Salcombe - *1·5M S of bar* ... 50°11'·65N 03°46'·67W
105 Bolt Tail - *1·3M SW of R Avon* .... 50°15'·55N 03°54'·25W
106 River Erme - *1·5M SSW of Battisborough Island* ...... 50°16'·80N 03°58'·50W
107 R Yealm - *1·2M SW of Yealm Head* .... 50°17'·48N 04°05'·77W
108 Plymouth - *0·9M S of W end of breakwater* .... 50°19'·17N 04°09'·57W
109 Rame Head - *0·2M S of* ..... 50°18'·17N 04°13'·39W
110 Eddystone - *1M S of* .... 50°09'·84N 04°15'·92W
111 Looe - *1·5M SE of entrance* .... 50°20'·26N 04°24'·80W

112 Polperro - *0·7M S of* .... 50°19'·04N 04°30'·87W
113 Fowey - *1·5M SSW of entrance* .... 50°18'·23N 04°39'·57W
114 Charlestown - *1M SE of* ...... 50°19'·03N 04°44'·17W
115 Mevagissey - *0·8M E of* ..... 50°16'·17N 04°45'·65W
116 Gwineas ECM - *0·2M E of* .. 50°14'·43N 04°45'·07W
117 Dodman Pt - *1·3M SSE of* ... 50°11'·90N 04°47'·00W
118 Falmouth - *0·8M S of St Anthony Head* .... 50°07'·67N 05°00'·97W
119 Helford River - *1M E of entrance* .... 50°05'·74N 05°04'·06W
120 Manacles - *0·2M E of* .... 50°02'·84N 05°01'·56W
121 Coverack - *1M E of* .... 50°01'·34N 05°04'·36W
122 Black Head - *0·7M SE of* ..... 49°59'·70N 05°05'·36W
123 Lizard - *3M S of* .... 49°54'·59N 05°12'·17W
124 Porth Mellin - *2M W of* .... 50°00'·90N 05°18'·78W
125 Porthleven - *0·4M SW of* ..... 50°04'·54N 05°19'·76W
126 Mountamopus SCM - *0·2M S of* .... 50°04'·44N 05°26'·26W
127 Penzance - *1·5M SE of and for Mousehole* .... 50°06'·04N 05°30'·06W
128 Tater Du light - *1·5M ESE of* .... 50°02'·54N 05°32'·67W
129 Runnel Stone SCM - *0·3M S of* .... 50°00'·88N 05°40'·37W
130 Wolf Rock - *2M S of* .... 49°54'·68N 05°48'·56W
131 St Mary's, Scilly - *2M E of St Mary's Sound* ... 49°54'·04N 06°15'·06W
216 Treguier - *4·1M N of Pointe de Chateau* .... 48°56'·43N 03°13'·49W
220 Roscoff - *6M NNE of entrance* .... 48°49'·14N 03°54'·36W
227 Ouessant Créac'h light - *3·5M NW of* .... 48°30'·00N 05°11'·30W

	1	2	3	4	5	6	7	8	9	10	11	12	13	14	15	16	17
1 Longships	1																
2 Scilly (Crow Sound)	22	2															
3 Penzance	15	35	3														
4 Lizard Point	23	42	16	4													
5 Falmouth	39	60	32	16	5												
6 Mevagissey	52	69	46	28	17	6											
7 Fowey	57	76	49	34	22	7	7										
8 Looe	63	80	57	39	29	16	11	8									
9 Plymouth (bkwtr)	70	92	64	49	39	25	22	11	9								
10 R. Yealm (ent)	72	89	66	49	39	28	23	16	4	10							
11 Salcombe	81	102	74	59	50	40	36	29	22	17	11						
12 Start Point	86	103	80	63	55	45	40	33	24	22	7	12					
13 Dartmouth	95	116	88	72	63	54	48	42	35	31	14	9	13				
14 Torbay	101	118	96	78	70	62	55	50	39	38	24	15	11	14			
15 Exmouth	113	131	107	90	82	73	67	61	49		33	27	24	12	15		
16 Lyme Regis	126	144	120	104	96	86	81	74	63	62	48	41	35	30	21	16	
17 Portland Bill	135	151	128	112	104	93	89	81	73	70	55	49	45	42	36	22	17

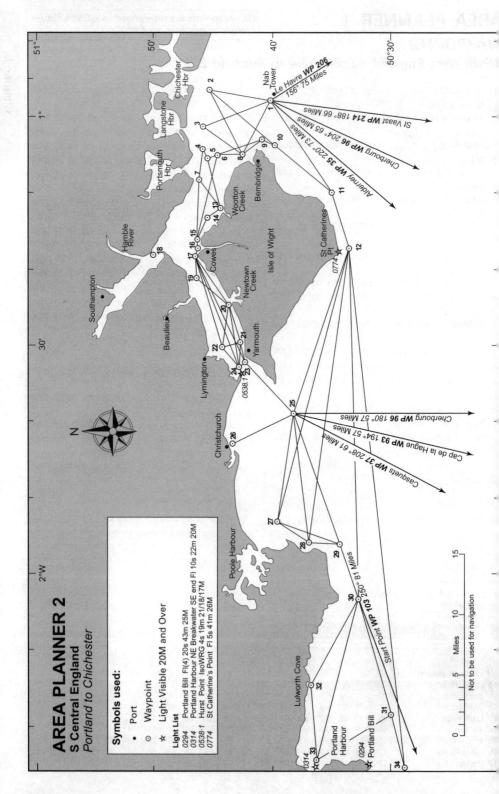

AREA PLANNER 2
S Central England
Portland to Chichester

Symbols used:

• Port
⊙ Waypoint
☆ Light Visible 20M and Over

Light List
0294 Portland Bill Fl(4) 20s 43m 25M
0314 Portland Harbour NE Breakwater SE end Fl 10s 22m 20M
0538·1 Hurst Point IsoWRG 4s 19m 21/18/17M
0774 St Catherine's Point Fl 5s 41m 26M

Miles

Not to be used for navigation

AREA PLANNER 2
WAYPOINTS
South Central England - *Portland to Chichester*

UK waypoints are referenced to WGS84 datum
French waypoints to ED50

Nab Tower - *0·5M NW of* ..... 50°40'·41N 00°57'·64W

West Pole Bn - *0·3M S of* ... 50°45'·41N 00°56'·46W

Langstone Fairway Beacon
- *0·5M S of* .... 50°45'·81N 01°01'·36W

Main Passage -
Dolphin gap off Southsea .... 50°46'·01N 01°04'·11W

Horse Sand PHM -
Portsmouth approach .... 50°45'·52N 01°05'·27W

Horse Sand/No Man's
Land Forts - *midway* .... 50°44'·73N 01°05'·09W

Gilkicker Point - *0·3M S of* .. 50°46'·03N 01°08'·49W

Bembridge Tide Gauge .... 50°42'·47N 01°05'·00W

Bembridge Ledge ECM .... 50°41'·16N 01°02'·78W

0 West Princessa WCM -
S of Bembridge .... 50°40'·15N 01°03'·64W

1 Dunnose Head - *1M off*....... 50°35'·03N 01°10'·09W

2 St Catherine's Point -
1M S of .... 50°33'·55N 01°17'·89W

3 Wootton Beacon .... 50°44'·54N 01°12'·14W

4 Peel Bank PHM - *E Solent* ... 50°45'·49N 01°13'·34W

5 Old Castle Point -
0·3M N of .... 50°46'·35N 01°16'·59W

6 Cowes ent .... 50°46'·23N 01°17'·95W

7 Egypt Point - *0·4M N of* ...... 50°46'·42N 01°18'·79W

8 Hamble Point SCM .... 50°50'·15N 01°18'·67W

9 Beaulieu Spit Bn - *0·3M off* .. 50°46'·85N 01°21'·69W

0 Newtown -
0·5M NW of ent .... 50°43'·90N 01°25'·29W

1 Yarmouth ent - *0·4M N of* ... 50°42'·83N 01°29'·96W

2 Lymington, Jack in the
basket - *seaward mark* .... 50°44'·27N 01°30'·57W

23 Hurst Narrows - *midway* ..... 50°42'·23N 01°32'·49W

24 Keyhaven - *0·2M E of ent* ... 50°42'·83N 01°32'·89W

25 Fairway Buoy -
Needles channel .... 50°38'·23N 01°38'·99W

26 Christchurch -
0·3M E of ent .... 50°43'·58N 01°43'·53W

27 Poole No 1 Bar Buoy -
1M E of .... 50°39'·32N 01°53'·58W

28 Swanage -
0·7M NE of pier .... 50°37'·03N 01°56'·08W

29 Anvil Point - *1·5M SE of* ...... 50°34'·33N 01°56'·08W

30 St Albans Head -
1·5M S of .... 50°33'·08N 02°03'·34W

31 East Shambles -
1M SE of .... 50°30'·03N 02°18'·98W

32 Lulworth Cove -
0·1M S of ent .... 50°36'·90N 02°14'·83W

33 Weymouth - *1M E of ent* .... 50°36'·63N 02°25'·00W

34 Portland Bill - *5M S of* .... 50°25'·76N 02°27'·38W

35 Alderney, Bray Hbr -
1M NE of .... 49°44'·60N 02°10'·63W

37 Casquets - *1M W of* .... 49°43'·38N 02°24'·06W

93 Cap de La Hague -
2M W of .... 49°43'·37N 02°00'·00W

96 Cherbourg -
0·5M N of W ent .... 49°40'·95N 01°39'·35W

103 Start Point - *2M S of* .... 50°11'·33N 03°38'·54W

206 Le Havre -
0·5M NE of Le Havre LHA .. 49°31'·79N 00°09'·23W

214 St-Vaast-la-Hougue -
3M ENE of ent .... 49°36'·40N 01°11'·00W

		1	2	3	4	5	6	7	8	9	10	11	12	13	14	15	16	17	18
1	Portland Bill	1																	
2	Weymouth	8	2																
3	Swanage	22	22	3															
4	Poole Hbr ent	28	26	6	4														
5	Needles Lt Ho	35	34	14	14	5													
6	Lymington	42	40	20	24	6	6												
7	Yarmouth (IOW)	40	39	18	22	4	2	7											
8	Beaulieu R. ent	46	45	25	29	11	7	7	8										
9	Cowes	49	46	28	27	14	10	9	2	9									
10	Southampton	55	54	34	34	20	16	16	9	9	10								
11	R. Hamble (ent)	53	51	32	34	18	12	13	6	6	5	11							
12	Portsmouth	58	57	37	35	23	19	19	12	10	18	13	12						
13	Langstone Hbr	61	59	39	39	25	21	21	14	12	21	18	5	13					
14	Chichester Bar	63	62	42	42	28	23	24	17	15	23	18	8	5	14				
15	Bembridge	59	58	38	39	24	18	19	13	10	18	15	5	6	8	15			
16	Nab Tower	64	63	43	44	29	23	24	18	15	24	19	10	7	6	6	16		
17	St Catherine's Pt	45	44	25	25	12	19	21	27	15	36	29	20	20	19	17	15	17	
18	Littlehampton	79	79	60	61	46	44	45	38	36	45	42	31	28	25	28	22	35	18

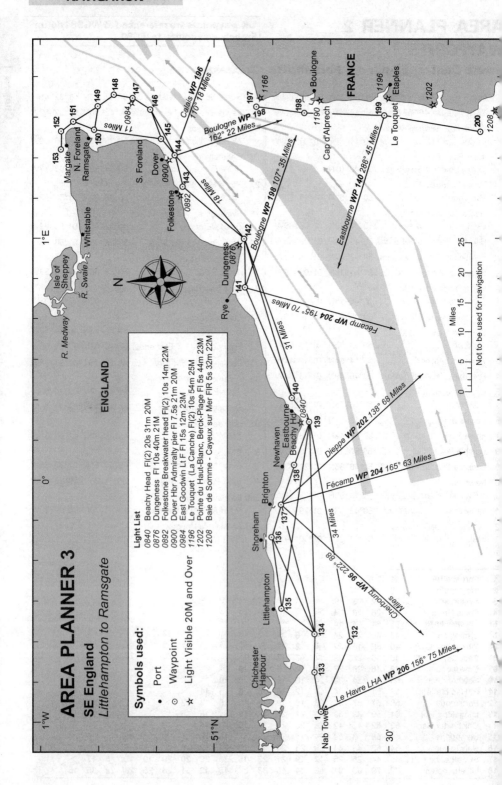

AREA PLANNER 3

SE England
Littlehampton to Ramsgate

Symbols used:

• Port
⊙ Waypoint
☆ Light Visible 20M and Over

Light List

0840	Beachy Head Fl(2) 20s 31m 20M
0876	Dungeness Fl 10s 40m 21M
0892	Folkestone Breakwater head Fl(2) 10s 14m 22M
0900	Dover Hbr Admiralty pier Fl 7.5s 21m 20M
0984	East Goodwin Lt F Fl 15s 12m 23M
1196	Le Touquet (La Canche) Fl(2) 10s 54m 25M
1202	Pointe du Haut-Blanc, Berck-Plage Fl 5s 44m 23M
1208	Baie de Somme - Cayeux sur Mer FIR 5s 32m 22M

Not to be used for navigation

AREA PLANNER 3
WAYPOINTS
South East England - *Littlehampton to Ramsgate*

> UK waypoints are referenced to WGS84 datum
> French waypoints to ED50

Nab Tower - *0·5M NW of* ..... 50°40'·41N 00°57'·64W

6 Cherbourg -
0·5M N of W entrance .... 49°40'·95N 01°39'·35W

32 Owers SCM - *1·8M SE of* .... 50°36'·83N 00°40'·69W

33 Boulder SHM - *0·1M N of* .... 50°41'·60N 00°49'·03W

34 East Borough Hd ECM -
0·1M N of .... 50°41'·63N 00°38'·83W

35 Littlehampton entrance -
1M 165°of on Ldg Lts .... 50°47'·03N 00°32'·11W

36 Shoreham entrance -
1M S of on Ldg Lts .... 50°48'·52N 00°14'·72W

37 Brighton entrance -
1M S of .... 50°47'·53N 00°06'·41W

38 Newhaven entrance -
1M S of .... 50°45'·56N 00°03'·56E

39 Beachy Hd - *1·5M S of* .... 50°42'·56N 00°14'·48E

40 Eastbourne - *1·2M SE
of Langney Point* .... 50°46'·29N 00°21'·00E

41 Rye - *0·1M S
of Rye Fairway Buoy* .... 50°53'·93N 00°48'·03E

42 Dungeness - *1M SE of* .... 50°54'·00N 00°59'·55E

43 Folkestone -
0·5M SE of breakwater .... 51°04'·20N 01°12'·25E

44 Dover - *1·2M SE
of Western entrance* .... 51°05'·83N 01°21'·00E

45 South Foreland - *2M E of* ..... 51°08·73N 01°26'·14E

146 South Goodwin PHM -
0·3M SE of .... 51°10'·43N 01°32'·59E

147 East Goodwin Lt Float -
0·8M W of .... 51°13'·26N 01°35'·14E

148 East Goodwin ECM -
0·2M E of .... 51°15'·77N 01°36'·02E

149 Goodwin Knoll - *1M SE of* .... 51°18'·88N 01°33'·37E

150 Ramsgate - *1M E of,
and for Pegwell Bay* .... 51°19'·51N 01°27'·04E

151 North Foreland - *1M E of* .... 51°22'·54N 01°28'·64E

152 Foreness Pt - *1M NNE of* .... 51°24'·50N 01°26'·30E

153 Margate - *0·7M N of* .... 51°24'·14N 01°22'·44E

197 Cap Gris-Nez -
2M NW of headland .... 50°53'·30N 01°32'·50E

198 Boulogne -
2M WNW of entrance .... 50°45'·22N 01°31'·11E

199 Étaples - *3M W
of Le Touquet Point* .... 50°32'·20N 01°30'·80E

200 St Valéry-sur-Somme -
5M WNW of Le Hourdel Pt . 50°15'·30N 01°27'·10E

202 Dieppe -
1M NW of entrance .... 49°57'·00N 01°04'·00E

204 Fécamp -
1M NW of entrance .... 49°46'·70N 00°20'·80E

206 Le Havre - *0·5M NE
of Le Havre LHA* .... 49°31'·79N 00°09'·23W

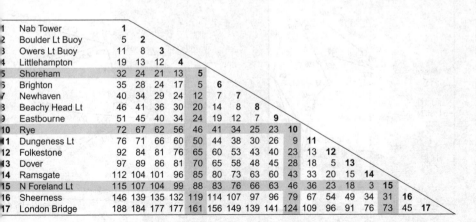

		1	2	3	4	5	6	7	8	9	10	11	12	13	14	15	16	17
1	Nab Tower	1																
2	Boulder Lt Buoy	5	2															
3	Owers Lt Buoy	11	8	3														
4	Littlehampton	19	13	12	4													
5	Shoreham	32	24	21	13	5												
6	Brighton	35	28	24	17	5	6											
7	Newhaven	40	34	29	24	12	7	7										
8	Beachy Head Lt	46	41	36	30	20	14	8	8									
9	Eastbourne	51	45	40	34	24	19	12	7	9								
10	Rye	72	67	62	56	46	41	34	25	23	10							
11	Dungeness Lt	76	71	66	60	50	44	38	30	26	9	11						
12	Folkestone	92	84	81	76	65	60	53	43	40	23	13	12					
13	Dover	97	89	86	81	70	65	58	48	45	28	18	5	13				
14	Ramsgate	112	104	101	96	85	80	73	63	60	43	33	20	15	14			
15	N Foreland Lt	115	107	104	99	88	83	76	66	63	46	36	23	18	3	15		
16	Sheerness	146	139	135	132	119	114	107	97	96	79	67	54	49	34	31	16	
17	London Bridge	188	184	177	177	161	156	149	139	141	124	109	96	91	76	73	45	17

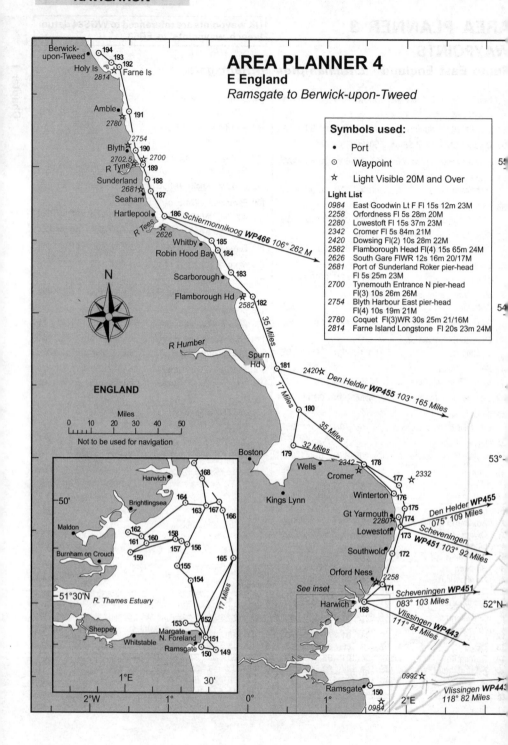

AREA PLANNER 4
E England
Ramsgate to Berwick-upon-Tweed

Symbols used:

- Port
- ⊙ Waypoint
- ☆ Light Visible 20M and Over

Light List

0984	East Goodwin Lt F Fl 15s 12m 23M
2258	Orfordness Fl 5s 28m 20M
2280	Lowestoft Fl 15s 37m 23M
2342	Cromer Fl 5s 84m 21M
2420	Dowsing Fl(2) 10s 28m 22M
2582	Flamborough Head Fl(4) 15s 65m 24M
2626	South Gare FIWR 12s 16m 20/17M
2681	Port of Sunderland Roker pier-head Fl 5s 25m 23M
2700	Tynemouth Entrance N pier-head Fl(3) 10s 26m 26M
2754	Blyth Harbour East pier-head Fl(4) 10s 19m 21M
2780	Coquet Fl(3)WR 30s 25m 21/16M
2814	Farne Island Longstone Fl 20s 23m 24M

ENGLAND

Miles
0 10 20 30 40 50
Not to be used for navigation

AREA PLANNER 4
WAYPOINTS

Waypoints are referenced to WGS84 datum

East England - *Ramsgate to Berwick-upon-Tweed*

9 Goodwin Knoll - *1M SE of* ......51°18'·88N 01°33'·37E

0 Ramsgate -
1M E of Pegwell Bay ....51°19'·47N 01°27'·04E

1 North Foreland - *1M E of* ..... 51°22'·54N 01°28'·64E

2 Foreness Point - *1M NNE of* 51°24'·50N 01°26'·30E

3 Margate - *0·7M N of* ....51°24'·14N 01°22'·44E

4 Fisherman's Gat -
SE turning waypoint ....51°33'·33N 01°24'·90E

5 Fisherman's Gat -
NW turning waypoint ....51°36'·33N 01°20'·60E

6 Black Deep/Sunk Sand -
turning waypoint ....51°40'·97N 01°24'·90E

7 Barrow No 2 PHM -
0·3M NE of........................51°42'·19N 01°23'·24E

8 Barrow No 3 ECM -
0·3M N of............................51°42'·32N 01°20'·25E

9 Whitaker Channel -
for River Crouch (6M) ....51°40'·43N 01°05'·20E

0 Swin Spitway SWM -
0·1M SSW of ....51°41'·84N 01°08'·26E

1 Spitway North -
turning waypoint ....51°43'·73N 01°07'·00E

2 Colne, Blackwater -
0·3M W of Eagle SHM ....51°44'·13N 01°03'·33E

3 NE Gunfleet ECM -
0·5M NW of ....51°50'·28N 01°27'·25E

4 Medusa SHM - *0·3M SW of* . 51°51'·03N 01°19'·90E

5 Kentish Knock ECM -
0·2M E of ....51°38'·53N 01°40'·70E

6 Trinity SCM - *0·6M N of* ....51°49'·68N 01°36'·35E

7 Sunk light F - *0·2M SW of* ... 51°50'·90N 01°34'·70E

8 Cork Sand Beacon NCM -
Harwich Yacht Channel ent .. 51°55'·24N 01°25'·19E

1 Orfordness - *1·5M ESE of* .... 52°04'·24N 01°36'·94E

172 Southwold - *2M ESE of ent* ... 52°18'·03N 01°43'·60E

173 Lowestoft - *2·8M E of ent* .... 52°28'·33N 01°50'·00E

174 Gt Yarmouth - *0·4M SSW
of S Corton SCM* ....52°32'·10N 01°49'·26E

175 Gt Yarmouth - *4·7M E of ent.* 52°34'·36N 01°52'·05E

176 Winterton -
0·5M NE of Cockle ECM .... 52°44'·40N 01°44'·20E

177 Winterton - *5·2M NE of* .... 52°46'·90N 01°48'·40E

178 Cromer light - *3M NNE of* .....52°58'·17N 01°21'·10E

179 North Well SWM -
0·5M NE .... 53°03'·37N 00°28'·50E

180 Inner Dowsing ECM -
0·5M NE of .... 53°19'·45N 00°35'·40E

181 Spurn Head - *2·6M NE
of Spurn Lightship* .... 53°34'·82N 00°17'·70E

182 Flamborough Hd - *2M E of* ....54°07'·12N 00°01'·20W

183 Scarborough - *1M E of ent* ....54°16'·88N 00°21'·66W

184 Robin Hood's Bay -
2·6M NE of .... 54°26'·41N 00°27'·40W

185 Whitby - *1·6M N of ent* .... 54°31'·11N 00°36'·70W

186 River Tees - *Fairway Buoy* ... 54°40'·94N 01°06'·48W

187 Seaham - *0·9M E of ent* .... 54°50'·24N 01°17'·75W

188 Sunderland - *1·7M E of ent* .. 54°55'·21N 01°18'·15W

189 R Tyne -
1·7M E by N of ent .... 55°01'·16N 01°21'·20W

190 Blyth - *1·5M E of ent* .... 55°07'·00N 01°26'·60W

191 Amble - *2·5M NE of ent* .... 55°21'·86N 01°30'·80W

192 Farne Island -
2M NE of Longstone light ..... 55°40'·01N 01°34'·05W

193 Holy Island -
1M NE of Emmanuel Hd .... 55°41'·95N 01°45'·60W

194 Berwick-upon-Tweed -
1·5M E of Breakwater .... 55°45'·90N 01°56'·40W

#	Port													Port	#
1	Ramsgate	1		11	31	61	78	91	107	126	189	205	205	232	Berwick-upon-Tweed	11
2	Sheerness	34	2		10	27	42	65	81	102	157	176	185	203	Amble	10
3	Gravesend	56	22	3		9	16	36	51	70	138	149	156	180	Sunderland	9
4	London Bridge	76	45	23	4		8	24	39	58	122	137	140	169	Hartlepool	8
5	Burnham-on-Crouch	44	34	53	76	5		7	16	35	88	114	121	143	Whitby	7
6	Brightlingsea	41	28	47	71	22	6		6	20	81	98	105	130	Scarborough	6
7	Harwich	40	50	65	83	31	24	7		5	58	83	87	114	Bridlington	5
8	River Deben (ent)	45	55	71	89	35	38	6	8		4	72	75	113	Hull	4
9	Southwold	62	80	95	113	58	63	30	23	9		3	34	83	Boston	3
10	Lowestoft	72	90	105	123	68	73	40	33	10	10		2	85	King's Lynn	2
11	Great Yarmouth	79	97	112	130	76	80	52	41	18	7	11		1	Great Yarmouth	1

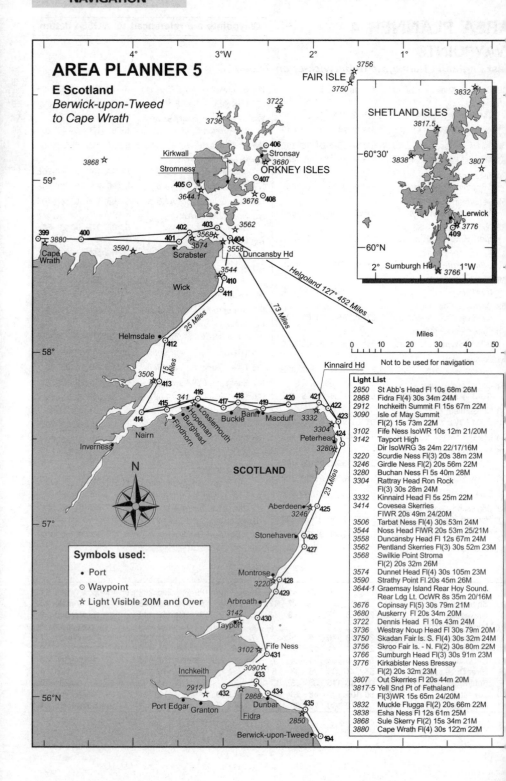

AREA PLANNER 5

E Scotland
*Berwick-upon-Tweed
to Cape Wrath*

FAIR ISLE

SHETLAND ISLES

ORKNEY ISLES

Kirkwall
Stromness
Stronsay

Cape Wrath
Scrabster
Duncansby Hd
Wick
Helmsdale
Kinnaird Hd

Lerwick
Sumburgh Hd

SCOTLAND

Inverness
Nairn
Buckie
Banff
Macduff
Peterhead

Aberdeen
Stonehaven

Montrose
Arbroath
Tayport
Fife Ness
Inchkeith
Port Edgar Granton
Dunbar
Fidra
Berwick-upon-Tweed

Symbols used:

- Port

⊙ Waypoint

☆ Light Visible 20M and Over

Miles
0   10   20   30   40   50

Not to be used for navigation

Light List

2850	St Abb's Head Fl 10s 68m 26M
2868	Fidra Fl(4) 30s 34m 24M
2912	Inchkeith Summit Fl 15s 67m 22M
3090	Isle of May Summit
	Fl(2) 15s 73m 22M
3102	Fife Ness IsoWR 10s 12m 21/20M
3142	Tayport High
	Dir IsoWRG 3s 24m 22/17/16M
3220	Scurdie Ness Fl(3) 20s 38m 23M
3246	Girdle Ness Fl(2) 20s 56m 22M
3280	Buchan Ness Fl 5s 40m 28M
3304	Rattray Head Ron Rock
	Fl(3) 30s 28m 24M
3332	Kinnaird Head Fl 5s 25m 22M
3414	Covesea Skerries
	FIWR 20s 49m 24/20M
3506	Tarbat Ness Fl(4) 30s 53m 24M
3544	Noss Head FIWR 20s 53m 25/21M
3558	Duncansby Head Fl 12s 67m 24M
3562	Pentland Skerries Fl(3) 30s 52m 23M
3568	Swilkie Point Stroma
	Fl(2) 20s 32m 26M
3574	Dunnet Head Fl(4) 30s 105m 23M
3590	Strathy Point Fl 20s 45m 26M
3644·1	Graemsay Island Rear Hoy Sound.
	Rear Ldg Lt. OcWR 8s 35m 20/16M
3676	Copinsay Fl(5) 30s 79m 21M
3680	Auskerry Fl 20s 34m 20M
3722	Dennis Head Fl 10s 43m 24M
3736	Westray Noup Head Fl 30s 79m 20M
3750	Skadan Fair Is. S. Fl(4) 30s 32m 24M
3756	Skroo Fair Is. - N. Fl(2) 30s 80m 22M
3766	Sumburgh Head Fl(3) 30s 91m 23M
3776	Kirkabister Ness Bressay
	Fl(2) 20s 32m 23M
3807	Out Skerries Fl 20s 44m 20M
3817·5	Yell Snd Pt of Fethaland
	Fl(3)WR 15s 65m 24/20M
3832	Muckle Flugga Fl(2) 20s 66m 22M
3838	Esha Ness Fl 12s 61m 25M
3868	Sule Skerry Fl(2) 15s 34m 21M
3880	Cape Wrath Fl(4) 30s 122m 22M

AREA PLANNER 5

WAYPOINTS

East Scotland - *Berwick-upon-Tweed to Cape Wrath*

94 Berwick-upon-Tweed -
1·5M E of .... 55°45'·90N 01°56'·40W

99 Cape Wrath - *2M NW of* ...... 58°38'·87N 05°02'·89W

00 Whiten Head - *4·4M N of* ...... 58°39'·18N 04°34'·90W

01 Scrabster -
1·4M NE of Holborn Head .... 58°38'·58N 03°30'·80W

02 Dunnet Head lt -
1·7M NW of .... 58°41'·58N 03°24'·39W

03 Pentland Firth -
1·5M NE by N of Stroma ...... 58°42'·98N 03°05'·31W

04 Duncansby Head -
2M NE of .... 58°39'·78N 02°58'·49W

05 Stromness - *2·8M NW
of Graemsay lt* .... 58°57'·07N 03°23'·80W

06 Stronsay -
0·8M NW of Ness lt .... 59°09'·97N 02°35'·90W

07 Kirkwall -
1·5M NW of Mull Hd .... 58°59'·37N 02°40'·50W

08 Copinsay light - *2·5M E of* ... 58°54'·07N 02°35'·20W

09 Lerwick -
1·1M SW of Bressay light ... 60°06'·57N 01°08'·50W

10 Wick - *1·6M E of South Hd* .. 58°25'·78N 03°01'·10W

11 Scarlet Head - *2M E by S of*. 58°21'·88N 03°02'·60W

12 Helmsdale - *1·8M SE of ent* 58°05'·48N 03°36'·90W

13 Tarbat Ness light - *2M E of* .. 57°51'·88N 03°42'·78W

14 Inverness -
0·5 NE of Fairway By .... 57°40'·28N 03°53'·40W

15 Findhorn -
2·2M NW of bay .... 57°41'·43N 03°40'·11W

416 Lossiemouth - *1·7M N of* ..... 57°45'·20N 03°16'·90W

417 Buckie - *2M WNW of* .... 57°41'·68N 03°00'·99W

418 Scar Nose - *1·6M N of* .... 57°43'·98N 02°51'·01W

419 Banff - *1·3M N of Meavie Pt* . 57°41'·64N 02°31'·30W

420 Troup Head - *1·8M N of* ...... 57°43'·50N 02°17'·75W

421 Kinnairds Head - *1·6M N of* . 57°43'·50N 02°00'·16W

422 Cairnbulg Point light -
1·9M NE of .... 57°42'·20N 01°53'·81W

423 Rattray Head light -
1·8M ENE of .... 57°37'·40N 01°46'·00W

424 Peterhead - *2·1M ESE* .... 57°29'·30N 01°42'·71W

425 Aberdeen -
2M E by N of Girdle Ness .... 57°08'·80N 01°59'·06W

426 Stonehaven - *2M E of* .... 56°57'·60N 02°08'·04W

427 Todhead Point light -
2·5M E of .... 56°53'·10N 02°08'·35W

428 Montrose - *2·1M E
of Scurdie Ness light* .... 56°42'·10N 02°22'·40W

429 Red Head - *1·8M E of* .... 56°37'·02N 02°25'·98W

430 Tayport -
0·5M E of Fairway By .... 56°29'·25N 02°37'·32W

431 Fife Ness - *2·8M ESE of* .... 56°15'·95N 02°30'·39W

432 Granton - *0·5M N
of Firth of Forth Fairway By*. 56°04'·00N 03°00'·09W

433 Bass Rock lt - *1·5M N of* ..... 56°06'·10N 02°38'·44W

434 Dunbar - *1·5M NNE of* .... 56°01'·76N 02°30'·30W

435 St Abb's Head lt -
1·5M NE of .... 55°56'·11N 02°06'·50W

1	Berwick-upon-Tweed	1		11	155	79	47	76	104	144	126	120	125	145	Cape Wrath	11
2	Eyemouth	10	2		10	95	124	120	148	190	170	162	156	160	Lerwick	10
3	Dunbar	26	17	3		9	50	46	74	114	104	90	95	115	Kirkwall	9
4	Port Edgar	58	50	34	4		8	31	59	99	89	75	80	100	Scrabster	8
5	Methil	45	36	20	20	5		7	29	69	58	44	50	72	Wick	7
6	Fife Ness	38	29	17	34	16	6		6	43	32	26	44	74	Helmsdale	6
7	Dundee	58	49	37	54	36	20	7		5	13	34	59	90	Inverness	5
8	Montrose	59	51	43	61	43	27	27	8		4	23	48	79	Nairn	4
9	Stonehaven	72	66	60	78	60	44	45	20	9		3	25	56	Lossiemouth	3
10	Aberdeen	82	78	73	90	72	56	57	32	13	10		2	33	Banff/Macduff	2
11	Peterhead	105	98	93	108	94	78	80	54	35	25	11		1	Peterhead	1

17

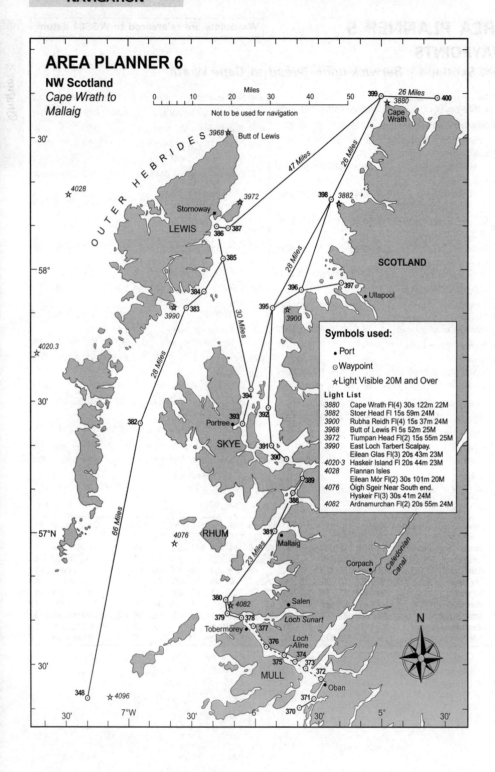

AREA PLANNER 6

NW Scotland
Cape Wrath to Mallaig

Miles

0   10   20   30   40   50

Not to be used for navigation

26 Miles

399   3880   400
Cape Wrath

3968 ☆ Butt of Lewis

O U T E R H E B R I D E S

☆ 4028

47 Miles   26 Miles

3972   398   3882

Stornoway

LEWIS ○─○ 387
386

385

28 Miles

SCOTLAND

58°

384 ○

396 ○   397 ○
● Ullapool

☆ 383   395 ○   ☆ 3900
3990   30 Miles

Symbols used:

● Port

○ Waypoint

☆ Light Visible 20M and Over

Light List

3880	Cape Wrath Fl(4) 30s 122m 22M
3882	Stoer Head Fl 15s 59m 24M
3900	Rubha Reidh Fl(4) 15s 37m 24M
3968	Butt of Lewis Fl 5s 52m 25M
3972	Tiumpan Head Fl(2) 15s 55m 25M
3990	East Loch Tarbert Scalpay.
	Eilean Glas Fl(3) 20s 43m 23M
4020·3	Haskeir Island Fl 20s 44m 23M
4028	Flannan Isles
	Eilean Mór Fl(2) 30s 101m 20M
4076	Òigh Sgeir Near South end.
	Hyskeir Fl(3) 30s 41m 24M
4082	Ardnamurchan Fl(2) 20s 55m 24M

☆ 4020.3

28 Miles

30'

394 ○

382 ○   Portree ●   392 ○

393 ○

SKYE   391 ○
390 ○

389 ○

388 ○

57°N

66 Miles   4076 ☆   RHUM   381 ○
Mallaig

23 Miles   Corpach ●   Caledonian Canal

380 ○   ☆ 4082   ● Salen
379 ○─○ 378   Loch Sunart
Tobermorey ●   377 ○
376 ○   Loch Aline
375 ○─○ 374   373 ○
MULL   372 ○
● Oban

348 ○   ☆ 4096   371 ○
370 ○

N

30'

30'   7°W   30'   6°   30'   5°   30'

348 Skerryvore lt -
    6·8M W by N of .... 56°20'·78N 07°18'·86W

370 Sound of Insh -
    1M SSW of Insh Island .... 56°17'·60N 05°41'·06W

371 Kerrera Sound - *0·7M SSW*
    of Rubha Seanach .... 56°21'·70N 05°33'·96W

372 Oban - *0·5M WNW*
    of Maiden Isle .... 56°26'·00N 05°30'·36W

373 Between Lady's Rock
    and Eilean Musdile .... 56°27'·19N 05°36'·75W

374 Sound of Mull -
    1·6M SE of Ardtornish Pt ..... 56°30'·15N 05°42'·81W

375 Loch Aline -
    0·7M S by W of ent .... 56°31'·30N 05°46'·86W

376 Sound of Mull -
    1·8M N of Salen .... 56°33'·00N 05°56'·36W

377 Tobermory -
    0·9M NE of harbour ent .... 56°38'·39N 06°02'·46W

378 Ardmore Point (Mull) -
    0·7M N of .... 56°40'·00N 06°07'·66W

379 Point of Ardnamurchan -
    2·8M S of .... 56°40'·90N 06°13'·36W

380 Point of Ardnamurchan -
    1·3M W of .... 56°43'·60N 06°15'·96W

381 Mallaig -
    1·5M WNW of hbr ent .... 57°00'·98N 05°52'·17W

382 Neist Point lt - *4M W of* .... 57°25'·42N 06°54'·57W

383 Sound of Shiant -
    2·2M E of Eilean Glas lt .... 57°51'·20N 06°34'·40W

384 Sound of Shiant -
    0·3M NW of Shiants PHM .... 57°54'·78N 06°26'·07W

385 Kebock Head - *2·3M E of* ..... 58°02'·38N 06°17'·10W

386 Stornoway -
    1·2M SE of harbour ent .... 58°10'·28N 06°20'·67W

387 Chicken Head - *1·2M S of* ... 58°09'·60N 06°15'·28W

388 Sandaig Islands lt -
    0·6M W by N of .... 57°10'·22N 05°43'·27W

389 Kyle Rhea (S approach) -
    0·6M W of Glenelg .... 57°12'·62N 05°38'·86W

390 Loch Alsh (W approach) -
    1M NW of ent .... 57°17'·18N 05°46'·17W

391 Crowlin Islands -
    1·5M W of .... 57°20'·68N 05°53'·87W

392 Inner Sound - *1·7M E*
    Rubha Ard Ghlaisen .... 57°29'·55N 05°55'·57W

393 Portree - *1·8M E of town* ..... 57°24'·98N 06°08'·07W

394 Sd of Raasay - *3·1M SE*
    of Rubha nam Brathairean ... 57°33'·28N 06°03'·86W

395 Rubha Reidh - *3M W of* .... 57°51'·58N 05°54'·40W

396 Greenstone Point -
    1·6M NW of .... 57°56'·58N 05°39'·27W

397 Ullapool - *1·7M NE*
    of Cailleach Head lt .... 57°56'·88N 05°21'·87W

398 Stoerhead light -
    2M NW of .... 58°15'·77N 05°26'·87W

399 Cape Wrath - *2M NW of* ...... 58°38'·87N 05°02'·89W

400 Whiten Head - *4·4M N of* ..... 58°39'·18N 04°34'·90W

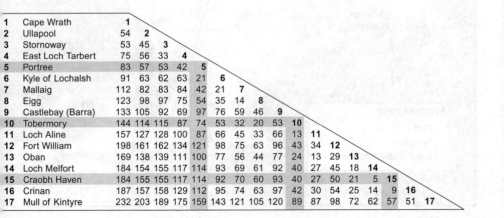

		1	2	3	4	5	6	7	8	9	10	11	12	13	14	15	16	17
1	Cape Wrath	1																
2	Ullapool	54	2															
3	Stornoway	53	45	3														
4	East Loch Tarbert	75	56	33	4													
5	Portree	83	57	53	42	5												
6	Kyle of Lochalsh	91	63	62	63	21	6											
7	Mallaig	112	82	83	84	42	21	7										
8	Eigg	123	98	97	75	54	35	14	8									
9	Castlebay (Barra)	133	105	92	69	97	76	59	46	9								
10	Tobermory	144	114	115	87	74	53	32	20	53	10							
11	Loch Aline	157	127	128	100	87	66	45	33	66	13	11						
12	Fort William	198	161	162	134	121	98	75	63	96	43	34	12					
13	Oban	169	138	139	111	100	77	56	44	77	24	13	29	13				
14	Loch Melfort	184	154	155	117	114	93	69	61	92	40	27	45	18	14			
15	Craobh Haven	184	155	155	117	114	92	70	60	93	40	27	50	21	5	15		
16	Crinan	187	157	158	129	112	95	74	63	97	42	30	54	25	14	9	16	
17	Mull of Kintyre	232	203	189	175	159	143	121	105	120	89	87	98	72	62	57	51	17

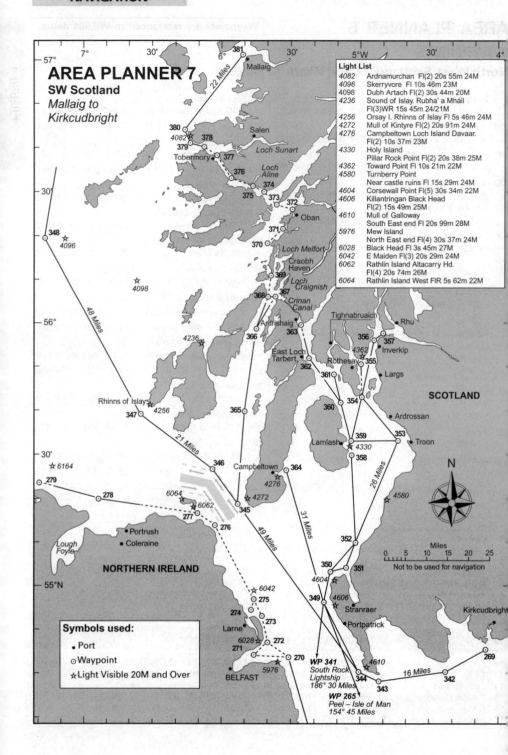

AREA PLANNER 7
SW Scotland
Mallaig to Kirkcudbright

Light List

4082	Ardnamurchan Fl(2) 20s 55m 24M
4096	Skerryvore Fl 10s 46m 23M
4098	Dubh Artach Fl(2) 30s 44m 20M
4236	Sound of Islay. Rubha' a Mháil Fl(3)WR 15s 45m 24/21M
4256	Orsay I. Rhinns of Islay Fl 5s 46m 24M
4272	Mull of Kintyre Fl(2) 20s 91m 24M
4276	Campbeltown Loch Island Davaar. Fl(2) 10s 37m 23M
4330	Holy Island Pillar Rock Point Fl(2) 20s 38m 25M
4362	Toward Point Fl 10s 21m 22M
4580	Turnberry Point Near castle ruins Fl 15s 29m 24M
4604	Corsewall Point Fl(5) 30s 34m 22M
4606	Killantringan Black Head Fl(2) 15s 49m 25M
4610	Mull of Galloway South East end Fl 20s 99m 28M
5976	Mew Island North East end Fl(4) 30s 37m 24M
6028	Black Head Fl 3s 45m 27M
6042	E Maiden Fl(3) 20s 29m 24M
6062	Rathlin Island Altacarry Hd. Fl(4) 20s 74m 26M
6064	Rathlin Island West FlR 5s 62m 22M

Symbols used:

• Port

⊙ Waypoint

☆ Light Visible 20M and Over

Waypoints are referenced to WGS84 datum

WAYPOINTS

South West Scotland - *Mallaig to Kirkcudbright*

329 Peel - *1M NW of hbr ent* .... 54°14'·50N 04°42'·57W
330 Kirkcudbright - *1·5M S of Little Ross lt* .... 54°44'·50N 04°05'·07W
331 Mew I lt - *1·5M ENE of* .... 54°42'·73N 05°28'·56W
332 Belfast - *0·7M ENE of No 1 Fairway Buoy* .... 54°42'·00N 05°45'·13W
333 Black Hd lt - *1·3M ENE of* .... 54°46'·50N 05°39'·26W
334 Isle of Muck - *1·1M NE of* ... 54°51'·70N 05°41'·91W
335 Larne Lough - *1M N of Barr's Point* .... 54°52'·53N 05°46'·81W
336 E Maiden lt - *1·7M SW of* .... 54°54'·50N 05°45'·57W
337 Torr Head - *0·6M ENE of* .... 55°12'·20N 06°02'·87W
338 Fair Head - *0·9M N of* .... 55°14'·60N 06°09'·00W
339 Lough Foyle - *4·1M NNE of Inishowen Head lt* .... 55°17'·90N 06°52'·27W
340 Malin Head - *3M NNE of* ..... 55°25'·00N 07°21'·26W
341 South Rock lt Vessel - *1·1M E of* .... 54°24'·52N 05°20'·13W
342 Burrow Head - *2M S of* .... 54°38'·60N 04°23'·65W
343 Mull of Galloway lt - *1·7M S of* .... 54°36'·40N 04°51'·50W
344 Crammag Head lt - *1·8M SW of* .... 54°38'·60N 05°00'·07W
345 Mull of Kintyre lt - *2·5M SW of* .... 55°16'·90N 05°51'·37W
346 Mull of Kintyre lt - *10·3M NW of* .... 55°25'·50N 06°01'·57W
347 Rhinns of Islay lt - *2·2M SW of* .... 55°38'·85N 06°33'·56W
348 Skerryvore lt - *6·8M W by N of* .... 56°20'·80N 07°18'·87W
349 Killantringan lt - *4·2M NW of* 54°54'·20N 05°14'·76W
350 Corsewall Pt lt - *1·8M WNW of* .... 55°01'·00N 05°12'·26W
351 Stranraer - *1M NNW of ent to Loch Ryan* .... 55°02'·40N 05°05'·17W
352 Bennane Hd - *1·5M NW of* ... 55°09'·25N 05°01'·87W
353 Troon - *2·1M W of hbr ent* .... 55°33'·10N 04°44'·77W
354 Little Cumbrae Island lt - *0·8M SW of* .... 55°42'·75N 04°59'·07W
355 Rothesay - *Ent to Rothesay Sound* .... 55°50'·90N 04°59'·67W
356 Firth of Clyde, Cloch Point lt - *1·3M WSW of* .... 55°55'·95N 04°54'·82W
357 R Clyde, Kempock Point - *0·9M WNW of* ....55°58'·10N 04°50'·57W

358 Lamlash - *1M SE of S ent* .... 55°29'·80N 05°03'·60W
359 Lamlash - *1M E of N ent* ..... 55°32'·90N 05°03'·07W
360 Isle of Arran - *2M NNE of Sannox Bay* .... 55°41'·60N 05°08'·07W
361 West Kyle - *1·3M SSE of Ardlamont Point* .... 55°48'·30N 05°11'·80W
362 East Loch Tarbert - *1M E of Loch* .... 55°52'·20N 05°22'·07W
363 Ardrishaig - *1·3M SSE of hbr ent* .... 55°59'·50N 05°25'·67W
364 Campbeltown - *1M NE of Loch ent* .... 55°26'·40N 05°31'·07W
365 Gigha Island - *1·5M W of Cath Sgeir WCM* .... 55°39'·69N 05°50'·07W
366 Sound of Jura - *2·5M NW of Island of Danna* .... 55°58'·80N 05°45'·56W
367 Loch Crinan - *0·6M NW of Ardnoe Point* .... 56°06'·00N 05°35'·46W
368 Sound of Jura - *2M SSW of Reisa an t-Sruith Is lt* .... 56°06'·00N 05°39'·97W
369 Sound of Luing - *0·5M WSW of Ardluing SHM* .... 56°11'·00N 05°39'·33W
370 Sound of Insh - *1M SSW of Insh Island* .... 56°17'·54N 05°41'·06W
371 Kerrera Sound - *0·7M SSW of Rubha Seanach* .... 56°21'·62N 05°33'·97W
372 Oban - *0·5M WNW of Maiden Isle* .. 56°26'·00N 05°30'·36W
373 Between Lady's Rock and Eilean Musdile ....56°27'·19N 05°36'·75W
374 Sound of Mull - *1·6M SE of Ardtornish Point* .... 56°30'·15N 05°42'·81W
375 Loch Aline - *0·7M S by W of ent* .... 56°31'·30N 05°46'·86W
376 Sound of Mull - *1·8M N of Salen* .... 56°33'·00N 05°56'·36W
377 Tobermory - *0·9M NE of hbr ent* .... 56°38'·39N 06°02'·46W
378 Ardmore Pt (Mull) - *0·7M N of* .... 56°40'·00N 06°07'·66W
379 Pt of Ardnamurchan - *2·8M S of* .... 56°40'·90N 06°13'·36W
380 Pt of Ardnamurchan - *1·3M W of* .... 56°43'·60N 06°15'·96W
381 Mallaig - *1·5M WNW of hbr ent* .... 57°00'·98N 05°52'·17W

	1	2	3	4	5	6	7	8	9	10	11	12	13	14
1 Loch Craignish	1													
2 Crinan	5	2												
3 Ardrishaig	14	9	3											
4 East Loch Tarbert	24	19	10	4										
5 Campbeltown	55	50	39	31	5									
6 Lamlash	48	43	34	25	24	6								
7 Largs	48	43	34	24	39	17	7							
8 Kip Marina	53	48	39	28	50	25	10	8						
9 Greenock	59	54	45	36	53	31	16	6	9					
10 Rhu (Helensburgh)	62	57	48	37	59	33	19	9	4	10				
11 Troon	54	49	40	33	33	16	20	29	34	38	11			
12 Girvan	67	62	53	43	29	20	33	46	49	51	21	12		
13 Stranraer	89	84	75	65	34	39	56	69	65	74	44	23	13	
14 Kirkcudbright	136	131	122	114	88	92	110	116	124	125	97	94	71	14

See table on page 19 for distances between Mallaig and Crinan

Chapter 1

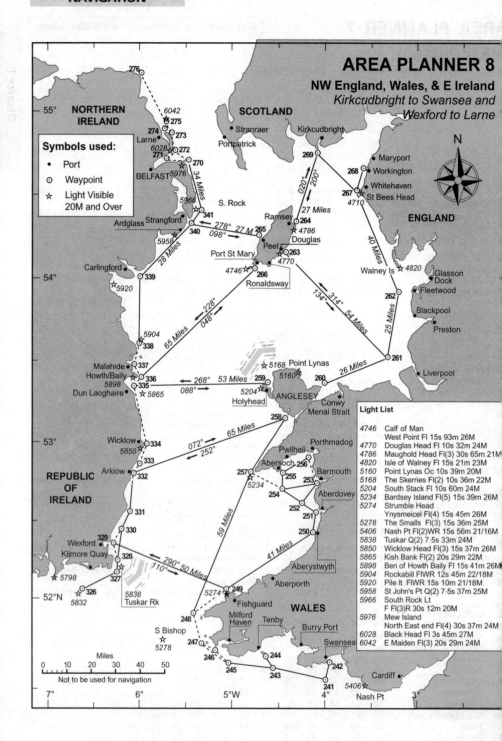

AREA PLANNER 8
NW England, Wales, & E Ireland
Kirkcudbright to Swansea and Wexford to Larne

Symbols used:
- • Port
- ⊙ Waypoint
- ☆ Light Visible 20M and Over

Light List

4746	Calf of Man West Point Fl 15s 93m 26M
4770	Douglas Head Fl 10s 32m 24M
4786	Maughold Head Fl(3) 30s 65m 21M
4820	Isle of Walney Fl 15s 21m 23M
5160	Point Lynas Oc 10s 39m 20M
5168	The Skerries Fl(2) 10s 36m 22M
5204	South Stack Fl 10s 60m 24M
5234	Bardsey Island Fl(5) 15s 39m 26M
5274	Strumble Head Ynysmeicel Fl(4) 15s 45m 26M
5278	The Smalls Fl(3) 15s 36m 25M
5406	Nash Pt Fl(2)WR 15s 56m 21/16M
5838	Tuskar Q(2) 7·5s 33m 24M
5850	Wicklow Head Fl(3) 15s 37m 26M
5865	Kish Bank Fl(2) 20s 29m 22M
5898	Ben of Howth Baily Fl 15s 41m 26M
5904	Rockabill FlWR 12s 45m 22/18M
5920	Pile lt FlWR 15s 10m 21/18M
5958	St John's Pt Q(2) 7·5s 37m 25M
5966	South Rock Lt F Fl(3)R 30s 12m 20M
5976	Mew Island North East end Fl(4) 30s 37m 24M
6028	Black Head Fl 3s 45m 27M
6042	E Maiden Fl(3) 20s 29m 24M

Miles
0 10 20 30 40 50
Not to be used for navigation

22

Waypoints are referenced to WGS84 datum

WAYPOINTS
W England, Wales & E Ireland - *Kirkcudbright to Swansea & Wexford to Larne*

41 Ledge SCM - *2M S of* .... 51°28'·00N 03°58'·84W
42 Swansea -
  1M SE of Mumbles Head ..... 51°33'·40N 03°57'·00W
43 Caldey Island - *7M SE of* ..... 51°32'·20N 04°35'·25W
44 Tenby - *1M SE of Caldey Is* . 51°37'·22N 04°39'·68W
45 Crow Rock - *1·3M S of* .... 51°35'·45N 05°03'·30W
46 Milford Haven -
  1·1M S of St Ann's Head .... 51°39'·74N 05°10'·68W
47 Skokholm Is It - *1·6M W of* . 51°41'·62N 05°19'·78W
48 S Bishop Is It - *3M NW of* ... 51°53'·35N 05°27'·90W
49 Fishguard -
  1·5M N of Strumble Head .... 52°03'·25N 05°04'·42W
50 Aberystwyth -
  1·5M W of ent .... 52°24'·40N 04°08'·00W
51 Aberdovey -
  1·5M W of hbr bar .... 52°31'·80N 04°07'·15W
52 Sarn-y-Bwch WCM -
  1·1M W of .... 52°34'·82N 04°15'·42W
53 Barmouth -
  1·2M W of hbr bar .... 52°42'·62N 04°05'·67W
54 Causeway WCM - *2M SW of* 52°39'·92N 04°28'·07W
55 Abersoch -
  1·2M SE St Tudwal's Is It ..... 52°47'·20N 04°26'·80W
56 Porthmadog -
  1·1M SW of Fairway Buoy ... 52°52'·65N 04°13'·05W
57 Bardsey I It - *4M NNW of* .... 52°48'·70N 04°50'·38W
58 Menai Strait -
  1·4M SW of Llanddwyn Is ... 53°07'·32N 04°26'·87W
59 Holyhead - *1M N of W Bkwtr* 53°20'·84N 04°37'·17W
60 Menai Strait -
  1·2M N of Puffin Is .... 53°20'·50N 04°01'·50W
61 Liverpool -
  0·7M S of Bar It Vessel .... 53°31'·30N 03°20'·97W
62 Fleetwood -
  2M SW of Lune Deep SCM .. 53°54'·04N 03°13'·07W
63 Douglas -
  1·1M E of Douglas Head ...... 54°08'·60N 04°26'·02W

264 Ramsey -
  1·3M ENE of S bkwtr .... 54°19'·90N 04°20'·27W
265 Peel - *1M NW of ent* .... 54°14'·50N 04°42'·57W
266 Pt St Mary -
  1·2M S of Kallow Pt .... 54°02'·90N 04°44'·05W
267 St Bees Head It - *2M W of* .. 54°30'·80N 03°41'·67W
268 Workington -
  1M WNW of bkwtr .... 54°39'·40N 03°36'·40W
269 Kirkcudbright -
  1·5M S of Little Ross It .... 54°44'·50N 04°05'·07W
270 Mew I It - *1·5M ENE of* .... 54°42'·75N 05°28'·59W
271 Belfast - *0·7M ENE*
  of No.1 Fairway Buoy .... 54°42'·00N 05°45'·13W
272 Black Head It - *1·3M ENE of*. 54°46'·50N 05°39'·26W
273 Isle of Muck - *1·1M NE of* ... 54°51'·70N 05°41'·91W
274 Larne Lough -
  1M N of Barr's Pt .... 54°52'·53N 05°46'·81W
275 East Maiden It -*1·7M SW of* 54°54'·50N 05°45'·57W
276 Torr Head - *0·6M ENE of* .... 55°12'·20N 06°02'·87W
326 Coningbeg It - *0·4M N of* ..... 52°02'·80N 06°39'·45W
327 Carnsore Pt - *3·2M ESE of* ... 52°09'·42N 06°16'·45W
328 Greenore Pt - *1·8M E of* .... 52°14'·43N 06°15'·90W
329 Wexford - *1·6M E of ent* ...... 52°20'·52N 06°19·30'W
330 W Blackwater SHM -
  0·4M W of .... 52°25'·82N 06°14'·06W
331 Cahore Point - *1·7M SE of*... 52°32'·52N 06°09'·96W
332 Arklow - *1·2M E by S of* .... 52°47'·42N 06°06'·36W
333 Mizen Head (E coast) -
  1M ESE of .... 52°51'·02N 06°01'·96W
334 Wicklow - *2·6M E of* .... 52°58'·92N 05°57'·86W
335 Dun Laoghaire - *2·2M NE of* .53°19'·62N 06°04'·66W
336 Ben of Howth - *1·4M E of* .... 53°22'·42N 06°00'·56W
337 Malahide - *1·5M E of Bar* ..... 53°27'·03N 06°04'·86W
338 Rockabill It - *1·2M WSW of* . 53°35'·32N 06°02'·06W
339 Carlingford Lough SWM .... 53°58'·70N 06°01'·12W
340 Strangford Lough SWM .... 54°18'·62N 05°28'·69W
341 S Rock It Vessel -*1·1M E of* . 54°24'·52N 05°20'·13W

#		1	2	3	4	5	6	7	8	9	10	11	12	13	14	15	16	17
1	Portpatrick	1																
2	Mull of Galloway	16	2															
3	Kirkcudbright	48	32	3														
4	Maryport	65	49	26	4													
5	Workington	63	47	25	6	5												
6	Ravenglass	70	54	40	30	23	6											
7	Point of Ayre	38	22	28	37	31	34	7										
8	Peel	41	26	46	55	49	52	18	8									
9	Douglas	60	42	46	50	44	39	19	30	9								
10	Glasson Dock	101	85	74	66	60	37	64	65	63	10							
11	Fleetwood	95	79	68	59	53	30	58	80	57	10	11						
12	Liverpool	118	102	97	89	83	60	80	86	70	52	46	12					
13	Conwy	111	95	95	92	86	58	72	72	59	62	56	46	13				
14	Beaumaris	109	93	94	95	89	72	71	73	58	66	60	49	12	14			
15	Caernarfon	117	103	104	105	99	82	81	73	68	76	70	59	22	10	15		
16	Holyhead	93	81	94	96	90	69	68	62	50	79	73	68	36	32	26	16	
17	Fishguard	171	158	175	175	169	160	153	140	134	153	147	136	100	88	78	89	17

ee table on page 25 and 27 for distances in Ireland, and page 25 for distances between Fishguard and Cardiff

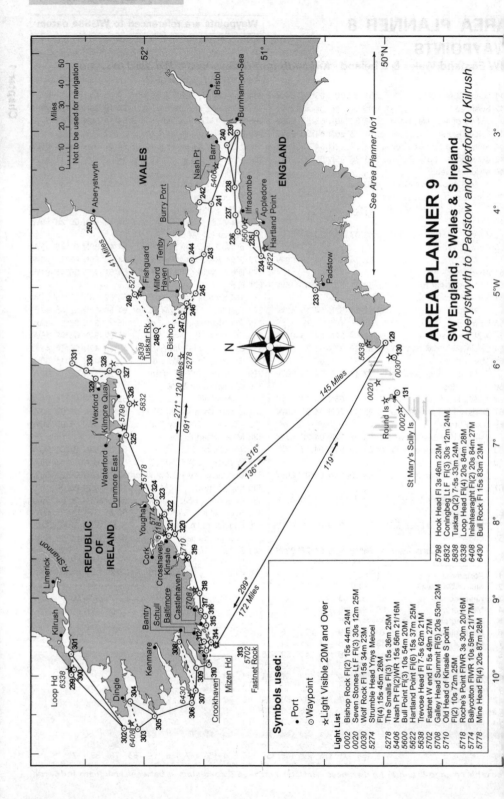

AREA PLANNER 9

SW England, S Wales & S Ireland
Aberystwyth to Padstow and Wexford to Kilrush

See Area Planner No1

Symbols used:

- Port
- ◎ Waypoint
- ★ Light Visible 20M and Over

Light List

0002	Bishop Rock Fl(2) 15s 44m 24M
0020	Seven Stones Lt F Fl(3) 30s 12m 25M
0030	Wolf Rock Fl 15s 34m 23M
5274	Strumble Head Ynys Meicel Fl(4) 15s 45m 26M
5278	The Smalls Fl(3) 15s 36m 25M
5406	Nash Pt Fl(2)WR 15s 56m 21/16M
5600	Bull Point Fl(3) 10s 54m 20M
5622	Hartland Point Fl(6) 15s 37m 25M
5638	Trevose Head Fl 7.5s 62m 21M
5702	Fastnet W end Fl 5s 49m 27M
5708	Galley Head Summit Fl(5) 20s 53m 23M
5710	Old Head of Kinsale S point Fl(2) 10s 72m 25M
5718	Roche's Point FlWR 3s 30m 20/16M
5774	Ballycotton FlWR 10s 59m 21/17M
5778	Mine Head Fl(4) 20s 87m 28M
5798	Hook Head Fl 3s 46m 23M
5832	Coningbeg Lt F Fl(3) 30s 12m 24M
5838	Tuskar Q(2) 7-5s 33m 24M
6338	Loop Head Fl(4) 20s 84m 28M
6408	Inishtearaght Fl(2) 20s 84m 27M
6430	Bull Rock Fl 15s 83m 23M

AREA PLANNER 9
WAYPOINTS

W England, S Wales and S Ireland - *Aberystwyth to Padstow & Wexford to Kilrush*

Chapter 1

29 Runnel Stone SCM - 0.3M S of .... 50°00'·88N 05°40'·37W
30 Wolf Rock It - 2M S of .... 49°54'·68N 05°48'·56W
31 St Mary's, Scilly - 2M E of St Mary's .... 49°54'·04N 06°15'.06W
33 Padstow - 2M NW of Stepper Pt .... 50°35'·70N 04°59'·16W
34 Hartland Pt - 2.5M NW of .... 51°02'·83N 04°34'·47W
35 River Taw - 1·6M NW of Bideford Fairway Buoy .... 51°06'·23N 04°18'·27W
36 Morte Point - 2.5M NNW of .. 51°13'·63N 04°15'·87W
37 Ilfracombe - 1·5M N of .... 51°14'·20N 04°06'·87W
38 Foreland Point - 1·5M N of .... 51°16'·20N 03°47'·25W
39 Burnham on Sea - 4.75M WNW of .... 51°15'·30N 03°07'·80W
40 Barry & R Severn - 2·9M SSW ent .... 51°21'·03N 03°17'·37W
41 Ledge SCM By - 2M S of ..... 51°28'·00N 03°58'·84W
42 Swansea - 1M SE of Mumbles Head ..... 51°33'·40N 03°57'·00W
43 Caldey I - 7M SE of .... 51°32'·20N 04°35'·25W
44 Tenby - 1M SE of Caldey I ... 51°37'·22N 04°39'·68W
45 Crow Rock - 1·3M S of .... 51°35'·45N 05°03'·30W
46 Milford Haven - 1·1M S of St Ann's Head .... 51°39'·74N 05°10'·68W
47 Skokholm I It - 1·6M W of ... 51°41'·62N 05°19'·78W
48 S Bishop I It - 3M NW of ..... 51°53'·35N 05°27'·90W
49 Fishguard - 1·5M N of Strumble Head .... 52°03'·25N 05°04'·42W
50 Aberystwyth - 1·5M W of ent .... 52°24'·40N 04°08'·00W
99 Loop Head It - 1·6M W of .... 52°33'·65N 09°58'·55W
00 Loop Head It - 1·4M S of ..... 52°32'·25N 09°55'·92W
01 Kilrush - 0.9M S of Kilcredaun It .... 52°33'·85N 09°42'·57W
02 Tearaght I It - 2·5M NW of... 52°06'·22N 10°42'·53W
03 Great Foze Rock - 1·8M SW of .... 52°00'·02N 10°43'·23W
04 Dingle - 1·2M S of Reenbeg Point ..... 52°05'·62N 10°15'·80W

305 Bray Head - 1·4M W of .... 51°52'·83N 10°28'·05W
306 The Bull I It - 1·7M SW of .... 51°34'·32N 10°20'·13W
307 Crow Head - 1·9M S of ...... 51°32'·92N 10°09'·44W
308 Bantry - 0.8M SW of Whiddy I .... 51°40'·03N 09°32'·83W
309 Sheep's Head It - 1·5M W of.......................... 51°32'·56N 09°53'·30W
310 Mizen Head It (SW) - 2M SSW of.......................... 51°25'·02N 09°50'·34W
311 Crookhaven - 1M ESE of Streek Head .... 51°27'·83N 09°40'·34W
312 Schull - 1M S of Long Is It ... 51°29'·22N 09°32'·03W
313 The Fastnet Rock It .... 51°23'·36N 09°36'·18W
314 Cape Clear - 1·6M SW of ..... 51°24'·23N 09°32'·93W
315 Baltimore - 1·5M S of hbr ent .... 51°26'·85N 09°23'·50W
316 Toe Head - 1·5M S of .... 51°27'·33N 09°13'·65W
317 Castle Haven - 1M SE of ent .... 51°30'.10N 09°09'.94W
318 Galley Head - 1·4M S of .... 51°30'·40N 08°57'·20W
319 Old Head of Kinsale It - 1·5M SSE of .... 51°34'·92N 08°30'·84W
320 Cork Landfall By - 0·4M E of .... 51°43'·03N 08°14'·84W
321 Roche's Point It - 1·2M S of . 51°46'·35N 08°15'·28W
322 Ballycotton I It - 1·5M S of .. 51°47'·99N 07°59'·25W
323 Youghal, S - 1M SE of Capel I .... 51°52'·26N 07°50'·08W
324 Youghal, SE - 2M SE of Blackball ECM ... 51°54'·77N 07°45'·28W
325 Waterford - 1·35M SSE of Dunmore E .... 52°07'·42N 06°58'·85W
326 Coningbeg It vessel - 0·4M N of .... 52°02'·80N 06°39'·45W
327 Carnsore Pt - 3·2M ESE of ... 52°09'·42N 06°16'·45W
328 Greenore Pt - 1·8M E of .... 52°14'·45N 06°15'·98W
329 Wexford - 1·6M E of ent ...... 52°20'·52N 06°19'·30W
330 W Blackwater SHM - 0·4M W of .... 52°25'·82N 06°14'·06W
331 Cahore Point - 1·7M SE of.... 52°32'·52N 06°09'·96W

Distance table (W England / S Wales ports)

#	Port	1	2	3	4	5	6	7	8	9	10	11	12
1	Aberystwyth	1											
2	Fishguard	40	2										
3	Milford Haven	84	48	3									
4	Tenby	107	71	28	4								
5	Swansea	130	94	55	36	5							
6	Cardiff	161	125	86	66	46	6						
7	Sharpness	192	156	117	106	75	33	7					
8	Avonmouth	175	139	100	89	58	20	18	8				
9	Burnham-on-Sea	169	133	94	70	48	53	50	33	9			
10	Ilfracombe	128	92	53	35	25	44	74	57	45	10		
11	Padstow	142	106	70	70	76	97	127	110	98	55	11	
12	Longships	169	133	105	110	120	139	169	152	140	95	50	12

Distance table (S Ireland ports)

12	11	10	9	8	7	6	5	4	3	2	1	Port	#
12	64	66	122	164	192	224	254	286	299	318	361	Kilrush	12
	11	13	69	111	139	171	201	233	246	265	308	Dingle	11
		10	56	102	131	165	188	227	242	252	295	Valentia	10
			9	42	70	102	132	164	177	196	239	Baltimore	9
				8	35	69	95	135	150	168	202	Kinsale	8
					7	34	65	100	115	133	172	Youghal	7
						6	32	69	84	102	139	Dunmore East	6
							5	34	47	66	108	Rosslare	5
								4	15	36	75	Arklow	4
									3	21	63	Wicklow	3
										2	48	Dun Laoghaire	2
											1	Carlingford Lough	1

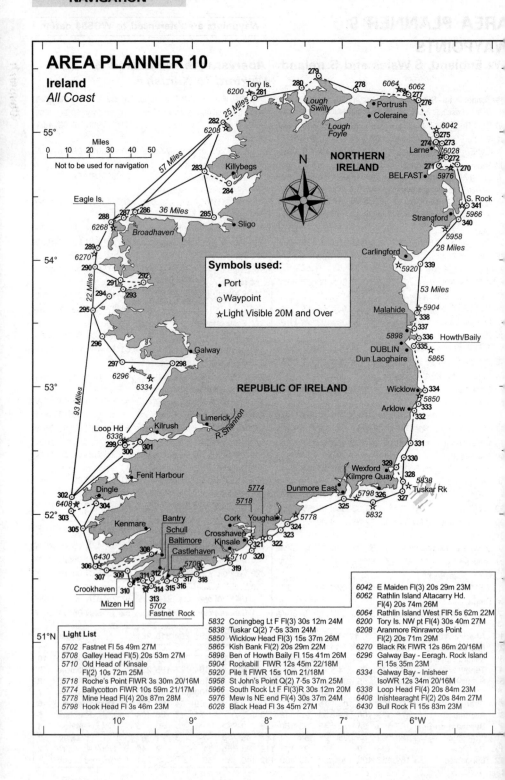

AREA PLANNER 10

Ireland
All Coast

Tory Is. 6200

55°

Miles
0 10 20 30 40 50

Not to be used for navigation

25 Miles
57 Miles

N

**NORTHERN
IRELAND**

Lough
Swilly

Portrush
Coleraine

Lough
Foyle

Killybegs

Larne
BELFAST

S. Rock

Strangford

Carlingford

28 Miles

Symbols used:

• Port

⊙ Waypoint

☆ Light Visible 20M and Over

Eagle Is.

36 Miles

Sligo

Broadhaven

54°

Malahide

53 Miles

Howth/Baily

DUBLIN
Dun Laoghaire

REPUBLIC OF IRELAND

Galway

53°

Wicklow

Arklow

Limerick

R. Shannon

Loop Hd
Kilrush

Wexford
Kilmore Quay

Fenit Harbour

Dunmore East

Tuskar Rk

Dingle

Cork Youghal

52°

Kenmare

Bantry
Schull
Baltimore
Castlehaven

Crosshaven
Kinsale

Crookhaven

Mizen Hd

Fastnet Rock

10°   9°   8°   7°   6°W

Light List

5702 Fastnet Fl 5s 49m 27M
5708 Galley Head Fl(5) 20s 53m 27M
5710 Old Head of Kinsale
      Fl(2) 10s 72m 25M
5718 Roche's Point FlWR 3s 30m 20/16M
5774 Ballycotton FlWR 10s 59m 21/17M
5778 Mine Head Fl(4) 20s 87m 28M
5798 Hook Head Fl 3s 46m 23M

5832 Coningbeg Lt F Fl(3) 30s 12m 24M
5838 Tuskar Q(2) 7·5s 33m 24M
5850 Wicklow Head Fl(3) 15s 37m 26M
5865 Kish Bank Fl(2) 20s 29m 22M
5898 Ben of Howth Baily Fl 15s 41m 26M
5904 Rockabill FlWR 12s 45m 22/18M
5920 Pile lt FlWR 15s 10m 21/18M
5958 St John's Point Q(2) 7·5s 37m 25M
5966 South Rock Lt F Fl(3)R 30s 12m 20M
5976 Mew Is NE end Fl(4) 30s 37m 24M
6028 Black Head Fl 3s 45m 27M

6042 E Maiden Fl(3) 20s 29m 23M
6062 Rathlin Island Altacarry Hd.
      Fl(4) 20s 74m 26M
6064 Rathlin Island West FlR 5s 62m 22M
6208 Aranmore Rinrawros Point
      Fl(2) 20s 71m 29M
6270 Black Rk FlWR 12s 86m 20/16M
6296 Galway Bay - Eeragh. Rock Island
      Fl 15s 35m 23M
6334 Galway Bay - Inisheer
      IsoWR 12s 34m 20/16M
6338 Loop Head Fl(4) 20s 84m 23M
6408 Inishtearaght Fl(2) 20s 84m 27M
6430 Bull Rock Fl 15s 83m 23M

51°N

AREA PLANNER 10

Waypoints are referenced to WGS84 datum

WAYPOINTS - Ireland

70 Mew Is Lt - *1·5M ENE of* ..... 54°42'·75N 05°28'·59W
71 Belfast - *0·7M ENE of*
   No.1 Fairway Buoy .... 54°42'·00N 05°45'·13W
72 Black Hd Lt -*1·3M ENE of* .... 54°46'·50N 05°39'·26W
73 Isle of Muck - *1·1M NE of* ... 54°51'·70N 05°41'·91W
74 Larne Lough -
   1M N of Barr's Point .... 54°52'·53N 05°46'·81W
75 E Maiden Lt - *1·7M SW of* ... 54°54'·50N 05°45'·57W
76 Torr Head - *0·6M ENE of* ..... 55°12'·20N 06°02'·87W
77 Fair Head - *0·9M N of* .... 55°14'·60N 06°09'·00W
78 L. Foyle
   4·1M NNE of Inishowen Lt ... 55°17'·90N 06°52'·27W
79 Malin Head - *3M NNE of* ..... 55°25'·00N 07°21'·26W
80 Lough Swilly -*1M N of ent* ... 55°18'·20N 07°34'·36W
81 Tory Island - *1·25M SE of* .... 55°14'·00N 08°11'·04W
82 Rinrawros Pt Lt,
   Aran - 1·3M NW of .... 55°01'·75N 08°35'·44W
83 Rathlin O'Birne I Lt -
   1·9M WSW of .... 54°39'·20N 08°52'·94W
84 Killibegs - *2·5M WNW*
   of St John's Point Lt .... 54°34'·70N 08°31'·84W
85 Sligo - *2·7M N of Aughris Hd* 54°19'·50N 08°45'·36W
86 The Stags rks - *1·3M N of* .... 54°23'·30N 09°47'·18W
87 Broadhaven - *1M N of bay* .. 54°20'·40N 09°56'·04W
88 Eagle Island -*1·4M NW of* ... 54°17'·81N 10°07'·43W
89 Black Rock -
   2·7M NE by N of .... 54°06'·20N 10°16'·63W
90 Achill Head - *1·8M SW of* .... 53°57'·30N 10°17'·93W
91 Clew Bay -
   1M SW of Achillbeg I Lt .... 53°50'·80N 09°57'·93W
92 Westport -
   1·5M WSW of Inishgort Lt ... 53°49'·00N 09°42'·63W
93 Clew Bay - *1·5M NW of*
   Roonah Head .... 53°46'·95N 09°55'·70W
94 Inishturk I - *1·2M NW of* ..... 53°43'·60N 10°08'·85W
95 Inishshark I - *1·8M W of* ..... 53°36'·50N 10°21'·05W
96 Slyne Hd Lt - *1·6M SW of* .... 53°22'·90N 10°16'·05W
97 Rock I Lt -
   5·3M NW by W of .... 53°11'·40N 09°58'·65W
98 Galway -
   2·3M N of Black Head Lt ..... 53°11'·55N 09°15'·84W
99 Loop Head Lt - *1·6M W of* ... 52°33'·65N 09°58'·55W
100 Loop Head Lt - *1·4M S of* ... 52°32'·25N 09°55'·92W
101 Kilrush - *0·9M S*
   of Kilcredaun Head Lt .... 52°33'·85N 09°42'·57W
102 Tearaght I Lt - *2·5M NW of* . 52°06'·22N 10°42'·53W
103 Gt Foze Rk - *1·8M SW of* ..... 52°00'·02N 10°43'·23W

304 Dingle -
   1·2M S of Reenbeg Pt .... 52°05'·62N 10°15'·80W
305 Bray Head - *1·4M W of* .... 51°52'·83N 10°28'·05W
306 The Bull I Lt - *1·7M SW of*... 51°34'·32N 10°20'·13W
307 Crow Head - *1·9M S of* .... 51°32'·92N 10°09'·44W
308 Bantry -
   0·8M SW of Whiddy I .... 51°40'·03N 09°32'·83W
309 Sheep's Hd Lt - *1·5M W of* . 51°32'·56N 09°53'·30W
310 Mizen Head Lt (SW) -
   2M SSW of .... 51°25'·02N 09°50'·34W
311 Crookhaven -
   1M ESE of Streek Head .... 51°27'·83N 09°40'·34W
312 Schull - *1M S of Long I Lt* ... 51°29'·22N 09°32'·03W
313 The Fastnet Rock .... 51°23'·36N 09°36'·18W
314 Cape Clear - *1·6M SW of* ... 51°24'·23N 09°32'·93W
315 Baltimore - *1·5M S of* .... 51°26'·85N 09°23'·50W
316 Toe Head - *1·5M S of* .... 51°27'·33N 09°13'·65W
317 Castle Haven - *1M SE of* ..... 51°30'·10N 09°09'·94W
318 Galley Head - *1·4M S of* ..... 51°30'·40N 08°57'·20W
319 Old Hd of Kinsale Lt -
   1·5M SSE of .... 51°34'·92N 08°30'·84W
320 Cork Landfall By - *0·4M E of* 51°43'·03N 08°14'·84W
321 Roche's Pt Lt - *1·2M S of*.... 51°46'·35N 08°15'·28W
322 Ballycotton I Lt - *1·5M S of* . 51°47'·95N 07°59'·17W
323 Youghal - *1M SE of Capel I*.. 51°52'·26N 07°50'·08W
324 Youghal, SE -
   2M SE of Blackball PHM ...... 51°54'·77N 07°45'·28W
325 Waterford -
   1·4M SSE of Dunmore E ...... 52°07'·42N 06°58'·85W
326 Coningbeg lt vsl - *0·4M N of* 52°02'·80N 06°39'·45W
327 Carnsore Pt - *3·2M ESE of* ... 52°09'·42N 06°16'·45W
328 Greenore Pt -*1·8M E of* ...... 52°14'·43N 06°15'·90W
329 Wexford - *1·6M E of* .... 52°20'·52N 06°19'·30W
330 W Blackwater SHM -
   0·4M W of .... 52°25'·82N 06°14'·06W
331 Cahore Point -*1·7M SE of* .... 52°32'·52N 06°09'·96W
332 Arklow - *1·2M E by S of* ...... 52°47'·42N 06°06'·36W
333 Mizen Head (E coast) -
   1M ESE of .... 52°51'·02N 06°01'·96W
334 Wicklow - *2·6M E of* .... 52°58'·92N 05°57'·86W
335 Dun Laoghaire - *2·2M NE of* . 53°19'·62N 06°04'·66W
336 Ben of Howth - *1·4M E of* ... 53°22'·42N 06°00'·56W
337 Malahide - *1·5M E of Bar*.... 53°27'·03N 06°04'·86W
338 Rockabill It- *1·2M WSW of* .. 53°35'·32N 06°02'·06W
339 Carlingford Lough SWM .... 53°58'·70N 06°01'·12W
340 Strangford Lough SWM .... 54°18'·62N 05°28'·69W
341 S Rock I vessel - *1·1M E of* . 54°24'·52N 05°20'·13W

1	Strangford Lough	**1**													
2	Bangor	34	**2**												
3	Carrickfergus	39	6	**3**											
4	Larne	45	16	16	**4**										
5	Carnlough	50	25	26	11	**5**									
6	Portrush	87	58	60	48	35	**6**								
7	Lough Foyle	92	72	73	55	47	11	**7**							
8	L Swilly (Fahan)	138	109	104	96	81	48	42	**8**						
9	Burtonport	153	130	130	116	108	74	68	49	**9**					
10	Killybegs	204	175	171	163	148	115	109	93	43	**10**				
11	Sligo	218	189	179	177	156	123	117	107	51	30	**11**			
12	Eagle Island	234	205	198	193	175	147	136	123	72	62	59	**12**		
13	Westport	295	266	249	240	226	193	187	168	120	108	100	57	**13**	
14	Galway	338	309	307	297	284	253	245	227	178	166	163	104	94	**14**
15	Kilrush	364	335	332	323	309	276	270	251	203	191	183	142	119	76	**15**

ee table on page 25 for distances anticlockwise between Kilrush and Carlingford Lough

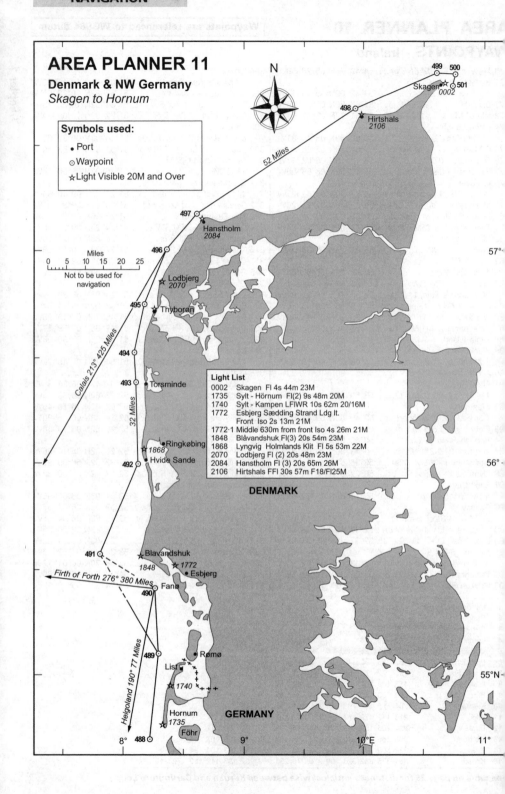

AREA PLANNER 11
Denmark & NW Germany
Skagen to Hornum

Symbols used:

- Port
- ⊙ Waypoint
- ☆ Light Visible 20M and Over

Miles
0 5 10 15 20 25
Not to be used for navigation

Light List

0002	Skagen	Fl 4s 44m 23M
1735	Sylt - Hörnum	Fl(2) 9s 48m 20M
1740	Sylt - Kampen	LFlWR 10s 62m 20/16M
1772	Esbjerg Sædding Strand Ldg lt. Front	Iso 2s 13m 21M
1772·1	Middle 630m from front	Iso 4s 26m 21M
1848	Blåvandshuk	Fl(3) 20s 54m 23M
1868	Lyngvig Holmlands Klit	Fl 5s 53m 22M
2070	Lodbjerg	Fl (2) 20s 48m 23M
2084	Hanstholm	Fl (3) 20s 65m 26M
2106	Hirtshals	FFl 30s 57m F18/Fl25M

Skagen 0002

Hirtshals 2106

52 Miles

Hanstholm 2084

Lodbjerg 2070

Thyborøn

Torsminde

Calais 213° 425 Miles

32 Miles

Ringkøbing

1868

Hvide Sande

DENMARK

Blavandshuk 1848

1772

Esbjerg

Fanø

Firth of Forth 276° 380 Miles

Helgoland 190° 77 Miles

Rømø

List

1740

Hornum 1735

Föhr

GERMANY

57°

56°

55°N

8° 9° 10°E 11°

AREA PLANNER 11

Waypoints are referenced to WGS84 datum

WAYPOINTS

Denmark & NW Germany - *Skagen to Hornum*

488 Hornum - *1·2M W*
of *Holtknobsloch landfall by* .54°40'·20N 08°08'·30E

489 Rømø - *0·4M W*
of *Lister Tief landfall by* .... 55°05'·34N 08°16'·00E

490 Esbjerg - *0·5M SW*
of *Grådyb landfall by* .... 55°24'·39N 08°11'·00E

491 Slugen Channel N - *9·6M W by N*
of *Blavands Huk lt* .... 55°35'·36N 07°48'·32E

492 Hvide Sande -
2·7M W of hbr ent .... 56°00'·00N 08°02'·42E

493 Torsminde -
2·7M W of hbr ent .... 56°22'·46N 08°02'·22E

494 Bovbjerg lt - *2·6M W of* .... 56°30'·76N 08°02'·52E

495 Thyborøn -
0·7M W of landfall by .... 56°42'·50N 08°07'·32E

496 Nørre Vorupør lt-
3·2M W of .... 56°57'·16N 08°16'·32E

497 Hanstholm -
1M NW of landfall by .... 57°08'·76N 08°33'·62E

498 Hirtshals -
2·3M N by W of hbr ent ...... 57°38'·00N 09°56'·50E

499 Skagen W lt - *2·2M N of* .... 57°47'·10N 10°35'·70E

500 Skagen SWM No1A -
1M S of .... 57°42'·43N 10°53'·43E

501 Skagen -
3·3M E of Skagen lt .... 57°44'·00N 10°43'·50E

		1	2	3	4	5	6	7	8	9	10	11	12	13	14	15	16	17	18
1	Skagen	1																	
2	Hirtshals	33	2																
3	Hanstholm	85	52	3															
4	Thyborøn	114	84	32	4														
5	Torsminde	141	108	56	24	5													
6	Hvide Sande	162	179	77	45	24	6												
7	Esbjerg	200	174	122	90	76	54	7											
8	Fanø	210	177	125	93	79	57	3	8										
9	Rømø	233	200	148	116	94	73	30	33	9									
10	Hörnum	248	215	163	131	108	86	70	73	29	10								
11	Husum	275	247	195	163	152	131	95	98	68	45	11							
12	Kiel/Holtenau	261	233	281	249	232	208	180	183	189	126	129	12						
13	Bremerhaven	306	285	233	201	185	163	127	129	107	83	82	123	13					
14	Wilhelmshaven	414	296	242	310	184	162	125	128	106	82	82	123	45	14				
15	Helgoland	259	238	186	154	141	119	83	85	63	39	47	104	44	43	15			
16	Cuxhaven	304	284	232	200	162	138	110	113	85	56	66	70	58	56	38	16		
17	Wangerooge	283	262	210	178	168	147	109	112	94	68	52	108	38	27	24	42	17	
18	Hamburg	338	317	265	233	216	192	163	167	139	99	113	90	81	110	88	54	61	18

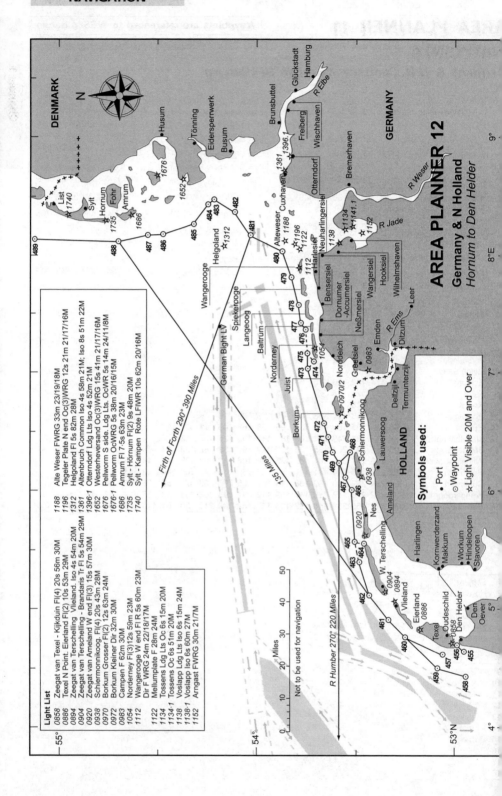

AREA PLANNER 12

Germany & N Holland
Hornum to Den Helder

Light List

0858	Zeegat van Texel - Kijkduin Fl(4) 20s 56m 30M
0886	Texel N Point. Eierland Fl(2) 10s 53m 29M
0894	Zeegat van Terschelling - Vlieland. Iso 4s 54m 20M
0904	Zeegat van Terschelling - Brandaris Tr Fl 5s 54m 29M
0920	Zeegat van Ameland W end Fl(3) 15s 57m 30M
0938	Schiermonnikoog. Fl(4) 20s 43m 28M
0970	Borkum Grosser Fl(2) 12s 63m 24M
0972	Borkum Kleiner Dir 32m 30M
0983	Campen F 62m 30M
1054	Norderney Fl(3)12s 59m 23M
1112	Wangerooge W end Fl R 5s 60m 23M
	Dir F WRG 24m 22/18/17M
1122	Mellumplate F 28m 24M
1134	Tossens Ldg Lts Oc 6s 15m 20M
1134·1	Tossens Oc 6s 51m 20M
1138	Voslapp Ldg Lts Iso 6s 15m 24M
1138·1	Voslapp Iso 6s 60m 27M
1152	Arngast FWRG 30m 21/7M

1188	Alte Weser FWRG 33m 23/19/18M
1196	Tegeler Plate N end Oc(3)WRG 12s 21m 21/17/16M
1312	Helgoland Fl 5s 82m 28M
1361	Altenbruch Common Iso 4s 58m 21M; Iso 8s 51m 22M
1396·1	Otterndorf Ldg Lts Iso 4s 52m 21M
1652	Westerheversand Oc(3)WRG 15s 41m 21/17/16M
1676	Pellworm S side. Ldg Lts. OcWR 5s 14m 24/11/8M
1676·1	Pellworm OcWRG 5s 38m 20/16/15M
1686	Amrum Fl 7·5s 63m 23M
1735	Sylt - Hörnum Fl(2) 9s 48m 20M
1740	Sylt - Kampen Rote LFlWR 10s 62m 20/16M

Symbols used:
- • Port
- ⊙ Waypoint
- ☆ Light Visible 20M and Over

Not to be used for navigation

DENMARK

GERMANY

HOLLAND

N

Waypoints are referenced to WGS84 datum

WAYPOINTS

Germany & N Holland - *Hornum to Den Helder*

5 Den Helder -
1·1M SW of Kijkduin lt .... 52°56'·90N 04°41'·90E

6 Den Helder -
1·1M N by E of Kijkduin lt .... 52°58'·40N 04°44'·10E

7 Molengat Channel - N ent .... 53°03'·00N 04°41'·00E

8 Noorderhaaks I -
3·2M WSW of .... 52°57'·30N 04°33'·70E

9 Texel -
0·3M W of Molengat NCM ... 53°00'·25N 04°34'·86E

10 Vlieland -
2·8M WNW of SW end of I ... 53°13'·50N 04°46'·60E

11 Vlieland -
W ent to Stortemelk chan. ... 53°19'·10N 04°55'·20E

12 Terschelling -
0·4M NW of Otto ECM .... 53°24'·82N 05°05'·94E

13 Terschelling - W ent
to Westgat buoyed chan. ...... 53°27'·80N 05°24'·00E

14 Borndiep Chan. -
1·3M WNW of Ameland lt.... 53°27'·60N 05°35'·60E

15 Ameland lt - 2·5M N of .... 53°29'·50N 05°37'·40E

16 Ameland -
2·9M NNE of E end .... 53°30'·40N 06°00'·00E

17 Schiermonnikoog N ent -
Westgat buoyed chan. .... 53°32'·50N 06°08'·40E

18 Schiermonnikoog E ent -
Lauwers buoyed chan. .... 53°33'·20N 06°17'·00E

19 Hubertgat SWM -
0·2M SSE of .... 53°34'·66N 06°14'·32E

20 Westerems SWM -
0·2M SE of ....53°36'·76N 06°19'·72E

21 Riffgat SWM - 0·2M SE of .... 53°38'·76N 06°27'·32E

22 Osterems SWM -
0·2M S of .... 53°41'·66N 06°36'·12E

473 Schluchter SWM - 0·2M S of 53°44'·25N 07°02'·17E

474 Norderney -
1·5M N by W of W end of I .. 53°43'·76N 07°06'·92E

475 Norderney - 0·5M S of Dovetief SWM
(frequently moved) .... 53°44'·77N 07°09'·80E

476 Baltrum - 1·4M N by E
of W end of Baltrum I .... 53°45'·00N 07°22'·40E

477 Langeoog - 0·2M N of Accumer Ee
SWM (frequently moved) ..... 53°47'·00N 07°24'·58E

478 Spiekeroog - 0·2M N of Otzumer Balje
SWM (frequently moved) ..... 53°48'·20N 07°37'·26E

479 Wangerooge -
0·2M N of Harle SWM .... 53°49'·48N 07°49'·00E

480 Neue Weser Chan. - 3·5M W by S
of Alte Weser lt .... 53°50'·86N 08°01'·82E

481 Elbe Chan. - 0·3M W
of Scharhörnriff NCM .... 53°59'·00N 08°10'·70E

482 Busum S Chan. -
0·2M W of Süderpiep SWM . 54°05'·88N 08°25'·32E

483 Busum N Chan. - 0·2M W
of Norderpiep SWM .... 54°11'·39N 08°28'·06E

484 Eidersperrwerk -
0·2M W of Eider SWM .... 54°14'·53N 08°27'·22E

485 Husum-
0·2M W of Hever SWM .... 54°20'·44N 08°18'·46E

486 Amrun -
0·2M W of Rütergat SWM ... 54°28'·22N 08°12'·89E

487 Hornum - 0·2M W
of Vortrapptief SWM .... 54°34'·87N 08°12'·61E

488 Hornum - 2M W
of Holtknobsloch SWM .... 54°40'·16N 08°06'·90E

489 Rømø - 0·4M W
of Lister Tief SWM .... 55°05'·34N 08°16'·00E

	1	2	3	4	5	6	7	8	9	10	11	12	13	14	15	16	17	18
Esbjerg	1																	
Hörnum Lt (Sylt)	47	2																
Husum	95	48	3															
Hamburg	163	112	113	4														
Kiel/Holtenau	179	128	129	90	5													
Brunsbüttel	126	75	76	37	53	6												
Cuxhaven	110	63	66	54	70	17	7											
Bremerhaven	127	80	82	81	131	78	58	8										
Wilhelmshaven	125	78	82	110	123	70	56	45	9									
Hooksiel	116	69	73	101	117	64	47	36	9	10								
Helgoland	83	38	47	88	104	51	38	44	43	35	11							
Wangerooge	109	60	52	61	108	55	42	38	27	19	24	12						
Langeoog	119	72	77	114	130	77	60	47	43	34	35	21	13					
Norderney	123	77	85	81	137	84	69	62	53	44	44	29	18	14				
Emden	165	129	137	174	190	137	120	115	106	97	85	80	63	47	15			
Borkum	133	97	105	104	163	110	95	88	80	71	67	55	46	31	32	16		
Delfzijl	155	119	127	159	173	120	105	100	89	83	81	65	56	41	10	22	17	
Den Helder	187	192	198	229	245	192	175	180	159	150	153	148	130	115	125	95	115	18

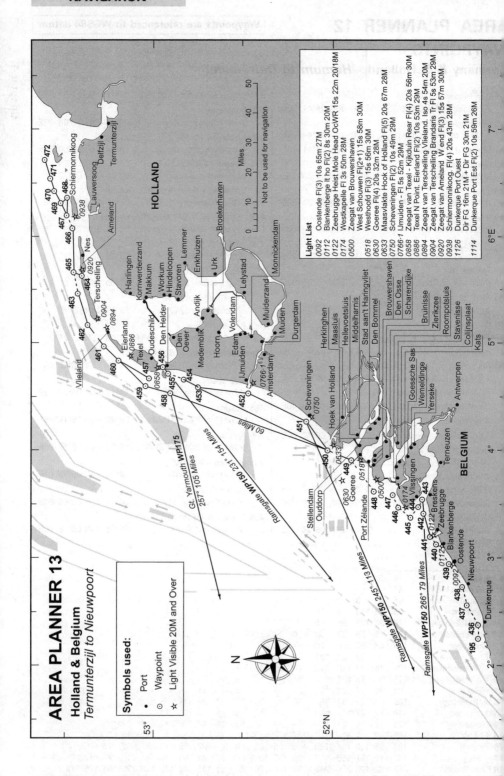

AREA PLANNER 13

Holland & Belgium
Termunterzijl to Nieuwpoort

Symbols used:

- Port
- ⊙ Waypoint
- ☆ Light Visible 20M and Over

Light List

0092	Oostende Fl(3) 10s 65m 27M
0112	Blankenberge lt ho Fl(2) 8s 30m 20M
0122	Zeebrugge Heist Mole Head OcWR 15s 22m 20/18M
0174	Westkapelle Fl 3s 50m 28M
0500	Zeegat van Brouwershaven
0518	West Schouwen Fl(2+1) 15s 58m 30M
0630	Westhoofd Fl(3) 15s 56m 30M
0633	Goeree Fl(4) 20s 32m 28M
0750	Maasvlakte Hook of Holland Fl(5) 20s 67m 28M
0766·1	Scheveningen Fl(2) 10s 49m 29M
0858	IJmuiden - Fl 5s 52m 29M
0886	Zeegat van Texel - Kijkduin Rear Fl(4) 20s 56m 30M
0894	Texel N Point. Eierland Fl(2) 10s 53m 29M
0904	Zeegat van Terschelling Vlieland. Iso 4s 54m 20M
0920	Zeegat van Terschelling Brandaris Tr Fl 5s 53m 29M
0938	Zeegat van Ameland W end Fl(3) 15s 57m 30M
1126	Schiermonnikoog. Fl(4) 20s 43m 28M
1114	Dunkerque Port Ouest
	Dir FG 16m 21M + Dir FG 30m 21M
	Dunkerque Port Est Fl(2) 10s 59m 26M

AREA PLANNER 13
WAYPOINTS

Waypoints for the UK, Holland & Belgium are referenced to WGS84 datum
French waypoints to ED50

Holland & Belgium - *Termunterzijl to Nieuwport*

50 Ramsgate - *1M E of* .... 51°19'·51N 01°27'·04E

75 Gt Yarmouth - *4·7M E of* ...... 52°34'·36N 01°52'·05E

95 Dunkerque - Port Est -
2M NW of .... 51°05'·00N 02°18'·40E

36 Dunkerque - Port Est -
1·7M NE by E of .... 51°04'·20N 02°23'·50E

37 Trapegeer SHM - *0·6M N of*. 51°09'·03N 02°34'·38E

38 Nieuwport -
0·9M NW by W of .... 51°09'·75N 02°41'·72E

39 Oostende - *0·5M NW of* ...... 51°14'·65N 02°54'·42E

40 Blankenberge -
0·8M NW of .... 51°19'·44N 03°05'·61E

41 Zeebrugge - *0·6M NW of* ..... 51°22'·27N 03°10'·73E

42 Ft Maisonnueve WCM -
0·3M NE of .... 51°24'·46N 03°21'·91E

43 Vlissingen -
1·4M NE of Niewe Sluis lt .... 51°25'·50N 03°32'·80E

44 Trawl SCM - *0·4M N of* .... 51°26'·70N 03°28'·22E

45 Westkapelle lt -
4M W by S of .... 51°31'·30N 03°20'·50E

46 Domburg - *2M NW of* .... 51°35'·60N 03°28'·00E

47 Roompotsluis -
S Channel 5M off .... 51°36'·20N 03°33'·20E

48 Geul Van de Banjaard -
N ent .... 51°44'·00N 03°33'·00E

49 Haringvlietsluizen -
ent to S Channel .... 51°51'·60N 03°53'·20E

50 Hoek van Holland -
1·2M WNW of ent to .... 51°59'·90N 04°00'·80E

51 Scheveningen -
0·7M NW of .... 52°07'·00N 04°14'·80E

52 IJmuiden -
0·7M W by N of ent .... 52°28'·10N 04°31'·10E

53 Petten WCM - *0·4M W of* ..... 52°47'·40N 04°36'·10E

454 Grote Kaap lt - *0·9M W of* .... 52°52'·90N 04°41'·40E

455 Den Helder -
1·1M SW of Kijkduin lt .... 52°56'·90N 04°41'·90E

456 Den Helder -
1·1M N by E of Kijkduin lt .... 52°58'·40N 04°44'·10E

457 Molengat Channel - *N ent* .... 53°03'·00N 04°41'·00E

458 Noorderhaaks I -
3·2M WSW of .... 52°57'·30N 04°33'·70E

459 Texel -
0·3M W of Molengat NCM ... 53°00'·25N 04°34'·86E

460 Vlieland -
2·8M WNW of SW end of I ... 53°13'·50N 04°46'·60E

461 Vlieland - *W of ent
to Stortemelk channel* .... 53°19'·10N 04°55'·20E

462 Terschelling -
0·4M NW of Otto ECM .... 53°24'·82N 05°05'·94E

463 Terschelling - *W ent
to Westgat buoyed channel*. 53°27'·80N 05°24'·00E

464 Borndiep Channel -
1·3M WNW of Ameland lt .... 53°27'·60N 05°35'·60E

465 Ameland lt - *2·5M N of* .... 53°29'·50N 05°37'·40E

466 Ameland -
2·9M NNE of E end .... 53°30'·40N 06°00'·00E

467 Schiermonnikoog *N ent -
Westgat buoyed channel* ..... 53°32'·50N 06°08'·40E

468 Schiermonnikoog *E ent -
Lauwers buoyed channel* ..... 53°33'·20N 06°17'·00E

469 Hubertgat SWM -
0·2M SSE of .... 53°34'·66N 06°14'·32E

470 Westereems SWM -
0·2M SE of .... 53°36'·76N 06°19'·72E

471 Riffgat SWM - *0·2M SE of* .... 53°38'·76N 06°27'·32E

472 Osterems SWM -
0·2M S of .... 53°41'·66N 06°36'·12E

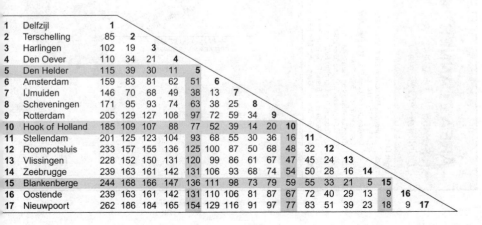

		1	2	3	4	5	6	7	8	9	10	11	12	13	14	15	16	17
1	Delfzijl	1																
2	Terschelling	85	2															
3	Harlingen	102	19	3														
4	Den Oever	110	34	21	4													
5	Den Helder	115	39	30	11	5												
6	Amsterdam	159	83	81	62	51	6											
7	IJmuiden	146	70	68	49	38	13	7										
8	Scheveningen	171	95	93	74	63	38	25	8									
9	Rotterdam	205	129	127	108	97	72	59	34	9								
10	Hook of Holland	185	109	107	88	77	52	39	14	20	10							
11	Stellendam	201	125	123	104	93	68	55	30	36	16	11						
12	Roompotsluis	233	157	155	136	125	100	87	50	68	48	32	12					
13	Vlissingen	228	152	150	131	120	99	86	61	67	47	45	24	13				
14	Zeebrugge	239	163	161	142	131	106	93	68	74	54	50	28	16	14			
15	Blankenberge	244	168	166	147	136	111	98	73	79	59	55	33	21	5	15		
16	Oostende	239	163	161	142	131	110	106	81	87	67	72	40	29	13	9	16	
17	Nieuwport	262	186	184	165	154	129	116	91	97	77	83	51	39	23	18	9	17

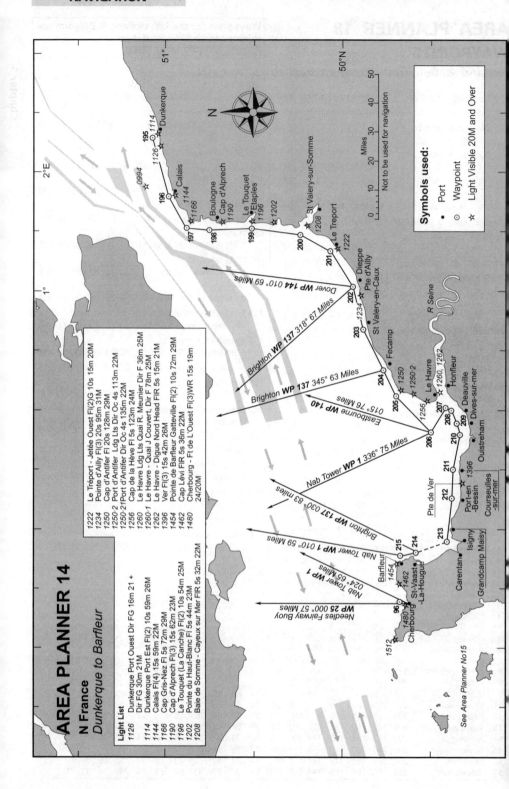

AREA PLANNER 14

N France
Dunkerque to Barfleur

Light List

1126	Dunkerque Port Ouest Dir FG 16m 21 +
	Dir FG 30m 21M
1114	Dunkerque Port Est Fl(2) 10s 59m 26M
1144	Calais Fl(4) 15s 59m 22M
1166	Cap Gris-Nez Fl 5s 72m 29M
1190	Cap d'Alprech Fl(3) 15s 62m 23M
1196	Le Touquet (La Canche) Fl(2) 10s 54m 25M
1202	Pointe du Haut-Blanc Fl 5s 44m 23M
1208	Baie de Somme - Cayeux sur Mer FIR 5s 32m 22M

1222	Le Tréport - Jetée Ouest Fl(2)G 10s 15m 20M
1234	Pointe d'Ailly Fl(3) 20s 95m 31M
1250	Cap d'Antifer Fl 20s 128m 29M
1250-2	Port d'Antifer Ldg Lts Dir Oc 4s 113m 22M
1256	Cap de la Hève Fl 5s 123m 24M
1260	Le Havre Ldg Lts Quai R. Meunier Dir F 36m 25M
1260-1	Le Havre - Qual J Couvert, Dir F 78m 25M
1262	Le Havre - Digue Nord Head FIR 5s 15m 21M
1396	Ver Fl(3) 15s 42m 26M
1454	Pointe de Barfleur Gatteville Fl(2) 10s 72m 29M
1462	Cap Lévi FIR 5s 36m 22M
1480	Cherbourg – Ft de L'Ouest Fl(3)WR 15s 19m 24/20M

Symbols used:

• Port

⊙ Waypoint

☆ Light Visible 20M and Over

Not to be used for navigation

Miles
0 10 20 30 40 50

See Area Planner No15

AREA PLANNER 14
WAYPOINTS
North France - *Dunkerque to Barfleur*

UK waypoints are referenced to WGS84 datum
French waypoints to ED50

1   Nab Tower - *0·5M NW of* ...... 50°40'·41N 00°57'·64W

25   Fairway Buoy -
  Needles Channel .... 50°38'·23N 01°38'·99W

96   Cherbourg -
  0·5M N of W ent .... 49°40'·95N 01°39'·35W

137   Brighton ent - *1M S of* .... 50°47'·53N 00°06'41W

140   Eastbourne -
  1·2M SE of Langney Point .... 50°46'·29N 00°21'·00E

141   Rye - *0·1M S*
  of Rye Fairway Buoy .... 50°53'·93N 00°48'·03E

144   Dover - *1·2M SE of W ent* .... 51°05'·83N 01°21'·00E

195   Dunkerque - *Port Est* -
  2M NW of ent .... 51°05'·00N 02°18'·40E

196   Calais - *2M NW of ent* .... 50°59'·25N 01°47'·78E

197   Cap Gris-Nez - *2M NW of* .... 50°53'·35N 01°32'·58E

198   Boulogne -
  2M WNW of ent .... 50°45'·30N 01°31'·50E

199   Étaples -
  3M W of Le Touquet Point .... 50°32'·20N 01°30'·80E

200   St Valéry-sur-Somme -
  5M WNW of Le Hourdel lt ..... 50°15'·30N 01°27'·10E

201   Le Trèport - *2M NW of ent* ... 50°05'·40N 01°20'·40E

202   Dieppe - *1M NW of ent* .... 49°57'·00N 01°04'·00E

203   St Valéry-en-Caux -
  2M N of ent .... 49°54'·50N 00°42'·30E

204   Fécamp - *1M NW of ent* ...... 49°46'·70N 00°20'·80E

205   Cap d'Antifer -
  1·8M NW of .... 49°42'·40N 00°07'·80E

206   Le Havre -
  0·5M NE of Le Havre LHA ... 49°31'·79N 00°09'·23W

207   Honfleur - *7·5M W of ent* ..... 49°27'·00N 00°02'·50E

208   Deauville -
  2·6M NNW of ent .... 49°24'·50N 00°02'·20E

209   Dives-sur-Mer -
  3M NNW of .... 49°20'·70N 00°07'·00W

210   Ouistreham -
  3·6M NNE of ent .... 49°21'·00N 00°11'·40W

211   Courseulles-sur-Mer -
  3M N of .... 49°23'·40N 00°27'·00W

212   Port-en-Bessin -
  3M NNE of .... 49°24'·00N 00°43'·60W

213   Grandcamp Maisy -
  4M NW of .... 49°26'·70N 01°06'·30W

214   St-Vaast-la-Hougue -
  3M ENE of .... 49°36'·40N 01°11'·00W

215   Barfleur - *2M NE of* .... 49°42'·00N 01°13'·30W

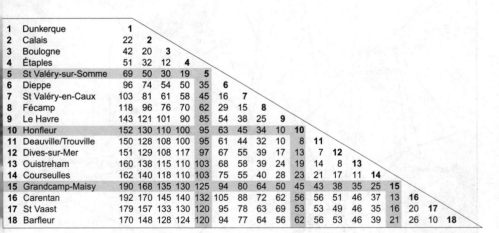

		1	2	3	4	5	6	7	8	9	10	11	12	13	14	15	16	17	18
1	Dunkerque	1																	
2	Calais	22	2																
3	Boulogne	42	20	3															
4	Étaples	51	32	12	4														
5	St Valéry-sur-Somme	69	50	30	19	5													
6	Dieppe	96	74	54	50	35	6												
7	St Valéry-en-Caux	103	81	61	58	45	16	7											
8	Fécamp	118	96	76	70	62	29	15	8										
9	Le Havre	143	121	101	90	85	54	38	25	9									
10	Honfleur	152	130	110	100	95	63	45	34	10	10								
11	Deauville/Trouville	150	128	108	100	95	61	44	32	10	8	11							
12	Dives-sur-Mer	151	129	108	117	97	67	55	39	17	13	7	12						
13	Ouistreham	160	138	115	110	103	68	58	39	24	19	14	8	13					
14	Courseulles	162	140	118	110	103	75	55	40	28	23	21	17	11	14				
15	Grandcamp-Maisy	190	168	135	130	125	94	80	64	50	45	43	38	35	25	15			
16	Carentan	192	170	145	140	132	105	88	72	62	56	56	51	46	37	13	16		
17	St Vaast	179	157	133	130	120	95	78	63	69	53	53	49	46	35	16	20	17	
18	Barfleur	170	148	128	124	120	94	77	64	56	62	56	53	46	39	21	26	10	18

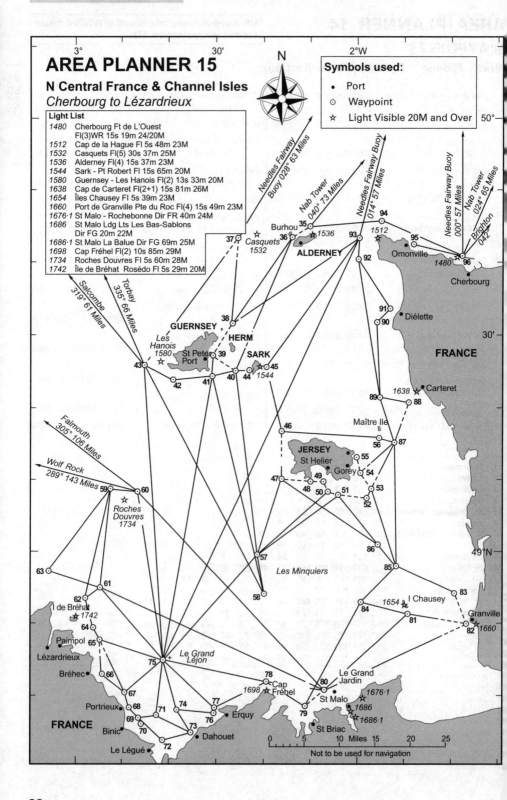

AREA PLANNER 15

N Central France & Channel Isles
Cherbourg to Lézardrieux

Light List
1480	Cherbourg Ft de L'Ouest Fl(3)WR 15s 19m 24/20M
1512	Cap de la Hague Fl 5s 48m 23M
1532	Casquets Fl(5) 30s 37m 25M
1536	Alderney Fl(4) 15s 37m 23M
1544	Sark - Pt Robert Fl 15s 65m 20M
1580	Guernsey - Les Hanois Fl(2) 13s 33m 20M
1638	Cap de Carteret Fl(2+1) 15s 81m 26M
1654	Îles Chausey Fl 5s 39m 23M
1660	Port de Granville Pte du Roc Fl(4) 15s 49m 23M
1676·1	St Malo - Rochebonne Dir FR 40m 24M
1686	St Malo Ldg Lts Les Bas-Sablons Dir FG 20m 22M
1686·1	St Malo La Balue Dir FG 69m 25M
1698	Cap Fréhel Fl(2) 10s 85m 29M
1734	Roches Douvres Fl 5s 60m 28M
1742	Île de Bréhat Rosédo Fl 5s 29m 20M

Symbols used:

- • Port
- ⊙ Waypoint
- ☆ Light Visible 20M and Over

Not to be used for navigation

AREA PLANNER 15
WAYPOINTS

*UK waypoints are referenced to WGS84 datum
Channel Is & French waypoints to ED50*

North Central France & Channel Is - *Cherbourg to Lezardrieux*

Chapter 1

Alderney, Bray Hbr -*1M NE of* .. 49°44'·60N 02°10'·63W
The Swinge - *trng wpt* .... 49°43'·50N 02°14'·40W
Casquets -*1M W of* .... 49°43'·38N 02°24'·06W
Guernsey NE -
1·2M E of Beaucette ....49°30'·13N 02°28'·30W
St Peter Port - *0·5M E of ent* . 49°27'·40N 02°30'·70W
Big Russel - *midway S*.......... 49°25'·30N 02°26'·00W
Guernsey -
1M SE of St Martin's Pt........ 49°24'·66N 02°30'·53W
Guernsey -
1·5M S of Pleinmont Pt .... 49°24'·00N 02°40'·00W
Guernsey -
1·8M W of Les Hanois.......... 49°26'·16N 02°45'·00W
Sark - *0·3M S of Brecou* .... 49°25'·47N 02°23'·30W
Sark - *1M E of Creux Hbr* ...... 49°25'·80N 02°19'·00W
Jersey -
1·75M NW of Grosnez Pt.......49°16'·60N 02°16'·75W
Jersey -
1M WSW of La Corbiere ....49°10'·46N 02°16'·32W
Jersey -
0·15M S of Noirmant Pt .... 49°09'·80N 02°10'·00W
St Helier - *0·3M S of bkwtr* ..... 49°09'·97N 02°07'·33W
St Helier -
0·3M S of Demie de Ras ...... 49°08'·73N 02°06'·11W
SE Jersey - *1st trng pt going E* 49°08'·05N 02°03'·35W
SE Jersey -
2nd trng pt to Gorey .... 49°07'·60N 01°57'·93W
SE Jersey -
3rd trng pt to Gorey .... 49°08'·70N 01°57'·20W
Gorey ent - *298°, 1·6M SE of* .. 49°11'·10N 01°59'·12W
St Catherine, Jersey -
0·5M SE of anchorage .... 49°13'·10N 02°00'·00W
Les Écrehou -
1·4M S of Maitre Ile Bn .... 49°15'·70N 01°55'·50W
NW Minquiers NCM -
0·1M W of .... 48°59'·70N 02°20'·65W
SW Minquiers WCM -
0·1M SW of .... 48°54'·34N 02°19'·42W
Roches Douvres lt - *3M NW of* 49°08'·60N 02°52'·10W
Roches Douvres lt - *2·5M NE of* 49°08'·10N 02°46'·20W
Lezardrieux -
1·5M N of La Horaire Bn .... 48°55'·07N 02°55'·15W
Lezardrieux appr - *1·7M NNE*. 48°53'·60N 02°58'·18W
Les Héaux de Brehat -
3M N of................................. 48°57'·60N 03°05'·10W

64 Rade de Brehat -
2·5M E by S of .... 48°49'·70N 02°56'·00W
65 Paimpol - *1M E of*
Les Charpentiers Bn .... 48°47'·90N 02°54'·40W
66 Bréhec -
0·8M E of Le Taureau Mk ...... 48°43'·60N 02°54'·00W
67 Ile Harbour lt - *1M NW of* ..... 48°40'·75N 02°49'·60W
68 St Quay Portrieux -
0·2M E of ent .... 48°38'·90N 02°48'·55W
69 La Roselière WCM - *0·3M S* .. 48°37'·25N 02°46'·40W
70 Binic - *2M 080° from bkwtr* .... 48°36'·50N 02°45'·85W
71 Caffa ECM By - *0·3M SE* ...... 48°37'·68N 02°42'·68W
72 Le Legué By - *0·2M NW of* .... 48°34'·52N 02°41'·28W
73 Dahouet - *1M NW of ent* ...... 48°35'·50N 02°35'·20W
74 Rohein WCM - *0·6M SW of*.... 48°38'·50N 02°38'·40W
75 Grand Léjon Lt Bn - *0·7M W of* 48°44'·90N 02°40'·80W
76 Erquy-*1M W of* .... 48°38'·10N 02°30'·00W
77 Cap d'Erquy - *0·6M WNW of* . 48°38'·95N 02°30'·00W
78 Cap Frehel Lt - *1·1M N of*..... 48°42'·50N 02°19'·07W
79 St Briac - *2M off on appr* ...... 48°38'·40N 02°10'·90W
80 St Malo - *1·3M NW of*
Le Grande Jardin Bn ....48°41'·10N 02°06'·40W
81 Iles Chausey - *1M S of ent* .... 48°51'·10N 01°49'·00W
82 Granville -
0·7M SW of Granville Lt .... 48°49'·62N 01°37'·55W
83 Iles Chausey -
0·5M E of Anvers ECM .... 48°54'·00N 01°40'·00W
84 SE Minquiers ECM - *1M SE of* . 48°52'·80N 01°58'·90W
85 Les Ardentes ECM Buoy -
0·2M E of............................. 48°57'·90N 01°51'·15W
86 NE Minquiers ECM -
0·1M NE of .... 49°00'·97N 01°55'·11W
87 Les Écrehou SE - *0·4M SE of*
Écrevière SCM .... 49°15'·10N 01°51'·65W
88 Cap de Carteret - *1·5M SW of* 49°20'·90N 01°49'·20W
89 Carteret - *0·3M SW of*
Trois Grunes WCM .... 49°21'·65N 01°55'·45W
90 Cap de Flamanville - *2M W of*.. 49°31'·65N 01°56'·30W
91 Diélette - *1M NW of*............. 49°34'·03N 01°52'·78W
92 Cap de la Hague - *4M SSW of* . 49°40'·54N 02°01'·55W
93 Cap de la Hague - *2·4M W of* .. 49°43'·49N 02°00'·17W
94 Cap de la Hague -
1·5M N of La Plate Lt .... 49°45'·50N 01°55'·70W
95 Omonville - *1M E of* .... 49°42'·55N 01°48'·25W
96 Cherbourg - *0·5M N of W ent*. 49°40'·95N 01°39'·35W

	1	2	3	4	5	6	7	8	9	10	11	12	13	14	15	16	17
1 Cherbourg	1																
2 Omonville	10	2															
3 Braye (Alderney)	25	15	3														
4 St Peter Port	44	34	23	4													
5 Creux (Sark)	37	29	22	10	5												
6 St Helier	64	51	46	29	24	6											
7 Carteret	41	29	28	31	23	26	7										
8 Portbail	49	33	32	35	27	25	5	8									
9 Iles Chausey	69	61	58	48	43	25	33	30	9								
10 Granville	75	67	66	55	50	30	38	35	9	10							
11 Dinan	102	91	85	66	64	50	62	59	29	35	11						
12 St Malo	90	79	73	54	52	38	50	47	17	23	12	12					
13 Dahouet	88	80	72	54	52	41	60	59	37	45	41	29	13				
14 Le Légué/St Brieuc	96	86	76	57	56	46	69	69	41	49	45	33	8	14			
15 Binic	95	84	75	56	55	46	70	70	43	51	45	33	10	8	15		
16 St Quay-Portrieux	88	80	73	56	51	46	64	64	47	54	47	35	11	7	4	16	
17 Lézardrieux	88	80	68	48	38	47	68	71	53	54	61	49	33	32	30	21	17

AREA PLANNER 16

NW France & Biscay
Ile de Bréhat to
Ile de Noirmoutier

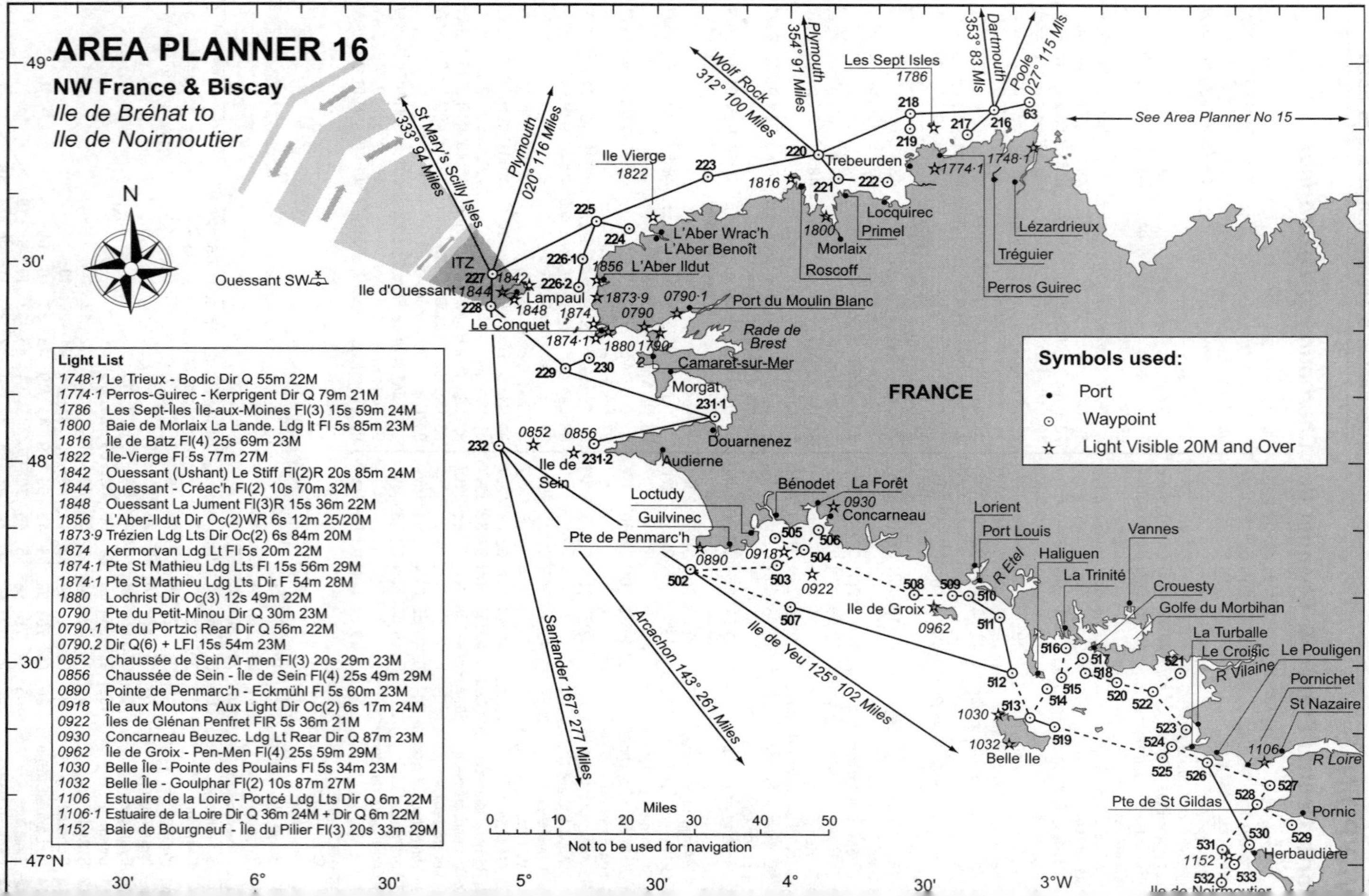

Symbols used:

- ● Port
- ◎ Waypoint
- ☆ Light Visible 20M and Over

FRANCE

Not to be used for navigation

Light List

1748·1 Le Trieux - Bodic Dir Q 55m 22M
1774·1 Perros-Guirec - Kerprigent Dir Q 79m 21M
1786 Les Sept-Iles Ile-aux-Moines Fl(3) 15s 59m 24M
1800 Baie de Morlaix La Lande. Ldg Lt Fl 5s 85m 23M
1816 Ile de Batz Fl(4) 25s 69m 23M
1822 Ile-Vierge Fl 5s 77m 27M
1842 Ouessant (Ushant) Le Stiff Fl(2)R 20s 85m 24M
1844 Ouessant - Créac'h Fl(2) 10s 70m 32M
1848 Ouessant La Jument Fl(3)R 15s 36m 22M
1856 L'Aber-Ildut Dir Oc(2)WR 6s 12m 25/20M
1873·9 Trézien Ldg Lts Dir Oc(2) 6s 84m 20M
1874 Kermorvan Ldg Lt Fl 5s 20m 22M
1874·1 Pte St Mathieu Ldg Lts Fl 15s 56m 29M
1874·1 Pte St Mathieu Ldg Lts Dir F 54m 28M
1880 Lochrist Dir Oc(3) 12s 49m 22M
1890 Ouessant SW
0790 Pte du Petit-Minou Dir Q 30m 23M
0790·1 Pte du Portzic Rear Dir Q 56m 22M
0790·2 Dir Q(6) + LFl 15s 54m 23M
0852 Chaussée de Sein Ar-men Fl(3) 20s 29m 23M
0856 Chaussée de Sein - Ile de Sein Fl(4) 25s 49m 29M
0890 Pointe de Penmarc'h - Eckmühl Fl 5s 60m 23M
0918 Ile aux Moutons Aux Light Dir Oc(2) 6s 17m 24M
0922 Iles de Glénan Penfret FlR 5s 36m 21M
0930 Concarneau Beuzec. Ldg Lt Rear Dir Q 87m 23M
0962 Ile de Groix - Pen-Men Fl(4) 25s 59m 29M
1030 Belle Ile - Pointe des Poulains Fl 5s 34m 23M
1032 Belle Ile - Goulphar Fl(2) 10s 87m 27M
1106 Estuaire de la Loire - Portcé Ldg Lts Dir Q 6m 22M
1106·1 Estuaire de la Loire Dir Q 36m 24M + Dir Q 6m 22M
1152 Baie de Bourgneuf - Ile du Pilier Fl(3) 20s 33m 29M

Plymouth 354° 91 Miles
Plymouth 020° 116 Miles
St Mary's Scilly Isles 333° 94 Miles
Poole 027° 115 Mls
Dartmouth 353° 83 Mls
Wolf Rock 312° 100 Miles
Ile de Yeu 125° 102 Miles
Arcachon 143° 261 Miles
Santander 167° 277 Miles

See Area Planner No 15

Miles

Ile d'Ouessant

N

38

Waypoints are referenced to ED50 datum

orth West France & Biscay - *Ile de Brehat to Ile de Noirmoutier*

Les Héaux de Brehat -
3M N of .... 48°57'·60N 03°05'·10W

6 Treguier - *4M NNW*
of Pte de Chateau .... 48°56'·20N 03°14'·30W

7 Perros Guirec -
2·3M NNW of Port Blanc ..... 48°52'·30N 03°20'·20W

8 Ile Bono lt - *4M NW of* .... 48°55'·50N 03°33'·90W

9 Ploumanach -
2·7M E of Les Triagoz .... 48°52'·32N 03°34'·67W

0 Roscoff - *6M NNE of ent* ...... 48°49'·10N 03°54'·30W

1 Morlaix & Primel - *2·2M NW*
of Pointe de Primel .... 48°45'·00N 03°51'·20W

2 Trebeurden - *1·5M S*
of Le Crapaud WCM .... 48°45'·23N 03°40'·50W

3 Pte de Beg-Pol lt - *4M N of* .. 48°44'·70N 04°20'·80W

4 L'Aber Wrach, L'Aber Benoit -
1M W of Libenter WCM .... 48°37'·60N 04°39'·90W

5 Gr Basse de Portsall WCM -
1·5M N of .... 48°38'·30N 04°45'·90W

6.1 Chenal du Four -
0.5M W of Le Four lt ho ...... 48°31'·50N 04°49'·00W

6.2 Chenal du Four -
Valbelle PHM buoy .... 48°26'·49N 04°49'·96W

7 Ouessant Créac'h lt -
3·5M NW of .... 48°30'·00N 05°11'·30W

8 Ouessant -
4·9M WSW of Lampaul .... 48°25'·30N 05°12'·30W

9 Vandrée WCM - *4·6M W of* ... 48°15'·30N 04°55'·00W

0 Chenal du Four, S Ent - *0·9M SW*
of Basse Royale SCM* .... 48°17'·20N 04°48'·20W

1.1 Douarnenez - *0.6M NW*
of Ile Tristan Lt (in R sector)* .... 48°06'·70N 04°20'·68W

1.2 Raz de Sein - *1M NW*
of La Plate* .... 48°02'·93N 04°46'·77W

2 Chaussée de Sein WCM -
1·6M SW of .... 48°02'·90N 05°09'·60W

2 Guilvinec -
5·5M SW of hbr ent .... 47°44'·30N 04°23'·50W

3 Concarneau appr - *2·3M SW*
of Ile aux Moutons lt* .... 47°44'·80N 04°03'·90W

4 Concarneau appr - *2·1M ENE*
of Ile aux Moutons lt* .... 47°47'·50N 03°58'·80W

5 Benodet -
3M S by E of river mouth ..... 47°48'·90N 04°05'·40W

6 Concarneau -
2M SSW of hbr ent .... 47°50'·40N 03°56'·50W

7 I de Glenan -*3M S*
of Jument de Glénan SCM* ... 47°35'·83N 04°01'·32W

508 Lorient -*3M NW by W*
of Pen Men lt* .... 47°40'·50N 03°34'·20W

509 Lorient Passe de L'Ouest - *0·9M SW*
of L Banc des Truies WCM* .. 47°40'·50N 03°25'·70W

510 Lorient S Chan -
2·3M S by W of ent .... 47°40'·40N 03°22'·50W

511 R Etel -
3M SW of river mouth .... 47°36'·60N 03°15'·70W

512 Quiberon Peninsula - *3
M W of* .... 47°28'·90N 03°11'·80W

513 Belle I - Le Palais -
1·3M NE of hbr ent .... 47°21'·60N 03°07'·50W

514 Pte de la Teignouse SW ent -
0·9M SW of .... 47°25'·20N 03°05'·20W

515 Pte de la Teignouse NE ent -
0·7M E of .... 47°26'·90N 03°00'·50W

516 La Trinite-sur-mer -
1·5M S by E of ent .... 47°32'·70N 02°59'·80W

517 Golfe du Morbihan -
2·2M S of ent channel .... 47°31'·00N 02°55'·20W

518 Chimère SCM - *0·5M SW of* . 47°28'·60N 02°54'·60W

519 Pte de Kerdonis lt - *2M NE of* 47°20'·20N 03°01'·50W

520 Pte de S Jacques lt -
1·8M S of .... 47°27'·40N 02°47'·40W

521 R Vilaine - *0·7M S*
of Les Mâts SCM* .... 47°28'·50N 02°34'·80W

522 Ile Dumet lt - *1·5M W of* ...... 47°24'·80N 02°39'·30W

523 La Turballe -
2M N of Pte du Croisic .... 47°19'·80N 02°32'·90W

524 Plateau du Four - *1·6M ESE*
of Le Four lt* .... 47°17'·40N 02°35'·80W

525 Plateau du Four -
0·4M S of Goué-Vas SCM ..... 47°14'·60N 02°38'·10W

526 Le Pouliguen - *2M W by S*
of Pt de Penchâteau* .... 47°15'·00N 02°27'·90W

527 St Nazaire -
3·5M SW of Pte Aiguillon lt ... 47°11'·40N 02°17'·60W

528 St Nazaire -
6·1M SW of Pte Aiguillon lt .. 47°09'·00N 02°19'·30W

529 Pornic - *2·1M WSW*
of Pornic hbr ent* .... 47°05'·70N 02°10'·00W

530 L'Herbaudière -
1·5M N by E of hbr ent .... 47°03'·10N 02°17'·50W

531 Ile du Pilier lt - *1·8M W of* .... 47°02'·60N 02°24'·10W

532 Chaussée des Boeufs -
SW ent .... 46°56'·70N 02°24'·10W

533 Ile Noirmoutier - *SW ent*
of Chenal de la Grise* .... 47°01'·10N 02°20'·80W

Lézardrieux 1	1	12	16	18	24	42	43	45	72	97	100	105	124	Pornic 12
Tréguier 2	22	2	11	12	24	39	40	41	66	87	90	95	113	St Nazaire 11
Perros-Guirec 3	28	21	3	10	13	30	30	34	55	78	80	85	106	La Baule/Pornichet 10
Trébeurden 4	40	32	17	4	9	18	22	27	48	73	75	79	100	Le Croisic 9
Morlaix 5	60	46	36	23	5	8	28	36	57	78	80	84	105	Arzal/Camoël 8
Roscoff 6	54	41	28	17	12	6	7	16	37	58	60	64	85	Crouesty 7
L'Aberwrac'h 7	84	72	60	49	48	32	7	6	26	47	48	54	74	Le Palais (Belle Ile) 6
Le Conquet 8	106	98	83	72	68	55	29	8	5	32	33	38	61	Lorient 5
Brest (marina) 9	114	107	92	83	79	67	42	18	9	4	4	12	37	Concarneau 4
Morgat 10	126	118	103	92	88	75	49	20	24	10	3	12	36	Port-la-Forêt 3
Douarnenez 11	131	123	108	97	93	80	54	25	29	11	11	2	30	Loctudy 2
Audierne 12	135	128	113	102	98	86	55	30	34	27	30	12	1	Audierne 1

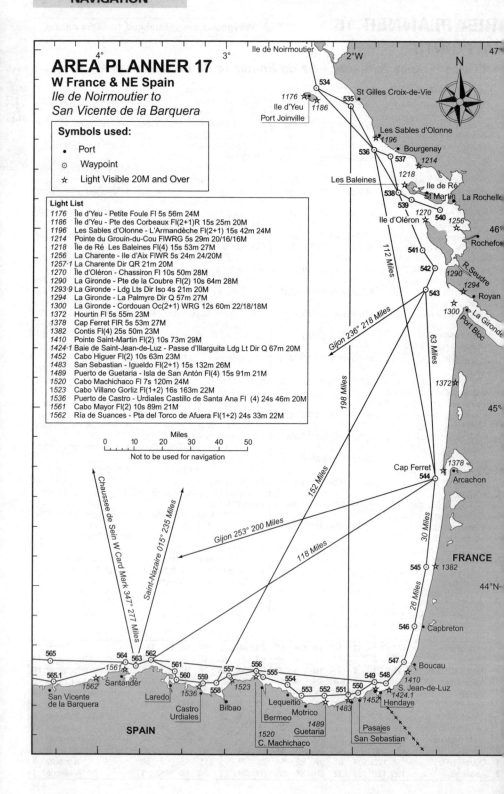

AREA PLANNER 17
W France & NE Spain
Ile de Noirmoutier to
San Vicente de la Barquera

Symbols used:

- • Port
- ⊙ Waypoint
- ☆ Light Visible 20M and Over

Light List

1176 Île d'Yeu - Petite Foule Fl 5s 56m 24M
1186 Île d'Yeu - Pte des Corbeaux Fl(2+1)R 15s 25m 20M
1196 Les Sables d'Olonne - L'Armandèche Fl(2+1) 15s 42m 24M
1214 Pointe du Grouin-du-Cou FlWRG 5s 29m 20/16/16M
1218 Île de Ré Les Baleines Fl(4) 15s 53m 27M
1256 La Charente - Ile d'Aix FlWR 5s 24m 24/20M
1257·1 La Charente Dir QR 21m 20M
1270 Île d'Oléron - Chassiron Fl 10s 50m 28M
1290 La Gironde - Pte de la Coubre Fl(2) 10s 64m 28M
1293·9 La Gironde - Ldg Lts Dir Iso 4s 21m 20M
1294 La Gironde - La Palmyre Dir Q 57m 27M
1300 La Gironde - Cordouan Oc(2+1) WRG 12s 60m 22/18/18M
1372 Hourtin Fl 5s 55m 23M
1378 Cap Ferret FlR 5s 53m 27M
1382 Contis Fl(4) 25s 50m 23M
1410 Pointe Saint-Martin Fl(2) 10s 73m 29M
1424·1 Baie de Saint-Jean-de-Luz - Passe d'Illarguita Ldg Lt Dir Q 67m 20M
1452 Cabo Higuer Fl(2) 10s 63m 23M
1483 San Sebastian - Igueldo Fl(2+1) 15s 132m 26M
1489 Puerto de Guetaria - Isla de San Antón Fl(4) 15s 91m 21M
1520 Cabo Machichaco Fl 7s 120m 24M
1523 Cabo Villano Gorliz Fl(1+2) 16s 163m 22M
1536 Puerto de Castro - Urdiales Castillo de Santa Ana Fl (4) 24s 46m 20M
1561 Cabo Mayor Fl(2) 10s 89m 21M
1562 Ría de Suances - Pta del Torco de Afuera Fl(1+2) 24s 33m 22M

Miles
0   10   20   30   40   50
Not to be used for navigation

Waypoints are referenced to ED50 datum

N France & NE Spain - *Ile de Nourmontier to San Vicente de la Barquera*

Chapter 1

34 Ile d'Yeu, Port Joinville -
2·4M N by E of hbr ent .... 46°46'·00N 02°19'·60W

35 St Gilles-Croix-de-Vie -
3M SW of ent .... 46°39'·70N 01°59'·60W

36 Les Sables-d'Olonne -
3·7M SW of ent .... 46°26'·30N 01°49'·60W

37 Bourgenay -
1·4M SW of SWM .... 46°24'·40N 01°43'·20W

38 Ile de Ré -
3M SW of Les Baleines lt ..... 46°12'·70N 01°37'·10W

39 La Rochelle appr chan. -
6·5M NW of Pte Chassiron .. 46°07'·40N 01°31'·60W

40 La Rochelle Ldg Lts -
6M SW by W of hbr ent ...... 46°06'·00N 01°17'·30W

41 Ile d'Oleron - *3·7M SW*
of Pte Chardonnière .... 45°54'·60N 01°26'·70W

42 R Seudre - *3M W*
of Pointe de Gatseau .... 45°47'·80N 01°18'·80W

43 R Gironde ent chan. - *7M SW*
of Pointe de la Coubre .... 45°38'·20N 01°22'·60W

44 Bassin d'Arcachon - *N ent -*
5M SW of Cap Ferret lt .... 44°35'·00N 01°19'·80W

45 Contis lt - *3·5M W of* .... 44°05'·70N 01°23'·80W

46 Capbreton -
1·9M W by N of hbr ent ...... 43°39'·80N 01°29'·50W

47 Boucau -
1·7M WNW of hbr bkwtr ...... 43°32'·80N 01°33'·70W

48 St Jean-de-Luz -
1·5M NNW of hbr ent .... 43°25'·50N 01°40'·80W

549 Hendaye -
1·8M N of Cabo Higuer lt ..... 43°25'·40N 01°47'·70W

550 Pasajes - *2M N of hbr ent* ... 43°22'·30N 01°55'·80W

551 San Sebastian -
2·2M N of ent to bay .... 43°21'·80N 01°59'·70W

552 Guetaria -
1·8M N of I de San Antón .... 43°20'·50N 02°11'·80W

553 Motrico -
1·8M NE of hbr ent .... 43°20'·10N 02°21'·00W

554 Lequeitio -
1·8M NNE of hbr ent .... 43°23'·60N 02°28'·60W

555 Bermeo - *2·2M NNE of* .... 43°27'·40N 02°41'·40W

556 Cabo Machichaco lt -
1·9M N of .... 43°29'·20N 02°45'·10W

557 Cabo Villano lt - *2·3M N of* ... 43°28'·30N 02°56'·60W

558 Abra de Bilbao -
2M N of hbr ent .... 43°24'·80N 03°04'·80W

559 Castro Urdiales -
1·9M NE of hbr ent .... 43°24'·40N 03°11'·00W

560 Laredo -
2M NE of Canto de Laredo .. 43°26'·80N 03°22'·50W

561 Punta del Pescador -
1·9M NE of .... 43°29'·10N 03°24'·20W

562 Cabo Ajo lt - *2·2M N of* .... 43°32'·90N 03°35'·30W

563 Santander -
1·7M N of I de St Marina ..... 43°30'·20N 03°43'·70W

564 Cabo Mayor lt - *1·7M N of* .... 43°31'·10N 03°47'·40W

565 St Vicente de la Barquera lt -
9·3M N of .... 43°33'·00N 04°23'·50W

		1	2	3	4	5	6	7	8	9	10	11	12	13	14	15	16
1	Port Joinville	1															
2	St Gilles-C-de-Vie	18	2														
3	Sables d'Olonne	31	16	3													
4	Bourgenay	40	25	9	4												
5	St Martin (I de Ré)	55	44	27	20	5											
6	La Rochelle	66	51	36	29	12	6										
7	Rochefort	84	75	61	54	36	26	7									
8	R La Seudre	89	71	58	52	33	24	30	8								
9	Port St Denis	59	48	33	30	21	13	26	22	9							
10	Port Bloc/Royan	97	85	71	60	56	52	68	27	42	10						
11	Bordeaux	152	140	126	115	111	107	123	82	97	55	11					
12	Cap Ferret	138	130	113	110	102	98	114	75	88	68	123	12				
13	Capbreton	192	186	169	166	165	156	172	131	145	124	179	58	13			
14	Anglet/Bayonne	200	195	181	178	177	168	184	143	157	132	187	70	12	14		
15	Santander	212	210	204	204	206	202	218	184	192	180	235	133	106	103	15	
16	Cabo Finisterre	377	395	393	394	406	407	423	399	397	401	456	376	370	373	274	16

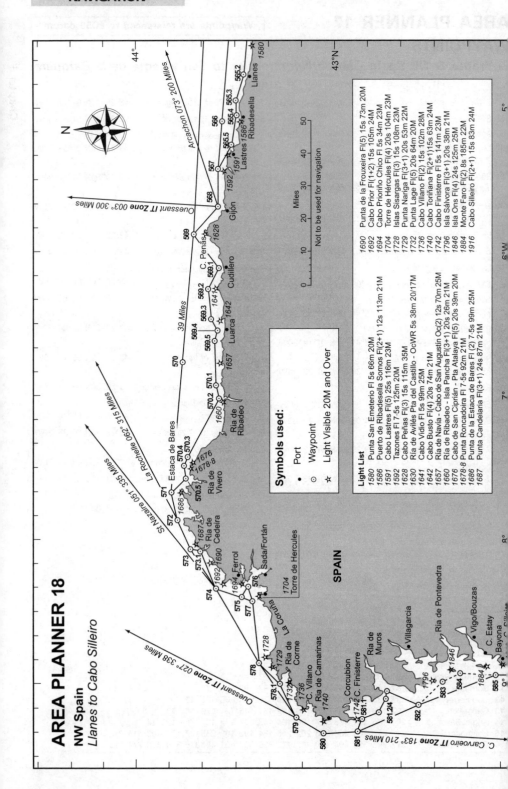

AREA PLANNER 18

NW Spain
Llanes to Cabo Silleiro

Symbols used:

- • Port
- ⊙ Waypoint
- ☆ Light Visible 20M and Over

Light List

1580	Punta San Emeterio Fl 5s 66m 20M
1586	Puerto de Ribadesella Somos Fl(2+1) 12s 113m 21M
1591	Cabo Lastres Fl(5) 25s 116m 23M
1592	Tazones Fl 7·5s 125m 20M
1628	Cabo Peñas Fl(3) 15s 115m 35M
1630	Ria de Avilés Pta del Castillo - OcWR 5s 38m 20/17M
1641	Cabo Vidio Fl 5s 99m 25M
1642	Cabo Busto Fl(4) 20s 74m 21M
1657	Ria de Navia - Cabo de San Augustín Oc(2) 12s 70m 25M
1660	Ria de Ribadeo - Isla Pancha Fl(3+1) 20s 26m 21M
1676	Cabo de San Ciprián - Pta Atalaya Fl(5) 20s 39m 20M
1678·8	Punta Roncadoira Fl 7·5s 92m 21M
1686	Punta de la Estaca de Bares Fl (2) 7·5s 99m 25M
1687	Punta Candelaria Fl(3+1) 24s 87m 21M

1690	Punta de la Frouxeira Fl(5) 15s 73m 20M
1692	Cabo Prior Fl(1+2) 15s 105m 24M
1694	Cabo Prioriño Chico Fl 5s 34m 23M
1704	Torre de Hércules Fl(4) 20s 104m 23M
1728	Islas Sisargas Fl(3) 15s 108m 23M
1729	Punta Nariga Fl(3+1) 20s 53m 22M
1732	Punta Lage Fl(5) 20s 64m 20M
1736	Cabo Villano Fl(2) 15s 102m 28M
1740	Cabo Toriñana Fl(2+1)15s 63m 24M
1742	Cabo Finisterre Fl 5s 141m 23M
1796	Isla Sálvora Fl(3+1) 20s 38m 21M
1846	Isla Ons Fl(4) 24s 125m 25M
1884	Monte Faro Fl(2) 8s 185m 22M
1916	Cabo Silleiro Fl(2+1) 15s 83m 24M

SPAIN

Not to be used for navigation

AREA PLANNER 18
WAYPOINTS
NW Spain - *Llanes to Cabo Silleiro*

65.2 Llanes -
1·5M N of hbr ent .... 43°26'·70N 04°44'·90W

65.3 Cabo de Mar -
1·5M N of headland .... 43°29'·20N 04°55'·70W

66 Punta de Somos lt -
6·3M N of .... 43°34'·70N 05°05'·00W

66.1 Ribadesella -
1·5M N of hbr ent .... 43°29'·60N 05°03'·90W

66.2 Lastres -
1·5M NE of hbr ent .... 43°32'·00N 05°14'·33W

67 Tazones lt - 2·7M N of ..... 43°35'·60N 05°24'·00W

68 Gijon -
1·9M ENE of bkwtr lt .... 43°35'·00N 05°38'·20W

69 Cabo Peñas lt - 3·1M N of. 43°42'·50N 05°50'·80W

69.1 Cudillero -
1·5M N of hbr ent .... 43°35'·47N 06°08'·86W

69.2 Cabo Vidio - 1·7M N of lt... 43°37'·30N 06°14'·82W

69.3 Cabo Busto - 1·5M N of lt. 43°35'·69N 06°28'·23W

69.4 Luarca - 1·5M N of hbr ent 43°34'·54N 06°32'·21W

69.5 Romanellas -
1·5M N of headland .... 43°35'·97N 06°37'·67W

70 Cabo San Augustin lt -
11·8M N of .... 43°45'·80N 06°44'·00W

70.1 Cabo S Sebastian -
1·75M N of lt .... 43°36'·23N 06°56'·81W

70.2 Ribadeo -
1·75M N of Ria ent........... 43°35'·21N 07°02'·21W

70.3 Los Farallones Is -
1·5M N of .... 43°44'·90N 07°26'·36W

70.4 Punta Roncadoira -
1·8M N of lt .... 43°45'·81N 07°31'·59W

70.5 Vivero -
3·5M N of Punta de Faro .. 43°46'·30N 07°35'·00W

71 Punta de la Estaca de Bares lt -
2M N of .... 43°49'·30N 07°41'·10W

72 Punta de los Aguillones lt -
2·5M N of .... 43°48'·80N 07°52'·10W

573 Punta Candelaria lt -
2·1M NW of .... 43°44'·30N 08°04'·70W

573.1 Cedeira -
0·5M W of Pta Lameda .... 43°40'·94N 08°05'·16W

574 Cabo Prior lt - 3·4M NW of 43°36'·70N 08°21'·50W

575 Cabo Prioriño Chico lt -
4·4M WNW of .... 43°29'·40N 08°25'·80W

576 El Ferrol approach - 1·4M SW
of Cabo Prioriño Chico lt ... 43°26'·70N 08°21'·80W

577 La Coruña - 3·3M NW
of Torre de Hercules lt .... 43°25'·10N 08°28'·00W

578 Sisargas I lt - 2·9M NW of 43°23'·70N 08°53'·50W

578.1 Corme - 1·8M W
of Pta del Roncundo .... 43°16'·57N 09°01'·86W

579 Cabo Villano lt -
3·6M NW of .... 43°11'·50N 09°16'·60W

579.1 Camariñas - 1·9M NW
of Punta de la Barca .... 43°08'·20N 09°14'·95W

580 Cabo Toriñana lt -
2·7M W of .... 43°03'·30N 09°21'·50W

581 Cabo Finisterre lt -
4M W of .... 42°52'·80N 09°21'·60W

581.1 Corcubion -
1·5M S of Cabo Finisterre. 42°51'·50N 09°16'·20W

581.2 Bajo de los Meixidos -
1M W of .... 42°45'·60N 09°14'·10W

581.3 Los Bruyos I - 2M SW of .. 42°42'·80N 09°10'·30W

581.4 Muros -
1·8M SSW of Pta Queixal . 42°42'·80N 09°05'·70W

582 Cabo Corrubedo lt -
4·2M WSW .... 42°33'·40N 09°10'·60W

583 Villagarcia -
2·5M S of Isla Salvora lt ... 42°25'·50N 09°00'·70W

584 Vigo - NW approach -
5M W of Pta Couso lt .... 42°18'·60N 08°58'·00W

585 Vigo/Bayona - SW approach -
3·8M NW of C Silleiro lt .... 42°08'·70N 08°57'·50W

		1	2	3	4	5	6	7	8	9
1	Bilbao (ent)	1								
2	Santander	36	2							
3	Gijón	116	90	3						
4	Cabo Peñas	126	96	10	4					
5	Ría de Ribadeo	179	149	63	53	5				
6	Cabo Ortegal	214	184	98	88	40	6			
7	La Coruña	252	222	136	126	78	38	7		
8	Cabo Villano	284	254	168	158	110	70	43	8	
9	Bayona	355	325	239	229	181	141	114	71	9

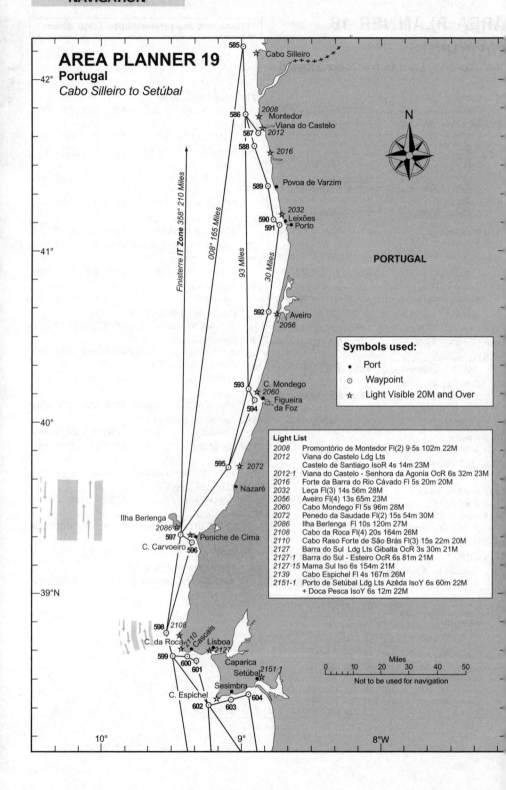

AREA PLANNER 19
Portugal
Cabo Silleiro to Setúbal

585
Cabo Silleiro

N

2008
586 ✦ Montedor
Viana do Castelo
587 ⊙ 2012
588 ⊙ ✦ 2016

589 ● Povoa de Varzim

2032
590 ✦ Leixões
591 ● Porto

PORTUGAL

592 ⊙ ✦ Aveiro
2056

Symbols used:

- ● Port
- ⊙ Waypoint
- ✦ Light Visible 20M and Over

593 ⊙ C. Mondego
✦ 2060
Figueira
594 ● da Foz

595 ⊙ ✦ 2072

● Nazaré

Ilha Berlenga
2086 ✦
597 ✦ Peniche de Cima
C. Carvoeiro 596

598 ⊙ 2108
● C. da Roca 2110 Cascais Lisboa
✦ 2127
599 ⊙ 600 ⊙ Caparica 2151·1
601 Setúbal ✦
Sesimbra
C. Espichel
602 603 604

Finisterre IT Zone 358° 210 Miles
008° 165 Miles
93 Miles
30 Miles

Light List
2008	Promontório de Montedor Fl(2) 9·5s 102m 22M
2012	Viana do Castelo Ldg Lts
	Castelo de Santiago IsoR 4s 14m 23M
2012·1	Viana do Castelo - Senhora da Agonia OcR 6s 32m 23M
2016	Forte da Barra do Rio Cávado Fl 5s 20m 20M
2032	Leça Fl(4) 13s 65m 23M
2056	Aveiro Fl(4) 13s 65m 23M
2060	Cabo Mondego Fl 5s 96m 28M
2072	Penedo da Saudade Fl(2) 15s 54m 30M
2086	Ilha Berlenga Fl 10s 120m 27M
2108	Cabo da Roca Fl(4) 20s 164m 26M
2110	Cabo Raso Forte de São Brás Fl(3) 15s 22m 20M
2127	Barra do Sul Ldg Lts Gibalta OcR 3s 30m 21M
2127·1	Barra do Sul - Esteiro OcR 6s 81m 21M
2127·15	Mama Sul Iso 6s 154m 21M
2139	Cabo Espichel Fl 4s 167m 26M
2151·1	Porto de Setúbal Ldg Lts Azêda IsoY 6s 60m 22M
	+ Doca Pesca IsoY 6s 12m 22M

Miles
0   10   20   30   40   50
Not to be used for navigation

42°
41°
40°
39°N

10°
9°
8°W

AREA PLANNER 19

Waypoints are referenced to ED50 datum

WAYPOINTS

Portugal - *Cabo Silleiro to Setúbal*

585 Vigo/Bayona - SW appr -
3·8M NW of Cabo Silleiro lt . 42°08'·70N 08°57'·50W

586 Montedor lt - *3·8M W of* ...... 41°44'·90N 08°57'·50W

587 Viano do Castelo (ldg lts) -
1·2M from bkwtr .... 41°39'·20N 08°51'·00W

588 Viano do Castelo (ldg lts) -
5·5M from bkwtr .... 41°35'·00N 08°52'·00W

589 Póvoa de Varzim -
1·6M WSW of hbr ent .... 41°21'·50N 08°48'·10W

590 Porto de Leixões -
2M W of bkwtr .... 41°10'·20N 08°45'·00W

591 Porto -
1·5M W of river mouth .... 41°08'·50N 08°42'·80W

592 Aveiro - *2M W of bkwtr* .... 40°38'·60N 08°48'·20W

593 Cabo Mondego lt -
3M W of .... 40°11'·30N 08°58'·10W

594 Figueira da Foz -
2·1M W of bkwtr .... 40°08'·60N 08°55'·00W

595 Nazaré - *2·8M W of hbr ent* . 39°35'·40N 09°08'·40W

596 Peniche de Cima -
1·5M SW of hbr ent .... 39°20'·00N 09°23'·84W

597 Cabo Carvoeiro lt -
3M W by N of .... 39°22'·50N 09°28'·30W

598 Cabo da Roca lt -
3·5M W of .... 38°47'·00N 09°34'·20W

599 Cabo Raso lt - *3·3M SW of* . 38°40'·40N 09°32'·10W

600 Cascais -
1·5M S of S Marta lt .... 38°40'·00N 09°25'·20W

601 Lisboa (ldg lts) -
5M SW of Gibalta lt .... 38°38'·60N 09°20'·50W

602 Cabo Espichel lt -
3·1M SW of .... 38°22'·50N 09°15'·40W

603 Sesimbra (ldg lts) -
1·5M S of hbr ent .... 38°24'·80N 09°06'·10W

604 Sétubal (ldg lts) -
3·5M SW of Outão lt .... 38°26'·80N 08°58'·60W

		1										
1	Longships	1										
2	Ushant (Créac'h)	100	2									
3	La Coruña	418	338	3								
4	Cabo Villano	439	365	43	4							
5	Bayona	510	436	114	71	5						
6	Viana do Castelo	537	468	141	98	32	6					
7	Leixões (Pôrto)	565	491	169	126	63	33	7				
8	Nazaré	659	585	263	220	156	127	97	8			
9	Cabo Carvoeiro	670	596	274	231	171	143	114	22	9		
10	Cabo Raso	710	636	314	271	211	183	154	62	40	10	
11	Lisboa (bridge)	686	652	330	287	227	199	170	78	56	16	11
12	Cabo Espichel	692	658	336	293	233	205	176	84	62	22	23	12

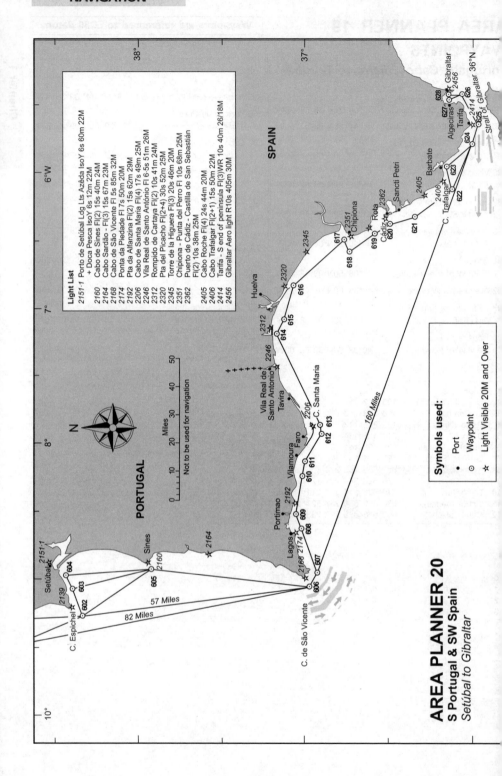

AREA PLANNER 20
S Portugal & SW Spain
Setúbal to Gibraltar

Light List

2151-1	Porto de Setúbal Ldg Lts Azêda IsoY 6s 60m 22M + Doca Pesca IsoY 6s 12m 22M
2160	Cabo de Sines Fl(2) 15s 40m 24M
2164	Cabo Sardão - Fl(3) 15s 67m 23M
2168	Cabo de São Vicente Fl 5s 85m 32M
2174	Ponta da Piedade Fl 7s 50m 20M
2192	Pta da Alfanzina Fl(2) 15s 62m 29M
2206	Cabo de Santa Maria Fl(4) 17s 49m 25M
2246	Vila Real de Santo António Fl 6.5s 51m 26M
2312	Rompido de Cartaya Fl(2) 10s 41m 24M
2320	Pta del Picacho Fl(2+4) 30s 52m 25M
2345	Torre de la Higuera Fl(3) 20s 46m 20M
2362	Chipiona - Punta del Perro Fl 10s 68m 25M Puerto de Cádiz - Castilla de San Sebastián Fl(2) 10s 38m 25M
2405	Cabo Roche Fl(4) 24s 44m 20M
2406	Cabo Trafalgar Fl(2+1) 15s 50m 22M
2414	Tarifa - S end of peninsula Fl(3)WR 10s 40m 26/18M
2456	Gibraltar Aero light R10s 405m 30M

Symbols used:

- ● Port
- ⊙ Waypoint
- ☆ Light Visible 20M and Over

SPAIN

PORTUGAL

Not to be used for navigation

Portugal & SW Spain - *Setúbal to Gibraltar*

2 Cabo Espichel -
3·1M SW of ....38°22'·50N 09°15'·40W

3 Sesimbra (ldg lts) -
1·5M S of hbr ent ....38°24'·80N 09°06'·10W

4 Sétubal (ldg lts) -
3·3M SW of Outão lt ....38°26'·80N 08°58'·60W

5 Sines - 1M W of bkwtr ....37°56'·30N 08°54'·60W

6 Cabo de São Vicente lt -
3M SW of ....36°59'·50N 09°02'·50W

7 Pta de Sagres lt -
2·5M S of ....36°57'·20N 08°56'·80W

8 Lagos - 1·4M SE
of Punta da Piedade lt .... 37°04'·00N 08°38'·80W

9 Portimão - 2M S of hbr ent ... 37°04'·40N 08°31'·50W

10 Albufeira lt - 2·6M S of ....37°02'·60N 08°14'·80W

11 Vilamoura -
1·6M SSW of hbr ent ....37°02'·60N 08°08'·20W

12 I da Barreta - 2M SW of ......36°56'·50N 07°57'·30W

13 Faro/Olhào -
1M SSW of ent chan. ....36°56'·70N 07°52'·60W

14 Santo António -
1.5M S of river mouth ....37°08'·50N 07°23'·60W

15 Fish Haven off Ria Higuerita -
1·7M S of ....37°05'·80N 07°20'·00W

616 Huelva -
1M S of river mouth ....37°05'·60N 06°49'·60W

617 Chipiona/Sanlúcar (ldg lts) -
0·5M WSW of SWM ....36°45'·70N 06°27'·50W

618 Punta del Perro lt -
3·2M W of ....36°44'·80N 06°30'·40W

619 Bahia de Cádiz - 2·2M SSW
of Punta Candor ....36°36'·10N 06°24'·80W

620 Cadiz - 1·6M W by S
of Castillo de San Sebastián .36°31'·40N 06°20'·80W

621 Sancti Petri -
3M SW of chan. ent .... 36°21'·00N 06°15'·30W

622 Cabo Trafalgar lt -
3·6M SW of ....36°08'·50N 06°05'·20W

623 Barbate -
1·1M S of end of bkwtr ....36°09'·70N 05°55'·40W

624 Pta Paloma lt - 4·6M SSW of .35°59'·50N 05°45'·00W

625 Tarifa -
1·3M S of I de Tarifa lt ....35°58'·80N 05°36'·60W

626 Pta Carnero lt - 1·8M SE of ..36°03'·40N 05°24'·00W

627 Algeciras -
1·2M SE of end of bkwtr ......36°08'·20N 05°24'·40W

628 Gibraltar -
0·8M SW of E Head pier ....36°08'·60N 05°22'·80W

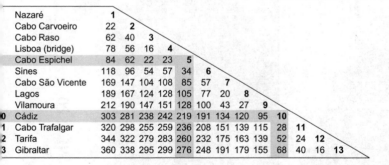

Nazaré	**1**												
Cabo Carvoeiro	22	**2**											
Cabo Raso	62	40	**3**										
Lisboa (bridge)	78	56	16	**4**									
Cabo Espichel	84	62	22	23	**5**								
Sines	118	96	54	57	34	**6**							
Cabo São Vicente	169	147	104	108	85	57	**7**						
Lagos	189	167	124	128	105	77	20	**8**					
Vilamoura	212	190	147	151	128	100	43	27	**9**				
Cádiz	303	281	238	242	219	191	134	120	95	**10**			
Cabo Trafalgar	320	298	255	259	236	208	151	139	115	28	**11**		
Tarifa	344	322	279	283	260	232	175	163	139	52	24	**12**	
Gibraltar	360	338	295	299	276	248	191	179	155	68	40	16	**13**

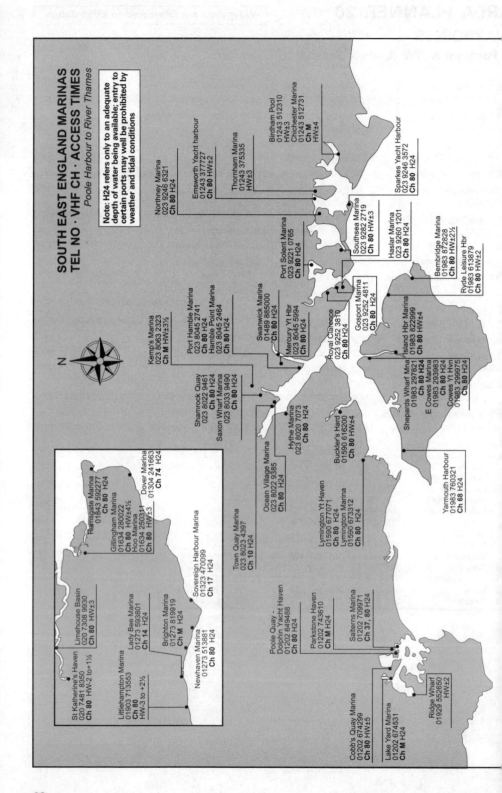

SOUTH EAST ENGLAND MARINAS
TEL NO · VHF CH · ACCESS TIMES
Poole Harbour to River Thames

Note: H24 refers only to an adequate depth of water being available; entry to certain ports may well be prohibited by weather and tidal conditions

N

Northney Marina
023 9246 6321
Ch 80 H24

Emsworth Yacht harbour
01243 377727
Ch 80 HW±2

Thornham Marina
01243 375335
HW±3

Birdham Pool
01243 512310
HW±3
Chichester Marina
01243 512731
Ch M
HW±4

Sparkes Yacht Harbour
023 9246 3572
Ch 80 H24

Port Solent Marina
023 9221 0765
Ch 80 H24

Southsea Marina
023 9282 2719
Ch 80 HW±3

Haslar Marina
023 9260 1201
Ch 80 H24

Bembridge Marina
01983 872828
Ch 80 HW±2½

Ryde Leisure Hbr
01983 613879
Ch 80 H24

Kemp's Marina
023 8063 2323
Ch M HW±3½

Port Hamble Marina
023 8045 2741
Ch 80 H24
Hamble Point Marina
023 8045 2464
Ch 80 H24

Swanwick Marina
01489 885000
Ch 80 H24

Mercury Yt Hbr
023 8045 5994
Ch 80 H24

Royal Clarence
023 9252 3810
Ch 80 H24

Gosport Marina
023 9252 4811
Ch 80 H24

Island Hbr Marina
01983 822999
Ch 80 HW±4

Shamrock Quay
023 8022 9461
Ch 80 H24
Saxon Wharf Marina
023 8033 9490
Ch 80 H24

Shepards Wharf Mna
01983 297821
Ch 80 H24
E Cowes Marina
01983 293983
Ch 80 H24
Cowes Yt Hvn
01983 299975
Ch 80 H24

Ocean Village Marina
023 8022 9385
Ch 80 H24

Hythe Marina
023 8020 7073
Ch 80 H24

Buckler's Hard
01590 616200
Ch 80 HW±4

Yarmouth Harbour
01983 760321
Ch 68 H24

Ramsgate Marina
01843 592277
Ch 80 H24

Gillingham Marina
01634 280022
Ch 80 HW±4½
Hoo Marina
01634 250311
Ch 80 HW±3

Dover Marina
01304 241663
Ch 74 H24

Town Quay Marina
023 8023 4397
Ch 10 H24

Lymington Yt Haven
01590 677071
Ch 80 H24
Lymington Marina
01590 673312
Ch 80 H24

Sovereign Harbour Marina
01323 470099
Ch 17 H24

St Katherine's Haven
020 7481 8350
Ch 80 HW-2 to+1½

Limehouse Basin
020 7308 9930
Ch 80 HW±3

Littlehampton Marina
01903 713553
Ch 80
HW-3 to +2½

Lady Bee Marina
01273 593801
Ch 14 H24

Brighton Marina
01273 819919
Ch M H24

Newhaven Marina
01273 513881
Ch 80 H24

Poole Quay –
Dolphin Yacht Haven
01202 649488
Ch 80 H24

Parkstone Haven
01202 743610
Ch M H24

Salterns Marina
01202 709971
Ch 37, 80 H24

Cobb's Quay Marina
01202 674299
Ch 80 HW±5

Lake Yard Marina
01202 674531
Ch M H24

Ridge Wharf
01929 552650
HW±2

Stromness Marina
01856 850744
Ch 12 H24

Kirkwall Marina
01856 872292
Ch 12 H24

ORKNEY Is.

SCOTLAND AND
EAST ENGLAND MARINAS
TEL NO · VHF CH · ACCESS TIMES
River Thames to the Firth of Clyde

Caley Marina
01463 236539
Ch 74 H24
Seaport Marina
01463 233140
Ch 74, 16
HW±4½

Lossiemouth 01343 813066
Ch 12 HW±4

Whitehills Marina
01261 861291
Ch 80 H24

Nairn Marina
01667 454330
Ch 10 HW±2

Peterhead Bay Marina
01779 474020
Ch 14 H24

SCOTLAND

Melfort Pier
01852 200333
Ch 80 H24

Dunstaffnage Marina
01631 566555 **Ch M** H24

Craobh Haven Marina
01852 500222
Ch 80 H24

> Note: H24 refers only to an adequate
> depth of water being available; entry to
> certain ports may well be prohibited by
> weather and tidal conditions

Ardfern Yacht Centre
01852 500247
Ch 80 H24

Sand Point Marina
01389 762396 H24

Port Edgar
0131 3313330
Ch 80 H24

NORTH SEA

Bellanoch
01546 603210
Ch 74 H24

Largs Yacht Haven
01475 675333
Ch 80 H24

Rhu Marina
01436 820238
Ch 80 H24

Clyde Marina
01294 607077
Ch 80 H24

Amble Marina 01665 712168
Ch 80 HW±4

Troon Yacht Haven
01292 315553
Ch 80 H24

North Shields Royal Quays Marina
0191 272 8282 **Ch 80** H24
St Peters Marina 0191 265 4472 **Ch 80** HW±3½

Holy Loch Marina
01369 701800
Ch 80, M H24

Sunderland Marina
0191 514 4721
Ch M H24

Hartlepool Marina
01429 865744
Ch M HW±5

Kip Marina
01475 521485
Ch 80 H24

Whitby Marina
01947 602354
Ch 11 HW±2

ENGLAND

Hull Marina
01482 330505
Ch 80 HW±3

South Ferriby Marina
01652 635620
Ch 74, 80 HW±3

Meridian Quay Marina
01472 268424
Ch 74 HW±2

Boston 01205 364420
Ch 12 HW±2

Wisbech Marina
01945 588059
Ch 9 HW±3

Fox's Marina 01473 689111 **Ch 80** H24
Neptune Marina 01473 236644 **Ch M, 80** H24
Ipswich Haven Marina 01473 215204 **Ch 80** H24
Woolverstone Marina 01473 780206 **Ch 80** H24
Suffolk Yacht Hbr 01473 659240 **Ch M** H24

Shotley Marina
01473 788982
Ch M H24

N

Bradwell Marina 01621 776235 **Ch 80, M** HW±4½
Blackwater Marina 01621 740264 **Ch M** HW±2
Burnham Yacht Harbour 01621 782150 **Ch M** H24
Tollesbury Marina 01621 869202 **Ch 80** HW-2
Essex Marina 01702 258531 **Ch M** H24
Heybridge Basin 01621 853506 **Ch 80** HW±1
West Wick Marina 01621 741268 **Ch M** HW±5
Bridge Marsh Marina 01621 740414 **Ch 80** HW±4

Titchmarsh Marina
01255 672185
Ch 80 HW±5

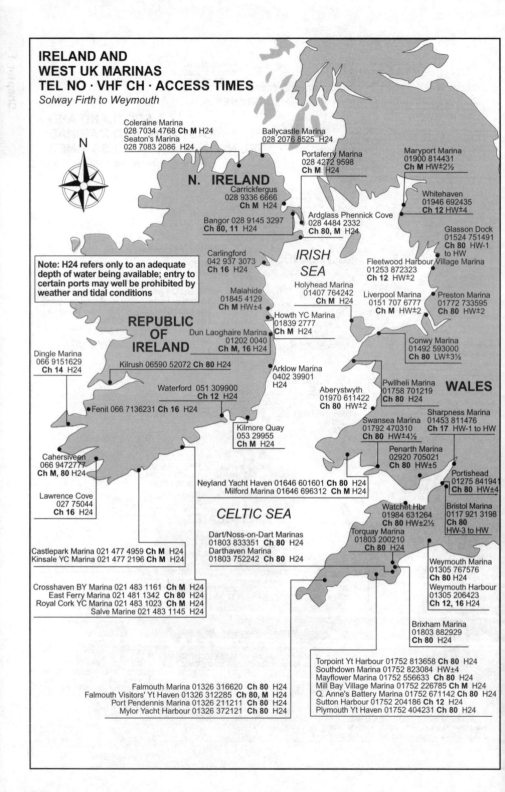

IRELAND AND
WEST UK MARINAS
TEL NO · VHF CH · ACCESS TIMES
Solway Firth to Weymouth

N

Coleraine Marina
028 7034 4768 **Ch M** H24
Seaton's Marina
028 7083 2086 H24

Ballycastle Marina
028 2076 8525 H24

Portaferry Marina
028 4272 9598
Ch M H24

Maryport Marina
01900 814431
Ch M HW±2½

N. IRELAND
Carrickfergus
028 9336 6666
Ch M H24

Whitehaven
01946 692435
Ch 12 HW±4

Bangor 028 9145 3297
Ch 80, 11 H24

Ardglass Phennick Cove
028 4484 2332
Ch 80, M H24

Glasson Dock
01524 751491
Ch 80 HW-1
to HW

Carlingford
042 937 3073
Ch 16 H24

*IRISH
SEA*

Fleetwood Harbour Village Marina
01253 872323
Ch 12 HW±2

Note: H24 refers only to an adequate
depth of water being available; entry to
certain ports may well be prohibited by
weather and tidal conditions

Malahide
01845 4129
Ch M HW±4

Holyhead Marina
01407 764242
Ch M H24

Liverpool Marina
0151 707 6777
Ch M HW±2

Preston Marina
01772 733595
Ch 80 HW±2

**REPUBLIC
OF
IRELAND**

Howth YC Marina
01839 2777
Ch M H24

Dun Laoghaire Marina
01202 0040
Ch M, 16 H24

Conwy Marina
01492 593000
Ch 80 LW±3½

Dingle Marina
066 9151629
Ch 14 H24

Kilrush 06590 52072 **Ch 80** H24

Arklow Marina
0402 39901
H24

Waterford 051 309900
Ch 12 H24

Aberystwyth
01970 611422
Ch 80 HW±2

Pwllheli Marina
01758 701219
Ch 80 H24

WALES

Fenit 066 7136231 **Ch 16** H24

Kilmore Quay
053 29955
Ch M H24

Swansea Marina
01792 470310
Ch 80 HW±4½

Sharpness Marina
01453 811476
Ch 17 HW-1 to HW

Cahersiveen
066 9472777
Ch M, 80 H24

Penarth Marina
02920 705021
Ch 80 HW±5

Lawrence Cove
027 75044
Ch 16 H24

Neyland Yacht Haven 01646 601601 **Ch 80** H24
Milford Marina 01646 696312 **Ch M** H24

Portishead
01275 841941
Ch 80 HW±4

CELTIC SEA

Watchet Hbr
01984 631264
Ch 80 HW±2½

Bristol Marina
0117 921 3198
Ch 80
HW-3 to HW

Castlepark Marina 021 477 4959 **Ch M** H24
Kinsale YC Marina 021 477 2196 **Ch M** H24

Dart/Noss-on-Dart Marinas
01803 833351 **Ch 80** H24
Darthaven Marina
01803 752242 **Ch 80** H24

Torquay Marina
01803 200210
Ch 80 H24

Weymouth Marina
01305 767576
Ch 80 H24

Crosshaven BY Marina 021 483 1161 **Ch M** H24
East Ferry Marina 021 481 1342 **Ch 80** H24
Royal Cork YC Marina 021 483 1023 **Ch M** H24
Salve Marine 021 483 1145 H24

Weymouth Harbour
01305 206423
Ch 12, 16 H24

Brixham Marina
01803 882929
Ch 80 H24

Torpoint Yt Harbour 01752 813658 **Ch 80** H24
Southdown Marina 01752 823084 HW±4
Mayflower Marina 01752 556633 **Ch 80** H24
Mill Bay Village Marina 01752 226785 **Ch M** H24
Q. Anne's Battery Marina 01752 671142 **Ch 80** H24
Sutton Harbour 01752 204186 **Ch 12** H24
Plymouth Yt Haven 01752 404231 **Ch 80** H24

Falmouth Marina 01326 316620 **Ch 80** H24
Falmouth Visitors' Yt Haven 01326 312285 **Ch 80, M** H24
Port Pendennis Marina 01326 211211 **Ch 80** H24
Mylor Yacht Harbour 01326 372121 **Ch 80** H24

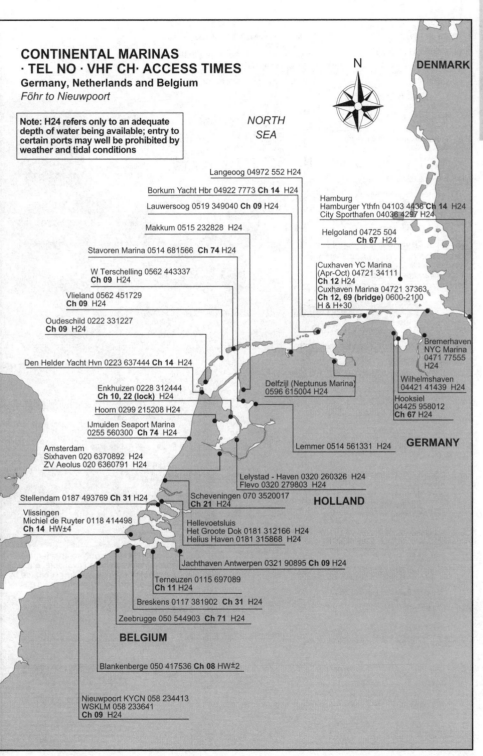

CONTINENTAL MARINAS
· TEL NO · VHF CH· ACCESS TIMES
Germany, Netherlands and Belgium
Föhr to Nieuwpoort

Note: H24 refers only to an adequate depth of water being available; entry to certain ports may well be prohibited by weather and tidal conditions

NORTH SEA

N

DENMARK

Langeoog 04972 552 H24

Borkum Yacht Hbr 04922 7773 **Ch 14** H24

Lauwersoog 0519 349040 **Ch 09** H24

Makkum 0515 232828 H24

Hamburg
Hamburger Ythfn 04103 4438 **Ch 14** H24
City Sporthafen 04036 4297 H24

Stavoren Marina 0514 681566 **Ch 74** H24

W Terschelling 0562 443337 **Ch 09** H24

Helgoland 04725 504 **Ch 67** H24

Cuxhaven YC Marina (Apr-Oct) 04721 34111 **Ch 12** H24
Cuxhaven Marina 04721 37363, **Ch 12, 69 (bridge)** 0600-2100 H & H+30

Vlieland 0562 451729 **Ch 09** H24

Oudeschild 0222 331227 **Ch 09** H24

Bremerhaven NYC Marina 0471 77555 H24

Den Helder Yacht Hvn 0223 637444 **Ch 14** H24

Enkhuizen 0228 312444 **Ch 10, 22 (lock)** H24

Delfzijl (Neptunus Marina) 0596 615004 H24

Wilhelmshaven 04421 41439 H24
Hooksiel 04425 958012 **Ch 67** H24

Hoorn 0299 215208 H24

IJmuiden Seaport Marina 0255 560300 **Ch 74** H24

Amsterdam
Sixhaven 020 6370892 H24
ZV Aeolus 020 6360791 H24

Lemmer 0514 561331 H24 GERMANY

Lelystad - Haven 0320 260326 H24
Flevo 0320 279803 H24

Stellendam 0187 493769 **Ch 31** H24

Scheveningen 070 3520017 **Ch 21** H24 HOLLAND

Vlissingen
Michiel de Ruyter 0118 414498 **Ch 14** HW±4

Hellevoetsluis
Het Groote Dok 0181 312166 H24
Helius Haven 0181 315868 H24

Jachthaven Antwerpen 0321 90895 **Ch 09** H24

Terneuzen 0115 697089 **Ch 11** H24

Breskens 0117 381902 **Ch 31** H24

Zeebrugge 050 544903 **Ch 71** H24

BELGIUM

Blankenberge 050 417536 **Ch 08** HW±2

Nieuwpoort KYCN 058 234413
WSKLM 058 233641 **Ch 09** H24

51

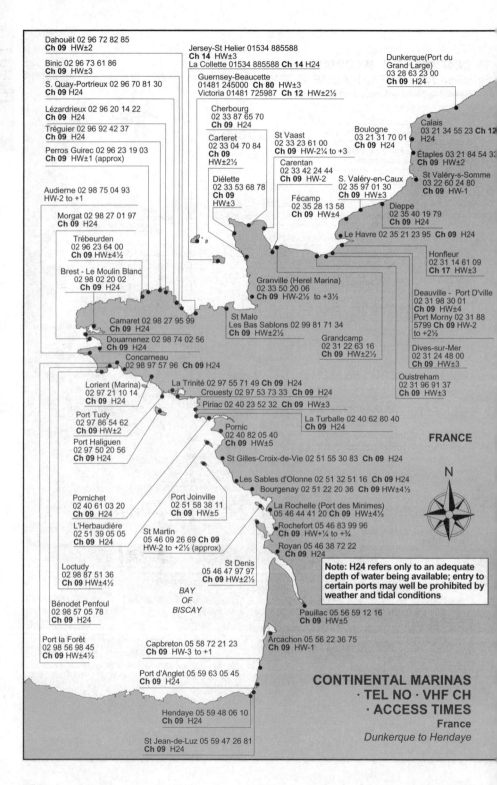

Dahouët 02 96 72 82 85
Ch 09 HW±2

Binic 02 96 73 61 86
Ch 09 HW±3

S. Quay-Portrieux 02 96 70 81 30
Ch 09 H24

Lézardrieux 02 96 20 14 22
Ch 09 H24

Tréguier 02 96 92 42 37
Ch 09 H24

Perros Guirec 02 96 23 19 03
Ch 09 HW±1 (approx)

Audierne 02 98 75 04 93
HW-2 to +1

Morgat 02 98 27 01 97
Ch 09 H24

Trébeurden
02 96 23 64 00
Ch 09 HW±4½

Brest - Le Moulin Blanc
02 98 02 20 02
Ch 09 H24

Camaret 02 98 27 95 99
Ch 09 H24
Douarnenez 02 98 74 02 56
Ch 09 H24

Concarneau
02 98 97 57 96 **Ch 09** H24

Lorient (Marina)
02 97 21 10 14
Ch 09 H24

Port Tudy
02 97 86 54 62
Ch 09 HW±2
Port Haliguen
02 97 50 20 56
Ch 09 H24

Pornichet
02 40 61 03 20
Ch 09 H24

L'Herbaudière
02 51 39 05 05
Ch 09 H24

Loctudy
02 98 87 51 36
Ch 09 HW±4½

Bénodet Penfoul
02 98 57 05 78
Ch 09 H24

Port la Forêt
02 98 56 98 45
Ch 09 HW±4½

Port Joinville
02 51 58 38 11
Ch 09 HW±5

St Martin
05 46 09 26 69 **Ch 09**
HW-2 to +2½ (approx)

Capbreton 05 58 72 21 23
Ch 09 HW-3 to +1

Port d'Anglet 05 59 63 05 45
Ch 09 H24

Hendaye 05 59 48 06 10
Ch 09 H24

St Jean-de-Luz 05 59 47 26 81
Ch 09 H24

Jersey-St Helier 01534 885588
Ch 14 HW±3
La Collette 01534 885588 **Ch 14** H24

Guernsey-Beaucette
01481 245000 **Ch 80** HW±3
Victoria 01481 725987 **Ch 12** HW±2½

Cherbourg
02 33 87 65 70
Ch 09 H24

Carteret
02 33 04 70 84
Ch 09
HW±2½

Diélette
02 33 53 68 78
Ch 09
HW±3

St Vaast
02 33 23 61 00
Ch 09 HW-2¼ to +3

Carentan
02 33 42 24 44
Ch 09 HW-2

Fécamp
02 35 28 13 58
Ch 09 HW±4

Granville (Herel Marina)
02 33 50 20 06
Ch 09 HW-2½ to +3½

St Malo
Les Bas Sablons 02 99 81 71 34
Ch 09 HW±2½

Grandcamp
02 31 22 63 16
Ch 09 HW±2½

La Trinité 02 97 55 71 49 **Ch 09** H24
Crouesty 02 97 53 73 33 **Ch 09** H24

Piriac 02 40 23 52 32 **Ch 09** HW±3

La Turballe 02 40 62 80 40
Ch 09 H24

Pornic
02 40 82 05 40
Ch 09 HW±5

St Gilles-Croix-de-Vie 02 51 55 30 83 **Ch 09** H24

Les Sables d'Olonne 02 51 32 51 16 **Ch 09** H24
Bourgenay 02 51 22 20 36 **Ch 09** HW±4½

La Rochelle (Port des Minimes)
05 46 44 41 20 **Ch 09** HW±4½
Rochefort 05 46 83 99 96
Ch 09 HW+¼ to +¾
Royan 05 46 38 72 22
Ch 09 H24

St Denis
05 46 47 97 97
Ch 09 HW±2½

Pauillac 05 56 59 12 16
Ch 09 HW±5

Arcachon 05 56 22 36 75
Ch 09 HW-1

Dunkerque(Port du
Grand Large)
03 28 63 23 00
Ch 09 H24

Calais
03 21 34 55 23 **Ch 12**
H24

Boulogne
03 21 31 70 01
Ch 09 H24

Étaples 03 21 84 54 33
Ch 09 HW±2

St Valéry-s-Somme
03 22 60 24 80
Ch 09 HW-1

S. Valéry-en-Caux
02 35 97 01 30
Ch 09 HW±3

Dieppe
02 35 40 19 79
Ch 09 H24

Le Havre 02 35 21 23 95 **Ch 09** H24

Honfleur
02 31 14 61 09
Ch 17 HW±3

Deauville - Port D'ville
02 31 98 30 01
Ch 09 HW±4
Port Morny 02 31 88
5799 **Ch 09** HW-2
to +2½

Dives-sur-Mer
02 31 24 48 00
Ch 09 HW±3

Ouistreham
02 31 96 91 37
Ch 09 HW±3

FRANCE

N

BAY
OF
BISCAY

Note: H24 refers only to an adequate
depth of water being available; entry to
certain ports may well be prohibited by
weather and tidal conditions

CONTINENTAL MARINAS
· TEL NO · VHF CH
· ACCESS TIMES
France
Dunkerque to Hendaye

CONTINENTAL MARINAS · TEL NO · VHF CH · ACCESS TIMES

Spain and Portugal
Bilbao to Gibraltar

BAY OF BISCAY

Ria deVivero 982 561014
Ch 16 H24

Ria de Ribadeo 982 110020
Ch 16 H24

La Coruña
981 203265
Ch 09 H24

Santander del Cantábrico
942 369288
Ch 09 H24

Portosin 981 826140
Ch 09 H24

Gijón 985 34 45 43
Ch 09 H24

Bilbao Getxo
94 4912367
Ch 09 H24

Bayona Monte Real Club de
ates 986 355576 **Ch 06** H24

Sangenjo 986 720517 **Ch 09** H24
Aguete 986 702373 H24

Ria de Arosa
Sta Eugenia Marina 981 873801 **Ch 09** H24
Puebla del Caraminal 981 877317 **Ch 09** H24
Villagarcia 986 511175 **Ch 09** H24
Piedras Negras 986 738430 H24

Viana do Castelo
258 359546
Ch 62 H24

Vigo Marina 986 224003
Ch 09 H24

Leixões
Porto Atlantico
229 964895 **Ch 62** H24

Povoa de Varzim
252 688212 **Ch 62** H24

Note: H24 refers only to an adequate
depth of water being available; entry to
certain ports may well be prohibited by
weather and tidal conditions

Figueira da Foz 233 402910
Ch 08 H24

Nazaré 262 561401
Ch 11 H24

SPAIN

Peniche
262 781153
Ch 16 H24

PORTUGAL

Lisboa
Bom Successo 213 631246 H24
Belém 213 631246 H24
Santo Amaro 213 631246 H24
Alcântara 213 631246 **Ch 12** H24
Doca de Terreiro do Trigo 218 876854 H24
Marina EXPO 218 985000 **Ch 62** H24

Cascais
214 824800
Ch 62 H24

Ayamonte 959 321694 **Ch 09** HW-3
Isla Canela 959 479000 **Ch 09** HW-3
Isla Cristina 959 343501 **Ch 09** HW-3

Vila Real de S. Antonio
281 541571 **Ch 12** HW-3

Sines 269 860612
Ch 11 H24

Mazagón 959 536251
Ch 09 H24

Rota 956 840069
Sherry 956 870303
Sta Maria 956 854400
Ch 09 H24

Lagos 282 770210
Ch 62 H24

Sancti-Petri 956 496169
Ch 09 HW-3

Barbate 956 431907
Ch 09 H24

Vilamoura 289 310560
Ch 62 H24

Gibraltar

Sheppards 350 75148 **Ch 71** H24
Marina Bay 350 73300 **Ch 73** H24
Queensway 350 44700 **Ch 71** H24

Chipiona 956 373844
Ch 09 H24

Cadiz RCN 956 253903 **Ch 09** H24
América 956 224240 **Ch 09** H24

Algeciras 956 572503
Ch 09 H24

MOROCCO

Times are in UT - add 1 hour in non-shaded areas to convert to DST

2004 Sunrise and Sunset Time

The times are based on **LAT 50°00'N   LONG 0°00'** - add 4 min for every degree West and subtract 4 min for every degree East

	Rise h m	Set h m	Rise h m	Set h m	Rise h m	Set h m	Rise h m	Set h m	Rise h m	Set h m	Rise h m	S h
	JANUARY		FEBRUARY		MARCH		APRIL		MAY		JUNE	
1	07 59	16 08	07 35	16 53	06 43	17 43	05 36	18 32	04 36	19 19	03 56	20
2	07 59	16 09	07 33	16 55	06 41	17 44	05 34	18 34	04 34	19 21	03 55	20
3	07 58	16 10	07 32	16 56	06 39	17 46	05 32	18 35	04 32	19 22	03 54	20
4	07 58	16 11	07 30	16 58	06 37	17 48	05 30	18 37	04 31	19 24	03 54	20
5	07 58	16 12	07 29	17 00	06 35	17 49	05 28	18 39	04 29	19 25	03 53	20
6	07 58	16 14	07 27	17 02	06 32	17 51	05 25	18 40	04 27	19 27	03 53	20
7	07 57	16 15	07 26	17 03	06 30	17 52	05 23	18 42	04 26	19 28	03 52	20
8	07 57	16 16	07 24	17 05	06 28	17 54	05 21	18 43	04 24	19 30	03 52	20
9	07 57	16 17	07 22	17 07	06 26	17 56	05 19	18 45	04 23	19 31	03 51	20
10	07 56	16 19	07 21	17 09	06 24	17 57	05 17	18 46	04 21	19 33	03 51	20
11	07 56	16 20	07 19	17 10	06 22	17 59	05 15	18 48	04 19	19 34	03 51	20
12	07 55	16 21	07 17	17 12	06 20	18 01	05 13	18 50	04 18	19 36	03 51	20
13	07 55	16 23	07 15	17 14	06 17	18 02	05 11	18 51	04 17	19 37	03 50	20
14	07 54	16 24	07 14	17 15	06 15	18 04	05 09	18 53	04 15	19 38	03 50	20
15	07 53	16 26	07 12	17 17	06 13	18 05	05 07	18 54	04 14	19 40	03 50	20
16	07 52	16 27	07 10	17 19	06 11	18 07	05 05	18 56	04 12	19 41	03 50	20
17	07 52	16 29	07 08	17 21	06 09	18 09	05 03	18 57	04 11	19 43	03 50	20
18	07 51	16 30	07 06	17 22	06 07	18 10	05 01	18 59	04 10	19 44	03 50	20
19	07 50	16 32	07 05	17 24	06 04	18 12	04 59	19 01	04 08	19 45	03 50	20
20	07 49	16 33	07 03	17 26	06 02	18 13	04 57	19 02	04 07	19 47	03 50	20
21	07 48	16 35	07 01	17 27	06 00	18 15	04 55	19 04	04 06	19 48	03 51	20
22	07 47	16 36	06 59	17 29	05 58	18 17	04 53	19 05	04 05	19 49	03 51	20
23	07 46	16 38	06 57	17 31	05 56	18 18	04 51	19 07	04 04	19 50	03 51	20
24	07 45	16 40	06 55	17 33	05 54	18 20	04 49	19 08	04 03	19 52	03 52	20
25	07 44	16 41	06 53	17 34	05 51	18 21	04 47	19 10	04 02	19 53	03 52	20
26	07 42	16 43	06 51	17 36	05 49	18 23	04 45	19 11	04 01	19 54	03 52	20
27	07 41	16 45	06 49	17 38	05 47	18 24	04 43	19 13	04 00	19 55	03 53	20
28	07 40	16 46	06 47	17 39	05 45	18 26	04 41	19 15	03 59	19 56	03 53	20
29	07 39	16 48	06 45	17 41	05 43	18 28	04 40	19 16	03 58	19 58	03 54	20
30	07 37	16 50			05 41	18 29	04 38	19 18	03 57	19 59	03 54	20
31	07 36	16 51			05 38	18 31			03 56	20 00		

	Rise h m	Set h m	Rise h m	Set h m	Rise h m	Set h m	Rise h m	Set h m	Rise h m	Set h m	Rise h m	Set h
	JULY		AUGUST		SEPTEMBER		OCTOBER		NOVEMBER		DECEMBER	
1	03 55	20 12	04 30	19 42	05 15	18 43	06 00	17 38	06 50	16 36	07 37	16
2	03 56	20 12	04 31	19 40	05 17	18 41	06 02	17 36	06 52	16 35	07 38	16
3	03 56	20 12	04 32	19 39	05 18	18 39	06 03	17 34	06 53	16 33	07 40	16
4	03 57	20 11	04 34	19 37	05 20	18 37	06 05	17 31	06 55	16 31	07 41	16
5	03 58	20 11	04 35	19 36	05 21	18 35	06 06	17 29	06 57	16 30	07 42	15
6	03 59	20 10	04 37	19 34	05 23	18 33	06 08	17 27	06 58	16 28	07 43	15
7	04 00	20 10	04 38	19 32	05 24	18 31	06 10	17 25	07 00	16 27	07 44	15
8	04 01	20 09	04 40	19 31	05 26	18 28	06 11	17 23	07 02	16 25	07 46	15
9	04 02	20 08	04 41	19 29	05 27	18 26	06 13	17 21	07 03	16 24	07 47	15
10	04 02	20 08	04 43	19 27	05 29	18 24	06 14	17 19	07 05	16 22	07 48	15
11	04 03	20 07	04 44	19 25	05 30	18 22	06 16	17 17	07 07	16 21	07 49	15
12	04 04	20 06	04 46	19 23	05 32	18 20	06 17	17 14	07 08	16 19	07 50	15
13	04 06	20 05	04 47	19 22	05 33	18 17	06 19	17 12	07 10	16 18	07 51	15
14	04 07	20 04	04 48	19 20	05 35	18 15	06 21	17 10	07 12	16 17	07 51	15
15	04 08	20 04	04 50	19 18	05 36	18 13	06 22	17 08	07 13	16 16	07 52	15
16	04 09	20 03	04 51	19 16	05 38	18 11	06 24	17 06	07 15	16 14	07 53	15
17	04 10	20 02	04 53	19 14	05 39	18 09	06 25	17 04	07 16	16 13	07 54	15
18	04 11	20 01	04 54	19 12	05 41	18 06	06 27	17 02	07 18	16 12	07 54	15
19	04 12	19 59	04 56	19 10	05 42	18 04	06 29	17 00	07 20	16 11	07 55	16
20	04 14	19 58	04 57	19 08	05 44	18 02	06 30	16 58	07 21	16 10	07 56	16
21	04 15	19 57	04 59	19 06	05 45	18 00	06 32	16 56	07 23	16 09	07 56	16
22	04 16	19 56	05 00	19 04	05 47	17 58	06 34	16 55	07 24	16 08	07 57	16
23	04 17	19 55	05 02	19 02	05 48	17 55	06 35	16 53	07 26	16 07	07 57	16
24	04 19	19 53	05 03	19 00	05 50	17 53	06 37	16 51	07 27	16 06	07 57	16
25	04 20	19 52	05 05	18 58	05 51	17 51	06 39	16 49	07 29	16 05	07 58	16
26	04 21	19 51	05 06	18 56	05 53	17 49	06 40	16 47	07 30	16 04	07 58	16
27	04 23	19 49	05 08	18 54	05 54	17 47	06 42	16 45	07 32	16 03	07 58	16
28	04 24	19 48	05 09	18 52	05 56	17 44	06 43	16 43	07 33	16 03	07 58	16
29	04 25	19 47	05 11	18 50	05 57	17 42	06 45	16 42	07 34	16 02	07 59	16
30	04 27	19 45	05 12	18 48	05 59	17 40	06 47	16 40	07 36	16 01	07 59	16
31	04 28	19 44	05 14	18 46			06 48	16 38			07 59	16

Times are in UT - add 1 hour in non-shaded areas to convert to DST

004 Moonrise and Moonset Time

The times are based on **LAT 50°00'N   LONG 0°00'** - add 4 min for every degree West and subtract 4 min for every degree East

Day	JANUARY Rise h m	Set h m	FEBRUARY Rise h m	Set h m	MARCH Rise h m	Set h m	APRIL Rise h m	Set h m	MAY Rise h m	Set h m	JUNE Rise h m	Set h m
1	12 31	01 52	12 02	04 15	11 20	04 07	13 32	04 33	15 02	03 31	18 11	02 40
2	12 47	03 01	12 41	05 19	12 17	04 57	14 50	04 54	16 23	03 46	19 43	03 04
3	13 06	04 10	13 32	06 15	13 25	05 36	16 10	05 11	17 47	04 01	21 11	03 38
4	13 31	05 19	14 34	07 01	14 39	06 07	17 30	05 26	19 16	04 18	22 24	04 27
5	14 04	06 27	15 45	07 37	15 57	06 30	18 53	05 41	20 47	04 40	23 17	05 34
6	14 48	07 28	17 00	08 05	17 16	06 50	20 19	05 58	22 17	05 09	23 54	06 55
7	15 42	08 21	18 17	08 27	18 35	07 06	21 47	06 16	23 37	05 49	** **	08 22
8	16 47	09 03	19 35	08 45	19 55	07 21	23 16	06 40	** **	06 45	00 20	09 46
9	17 59	09 36	20 52	09 00	21 17	07 37	** **	07 13	00 39	07 56	00 40	11 07
10	19 14	10 01	22 10	09 15	22 41	07 53	00 39	07 57	01 23	09 18	00 55	12 22
11	20 30	10 21	23 31	09 31	** **	08 13	01 50	08 58	01 54	10 41	01 09	13 35
12	21 46	10 38	** **	09 48	00 07	08 39	02 43	10 11	02 16	12 02	01 22	14 46
13	23 02	10 54	00 54	10 09	01 32	09 15	03 21	11 32	02 33	13 19	01 35	15 57
14	** **	11 09	02 19	10 38	02 50	10 03	03 49	12 54	02 48	14 33	01 51	17 08
15	00 21	11 25	03 42	11 17	03 54	11 07	04 09	14 13	03 01	15 44	02 09	18 19
16	01 42	11 43	04 57	12 11	04 42	12 23	04 25	15 29	03 14	16 56	02 33	19 28
17	03 07	12 07	05 58	13 20	05 17	13 45	04 39	16 43	03 28	18 07	03 03	20 31
18	04 34	12 40	06 42	14 41	05 42	15 07	04 52	17 55	03 44	19 18	03 44	21 25
19	05 58	13 25	07 14	16 06	06 02	16 27	05 06	19 07	04 04	20 29	04 35	22 08
20	07 11	14 28	07 38	17 29	06 17	17 44	05 20	20 19	04 29	21 37	05 37	22 41
21	08 07	15 45	07 56	18 48	06 31	18 58	05 38	21 31	05 03	22 37	06 45	23 06
22	08 47	17 10	08 12	20 04	06 45	20 11	05 59	22 41	05 46	23 28	07 57	23 26
23	09 15	18 35	08 26	21 17	06 59	21 23	06 27	23 47	06 41	** **	09 10	23 42
24	09 36	19 56	08 40	22 29	07 15	22 35	07 04	** **	07 45	00 08	10 24	23 57
25	09 53	21 13	08 54	23 41	07 34	23 46	07 52	00 44	08 55	00 38	11 38	** **
26	10 08	22 26	09 11	** **	07 58	** **	08 50	01 31	10 08	01 02	12 55	00 11
27	10 21	23 37	09 32	00 52	08 29	00 54	09 58	02 08	11 23	01 20	14 15	00 25
28	10 35	** **	09 59	02 01	09 10	01 57	11 10	02 36	12 38	01 36	15 40	00 42
29	10 51	00 47	10 34	03 07	10 02	02 51	12 26	02 58	13 56	01 51	17 09	01 02
30	11 09	01 57			11 05	03 34	13 43	03 15	15 16	02 05	18 38	01 31
31	11 32	03 07			12 16	04 07			16 41	02 21		

Day	JULY Rise	Set	AUGUST Rise	Set	SEPTEMBER Rise	Set	OCTOBER Rise	Set	NOVEMBER Rise	Set	DECEMBER Rise	Set
1	19 59	02 11	20 43	04 48	19 52	07 54	18 43	09 20	18 47	11 44	19 40	11 48
2	21 03	03 09	21 03	06 17	20 06	09 11	19 04	10 35	19 41	12 36	20 50	12 13
3	21 49	04 25	21 19	07 41	20 21	10 26	19 32	11 48	20 44	13 16	22 02	12 33
4	22 20	05 52	21 33	09 01	20 40	11 41	20 08	12 55	21 54	13 47	23 14	12 49
5	22 43	07 21	21 47	10 18	21 04	12 54	20 55	13 54	23 06	14 10	** **	13 03
6	23 00	08 46	22 02	11 32	21 35	14 04	21 54	14 41	** **	14 28	00 27	13 16
7	23 15	10 06	22 18	12 45	22 15	15 07	23 00	15 18	00 19	14 44	01 42	13 29
8	23 28	11 22	22 38	13 57	23 07	16 01	** **	15 45	01 34	14 57	03 00	13 44
9	23 42	12 35	23 04	15 08	** **	16 44	00 12	16 06	02 49	15 11	04 23	14 02
10	23 57	13 47	23 38	16 15	00 09	17 17	01 27	16 24	04 08	15 25	05 51	14 27
11	** **	14 58	** **	17 15	01 19	17 42	02 42	16 38	05 30	15 42	07 21	15 02
12	00 14	16 10	00 23	18 05	02 33	18 02	03 58	16 52	06 57	16 03	08 47	15 54
13	00 36	17 19	01 19	18 43	03 48	18 18	05 16	17 06	08 27	16 32	09 57	17 04
14	01 04	18 24	02 24	19 15	05 03	18 32	06 36	17 21	09 55	17 14	10 47	18 30
15	01 42	19 21	03 36	19 38	06 19	18 46	07 59	17 39	11 12	18 13	11 22	19 59
16	02 30	20 07	04 50	19 56	07 37	19 00	09 26	18 03	12 11	19 29	11 46	21 27
17	03 29	20 43	06 04	20 11	08 56	19 15	10 54	18 36	12 53	20 53	12 05	22 49
18	04 36	21 11	07 18	20 25	10 19	19 35	12 16	19 22	13 21	22 19	12 20	** **
19	05 48	21 32	08 33	20 38	11 44	20 01	13 24	20 26	13 42	23 42	12 33	00 07
20	07 01	21 49	09 50	20 53	13 08	20 37	14 15	21 43	13 58	** **	12 46	01 23
21	08 15	22 04	11 09	21 09	14 25	21 28	14 50	23 07	14 12	01 02	13 00	02 37
22	09 28	22 17	12 31	21 31	15 27	22 36	15 16	** **	14 25	02 18	13 17	03 50
23	10 43	22 31	13 56	21 59	16 13	23 56	15 35	00 32	14 39	03 32	13 38	05 04
24	12 00	22 46	15 19	22 40	16 46	** **	15 50	01 54	14 53	04 46	14 05	06 16
25	13 20	23 05	16 33	23 37	17 10	01 22	16 04	03 13	15 11	06 01	14 40	07 24
26	14 45	23 28	17 31	** **	17 28	02 48	16 17	04 29	15 34	07 15	15 27	08 23
27	16 12	** **	18 14	00 51	17 43	04 11	16 31	05 45	16 03	08 27	16 24	09 12
28	17 35	00 02	18 44	02 17	17 57	05 30	16 47	07 01	16 42	09 33	17 29	09 49
29	18 46	00 50	19 06	03 46	18 11	06 48	17 06	08 16	17 32	10 29	18 39	10 17
30	19 39	01 56	19 23	05 12	18 26	08 04	17 31	09 30	18 32	11 14	19 51	10 38
31	20 17	03 18	19 38	06 35			18 04	10 41			21 02	10 55

Times are in UT - add 1 hour in non-shaded areas to convert to DST

2004 Sunrise and Sunset Time

The times are based on LAT 55°00'N LONG 0° - add 4 min for every degree West and subtract 4 min for every degree East

	Rise h m	Set h m	Rise h m	Set h m	Rise h m	Set h m	Rise h m	Set h m	Rise h m	Set h m	Rise h m	Set h m
	JANUARY		FEBRUARY		MARCH		APRIL		MAY		JUNE	
1	08 45	16 02	08 12	16 56	07 09	17 56	05 51	18 58	04 39	19 56	03 48	20 48
2	08 45	16 03	08 10	16 58	07 07	17 58	05 49	19 00	04 37	19 58	03 47	20 49
3	08 45	16 04	08 08	17 00	07 04	18 00	05 46	19 02	04 35	20 00	03 46	20 51
4	08 44	16 05	08 07	17 02	07 02	18 02	05 43	19 03	04 33	20 02	03 46	20 52
5	08 44	16 07	08 05	17 04	06 59	18 04	05 41	19 05	04 31	20 04	03 45	20 53
6	08 43	16 08	08 03	17 06	06 57	18 06	05 38	19 07	04 29	20 06	03 44	20 54
7	08 43	16 10	08 01	17 08	06 54	18 08	05 36	19 09	04 27	20 07	03 43	20 55
8	08 42	16 11	07 59	17 10	06 52	18 10	05 33	19 11	04 25	20 09	03 43	20 56
9	08 42	16 13	07 57	17 12	06 50	18 12	05 31	19 13	04 23	20 11	03 42	20 57
10	08 41	16 14	07 55	17 15	06 47	18 14	05 28	19 15	04 21	20 13	03 42	20 58
11	08 40	16 16	07 53	17 17	06 44	18 16	05 26	19 17	04 19	20 15	03 41	20 58
12	08 39	16 17	07 50	17 19	06 42	18 18	05 24	19 19	04 17	20 17	03 41	20 59
13	08 38	16 19	07 48	17 21	06 39	18 20	05 21	19 21	04 15	20 18	03 41	21 00
14	08 37	16 21	07 46	17 23	06 37	18 22	05 19	19 23	04 14	20 20	03 40	21 00
15	08 36	16 22	07 44	17 25	06 34	18 24	05 16	19 25	04 12	20 22	03 40	21 01
16	08 35	16 24	07 42	17 27	06 32	18 26	05 14	19 27	04 10	20 24	03 40	21 01
17	08 34	16 26	07 40	17 29	06 29	18 28	05 11	19 29	04 08	20 25	03 40	21 02
18	08 33	16 28	07 37	17 31	06 27	18 30	05 09	19 31	04 07	20 27	03 40	21 02
19	08 32	16 30	07 35	17 34	06 24	18 32	05 07	19 33	04 05	20 29	03 40	21 03
20	08 31	16 32	07 33	17 36	06 22	18 34	05 04	19 35	04 04	20 31	03 40	21 03
21	08 29	16 34	07 31	17 38	06 19	18 36	05 02	19 37	04 02	20 32	03 41	21 03
22	08 28	16 35	07 28	17 40	06 17	18 38	05 00	19 39	04 01	20 34	03 41	21 03
23	08 27	16 37	07 26	17 42	06 14	18 40	04 57	19 41	03 59	20 35	03 41	21 03
24	08 25	16 39	07 24	17 44	06 11	18 42	04 55	19 42	03 58	20 37	03 41	21 03
25	08 24	16 41	07 21	17 46	06 09	18 44	04 53	19 44	03 56	20 38	03 42	21 03
26	08 22	16 43	07 19	17 48	06 06	18 46	04 50	19 46	03 55	20 40	03 42	21 03
27	08 21	16 45	07 16	17 50	06 04	18 48	04 48	19 48	03 54	20 41	03 43	21 03
28	08 19	16 47	07 14	17 52	06 01	18 50	04 46	19 50	03 53	20 43	03 44	21 03
29	08 17	16 49	07 12	17 54	05 59	18 52	04 44	19 52	03 51	20 44	03 44	21 02
30	08 16	16 52			05 56	18 54	04 42	19 54	03 50	20 46	03 45	21 02
31	08 14	16 54			05 54	18 56			03 49	20 47		

	Rise h m	Set h m	Rise h m	Set h m	Rise h m	Set h m	Rise h m	Set h m	Rise h m	Set h m	Rise h m	Set h m
	JULY		AUGUST		SEPTEMBER		OCTOBER		NOVEMBER		DECEMBER	
1	03 46	21 02	04 29	20 22	05 27	19 12	06 23	17 55	07 24	16 42	08 22	15 56
2	03 47	21 01	04 31	20 20	05 29	19 09	06 25	17 53	07 26	16 40	08 23	15 56
3	03 47	21 01	04 33	20 18	05 30	19 07	06 27	17 50	07 28	16 38	08 25	15 55
4	03 48	21 00	04 35	20 16	05 32	19 04	06 29	17 48	07 30	16 36	08 26	15 54
5	03 49	20 59	04 36	20 14	05 34	19 02	06 31	17 45	07 32	16 34	08 27	15 54
6	03 50	20 59	04 38	20 12	05 36	18 59	06 32	17 43	07 34	16 32	08 29	15 53
7	03 51	20 58	04 40	20 10	05 38	18 57	06 34	17 40	07 37	16 30	08 30	15 53
8	03 53	20 57	04 42	20 08	05 40	18 54	06 36	17 38	07 39	16 28	08 32	15 52
9	03 54	20 56	04 44	20 06	05 42	18 52	06 38	17 35	07 41	16 26	08 33	15 52
10	03 55	20 55	04 46	20 04	05 43	18 49	06 40	17 33	07 43	16 25	08 34	15 52
11	03 56	20 54	04 47	20 01	05 45	18 46	06 42	17 30	07 45	16 23	08 35	15 52
12	03 57	20 53	04 49	19 59	05 47	18 44	06 44	17 28	07 47	16 21	08 36	15 51
13	03 59	20 52	04 51	19 57	05 49	18 41	06 46	17 25	07 49	16 19	08 37	15 51
14	04 00	20 51	04 53	19 55	05 51	18 39	06 48	17 23	07 51	16 18	08 38	15 51
15	04 02	20 49	04 55	19 53	05 53	18 36	06 50	17 20	07 53	16 16	08 39	15 51
16	04 03	20 48	04 57	19 50	05 55	18 34	06 52	17 18	07 55	16 15	08 40	15 52
17	04 04	20 47	04 59	19 48	05 57	18 31	06 54	17 16	07 57	16 13	08 41	15 52
18	04 06	20 46	05 01	19 46	05 58	18 28	06 56	17 13	07 58	16 12	08 41	15 52
19	04 07	20 44	05 02	19 43	06 00	18 26	06 58	17 11	08 00	16 10	08 42	15 52
20	04 09	20 43	05 04	19 41	06 02	18 23	07 00	17 09	08 02	16 09	08 43	15 53
21	04 11	20 41	05 06	19 39	06 04	18 21	07 02	17 06	08 04	16 07	08 43	15 53
22	04 12	20 40	05 08	19 36	06 06	18 18	07 04	17 04	08 06	16 06	08 44	15 53
23	04 14	20 38	05 10	19 34	06 08	18 16	07 06	17 02	08 08	16 05	08 44	15 54
24	04 15	20 36	05 12	19 31	06 10	18 13	07 08	16 59	08 10	16 03	08 45	15 55
25	04 17	20 35	05 14	19 29	06 12	18 10	07 10	16 57	08 11	16 02	08 45	15 56
26	04 19	20 33	05 15	19 27	06 13	18 08	07 12	16 55	08 13	16 01	08 45	15 57
27	04 20	20 31	05 17	19 24	06 15	18 05	07 14	16 53	08 15	16 00	08 45	15 57
28	04 22	20 30	05 19	19 22	06 17	18 03	07 16	16 51	08 17	15 59	08 45	15 58
29	04 24	20 28	05 21	19 19	06 19	18 00	07 18	16 49	08 18	15 58	08 45	15 59
30	04 26	20 26	05 23	19 17	06 21	17 58	07 20	16 46	08 20	15 57	08 45	16 00
31	04 27	20 24	05 25	19 14			07 22	16 44			08 45	16 02

Times are in UT - add 1 hour in non-shaded areas to convert to DST

004 Moonrise and Moonset Time

The times are based on **LAT 55°00'N   LONG 0°** - add 4 min for every degree West and subtract 4 min for every degree East

Day	JAN Rise h m	JAN Set h m	FEB Rise h m	FEB Set h m	MAR Rise h m	MAR Set h m	APR Rise h m	APR Set h m	MAY Rise h m	MAY Set h m	JUN Rise h m	JUN Set h m
1	12 39	02 22	11 49	05 08	11 01	05 07	13 32	05 17	15 19	03 58	18 55	02 43
2	12 50	03 37	12 24	06 17	12 01	05 55	14 57	05 30	16 47	04 06	20 36	03 00
3	13 03	04 53	13 14	07 14	13 14	06 30	16 23	05 41	18 19	04 15	22 11	03 26
4	13 22	06 09	14 20	07 58	14 35	06 54	17 51	05 50	19 56	04 26	23 25	04 08
5	13 50	07 22	15 37	08 28	16 00	07 10	19 21	05 59	21 36	04 40		05 15
6	14 30	08 27	16 59	08 49	17 26	07 23	20 54	06 08	23 15	05 00	00 14	06 42
7	15 26	09 19	18 23	09 04	18 52	07 33	22 31	06 20		05 32	00 42	08 17
8	16 35	09 58	19 47	09 15	20 19	07 42		06 36	00 39	06 24	01 00	09 50
9	17 53	10 24	21 12	09 25	21 48	07 51	00 09	07 00	01 39	07 39	01 13	11 17
10	19 15	10 43	22 36	09 34	23 20	08 01	01 39	07 39	02 16	09 08	01 22	12 39
11	20 38	10 57		09 43		08 14	02 52	08 38	02 39	10 39	01 30	13 58
12	22 00	11 07	00 04	09 54	00 54	08 33	03 41	09 56	02 54	12 08	01 37	15 16
13	23 23	11 17	01 34	10 09	02 27	09 00	04 12	11 24	03 04	13 31	01 45	16 33
14		11 26	03 07	10 29	03 50	09 44	04 31	12 54	03 13	14 52	01 55	17 51
15	00 48	11 36	04 38	11 01	04 55	10 48	04 44	14 21	03 20	16 09	02 07	19 08
16	02 17	11 48	05 58	11 52	05 38	12 10	04 54	15 44	03 27	17 27	02 24	20 23
17	03 50	12 04	06 57	13 04	06 05	13 40	05 02	17 04	03 36	18 44	02 49	21 30
18	05 26	12 29	07 35	14 31	06 22	15 10	05 10	18 22	03 46	20 03	03 25	22 25
19	06 56	13 08	07 59	16 04	06 35	16 37	05 17	19 40	03 59	21 20	04 17	23 05
20	08 11	14 09	08 15	17 35	06 44	18 00	05 26	20 59	04 18	22 34	05 22	23 32
21	09 03	15 31	08 27	19 01	06 52	19 21	05 38	22 18	04 46	23 38	06 37	23 50
22	09 36	17 04	08 36	20 24	07 00	20 40	05 53	23 35	05 27		07 56	
23	09 56	18 37	08 44	21 43	07 09	21 59	06 14		06 23	00 28	09 16	00 04
24	10 10	20 05	08 53	23 01	07 18	23 17	06 46	00 45	07 32	01 03	10 36	00 14
25	10 21	21 29	09 02		07 31		07 32	01 45	08 49	01 27	11 57	00 22
26	10 30	22 48	09 13	00 19	07 49	00 35	08 34	02 30	10 09	01 44	13 20	00 30
27	10 38		09 27	01 37	08 14	01 50	09 47	03 01	11 31	01 56	14 47	00 39
28	10 46	00 05	09 48	02 53	08 51	02 57	11 07	03 22	12 53	02 06	16 20	00 49
29	10 56	01 21	10 18	04 05	09 43	03 51	12 29	03 37	14 17	02 14	17 57	01 02
30	11 08	02 38			10 51	04 31	13 53	03 48	15 44	02 23	19 35	01 22
31	11 25	03 54			12 09	04 58			17 17	02 32		

Day	JUL Rise h m	JUL Set h m	AUG Rise h m	AUG Set h m	SEP Rise h m	SEP Set h m	OCT Rise h m	OCT Set h m	NOV Rise h m	NOV Set h m	DEC Rise h m	DEC Set h m
1	21 01	01 55	21 23	04 43	20 08	08 16	18 43	10 00	18 26	12 46	19 29	12 41
2	22 03	02 49	21 35	06 21	20 16	09 40	18 57	11 22	19 21	13 37	20 47	12 59
3	22 41	04 08	21 45	07 53	20 25	11 02	19 18	12 42	20 29	14 13	22 06	13 12
4	23 04	05 43	21 53	09 20	20 38	12 23	19 49	13 55	21 46	14 37	23 25	13 22
5	23 19	07 21	22 01	10 43	20 54	13 43	20 34	14 56	23 05	14 54		13 30
6	23 29	08 54	22 09	12 03	21 19	15 00	21 35	15 41		15 05	00 44	13 37
7	23 38	10 21	22 20	13 23	21 55	16 08	22 48	16 12	00 26	15 14	02 05	13 44
8	23 46	11 43	22 33	14 42	22 47	17 03		16 33	01 47	15 22	03 30	13 53
9	23 53	13 03	22 53	16 00	23 54	17 42	00 07	16 47	03 09	15 29	05 00	14 04
10		14 21	23 21	17 13		18 08	01 29	16 58	04 34	15 37	06 37	14 21
11	00 02	15 39		18 16	01 10	18 26	02 51	17 06	06 04	15 47	08 17	14 47
12	00 14	16 57	00 03	19 05	02 31	18 39	04 14	17 14	07 39	16 01	09 49	15 33
13	00 29	18 13	01 01	19 40	03 54	18 49	05 38	17 21	09 18	16 21	10 59	16 44
14	00 51	19 23	02 12	20 03	05 16	18 57	07 06	17 30	10 55	16 55	11 43	18 17
15	01 24	20 21	03 30	20 19	06 38	19 05	08 37	17 41	12 16	17 51	12 09	19 56
16	02 11	21 05	04 51	20 31	08 02	19 13	10 13	17 57	13 11	19 11	12 25	21 32
17	03 13	21 36	06 12	20 40	09 29	19 22	11 49	18 21	13 45	20 44	12 36	23 02
18	04 26	21 57	07 33	20 48	10 59	19 34	13 18	19 02	14 05	22 19	12 44	
19	05 45	22 11	08 55	20 55	12 33	19 52	14 27	20 05	14 18	23 50	12 52	00 27
20	07 05	22 22	10 17	21 04	14 06	20 20	15 12	21 28	14 28		12 59	01 48
21	08 25	22 31	11 43	21 14	15 28	21 07	15 40	23 01	14 35	01 16	13 07	03 09
22	09 45	22 39	13 14	21 28	16 29	22 16	15 57		14 43	02 39	13 18	04 29
23	11 06	22 47	14 47	21 48	17 09	23 44	16 09	00 34	14 50	04 00	13 32	05 50
24	12 29	22 56	16 18	22 22	17 33		16 18	02 04	14 59	05 20	13 52	07 09
25	13 57	23 07	17 35	23 16	17 49	01 19	16 25	03 29	15 10	06 42	14 22	08 23
26	15 30	23 23	18 31		18 00	02 53	16 33	04 53	15 25	08 03	15 06	09 25
27	17 05	23 48	19 06	00 34	18 08	04 23	16 41	06 15	15 48	09 22	16 06	10 12
28	18 36		19 27	02 08	18 16	05 50	16 50	07 37	16 23	10 33	17 17	10 43
29	19 48	00 30	19 41	03 46	18 24	07 14	17 03	09 00	17 12	11 31	18 34	11 05
30	20 36	01 36	19 52	05 21	18 32	08 37	17 20	10 21	18 15	12 13	19 52	11 19
31	21 05	03 05	20 00	06 51			17 47	11 39			21 10	11 30

RACONS (RADAR BEACONS)

Radar beacons within the main areas covered in this Almanac are listed below in WGS 84 datum. See the *Reeds Nautical Almanac* for those within Denmark, Spain and Portugal as well as for more information on racons.

Details given in the table are: The name of the beacon; latitude and longitude; approximate range in nautical miles (this to some extent depends on the effective range of the yacht's radar set); the Morse identification signal (racons coded 'D' are used to mark new dangers such as wrecks); the sector within which signals may be received, if not 360°. Note that most racons respond throughout 360°, but a few respond only within an angular sector, bearings quoted always being towards the beacon, clockwise from 000° to 359°.

Name	Position		Range	Ident	Sector
ENGLAND – SOUTH AND EAST COAST					
Bishop Rock Lt	49°52'·37N	06°26'·74W	18M	T	254°-215
Round Island Lt	49°58'·74N	06°19'·40W	10M	M	
Seven Stones Lt F	50°03'·62N	06°04'·34W	15M	O	360°
Wolf Rock Lt	49°56'·72N	05°48'·57W	10M	T	360°
Eddystone Lt	50°10'·85N	04°15'·94W	10M	T	360°
Bridge Lt By	50°39'·63N	01°36'·88W	10M	T	
West Bramble Lt By	50°47'·20N	01°18'·65W	3M	T	360°
Nab Lt	50°40'·08N	00°57'·15W	10M	T	360°
Owers Lt By	50°38'·63N	00°41'·19W	10M	O	360°
North East Goodwin Lt By	51°20'·31N	01°34'·16E	10M	M	360°
Dover Strait TSS Foxtrot 3 Lt V	51°23'·85N	02°00'·51E	10M	T	360°
Thames Barrier Pier No. 4 E end*	51°29'·90N	00°02'·24E		T	
Thames Barrier Pier No. 4 W end*	51°29'·89N	00°02'·18E		T	
Thames Barrier Pier No. 8 E end*	51°29'·74N	00°02'·26E		T	
Thames Barrier Pier No. 8 W end*	51°29'·74N	00°02'·20E		T	

* Operational only when visibility in Woolwich Reach is reduced to 1M or less, or for test purposes or training. Information about Racon operation is included in routine bcsts on VHF Ch 14.

Name	Position		Range	Ident	Sector
Outer Tongue Lt By	51°30'·73N	01°26'·40E	10M	T	360°
Barrow Lt By No. 3	51°42'·02N	01°20'·24E	10M	M	360°
South Galloper Lt By	51°43'·98N	01°56'·39E	10M	T	360°
Sunk Lt F	51°51'·03N	01°34'·89E	10M	T	360°
Harwich Channel No 1 Lt By	51°56'·13N	01°27'·06E	10M	T	360°
Outer Gabbard Lt By	51°57'·83N	02°04'·19E	10M	O	360°
North Shipwash Lt By	52°01'·73N	01°38'·27E	10M	M	360°
Orfordness Lt	52°05'·03N	01°34'·46E	18M	T	
Cross Sand Lt By	52°37'·03N	01°59'·14E	10M	T	360°
Winterton Church Tower	52°42'·92N	01°41'·21E	10M	T	360°
Smiths Knoll Lt By	52°43'·52N	02°17'·89E	10M	T	360°
Newarp Lt V	52°48'·37N	01°56'·69E	10M	O	360°
Cromer Lt	52°55'·45N	01°19'·01E	25M	O	360°
North Haisbro Lt By	53°00'·22N	01°32'·29E	10M	T	360°
North Well Lt By	53°03'·02N	00°27'·90E	10M	T	360°
Dudgeon Lt By	53°16'·62N	01°16'·90E	10M	O	360°
Inner Dowsing ECM	53°19'·10N	00°34'·80E	10M	T	360°
Spurn Lt F	53°33'·56N	00°14'·20E	5M	M	360°
Humber Lt F	53°39'·06N	00°19'·98E	7M	T	360°
Tees Fairway Lt By	54°40'·94N	01°06'·48W		B	360°
SCOTLAND – EAST TO WEST COAST					
St Abb's Head Lt	55°54'·96N	02°08'·29W	18M	T	360°
Inchkeith Fairway Lt By	56°03'·49N	03°00'·10W	5M	T	360°
Firth of Forth N Channel Lt By	56°02'·80N	03°10'·97W	5M	T	360°
Bell Rock Lt	56°26'·07N	02°23'·20W	18M	M	360
Abertay Lt By	56°27'·39N	02°40'·36W	8M	T	360°
Scurdie Ness Lt	56°42'·10N	02°26'·24W	14-16M	T	360
Girdle Ness Lt	57°08'·34N	02°02'·91W	25M	G	360°
Aberdeen Fairway Lt By	57°09'·31N	02°01'·94W	7M	T	360°

Name	Position		Range	Ident	Sector
Buchan Ness Lt	57°28'·23N	01°46'·51W	14-16M	O	360°
Rattray Head Lt	57°36'·61N	01°49'·03W	15M	M	360°
Kessock Bridge Centre Mark	57°29'·97N	04°13'·81W	6M	K	
Cromarty Firth Fairway Lt By	57°39'·96N	03°54'·19W	5M	M	360°
Tarbat Ness Lt	57°51'·88N	03°46'·76W	14-16M	T	360
Duncansby Head Lt	58°38'·65N	03°01'·58W	16M	T	360°
Lother Rock Lt	58°43'·80N	02°58'·68W	10M	M	360°
North Ronaldsay Lt	59°23'·37N	02°23'·03W	14-17M	T	360°
Rumble Rock Lt Bn	60°28'·17N	01°07'·25W	8-10M	O	360°
Gruney Island Lt	60°39'·15N	01°18'·16W	14M	T	360
Ve Skerries Lt	60°22'·36N	01°48'·78W	15M	T	360°
Eilean Glas Lt	57°51'·40N	06°38'·55W	16-18M	T	360°
Ardivachar Pt	57°22'·92N	07°25'·54W	16M	T	360°
Carrach Rocks Lt By	57°17'·18N	05°45'·36W	5M	T	360°
Hyskeir Lt	56°58'·14N	06°40'·87W	14-17M	T	360°
Castlebay South By	56°56'·09N	07°27'·21W	7M	T	360°
Bo Vich Chuan Lt By	56°56'·15N	07°23'·31W	5M	M	360°
Skerryvore Lt	56°19'·36N	07°06'·88W	18M	M	360°
Dubh Sgeir Lt	56°14'·76N	05°40'·20W	5M	M	360
ENGLAND – WEST COAST AND WALES					
Point of Ayre Lt	54°24'·94N	04°22'·13W	13-15M	M	360°
Halfway Shoal Lt Bn	54°01'·46N	03°11'·88W	10M	B	360°
Lune Deep Lt By	53°55'·81N	03°11'·08W	10M	T	360°
Bar Lt F	53°32'·01N	03°20'·98W	10M	T	360°
West Constable Lt By	53°23'·14N	03°49'·26W	10M	M	
The Skerries Lt	53°25'·27N	04°36'·50W	25M	T	360°
South Bishop Lt	51°51'·14N	05°24'·74W	10M	O	
The Smalls Lt	51°43'·28N	05°40'·19W	25M	T	360°
Watwick Pt Rear Ldg Lt Bn	51°41'·78N	05°09'·24W		Y	360°
West Blockhouse Front Middle Ldg Lt Bn	51°41'·31N	05°09'·56W		Q	010°-230°
S. Gowan Lt By	51°31'·93N	04°59'·77W	10M	T	360°
West Helwick Lt By W.HWK	51°31'·40N	04°23'·65W	10M	T	360°
Swansea Bar Lt By W. Scar	51°28'·31N	03°55'·57W	10M	T	360°
Cabenda Lt By	51°33'·36N	03°52'·23W		C	
English & Welsh Grounds Lt By	51°27'·13N	02°59'·94W	7M	T	360°
Second Severn Crossing Centre Lt SW	51°34'·45N	02°42'·03W		O	
Breaksea Lt F	51°19'·88N	03°19'·08W	10M	T	360°
IRELAND					
Hellyhunter Lt By	54°00'·34N	06°02'·06W	5-14M	K	
South Rock Lt F	54°24'·49N	05°22'·02W	13M	T	360°
Mew Island Lt	54°41'·91N	05°30'·81W	14M	O	360°
Belfast Fairway Lt By	54°41'·70N	05°46'·24W		G	
East Maiden Lt	54°55'·73N	05°43'·67W	11-21M	M	360°
Rathlin East Lt	55°18'·06N	06°10'·30W	15-27M	G	089°-003°
Bull Rock Lt	51°35'·51N	10°18'·07W	16-27M	N	360°
Fastnet Lt	51°23'·35N	09°36'·19W	18M	G	360°
Cork Lt By	51°42'·92N	08°15'·60W	7M	T	360°
Hook Head Lt	52°07'·32N	06°55'·85W	10M	K	237°-177°
Coningbeg Lt F	52°02'·40N	06°39'·49W	13M	M	360°
Tuskar Rock Lt	52°12'·17N	06°12'·42W	18M	T	360°
Arklow Lanby	52°39'·52N	05°58'·16W	10M	O	360°
Codling Lanby	53°03'·02N	05°40'·76W	10M	G	360°
Dublin Bay Lt By	53°19'·92N	06°04'·64W		M	
Kish Bank Lt	53°18'·70N	05°55'·44W	15M	T	360°
GERMANY					
Westerems Lt By	53°36'·91N	06°19'·40E	8M	T	360°
Borkumriff Lt By	53°47'·44N	06°22'·02E	8M	T	360°

Name	Position		Range	Ident	Sector
GW/EMS Lt F	54°09'·96N	06°20'·72E	8M	T	360°
German Bight Lt V	54°10'·72N	07°27'·53E	8M	T	360°
Jade/Weser Lt By	53°58'·24N	07°38'·76E	8M	T	360°
Tonne 3/Jade 2 Lt By	53°52'·05N	07°47'·30E	8M	T	360°
Elbe Lt By	53°59'·92N	08°06'·56E	8M	T	360°
NETHERLANDS					
Keeten B Lt By	51°36'·35N	03°58'·05E	3-10M	K	360°
Zuid Vlije Lt By ZV11/SRK 4	51°38'·23N	04°14'·56E	3-10M	K	360°
Noord Hinder Lt By	52°00'·04N	02°51'·03E	12-15M	T	
Noord Hinder Noord NHR-N Lt By	52°10'·78N	03°04'·69E	10M	K	
Schouwenbank Lt By	51°44'·94N	03°14'·31E	10M	O	360°
Goeree Lt	51°55'·42N	03°40'·03E	12-15M	T	360°
Maas Centre Lt By (MC)	52°01'·12N	03°53'·44E	10M	M	360°
IJmuiden (IJM) Lt By	52°28'·44N	04°23'·78E	10M	Y	360°
Schulpengat Fairway Lt By SG	52°52'·90N	04°37'·90E		Z	
DW Route Lt By BR/S	52°54'·89N	03°18'·06E		G	
Vlieland Lanby VL-CENTER	53°26'·93N	04°39'·88E	12-15M	C	360°
ZS Lt By	53°19'·78N	04°55'·88E		T	
Westgat Schiermonnikoog WG Lt By	53°32'·56N	06°10'·71E		N	
Botney Ground BG/S Lt By	53°35'·69N	03°00'·96E		T	
DW Route Lt By FR/A	54°00'·28N	04°21'·30E	10M	T	
DW Route Lt By EF	54°03'·29N	04°59'·70E		T	
DW Route Lt By EF/B	54°06'·59N	05°39'·86E		M	
DW Route Lt By EF/C	54°08'·24N	05°59'·89E		O	
BELGIUM					
West Hinder Lt	51°23'·31N	02°26'·27E	10M	W	
West Hinder Route Lt By KB	51°21'·03N	02°42'·83E		K	
FRANCE					
Dyck (Dunkerque Approach) Lt By	51°02'·98N	01°51'·76E		B	360°
Vergoyer Lt By N	50°39'·64N	01°22'·18E	5-8M	C	360°
Bassurelle Lt By	50°32'·74N	00°57'·69E	5-8M	B	360°
Antifer Approach Lt By A5	49°45'·83N	00°17'·40W		K	360°
Le Havre LHA Lanby	49°31'·38N	00°09'·88W	8-10M		360°
Ouessant NE Lt By	48°59'·48N	05°23'·94W	20M	B	360°
Ouessant SW Lanby	48°30'·10N	05°45'·10W	10M	M	360°
Pointe de Créac'h Lt (Ile Ouessant)	48°27'·55N	05°07'·76W	20M	C	030°-248
Chausée de Sein Lt By	48°03'·75N	05°07'·78W	10M	O	360°
S. Nazaire Lt By SN1	47°00'·07N	02°39'·84W	3-8M	Z	360°
S. Nazaire La Couronnée	47°07'·59N	02°20'·05W	3-5M		360°
BXA Lanby	45°37'·53N	01°28'·69W		B	360°
MID CHANNEL					
Channel Lt F	49°54'·46N	02°53'·74W	15M	O	360°
East Channel Lt By	49°58'·66N	02°28'·98W	10M	T	360°
EC2 Lt By	50°12'·13N	01°12'·49W	10M	T	360°
Greenwich Lt V	50°24'·54N	00°00'·10W	10M	M	360°
Varne Lt V	51°01'·29N	01°23'·90E	10M	T	360°
MPC Lt By	51°06'·13N	01°38'·25E	10M	O	360°
East Goodwin Lt F	51°13'·25N	01°36'·38E	10M	T	360°
Sandettié Lt F	51°09'·34N	01°47'·10E	10M	T	360°
Inter Bank Lt By	51°16'·47N	01°52'·23E	10M	M	
CHANNEL ISLANDS					
Casquets Lt	49°43'·32N	02°22'·62W	25M	T	360°
Platte Fougère Lt	49°30'·82N	02°29'·14W		P	
St Helier Demi de Pas Lt	49°09'·00N	02°06'·15W	10M	T	360°

SPEED, TIME AND DISTANCE IN NAUTICAL MILES

Speed in knots

Time in minutes	1	2	3	4	5	6	7	8	9	10	15	20
1	0·0	0·0	0·1	0·1	0·1	0·1	0·1	0·1	0·2	0·2	0·3	0·3
2	0·0	0·1	0·1	0·1	0·2	0·2	0·2	0·3	0·3	0·3	0·5	0·7
3	0·1	0·1	0·2	0·2	0·3	0·3	0·4	0·4	0·5	0·5	0·8	1·0
4	0·1	0·1	0·2	0·3	0·3	0·4	0·5	0·5	0·6	0·7	1·0	1·3
5	0·1	0·2	0·3	0·3	0·4	0·5	0·6	0·7	0·8	0·8	1·3	1·7
6	0·1	0·2	0·3	0·4	0·5	0·6	0·7	0·8	0·9	1·0	1·5	2·0
7	0·1	0·2	0·4	0·5	0·6	0·7	0·8	0·9	1·1	1·2	1·8	2·3
8	0·1	0·3	0·4	0·5	0·7	0·8	0·9	1·1	1·2	1·3	2·0	2·7
9	0·2	0·3	0·5	0·6	0·8	0·9	1·1	1·2	1·4	1·5	2·3	3·0
10	0·2	0·3	0·5	0·7	0·8	1·0	1·2	1·3	1·5	1·7	2·5	3·3
11	0·2	0·4	0·6	0·7	0·9	1·1	1·3	1·5	1·7	1·8	2·8	3·7
12	0·2	0·4	0·6	0·8	1·0	1·2	1·4	1·6	1·8	2·0	3·0	4·0
13	0·2	0·4	0·7	0·9	1·1	1·3	1·5	1·7	2·0	2·2	3·3	4·3
14	0·2	0·5	0·7	0·9	1·2	1·4	1·6	1·9	2·1	2·3	3·5	4·7
15	0·3	0·5	0·8	1·0	1·3	1·5	1·8	2·0	2·3	2·5	3·8	5·0
16	0·3	0·5	0·8	1·1	1·3	1·6	1·9	2·1	2·4	2·7	4·0	5·3
17	0·3	0·6	0·9	1·1	1·4	1·7	2·0	2·3	2·6	2·8	4·3	5·7
18	0·3	0·6	0·9	1·2	1·5	1·8	2·1	2·4	2·7	3·0	4·5	6·0
19	0·3	0·6	1·0	1·3	1·6	1·9	2·2	2·5	2·9	3·2	4·8	6·3
20	0·3	0·7	1·0	1·3	1·7	2·0	2·3	2·7	3·0	3·3	5·0	6·7
21	0·4	0·7	1·1	1·4	1·8	2·1	2·5	2·8	3·2	3·5	5·3	7·0
22	0·4	0·7	1·1	1·5	1·8	2·2	2·6	2·9	3·3	3·7	5·5	7·3
23	0·4	0·8	1·2	1·5	1·9	2·3	2·7	3·1	3·5	3·8	5·8	7·7
24	0·4	0·8	1·2	1·6	2·0	2·4	2·8	3·2	3·6	4·0	6·0	8·0
25	0·4	0·8	1·3	1·7	2·1	2·5	2·9	3·3	3·8	4·2	6·3	8·3
30	0·5	1·0	1·5	2·0	2·5	3·0	3·5	4·0	4·5	5·0	7·5	10·0
35	0·6	1·2	1·8	2·3	2·9	3·5	4·1	4·7	5·3	5·8	8·8	11·7
40	0·7	1·3	2·0	2·7	3·3	4·0	4·7	5·3	6·0	6·7	10·0	13·3
45	0·8	1·5	2·3	3·0	3·8	4·5	5·3	6·0	6·8	7·5	11·3	15·0
50	0·8	1·7	2·5	3·3	4·2	5·0	5·8	6·7	7·5	8·3	12·5	16·7

DISTANCE FROM DIPPING LIGHT IN NAUTICAL MILES

Height of eye in feet

Height of light in metres	2	3	4	5	6	7	8	9	10	20	30	40	50
2	4·6	4·9	5·2	5·5	5·7	6·0	6·2	6·4	6·6	8·1	9·2	10·2	11·0
3	5·2	5·6	5·9	6·2	6·4	6·6	6·8	7·0	7·2	8·7	9·9	10·8	11·7
4	5·8	6·1	6·4	6·7	6·9	7·2	7·4	7·6	7·8	9·3	10·4	11·4	12·2
5	6·3	6·6	6·9	7·2	7·4	7·7	7·9	8·1	8·3	9·8	10·9	11·9	12·7
6	6·7	7·1	7·4	7·6	7·9	8·1	8·3	8·5	8·7	10·2	11·3	12·3	13·2
7	7·1	7·5	7·8	8·0	8·3	8·5	8·7	8·9	9·1	10·6	11·8	12·7	13·6
8	7·5	7·8	8·2	8·4	8·7	8·9	9·1	9·3	9·5	11·0	12·1	13·1	14·0
9	7·8	8·2	8·5	8·8	9·0	9·2	9·5	9·7	9·8	11·3	12·5	13·5	14·3
10	8·2	8·5	8·8	9·1	9·4	9·6	9·8	10·0	10·2	11·7	12·8	13·8	14·6
11	8·5	8·9	9·2	9·4	9·7	9·9	10·1	10·3	10·5	12·0	13·1	14·1	15·0
12	8·8	9·2	9·5	9·7	10·0	10·2	10·4	10·6	10·8	12·3	13·4	14·4	15·3
13	9·1	9·5	9·8	10·0	10·3	10·5	10·7	10·9	11·1	12·6	13·7	14·7	15·6
14	9·4	9·7	10·0	10·3	10·6	10·8	11·0	11·2	11·4	12·9	14·0	15·0	15·8
15	9·6	10·0	10·3	10·6	10·8	11·1	11·3	11·5	11·6	13·1	14·3	15·3	16·1
16	9·9	10·3	10·6	10·8	11·1	11·3	11·5	11·7	11·9	13·4	14·6	15·5	16·4
17	10·2	10·5	10·8	11·1	11·3	11·6	11·8	12·0	12·2	13·7	14·8	15·8	16·6
18	10·4	10·8	11·1	11·4	11·6	11·8	12·0	12·2	12·4	13·9	15·1	16·0	16·9
19	10·7	11·0	11·3	11·6	11·8	12·1	12·3	12·5	12·7	14·2	15·3	16·3	17·1
20	10·9	11·3	11·6	11·8	12·1	12·3	12·5	12·7	12·9	14·4	15·5	16·5	17·3
25	12·0	12·3	12·6	12·9	13·2	13·4	13·6	13·8	14·0	15·5	16·6	17·6	18·4
30	13·0	13·3	13·6	13·9	14·1	14·4	14·6	14·8	15·0	16·5	17·6	18·6	19·4
40	14·7	15·1	15·4	15·7	15·9	16·1	16·3	16·5	16·7	18·2	19·4	20·3	21·2
50	16·3	16·6	16·9	17·2	17·4	17·7	17·9	18·1	18·3	19·8	20·9	21·9	22·7
60	17·7	18·0	18·3	18·6	18·8	19·1	19·3	19·5	19·7	21·2	22·3	23·3	24·1

CHAPTER 2 - WEATHER

CONTENTS

Map of UK shipping forecast areas 64

Shipping forecast record 65

Beaufort scale & Met terminology 66

Weather sources in the UK
BBC Radio 4 broadcasts 67
BBC local radio station broadcasts 68
Broadcasts by HM Coastguard 70
Navtex 72
Telephone recordings 74
Fax messages 75
Mobile 'phones 76
Other sources 77

Weather sources abroad
Channel Islands 78
Ireland 79
Denmark 80
Germany 81
Netherlands 82
Belgium 83
France 83
North and North West Spain 86
Portugal 88
South West Spain 88
Gibraltar 89

Five language weather glossary 89

MAP OF UK SHIPPING FORECAST AREAS

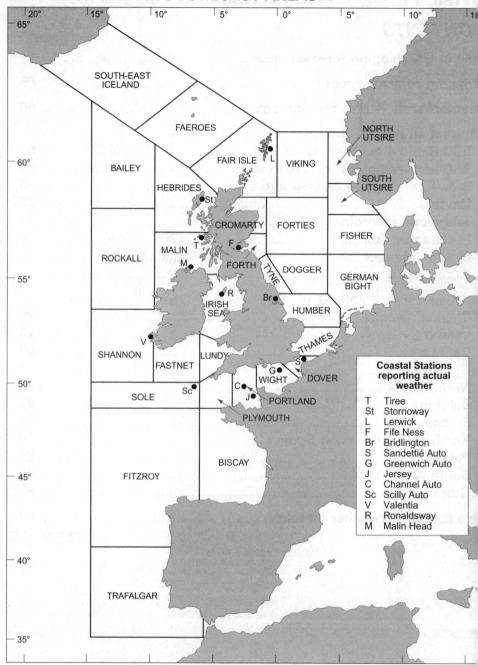

Coastal Stations reporting actual weather

T Tiree
St Stornoway
L Lerwick
F Fife Ness
Br Bridlington
S Sandettié Auto
G Greenwich Auto
J Jersey
C Channel Auto
Sc Scilly Auto
V Valentia
R Ronaldsway
M Malin Head

SHIPPING FORECAST RECORD Time/Day/Date ....

GENERAL SYNOPSIS

at .... UTC/BST

System position	Present position at	Movement	Forecast	

Gales	SEA AREA FORECAST	Wind (At first)	(Later)	Weather	Visibility
	VIKING				
	NORTH UTSIRE				
	SOUTH UTSIRE				
	FORTIES				
	CROMARTY				
	FORTH				
	TYNE				
	DOGGER				
	FISHER				
	GERMAN BIGHT				
	HUMBER				
	THAMES				
	DOVER				
	WIGHT				
	PORTLAND				
	PLYMOUTH				
	BISCAY				
	FITZROY				
	TRAFALGAR				
	SOLE				
	LUNDY				
	FASTNET				
	IRISH SEA				
	SHANNON				
	ROCKALL				
	MALIN				
	HEBRIDES				
	BAILEY				
	FAIR ISLE				
	FAEROES				
	S E ICELAND				

COASTAL REPORTS BST at .... UTC	Wind Direction	Force	Weather	Visibility	Pressure	Change	COASTAL REPORTS	Wind Direction	Force	Weather	Visibility	Pressure	Change
Tiree (T)							Greenwich Lt V (G)						
Stornoway (St)							Jersey (J)						
Lerwick (L)							Channel auto (C)						
Fife Ness (F)							Scilly auto (Sc)						
Bridlington (Br)							Valentia (V)						
Sandettie auto (S)							Ronaldsway (R)						

Beaufort scale

Force	Wind speed (knots)	(km/h)	(m/sec)	Description	State of sea	Probable wave ht(m)
0	0–1	0–2	0–0·5	Calm	Like a mirror	0
1	1–3	2–6	0·5–1·5	Light air	Ripples like scales are formed	0
2	4–6	7–11	2–3	Light breeze	Small wavelets, still short but more pronounced, not breaking	0·1
3	7–10	13–19	4–5	Gentle breeze	Large wavelets, crests begin to break; a few white horses	0·4
4	11–16	20–30	6–8	Moderate breeze	Small waves growing longer; fairly frequent white horses	1
5	17–21	31–39	8–11	Fresh breeze	Moderate waves, taking more pronounced form; many white horses, perhaps some spray	2
6	22–27	41–50	11–14	Strong breeze	Large waves forming; white foam crests more extensive; probably some spray	3
7	28–33	52–61	14–17	Near gale	Sea heaps up; white foam from breaking waves begins to blow in streaks	4
8	34–40	63–74	17–21	Gale	Moderately high waves of greater length; edge of crests break into spindrift; foam blown in well-marked streaks	5·5

Terms used in weather bulletins

a. Speed of movement of pressure systems

Slowly: Moving at less than 15 knots
Steadily: Moving at 15 to 25 knots
Rather quickly: Moving at 25 to 35 knots
Rapidly: Moving at 35 to 45 knots
Very rapidly: Moving at more than 45 knots

b. Visibility

Good: More than 5 miles
Moderate: 2 – 5 miles
Poor: 1000 metres – 2 miles
Fog: Less than 1000 metres

c. Barometric pressure changes (tendency)

Rising or falling slowly: Pressure change of 0·1 to 1·5 millibars in the preceding 3 hours.

Rising or falling: Pressure change of 1·6 to 3·5 millibars in the preceding 3 hours.

Rising or falling quickly: Pressure change of 3·6 to 6 millibars in the preceding 3 hours.

Rising or falling very rapidly: Pressure change of more than 6 millibars in the preceding 3 hours.

Now rising (or falling): Pressure has been falling (rising) or steady in the preceding 3 hours, but at the time of observation was definitely rising (falling).

d. Gale warnings

A **'Gale'** warning means that winds of at least force 8 (34-40 knots) or gusts reaching 43-51 knots are expected somewhere within the area, but no necessarily over the whole area. **'Severe Gale'** mean winds of at least force 9 (41-47 knots) or gusts reachin 52-60 knots. **'Storm'** means winds of force 10 (48-5 knots) or gusts of 61-68 knots. **'Violent Storm'** mean winds of force 11 (56-63 kn) or gusts of 69 kn or more and **'Hurricane Force'** means winds of force 12 (6 knots or more).

Gale warnings remain in force until amended o cancelled ('gales now ceased'). If a gale persists fo more than 24 hours the warning is re-issued.

e. Timing of gale warnings

Imminent   Within 6 hrs of time of issue

Soon   Within 6 – 12 hrs of time of issue

Later   More than 12 hrs from time of issu

f. Strong wind warnings

Issued, if possible 6 hrs in advance, when winds F6 c more are expected up to 5M offshore; valid for 12 hrs

g. Wind

Wind direction: Indicates the direction from whicl the wind is blowing.

Winds becoming cyclonic: Indicates that there wi be considerable changes in wind direction across th path of a depression within the forecast area.

Veering: The changing of the wind in a clockwis direction, i.e. SW to W.

Backing: The changing of the wind in an anti clockwise direction, i.e. W to SW.

WEATHER SOURCES IN THE UK

RADIO BROADCASTING

Shipping forecasts are broadcast by BBC Radio 4 at the following local times:

0048[1]	LW, MW, FM
0536[1]	LW, MW, FM
1201	LW only
1754	LW, FM (Sat/Sun)

Followed by the forecast for Inshore waters and weather reports from coastal stations.

The bands/frequencies used are:

LW	198 kHz
MW	
Newcastle:	603 kHz
Crystal Palace, Lisnagarvey	
and Londonderry:	720 kHz
Redruth:	756 kHz
Enniskillen & Plymouth:	774 kHz;
Aberdeen (Redmoss):	1449 kHz
Carlisle:	1485 kHz
FM	92·4-105 MHz

Contents of the shipping forecast

The forecast contains:

a summary of gale warnings in force. (Gale warnings are also broadcast at the earliest break in Radio 4 programmes after receipt, and after the next news bulletin).

a general synopsis for the next 24 hours with changes expected during that period; and

a forecast for each sea area for the next 24 hours, giving wind direction and force, weather and visibility. Sea area **Trafalgar** is included only in the 0048 forecast.

2. Weather reports from coastal stations follow the 0048 and 0535 shipping forecasts, but not those at 1201 and 1754.

The reporting stations are: Tiree, Stornoway, Lerwick, Fife Ness, Bridlington, Sandettie*, Jersey, Channel Lt V*, Greenwich Lt V*, Scilly*, Valentia, Ronaldsway, Malin Head. * Automatic station.

They are shown on the shipping forecast map and a block is provided for their contents. These reports include wind direction and Beaufort force, present weather, visibility, and sea-level pressure and tendency (if available).

Shipping forecasts cover large sea areas and cannot readily include the detailed variations that may occur inshore. If coasting, the Inshore waters forecast (see opposite) may be more helpful.

3. Inshore waters forecast, BBC Radio 4

The inshore waters forecast (up to 12M offshore around the UK and N Ireland) is broadcast after the 0048 and 0535 forecasts at approx 0053 and 0539 respectively. It is valid until 2359 on the day of issue and includes a general synopsis, forecasts of wind direction and force, visibility and weather.

It covers 9 stretches of inshore waters defined by places and headlands: clockwise from Duncansby Hd via Berwick-upon-Tweed, Whitby, N Foreland, St Catherine's Pt, Land's End, Colwyn Bay, Mull of Kintyre (inc L. Foyle to Carlingford Lough), Cape Wrath, Orkney and Shetland.

Strong Wind Warnings are issued by the Met Office to HM Coastguard, the BBC and local radio stations. Such warnings are issued whenever winds of Force 6 or more are expected over coastal waters up to 5M offshore. Whenever possible they are issued 6 hrs before the onset of strong winds and cover a period 12 hrs ahead.

4. After the 0048 inshore waters forecast, reports are broadcast of **actual weather** at: Boulmer, *Bridlington*, Sheerness, St Catherine's Point*, *Scilly**, Milford Haven, Aberporth, Valley, Liverpool (Crosby), *Ronaldsway*, Larne, Machrihanish*, Greenock, *Stornoway*, *Lerwick*, Wick*, Aberdeen and Leuchars. * Automatic station.

Stations in italics also feature in the 0048 and 0535 shipping forecasts.

5. BBC general (land) forecasts

Land area forecasts may include an outlook period up to 48 hours beyond the shipping forecast, more details of frontal systems and weather along the coasts. The most comprehensive land area forecasts are broadcast by BBC Radio 4 at the times of most News bulletins.

Wind strength in land area forecasts

Wind, as described in land forecasts, equates to the following Beaufort wind forces:

Calm:	0	Fresh:	5
Light:	1–3	Strong:	6–7
Moderate:	4	Gale:	8

Visibility in land area forecasts

Visibility, as described in land forecasts, equates to the following distances:

Mist:	Between 2000m and 1000m
Fog:	Less than 1000m
Dense fog:	Less than 50m.

6. The UK Met Office has moved from Bracknell to: FitzRoy Road, Exeter, Devon EX1 3PB. Tel and Fax numbers remain 0845 300 0300 and 0845 300 1300 respectively. Enquiries@metoffice.com www.met-office.gov.uk

Chapter 2

FORECASTS FROM LOCAL RADIO STATIONS

Many local radio stations broadcast local weather reports and forecasts. This information varies from present conditions to Small Craft Warnings when Force 6 or more winds are expected. Some local and regional BBC radio stations are listed below, but note that broadcast times (LT) tend to be a little approximate and the information is subject to change.

STATIONS +TIMES	FREQUENCIES
RADIO CORNWALL	**630, 657 kHz, 95.2, 96.0, 103.9 MHz**
Shipping	*Coastal Conditions*
Mon - Fri 0645	Mon - Fri 0725, 0825, 1225
Sat 0645	Sat 0725, 0825, 1310
Sun 0845 (*Tides and Shipping*)	Sun 0825
TideTimes	*Inshore waters*
Mon - Fri 0745	Mon - Fri 0610, 0715, 0815, 1030, 1225, 1725
Sat 0745	Sat 0610, 0715, 0815, 0930, 1130, 1310
Sun 0845 (*Tides and Shipping*)	Sun 0705, 0815, 0915, 1305

BBC RADIO DEVON **801, 855, 990, 1458 kHz, 94.8, 95.8, 96.0, 103.4, 104.3 MHz**
Shipping Forecast
Mon - Fri 0533, 0633, 0833, 1733
Sat 0645, 0735, 0845
Sun 0633, 0733

BBC RADIO SOLENT **1359, 999 kHz, 96.1, 103.8 MHz**
Weather, Shipping Forecast and Tide times
Mon-Fri Approx 0535
Shipping Forecast, Local sea conditions and Tide times
Mon - Fri 0645
Sat 0645, 0745
Sun 0645, 0745
Inshore Waters
Daily from 0630-1830 on every half hour
Shipping Movements
Mon - Fri 0533, 0645, 0845
Sat 0645
Sun 0645
'Solent Sea-Dog'
Mon - Sat 0650
Gunfacts
Tipnor Coastal Gunnery Range & Lulworth Range
Mon - Fri 0535, 0645
Sat - Sun 0745

BBC RADIO KENT **96.7, 97.6, 104.2 MHz**
Inshore Forecast, Tide times
Mon - Fri 0633, 0733, 0833, 1230, 1630, 1730, 1830
Inshore Forecast, Tide times
Sat 0733, 0833, 1305
Sun 0633, 0733, 0833, 0933, 1305

BBC RADIO ESSEX **765 kHz, 95.3, 103.5 MHz**
Inshore Forecast, Tide times
Mon - Fri 0744, 0844, 1744, 1844
Sat 0744, 0844, 1206, 1306
Sun 0744, 0844

BC RADIO SUFFOLK   **95.5,103.9 MHz**
nshore Forecast, Tide Times
Mon - Fri 0700, 0800, 1300, 1700, 1800
Sat - Sun 0600, 0700, 1300

BC RADIO HUMBERSIDE   **95.9 MHz, 1485 kHz**
Coastal Forecast
Mon - Fri 0633, 0733, 0833, 1230, 1633, 1833
at 0833; Sun 0915

BC RADIO YORK   **95.5 MHz, 1260 kHz (E Coast), 103.7 MHz 666 kHz Central), 104.3 MHz (Dales)**
nshore Forecast (Whitby to The Wash)
Mon - Fri 0635, 0735, 0835, 1800
at - Sun approx 0630, 0730

BC RADIO CLEVELAND   **95.0 & 95.8 MHz**
nshore Forecast (Hartlepool to Flamborough Hd)
Mon - Fri 0645, 0745, 0845, 1645, 1745, 1845
at - Sun 0745, 0845, 0945, 1230* (*Sun only)

BC RADIO NEWCASTLE   **1458 kHz, 95.4, 96.0, 103.7, 104.4 MHz**
nshore Forecast (Berwick to Flamborough Hd) Tide Times
Mon - Fri 0555, 0655, 0755, 0855, 1155, 1255, 1655, 1755
at - Sun 0754, 0854, 0954, 1154* (* Sun only)

BC RADIO SCOTLAND   **810 kHz, 92.7 - 94.3 MHz**
aily Weather Forecasts for Scotland
Mon - Fri 0658, 0758, 1258, 2158
at - Sun 0758, 1258
utdoor conditions
at - Sun 0658, 1858

BC RADIO CUMBRIA   **95.6, 96.1 MHz**
oastal Forecast
Mon - Fri 0632, 0732, 0832, 1732, 1832
at - Sun 0730, 0830

BC RADIO LANCASHIRE   **855, 1557 kHz, 95.5, 103.9, 104.5 MHz**
shore Waters Forecast
on - Fri 0750, 0850
ng Range Weather Forecast
un 0805, 1230

ADIO MERSEYSIDE   **1485 kHz, 95.8 MHz**
shore Waters Forecast
on - Fri 0700, 0800, 1200, 1300, 1715, 1745
at - Sun 0800, 0900, 1200, 1300, 1800

BC RADIO WALES   **657, 882, 1125 kHz, 92.4-94.6, 96.8, 103.5-105 MHz**
eneral Forecast, in English
on - Fri 0606, 0658, 0903, 1003, 1150, 1359, 1629*, 1729* (*also includes a weekly outlook)
at 0859, 1259, 1759
un 0859, 1759

BROADCASTS BY HM COASTGUARD

Coastguard	Shipping forecast areas	Local Inshore forecast areas	Broadcast times UT					
SOUTH COAST								
Falmouth	Plymouth, Lundy, Fastnet, Sole	8 & 9	0140	0540	*0940*	1340	1740	*2140*
Brixham	Plymouth, Portland	8	0050	0450	*0850*	1250	1650	*2050*
Portland	Plymouth, Portland, Wight	7 & 8	0220	0620	*1020*	1420	1820	*2220*
Solent	Portland, Wight	6 & 7	0040	0440	*0840*	1240	1640	*2040*
Dover	Thames, Dover, Wight	5, 6 & 7	0105	0505	*0905*	1305	1707	*2105*
EAST COAST								
Thames	Thames, Dover	5	0010	0410	*0810*	1210	1610	*2010*
Yarmouth	Humber, Thames	5	0040	0440	*0840*	1240	1640	*2040*
Humber	Humber, Tyne, Dogger, German Bight	3 & 4	0340	*0740*	1140	1540	*1940*	2340
Forth	Forth, Tyne, Dogger, Forties	2	0205	0605	*1005*	1405	1805	*2205*
Aberdeen	Fair I, Cromarty, Forth, Forties	1 & 2	0320	*0720*	1120	1520	*1920*	2320
Shetland	Faeroes, Fair I, Viking	1 & 16	0105	0505	*0905*	1305	1705	*2105*
WEST COAST								
Stornoway	Fair I, Faeroes, Bailey, Hebrides, Malin, Rockall	15	0110	0510	*0910*	1310	1710	*2110*
Clyde	Bailey, Hebrides, Rockall, Malin	13, 14 & 15	0020	0420	*0820*	1220	1620	*2020*
Belfast	Irish Sea, Malin	12	0305	*0705*	1105	1505	*1905*	2305
Liverpool	Irish Sea, Malin	11	0210	0610	*1010*	1410	1810	*2210*
Holyhead	Irish Sea	10	0235	*0635*	1035	1435	*1835*	2235
Milford Haven	Lundy, Irish Sea, Fastnet	9 & 10	0335	*0735*	1135	1535	*1935*	2335
Swansea	Lundy, Irish Sea, Fastnet	9	0005	0405	*0805*	1205	1605	*2005*

COASTGUARD BROADCASTS OF SHIPPING AND INSHORE WATERS FORECASTS

Shipping & Inshore waters forecasts

CG Centres routinely broadcast the Shipping forecast for their adjacent sea areas, twice daily at the times given above in italics.

Inshore waters forecasts are broadcast every 4 hours as given above. The boundaries of the 16 areas used by the CG for these forecasts are shown opposite. These areas are not referred to by their numbers in the actual forecast.

VHF working channels 10, 23, 73, 84 and 86 are used for all such broadcasts. The channel to select is first announced on VHF Ch 16.

But the locations of remote transmitters and their working channels are slowly being published. Thus far (Oct 2003) they include:

Aberdeen MRCC

Dunnet Head	84	58°40'N 03°22'W
Ben Tongue	23	58°30'N 04°24'W
Noss Head	84	58°29'N 03°03'W
Thrumster	84	58°24'N 03°07'W
Windyhead	23	57°39'N 02°14'W
Rosemarkie	86	57°38'N 04°05'W
Banff	23	57°38'N 02°31'W
Peterhead	86	57°31'N 01°46'W
Foyers	86	57°14'N 04°31'W
Gregness	86	57°08'N 02°03'W

Brixham MRSC

Beer Head	84	50°41'N 03°05'
Teignmouth	10	50°34'N 03°32''
Berry Head	86	50°24'N 03°29''
Dartmouth	23	50°21'N 03°35'W
East Prawle	73	50°13'N 03°42''
Salcombe	84	50°15'N 03°45''
Rame Head	10	50°19'N 04°13''
Fowey	86	50°20'N 04°38''

Falmouth MRCC

Falmouth	23	50°09'N 05°06''
Lizard	86	49°58'N 05°12''
St Mary's	23	49°56'N 06°18''
Trevose Head	86	50°33'N 05°02''

Humber MRSC

Newton	23	55°31'N 01°37''
Whitby	84	55°29'N 00°36''
Cullercoats	84	55°04'N 01°28''
Hartlepool	23	54°42'N 01°10''
Flamborough	23	54°07'N 00°05''
Easington	84	53°39'N 00°06''

Shetland MRSC

Saxa Vord	23	60°42'N 00°51''
Collafirth	73	60°32'N 01°23''
Shetland	84	60°10'N 01°08''
Fitful Head	10	59°54'N 01°23''
Wideford	23	58°59'N 03°01''

The following MF frequencies are also used, after an announcement on 2182 kHz: **Falmouth** 2226 kHz; **Solent** 1641 kHz; **Yarmouth** 1869 kHz; **Humber** 2226 kHz; **Aberdeen** 2226 kHz; **Shetland** 1770 kHz; **Stornoway** 1743 kHz; **Clyde** 1883 kHz; **Holyhead** 1880 kHz; and **Milford Haven** 1767 kHz.

Gale or strong wind warnings, weather messages and shipping forecasts are broadcast after initial announcements on VHF Ch 16 and 2182 kHz.

Actual weather On request, CG Centres may report the actual weather in their vicinity. But the CG stress that they are not qualified Met observers and such reports may be simply a look out of the window or originate from passing ships and yachts.

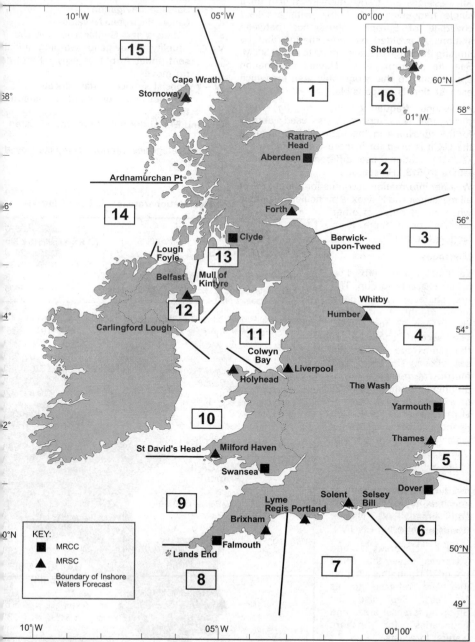

KEY:
- ■ MRCC
- ▲ MRSC
- —— Boundary of Inshore Waters Forecast

Inshore waters forecasts: Area boundaries used by the Coastguard

NAVTEX

Navtex uses a dedicated aerial, receiver and integral printer or LCD screen. The user programmes the receiver for the required station(s) and message categories. It automatically prints or displays MSI, ie weather, navigational and safety data.

All messages are transmitted in English on a single frequency of 518 kHz, with excellent coverage of Europe. Interference between stations is avoided by time sharing and by limiting the range of transmitters to about 300M. See the diagram below. Navtex information applies only to the geographic area for which each station is responsible.

A second frequency, *490 kHz (in italics throughout this chapter)*, is used abroad for transmissions in the national language; in the UK it is used for inshore waters forecasts. *490 kHz* stations use different identification letters to 518 kHz stations.

Weather information accounts for about 75% of all messages and Navtex is particularly valuable when out of range of other sources, or if there is a language problem.

Messages

Each message is prefixed by a four-character group. The first character is the code letter of the transmitting station (eg **E** for Niton). The second character is the message category, see above. The third and fourth are message serial numbers, running from 01 to 99 and then re-starting at 01. The serial number 00 denotes urgent messages which are always printed. Messages which are corrupt or have already been printed are rejected. Weather messages, and certain other message types, are dated and timed. All Navtex messages end with NNNN.

Note: Navareas and Metareas have the same boundaries; in this chapter they are referred to as Metareas. See also the Shipping forecast areas and boundaries for Inshore waters forecasts.

Message categories

A*	Navigational warnings
B*	Meteorological warnings
C	Ice reports
D*	SAR info and Piracy attack warnings
E	Weather forecasts
F	Pilot service
H	Loran-C
J	Satellite navigation
K	Other electronic Navaids
L	Subfacts and Gunfacts for the UK
V	Amplifying navigation warnings initial sent under A; plus weekly oil and g rig moves
W – Y	Special service – trial allocation
Z	No messages on hand at schedule time

G, I and **M – U** are not at present allocated

* These categories cannot be rejected by th receiver.

Navtex stations/areas – UK & W Europe

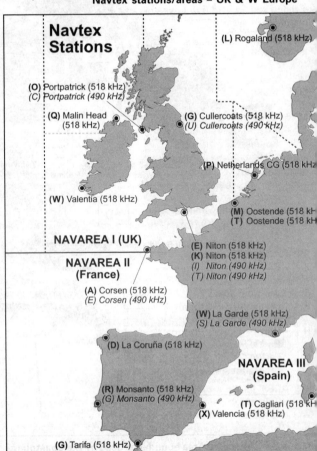

Navtex Stations

(L) Rogaland (518 kHz)

(O) Portpatrick (518 kHz)
(C) Portpatrick (490 kHz)

(Q) Malin Head (518 kHz)

(G) Cullercoats (518 kHz)
(U) Cullercoats (490 kHz)

(P) Netherlands CG (518 kHz)

(W) Valentia (518 kHz)

(M) Oostende (518 kH
(T) Oostende (518 kH

NAVAREA I (UK)

NAVAREA II (France)

(E) Niton (518 kHz)
(K) Niton (518 kHz)
(I) Niton (490 kHz)
(T) Niton (490 kHz)

(A) Corsen (518 kHz)
(E) Corsen (490 kHz)

(W) La Garde (518 kHz)
(S) La Garde (490 kHz)

(D) La Coruña (518 kHz)

NAVAREA III (Spain)

(R) Monsanto (518 kHz)
(G) Monsanto (490 kHz)

(T) Cagliari (518 kH
(X) Valencia (518 kHz)

(G) Tarifa (518 kHz)

UK 518 kHz stations

The times (UT) of weather messages are in bold; the times of an extended outlook (a further 2 or 3 days beyond the shipping forecast period) are in italics. The Sea Areas covered follow the sequence on page 70.

G – Cullercoats   *0100* 0500 **0900** 1300 1700 **2100**
Fair Isle clockwise to Thames, excluding N & S Utsire, Fisher and German Bight.

O – Portpatrick   *0220* **0620** 1020 1420 **1820** 2220
Lundy clockwise to SE Iceland.

E – Niton   *0040* 0440 **0840** 1240 1640 **2040**
Thames clockwise to Fastnet, excluding Trafalgar.

UK 490 kHz stations

These provide forecasts for the Inshore waters (12M offshore) of the UK, including Shetland, plus a national 3 day outlook for inshore waters. Times are UT.

U – Cullercoats	*Cape Wrath to North Foreland*	*0720*		*1920*
C – Portpatrick	*St David's Head to Cape Wrath*		*0820*	*2020*
I – Niton	*The Wash to Colwyn Bay*	*0520*		*1720*

Navtex coverage abroad

Selected Navtex stations in Metareas I to III, with their identity codes and transmission times, are listed below. Times of weather messages are shown in **bold**. Gale warnings are usually transmitted 4 hourly.

METAREA I (Co-ordinator – UK) Transmission times (UT)

K – **Niton** (Note 1)	0140	0540	0940	1340	1740	2140
T – Niton (Note 2)	*0310*	*0710*	*1110*	*1510*	*1910*	*2310*
W – **Valentia**, Eire	0340	**0740**	**1140**	1540	**1940**	2340
Q – **Malin Head**, Eire	0240	**0640**	**1040**	1440	**1840**	2240
P – **Netherlands CG**, Den Helder	**0230**	0630	1030	**1430**	1830	2230
M – **Oostende**, Belgium (Note 3)	0200	0600	1000	1400	1800	2200
T – **Oostende**, Belgium (Note 4)	0310	**0710**	1110	1510	**1910**	2310
L – **Rogaland**, Norway	**0150**	0550	0950	**1350**	1750	2150

Note 1 In English, no weather; only Nav warnings for the French coast from Cap Gris Nez to Île de Bréhat.
2 *In French, weather info (and Nav warnings) for sea areas Humber to Ouessant (Plymouth).*
3 No weather information, only Nav warnings for NavArea Juliett.
4 Forecasts and strong wind warnings for Thames and Dover, plus Nav info for the Belgian coast.

METAREA II (Co-ordinator – France)

A – **Corsen**, Le Stiff, France	0000	0400	0800	**1200**	1600	2000
E – Corsen, Le Stiff, France (In French)	*0040*	*0440*	*0840*	*1240*	*1640*	*2040*
D – **Coruña**, Spain	0030	0430	**0830**	1230	1630	**2030**
R – **Monsanto**, Portugal	**0250**	**0650**	**1050**	**1450**	**1850**	**2250**
G – Monsanto, Portugal (In Portuguese)	*0100*	*0500*	*0900*	*1300*	*1700*	*2100*
F – **Horta**, A ores, Portugal	**0050**	**0450**	**0850**	**1250**	**1650**	**2050**
J – Horta, Açores, (In Portuguese)	*0130*	*0530*	*0930*	*1330*	*1730*	*2130*
G – **Tarifa**, Spain (English & Spanish)	0100	0500	**0900**	1300	1700	**2100**
I – **Las Palmas**, Islas Canarias, Spain	0120	0520	**0920**	**1320**	**1720**	2120

METAREA III (Co-ordinator – Spain)

X – **Valencia**, Spain (English & Spanish)	0350	**0750**	1150	1550	**1950**	2350
W – **La Garde**, (Toulon), France	0340	**0740**	**1140**	1540	1940	**2340**
S – La Garde, (Toulon), France (In French)	*0300*	*0700*	*1100*	*1500*	*1900*	*2300*
T – **Cagliari**, Sardinia, Italy	0310	**0710**	1110	1510	**1910**	2310

WEATHER BY TELEPHONE

Marinecall recorded forecasts for Inshore waters

For any of 16 UK inshore areas, call **09066 526 + the Area number** shown below. For a National inshore waters forecast for 3 to 5 days dial the suffix 234. 09066 calls cost 60p per minute at all times.

Forecasts cover the waters out to 12M offshore for up to 5 days and include: General situation, any strong wind or gale warnings in force, wind, weather, visibility, sea state, maximum air and sea temperatures. The initial 2 day forecast is followed by a forecast for days 3 to 5. Forecasts are updated at 0700 and 1900 daily. Area 250 (Channel Islands) is additionally updated at 1300.

The local inshore forecast for Shetland is only available from Shetland CG on ☎ 01595 692976.

Recorded forecasts for offshore planning

For 2 to 5-day planning forecasts for offshore areas, updated 0800 daily, call **09066 526** plus the 3-digit number: **251** English Channel; **252** Southern North Sea; **253** Irish Sea; **254** Biscay; **255** NW Scotland; **256** Northern North Sea.

Recorded actual weather (Marinecall)

For reports of the actual weather at 47 coastal stations call ☎ **09068 226** plus the three-digit number below.

These reports are updated hourly and include air temperature, weather, cloud, wind/gusts, visibility, pressure and tendency.

Inshore & Offshore forecast areas by Telephone

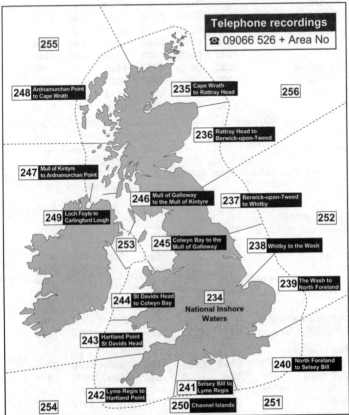

432	Channel Lt V	**453**	Boulmer
	Guernsey		Tynemouth
	Bréhat	**454**	Bridlington
451	Cape Wrath		Holbeach
	Wick	**455**	Walton-o-t-Naze
	Lossiemouth		Weybourne
452	Peterhead		Sheerness
	Aberdeen	**456**	Greenwich Lt V
	Fife Ness		Dover
			Newhaven
		457	Thorney Island
			Lee-on-Solent
			St Catherine's Pt
		458	Brixham
			Plymouth
			Falmouth
			St. Mary's (Scilly)
		459	Cardiff
			Mumbles
			Milford Haven
		460	Aberdaron
			Aberporth
			Valley
		461	Rhyl
			Crosby
			Walney Island
		462	Machrihanish
			Prestwick
			Greenock
		463	Oban
			Tiree
		464	Benbecula
			Aultbea
			Butt of Lewis
		465	Ballycastle
			Bangor
			Malin Head

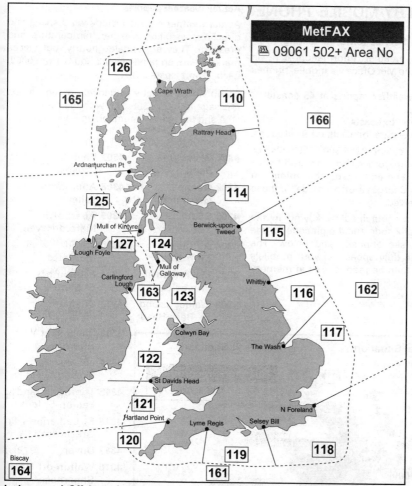

MetFAX
📠 09061 502+ Area No

126
165
Cape Wrath
110
166
Rattray Head
Ardnamurchan Pt
114
125
Berwick-upon-Tweed
115
Mull of Kintyre
127 124
Lough Foyle
Mull of Galloway
Carlingford Lough
163 123
Whitby
116
162
Colwyn Bay
The Wash
117
122
St Davids Head
121
N Foreland
Hartland Point
Lyme Regis Selsey Bill
120
Biscay
164
119
161
118

Inshore and Offshore forecast areas and codes by Fax

WEATHER BY FAX (MetFAX)

Inshore waters forecasts

For 2 day forecasts and synoptic charts for inshore waters dial 09061 502 + Area No required, as shown above. For a National inshore 3-5 day forecast the suffix is 109. Press the 'Start' key after the introductory remarks. 09061 calls cost £1.50 per minute and the length of call is about three minutes.

Offshore areas' planning forecasts

For 2 – 5 day forecasts and 48/72 hour synoptic charts for the offshore Areas shown above dial 09061 502 + Number of the area required:

161	English Channel
162	Southern North Sea
163	Irish Sea
164	Biscay
165	North West Scotland
166	Northern North Sea

Other MetFAX services

For other MetFAX services dial 09060 100 plus:

401	Marine index
426	Forecast charts for 2, 3, 4 and 5 days
441	Shipping forecast (updated 0030, 0600, 1400, 1800)
444	Surface analysis charts
445	24 hr surface forecast chart
446	Guide to surface charts
447	Chart of latest UK weather reports
450	3-5 days inshore waters forecast
474	Med/European plotted chart
498	Users guide to satellite image
499	Satellite image

Further details from the Met Office Customer Centre, ☎ 0845 300 0300; 📠 0845 300 1300. www.metoffice.com

WEATHER BY MOBILE 'PHONE

Short Message Service (SMS, or texting)

The following weather information can be obtained from the Met Office via mobile 'phones using SMS:

a. Actual weather reports at 45 coastal stations.
b. Shipping forecasts.
c. Inshore waters forecasts for 9 UK areas.

First register by calling 0845 300 0300 (H24) or on line at www.metoffice.com and credit your account with a credit card; the minimum payment is £10. Charges are only made for those messages received.

Forecasts etc are obtained by keying in the appropriate prefix code and 4 digit code for the area required; see opposite and below. The information will duly appear on your mobile's screen. It can then be read, stored in memory or deleted.

Actual weather reports

Actual weather reports include wind speed and direction, visibility, weather, temperature and pressure. They are updated hourly, but places marked * are updated every 3 hours from 0000. Each report costs 30p.

To obtain an actual weather report send a text message to 07712 396 853, with the prefix MET CRA and the relevant number, eg MET CRA 4317 for Dover.

4301	Ballycastle Bangor Hbr*	4307	Rhyl Crosby
4302	Oban* Greenock	4308	Aberdaron Valley
4303	South Uist Tiree	4309	Aberporth Milford Haven
4304	Aultbea Stornoway	4310	Cardiff Mumbles
4305	Machrihanish Prestwick	4311	Falmouth* St Mary's
4306	Walney Island St. Bees Head	4312	Brixham Plymouth
		4313	Channel Lt V Guernsey
		4314	Jersey Bréhat*
		4315	Thorney Island Lee-on-Solent
		4316	St Catherine's Pt Greenwich Lt V
		4317	Dover
		4318	Walton-o-t-Naze Sheerness*
		4319	Weybourne Holbeach
		4320	Bridlington Donna Nook
		4322	Aberdeen Fife Ness
		4323	Peterhead* Lossiemouth
		4324	Sule Skerry Wick

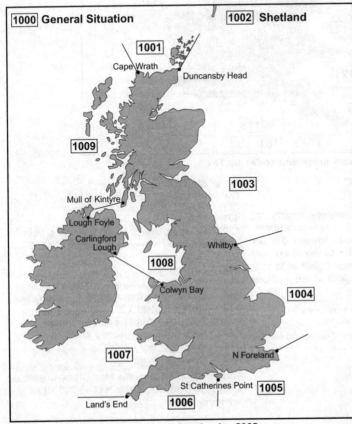

Inshore waters forecast areas and codes by SMS

Shipping forecast and gale warnings

To obtain a Shipping forecast send a text message to 07712 396 853, with the prefix MET SAF and the relevant number, eg MET SAF 4424 for sea area Wight. To obtain a gale warning, if any are in force: As above, with the prefix MET SAG, eg MET SAG 4427 for Biscay.

Forecasts are updated at 0001, 0500, 1100 and 1700 UT. Forecasts & gale warnings cost 10p/message.

4411	Viking	4426	Plymouth
4412	North Utsire	4427	Biscay
4413	South Utsire	4428	Fitzroy
4414	Forties	4429	Sole
4415	Cromarty	4430	Lundy
4416	Forth	4431	Fastnet
4417	Tyne	4432	Irish Sea
4418	Dogger	4433	Shannon
4419	Fisher	4434	Rockall
4420	German Bight	4435	Malin
4421	Humber	4436	Hebrides
4422	Thames	4437	Bailey
4423	Dover	4438	Fair Isle
4424	Wight	4439	Faeroes
4425	Portland	4440	SE Iceland

Inshore waters forecast

The Inshore waters forecast is issued twice daily at 0500 and 2300 UT and covers the next 24 hours. It includes wind speed and direction, weather and visibility, plus sea state for the first 6 hours of the forecast. The forecast areas are shown opposite. The cost is 50p/message.

To obtain an Inshore waters forecast, send a text message to 07712 396 853 using the prefix MET IWF and the number required, eg MET IWF 006 for St Catherine's Point to Land's End.

1000	General situation
1001	Cape Wrath to Duncansby Head, including Orkney
1002	Shetland
1003	Duncansby Head to Whitby
1004	Whitby to North Foreland
1005	North Foreland to St Catherine's Point
1006	St Catherine's Point to Land's End
1007	Land's End to Colwyn Bay
1008	Colwyn Bay to Mull of Kintyre, including Lough Foyle to Carlingford Lough
1009	Mull of Kintyre to Cape Wrath

OTHER SOURCES

Internet

A range of meteorological information is available over the Internet including MetFAX marine services, 2 and 3 to 5 day inshore forecasts, shipping forecasts, gale warnings; coastal reports charts and satellite images. Visit the Meteorological Office site at:

www.met-office.gov.uk

More information is available from the MetWEB Helpline ☎ 0845 300 0300 or e-mail:

sales@meto.gov.uk

Press forecasts

The better papers include a synoptic chart which, in the absence of any other chart, can help to interpret the shipping forecast. However, the interval between the time of issue and the time at which they are available next day may make press forecasts of only limited value to yachtsmen.

Television forecasts

Some TV forecasts show a synoptic chart which, with the satellite pictures, can be a useful guide to the weather situation.

In the UK Ceefax (BBC) gives the weather index on page 400, inshore waters forecasts on page 409 and 5 day forecasts on page 405. Teletext (ITN) has a weather index on page 151, shipping forecasts on page 157 and inshore waters forecasts on page 158. Antiope is the equivalent French system.

In some remote areas abroad a TV forecast in a bar, cafe or even shop window may be the best or only source of weather information.

UK Weather Centres and Met Offices

London	020 7696 0573/020 7405 4356
Norwich	01603 763898
Newcastle	0191 232 3808
Aberdeen Airport	01224 210575
Kirkwall Airport, Orkney	01856 873802
Sella Ness, Shetland	01806 242069
Glasgow	0141 248 7272
Manchester	0161 4771017
Cardiff	029 2022 5746
Bristol	0117 927 6265

Forecasters direct

A Met Office forecaster in the UK can be called H24 on ☎ + 44 (0) 8700 767 888 for a detailed briefing on, for example, the synoptic situation, specific weather windows or the longer term outlook, plus answers to any questions. Pay a flat rate of £17·00 by credit card.

To call a forecaster in Gibraltar for weather in the Mediterranean or Canary Islands dial ☎ + 44 (0) 8700 767 818. Pay by credit card at a flat rate of £15·00; no time limit is specified, but 5-10 mins is average. For a Fax forecast, £3 by credit card, dial 🖷 + 44 (0)8700 767 818.

CHANNEL ISLANDS

Jersey Met Dept. For the recorded CI shipping forecast for the area bounded by 50°N, the French coast from Cap de la Hague to Ile de Brehat and 03°W, call ☎ 0900 665 0022 (069 69 88 00 if calling from Guernsey). The forecast includes: general situation, 24hr forecast for wind/weather/ visibility/sea state/swell/sea temperature and St Helier tide times and heights, plus 2 to 4 day outlooks. For credit card charges call ☎ +44 (0)1534 745550 or 🖷 +44 (0)1534 746351.
Briefing by a forecaster costs £5.00 for unlimited time: Call ☎ +44 (0)1534 745550 with credit card details and transfer to the forecaster on ☎ +44 (0)1534 492256.

Jersey Radio 1659 kHz and Ch 25, 82. Storm warnings on receipt and at 0307, 0907, 1507 and 2107 UT. Near gale warnings, synopsis, 24hr forecast and outlook for next 24 hrs for CI south of 50°N and east of 03°W. Station reports at 0645[1], 0745[1], 0845[1], 1245 ,1845 and 2245 UT ([1] hr earlier when DST in force).

Saint Helier Pierheads Ch 18. Wind speed/direction/gusts (meaned over 10 minute period) is automatically broadcast every 2 minutes.

BBC Radio Jersey 1026 kHz and 88·8 MHz. Storm warnings on receipt. Wind information at 0635, 0710, 0735, 0810, 0835, 1710, 1735 and 1835 LT. Shipping forecast, synopsis, visibility, reports from selected stations, wind direction/force for local Jersey waters at 0635 and 1800 LT Mon-Fri; 0735 LT Sat/Sun.

BBC Radio Guernsey 1116 kHz and 93·2 MHz. Coastal forecast, synopsis, storm warnings, wind strength, plus shipping movements are broadcast for the waters around Guernsey, Herm and Sark at 0630, 0730, 0830 LT Mon-Sun; and 1730 M-F. In the summer actual weather at the following stations is included: Alderney, Guernsey, Jersey, Cap de la Hague, Cherbourg, Dinard, Portland & Channel Lt V

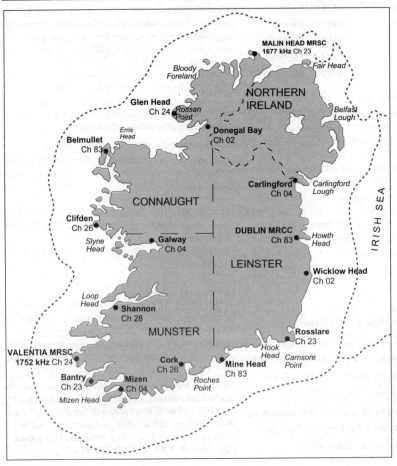

Provinces, headlands, sea areas and coastal stations referred to in weather broadcasts are shown here. Forecasts for coastal waters cover areas within 30M of the shore.

IRELAND

COAST RADIO STATIONS (All broadcasts are given 1hr earlier when DST is in force).

Gale warnings, a synopsis and 24-hour forecasts for up to 30M offshore and for the Irish Sea are broadcast on VHF at 0103, 0403, 0703, 1003, 1303, 1603, 1903 & 2203 (UT) after an initial announcement on Ch 16. The broadcasting stations (anti-clockwise) and VHF channels are:

MALIN HEAD 23, Glen Head 24, Donegal Bay 02, Belmullet 83 and Clifden 26.

Galway 04, Shannon 28, VALENTIA 24, Bantry 23, Mizen 04 and Cork 26.

Mine Head 83, Rosslare 23, Wicklow Head 02, DUBLIN 83 and Carlingford 04.

Gale warnings are broadcast on these VHF channels on receipt and at 0033, 0633, 1233 & 1833 (UT), after an initial announcement on Ch 16. Small craft warnings are broadcast if F6 winds are expected within 30M of the coast, Apr-Sep.

MF broadcasts. Valentia Radio broadcasts on 1752 kHz: (a) forecasts for sea areas Shannon and Fastnet at 0833, 2033 UT, and on request. (b) Gale warnings at the end of the next silence period after receipt and at 0303, 0903, 1503 and 2103 (UT), after an initial announcement on 2182 kHz.

NATIONAL AND LOCAL RADIO STATIONS

RTE (Radio Telefís Éireann) Radio 1 on 567 & 729 kHz and FM (see below), broadcasts a synopsis, detailed forecast and gale warnings in force for coastal waters and the Irish Sea; plus a 24 hour outlook at 0605, 1955, 2355 Mon-Thu; 0605, 2355 Fri; and 0605, 1250, 1955, 2355 Sat, Sun and public Holidays; all times UT. Broadcasts are 1hr earlier when DST is in force.

The main transmitters and FM frequencies are:

East Coast Radio: Bray Head 96·2 MHz (covering South Dublin area) and Ballyguile 102·9 MHz (covering Wicklow area). Broadcasts a general forecast, storm warnings and wind strength for area from Dublin Bay to Arklow Head at every H+06 (0700-1800 LT) after the news bulletin.

South Coast Radio: Mount Leinster 95·6 MHz, Gorey 96·2 MHz, Wexford 96·4 MHz. Broadcasts at 0712 LT (Mon-Fri) and every H+30 (0700-1800 LT) H24 after the commercial break include a detailed general forecast and synopsis for coastal waters, plus storm warnings if adverse weather is forecast.

WLR FM: Faha Ring 95·1 MHz, Carrickpherish 97·5 MHz. Broadcasts at every H+04 and 1315 1815 LT include a general forecast, gale warnings, wind strength for area from Youghal to Kilmore Quay. Tidal information is included from Jun-Sep.

Radio Kerry: The transmitters are at Mullaghanish 97·0 MHz (650m mountain, 16 miles SE of Killarney), Ballybunnion 97·6 MHz (mouth of the River Shannon), Portmagee 96·2MHz (by Valentia), Tralee 96·2 MHz (head of Tralee Bay) and Killarney 96·6 MHz (20 miles SSE of Tralee).

Broadcasts at 0004, 0104, 0704, 0804, 0835, 0910, 1004, 1104, 1204, 1330, 1404, 1504, 1604, 1704, 1740, 1904, 2104, 2204 and 2304 (all LT) include a general forecast, synopsis, gale warnings and wind strength for the coastal area from Cork to Shannon.

Broadcasts at 0755 and 1155 LT include a synopsis and forecast visibility, sea state and wind strength for sea areas Fastnet and Shannon.

Storm warnings

Gale warnings are broadcast by RTE Radio 1 on 567 kHz at the first programme juncture after receipt and with news bulletins; also by RTE 2 from Athlone 612 kHz, Dublin 1278 kHz and Cork 1278 kHz.

Telephone and Fax

The latest Sea area forecast and gale warnings can be obtained from Weatherdial ☎ 1550 123 855. The same information, plus isobaric, swell and wave charts are available by Fax on 1570 131 838.

It may be possible to speak to a forecaster at:

Central Forecast Office, Dublin (H24) (01) 424655
Dublin Airport Met   (01) 379900 ext 4531
Cork Airport Met (0900–2000)   (021) 965974
Shannon Airport Met (H24)   (061) 61333
Belfast International Airport   028 9031 2353

DENMARK

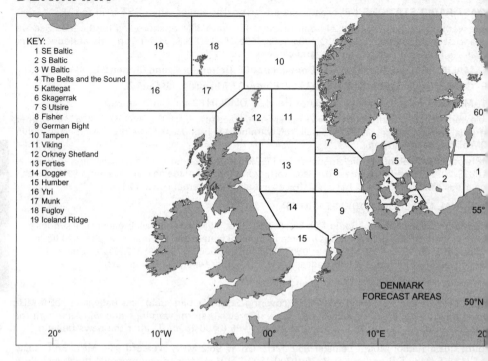

KEY:
1 SE Baltic
2 S Baltic
3 W Baltic
4 The Belts and the Sound
5 Kattegat
6 Skagerrak
7 S Utsire
8 Fisher
9 German Bight
10 Tampen
11 Viking
12 Orkney Shetland
13 Forties
14 Dogger
15 Humber
16 Ytri
17 Munk
18 Fugloy
19 Iceland Ridge

DENMARK
FORECAST AREAS

Lyngby Radio broadcasts gale warnings, synopsis and forecasts in Danish/English on receipt or on request from the following remote CRS, all using callsign *Lyngby Radio*:

Skagen	Ch 04, 1758 kHz	Areas 5 & 6.
Hirtshals	Ch 66	Areas 5, 6 & 8.
Hanstholm	Ch 01	Areas 6 & 8.
Bovbjerg	Ch 02	Areas 6, 8 & 9.
Blåvand	Ch 23, 1734 kHz	Areas 8 & 9.

National Radio – Danmarks Radio
Programme 1 (**Kalundborg** 243 and 1062 kHz) broadcasts in Danish every hour after the news strong wind warnings for Danish Areas 2-5, Limfjorden and, only 1 May to 31 Oct, Area 9.

Programme 3 (Stations/freqs below) broadcasts at 0445, 0745, 1045, 1645 and 2145 UT the synoptic situation and outlook for all Danish areas. Plus a 5 day outlook for Areas 2-9 & 13-15; and a 7 day outlook for Jutland, The Islands and Bornholm, followed by reports from coastal stations.

North Jutland	96·6 MHz
West Jutland	92·9 MHz
SW Jutland	92·3 MHz
South Jutland	97·2 MHz

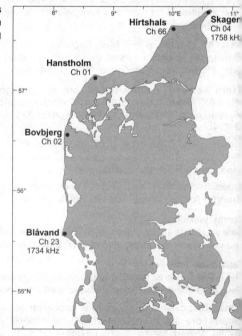

GERMANY

Deutsche Wetterdienst (DWD)

The German weather service provides weather info through a databank which is updated twice daily; more often for weather reports and text forecasts. German Weather Service, Frankfurter Str 135, 63067 Offenbach. ☎ + 49 (0) 69 8062-0 ⌨ + 49 (0) 69 8062 4484 www.dwd.de seeschifffahrt@dwd.de. SEEWIS (Marine weather information system) allows data to be accessed by telephone/modem and fed into an onboard computer.

Traffic Centres

Traffic Centres broadcast local storm warnings, weather messages, visibility and ice reports (when appropriate) in German. (E) = in **English** and German.

Traffic Centre	VHF Ch	Every
German Bight Traffic (E)	80	H+00
Ems Traffic	15, 18, 20, 21	H+50
Jade Traffic	20, 63	H+10
Bremerhaven Weser	02, 04, 05, 07, 21, 22, 82	H+20
Bremen Weser Traffic	19, 78, 81	H+30
Hunte Traffic	63	H+30
Cuxhaven Elbe Traffic (E)	71 (outer Elbe)	H+35
Brunsbüttel Elbe Traffic (E)	68 (lower Elbe)	H+05
Kiel Kanal II (E-bound)	02	H+15 & H+45
KielKanal III (W-bound)	03	H+20 & H+50

CRS – Seefunk (DPO7)

Seefunk CRS broadcast gale and strong wind warnings, synopsis, 12hr forecast, outlook for a further 12hr and coastal reports, in German, for areas B10-B12 and N9-N11 at 0745[A], **0945**, 1245, **1645** and **1945**[A] UT. [A]only in summer.

Hamburg (Control centre)	Ch 83
Borkum	Ch 28
Bremen	Ch 25
Elber-Weser	Ch 24
Nordfriesland	Ch 26

A 4-5 day outlook for the North and Baltic Seas is broadcast at the times above in bold.

Radio broadcasting
North German Radio (NDR)
a. NDR 1 Welle Nord (FM)

A synopsis, 12hrs forecast and 24hrs outlook are broadcast in German at 0730 UT (1 May – 30 Sep) for Helgoland, Elbe and North Frisian coast by: **Helgoland** 88·9 MHz; **Hamburg** 89·5 & 90·3 MHz; **Flensburg** 89·6 MHz; **Heide** 90·5 MHz; **Sylt** 90·9 MHz; **Kiel** 91·3 MHz.

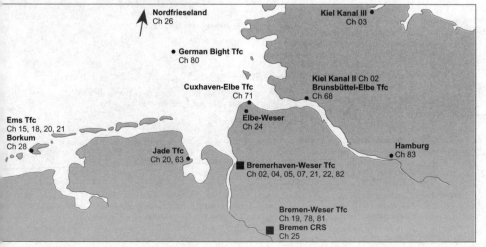

Chapter 2

b. NDR 4 Hamburg (MW)
A synopsis, 12hrs forecast and outlook for a further 12hrs are broadcast in German at 0005, 083(
and 2200 UT on 702 (Flensburg) & 972 (Hamburg) kHz for areas B10-B14 and N9-N12; plus Nortl
Sea station reports.

Radio Bremen (MW and FM)
A 12hrs wind forecast for Areas B11 and N10 is broadcast in German on receipt by: **Bremerhavel**
936 kHz; 89·3, 92·1, 95·4 & 100·8 MHz; and **Bremen** 88·3, 93·8, 96·7 & 101·2 MHz.

HF Radio
Offenbach (Main) broadcasts in **English** on 4583, 7646 and 10100·8 kHz at 0305, 0535, 0835,
1135, 1435, 1735 and 2035 UT: Weather reports for the North and Baltic Seas. At 0355,1530
UT: Medium term weather reports for the North Sea and 5 day prognosis for areas N1-12, A5,
A6 and IJsselmeer.

Telephone forecasts
For forecast and outlook (1 April – 30 Sep) call 0190 1160 (only within Germany) plus two digits
for the following areas:

45 North Frisian Islands and Helgoland	46 R Elbe to Hamburg
47 Weser Estuary and Jade Bay	48 E Frisian Islands and Ems Estuary
53 For inland pleasure craft	54 Denmark
55 Netherlands, IJsselmeer, Schelde, Maas	

For year-round weather synopsis, forecast and outlook, call 0190 1169 plus two digits as follows

20 General information	21 North Sea and Baltic
22 German Bight and SW North Sea	31 Reports for North Sea and Baltic
59 Current wind strength for North Sea coasts	

For the latest wind and storm warnings for individual areas of the North Sea coasts, call +49 4(
3196 628 (H24). If no warning is in force, a wind forecast for the German Bight is given.

NETHERLANDS

Netherlands Coastguard

a. VHF weather broadcasts
Forecasts for Dutch coastal waters up to 30M offshore (including IJsselmeer) are transmitted ir
English and Dutch at 0805, 1305, 1905, 2305 LT on the VHF channels shown below, without prio
announcement on Ch 16. Gale warnings are broadcast on receipt and at 0333, 0733, 1133, 1533
1933 and 2333 UT.

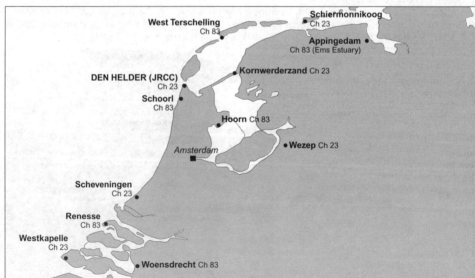

Westkapelle	Ch 23	Hoorn	Ch 83	Woensdrecht	Ch 83
Wezep	Ch 23	Renesse	Ch 83	Kornwerderzand	Ch 23
Scheveningen	Ch 23	West Terschelling	Ch 83	Schoorl	Ch 83
Schiermonnikoog	Ch 23	Den Helder	Ch 23	Appingedam	Ch 83

●. MF weather broadcasts

A forecast for sea areas Dover, Thames, Humber, German Bight, Dogger, Fisher, Forties and Viking is broadcast in **English** at 0940 & 2140 UT on 3673 kHz.

Gale warnings for these sea areas are broadcast in **English** on receipt and at 0333, 0733, 1133, 1533, 1933 and 2333 UT.

Radio Noord-Holland (FM)

Coastal forecasts, gale warnings and wind strength are broadcast in Dutch, Mon-Fri at 0730, 0838, 1005,1230 and 1705LT; Sat/Sun 1005, by:
Wieringermeer 93.9 MHz and **Haarlem** 97.6 MHz. In summer additional info is broadcast for leisure craft and beach areas.

BELGIUM

Coast Radio Stations

Oostende Radio broadcasts strong wind warnings and a forecast valid for sea areas Thames and Dover in **English** and Dutch on VHF Ch 27 and 2761 kHz at 0820 and 1720 UT. Strong wind warnings are also broadcast on receipt and at the end of the next two silent periods.

Antwerpen Radio broadcasts on VHF Ch 24 in **English** and Dutch for the Schelde estuary: Gale warnings on receipt, at the end of the next two silent periods and every odd H+05. Also strong wind warnings (F6+) on receipt and at every H+03 and H+48.

FRANCE

The French Met Office (Météo-France) issues a free annual booklet *Le Guide Marine* which summarises the various means by which weather forecasts and warnings are broadcast or otherwise disseminated. It can often be obtained from marina offices, on the internet (www.meteo.fr) or from Météo-France, Direction de la Production, Service de prévision marine, 42 ave Gaspard-Coriolis, 31057 Toulouse-Cedex; ☎ 05 61 07 80 80.

CROSS VHF broadcasts

CROSS broadcasts in French, after an announcement on Ch 16: Gale warnings, synopsis, a 12hrs forecast, 48hrs outlook for coastal waters. VHF working channels, coastal areas covered to 20M offshore, remote stations and local times are shown below. In the English Channel broadcasts can also be given in English, on request Ch 16. Gale warnings are routinely broadcast in French and **English** by all stations at H+03 and at other times as shown.

CROSS GRIS-NEZ - Ch 79   Belgian border to Baie de la Somme
Dunkerque	0720, 1603, 1920
Gris-Nez	0710, 1545, 1910
Ailly	0703, 1533, 1903

CROSS JOBOURG - Ch 80   Baie de la Somme to Cap de la Hague
Antifer	0803, 1633, 2003
Port-en-Bessin	0745, 1615, 1945
Jobourg	0733, 1603, 1933

Cap de la Hague to Pointe de Penmarc'h
Jobourg	0715, 1545, 1915
Granville	0703, 1533, 1903

Gale warnings for areas 13-15 in French and **English** on receipt, on request and at H+03, H+20 and H+50. 'Jobourg Traffic' (VTS) broadcasts traffic info and special weather bulletins at H+20 and H+50, Ch 20.

CROSS CORSEN - Ch 79   Cap de la Hague to Pointe de Penmarc'h
(Times in **bold** = 1 May to 30 Sep).

Cap Fréhel	0545, 0803, **1203**, 1633, 2003	Bodic	0533, 0745, **1145**, 1615, 1945
Ile de Batz	0515, 0733, **1133**, 1603, 1933	Le Stiff	0503, 0715, **1115**, 1545, 1915
Pte du Raz	0445, 0703, **1103**, 1533, 1903		

Gale warnings for areas 14-17 in French & **English** on receipt and at every even H+10 and H+50. Also a 24hr forecast for areas 14-17 in French and **English** at 0750, 1050, 1350, 1650, 1950 and 2250 UT.

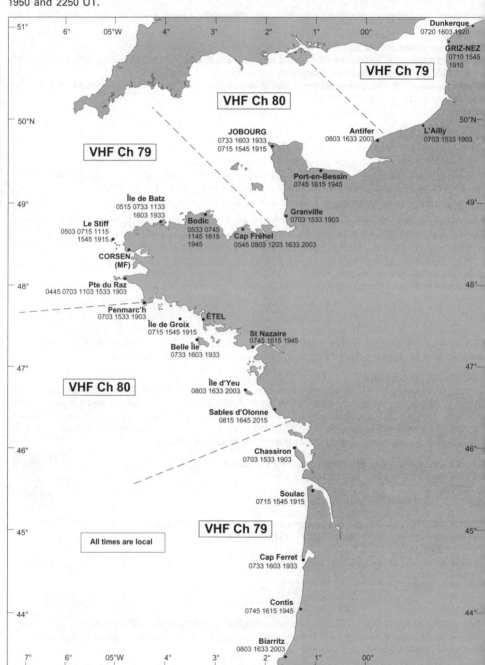

CROSS ÉTEL

Ch 80 Pte de Penmarc'h to Anse de l'Aiguillon		Ch 79 L'Anse de l'Aiguillon to Spanish border	
Penmarc'h	0703, 1533, 1903	Chassiron	0703, 1533, 1903
Ile de Groix	0715, 1545, 1915	Soulac	0715, 1545, 1915
Belle Ile	0733, 1603, 1933	Cap Ferret	0733, 1603, 1933
St Nazaire	0745, 1615, 1945	Contis	0745, 1615, 1945
Ile d'Yeu	0803, 1633, 2003	Biarritz	0803, 1633, 2003
Les Sables d'Olonne	0815, 1645, 2015		

CROSS MF broadcasts

CROSS Gris Nez and Corsen broadcast routine weather bulletins and gale warnings on 1650 kHz and 2677kHz in French; a prior announcement on 2182 kHz states the working frequency to be used. Gale warnings are broadcast on receipt and at every H+03.

CROSS	Routine bulletins	Areas
Gris Nez	0833, 2033 LT	10-15
Corsen	0815, 2015 LT	14-24

Radio broadcasting

France Inter (LW)   162 kHz (1852m)
For all areas: storm warnings, synopsis, 24hr fcst and outlook, broadcast in French for Areas 1 to 24 at 2003 LT daily. Additional stations which broadcast on MW at 0640 LT include Paris 864 kHz, Bordeaux 1206 kHz & Brest 1404 kHz.

RADIO FRANCE INTERNATIONALE (RFI)

RFI broadcasts weather messages in French on HF at 1130 UT daily. Frequencies and reception areas are: 6175 kHz North Sea, English Channel, Bay of Biscay; 15300, 15515, 17570 and 21645 kHz the North Atlantic, E of 50°W. Engineering bulletins indicating frequency changes are transmitted between H+53 and H+00.

Radio Bleue (MW)

Essentially a music programme, but with forecasts in French at 0655 LT covering:

English Channel & North Sea:	Paris	864 kHz	Lille	1377 kHz
English Channel & E Atlantic:	Rennes	711 kHz	Brest	1404 kHz
Bay of Biscay & E Atlantic:	Bordeaux	1206 kHz	Bayonne	1494 kHz

Local radio (FM)

Radio France Cherbourg   100·7 MHz
Coastal forecast, storm warnings, visibility, wind strength, tidal information, small craft warnings, in French, for the Cherbourg peninsula, broadcast 0829 LT by:

St Vaast-la-Hougue	85·0 MHz	Cherbourg	100·7 MHz
Cap de la Hague	99·8 MHz	Carteret	99·9 MHz

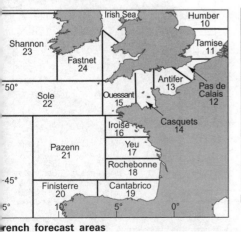

French forecast areas

Metarea II – SafetyNET forecast areas

Recorded forecasts by telephone

a. MÉTÉO (Weather). The BQR (*Bulletin Quotidien des Renseignements*) is a very informativ daily bulletin displayed in Hr Mr offices and YC's. For each French port, under TELEPHONE, Météᵉ is the ☎ of a local Met Office. Auto gives the ☎ for recorded inshore and Coastal forecasts; diᵃ 08 36 68 08 dd (dd is the Départment No, shown under each port). To select the inshore (*rivage* or Coastal (*Côte*; out to 20M offshore) bulletin, say "STOP" as your choice is spoken. Inshor bulletins contain 5 day forecasts, local tides, signals, sea temperature, surf conditions, etc. stron wind/gale warnings, general synopsis, 24hrs forecast and outlook.

b. For Offshore bulletins (*zones du large*) for Channel and North Sea, Atlantic or Mediterraneaᵣ dial ☎ 08 36 68 08 08. To select desired offshore area say "STOP" as it is named. Offshore bulletiᵣ contain strong wind/gale warnings, the general synopsis and forecast, and the 5 day outlook.

NORTH AND NORTH WEST SPAIN

Coast Radio Stations

VHF weather warnings and 48hr coastal forecasts are broadcast in Spanish at 0840, 1240 & 201 (UT) by:

Pasajes Ch 27; **Bilbao** Ch 26; **Santander** Ch 24; **Cabo Peñas** Ch 26; **Navia** Ch 60; **Cabo Ortegᵃ** Ch 02; **La Coruña** Ch 26; **Finisterre** Ch 22; **Vigo** Ch 65; and **La Guardia** Ch 21 .

MF gale warnings, synopsis and 24/48hr forecasts for Atlantic areas are broadcast at 0703 1303 190₁ (UT) by: **Machichaco** 1707 kHz; **Cabo Peñas** 1677 kHz; **La Coruña** 1698 kHz; and **Finisterre** 1764 kHᵢ

Recorded telephone forecasts

For a telephone weather recording in Spanish, call:

☎ 906 365 372 for Cantábrico and Galicia coasts.

☎ 906 365 374 for High Seas bulletins. This service is only available within Spain or foᵣ Autolink-equipped   vessels.

Coastguard MRCC/MRSC

Gale warnings and coastal forecasts are broadcast in Spanish and English on receipt and as listeᵈ

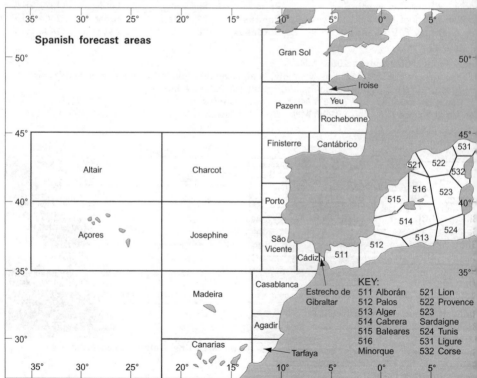

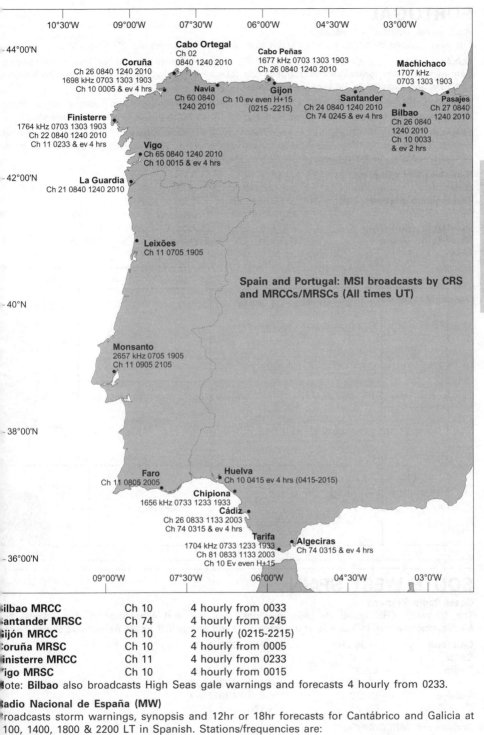

Spain and Portugal: MSI broadcasts by CRS and MRCCs/MRSCs (All times UT)

Cabo Ortegal
Ch 02
0840 1240 2010

Cabo Peñas
1677 kHz 0703 1303 1903
Ch 26 0840 1240 2010

Coruña
Ch 26 0840 1240 2010
1698 kHz 0703 1303 1903
Ch 10 0005 & ev 4 hrs

Machichaco
1707 kHz
0703 1303 1903

Navia
Ch 60 0840
1240 2010

Gijon
Ch 10 ev even H+15
(0215 -2215)

Santander
Ch 24 0840 1240 2010
Ch 74 0245 & ev 4 hrs

Pasajes
Ch 27 0840
1240 2010

Finisterre
1764 kHz 0703 1303 1903
Ch 22 0840 1240 2010
Ch 11 0233 & ev 4 hrs

Bilbao
Ch 26 0840
1240 2010
Ch 10 0033
& ev 2 hrs

Vigo
Ch 65 0840 1240 2010
Ch 10 0015 & ev 4 hrs

La Guardia
Ch 21 0840 1240 2010

Leixões
Ch 11 0705 1905

Monsanto
2657 kHz 0705 1905
Ch 11 0905 2105

Faro
Ch 11 0805 2005

Huelva
Ch 10 0415 ev 4 hrs (0415-2015)

Chipiona
1656 kHz 0733 1233 1933

Cádiz
Ch 26 0833 1133 2003
Ch 74 0315 & ev 4 hrs

Tarifa
1704 kHz 0733 1233 1933
Ch 81 0833 1133 2003
Ch 10 Ev even H±15

Algeciras
Ch 74 0315 & ev 4 hrs

Bilbao MRCC	Ch 10	4 hourly from 0033
Santander MRSC	Ch 74	4 hourly from 0245
Gijón MRCC	Ch 10	2 hourly (0215-2215)
Coruña MRSC	Ch 10	4 hourly from 0005
Finisterre MRCC	Ch 11	4 hourly from 0233
Vigo MRSC	Ch 10	4 hourly from 0015

Note: **Bilbao** also broadcasts High Seas gale warnings and forecasts 4 hourly from 0233.

Radio Nacional de España (MW)
Broadcasts storm warnings, synopsis and 12hr or 18hr forecasts for Cantábrico and Galicia at 100, 1400, 1800 & 2200 LT in Spanish. Stations/frequencies are:

San Sebastián	774 kHz	**Bilbao**	639 kHz
Santander	855 kHz	**Oviedo**	729 kHz
a Coruña	639 kHz		

PORTUGAL

Radionaval weather broadcasts
The three stations broadcast bulletins at the times (UT), VHF channels and MF frequencies listed below

Leixões (Porto)   Ch 11   0705, 1905   Storm, gale and poor visibility warnings
Synopsis and 24hr forecast for Portuguese coastal waters within 20M, covering area Rio Minho to Cabo de São Vicente. In Portuguese, repeated in **English**.

Monsanto (Lisbon)   Ch 11, 2657 kHz   0905, 2105   Storm, gale and poor visibility warnings
Synopsis and 24hr forecast for Areas 4, 6 and 16-19. In Portuguese, repeated in **English**.

Faro   Ch 11   0805, 2005   Storm, gale and poor visibility warnings
Synopsis and 24hr fcst for Portuguese coastal waters within 20M, covering area Cabo Carvoeiro to Rio Guadiana. In Portuguese, repeated in **English**.

Radiofusão Portuguesa
Broadcasts weather bulletins for the coastal waters of Portugal in Portuguese at 1100 UT
Transmitters and frequencies are:

Porto	720 kHz	**Viseu**	666 kHz
Montemor (Coimbra)	630 kHz	**Lisboa 1**	666 kHz
Miranda do Douro	630 kHz	**Elvas**	720 kHz
Faro	720 kHz, 97·6 MHz		

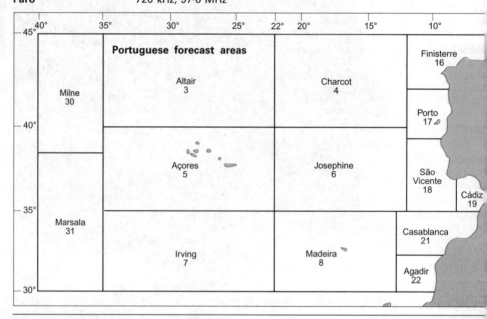

SOUTH WEST SPAIN

Coast Radio Stations
The following CRS broadcast gale warnings, synopsis and 48hr forecasts for Atlantic and Mediterranean areas, in Spanish, at the times (UT) and on the VHF or MF frequencies shown below

Chipiona	1656 kHz	0733 1233 1933
Cadiz	Ch 26	0833 1133 2003
Tarifa	Ch 81	0833 1133 2003
	1704kHz	0733 1233 1933
Malaga	Ch 26	0833 1133 2003
Cabo Gata	Ch 27	0833 1133 2003

Coastguard MRCC/MRSC
Broadcast in Spanish and **English** weather bulletins at the times (UT) and VHF channels listed below

Huelva MRSC	Ch 10	4 hourly (0415-2015)
Cadiz MRSC	Ch 74	0315, 0515, 0715, 1115, 1515, 1915, 2315

Tarifa MRCC   Ch 10, 67   Every even H+15. Actual wind and visibility at Tarifa, followed by a forecast for Strait of Gibraltar, Cádiz Bay and Alborán, in **English** and Spanish. Fog (visibility) warnings are broadcast every even H+15, and more frequently when visibility falls below 2M.

Algeciras MRSC   Ch 74   0315, 0515, 0715, 1115, 1515, 1915, 2315
Recorded telephone forecasts
Call ☎ 906 365 373 for a coastal waters bulletin for the Atlantic coast of Andalucia. ☎ 906 365 374 or High Seas bulletins. Bulletins are in Spanish. The service is only available within Spain and to Autolink-equipped vessels.

GIBRALTAR

Radio Gibraltar (Gibraltar Broadcasting Corporation)
Broadcasts in English: General synopsis, wind force and direction, visibility and sea state, radius 5M from Gibraltar. Frequencies are 1458 kHz, 91·3 MHz, 92·6 MHz and 100·5 MHz. Times (UT):
Mon-Fri: 0530, 0630, 0730, 1030, 1230
Sat: 0530, 0630, 0730, 1030
Sun: 0630, 0730, 1030

British Forces Broadcasting Service (BFBS)   **Gibraltar**
Gale warnings for the Gibraltar area are broadcast on receipt by BFBS 1 and 2. All broadcasts are in English and comprise: Shipping forecast, wind, weather, visibility, sea state, swell, HW & LW times for waters within 5M of Gibraltar.

BFBS 1 frequencies and times (Local):
93·5, 97·8* MHz FM.
Mon-Fri: 0745   0845   1005   1605
Sat: 0845   0945   1202
Sun: 0845   0945   1202   1602
*This frequency is reported to have greater range.

BFBS 2 frequencies and time:
89·4, 99·5 MHz FM. Mon-Fri: 1200 **UK Local time**

Talk to a forecaster
To talk to a forecaster in Gibraltar about localised weather in the Mediterranean or Canary Islands call ☎ + 44 (0) 8700 767 818. Calls are paid by credit card at a flat rate of £15·00; there is no specified time limit, but 5-10 minutes is average.

Mediterranean forecasts by Fax
From the UK dial 🖷 09060 100 + area numbers:
435   Gibraltar to Malaga   436   Malaga to Cartagena
437   Cartagena to Valencia   438   Valencia to Barcelona
439   Balearic Islands

FOREIGN WEATHER TERMS

English	German	French	Spanish	Dutch
air mass	Luftmasse	Masse d'air	Massa de aire	Luchtmassa
anticyclone	Antizyklonisch	Anticyclone	Anticiclón	Hogedrukgebied
area	Gebiet	Zone	Zona	Gebied
backing wind	Rückdrehender Wind	Vent reculant	Rolar el viento	Krimpende wind
barometer	Barometer	Baromètre	Barómetro	Barometer
breeze	Brise	Brise	Brisa	Bries
calm	Flaute	Calme	Calma	Kalmte
centre	Zentrum	Centre	Centro	Centum
clouds	Wolken	Nuages	Nube	Wolken
cold	Kalt	Froid	Frio	Koud
cold front	Kaltfront	Front froid	Frente frio	Kou front
cyclonic	Zyklonisch	Cyclonique	Ciclonica	Cycloonachtig
decrease	Abnahme	Affaiblissement	Disminución	Afnemen
deep	Tief	Profond	Profundo	Diep
deepening	Vertiefend	Approfondissant	Ahondamiento	Verdiepend
depression	Sturmtief	Dépression	Depresión	Depressie

English	German	French	Spanish	Dutch
Direction	Richtung	Direction	Direción	Richting
Dispersing	Auflösend	Se dispersant	Disipación	Oplossend
Disturbance	Störung	Perturbation	Perturbación	Verstoving
Drizzle	Niesel	Bruine	Lioviena	Motregen
East	Ost	Est	Este	Oosten
Extending	Ausdehnung	S'étendant	Extension	Uitstrekkend
Extensive	Ausgedehnt	Etendu	General	Uitgebreid
Falling	Fallend	Descendant	Bajando	Dalen
Filling	Auffüllend	Secomblant	Relleno	Vullend
Fog	Nebel	Brouillard	Niebla	Nevel
Fog bank	Nebelbank	Ligne de brouillard	Banco de niebla	Mist bank
Forecast	Vorhersage	Prévision	Previsión	Vooruitzicht
Frequent	Häufig	Fréquent	Frecuenta	Veelvuldig
Fresh	Frisch	Frais	Fresco	Fris
Front	Front	Front	Frente	Front
Gale	Sturm	Coup de vent	Temporal	Storm
Gale warning	Sturmwarnung	Avis de coup de vent	Aviso de temporal	Stormwaarschuwing
Good	Gut	Bon	Bueno	Goed
Gradient	Druckunterschied	Gradient	Gradiente	Gradiatie
Gust, squall	Bö	Rafalle	Ráfaga	Windvlaag
Hail	Hagel	Grêle	Granizo	Hagel
Haze	Diesig	Brume	Calina	Nevel
Heavy	Schwer	Abondant	Abunante	Zwaar
High	Hoch	Anticyclone	Alta presión	Hoog
Increasing	Zunehmend	Augmentant	Aumentar	Toenemend
Isobar	Isobar	Isobare	Isobara	Isobar
Isolated	Vereinzelt	Isolé	Aislado	Verspreid
Lightning	Blitze	Eclair de foudre	Relampago	Bliksem
Local	Örtlich	Locale	Local	Plaatselijk
Low	Tief	Dépression	Baja presión	Laag
Mist	Dunst	Brume légere	Nablina	Mist
Moderate	Mäßig	Modéré	Moderado	Matig
Moderating	Abnehmend	Se modérant	Medianente	Matigend
Moving	Bewegend	Se déplacant	Movimiento	Bewegend
North	Nord	Nord	Septentrional	Noorden
Occluded	Okklusion	Couvert	Okklusie	Bewolkt
Poor	Schlecht	Mauvais	Mal	Slecht
Precipitation	Niederschlag	Précipitation	Precipitación	Neerslag
Pressure	Druck	Pression	Presión	Druk
Rain	Regen	Pluie	lluvia	Regen
Ridge	Hochdruckbrücke	Crête	Cresta	Rug
Rising	Ansteigend	Montant	Subiendo	Stijgen
Rough	Rauh	Agitée	Bravo o alborotado	Ruw
Sea	See	Mer	Mar	Zee
Seaway	Seegang	Haute mer	Alta mar	Zee
Scattered	Vereinzelt	Sporadiques	Difuso	Verspreid
Shower	Schauer	Averse	Aguacero	Bui
Slight	Leicht	Un peu	Leicht	Licht
Slow	Langsam	Lent	Lent	Langzaam
Snow	Schnee	Neige	Nieve	Sneeuw
South	Süd	Sud	Sur	Zuiden
Storm	Sturm	Tempête	Temporal	Storm
Sun	Sonne	Soleil	Sol	Zon
Swell	Schwell	Houle	Mar de fondo	Deining
Thunder	Donner	Tonnerre	Tormenta	Donder
Thunderstorm	Gewitter	Orage	Tronada	Onweer
Trough	Trog, Tiefausläufer	Creux	Seno	Trog
Variable	Umlaufend	Variable	Variable	Veranderlijk
Veering	Rechtdrehend	Virement de vent	Dextrogiro	Ruimende wind
Warm front	Warmfront	Front chaud	Frente calido	Warm front
Weather	Wetter	Temps	Tiempo	Weer
Wind	Wind	Vent	Viento	Wind
Weather report	Wetterbericht	Météo	Previsión meteorologica	Weer bericht

CHAPTER 3 - COMMUNICATIONS

CONTENTS

Radio operation 92

Radio data 94

Port Radio Stations 96
  England - South coast 96
  England - East coast 97
  Scotland 98
  England - West coast & Wales 99
  Ireland 99
  Denmark 100
  Germany 100
  Netherlands 101
  Belgium 102
  North France 103
  Channel Islands 103
  West France 103
  Spain 104
  Portugal 104
  Gibraltar 104

VTS Charts 105
  Thames & Medway 105
  Humber Estuary 106
  Netherlands - Scheldemond & Westerschelde 107
  Netherlands - Approaches to Nieuwe Waterweg 108

VHF & MF Coast Radio Stations 109
  Channel Islands 109
  Republic of Ireland 109
  Denmark 110
  Germany 110
  North Spain 110
  Portugal 111
  South West Spain 111

Sound signals and shapes 112

Chapter 3

RADIO OPERATION

Avoiding interference

Before transmitting, first listen on the VHF channel. If occupied, wait for a break before transmitting, or choose another channel. If you cause interference you must comply immediately with any request from a Coastguard or Coast Radio Station to stop transmitting. The request will state how long to desist.

Control of communications

Ship-to-Shore: Except in the case of distress, urgency or safety, communications between ship and shore-based stations are controlled by the latter.

Intership: The ship *called* controls communication. If you call another ship, then it has control. If you are called by a ship, you assume control. If a shore-based station breaks in, both ships must comply with instructions given. A shore-based station has better aerials and equipment and so its transmission and reception ranges are greater.

Radio confidentiality

Inevitably you will overhear private conversations on VHF. It is illegal to reproduce them, pass them on or use them for any purpose.

Voice technique

There are two considerations when speaking:

What to say – *i.e. voice procedure*

How to say it – *i.e. voice technique*

Clear R/T speech is vital. If a message cannot be understood by the receiving operator it is useless.

Anyone can become a good operator by following a few rules: The voice should be pitched at a higher level than for normal conversation. Avoid dropping the voice pitch at the end of a word or phrase. Hold the microphone a few inches in front of the mouth and speak directly into it at a normal level. Speak clearly so that there can be no confusion. Emphasise words with weak syllables; 'Tower', if badly pronounced, could sound like 'tar'. People with strong accents must try to use as understandable a pronunciation as possible.

Messages which have to be written down at the receiving station should be spoken slowly. This gives time for it to be written down by the receiving operator. Remember, the average reading speed is 250 words a minute, whilst average writing speed is only 20. If the transmitting operator himself writes it down all should be well.

Difficult words may be spelled phonetically. Operators precede this with 'I spell'. If the word is pronounceable include it before and after it has been spelt. For example, if an operator sends the message 'I will moor alongside the yacht *Coila*' he would transmit: 'I will moor alongside the yacht *Coila* – I spell – Charlie Oscar India Lima Alfa – *Coila*'. When asked for your international callsign – say it is MGLA4 – transmit 'My callsign is Mike Golf Lima Alfa Four.'

The phonetic alphabet

The syllables to emphasise are underlined

Letter	Morse	Phonetic	Spoken as
A	•–	Alfa	AL-fah
B	–•••	Bravo	BRAH-voh
C	–•–•	Charlie	CHAR-lee
D	–••	Delta	DELL-tah
E	•	Echo	ECK-oh
F	••–•	Foxtrot	FOKS-trot
G	––•	Golf	GOLF
H	••••	Hotel	hoh-TELL
I	••	India	IN-dee-ah
J	•–––	Juliett	JEW-lee-ett
K	–•–	Kilo	KEY-loh
L	•–••	Lima	LEE-mah
M	––	Mike	MIKE
N	–•	November	no-VEM-ber
O	–––	Oscar	OSS-car
P	•––•	Papa	pa-PAH
Q	––•–	Quebec	keh-BECK
R	•–•	Romeo	ROW-me-oh
S	•••	Sierra	see-AIR-rah
T	–	Tango	TANG-go
U	••–	Uniform	YOU-nee-form or OO-nee-form
V	•••–	Victor	VIK-tah
W	•––	Whiskey	WISS-key
X	–••–	X-Ray	ECKS-ray
Y	–•––	Yankee	YANG-key
Z	––••	Zulu	ZOO-loo

Phonetic numerals

When numerals are transmitted, the following pronunciations make them easier to understand

No	Morse	Spoken as	No	Morse	Spoken as
1	•––––	WUN	6	–••••	SIX
2	••–––	TOO	7	––•••	SEV-EN
3	•••––	TREE	8	–––••	AIT
4	••••–	FOW-ER	9	––––•	NIN-ER
5	•••••	FIFE	0	–––––	ZERO

umerals are transmitted digit by digit except at multiples of thousands may be spoken s follows:

umeral	Spoken as
1	FOW-ER FOW-ER
9	NIN-ER ZERO
36	WUN TREE SIX
00	FIFE ZERO ZERO
478	WUN FOW-ER SEV-EN AIT
000	SEV-EN THOU-SAND

unctuation

unctuation marks should be used only where eir omission would cause confusion.

lark	Word	Spoken as
	Decimal	DAY-SEE-MAL
	Comma	COMMA
	Stop	STOP

rocedure words or 'prowords'

hese are used to shorten transmissions

ll after: Used after proword *'say again'* to equest repetition of a portion of a message

ll before: Used after proword *'say again'* to equest repetition of a portion of message

orrect: Reply to repetition of message that was receded by prowords *'read back for check'* hen it has been correctly repeated. Often aid twice

orrection: Spoken during the transmission of message means an error has been made in this ansmission. Cancel the last word or group of ords. The correct word or group follows

figures: Following numeral or group of umerals to be written as figures

letters: Following numeral or group of numerals be written as figures as spoken

say again: I am repeating transmission or ortion indicated

spell: I shall spell the next word or group of tters phonetically

ut: This is the end of working to you

ver: Invitation to reply

ead back: If receiving station is doubtful about ccuracy of whole or part of message it may epeat it back to the sending station, preceding e repetition with prowords *'I read back'*

ay again: Repeat your message or portion referred ie *'Say again all after'*, *'Say again address'*, etc

tation calling: Used when a station is uncertain f the calling station's identification

his is: This transmission is from the station hose callsign or name immediately follows

ait: If a called station is unable to accept traffic

immediately, it will reply 'WAIT.......MINUTES'. If probable delay exceeds 10 minutes the reason will be given

Word after or Word before: Used after the proword *'say again'* to request repetition

Wrong: Reply to repetition of message preceded by prowords *'read back'* when it has been incorrectly repeated

Calls, calling and callsigns

Shore-based stations normally identify themselves by using their geographical name followed by the word Radio, eg Solent Coastguard, Humber Radio, etc. Vessels usually identify themselves by the name on their licence but the International callsign assigned to the ship may be used in certain cases. If two yachts bear the same name or where some confusion may result, you should give your International callsign when starting communications, and thereafter use your ship's name as callsign.

'All ships' broadcast

Information to be received or used by all who intercept it, eg gale warnings, navigational warnings, weather forecasts etc, is generally broadcast by Coastguard Radio and addressed 'All stations'. No reply is needed.

Establishing communication with a shore-based station

The initial call is usually made on a working channel. Channel 16 should not be used except for distress, urgency or very briefly to establish a working channel.

- Switch to one of the station's working channels, pausing to check no-one is transmitting
- Are you close enough to try low power *(1 watt)* first? Possible at ranges up to 10 miles. Otherwise use high power *(25 watts)* with more battery drain. Then give the callsign of the station called *(up to three times only)* and prowords 'This is'
- The callsign of calling station up to three times only
- Indication of number of R/T calls you have to make
- Proword 'Over'

Small faults can drastically reduce your transmitting range. Possibly the aerial for the channel chosen has been optimised for areas east of the station and you are to the west. If approaching the station wait 15 minutes and call again. If the range is opening, either try again in hope, or try another station within range.

Every time you call at high power, you are decreasing battery state and the range your VHF will achieve.

Chapter 3

RADIO DATA

SHORT, MEDIUM and LONG RANGE RADIO COMMUNICATIONS

A suitable radio receiver on board will provide weather forecasts and time signals at scheduled times on a number of frequencies in various wavebands. With a maritime receiver you are not limited to the familiar BBC and commercial broadcasts. HM Coastguard transmit navigation warnings, storm warnings and weather messages for shipping in their respective sea areas.

Short range radiotelephony (RT) transmits and receives on VHF channels in the marine VHF (Very High Frequency) band. The equipment and procedures are simple, but range is normally limited to about 20 miles from ship to shore, rather less from ship to ship. Interconnection with national telephone systems is possible on certain VHF/RT channels when a yacht is within range of a Coast Radio Station, although there are now no such stations on the mainland of the UK, France or the Netherlands. Mobile telephones are now by far the most common form of ship to shore communication.

Medium range two-way communication operate in the marine MF (medium frequency) RT band, the 2MHz 'trawler band'. Single sideband techniques are employed on these medium frequencies and SSB equipment is essential. The effective range depends on the power of the transmitter on board and the sensitivity of the associated receiver; in general this might be up to 200 miles from certain (but not all) Coast Radio Stations.

Each channel in the VHF/RT band and each frequency in the MF/RT band has its specific purpose and may not be used at random for general conversation. Calling on the wrong channel merely wastes time and causes annoyance to other users.

THE MARINE VHF BAND

VHF is used by most vessels, Coast Radio Stations, ports, coastguard centres and other rescue services. Its range is slightly better than the line of sight between the transmitting and receiving aerials. It pays to fit a good aerial, as high as possible.

In the Marine VHF/RT band the individual frequencies are separated from their neighbours by exactly 25kHz 'elbow-room'

to eliminate mutual interference. Fo convenience each working frequency is give a channel number; the numbers do not ru consecutively because the channels wer originally spaced 50kHz apart. But it has sinc become possible to fit another channel i between each original one and so make full use of the waveband. Marine VHF frequencie are in the band 156·00 –174·00 MHz. Channe 29 to 59 are allocated to other purposes. Thu 55 channels are available, plus some wit special purposes (see below).

Of the 55 channels available in the Marine VHl RT band, small craft are unlikely to need mor than a selected dozen, some of which may var with the area in which a boat operates.

The simplest and earliest VHF/RT transmitte receivers operated only in the 'simplex' mod ie transmit and receive on the same channe so that only one person can talk at a time. Th channel numbers are 06 (mandatory), 08 to 1 67 to 74 and 77.

All other channels are for 'duplex' working, i transmit and receive on different frequencie so that conversation is normal.

For full duplex operation a more elaborate an expensive transmitter-receiver with either tw aerials or a special filter is needed, but it ca interconnect with the shore telephone syster so as to converse with subscribers who hav no knowledge of radio procedures.

More common among yachtsmens' VHF/RT however, are the semi-duplex operating set which, although involving simplex procedure allow you to communicate with station operating duplex systems and to link wit shore telephones via Coast Radio Stations.

VHF Channel Grouping

Channels are grouped for three main purpose but some can be used for more than on purpose. They are listed below in their preferre order of usage:

(1) *Public correspondence* (ie used to acces the shore telephone system via Coast Radi Stations): Ch 26, 27, 25, 24, 23, 28, 04, 01, 03, 0: 07, 05, 84, 87, 86, 83, 85, 88, 61, 64, 65, 62, 66, 6: 60, 82, 78, 81. All channels are duplex.

(2) *Inter-ship:* Ch 06, 08, 10, 13, 09, 72, 73, 67, 6! 77, 15, 17. These are all simplex channels. It is a well to know them, so that if another vesse calls you, you can swiftly nominate a workin channel from within this group.

Port Operations:

...mplex: Ch 12, 14, 11, 13, 09, 68, 71, 74, 69, 73, ...15.

...plex: Ch 20, 22, 18, 19, 21, 05, 07, 02, 03, 01, 04, ...82, 79, 81, 80, 60, 63, 66, 62, 65, 64, 61, 84.

...ecial purposes. The following channels have ...e specific purpose only:

...0 (156·00 MHz): SAR ops, not available ...yachts.

...13 (156·650 MHz): Intership safety of ...vigation (sometimes referred to as bridge- ...-bridge); a possible channel for calling a ...erchant ship if no contact on Ch 16.

...16 (156·80 MHz): Distress, Safety and calling. ...e *Chapter 4 for Distress and Safety*. Ch 16 ...ill be monitored by ships, CG centres (and, in ...me areas, any remaining Coast Radio ...tations) for Distress and Safety until at least ...05, in parallel with DSC Ch 70. Yachts should ...onitor Ch 16. After an initial call, the stations ...ncerned **must** switch to a working channel, ...cept for Safety matters.

...'s **10** (156·500 MHz), **23** (161·750 MHz), **73** ...56·675 MHz), **84** (161·825 MHz) and **86** (161·925 ...Hz): for MSI broadcasts by HMCG.

...**67** (156·375 MHz): the Small Craft Safety ...annel in the UK, accessed via Ch 16.

...**70** (156·525 MHz): exclusively for digital ...lective calling for Distress and Safety ...urposes.

...**80** (157·025 MHz): the primary working ...annel between yachts and UK marinas.

...**M** (157·85 MHz): the secondary working ...annel between yachts and UK marinas; ...reviously known as Ch 37.

...**M2** (161·425 MHz): for race control, with Ch ...4 as stand-by. YCs may apply to use Ch M2.

MEDIUM RANGE MF/RT

...he limited line-of-sight range of VHF/RT makes ...longer-range system desirable for small craft ...hich need to maintain contact with shore ...tations when offshore or in a coastal area to ...hich VHF cover does not extend.

...ingle sideband MF/RT provides such contact ...ll around the waters of the UK and Western ...urope. A receiver alone gives the ability to ...ear weather bulletins, storm and navigation ...arnings for local sea areas broadcast from ...oast Radio Stations in the 1.6 to 4.0MHz ...aritime band, ie on frequencies between

1605 and 4200 kHz. Not all radio stations are equipped to deal with this traffic but there are sufficient stations adequately spaced around the coast to cover all UK coastal waters.

Unlike VHF and HF, MF transmissions tend to follow the curvature of the earth, which makes them suitable for direction-finding equipment. For this reason, and because of their good range, the marine Distress radiotelephone frequency is in the MF band (2182 kHz).

TRAFFIC LISTS

Coast stations wishing to contact a vessel at sea will first attempt to do so by a direct call on Channel 16 which will be heard if a loudspeaker watch is kept and the vessel is within range. Failing this, the vessel's name will be added to the Traffic List broadcast at (usually) two hour intervals at the times and on the frequencies (channels) shown elsewhere in Coast Radio Stations section, pages 109 - 111. Unless you monitor that frequency at the appropriate time you may never know that there is incoming traffic awaiting attention. When such a call is received, the response is to call the station concerned on the working channel.

SILENCE PERIODS

Although there is no official silence period for VHF, it is generally advised that no transmission be made during the silence periods which are enforced for the 2182kHz distress frequency. The periods are the three minutes immediately after the whole and half hours, ie H to H+03 and H+30 to H+33.

LONG RANGE HF RADIO

HF radiotelephones use frequencies in the 4, 8, 12, 16 and 22 MHz bands (short wave) that are chosen to suit propagation conditions. HF is more expensive than MF and requires more power, but can provide worldwide coverage. A good installation and skilled operating techniques are essential for satisfactory results.

HF waves travel upwards and bounce off the ionosphere back to earth. Reception is better at night when the ionosphere is denser. The directional properties of HF transmissions are poor, so there is no HF Distress frequency.

PORT RADIO STATIONS

The following listings are derived from ALRS (Admiralty List of Radio Signals). They are therefore biassed towards 'Big Ships'. However if read in conjunction with Marina R/T details which appear in Chapter 1, pages 48 - 53, the most complete picture will emerge. (It is hoped to combine the two listings in a later edition).

Annotations: Ch 16 is almost universally guarded; it is therefore omitted. *Call on a working channel if essential. In many larger ports it is sensible to monitor the primary port channel (in bold) before changing to a marina channel.* Times are local, unless marked **UT. H24** = continuous watch. **HJ** = day only. **HX** = no specific hours.

ENGLAND – SOUTH COAST

ST MARY'S, Isles of Scilly: Ch 14 69
Summer only 0800-1700, Sat 0800-1200
NEWLYN:
Hbr office: Ch 09 **12**
Mon-Fri: 0800-1700, Sat: 0800-1200
PENZANCE:
Hbr office: Ch 09 **12** Mon-Fri: 0800-1730 Sat: 0830-1230. Access −2HW+1
FALMOUTH:
Falmouth Hbr Radio: Ch 12 14 (Mon-Fri 0800-1700). Harbour Launch *Killigrew:* **Ch 12**
Truro Hbr office: Call *Carrick One* **Ch 12**
MEVAGISSEY:
Hbr office: Ch 14
Summer: 0900-2100, Winter: 0900-1700
CHARLESTOWN:
Hbr office: Ch 14 Access −2HW+1, when vessel expected
PAR:
Hbr office: Ch 12 Access HW±2
FOWEY:
Fowey Hbr Radio and (0900-2200) **Hbr Patrol: Ch 12.** Water Taxi: Ch 06. Refueller: Ch 10
LOOE: Ch 16 HX
PLYMOUTH:
Naval: *Long Room Port Control* **Ch** 08 12 **14**
Sutton Hbr Lock: Ch 12 H24
Cattewater Hbr: Ch 14 (Mon-Fri 0900-1700)
SALCOMBE:
Salcombe Hbr or launch: Ch 14 May to mid-Sep: 7/7, 0600-2200; otherwise: M-F 0900-1600
Salcombe Hbr Taxi **Ch 12.** Fuel barge: **Ch 06**
Egremont (ICC Floating HQ): **Ch M**
DARTMOUTH:
Dart Nav Ch 11 M-F: 0830-1800, Sat: 0900-1200
Fuel barge: **Ch 06.** Water taxi: **Ch 08**
TORBAY HARBOURS:
Call *Brixham Port* or *Torquay Port* **Ch 14** May-Sep: 0800-1800; Oct-Apr: Mon-Fri: 0900-1700

TEIGNMOUTH:
Teignmouth Hbr Radio Ch 12 Mon-Fri 0800-1700; Sat 0900-1200 and when vessel due
EXETER:
Port of Exeter Ch 12 Mon-Fri: 0730-1730 and when vessel expected. **Exmouth Dock Ch 14**
Retreat Boatyard: Ch M HW±2
LYME REGIS:
Ch 14. Summer: 0800-2000, Winter: 1000-1500 Access HW±2½
BRIDPORT:
Bridport Radio Ch 11
PORTLAND:
Portland Harbour Radio Ch 74 (H24)
WEYMOUTH:
Hbr Office & Town Bridge: Ch 12 Mon-Fri: 0800-2000 (summer & when vessel is due)
Fuel: Ch 60
POOLE:
Harbour Control & Bridge Ch 14 (H24)
Poole Bay Fuels: Ch M Mon-Fri: 0900-1730, weekends in season 0830-1800
YARMOUTH (IoW):
Hbr office: Ch 68 H24. **Water taxi: Ch 15**
NEWPORT (IoW):
Hr Mr: 69 0800-1600
COWES:
Hbr Office & Chain Ferry Ch 69
Mon-Fri: 0800-1700 and by arrangement
Water Taxi: Ch 77
RYDE:
Hbr office: Ch 80
Summer 0900-2000 Winter HX. Access HW±2
BEMBRIDGE:
Harbour launch **Ch M**
SOUTHAMPTON:
Monitor Port operations Ch 12 14
VTS Broadcasts Ch 12 Every H 0600-2200, 1 Jun-30 Sep
HAMBLE:
Hbr Radio: Ch 68 Apr-Sep daily: 0600-2200, Oct-Mar 0700-1830
Water Taxi: Call *Blue Star Boats* **Ch 77 06**
PORTSMOUTH:
Monitor Ch 11. Call *QHM* **Ch 11** if essential
PORTSMOUTH COMMERCIAL HARBOUR:
Call *Portsmouth Hbr Radio* **Ch 11** 14 **(H24)**
LANGSTONE:
Hbr office: Ch 12. Summer: daily 0830-1700; Winter: Mon-Fri 0830-1700; Sat-Sun 0830-1300
CHICHESTER:
Hbr office: Ch 14. 1 Apr - 30 Sep: M-Fri: 0900-1300, 1400-1700. Sat: 0900-1300. 1 Oct - 31 March: 0900-1300, 1400-1700
Water taxi **Ch 08** 0900-1800, mobile 07970 378350
LITTLEHAMPTON:
Hbr office & Bridge: Ch 71 HX
Arun Yacht Club: Ch M Access HW±3

SHOREHAM:
Shoreham Hbr Radio: Ch 14 (H24) and lock
BRIGHTON:
Call Brighton Control: Ch M 80. Inner hbr only,
access 0800-1800 via lock
NEWHAVEN:
Newhaven Radio Ch 12; ditto Swing bridge
EASTBOURNE:
Sovereign Hbr, inc Lock/berthing: Ch 17
RYE:
Hbr radio: Ch 14 0900-1700 or when ship due
FOLKESTONE:
Call Port Control: Ch 15 for clearance to enter
DOVER:
Call Port Control Ch 74 for clearance to enter
Diesel fuel & Water Taxi: via marina Ch 80
DOVER STRAIT:
Channel Navigation Information Service
CNIS: Dover Coastguard Ch 11 67 80
Ch 11 bcsts Info H+40 plus extra bcst when
visibility <2M; ditto Gris Nez Traffic Ch 79 at
H+10, plus additional bcst every H+25 when
visibility <2M
RAMSGATE:
Port Control Ch 14

ENGLAND – EAST COAST
MEDWAY:
Monitor Medway Radio Ch 74
Kingsferry Bridge (W Swale): Ch 10 H24
WHITSTABLE:
Hbr Radio: Ch 09 12, Mon-Fri: 0830-1700 and
3HW+1
PORT OF LONDON:
Port Control London: Ch 12 (from seaward
approaches to Sea Reach No 4 buoy)
Port Control London: Ch 68
Sea Reach No 4 Lt buoy to Crayford Ness
Woolwich Radio: Ch 14, 22
Above Crayford Ness
Thames Barrier: Ch 14
All VHF-equipped vessels intending to navigate
the Thames Barrier Control Zone must report
to Woolwich Radio on Ch 14
RIVER THAMES:
Patrol Launches: Call Thames Patrol Ch 06 12 13
14 16
King George V Dock Lock: Call KG Control
Ch 13
West India Dock Lock: Ch 13
Greenwich Yacht Club: Ch M
Thames Lock (Brentford): Ch 74
Summer 0800-1800 Winter 0800-1630
Cadogan Pier: Ch 14 0900-1700
RIVER ROACH:
Havengore Bridge: Ch 72 HJ, Access HW±2
RIVER BLACKWATER:
River Bailiff: Ch 16 0900-1700
Heybridge Lock: Ch 80 –2HW+1

RIVER COLNE, BRIGHTLINGSEA:
Hbr Radio: Ch 68 0800-2000
RIVERS STOUR AND ORWELL:
HARWICH VTS: Ch 71 09 11 20 H24
SUNK VTS Ch 14 H24
Harwich International Port Ch 13
Ipswich Port Radio: Ch 68 H24
RIVER DEBEN:
Hbr office: Ch 08
SOUTHWOLD:
Port Radio: Ch 09 12;
LOWESTOFT:
Hbr Control: Ch 11 14
Royal Norfolk & Suffolk YC: Ch 80 Access
HW±4
Mutford Lock and Road Bridge: Ch 09 14
GREAT YARMOUTH:
Port Control/VTS: Ch 09 11 12 H24
Haven Bridge: Ch 12
WELLS-NEXT-THE-SEA:
Wells Hbr Radio: Ch 12
HJ and HW–3 when vessel expected
WISBECH:
Ch 09 HW–3 when vessel expected
Sutton Bridge: Ch 09
KING'S LYNN:
Call KLCB Ch 14 11
Mon-Fri: 0800-1730 and –4HW+1
BOSTON:
Dock: Ch 11 12
Grand Sluice: Ch 74 only when lock operates
Denver Sluice: Ch 73 when vessel expected
RIVER HUMBER:
VTS Area 1: Ch 14 (from sea to Clee Ness Lt F)
VTS Area 2: Ch 12 (up-river to Garleston on R
Trent and Goole on R Ouse). MSI broadcasts
on Ch 12 & 14 every 2hrs from 0103
Grimsby Docks: Ch 74; 18 79 H24
South Ferriby sluice: Ch 74 80
Mon-Fri: 0930-1700; Sat, Sun & Holidays:
1030-1700. Access HW±3
RIVER TRENT TO NEAR NEWARK
Burton-upon-Stather, Flixborough, Grove,
Keadby, Gunness, Gainsborough: All Ch 17.
Locks at Keadby, West Stockwith, Torksey and
Cromwell: All Ch 74
RIVER OUSE TO NABURN
Blacktoft Jetty: Ch 14
Goole Docks: Ch 14 H24
Goole Railway Bridge: Ch 09
Howdendyke: Ch 09
Boothferry bridge: Ch 09
Selby lock: Ch 74 HJ
Selby railway and Toll bridges: Ch 09 contact
10 mins in advance
Naburn Lock: Ch 74
BRIDLINGTON:
Hbr office: Ch 12 HX. Access HW±3
SCARBOROUGH:
Scarborough Lt Ho Ch 12 H24. Access HW±3

WHITBY:
HM & Bridge: **Ch 11**, 12 H24. Access HW±2
TEES and HARTLEPOOL:
Tees Port control: **Ch** 08, 11, 12, **14, 22**
R. Tees Barrage: **Ch M** H24
SEAHAM:
Hbr office: **Ch 12** Mon-Fri: 0800-1800
Access HW $-2\frac{1}{2}$ to $+1\frac{1}{2}$
SUNDERLAND:
Hbr Radio: **Ch 14** (H24)
TYNE, PORT OF:
Tyne Hbr Radio: **Ch 11 12** 14, inc Info service
Harbour Launch: **Ch** 06 08 11 12 14
BLYTH:
Port control: **Ch 11 12**
WARKWORTH HARBOUR (Amble):
Hbr office: **Ch 14** (Mon-Fri 0900-1700)
BERWICK-UPON-TWEED:
Hbr office: **Ch 12** Mon-Fri 0800-1700

SCOTLAND
EYEMOUTH:
Ch 12 office hours
FORTH PORTS:
Call *Forth Navigation* **Ch 71**; 12, **20** on request
Leith: **Ch 12**
Granton, Royal Forth YC: Call *Boswell* **Ch M**
Access HW±4
Grangemouth Docks: **Ch 14**
Methil Docks: **Ch 14** Access −3HW+1
Anstruther: **Ch 11** Access HW±2
PERTH:
Perth Harbour **Ch 09**
DUNDEE:
Dundee Harbour Radio **Ch 12**
Royal Tay YC: **Ch M**
ARBROATH:
Arbroath Port Control **Ch 11**
MONTROSE:
Montrose Port Control **Ch 12**
STONEHAVEN:
Stonehaven **Ch 11**
ABERDEEN:
Aberdeen Port Control **Ch** 06 11 **12** 13
PETERHEAD:
Peterhead Hbrs **Ch 14** for cl'nce to enter/exit
FRASERBURGH: Ch 12 H24
MACDUFF: Ch 12 H24
BANFF: Ch 14 HX, access HW±4
WHITEHILLS: *Whitehills Hbr Radio* **Ch 14**
BUCKIE: Ch 12 (Ch 16 is H24)
LOSSIEMOUTH:
Ch 12 0700-1700 & 1hr before vessel is due
HOPEMAN and BURGHEAD:
Burghead Radio **Ch 14** HX or when vessel due
INVERNESS:
Inverness Hbr Office: **Ch 12**
M-Fri: 0900-1700 and when vessel expected
Clachnaharry Sea Lock **Ch 74** HW±4 in HO

CROMARTY FIRTH, inc Invergordon: Ch 11
HELMSDALE: Ch 13
WICK: Ch 14 HX
SCRABSTER:
Port: **Ch 12** H24. Call on entry and exit.
ORKNEY HARBOURS NAVIGATION SERVICE
Orkney Harbour Radio **Ch** 09 **11** 12
Kirkwall: Ch 12
M-Fri: 0800-1700 and when vessel expected
Stromness Harbour: Ch 12 M-Fri: 0900-1700
Pierowall (Westray Pier): Ch 14 when vessel is expected
FAIR ISLE:
Call *Shetland Coastguard* **Ch 16**
SHETLAND
Lerwick Hbr: **Ch 11 12**
Scalloway Hbr Radio: **Ch** 09 **12**
Mon-Fri: 0600-1800, Sat: 0600-1230
Sullom Voe VTS: **Ch 14** for traffic info, weather and radar assistance on request
Balta Sound Harbour: **Ch 16** HO
OUTER HEBRIDES
STORNOWAY: Hbr office **Ch 12** H24
Loch Maddy, N Uist: **Ch 12** HX
St Kilda: Call *Kilda Radio* **Ch 16** HJ
MAINLAND
Kinlochbervie: **Ch 14** HX
Lochinver: **Ch 09** HX
ULLAPOOL: Ch 14 12 H24 fishing season, otherwise HO
Gairloch Harbour: **Ch 16** 0900-1400; 1900-2300
ISLE OF SKYE
Uig: **Ch 08** HX. Portree Harbour: **Ch 12** HX
Skye Bridge Crossing: **Ch 12**
KYLE OF LOCH ALSH: Ch 11
Mallaig: **Ch 09** HO
Tiree, Gott Bay Pier, : **Ch 31** HX
Isle of Coll, Arinagour Pier: **Ch 31**
Loch Sunart, Salen Jetty: **Ch 16**
ISLAND OF MULL
Tobermory: **Ch 12** HJ
Craignure Pier: **Ch 31** HX
Corpach/Caledonian Canal: **Ch 16** 74
Summer: 0700-2200; Spring/Autumn: 0830-1650; Winter: 0930-1530
OBAN:
Port **Ch 12** 0900-1700. Oban Bay, monitor **16**
CRINAN CANAL: Ch 74
May-Sep: 0800-1200, 1230-1600, 1620-1800; Oct: Mon-Sat: 0800-1200, 1230-1600; Nov-Apr Mon-Fri: 0900-1530
Tarbert, Loch Fyne: **Ch 14**
CAMPBELTOWN: Ch 12 13
Mon-Fri: 0900-1700
ROTHESAY, Bute: Ch 12
May-Sep: 0600-2100; Oct-Apr: 0600-1900
ARDROSSAN:
Hbr office: **Ch 12 14**

CLYDEPORT:
Clydeport Estuary Radio: Ch 12 H24
QHM Faslane: Ch 73 13
Greenock Control: Ch 73
IRVINE: Ch 12
Port & Bridge: Ch 12 HX, Mon-Fri: 0800-1600
TROON: Ch 14
Seacat, daily Arr: 0930, 2030; Dep 1015, 2100
AYR: Ch 14 H24
GIRVAN: Ch 12 Mon-Fri: 0900-1700
STRANRAER: Ch 14 (H24) Monitor for ferries
KIRKCUDBRIGHT: Ch 12 0800-1700
Access HW±3

ENGLAND W COAST & WALES

Silloth Docks: Ch 12 Access -2½HW+1
WORKINGTON:
Hbr Radio: Ch 11 14 Access -2½HW+2
WHITEHAVEN:
Ch 12 Access HW±3
ISLE OF MAN
Douglas Port Control and Info: Ch 12 H24.
Note: if unable to contact other IoM hbrs
below, call Douglas
Castletown: Ch 12 0830-1700
Port St Mary: Ch 12 HJ and when vessel due
Peel: Ch 12 HJ and when vessel expected
Ramsey: Ch 12 HO and when vessel due
MAINLAND
Barrow Port Control: Ch 12
Heysham Port: Ch 14 74
GLASSON DOCK Ch 69
Access -1½HW through lock
FLEETWOOD:
Fleetwood Dock Radio: Ch 12 0900-1700
Access HW±2 through lock
LIVERPOOL:
Call Mersey Radio Ch 12 for port operations
Information broadcasts: Ch 09 at 3h and 2h
before HW. Radar assistance Ch 18
Brunswick Dock: Ch M for Liverpool marina
Canning Dock: Ch M 0900-1700. Access -2HW
through lock to Albert Dock
CONWY:
Ch 12 14 Apr-Sep: 0900-1800; Oct-Mar: Mon-
Fri: 0900-1800. Access -3HW+2
MENAI STRAIT
Beaumaris & Menai Bridge: Ch 69
Mon-Fri: 0800-1700
Caernarfon: Call Caernarfon Hbr Ch 14
Mon-Fri: 0900-1700 Sat: 0900-1200
HOLYHEAD
Port Control: Ch 14 H24
PWLLHELI
Hbr office Ch 08 0900-1715. Access -2HW+1¾
PORTHMADOG
Call Portmadog Hbr Ch 12 14 0900-1700, and
when vessel expected. Access HW±1½

BARMOUTH
Ch 12 May-Sept: 0900-2200; Oct-April: 0900-
1700 weekdays only
ABERDOVEY: Ch 12 0900-1700 Access HW±3
ABERYSTWYTH: Ch 14 Access HW±3
ABERAERON: Ch 14 Served by NEW QUAY
Harbourmaster. 0900-1700. Access HW±3
FISHGUARD: Hbr office: Ch 14
MILFORD HAVEN
Port Control & Patrol launch: Ch 12, monitor
continuously whilst under way
Milford Docks: Call Pierhead Ch 14 09 12
Locking approx HW±3; freeflow HW -2 to HW
Tenby: Ch 80 Access HW±2½
Saundersfoot: Ch 11 Summer: 0800-2100,
Winter: Mon-Fri: 0800-1800. Access HW±2
SWANSEA BAY
Docks Radio: Ch 14 H24
Tawe Lock for marina: Ch 18
River Neath: Ch 77 H24 Port Talbot: Ch 12 H24
BARRY: Barry Radio Ch 11 Access -4HW+3
CARDIFF
Cardiff Radio Ch 14. Barrage control: Ch 18
NEWPORT:
Port: Ch 09 69 71 Access HW±4
SHARPNESS
Call Sharpness Radio Ch 13 for locking in
Canal operations: Ch 74 Access -5HW+1
BRISTOL
Avonmouth Sig Stn Avonmouth Radio: Ch 12
09 11 for reporting and VTS info on request
City Docks Radio: Ch 11 14 Access -3HW+1
Bristol Floating Hbr: Ch 73 Mon-Thu 0800-
1700; Fri 0800-1630; other times 0800-sunset.
Access -3HW+1 through lock
Prince Street Bridge and Netham Lock: Ch 73
BURNHAM-ON-SEA/BRIDGWATER
Hbr office: Ch 08 Access -3HW when vessel
is expected
ILFRACOMBE:
Hbr office: Ch 12 Apr-Oct: 0815-1700, when
manned; Nov-Mar: HX. Access HW±2
APPLEDORE-BIDEFORD:
Call Port/PV 'Two Rivers' Ch 12 Access -2HW
BUDE:
Hbr office: Ch 12 When vessel expected
PADSTOW:
Ch 12 M-Fri: 0800-1700 and HW±2
ST IVES: Ch 14 HX
Hayle Harbour: Ch 18 0900-1700

IRELAND

SHANNON ESTUARY: Ch 12 13
Galway: Ch 12 Access -2½HW+1
Rossaveel: Ch 12 14 Office Hours
CORK:
Port Ops: Ch 12 14
Kinsale: Ch 14. HO and when vessel expected

Bantry: Ch 06 11 12 14 H24
Castletown Bearhaven: Ch 14
Dingle Ch 11 M
Limerick: Ch 12 13
Office hours & when vessel expected
Fenit: Ch 12 14 HX
ROSSLARE EUROPORT:
Hbr office: Ch 06 12 14 H24
Waterford & New Ross: Ch 12 14 HJ &
when vessel expected
Youghal: Ch 14 Access HW±3
ARKLOW:
Port: Ch 14
WICKLOW:
Port: Ch 14 12
DUN LAOGHAIRE:
Hbr office: Ch 14
DUBLIN:
Port Radio: Ch 12 13
Lifting Bridge: Call Eastlink Ch 12 13
HOWTH:
Hr Mr: Ch 13 Mon-Fri: 0700-2300
Sat/Sun: HX
STRANGFORD HARBOUR:
Ch 12 14 M
Ardglass Harbour: Ch 14 12
Mon-Fri 0900-1700
Killyleagh: Ch 12 HX
Kilkeel: Ch 12 14 Mon-Fri: 0900-2000
Warrenpoint: Ch 12 H24
Greenore: Ch 16 HJ
Dundalk: Ch 14 Mon-Fri: 0900-1700
Drogheda: Ch 11 Mon-Fri: 0800-1700. HX
BELFAST:
VTS: Ch 12
Portavogie: Ch 12 14 Mon-Fri 0900-1700
LARNE:
Hr Mr: Ch 14
Cloghan Point: Ch 10
COLERAINE:
Ch 12 Mon-Fri 0900-1700
Portrush: Ch 12 Mon-Fri 0900-1700; Sat-Sun
0900-1700, Jun-Sep only
LONDONDERRY:
Hbr radio: Ch 14 12
SLIGO:
Hr Mr: Ch 12 14
0900-1700 and when vessel expected
Killybegs: Ch 14 when vessel expected
Burton Port: Ch 14 06 12

DENMARK
Skagen: Ch 12 13 H24
Hirtshals Havn: Ch 12 13 HX
Torup Strand: Ch 12 13 HX
Hanstholm Havn: Ch 12 13 HX
THYBORØN: Ch 12 13 H24

Torsminde: Ch 12 13 0300-1300, 1400-2400
Hvide Sande: Ch 12 13 HX
Esbjerg: Ch 12 H24 (HJ during ice)
Rømø Havn: Ch 10 12 13 HX

GERMANY
HELGOLAND:
Port: Ch 67
May-Aug: Mon-Thu: 0700-1200 1300-2000
Fri-Sat: 0700-2000 Sun: 0700-1200
Sep-Apr: Mon-Thu: 0700-1200 1300-1600
Fri: 0700-1200
INNER DEUTSCHE BUCHT
(GERMAN BIGHT):
VTS: Eastern part: Ch 80
VTS: Western part: Ch 79
NORD-OSTSEE KANAL:
KIEL KANAL:
VTS Canal 1 Ch 09 13
VTS Canal 2 Ch 02
VTS Canal 3 Ch 03
VTS Canal 4 Ch 12
Brieholz: Ch 73
Ostermoor: Ch 73
Friedrichskoog: Ch 10 Access HW±2
Büsum Port: Ch 11
Eider Lock: Ch 14
Husum Port: Ch 11
Information bcsts: Ch 11 every H+00. Access
–4HW+2
Pellworm Port: Ch 11 0700-1700
Wyk Port: Ch 11
List Port: Ch 11 0800-1200 1600-1800
BRUNSBÜTTEL ELBE PORT:
Port: Ch 12
Oste Bridge (flood barrage): Ch 69
Apr-Sep the bridge is opened on request
Ch 69. Oct-Mar request through Ch 03 or 16
Belum Radar or Ch 21 Cuxhaven Radar
Oste Bridge Geversdorf: Ch 69; The bridge
opens on request for small craft Apr-Sep:
0730-1930 and every H+00 and H+30
Oberndorf Bridge: Ch 69 Oct-Mar H24,
Apr-Sep 1930-0730. The bridge is opened on
request by telephone 04772 86 10 11
Stör Llock: Ch 09 The bridge is opened
on request
Glückstadt Lock: Ch 11 0700-1600 and during
HW
Stadersand Elbe Port: Ch 12
Este Lock: Ch 10
Este Bridge: Ch 10 Opened on request
DIE ELBE:
VTS: Ch 71
Brunsbüttel Elbe Traffic: Ch 68
HAMBURG:
VTS: Ch 74 13 14
Port Traffic: Ch 74 13 14

be Port: Ch 12
the Bridge: Ch 13
attwyk Bridge: Ch 13
arburg Lock: Ch 13
efstack Lock: Ch 11
UXHAVEN ELBE:
uxhaven Elbe Port: Ch 12 HX
uxhaven Lock: Ch 69
REMERHAVEN:
ort: Ch 12
schereihafen Lock: Ch 69 70
emerhaven Nord Lock: 69 70
emerhaven Weser:
ort: Ch 14
ake Lock: Ch 10
sfleth-Ohrt Railway Bridge: Ch 73 –
h before sunrise to 2h after sunset
unte Lock: Ch 73
unte lifting bridge: Ch 73 – 2h before
nrise to 2h after sunset
denburg:
ailway Bridge: Ch 73
24 except Sun and public holidays
30-0630
ck: Ch 20 Mon-Sat: 0500-2100
un: 0900-1200
äcilien Bridge: Ch 73
slebshausen Lock: Ch 12
REMEN:
ort: Ch 03
ck: Ch 20 Mon-Sat: 0600-2200, Sun: Oct-Apr
300-1100 May-Sep: 0800-1400 1730-1930
E WESER AND DIE HUNTE:
remerhaven Weser Tfc: Ch 02 04 05 07 21 22 82
remen Weser Traffic: Ch 19 78 81
unte Traffic:
TS: Ch 63
fo in German: Ch 02 04 05 07 21 22 82 every
+20 by Bremerhaven Weser Traffic
fo in German: Ch 19 78 81 H+30 by Bremen
eser Traffic
fo in German: Ch 63 H+30 by Hunte Traffic
E JADE:
TS: Ch 20 63
fo bcsts (in German): Ch 20 63 every H+10
ILHEMSHAVEN:
ort: Ch 11. Lock: Ch 13
ridges: Ch 11
AREL Lock: Ch 13 HW±2
ORKUM:
ort: Ch 14 All year Mon-Fri: 0700-2200,
ep-Apr Sat & Sun: 0700-1700, May-Aug Sat:
300-1200 1500-2100 Sun: 0700-1100 1400-2000
orddeich: Ch 17
on: 0730-1900, Tue-Fri: 0700-1300 1330-1900,
at & Sun: 0800-1200 1230-1730
orderney: Ch 17 Mon: 0700-1200 1230-1730,
ues: 0900-1200 1230-1900, Wed-Sun: 0700-
200 1230-1900

Langeoog: Ch 17 0700-1700
Benersiel: Ch 17 Oct-Mar Mon-Fri: 0700-1230
1330-1700, Apr-Sep Mon-Fri: 0700-1900 Sat &
Sun: 0700-1100 1300-1700
Harlesiel: lock Ch 17 0700-2100
Wangerooge: Ch 17 0700-1700
DIE EMS VTS: Call Ems Traffic Ch 15 18 20 21
Ems Traffic broadcasts every H+50 on
Ch 15 18 20 and 21 in German. All vessels
must keep a continuous watch on the
appropriate channel
Emden Locks: Ch 13
Oldersum Lock: Ch 13 May-Sep Mon-Fri 0700-
2000 Sat & Sun 0800-2000, Oct-Apr Mon-Thu
0700-1530 Fri 0700-1400
Leer Bridge: Ch 15
Leer Lock: Ch 13 16
Weener Bridge: Ch 15
Weener Lock: Ch 13 1 Apr- 31 Oct only: Mon-
Thu 0700-1600 Fri: 0700-sunset Sat & Sun:
sunrise-sunset
Papenburg Lock: Ch 13

NETHERLANDS

DELFZIJL:
Hbr office: Ch 14 Radar assistance given when
visibility falls below 2000m
Info broadcasts: Ch 66 Every even H+10
Locks: Ch 11 Mon-Sat: H24, Sun & holidays
on request
Weiwerder Bridge: Ch 11
Heemskes and Handelshaven Bridges: Ch 14
Mon-Sat: 0600-1400
Farmsumerhaven: Ch 14
EEMSHAVEN:
Hbr office: Ch 14. Radar: Ch 01 19
VTS DELFZIJL/EEMSHAVEN
Delfzijl Radar: Ch 03
Eemshaven Radar: Ch 01
Port Control: Ch 66
Intership: Ch 10
DEN HELDER: VTS Tfc Centre Ch 12
Port Control: Ch 14
Moormanbrug Bridge: Ch 18
Koopvaarders Lock: Ch 22
IJSSELMEER
Den Oever Lock: Ch 20
Kornwerderzand: locks Ch 18
Harlingen: Ch 11 Mon 0000-Sat 2200
Terschelling: Call Brandaris VTS Ch 02
All vessels must keep a listening watch Ch 02
AMSTERDAM:
Port Control: Ch 04 68
Port Information: Ch 14
Beverwijk: Ch 71
Wilhelminasluis: Ch 20
Westerkeersluis: Ch 22
Haarlem: Ch 18
Oranjesluisen: Ch 18

COMMUNICATIONS

Enkhuizen or Krabbersgat: Ch 22
Lock operates weekdays 0300-2300, Sun and holidays 0800-2000
NORDZEE KANAAL:
VTS: Ch 68
From Ijmuiden Lt By to the IJmuiden Sluices
Noordzee sluizen: Call Sluis IJmuiden Ch 22
Noordzee kanaal: Ch 03 From IJmuiden Sluices to km 11·2
Zijkanaal C Sluice: Call Sluis IJmuiden Ch 18
IJMUIDEN:
Traffic Centre: Ch 07 West of IJmuiden lt buoy
Port Control: Ch 61 From IJmuiden Lt buoy to the North Sea Locks
SCHEVENINGEN:
Traffic Centre: Ch 21
Port: Ch 14
MAAS APPROACH: Ch 01
Oude Maas: Ch 62
Bridges and locks:
Botlebrug: Ch 18
Koninginnebrug: Ch 18
Spijkenisserbrug: Ch 18
Brienenoordbrug: Ch 20
Sluis Weurt: Ch 18
Prins Bernhardsluis: Ch 18
Sluis S. Andries: Ch 20
Maassluis (Buitehaven ent): Ch 80
Manderssluis: Ch 20
NIEUWE WATERWEG:
HCC Central Traffic Control Ch 11 14 19 See VTS Chart No 4. Report to and keep a continuous listening watch on the appropriate Tfc Centre
DORDRECHT:
Tfc Control: Dordrecht Ch 79, Heerjansdam Ch 04
Port: Ch 74
General nautical information: Ch 71
Bruggen Dordrecht: Ch 19
Alblasserdamse brug: Ch 22
Papendrechtse brug: Ch 19
Merwedesluis en Verkeersbrug: Ch 18
Algera sluis en Stuw: Ch 22
Julianasluis: Ch 18
Grote Sluis Vianen: Ch 22
Andel Wilhelminasluis: Ch 22
Dordrecht Railway and Rd Bridge: Ch 71
Broombrug/Wijnhavn: Ch 74
HOEK VAN HOLLAND ROADSTEAD:
VTS: Call Maasmond Entrance Ch 03. Follow a track close W of a line joining buoys MV, MVN and Indusbank N. Before crossing, report vessel's name, position and course. Whilst crossing, maintain continuous listening watch.
OOSTERSCHELDE:
Call Roompotsluis Ch 18 Lock operating times: Mon and Thu: 0000-2200, Tue and Sun: 0600-0000, Wed: H24, Fri and Sat: 0600-2200
Roompot Harbour: Ch 31
Ouddorp Coastguard: Ch 25

Wemeldinge Bridge and Locks: Ch 68
Zeelandbrug Bridge: Ch 18
Krammer Locks: Ch 22
Kreekraksluizen: Ch 20 Vessels should repo to the locks as follows: S bound: after Thole Hr; N bound: after Bath bridge
Harlingvliet-Sluizen: Ch 20 Operating time Mon-Fri 0000-2200; 1 Nov - 1 April Sat 0800-220 Sun 0800-1000, 1600-1800; 1 April - 1 Nov Sat Sun 0800-2000
WESTERSCHELDE:
VTS: See VTS Chart No 3. Reporting, in Englis or Dutch, is compulsory for all Inward an Outward-Bound vessels. All vessels, includir those at anchor, must keep a continuou listening watch on the VHF channel for th appropriate Traffic Area. The boundaries each Traffic Area are marked by buoys. emergency call the Traffic Centre: Ch 67
STEENBANK TRAFFIC AREA:
VTS Tfc Centre: Ch 64
VLISSINGEN TRAFFIC AREA:
VTS Tfc Centre: Ch 14. Info: Ch 14 every H+50
HANSWEERT TRAFFIC AREA:
VTS Tfc Centre: Ch 65
TERNEUZEN TRAFFIC AREA:
VTS Tfc Centre: Ch 03. Info: Ch 11 every H+00
GENT/TERNEUZEN TRAFFIC AREA:
VTS Tfc Centre: Ch 11
VLISSINGEN:
Call Flushing Port Control Ch 09
Locks & Bridge: Ch 18
TERNEUZEN:
Hr office: Ch 11
Locks: Ch 69
Westsluis and Middensuis: Ch 06
Oostsluis: Ch 18
Gent: Ch 05 11
Hansweert Locks: Ch 22

BELGIUM

ANTWERPEN TRAFFIC AREA:
VTS: Tfc Centre: Ch 12. Info: Ch 12 every H+30
ANTWERPEN:
Calling and safety: Ch 74
VTS Centre: Ch 18
Bridges: Ch 62
Boudewijnsluis & Van Cauwelaertsluis: Ch 08 71
Royerssluis Ch 74
Kattendijksluis: Ch 22
Kallosluis: Ch 08 74
Zandvlietsluis and Berendrechtsluis: Ch 06 75
Winthamsluis: Ch 68
ZEEBRUGGE TRAFFIC AREA:
VTS Tfc Centre: Ch 69. Info: Ch 69 every H+10
WANDELAAR TRAFFIC AREA:
VTS Tfc Centre: Ch 65
ZEEBRUGGE:
Port Control: Ch 71 H24. Locks: Ch 68

OSTENDE:
Port Control: Ch 09 H24. Lock: Ch 14
NIEUWPOORT:
Hbr office: Ch 09 H24

NORTH FRANCE

DUNKERQUE
Port: Ch 73 H24
CALAIS:
Port: Call Calais Port Traffic Ch 12 H24
Ecluse Carnot: Ch 12 HX
BOULOGNE:
Call Control Tower, Boulogne Port Ch 12
Le Touquet: Ch 09; 77 Access –2HW+1
Etaples-Sur-Mer: Ch 09 Access HW±2
LE TREPORT: Ch 12 72 Access HW±3
DIEPPE:
Port: Ch 12 HO
ST VALÉRY-EN-CAUX: lock Ch 09 Day: HW±2¼,
Night: HW±½ (Bridge opens H & H+30 during
these periods)
FÉCAMP: Ch 10 12 Access –3HW+1
Antifer Port: Ch 22
LE HAVRE:
Port Operations: Ch 67 69
Control Tower: Ch 12 20
Tancarville Port: Ch 16 H24. Lock: Ch 18 HX
LA SEINE:
VTS: Ch 15 (Estuary) 68 (River) 73
Radar Ch 13 73 82
HONFLEUR: Port: Ch 17 73
Locks and Bridges: Ch 17 H24
Port Jérome: Call PR Ch 73 H24
ROUEN:
Port: Ch 73 68
ROUEN TO PARIS – LOCKS:
Poses-Amfreville: Ch 18
Notre-Dame-de-la-Garenne: Ch 22
Mericourt: Ch 18
Andrésy: Ch 22
Bougival: Ch 22
Chatou: Ch 18
Suresnes: Ch 22
Paris-Arsenal: Ch 09
DEAUVILLE-TROUVILLE: Ch 09 0800-1730
OUISTREHAM-CAEN:
Port: Ch 68 74. Lock: Ch 12 68 Access –2HW+3
Canal de Caen: Monitor Ch 68 H24
Courseulles-sur-Mer: Ch 09 HW±3
Port-en-Bessin Lock & Bridge: Ch 18 HW±2
CHERBOURG:
Call Vigie du Homet Ch 12 H24
Lock: Ch 06 Access HW±¾
GRANVILLE:
Hbr office: Ch 12 HW±1½
ST MALO:
Hbr office: Ch 12 H24
Rance barrage lock: Ch 13
DAHOUËT: Marina: Ch 09

LE LÉGUÉ – SAINT BRIEUC:
Call Légué Port Ch 12 Approx –2HW+1½
Pontrieux Lock: Ch 12 Access –2HW+1
ROSCOFF-BLOSCON:
Port: Ch 12
0830-1200 1330-1800

CHANNEL ISLANDS

BRAYE, Alderney:
Port: Ch 12 74
May-Sep daily: 0800-1800 Oct daily: 0800-1800
Nov-Apr: Mon-Fri: 0800-1700. Outside these
hours, call St Peter Port
GUERNSEY:
St Peter Port: Ch 12 H24. Access HW±3
St Sampson: Ch 12 Via St Peter Port
Port Control
JERSEY:
St Helier: Ch 14 H24. Access HW±3
(Note: Do not use Ch M in St Helier)
Gorey: Ch 74 HW±3

WEST FRANCE

LE CONQUET:
Port: Ch 08 Season 0830-1200 1330-1800;
BREST:
Port de Commerce: Ch 12. Naval Port: Ch 74
CAMARET: Ch 09 Season 0730-2200; out of
season: 0830-1200 1330-1730
DOUARNENEZ:
Hbr office: Ch 12 0800-1200 1330-1730
SAINT GUÉNOLE: Ch 12 HJ
LE GUILVINEC:
Port: Ch 12 HX
LOCTUDY:
Hbr office: Ch 12 Mon-Fri: 0630-1200 1400-
1900; Sat: 0800-1200
CONCARNEAU:
Port: Ch 12
LORIENT:
Hbr office: Call Vigie Port Louis Ch 12
SAINT-NAZAIRE:
PORT: Ch 06 12 14 67 69
Loire VTS: Saint–Nazaire Port Control Ch 12
DONGES: Port: Ch 12 69 H24
Nantes: Ch 12 06 14 67 69
LES SABLES D'OLONNE:
Lock: Ch 12 HM Mon-Fri: 0800-1800
LA ROCHELLE
Port: Ch 12 H24
ROCHEFORT:
Hr office: Ch 12 0800-1200 1400-1800LT
Tonnay-Charente: Ch 12 HX
LA GIRONDE:
VTS: Ch 12 Compulsory from BXA Lt buoy to
Bordeaux, but not for leisure craft which may
monitor. Radar: Ch 12. Tidal Info: Ch 17
Height of water between Le Verdon and
Bordeaux bcst automatically every 5 mins

PAUILLAC:
Hbr office: Ch 12
BLAYE:
Port: Ch 12
Ambès: Ch 12
BORDEAUX:
Hbr office: Ch 12 H24
BAYONNE: Ch 12 H24

NW SPAIN

BILBAO:
VTS: Ch 10
Signal Station: Ch 12 13 HX
SANTANDER:
Port: Ch 06 12 14
PUERTO DE SAN CIPRIÄN: Ch 14
EL FERROL: Ch 14 (H24) 10 11 12 13
LA CORUÑA:
Port: Ch 12 13 HX
CORCUBIÓN: Ch 14 when vessel is expected
FINISTERRE:
VTS: Ch 11 74
VILLAGARCIA DE AROSA:
Port: Ch 12 HX
VIGO:
VTS: Call Vigo Traffic Ch 10 H24
Port: Call Vigo Prácticos Ch 14 HX

PORTUGAL

VIANA DO CASTELO:
Ch 11 Mon-Fri 0900-1200 1400-1700
PÓVOA DE VARZIM:
Ch 11 Mon-Fri 0900-1200 1400-1700
VILA DO CONDE: Ch 11 Mon-Fri 0900-1200
1400-1700
LEIXÕES: Ch 12 11 13 19 60
Marina: Ch 62
Radar Station: Ch 12 01 04 09 10 11 12 14 18 20
61 63 67 68 69 71 79 80 84, H24
DOURO: Ch 11 Mon-Fri 0900-1200 1400-1700
AVEIRO: Ch 11 Mon-Fri 0900-1200 1400-1700
FIGUEIRA DA FOZ: Ch 11 Mon-Fri 0900-1200
1400-1700

NAZARÉ: Ch 11 Mon-Fri 0900-1200 1400-1700
PENICHE: Ch 11
LISBOA: Call Lisboa Port Control Ch 74
Doca de Alcântara: Ch 12 05
SESIMBRA: Ch 11
Mon-Fri 0900-1200 1400-1700
SETÚBAL: Ch 11 H24
SINES: Ch 12 11 13
LAGOS: Ch 11 Mon-Fri 0900-1200 1400-1700
PORTIMÃO: Ch 11 Mon-Fri 0900-1200
1400-1700
VILAMOURA: Ch 62 H24
FARO: Ch 11
OLHÃO: Ch 11
VILA REAL DE SANTO ANTÓNIO: Ch 11
Mon-Fri 0900-1200 1400-1700

SW SPAIN

EL ROMPIDO: Marina: Ch 09 HX
PUNTA UMBRÍA: Club: Ch 09 HX
RÍO GUADALQUIVIR:
Call Obras Puerto Sevilla Ch 12
CÁDIZ:
Call Cádiz Prácticos Ch 11 12 14 H24
Rota: Ch 09

STRAIT OF GIBRALTAR

TARIFA:
VTS: Call Tarifa Traffic Ch 10
Information (on request): Ch 67
Urgent messages will be bcst at any time on
Ch 10 and Ch 16. Routine messages will be
bcst every even H+15 on Ch 10
ALGECIRAS:
Port: Call Algeciras Prácticos Ch 09 12
13 HX

GIBRALTAR

GIBRALTAR BAY Ch 12 Yachts to monitor this
working channel whilst under way.
Commercial Port: Ch 06 13 14
Queen's Harbour Master: Ch 08 Mon-Thu:
0800-1630; Fri: 0800-1600

NOTES

_____

_____

_____

_____

_____

_____

_____

_____

_____

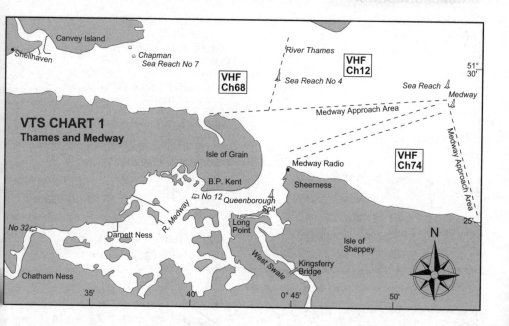

VTS CHART 1
Thames and Medway

Canvey Island
Shellhaven
Chapman
Sea Reach No 7
River Thames
VHF Ch12
Sea Reach No 4
VHF Ch68
Sea Reach
Medway
Medway Approach Area
51° 30'
Isle of Grain
B.P. Kent
No 12
Queenborough Spit
Medway Radio
Sheerness
VHF Ch74
Medway Approach Area
No 32
Darnett Ness
R. Medway
Long Point
West Swale
Kingsferry Bridge
Isle of Sheppey
25'
Chatham Ness
35'   40'   0° 45'   50'
N

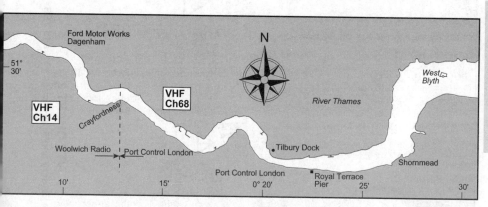

Ford Motor Works
Dagenham
N
51° 30'
West Blyth
VHF Ch14
VHF Ch68
Crayfordness
River Thames
Woolwich Radio
Port Control London
Tilbury Dock
Shornmead
Port Control London
Royal Terrace Pier
10'   15'   0° 20'   25'   30'

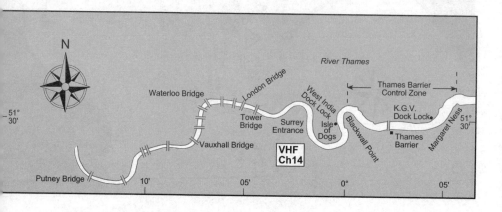

N
River Thames
Waterloo Bridge
London Bridge
West India Dock Lock
Thames Barrier Control Zone
51° 30'
Tower Bridge
Surrey Entrance
Isle of Dogs
Blackwall Point
K.G.V. Dock Lock
51° 30'
Vauxhall Bridge
VHF Ch14
Thames Barrier
Margaret Ness
Putney Bridge
10'   05'   0°   05'

VTS CHART 2

Humber Estuary and Approaches VTS and TSS

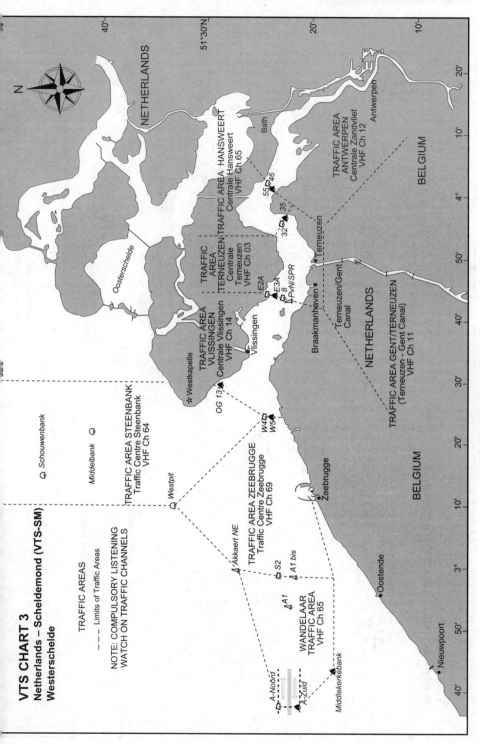

VTS CHART 3
Netherlands – Scheldemond (VTS-SM)
Westerschelde

TRAFFIC AREAS

– – – Limits of Traffic Areas

NOTE: COMPULSORY LISTENING
WATCH ON TRAFFIC CHANNELS

TRAFFIC AREA STEENBANK
Traffic Centre Steenbank
VHF Ch 64

TRAFFIC AREA ZEEBRUGGE
Traffic Centre Zeebrugge
VHF Ch 69

WANDELAAR
TRAFFIC AREA
VHF Ch 65

TRAFFIC AREA
VLISSINGEN
Centrale Vlissingen
VHF Ch 14

TRAFFIC
AREA
TERNEUZEN
Centrale
Terneuzen
VHF Ch 03

TRAFFIC AREA HANSWEERT
Centrale Hansweert
VHF Ch 65

TRAFFIC AREA
ANTWERPEN
Centrale Zandvliet
VHF Ch 12

TRAFFIC AREA GENT/TERNEUZEN
(Terneuzen - Gent Canal)
VHF Ch 11

NETHERLANDS

BELGIUM

Schouwenbank

Middelbank

Oosterschelde

★ Westkapelle

Vlissingen

Braakmanhaven

Terneuzen

Bath

Antwerpen

Terneuzen/Gent
Canal

Westpit

Westkapelle

OG 13

E2A

E3A

8

PvN/SPR

55·46

35

32

W4
W5

Akkaert NE

S2

A1 bis

A1

A-Noord

A-Zuid

Middelkerkebank

Zeebrugge

Oostende

Nieuwpoort

51°30'N

40'

20'

10'

20'

10'

4°

50'

40'

30'

20'

10'

3°

50'

40'

N

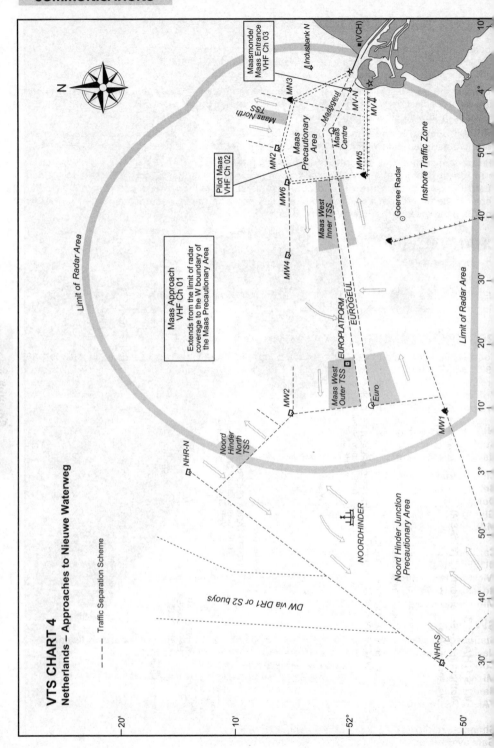

VTS CHART 4
Netherlands – Approaches to Nieuwe Waterweg

– – – – Traffic Separation Scheme

Maasmonde/Maas Entrance VHF Ch 03

Pilot Maas VHF Ch 02

Maas Approach VHF Ch 01
Extends from the limit of radar coverage to the W boundary of the Maas Precautionary Area

Limit of Radar Area

Maas North TSS

Maas Precautionary Area

Maas Centre

Maas West Inner TSS

Maas West Outer TSS

Inshore Traffic Zone

Goeree Radar

Limit of Radar Area

EUROPLATFORM

EUROGEUL

Euro

Noord Hinder North TSS

NOORDHINDER

Noord Hinder Junction Precautionary Area

DW via DR1 or S2 buoys

Indusbank N

(VCH)

MN3

MN2

MV-N

MV

MW5

MW6

MW4

MW2

MW1

NHR-N

NHR-S

HF & MF COAST RADIO STATIONS

oast Radio Stations* (CRS) deal with public correspondence (and a few other things). They nable a yachtsman to be linked by radio into the public telephone system in order to converse ith a subscriber ashore, ie he can make or receive a Link call.

owever the immensely popular and convenient mobile 'phone has to a great extent rendered nk calls obsolescent. Thus there are no longer any CRS in the UK, France and Netherlands. In ermany a limited service is provided by a commercial company (see below).

RS still operate in the Channel Islands, Republic of Ireland, Denmark, Belgium, Spain and ortugal, as listed below. But they too may gradually be withdrawn from service.

Readers of such arcane documents as the Admiralty List of Radio Signals will be aware that the rm 'Coast Radio Station' is now used to embrace, not only the original CRS, but also Coast-uard Centres, both in the UK and abroad. This is ambiguous and therefore confusing. As a eneral rule the CG does **not** handle Link calls, except in those countries (eg Ireland, Denmark nd Belgium) where the functions of CG and CRS have always been co-located.

CHANNEL ISLANDS

T PETER PORT RADIO 49°27'·00N 02°32'00W ☎ 01481 720672 ▨ 01534 714177
nk calls on **Ch 62** only

ERSEY RADIO 49°10'·85N 02°14'30W ☎ 01534 741121 ▨ 01534 499089
nk calls on **Ch 25** only

REPUBLIC OF IRELAND

oast Radio is provided by the Dept of the Marine, Leeson Lane, Dublin 2, Eire. ☎ +353 (0)1 662 922; ext 670 for enquiries. Broadcasts are made on a working channel/frequency following a reliminary announcement on Ch 16 and 2182 kHz. Ch 67 is used for Safety messages only. HF calls to an Irish Coast Radio Station should be made on a working channel. Only use Ch 16 case of difficulty or in emergency.

W and SE Ireland

tations broadcast at 0033, 0433, 0833, 1233, 1633 and 2033 UT on VHF Channels listed. avigational warnings and Traffic Lists are broadcast at every odd H+03 (except 0303 0703).

lifden Radio	53°30'N 09°56'W	VHF 26
elmullet Radio	54°16'N 10°03'W	VHF 83
onegal Bay	54°22'N 08°31'W	VHF 02
ilen Head Radio	54°44'N 08°43'W	VHF 24
1ALIN HEAD RADIO	55°22'N 07°21'W	VHF 23 MF 1677 kHz, ☎ +353 (0) 77 70103
		MMSI 002500100 DSC: 2187·5 kHz
arlingford Radio	54°05'N 06°19'W	VHF 04
UBLIN RADIO	53°23'N 06°04'W	VHF 83
/icklow Head Radio	52°58'N 06°00'W	VHF 02
osslare Radio	52°15'N 06°20'W	VHF 23
line Head Radio	52°00'N 07°35'W	VHF 83

W Ireland

tations broadcast at 0233, 0633, 1033, 1433, 1833 and 2233 UT on VHF Channels listed. avigational warnings and Traffic Lists are broadcast at every odd H+33 (not 0133 0533).

ork Radio	51°51'N 08°29'W	VHF 26
lizen Radio	51°34'N 09°33'W	VHF 04
antry Radio	51°38'N 10°00'W	VHF 23
ALENTIA RADIO	51°56'N 10°21'W	VHF 24 MF 1752 kHz, ☎ + 353 (0) 66947 6109
		MMSI 002500200, DSC: 2187·5 kHz
hannon Radio	52°31'N 09°36'W	VHF 28
ialway Bay Radio	53°18'N 09°07'W	VHF 04

DENMARK

All VHF/MF Coast Radio Stations are remotely controlled from Lyngby Radio (55°50N 11°25'E) (MMSI 002191000). Call on working frequencies to help keep Ch 16 clear. The callsign for all stations is Lyngby Radio. Traffic lists are broadcast on all VHF channels every odd H+05. All MF stations, except Skagen, keep watch H24 on 2182 kHz. The stations listed below monitor Ch 16 H24 and Ch 70 DSC. Blåvand, Skagen and Lyngby also monitor MF 2187·5 kHz DSC. MF DSC Public correspondence facilities are available from Blåvand and Skagen on 1624·5 and 2177 kHz.

VHF AND MF

Lyngby	55°50'N 11°25'E	VHF Ch **07**, 85	MF 1704, 2170·5 kHz
Blåvand	55°33'N 08°07'E	VHF Ch 23	MF 1734, 1767, 2593
Bovbjerg	56°32'N 08°10'E	VHF Ch 02	MF 1734, 1767, 2593
Hanstholm	57°07'N 08°39'E	VHF Ch 01	
Hirtshals	57°31'N 09°57'E	VHF Ch 66	
Skagen	57°44'N 10°35'E	VHF Ch 04	MF 1758

GERMANY

Coast Radio Stations: DPO7 – Seefunk (Hamburg) *(MMSI 002113100)*

Hamburg	53°33'N 09°58'E	VHF Ch 27, 83	DSC Ch 70 & 16
Borkum	53°35'N 06°40'E	VHF Ch 28	DSC Ch 70 & 16
Bremen	53°05'N 08°48'E	VHF Ch 25	DSC Ch 70 & 16
Elbe Weser	53°50'N 08°39'E	VHF Ch 01, 24	DSC Ch 70 & 16
Nordfriesland	54°31'N 08°41'E	VHF Ch 26	DSC Ch 70 & 16
Traffic Lists:	0745, 0945, 1245, 1645, 1945 and every H & H+30 on request Ch 16		

NORTH SPAIN

Call on the working channel as listed below, using the callsign of the remotely controlled station; Ch 16 is not continuously guarded. Stations are remotely controlled by Bilbao and Coruna Communications Centres.

Traffic lists are broadcast only on MF, every odd H+33, 0333-2333, except 2133. All times UT.

Pasajes   43°17'N 01°55'W *VHF 27*

Machichaco Radio 43°27'N 02°45'W *No VHF*
MF: Transmits 1707, 2182 kHz (H24);
receives on 2132, 2045, 2048, 2182 (H24).
Traffic lists: *1707 kHz;* every odd H+33
Navigation warnings: *1707 kHz* Urgent warnings on receipt, after next silence period and at 0703 1903 in English and Spanish

BILBAO   43°22'N 03°02'W *VHF 26*. Controls Pasajes to Navia

Santander   43°25'N 03°36'W *VHF 24*

Cabo Peñas   43°26'N 05°35'W   *VHF 23, MF 1677 kHz*
Navigation warnings: 1677 kHz. Urgent warnings on receipt, after next silence period and at 0703 1903 in English and Spanish

Navia   43°25'N 06°50'W *VHF 60*

Cabo Ortegal   43°35'N 07°47'W *VHF 02*
Navigation warnings: *VHF 02* at 0840 and 2010

CORUÑA   43°22'N 08°27'W *VHF 26, MF 1698 kHz*
Navigation warnings: *VHF 26* at 0840 and 2010; *1698 kHz* at 0703, 1903

Finisterre   42°54'N 09°16'W *VHF 22, MF 1764 kHz*
Navigation warnings: *VHF 22* at 0840 and 2010; *1764 kHz* at 0703, 1903

Vigo   42°10'N 08°41'W *VHF 65.* Nav warnings: *VHF 20* at 0840 and 2010

La Guardia   41°53'N 08°52'W *VHF 21.* Nav warnings: *VHF 82* at 0840 and 2010

PORTUGAL

Stations are remotely controlled from Lisboa. All monitor Ch 16 H24

Arga Radio	41°48'N 08°41'W	*VHF 25 28*
Arestal Radio	40°46'N 08°21'W	*VHF 24 26*
Montejunto Radio	39°10'N 09°03'W	*VHF 25 26*
LISBOA RADIO	38°33'N 09°11'W	*VHF 23 26. MF: Transmits on 2182, 2578, 2640, 2691, 2781, 3607, 2778, 2693 kHz. Receives on 2182 (kHz) (H24)*
		Traffic lists: 2693 kHz every even H+05, after announcement on 2182 kHz
Atalaia Radio	38°10'N 08°38'W	*VHF 24 25*
Picos Radio	37°50'N 08°35'W	*VHF 23 28*
Estoi Radio	37°10'N 07°50'W	*VHF 24 28*

SOUTH WEST SPAIN

Stations are remotely controlled from Malaga. Initially call Ch 16 H24 using station callsign

Chipiona Radio	36°41'N 06°25'W	*No VHF. MF: Transmits 1656, 2182 kHz (H24); receives on 2081 2182*
		Traffic lists: 1656 kHz every odd H+33 (except 0133 & 2133). Navigation warnings: 1656 kHz. Urgent warnings on receipt, and at 0733 1933, *in Spanish*
Cádiz Radio	36°21'N 06°17'W	*VHF 83*
		Navigation warnings: *Ch 26* on receipt, after next silence period, and at 0833, 2003, *in Spanish*
Tarifa Radio	36°03'N 05°33'W	*VHF 81; MF 1704 kHz: Transmits kHz 1704, 2182, (H24). Receives 2129, 2182 (H24), 2045, 2048, 2610, 3290 (Autolink)*
		Traffic lists: *1704 kHz*. Navigation warnings: *VHF 81* at 0833 and 2003. *1704 kHz* on receipt, at 0733 1933, *in Spanish*

NOTES

SOUND SIGNALS

MANOEUVRING AND WARNING SIGNALS (Rule 34)

Short blast ● = about 1 second. Long blast ▬ = about 5 seconds

●   I am altering course to **Starboard**
●●   I am altering course to **Port**
●●●   My engines are going **Astern**
●●●●●   I do not understand your intentions/actions

In a narrow channel

▬ ▬●   I intend to overtake you on your **Starboard** side
▬ ▬●●   I intend to overtake you on your **Port** side
▬●▬●   In response to the above two signals - **Agreed**

Nearing a bend in the channel or an area where other vessels may be hidden by obstructions

▬   Warns of a vessel's presence
▬   Acknowledgement by any approaching vessel

VESSELS IN RESTRICTED VISIBILITY (Rule 35)

▬   Power vessel underway (every 2 mins)
▬ ▬   Power vessel underway but stopped (every 2 mins)
▬●●   Vessels not under command, restricted in their ability to manoeuvre, constrained by draught, sailing, fishing or towing - (every 2 mins)
▬●●●   Last vessel in tow (immediately after tug signal)

🔔 *5 seconds*   At ⚓ (bell, every minute)

🔔 *5 seconds +*
🔔 *5 seconds*   At anchor over 100m (bell forward, gong aft, every minute)

●▬●   At ⚓, as well as above, to warn an approaching vessel

Yachts under 12m are not obliged to sound the fog signals listed above, but if they do not, they *must* make some efficient noise every two minutes

SHAPES

▼	Sailing vessel under sail *and* power. **Rule 25**	◆	Towing vessel - length of tow over 200m. **Rule 24**
●	Vessel at anchor. **Rule 30**	●◆●	Vessel restricted in her ability to manoeuvre. **Rule 27**
▼▲	Vessel fishing or trawling. **Rule 26**	●●	Vessel not under command. **Rule 27**
▼▲ + ▲	Vessel fishing with outlying gear over 150m long.	⬛	Vessel constrained by her draught **Rule 28**

CHAPTER 4 - SAFETY

CONTENTS

Think about Safety 114

How to make a distress call 115

MAYDAY relay 115

Helicopter rescue 116

Medical help 116

First aid 117
  Essential information 117
  General medical information 118
  First Aid Kit 120

Coastguard services in the UK and abroad 121

Emergency VHF Direction Finding in the UK 129

UK & France VHF Direction Finding map 130

Emergency VHF Direction Finding in France 131

Diagrams of Military exercise areas 132

GMDSS 136
  Introduction 136
  Objective 136
  Maritime Safety Information 136
  Functions 136
  Distress alerting 136
  Communications 137
  Digital selective calling 137
  Inmarsat 137
  Cospas/Sarsat 137
  Sea areas 137

Glossary of foreign terms 138
  Ashore 138
  Navigation 138
  Officialdom 139
  Safety/Distress 140

THINK ABOUT SAFETY – then do something to enhance it

Safety at sea is no mere abstract concept. It is very real and may save the lives c yourself and your crew, as well as your boat. It may also avoid having to ca upon the safety services. There are three main requirements, all of which are i your power to implement:

KNOWLEDGE. This means knowledge of the weather (above all else) and c the sea; of the Collision Regulations; of your boat and its systems; of the water in which you are navigating; and not least of yourself, your strengths an weaknesses. Knowledge requires training, whether it be in navigatior meteorology, boat handling, engines or electrics – and lastly survival technique when all else has failed and you have abandoned ship for the liferaft. We shoul all tackle GMDSS which will acquire increasing relevance to yachtsmen a VHF Channel 16 becomes less widely monitored in the near future.

EXPERIENCE. Nobody ever became experienced overnight. It is a long an sometimes painful process of finding out for yourself, learning an decision-making. At every stage be aware of your limitations and arrange, a far as possible, to stay within them. Read everything you can on the subjec Learn from other people's mistakes. Knowledge and experience make fc sound judgement.

Recently a yacht was lost (and very nearly her crew) whilst trying to enter harbour in an onshore gale. The skipper had been told not to attempt entry, bt he was tired and desperate to find shelter. He knew conditions were marginal, t say the least, but he still persisted in his attempt. It's called "Get-home-itis" an in all its forms is a potential killer. He and his crew owe their lives to the RNLI. D not do the same; stay at sea, however daunting the prospect – or better still avoi getting into that predicament. There are no medals for staying in harbour, bt there is life.

EQUIPMENT. Shun fancy toys. Go for proven gear, whether it be the correct siz of anchor, a stable dinghy (scene of so many tragic accidents), a trysail an storm jib for those sailing out of range of a safe haven, replacements for worr out rigging, a properly maintained engine or a decent VHF radio – and don forget that GMDSS is now affordable and training courses are widely availabl(

DEFINITIONS OF DISTRESS, URGENCY AND SAFETY

Yachts should keep watch on VHF Channel 16 at all times when at sea. Otherwis a distress call from another nearby craft may be missed; likewise broadcasts c navigation and weather warnings. Apart from distress, urgency and safety call only transmit on Channel 16 when calling/answering the Coastguard, Coast Rad Stations or other ships before transferring asap to a working channel.

The distress call 'MAYDAY' requests immediate assistance for a ship or perso in grave and imminent danger. This includes a man overboard, if he is n(immediately recovered. Yachts hearing a MAYDAY must give what assistanc they can, provided it does not endanger their own yacht or crew.

The urgency prefix 'PAN-PAN' is used when the safety of a ship or person is ¡ risk, or medical advice is urgently required (see PAN-PAN MEDICO overleaf).

The safety prefix 'SECURITE' is used by coast stations before navigation or weath(warnings. Or ships at sea might use it to report hazards, eg a buoy adrift.

HOW TO MAKE A DISTRESS CALL

Switch on the VHF Radio
Select Channel 16
Select **HIGH POWER (25W)**
Switch off DUAL WATCH
Holding down the button on microphone or handset, say slowly and clearly:
MAYDAY, MAYDAY, MAYDAY
This is.....................................(Say your boat's name 3 times)
MAYDAY...........(Say the boat's name once only)
My position is..................

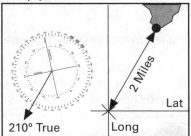

210° True   Long

Give your position either as:

Lat and Long (from the GPS); or as

Bearing and distance <u>from</u> a known landmark or feature:

For example 'My position is 2 miles SSW of Portland Bill'

Say if you are not sure of position– do not guess!

). **Tell them what is wrong:** For example, the boat is sinking; how many people (including you) on board; if you have fired flares; if you are abandoning ship, etc. If there is time, repeat your position
. **I require immediate assistance. Over -** This means: please reply
2. Release the microphone button and listen
3. Only if you can't hear clearly, adjust the *VOLUME* and/or *SQUELCH*

If there is no reply, check the radio switches and repeat the message

MAYDAY RELAY

If you hear a MAYDAY CALL, write it down
If practicable, give assistance

If the MAYDAY is not answered, pass it on like this:
Select VHF Channel 16
Select HIGH POWER (25W)
Switch off DUAL WATCH

Then, holding down the button on microphone or handset, say slowly and clearly:
  MAYDAY RELAY, MAYDAY RELAY, MAYDAY RELAY
This is......................(say your boat's name 3 times)
State the MAYDAY message, exactly as you wrote it down
). **Over -** This means: please reply
. Release the button and listen

HELICOPTER RESCUE

1. **COMMUNICATE ON (CH 16) VHF**
2. Use flares or smoke when helicopter is seen or heard
3. Pilot may ask you to drop sails and motor an **EXACT COURSE**
4. You may be asked to stream tender astern with casualty in
5. Brief crew early (too noisy when helicopter is close)
6. **HELM MUST KEEP ON COURSE** and not be distracted
7. Weighted line lowered
8. Let it touch boat or water first (to earth any static charge)
9. Take in slack line only
10. **PULL IN AS DIRECTED**
11. **DO NOT SECURE IT TO THE BOAT**
12. **DO AS YOU ARE TOLD**

Note: The text and sketch relate to a Hi-line transfer, one of several techniques which may be used

MEDICAL HELP

1. **CH 16, High power, Dual watch off**
2. **PAN PAN MEDICO** .... (repeat 3 times)
3. **ALL STATIONS** .... (repeat 3 times)
4. **This is** .... (repeat 3 times)
5. **Over**
    Next message should contain:
    Yacht's name, callsign, nationality
    Yacht's position and nearest harbour
    Patient's details, symptoms and advice wanted
    The medication you have on board

MEDICAL ADVICE BY RADIO

European countries covered by this Almanac will give free medical advice on request. Messages are usually sent via Coastguard or Coast Radio Stations of the country concerned.

UK Yachts should call nearest Coastguard Centre by name on VHF Ch 16 using the prefix PAN-PAN MEDICO. If your casualty is in grave and imminent danger requiring immediate assistance make a MAYDAY call. The CG will nominate Ch 67 for full details and then arrange priority allocation of a working channel and will connect you to a doctor on that channel.

The CG may monitor the call to the doctor and contact the appropriate rescue service. If not, in cases of emergency, call the CG again on Ch 16 to arrange a helicopter or lifeboat.

REPUBLIC OF IRELAND Call nearest Coast Radio Station by name. Procedures are similar to UK.

DENMARK Call 'Radiomedical Lyngby': English, Danish, Norwegian, Swedish, French or German are spoken.

GERMANY Call nearest Coast Radio Station using 'Funkarzt. . . (name of station)'. English or German are spoken.

NETHERLANDS Call 'Netherlands Coastguard, radio medical advice'. English and Dutch are spoken. Expect transfer to working Ch 23 or 83 or duty doctor.

BELGIUM Call 'Radiomedical Ostend': English, French, Dutch or German are spoken.

FRANCE Call nearest CROSS, eg 'Radiomedical CROSS Jobourg' with PAN-PAN prefix. French, English or International Code of Signals. SAMU (Urgent Medical Aid Service) in Toulouse may be contacted by the CROSS to advise on treatment and/or possible evacuation. CROSS Etel specialises in providing medical advice.

SPAIN Call 'Medrad ... (any Coast Radio Station)': Spanish.

PORTUGAL Call 'Radiomedical Lisboa': English, French, Portuguese are spoken.

FIRST AID
ESSENTIAL INFORMATION:

First ensure your own safety and that of the vessel.

GETTING HELP

Recognising signs of serious injury is not usually difficult, but it is always better to ask advice if not sure. This is available by making a **PAN-PAN** call by R/T or VHF radio, which will normally be processed by a Coast Radio Station and/or the Coastguard. You will be connected to a local doctor or hospital for advice and, if assistance is required, it will be co-ordinated by the Coastguard (see LH column).

FIRST STEPS

A - AIRWAY - NOT BREATHING: Know how to achieve and maintain an airway in all unconscious patients, by:
(1) Clearing any seaweed, excess saliva, vomit, false teeth, etc from mouth and nose.
(2) Lifting the chin to prevent choking by tongue and soft palate falling back.

B - BREATHING - Sealing mouth with own mouth and pinching nose, then blow slowly and gently until the casualty's chest rises. Ten inflations should improve colour, then continue after 2-4 seconds another 10 ventilations, then re-assess. You can use mouth to nose ventilation if the casualty's mouth cannot be opened enough to breath into. The best position for maintaining spontaneous breathing after restarting is in the semi-prone or coma position. The casualty is rolled carefully on his side keeping head and neck in line.

C - CIRCULATION - HEART NOT BEATING: You can revive an unconscious or possibly near dead patient by external cardiac massage, if there is no pulse. The best place to find a pulse is in the neck beside the Trachea (Windpipe).

The patient must be lying on a firm surface. First ventilate 1 - 2 breaths. Then apply cardiac massage by pressure over the lower third of the sternum (breastbone). The heel of one hand should be placed two fingers width above the lower extremity of the sternum, and the heel of the other hand placed on top, with the fingers interlocked, keeping the elbows straight. Press down firmly on the sternum using just enough force to depress it (4.5cm), then release keeping hands in place. Continue by pressing firmly over the sternum with both hands, one on top of the other, with intermittent mouth to mouth respiration. The rate should be 80 compresses per minute, and the ratio of breaths to pressure should be 2:15. This should be continued until either colour improves, breathing starts or a pulse becomes palpable in the neck. Then place the patient in the recovery position.

BLEEDING: Know how to deal with severe haemorrhage.

EXTERNAL BLEEDING:- 1: Remove any loose foreign bodies from wounds. 2: Press a folded handkerchief or soft pad directly on to wound, adding more padding if this becomes soaked. 3: If possible raise bleeding part. 4: If pressure is used to control bleeding check colour and temperature of parts distal to pressure pad to ensure adequate blood supply, releasing pressure frequently.

INTERNAL BLEEDING: Apparent when blood appears from the mouth or rectum, or suspected when a person collapses with pallor, sweating and a fast pulse.

All that can be done is to place the victim in the semi-prone position and prevent heat loss by covering with a blanket or sleeping bag. Supervision is necessary. *ADVICE SHOULD BE SOUGHT AS SOON AS POSSIBLE BY RADIO* (Make VHF **PAN-PAN** call).

LIVES CAN BE SAVED in all cases of injury by attending to the **A**IRWAY, **B**REATHING, **C**IRCULATION AND CONSCIOUS LEVEL of injured crew and doing this in an organised method. Using a check list prevents less important factors taking precedent. Always keep checking on anyone who has had an injury or been in the water.

GENERAL MEDICAL INFO

ARREST - of heart's action can be caused by near drowning, by blood loss and by illness such as heart attack. It is not hard to recognise as the victim is obviously near death and a pulse cannot be found.

Refer to resuscitation above and perform external cardiac massage with patient on a firm surface such as deck or cabin sole, and with mouth to mouth resuscitation in a ratio of roughly 2 breaths to 15 chest pressings. Start with 2 breaths of expired air.

BREATHING - In conscious patients, problems can be caused by pain from injured ribs or chest infection. Help is given by pain killing tablets and/or antibiotics. Crew members with asthma will usually have their own medication and should be kept propped up. Keep checking. In an unconscious patient the airway must be cleared, the jaw tipped up and mouth to mouth breathing started if necessary, or if the patient is able to breath by himself he must be placed in the semi-prone position and carefully watched in case the airway gets blocked by his tongue or by vomit or saliva.

CIRCULATION: Problems of central (the heart/pump) and peripheral (blood vessels/distribution) should be tackled as follows:

(1) Central: Failure of the Heart's Action - dealt with by External Cardiac Massage (see above)

(2) Peripheral: Attempt to stop haemorrhage by method described above (see Bleeding)

BROKEN BONES - principles are immobilisation and observation of circulation to the part beyond the probable fracture.

Skull: suspect fracture in severe blows to the head, especially if the patient is unconscious. Priorities are (a) airway clearance and maintenance and cardiac massage if required (b) pressure if scalp bleeding is severe (c) monitoring of conscious or unconscious state (d) remember the possibility of neck injuries, keep neck and shoulders in line.

Spine: possible in falls from a height. Priority is always airway clearance and maintenance. *DO NOT USE EXCESSIVE CHIN TILT*, but if possible try to roll or lift patient from danger with head and back in a straight line – for example on a board large enough to stretch from head to buttocks with a rolled towel around the neck to minimise movement. The head should be held steady at all times in line with body in horizontal and vertical planes. *THIS IS ESSENTIAL TO PROTECT THE SPINAL CORD.*

Ribs: are often fractured in crush injuries and falls and do not take precedent over skull or spine injuries. If they appear to be the only injury then pain relief is essential to allow free movement of the chest for efficient breathing. Consider internal bleeding if patient becomes pale, clammy and collapsed. Possible internal damage if he becomes breathless.

Upper Limbs: can be splinted to the trunk whether the fracture is closed or if bone is protruding. The bone should be immobilised at the joint above and below the fracture and padding should be inserted below any bandage or strapping. This should not be too tight and the part of the limb beyond should be checked regularly for changes in colour and temperature and for swelling which can restrict the blood flow. If this happens the bindings must be loosened. If the bone is protruding, cut clothing away and if possible cover with sterile gauze. Pain killers and, in the case of open fracture antibiotics should be given as soon as possible.

Lower Limbs: immobilise at point above and below fracture if possible. Check circulation in limb. Give pain relief or antibiotic cover for open fractures. The other limb, or an oar, is a suitable splint. Strapping should be added and distal circulation monitored.

BURNS - best treatment is immediate immersion of affected part in clean, cold sea water for at least 10 minutes. Severe burns will swell a lot so any tight clothing or jewellery should be cut open or removed. The swelling around the burn is fluid from the body, which is then lost from the circulation so the victim can be shocked and dehydrated and fluid replacement is essential.

Burned tissue is easily infected and should not be handled, removed or blisters pricked. If clothing is stuck it should be left. Sunburn is a form of burn and can result in severe dehydration and shock.

BRUISES - can cause a lot of pain under a finger or toenail. These can be treated safely by flaming the end of a piece of wire (such as a paper clip) and burning through the nail, just enough to release the blood.

COLD INJURY - hypothermia should be suspected after any accidental immersion. Treat, whether apparent or not, by gradual re-warming. Shelter, dry clothes, gentle warmth from another person or handwarm heat source in a sleeping bag will help. *RESUSCITATION MAY BE REQUIRED.* Continual observation is essential.

CHOKING - can be relieved by a sharp blow to the back preferably in the head down position. Alternatively grasp the victim from behind and pull clasped hands into the upper abdomen.

COLLAPSE - can complicate injuries involving loss of blood, pain and loss of fluid. If the patient is unconscious then airway clearance, resuscitation and treatment of blood loss, followed by maintenance in the semi-prone position is paramount. Heat loss must be prevented but no active heating should be used. If the patient is conscious, loosen tight clothes and elevate the lower limbs. Fluids should be given (if conscious) frequently in small amounts.

CUTS - if deep, remove any foreign body and treat bleeding with compression. Clean and dry cut. Bring the edges together using Steristrips (or adhesive tape) to hold them closed, starting in mid-cut and working to ends. Reinforce middle strips to prevent bursting.

DROWNING - Try all the resuscitation techniques in the introduction, according to need.
A - Airway: clearance and maintenance
B - Breathing: by mouth to mouth or mouth to nose
C - Circulation: External Cardiac Massage may be required.

If successful, remember to monitor level of consciousness and check airway. Maintain semi-prone position and keep under observation.

Hypothermia: usually complicates cold water immersion. Remove wet clothes and put patient in a dry sleeping bag with either a handwarm hot water bottle or a warm dry person. Look after patient out of wind, chill and rain and warm the cabin if possible. It can help to raise lower limbs and wrap towel round abdomen. Remember to watch for deterioration during warming.

DIARRHOEA - should be treated by oral fluids only; no solid food for 24/48 hours.

EYE INJURIES - Foreign body(ies) -
(a) Try to flush out with plenty of clean water. (b) Try pulling upper lid over lower then releasing to remove foreign body from under upper lid. (c) Raise upper, then lower lid, asking casualty to look all around. The upper lid can be turned back on itself over a matchstick. The speck can usually be seen and removed with a Q-tip or clean handkerchief.

If the foreign body cannot be removed it may have penetrated the eye and no further attempts should be made to remove it. The eye should be covered and both eyes rested. If pain persists after the speck is removed there may be a concealed abrasion and the eyes should be rested and Chloromycetin eye drops or a solution of 1 teaspoonful salt to 1 pint of boiled cooled water inserted.

Lost contact lenses can sometimes be lodged under upper lid in upper outer part of eye. It is possible to see them by turning back the lid and massaging them back into position through the lid.

FISH HOOKS - can penetrate the skin and may have to be pushed right through until the barb can be cut off with pliers and the hook withdrawn.

HEART ATTACK - though often hard to be sure, the following treatment should at least do no harm. If the patient is conscious, make them comfortable in the half-sitting position and give the strongest available pain killers. If the patient becomes semi-conscious place them in the recovery position, and observe carefully for maintenance of clear airway, and commence resuscitation should it be necessary.

HYPOTHERMIA - nearly always complicates cold water immersion and should be considered even when not apparent. If conscious the victim may be confused and appear drunk, seeming lethargic and remote from what is going on. Shivering fits may or may not occur and poor colour, vomiting or faintness can develop. The treatment is mentioned under Cold Injury above and consists of gradual rewarming by removal from wet and cold, replacement of wet clothing and if conscious rewarming in a warm sleeping bag. Priority must be given to attention to airway and the semi-prone position if the victim is unconscious.

INTERNAL INJURIES - may occur in any of the accidents which cause broken bones and bleeding and should be suspected when the patient seems unduly distressed, collapsed or blood appears from the body openings. The abdomen may appear rigid.

The priorities are airway clearance and maintenance and the adoption of the semi-prone position with careful observation to ensure prompt treatment of respiratory or cardiac arrest. The victim should be covered to prevent heat loss.

JOINTS - can be strained and sprained on decks and winches. The treatment is rest and time, but supporting crepe bandages can be comforting.

SEASICKNESS - is best avoided by starting treatment such as Stugeron or your favourite at least 12 hours before sailing. All these drugs may cause drowsiness. Alcohol must be avoided and hangovers predispose to seasickness.

ALL SEASICK CREW ON DECK SHOULD WEAR A HARNESS and should not be allowed to vomit over the side. Oral rehydration with very small amounts of rehydration fluids should be started, and fresh air and the ability to see the horizon can help.

The danger of cold should not be ignored. Stemetil anti-sickness suppositories can be useful.

SWALLOWING - Accidentally swallowed objects can usually be left to nature. Dangerous objects such as watch batteries and open safety pins should be treated as emergencies.

STINGS - from jellyfish are treated by oral antihistamines.

TOOTHACHE - caused by abscess and accompanied by swelling can be treated with antibiotics and painkillers. You can buy (OTC) dental kits.

VOMITING - Attempts should be made at rehydration using small amounts of fluid, preferably oral rehydration packs.

The information in the above list should give a casualty the best possibility of recovering until help arrives.

NOTE: It is so far unknown to contract AIDS from saliva, for although the virus may be present, the concentration is low. Intact skin is believed to be a secure protection from the virus present in blood and the risk in dealing with an unknown person is still very small.

The Yachtsman's Handbook, published by Nautical Data, offers more comprehensiv coverage of this subject.

FIRST AID KIT

Items marked Rx require a prescription fror a General Practitioner, who will have his her own preferences and opinion on the nee for a prescription. The following are main for guidance:

ANALGESICS - for pain relief
Paracetamol (Panadol) tabs 500mg. Dose; tabs 4-6 hours for medium to moderate pair Dihydrocodeine tabs (Rx). Dose: 1 tab 4-6 hour for moderate to severe pain. Cause constipatio with long term use. Can be used at nigh for cough or in the treatment of diarrhoea Pharmacists will discuss other (OTC) painkiller which are used for moderate pain.

ANTACIDS - for heartburn and indigestior Gaviscon tabs. Dose; 2 tabs chewed an swallowed 3/4 times daily.

ANTIBIOTICS - for infections

Amoxycillin capsules 250mg (Rx). Dose: 2 cap three times daily. Check for allergy, otherwis safe. Erythromycin tablets 250mg (Rx) Fo infection if allergic to Penicillin. Dose: 1 tab fou times daily.

DIARRHOEALS - Imodium capsules after eac loose stool. Up to 6 per day in conjunction wit oral rehydration and avoiding solid food.

ANTIEMETICS - for seasickness. Prevention Stugeron or other proprietory preparatior Stemetil suppositories (Rx) along with ora rehydration in severe cases.

ANTIHISTAMINES - for stings, bites and ha fever. Newer Antihistamine - Loratadine, 1 table daily is less likely to cause drowsiness.

Piriton tablets 4mg - cause drowsiness

ANTISEPTICS - Savlon, TCP, Dettol etc.

DRESSINGS - Melolin Sterile Squares 10cm 10cm. Put shiny side to wound, can be cut u and secured with Elastoplast or Micropore Tape Crepe bandages - assorted widths for dressings sprains or for securing splints. Steristrips fo wound closure.

EYE DROPS - for sticky, gritty or red eyes Chloromycetin drops (Rx).

ORAL REHYDRATION - for vomiting and diarrhoea Rehidrat or Diarolyte Powders in sachets with instructions. Start with small amounts ther give freely to replace lost fluid in vomiting diarrhoea, burns and sunburn.

HM Coastguard MRCCs and MRSCs

All Centres have operational A1 DSC VHF CH 70. All A2 DSC stations are operational, as indicated by 2187·5 kHz. WZ (Coastal) Navigation Warnings, Gale Warnings and Inshore Forecasts are as follows: Stations additionally broadcasting Gunfacts and Subfacts are indicated by *.

FALMOUTH COASTGUARD (MRCC)
50°09'N 05°03'W.
DSC MMSI 002320014 (2187·5 kHz)
Pendennis Pt, Castle Dr, Falmouth TR11 4WZ.
☎ 01326 317575l; ✉ 01326 318342.
Area from Marsland Mouth to Dodman Point.
On VHF Ch 16*, MF 2226 kHz Navigation Warnings at: 0140 0540 0940 1340 1740 and 2140 UT.

BRIXHAM COASTGUARD (MRSC)
50°24'N 03°31'W. DSC MMSI 002320013
King's Quay, Brixham TQ5 9TW.
☎ 01803 882704; ✉ 01803 882780.
Area from Dodman Point to Topsham.
On VHF Ch 16* Navigation Warnings at:
0050 0450 0850 1250 1650 2050 UT

PORTLAND COASTGUARD (MRSC)
50°36'N 02°27'W. DSC MMSI 002320012
Custom House Quay, Weymouth DT4 8BE.
☎ 01305 760439; ✉ 01305 760452.
Area from Topsham to Chewton Bunney.
On VHF Ch 16 Navigation Warnings at: 0220 0620 1020 1420 1820 and 2220 UT

SOLENT COASTGUARD (MRSC)
50°48'N 01°12'W. DSC MMSI 002320011
44A Marine Parade West, Lee-on-Solent, Gosport PO13 9NR.
☎ 02392 552100; ✉ 02392 551763.
Area from Chewton Bunney to Beachy Head.
Call Ch 67 (H24) for safety traffic.
On VHF Ch 16, MF 1641 kHz Navigation Warnings at: 0040 0440 0840 1240 1640 and 2040 UT

DOVER COASTGUARD (MRCC)
50°08'N 01°20'E. DSC MMSI 002320010
Langdon Battery, Swingate, Dover CT15 5NA.
☎ 01304 210008; ✉ 01304 202137.
Area from Beachy Head to Reculver Towers.
On VHF Ch 16, Navigation Warnings at: 0105 0505 0905 1305 1705 and 2105 UT
Operates Channel Navigation Information Service (CNIS) which broadcasts nav and tfc info on Ch 11 every H+40 (and H+55 in bad vis).

LONDON COASTGUARD
51°30'N 00°05'E. DSC MMSI 002320063
Thames Barrier Navigation Centre, Unit 28, 34 Bowater Road, Woolwich, London SE18 5TF.
☎ 0208 312 7380; ✉ 0208 312 7679.
Area River Thames from Shell Haven Pt (North Bank) and Egypt (South Bank) to Teddington.
NOTE: Does not broadcast MSI. Call on VHF Ch 16 *London Coastguard.*

THAMES COASTGUARD (MRSC)
51°51'N 01°17'E. DSC MMSI 002320009
East Terrace, Walton-on-the-Naze CO14 8PY.
☎ 01255 675518; ✉ 01255 675249.
Area from Reculver Towers to Southwold.
On VHF Ch 16 Navigation Warnings at: 0010 0410 0810 1210 1610 and 2010 UT

YARMOUTH COASTGUARD (MRCC)
52°37'N 01°43'E. DSC MMSI 002320008
Haven Bridge Hse, Great Yarmouth NR30 1HZ.
☎ 01493 851338; ✉ 01493 852307.
Area from Southwold to Haile Sand Fort.
On VHF Ch 16, MF 1869 kHz Navigation Warnings at: 0040 0440 0840 1240 1640 and 2040 UT

HUMBER COASTGUARD (MRSC)
54°06'N 00°11'W.
DSC MMSI 002320007 (2187·5 kHz)
Lime Kiln Lane, Bridlington, N Humberside YO15 2LX.
☎ 01262 672317; ✉ 01262 606915.
Area from Haile Sand Fort to the Scottish border.
On VHF Ch 16, MF 2226 kHz Navigation Warnings at: 0340 0740 1140 1540 1940 and 2340 UT

FORTH COASTGUARD (MRSC)
56°17'N 02°35'W. DSC MMSI 002320005
Fifeness, Crail, Fife KY10 3XN.
☎ 01333 450666; ✉ 01333 450725.
Area from English border to Doonies Point.
On VHF Ch 16 Navigation Warnings at: 0205 0605 1005 1405 1805 and 2205 UT

ABERDEEN COASTGUARD (MRCC)
57°08'N 02°05'W.
DSC MMSI 002320004 (2187·5 kHz)
Marine Hse, Blaikies Quay, Aberdeen AB11 5PB.
☎ 01224 592334; ✉ 01224 575920.
Area from Doonies Pt to Cape Wrath, incl Pentland Firth.
On VHF Ch 16, On MF 2226 kHz Navigation Warnings at: 0320 0720 1120 1520 1920 and 2320 UT

SHETLAND COASTGUARD (MRSC)
60°09'N 01°08'W.
DSC MMSI 002320001(2187·5 kHz)
The Knab, Knab Rd, Lerwick ZE1 0AX.
☎ 01595 692976; ✉ 01595 694810.
Area from Covers Shetland, Orkney and Fair Isle. On VHF Ch 16, MF 1770 kHz Navigation Warnings at: 0105 0505 0905 1305 1705 2105 UT

STORNOWAY COASTGUARD (MRSC)
58°12'N 06°22'W.
DSC MMSI 002320024 (2187·5 kHz)
Battery Point, Stornoway, Isle of Lewis HS1 2RT.
☎ 01851 702013; ✉ 01851 704387.
Area from Cape Wrath to Ardnamurchan Pt. Mainland, Narra to Butt of Lewis, Western Is and St Kilda.
On VHF Ch 16, MF 1743 kHz Navigation Warnings at: 0110 0510 0910 1310 1710 2110 UT

CLYDE COASTGUARD (MRCC)
55°58'N 04°48'W.
DSC MMSI 002320022 (2187·5 kHz)
Navy Buildings, Eldon St, Greenock PA16 7QY.
☎ 01475 729988; 🖷 01475 786955.
Area from Ardnamurchan Point to Mull
of Galloway.
On VHF Ch 16*, MF 1883 kHz Navigation
Warnings, strong wind warnings and gale
warnings at: 0020 0420 0820 1220 1620 2020 UT

BELFAST COASTGUARD (MRSC)
54°40'N 05°40'W.
DSC MMSI 002320021
Bregenz House, Quay St, Bangor, Co Down
BT20 5ED.
☎ 02891 463933; 🖷 02891 465886.
Area covers Northern Ireland.
On VHF Ch 16* Navigation Warnings at:
0305 0705 1105 1505 1905 and 2305 UT

LIVERPOOL COASTGUARD (MRSC)
53°30'N 03°03'W.
DSC MMSI 002320019
Hall Road West, Crosby, Liverpool L23 8SY
☎ 0151 9313341; 🖷 0151 9313347
Area from Mull of Galloway to Queensferry.
On VHF Ch 16 Navigation Warnings at:
0210 0610 1010 1410 1810 and 2210 UT

HOLYHEAD COASTGUARD (MRSC)
53°19'N 04°38'W.
DSC MMSI 002320018 (2187·5 kHz)
Holyhead, Anglesey, Gwynedd LL65 1ET
☎ 01407 762051; 🖷 01407 764373
Area from Queensferry to Friog
On VHF Ch 16 Navigation Warnings at: 0235
0635 1035 1435 1835 and 2235 UT

MILFORD HAVEN COASTGUARD (MRSC)
51°41'N 05°10'W.
DSC MMSI 002320017 (2187·5 kHz)
Gorsewood Drive, Hakin, Milford Haven,
Pembs SA73 2HB.
☎ 01646 690909; 🖷 01646 692176.
Area from Friog to River Towy.
On VHF Ch 16, MF 1767 kHz Navigation
Warnings at: 0335 0735 1135 1535 1935 and
2335 UT

SWANSEA COASTGUARD (MRCC)
51°34'N 03°58'W.
DSC MMSI 002320016
Tutt Head, Mumbles, Swansea SA3 4EX.
☎ 01792 366534; 🖷 01792 369005.
Area from River Towy to Marsland Mouth.
On VHF Ch 16 Navigation Warnings at: 000▮
0405 0805 1205 1605 and 2005 UT

CHANNEL ISLANDS
ST PETER PORT RADIO (CRS)
49°27'·00N 02°32'00W.
DSC MMSI 002320064
☎ 01481 720672; 🖷 01534 714177
Area covers the Channel Islands Northern
area; Alderney Radio keeps watch Ch 16 HJ.
On VHF Ch 20, MF 1764 kHz Navigation
Warnings at: 0133 0533 0933 1333 1733 and
2133 UT

JERSEY RADIO (CRS)
49°10'·85N 02°14'30W.
DSC MMSI 002320060
☎ 01534 741121. 🖷 01534 499089
Area covers the Channel Is Southern area.
On VHF Ch 25 82, MF 1658 kHz Navigation
Warnings at: 0645 0433 0745 0845 1245 1633
1845 2033 2245 UT

IRISH COASTGUARD

The Irish Coastguard is part of the Department of
Marine, Leeson Lane, Dublin 2. ☎ (01) 6620922;
🖷 (01) 662 0795.

The Coastguard co-ordinates all SAR
operations around the coast of Ireland through
Dublin MRCC, Malin Head MRSC and Valentia
MRSC. It liaises with UK and France during any
rescue operation within 100M of the Irish coast.

The MRCC/MRSCs are co-located with the Coast
Radio Stations of the same name and manned
by the same staff. All stations maintain H24
listening watch on VHF Ch 16. If ashore dial 999
and ask for Marine Rescue in an emergency.

Details of the MRCC/MRSCs are as follows:

DUBLIN (MRCC)
53°20'N 06°15W.
DSC MMSI 002500300 (+2187·5 kHz).
☎ +353 1 662 0922/3; 🖷 +353 1 662 0795.
Covers Carlingford Lough to Youghal.

VALENTIA (MRSC)
51°56'N 10°21'W.
DSC MMSI 002500200 (+2187·5 kHz).
☎ +353 669 476 109; 🖷 +353 669 476 289.
Covers Youghal to Slyne Head.

MALIN HEAD (MRSC)
55°22'N 07°20W.
DSC MMSI 002500100 (+2187·5 kHz).
☎ +353 77 70103; 🖷 +353 77 70221.
Covers Slyne Head to Lough Foyle.

AR RESOURCES

he Irish Coastguard provides some 50 units
ound the coast and is on call 24 hours a day.
ome of these units have a specialist cliff
imbing capability.

helicopter, based at Shannon, can respond
ithin 15 to 45 minutes and operate to a radius
200M. It is equipped with infrared search
quipment and can uplift 14 survivors. In
ddition helicopters (based at Finner Camp in
onegal and at Baldonnel, Dublin) can operate
150 miles by day and 70 miles at night.

ther military and civilian aircraft and vessels,
gether with the Garda and lighthouse
rvice, can be called upon.

he RNLI maintains four stations around the
ast and some 26 lifeboats. Additionally, six
dividually community-run inshore rescue
ats are available.

OAST AND CLIFF RESCUE SERVICES

his comprises about 50 stations manned by
lunteers, who are trained in first aid and
quipped with inflatables, breeches buoys,
iff ladders etc. Their ☎ numbers (the Leader's
sidence) are given, where appropriate, under
ch port.

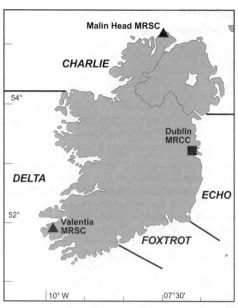

Irish Coastguard centres

ANISH COASTGUARD

he Danish Coastguard is controlled remotely
om Lyngby through Blavand and Skagen CRS.

yngby is an operational Coast DSC station
orking via Blavand and Skagen on VHF Ch 70
MSI 002191000.

here are at least 12 lifeboats stationed at the
ajor harbours along this west facing coast.

SI Navigational Warnings are broadcast on
HF from Lyngby at 0133 0533 0933 1333 1733
133 on channels shown.

F broadcasts are transmitted on 1758KHz from
kajen and 1734KHz from Blavand.

ring Practice areas exist at:

Tranum and Blokhus ☎ 98235088 or call
Tranum on VHF Ch 16.

Nymindegab ☎ 75289355 or call *Nymindegab*
on VHF Ch 16.

Oksbøl ☎ 76541213 or call *Oksbøl* on VHF
Ch 16; (Lyngby Radio broadcasts firing
warnings at 0705 1705).

Rømø E ☎ 74755219 or call *Fly Rømø* on
VHF Ch 16; Rømø W ☎ 74541340.

Danish Coastguard centres

GERMANY

SAFETY SERVICES

Maritime Rescue Co-ordination Centre Bremen MRCC (☎ 0421 536870; 🖷 0421 5368714; MMSI 002111240) callsign *Bremen Rescue Radio,* coordinates SAR operations in the Search & Rescue Region (SRR) which abuts the UK SRR at about 55°12'N 03°30'E. A 24 hrs watch is kept on VHF Ch 16 and DSC Ch 70 via remote stations at Norddeich, Elbe Weser, Bremen, Helgoland, Hamburg, Eiderstedt and Nordfriesland.

DGzRS, the German Sea Rescue Service *(Deutsch Gesellschaft zur Rettung Schiffbrüchiger),* is also based at Bremen (☎ 0421 537 0777; 🖷 0421 537 0714). It monitors Ch 16 H24. Offshore lifeboats are based at Borkum, Norderney, Langeoog, Wilhelmshaven, Bremerhaven, Cuxhaven, Helgoland, Amrum and List. There are also many inshore lifeboats. The German Navy provides ships and SAR helicopters.

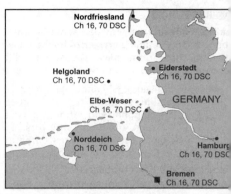

German Coastguard Radio Stations

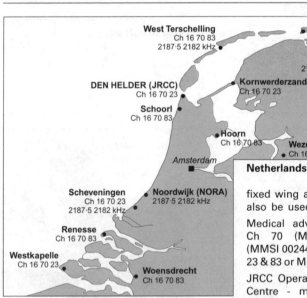

Netherlands Coastguard Radio Stations

NETHERLANDS AND BELGIUM

Netherlands

The Netherlands Coastguard (JRCC Den Helder) coordinates SAR operations using callsign *Den Helder Rescue.* A JRCC is a Joint Rescue Coordination Centre (marine and aeronautical).

The JRCC keeps a listening watch H24 on Ch 16 (until 1 Feb 2005), DSC Ch 70, and MF DSC 2187·5kHz (but not on 2182kHz); MMSI 002442000. Working channels are VHF 67 & 73.

There are 24 lifeboat stations along the coast and 10 inshore lifeboat stations. Helicopters,

fixed wing aircraft and ships of the RNLN ca also be used.

Medical advice: initial call on Ch 16, DS Ch 70 (MMSI 002442000) or 2187·5 kł (MMSI 002442000). Working chans are VHF C 23 & 83 or MF 2824 kHz transmit, 2520 kHz liste

JRCC Operations (Joint Rescue Coordinatic Centre - marine and aeronautical) can t contacted H24 through the following:

For emergency:
☎ + 31 (0) 900 0111; 🖷 + 31 (0) 223 658358.

Operational telephone number:
☎ + 31 (0) 223 542300.

or HO for Admin/info
☎+ 31 (0) 255 546546; 🖷+31 223 658300.

Inmarsat 'C': 424477710

Navigational warnings
Navigational warnings *(Nautische Warnnachrich* for the North Sea coast are contained in IJmuide Navtex (P) transmissions. Dangers to navigatic should be reported to Seewarn Cuxhaven.

Belgium

SAR GENERAL

The Belgian Pilotage Service coordinates SAR operations from Oostende MRCC. The MRCC is connected by telephone to the Oostende Coast Radio Station (OST) which maintains listening watch H24 on Ch 16, 2182kHz and DSC Ch 70 and 187·5kHz. MMSI 002050480. ☎ 059 706565; ᐧ 059 701339. Antwerpen CRS, remotely controlled by Oostende CRS, has MMSI 002050485. DSC Ch 70.

Telephone and Fax numbers are:

MRCC Oostende ☎ +32(0) 59 701000; ᐧ +32(0) 59 703605.

MRSC Nieuwpoort ☎ +32(0) 58 230000; ᐧ +32(0) 58 231575.

MRSC Zeebrugge ☎ +32(0) 50 550801; ᐧ +32(0) 50 547400.

RCC Brussels (Point of contact for Cospas/Sarsat):

☎ +32(0) 2 226 8856 (Mon-Fri 0600-1500 UT).

Offshore and inshore lifeboats are based at Nieuwpoort, Oostende and Zeebrugge.

The Belgian Air Force provides helicopters from Koksijde near the French border. The Belgian Navy also cooperates in SAR operations.

Navigational warnings are broadcast by Oostende Radio on receipt and at scheduled times on 2761 kHz and VHF Ch 27. Also by Oostende Navtex (M) at: 0200, 0600, 1000, 1400, 1800, 2200 UT for the SW part of the North Sea.

FRANCE – CROSS

Four Centres Régionaux Opérationnels de Surveillance et de Sauvetage (CROSS) cover the Channel and Atlantic coasts; see below. CROSS is an MRCC. CROSS provides a permanent, H24, all weather operational presence along the French coast and liaises with foreign CGs. CROSS' main functions include:

(1)   Co-ordinating Search and Rescue.
(2)   Navigational surveillance.
(3)   Broadcasting navigational warnings.
(4)   Broadcasting weather information.
(5)   Anti-pollution control.
(6)   Marine and fishery surveillance.

CROSS and sous-Cross centres

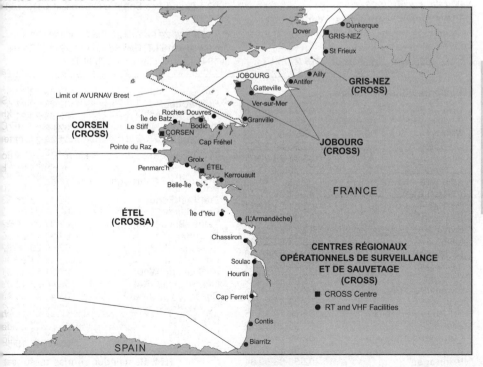

All centres keep watch on VHF Ch 16 as well as Ch 70 (DSC), and broadcast gale warnings along with weather forecasts and local navigational warnings.

CROSSA Étel specialises in providing medical advice and responds to alerts from Cospas/Sarsat satellites.

CROSS can be contacted by R/T, by ☎, through Coast Radio Stations, via the National Gendarmerie or Affaires Maritimes, or via a Semaphore station. Call *Semaphore* station on Ch 16 (working Ch 10) or by ☎ as listed late in this section.

In addition to their safety and SAR functions CROSS stations using, for example, the callsig *Corsen Traffic* monitor Traffic Separatio Schemes in the Dover Strait, off Casquets an off Ouessant. They also broadcast navigation warnings and weather forecasts. See Chapter for times and VHF channels.

CROSS stations
All stations co-ordinate SAR on VHF Ch 15 67 68 73. DSC Ch 70

CROSS Gris-Nez
50°52'N 01°35'E   MMSI 002275100
☎ 03 21 87 21 87; ✉ 03 21 87 78 55
Belgian Border to Cap d'Antifer
DSC Ch 70 MF 2187·5 kHz

Navigation Warnings

On VHF Ch 79: From: Dunkerque, Gris-Nez, Saint-Frieux and L'Ailly every H+10

On MF 1650 kHz: Gris-Nez at 0833 2033 UT

CROSS Jobourg
49°41'N 01°54'W   MMSI 002275200
☎ 02 33 52 72 13; ✉ 02 33 52 71 72
Cap de la Hague to Mont St Michel

Navigation Warnings

On VHF Ch 80: From: Antifer, Ver-sur-Mer, Gatteville, Jobourg, Granville and Roche Douvres every H+20/H+50.

On MF 1650 kHz: Gris-Nez at 0915 2115 LT

CROSS Corsen
48°24'N 04°47'W   MMSI 002275300
☎ 02 98 89 31 31; ✉ 02 98 89 65 75
Mont St Michel to Pointe de Penmarc'h

Navigation Warnings

On MF 2677 kHz: From CROSS Corsen at 0735 1935 LT

CROSS Étel
47°39'N 03°12'W   MMSI 002275000
☎ 02 97 55 35 35; ✉ 02 97 55 49 34
Pointe de Penmarc'h to the Spanish Border

Navigation Warnings

On VHF Ch 80: From: Penmarc'h 0703 1533 1903 LT, Ile de Groix at 0715 1545 1915 LT. Belle-Ile at 0733 1603 1933 LT, Saint-Nazaire at 0745 1615 1945 LT, Ile d'Yeu at 0803 1633 2003 LT, and Les Sable d'Olonne at 0815 164! 2015 LT.

On VHF Ch 79 From: Chassiron at 1903 LT, Soulac at 1915 LT, Cap Ferrat at 1933 LT, Contis at 1945 LT and Biarritz at 2003 LT.

Semaphore (Signal) stations

*	Dunkerque	03·28·66·86·18	
	Boulogne	03·21·31·32·10	
	Ault	03·22·60·47·33	
	Dieppe	02·35·84·23·82	
*	Fécamp	02·35·28·00·91	
*	La Hève	02·35·46·07·81	
*	Le Havre	02·35·21·74·39	
	Villerville	02·31·88·11·13	
*	Port-en-Bessin	02·31·21·81·51	
	St-Vaast	02·33·54·44·50	
*	Barfleur	02·33·54·04·37	
	Lévy	02·33·54·31·17	
*	Le Homet	02·33·92·60·08	
	La Hague	02·33·52·71·07	
	Carteret	02·33·53·85·08	
	Barneville Le Roc	02·33·50·05·85	
	St-Cast	02·96·41·85·30	
*	St Quay-Portrieux	02·96.70.42.18	
	Bréhat	02·96·20·00·12	
*	Ploumanac'h	02·96·91·46·51	
	Batz	02·98·61·76·06	
*	Brignogan	02·98·83·50·84	

*	Ouessant Stiff	02·98·48·81·5C	
*	St-Mathieu	02·98·89·01·59	
*	Portzic (Ch 08)	02·98·22·21·47	
	Toulinguet	02·98·27·90·02	
	Cap-de-la-Chèvre	02·98·27·09·5E	
*	Pointe-du-Raz	02·98·70·66·57	
*	Penmarc'h	02·98·58·61·0C	
	Beg Meil	02·98·94·98·92	
*	Port-Louis	02·97·82·52·1C	
	Étel Mât Fenoux	02·97·55·35·3E	
	Beg Melen (Groix)	02·97·86·80·13	
	Talut (Belle-Île)	02·97·31·85·07	
	St-Julien	02·97·50·09·3E	
	Piriac-sur-Mer	02·40·23·59·87	
*	Chemoulin	02·40·91·99·0C	
	St-Sauveur (Yeu)	02·51·58·31·01	
	Les Baleines (Ré)	05·46·29·42·06	
	Chassiron (Oléron)	05·46·47·85·43	
*	Pointe-de-Grave	05·56·09·60·03	
	Cap Ferret	05·56·60·60·03	
	Messanges	05·58·48·94·1C	
*	Socoa	05·59·47·18·54	

* H24. Remainder sunrise to sunset

EMERGENCY VHF DF SERVICE

A yacht in emergency can call CROSS on VHF Ch 16, 11 or 67 to obtain a bearing. This will be passed as the true bearing of the yacht *from* the DF station. The Semaphore stations listed above are also equipped with VHF DF. They keep watch on Ch 16 and other continuously scanned frequencies, which include Ch 1-29, 36, 39, 48, 50, 52, 55, 56 and 60-88.

MEDICAL

The Service d'Aide Médicale Urgente (SAMU) can be contacted via CROSS. CROSS Étel specialises in providing medical advice. It can be contacted via:

Lille – 03·20·54·22·22

Le Havre – 02·35·47·15·15

Caen – 02·31·44·88·88

Saint Brieuc – 02·96·94·28·95

Brest – 02·98·46·11·33

Rennes – 02·97·54·22·11

Nantes – 02·40·08·37·77

La Rochelle – 05·46·27·32·15

Bordeaux – 05·56·96·70·70

Bayonne – 05·59·63·33·33

Semaphore stations

These stations keep a visual, radar and radio watch (VHF Ch 16) around the coast. They show visual gale warning signals, will repeat forecasts and offer local weather reports. They relay emergency calls to CROSS and are equipped with VHF DF; see above.

Lifeboats

The lifeboat service Société National de Sauvetage en Mer (SNSM) comes under CROSS, but ashore it is best to contact local lifeboat stations direct. A hefty charge may be levied if a SNSM lifeboat attends a vessel not in distress.

Navigation warnings

Long-range warnings are broadcast by Inmarsat SafetyNet for Navarea II, which includes the west coast of France. The north coast lies in Navarea I.

Avurnavs (AVis URgents aux NAVigateurs) are regional Coastal and Local warnings issued by two regional authorities:

(1) **Brest** – for the west coast of France and the western Channel to Mont St Michel; and

(2) **Cherbourg** – for the eastern Channel from Mont St Michel to the Belgian frontier.

Avurnavs are broadcast by Niton and Brest on Navtex, and on MF by Jobourg and CROSS Gris Nez; urgent ones on receipt and after next silence period, and at scheduled times. Warnings are prefixed by '*Sécurité Avurnav*', followed by the name of the station.

Local warnings for coastal waters are broadcast in French and **English** by CROSS as follows:

CROSS	VHF Ch	Times (local)
Dunkerque	79	H+10
CROSS Gris Nez	79	H+10
	1650 kHz	0833 2033 LT
Saint Frieux	79	H+10
L'Ailly	79	H+10
CROSS Jobourg	80	H+20 & H+50
	1650 kHz	0915 2115 LT
Granville	80	H+20
Roche Douvre	80	H+20 & H+50
CROSS Corsen	79	H+10 & H+40
	2677 kHz	0735 1935 LT
Bodic	79	H+10 & H+40
Ile de Batz	79	H+10 & H+40
Le Stiff	79	H+10 & H+40
Pointe du Raz	79	H+10 & H+40
CROSS Étel	80	On receipt

SPAIN AND PORTUGAL

Spain and Portugal – MRCC/MRSC

MRCCs and MRSCs are primarily responsible for handling Distress, Safety and Urgency communications. Madrid MRCC coordinates SAR on the N and NW coasts of Spain through six MRCC/MRSCs. All stations monitor VHF Ch 16 and 2182 kHz H24 and VHF DSC Ch 70 (H24).

In Portugal, the Portuguese Navy coordinates SAR in two regions, Lisboa and Santa Maria (Azores).

In SW Spain and the Gibraltar Strait MRCC Tarifa coordinates SAR.

Digital Selective Calling (DSC) is operational as shown below. MRCC/MRSCs also broadcast weather as shown in Chapter 2. MRCC/MRSCs do not handle commercial link calls.

Search and Rescue operations and the prevention of pollution in Spain are undertaken by the National Society for Maritime Rescue and Safety (Salvamento y Seguridad – SASEMA).

A shipping forecast is broadcast, in Spanish, every two hours from Salvamento Marítimao's regional centres and copies of this can usually be obtained from most yacht clubs.

NORTH AND NORTH-WEST SPAIN

Bilbao MRCC MMSI 002240996	43°21'N 03°02'W ☎ 94 483 9286; 🖷 94 483 9161	Ch 10: Nav warnings every 4 hours from 0233 UT. DSC Ch 70, 2187·5 kHz
Santander MRSC MMSI 002241009	43°28'N 03°43'W ☎ 942 213 030; 🖷 942 213 638	Ch 11: Nav warnings every 4 hours from 0045 UT. DSC Ch 70 2187·5 kHz
Gijón MRCC MMSI 002240997	43°37'N 05°42'W ☎ 985 326 050; 🖷 985 320 908	Ch 10 Nav warnings every H+15 DSC Ch 70, 2187·5 kHz
Coruña MRSC MMSI 002241022	43°22'N 08°23'W ☎ 981 209 548; 🖷 981 209 518 Call: *Coruña Traffic*	Ch 13, 16, 67 Ch 13: Nav warnings every 4 hours from 0205 UT. DSC Ch 70, 2187·5 kHz
Finisterre MRCC MMSI 002240993	42°42'N 08°59'W ☎ 981 767 320; 🖷 981 767 740 Call: *Finisterre Traffic*	Ch 11, 16 2182 kHz Ch 11: Nav warnings every 4 hours from 0033 UT. DSC Ch 70, 2187·5 kHz
Vigo MRSC MMSI 002240998	42°10'N 08°41'W ☎ 986 297 403; 🖷 986 290 455	Ch 11, 16 2182 kHz DSC Ch 70, 2187·5 kHz Ch 10: Nav warnings every 4 hours from 0215 UT

PORTUGAL

Lisboa MRCC 38°41'N 09°19'W
Ch 23 25 26 27 28 MF 2182 2578 2693 kHz.
MMSI 002630100
☎ 351 21 419 0098
🖷 351 21 419 9900
DSC Ch 70; 2187·5 kHz
VHF Services controlled from Lisboa:

Arga	Ch 25 28 83
Arestal	Ch 24 26 85
Montejunto	Ch 23 27 87
Atalaia	Ch 24 26 85
Picos	Ch 23 27 85
Estoi	Ch 24 28 86

Spanish & Portuguese Coastguard Radio Stations

SOUTH WEST SPAIN

Tarifa MRCC MMSI 002240994	36°01'N 05°35'W ☎ 956 681 452; 🖷 956 680 606	Ch 16 10 74, 2182 kHz (all H24); Call: *Tarifa Traffic* Ch 10 74: Nav warnings every even H+15 and on receipt DSC Ch 70, 2187·5 kHz (H24)
Algeciras MRSC MMSI 002241001	36°08'N 05°26'W ☎ 956 585 404; 🖷 956 585 402	Ch 15 16 74 DSC Ch 70 Nav warnings on request

emotely controlled H24 by a Coastguard Maritime Rescue Co-ordination Centre (MRCC) or aritime Rescue Sub-Centre (MRSC), this equipment is for emergency use only. It is not a free avigational service and should only be used 'one stage down' from real distress. It is in all achtsmen's interests not to abuse the service.

fter contact on Ch 16, invariably Ch 67 is used for the DF procedure; this may be a count from 10. Note that the bearing obtained is from the station to the vessel.

HF-DF stations are marked on charts by a dot and magenta circle, suffixed 'RG'.

TATION	CONTROLLED BY	POSITION	
arra	MRSC Stornoway	57°00'·81N	07°30'·42W
awdsey	MRSC Thames	51°59'·60N	01°25'·00E
erry Head	MRSC Brixham	50°23'·97N	03°29'·05W
oniface	MRSC Solent	50°36'·21N	01°12'·03W
ompass Head	MRSC Shetland	59°52'·05N	01°16'·30W
rosslaw	MRSC Forth	55°54'·48N	02°12'·31W
ullercoats	MRSC Humber	55°04'·00N	01°28'·00W
unnet Head	MRCC Aberdeen	58°40'·31N	03°22'·52W
asington	MRSC Humber	53°39'·13N	00°05'·90E
ast Prawle	MRSC Brixham	50°13'·10N	03°42'·50W
airlight	MRCC Dover	50°52'·19N	00°38'·74E
fe Ness	MRSC Forth	56°16'·70N	02°35'·30W
amborough	MRSC Humber	54°07'·08N	00°05'·21W
reat Ormes Head	MRSC Holyhead	53°19'·96N	03°51'·25W
rove Point	MRSC Portland	50°32'·93N	02°25'·20W
artland Pt	MRCC Swansea	51°01'·22N	04°31'·40W
artlepool	MRSC Humber	54°41'·79N	01°10'·57W
engistbury Head	MRSC Portland	50°42'·95N	01°45'·64W
verbervie	MRSC Forth	56°51'·10N	02°15'·65W
ilchiaran	MRCC Clyde	55°45'·90N	06°27'·19W
ands End	MRCC Falmouth	50°08'·13N	05°38'·19W
andgon Battery	MRCC Dover	51°07'·97N	01°20'·59E
aw Hill	MRCC Clyde	55°41'·76N	04°50'·46W
zard	MRCC Falmouth	49°57'·60N	05°12'·06W
owestoft	MRCC Yarmouth	52°28'·60N	01°42'·20E
ewhaven	MRSC Solent	50°46'·93N	00°03'·01E
ewton	MRSC Humber	55°31'·01N	01°37'·10W
orth Foreland	MRCC Dover	51°22'·53N	01°26'·72E
oss Head	MRCC Aberdeen	58°28'·80N	03°03'·00W
ame Head	MRSC Brixham	50°19'·03N	04°13'·20W
hiw	MRSC Holyhead	52°50'·00N	04°37'·82W
odel	MRSC Stornoway	57°44'·90N	06°57'·41W
t Ann's Head	MRSC Milford Haven	51°40'·97N	05°10'·52W
t Mary's, Isles of Scilly	MRCC Falmouth	49°55'·73N	06°18'·25W
andwick	MRSC Stornoway	58°12'·65N	06°21'·27W
elsey	MRSC Solent	50°43'·80N	00°48'·22W
hoeburyness	MRSC Thames	51°31'·38N	00°46'·50E
kegness	MRCC Yarmouth	53°09'·00N	00°21'·00E
naefell	MRSC Liverpool	54°15'·84N	04°27'·66W
iree	MRSC Clyde	56°30'·62N	06°57'·68W
evose Head	MRCC Falmouth	50°32'·91N	05°01'·99W
imingham	MRCC Yarmouth	52°54'·57N	01°20'·60E
ynemouth	MRSC Humber	55°01'·07N	01°24'·99W
alney Island	MRSC Liverpool	54°06'·61N	03°16'·00W
hitby	MRSC Humber	54°29'·40N	00°36'·30W
ideford Hill	MRSC Shetland	58°59'·29N	03°01'·40W
indyhead	MRCC Aberdeen	57°38'·90N	02°14'·50W

HANNEL ISLANDS

uernsey	Ship transmits on Ch 16 (Distress only)	49°26'·27N	02°35'·77W
ersey	or Ch 67 (Guernsey) or Ch 82 (Jersey)	49°10'·85N	02°14'·30W

RELAND

rlock Head	MRSC Belfast	54°40'·41N	05°34'·97W
est Torr	MRSC Belfast	55°11'·70N	06°05'·20W

Chapter 4

VHF EMERGENCY DIRECTION FINDING SERVICES

United Kingdom	Ch 16 (Distress only) Ch 67
Guernsey	Ch 16 (Distress) Ch 67
Jersey	Ch 16 (Distress) Ch 82
France	Ch 16 11 67

FRENCH EMERGENCY VHF DIRECTION FINDING SERVICE

his service is for EMERGENCY USE ONLY. Each VHF direction-finding station is remotely ontrolled either by a Centre Régional Opérationnel de Surveillance et du Sauvetage (CROSS), ignal Station or Naval Lookout Station. See associated diagram. CROSS Stations guard Ch 16 r 11; (if a maritime rescue operation is already underway on Ch 11, then Ch 67 is used). ignal Stations and Lookout Stations keep a priority watch on Ch 16. Seven additional equencies are retained in memory (scanner sweeping) from amongst the following channels:

1-29	:	156.050 MHz-157.450 MHz	52	:	155.625 MHz
36	:	162.400 MHz	55	:	155.775 MHz
39	:	162.550 MHz	56	:	155.825 MHz
48	:	121.500 MHz	60-88	:	156.025 MHz-157.425 MHz
50	:	155.525 MHz			

hip transmits on Ch 16 (distress only) or Ch 11 in order that the station can determine its earing. Ship's bearing from the station is transmitted on Ch 16 (distress only) or Ch 11

TATION	HOURS	CONTROLLED BY	POSITION	
ult	HJ	Sig Stn	50°06'·50N	01°27'·50E
arfleur	H24	Sig Stn	49°41'·90N	01°15'·90W
atz	HJ	Sig Stn	48°44'·80N	04°00'·60W
eg-Meil	HJ	Sig Stn	47°51'·30N	03°58'·40W
eg Melen	HJ	Sig Stn	47°39'·20N	03°30'·10W
oulogne	HJ	Sig Stn	50°44'·00N	01°36'·00E
réhat	HJ	Sig Stn	48°51'·30N	03°00'·10W
rignogan	H24	Sig Stn	48°40'·60N	04°19'·70W
ap de La Chèvre	HJ	Sig Stn	48°10'·20N	04°33'·00W
ap Ferret	HJ	Sig Stn	44°37'·50N	01°15'·00W
arteret	HJ	Sig Stn	49°22'·40N	01°48'·30W
hassiron	HJ	Sig Stn	46°02'·80N	01°24'·50W
hemoulin	H24	Sig Stn	47°14'·10N	02°17'·80W
réach (Ouessant)	H24	CROSS Corsen	48°27'·60N	05°07'·80W
réach (Ouessant)	HJ	Sig Stn	48°27'·60N	05°07'·70W
ieppe	HJ	Sig Stn	49°56'·00N	01°05'·20E
unkerque	H24	Sig Stn	51°03'·40N	02°20'·40E
tel	H24	CROSS Étel	47°39'·80N	03°12'·00W
écamp	H24	Sig Stn	49°46'·10N	00°22'·20E
ris-Nez	H24	CROSS Gris Nez	50°52'·20N	01°35'·01E
rouin (Cancale)	HJ	Sig Stn	48°42'·60N	01°50'·60W
omet	H24	Lookout Stn	49°39'·50N	01°37'·90W
obourg	H24	CROSS Jobourg	49°41'·50N	01°54'·50W
a Coubre	H24	Sig Stn	45°41'·90N	01°13'·40W
a Hague	HJ	Sig Stn	49°43'·60N	01°56'·30W
a Hève	H24	Sig Stn	49°30'·60N	00°04'·20E
e Roc	HJ	Sig Stn	48°50'·10N	01°36'·90W
e Talut	HJ	Sig Stn	47°17'·70N	03°13'·00W
es Baleines	HJ	Sig Stn	46°14'·60N	01°33'·70W
evy	HJ	Sig Stn	49°41'·70N	01°28'·20W
lessanges	HJ	Sig Stn	43°48'·80N	01°23'·90W
enmarc'h	H24	Sig Stn	47°47'·90N	04°22'·40W
iriac	H24	Sig Stn	47°22'·50N	02°33'·40W
loumanach	H24	Sig Stn	48°49'·50N	03°28'·20W
ointe de Grave	HJ	Sig Stn	45°34'·30N	01°03'·90W
ointe du Raz	H24	Sig Stn	48°02'·30N	04°43·80W
ort-en-Bessin	H24	Sig Stn	49°21'·10N	00°46'·30W
ort-Louis	H24	Lookout Stn	47°42'·60N	03°21'·80W
oches-Douvres	H24	CROSS Jobourg	49°06'·39N	02°48'·80W
aint-Cast	HJ	Sig Stn	48°38'·60N	02°14'·70W
aint-Julien	HJ	Sig Stn	47°29'·70N	03°07'·50W
aint-Mathieu	H24	Lookout Stn	48°19'·80N	04°46'·20W
aint-Quay-Portrieux	H24	Sig Stn	48°39'·30N	02°49'·50W
aint-Sauveur	HJ	Sig Stn	46°41'·70N	02°18'·80W
aint-Vaast	HJ	Sig Stn	49°34'·50N	01°16'·50W
angatte	H24	Sig Stn	50°57'·10N	01°46'·39E
ocoa	H24	Sig Stn	43°23'·30N	01°41'·10W
aillefer	HJ	Sig Stn	47°21'·80N	03°09'·00W
oulinguet (Camaret)	HJ	Sig Stn	48°16'·80N	04°37'·50W
illerville	HJ	Sig Stn	49°23'·20N	00°06'·50E

MILITARY EXERCISE AREAS

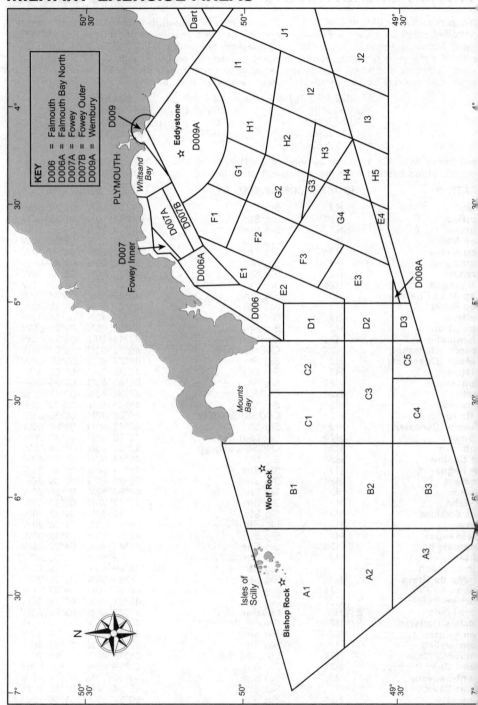

KEY

D006 = Falmouth
D006A = Falmouth Bay North
D007A = Fowey
D007B = Fowey Outer
D009A = Wembury

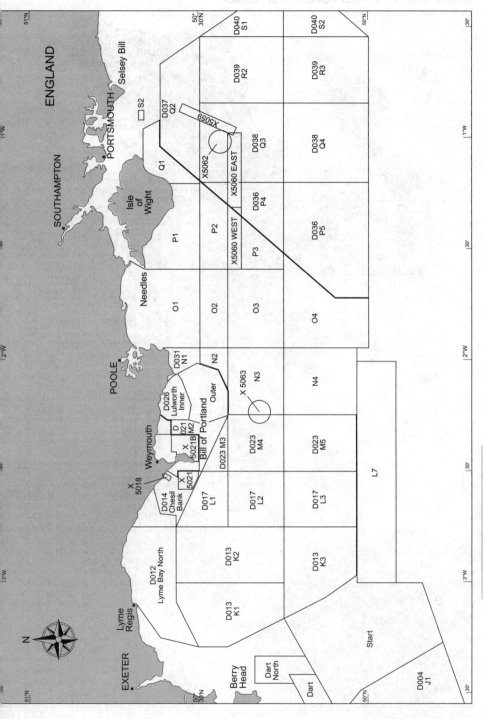

MILITARY EXERCISE AREAS

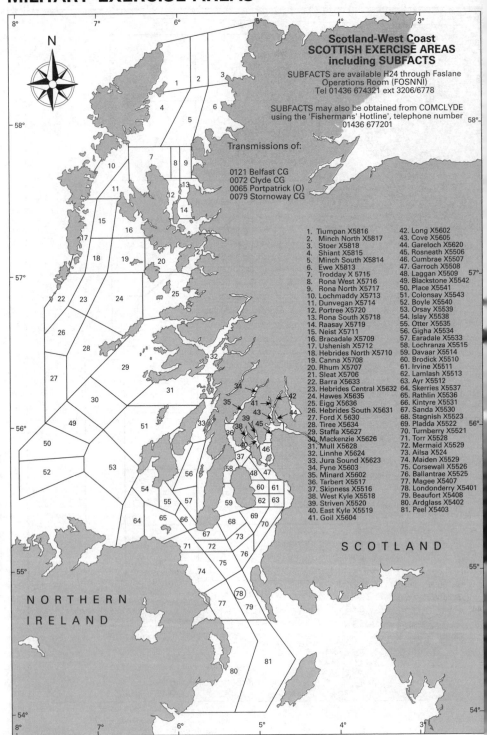

Scotland-West Coast
SCOTTISH EXERCISE AREAS
including SUBFACTS

SUBFACTS are available H24 through Faslane
Operations Room (FOSNNI)
Tel 01436 674321 ext 3206/6778

SUBFACTS may also be obtained from COMCLYDE
using the 'Fishermans' Hotline', telephone number
01436 677201

Transmissions of:

0121 Belfast CG
0072 Clyde CG
0065 Portpatrick (O)
0079 Stornoway CG

1. Tiumpan X5816
2. Minch North X5817
3. Stoer X5818
4. Shiant X5815
5. Minch South X5814
6. Ewe X5813
7. Trodday X 5715
8. Rona West X5716
9. Rona North X5717
10. Lochmaddy X5713
11. Dunvegan X5714
12. Portree X5720
13. Rona South X5718
14. Raasay X5719
15. Neist X5711
16. Bracadale X5709
17. Ushenish X5712
18. Hebrides North X5710
19. Canna X5708
20. Rhum X5707
21. Sleat X5706
22. Barra X5633
23. Hebrides Central X5632
24. Hawes X5635
25. Eigg X5636
26. Hebrides South X5631
27. Ford X 5630
28. Tiree X5634
29. Staffa X5627
30. Mackenzie X5626
31. Mull X5628
32. Linnhe X5624
33. Jura Sound X5623
34. Fyne X5603
35. Minard X5602
36. Tarbert X5517
37. Skipness X5516
38. West Kyle X5518
39. Striven X5520
40. East Kyle X5519
41. Goil X5604

42. Long X5602
43. Cove X5605
44. Gareloch X5620
45. Rosneath X5506
46. Cumbrae X5507
47. Garroch X5508
48. Laggan X5509
49. Blackstone X5542
50. Place X5541
51. Colonsay X5543
52. Boyle X5540
53. Orsay X5539
54. Islay X5538
55. Otter X5535
56. Gigha X5534
57. Earadale X5533
58. Lochranza X5515
59. Davaar X5514
60. Brodick X5510
61. Irvine X5511
62. Lamlash X5513
63. Ayr X5512
64. Skerries X5537
65. Rathlin X5536
66. Kintyre X5531
67. Sanda X5530
68. Stagnish X5523
69. Pladda X5522
70. Turnberry X5521
71. Torr X5528
72. Mermaid X5529
73. Ailsa X524
74. Maiden X5529
75. Corsewall X5526
76. Ballantrae X5525
77. Magee X5407
78. Londonderry X5401
79. Beaufort X5408
80. Ardglass X5402
81. Peel X5403

SCOTLAND

NORTHERN
IRELAND

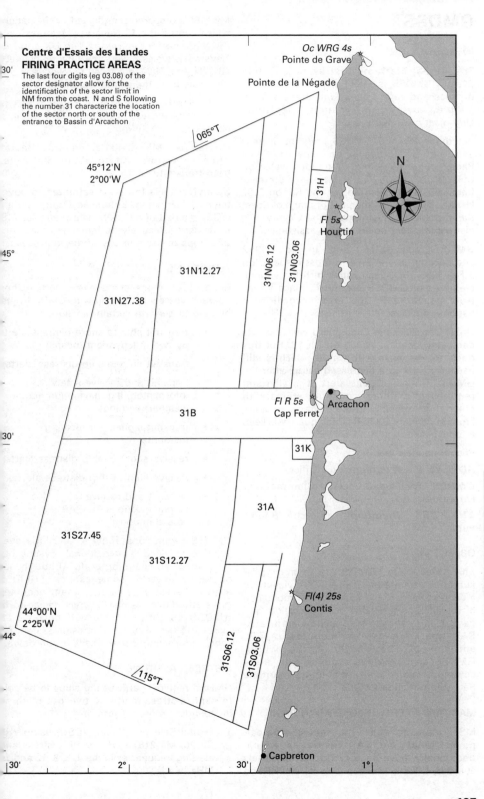

Centre d'Essais des Landes
FIRING PRACTICE AREAS

The last four digits (eg 03.08) of the sector designator allow for the identification of the sector limit in NM from the coast. N and S following the number 31 characterize the location of the sector north or south of the entrance to Bassin d'Arcachon

Oc WRG 4s
Pointe de Grave

Pointe de la Négade

065°T

45°12'N
2°00'W

31H

N

Fl 5s
Hourtin

31N12.27

31N06.12

31N03.06

31N27.38

31B

Fl R 5s
Cap Ferret

Arcachon

31K

31A

31S27.45

31S12.27

44°00'N
2°25'W

Fl(4) 25s
Contis

115°T

31S06.12

31S03.06

Capbreton

GMDSS

INTRODUCTION

The Global Maritime Distress and Safety System (GMDSS) is a third generation maritime distress and safety communications system adopted by the International Maritime Organisation (IMO).

Before the advent of GMDSS, maritime distress and safety relied heavily on ships and Coast Radio Stations keeping continuous watch on the three main international distress frequencies: 500 kHz (Morse) and R/T on 2182 kHz and VHF Ch 16. When out of range of Coast Radio Stations, only ships in the vicinity of a distress incident could render assistance.

GMDSS was introduced in Feb 1992 and became operational in most respects on 1 Feb 1999. The speed with which the various elements of GMDSS are put in place varies from sea area to sea area according to national policies.

On 31 Jan 2005 the Coastguard will cease its dedicated headset Watch on Ch 16. But this does not dispense with Ch 16, which is still needed to talk to a distressed vessel after the GMDSS DSC electronic alert. It is also still required to maintain communications with other ships assisting in the distress situation. From 31 January 2005 HM Coastguard will keep a loudspeaker watch on Ch 16.

Recommended reading:

ALRS, Vol 5 (UK Hydrographic Office).

GMDSS for small craft (Clemmetsen/ Fernhurst).

VHF DSC Handbook (Fletcher/Reed's Publications).

OBJECTIVE

The objective of GMDSS is to alert SAR authorities ashore and ships in the vicinity to a distress incident by means of a combination of satellite and terrestrial communication, and navigation systems. As a result a coordinated SAR operation can be mounted rapidly and reliably anywhere in the world. GMDSS also provides urgency and safety communications, and promulgates Maritime Safety Information (MSI).

MARITIME SAFETY INFORMATION (MSI)

MSI refers to the vital meteorological, navigational and SAR messages which, traditionally, have been broadcast to vessels at sea by CRSs in Morse and by RT on VHF and

MF. MSI is prepared/coordinated by the nations which control the 16 Navareas/Metareas used for Nav and Met warnings. The UK controls Navarea 1, which covers the Atlantic between 48°27N and 71°N, out to 40°W. Navareas and Metareas have the same boundaries.

GMDSS broadcasts MSI in English by two independent but complementary means, Navtex and SafetyNet:

Navtex on MF (518kHz) covers coastal offshore waters out to about 300 miles from transmitters.

SafetyNet uses Inmarsat satellites to cover beyond MF range. Enhanced Group Calling (EGC) is a part of SafetyNet which enables MSI to be sent selectively by Inmarsat-C satellites to groups of users in any of the four oceans.

FUNCTIONS

Regardless of the sea areas in which they operate, vessels complying with GMDSS must be able to perform certain functions:

- transmit ship-to-shore distress alerts by two independent means;

- transmit ship-to-ship distress alerts;

- transmit and receive safety information, e.g. navigation and weather warnings;

- transmit signals for locating incidents;

- receive shore-to-ship distress alerts;

- receive ship-to-ship distress alerts;

- transmit and receive communications for SAR co-ordination.

GMDSS regulations apply to all ships over 300 tons engaged in international voyages, but they affect all seagoing craft. Although not obligatory for yachts, some features of GMDSS are of interest and, as equipment becomes more affordable, yachtsmen may decide to fit GMDSS voluntarily. This will become an increasing necessity as the present system for sending/receiving distress calls is run down.

DISTRESS ALERTING

GMDSS requires participating ships to be able to send distress alerts by two out of three independent means. These are:

1 Digital Selective Calling (DSC) using VHF Ch 70, MF 2187.5 kHz, or HF distress and alerting frequencies in the 4, 6, 8, 12 and 16 MHz bands.

EPIRBs (406 MHz via Cospas/Sarsat satellites;121.5 MHz aeronautical civil distress; and 243MHz UHF aeronautical military distress; float-free or manually operated); or the Inmarsat system in the 1.6 GHz band. All types transmit distress messages which include the position and identification of the vessel in distress.

Inmarsat, via ship terminals.

COMMUNICATIONS

GMDSS uses both terrestrial and satellite based communications. Terrestrial communications, ie VHF, MF and HF, are employed in Digital Selective Calling (see below). Satellite communications come in the form of INMARSAT and Cospas/Sarsat.

DIGITAL SELECTIVE CALLING (DSC)

DSC is a fundamental part of GMDSS. It is so called because information is sent by a burst of digital code; selective because it is addressed to another DSC radio-telephone.

Under GMDSS, every vessel and relevant shore stations have a 9-digit identification number, known as an MMSI (Maritime Mobile Service Identity) that is used for identification in all DSC messages.

DSC is used to transmit distress alerts from ships, and to receive distress acknowledgments from ships or shore stations. DSC can also be used for relay purposes and for Urgency, Safety and Routine calling and answering.

In practice, a DSC distress call sent on VHF works broadly as follows:

Yachtsman presses the distress button; the set automatically switches to Ch 70 and transmits a coded distress message before reverting to Ch 16.

Any ship will reply directly by voice on Ch 16. But a CRS would send a distress acknowledgment on Ch 70 (automatically turning off the distress transmission), before replying on Ch 16. If a distress acknowledgment is not received from a CRS, the call will automatically be repeated about every 4 mins.

INMARSAT

Inmarsat (International Maritime Satellite System), via four geostationary satellites, provides near-global communications except in the polar regions above about 70°N and 70°S.

1.6 GHz satellite EPIRBs, operating through Inmarsat, can also be used for alerting, in addition to 406 MHz EPIRBs which use Cospas/Sarsat.

COSPAS/SARSAT

The US/Russian Cospas/Sarsat satellites complement the various other Satcom systems. They not only detect an emergency signal transmitted by an EPIRB, but also locate it with a high degree of accuracy.

There are four Cospas/Sarsat satellites operating in low polar orbits. In addition to these, there are four GEOSAR geostationary earth orbit satellites capable of receiving alerts from 406 MHz beacons.

SEA AREAS

For the purposes of GMDSS, the world's sea areas are divided into four categories in each of which ships must carry certain types of radio equipment.

The categories of areas are:

A1 an area within RT coverage of at least one VHF Coast Radio Station or Coastguard Centre in which continuous alerting via DSC is available. Range: roughly 40 miles from the CRS/CG.

A2 an area, excluding sea area A1, within RT coverage of at least one MF CRS/CG in which continuous DSC alerting is available. Range: roughly 100-150 miles from the CRS/CG.

A3 an area, excluding sea areas A1 and A2, within coverage of an Inmarsat satellite between 70°N and 70°S in which continuous alerting is available.

A4 an area outside sea areas A1, A2 and A3; ie in practice the polar regions.

The UK has declared its coastal waters to be an A1 area, but intends to continue guarding VHF Channel 16 until 01 Feb 2005. VHF DSC is fully operational at all UK Coastguard Radio Stations. France declared the English Channel to be an A1 area.

As most UK yachtsmen will operate in an A1 area, a VHF radio and a Navtex receiver will initially meet GMDSS requirements. As suitable VHF DSC sets become available (and affordable) it will make sense to re-equip with DSC equipment.

GLOSSARY OF FOREIGN TERMS

ENGLISH	GERMAN	FRENCH	SPANISH	DUTCH
ASHORE				
Ashore	An Land	A terre	A tierra	Aan land
Airport	Flughafen	Aéroport	Aeropuerto	Vliegveld
Bank	Bank	Banque	Banco	Bank
Boathoist	Bootskran	Travelift	Travelift	Botenlift
Boatyard	Bootswerft	Chantier naval	Astilleros	Jachtwerf
Bureau de change	Wechselstelle	Bureau de change	Cambio	Geldwisselkantoor
Bus	Bus	Autobus	Autobús	Bus
Chandlery	Yachtausrüster	Shipchandler	Efectos navales	Scheepswinkel
Chemist	Apotheke	Pharmacie	Farmacia	Apotheek
Dentist	Zahnarzt	Dentiste	Dentista	Tandarts
Doctor	Arzt	Médecin	Médico	Dokter
Engineer	Motorenservice	Ingénieur/mécanique	Mecánico	Ingenieur
Ferry	Fähre	Ferry/transbordeur	Ferry	Veer/Pont
Garage	Autowerkstatt	Station service	Garage	Garage
Harbour	Hafen	Port	Puerto	Haven
Hospital	Krankenhaus	Hôpital	Hospital	Ziekenhuis
Mast crane	Mastenkran	Grue	Grúa	Masten kraan
Post office	Postamt	Bureau de poste/PTT	Correos	Postkantoor
Railway station	Bahnhof	Gare de chemin de fer	Estación de ferrocanil	Station
Sailmaker	Segelmacher	Voilier	Velero	Zeilmaker
Shops	Geschäfte	Boutiques	Tiendas	Winkels
Slip	Slip	Cale	Varadero	Helling
Supermarket	Supermarkt	Supermarché	Supermercado	Supermarkt
Taxi	Taxi	Taxi	Taxis	Taxi
Village	Ort	Village	Pueblo	Dorp
Yacht club	Yachtclub	Club nautique	Club náutico	Jacht club
NAVIGATION				
Abeam	Querab	A côté	Por el través	Naast
Ahead	Voraus	Avant	Avante	Voor
Astern	Achteraus	Arrière	Atrás	Achter
Bearing	Peilung	Cap	Maración	Peiling
Buoy	Tonne	Bouée	Boya	Boei
Binoculars	Fernglas	Jumelles	Prismáticos	Verrekijker
Channel	Kanal	Chenal	Canal	Kanaal
Chart	Seekarte	Carte	Carta náutica	Zeekaart
Compass	Kompass	Compas	Compás	Kompas
Compass course	Kompass Kurs	Cap du compas	Rumbo de aguja	Kompas koers
Current	Strömung	Courant	Coriente	Stroom
Dead reckoning	Koppelnavigation	Estime	Estimación	Gegist bestek
Degree	Grad	Degré	Grado	Graden
Deviation	Deviation	Déviation	Desvio	Deviatie
Distance	Entfernung	Distance	Distancia	Afstand
Downstream	Flußabwärts	En aval	Río abajo	Stroom afwaards
East	Ost	Est	Este	Oost
Ebb	Ebbe	Jusant	Marea menguante	Eb

ENGLISH	GERMAN	FRENCH	SPANISH	DUTCH
chosounder	Echolot	Sondeur	Sonda	Dieptemeter
stimated position	Gegißte Position	Point estimé	Posición estimado	Gegiste positie
athom	Faden	Une brasse	Braza	Vadem
eet	Fuß	Pieds	Pie	Voet
ood	Flut	Flot	Flujo de marea	Vloed
andbearing compass	Handpeilkompass	Compas de relèvement	Compás de marcaciones	Handpeil kompas
arbour guide	Hafenhandbuch	Guide du port	Guia del Puerto	Havengids
igh water	Hochwasser	Peine mer	Altamer	Hoog water
atitude	Geographische Breite	Latitude	Latitud	Breedte
eading lights	Feuer in Linie	Alignement	Luz de enfilación	Geleide lichten
eeway	Abdrift	Dérive	Hacia sotavento	Drift
ghthouse	Leuchtturm	Phare	Faro	Vuurtoren
ist of lights	Leuchtfeuer Verzeichnis	Liste des feux	Listude de Luces	Lichtenlijst
og	Logge	Loch	Corredera	Log
ongitude	Geographische Länge	Longitude	Longitud	Lengte
ow water	Niedrigwasser	Basse mer	Bajamar	Laag water
letre	Meter	Mètre	Metro	Meter
linute	Minute	Minute	Minuto	Minuut
autical almanac	Nautischer Almanach	Almanach nautique	Almanaque náutico	Almanak
autical mile	Seemeile	Mille nautique	Milla marina	Zeemijl
eap tide	Nipptide	Morte-eau	Marea muerta	Dood tij
orth	Nord	Nord	Norte	Noord
ilot	Lotse	Pilote	Práctico	Loods/Gids
ilotage book	Handbuch	Instructions nautiques	Derrotero	Vaarwijzer
DF	Funkpeiler	Radio gonio	Radio-gonió	Radio richtingzoeker
adar	Radar	Radar	Radar	Radar
adio receiver	Radio, Empfänger	Récepteur radio	Receptor de radio	Radio ontvanger
adio transmitter	Sender	Emetteur radio	Radio-transmisor	Radio zender
iver outlet	Flußmündung	Embouchure	Embocadura	Riviermond
outh	Süd	Sud	Sud, Sur	Zuid
pring tide	Springtide	Vive-eau	Marea viva	Springtij/springvloed
ide	Tide, Gezeit	Marée	Marea	Getijde
ide tables	Tidenkalender	Annuaire des marées	Anuario de mareas	Getijdetafel
rue course	Wahrer Kurs	Vrai cap	Rumbo	Ware Koers
pstream	Flußaufwärts	En amont	Río arriba	Stroom opwaards
HF	UKW	VHF	VHF	Marifoon
ariation	Mißweisung	Variation	Variación	Variatie
Vaypoint	Wegpunkt	Point de rapport	Waypoint	Waypoint/Route punt
Vest	West	Ouest	Oeste	West

FFICIALDOM

ENGLISH	GERMAN	FRENCH	SPANISH	DUTCH
ertificate of registry	Schiffszertifikat	Acte de franchisation	Documentos de matrícuia	Zeebrief
heck in	Einklarieren	Enregistrement	Registrar	Check-in
ustoms	Zoll	Douanes	Aduana	Douane
eclare	Verzollen	Déclarer	Declarar	Aangeven
arbour master	Hafenmeister	Capitaine du port	Capitán del puerto	Havenmeester
asurance	Versicherung	Assurance	Seguro	Verzekering
asurance certificate	Versicherungspolice	Certificat d'assurance	Certificado deseguro	Verzekeringsbewijs
assport	Paß	Passeport	Pasaporte	Paspoort

ENGLISH	GERMAN	FRENCH	SPANISH	DUTCH
Police	Polizei	Police	Policía	Politie
Pratique	Verkehrserlaubnis	Pratique	Prático	Verlof tot ontscheping
Prohibited area	Sperrgebiet	Zone interdite	Zona de prohibida	Verboden gebied
Register	Register	Liste de passagers	Lista de tripulantes/rol	Register
Ship's log	Logbuch	Livre de bord	Cuaderno de bitácora	Logboek
Ship's papers	Schiffspapiere	Papiers de bateau	Documentos del barco	Scheepspapieren
Surveyor	Gutachter	Expert maritime	Inspector	Opzichter

SAFETY/DISTRESS

ENGLISH	GERMAN	FRENCH	SPANISH	DUTCH
Assistance	Hilfeleistung	Assistance	Asistencia	Assistentie
Bandage	Verband	Pansement	Vendas	Verband
Burns	Verbrennung	Brûlures	Quemadura	Brand wond
Capsize	Kentern	Chavirage	Volcó	Omslaan
Coastguard	Küstenwache	Garde de côte	Guarda costas	Kust wacht
Dismasted	Mastbruch	Démâtè	Desarbolar	Mastbreuk
Distress	Seenot	Détresse	Pena	Nood
Distress flares	Signalraketen	Fusées de détresse	Bengalas	Nood signaal
Doctor	Doktor	Médecin	Médico	Doktor/Arts
EPIRB	EPIRB	Balise	Baliza	EPIRB
Emergency	Notfall	Urgence	Emergencias	Noodgeval
Exhaustion	Erschöpfung	Epuisement	Agotamiento	Uitputting
Fever	Fieber	Fièvre	Fiebre	Koorts
Fire extinguisher	Feuerlöscher	Extincteur	Extintor	Brand blusser
First aid	Erste Hilfe	Premier secours	Primeros auxillos	Eerste hulp
Fracture	Fraktur	Cassure	Fractura	Breuk
Grounded	Aufgelaufen	Echoué	Encallado	Vastgelopen
Harness	Lifebelt	Harnais	Arnés de seguridad	Harnas/Tuig
Headache	Kopfschmerz	Mal à la tête	Dolor de cabeza	Hoofdpijn
Heart attack	Herzanfall	Crise cardiaque	Ataque corazón	Hartaanval
Helicopter	Hubschrauber	Hélicoptère	Helicóptero	Helikopter
Hospital	Krankenhaus	Hôpital	Hospital	Ziekenhuis
Illness	Krankheit, Übelkeit	Maladie	Enfermo	Ziekte
Injury	Verletzung	Blessure	Lesión	Verwonding
Jackstay	Strecktau	Contre-étai	Violín	Veiligheidstag
Lifeboat	Rettungsboot	Canot de sauvetage	Lancha de salvamento	Reddingsboot
Liferaft	Rettungsinsel	Radeau de sauvetage	Balsa salvavidas	Reddingsvlot
Lifejacket	Schwimmweste	Gilet de sauvetage	Chaleco salvavidas	Reddingsvest
Man overboard	Mann über Bord	Homme à la mer	Hombre al agua	Man over boord
Pulse	Puls	Poux	Pulso	Hartslag
Rest	Ruhen	Repos	Reposo	Rust
Seacock	Seeventil	Vanne	Grifos de fondo	Afsluiter
Seasickness	Seekrankheit	Mal de mer	Mareo	Zeeziekte
Seaworthy	Seetüchtig	Marin	Marinero	Zeewaardig
Shock	Schock	Choc	Choque	Shock
Sinking	Sinken	En train de couler	Hundiendo	Zinken
Sleep	Schlaf	Sommeil	Sueño	Slaap
Tow line	Schleppleine	Filin de remorque	Cabo	Sleeplijn
Unconscious	Bewußtlos	Inconscient	Inconsciente	Buiten bewustzijn
Wound	Wunde	Blessure	Herida	Wond

140

CHAPTER 5 - TIDES

CONTENTS

Dover tidal ranges 142

Brest tidal coefficients 143

Tidal Calculations 144

Special instructions: Christchurch to Selsey Bill 148

Secondary ports & tidal differences 150

Tidal gates 169

Tidal stream charts 178

Tidal curves & predictions

Southern England 216
Falmouth, Plymouth, Dartmouth, Portland, Poole Harbour, Southampton,
(tidal curves Christchurch to Selsey Bill) Portsmouth, Shoreham, Dover

Eastern England 254
Sheerness, London Bridge, Burnham-on-Crouch, Walton-on-the-Naze,
Lowestoft, Immingham, R.Tyne

Scotland 282
Leith, Aberdeen, Wick, Lerwick, Stornoway, Ullapool, Oban, Greenock

Western England and Wales 314
Liverpool, Holyhead, Milford Haven, Avonmouth

Ireland 330
Dublin, Belfast, Galway, Cobh

Denmark 346
Esbjerg

Germany 350
Helgoland, Cuxhaven, Wilhelmshaven

Netherlands 362
Hoek van Holland, Vlissingen

Northern France 370
Dunkerque, Dieppe, Le Havre, Cherbourg, St Malo

Channel Islands 390
St Peter Port, St Helier

Western France 398
Brest, Pointe de Grave

Portugal & Gibraltar 406
Lisboa, Gibraltar

Chapter 5

DOVER TIDAL RANGES 2004

January

Day	HW	Range	HW
1	0552	3.3	1842
2	0700	3.3	1944
3	0802	3.5	2039
4	0856	3.8	2126
5	0941	4.3	2208
6	1021	4.5	2245
7	1057	4.8	2320
8	1132	4.9	2353
9	1206	4.9	
10	0025	4.9	1239
11	0058	4.9	1312
12	0133	4.9	1348
13	0212	4.8	1430
14	0257	4.6	1518
15	0349	4.2	1617
16	0452	3.9	1731
17	0606	3.8	1854
18	0723	3.9	2007
19	0833	4.3	2110
20	0937	4.8	2208
21	1034	5.3	2259
22	1126	5.6	2345
23	1212	5.8	
24	0028	5.8	1255
25	0110	5.7	1336
26	0151	5.4	1416
27	0232	4.9	1458
28	0314	4.4	1542
29	0358	3.8	1634
30	0450	3.3	1736
31	0556	2.9	1846

February

Day	HW	Range	HW
1	0709	2.8	1956
2	0818	3.2	2056
3	0915	3.8	2145
4	1000	4.3	2225
5	1038	4.7	2300
6	1114	5.1	2334
7	1149	5.3	
8	0007	5.4	1223
9	0041	5.6	1255
10	0115	5.6	1330
11	0152	5.4	1407
12	0232	5.2	1451
13	0319	4.6	1542
14	0416	3.9	1650
15	0533	3.5	1828
16	0710	3.3	1958
17	0836	3.8	2111
18	0946	4.5	2209
19	1042	5.2	2256
20	1126	5.7	2337
21	1205	5.9	
22	0014	6.0	1240
23	0052	5.9	1313
24	0127	5.6	1347
25	0201	5.3	1420
26	0233	4.7	1454
27	0305	4.1	1532
28	0345	3.3	1628
29	0452	2.6	1753

March

Day	HW	Range	HW
1	0622	2.5	1914
2	0742	2.8	2024
3	0848	3.4	2118
4	0936	4.2	2158
5	1015	4.8	2234
6	1051	5.3	2308
7	1126	5.7	2342
8	1159	5.8	
9	0017	6.0	1233
10	0052	6.1	1307
11	0129	5.8	1346
12	0209	5.4	1429
13	0256	4.7	1521
14	0355	3.7	1634
15	0523	3.0	1817
16	0710	3.1	1953
17	0843	3.6	2107
18	0948	4.5	2200
19	1035	5.3	2242
20	1113	5.8	2319
21	1145	6.0	2354
22	1216	6.0	
23	0028	5.8	1247
24	0101	5.6	1318
25	0130	5.3	1346
26	0154	4.8	1411
27	0218	4.2	1437
28	0251	3.5	1516
29	0345	2.7	1700
30	0544	2.3	1832
31	0706	2.5	1944

April

Day	HW	Range	HW
1	0813	3.3	2040
2	0903	4.1	2123
3	0944	4.9	2201
4	1021	5.4	2237
5	1057	5.8	2314
6	1132	6.2	2350
7	1208	6.3	
8	0028	6.2	1246
9	0108	6.0	1328
10	0152	5.4	1415
11	0244	4.4	1514
12	0353	3.6	1632
13	0523	3.0	1803
14	0709	3.2	1938
15	0835	3.9	2048
16	0931	4.7	2137
17	1013	5.3	2217
18	1047	5.6	2254
19	1118	5.8	2329
20	1149	5.7	
21	0002	5.6	1220
22	0034	5.3	1251
23	0101	5.1	1318
24	0122	4.8	1340
25	0146	4.3	1406
26	0220	3.6	1446
27	0312	3.0	1603
28	0507	2.6	1744
29	0627	2.7	1857
30	0732	3.4	1955

May

Day	HW	Range	HW
1	0824	4.1	2042
2	0908	4.9	2124
3	0947	5.5	2204
4	1026	5.9	2244
5	1105	6.2	2324
6	1146	6.3	
7	0007	6.2	1230
8	0053	5.8	1318
9	0143	5.2	1412
10	0243	4.5	1513
11	0353	3.8	1622
12	0514	3.5	1738
13	0648	3.5	1904
14	0804	4.0	2013
15	0857	4.5	2104
16	0939	4.8	2146
17	1014	5.2	2225
18	1048	5.2	2302
19	1121	5.2	2336
20	1155	5.1	
21	0009	5.1	1228
22	0038	4.9	1258
23	0104	4.6	1325
24	0131	4.3	1354
25	0207	3.8	1436
26	0258	3.5	1533
27	0416	3.2	1647
28	0538	3.3	1800
29	0644	3.5	1903
30	0740	4.1	1957
31	0828	4.7	2045

June

Day	HW	Range	HW
1	0914	5.3	2132
2	0958	5.7	2218
3	1045	5.8	2306
4	1132	5.9	2355
5	1222	5.8	
6	0046	5.7	1314
7	0142	5.3	1407
8	0241	4.8	1503
9	0343	4.4	1601
10	0449	4.0	1703
11	0602	3.8	1812
12	0712	3.8	1922
13	0810	4.0	2021
14	0857	4.2	2111
15	0940	4.4	2156
16	1019	4.7	2236
17	1057	4.7	2314
18	1134	4.8	2348
19	1209	4.8	
20	0021	4.8	1242
21	0053	4.6	1313
22	0124	4.4	1344
23	0158	4.3	1421
24	0238	4.1	1505
25	0328	4.0	1558
26	0429	3.8	1700
27	0541	3.8	1807
28	0651	4.0	1913
29	0752	4.3	2013
30	0849	4.8	2110

July

Day	HW	Range	HW
1	0943	5.2	2206
2	1037	5.6	2301
3	1129	5.7	2355
4	1219	5.8	
5	0046	5.8	1307
6	0138	5.6	1355
7	0228	5.3	1443
8	0318	4.9	1532
9	0410	4.3	1623
10	0505	3.8	1720
11	0607	3.7	1823
12	0713	3.4	1932
13	0814	3.5	2035
14	0908	3.8	2130
15	0956	4.2	2216
16	1037	4.4	2255
17	1115	4.7	2330
18	1149	4.8	
19	0003	4.8	1222
20	0036	4.9	1254
21	0107	4.9	1325
22	0137	4.8	1358
23	0212	4.8	1437
24	0253	4.5	1521
25	0342	4.3	1615
26	0444	3.9	1722
27	0606	3.7	1840
28	0730	3.8	1958
29	0841	4.2	2109
30	0943	4.8	2212
31	1038	5.3	2308

August

Day	HW	Range	HW
1	1126	5.7	2357
2	1211	5.9	
3	0041	6.0	1254
4	0123	5.9	1335
5	0203	5.6	1417
6	0243	5.1	1458
7	0326	4.5	1542
8	0414	3.8	1631
9	0512	3.2	1731
10	0620	2.9	1843
11	0734	2.8	2001
12	0842	3.3	2110
13	0936	3.8	2159
14	1018	4.4	2236
15	1052	4.8	2308
16	1125	5.1	2340
17	1156	5.2	
18	0011	5.3	1228
19	0041	5.4	1259
20	0111	5.3	1332
21	0144	5.3	1408
22	0223	5.0	1450
23	0309	4.3	1541
24	0409	3.6	1651
25	0543	3.2	1830
26	0725	3.3	2002
27	0841	3.9	2118
28	0943	4.7	2218
29	1032	5.4	2306
30	1115	5.9	2346
31	1155	6.2	

September

Day	HW	Range	HW
1	0023	6.2	1233
2	0057	6.0	1310
3	0131	5.7	1346
4	0206	5.2	1422
5	0243	4.5	1458
6	0325	3.7	1542
7	0422	2.9	1645
8	0536	2.4	1804
9	0656	2.4	1927
10	0813	3.0	2045
11	0910	3.7	2133
12	0949	4.4	2207
13	1022	4.9	2238
14	1054	5.3	2310
15	1126	5.5	2341
16	1157	5.7	
17	0012	5.7	1230
18	0043	5.7	1304
19	0118	5.4	1341
20	0158	5.0	1424
21	0246	4.2	1519
22	0352	3.3	1645
23	0542	2.8	1835
24	0719	3.2	2008
25	0836	4.0	2118
26	0932	4.9	2209
27	1016	5.5	2250
28	1055	5.9	2324
29	1132	6.1	2356
30	1207	6.0	

October

Day	HW	Range	HW
1	0028	5.8	1242
2	0100	5.5	1315
3	0132	5.1	1345
4	0203	4.4	1415
5	0235	3.8	1450
6	0325	2.9	1602
7	0455	2.3	1731
8	0616	2.3	1851
9	0731	2.7	2002
10	0828	3.5	2051
11	0909	4.3	2129
12	0944	5.0	2203
13	1018	5.4	2236
14	1051	5.7	2309
15	1126	5.9	2342
16	1201	6.0	
17	0018	5.9	1239
18	0057	5.4	1321
19	0142	4.9	1410
20	0238	4.0	1517
21	0357	3.2	1652
22	0531	3.1	1831
23	0703	3.3	1959
24	0816	4.2	2101
25	0909	4.9	2146
26	0951	5.4	2224
27	1029	5.7	2256
28	1106	5.8	2327
29	1141	5.7	
30	0000	5.5	1215
31	0033	5.2	1246

November

Day	HW	Range	HW
1	0104	4.9	1314
2	0133	4.4	1341
3	0201	3.8	1414
4	0239	3.2	1515
5	0403	2.6	1653
6	0527	2.4	1808
7	0638	2.8	1913
8	0736	3.4	2005
9	0822	4.2	2048
10	0902	4.8	2125
11	0940	5.3	2202
12	1018	5.7	2239
13	1057	5.9	2318
14	1138	6.0	
15	0000	5.8	1223
16	0046	5.4	1311
17	0138	4.8	1409
18	0240	4.2	1521
19	0350	3.7	1643
20	0505	3.5	1810
21	0627	3.6	1927
22	0739	4.1	2027
23	0834	4.6	2113
24	0920	4.9	2152
25	1001	5.1	2227
26	1040	5.2	2301
27	1116	5.2	2336
28	1151	5.1	
29	0011	4.9	1225
30	0045	4.7	1256

December

Day	HW	Range	HW
1	0116	4.4	1325
2	0145	4.0	1358
3	0220	3.7	1442
4	0308	3.3	1547
5	0415	3.0	1708
6	0529	3.1	1817
7	0635	3.4	1915
8	0731	3.9	2004
9	0819	4.5	2049
10	0905	5.1	2133
11	0951	5.5	2218
12	1038	5.7	2306
13	1126	5.8	2353
14	1217	5.7	
15	0043	5.5	1310
16	0137	5.2	1408
17	0232	4.8	1510
18	0330	4.4	1615
19	0431	4.1	1724
20	0537	3.9	1834
21	0647	3.8	1937
22	0751	3.9	2032
23	0846	4.1	2119
24	0935	4.3	2202
25	1019	4.6	2241
26	1058	4.8	2319
27	1135	4.8	2355
28	1209	4.8	
29	0029	4.8	1242
30	0100	4.6	1312
31	0129	4.4	1342

BREST TIDAL COEFFICIENTS 2004

Date	Jan am	Jan pm	Feb am	Feb pm	Mar am	Mar pm	Apr am	Apr pm	May am	May pm	June am	June pm	July am	July pm	Aug am	Aug pm	Sept am	Sept pm	Oct am	Oct pm	Nov am	Nov pm	Dec am	Dec pm
1		41	32	34		25	40	48	55	63	80	85	80	85	94	97	102	100	93	88	68	63	60	56
2	41	43	38	43	30	36	56	64	71	78	90	94	89	92	99	100	96	91	83	77	57	51	52	48
3	45	48	48	53	42	49	72	79	85	91	97	98	94	95	99	97	86	79	71	64	46	40	45	41
4	51	54	58	63	56	64	86	92	96	101	99	98	96	95	94	89	73	65	57	50	34	30	39	37
5	57	61	68	73	70	77	98	102	103	105	96	93	93	91	84	78	58	50	43	36	27	26	36	37
6	64	66	77	81	83	88	105	106	105	103	90	85	87	83	72	65	43	36	30	24	28		39	
7	69	71	84	87	93	97	107	105	100	96	80	74	78	72	58	51	30	25	22		32	38	43	47
8	73	74	88	89	99	101	103	98	90	84	69	64	67	61	45	39	23		22	26	45	51	53	58
9	75	76	90	89	101	101	93	86	77	69	60	56	56	52	35	32	25	29	33	40	59	65	64	70
10	76	76	88	85	99	95	78	70	63	56	53	51	48	45		31	35	41	47	54	72	79	76	81
11	75	74	82	78	91	85	61	53	51	48		50		43	32	36	48	55	62	69	85	90	86	90
12	72	70	73	68	79	71	47	42	47		51	52	42	43	40	45	62	68	76	82	94	97	93	95
13	67	64	62	57	63	55	41		48	51	54	56	44	47	50	55	74	80	88	92	99	99	96	96
14	62	59	51	47	48	42	44	48	55	59	58	60	49	52	60	65	84	89	96	99	99	97	95	93
15	56	54		45	40		55	61	63	67	62	64	56	59	70	74	92	94	100	101	94	90	89	86
16	52	52	46	49	41	46	68	74	70	73	66	67	62	64	77	81	96	97	100	98	84	78	81	76
17		53	55	61	53	60	79	83	76	78	68	69	67	69	83	85	96	94	94	90	72	65	71	66
18	55	59	69	76	68	75	87	89	79	79	70	70	71	73	86	87	92	88	84	77	59	54	61	57
19	64	69	83	88	82	88	91	91	79	79	70	69	74	75	87	86	83	77	69	62	50	49	54	51
20	75	80	93	97	92	96	91	90	78	76	68	67	75	75	84	81	70	63	54	47	49			50
21	85	90	99	100	98	99	88	85	74	72	66	64	74	73	77	73	55	48	42	41	51	54	50	51
22	93	96	100	99	99	97	82	78	69	66	62	60	71	69	68	63	42	39		43	58	62	53	55
23	97	97	96	92	95	92	74	69	63	59	58	56	67	64	57	52		39	47	53	66	70	57	60
24	96	94	88	82	87	83	64	58	55	51	54	52	61	58	47	44	43	50	60	67	73	75	62	65
25	91	87	76	70	77	71	52	47	47	44	50	49	55	53		43	58	66	73	79	77	79	66	68
26	82	77	63	57	65	58	41	36	41	39	49	49	51	50	45	50	74	81	84	87	80	80	69	70
27	70	64	49	43	51	45	31	28	38	38	51			50	56	64	88	93	90	92	79	78	71	71
28	58	52	36	30	38	32	28	30	41		53	57	52	56	72	79	97	99	92	92	77	75	71	71
29	46	40	26	24	26	23		35	44	49	61	66	61	67	86	92	100	100	91	88	73	70	70	69
30	36	33				23	41	48	55	61	71	76	73	79	97	100	99	96	86	82	67	63	68	66
31		31			27	33			67	74			85	90	102	103			78	73			64	62

These tidal coefficients indicate at a glance the magnitude of the tide on any particular day by assigning a non-dimensional coefficient to the twice-daily range of tide. The coefficient is based on a scale of 45 for mean neap (morte eau) and 95 for mean spring (vive eau) ranges at Brest. The coefficient is 70 for an average tide. A very small neap tide may have a coefficient of only 20, whilst a very big spring tide might be as high as 120. The ratio of the coefficients of different tides equals the ratio of their ranges; the range, for example, of the largest spring tide (120) is six times that of the smallest neap tide (20). The table above is for Brest, but holds good elsewhere along the Channel and Atlantic coasts of France.

French translations of common tidal terms are as follows:

HW	Pleine mer (PM)	MHWS	Pleine mer moyenne de VE
LW	Basse mer (BM)	MHWN	Pleine mer moyenne de ME
Springs	Vive eau (VE)	MLWN	Basse mer moyenne de ME
Neaps	Morte eau (ME)	MLWS	Basse mer moyenne de VE

Chapter 5

TIDAL CALCULATIONS

Find the height at a given time (STANDARD PORT)

1. On Standard Curve diagram, plot heights of H.W. and L.W. occuring either side of required time and join by sloping line.
2. Enter H.W. Time and sufficient others to bracket required time.
3. From required time, proceed vertically to curves, using heights plotted in (1) to help interpolation between Spring and Neaps. Do NOT extrapolate.
4. Proceed horizontally to sloping line, thence vertically to Height scale.
5. Read off height.

EXAMPLE:

Find the height of tide at ULLAPOOL at 1900 on 6th January

From tables	JANUARY	
ULLAPOOL	**6** 0420	4.6
	1033	1.6
	1641	4.6
	F 2308	1.2

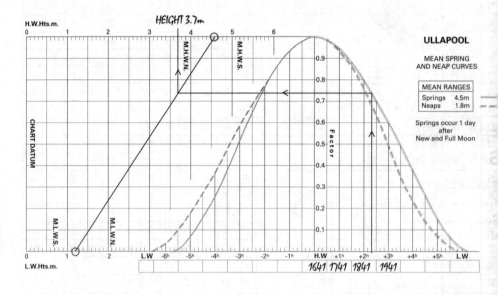

HEIGHT 3.7m

H.W.Hts.m.

ULLAPOOL

MEAN SPRING AND NEAP CURVES

MEAN RANGES
Springs 4.5m
Neaps 1.8m

Springs occur 1 day after New and Full Moon

Factor

L.W.Hts.m.   1641 1741 1841 1941

Find the time for a given height (STANDARD PORT)

1. On Standard Curve diagram, plot heights of H.W. and L.W. occurring either side of require event and join by sloping line.
2. Enter H.W. time and those for half-tidal cycle covering required event.
3. From required height, proceed vertically to sloping line, thence horizontally to curves, usin heights plotted in (1) to assist interpolation between Spring and Neaps. Do NOT extrapolate
4. Proceed vertically to Time scale.
5. Read off time.

EXAMPLE:

Find the time at which the afternoon tide at ULLAPOOL falls to 3.7m on 6 January

From tables	JANUARY	
ULLAPOOL	**6** 0420	4.6
	1033	1.6
	1641	4.6
	F 2308	1.2

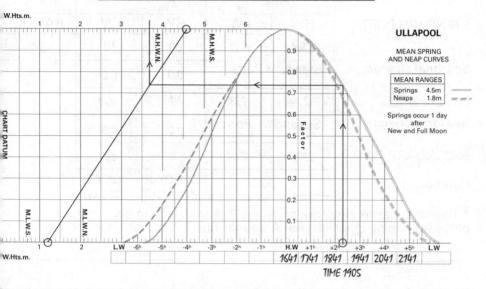

ULLAPOOL

MEAN SPRING
AND NEAP CURVES

MEAN RANGES
Springs 4.5m
Neaps 1.8m

Springs occur 1 day
after
New and Full Moon

TIME 1905

Find the time and height of H.W. and L.W. at a Secondary Port

EXAMPLE:

Find the time and height of the afternoon H.W. and L.W. at ST MARY's (Isles of Scilly) on 14th July (BST)

Note: The data used in this example do not refer to the year of these tables.

from tables	JULY	
PLYMOUTH (DEVONPORT)	**14** 0309	1.0
	0927	5.3
	1532	1.1
	SA 2149	5.0

From tables

Location	Lat	Long	High Water		Low Water		MHWS	MHWN	MLWN	MLWS
			0000 and 1200	0600 and 1800	0000 and 1200	0600 and 1800				
DEVONPORT *Standard port*	50°22'N	4°11'W					5.5	4.4	2.2	0.8
St. Mary's, *Scilly*	49° 55'N	6°19'W	−0035	−0100	−0040	−0025	+0.2	−0.1	−0.2	−0.1

TIDAL PREDICTION FORM (NP 204)

STANDARD PORT _Devonport_   TIME/HEIGHT REQUIRED _pm_

SECONDARY PORT _St Mary's_   DATE _14 July_ TIME ZONE _B.S.T_

	TIME		HEIGHT		
STANDARD PORT	HW	LW	HW	LW	RANGE
	1 2149	2 1532	3 5·0	4 1·1	5 3·9
Seasonal change	Standard Ports -		6 0·0	6 0·0	
DIFFERENCES	7* -0044	8 -0032	9 0·1	10 -0·1	
Seasonal change *	Secondary Ports +		11 0·0	11 0·0	
SECONDARY PORT	12 2105	13 1500	14 5·1	15 1·0	
Duration	16 0605		LW 1500 UT = 1600 BST HW 2105 UT = 2205 BST		

* The seasonal changes are generally less than ± 0.1m and for most purposes can be ignored. See Admiraly Tide Tables Vol 1. for details

INTERMEDIATE TIMES/HEIGHTS (SECONDARY PORT)

These are the same as the appropriate calculations for a Standard Port except that the Standard Curve diagram for the Standard Port must be entered with H.W. and L.W. heights and times for the Secondary Port obtained on Form N.P. 204. When interpolating between the Spring and Neap curves the Range at the Standard Port must be used.

EXAMPLES:

Find the height of the tide at PADSTOW at 1100 on 28th February. Find the time at which the morning tide at PADSTOW falls to 4.9m on 28th February.

Notes:
The data in these examples do not refer to the year of these tables.

From tables	FEBRUARY		
MILFORD HAVEN	**28**	0315	1.1
		0922	6.6
		1538	1.3
	TU	2145	6.3

Location	Lat	Long	High Water		Low Water		MHWS	MHWN	MLWN	MLWS
MILFORD HAVEN	51°42'N	5°03'W	0100 and 1300	0700 and 1900	0100 and 1300	0700 and 1900	7.0	5.2	2.5	0.7
Standard port										
River Camel										
Padstow	50°33'N	4°56'W	-0055	-0050	-0040	-0050	+0.3	+0.4	+0.1	+0.1
Wadebridge	50°31'N	4°50'W	-0052	-0052	+0235	+0245	-3.8	-3.8	-2.5	-0.4

TIDAL PREDICTION FORM (NP 204)

STANDARD PORT ....*Milford Haven*.... TIME/HEIGHT REQUIRED .....*1100 : 4.9*.....

SECONDARY PORT ...*Padstow*.... DATE *28 Feb*.... TIME ZONE ...*UT*....

	TIME		HEIGHT		
STANDARD PORT	HW	LW	HW	LW	RANGE
	1 *0922*	2 *1538*	3 *6·6*	4 *1·3*	5 *5·3*
Seasonal change	Standard Ports +		6 *0·0*	6 *0·0*	
DIFFERENCES	7* *-0052*	8 –	9 *+0·3*	10 *+0·1*	
Seasonal change *	Secondary Ports -		11 *0·0*	11 *0·0*	
SECONDARY PORT	12 *0830*	13 –	14 *6·9*	15 *1·4*	
Duration	16 –				

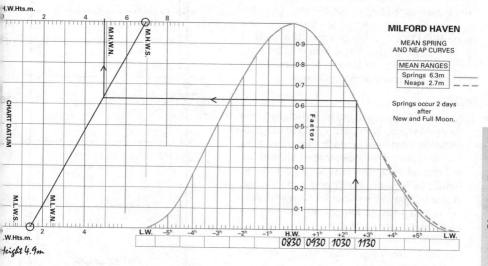

H.W.Hts.m.

CHART DATUM

M.H.W.N. M.H.W.S. M.L.W.N. M.L.W.S.

MILFORD HAVEN

MEAN SPRING AND NEAP CURVES

MEAN RANGES
Springs 6.3m
Neaps 2.7m

Springs occur 2 days after New and Full Moon.

Factor
0·9 0·8 0·7 0·6 0·5 0·4 0·3 0·2 0·1

L.W. -5ʰ -4ʰ -3ʰ -2ʰ -1ʰ H.W. +1ʰ +2ʰ +3ʰ +4ʰ +5ʰ L.W.

0830 0930 1030 1130

.W.Hts.m.

Height 4.9m

SPECIAL INSTRUCTIONS FOR PLACES BETWEEN CHRISTCHURCH AND SELSEY BILL

- Owing to the rapid change of tidal characteristics and distortion of the tidal curve in this area, curves are shown for individual ports. It is a characteristic of the tide here that Low Water is more sharply defined than High Water and these curves have therefore been drawn with their times relative to that of Low Water.
- Apart from differences caused by referring the times to Low Water the procedure for obtaining intermediate heights at places whose curves are shown is identical to that used for normal Secondary Ports.
- The **height** differences for ports between Christchurch and Yarmouth always refer to the higher High Water, i.e. that which is shown as reaching a factor of 1.0 on the curves. Note that the **time** differences, which are not required for this calculation, also refer to the higher High Water.
- The tide at ports between Christchurch and Yarmouth shows considerable change of shape and duration between Springs and Neaps and it is not practical to define the tide with only two curves. A third curve has therefore been drawn for the range at Portsmouth at which the two High Waters are equal at the port concerned – this range being marked on the body of the graph. Interpolation here should be between this "critical" curve and either the Spring or Neap curve as appropriate.

Note that while the critical curve extends throughout the tidal cycle the Spring and Neap curves stop at the higher High Water. Thus for a range at Portsmouth of 3.5m the factor for 7 hours after LW at Lymington should be referred to the following Low Water, whereas had the range at Portsmouth been 2.5, it should be referred to the preceding Low Water.

NOTES

1. NEWPORT. Owing to the constriction of the River Medina, Newport requires slightly different treatment since the harbour dries out at 1.4m. The calculation should be performed using the Low Water Time and Height Differences for Cowes and the High Water Height Differences for Newport. Any calculated heights which fall below 1.4m should be treated as 1.4m
2. CHRISTCHURCH (Tuckton). Low Waters do not fall below 0.7m except under very low river flow conditions.

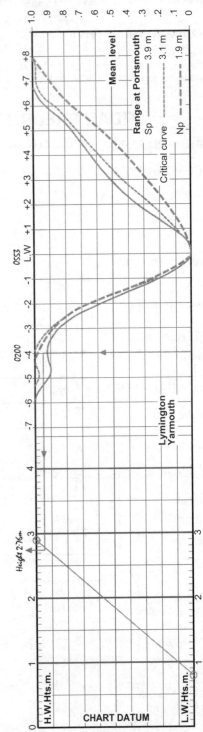

To find the Height of tide at a given time at any Secondary Port between Christchurch and Selsey Bill

1. Complete top section of N.P. 204 (as below). Omit H.W. time column (Boxes 1,7,12)
2. On Standard Curve diagram (previous page), plot Secondary Port H.W. and L.W. heights and join by sloping line.
3. From the time required, using Secondary Port L.W. time, proceed vertically to curve, interpolating as necessary using Range at Portsmouth. Do NOT extrapolate.
4. Proceed horizontally to sloping line, thence vertically to Height Scale.
5. Read off height.

EXAMPLE:

Find the height of tide at LYMINGTON at 0200 UT on 18th November

From tables	NOVEMBER	
PORTSMOUTH	**18** 0110	4.6
	0613	1.1
	1318	4.6
	SA 1833	1.0

From tables

Location	Lat	Long	High Water		Low Water		MHWS	MHWN	MLWN	MLWS
			0000	0600	0500	1100				
PORTSMOUTH	50°48'N	1°07'W	and	and	and	and	4.7	3.8	1.9	0.8
Standard port			1200	1800	1700	2300				
Lymington	50°46'N	1°32'W	-0110	+0005	-0020	-0020	-1.7	-1.2	-0.5	-0.1

STANDARD PORT ..*Portsmouth*.. TIME/HEIGHT REQUIRED ... *0200*

SECONDARY PORT *Lymington* ... DATE *18 Nov* TIME ZONE ... *UT*

	TIME		HEIGHT		
STANDARD PORT	HW	LW	HW	LW	RANGE
	1 –	2 0613	3 4.6	4 1.1	5 3.5
Seasonal change	Standard Ports -		6 0.0	6 0.0	
DIFFERENCES	7* –	8 -0020	9 -1.7	10 -0.2	
Seasonal change *	Secondary Ports +		11 0.0	11 0.0	
SECONDARY PORT	12 –	13 0553	14 2.9	15 0.9	
Duration	16 –				

* The Seasonal changes are generally less than ± 0.1m and for most purposes can be ignored. See Admiralty Tide Tables Vol 1 for full details.

SECONDARY PORTS & TIDAL DIFFERENCES
SOUTH COAST ENGLAND *Time Zone UT*

Location	Lat	Long	High Water		Low Water		MHWS	MHWN	MLWN	MLWS
			0000	0600	0000	0600				
PLYMOUTH, DEVONPORT	50 22N	4 11W	and	and	and	and	5.5	4.4	2.2	0.8
standard port			1200	1800	1200	1800				
Isles of Scilly, St. Mary's	49 55N	6 19W	−0035	−0100	−0040	−0025	+0.2	−0.1	−0.2	−0.1
Penzance *Newlyn*	50 06N	5 33W	−0040	−0110	−0035	−0025	+0.1	0.0	−0.2	0.0
Porthleven	50 05N	5 19W	−0045	−0105	−0030	−0025	0.0	−0.1	−0.2	0.0
Lizard Point	49 57N	5 12W	−0045	−0100	−0030	−0030	−0.2	−0.2	−0.3	−0.2
Coverack	50 01N	5 05W	−0030	−0050	−0020	−0015	−0.2	−0.2	−0.3	−0.2
Helford River *Entrance*	50 05N	5 05W	−0030	−0035	−0015	−0010	−0.2	−0.2	−0.3	−0.2
FALMOUTH	50 09N	5 03W	*standard port*							
Truro	50 16N	5 03W	−0020	−0025	*dries*	*dries*	−2.0	−2.0	*dries*	
Mevagissey	50 16N	4 47W	−0015	−0020	−0010	−0005	−0.1	−0.1	−0.2	−0.1
Par	50 21N	4 42W	−0010	−0015	−0010	−0005	−0.4	−0.4	−0.4	−0.2
Fowey	50 20N	4 38W	−0010	−0015	−0010	−0005	−0.1	−0.1	−0.2	−0.2
Lostwithiel	50 24N	4 40W	+0005	−0010	*dries*	*dries*	−4.1	−4.1	*dries*	
Looe	50 21N	4 27W	−0010	−0010	−0005	−0005	−0.1	−0.2	−0.2	−0.2
Whitsand Bay	50 20N	4 15W	0000	0000	0000	0000	0.0	+0.1	−0.1	+0.2
Saltash	50 24N	4 12W	0000	+0010	0000	−0005	+0.1	+0.1	+0.1	+0.1
Cargreen	50 26N	4 12W	0000	+0010	+0020	+0020	0.0	0.0	−0.1	0.0
Cotehele Quay	50 29N	4 13W	0000	+0020	+0045	+0045	−0.9	−0.9	−0.8	−0.4
Lopwell	50 28N	4 09W	*no data*	*no data*	*dries*	*dries*	−2.6	−2.7	*dries*	
Jupiter Point	50 23N	4 14W	+0010	+0005	0000	−0005	0.0	0.0	+0.1	0.0
St. Germans	50 23N	4 18W	0000	0000	+0020	+0020	−0.3	−0.1	0.0	+0.2
Turnchapel	50 22N	4 07W	0000	0000	+0010	−0015	0.0	+0.1	+0.2	+0.1
Bovisand Pier	50 20N	4 08W	0000	−0020	0000	−0010	−0.2	−0.1	0.0	+0.1
River Yealm Entrance	50 18N	4 04W	+0006	+0006	+0002	+0002	−0.1	−0.1	−0.1	−0.1
			0100	0600	0100	0600				
PLYMOUTH, DEVONPORT	50 22N	4 11W	and	and	and	and	5.5	4.4	2.2	0.8
standard port			1300	1800	1300	1800				
Salcombe	50 13N	3 47W	0000	+0010	+0005	−0005	−0.2	−0.3	−0.1	−0.1
Start Point	50 13N	3 39W	+0015	+0015	+0005	+0010	−0.1	−0.2	+0.1	+0.2
River Dart										
DARTMOUTH	50 21N	3 34W	*standard port*							
Greenway Quay	50 23N	3 35W	+0030	+0045	+0025	+0005	−0.6	−0.6	−0.2	−0.2
Totnes	50 26N	3 41W	+0030	+0040	+0115	+0030	−2.0	−2.1	*dries*	
Torquay	50 28N	3 31W	+0025	+0045	+0010	0000	−0.6	−0.7	−0.2	−0.1
Teignmouth *Approaches*	50 33N	3 29W	+0020	+0050	+0025	0000	−0.9	−0.8	−0.2	−0.1
Teignmouth *New Quay*	50 33N	3 30W	+0025	+0055	+0040	+0005	−0.8	−0.8	−0.2	+0.1
Exmouth *Approaches*	50 36N	3 23W	+0030	+0050	+0015	+0005	−0.9	−1.0	−0.5	−0.3
River Exe										
Exmouth Dock	50 37N	3 25W	+0035	+0055	+0050	+0020	−1.5	−1.6	−0.9	−0.6
Starcross	50 38N	3 27W	+0040	+0110	+0055	+0025	−1.4	−1.5	−0.8	−0.1
Topsham	50 41N	3 28W	+0045	+0105	*no data*	*no data*	− 1.5	−1.6	*no data*	
Lyme Regis	50 43N	2 56W	+0040	+0100	+0005	−0005	−1.2	−1.3	−0.5	−0.2
Bridport *West Bay*	50 42N	2 45W	+0025	+0040	0000	0000	−1.4	−1.4	−0.6	−0.2
Chesil Beach	50 37N	2 33W	+0040	+0055	−0005	+0010	−1.6	−1.5	−0.5	0.0
Chesil Cove	50 34N	2 28W	+0035	+0050	−0010	+0005	−1.5	−1.6	−0.5	−0.2
			0100	0700	0100	0700				
PORTLAND	50 34N	2 26W	and	and	and	and	2.1	1.4	0.8	0.1
standard port			1300	1900	1300	1900				
Lulworth Cove	50 37N	2 15W	+0005	+0015	−0005	0000	+0.1	+0.1	+0.2	+0.1
Mupe Bay	50 37N	2 13W	+0005	+0015	−0005	0000	+0.1	+0.1	+0.2	+0.1
			0000	0600	0500	1100				
PORTSMOUTH	50 48N	1 07W	and	and	and	and	4.7	3.8	1.9	0.8
standard port			1200	1800	1700	2300				
Swanage	50 37N	1 57W	−0250	+0105	−0105	−0105	−2.7	−2.2	−0.7	−0.3
Poole Harbour Entrance	50 41N	1 57W	−0230	+0115	−0045	−0020	−2.5	−2.1	−0.6	−0.2
POOLE, TOWN QUAY	50 43N	1 59W	*standard port*							
Pottery Pier	50 42N	1 59W	−0150	+0200	−0010	0000	−2.7	−2.1	−0.6	0.0
Wareham *River Frome*	50 41N	2 06W	−0140	+0205	+0110	+0035	−2.5	−2.1	−0.7	+0.1
Cleavel Point	50 40N	2 00W	−0220	+0130	−0025	−0015	−2.6	−2.3	−0.7	−0.3
Bournemouth	50 43N	1 52W	−0240	+0055	−0050	−0030	−2.7	−2.2	−0.8	−0.3
Christchurch *Entrance*	50 43N	1 45W	−0230	+0030	−0035	−0035	−2.9	−2.4	−1.2	−0.2
Christchurch *Quay*	50 44N	1 46W	−0210	+0100	+0105	+0055	−2.9	−2.4	−1.0	0.0
Christchurch *Tuckton*	50 44N	1 47W	−0205	+0110	+0110	+0105	−3.0	−2.5	−1.0	+0.1

Location	Lat	Long	High Water		Low Water		MHWS	MHWN	MLWN	MLWS
Hurst Point	50 42N	1 33W	−0115	−0005	−0030	−0025	−2.0	−1.5	−0.5	−0.1
Lymington	50 46N	1 32W	−0110	+0005	−0020	−0020	−1.7	−1.2	−0.5	−0.1
Bucklers Hard	50 48N	1 25W	−0040	−0010	+0010	−0010	−1.0	−0.8	−0.2	−0.3
Stansore Point	50 47N	1 21W	−0050	−0010	−0005	−0010	−0.8	−0.5	−0.3	−0.1
Isle of Wight										
Yarmouth	50 42N	1 30W	−0105	+0005	−0025	−0030	−1.7	−1.2	−0.3	0.0
Totland Bay	50 41N	1 33W	−0130	−0045	−0035	−0045	−2.2	−1.7	−0.4	−0.1
Freshwater	50 40N	1 31W	−0210	+0025	−0040	−0020	−2.1	−1.5	−0.4	0.0
Ventnor	50 36N	1 12W	−0025	−0030	−0025	−0030	−0.8	−0.6	−0.2	+0.2
Sandown	50 39N	1 09W	0000	+0005	+0010	+0025	−0.6	−0.5	−0.2	0.0
Foreland *Lifeboat Slip*	50 41N	1 04W	−0005	0000	+0005	+0010	+0.1	+0.1	0.0	+0.1
Bembridge Harbour	50 42N	1 06W	+0020	0000	+0100	+0020	−1.5	−1.4	−1.3	−1.0
Ryde	50 44N	1 07W	−0010	+0010	−0005	−0010	−0.2	−0.1	0.0	+0.1
Medina River										
Cowes	50 46N	1 18W	−0015	+0015	0000	−0020	−0.5	−0.3	−0.1	0.0
Folly Inn	50 44N	1 17W	−0015	+0015	0000	−0020	−0.6	−0.4	−0.1	+0.2
Newport	50 42N	1 17W	no data	no data	no data	no data	−0.6	−0.4	+0.1	+0.8
			0400	1100	0000	0600				
SOUTHAMPTON	50 54N	1 24W	and	and	and	and	4.5	3.7	1.8	0.5
standard port			1600	2300	1200	1800				
Calshot Castle	50 49N	1 18W	0000	+0025	0000	0000	0.0	0.0	+0.2	+0.3
Redbridge	50 55N	1 28W	−0020	+0005	0000	−0005	−0.1	−0.1	−0.1	−0.1
River Hamble										
Warsash	50 51N	1 18W	+0020	+0010	+0010	0000	0.0	+0.1	+0.1	+0.3
Bursledon	50 53N	1 18W	+0020	+0020	+0010	+0010	+0.1	+0.1	+0.2	+0.2
			0500	1000	0000	0600				
PORTSMOUTH	50 48N	1 07W	and	and	and	and	4.7	3.8	1.9	0.8
standard port			1700	2200	1200	1800				
Lee–on–the–Solent	50 48N	1 12W	−0005	+0005	−0015	−0010	−0.2	−0.1	+0.1	+0.2
Chichester Harbour										
Entrance	50 47N	0 56W	−0010	+0005	+0015	+0020	+0.2	+0.2	0.0	+0.1
Northney	50 50N	0 58W	+0010	+0015	+0015	+0025	+0.2	0.0	−0.2	−0.3
Bosham	50 50N	0 52W	0000	+0010	no data	no data	+0.2	+0.1	no data	
Itchenor	50 48N	0 52W	−0005	+0005	+0005	+0025	+0.1	0.0	−0.2	−0.2
Dell Quay	50 49N	0 49W	+0005	+0015	no data	no data	+0.2	+0.1	no data	
Selsey Bill	50 43N	0 47W	+0010	−0010	+0035	+0020	+0.5	+0.2	−0.2	−0.2
Nab Tower	50 40N	0 57W	+0015	0000	+0015	+0015	−0.2	0.0	+0.2	0.0
			0500	1000	0000	0600				
SHOREHAM	50 50N	0 15W	and	and	and	and	6.3	4.8	1.9	0.6
standard port			1700	2200	1200	1800				
Pagham	50 46N	0 43W	+0015	0000	−0015	−0025	−0.7	−0.5	−0.1	−0.1
Bognor Regis	50 47N	0 40W	+0010	−0005	−0005	−0020	−0.6	−0.5	−0.2	−0.1
River Arun										
Littlehampton *Entrance*	50 48N	0 32W	+0010	0000	−0005	−0010	−0.4	−0.4	−0.2	−0.2
Littlehampton *UMA wharf*	50 48N	0 33W	+0015	+0005	0000	+0045	−0.7	−0.7	−0.3	+0.2
Arundel	50 51N	0 33W	no data	+0120	no data	no data	−3.1	−2.8	no data	
Worthing	50 48N	0 22W	+0010	0000	−0005	−0010	−0.1	−0.2	0.0	0.0
Brighton	50 49N	0 08W	0000	−0005	0000	0000	+0.3	+0.2	+0.1	0.0
Newhaven	50 47N	0 04E	−0015	−0010	0000	0000	+0.2	+0.1	−0.1	−0.2
Eastbourne	50 46N	0 17E	−0010	−0005	+0015	+0020	+1.1	+0.6	+0.2	+0.1
			0000	0600	0100	0700				
DOVER	51 07N	1 19E	and	and	and	and	6.8	5.3	2.1	0.8
standard port			1200	1800	1300	1900				
Hastings	50 51N	0 35E	0000	−0010	−0030	−0030	+0.8	+0.5	+0.1	−0.1
Rye *Approaches*	50 55N	0 47E	+0005	−0010	no data	no data	+1.0	+0.7	no data	
Rye *Harbour*	50 56N	0 46E	+0005	−0010	dries	dries	−1.4	−1.7	dries	
Dungeness	50 54N	0 58E	−0010	−0015	−0020	−0010	+1.0	+0.6	+0.4	+0.1
Folkestone	51 05N	1 12E	−0020	−0005	−0010	−0010	+0.4	+0.4	0.0	−0.1
Deal	51 13N	1 25E	+0010	+0020	+0010	+0005	−0.6	−0.3	0.0	0.0
Richborough	51 18N	1 21E	+0015	+0015	+0030	+0030	−3.4	−2.6	−1.7	−0.7
Ramsgate	51 20N	1 25E	+0030	+0030	+0017	+0007	−1.6	−1.3	−0.7	−0.2
EAST COAST ENGLAND *Time Zone UT*										
			0200	0800	0200	0700				
SHEERNESS	51 27N	0 45E	and	and	and	and	5.8	4.7	1.5	0.6
standard port			1400	2000	1400	1900				
Margate	51 23N	1 23E	−0050	−0040	−0020	−0050	−0.9	−0.9	−0.1	0.0
Herne Bay	51 23N	1 07E	−0025	−0015	0000	−0025	−0.5	−0.5	−0.1	−0.1
Whitstable	51 22N	1 02E	−0008	−0011	+0005	0000	−0.3	−0.3	0.0	−0.1

Location	Lat	Long	High Water		Low Water		MHWS	MHWN	MLWN	MLWS
River Swale										
Grovehurst Jetty	51 22N	0 46E	−0007	0000	0000	+0016	0.0	0.0	0.0	−0.1
Faversham	51 19N	0 54E	no data	no data	no data	no data	−0.2	−0.2	no data	
River Medway										
Bee Ness	51 25N	0 39E	+0002	+0002	0000	+0005	+0.2	+0.1	0.0	0.0
Bartlett Creek	51 23N	0 38E	+0016	+0008	no data	no data	+0.1	0.0	no data	
Darnett Ness	51 24N	0 36E	+0004	+0004	0000	+0010	+0.2	+0.1	0.0	−0.1
Chatham *Lock approaches*	51 24N	0 33E	+0010	+0012	+0012	+0018	+0.3	+0.1	−0.1	−0.2
Upnor	51 25N	0 32E	+0015	+0015	+0015	+0025	+0.2	+0.2	−0.1	−0.1
Rochester *Strood Pier*	51 24N	0 30E	+0018	+0018	+0018	+0028	+0.2	+0.2	−0.2	−0.3
Wouldham	51 21N	0 27E	+0030	+0025	+0035	+0120	−0.2	−0.3	−1.0	−0.3
New Hythe	51 19N	0 28E	+0035	+0035	+0220	+0240	−1.6	−1.7	−1.2	−0.3
Allington Lock	51 17N	0 30E	+0050	+0035	no data	no data	−2.1	−2.2	−1.3	−0.4
River Thames										
Southend−on−Sea	51 31N	0 43E	−0005	0000	0000	+0005	0.0	0.0	−0.1	−0.1
Coryton	51 30N	0 31E	+0005	+0010	+0010	+0015	+0.4	+0.3	+0.1	−0.1
			0300	**0900**	**0400**	**1100**				
LONDON BRIDGE	51 30N	0 05W	and	and	and	and	7.1	5.9	1.3	0.5
standard port			**1500**	**2100**	**1600**	**2300**				
Albert Bridge	51 29N	0 10W	+0025	+0020	+0105	+0110	−0.9	−0.8	−0.7	−0.4
Hammersmith Bridge	51 29N	0 14W	+0040	+0035	+0205	+0155	−1.4	−1.3	−1.0	−0.5
Kew Bridge	51 29N	0 17W	+0055	+0050	+0255	+0235	−1.8	−1.8	−1.2	−0.5
Richmond Lock	51 28N	0 19W	+0105	+0055	+0325	+0305	−2.2	−2.2	−1.3	−0.5
			0200	**0700**	**0100**	**0700**				
SHEERNESS	51 27N	0 45E	and	and	and	and	5.8	4.7	1.5	0.6
standard port			**1400**	**1900**	**1300**	**1900**				
Thames Estuary Shivering Sand	51 30N	1 05E	−0025	−0019	−0008	−0026	−0.6	−0.6	−0.1	−0.1
			0000	**0600**	**0500**	**1100**				
WALTON−ON−THE−NAZE	51 51N	1 17E	and	and	and	and	4.2	3.4	1.1	0.4
standard port			**1200**	**1800**	**1700**	**2300**				
Whitaker Beacon	51 40N	1 06E	+0022	+0024	+0033	+0027	+0.6	+0.5	+0.2	+0.1
Holliwell Point	51 38N	0 56E	+0034	+0037	+0100	+0037	+1.1	+0.9	+0.3	+0.1
River Roach Rochford	51 35N	0 43E	+0050	+0040	dries	dries	−0.8	−1.1	dries	
River Crouch										
BURNHAM−ON−CROUCH	51 37N	0 48E		*standard port*						
North Fambridge	51 38N	0 41E	+0115	+0050	+0130	+0100	+1.1	+0.8	0.0	−0.1
Hullbridge	51 38N	0 38E	+0115	+0050	+0135	+0105	+1.1	+0.8	0.0	−0.1
Battlesbridge	51 37N	0 34E	+0120	+0110	dries	dries	−1.8	−2.0	dries	
River Blackwater										
Bradwell Waterside	51 45N	0 53E	+0035	+0023	+0047	+0004	+1.0	+0.8	+0.2	0.0
Osea Island	51 43N	0 46E	+0057	+0045	+0050	+0007	+1.1	+0.9	+0.1	0.0
Maldon	51 44N	0 42E	+0107	+0055	no data	no data	−1.3	−1.1	no data	
West Mersea	51 47N	0 54E	+0035	+0015	+0055	+0010	+0.9	+0.4	+0.1	+0.1
River Colne										
Brightlingsea	51 48N	1 00E	+0025	+0021	+0046	+0004	+0.8	+0.4	+0.1	0.0
Colchester	51 53N	0 56E	+0035	+0025	dries	dries	0.0	−0.3	dries	
Clacton−on−Sea	51 47N	1 09E	+0012	+0010	+0025	+0008	+0.3	+0.1	+0.1	+0.1
Bramble Creek	51 53N	1 14E	+0010	−0007	−0005	+0010	+0.3	+0.3	+0.3	+0.3
Sunk Head	51 46N	1 30E	0000	+0002	−0002	+0002	−0.3	−0.3	−0.1	−0.1
Harwich	51 57N	1 17E	+0007	+0002	−0010	−0012	−0.2	0.0	0.0	0.0
Wrabness	51 57N	1 10E	+0017	+0015	−0010	−0012	−0.1	0.0	0.0	0.0
Mistley	51 57N	1 05E	+0032	+0027	−0010	−0012	0.0	0.0	−0.1	−0.1
Pin Mill	52 00N	1 17E	+0012	+0015	−0008	−0012	−0.1	0.0	0.0	0.0
Ipswich	52 03N	1 10E	+0022	+0027	0000	−0012	0.0	0.0	−0.1	−0.1
			0100	**0700**	**0100**	**0700**				
WALTON−ON−THE−NAZE	51 51N	1 17E	and	and	and	and	4.2	3.4	1.1	0.4
standard port			**1300**	**1900**	**1300**	**1900**				
Felixstowe Pier	51 57N	1 21E	−0005	−0007	−0018	−0020	−0.5	−0.4	0.0	0.0
River Deben										
Woodbridge Haven	51 59N	1 24E	0000	−0005	−0020	−0025	−0.5	−0.5	−0.1	+0.1
Woodbridge	52 05N	1 19E	+0045	+0025	+0025	−0020	−0.2	−0.3	−0.2	0.0
Bawdsey	52 00N	1 26E	−0016	−0020	−0030	−0032	−0.8	−0.6	−0.1	−0.1
Orford Haven										
Bar	52 02N	1 28E	−0026	−0030	−0036	−0038	−1.0	−0.8	−0.1	0.0
Orford Quay	52 05N	1 32E	+0040	+0040	+0055	+0055	−1.4	−1.1	0.0	+0.2
Slaughden Quay	52 08N	1 36E	+0105	+0105	+0125	+0125	−1.3	−0.8	−0.1	+0.2
Iken Cliffs	52 09N	1 31E	+0130	+0130	+0155	+0155	−1.3	−1.0	0.0	+0.2

Location	Lat	Long	High Water		Low Water		MHWS	MHWN	MLWN	MLWS
			0300	0900	0200	0800				
LOWESTOFT	52 28N	1 45E	and	and	and	and	2.4	2.1	1.0	0.5
standard port			1500	2100	1400	2000				
Orford Ness	52 05N	1 35E	+0135	+0135	+0135	+0125	+0.4	+0.6	−0.1	0.0
Aldeburgh	52 09N	1 36E	+0130	+0130	+0115	+0120	+0.3	+0.2	−0.1	−0.2
Minsmere Sluice	52 14N	1 38E	+0110	+0110	+0110	+0110	0.0	−0.1	−0.2	−0.2
Southwold	52 19N	1 40E	+0105	+0105	+0055	+0055	0.0	0.0	−0.1	0.0
Great Yarmouth										
Gorleston-on-Sea	52 34N	1 44E	−0035	−0035	−0030	−0030	0.0	0.0	0.0	0.0
Britannia Pier	52 36N	1 45E	−0105	−0100	−0040	−0055	+0.1	+0.1	0.0	0.0
Caister-on-Sea	52 39N	1 44E	−0120	−0120	−0100	−0100	0.0	−0.1	0.0	0.0
Winterton-on-Sea	52 43N	1 42E	−0225	−0215	−0135	−0135	+0.8	+0.5	+0.2	+0.1
			0100	0700	0100	0700				
IMMINGHAM	53 38N	0 11E	and	and	and	and	7.3	5.8	2.6	0.9
standard port			1300	1900	1300	1900				
Cromer	52 56N	1 18E	+0050	+0030	+0050	+0130	−2.1	−1.7	−0.5	−0.1
Blakeney Bar	52 59N	0 59E	+0035	+0025	+0030	+0040	−1.6	−1.3	no data	
Blakeney	52 57N	1 01E	+0115	+0055	no data	no data	−3.9	−3.8	no data	
Wells Bar	52 59N	0 49E	+0020	+0020	+0020	+0020	−1.3	−1.0	no data	
Wells	52 57N	0 51E	+0035	+0045	+0340	+0310	−3.8	−3.8	not below CD	
Burnham Overy Staithe	52 58N	0 48E	+0045	+0055	no data	no data	−5.0	−4.9	no data	
The Wash										
Hunstanton	52 56N	0 29E	+0010	+0020	+0105	+0025	+0.1	−0.2	−0.1	0.0
West Stones	52 50N	0 21E	+0025	+0025	+0115	+0040	−0.3	−0.4	−0.3	+0.2
King's Lynn	52 45N	0 24E	+0030	+0030	+0305	+0140	−0.5	−0.8	−0.8	+0.1
Wisbech Cut	52 48N	0 13E	+0020	+0025	+0200	+0030	−0.3	−0.7	−0.4 no data	
Lawyer's Creek	52 53N	0 05E	+0010	+0020	no data	no data	−0.3	−0.6	no data	
Tabs Head	52 56N	0 05E	0000	+0005	+0125	+0020	+0.2	−0.2	−0.2	−0.2
Boston	52 58N	0 01W	0000	+0010	+0140	+0050	−0.5	−1.0	−0.9	−0.5
Skegness	53 09N	0 21E	+0010	+0015	+0030	+0020	−0.4	−0.5	−0.1	0.0
Inner Dowsing Light Tower	53 20N	0 34E	0000	0000	+0010	+0010	−0.9	−0.7	−0.1	+0.3
River Humber										
Bull Sand Fort	53 34N	0 04E	−0020	−0030	−0035	−0015	−0.4	−0.3	+0.1	+0.2
Grimsby	53 35N	0 04W	−0012	−0012	−0015	−0015	−0.2	−0.1	0.0	+0.2
Hull King George Dock	53 44N	0 16W	+0010	+0010	+0021	+0017	+0.3	+0.2	−0.1	−0.2
Hull Albert Dock	53 44N	0 21W	+0019	+0019	+0033	+0027	+0.3	+0.1	−0.1	−0.2
Humber Bridge	53 43N	0 27W	+0027	+0022	+0049	+0039	−0.1	−0.4	−0.7	−0.6
River Trent										
Burton Stather	53 39N	0 42W	+0105	+0045	+0335	+0305	−2.1	−2.3	−2.3	dries
Flixborough Wharf	53 37N	0 42W	+0120	+0100	+0400	+0340	−2.3	−2.6	dries	
Keadby	53 36N	0 44W	+0135	+0120	+0425	+0410	−2.5	−2.8	dries	
Owston Ferry	53 29N	0 46W	+0155	+0145	dries	dries	−3.5	−3.9	dries	
River Ouse										
Blacktoft	53 42N	0 43W	+0100	+0055	+0325	+0255	−1.6	−1.8	−2.2	−1.1
Goole	53 42N	0 52W	+0130	+0115	+0355	+0350	−1.6	−2.1	−1.9	−0.6
			0200	0800	0100	0800				
R. TYNE, N. SHIELDS	55 01N	1 26W	and	and	and	and	5.0	3.9	1.8	0.7
standard port			1400	2000	1300	2000				
Cridlington	54 05N	0 11W	+0119	+0109	+0109	+0104	+1.1	+0.8	+0.5	+0.4
Filey Bay	54 13N	0 16W	+0101	+0101	+0101	+0048	+0.8	+1.0	+0.6	+0.3
Scarborough	54 17N	0 23W	+0059	+0059	+0044	+0044	+0.7	+0.7	+0.5	+0.2
Whitby	54 29N	0 37W	+0034	+0049	+0034	+0019	+0.6	+0.4	+0.1	+0.1
Middlesborough	54 35N	1 13W	+0019	+0021	+0014	+0011	+0.6	+0.6	+0.3	+0.1
Hartlepool	54 41N	1 11W	+0015	+0015	+0008	+0008	+0.4	+0.3	0.0	+0.1
Seaham	54 50N	1 19W	+0004	+0004	−0001	−0001	+0.2	+0.2	+0.2	0.0
Sunderland	54 55N	1 21W	+0002	−0002	−0002	−0002	+0.2	+0.3	+0.2	+0.1
Newcastle-upon-Tyne	54 58N	1 36W	+0003	+0003	+0008	+0008	+0.3	+0.2	+0.1	+0.1
Blyth	55 07N	1 29W	+0005	−0007	−0001	+0009	0.0	0.0	−0.1	+0.1
Coquet Island	55 20N	1 32W	−0010	−0010	−0020	−0020	+0.1	+0.1	0.0	+0.1
Amble	55 20N	1 34W	−0013	−0013	−0016	−0020	0.0	0.0	+0.1	+0.1
North Sunderland	55 34N	1 38W	−0048	−0044	−0058	−0102	−0.2	−0.2	−0.2	0.0
Holy Island	55 40N	1 47W	−0043	−0039	−0105	−0110	−0.2	−0.2	−0.3	−0.1
Berwick	55 47N	2 00W	−0053	−0053	−0109	−0109	−0.3	−0.1	−0.5	−0.1
SCOTLAND Time Zone UT			0300	0900	0300	0900				
LEITH	55 59N	3 11W	and	and	and	and	5.6	4.4	2.0	0.8
standard port			1500	2100	1500	2100				
Eyemouth	55 52N	2 05W	−0003	+0008	+0011	+0005	−0.5	−0.4	−0.1	0.0
Dunbar	56 00N	2 31W	−0003	+0003	+0003	−0003	−0.3	−0.3	0.0	+0.1
Fidra	56 04N	2 47W	−0001	0000	−0002	+0001	−0.2	−0.2	0.0	0.0

TIDES

Location	Lat	Long	High Water		Low Water		MHWS	MHWN	MLWN	MLWS
Cockenzie	55 58N	2 57W	−0007	−0015	−0013	−0005	−0.2	0.0	no data	
Granton	55 59N	3 13W	0000	0000	0000	0000	0.0	0.0	0.0	0.0
Grangemouth	56 02N	3 41W	+0025	+0010	−0052	−0015	−0.1	−0.2	−0.3	−0.3
Kincardine	56 04N	3 43W	+0015	+0030	−0030	−0030	0.0	−0.2	−0.5	−0.3
Alloa	56 07N	3 48W	+0040	+0040	+0025	+0025	−0.2	−0.5	no data	−0.7
Stirling	56 07N	3 56W	+0100	+0100	No data		−2.9	−3.1	−2.3	−0.7
Firth of Forth										
Burntisland	56 03N	3 14W	+0013	+0004	−0002	+0007	+0.1	0.0	+0.1	+0.2
Kirkcaldy	56 09N	3 09W	+0005	0000	−0004	−0001	−0.3	−0.3	−0.2	−0.2
Methil	56 11N	3 00W	−0005	−0001	−0001	−0001	−0.1	−0.1	−0.1	−0.1
Anstruther Easter	56 13N	2 42W	−0018	−0012	−0006	−0008	−0.3	−0.2	0.0	0.0
			0000	**0600**	**0100**	**0700**				
ABERDEEN	57 09N	2 05W	and	and	and	and	4.3	3.4	1.6	0.6
standard port			1200	1800	1300	1900				
River Tay										
Bar	56 27N	2 38W	+0100	+0100	+0050	+0110	+0.9	+0.8	+0.3	+0.1
Dundee	56 27N	2 58W	+0140	+0120	+0055	+0145	+1.1	+0.9	+0.3	+0.1
Newburgh	56 21N	3 14W	+0215	+0200	+0250	+0335	−0.2	−0.4	−1.1	−0.5
Perth	56 24N	3 27W	+0220	+0225	+0510	+0530	−0.9	−1.4	−1.2	−0.3
Arbroath	56 33N	2 35W	+0056	+0037	+0034	+0055	+0.7	+0.7	+0.2	+0.1
Montrose	56 42N	2 27W	+0055	+0055	+0030	+0040	+0.5	+0.4	+0.2	0.0
Stonehaven	56 58N	2 12W	+0013	+0008	+0013	+0009	+0.2	+0.2	+0.1	0.0
Peterhead	57 30N	1 46W	−0035	−0045	−0035	−0040	−0.5	−0.3	−0.1	−0.1
Fraserburgh	57 41N	2 00W	−0105	−0115	−0120	−0110	−0.6	−0.5	−0.2	0.0
			0200	**0900**	**0400**	**0900**				
ABERDEEN	57 09N	2 05W	and	and	and	and	4.3	3.4	1.6	0.6
standard port			1400	2100	1600	2100				
Banff	57 40N	2 31W	−0100	−0150	−0150	−0050	−0.4	−0.2	−0.1	+0.2
Whitehills	57 41N	2 35W	−0122	−0137	−0117	−0127	−0.4	−0.3	+0.1	+0.1
Buckie	57 40N	2 58W	−0130	−0145	−0125	−0140	−0.2	−0.2	0.0	+0.1
Lossiemouth	57 43N	3 18W	−0125	−0200	−0130	−0130	−0.2	−0.2	0.0	0.0
Burghead	57 42N	3 29W	−0120	−0150	−0135	−0120	−0.2	−0.2	0.0	0.0
Nairn	57 36N	3 52W	−0120	−0150	−0135	−0130	0.0	−0.1	0.0	+0.1
McDermott Base	57 36N	3 59W	−0110	−0140	−0120	−0115	−0.1	−0.1	+0.1	+0.3
			0300	**1000**	**0000**	**0700**				
ABERDEEN	57 09N	2 05W	and	and	and	and	4.3	3.4	1.6	0.6
standard port			1500	2200	1200	1900				
Inverness Firth										
Fortrose	57 35N	4 08W	−0125	−0125	−0125	−0125	0.0	0.0	no data	
Inverness	57 30N	4 15W	−0050	−0150	−0200	−0150	+0.5	+0.3	+0.2	+0.1
Cromarty Firth										
Cromarty	57 42N	4 03W	−0120	−0155	−0155	−0120	0.0	0.0	+0.1	+0.2
Invergordon	57 41N	4 10W	−0105	−0200	−0200	−0110	+0.1	+0.1	+0.1	+0.1
Dingwall	57 36N	4 25W	−0045	−0145	no data	no data	+0.1	+0.2	no data	
			0300	**0800**	**0200**	**0800**				
ABERDEEN	57 09N	2 05W	and	and	and	and	4.3	3.4	1.6	0.6
standard port			1500	2000	1400	2000				
Dornoch Firth										
Portmahomack	57 50N	3 50W	−0120	−0210	−0140	−0110	−0.2	−0.1	+0.1	+0.1
Meikle Ferry	57 51N	4 08W	−0100	−0140	−0120	−0055	+0.1	0.0	−0.1	0.0
Golspie	57 58N	3 59W	−0130	−0215	−0155	−0130	−0.3	−0.3	−0.1	0.0
			0000	**0700**	**0200**	**0700**				
WICK	58 26N	3 05W	and	and	and	and	3.5	2.8	1.4	0 .7
standard port			1200	1900	1400	1900				
Helmsdale	58 07N	3 39W	+0025	+0015	+0035	+0030	+0.4	+0.3	+0.1	0.0
Duncansby Head	58 39N	3 02W	−0115	−0115	−0110	−0110	−0.4	−0.4	no data	
Orkney Islands										
Muckle Skerry	58 41N	2 55W	−0025	−0025	−0020	−0020	−0.9	−0.8	−0.4	−0.3
Burray Ness	58 51N	2 52W	+0005	+0005	+0015	+0015	−0.2	−0.3	−0.1	−0.1
Deer Sound	58 58N	2 50W	−0040	−0040	−0035	−0035	−0.3	−0.3	−0.1	−0.1
Kirkwall	58 59N	2 58W	−0042	−0042	−0041	−0041	−0.5	−0.4	−0.1	−0.1
Loth	59 12N	2 42W	−0052	−0052	−0058	−0058	−0.1	0.0	+0.3	+0.4
Kettletoft Pier	59 14N	2 36W	−0025	−0025	−0015	−0015	0.0	0.0	+0.2	+0.2
Rapness	59 15N	2 52W	−0205	−0205	−0205	−0205	+0.1	0.0	+0.2	0.0
Pierowall	59 19N	2 58W	−0150	−0150	−0145	−0145	+0.2	0.0	0.0	−0.1

●cation	Lat	Long	High Water		Low Water		MHWS	MHWN	MLWN	MLWS
Tingwall	59 05N	3 02W	−0200	−0125	−0145	−0125	−0.4	−0.4	−0.1	−0.1
Stromness	58 58N	3 18W	−0225	−0135	−0205	−0205	+0.1	−0.1	0.0	0.0
St. Mary's	58 54N	2 55W	−0140	−0140	−0140	−0140	−0.2	−0.2	0.0	−0.1
Widewall Bay	58 49N	3 01W	−0155	−0155	−0150	−0150	+0.1	−0.1	−0.1	−0.3
Bur Wick	58 44N	2 58W	−0100	−0100	−0150	−0150	−0.1	−0.1	+0.2	+0.1
			0000	**0600**	**0100**	**0800**				
RWICK	60 09N	1 08W	and	and	and	and	**2.1**	**1.7**	**0.9**	**0.5**
andard port			**1200**	**1800**	**1300**	**2000**				
●r Isle	59 32N	1 36W	−0006	−0015	−0031	−0037	+0.1	0.0	+0.1	+0.1
●etland Islands										
Sumburgh *Grutness Voe*	59 53N	1 17W	+0006	+0008	+0004	−0002	−0.3	−0.3	−0.2	−0.1
Dury Voe	60 21N	1 10W	−0015	−0015	−0010	−0010	0.0	−0.1	0.0	−0.2
Out Skerries	60 25N	0 45W	−0025	−0025	−0010	−0010	+0.1	0.0	0.0	−0.1
Toft Pier	60 28N	1 12W	−0105	−0100	−0125	−0115	+0.2	+0.1	−0.1	−0.1
Burra Voe *Yell Sound*	60 30N	1 03W	−0025	−0025	−0025	−0025	+0.2	+0.1	0.0	−0.1
Mid Yell	60 36N	1 03W	−0030	−0020	−0035	−0025	+0.3	+0.2	+0.2	+0.1
Balta Sound	60 45N	0 50W	−0055	−0055	−0045	−0045	+0.2	+0.1	0.0	−0.1
Burra Firth	60 48N	0 52W	−0110	−0110	−0115	−0115	+0.4	+0.2	0.0	0.0
Bluemull Sound	60 42N	1 00W	−0135	−0135	−0155	−0155	+0.5	+0.2	+0.1	0.0
Sullom Voe	60 27N	1 18W	−0135	−0125	−0135	−0120	0.0	0.0	−0.2	−0.2
Hillswick	60 29N	1 29W	−0220	−0220	−0200	−0200	−0.1	−0.1	−0.1	−0.1
Scalloway	60 08N	1 16W	−0150	−0150	−0150	−0150	−0.5	−0.4	−0.3	0.0
Bay of Quendale	59 54N	1 20W	−0025	−0025	−0030	−0030	−0.4	−0.3	0.0	+0.1
Foula	60 07N	2 03W	−0140	−0130	−0140	−0120	−0.1	−0.1	0.0	0.0
			0200	**0700**	**0100**	**0700**				
●CK	58 26N	3 05W	and	and	and	and	**3.5**	**2.8**	**1.4**	**0.7**
andard port			**1400**	**1900**	**1300**	**1900**				
●oma	58 40N	3 08W	−0115	−0115	−0110	−0110	−0.4	−0.5	−0.1	−0.2
●ls Bay	58 38N	3 10W	−0150	−0150	−0202	−0202	+0.7	+0.7	+0.6	+0.3
●rabster	58 37N	3 33W	−0255	−0225	−0240	−0230	+1.5	+1.2	+0.8	+0.3
●le Skerry	59 05N	4 24W	−0320	−0255	−0315	−0250	+0.4	+0.3	+0.2	+0.1
●ch Eriboll Portnancon	58 30N	4 42W	−0340	−0255	−0315	−0255	+1.6	+1.3	+0.8	+0.4
●le of Durness	58 36N	4 47W	−0350	−0350	−0315	−0315	+1.1	+0.7	+0.4	−0.1
●na	59 08N	5 49W	−0410	−0345	−0330	−0340	−0.1	−0.2	−0.2	−0.1
			0100	**0700**	**0300**	**0900**				
●ORNOWAY	58 12N	6 23W	and	and	and	and	**4.8**	**3.7**	**2.0**	**0.7**
andard port			**1300**	**1900**	**1500**	**2100**				
●ter Hebrides										
Loch Shell	58 00N	6 25W	−0013	0000	0000	−0017	0.0	−0.1	−0.1	0.0
E. Loch Tarbert	57 54N	6 48W	−0025	−0010	−0010	−0020	+0.2	0.0	+0.1	+0.1
Loch Maddy	57 36N	7 06W	−0044	−0014	−0016	−0030	0.0	−0.1	−0.1	0.0
Loch Carnan	57 22N	7 16W	−0050	−0010	−0020	−0040	−0.3	−0.5	−0.1	−0.1
Loch Skiport	57 20N	7 16W	−0100	−0025	−0024	−0024	−0.2	−0.4	−0.3	−0.2
Loch Boisdale	57 09N	7 16W	−0055	−0030	−0020	−0040	−0.7	−0.7	−0.3	−0.2
Barra *North Bay*	57 00N	7 24W	−0103	−0031	−0034	−0048	−0.6	−0.5	−0.2	−0.1
Castle Bay	56 57N	7 29W	−0115	−0040	−0045	−0100	−0.5	−0.6	−0.3	−0.1
Barra Head	56 47N	7 38W	−0115	−0040	−0045	−0055	−0.8	−0.7	−0.2	+0.1
Shillay	57 31N	7 41W	−0103	−0043	−0047	−0107	−0.6	−0.7	−0.7	−0.3
Balivanich	57 29N	7 23W	−0103	−0017	−0031	−0045	−0.7	−0.6	−0.5	−0.2
Scolpaig	57 39N	7 29W	−0033	−0033	−0040	−0040	−1.0	−0.9	−0.5	0.0
Leverburgh	57 46N	7 01W	−0025	−0025	−0015	−0025	−0.2	−0.2	−0.1	−0.1
W. Loch Tarbert	57 55N	6 55W	−0015	−0015	−0046	−0046	−1.1	−0.9	−0.5	0.0
Little Bernera	58 16N	6 52W	−0021	−0011	−0017	−0027	−0.5	−0.6	−0.4	−0.2
Carloway	58 17N	6 47W	−0040	+0020	−0035	−0015	−0.6	−0.5	−0.4	−0.1
Kilda Village Bay	57 48N	8 34W	−0040	−0040	−0045	−0045	−1.4	−1.2	−0.8	−0.3
●nnan Isles	58 16N	7 36W	−0026	−0016	−0016	−0026	−0.9	−0.7	−0.6	−0.2
●ckall	57 36N	13 41W	−0055	−0055	−0105	−0105	−1.8	−1.5	−0.9	−0.2
			0000	**0600**	**0300**	**0900**				
LAPOOL	57 54N	5 10W	and	and	and	and	**5.2**	**3.9**	**2.1**	**0.7**
andard port			**1200**	**1800**	**1500**	**2100**				
●ch Bervie	58 27N	5 03W	+0030	+0010	+0010	+0020	−0.3	−0.3	−0.2	0.0
●ch Laxford	58 24N	5 05W	+0015	+0015	+0005	+0005	−0.3	−0.4	−0.2	0.0
●drachillis Bay										
Badcall Bay	58 19N	5 08W	+0005	+0005	+0005	+0005	−0.7	−0.5	−0.5	+0.2
Loch Nedd	58 14N	5 10W	0000	0000	0000	0000	−0.3	−0.2	0.0	0.0
●ch Inver	58 09N	5 18W	−0005	−0005	−0005	−0005	−0.2	0.0	0.0	+0.1

Location	Lat	Long	High Water		Low Water		MHWS	MHWN	MLWN	MLWS
Summer Isles Tanera Mor	58 01N	5 24W	−0005	−0005	−0010	−0010	−0.1	+0.1	0.0	+0.1
Loch Ewe Mellon Charles	57 51N	5 38W	−0010	−0010	−0010	−0010	−0.1	−0.1	−0.1	0.0
Loch Gairloch Gairloch	57 43N	5 41W	−0020	−0020	−0010	−0010	0.0	+0.1	−0.3	−0.1
Loch Torridon Shieldaig	57 31N	5 39W	−0020	−0020	−0015	−0015	+0.4	+0.3	+0.1	0.0
Inner Sound Applecross	57 26N	5 49W	−0010	−0015	−0010	−0010	0.0	0.0	0.0	+0.1
Loch Carron Plockton	57 20N	5 39W	+0005	−0025	−0005	−0010	+0.5	+0.5	+0.5	+0.2
Rona Loch a' Bhraige	57 35N	5 58W	−0020	0000	−0010	0000	−0.1	−0.1	−0.1	−0.2
Skye										
Broadford Bay	57 15N	5 54W	−0015	−0015	−0010	−0015	+0.2	+0.1	+0.1	0.0
Portree	57 24N	6 11W	−0025	−0025	−0025	−0025	+0.1	−0.2	−0.2	0.0
Loch Snizort (Uig Bay)	57 35N	6 22W	−0045	−0020	−0005	−0025	+0.1	−0.4	−0.2	0.0
Loch Dunvegan	57 27N	6 38W	−0105	−0030	−0020	−0040	0.0	−0.1	0.0	0.0
Loch Harport	57 20N	6 25W	−0115	−0035	−0020	−0100	−0.1	−0.1	0.0	+0.1
Soay Camus nan Gall	57 09N	6 13W	−0055	−0025	−0025	−0045	−0.4	−0.2	*no data*	
Loch Alsh										
Kyle of Lochalsh	57 17N	5 43W	−0040	−0020	−0005	−0025	+0.1	0.0	0.0	−0.1
Dornie Bridge	57 17N	5 31W	−0040	−0010	−0005	−0020	+0.1	−0.1	0.0	0.0
Kyle Rhea Glenelg Bay	57 13N	5 38W	−0105	−0035	−0035	−0055	−0.4	−0.4	−0.9	−0.1
Loch Hourn	57 06N	5 34W	−0125	−0050	−0040	−0110	−0.2	−0.1	−0.1	+0.1
			0000	**0600**	**0100**	**0700**				
OBAN	56 25N	5 29W	and	and	and	and	**4.0**	**2.9**	**1.8**	**0.7**
standard port			**1200**	**1800**	**1300**	**1900**				
Loch Nevis										
Inverie Bay	57 02N	5 41W	+0030	+0020	+0035	+0020	+1.0	+0.9	+0.2	0.0
Mallaig	57 00N	5 50W	+0017	+0017	+0017	+0017	+1.0	+0.7	+0.3	+0.1
Eigg Bay of Laig	56 55N	6 10W	+0015	+0030	+0040	+0005	+0.7	+0.6	−0.2	− 0.2
Loch Moidart	56 47N	5 53W	+0015	+0015	+0040	+0020	+0.8	+0.6	− 0.2	−0.2
Coll Loch Eatharna	56 37N	6 31W	+0025	+0010	+0015	+0025	+0.4	+0.3	*no data*	
Tiree Gott Bay	56 31N	6 48W	0000	+0010	+0005	+0010	0.0	+0.1	0.0	0.0
			0100	**0700**	**0100**	**0800**				
OBAN	56 25N	5 29W	and	and	and	and	**4.0**	**2.9**	**1.8**	**0.7**
standard port			**1300**	**1900**	**1300**	**2000**				
Mull										
Carsaig Bay	56 19N	5 59W	−0015	−0005	−0030	+0020	+0.1	+0.2	0.0	−0.1
Iona	56 19N	6 23W	−0010	−0005	−0020	+0015	0.0	+0.1	−0.3	−0.2
Bunessan	56 19N	6 14W	−0015	−0015	−0010	−0015	+0.3	+0.1	0.0	−0.1
Ulva Sound	56 29N	6 08W	−0010	−0015	0000	−0005	+0.4	+0.3	0.0	−0.1
Loch Sunart Salen	56 42N	5 47W	−0015	+0015	+0010	+0005	+0.6	+0.5	−0.1	−0.1
Sound of Mull										
Tobermory	56 37N	6 04W	+0025	+0010	+0015	+0025	+0.4	+0.4	0.0	0.0
Salen	56 31N	5 57W	+0045	+0015	+0020	+0030	+0.2	+0.2	−0.1	0.0
Loch Aline	56 32N	5 46W	+0012	+0012	*no data*	*no data*	+0.5	+0.3	*no data*	
Craignure	56 28N	5 42W	+0030	+0005	+0010	+0015	0.0	+0.1	−0.1	−0.1
Loch Linnhe										
Corran	56 43N	5 14W	+0007	+0007	+0004	+0004	+0.4	+0.4	−0.1	0.0
Corpach	56 50N	5 07W	0000	+0020	+0040	0000	0.0	0.0	−0.2	−0.2
Loch Eil Head	56 51N	5 20W	+0025	+0045	+0105	+0025	*no data*		*no data*	
Loch Leven Head	56 43N	5 00W	+0045	+0045	+0045	+0045	*no data*		*no data*	
Loch Linnhe Port Appin	56 33N	5 25W	−0005	−0005	−0030	0000	+0.2	+0.2	+0.1	+0.1
Loch Creran										
Barcaldine Pier	56 32N	5 19W	+0010	+0020	+0040	+0015	+0.1	+0.1	0.0	+0.1
Loch Creran Head	56 33N	5 16W	+0015	+0025	+0120	+0020	−0.3	−0.3	−0.4	−0.3
Loch Etive										
Dunstaffnage Bay	56 27N	5 26W	+0005	0000	0000	+0005	+0.1	+0.1	+0.1	+0.1
Connel	56 27N	5 24W	+0020	+0005	+0010	+0015	−0.3	−0.2	−0.1	+0.1
Bonawe	56 27N	5 13W	+0150	+0205	+0240	+0210	−2.0	−1.7	−1.3	−0.5
Seil Sound	56 18N	5 35W	−0035	−0015	−0040	−0015	−1.3	−0.9	−0.7	−0.3
Colonsay Scalasaig	56 04N	6 10W	−0020	−0005	−0015	+0005	−0.1	−0.2	−0.2	−0.2
Jura Glengarrisdale Bay	56 06N	5 47W	−0020	0000	−0010	0000	−0.4	−0.2	0.0	−0.2
Islay										
Rubha A'Mhail	55 56N	6 07W	−0020	0000	+0005	−0015	−0.3	−0.1	−0.3	−0.1
Ardnave Point	55 52N	6 20W	−0035	+0010	0000	−0025	−0.4	−0.2	−0.3	−0.1
Orsay	55 41N	6 31W	−0110	−0110	−0040	−0040	−1.4	−0.6	−0.5	−0.2
Bruichladdich	55 48N	6 22W	−0105	−0035	−0110	−0110	−1.8	−1.3	−0.4	+0.1
Port Ellen	55 38N	6 11W	−0530	−0050	−0045	−0530	−3.1	−2.1	−1.3	−0.4
Port Askaig	55 51N	6 06W	−0110	−0030	−0020	−0020	−1.9	−1.4	−0.8	−0.3
Sound of Jura										
Craighouse	55 50N	5 57W	−0230	−0250	−0150	−0230	−3.0	−2.4	−1.3	−0.6

Location	Lat	Long	High Water		Low Water		MHWS	MHWN	MLWN	MLWS
Loch Melfort	56 15N	5 29W	−0055	−0025	−0040	−0035	−1.2	−0.8	−0.5	−0.1
Loch Beag	56 09N	5 36W	−0110	−0045	−0035	−0045	−1.6	−1.2	−0.8	−0.4
Carsaig Bay	56 02N	5 38W	−0105	−0040	−0050	−0050	−2.1	−1.6	−1.0	−0.4
Sound of Gigha	55 41N	5 44W	−0450	−0210	−0130	−0410	−2.5	−1.6	−1.0	−0.1
Machrihanish	55 25N	5 45W	−0520	−0350	−0340	−0540	Mean range 0.5 metres			
			0000	**0600**	**0000**	**0600**				
GREENOCK	55 57N	4 46W	and	and	and	and	**3.4**	**2.8**	**1.0**	**0.3**
standard port			**1200**	**1800**	**1200**	**1800**				
Firth of Clyde										
Southend, Kintyre	55 19N	5 38W	−0030	−0010	+0005	+0035	−1.3	−1.2	−0.5	−0.2
Campbeltown	55 25N	5 36W	−0025	−0005	−0015	+0005	−0.5	−0.3	+0.1	+0.2
Carradale	55 36N	5 28W	−0015	−0005	−0005	+0005	−0.3	−0.2	+0.1	+0.1
Loch Ranza	55 43N	5 18W	−0015	−0005	−0010	−0005	−0.4	−0.3	−0.1	0.0
Loch Fyne										
East Loch Tarbert	55 52N	5 24W	−0005	−0005	0000	−0005	+0.2	+0.1	0.0	0.0
Inveraray	56 14N	5 04W	+0011	+0011	+0034	+0034	−0.1	+0.1	−0.5	−0.2
Kyles of Bute										
Rubha a'Bhodaich	55 55N	5 09W	−0020	−0010	−0007	−0007	−0.2	−0.1	+0.2	+0.2
Tighnabruich	55 55N	5 13W	+0007	−0010	−0002	−0015	0.0	+0.2	+0.4	+0.5
Firth of Clyde – continued										
Millport	55 45N	4 56W	−0005	−0025	−0025	−0005	0.0	−0.1	0.0	+0.1
Rothesay Bay	55 51N	5 03W	−0020	−0015	−0010	−0002	+0.2	+0.2	+0.2	+0.2
Wemyss Bay	55 53N	4 53W	−0005	−0005	−0005	−0005	0.0	0.0	+0.1	+0.1
Loch Long										
Coulport	56 03N	4 53W	−0011	−0011	−0008	−0008	0.0	0.0	0.0	0.0
Lochgoilhead	56 10N	4 54W	+0015	0000	−0005	−0005	−0.2	−0.3	−0.3	−0.3
Arrochar	56 12N	4 45W	−0005	−0005	−0005	−0005	0.0	0.0	−0.1	−0.1
Gareloch										
Rosneath	56 01N	4 47W	−0005	−0005	−0005	−0005	0.0	−0.1	0.0	0.0
Faslane	56 04N	4 49W	−0010	−0010	−0010	−0010	0.0	0.0	−0.1	−0.2
Garelochhead	56 05N	4 50W	0000	0000	0000	0000	0.0	0.0	0.0	−0.1
River Clyde										
Helensburgh	56 00N	4 44W	0000	0000	0000	0000	0.0	0.0	0.0	0.0
Port Glasgow	55 56N	4 41W	+0010	+0005	+0010	+0020	+0.2	+0.1	0.0	0.0
Bowling	55 56N	4 29W	+0020	+0010	+0030	+0055	+0.6	+0.5	+0.3	+0.1
Clydebank *Rothesay Dock*	55 54N	4 24W	+0025	+0015	+0035	+0100	+1.0	+0.8	+0.5	+0.4
Glasgow	55 51N	4 16W	+0025	+0015	+0035	+0105	+1.3	+1.2	+0.6	+0.4
Firth of Clyde – continued										
Brodick Bay	55 35N	5 08W	0000	0000	+0005	+0005	−0.2	−0.2	0.0	0.0
Lamlash	55 32N	5 07W	−0016	−0036	−0024	−0004	−0.2	−0.2	*no data*	
Ardrossan	55 38N	4 49W	−0020	−0010	−0010	−0010	−0.2	−0.2	+0.1	+0.1
Irvine	55 36N	4 41W	−0020	−0020	−0030	−0010	−0.3	−0.3	−0.1	0.0
Troon	55 33N	4 41W	−0025	−0025	−0020	−0020	−0.2	−0.2	0.0	0.0
Ayr	55 28N	4 39W	−0025	−0025	−0030	−0015	−0.4	−0.3	+0.1	+0.1
Girvan	55 15N	4 52W	−0025	−0040	−0035	−0010	−0.3	−0.3	−0.1	0.0
Loch Ryan Stranraer	54 55N	5 03W	−0030	−0025	−0010	−0010	−0.2	−0.1	0.0	+0.1

WEST COAST ENGLAND *Time Zone UT*

Location	Lat	Long	High Water		Low Water		MHWS	MHWN	MLWN	MLWS
			0000	**0600**	**0200**	**0800**				
LIVERPOOL	53 24N	3 01W	and	and	and	and	**9.3**	**7.4**	**2.9**	**0.9**
standard port			**1200**	**1800**	**1400**	**2000**				
Portpatrick	54 50N	5 07W	+0018	+0026	0000	−0035	−5.5	−4.4	−2.0	−0.6
Luce Bay										
Drummore	54 41N	4 53W	+0030	+0040	+0015	+0020	−3.4	−2.5	−0.9	−0.3
Port William	54 46N	4 35W	+0030	+0030	+0025	0000	−2.9	−2.2	−0.8	*no data*
Wigtown Bay										
Isle of Whithorn	54 42N	4 22W	+0020	+0025	+0025	+0005	−2.4	−2.0	−0.8	−0.2
Garlieston	54 47N	4 22W	+0025	+0035	+0030	+0005	−2.3	−1.7	−0.5	*no data*
Solway Firth										
Kirkcudbright Bay	54 48N	4 04W	+0015	+0015	+0010	0000	−1.8	−1.5	−0.5	−0.1
Hestan Islet	54 50N	3 48W	+0025	+0025	+0020	+0025	−1.0	−1.1	−0.5	0.0
Southerness Point	54 52N	3 36W	+0030	+0030	+0030	+0010	−0.7	−0.7	*no data*	
Annan Waterfoot	54 58N	3 16W	+0050	+0105	+0220	+0310	−2.2	−2.6	−2.7	
Torduff Point	54 58N	3 09W	+0105	+0140	+0520	+0410	−4.1	−4.9		
Redkirk	54 59N	3 06W	+0110	+0215	+0715	+0445	−5.5	−6.2		
Silloth	54 52N	3 24W	+0030	+0040	+0045	+0055	−0.1	−0.3	−0.6	−0.1
Maryport	54 43N	3 30W	+0017	+0032	+0020	+0005	−0.7	−0.8	−0.4	0.0
Workington	54 39N	3 34W	+0020	+0020	+0020	+0010	−1.2	−1.1	−0.3	0.0
Whitehaven	54 33N	3 36W	+0005	+0015	+0010	+0005	−1.3	−1.1	−0.5	+0.1
Tarn Point	54 17N	3 25W	+0005	+0005	+0010	0000	−1.0	−1.0	−0.4	0.0
Duddon Bar	54 09N	3 20W	+0003	+0003	+0008	+0002	−0.8	−0.8	−0.3	0.0

Chapter 5

157

TIDES

Location	Lat	Long	High Water		Low Water		MHWS	MHWN	MLWN	MLWS
			0000	0600	0200	0700				
LIVERPOOL	53 24N	3 01W	and	and	and	and	9.3	7.4	2.9	0.9
standard port			1200	1800	1400	1900				
Barrow–in–Furness	54 06N	3 12W	+0015	+0015	+0015	+0015	0.0	−0.3	+0.1	+0.2
Ulverston	54 11N	3 04W	+0020	+0040	no data	no data	0.0	−0.1	no data	
Arnside	54 12N	2 51W	+0100	+0135	no data	no data	+0.5	+0.2	no data	
Morecambe	54 04N	2 52W	+0005	+0010	+0030	+0015	+0.2	0.0	0.0	+0.2
Heysham	54 02N	2 55W	+0005	+0005	+0015	0000	+0.1	0.0	0.0	+0.2
River Lune Glasson Dock	54 00N	2 51W	+0020	+0030	+0220	+0240	−2.7	−3.0	no data	
Lancaster	54 03N	2 49W	+0110	+0030	dries	dries	−5.0	−4.9	dries	
River Wyre										
Wyre Lighthouse	53 57N	3 02W	−0010	−0010	+0005	0000	−0.1	−0.1	no data	
Fleetwood	53 56N	3 00W	−0008	−0008	−0003	−0003	−0.1	−0.1	+0.1	+0.3
Blackpool	53 49N	3 04W	−0015	−0005	−0005	−0015	−0.4	−0.4	−0.1	+0.1
River Ribble Preston	53 46N	2 45W	+0010	+0010	+0335	+0310	−4.0	−4.1	−2.8	−0.8
Liverpool Bay										
Southport	53 39N	3 01W	−0020	−0010	no data	no data	−0.3	−0.3	no data	
Formby	53 32N	3 07W	−0015	−0010	−0020	−0020	−0.3	−0.1	0.0	+0.1
River Mersey										
Gladstone Dock	53 27N	3 01W	−0003	−0003	−0003	−0003	−0.1	−0.1	0.0	−0.1
Eastham	53 19N	2 57W	+0010	+0010	+0009	+0009	+0.3	+0.1	−0.1	−0.3
Hale Head	53 19N	2 48W	+0030	+0025	no data	no data	−2.4	−2.5	no data	
Widnes	53 21N	2 44W	+0040	+0045	+0400	+0345	−4.2	−4.4	−2.5	−0.3
Fiddler's Ferry	53 22N	2 39W	+0100	+0115	+0540	+0450	−5.9	−6.3	−2.4	−0.4
River Dee										
Hilbre Island	53 23N	3 13W	−0015	−0012	−0010	−0015	−0.3	−0.2	+0.2	+0.4
Mostyn Docks	53 19N	3 16W	−0020	−0015	−0020	−0020	−0.8	−0.7	no data	
Connah's Quay	53 13N	3 03W	0000	+0015	+0355	+0340	−4.6	−4.4	dries	
Chester	53 12N	2 54W	+0105	+0105	+0500	+0500	−5.3	−5.4	dries	
Isle of Man										
Peel	54 14N	4 42W	+0005	+0005	−0015	−0025	−4.1	−3.1	−1.4	−0.5
Ramsey	54 19N	4 22W	+0005	+0015	−0005	−0015	−1.9	−1.5	−0.6	0.0
Douglas	54 09N	4 28W	+0005	+0015	−0015	−0025	−2.4	−2.0	−0.5	−0.1
Port St. Mary	54 04N	4 44W	+0005	+0015	−0010	−0030	−3.4	−2.6	−1.3	−0.4
Calf Sound	54 04N	4 48W	+0005	+0005	−0015	−0025	−3.2	−2.6	−0.9	−0.3
Port Erin	54 05N	4 46W	−0005	+0015	−0010	−0050	−4.1	−3.2	−1.3	−0.5

WALES *Time Zone UT*

Location	Lat	Long	High Water		Low Water		MHWS	MHWN	MLWN	MLWS
Colwyn Bay	53 18N	3 43W	−0020	−0020	no data	no data	−1.5	−1.3	no data	
Llandudno	53 20N	3 50W	−0020	−0020	−0035	−0040	−1.7	−1.4	−0.7	−0.3
			0000	0600	0500	1100				
HOLYHEAD	53 19N	4 37W	and	and	and	and	5.6	4.4	2.0	0.7
standard port			1200	1800	1700	2300				
Conwy	53 17N	3 50W	+0025	+0035	+0120	+0105	+2.3	+1.8	+0.6	+0.4
Menai Strait										
Beaumaris	53 16N	4 05W	+0025	+0010	+0055	+0035	+2.0	+1.6	+0.5	+0.1
Menai Bridge	53 13N	4 09W	+0030	+0010	+0100	+0035	+1.7	+1.4	+0.3	0.0
Port Dinorwic	53 11N	4 13W	−0015	−0025	+0030	0000	0.0	0.0	0.0	+0.1
Caernarfon	53 09N	4 16W	−0030	−0030	+0015	−0005	−0.4	−0.4	−0.1	−0.1
Fort Belan	53 07N	4 20W	−0040	−0015	−0025	−0005	−1.0	−0.9	−0.2	−0.1
Trwyn Dinmor	53 19N	4 03W	+0025	+0015	+0050	+0035	+1.9	+1.5	+0.5	+0.2
Moelfre	53 20N	4 14W	+0025	+0020	+0050	+0035	+1.9	+1.4	+0.5	+0.2
Amlwch	53 25N	4 20W	+0020	+0010	+0035	+0025	+1.6	+ 1.3	+0.5	+0.2
Cemaes Bay	53 25N	4 27W	+0020	+0025	+0040	+0035	+1.0	+0.7	+0.3	+0.1
Trearddur Bay	53 16N	4 37W	−0045	−0025	−0015	−0015	−0.4	−0.4	0.0	+0.1
Porth Trecastell	53 12N	4 30W	−0045	−0025	−0005	−0015	−0.6	−0.6	0.0	0.0
Llanddwyn Island	53 08N	4 25W	−0115	−0055	−0030	−0020	−0.7	−0.5	−0.1	0.0
Trefor	53 00N	4 25W	−0115	−0100	−0030	−0020	−0.8	−0.9	−0.2	−0.1
Porth Dinllaen	52 57N	4 34W	−0120	−0105	−0035	−0025	−1.0	−1.0	−0.2	−0.2
Porth Ysgaden	52 54N	4 39W	−0125	−0110	−0040	−0035	−1.1	−1.0	−0.1	−0.1
Bardsey Island	52 46N	4 47W	−0220	−0240	−0145	−0140	−1.2	−1.2	−0.5	−0.1
			0100	0800	0100	0700				
MILFORD HAVEN	51 42N	5 03W	and	and	and	and	7.0	5.2	2.5	0.7
standard port			1300	2000	1300	1900				
Cardigan Bay										
Aberdaron	52 48N	4 43W	+0210	+0200	+0240	+0310	−2.4	−1.9	−0.6	−0.2
St. Tudwal's Roads	52 49N	4 29W	+0155	+0145	+0240	+0310	−2.2	−1.9	−0.7	−0.2
Pwllheli	52 53N	4 24W	+0210	+0150	+0245	+0320	−2.0	− 1.8	−0.6	−0.2
Criccieth	52 55N	4 14W	+0210	+0155	+0255	+0320	−2.0	−1.8	−0.7	−0.3
Porthmadog	52 55N	4 08W	+0235	+0210	no data	no data	−1.9	−1.8	no data	

158

Location	Lat	Long	High Water		Low Water		MHWS	MHWN	MLWN	MLWS
Barmouth	52 43N	4 03W	+0215	+0205	+0310	+0320	-2.0	-1.7	-0.7	0.0
Aberdovey	52 32N	4 03W	+0215	+0200	+0230	+0305	-2.0	-1.7	-0.5	0.0
Aberystwyth	52 24N	4 05W	+0145	+0130	+0210	+0245	-2.0	-1.7	-0.7	0.0
New Quay	52 13N	4 21W	+0150	+0125	+0155	+0230	-2.1	-1.8	-0.6	-0.1
Aberporth	52 08N	4 33W	+0135	+0120	+0150	+0220	-2.1	-1.8	-0.6	-0.1
Port Cardigan	52 07N	4 42W	+0140	+0120	+0220	+0130	-2.3	-1.8	-0.5	0.0
Cardigan *Town*	52 05N	4 40W	+0220	+0150	*no data*	*no data*	-2.2	-1.6	*no data*	
Fishguard	52 00N	4 58W	+0115	+0100	+0110	+0135	-2.2	-1.8	-0.5	+0.1
Porthgain	51 57N	5 11W	+0055	+0045	+0045	+0100	-2.5	-1.8	-0.6	0.0
Ramsey Sound	51 53N	5 19W	+0030	+0030	+0030	+0030	-1.9	-1.3	-0.3	0.0
Solva	51 52N	5 12W	+0015	+0010	+0035	+0015	-1.5	-1.0	-0.2	0.0
Little Haven	51 46N	5 06W	+0010	+0010	+0025	+0015	-1.1	-0.8	-0.2	0.0
Martin's Haven	51 44N	5 15W	+0010	+0010	+0015	+0015	-0.8	-0.5	+0.1	+0.1
Skomer Island	51 44N	5 17W	-0005	-0005	+0005	+0005	-0.4	-0.1	0.0	0.0
Dale Roads	51 42N	5 09W	-0005	-0005	-0008	-0008	0.0	0.0	0.0	-0.1
Cleddau River										
Neyland	51 42N	4 57W	+0002	+0010	0000	0000	0.0	0.0	0.0	0.0
Black Tar	51 45N	4 54W	+0010	+0020	+0005	0000	+0.1	+0.1	0.0	-0.1
Haverfordwest	51 48N	4 58W	+0010	+0025	*dries*	*dries*	-4.8	-4.9	*dries*	
Stackpole Quay	51 37N	4 54W	-0005	+0025	-0010	-0010	+0.9	+0.7	+0.2	+0.3
Tenby	51 40N	4 42W	-0015	-0010	-0015	-0020	+1.4	+1.1	+0.5	+0.2
Towy River										
Ferryside	51 46N	4 22W	0000	-0010	+0220	0000	-0.3	-0.7	-1.7	-0.6
Carmarthen	51 51N	4 18W	+0010	0000	*dries*	*dries*	-4.4	-4.8	*dries*	
Burry Inlet										
Burry Port	51 41N	4 15W	+0003	+0003	+0007	+0007	+1.6	+1.4	+0.5	+0.4
Llanelli	51 40N	4 10W	-0003	-0003	+0150	+0020	+0.8	+0.6	*no data*	
Mumbles	51 34N	3 58W	+0005	+0010	-0020	-0015	+2.3	+1.7	+0.6	+0.2
River Neath Entrance	51 37N	3 51W	+0002	+0011	*dries*	*dries*	+2.7	+2.2	*dries*	
Port Talbot	51 35N	3 49W	+0003	+0005	-0010	-0003	+2.6	+2.2	+1.0	+0.5
Porthcawl	51 28N	3 42W	+0005	+0010	-0010	-0005	+2.9	+2.3	+0.8	+0.3

			0600	1100	0300	0800				
BRISTOL, AVONMOUTH	51 30N	2 44W	and	and	and	and	**13.2**	**9.8**	**3.8**	**1.0**
standard port			1800	2300	1500	2000				
Barry	51 23N	3 16W	-0030	-0015	-0125	-0030	-1.8	-1.3	+0.2	0.0
Flat Holm	51 23N	3 07W	-0015	-0015	-0045	-0045	-1.3	-1.1	-0.2	+0.2
Steep Holm	51 20N	3 06W	-0020	-0020	-0050	-0050	-1.6	-1.2	-0.2	-0.2
Cardiff	51 27N	3 09W	-0015	-0015	-0100	-0030	-1.0	-0.6	+0.1	0.0
Newport	51 33N	2 59W	-0020	-0010	0000	-0020	-1.1	-1.0	-0.6	-0.7
River Wye Chepstow	51 39N	2 40W	+0020	+0020	*no data*	*no data*	*no data*		*no data*	

			0000	0600	0000	0700				
BRISTOL, AVONMOUTH	51 30N	2 44W	and	and	and	and	**13.2**	**9.8**	**3.8**	**1.0**
standard port			1200	1800	1200	1900				

WEST COAST ENGLAND *Time Zone UT*

Location	Lat	Long	High Water		Low Water		MHWS	MHWN	MLWN	MLWS
River Severn										
Sudbrook	51 35N	2 43W	+0010	+0010	+0025	+0015	+0.2	+0.1	-0.1	+0.1
Beachley *Aust*	51 36N	2 38W	+0010	+0015	+0040	+0025	-0.2	-0.2	-0.5	-0.3
Inward Rocks	51 39N	2 37W	+0020	+0020	+0105	+0045	-1.0	-1.1	-1.4	-0.6
Narlwood Rocks	51 39N	2 36W	+0025	+0025	+0120	+0100	-1.9	-2.0	-2.3	-0.8
White House	51 40N	2 33W	+0025	+0025	+0145	+0120	-3.0	-3.1	-3.6	-1.0
Berkeley	51 42N	2 30W	+0030	+0045	+0245	+0220	-3.8	-3.9	-3.4	-0.5
Sharpness Dock	51 43N	2 29W	+0035	+0050	+0305	+0245	-3.9	-4.2	-3.3	-0.4
Wellhouse Rock	51 44N	2 29W	+0040	+0055	+0320	+0305	-4.1	-4.4	-3.1	-0.2
Epney	51 42N	2 24W	+0130	*no data*	*no data*	*no data*	-9.4	*no data*	*no data*	
Minsterworth	51 50N	2 23W	+0140	*no data*	*no data*	*no data*	-10.1	*no data*	*no data*	
Llanthony	51 51N	2 21W	+0215	*no data*	*no data*	*no data*	-10.7	*no data*	*no data*	

			0200	0800	0300	0800				
BRISTOL, AVONMOUTH	51 30N	2 44W	and	and	and	and	**13.2**	**9.8**	**3.8**	**1.0**
standard port			1400	2000	1500	2000				
River Avon										
Shirehampton	51 29N	2 41W	0000	0000	+0035	+0010	-0.7	-0.7	-0.8	0.0
Sea Mills	51 29N	2 39W	+0005	+0005	+0105	+0030	-1.4	-1.5	-1.7	-0.1
Cumberland Basin *Entrance*	51 27N	2 37W	+0010	+0010	*dries*	*dries*	-2.9	-3.0	*dries*	
Portishead	51 30N	2 45W	-0002	0000	*no data*	*no data*	-0.1	-0.1	*no data*	
Clevedon	51 27N	2 52W	-0010	-0020	-0025	-0015	-0.4	-0.2	+0.2	0.0
St Thomas Head	51 24N	2 56W	0000	0000	-0030	-0030	-0.4	-0.2	+0.1	+0.1
English & Welsh Grounds	51 28N	2 59W	-0008	-0008	-0030	-0030	-0.5	-0.8	-0.3	0.0
Weston–super–Mare	51 21N	2 59W	-0020	-0030	-0130	-0030	-1.2	-1.0	-0.8	-0.2
River Parrett										
Burnham-on-Sea	51 14N	3 00W	-0020	-0025	-0030	0000	-2.3	-1.9	-1.4	-1.1
Bridgwater	51 08N	3 00W	-0015	-0030	+0305	+0455	-8.6	-8.1	*dries*	

Location	Lat	Long	High Water		Low Water		MHWS	MHWN	MLWN	MLWS
Hinkley Point	51 13N	3 08W	−0020	−0025	−0100	−0040	−1.7	−1.4	−0.2	−0.2
Watchet	51 11N	3 20W	−0035	−0050	−0145	−0040	−1.9	−1.5	+0.1	+0.1
Minehead	51 13N	3 28W	−0037	−0052	−0155	−0045	−2.6	−1.9	−0.2	0.0
Porlock Bay	51 13N	3 38W	−0045	−0055	−0205	−0050	−3.0	−2.2	−0.1	−0.1
Lynmouth	51 14N	3 49W	−0055	−0115	no data	no data	−3.6	−2.7	no data	
			0100	**0700**	**0100**	**0700**				
MILFORD HAVEN	51 42N	5 03W	and	and	and	and	**7.0**	**5.2**	**2.5**	**0.7**
standard port			**1300**	**1900**	**1300**	**1900**				
Ilfracombe	51 13N	4 07W	−0016	−0016	−0041	−0031	+2.3	+1.8	+0.6	+0.3
Rivers Taw & Torridge										
Appledore	51 03N	4 12W	−0020	−0025	+0015	−0045	+0.5	0.0	−0.9	−0.5
Yelland Marsh	51 04N	4 10W	−0010	−0015	+0100	−0015	+0.1	−0.4	−1.2	−0.6
Fremington	51 05N	4 07W	−0010	−0015	+0030	−0030	−1.1	−1.8	−2.2	−0.5
Barnstaple	51 05N	4 04W	0000	−0015	−0155	−0245	−2.9	−3.8	−2.2	−0.4
Bideford	51 01N	4 12W	−0020	−0025	0000	0000	−1.1	−1.6	−2.5	−0.7
Clovelly	51 00N	4 24W	−0030	−0030	−0020	−0040	+1.3	+1.1	+0.2	+0.2
Lundy	51 10N	4 40W	−0025	−0025	−0020	−0035	+1.0	+0.7	+0.2	0.0
Bude	50 50N	4 33W	−0040	−0040	−0035	−0045	+0.7	+0.6	no data	
Boscastle	50 41N	4 42W	−0045	−0010	−0110	−0100	+0.3	+0.4	+0.2	+0.2
Port Isaac	50 35N	4 50W	−0100	−0100	−0100	−0100	+0.5	+0.6	0.0	+0.2
River Camel										
Padstow	50 33N	4 56W	−0055	−0050	−0040	−0050	+0.3	+0.4	+0.1	+0.1
Wadebridge	50 31N	4 50W	−0052	−0052	+0235	+0245	−3.8	−3.8	−2.5	−0.4
Newquay	50 25N	5 05W	−0100	−0110	−0105	−0050	0.0	+0.1	0.0	−0.1
Perranporth	50 21N	5 09W	−0100	−0110	−0110	−0050	−0.1	0.0	0.0	+0.1
St. Ives	50 13N	5 28W	−0050	−0115	−0105	−0040	−0.4	−0.3	−0.1	+0.1
Cape Cornwall	50 08N	5 42 W	−0130	−0145	−0120	−0120	−1.0	−0.9	−0.5	−0.1
Sennen Cove	50 04N	5 42W	−0130	−0145	−0125	−0125	−0.9	−0.4	no data	

IRELAND *Time Zone UT*

Location	Lat	Long	High Water		Low Water		MHWS	MHWN	MLWN	MLWS
			0000	**0700**	**0000**	**0500**				
DUBLIN, NORTH WALL	53 21N	6 13W	and	and	and	and	**4.1**	**3.4**	**1.5**	**0.7**
standard port			**1200**	**1900**	**1200**	**1700**				
Courtown	52 39N	6 13W	−0328	−0242	−0158	−0138	−2.8	−2.4	−0.5	0.0
Arklow	52 47N	6 08W	−0315	−0201	−0140	−0134	−2.7	−2.2	−0.6	−0.1
Wicklow	52 59N	6 02W	−0019	−0019	−0024	−0026	−1.4	−1.1	−0.4	0.0
Greystones	53 09N	6 04W	−0008	−0008	−0008	−0008	−0.5	−0.4	no data	
Dun Laoghaire	53 18N	6 08W	−0006	−0001	−0002	−0003	0.0	0.0	0.0	+0.1
Dublin Bar	53 21N	6 09W	−0006	−0001	−0002	−0003	0.0	0.0	0.0	+0.1
Howth	53 23N	6 04W	−0007	−0005	+0001	+0005	0.0	−0.1	−0.2	−0.2
Malahide	53 27N	6 09W	+0002	+0003	+0009	+0009	+0.1	−0.2	−0.4	−0.2
Balbriggan	53 37N	6 11W	−0021	−0015	+0010	+0002	+0.3	+0.2	no data	
River Boyne Bar	53 43N	6 14W	−0005	0000	+0020	+0030	+0.4	+0.3	−0.1	−0.2
Dunany Point	53 52N	6 14W	−0028	−0018	−0008	−0006	+0.7	+0.9	no data	
Dundalk Soldiers Point	54 00N	6 21W	−0010	−0010	0000	+0045	+1.0	+0.8	+0.1	−0.1

NORTHERN IRELAND *Time Zone UT*

Location	Lat	Long	High Water		Low Water		MHWS	MHWN	MLWN	MLWS
Carlingford Lough										
Cranfield Point	54 01N	6 03W	−0027	−0011	+0005	−0010	+0.7	+0.9	+0.3	+0.2
Warrenpoint	54 06N	6 15W	−0020	−0010	+0025	+0035	+1.0	+0.7	+0.2	+0.0
Newry *Victoria Lock*	54 09N	6 19W	+0005	+0015	+0045	dries	+1.2	+0.9	+0.1	dries
			0100	**0700**	**0000**	**0600**				
BELFAST	54 36N	5 55W	and	and	and	and	**3.5**	**3.0**	**1.1**	**0.4**
standard port			**1300**	**1900**	**1200**	**1800**				
Kilkeel	54 03N	5 59W	+0040	+0030	+0010	+0010	+1.2	+1.1	+0.4	+0.4
Newcastle	54 12N	5 53W	+0025	+0035	+0020	+0040	+1.6	+1.1	+0.4	+0.1
Killough Harbour	54 15N	5 38W	0000	+0020	no data	no data	+1.8	+1.6	no data	
Ardglass	54 16N	5 36W	+0010	+0015	+0005	+0010	+1.7	+1.2	+0.6	+0.3
Strangford Lough										
Killard Point	54 19N	5 31W	+0011	+0021	+0005	+0025	+1.0	+0.8	+0.1	+0.1
Strangford	54 22N	5 33W	+0147	+0157	+0148	+0208	+0.1	+0.1	−0.2	0.0
Quoile Barrier	54 22N	5 41W	+0150	+0200	+0150	+0300	+0.2	+0.2	−0.3	−0.1
Killyleagh	54 24N	5 39W	+0157	+0207	+0211	+0231	+0.3	+0.3	no data	
South Rock	54 24N	5 25W	+0023	+0023	+0025	+0025	+1.0	+0.8	+0.1	+0.1
Portavogie	54 28N	5 26W	+0010	+0020	+0010	+0020	+1.2	+0.9	+0.3	+0.2
Donaghadee	54 38N	5 32W	+0020	+0020	+0023	+0023	+0.5	+0.4	0.0	+0.1
Carrickfergus	54 43N	5 48W	+0005	+0005	+0005	+0005	−0.3	−0.3	−0.2	−0.1
Larne	54 51N	5 47W	+0005	0000	+0010	−0005	−0.7	−0.5	−0.3	0.0
Red Bay	55 04N	6 03W	+0022	−0010	+0007	−0017	−1.9	−1.5	−0.8	−0.2
Cushendun	55 08N	6 02W	+0010	−0030	0000	−0025	−1.7	−1.5	−0.6	−0.2
Portrush	55 12N	6 40W	−0433	−0433	−0433	−0433	−1.6	−1.6	−0.3	0.0
Coleraine	55 08N	6 40W	−0403	−0403	−0403	−0403	−1.3	−1.2	−0.2	0.0

Location	Lat	Long	High Water		Low Water		MHWS	MHWN	MLWN	MLWS
			0200	0900	0200	0800				
GALWAY	53 16N	9 03W	and	and	and	and	5.1	3.9	2.0	0.6
standard port			1400	2100	1400	2000				
Londonderry	55 00N	7 19W	+0254	+0319	+0322	+0321	−2.4	−1.8	−0.8	−0.1

IRELAND *Time Zone UT*

Location	Lat	Long	High Water		Low Water		MHWS	MHWN	MLWN	MLWS
Inishtrahull	55 26N	7 14W	+0100	+0100	+0115	+0200	−1.8	−1.4	−0.4	−0.2
Portmore	55 22N	7 20W	+0120	+0120	+0135	+0135	−1.3	−1.1	−0.4	−0.1
Trawbreaga Bay	55 19N	7 23W	+0115	+0059	+0109	+0125	−1.1	−0.8	*no data*	
Lough Swilly										
Rathmullan	55 05N	7 31W	+0125	+0050	+0126	+0118	−0.8	−0.7	−0.1	−0.1
Fanad Head	55 16N	7 38W	+0115	+0040	+0125	+0120	−1.1	−0.9	−0.5	−0.1
Mulroy Bay										
Bar	55 15N	7 46W	+0108	+0052	+0102	+0118	−1.2	−1.0	*no data*	
Fanny's Bay	55 12N	7 49W	+0145	+0129	+0151	+0207	−2.2	−1.7	*no data*	
Seamount Bay	55 11N	7 44W	+0210	+0154	+0226	+0242	−3.1	−2.3	*no data*	
Cranford Bay	55 09N	7 42W	+0329	+0313	+0351	+0407	−3.7	−2.8	*no data*	
Sheephaven										
Downies Bay	55 11N	7 50W	+0057	+0043	+0053	+0107	−1.1	−0.9	*no data*	
Inishbofin Bay	55 10N	8 10W	+0040	+0026	+0032	+0046	−1.2	−0.9	*no data*	

Location	Lat	Long	High Water		Low Water		MHWS	MHWN	MLWN	MLWS
			0600	1100	0000	0700				
GALWAY	53 16N	9 03W	and	and	and	and	5.1	3.9	2.0	0.6
standard port			1800	2300	1200	1900				
Gweedore Harbour	55 04N	8 19W	+0048	+0100	+0055	+0107	−1.3	−1.0	−0.5	−0.1
Burtonport	54 59N	8 26W	+0042	+0055	+0115	+0055	−1.2	−1.0	−0.6	−0.1
Loughros More Bay	54 47N	8 30W	+0042	+0054	+0046	+0058	−1.1	−0.9	*no data*	
Donegal Bay										
Killybegs	54 38N	8 26W	+0040	+0050	+0055	+0035	−1.0	−0.9	−0.5	0.0
Donegal Hbr *Salt Hill Quay*	54 38N	8 13W	+0038	+0050	+0052	+0104	−1.2	−0.9	*no data*	
Mullaghmore	54 28N	8 27W	+0036	+0048	+0047	+0059	−1.4	−1.0	−0.4	−0.2
Sligo Harbour *Oyster Island*	54 18N	8 34W	+0043	+0055	+0042	+0054	−1.0	−0.9	−0.5	−0.1
Ballysadare Bay *Culleenamore*	54 16N	8 36W	+0059	+0111	+0111	+0123	−1.2	−0.9	*no data*	
Killala Bay *Inishcrone*	54 13N	9 06W	+0035	+0055	+0030	+0050	−1.3	−1.2	−0.7	−0.2
Broadhaven	54 16N	9 53W	+0040	+0050	+0040	+0050	−1.4	−1.1	−0.4	−0.1
Blacksod Bay										
Blacksod Quay	54 06N	10 03W	+0025	+0035	+0040	+0040	−1.2	−1.0	−0.6	−0.2
Bull's Mouth	54 02N	9 55W	+0101	+0057	+0109	+0105	−1.5	− 1.0	−0.6	−0.1
Clare Island	53 48N	9 57W	+0019	+0013	+0029	+0023	−1.0	−0.7	−0.4	−0.1
Westport Bay										
Inishraher	53 48N	9 38W	+0030	+0012	+0058	+0026	−0.6	−0.5	−0.3	−0.1
Killary Harbour	53 38N	9 53W	+0021	+0015	+0035	+0029	−1.0	−0.8	−0.4	−0.1
Inishbofin Bofin Harbour	53 37N	10 13W	+0013	+0009	+0021	+0017	−1.0	−0.8	−0.4	−0.1
Clifden Bay	53 29N	10 04W	+0005	+0005	+0016	+0016	−0.7	−0.5	*no data*	
Slyne Head	53 24N	10 14W	+0002	+0002	+0010	+0010	−0.7	−0.5	*no data*	
Roundstone Bay	53 23N	9 55W	+0003	+0003	+0008	+0008	−0.7	−0.5	−0.3	−0.1
Kilkieran Cove	53 20N	9 44W	+0005	+0005	+0016	+0016	−0.3	−0.2	−0.1	0.0
Aran Islands Killeany Bay	53 07N	9 39W	−0008	−0008	+0003	+0003	−0.4	−0.3	−0.2	−0.1
Liscannor	52 56N	9 23W	−0003	−0007	+0006	+0002	−0.4	−0.3	*no data*	
Seafield Point	52 48N	9 30W	−0006	−0014	+0004	−0004	−0.5	−0.4	*no data*	
Kilrush	52 38N	9 30W	−0006	+0027	+0057	−0016	−0.1	−0.2	−0.3	−0.1
Limerick Dock	52 40N	8 38W	+0135	+0141	+0141	+0219	+1.0	+0.7	−0.8	−0.2

Location	Lat	Long	High Water		Low Water		MHWS	MHWN	MLWN	MLWS
			0500	1100	0500	1100				
COBH	51 51N	8 18 W	and	and	and	and	4.1	3.2	1.3	0.4
standard port			1700	2300	1700	2300				
Tralee Bay *Fenit Pier*	52 16N	9 52W	−0057	−0017	−0029	−0109	+0.5	+0.2	+0.3	+0.1
Smerwick Harbour	52 12N	10 24W	−0107	−0027	−0041	−0121	−0.3	−0.4	*no data*	
Dingle Harbour	52 07N	10 15W	−0111	−0041	−0049	−0119	−0.1	0.0	+0.3	+0.4
Castlemaine Hbr										
Cromane Point	52 09N	9 54W	−0026	−0006	−0017	−0037	+0.4	+0.2	+0.4	+0.2
Valentia Harbour										
Knights Town	51 56N	10 18W	−0118	−0038	−0056	−0136	−0.6	−0.4	−0.1	0.0
Ballinskelligs Bay										
Castle	51 49N	10 16W	−0119	−0039	−0054	−0134	−0.5	−0.5	−0.1	0.0
Kenmare River										
West Cove	51 46N	10 03W	−0113	−0033	−0049	−0129	−0.6	−0.5	−0.1	0.0
Dunkerron Harbour	51 52N	9 38W	−0117	−0027	−0050	−0140	−0.2	−0.3	+0.1	0.0
Coulagh Bay										
Ballycrovane Hbr	51 43N	9 57W	−0116	−0036	−0053	−0133	−0.6	−0.5	−0.1	0.0

Location	Lat	Long	High Water		Low Water		MHWS	MHWN	MLWN	MLWS
Black Ball Harbour	51 36N	10 02W	−0115	−0035	−0047	−0127	−0.7	−0.6	−0.1	+0.1
Bantry Bay										
Castletown Bearhaven	51 39N	9 54W	−0048	−0012	−0025	−0101	−0.9	−0.6	−0.1	0.0
Bantry	51 41N	9 28W	−0045	−0025	−0040	−0105	−0.9	−0.8	−0.2	0.0
Dunmanus Bay										
Dunbeacon Harbour	51 37N	9 33W	−0057	−0025	−0032	−0104	−0.8	−0.7	−0.3	−0.1
Dunmanus Harbour	51 32N	9 40W	−0107	−0031	−0044	−0120	−0.7	−0.6	−0.2	0.0
Crookhaven	51 28N	9 43W	−0057	−0033	−0048	−0112	−0.8	−0.6	−0.4	−0.1
Schull	51 31N	9 32W	−0040	−0015	−0015	−0110	−0.9	−0.6	−0.2	0.0
Baltimore	51 29N	9 23W	−0025	−0005	−0010	−0050	−0.6	−0.3	+0.1	+0.2
Castletownshend	51 32N	9 10W	−0020	−0030	−0020	−0050	−0.4	−0.2	+0.1	+0.3
Clonakilty Bay	51 35N	8 50W	−0033	−0011	−0019	−0041	−0.3	−0.2	no data	
Courtmacsherry	51 38N	8 42W	−0029	−0007	+0005	−0017	−0.4	−0.3	−0.2	−0.1
Kinsale	51 42N	8 31W	−0019	−0005	−0009	−0023	−0.2	0.0	+0.1	+0.2
Roberts Cove	51 45N	8 19W	−0005	−0005	−0005	−0005	−0.1	0.0	0.0	+0.1
Cork Harbour										
Ringaskiddy	51 50N	8 19W	+0005	+0020	+0007	+0013	+0.1	+0.1	+0.1	+0.1
Marino Point	51 53N	8 20W	0000	+0010	0000	+0010	+0.1	+0.1	0.0	0.0
Cork City	51 54N	8 27W	+0005	+0010	+0020	+0010	+0.4	+0.4	+0.3	+0.2
Ballycotton	51 50N	8 01W	−0011	+0001	+0003	−0009	0.0	0.0	−0.1	0.0
Youghal	51 57N	7 51W	0000	+0010	+0010	0000	−0.2	−0.1	−0.1	−0.1
Dungarvan Harbour	52 05N	7 34W	+0004	+0012	+0007	−0001	0.0	+0.1	−0.2	0.0
Waterford Harbour										
Dunmore East	52 09N	6 59W	+0008	+0003	0000	0000	+0.1	0.0	+0.1	+0.2
Cheekpoint	52 16N	7 00W	+0022	+0020	+0020	+0020	+0.3	+0.2	+0.2	+0.1
Kilmokea Point	52 17N	7 00W	+0026	+0022	+0020	+0020	+0.2	+0.1	+0.1	+0.1
Waterford	52 16N	7 07W	+0057	+0057	+0046	+0046	+0.4	+0.3	−0.1	+0.1
New Ross	52 24N	6 57W	+0100	+0030	+0055	+0130	+0.3	+0.4	+0.3	+0.4
Baginbun Head	52 10N	6 50W	+0003	+0003	−0008	−0008	−0.2	−0.1	+0.2	+0.2
Great Saltee	52 07N	6 38W	+0019	+0009	−0004	+0006	−0.3	−0.4	no data	
Carnsore Point	52 10N	6 22W	+0029	+0019	−0002	+0008	−1.1	−1.0	no data	
Rosslare Harbour	52 15N	6 21W	+0045	+0035	+0015	−0005	−2.2	−1.8	−0.5	−0.1
Wexford Harbour	52 20N	6 27W	+0126	+0126	+0118	+0108	−2.1	−1.7	−0.3	+0.1

DENMARK *Time Zone −0100*

			0300	0700	0100	0800				
ESBJERG	55 28N	8 27E	and	and	and	and	**1.9**	**1.5**	**0.5**	**0.1**
standard port			1500	1900	1300	2000				
Hirtshals	57 36N	9 58E	+0055	+0320	+0340	+0100	−1.6	−1.3	−0.4	−0.1
Hanstholm	57 08N	8 36E	+0100	+0340	+0340	+0130	−1.6	−1.2	−0.4	−0.1
Thyborøn	56 42N	8 13E	+0120	+0230	+0410	+0210	−1.5	−1.2	−0.4	−0.1
Torsminde	56 22N	8 07E	+0045	+0050	+0040	+0010	−1.3	−1.0	−0.4	−0.1
Hvide Sande	56 00N	8 07E	0000	+0010	−0015	−0025	−1.1	−0.8	−0.3	−0.1
Blavandshuk	55 33N	8 05E	−0120	−0110	−0050	−0100	−0.1	−0.1	−0.2	−0.1
Gradyb Bar	55 26N	8 15E	−0130	−0115	no data	no data	−0.4	−0.3	−0.2	−0.1
Rømø Havn	55 05N	8 34E	−0040	−0005	0000	−0020	0.0	+0.1	−0.2	−0.2
Hojer	54 58N	8 40E	−0020	+0015	no data	no data	+0.5	+0.6	−0.1	−0.1

GERMANY *Time Zone −0100*

			0100	0600	0100	0800				
HELGOLAND	54 11N	7 53E	and	and	and	and	**2.7**	**2.4**	**0.4**	**0.0**
standard port			1300	1800	1300	2000				
Lister Tief List	55 01N	8 27E	+0252	+0240	+0201	+0210	−0.8	−0.6	−0.2	0.0
Hörnum	54 45N	8 18E	+0223	+0218	+0131	+0137	−0.5	−0.4	−0.2	0.0
Amrum–Hafen	54 38N	8 23E	+0138	+0137	+0128	+0134	+0.1	+0.2	−0.1	0.0
Dagebüll	54 44N	8 41E	+0226	+0217	+0211	+0225	+0.5	+0.5	−0.1	−0.1
Suderoogsand	54 25N	8 30E	+0116	+0102	+0038	+0122	+0.4	+0.3	−0.1	0.0
Hever Husum	54 28N	9 01E	+0205	+0152	+0118	+0200	+1.1	+1.0	0.0	0.0
Suederhoeft	54 16N	8 42E	+0103	+0056	+0051	+0112	+0.7	+0.6	0.0	0.0
Eidersperrwerk	54 16N	8 51E	+0120	+0115	+0130	+0155	+0.7	+0.6	−0.1	0.0
Linnenplate	54 13N	8 40E	+0047	+0046	+0034	+0046	+0.7	+0.6	0.0	−0.1
Büsum	54 07N	8 52E	+0054	+0049	−0001	+0027	+0.9	+0.8	0.0	0.0

			0200	0800	0200	0900				
CUXHAVEN	53 52N	8 43E	and	and	and	and	**3.3**	**2.9**	**0.4**	**0.0**
standard port			1400	2000	1400	2100				
River Elbe										
Grober Vogelsand	54 00N	8 29E	−0044	−0046	−0101	−0103	0.0	0.0	+0.1	−0.1
Scharhörn	53 58N	8 28E	−0045	−0047	−0101	−0103	+0.1	+0.1	+0.1	0.0
Otterndorf	53 50N	8 52E	+0025	+0025	+0022	+0022	−0.1	−0.1	−0.1	0.0
Brunsbüttel	53 53N	9 08E	+0057	+0105	+0121	+0112	0.0	0.0	0.0	0.0

Location	Lat	Long	High Water		Low Water		MHWS	MHWN	MLWN	MLWS
Glückstadt	53 47N	9 25E	+0205	+0214	+0220	+0213	-0.2	-0.2	-0.2	0.0
Stadersand	53 38N	9 32E	+0241	+0245	+0300	+0254	-0.1	0.0	-0.2	0.0
Schulau	53 34N	9 42E	+0304	+0315	+0337	+0321	+0.1	+0.1	-0.3	-0.1
Seemannshoeft	53 32N	9 53E	+0324	+0332	+0403	+0347	+0.2	+0.2	-0.4	-0.2
Hamburg	53 33N	9 58E	+0338	+0346	+0422	+0406	+0.3	+0.4	-0.4	-0.2
Harburg	53 28N	10 00E	+0344	+0350	+0430	+0416	+0.4	+0.3	-0.4	-0.2

			0200	0800	0200	0900				
WILHELMSHAVEN	53 31N	8 09E	and	and	and	and	4.3	3.8	0.6	0.0
standard port			1400	2000	1400	2100				
River Weser										
Alter Weser Lt Hse	53 32N	8 08E	-0055	-0048	-0015	-0029	-1.1	-1.0	-0.2	-0.1
Bremerhaven	53 33N	8 34E	+0029	+0046	+0033	+0038	-0.2	-0.2	-0.2	-0.1
Nordenham	53 28N	8 29E	+0051	+0109	+0055	+0058	-0.2	-0.1	-0.4	-0.3
Brake	53 19N	8 29E	+0120	+0119	+0143	+0155	-0.2	-0.2	-0.4	-0.2
Elsfleth	53 16N	8 29E	+0137	+0137	+0206	+0216	-0.2	-0.1	-0.3	-0.1
Vegesack	53 10N	8 37E	+0208	+0204	+0250	+0254	-0.3	-0.2	-0.5	-0.2
Bremen	53 07N	8 43E	+0216	+0211	+0311	+0314	-0.2	-0.2	-0.6	-0.3
River Jade										
Wangerooge East	53 46N	7 59E	-0058	-0053	-0024	-0034	-0.9	-0.9	-0.1	0.0
Wangerooge West	53 47N	7 52E	-0101	-0058	-0035	-0045	-1.0	-1.0	-0.2	0.0
Schillig	53 42N	8 03E	-0031	-0025	-0006	-0014	-0.7	-0.6	0.0	0.0
Hooksiel	53 39N	8 05E	-0023	-0022	-0008	-0012	-0.5	-0.4	0.0	0.0

			0200	0700	0200	0800				
HELGOLAND	54 11N	7 53E	and	and	and	and	2.7	2.4	0.4	0.0
standard port			1400	1900	1400	2000				
East Frisian Islands and coast										
Spiekeroog	53 45N	7 41E	+0003	-0003	-0031	-0012	+0.4	+0.3	0.0	0.0
Neuharlingersiel	53 42N	7 42E	+0014	+0008	-0024	-0013	+0.5	+0.4	0.0	0.0
Langeoog	53 43N	7 30E	+0003	-0001	-0034	-0018	+0.4	+0.2	0.0	0.0
Norderney Riffgat	53 42N	7 09E	-0024	-0030	-0056	-0045	+0.1	0.0	0.0	0.0
Norddeich Hafen	53 37N	7 10E	-0018	-0017	-0029	-0012	+0.2	+0.1	0.0	0.0
Juist	53 40N	7 00E	-0026	-0032	-0019	-0008	+0.2	+0.1	0.0	0.0
River Ems										
Memmert	53 38N	6 54E	-0032	-0038	-0114	-0103	+0.1	+0.1	0.0	0.0
Borkum Fischerbalje	53 33N	6 45E	-0048	-0052	-0124	-0105	0.0	0.0	0.0	0.0
Emshorn	53 30N	6 50E	-0037	-0041	-0108	-0047	+0.1	+0.1	0.0	0.0
Knock	53 20N	7 02E	+0018	+0005	-0028	+0004	+0.6	+0.6	0.0	0.0
Emden	53 20N	7 11E	+0041	+0028	-0011	+0022	+0.8	+0.8	0.0	0.0

NETHERLANDS Time Zone –0100

			0200	0700	0200	0800				
HELGOLAND	54 11N	7 53E	and	and	and	and	2.7	2.4	0.4	0.0
standard port			1400	1900	1400	2000				
Nieuwe Statenzijl	53 14N	7 13E	+0110	+0135	no data	no data	+1.1	+1.0	no data	
Delfzijl	53 20N	6 56E	+0020	-0005	-0040	0000	+0.8	+0.8	+0.2	+0.2
Eemshaven	53 26N	6 52E	-0025	-0045	-0115	-0045	+0.5	+0.4	+0.3	+0.3
Schiermonnikoog	53 28N	6 12E	-0120	-0130	-0240	-0220	+0.1	+0.1	+0.3	+0.3
Waddenzee										
Lauwersoog	53 25N	6 12E	-0130	-0145	-0235	-0220	+0.1	+0.1	+0.2	+0.2
Nes	53 26N	5 47E	-0135	-0150	-0245	-0225	+0.1	0.0	+0.2	+0.2
Holwerd	53 24N	5 53E	-0120	-0135	-0155	-0135	+0.2	+0.2	+0.4	+0.3
West Terschelling	53 22N	5 13E	-0220	-0250	-0335	-0310	-0.4	-0.4	+0.1	+0.2
Vlieland–Haven	53 18N	5 06E	-0250	-0320	-0355	-0330	-0.4	-0.4	+0.1	+0.2
Harlingen	53 10N	5 25E	-0155	-0245	-0210	-0130	-0.5	-0.5	-0.1	+0.2
Kornwerderzand	53 04N	5 20E	-0210	-0315	-0300	-0215	-0.5	-0.5	-0.1	+0.2
Den Oever	52 56N	5 02E	-0245	-0410	-0400	-0305	-0.8	-0.7	0.0	+0.2
Oude Schild	53 02N	4 51E	-0310	-0420	-0445	-0400	-1.0	-0.8	0.0	+0.2
Den Helder	52 58N	4 45E	-0410	-0520	-0520	-0430	-1.0	-0.8	0.0	+0.2
Noordwinning Platform K13–A	53 13N	3 13E	-0420	-0430	-0520	-0530	-1.1	-1.1	+0.1	+0.1

			0300	0900	0400	1000				
VLISSINGEN	51 27N	3 36E	and	and	and	and	4.7	3.8	0.8	0.2
standard port			1500	2100	1600	2200				
Jmuiden	52 28N	4 35E	+0145	+0140	+0305	+0325	-2.6	-2.1	-0.5	0.0
Scheveningen	52 06N	4 16E	+0105	+0100	+0220	+0245	-2.6	-2.1	-0.6	0.0
Europlatform	52 00N	3 17E	+0005	-0005	-0030	-0055	-2.6	-2.1	-0.5	0.0

TIDES

Location	Lat	Long	High Water		Low Water		MHWS	MHWN	MLWN	MLWS
Nieuwe Waterweg										
HOEK VAN HOLLAND			*standard port*							
Maassluis	51 55N	4 15E	+0155	+0115	+0100	+0310	-2.7	-2.1	-0.6	0.0
Nieuwe Maas Vlaardingen	51 54N	4 21E	+0150	+0120	+0130	+0330	-2.6	-2.1	-0.6	0.0
Lek										
Krimpen Aan de Lek	51 53N	4 38E	+0225	+0200	+0325	+0445	-3.1	-2.5	-0.7	-0.1
Schoonhoven	51 57N	4 51E	+0415	+0315	+0435	+0545	-3.1	-2.3	-0.4	+0.2
Oude Maas										
Spijkenisse	51 52N	4 20E	+0145	+0120	+0145	+0310	-2.9	-2.3	-0.6	0.0
Goidschalxoord	51 50N	4 27E	+0200	+0140	+0240	+0410	-3.3	-2.7	-0.7	0.0
Merwede										
Dordrecht	51 49N	4 39E	+0220	+0210	+0420	+0510	-3.7	-3.0	-0.7	-0.1
Werkendam	51 49N	4 53E	+0425	+0410	+0550	+0650	-4.0	-3.2	-0.5	+0.1
Moerdijk	51 42N	4 36E	+0525	+0450	+0520	-0605	-4.2	-3.3	-0.6	+0.1
Haringvlietsluizen	51 50N	4 02E	+0015	+0015	+0015	-0020	-1.7	-1.6	-0.4	+0.1
Brouwershavensche gat	51 45N	3 49E	0000	+0010	0000	-0030	-1.5	-1.3	-0.3	+0.1
Ooster Schelde										
Roompot Buiten	51 37N	3 40E	-0015	+0005	+0005	-0020	-1.1	-0.9	-0.2	+0.1
Stavenisse	51 36N	4 01E	+0150	+0120	+0055	+0115	-1.2	-0.8	-0.4	+0.1
Lodijkse Gat	51 30N	4 12E	+0145	+0125	+0105	+0115	-0.6	-0.3	-0.2	+0.1
Zijpe Philipsdam *West*	51 40N	4 11E	+0215	+0125	+0100	+0110	-1.1	-0.7	-0.4	0.0
Walcheren Westkapelle	51 31N	3 27E	-0025	-0015	-0010	-0025	-0.5	-0.5	-0.1	+0.1
Westerschelde										
Terneuzen	51 20N	3 50E	+0020	+0020	+0020	+0030	+0.4	+0.4	0.0	+0.1
Hansweert	51 27N	4 00E	+0100	+0050	+0040	+0100	+0.6	+0.7	0.0	+0.1
Bath	51 24N	4 13E	+0125	+0115	+0115	+0140	+1.0	+1.0	0.0	+0.1

BELGIUM *Time Zone –0100*

Location	Lat	Long	High Water		Low Water		MHWS	MHWN	MLWN	MLWS
Antwerpen	51 21N	4 14E	+0128	+0116	+0121	+0144	+1.2	+1.0	+0.1	+0.1
Zeebrugge	51 21N	3 12E	-0035	-0015	-0020	-0035	+0.2	+0.2	+0.4	+0.2
Blankenberge	51 19N	3 07E	-0040	-0040	-0040	-0040	-0.3	0.0	+0.3	+0.2
Oostende	51 14N	2 56E	-0055	-0040	-0030	-0045	+0.5	+0.5	+0.4	+0.2
Nieuwpoort	51 09N	2 43E	-0110	-0050	-0035	-0045	+0.7	+0.6	+0.5	+0.2

FRANCE *Time Zone –0100*

Location	Lat	Long	High Water		Low Water		MHWS	MHWN	MLWN	MLWS
DUNKERQUE	51 03N	2 22E	0200 and 1400	0800 and 2000	0200 and 1400	0900 and 2100	6.0	5.0	1.5	0.6
standard port										
Gravelines	51 01N	2 06E	-0005	-0015	-0005	+0005	+0.3	+0.1	-0.1	-0.1
Sandettie Bank	51 09N	1 47E	-0015	-0025	-0020	-0005	+0.1	-0.1	-0.1	-0.1
Calais	51 58N	1 51E	-0020	-0030	-0015	-0005	+1.2	+0.9	+0.6	+0.3
Wissant	50 53N	1 40E	-0035	-0050	-0030	-0010	+1.9	+1.5	+0.8	+0.4
DIEPPE	49 56N	1 05E	0100 and 1300	0600 and 1800	0100 and 1300	0700 and 1900	9.3	7.4	2.5	0.8
standard port										
Boulogne	50 44N	1 35E	+0014	+0027	+0035	+0033	-0.4	-0.2	+0.1	+0.3
Le Touquet, Étaples	50 31N	1 35E	+0007	+0017	+0032	+0032	+0.2	+0.3	+0.4	+0.4
Berck	50 24N	1 34E	+0007	+0017	+0028	+0028	+0.5	+0.5	+0.4	+0.4
La Somme										
Le Hourdel	50 13N	1 34E	+0020	+0020	no data	no data	+0.8	+0.6	no data	
St Valéry	50 11N	1 37E	+0035	+0035	no data	no data	+0.9	+0.7	no data	
Cayeux	50 11N	1 29E	0000	+0005	+0015	+0010	+0.4	+0.5	+0.5	+0.5
Le Tréport	50 04N	1 22E	+0005	0000	+0007	+0007	+0.1	+0.1	0.0	+0.1
St. Valéry–en–Caux	49 52N	0 42E	-0005	-0005	-0015	-0020	-0.5	-0.4	-0.1	-0.1
Fécamp	49 46N	0 22E	-0015	-0010	-0030	-0040	-1.0	-0.6	+0.3	+0.4
Etretat	49 42N	0 12E	-0020	-0020	-0045	-0050	-1.2	-0.8	+0.3	+0.4
LE HAVRE	49 29N	0 07E	0000 and 1200	0500 and 1700	0000 and 1200	0700 and 1900	7.9	6.6	2.8	1.2
standard port										
Antifer *Le Havre*	49 39N	0 09E	+0025	+0015	+0005	-0007	+0.1	0.0	0.0	0.0
La Seine										
Honfleur	49 25N	0 14E	-0135	-0135	+0015	+0040	+0.1	+0.1	+0.1	+0.3
Tancarville	49 28N	0 28E	-0105	-0100	+0105	+0140	-0.1	-0.1	0.0	+1.0
Quillebeuf	49 28N	0 32E	-0045	-0050	+0120	+0200	0.0	0.0	+0.2	+1.4
Vatteville	49 29N	0 40E	+0005	-0020	+0225	+0250	0.0	-0.1	+0.8	+2.3
Caudebec	49 32N	0 44E	+0020	-0015	+0230	+0300	-0.3	-0.2	+0.9	+2.4
Heurteauville	49 27N	0 49E	+0110	+0025	+0310	+0330	-0.5	-0.2	+1.1	+2.7

Location	Lat	Long	High Water		Low Water		MHWS	MHWN	MLWN	MLWS
Duclair	49 29N	0 53E	+0225	+0150	+0355	+0410	−0.4	−0.3	+1.4	+3.3
Rouen	49 27N	1 06E	+0440	+0415	+0525	+0525	−0.2	−0.1	+1.6	+3.6
Trouville	49 22N	0 05E	−0100	−0010	0000	+0005	+0.4	+0.3	+0.3	+0.1
Dives	49 18N	0 05W	−0100	−0010	0000	0000	+0.3	+0.2	+0.2	+0.1
Ouistreham	49 17N	0 15W	−0045	−0010	−0005	0000	−0.3	−0.3	−0.2	−0.3
Courseulles−sur−Mer	49 20N	0 27W	−0045	−0015	−0020	−0025	−0.5	−0.5	−0.1	−0.1
Arromanches	49 21N	0 37W	−0055	−0025	−0027	−0035	−0.6	−0.6	−0.2	−0.2
Port−en−Bessin	49 21N	0 45W	−0055	−0030	−0030	−0035	−0.7	−0.7	−0.2	−0.1
Alpha−Baie de Seine	49 49N	0 20W	+0030	+0020	−0005	−0020	−1.0	−0.9	−0.4	−0.2
			0300	1000	0400	1000				
CHERBOURG	49 39N	1 38W	and	and	and	and	**6.4**	**5.0**	**2.5**	**1.1**
standard port			1500	2200	1600	2200				
Rade de la Capelle	49 25N	1 05W	+0115	+0050	+0130	+0117	+0.8	+0.9	+0.1	+0.1
Iles Saint Marcouf	49 30N	1 08W	+0118	+0052	+0125	+0110	+0.6	+0.7	+0.1	+0.1
St. Vaast−la−Hougue	49 34N	1 16W	+0120	+0050	+0120	+0115	+0.3	+0.5	0.0	−0.1
Barfleur	49 40N	1 15W	+0110	+0055	+0052	+0052	+0.1	+0.3	0.0	0.0
Omonville	49 42N	1 50W	−0010	−0010	−0015	−0015	−0.1	−0.1	0.0	0.0
Goury	49 43N	1 57W	−0100	−0040	−0105	−0120	+1.7	+1.6	+1.0	+0.3

CHANNEL ISLANDS *Time Zone UT*

	Lat	Long	High Water		Low Water		MHWS	MHWN	MLWN	MLWS
			0300	0900	0200	0900				
ST. HELIER	49 11N	2 07W	and	and	and	and	**11.0**	**8.1**	**4.0**	**1.4**
standard port			1500	2100	1400	2100				
Alderney Braye	49 43N	2 12W	+0050	+0040	+0025	+0105	−4.8	−3.4	−1.5	−0.5
Sark Maseline Pier	49 26N	2 21W	+0005	+0015	+0005	+0010	−2.1	−1.5	−0.6	−0.3
Guernsey St PETER PORT	49 27N	2 31W		*standard port*						
Jersey										
St. Catherine Bay	49 13N	2 01W	0000	+0010	+0010	+0010	0.0	−0.1	0.0	+0.1
Bouley Bay	49 14N	2 05W	+0002	+0002	+0004	+0004	−0.3	−0.3	−0.1	−0.1
Les Ecrehou	49 17N	1 56W	+0005	+0009	+0011	+0009	−0.2	+0.1	−0.2	0.0
Les Minquiers	48 57N	2 08W	−0014	−0018	−0001	−0008	+0.5	+0.6	+0.1	+0.1

FRANCE *Time Zone −0100*

	Lat	Long	High Water		Low Water		MHWS	MHWN	MLWN	MLWS
			0100	0800	0300	0800				
ST. MALO	48 38N	2 02W	and	and	and	and	**12.2**	**9.3**	**4.2**	**1.5**
standard port			1300	2000	1500	2000				
Iles Chausey	48 52N	1 49W	+0005	+0005	+0015	+0015	+0.8	+0.7	+0.6	+0.4
Diélette	49 33N	1 52W	+0045	+0035	+0020	+0035	−2.5	−1.9	−0.7	−0.3
Carteret	49 22N	1 47W	+0030	+0020	+0015	+0030	−1.6	−1.2	−0.5	−0.2
Portbail	49 18N	1 45W	+0030	+0025	+0025	+0030	−0.8	−0.6	−0.2	−0.1
St. Germain sur Ay	49 14N	1 36W	+0025	+0025	+0035	+0035	−0.7	−0.5	0.0	+0.1
Le Sénéquet	49 05N	1 40W	+0015	+0015	+0023	+0023	−0.3	−0.3	+0.1	+0.1
Regnéville sur Mer	49 01N	1 33W	+0010	+0010	+0030	+0020	+0.4	+0.3	+0.2	0.0
Granville	48 50N	1 36W	+0005	+0005	+0020	+0010	+0.7	+0.5	+0.3	+0.1
Cancale	48 40N	1 51W	−0002	−0002	+0010	+0010	+0.8	+0.6	+0.3	+0.1
Ile des Hebihens	48 37N	2 11W	−0002	−0002	−0005	−0005	−0.2	−0.2	−0.1	−0.1
St. Cast	48 38N	2 15W	−0002	−0002	−0005	−0005	−0.2	−0.2	−0.1	−0.1
Erquy	48 38N	2 28W	−0010	−0005	−0023	−0017	−0.6	−0.5	0.0	0.0
Dahouët	48 35N	2 34W	−0010	−0010	−0025	−0020	−0.9	−0.7	−0.2	−0.2
Le Légué *(buoy)*	48 34N	2 41W	−0010	−0005	−0020	−0015	−0.8	−0.5	−0.2	−0.1
Binic	48 36N	2 49W	−0008	−0008	−0030	−0015	−0.8	−0.7	−0.2	−0.2
Portrieux	48 38N	2 49W	−0010	−0005	−0025	−0020	−0.9	−0.7	−0.2	−0.2
Paimpol	48 47N	3 02W	−0010	−0005	−0035	−0025	−1.4	−1.0	−0.4	−0.2
Ile de Bréhat	48 51N	3 00W	−0015	−0010	−0045	−0035	−1.9	−1.4	−0.6	−0.3
Les Héaux de Bréhat	48 55N	3 05W	−0020	−0015	−0055	−0035	−2.4	−1.7	−0.7	−0.3
Lézardrieux	48 47N	3 06W	−0020	−0015	−0055	−0045	−1.7	−1.3	−0.5	−0.2
Port−Béni	48 51N	3 10W	−0025	−0025	−0105	−0050	−2.4	−1.7	−0.6	−0.2
Tréguier	48 47N	3 13W	−0020	−0020	−0100	−0045	−2.3	−1.6	−0.6	−0.2
Perros−Guirec	48 49N	3 28W	−0040	−0045	−0120	−0105	−2.9	−2.0	−0.8	−0.3
Ploumanac'h	48 50N	3 29W	−0035	−0040	−0120	−0100	−2.9	−2.0	−0.7	−0.2
			0000	0600	0000	0600				
BREST	48 23N	4 30W	and	and	and	and	**6.9**	**5.4**	**2.6**	**1.0**
standard port			1200	1800	1200	1800				
Trébeurden	48 46N	3 35W	+0100	+0110	+0120	+0100	+2.3	+1.9	+0.9	+0.4
Locquirec	48 42N	3 38W	+0058	+0108	+0120	+0100	+2.2	+1.8	+0.8	+0.3
Anse de Primel	48 43N	3 50W	+0100	+0110	+0120	+0100	+2.1	+1.7	+0.8	+0.3
Rade de Morlaix Morlaix	48 41N	3 53W	+0055	+0105	+0115	+0055	+2.0	+1.7	+0.8	+0.3
Roscoff	48 43N	3 58W	+0055	+0105	+0115	+0055	+1.9	+1.6	+0.8	+0.3

Location	Lat	Long	High Water		Low Water		MHWS	MHWN	MLWN	MLWS
Ile de Batz	48 44N	4 00W	+0045	+0100	+0105	+0055	+2.0	+1.6	+0.9	+0.4
Brignogan	48 40N	4 19W	+0040	+0045	+0058	+0038	+1.5	+1.2	+0.6	+0.2
L'Aber Vrac'h Ile Cézon	48 36N	4 34W	+0030	+0030	+0040	+0035	+0.8	+0.7	+0.2	0.0
Aber Benoit	48 35N	4 37W	+0022	+0025	+0035	+0020	+0.9	+0.7	+0.3	+0.1
Portsall	48 34N	4 43W	+0015	+0020	+0025	+0015	+0.6	+0.5	+0.1	0.0
L'Aber Ildut	48 28N	4 45W	+0010	+0010	+0023	+0010	+0.4	+0.3	0.0	0.0
Ouessant Baie de Lampaul	48 27N	5 06W	+0005	+0005	−0005	+0003	0.0	−0.1	−0.1	0.0
Molene	48 24N	4 58W	+0012	+0012	+0017	+0017	+0.4	+0.3	+0.2	+0.1
Le Conquet	48 22N	4 47W	−0005	0000	+0007	+0007	−0.1	−0.1	−0.1	0.0
Le Trez Hir	48 21N	4 42W	−0010	−0005	−0008	−0008	−0.3	−0.3	−0.1	0.0
Camaret	48 17N	4 35W	−0010	−0010	−0013	−0013	−0.3	−0.3	−0.1	0.0
Morgat	48 13N	4 30W	−0008	−0008	−0020	−0010	−0.4	−0.4	−0.2	0.0
Douarnenez	48 06N	4 19W	−0010	−0015	−0018	−0008	−0.5	−0.5	−0.3	−0.1
Ile de Sein	48 02N	4 51W	−0005	−0005	−0010	−0005	−0.7	−0.6	−0.2	−0.1
Audierne	48 01N	4 33W	−0035	−0030	−0035	−0030	−1.7	−1.3	−0.6	−0.2
Le Guilvinec	47 48N	4 17W	−0010	−0025	−0025	−0015	−1.8	−1.4	−0.6	−0.1
Lesconil	47 48N	4 13W	−0008	−0028	−0028	−0018	−1.9	−1.4	−0.6	−0.1
Pont l'Abbe River Loctudy	47 50N	4 10W	−0010	−0030	−0030	−0020	−2.0	−1.6	−0.7	−0.3
Odet River										
Bénodet	47 53N	4 07W	0000	−0020	−0023	−0013	−1.8	−1.4	−0.6	−0.2
Corniguel	47 58N	4 06W	+0015	+0010	−0015	−0010	−2.0	−1.6	−1.0	−0.7
Concarneau	47 52N	3 55W	−0010	−0030	−0030	−0020	−1.9	−1.5	−0.7	−0.2
Iles de Glenan Ile de Penfret	47 44N	3 57W	−0005	−0030	−0028	−0018	−1.9	−1.5	−0.7	−0.2
Port Louis	47 42N	3 21W	+0004	−0021	−0022	−0012	−1.8	−1.4	−0.6	−0.1
Lorient	47 45N	3 21W	+0003	−0022	−0020	−0010	−1.8	−1.4	−0.6	−0.2
Hennebont	47 48N	3 17W	+0015	−0017	+0005	+0003	−1.9	−1.5	−0.8	−0.2
Ile de Groix Port Tudy	47 39N	3 27W	0000	−0025	−0025	−0015	−1.8	−1.4	−0.6	−0.1
Port d'Etel	47 39N	3 12W	+0020	−0010	+0030	+0010	−2.0	−1.3	−0.4	+0.5
Port–Haliguen	47 29N	3 06W	+0015	−0020	−0015	−0010	−1.7	−1.3	−0.6	−0.3
Port Maria	47 29N	3 08W	+0010	−0025	−0025	−0015	−1.6	−1.3	−0.6	−0.1
Belle–Ile Le Palais	47 21N	3 09W	+0007	−0028	−0025	−0020	−1.8	−1.4	−0.7	−0.3
Crac'h River La Trinité	47 35N	3 01W	+0020	−0020	−0015	−0005	−1.5	−1.1	−0.5	−0.2
Morbihan										
Port–Navalo	47 33N	2 55W	+0030	−0005	−0010	−0005	−2.0	−1.5	−0.8	−0.3
Auray	47 40N	2 59W	+0055	0000	+0020	+0005	−2.0	−1.4	−0.8	−0.2
Arradon	47 37N	2 50W	+0155	+0145	+0145	+0130	−3.7	−2.7	−1.6	−0.5
Vannes	47 39N	2 46W	+0220	+0200	+0200	+0125	−3.6	−2.7	−1.6	−0.5
Le Logeo	47 33N	2 51W	+0155	+0140	+0145	+0125	−3.7	−2.7	−1.6	−0.5
Port du Crouesty	47 32N	2 54W	+0013	−0022	−0017	−0012	−1.6	−1.2	−0.6	−0.3
Ile de Houat	47 24N	2 57W	+0010	−0025	−0020	−0015	−1.7	−1.3	−0.6	−0.3
Ile de Hoedic	47 20N	2 52W	+0010	−0035	−0027	−0022	−1.8	−1.4	−0.7	−0.3
Pénerf	47 31N	2 37W	+0020	−0025	−0015	−0015	−1.5	−1.1	−0.6	−0.3
Tréhiguier	47 30N	2 27W	+0035	−0020	−0005	−0010	−1.4	−1.0	−0.5	−0.3
Le Croisic	47 18N	2 31W	+0015	−0040	−0020	−0015	−1.5	−1.1	−0.6	−0.3
Le Pouliguen	47 17N	2 25W	+0020	−0025	−0020	−0025	−1.5	−1.1	−0.6	−0.3
Le Grand–Charpentier	47 13N	2 19W	+0015	−0045	−0025	−0020	−1.5	−1.1	−0.6	−0.2
Pornichet	47 16N	2 21W	+0020	−0045	−0022	−0022	−1.4	−1.0	−0.5	−0.2
La Loire										
St. Nazaire	47 16N	2 12W	+0030	−0040	−0010	−0010	−1.1	−0.8	−0.4	−0.2
Donges	47 18N	2 05W	+0035	−0035	+0005	+0005	−1.0	−0.7	−0.5	−0.4
Cordemais	47 17N	1 54W	+0055	−0005	+0105	+0030	−0.7	−0.5	−0.7	−0.4
Le Pellerin	47 12N	1 46W	+0110	+0010	+0145	+0100	−0.7	−0.5	−0.9	−0.4
Nantes Chantenay	47 12N	1 35W	+0135	+0055	+0215	+0125	−0.6	−0.3	−0.8	−0.1
			0500	1100	0500	1100				
BREST	48 23N	4 30W	and	and	and	and	**6.9**	**5.4**	**2.6**	**1.0**
standard port			1700	2300	1700	2300				
Pointe de Saint–Gildas	47 08N	2 15W	−0045	+0025	−0020	−0020	−1.3	−1.0	−0.5	−0.2
Pornic	47 06N	2 07W	−0050	+0030	−0010	−0010	−1.1	−0.8	−0.4	−0.2
Ile de Noirmoutier L'Herbaudière	47 02N	2 18W	−0047	+0023	−0020	−0020	−1.4	−1.0	−0.5	−0.2
Fromentine	46 54N	2 10W	−0050	+0020	−0020	+0010	−1.6	−1.2	−0.7	−0.0
Ile de Yeu Port Joinville	46 44N	2 21W	−0040	+0015	−0030	−0035	−1.9	−1.4	−0.7	−0.3
St. Gilles–Croix–de–Vie	46 41N	1 56W	−0030	+0015	−0032	−0032	−1.8	−1.3	−0.6	−0.3
Les Sables d'Olonne	46 30N	1 48W	−0030	+0015	−0035	−0035	−1.7	−1.3	−0.6	−0.3
			0000	0600	0500	1200				
POINTE DE GRAVE	45 34N	1 04W	and	and	and	and	**5.4**	**4.4**	**2.1**	**1.0**
standard port			1200	1800	1700	2400				
Ile de Ré St Martin	46 12N	1 22W	+0015	−0030	−0025	−0020	+0.6	+0.5	+0.3	−0.1
La Pallice	46 10N	1 13W	+0015	−0030	−0025	−0020	+0.6	+0.5	+0.3	−0.1
La Rochelle	46 09N	1 09W	+0015	−0030	−0025	−0020	+0.6	+0.5	+0.3	−0.1

Location	Lat	Long	High Water		Low Water		MHWS	MHWN	MLWN	MLWS
Ile d'Aix	46 01N	1 10W	+0015	−0040	−0030	−0025	+0.7	+0.5	+0.3	−0.1
La Charente Rochefort	45 57N	0 58W	+0035	−0010	+0030	+0125	+1.1	+0.9	+0.1	−0.2
Le Chapus	45 51N	1 11W	+0015	−0040	−0025	−0015	+0.6	+0.6	+0.4	+0.2
La Cayenne	45 47N	1 08W	+0030	−0015	−0010	−0005	+0.2	+0.2	+0.3	0.0
Pointe de Gatseau	45 48N	1 14W	+0005	−0005	−0015	−0025	−0.1	−0.1	+0.2	+0.2
La Gironde										
Royan	45 37N	1 01W	0000	−0005	−0005	−0005	−0.3	−0.2	0.0	0.0
Richard	45 27N	0 56W	+0018	+0018	+0028	+0033	−0.1	−0.1	−0.4	−0.5
Lamena	45 20N	0 48W	+0035	+0045	+0100	+0125	+0.2	+0.1	−0.5	−0.3
Pauillac	45 12N	0 45W	+0100	+0100	+0135	+0205	+0.1	0.0	−1.0	−0.5
La Reuille	45 03N	0 36W	+0135	+0145	+0230	+0305	−0.2	−0.3	−1.3	−0.7
La Garonne										
Le Marquis	45 00N	0 33W	+0145	+0150	+0247	+0322	−0.3	−0.4	− 1.5	−0.9
Bordeaux	44 52N	0 33W	+0200	+0225	+0330	+0405	−0.1	−0.2	−1.7	−1.0
La Dordogne Libourne	44 55N	0 15W	+0250	+0305	+0525	+0540	−0.7	−0.9	−2.0	−0.4
Bassin d' Arcachon										
Cap Ferret	44 37N	1 15W	−0015	+0005	−0005	+0015	−1.4	−1.2	−0.8	−0.5
Arcachon *Eyrac*	44 40N	1 10W	+0010	+0025	0000	+0020	−1.1	−1.0	−0.8	−0.6
L'Adour Boucau	43 31N	1 31W	−0030	−0035	−0025	−0040	−1.2	−1.1	−0.4	−0.3
St Jean de Luz Socoa	43 23N	1 40W	−0040	−0045	−0030	−0045	−1.1	−1.1	−0.6	−0.4

SPAIN *Time Zone −0100*

Location	Lat	Long	High Water		Low Water		MHWS	MHWN	MLWN	MLWS
Pasajes	43 20N	1 56W	−0050	−0030	−0015	−0045	−1.2	−1.3	−0.5	−0.5
San Sebastian	43 19N	1 59W	−0110	−0030	−0020	−0040	−1.2	−1.2	−0.5	−0.4
Guetaria	43 18N	2 12W	−0110	−0030	−0020	−0040	−1.0	−1.0	−0.5	−0.4
Lequeitio	43 22N	2 30W	−0115	−0035	−0025	−0045	−1.2	−1.2	−0.5	−0.4
Bermeo	43 25N	2 43W	−0055	−0015	−0005	−0025	−0.8	−0.7	−0.5	−0.4
Abra de Bilbao	43 21N	3 02W	−0125	−0045	−0035	−0055	−1.2	−1.2	−0.5	−0.4
Portugalete *Bilbao*	43 20N	3 02W	−0100	−0020	−0010	−0030	−0.7	−1.2	−0.2	−0.6
Castro Urdiales	43 23N	3 13W	−0040	−0120	−0020	−0110	−1.4	−1.5	−0.6	−0.6
Ria de Santona	43 26N	3 28W	−0005	−0045	+0015	−0035	−0.7	−1.2	−0.3	−0.7
Santander	43 28N	3 47W	−0020	−0100	0000	−0050	−0.7	−1.2	−0.3	−0.7
Ria de Suances	43 27N	4 03W	0000	−0030	+0020	−0020	−1.5	−1.5	−0.6	−0.6
San Vicente de la Barquera	43 23N	4 24W	−0020	−0100	0000	−0050	−1.5	−1.5	−0.6	−0.6
Ria de Tina Mayor	43 24N	4 31W	−0020	−0100	0000	−0050	−1.4	−1.5	−0.6	−0.6
Ribadesella	43 28N	5 04W	+0005	−0020	+0020	−0020	−1.4	−1.3	−0.6	−0.4
Gijon	43 34N	5 42W	−0005	−0030	+0010	−0030	−1.0	−1.4	−0.4	−0.7
Luanco	43 37N	5 47W	−0010	−0035	+0005	−0035	−1.4	−1.3	−0.6	−0.4
Aviles	43 35N	5 56W	−0100	−0040	−0015	−0050	−1.2	−1.6	−0.5	−0.7
San Esteban de Pravia	43 34N	6 05W	−0005	−0030	+0010	−0030	−1.2	−1.3	−0.6	−0.4
Luarca	43 33N	6 32W	+0010	−0015	+0025	−0015	−1.2	−1.1	−0.5	−0.3
Ribadeo	43 33N	7 02W	+0010	−0015	+0025	−0015	−1.3	−1.5	−0.7	−0.8
Burela	43 39N	7 21W	+0010	−0015	+0025	−0015	−1.5	−1.5	−0.7	−0.6
Ria de Vivero	43 43N	7 36W	+0010	−0015	+0025	−0015	−1.4	−1.3	−0.6	−0.4
Santa Marta de Ortigueira	43 41N	7 51W	−0020	0000	+0020	−0010	−1.3	−1.2	−0.6	−0.4
El Ferrol del Caudillo	43 28N	8 16W	−0045	−0100	−0010	−0105	−1.6	−1.4	−0.7	−0.4
La Coruna	43 22N	8 24W	−0110	−0050	−0030	−0100	−1.6	−1.6	−0.6	−0.5
Ria de Corme	43 16N	8 58W	−0025	−0005	+0015	−0015	−1.7	−1.6	−0.6	−0.5
Ria de Camarinas	43 08N	9 11W	−0115	−0055	0000	−0105	−1.6	−1.6	−0.6	−0.5

Location	Lat	Long	High Water		Low Water		MHWS	MHWN	MLWN	MLWS
LISBOA	38 42N	9 07W	0500 and 1700	1000 and 2200	0300 and 1500	0800 and 2000	3.8	3.0	1.5	0.6
standard port										
Corcubion	42 57N	9 12W	+0055	+0110	+0120	+0135	−0.5	−0.4	−0.3	−0.1
Muros	42 46N	9 03W	+0050	+0105	+0115	+0130	−0.3	−0.3	−0.2	−0.1
Ria de Arosa Villagarcia	42 37N	8 47W	+0040	+0100	+0110	+0120	−0.3	−0.2	−0.2	−0.1
Ria de Pontevedra Marin	42 24N	8 42W	+0050	+0110	+0120	+0130	−0.5	−0.4	−0.2	−0.1
Vigo	42 15N	8 43W	+0040	+0100	+0105	+0125	−0.4	−0.3	−0.2	−0.1
Bayona	42 07N	8 51W	+0035	+0050	+0100	+0115	−0.3	−0.3	−0.2	−0.1
La Guardia	41 54N	8 53W	+0040	+0055	+0105	+0120	−0.5	−0.4	−0.3	−0.2

Location	Lat	Long	High Water		Low Water		MHWS	MHWN	MLWN	MLWS
LISBOA	38 42N	9 07W	0400 and 1600	0900 and 2100	0400 and 1600	0900 and 2100	3.8	3.0	1.5	0.6
standard port										

PORTUGAL *Time Zone UT*

Location	Lat	Long	High Water		Low Water		MHWS	MHWN	MLWN	MLWS
Viana do Castelo	41 41N	8 50W	−0020	0000	+0010	+0015	−0.3	−0.4	−0.1	−0.1
Esposende	41 32N	8 47W	−0020	0000	+0010	+0015	−0.6	−0.5	−0.2	−0.1
Povoa de Varzim	41 22N	8 46W	−0020	0000	+0010	+0015	−0.3	−0.3	−0.1	−0.1

TIDES

Location	Lat	Long	High Water		Low Water		MHWS	MHWN	MLWN	MLWS
Porto de Leixoes	41 11N	8 42W	-0025	-0010	0000	+0010	-0.3	-0.4	-0.1	-0.1
Rio Douro										
Entrance	41 09N	8 40W	-0010	+0005	+0015	+0025	-0.6	-0.5	-0.2	-0.1
Oporto *Porto*	41 08N	8 37W	+0002	+0002	+0040	+0040	-0.5	-0.4	-0.2	0.0
Porto de Aveiro	40 39N	8 45W	+0005	+0010	+0010	+0015	-0.6	-0.4	-0.1	+0.1
Figueira da Foz	40 09N	8 51W	-0015	0000	+0010	+0020	-0.4	-0.4	-0.1	-0.1
Nazare *Pederneira*	39 35N	9 04W	-0030	-0015	-0005	+0005	-0.5	-0.4	-0.1	0.0
Peniche	39 21N	9 22W	-0035	-0015	-0005	0000	-0.3	-0.4	-0.1	0.0
Ericeira	38 58N	9 25W	-0040	-0025	-0010	-0010	-0.4	-0.3	-0.1	0.0
River Tagus (Rio Tejo)										
Cascais	38 42N	9 25W	-0040	-0025	-0015	-0010	-0.3	-0.3	+0.1	+0.1
Paco de Arcos	38 41N	9 18W	-0020	-0030	-0005	-0005	-0.4	-0.4	-0.2	-0.1
Pedroucos	38 42N	9 13W	-0010	-0015	0000	0000	-0.2	-0.1	-0.1	-0.1
Alfeite	38 40N	9 09W	+0005	0000	0000	+0005	0.0	0.0	-0.1	0.0
Alcochete	38 45N	8 58W	+0010	+0010	+0010	+0010	+0.5	+0.4	+0.1	0.0
Vila Franca de Xira	38 57N	8 59W	+0045	+0040	+0100	+0140	+0.3	+0.2	-0.2	+0.3
Sesimbra	38 26N	9 07W	-0045	-0030	-0020	-0010	-0.4	-0.4	-0.1	0.0
Setubal	38 30N	8 54W	-0020	-0015	-0005	+0005	-0.4	-0.4	-0.1	-0.1
Porto de Sines	37 57N	8 53W	-0050	-0030	-0020	-0010	-0.4	-0.4	-0.1	0.0
Milfontes	37 43N	8 47W	-0040	-0030	*no data*	*no data*	-0.1	-0.1	0.0	+0.1
Arrifana	37 17N	8 52W	-0030	-0020	*no data*	*no data*	-0.1	0.0	-0.1	+0.1
Enseada de Belixe	37 01N	8 58W	-0050	-0030	-0020	-0015	+0.3	+0.2	+0.2	+0.2
Lagos	37 06N	8 40W	-0100	-0040	-0030	-0025	-0.4	-0.4	-0.1	0.0
Portimao	37 07N	8 32W	-0100	-0040	-0030	-0025	-0.5	-0.4	-0.1	+0.1
Ponta do Altar	37 06N	8 31W	-0100	-0040	-0030	-0025	-0.3	-0.3	-0.1	0.0
Enseada de Albufeira	37 05N	8 15W	-0035	+0015	-0005	0000	-0.2	-0.2	0.0	+0.1
Porto de Faro-Olhao	36 59N	7 52W	-0050	-0030	-0015	+0005	-0.4	-0.4	-0.1	0.0
Rio Guadiana										
Vila Real de Santo António	37 12N	7 25W	-0050	-0015	-0010	0000	-0.4	-0.4	-0.1	+0.1

LISBOA	38 42N	9 07W	0500 and 1700	1000 and 2200	0500 and 1700	1100 and 2300	3.8	3.0	1.5	0.6
standard port										

SPAIN *Time Zone -0100*

Location	Lat	Long	High Water		Low Water		MHWS	MHWN	MLWN	MLWS
Ayamonte	37 13N	7 25W	+0005	+0015	+0025	+0045	-0.7	-0.6	-0.1	-0.2
Ria de Huelva										
Bar	37 08N	6 52W	0000	+0015	+0035	+0030	-0.1	-0.6	-0.1	-0.4
Huelva, Muelle de Fabrica	37 15N	6 58W	+0010	+0025	+0045	+0040	-0.3	-0.3	-0.3	-0.1
Rio Guadalquivir										
Bar	36 45N	6 26W	-0005	+0005	+0020	+0030	-0.6	-0.5	-0.2	-0.2
Bonanza	36 48N	6 20W	+0025	+0040	+0100	+0120	-0.8	-0.6	-0.4	-0.1
Corta de los Jerónimos	37 08N	6 06W	+0210	+0230	+0255	+0345	-1.2	-0.9	-0.5	-0.1
Sevilla	37 23N	6 00W	+0400	+0430	+0510	+0545	-1.7	-1.2	-0.6	-0.1
Rota	36 37N	6 21W	-0010	+0010	+0025	+0015	-0.7	-0.6	-0.3	-0.1
Puerto de Santa Maria	36 36N	6 13W	+0006	+0006	+0027	+0027	-0.6	-0.4	-0.3	-0.1
Cadiz										
Puerto Cadiz	36 32N	6 17W	0000	+0020	+0040	+0025	-0.5	-0.5	-0.3	0.0
La Carraca	36 30N	6 11W	+0020	+0050	+0100	+0040	-0.5	-0.4	-0.1	0.0
Cabo Trafalgar	36 11N	6 02W	-0003	-0003	+0026	+0026	-1.4	-1.1	-0.6	-0.1
Barbate	36 11N	5 56W	+0016	+0016	+0045	+0045	-1.9	-1.5	-0.5	+0.1
Punta Camarinal	36 05N	5 48W	-0007	-0007	+0013	+0013	-1.7	-1.4	-0.7	-0.2

GIBRALTAR *Time Zone -0100*

Location	Lat	Long	High Water		Low Water		MHWS	MHWN	MLWN	MLWS
GIBRALTAR	36 08N	5 21W	0000 and 1200	0700 and 1900	0100 and 1300	0600 and 1800	1.0	0.7	0.3	0.1
standard port										
Tarifa	36 00N	5 36W	-0038	-0038	-0042	-0042	+0.4	+0.3	+0.3	+0.2
Punta Carnero	36 04N	5 26W	-0010	-0010	0000	0000	0.0	+0.1	+0.1	+0.1
Algeciras	36 07N	5 27W	-0010	-0010	-0010	-0010	+0.1	+0.2	+0.1	+0.1

TIDAL GATES - SOUTHERN ENGLAND

A guide to the time of tide turn at tidal gates, the approximate maximum strength of the tidal flow (spring rates shown - neaps are approximately 60% of these), and the position and timing of races, counter tides, etc.

LAND'S END (AC 1148)

Tidal streams set hard north/south round Land's End, and east/west around Gwennap and Pendeen. But the inshore currents run counter to the tidal streams. By staying close inshore, this tidal gate favours a N-bound passage. With careful timing nearly 9½hrs of fair tide can be carried, from HWD−3 to HWD+5. The chartlets, referenced to HW Dover, depict both tidal streams and inshore currents.

FLOOD	EBB

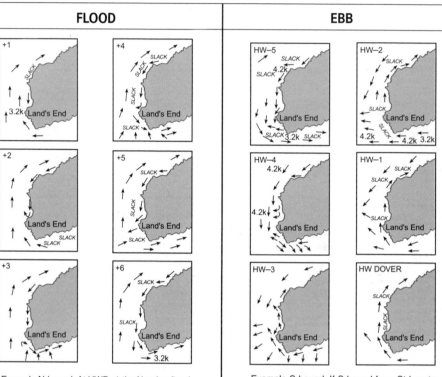

Example N-bound: At HWD+1 the N-going flood starts off Gwennap and does not turn NE along the N Cornish coast until HWD+3. But as early as HWD−3 an inshore current is beginning to set north. Utilise this by arriving off Runnel Stone at HWD−2 and then keeping within ¼M of the shore. If abeam the Brisons at HWD, the tide and current should serve for the next 6 or 7 hours to make good St Ives, or even Newquay and Padstow.

Example S-bound: If S-bound from St Ives to Newlyn, aim to reach the Runnel Stone by HWD+5, ie with 2hrs of E-going tide in hand for the remaining 9M to Newlyn. To achieve this 20M passage, leave St Ives 5 hours earlier, ie at HWD. Buck a foul tide for the first 3 hours, then use the S-going inshore current, keeping as close inshore as is prudent, only moving seaward to clear the Wra and the Brisons. This timing would also suit a passage from S Wales or the Bristol Channel, going inshore of Longships if conditions allow.

From Ireland, ie Cork or further W, the inshore passage would not benefit. But aim to be off the Runnel Stone at HWD+5 if bound for Newlyn; or at HWD+3 if bound for Helford/Falmouth, with the W-going stream slackening and 5hrs of fair tide to cover the remaining 20M past the Lizard.

With acknowledgements to the Royal Cruising Club Pilotage Foundation for their kind permission to use the tidal stream chartlets and text written by Hugh Davies, as first published in Yachting Monthly magazine.

Chapter 5

TIDAL GATES - SOUTHERN ENGLAND

A guide to the time of tide turn at tidal gates, the approximate maximum strength of the tidal flow (spring rates shown - neaps are approximately 60% of these), and the position and timing of races, counter tides, etc.

FLOOD	EBB

THE LIZARD (AC 777, 2345)

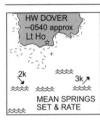

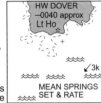

Drying rocks lie approx 5 cables S of the Lizard lt ho and extend westwards. 49°57'N is about as far N as yachts may safely pass inshore of the Race, which extends 2-3M to seaward of these rocks. Race conditions may also exist SE of the Lizard with short, heavy seas in westerlies. If passing S of the Race, route via 49°55'N 05°13'W to clear the worst of the Race.

Inshore the E-going Channel flood, 2kn max @ springs, begins at HW Dover +0145; and outside the Race at approx HWD +0300.	Inshore the W-going Channel ebb, 3kn max @ springs, begins at HW Dover –0345; and outside the Race at HWD –0240.

START POINT (AC 1634)

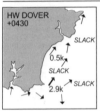

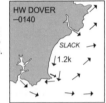

Start Pt, and to a lesser extent Prawle Pt (3.3M WSW), can be slow to round when W-bound with a fair tide against a W'ly wind raising a bad sea. Drying rocks extend 3 cables SSE of the lt ho and a Race may extend up to 1.7M ESE and 1.0M S of the lt ho. It is safe to pass between the Race and the rocks, but in bad weather wiser to go outside the Race. The Skerries Bank (least depth 2.1m) lies 8 cables NE of Start Pt. On both the flood and the ebb back eddies form between Start Pt and Hallsands, 1M NW.

The NE-going Channel flood, 3.1kn max @ springs, begins at HW Dover +0430.	The SW-going Channel ebb, 2.2kn max @ springs, begins at HW Dover –0140, but an hour earlier it is possible to round Start Pt close inshore using the back eddy.

PORTLAND (AC 2255)

A dangerous Race forms between 200 metres and 2 miles south of Portland Bill. The Race shifts westward on the W-going stream and eastward on the E-going stream. In the latter case it is not advisable to pass between the Race and the Shambles Bank. Study carefully the hourly tidal stream chartlets on pp.184-185 or in NP 257. The Race may be avoided either by passing to seaward of it, ie 3-5M south of the Bill and east of the Shambles; or by using the inshore passage – if conditions suit.

Seaward of the Race.

E-bound: The Channel flood sets east from HW Dover +6 to HWD –1.	W-bound: The ebb sets west from HW Dover to HWD +5½.

The inshore passage, (a narrow stretch of relatively smooth water between the Bill and the Race), should be started, in either direction, from a position 2M north of the Bill, keeping close inshore to the Portland peninsula. It should not be used at night (due to pot floats), nor in winds >F4/5, nor at springs especially with wind against tide.

If E-bound via the inshore passage, slackish water or a fair stream occurs around the Bill from HW Portland –3 to +1. The passage across Lyme Bay should be specifically timed to meet this critical window.	W-bound, similar conditions occur from HW Portland +4 to –6. The W-bound timing is easy if you have started from Weymouth, Portland harbour or Lulworth Cove.

ST ALBAN'S HEAD (AC 2610)

A sometimes vicious Race forms over St Alban's Ledge, a rocky dorsal ridge (least depth 8.5m) which extends approx 4M SW from St Alban's Head. Three yellow naval target buoys (DZ A, B and C) straddle the middle and outer sections, but are only occasionally used. In settled weather and at neaps the Race may be barely perceptible in which case it can be crossed with impunity. Avoid it either by keeping to seaward via 50°31'.40N 02°07'.80W; or by using the narrow inshore passage at the foot of St Alban's Head.

Based on a position 1M S of St Alban's Head, the tidal stream windows are:

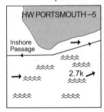

ESE-going stream starts at HW Portsmouth +0530. Spring rates are the same, max 4kn. Along the W side of St Alban's Head the stream runs almost continuously SE due to a back eddy.	WNW-going stream starts at HW Portsmouth. Overfalls extend 2.5M further SW than on the E-going stream and are more dangerous to small craft. Slack water lasts barely half an hour.

The inshore passage lies as close to the foot of St Alban's Head as feels comfortable. It may be hard to see the width of clear water in the inshore passage until committed to it, but except in onshore gales when it is better to stay offshore, the passage will be swiftly made with only a few, if any, overfalls. The NCI station on the Head (☎ 01929 439220) may advise on conditions.

TIDAL GATES - SOUTHERN ENGLAND

A guide to the time of tide turn at tidal gates, the approximate maximum strength of the tidal flow (spring rates shown - neaps are approximately 60% of these), and the position and timing of races, counter tides, etc.

FLOOD	EBB

THE NEEDLES CHANNEL (AC 2035)

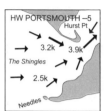

The Needles Channel lies between the SW Shingles PHM buoy and the Bridge WCM buoy. Once through this narrow section the channel widens with the Island shore to starboard and the long, drying 1.2m, Shingles bank to port. Abeam Hurst Castle the channel again narrows (assisted by The Trap, a shoal spit south of Hurst Castle) before opening out into the west Solent.

Study carefully the hourly tidal stream chartlets for the Isle of Wight on pp.186-191 and the values shown on AC 2035 at tidal diamonds B, C, D and E.

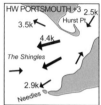

The ENE-going flood runs from HW Portsmouth +5 until HW P −1½, at springs reaching 3.1kn at The Bridge and 3.9kn at Hurst.

The WSW-going ebb runs from HW P −1 until HW P +4½, reaching 4.4kn at Hurst and 3.4kn at The Bridge, both spring rates. The ebb sets strongly WSW across the Shingles which with adequate rise is routinely crossed by racing yachts; but cruisers should stay clear even in calm conditions when any swell causes the sea to break heavily.

Prevailing W/SW winds, even if only F4, against the ebb raise dangerous breaking seas in the Needles Channel and at The Bridge extending 9 cables west from the Needles light. Worst conditions are often found just after LW slack. In such conditions it is safer to go via the North Channel to Hurst. In W/SW gales avoid the Needles altogether by sheltering at Poole or going east-about via Nab Tower.

ON PASSAGE UP CHANNEL

The following 3 tidal gates (The Looe, Beachy Head and Dungeness) are components in the tidal conveyor belt which, if stepped onto at the outset, can enable a fastish yacht to carry a fair tide for 88M from Selsey Bill to Dover. Go through the Looe at slackish water, HW Portsmouth +4½ (HW Dover +5). Based on a mean SOG of 7 knots, Beachy Head will be passed at HW D −1, Dungeness at HW D +3 and Dover at HW +5½, only bucking the first of the ebb in the last hour. A faster boat could make Ramsgate. The down-Channel passage is less rewarding and many yachts will pause at Brighton.

THE LOOE (AC 2045, 1652)

This channel is little shorter than the detour south of the Owers, but is much used by yachts on passage from/to points east of the Solent. Although adequately lit, it is best not attempted at night due to many lobster floats; nor in onshore gales as searoom is limited by extensive shoals on which the sea breaks.

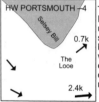

The E-going flood runs from HW Portsmouth +4½ (HW Dover +5) until HW P −1½ (HW D −1), at springs reaching 2.4kn near the Boulder and Street light buoys which mark its narrow western end; they may be hard to see in other than good visibility. Max neap rate is 1.2kn.

The W-going ebb runs from HW P −1½ (HW D −1) until HW P +4½ (HW D +5), at springs reaching 2.6kn near Boulder and Street. Max neap rate is 1.3kn.

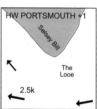

At the wider eastern end of the channel (near E Borough Head buoy) rates are greatly reduced.

BEACHY HEAD (AC 1652, 536)

Stay at least 5 cables to seaward of the towering chalk cliffs to avoid isolated boulders and rocky, part-drying ridges such as Head Ledge. The lt stands on a drying rock ledge. Close inshore many fishing floats are a trap for the unwary. In bad weather stay 2M offshore to avoid overfalls caused by a ridge of uneven ground which extends 1M SSE from Beachy Head.

2M south of Beachy Head the E-going flood starts at HW Dover +0530, max spring rate 2.6kn.

The W-going ebb starts at HW Dover +0030, max spring rate 2.0kn.

Between 5M and 7M east of Beachy Head avoid breakers and eddies caused by the Horse of Willingdon, Royal Sovereign and other shoals.

DUNGENESS (AC 536, 1892)

Tidal stream atlases: Dungeness is on the east and west edges respectively of NP 250 (English Channel) and NP 233 (Dover Strait). The nearest tidal stream diamond (2.2M SE of Dungeness) is 'H' on AC 536 and 'B' on AC 1892; their positions and values are the same.

The NE-going flood starts at HW Dover −0100, max spring rate 1.9kn.

The SW-going ebb starts at HW Dover +0430, max spring rate 2.1kn.

TIDAL GATES - NORTH EAST SCOTLAND

A guide to the time of tide turn at tidal gates, and in straits and estuaries, showing the approximate strength of the tidal flow (spring rates shown - neaps are approximately 60% of these), and the position and timing of races, counter tides etc.

FLOOD	EBB

FIRTHS of FORTH (AC 175) & TAY (AC 1481)

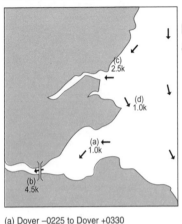

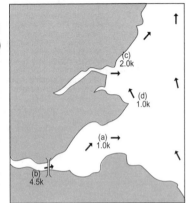

Tidal streams are quite weak in the outer part of the Firth, increasing as the narrows at islands and the bridges are approached. Apart from the stream of the Tay, which attains 5 knots in most places, the coastwise tidal streams between Fife Ness and Arbroath are weak.

(a) Dover −0225 to Dover +0330
(b) Dover −0200 to Dover +0400
(c) Dover −0210 to Dover +0420
(d) Dover −0110 to Dover +0520

(a) Dover +0330 to Dover −0225
(b) Dover +0400 to Dover −0200
(c) Dover +0420 to Dover −0210
(d) Dover +0520 to Dover −0110

PASSAGES FROM FORTH & TAY

Northbound. Leave before HW (Dover +0400) to be at N Carr at Dover +0600. Bound from Forth to Tay aim to arrive at Abertay By at LW slack (Dover −0200).
Southbound. Leave before LW (Dover -0200) to be at Bass Rk at HW Dover. Similar timings if bound from Tay to Forth, leave late in ebb to pick up early flood off St Andrews to N Carr and into Forth.

INVERNESS & CROMARTY FIRTHS (AC 1077)

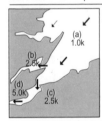

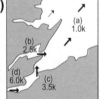

Tidal streams in the Inverness Firth and approaches are not strong, except in the Cromarty Firth Narrows, the Fort George Narrows and the Kessock Road, including off the entrance to the Caledonian Canal.

(a) Dover −0555 to Dover +0030	(a) Dover +0030 to Dover −0555
(b) Dover −0400 to Dover +0115	(b) Dover +0115 to Dover −0400
(c) Dover −0400 to Dover −0220	(c) Dover +0115 to Dover −0440
(d) Dover −0430 to Dover +0100	(d) Dover −0130 to Dover +0545

PENTLAND FIRTH & ORKNEYS (AC 1954)

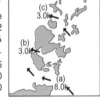

The tide flows strongly around and through the Orkney Islands. The Pentland Firth is a dangerous area for all craft, tidal flows reach 12 knots between Duncansby Head and S Ronaldsay. W of Dunnet Hd & Hoy is less violent. There is little tide within Scapa Flow.

(a) Dover −0500 to Dover +0100	(a) Dover +0115 to Dover −0535
(b) Dover +0500 to Dover −0110	(b) Dover −0115 to Dover +0050
(c) Dover −0530 to Dover +0040	(c) Dover +0040 to Dover −0530

SHETLAND ISLANDS (AC 219)

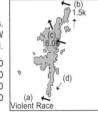

The tidal flow around the Shetland Islands rotates as the cycle progresses. When the flood begins, at −0400 HW Dover, the tidal flow is to the E, at HW Dover it is S, at Dover +0300 it is W, and at −0600 Dover it is N.

(a) Dover −0410 to Dover +0020	(a) Dover +0050 to Dover −0410
(b) Dover −0400 to Dover +0030	(b) Dover +0130 to Dover −0500
(c) Dover −0530 to Dover +0100	(c) Dover +0100 to Dover −0530
(d) Dover −0400 to Dover −0200	(d) Dover +0200 to Dover +0500

TIDAL GATES - NORTH WEST SCOTLAND

A guide to the time of tide turn at tidal gates, the approximate maximum strength of the tidal flow (spring rates shown - neaps are approximately 60% of these), and the position and timing of races, counter tides, etc.

FLOOD	EBB

SOUND OF HARRIS (AC 2642)

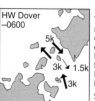

HW Dover −0600

The behaviour of tidal streams in the Sd of Harris varies from day to night, springs to neaps, and winter to summer. The following data applies to daylight, in summer at spring tides in the Cope Channel. Further information can be sought in the Admiralty West of Scotland Pilot.
HW Dover - HW D +0200: SE stream.
HW D +0300 - HW D +0600: Incoming stream from both ends.
HW D −0600 - HW D −0500: NW stream.
HW D −0500 - HW Dover: Outgoing stream from both ends.
At neaps in summer the stream will run SE for most of the day.
Tide rates shown are the maxima likely to be encountered at any time.

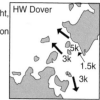

HW Dover

THE LITTLE MINCH (AC 1795)

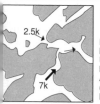

The N going stream on both shores begins at HW Dover +0430 (HW Ullapool −0345), with the strongest flow from mid channel to the Skye coast. There is a W going counter tide E of Vaternish Point.

The S going stream on both shores begins at HW Dover −0130 (HW Ullapool +0240), with the strongest flow from mid channel to the Skye coast. The E going stream in Sound of Scalpay runs at up to 2k. The E going flood and W going ebb in Sound of Scalpay run at up to 2k.

KYLE OF LOCHALSH & KYLERHEA (AC 2540)

NOTE: THESE STREAMS ARE SUBJECT TO VARIATION

N going stream in Kyle Rhea begins HW Dover +0140 (HW Ullapool +0555) and runs for 6 hours. The E going stream in Kyle Akin begins (Sp) HW Dover +0350 (HW Ullapool −0415). (Nps) HW Dover −0415 (HW Ullapool).

S going stream in Kyle Rhea begins HW Dover −0415 (HW Ullapool) and runs for 6 hours. The W going stream in Kyle Akin begins (Sp) HW Dover −0015 (HW Ullapool +0400). (Nps) HW Dover +0140 (HW Ullapool +0555).

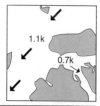

SOUND OF MULL - WEST (AC 2171)

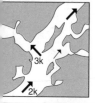

The N going stream off Ardnamurchan begins at HW Dover +0130 (HW Oban −0525). The E going stream in the Sound of Mull begins at HW Dover +0555 (HW Oban −0100).

The S going stream off Ardnamurchan begins at HW Dover −0430 (HW Oban +0100). The W going stream in the Sound of Mull begins at HW Dover −0130 (HW Oban +0400).

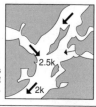

SOUND OF MULL - EAST (AC 2171)

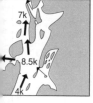

The N going stream in the Firth of Lorne begins at HW Dover −0100 (HW Oban −0430). The W going stream in the Sound of Mull begins at HW Dover +0105 (HW Oban −0550). The ingoing tides at Lochs Feochan, Etive and Creran begin at HW Dover +0300, −0100 & +0030.

The S going stream in the Firth of Lorne begins at HW Dover +0500 (HW Oban −0155). The E going stream in the Sound of Mull begins at HW Dover +0555 (HW Oban −0025). The outgoing tides at Lochs Feochan, Etive and Creran begin at HW Dover −0500, −0520 & −0505.

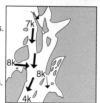

SOUND OF LUING & DORUS MOR (AC 2343)

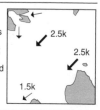

The N or W going stream begins as follows:
Dorus Mor: HW Dover −0200 (HW Oban +0330). Springs: 8 knots.
Corryvreckan: HW D −0120 (HW O +0410). Sp: 8.5 knots.
Cuan Sound: HW D −0110 (HW O +0420). Sp: 6 knots.
Sound of Jura: HW D −0130 (HW O +0400). Sp: 4 knots.
Sound of Luing: HW D −0100 (HW O +0430). Sp: 7 knots.
The S or E going stream begins as follows:
Dorus Mor: HW Dover +0440 (HW Oban −0215). Springs: 8 knots.
Corryvreckan: HW D +0445 (HW O −0210). Sp: 8.5 knots.
Cuan Sound: HW D +0455 (HW O −0200). Sp: 6 knots.
Sound of Jura: HW D +0450 (HW O −0205). Sp: 4 knots.
Sound of Luing: HW D +0500 (HW O −0155). Sp: 7 knots.

Chapter 5

TIDAL GATES - SOUTH WEST SCOTLAND

A guide to the time of tide turn at tidal gates, the approximate maximum strength of the tidal flow (spring rates shown - neaps are approximately 60% of these), and the position and timing of races, counter tides, etc.

FLOOD	EBB

SOUNDS OF ISLAY AND GIGHA (AC 2168)

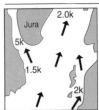

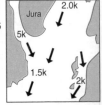

Main flood begins +0015 HW Dover (HW Oban +0545). Streams turn approx 1 hr earlier in Gigha Sd & at Kintyre & Jura shores. S going stream for 9hrs close inshore between Gigha and Machrihanish starting HW Dover (HW Oban −0530).

Main ebb begins HW Dover −0545 (HW Oban −0015). Streams turn 1 hr earlier in Gigha Sd, Kintyre & Jura shores. Overfalls off McArthur's Hd.

NORTH CHANNEL - NORTH (AC 2798)

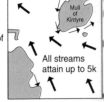

Main flood begins HW Dover −0600 (HW Greenock +0505). Races off Mull of Kintyre, Altacarry Hd & Fair Hd. Counter tides in bays of Antrim coast. W-going streams in Rathlin Sd, counter tide from Sanda Sd to Machrihanish last 1h30 - 2 hrs.

Main ebb begins HW Dover (HW Greenock −0120). Races off Mull of Kintyre & Altacarry Hd. Counter tides in bays of Antrim coast, counter tide from Macrihanish to Sanda Sd last 1h30 - 2 hrs.

NORTH CHANNEL - SOUTH (AC 2198)

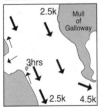

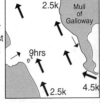

Irish coast - flood begins HW Dover +0610 (HW Belfast −0600). Scottish coast - HW Dover +0430 (HW Greenock +0310). Races off Copeland Is. & Mull of Galloway. Counter tide off Donaghadee and Island Magee last 3 hrs of flood.

Irish coast - ebb begins HW Dover −0015 (HW Belfast). Scottish coast - HW Dover −0130 (HW Greenock −0250). Races off Copeland Is. & Mull of Galloway. Flood begins 2 hrs early close inshore N of Mull of Galloway.

APPROACHES TO STRANGFORD LOUGH (AC 2156)

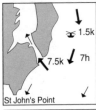

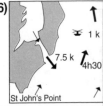

The tide cycle is approx 3 hours later than in the N Channel

Flood runs for 6 hours from HW Dover −0345 (HW Belfast −0330), with a maximum rate of 7.5 knots at Rue Point. The strong flow flattens the sea in onshore winds and entrance can be made in strong winds.

Ebb runs for 6 hours from HW Dover +0215 (HW Belfast +0230), max rate 7.5k, E of Angus Rk. If entering against ebb use West Channel with care. Smoothest water near Bar Pladdy Buoy when leaving.

ISLE OF MAN - NORTH (AC 2094)

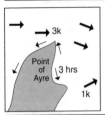

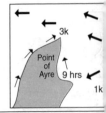

E going stream at Point of Ayre begins HW Dover −0545 (HW Liverpool −0600). Counter tide inside banks E of Point. In Ramsey Bay the S Going tide runs for 3h from +0530 Dover (+0515 Liverpool).

W going stream at Point of Ayre begins HW Dover +0015 (HW Liverpool). Counter tide inside banks W of Point. In Ramsey Bay the N going tide runs for 9h from −0330 Dover (−0345 Liverpool).

ISLE OF MAN - SOUTH (AC 2094)

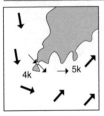

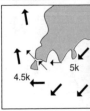

E going stream begins −0600 Dover (Liverpool +0610). Overfalls and race E of Chicken Rock. Calf Sound: The E going stream begins earlier, at approximately Dover +0400 (Liverpool +0345).

W going stream begins +0015 Dover (HW Liverpool). Overfalls and race N of Chicken Rock. Calf Sound:The W going stream begins earlier, at approximately −0130 Dover (−0145 Liverpool). Note: all times may vary due to weather conditions.

TIDAL GATES - IRISH SEA

A guide to the time of tide turn at tidal gates, the approximate strength of the tidal flow (spring rates shown — neaps are approximately 60% of these), and the position and timing of races, counter tides, etc.

FLOOD	EBB

DUBLIN BAY (AC 1415)

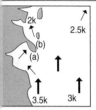

Tide between Rosbeg bank and Howth Hd (a) runs NE from HW Dublin +0300 for 9h30. In Howth Sd (b) the stream is NW going from +0430 to –0130. New flood and ebb tides begin close to the S shore and N of Baily up to 1h before HW Dublin .

The tide between Rosbeg bank and Howth Hd (a) runs SW from HW Dublin for 3h. In Howth Sd (b) the stream is SE going from –0130 to +0430. Strengths of streams increase S of Dublin Bay, and decrease N of it.

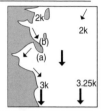

N W ANGLESEY (AC 1977)

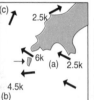

Flood tide close to the coast runs at over 5k springs, and at about 2.5k 7 miles offshore. The brief period of slack water offshore is 1h before HW Dover (1h15 before HW L'pool). Slack water lasts longer in Holyhead Bay.

Ebb tide close to the coast runs at over 5k springs, and at about 2.5k 7 miles offshore. Slack water is 5h after HW Dover (4h45 after HW L'pool). There is no significant counter tide in Holyhead Bay, but the ebb starts first there, giving about 9h W-going tide N of the harbour (a).

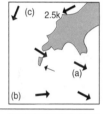

BARDSEY SOUND (AC 1971)

The tide turns to the NW or NE (flood) as follows:
at (a): HW Dover +0300;
at (b): HW D +0500;
at (c): –0545 HW D.
These times are approximate.
There is a strong eddy down tide of Bardsey Island and overfalls throughout the area.

The tide turns to the SW or SE (ebb) as follows:
at (a): HW Dover –0300;
at (b): HW D –0100 ;
at (c): at HW D –0030.
These times are approximate.
There is a strong eddy down tide of Bardsey Island and overfalls throughout the area.

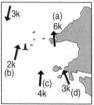

S W WALES (AC 1478)

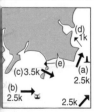

The tide turns to the S or SE (Bristol Channel flood) as follows:
at (a): HW Dover –0200;
at (b) & (c): HW D –0100 ;
at (d): –0300 HW D

The tide turns to the N or NW (Bristol Channel ebb) as follows:
at (a): HW Dover +0400;
at (b) & (c): HW D +0500 ;
at (d): +0300 HW D

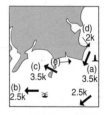

CARNSORE POINT (AC 2049)

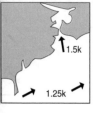

The tide turns to the NE or N (Irish Sea flood) as follows:
at (a): HW Dover +0500; at (b): HW D +0520; at (c): HW D +0600; at (d): –0600 HW D. NE going streams are shorter in duration and weaker than SE going - careful passage planning is essential.

The tide turns to the SW or S as follows:
at (a): –0200 HW D ; at (b): HW D –0020; at (c): –0015 HW D; at (d): –0300 HW Dover. Leaving Rosslare at –0300 HW D a yacht can carry a fair tide for about 8h until HW D +0515 off Hook Head.

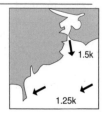

NOTE: The tide turns on St Patrick's Bridge (e) up to 2 hours earlier than in Saltee Sound

CORK COAST (AC 2049)

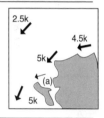

The tide, which flows coastwise, turns to the NE at HW Dover +0045. There is an eddy 5 miles ESE of Old Head of Kinsale at HW Dover +0400. The ingoing Cork Harbour tide begins at HW Dover +0055.

The tide turns SW at HW Dover +0500. The outgoing Cork Harbour tide begins at HW Dover –0540.

MENAI STRAIT (AC 1464) FLOOD

 (T): turning → : < 2k ➡ : 2-4k ⫸ : 4k +

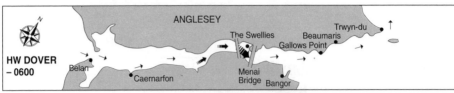

LOCAL LW: Caernarfon: HW Dover –0555. Port Dinorwic: –0620. Menai: –0540. Beaumaris: –0605.

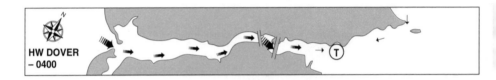

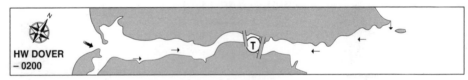

SLACK WATER IN THE SWELLIES: HW Dover –0200 to –0230.

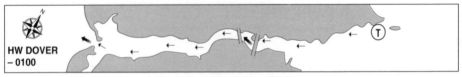

LOCAL HW: Belan: HW Dover –0115. Caernarfon: –0105. Port Dinorwic: –0050.

THE SWELLIES

WESTBOUND: Leave or pass Beaumaris in time to arrive at the Swellies by HW Dover –0230 to –0200. If in doubt about passage speed, leave early; the adverse tide will check your progress. For a first time passage this is useful, as the yacht's speed over the ground is reduced. Late arrival will mean a faster passage, but with perhaps less control.

EASTBOUND: Leave or pass Port Dinorwic in time to arrive at Menai Bridge by HW Dover –0230 to –0200. Progress towards the Swellies should be closely monitored, as you are travelling with the last of the flood. Early arrival will mean a fast, perhaps dangerous passage, being late may make it impossible.

MENAI STRAIT contd EBB

(T) : turning → : < 2k ➡ : 2-4k �➡ : 4k +

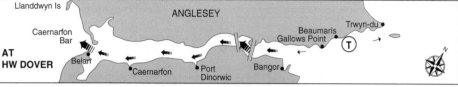

LOCAL HW TIMES: Menai: Dover − 0005. Beaumaris: Dover − 0010

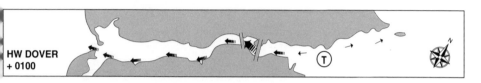

HW DOVER + 0100

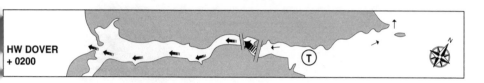

HW DOVER + 0200

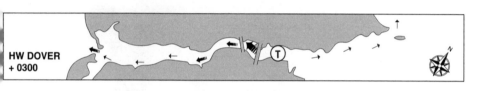

HW DOVER + 0300

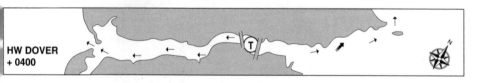

HW DOVER + 0400

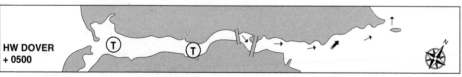

HW DOVER + 0500

LOCAL LW TIMES: Belan: Dover + 0520.

CAERNARFON BAR

CAERNARFON BAR is without question highly dangerous in certain conditions. Buoys are located to suit changing channel; positions obtainable from Caernarfon Port Radio - VHF Ch 16; 06, 12: 2h–HW, or when vessel expected. Beware cross track tides near high water. Bar impassable during or after fresh or strong onshore weather. Keep strictly in channel.

OUTWARD BOUND: Do not leave Belan Narrows after half tide, better as soon as possible after the ebb commences, which gives maximum depth and duration of fair tide if bound S & W.

INWARD BOUND: Locating the bar buoys may be difficult; head for Llanddwyn I. until they are located. Only cross after half tide (HW Dover −0400), which inevitably limits onward passage to max of 3 hours.

ENGLISH CHANNEL AND SOUTH BRITTANY

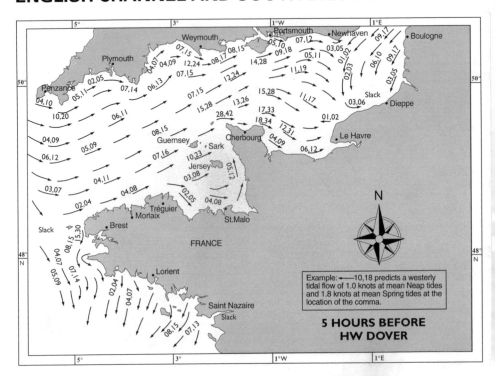

Example: ◄——10,18 predicts a westerly tidal flow of 1.0 knots at mean Neap tides and 1.8 knots at mean Spring tides at the location of the comma.

5 HOURS BEFORE HW DOVER

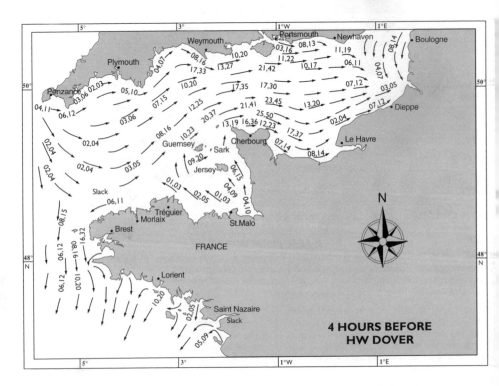

4 HOURS BEFORE HW DOVER

ENGLISH CHANNEL AND SOUTH BRITTANY

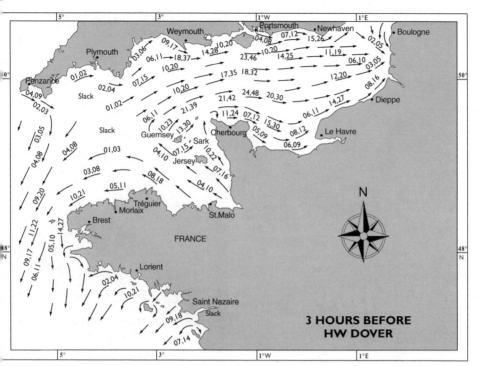

3 HOURS BEFORE HW DOVER

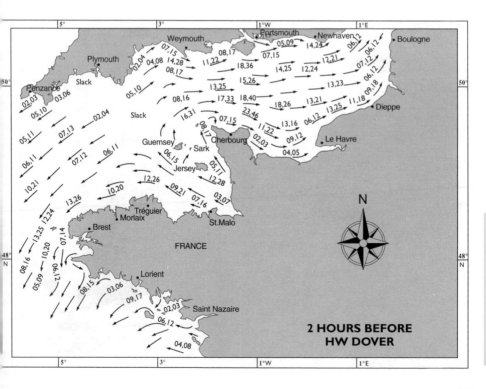

2 HOURS BEFORE HW DOVER

ENGLISH CHANNEL AND SOUTH BRITTANY

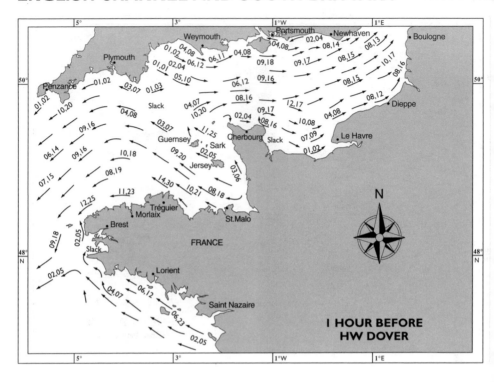

I HOUR BEFORE HW DOVER

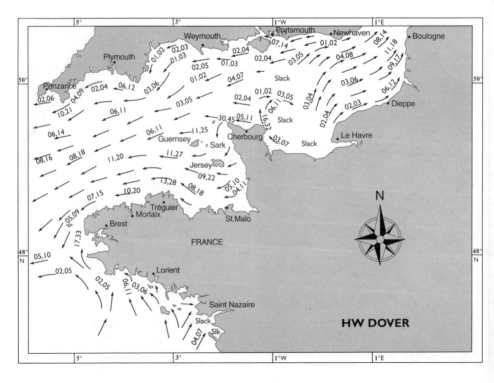

HW DOVER

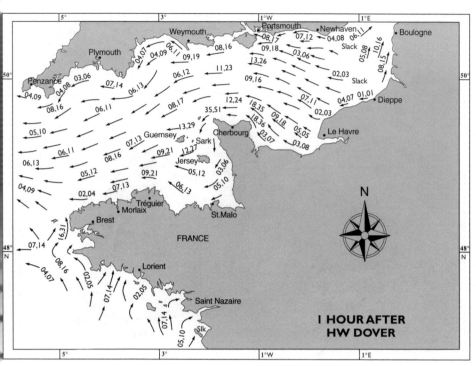

1 HOUR AFTER
HW DOVER

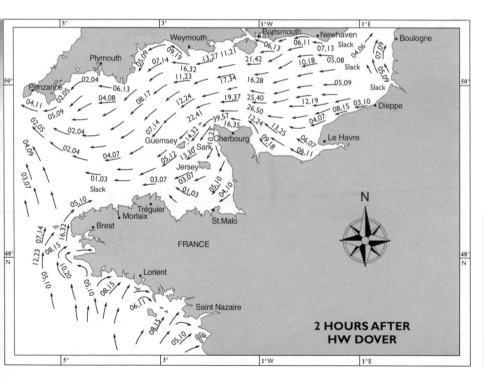

2 HOURS AFTER
HW DOVER

ENGLISH CHANNEL AND SOUTH BRITTANY

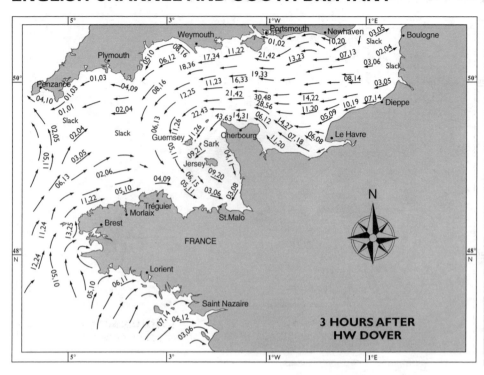

3 HOURS AFTER HW DOVER

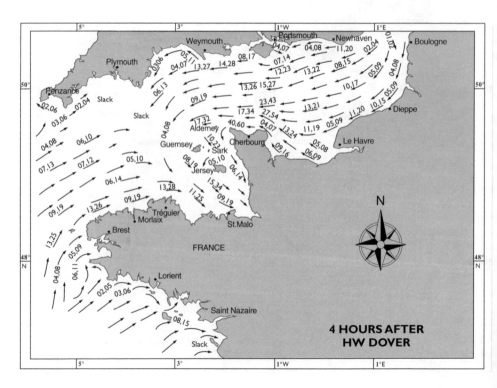

4 HOURS AFTER HW DOVER

ENGLISH CHANNEL AND SOUTH BRITTANY

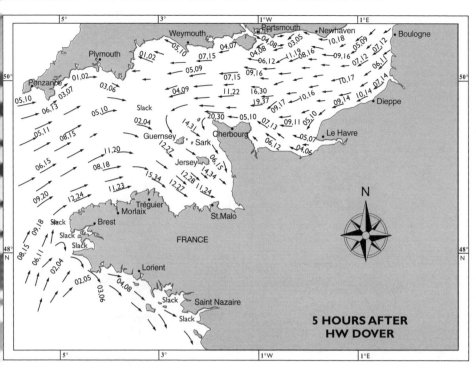

5 HOURS AFTER HW DOVER

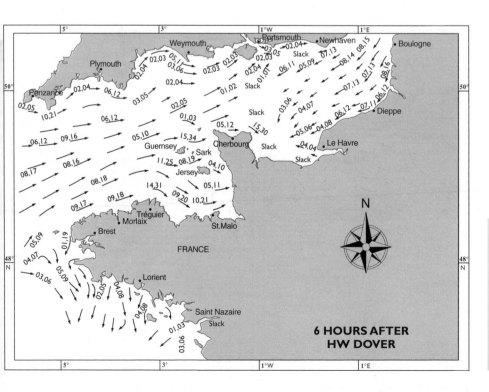

6 HOURS AFTER HW DOVER

PORTLAND

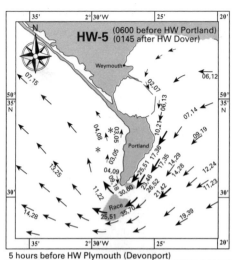

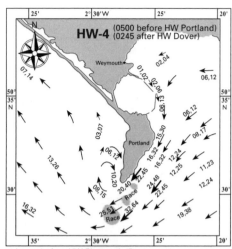

5 hours before HW Plymouth (Devonport)

4 hours before HW Plymouth (Devonport)

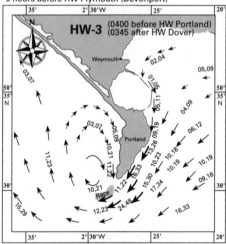

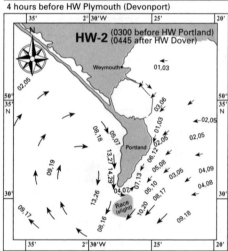

3 hours before HW Plymouth (Devonport)

2 hours before HW Plymouth (Devonport)

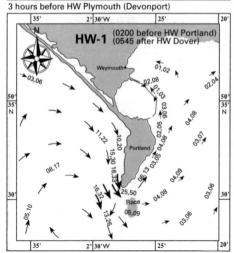

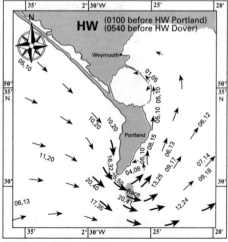

1 hour before HW Plymouth (Devonport)

HW Plymouth (Devonport)

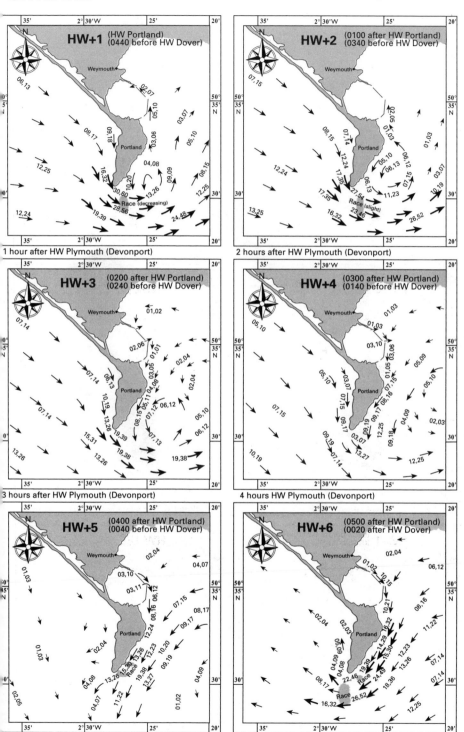

ISLE OF WIGHT

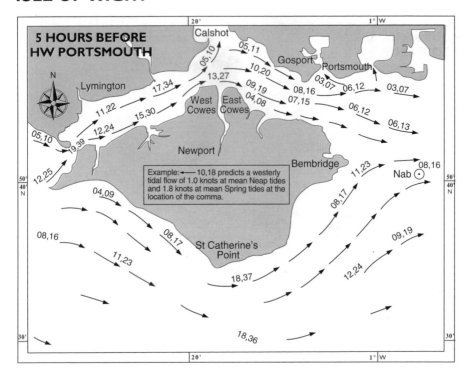

5 HOURS BEFORE HW PORTSMOUTH

Calshot
Gosport
Portsmouth
Lymington
West Cowes
East Cowes
Newport
Bembridge
Nab ⊙
St Catherine's Point

Example: ◄——10,18 predicts a westerly tidal flow of 1.0 knots at mean Neap tides and 1.8 knots at mean Spring tides at the location of the comma.

05,10 · 05,11 · 13,27 · 10,20 · 03,07 · 06,12 · 03,07 · 17,34 · 09,19 · 08,16 · 07,15 · 06,12 · 04,08 · 06,13 · 11,22 · 15,30 · 12,24 · 05,10 · 19,39 · 12,25 · 04,09 · 08,17 · 11,23 · 08,16 · 08,16 · 11,23 · 08,17 · 18,37 · 12,24 · 09,19 · 18,36

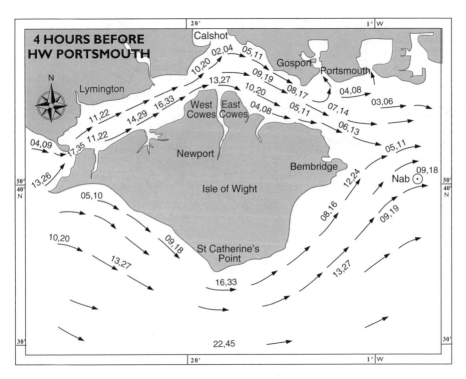

4 HOURS BEFORE HW PORTSMOUTH

Calshot
Gosport
Portsmouth
Lymington
West Cowes
East Cowes
Newport
Isle of Wight
Bembridge
Nab ⊙
St Catherine's Point

02,04 · 05,11 · 10,20 · 09,19 · 13,27 · 10,20 · 08,17 · 04,08 · 04,08 · 05,11 · 07,14 · 03,06 · 11,22 · 16,33 · 06,13 · 11,22 · 14,29 · 04,09 · 11,22 · 05,11 · 17,35 · 13,26 · 05,10 · 09,18 · 12,24 · 09,18 · 10,20 · 08,16 · 09,19 · 13,27 · 16,33 · 13,27 · 22,45

ISLE OF WIGHT

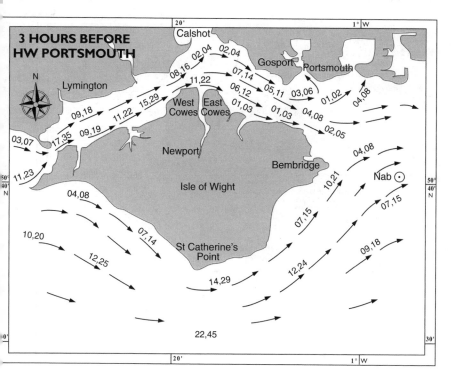

3 HOURS BEFORE HW PORTSMOUTH

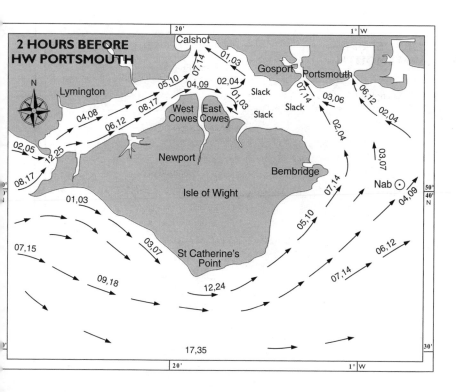

2 HOURS BEFORE HW PORTSMOUTH

ISLE OF WIGHT

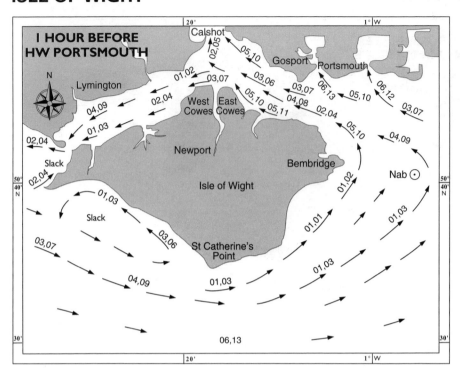

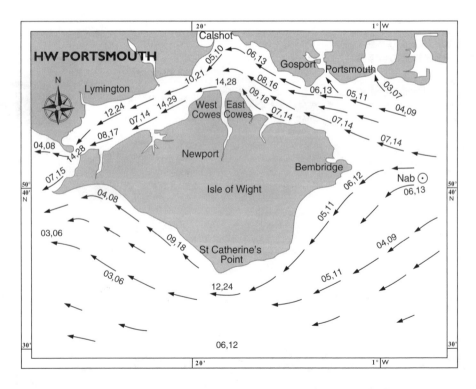

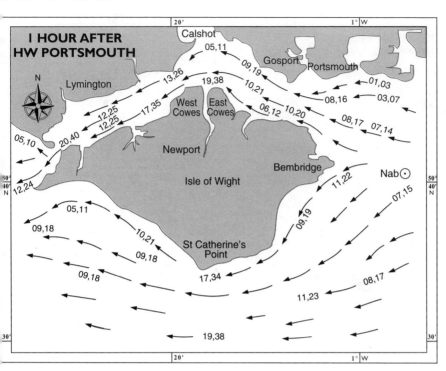

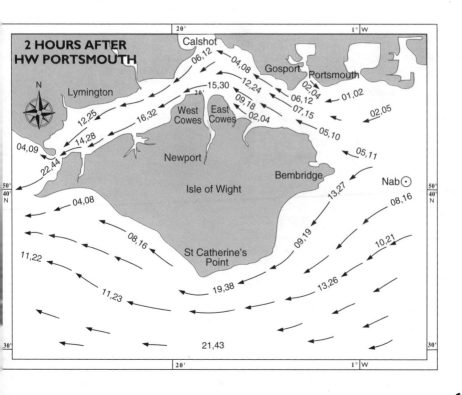

ISLE OF WIGHT

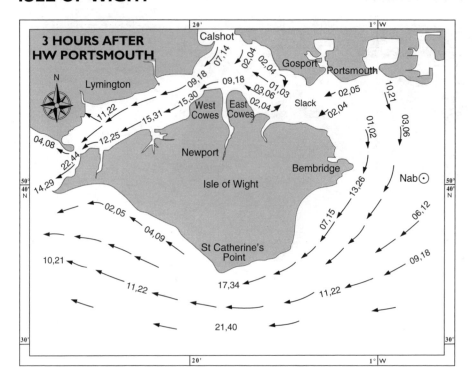

3 HOURS AFTER HW PORTSMOUTH

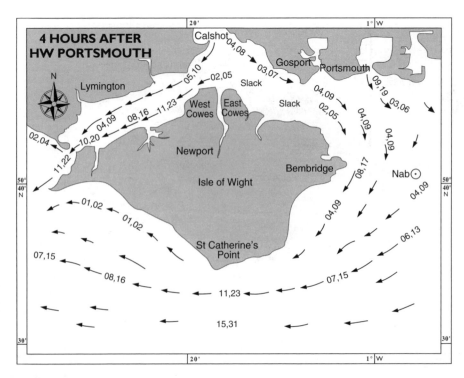

4 HOURS AFTER HW PORTSMOUTH

SLE OF WIGHT

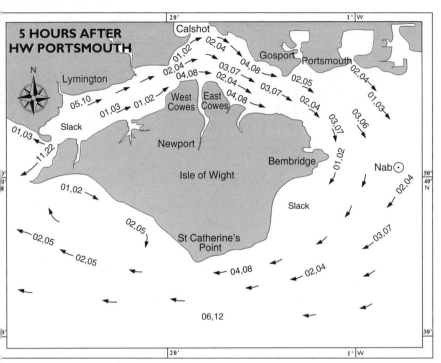

5 HOURS AFTER HW PORTSMOUTH

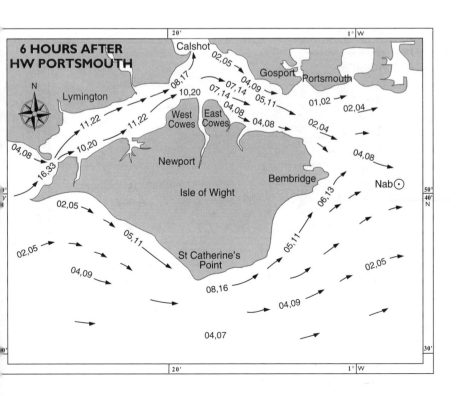

6 HOURS AFTER HW PORTSMOUTH

CHANNEL ISLES

Example: ←—10,18 predicts a westerly tidal flow of 1.0 knots at mean Neap tides and 1.8 knots at mean Spring tides at the location of the comma.

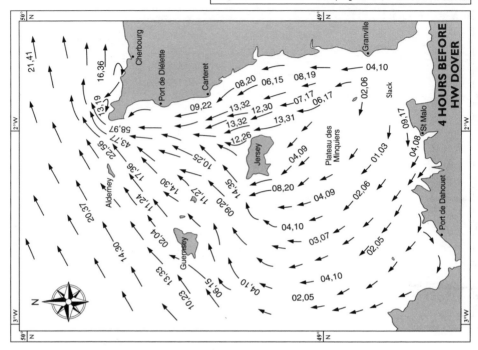

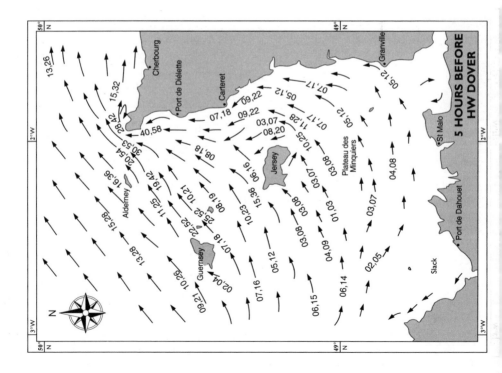

CHANNEL ISLES

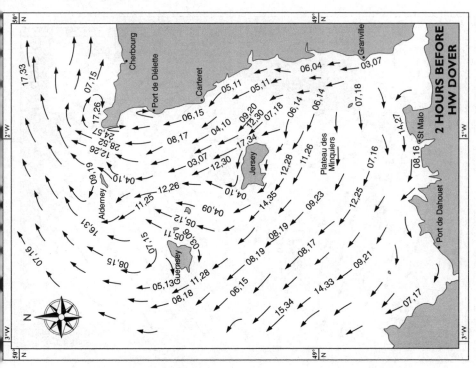

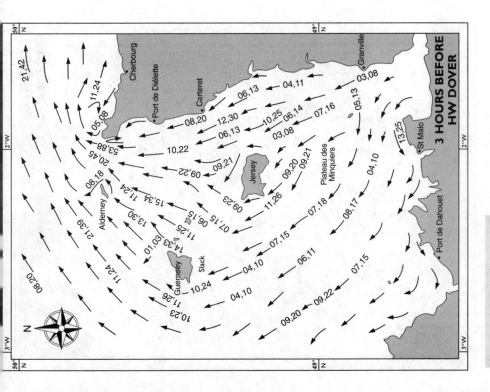

CHANNEL ISLES

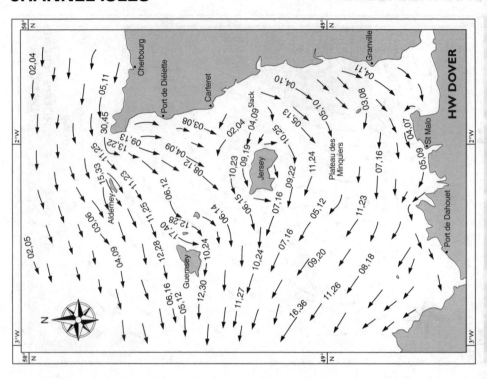

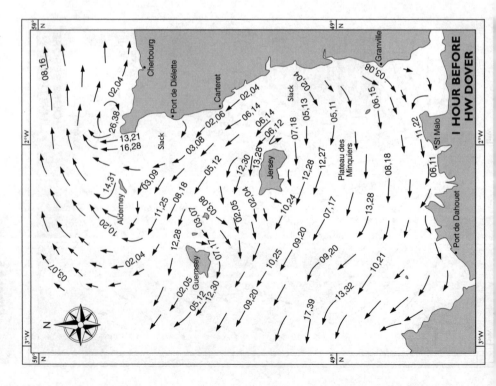

CHANNEL ISLES

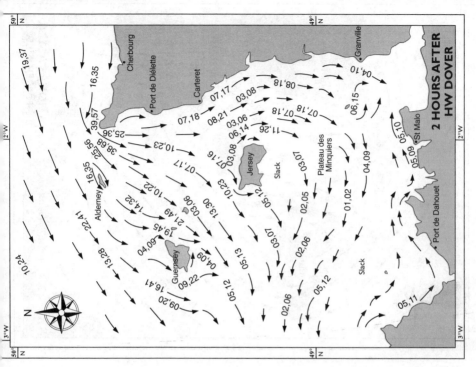

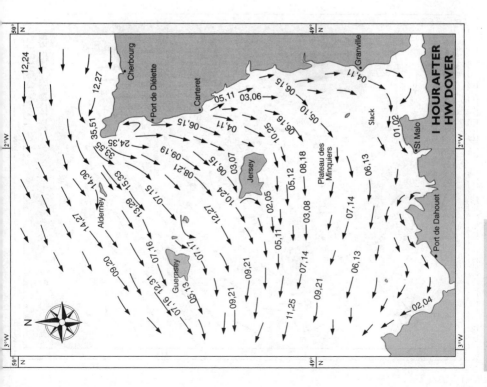

CHANNEL ISLES

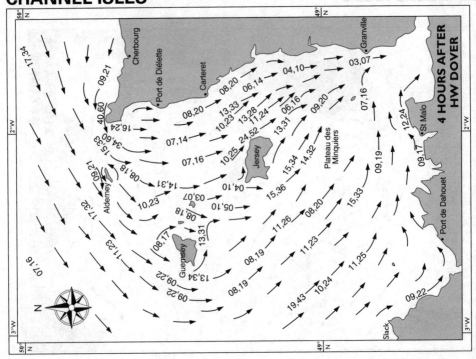

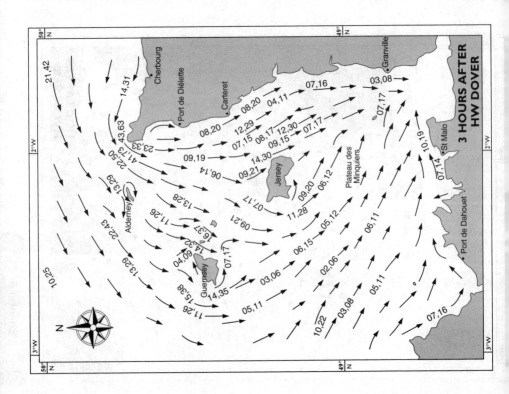

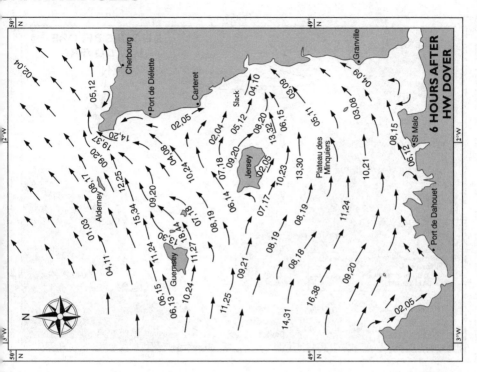

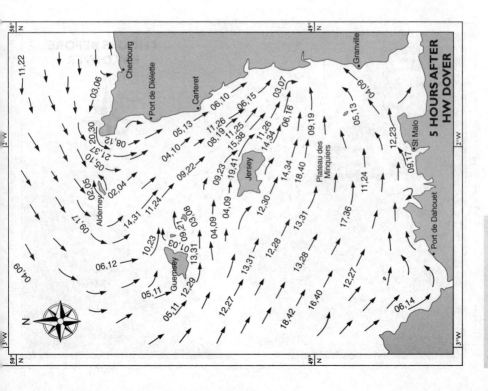

NORTH SEA

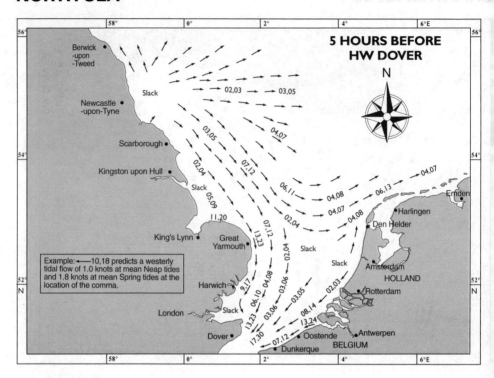

5 HOURS BEFORE HW DOVER

Example: ←—10,18 predicts a westerly tidal flow of 1.0 knots at mean Neap tides and 1.8 knots at mean Spring tides at the location of the comma.

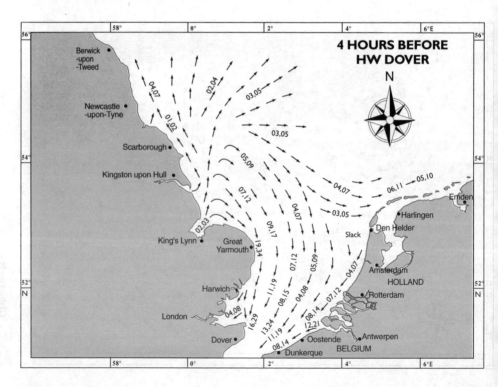

4 HOURS BEFORE HW DOVER

NORTH SEA

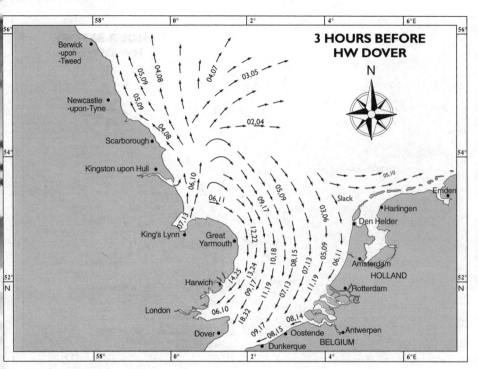

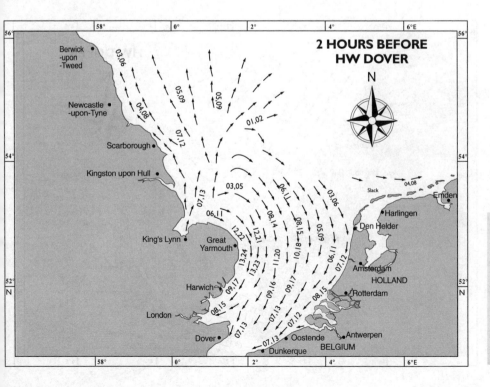

NORTH SEA

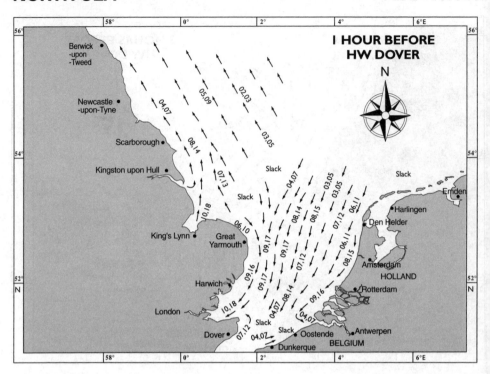

I HOUR BEFORE HW DOVER

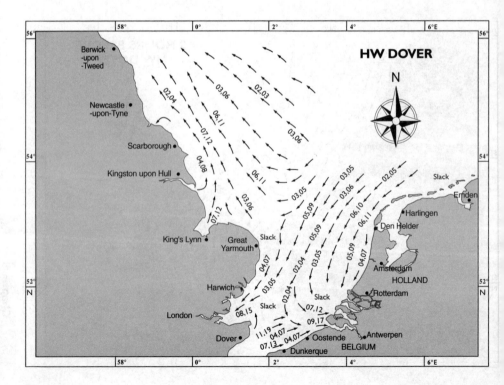

HW DOVER

200

NORTH SEA

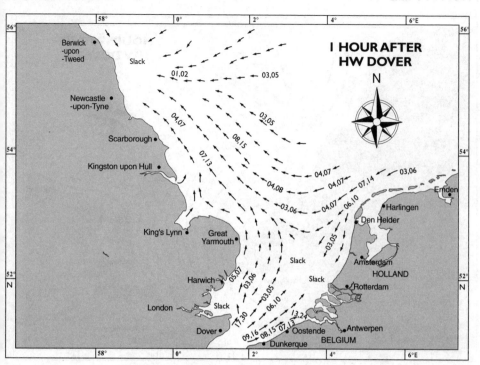

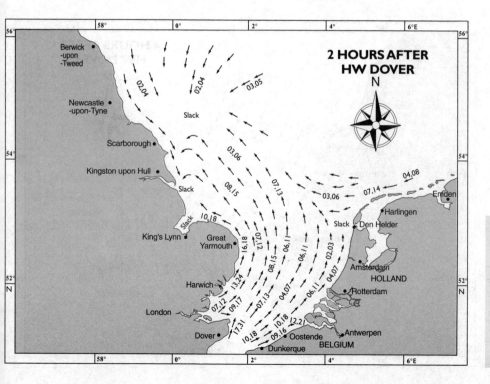

Chapter 5

NORTH SEA

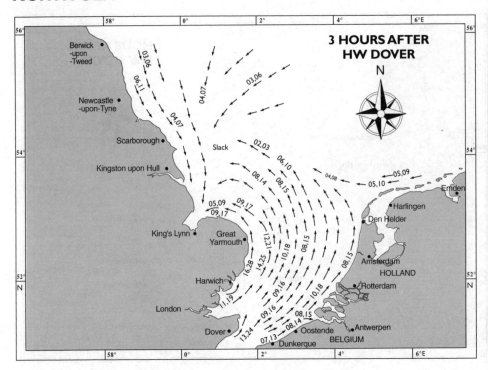

3 HOURS AFTER HW DOVER

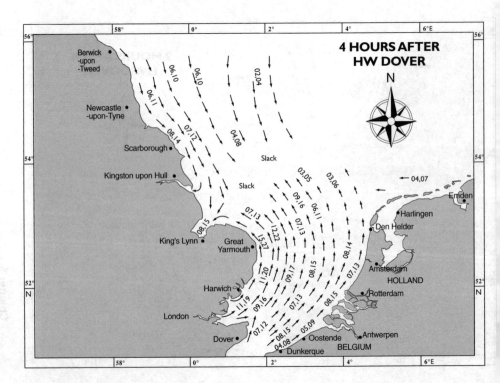

4 HOURS AFTER HW DOVER

NORTH SEA

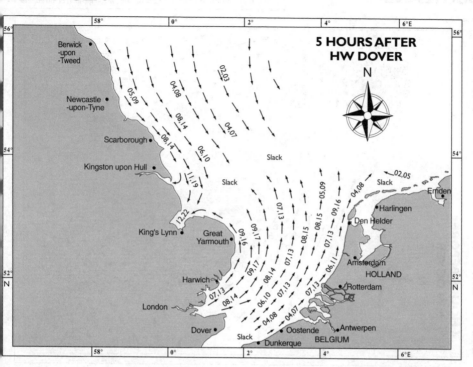

5 HOURS AFTER HW DOVER

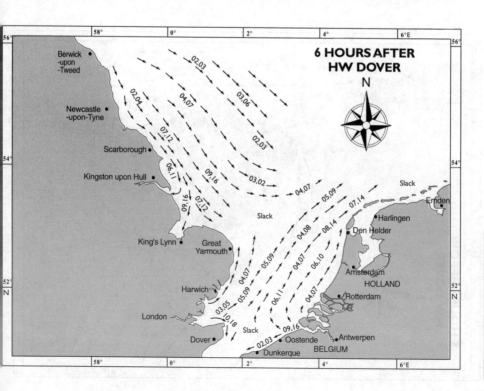

6 HOURS AFTER HW DOVER

Chapter 5

SCOTLAND

Example: ←—10,18 predicts a westerly tidal flow of 1.0 knots at mean Neap tides and 1.8 knots at mean Spring tides at the location of the comma.

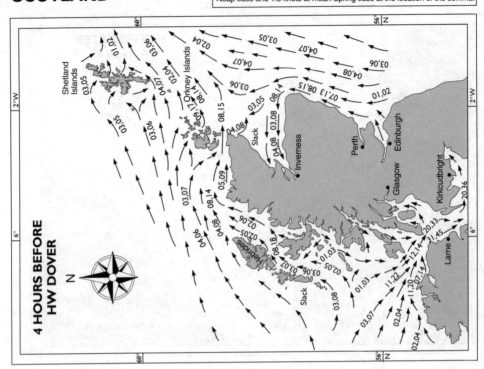

4 HOURS BEFORE HW DOVER

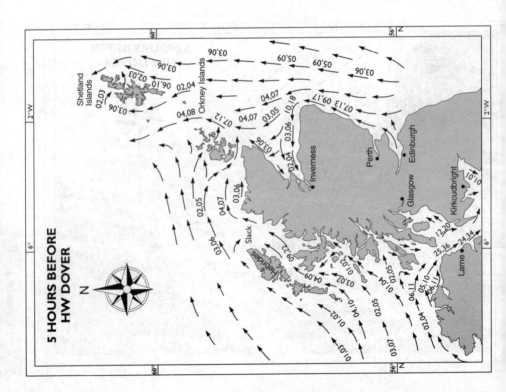

5 HOURS BEFORE HW DOVER

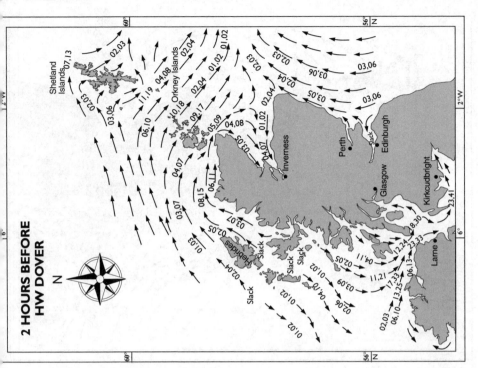

2 HOURS BEFORE HW DOVER

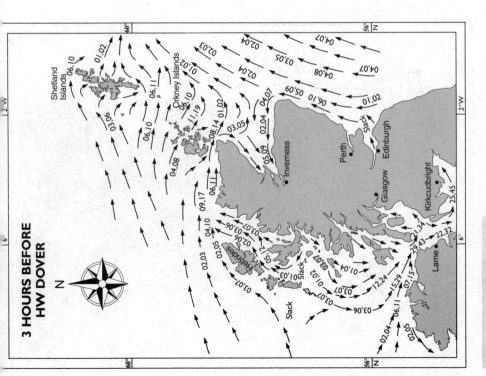

3 HOURS BEFORE HW DOVER

Chapter 5

205

SCOTLAND

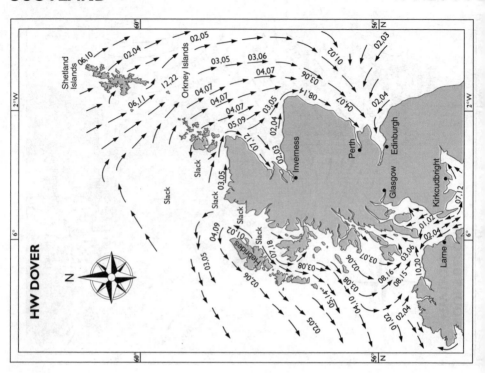

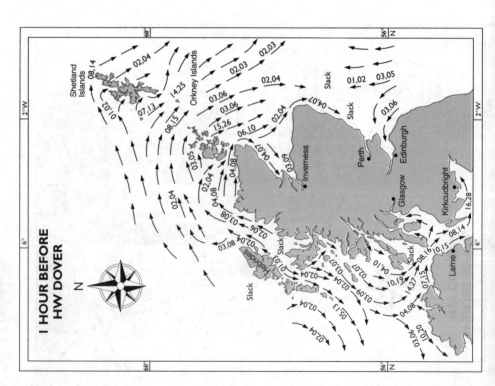

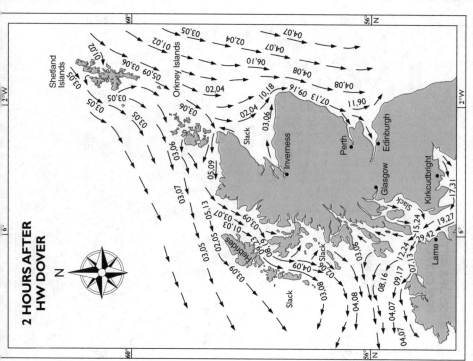

2 HOURS AFTER HW DOVER

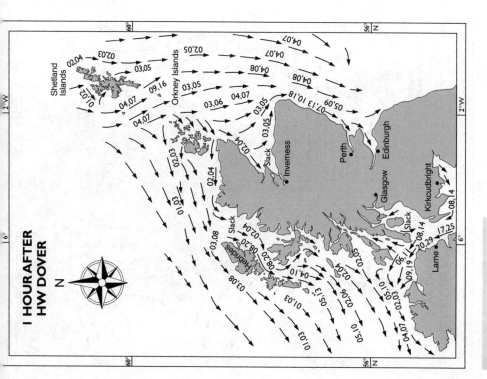

1 HOUR AFTER HW DOVER

SCOTLAND

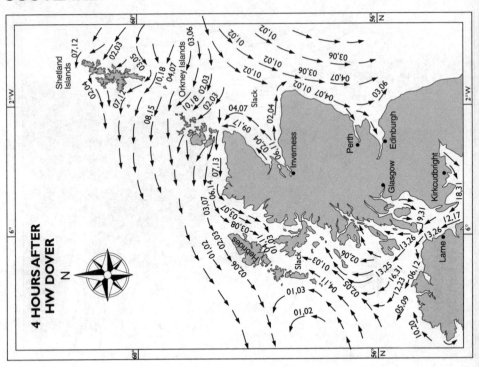

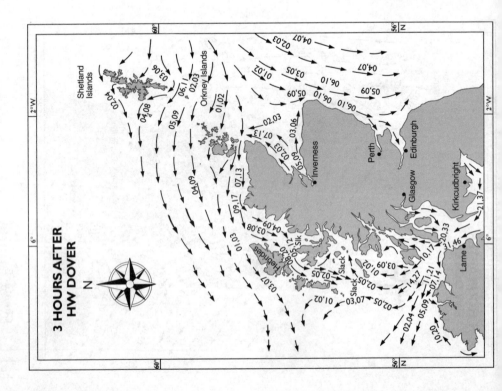

SCOTLAND

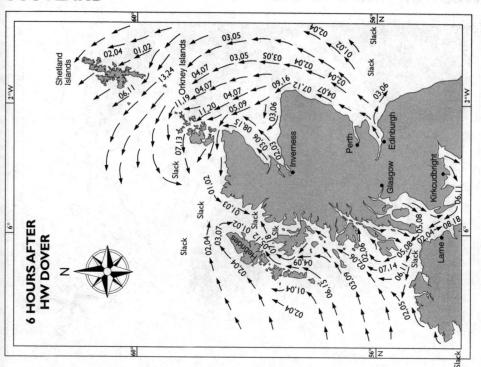

6 HOURS AFTER HW DOVER

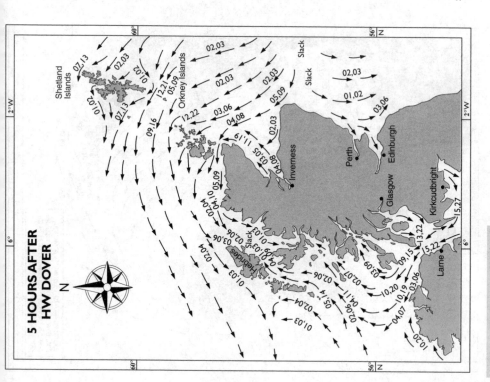

5 HOURS AFTER HW DOVER

WEST UK AND IRELAND

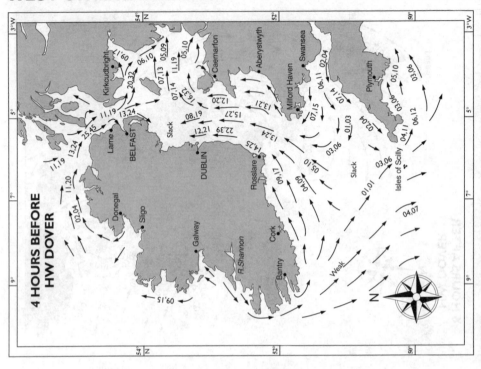

4 HOURS BEFORE HW DOVER

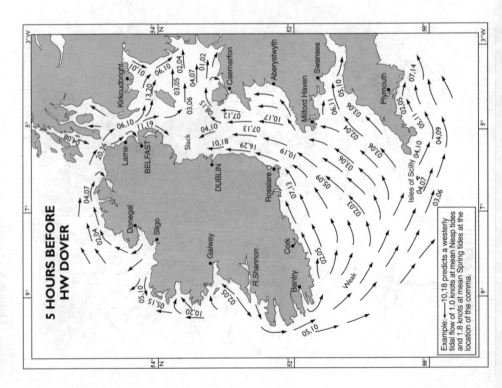

5 HOURS BEFORE HW DOVER

Example:— →10,18 predicts a westerly tidal flow of 1.0 knots at mean Neap tides and 1.8 knots at mean Spring tides at the location of the comma.

WEST UK AND IRELAND

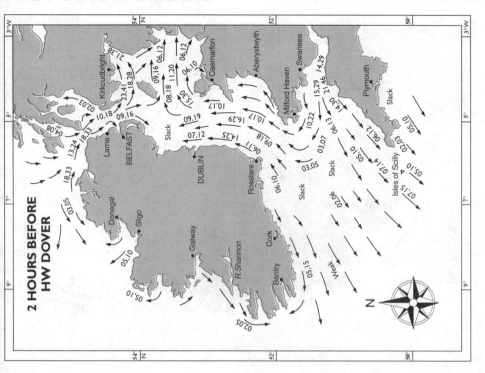

2 HOURS BEFORE HW DOVER

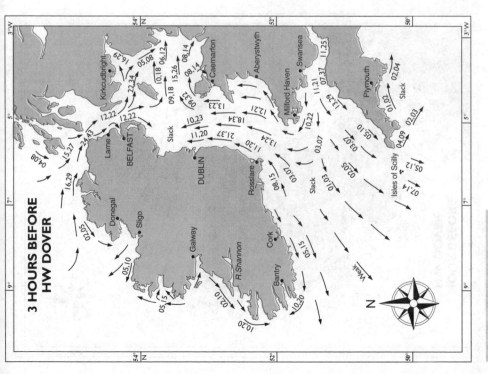

3 HOURS BEFORE HW DOVER

WEST UK AND IRELAND

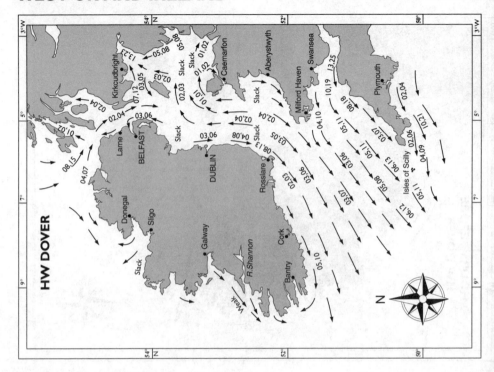

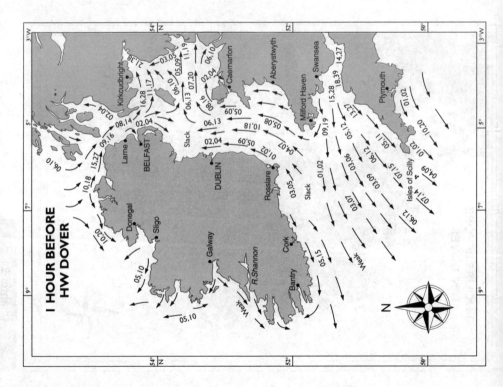

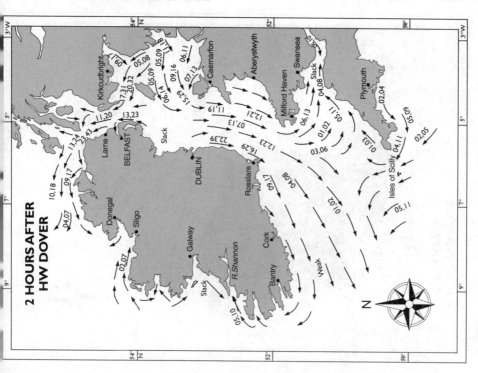

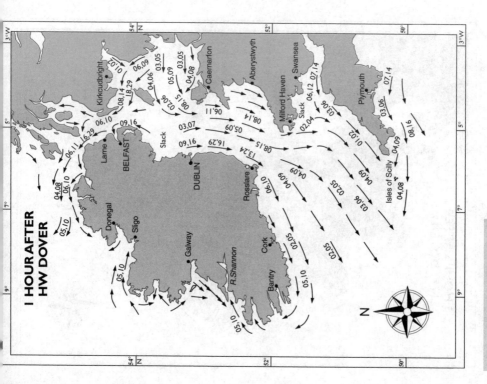

WEST UK AND IRELAND

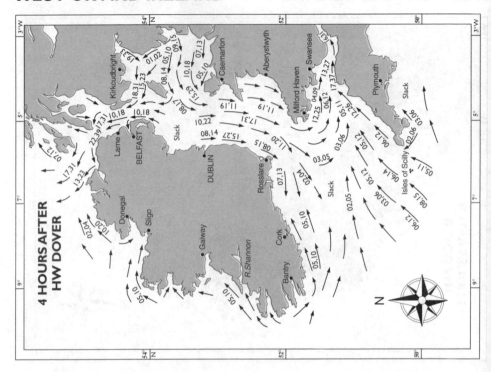

4 HOURS AFTER HW DOVER

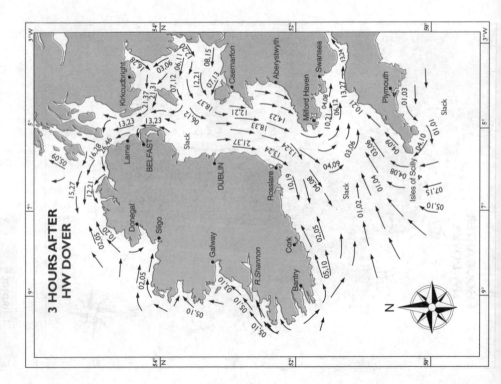

3 HOURS AFTER HW DOVER

WEST UK AND IRELAND

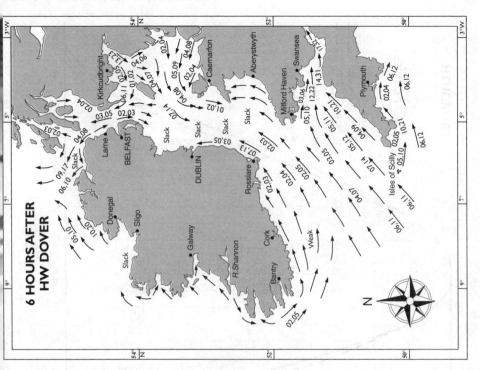

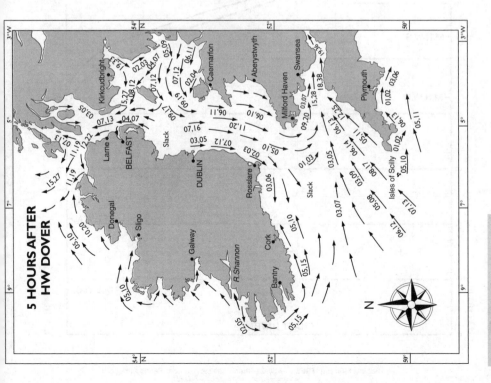

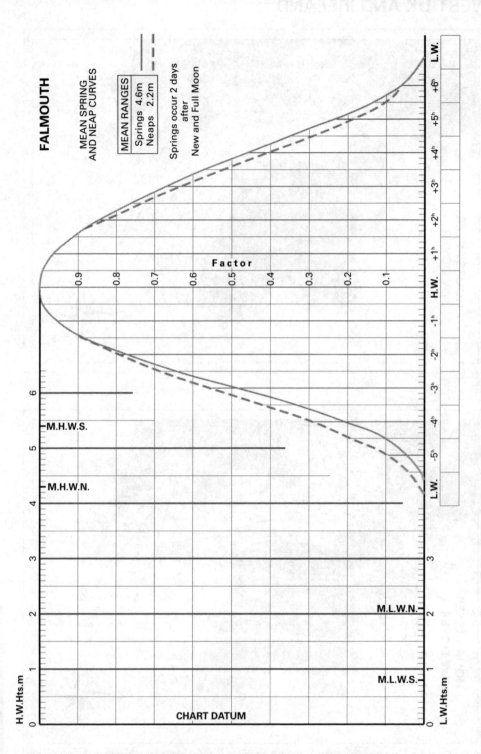

FALMOUTH

MEAN SPRING
AND NEAP CURVES

MEAN RANGES
Springs 4.6m
Neaps 2.2m

Springs occur 2 days
after
New and Full Moon

Factor

0.9 0.8 0.7 0.6 0.5 0.4 0.3 0.2 0.1

L.W. +6ʰ +5ʰ +4ʰ +3ʰ +2ʰ +1ʰ H.W. -1ʰ -2ʰ -3ʰ -4ʰ -5ʰ L.W.

M.H.W.S.
M.H.W.N.

M.L.W.N.
M.L.W.S.

H.W.Hts.m

L.W.Hts.m

CHART DATUM

ENGLAND – FALMOUTH

LAT 50°09′N   LONG 5°03′W

TIMES AND HEIGHTS OF HIGH AND LOW WATERS

YEAR **2004**

JANUARY

Day	Time m	Day	Time m
1 TH	0606 2.1 / 1209 4.4 / 1845 2.0	16 F	0512 1.8 / 1115 4.6 / 1757 1.8 / 2358 4.4
2 F	0051 4.2 / 1312 4.3 / 1949 2.0	17 SA	0632 1.9 / 1230 4.5 / 1919 1.8
3 SA	0148 4.3 / 0821 2.0 / 1412 4.4 / 2049 1.9	18 SU	0115 4.5 / 0757 1.8 / 1348 4.6 / 2036 1.6
4 SU	0242 4.5 / 0919 1.9 / 1504 4.6 / 2140 1.7	19 M	0228 4.7 / 0912 1.5 / 1500 4.7 / 2145 1.5
5 M	0329 4.7 / 1009 1.6 / 1552 4.7 / 2226 1.5	20 TU	0333 5.0 / 1018 1.3 / 1603 4.9 / 2245 1.2
6 TU	0413 4.9 / 1053 1.5 / 1635 4.8 / 2307 1.5	21 W	0430 5.2 / 1115 1.0 / ● 1659 5.1 / 2339 1.0
7 W	0453 5.1 / 1132 1.4 / 1714 4.9 / ○ 2345 1.4	22 TH	0519 5.4 / 1207 0.8 / 1750 5.2
8 TH	0531 5.1 / 1210 1.3 / 1754 4.9	23 F	0028 0.8 / 0608 5.5 / 1255 0.6 / 1839 5.2
9 F	0022 1.3 / 0609 5.2 / 1246 1.3 / 1833 4.9	24 SA	0114 0.8 / 0656 5.5 / 1340 0.6 / 1926 5.1
10 SA	0058 1.3 / 0647 5.1 / 1322 1.4 / 1911 4.9	25 SU	0155 0.8 / 0740 5.4 / 1420 0.7 / 2007 5.0
11 SU	0133 1.3 / 0724 5.1 / 1358 1.3 / 1948 4.8	26 M	0233 1.0 / 0820 5.3 / 1457 0.9 / 2043 4.9
12 M	0208 1.4 / 0800 5.0 / 1434 1.3 / 2025 4.7	27 TU	0308 1.2 / 0854 5.1 / 1531 1.2 / 2115 4.7
13 TU	0244 1.4 / 0839 5.0 / 1511 1.4 / 2105 4.6	28 W	0341 1.5 / 0926 4.8 / 1605 1.5 / 2146 4.5
14 W	0324 1.5 / 0922 4.9 / 1554 1.5 / 2151 4.5	29 TH	0416 1.7 / 1000 4.6 / 1641 1.8 / ◐ 2225 4.3
15 TH	0411 1.6 / 1013 4.7 / 1647 1.6 / ◑ 2249 4.4	30 F	0458 2.0 / 1045 4.3 / 1729 2.1 / 2321 4.2
		31 SA	0558 2.2 / 1151 4.1 / 1834 2.2

FEBRUARY

Day	Time m	Day	Time m
1 SU	0037 4.1 / 0713 2.3 / 1316 4.1 / 1947 2.2	16 M	0051 4.3 / 0737 2.0 / 1338 4.3 / 2024 1.9
2 M	0157 4.2 / 0831 2.2 / 1431 4.2 / 2058 2.0	17 TU	0217 4.5 / 0908 1.7 / 1459 4.5 / 2141 1.6
3 TU	0300 4.5 / 0939 1.9 / 1529 4.4 / 2158 1.7	18 W	0326 4.8 / 1015 1.3 / 1601 4.8 / 2240 1.3
4 W	0352 4.7 / 1031 1.6 / 1618 4.7 / 2247 1.5	19 TH	0421 5.1 / 1109 0.9 / 1653 5.0 / 2330 0.9
5 TH	0436 5.0 / 1116 1.4 / 1701 4.8 / 2331 1.3	20 F	0509 5.4 / 1157 0.6 / ● 1738 5.2
6 F	0516 5.1 / 1157 1.2 / 1742 4.9 / ○	21 SA	0015 0.7 / 0553 5.5 / 1241 0.5 / 1822 5.2
7 SA	0011 1.1 / 0557 5.2 / 1236 1.0 / 1822 5.0	22 SU	0057 0.6 / 0636 5.5 / 1321 0.4 / 1902 5.2
8 SU	0049 1.0 / 0636 5.3 / 1313 0.9 / 1900 5.0	23 M	0135 0.6 / 0715 5.4 / 1357 0.5 / 1936 5.1
9 M	0124 0.9 / 0713 5.3 / 1348 0.9 / 1934 5.0	24 TU	0209 0.7 / 0748 5.3 / 1429 0.7 / 2004 5.0
10 TU	0158 0.9 / 0748 5.2 / 1421 0.9 / 2008 5.0	25 W	0238 1.0 / 0817 5.1 / 1456 1.1 / 2030 4.8
11 W	0231 1.0 / 0823 5.2 / 1454 1.0 / 2043 4.9	26 TH	0305 1.3 / 0843 4.8 / 1522 1.4 / 2057 4.6
12 TH	0306 1.2 / 0900 5.0 / 1530 1.3 / 2123 4.7	27 F	0330 1.5 / 0913 4.6 / 1547 1.7 / 2131 4.4
13 F	0346 1.4 / 0944 4.8 / 1613 1.5 / ◑ 2212 4.5	28 SA	0358 1.9 / 0951 4.3 / 1620 2.0 / 2216 4.2
14 SA	0437 1.7 / 1042 4.5 / 1712 1.8 / 2323 4.3	29 SU	0445 2.2 / 1045 4.0 / 1725 2.3 / 2325 4.0
15 SU	0552 2.0 / 1204 4.3 / 1842 2.0		

MARCH

Day	Time m	Day	Time m
1 M	0617 2.4 / 1214 3.9 / 1858 2.4	16 TU	0042 4.2 / 0739 2.1 / 1342 4.1 / 2026 2.0
2 TU	0108 4.0 / 0747 2.3 / 1403 4.0 / 2021 2.2	17 W	0214 4.4 / 0908 1.6 / 1500 4.4 / 2136 1.6
3 W	0231 4.3 / 0909 2.0 / 1508 4.3 / 2131 1.8	18 TH	0318 4.8 / 1006 1.2 / 1556 4.8 / 2228 1.2
4 TH	0326 4.6 / 1007 1.5 / 1557 4.6 / 2225 1.5	19 F	0408 5.1 / 1054 0.8 / 1640 5.0 / 2313 0.8
5 F	0413 4.9 / 1054 1.3 / 1641 4.8 / 2310 1.2	20 SA	0452 5.3 / 1138 0.5 / 1718 5.2 / ● 2355 0.6
6 SA	0455 5.1 / 1136 0.9 / 1720 5.0 / ○ 2351 0.9	21 SU	0530 5.4 / 1218 0.4 / 1755 5.2
7 SU	0534 5.3 / 1216 0.7 / 1759 5.1	22 M	0034 0.5 / 0609 5.4 / 1255 0.4 / 1830 5.2
8 M	0031 0.7 / 0615 5.4 / 1254 0.6 / 1837 5.2	23 TU	0109 0.6 / 0643 5.3 / 1328 0.6 / 1859 5.2
9 TU	0107 0.6 / 0652 5.4 / 1329 0.5 / 1913 5.2	24 W	0139 0.7 / 0712 5.2 / 1356 0.8 / 1923 5.1
10 W	0141 0.6 / 0729 5.4 / 1403 0.6 / 1947 5.2	25 TH	0206 1.0 / 0738 5.0 / 1420 1.1 / 1949 4.9
11 TH	0214 0.7 / 0804 5.2 / 1435 0.8 / 2021 5.0	26 F	0228 1.2 / 0805 4.8 / 1441 1.4 / 2016 4.7
12 F	0249 0.9 / 0841 5.0 / 1510 1.1 / 2059 4.8	27 SA	0248 1.5 / 0834 4.5 / 1500 1.6 / 2049 4.5
13 SA	0328 1.3 / 0925 4.7 / 1551 1.5 / ◑ 2146 4.5	28 SU	0310 1.8 / 0910 4.2 / 1524 1.9 / ◐ 2132 4.3
14 SU	0417 1.6 / 1023 4.3 / 1648 1.9 / 2257 4.3	29 M	0347 2.1 / 1005 4.0 / 1610 2.3 / 2235 4.1
15 M	0534 2.0 / 1156 4.0 / 1827 2.2	30 TU	0527 2.4 / 1125 3.8 / 1818 2.5
		31 W	0007 4.0 / 0711 2.3 / 1330 3.9 / 1946 2.2

APRIL

Day	Time m	Day	Time m
1 TH	0154 4.2 / 0831 1.9 / 1438 4.2 / 2056 1.8	16 F	0258 4.8 / 0942 1.2 / 1534 4.8 / 2203 1.2
2 F	0253 4.6 / 0931 1.5 / 1527 4.6 / 2151 1.5	17 SA	0346 5.0 / 1028 0.9 / 1615 5.0 / 2247 0.9
3 SA	0341 4.9 / 1020 1.1 / 1610 4.8 / 2239 1.1	18 SU	0427 5.2 / 1110 0.7 / 1651 5.1 / 2328 0.7
4 SU	0424 5.1 / 1105 0.8 / 1651 5.1 / 2323 0.8	19 M	0504 5.3 / 1149 0.6 / ● 1724 5.2
5 M	0506 5.3 / 1147 0.6 / 1730 5.2 / ○	20 TU	0005 0.7 / 0537 5.3 / 1224 0.6 / 1754 5.2
6 TU	0004 0.6 / 0547 5.4 / 1228 0.4 / 1809 5.3	21 W	0038 0.7 / 0609 5.2 / 1255 0.8 / 1822 5.2
7 W	0044 0.5 / 0628 5.5 / 1307 0.4 / 1848 5.4	22 TH	0108 0.9 / 0638 5.1 / 1322 1.0 / 1847 5.1
8 TH	0122 0.5 / 0709 5.4 / 1343 0.5 / 1925 5.3	23 F	0133 1.1 / 0706 4.9 / 1345 1.2 / 1915 5.0
9 F	0159 0.6 / 0749 5.2 / 1419 0.8 / 2003 5.2	24 SA	0156 1.3 / 0734 4.7 / 1406 1.5 / 1945 4.8
10 SA	0236 0.9 / 0830 5.0 / 1456 1.2 / 2044 4.9	25 SU	0217 1.5 / 0806 4.5 / 1427 1.6 / 2019 4.6
11 SU	0318 1.3 / 0918 4.6 / 1540 1.6 / 2134 4.6	26 M	0243 1.7 / 0846 4.2 / 1456 1.9 / 2103 4.4
12 M	0412 1.7 / 1020 4.2 / 1641 2.0 / ◐ 2246 4.3	27 TU	0324 2.0 / 0940 4.0 / 1544 2.2 / ◐ 2203 4.2
13 TU	0534 2.0 / 1201 4.0 / 1826 2.2	28 W	0450 2.2 / 1053 3.9 / 1738 2.4 / 2321 4.1
14 W	0036 4.2 / 0734 1.9 / 1336 4.2 / 2011 2.0	29 TH	0634 2.2 / 1235 4.0 / 1908 2.2
15 TH	0158 4.5 / 0849 1.5 / 1444 4.5 / 2113 1.5	30 F	0055 4.3 / 0747 1.8 / 1352 4.2 / 2014 1.8

Chapter 5

TIME ZONE (UT)
For Summer Time add ONE hour in **non-shaded areas**

ENGLAND – FALMOUTH

LAT 50°09′N   LONG 5°03′W

TIMES AND HEIGHTS OF HIGH AND LOW WATERS

YEAR 2004

MAY

Day	Time	m	Day	Time	m
1 SA	0206 / 0847 / 1445 / 2111	4.6 / 1.5 / 4.6 / 1.5	**16** SU	0313 / 0954 / 1540 / 2214	4.8 / 1.1 / 4.8 / 1.2
2 SU	0259 / 0940 / 1532 / 2202	4.8 / 1.1 / 4.8 / 1.1	**17** M	0356 / 1037 / 1618 / 2256	5.0 / 1.0 / 5.0 / 1.0
3 M	0347 / 1029 / 1616 / 2250	5.1 / 0.8 / 5.1 / 0.8	**18** TU	0434 / 1116 / 1651 / 2333	5.0 / 0.9 / 5.1 / 1.0
4 TU	0434 / 1116 / 1659 / 2337 ○	5.2 / 0.6 / 5.2 / 0.6	**19** W	0508 / 1151 / 1721 ●	5.0 / 1.0 / 5.1
5 W	0519 / 1201 / 1743	5.4 / 0.5 / 5.4	**20** TH	0008 / 0538 / 1223 / 1751	1.0 / 5.0 / 1.0 / 5.1
6 TH	0021 / 0605 / 1245 / 1826	0.5 / 5.4 / 0.5 / 5.4	**21** F	0039 / 0610 / 1252 / 1821	1.1 / 4.9 / 1.2 / 5.1
7 F	0104 / 0652 / 1327 / 1909	0.5 / 5.3 / 0.7 / 5.4	**22** SA	0107 / 0643 / 1318 / 1852	1.2 / 4.8 / 1.3 / 5.0
8 SA	0147 / 0738 / 1408 / 1952	0.7 / 5.2 / 0.9 / 5.2	**23** SU	0134 / 0716 / 1345 / 1925	1.4 / 4.7 / 1.5 / 4.8
9 SU	0230 / 0826 / 1451 / 2038	0.9 / 4.9 / 1.3 / 5.0	**24** M	0202 / 0752 / 1413 / 2001	1.5 / 4.5 / 1.6 / 4.7
10 M	0318 / 0920 / 1539 / 2131	1.3 / 4.6 / 1.5 / 4.7	**25** TU	0235 / 0833 / 1448 / 2046	1.6 / 4.3 / 1.8 / 4.5
11 TU	0414 / 1025 / 1641 / ◐ 2242	1.5 / 4.3 / 1.9	**26** W	0319 / 0925 / 1538 / 2140	1.8 / 4.2 / 2.0 / 4.4
12 W	0530 / 1152 / 1807	1.8 / 4.2 / 2.0	**27** TH	0424 / 1026 / ◐ 2243	2.0 / 4.1 / 4.3
13 TH	0016 / 0702 / 1307 / 1933	4.4 / 1.8 / 4.2 / 1.9	**28** F	0548 / 1140 / 1821 / 2356	1.9 / 4.1 / 2.0 / 4.4
14 F	0128 / 0812 / 1408 / 2036	4.5 / 1.6 / 4.4 / 1.6	**29** SA	0701 / 1253 / 1929	1.7 / 4.3 / 1.8
15 SA	0224 / 0907 / 1457 / 2128	4.7 / 1.4 / 4.7 / 1.4	**30** SU	0108 / 0802 / 1354 / 2029	4.6 / 1.5 / 4.5 / 1.5
			31 M	0211 / 0859 / 1449 / 2125	4.8 / 1.2 / 4.8 / 1.3

JUNE

Day	Time	m	Day	Time	m
1 TU	0309 / 0954 / 1541 / 2219	5.0 / 1.0 / 5.0 / 1.0	**16** W	0401 / 1043 / 1620 / 2303	4.7 / 1.3 / 4.9 / 1.3
2 W	0403 / 1047 / 1632 / 2312	5.1 / 0.9 / 5.2 / 0.8	**17** TH	0440 / 1121 / 1655 / ● 2341	4.8 / 1.3 / 5.0 / 1.3
3 TH	0456 / 1138 / 1719 / ○	5.2 / 0.7 / 5.3	**18** F	0516 / 1156 / 1729	4.8 / 1.3 / 5.1
4 F	0002 / 0548 / 1227 / 1808	0.7 / 5.3 / 0.7 / 5.4	**19** SA	0016 / 0553 / 1230 / 1804	1.3 / 4.8 / 1.3 / 5.0
5 SA	0052 / 0640 / 1315 / 1858	0.6 / 5.2 / 0.8 / 5.4	**20** SU	0049 / 0630 / 1302 / 1840	1.3 / 4.8 / 1.4 / 5.0
6 SU	0140 / 0732 / 1402 / 1946	0.7 / 5.1 / 0.9 / 5.3	**21** M	0122 / 0708 / 1334 / 1916	1.4 / 4.7 / 1.5 / 4.9
7 M	0228 / 0825 / 1448 / 2036	0.9 / 4.9 / 1.2 / 5.1	**22** TU	0155 / 0747 / 1408 / 1953	1.5 / 4.5 / 1.5 / 4.8
8 TU	0317 / 0920 / 1537 / 2128	1.1 / 4.7 / 1.4 / 4.9	**23** W	0231 / 0827 / 1443 / 2033	1.5 / 4.4 / 1.6 / 4.7
9 W	0409 / 1017 / 1629 / ◐ 2227	1.4 / 4.5 / 1.6 / 4.7	**24** TH	0310 / 0909 / 1525 / 2119	1.5 / 4.4 / 1.7 / 4.6
10 TH	0507 / 1122 / 1731 / 2338	1.5 / 4.4 / 1.8 / 4.5	**25** F	0357 / 0958 / 1616 / ◐ 2210	1.6 / 4.3 / 1.8 / 4.6
11 F	0613 / 1224 / 1840	1.6 / 4.3 / 1.8	**26** SA	0456 / 1056 / 1723 / 2311	1.7 / 4.3 / 1.8 / 4.5
12 SA	0043 / 0720 / 1321 / 1945	4.5 / 1.6 / 4.4 / 1.8	**27** SU	0607 / 1200 / 1838	1.6 / 4.4 / 1.8
13 SU	0141 / 0819 / 1413 / 2043	4.5 / 1.6 / 4.5 / 1.6	**28** M	0018 / 0716 / 1307 / 1948	4.6 / 1.5 / 4.5 / 1.6
14 M	0232 / 0912 / 1500 / 2135	4.6 / 1.5 / 4.6 / 1.5	**29** TU	0130 / 0822 / 1413 / 2053	4.6 / 1.5 / 4.7 / 1.5
15 TU	0318 / 1000 / 1542 / 2222	4.6 / 1.4 / 4.8 / 1.4	**30** W	0238 / 0925 / 1513 / 2155	4.8 / 1.3 / 4.9 / 1.2

JULY

Day	Time	m	Day	Time	m
1 TH	0342 / 1025 / 1611 / 2254	4.9 / 1.1 / 5.1 / 1.0	**16** F	0418 / 1057 / 1636 / 2321	4.6 / 1.5 / 4.9 / 1.4
2 F	0441 / 1122 / 1704 / ○ 2350	5.0 / 1.0 / 5.3 / 0.8	**17** SA	0500 / 1137 / 1714 ●	4.7 / 1.4 / 5.0
3 SA	0535 / 1216 / 1756	5.1 / 0.8 / 5.4	**18** SU	0000 / 0539 / 1216 / 1753	1.3 / 4.8 / 1.3 / 5.1
4 SU	0043 / 0631 / 1307 / 1847	0.7 / 5.2 / 0.8 / 5.5	**19** M	0037 / 0621 / 1251 / 1832	1.3 / 4.8 / 1.3 / 5.1
5 M	0134 / 0726 / 1355 / 1938	0.6 / 5.1 / 0.8 / 5.4	**20** TU	0112 / 0701 / 1325 / 1909	1.2 / 4.8 / 1.3 / 5.0
6 TU	0221 / 0817 / 1439 / 2026	0.7 / 5.0 / 0.9 / 5.3	**21** W	0146 / 0737 / 1358 / 1944	1.2 / 4.7 / 1.3 / 5.0
7 W	0306 / 0905 / 1522 / 2111	0.8 / 4.9 / 1.1 / 5.1	**22** TH	0219 / 0813 / 1430 / 2018	1.2 / 4.7 / 1.4 / 4.9
8 TH	0349 / 0950 / 1604 / 2155	1.1 / 4.7 / 1.4 / 4.9	**23** F	0253 / 0849 / 1504 / 2055	1.3 / 4.6 / 1.4 / 4.8
9 F	0432 / 1035 / 1649 / 2241	1.4 / 4.5 / 1.6 / 4.6	**24** SA	0329 / 0928 / 1544 / 2138	1.4 / 4.5 / 1.5 / 4.7
10 SA	0519 / 1127 / 1741 / 2338	1.6 / 4.3 / 1.8 / 4.4	**25** SU	0413 / 1015 / 1635 / ◐ 2231	1.5 / 4.4 / 1.7 / 4.6
11 SU	0613 / 1222 / 1841	1.8 / 4.2 / 2.0	**26** M	0511 / 1105 / 1745 / 2342	1.6 / 4.3 / 1.8 / 4.5
12 M	0042 / 0715 / 1321 / 1948	4.3 / 1.9 / 4.3 / 2.0	**27** TU	0629 / 1231 / 1913	1.8 / 4.4 / 1.8
13 TU	0145 / 0819 / 1417 / 2052	4.3 / 1.9 / 4.4 / 1.9	**28** W	0102 / 0754 / 1349 / 2033	4.4 / 1.7 / 4.5 / 1.6
14 W	0242 / 0919 / 1509 / 2150	4.3 / 1.8 / 4.6 / 1.7	**29** TH	0223 / 0909 / 1459 / 2144	4.5 / 1.5 / 4.8 / 1.4
15 TH	0333 / 1012 / 1555 / 2239	4.5 / 1.6 / 4.8 / 1.5	**30** F	0333 / 1016 / 1600 / 2247	4.8 / 1.3 / 5.1 / 1.1
			31 SA	0433 / 1114 / 1654 / ○ 2343	5.0 / 1.0 / 5.3 / 0.8

AUGUST

Day	Time	m	Day	Time	m
1 SU	0526 / 1207 / 1744	5.1 / 0.8 / 5.5	**16** M	0524 / 1159 / 1736 ●	4.9 / 1.2 / 5.2
2 M	0034 / 0620 / 1256 / 1834	0.6 / 5.2 / 0.6 / 5.5	**17** TU	0021 / 0604 / 1235 / 1816	1.1 / 4.9 / 1.1 / 5.2
3 TU	0121 / 0710 / 1340 / 1921	0.5 / 5.2 / 0.6 / 5.5	**18** W	0056 / 0642 / 1309 / 1851	1.0 / 5.0 / 1.0 / 5.2
4 W	0204 / 0755 / 1420 / 2004	0.5 / 5.1 / 0.7 / 5.4	**19** TH	0129 / 0718 / 1340 / 1925	0.9 / 5.0 / 1.0 / 5.2
5 TH	0244 / 0835 / 1457 / 2041	0.7 / 5.0 / 0.9 / 5.2	**20** F	0200 / 0750 / 1410 / 1957	1.0 / 4.9 / 1.1 / 5.1
6 F	0319 / 0909 / 1532 / 2112	0.9 / 4.8 / 1.2 / 4.9	**21** SA	0230 / 0822 / 1442 / 2031	1.1 / 4.8 / 1.2 / 5.0
7 SA	0353 / 0939 / 1606 / ◐ 2143	1.3 / 4.6 / 1.5 / 4.6	**22** SU	0303 / 0857 / 1518 / 2110	1.2 / 4.6 / 1.4 / 4.8
8 SU	0427 / 1012 / 1644 / 2221	1.6 / 4.4 / 1.8 / 4.4	**23** M	0341 / 0941 / 1603 / ◐ 2201	1.5 / 4.5 / 1.6 / 4.5
9 M	0509 / 1058 / 1737 / 2317	1.9 / 4.2 / 2.1 / 4.1	**24** TU	0432 / 1043 / 1709 / 2316	1.8 / 4.4 / 2.0 / 4.3
10 TU	0608 / 1212 / 1850	2.2 / 4.1 / 2.3	**25** W	0553 / 1209 / 1856	2.1 / 4.3 / 2.1
11 W	0050 / 0722 / 1338 / 2011	4.0 / 2.2 / 4.2 / 2.2	**26** TH	0054 / 0745 / 1342 / 2032	4.2 / 2.0 / 4.4 / 1.8
12 TH	0213 / 0842 / 1442 / 2125	4.1 / 2.1 / 4.4 / 1.9	**27** F	0226 / 0909 / 1456 / 2144	4.4 / 1.7 / 4.8 / 1.5
13 F	0312 / 0948 / 1533 / 2220	4.3 / 1.8 / 4.7 / 1.6	**28** SA	0334 / 1012 / 1555 / 2241	4.7 / 1.3 / 5.0 / 1.0
14 SA	0400 / 1038 / 1617 / 2304	4.6 / 1.5 / 4.9 / 1.4	**29** SU	0428 / 1105 / 1643 / 2331	5.0 / 1.0 / 5.4 / 0.7
15 SU	0443 / 1120 / 1658 / 2344	4.7 / 1.4 / 5.1 / 1.2	**30** M	0514 / 1153 / 1728 ○	5.2 / 0.7 / 5.6
			31 TU	0017 / 0600 / 1237 / 1813	0.4 / 5.3 / 0.5 / 5.6

Chart Datum: 2·91 metres below Ordnance Datum (Newlyn)

TIME ZONE (UT)
For Summer Time add ONE hour in **non-shaded areas**

ENGLAND – FALMOUTH
LAT 50°09'N   LONG 5°03'W
TIMES AND HEIGHTS OF HIGH AND LOW WATERS

YEAR 2004

SEPTEMBER

Day	Time m	Time m	Time m	Time m		Day	Time m	Time m	Time m	Time m
1 W	0100 0.4	0643 5.3	1854 5.5			16 TH	0031 0.8	0616 5.2	1245 0.8	1827 5.4
2 TH	0139 0.5	0721 5.2	1353 0.6	1930 5.4		17 F	0104 0.7	0650 5.2	1318 0.8	1902 5.3
3 F	0213 0.7	0754 5.1	1426 0.9	2001 5.2		18 SA	0136 0.8	0723 5.2	1349 0.9	1935 5.2
4 SA	0243 1.0	0820 4.9	1454 1.2	2027 4.9		19 SU	0207 1.0	0756 5.1	1422 1.1	2011 5.0
5 SU	0310 1.4	0844 4.7	1521 1.5	2054 4.6		20 M	0240 1.3	0833 4.9	1458 1.4	2053 4.8
6 M	0336 1.7	0914 4.5	1550 1.9	2128 4.3 ☽		21 TU	0318 1.5	0919 4.6	1544 1.7	2146 4.4 ☽
7 TU	0406 2.1	0957 4.3	1633 2.3	2218 4.0		22 W	0409 2.0	1023 4.4	1654 2.1	2307 4.1
8 W	0504 2.4	1101 4.1	1758 2.5	2342 3.9		23 TH	0541 2.3	1159 4.2	1900 2.2	
9 TH	0637 2.5	1255 4.1	1935 2.4			24 F	0104 4.1	0752 2.2	1343 4.5	2035 1.8
10 F	0150 4.0	0811 2.3	1416 4.3	2102 2.1		25 SA	0232 4.5	0906 1.7	1452 4.9	2136 1.4
11 SA	0252 4.3	0924 1.9	1511 4.6	2155 1.6		26 SU	0330 4.8	1000 1.3	1543 5.2	2226 0.9
12 SU	0340 4.6	1013 1.5	1555 4.9	2238 1.4		27 M	0415 5.1	1048 0.9	1627 5.5	2311 0.6
13 M	0422 4.8	1055 1.3	1635 5.1	2317 1.1		28 TU	0456 5.3	1131 0.7	1707 5.6	2353 0.5
14 TU	0501 5.0	1134 1.1	1712 5.3	2355 0.9		29 W	0533 5.4	1212 0.6	1746 5.6	
15 W	0538 5.1	1211 0.9	1751 5.4			30 TH	0032 0.5	0610 5.4	1249 0.6	1822 5.5

OCTOBER

Day	Time m	Time m	Time m	Time m		Day	Time m	Time m	Time m	Time m
1 F	0107 0.6	0642 5.3	1322 0.8	1852 5.3		16 SA	0038 0.7	0623 5.4	1256 0.8	1839 5.4
2 SA	0138 0.9	0710 5.2	1351 1.0	1919 5.1		17 SU	0114 0.8	0700 5.4	1331 0.9	1918 5.3
3 SU	0204 1.2	0733 5.0	1416 1.3	1946 4.9		18 M	0149 1.0	0737 5.2	1408 1.1	1959 5.0
4 M	0227 1.5	0800 4.9	1439 1.6	2013 4.6		19 TU	0225 1.4	0819 5.0	1449 1.5	2046 4.7
5 TU	0247 1.8	0833 4.6	1500 1.9	2050 4.3		20 W	0308 1.7	0908 4.8	1540 1.8	2144 4.4 ☽
6 W	0307 2.1	0915 4.4	1531 2.3	2140 4.1		21 TH	0404 2.1	1014 4.5	1657 2.2	2313 4.1
7 TH	0345 2.5	1016 4.1	1707 2.6	2256 3.9		22 F	0543 2.4	1155 4.4	1858 2.1	
8 F	0555 2.7	1149 4.1	1858 2.5			23 SA	0103 4.2	0739 2.2	1329 4.6	2018 1.7
9 SA	0118 3.9	0734 2.5	1342 4.3	2022 2.1		24 SU	0216 4.5	0845 1.7	1432 4.9	2113 1.4
10 SU	0223 4.3	0846 2.0	1438 4.6	2116 1.7		25 M	0309 4.9	0936 1.4	1521 5.2	2201 1.0
11 M	0310 4.6	0936 1.6	1522 4.9	2200 1.4		26 TU	0353 5.1	1022 1.1	1604 5.4	2244 0.8
12 TU	0352 4.9	1020 1.3	1604 5.2	2242 1.1		27 W	0430 5.3	1104 0.9	1642 5.4	2324 0.7
13 W	0431 5.1	1101 1.1	1643 5.3	2322 0.8		28 TH	0505 5.4	1143 0.8	1717 5.4 ○	
14 TH	0509 5.2	1141 0.9	1722 5.4 ●			29 F	0001 0.8	0536 5.4	1219 0.8	1749 5.4
15 F	0001 0.7	0546 5.3	1219 0.8	1801 5.5		30 SA	0035 0.9	0605 5.3	1251 1.0	1819 5.2
						31 SU	0103 1.1	0632 5.3	1319 1.2	1845 5.1

NOVEMBER

Day	Time m	Time m	Time m	Time m		Day	Time m	Time m	Time m	Time m
1 M	0129 1.3	0700 5.1	1344 1.5	1914 4.9		16 TU	0139 1.1	0728 5.4	1404 1.1	1956 5.0
2 TU	0151 1.5	0729 5.0	1407 1.6	1946 4.6		17 W	0222 1.4	0815 5.2	1451 1.4	2048 4.8
3 W	0212 1.8	0804 4.7	1432 1.9	2025 4.4		18 TH	0309 1.6	0907 4.9	1545 1.6	2148 4.5
4 TH	0238 2.1	0849 4.5	1508 2.2	2118 4.1		19 F	0407 2.0	1011 4.7	1655 1.9	2309 4.3 ☽
5 F	0320 2.4	0945 4.3	1621 2.5	2226 4.0 ☽		20 SA	0527 2.2	1137 4.6	1825 1.9	
6 SA	0502 2.6	1100 4.2	1809 2.4			21 SU	0033 4.3	0659 2.1	1256 4.6	1940 1.7
7 SU	0009 4.0	0644 2.5	1237 4.3	1928 2.1		22 M	0140 4.5	0807 1.8	1358 4.8	2038 1.5
8 M	0134 4.3	0755 2.1	1347 4.6	2026 1.7		23 TU	0233 4.7	0902 1.5	1449 4.9	2128 1.4
9 TU	0226 4.6	0850 1.7	1439 4.8	2116 1.5		24 W	0318 4.9	0951 1.4	1535 5.1	2213 1.2
10 W	0312 4.8	0939 1.5	1525 5.1	2203 1.2		25 TH	0359 5.1	1034 1.2	1615 5.2	2254 1.1
11 TH	0355 5.1	1026 1.2	1610 5.3	2248 1.0		26 F	0436 5.2	1114 1.1	1650 5.3	2331 1.1 ○
12 F	0437 5.3	1111 1.0	1654 5.4	2332 0.8 ●		27 SA	0508 5.3	1151 1.1	1722 5.1	
13 SA	0518 5.4	1154 0.8	1737 5.4			28 SU	0005 1.2	0536 5.3	1224 1.2	1753 5.1
14 SU	0015 0.8	0600 5.5	1238 0.8	1823 5.4		29 M	0035 1.3	0607 5.2	1255 1.4	1825 5.0
15 M	0057 0.9	0643 5.5	1320 0.9	1909 5.3		30 TU	0103 1.5	0639 5.1	1323 1.5	1858 4.8

DECEMBER

Day	Time m	Time m	Time m	Time m		Day	Time m	Time m	Time m	Time m
1 W	0131 1.5	0713 5.0	1352 1.6	1933 4.6		16 TH	0222 1.2	0813 5.4	1452 1.1	2049 4.9
2 TH	0159 1.7	0750 4.8	1423 1.8	2013 4.4		17 F	0309 1.4	0904 5.2	1541 1.3	2142 4.7
3 F	0231 1.9	0832 4.7	1501 2.0	2102 4.3		18 SA	0359 1.5	0958 5.0	1634 1.5	2241 4.5 ☽
4 SA	0312 2.1	0922 4.5	1554 2.1	2158 4.2		19 SU	0454 1.8	1100 4.8	1736 1.7	2347 4.4
5 SU	0413 2.3	1020 4.4	1709 2.2	2306 4.2 ☽		20 M	0600 1.9	1208 4.6	1843 1.8	
6 M	0539 2.3	1129 4.4	1828 2.1			21 TU	0049 4.4	0712 2.0	1310 4.6	1949 1.8
7 TU	0018 4.3	0657 2.1	1239 4.5	1933 1.8		22 W	0146 4.5	0817 1.9	1408 4.6	2048 1.7
8 W	0125 4.5	0801 1.9	1344 4.7	2031 1.5		23 TH	0239 4.6	0915 1.7	1500 4.7	2140 1.6
9 TH	0222 4.7	0858 1.6	1443 4.9	2126 1.4		24 F	0326 4.8	1005 1.5	1547 4.8	2226 1.5
10 F	0316 4.9	0953 1.4	1538 5.1	2218 1.2		25 SA	0408 5.0	1050 1.5	1627 4.9	2306 1.4
11 SA	0408 5.2	1046 1.1	1631 5.2	2310 1.0		26 SU	0444 5.1	1130 1.4	1704 4.9	2343 1.4 ○
12 SU	0457 5.3	1136 0.9	1721 5.3	2359 0.9 ●		27 M	0518 5.2	1210 1.4	1738 4.9	
13 M	0545 5.5	1226 0.8	1813 5.3			28 TU	0017 1.4	0554 5.2	1241 1.4	1815 4.9
14 TU	0048 0.9	0634 5.5	1315 0.8	1904 5.2		29 W	0050 1.4	0630 5.1	1313 1.4	1852 4.8
15 W	0135 1.0	0724 5.5	1404 0.9	1956 5.1		30 TH	0122 1.5	0707 5.0	1345 1.5	1929 4.7
						31 F	0153 1.5	0744 4.9	1417 1.5	2007 4.6

Chart Datum: 2·91 metres below Ordnance Datum (Newlyn)

Chapter 5

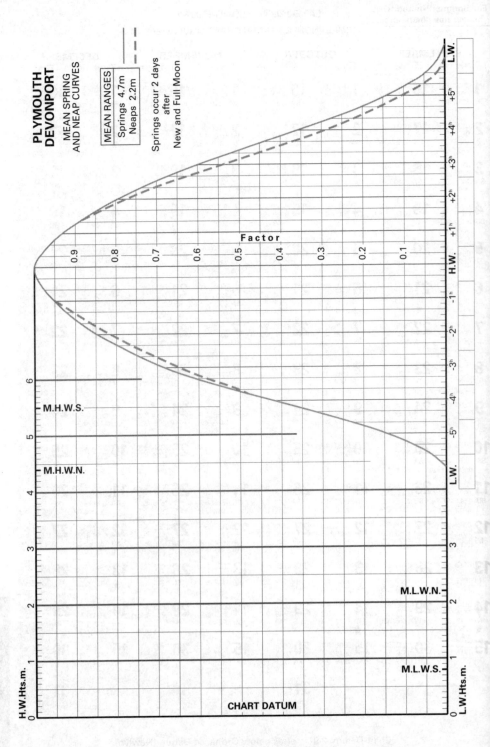

PLYMOUTH DEVONPORT
MEAN SPRING AND NEAP CURVES

MEAN RANGES	
Springs	4.7m
Neaps	2.2m

Springs occur 2 days after New and Full Moon

Factor

ENGLAND – PLYMOUTH

LAT 50°22'N   LONG 4°11'W

TIMES AND HEIGHTS OF HIGH AND LOW WATERS

YEAR **2004**

JANUARY

Time	m	Time	m
1 TH 0016 / 0616 / 1235 / 1855	4.3 / 2.2 / 4.5 / 2.1	**16** 0522 / 1141 / F 1807	1.9 / 4.7 / 1.9
2 F 0118 / 0724 / 1340 / 1959	4.3 / 2.3 / 4.4 / 2.1	**17** SA 0024 / 0642 / 1257 / 1929	4.5 / 2.0 / 4.6 / 1.9
3 SA 0217 / 0831 / 1441 / 2059	4.4 / 2.1 / 4.5 / 2.0	**18** SU 0143 / 0807 / 1417 / 2046	4.6 / 1.9 / 4.7 / 1.7
4 SU 0312 / 0929 / 1535 / 2150	4.6 / 2.0 / 4.7 / 1.8	**19** M 0258 / 0922 / 1531 / 2155	4.8 / 1.6 / 4.8 / 1.5
5 M 0401 / 1019 / 1624 / 2236	4.8 / 1.7 / 4.8 / 1.6	**20** TU 0405 / 1028 / 1636 / 2255	5.1 / 1.3 / 5.0 / 1.2
6 TU 0446 / 1103 / 1708 / 2317	5.0 / 1.6 / 4.9 / 1.5	**21** W 0503 / 1125 / 1733 / ● 2349	5.3 / 1.0 / 5.2 / 1.0
7 W 0527 / 1142 / 1749 / ○ 2355	5.2 / 1.4 / 5.0 / 1.4	**22** TH 0554 / 1217 / 1824	5.5 / 0.8 / 5.3
8 TH 0606 / 1220 / 1828	5.2 / 1.3 / 5.0	**23** F 0038 / 0642 / 1305 / 1912	0.8 / 5.6 / 0.6 / 5.3
9 F 0032 / 0643 / 1256 / 1906	1.3 / 5.3 / 1.3 / 5.0	**24** SA 0124 / 0729 / 1350 / 1958	0.8 / 5.6 / 0.6 / 5.2
10 SA 0108 / 0720 / 1332 / 1943	1.3 / 5.2 / 1.3 / 5.0	**25** SU 0205 / 0812 / 1430 / 2038	0.8 / 5.5 / 0.7 / 5.1
11 SU 0143 / 0756 / 1408 / 2019	1.3 / 5.2 / 1.3 / 4.9	**26** M 0243 / 0850 / 1507 / 2113	1.0 / 5.4 / 0.9 / 5.0
12 M 0218 / 0831 / 1444 / 2055	1.4 / 5.1 / 1.3 / 4.8	**27** TU 0318 / 0923 / 1541 / 2144	1.2 / 5.2 / 1.2 / 4.8
13 TU 0254 / 0909 / 1521 / 2134	1.4 / 5.1 / 1.4 / 4.7	**28** W 0351 / 0954 / 1615 / 2214	1.5 / 4.9 / 1.6 / 4.6
14 W 0334 / 0950 / 1604 / 2219	1.6 / 5.0 / 1.6 / 4.6	**29** TH 0426 / 1028 / 1653 / ◑ 2252	1.8 / 4.7 / 1.9 / 4.4
15 TH 0421 / 1040 / 1657 / ◑ 2315	1.7 / 4.8 / 1.7 / 4.5	**30** F 0508 / 1112 / 1739 / 2346	2.1 / 4.4 / 2.2 / 4.3
		31 SA 0608 / 1217 / 1844	2.3 / 4.2 / 2.3

FEBRUARY

Time	m	Time	m
1 SU 0104 / 0723 / 1344 / 1957	4.2 / 2.4 / 4.2 / 2.3	**16** M 0118 / 0747 / 1406 / 2034	4.4 / 2.1 / 4.4 / 2.0
2 M 0226 / 0841 / 1501 / 2108	4.3 / 2.3 / 4.3 / 2.1	**17** TU 0247 / 0918 / 1530 / 2151	4.6 / 1.8 / 4.6 / 1.7
3 TU 0331 / 0949 / 1601 / 2208	4.6 / 2.0 / 4.5 / 1.8	**18** W 0358 / 1025 / 1634 / 2250	4.9 / 1.3 / 4.9 / 1.3
4 W 0424 / 1041 / 1651 / 2257	4.8 / 1.7 / 4.8 / 1.6	**19** TH 0454 / 1119 / 1727 / 2340	5.2 / 0.9 / 5.1 / 0.9
5 TH 0509 / 1126 / 1735 / 2341	5.1 / 1.4 / 4.9 / 1.3	**20** F 0543 / 1207 / ● 1813	5.5 / 0.6 / 5.3
6 F 0551 / 1207 / 1816	5.2 / 1.2 / 5.0	**21** SA 0025 / 0627 / 1251 / 1855	0.7 / 5.6 / 0.5 / 5.3
7 SA 0021 / 0631 / 1246 / ○ 1855	1.1 / 5.3 / 1.0 / 5.1	**22** SU 0107 / 0709 / 1331 / 1934	0.6 / 5.6 / 0.4 / 5.3
8 SU 0059 / 0709 / 1323 / 1932	1.0 / 5.4 / 0.9 / 5.1	**23** M 0145 / 0747 / 1407 / 2008	0.6 / 5.5 / 0.5 / 5.2
9 M 0134 / 0745 / 1358 / 2006	0.9 / 5.4 / 0.9 / 5.1	**24** TU 0219 / 0819 / 1439 / 2035	0.7 / 5.4 / 0.8 / 5.1
10 TU 0208 / 0819 / 1431 / 2039	0.9 / 5.3 / 0.9 / 5.1	**25** W 0248 / 0847 / 1506 / 2100	1.0 / 5.2 / 1.1 / 4.9
11 W 0241 / 0853 / 1504 / 2113	1.0 / 5.3 / 1.0 / 5.0	**26** TH 0315 / 0913 / 1532 / 2126	1.3 / 4.9 / 1.4 / 4.7
12 TH 0316 / 0929 / 1540 / 2151	1.2 / 5.1 / 1.3 / 4.8	**27** F 0340 / 0942 / 1557 / 2159	1.6 / 4.7 / 1.8 / 4.5
13 F 0356 / 1012 / 1623 / ◑ 2239	1.4 / 4.9 / 1.6 / 4.6	**28** SA 0408 / 1019 / 1630 / 2243	2.0 / 4.4 / 2.1 / 4.3
14 SA 0447 / 1109 / 1722 / 2348	1.8 / 4.6 / 1.9 / 4.4	**29** SU 0455 / 1112 / 1735 / 2350	2.3 / 4.1 / 2.4 / 4.1
15 SU 0602 / 1230 / 1852	2.1 / 4.4 / 2.1		

MARCH

Time	m	Time	m
1 M 0627 / 1240 / 1908	2.5 / 4.0 / 2.5	**16** TU 0109 / 0749 / 1410 / 2036	4.3 / 2.2 / 4.2 / 2.1
2 TU 0136 / 0757 / 1432 / 2031	4.1 / 2.4 / 4.1 / 2.3	**17** W 0243 / 0918 / 1531 / 2146	4.5 / 1.7 / 4.5 / 1.7
3 W 0301 / 0919 / 1539 / 2141	4.4 / 2.1 / 4.4 / 1.9	**18** TH 0350 / 1016 / 1628 / 2238	4.9 / 1.2 / 4.9 / 1.2
4 TH 0358 / 1017 / 1630 / 2235	4.7 / 1.6 / 4.7 / 1.5	**19** F 0441 / 1104 / 1713 / 2323	5.2 / 0.8 / 5.1 / 0.8
5 F 0446 / 1104 / 1714 / 2320	5.0 / 1.3 / 4.9 / 1.2	**20** SA 0526 / 1148 / ● 1753	5.4 / 0.5 / 5.3
6 SA 0529 / 1146 / ○ 1755	5.2 / 0.9 / 5.1	**21** SU 0005 / 0605 / 1228 / 1829	0.6 / 5.5 / 0.4 / 5.3
7 SU 0001 / 0609 / 1226 / 1833	0.9 / 5.4 / 0.7 / 5.2	**22** M 0044 / 0643 / 1305 / 1903	0.5 / 5.5 / 0.4 / 5.3
8 M 0041 / 0648 / 1304 / 1910	0.7 / 5.5 / 0.6 / 5.3	**23** TU 0119 / 0716 / 1338 / 1931	0.6 / 5.4 / 0.6 / 5.3
9 TU 0117 / 0725 / 1339 / 1945	0.6 / 5.5 / 0.5 / 5.3	**24** W 0149 / 0744 / 1406 / 1955	0.7 / 5.3 / 0.8 / 5.2
10 W 0151 / 0801 / 1413 / 2018	0.6 / 5.5 / 0.6 / 5.3	**25** TH 0216 / 0810 / 1430 / 2020	1.0 / 5.1 / 1.1 / 5.0
11 TH 0224 / 0835 / 1445 / 2051	0.7 / 5.3 / 0.8 / 5.1	**26** F 0238 / 0836 / 1451 / 2046	1.2 / 4.9 / 1.4 / 4.8
12 F 0259 / 0911 / 1520 / 2128	0.9 / 5.1 / 1.1 / 4.9	**27** SA 0258 / 0904 / 1510 / 2118	1.5 / 4.6 / 1.7 / 4.6
13 SA 0338 / 0953 / 1601 / ◑ 2214	1.3 / 4.8 / 1.6 / 4.6	**28** SU 0320 / 0939 / 1534 / ● 2200	1.9 / 4.3 / 2.0 / 4.4
14 SU 0427 / 1050 / 1658 / 2323	1.7 / 4.4 / 2.0 / 4.2	**29** M 0357 / 1032 / 1620 / 2302	2.2 / 4.1 / 2.4 / 4.2
15 M 0544 / 1222 / 1837	2.1 / 4.1 / 2.3	**30** TU 0537 / 1150 / 1828	2.5 / 3.9 / 2.6
		31 W 0033 / 0721 / 1358 / 1956	4.1 / 2.4 / 4.0 / 2.3

APRIL

Time	m	Time	m
1 TH 0223 / 0841 / 1508 / 2106	4.3 / 2.0 / 4.3 / 1.9	**16** F 0329 / 0952 / 1606 / 2213	4.9 / 1.2 / 4.9 / 1.2
2 F 0324 / 0941 / 1559 / 2201	4.7 / 1.6 / 4.7 / 1.5	**17** SA 0418 / 1038 / 1648 / 2257	5.1 / 0.9 / 5.1 / 0.9
3 SA 0413 / 1030 / 1643 / 2249	5.0 / 1.1 / 4.9 / 1.1	**18** SU 0500 / 1120 / 1725 / 2338	5.3 / 0.7 / 5.2 / 0.7
4 SU 0457 / 1115 / 1725 / 2333	5.2 / 0.8 / 5.2 / 0.8	**19** M 0538 / 1159 / 1759 ●	5.4 / 0.6 / 5.3
5 M 0540 / 1157 / ○ 1805	5.4 / 0.6 / 5.3	**20** TU 0015 / 0612 / 1234 / 1828	0.7 / 5.4 / 0.6 / 5.3
6 TU 0014 / 0621 / 1238 / 1843	0.6 / 5.5 / 0.4 / 5.4	**21** W 0048 / 0643 / 1305 / 1855	0.7 / 5.3 / 0.8 / 5.3
7 W 0054 / 0701 / 1317 / 1921	0.5 / 5.6 / 0.4 / 5.5	**22** TH 0118 / 0711 / 1332 / 1920	0.9 / 5.2 / 1.0 / 5.2
8 TH 0132 / 0741 / 1353 / 1957	0.5 / 5.5 / 0.5 / 5.4	**23** F 0143 / 0738 / 1355 / 1947	1.1 / 5.0 / 1.2 / 5.1
9 F 0209 / 0820 / 1429 / 2034	0.6 / 5.3 / 0.8 / 5.3	**24** SA 0206 / 0806 / 1416 / 2016	1.3 / 4.8 / 1.5 / 4.9
10 SA 0246 / 0900 / 1506 / 2114	0.9 / 5.1 / 1.2 / 5.0	**25** SU 0227 / 0837 / 1437 / 2049	1.6 / 4.6 / 1.7 / 4.7
11 SU 0328 / 0946 / 1550 / 2202	1.3 / 4.7 / 1.7 / 4.7	**26** M 0253 / 0915 / 1506 / 2132	1.8 / 4.3 / 2.0 / 4.5
12 M 0422 / 1047 / 1651 / ◑ 2313	1.8 / 4.3 / 2.1 / 4.4	**27** TU 0334 / 1008 / 1554 / ◑ 2230	2.1 / 4.1 / 2.3 / 4.3
13 TU 0544 / 1227 / 1836	2.1 / 4.1 / 2.3	**28** W 0500 / 1119 / 1748 / 2346	2.5 / 4.0 / 2.5 / 4.2
14 W 0103 / 0744 / 1404 / 2021	4.3 / 2.0 / 4.3 / 2.1	**29** TH 0644 / 1302 / 1918	2.3 / 4.1 / 2.3
15 TH 0227 / 0859 / 1514 / 2123	4.6 / 1.6 / 4.6 / 1.6	**30** F 0122 / 0757 / 1421 / 2024	4.4 / 1.9 / 4.3 / 1.9

Chapter 5

Chart Datum: 3·22 metres below Ordnance Datum (Newlyn)

ENGLAND – PLYMOUTH

TIME ZONE (UT)
For Summer Time add ONE hour in **non-shaded areas**

LAT 50°22'N   LONG 4°11'W

TIMES AND HEIGHTS OF HIGH AND LOW WATERS

YEAR 2004

MAY

Time	m		Time	m
1 0235	4.7	**16**	0344	4.9
0857	1.5		1004	1.1
SA 1516	4.7	SU	1612	4.9
2121	1.5		2224	1.2
2 0330	4.9	**17**	0428	5.1
0950	1.1		1047	1.0
SU 1604	4.9	M	1651	5.1
2212	1.1		2306	1.0
3 0419	5.2	**18**	0507	5.1
1039	0.8		1126	0.9
M 1649	5.2	TU	1725	5.2
2300	0.8		2343	1.0
4 0507	5.3	**19**	0542	5.1
1126	0.6		1201	1.0
TU 1733	5.3	W	1756	5.2
○ 2347	0.6	●		
5 0554	5.5	**20**	0018	1.0
1211	0.5		0613	5.1
W 1817	5.5	TH	1233	1.0
			1825	5.2
6 0031	0.5	**21**	0049	1.1
0639	5.5		0644	5.0
TH 1255	0.5	F	1302	1.2
1859	5.5		1854	5.2
7 0114	0.5	**22**	0117	1.2
0725	5.4		0716	4.9
F 1337	0.7	SA	1328	1.3
1941	5.5		1925	5.1
8 0157	0.7	**23**	0144	1.4
0810	5.3		0748	4.8
SA 1418	0.9	SU	1355	1.5
2023	5.3		1957	4.9
9 0240	0.9	**24**	0212	1.6
0856	5.0		0823	4.6
SU 1501	1.3	M	1423	1.7
2108	5.1		2032	4.8
10 0328	1.3	**25**	0245	1.7
0948	4.7		0903	4.4
M 1549	1.6	TU	1458	1.9
2159	4.8		2115	4.6
11 0424	1.6	**26**	0329	1.9
1052	4.4		0953	4.3
TU 1651	2.0	W	1548	2.1
◑ 2309	4.6		2208	4.5
12 0540	1.9	**27**	0434	2.1
1218	4.3		1053	4.2
W 1817	2.1	TH	1705	2.2
		◑	2310	4.4
13 0042	4.5	**28**	0558	2.0
0712	1.9		1205	4.2
TH 1335	4.3	F	1831	2.1
1943	2.0			
14 0156	4.6	**29**	0022	4.5
0822	1.6		0711	1.8
F 1437	4.5	SA	1320	4.4
2046	1.7		1939	1.9
15 0254	4.8	**30**	0136	4.7
0917	1.4		0812	1.5
SA 1528	4.8	SU	1423	4.6
2138	1.4		2039	1.6
		31	0240	4.9
			0909	1.2
		M	1520	4.9
			2135	1.3

JUNE

Time	m		Time	m
1 0340	5.1	**16**	0434	4.8
1004	1.0		1053	1.3
TU 1613	5.1	W	1653	5.0
2229	1.0		2313	1.3
2 0436	5.2	**17**	0513	4.9
1057	0.9		1131	1.3
W 1705	5.3	TH	1729	5.1
2322	0.8	●	2351	1.3
3 0530	5.3	**18**	0551	4.9
1148	0.7		1206	1.3
TH 1754	5.4	F	1804	5.2
○				
4 0012	0.7	**19**	0026	1.3
0622	5.4		0627	4.9
F 1237	0.7	SA	1240	1.3
1842	5.5		1838	5.1
5 0102	0.6	**20**	0059	1.3
0713	5.3		0703	4.9
SA 1325	0.8	SU	1312	1.4
1930	5.5		1913	5.1
6 0150	0.7	**21**	0132	1.4
0804	5.2		0740	4.8
SU 1412	0.9	M	1344	1.5
2017	5.4		1948	5.0
7 0238	0.9	**22**	0205	1.5
0855	5.0		0818	4.6
M 1458	1.2	TU	1418	1.6
2106	5.2		2024	4.9
8 0327	1.1	**23**	0241	1.5
0948	4.8		0857	4.5
TU 1547	1.4	W	1453	1.7
2156	5.0		2103	4.8
9 0419	1.4	**24**	0320	1.6
1044	4.6		0938	4.5
W 1639	1.7	TH	1535	1.8
2254	4.8		2147	4.7
10 0517	1.6	**25**	0407	1.7
1147	4.5		1026	4.4
TH 1741	1.9	F	1626	1.9
		◑	2237	4.7
11 0003	4.6	**26**	0506	1.8
0623	1.7		1122	4.4
F 1251	4.4	SA	1733	1.9
1850	1.9		2337	4.6
12 0110	4.6	**27**	0617	1.7
0730	1.7		1226	4.5
SA 1349	4.5	SU	1848	1.9
1955	1.9			
13 0209	4.6	**28**	0045	4.7
0829	1.7		0726	1.6
SU 1442	4.6	M	1335	4.6
2053	1.7		1958	1.7
14 0302	4.7	**29**	0158	4.7
0922	1.6		0832	1.5
M 1531	4.7	TU	1442	4.8
2145	1.6		2103	1.5
15 0350	4.7	**30**	0308	4.9
1010	1.4		0935	1.2
TU 1614	4.9	W	1545	5.0
2232	1.4		2205	1.2

JULY

Time	m		Time	m
1 0414	5.0	**16**	0451	4.7
1035	1.1		1107	1.5
TH 1644	5.2	F	1709	5.0
2304	1.0		2331	1.4
2 0514	5.1	**17**	0534	4.8
1132	1.0		1147	1.4
F 1738	5.4	SA	1749	5.1
○		●		
3 0000	0.8	**18**	0010	1.3
0610	5.2		0614	4.9
SA 1226	0.8	SU	1226	1.3
1830	5.5		1827	5.2
4 0053	0.7	**19**	0047	1.3
0704	5.3		0654	4.9
SU 1317	0.8	M	1301	1.3
1920	5.6		1905	5.2
5 0144	0.6	**20**	0122	1.2
0758	5.2		0733	4.9
M 1405	0.8	TU	1335	1.3
2010	5.5		1941	5.1
6 0231	0.7	**21**	0156	1.2
0847	5.1		0809	4.8
TU 1449	0.9	W	1408	1.3
2056	5.4		2015	5.1
7 0316	0.8	**22**	0229	1.2
0934	5.0		0844	4.8
W 1532	1.1	TH	1440	1.4
2140	5.2		2048	5.0
8 0359	1.1	**23**	0303	1.3
1018	4.8		0918	4.7
TH 1614	1.4	F	1514	1.4
2223	5.0		2124	4.9
9 0442	1.4	**24**	0339	1.4
1102	4.6		0956	4.6
F 1659	1.7	SA	1554	1.6
◑ 2308	4.7		2206	4.8
10 0529	1.7	**25**	0423	1.6
1152	4.4		1042	4.5
SA 1751	1.9	SU	1645	1.8
		◑	2258	4.7
11 0003	4.5	**26**	0521	1.7
0623	1.9		1143	4.5
SU 1249	4.3	M	1755	1.9
1851	2.1			
12 0109	4.4	**27**	0007	4.6
0725	2.0		0639	1.9
M 1349	4.4	TU	1258	4.5
1958	2.1		1923	1.9
13 0213	4.4	**28**	0130	4.5
0829	2.0		0804	1.8
TU 1447	4.5	W	1418	4.6
2102	2.0		2043	1.7
14 0312	4.6	**29**	0253	4.6
0929	1.9		0919	1.6
W 1540	4.7	TH	1530	4.9
2200	1.8		2154	1.4
15 0405	4.6	**30**	0405	4.9
1022	1.7		1026	1.3
TH 1627	4.9	F	1633	5.2
2249	1.6		2257	1.1
		31	0506	5.1
			1124	1.0
		SA	1728	5.4
		○	2353	0.8

AUGUST

Time	m		Time	m
1 0601	5.2	**16**	0559	5.0
1217	0.8		1209	1.2
SU 1818	5.6	M	1811	5.3
2 0044	0.6	**17**	0031	1.1
0653	5.3		0638	5.0
M 1306	0.6	TU	1245	1.1
1907	5.6		1849	5.3
3 0131	0.5	**18**	0106	1.0
0742	5.3		0715	5.1
TU 1350	0.6	W	1319	1.0
1953	5.6		1924	5.3
4 0214	0.5	**19**	0139	0.9
0826	5.2		0750	5.1
W 1430	0.7	TH	1350	1.0
2035	5.5		1957	5.3
5 0254	0.7	**20**	0210	1.0
0905	5.1		0821	5.0
TH 1507	0.9	F	1420	1.1
2111	5.3		2028	5.2
6 0329	0.9	**21**	0240	1.1
0938	4.9		0852	4.9
F 1542	1.2	SA	1452	1.3
2141	5.0		2101	5.1
7 0403	1.3	**22**	0313	1.2
1007	4.7		0926	4.8
SA 1616	1.6	SU	1528	1.4
◑ 2211	4.7		2139	4.9
8 0437	1.7	**23**	0351	1.5
1039	4.5		1009	4.6
SU 1654	1.9	M	1613	1.7
2248	4.5	◑	2229	4.6
9 0519	2.0	**24**	0442	1.9
1124	4.3		1110	4.5
M 1747	2.2	TU	1719	2.1
2343	4.2		2342	4.4
10 0618	2.3	**25**	0603	2.2
1238	4.2		1235	4.4
TU 1900	2.4	W	1906	2.2
11 0117	4.1	**26**	0121	4.3
0732	2.3		0755	2.1
W 1406	4.3	TH	1410	4.5
2021	2.3		2042	1.9
12 0242	4.2	**27**	0256	4.5
0852	2.2		0919	1.8
TH 1512	4.5	F	1527	4.9
2135	2.0		2154	1.5
13 0343	4.4	**28**	0406	4.8
0958	1.9		1022	1.3
F 1605	4.8	SA	1627	5.2
2230	1.7		2251	1.0
14 0433	4.7	**29**	0501	5.1
1048	1.6		1115	1.0
SA 1650	5.0	SU	1717	5.5
2314	1.4		2341	0.7
15 0517	4.8	**30**	0549	5.3
1130	1.4		1203	0.7
SU 1732	5.2	M	1803	5.7
2354	1.2	○		
		31	0027	0.4
			0634	5.4
		TU	1247	0.5
			1846	5.7

Chart Datum: 3·22 metres below Ordnance Datum (Newlyn)

TIME ZONE (UT)
For Summer Time add ONE hour in **non-shaded areas**

ENGLAND – PLYMOUTH

YEAR 2004

LAT 50°22'N   LONG 4°11'W

TIMES AND HEIGHTS OF HIGH AND LOW WATERS

SEPTEMBER

Day	Time	m	Time	m	Day	Time	m	Time	m
1 W	0110	0.4	0716	5.4	16 TH	0041	0.8	0649	5.3
	1327	0.5	1927	5.6		1255	0.8	1900	5.5
2 TH	0149	0.5	0753	5.3	17 F	0114	0.7	0723	5.3
	1403	0.6	2002	5.5		1328	0.8	1934	5.4
3 F	0223	0.7	0825	5.2	18 SA	0146	0.8	0755	5.3
	1436	0.9	2032	5.3		1359	0.9	2007	5.3
4 SA	0253	1.0	0850	5.0	19 SU	0217	1.0	0827	5.2
	1504	1.2	2057	5.0		1432	1.1	2042	5.1
5 SU	0320	1.4	0914	4.8	20 M	0250	1.3	0903	5.0
	1531	1.6	2123	4.8		1508	1.4	2122	4.9
6 M	0346	1.8	0943	4.6	21 TU	0328	1.6	0947	4.7
	1600	2.0	2156	4.4		1554	1.8	2214	4.5
7 TU	0416	2.2	1025	4.4	22 W	0419	2.1	1050	4.5
	1643	2.4	2245	4.1		1704	2.2	2333	4.2
8 W	0514	2.5	1127	4.2	23 TH	0551	2.4	1225	4.3
	1808	2.6				1910	2.3		
9 TH	0007	4.0	0647	2.6	24 F	0132	4.2	0802	2.3
	1322	4.2	1945	2.5		1411	4.6	2045	1.9
10 F	0219	4.1	0821	2.4	25 SA	0302	4.6	0916	1.8
	1446	4.4	2112	2.2		1523	5.0	2146	1.4
11 SA	0323	4.6	0934	2.0	26 SU	0402	4.9	1010	1.3
	1542	4.7	2205	1.7		1615	5.3	2236	0.9
12 SU	0412	4.7	1023	1.6	27 M	0448	5.2	1058	0.9
	1627	4.9	2248	1.4		1700	5.6	2321	0.6
13 M	0455	4.9	1105	1.3	28 TU	0530	5.4	1141	0.7
	1708	5.0	2327	1.1		1741	5.7	O	
14 TU	0535	5.1	1144	1.1	29 W	0003	0.5	0608	5.5
	1747	5.4				1222	0.6	1820	5.7
15 W	0005	0.9	0613	5.2	30 TH	0042	0.5	0644	5.5
	1221	0.9	1825	5.5		1259	0.6	1855	5.6

OCTOBER

Day	Time	m	Time	m	Day	Time	m	Time	m
1 F	0117	0.6	0715	5.4	16 SA	0048	0.7	0656	5.5
	1332	0.8	1925	5.4		1306	0.8	1912	5.5
2 SA	0148	0.9	0742	5.3	17 SU	0124	0.8	0732	5.5
	1401	1.0	1951	5.2		1341	0.9	1950	5.4
3 SU	0214	1.2	0805	5.1	18 M	0159	1.0	0809	5.3
	1426	1.3	2017	5.0		1418	1.1	2030	5.1
4 M	0237	1.5	0831	5.0	19 TU	0235	1.4	0849	5.1
	1449	1.7	2044	4.7		1459	1.5	2115	4.8
5 TU	0257	1.9	0903	4.7	20 W	0318	1.8	0937	4.9
	1510	2.0	2119	4.4		1550	1.9	2212	4.5
6 W	0317	2.2	0944	4.5	21 TH	0414	2.2	1041	4.6
	1541	2.4	2208	4.2		1707	2.3	2339	4.2
7 TH	0355	2.6	1043	4.2	22 F	0553	2.5	1221	4.5
	1717	2.7	2322	4.0		1908	2.2		
8 F	0605	2.8	1215	4.2	23 SA	0131	4.3	0749	2.3
	1908	2.6				1357	4.7	2028	1.8
9 SA	0146	4.0	0744	2.6	24 SU	0246	4.6	0855	1.8
	1410	4.4	2032	2.2		1502	5.0	2123	1.4
10 SU	0253	4.4	0856	2.1	25 M	0340	5.0	0946	1.4
	1508	4.7	2126	1.8		1553	5.3	2211	1.0
11 M	0341	4.7	0946	1.7	26 TU	0425	5.2	1032	1.1
	1554	5.0	2210	1.4		1637	5.5	2254	0.8
12 TU	0424	5.0	1030	1.3	27 W	0503	5.4	1114	0.9
	1637	5.3	2252	1.1		1716	5.5	2334	0.7
13 W	0504	5.2	1111	1.1	28 TH	0539	5.5	1153	0.8
	1717	5.4	2332	0.8		1752	5.5		
14 TH	0543	5.3	1151	0.9	29 F	0011	0.8	0611	5.5
	1757	5.5				1223	0.9	1823	5.5
15 F	0011	0.7	0620	5.4	30 SA	0045	0.9	0639	5.4
	1229	0.8	1835	5.6		1301	1.0	1852	5.3
					31 SU	0113	1.1	0705	5.4
						1329	1.2	1918	5.2

NOVEMBER

Day	Time	m	Time	m	Day	Time	m	Time	m
1 M	0139	1.3	0732	5.2	16 TU	0149	1.1	0800	5.5
	1354	1.5	1946	5.0		1414	1.1	2027	5.1
2 TU	0201	1.6	0801	5.1	17 W	0232	1.4	0845	5.3
	1417	1.7	2017	4.7		1501	1.4	2117	4.9
3 W	0222	1.9	0835	4.8	18 TH	0319	1.7	0936	5.0
	1442	2.0	2055	4.5		1555	1.7	2216	4.6
4 TH	0248	2.2	0918	4.6	19 F	0417	2.1	1038	4.8
	1518	2.3	2146	4.2		1705	2.0	2335	4.4
5 F	0330	2.5	1013	4.4	20 SA	0537	2.3	1202	4.7
	1631	2.6	2253	4.1		1835	2.0		
6 SA	0512	2.7	1126	4.3	21 SU	0100	4.4	0709	2.2
	1819	2.5				1323	4.7	1950	1.8
7 SU	0035	4.1	0654	2.6	22 M	0208	4.6	0817	1.9
	1304	4.4	1938	2.2		1427	4.9	2048	1.6
8 M	0202	4.4	0805	2.2	23 TU	0303	4.8	0912	1.6
	1416	4.7	2036	1.8		1520	5.0	2138	1.4
9 TU	0256	4.7	0900	1.8	24 W	0350	5.0	1001	1.4
	1509	4.9	2126	1.5		1607	5.2	2223	1.2
10 W	0343	4.9	0949	1.5	25 TH	0432	5.2	1044	1.2
	1557	5.2	2213	1.2		1648	5.3	2304	1.1
11 TH	0427	5.2	1036	1.2	26 F	0509	5.3	1124	1.1
	1643	5.4	2258	1.0		1724	5.3	2341	1.1
12 F	0510	5.4	1121	1.0	27 SA	0542	5.4	1201	1.1
	1728	5.5	2342	0.8		1757	5.2		
13 SA	0553	5.5	1204	0.8	28 SU	0015	1.2	0611	5.4
	1812	5.5				1234	1.2	1827	5.2
14 SU	0025	0.8	0634	5.6	29 M	0045	1.3	0641	5.3
	1248	0.8	1856	5.5		1305	1.4	1858	5.1
15 M	0107	0.9	0716	5.6	30 TU	0113	1.5	0712	5.2
	1330	0.9	1941	5.4		1333	1.5	1930	4.9

DECEMBER

Day	Time	m	Time	m	Day	Time	m	Time	m
1 W	0141	1.6	0745	5.1	16 TH	0232	1.2	0844	5.5
	1402	1.7	2005	4.7		1502	1.1	2118	5.0
2 TH	0209	1.8	0821	4.9	17 F	0319	1.4	0933	5.3
	1433	1.9	2044	4.5		1551	1.3	2210	4.8
3 F	0241	2.0	0902	4.8	18 SA	0409	1.6	1026	5.1
	1511	2.1	2131	4.4		1644	1.6	2308	4.6
4 SA	0322	2.2	0950	4.6	19 SU	0504	1.9	1126	4.9
	1604	2.2	2226	4.3		1746	1.8		
5 SU	0423	2.4	1047	4.5	20 M	0012	4.5	0610	2.0
	1719	2.3	2332	4.3		1234	4.7	1853	1.9
6 M	0549	2.4	1154	4.5	21 TU	0116	4.5	0722	2.1
	1838	2.2				1338	4.7	1959	1.9
7 TU	0045	4.4	0707	2.2	22 W	0215	4.6	0827	2.0
	1306	4.6	1943	1.9		1437	4.7	2058	1.8
8 W	0153	4.6	0811	2.0	23 TH	0309	4.7	0925	1.8
	1412	4.8	2041	1.6		1531	4.8	2150	1.7
9 TH	0252	4.8	0908	1.7	24 F	0358	4.9	1015	1.6
	1513	5.0	2136	1.4		1619	4.9	2236	1.5
10 F	0348	5.0	1003	1.4	25 SA	0441	5.1	1100	1.5
	1610	5.2	2228	1.3		1700	5.0	2316	1.4
11 SA	0441	5.3	1056	1.1	26 SU	0518	5.2	1140	1.4
	1704	5.3	2320	1.0		1738	5.0	2353	1.4
12 SU	0531	5.4	1146	0.9	27 M	0553	5.3	1217	1.4
	1756	5.4				1813	5.0		
13 M	0009	0.9	0619	5.6	28 TU	0027	1.4	0628	5.3
	1236	0.8	1846	5.4		1251	1.4	1848	5.0
14 TU	0058	0.9	0707	5.6	29 W	0100	1.4	0703	5.2
	1325	0.8	1936	5.3		1323	1.4	1925	4.9
15 W	0145	1.0	0756	5.6	30 TH	0132	1.5	0739	5.1
	1414	0.9	2027	5.2		1355	1.5	2001	4.8
					31 F	0203	1.6	0815	5.0
						1427	1.6	2038	4.7

Chart Datum: 3·22 metres below Ordnance Datum (Newlyn)

Chapter 5

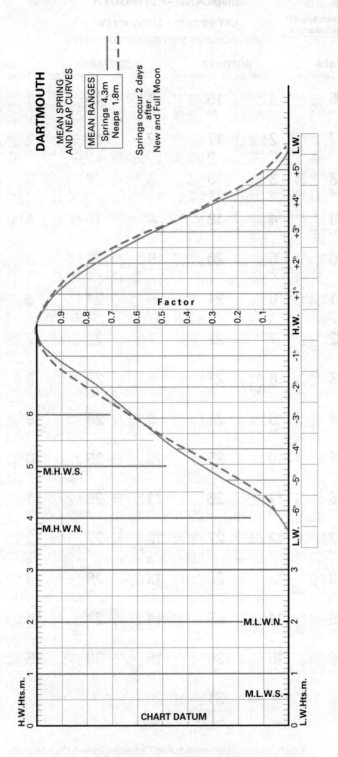

DARTMOUTH

MEAN SPRING
AND NEAP CURVES

MEAN RANGES
Springs 4.3m
Neaps 1.8m

Springs occur 2 days
after
New and Full Moon

Factor

0.9 0.8 0.7 0.6 0.5 0.4 0.3 0.2 0.1

L.W. +5ʰ +4ʰ +3ʰ +2ʰ +1ʰ H.W. -1ʰ -2ʰ -3ʰ -4ʰ -5ʰ -6ʰ L.W.

M.H.W.S.

M.H.W.N.

M.L.W.N.

M.L.W.S.

CHART DATUM

H.W.Hts.m.

L.W.Hts.m.

ENGLAND - DARTMOUTH

YEAR **2004**

LAT 50°21'N   LONG 3°34'W

TIMES AND HEIGHTS OF HIGH AND LOW WATERS

JANUARY

Time m		Time m	
1 TH 0032 3.7 / 0611 2.0 / 1250 3.9 / 1851 1.9		**16** F 0518 1.7 / 1158 4.1 / 1802 1.7	
2 F 0134 3.7 / 0720 2.1 / 1356 3.8 / 1955 1.9		**17** SA 0040 3.9 / 0638 1.8 / 1312 4.0 / 1925 1.7	
3 SA 0235 3.8 / 0828 1.9 / 1459 3.9 / 2056 1.8		**18** SU 0159 4.0 / 0803 1.7 / 1435 4.1 / 2043 1.5	
4 SU 0331 4.0 / 0926 1.8 / 1555 4.1 / 2148 1.6		**19** M 0317 4.2 / 0919 1.4 / 1551 4.2 / 2153 1.3	
5 M 0422 4.2 / 1017 1.5 / 1646 4.2 / 2235 1.4		**20** TU 0426 4.5 / 1026 1.1 / 1658 4.4 / 2254 1.0	
6 TU 0509 4.4 / 1102 1.4 / 1731 4.3 / 2316 1.3		**21** W 0526 4.7 / 1124 0.8 / 1757 4.6 / ● 2348 0.8	
7 W 0551 4.6 / 1141 1.2 / 1814 4.4 / O 2354 1.2		**22** TH 0619 4.9 / 1216 0.6 / 1849 4.7	
8 TH 0631 4.6 / 1219 1.1 / 1853 4.4		**23** F 0038 0.6 / 0706 5.0 / 1305 0.4 / 1936 4.7	
9 F 0032 1.1 / 0707 4.7 / 1256 1.1 / 1930 4.4		**24** SA 0124 0.6 / 0752 5.0 / 1349 0.4 / 2020 4.6	
10 SA 0108 1.1 / 0743 4.6 / 1331 1.1 / 2006 4.4		**25** SU 0204 0.6 / 0834 4.9 / 1428 0.5 / 2059 4.5	
11 SU 0142 1.1 / 0818 4.6 / 1407 1.1 / 2041 4.3		**26** M 0241 0.8 / 0911 4.8 / 1505 0.7 / 2134 4.4	
12 M 0217 1.2 / 0852 4.5 / 1442 1.1 / 2116 4.2		**27** TU 0316 1.0 / 0943 4.6 / 1538 1.0 / 2204 4.2	
13 TU 0252 1.2 / 0930 4.5 / 1519 1.2 / 2154 4.1		**28** W 0348 1.3 / 1013 4.3 / 1612 1.4 / 2233 4.0	
14 W 0331 1.4 / 1009 4.4 / 1601 1.4 / 2238 4.0		**29** TH 0423 1.6 / 1047 4.1 / 1647 1.7 / ◑ 2310 3.8	
15 TH 0418 1.5 / 1058 4.2 / 1653 1.5 / ◑ 2332 3.9		**30** F 0504 1.9 / 1130 3.8 / 1734 2.0	
		31 SA 0002 3.7 / 0603 2.1 / 1233 3.6 / 1840 2.1	

FEBRUARY

Time m		Time m	
1 SU 0119 3.6 / 0719 2.2 / 1400 3.6 / 1953 2.1		**16** M 0134 3.8 / 0743 1.9 / 1423 3.8 / 2031 1.8	
2 M 0244 3.7 / 0838 2.1 / 1520 3.7 / 2105 1.9		**17** TU 0306 4.0 / 0915 1.6 / 1550 4.0 / 2149 1.5	
3 TU 0351 4.0 / 0947 1.8 / 1622 3.9 / 2206 1.6		**18** W 0419 4.3 / 1023 1.1 / 1656 4.3 / 2249 1.1	
4 W 0446 4.2 / 1040 1.5 / 1714 4.2 / 2256 1.4		**19** TH 0517 4.6 / 1118 0.7 / 1751 4.5 / 2339 0.7	
5 TH 0532 4.5 / 1125 1.2 / 1759 4.3 / 2340 1.1		**20** F 0607 4.9 / 1206 0.4 / ● 1838 4.7	
6 F 0616 4.6 / 1206 1.0 / 1841 4.4		**21** SA 0024 0.5 / 0652 5.0 / 1251 0.3 / 1919 4.7	
7 SA 0020 0.9 / 0655 4.7 / 1246 0.8 / 1919 4.5		**22** SU 0107 0.4 / 0733 5.0 / 1330 0.2 / 1957 4.7	
8 SU 0059 0.6 / 0733 4.8 / 1323 0.7 / 1955 4.5		**23** M 0144 0.4 / 0809 4.9 / 1406 0.3 / 2030 4.6	
9 M 0133 0.7 / 0807 4.8 / 1357 0.7 / 2028 4.5		**24** TU 0218 0.5 / 0841 4.8 / 1437 0.6 / 2056 4.5	
10 TU 0207 0.7 / 0841 4.7 / 1429 0.7 / 2100 4.5		**25** W 0246 0.8 / 0908 4.6 / 1504 0.9 / 2121 4.3	
11 W 0239 0.8 / 0914 4.7 / 1502 0.8 / 2134 4.4		**26** TH 0313 1.1 / 0934 4.3 / 1529 1.2 / 2146 4.1	
12 TH 0314 1.0 / 0949 4.5 / 1537 1.1 / 2210 4.2		**27** F 0337 1.4 / 1002 4.1 / 1554 1.6 / 2218 3.9	
13 F 0353 1.2 / 1031 4.3 / 1620 1.4 / ◑ 2257 4.0		**28** SA 0405 1.8 / 1038 3.8 / 1626 1.9 / 2301 3.7	
14 SA 0443 1.6 / 1127 4.0 / 1718 1.7		**29** SU 0451 2.1 / 1130 3.5 / 1730 2.2	
15 SU 0004 3.8 / 0557 1.9 / 1245 3.8 / 1848 1.9			

MARCH

Time m		Time m	
1 M 0006 3.5 / 0622 2.3 / 1255 3.4 / 1904 2.3		**16** TU 0124 3.7 / 0745 2.0 / 1427 3.6 / 2033 1.9	
2 TU 0152 3.5 / 0753 2.2 / 1450 3.5 / 2028 2.1		**17** W 0301 3.9 / 0915 1.5 / 1551 3.9 / 2144 1.5	
3 W 0320 3.8 / 0916 1.9 / 1559 3.8 / 2139 1.7		**18** TH 0411 4.3 / 1014 1.0 / 1650 4.3 / 2237 1.0	
4 TH 0419 4.1 / 1015 1.4 / 1652 4.1 / 2234 1.3		**19** F 0503 4.6 / 1103 0.6 / 1736 4.5 / 2322 0.6	
5 F 0509 4.4 / 1103 1.1 / 1737 4.3 / 2319 1.0		**20** SA 0550 4.8 / 1147 0.3 / ● 1818 4.7	
6 SA 0553 4.6 / 1145 0.7 / 1820 4.5 / O		**21** SU 0004 0.4 / 0630 4.9 / 1227 0.2 / 1854 4.7	
7 SU 0000 0.7 / 0634 4.8 / 1225 0.5 / 1857 4.6		**22** M 0044 0.3 / 0707 4.9 / 1305 0.2 / 1927 4.7	
8 M 0041 0.5 / 0712 4.9 / 1304 0.4 / 1934 4.7		**23** TU 0119 0.4 / 0739 4.8 / 1337 0.4 / 1954 4.7	
9 TU 0117 0.4 / 0748 4.9 / 1338 0.3 / 2007 4.7		**24** W 0148 0.5 / 0807 4.7 / 1405 0.6 / 2017 4.6	
10 W 0150 0.4 / 0823 4.9 / 1412 0.4 / 2040 4.7		**25** TH 0215 0.8 / 0832 4.5 / 1428 0.9 / 2042 4.4	
11 TH 0223 0.5 / 0856 4.7 / 1443 0.6 / 2112 4.5		**26** F 0236 1.0 / 0857 4.3 / 1449 1.2 / 2107 4.2	
12 F 0257 0.7 / 0932 4.5 / 1518 0.9 / 2148 4.3		**27** SA 0256 1.3 / 0925 4.0 / 1508 1.5 / 2138 4.0	
13 SA 0335 1.1 / 1012 4.2 / 1552 1.3 / ◑ 2233 4.0		**28** SU 0318 1.7 / 0959 3.7 / 1531 1.8 / ◑ 2219 3.8	
14 SU 0424 1.5 / 1108 3.8 / 1654 1.8 / 2340 3.8		**29** M 0354 2.0 / 1050 3.5 / 1617 2.2 / 2320 3.6	
15 M 0539 1.9 / 1238 3.5 / 1833 2.1		**30** TU 0532 2.3 / 1206 3.3 / 1823 2.4	
		31 W 0048 3.5 / 0717 2.2 / 1415 3.4 / 1952 2.1	

APRIL

Time m		Time m	
1 TH 0241 3.7 / 0838 1.8 / 1527 3.7 / 2103 1.7		**16** F 0349 4.3 / 0950 1.0 / 1627 4.3 / 2211 1.0	
2 F 0344 4.1 / 0939 1.4 / 1620 4.1 / 2159 1.3		**17** SA 0440 4.5 / 1037 0.7 / 1711 4.5 / 2256 0.7	
3 SA 0434 4.4 / 1029 0.9 / 1705 4.3 / 2248 0.9		**18** SU 0523 4.7 / 1119 0.5 / 1749 4.6 / 2337 0.5	
4 SU 0520 4.6 / 1114 0.6 / 1749 4.6 / 2332 0.6		**19** M 0602 4.8 / 1158 0.4 / ● 1824 4.7	
5 M 0604 4.8 / 1156 0.4 / 1830 4.7 / O		**20** TU 0014 0.5 / 0637 4.8 / 1234 0.4 / 1853 4.7	
6 TU 0013 0.4 / 0646 4.9 / 1238 0.2 / 1907 4.8		**21** W 0048 0.5 / 0707 4.7 / 1305 0.6 / 1919 4.7	
7 W 0054 0.3 / 0725 5.0 / 1317 0.2 / 1944 4.9		**22** TH 0118 0.7 / 0735 4.6 / 1331 0.8 / 1943 4.6	
8 TH 0131 0.3 / 0804 4.9 / 1352 0.3 / 2019 4.8		**23** F 0142 0.9 / 0801 4.4 / 1354 1.0 / 2009 4.5	
9 F 0208 0.4 / 0842 4.7 / 1428 0.6 / 2055 4.7		**24** SA 0205 1.1 / 0828 4.2 / 1415 1.3 / 2038 4.3	
10 SA 0244 0.7 / 0921 4.5 / 1504 1.0 / 2135 4.4		**25** SU 0226 1.4 / 0858 4.0 / 1435 1.5 / 2110 4.1	
11 SU 0326 1.1 / 1005 4.1 / 1547 1.5 / 2221 4.1		**26** M 0251 1.6 / 0935 3.7 / 1504 1.8 / 2152 3.9	
12 M 0419 1.6 / 1105 3.7 / 1647 1.9 / ◑ 2331 3.7		**27** TU 0331 1.9 / 1027 3.5 / 1551 2.1 / ◑ 2248 3.7	
13 TU 0539 1.9 / 1243 3.5 / 1832 2.1		**28** W 0456 2.1 / 1136 3.4 / 1743 2.3	
14 W 0118 3.7 / 0740 1.8 / 1421 3.7 / 2017 1.9		**29** TH 0002 3.6 / 0640 2.1 / 1317 3.5 / 1914 2.1	
15 TH 0245 4.0 / 0856 1.4 / 1533 4.0 / 2120 1.4		**30** F 0138 3.8 / 0753 1.7 / 1439 3.7 / 2020 1.7	

Chart Datum: 2·62 metres below Ordnance Datum (Newlyn)

Chapter 5

TIME ZONE (UT)
For Summer Time add ONE hour in **non-shaded areas**

ENGLAND - DARTMOUTH

LAT 50°21'N   LONG 3°34'W

TIMES AND HEIGHTS OF HIGH AND LOW WATERS

YEAR **2004**

MAY

Day	Time m	Time m		Day	Time m	Time m
1 SA	0253 4.1 / 0854 1.3	1536 4.1 / 2118 1.3		**16** SU	0404 4.3 / 1002 0.9	1633 4.3 / 2222 1.0
2 SU	0350 4.3 / 0948 0.9	1625 4.3 / 2210 0.9		**17** M	0450 4.5 / 1046 0.8	1714 4.5 / 2305 0.8
3 M	0441 4.6 / 1038 0.6	1712 4.6 / 2259 0.6		**18** TU	0530 4.5 / 1125 0.7	1749 4.6 / 2342 0.8
4 TU	0530 4.7 / 1125 0.4	1757 4.7 / ○2346 0.4		**19** W	0606 4.5 / 1200 0.8	1821 4.6 ●
5 W	0619 4.9 / 1210 0.3	1842 4.9		**20** TH	0017 0.8 / 0638 4.5	1233 0.8 / 1850 4.6
6 TH	0031 0.3 / 0703 4.9	1255 0.3 / 1923 4.9		**21** F	0049 0.9 / 0708 4.4	1302 1.0 / 1918 4.6
7 F	0114 0.3 / 0748 4.8	1336 0.5 / 2004 4.9		**22** SA	0117 1.0 / 0739 4.3	1328 1.1 / 1948 4.5
8 SA	0156 0.5 / 0832 4.7	1417 0.7 / 2045 4.7		**23** SU	0143 1.2 / 0810 4.2	1354 1.3 / 2019 4.3
9 SU	0238 0.7 / 0917 4.4	1459 1.1 / 2129 4.5		**24** M	0211 1.4 / 0845 4.0	1422 1.5 / 2053 4.2
10 M	0326 1.1 / 1007 4.1	1546 1.4 / 2218 4.2		**25** TU	0243 1.5 / 0924 3.8	1456 1.7 / 2135 4.0
11 TU	0421 1.4 / 1104 3.8	1647 1.8 / ◑2327 4.0		**26** W	0327 1.7 / 1012 3.7	1545 1.9 / 2227 3.9
12 W	0535 1.7 / 1234 3.7	1812 1.9		**27** TH	0430 1.9 / 1111 3.6	1701 2.0 / ◑2328 3.8
13 TH	0057 3.9 / 0708 1.7	1351 3.7 / 1939 1.8		**28** F	0553 1.8 / 1221 3.6	1827 1.9
14 F	0213 4.0 / 0818 1.4	1455 3.9 / 2043 1.5		**29** SA	0038 3.9 / 0707 1.6	1336 3.8 / 1935 1.7
15 SA	0313 4.2 / 0914 1.2	1548 4.2 / 2136 1.2		**30** SU	0152 4.1 / 0808 1.3	1441 4.0 / 2036 1.4
				31 M	0258 4.3 / 0906 1.0	1540 4.3 / 2133 1.1

JUNE

Day	Time m	Time m		Day	Time m	Time m
1 TU	0400 4.5 / 1002 0.8	1634 4.5 / 2227 0.8		**16** W	0456 4.2 / 1052 1.1	1716 4.4 / 2312 1.1
2 W	0458 4.6 / 1056 0.7	1728 4.7 / 2321 0.6		**17** TH	0536 4.3 / 1130 1.1	1753 4.5 / ●2350 1.1
3 TH	0554 4.7 / 1147 0.5	1819 4.8 ○		**18** F	0616 4.3 / 1205 1.1	1829 4.6
4 F	0011 0.5 / 0647 4.8	1237 0.5 / 1906 4.9		**19** SA	0025 1.1 / 0652 4.3	1240 1.1 / 1902 4.5
5 SA	0102 0.4 / 0737 4.7	1325 0.6 / 1953 4.9		**20** SU	0059 1.1 / 0727 4.3	1312 1.2 / 1937 4.5
6 SU	0149 0.5 / 0826 4.6	1411 0.7 / 2039 4.8		**21** M	0131 1.2 / 0803 4.2	1343 1.3 / 2010 4.4
7 M	0236 0.7 / 0916 4.4	1456 1.0 / 2127 4.6		**22** TU	0204 1.3 / 0840 4.0	1417 1.4 / 2046 4.3
8 TU	0325 0.9 / 1007 4.2	1544 1.2 / 2215 4.4		**23** W	0239 1.3 / 0918 3.9	1451 1.5 / 2124 4.2
9 W	0416 1.2 / 1102 4.0	1635 1.5 / ◑2312 4.2		**24** TH	0318 1.4 / 0958 3.9	1532 1.6 / 2206 4.1
10 TH	0513 1.4 / 1203 3.9	1736 1.7		**25** F	0404 1.5 / 1045 3.8	1623 1.7 / ◑2255 4.1
11 F	0019 4.0 / 0618 1.5	1306 3.8 / 1846 1.7		**26** SA	0502 1.6 / 1139 3.8	1728 1.7 / 2354 4.0
12 SA	0125 4.0 / 0726 1.5	1406 3.9 / 1951 1.7		**27** SU	0612 1.5 / 1242 3.9	1844 1.7
13 SU	0226 4.0 / 0825 1.5	1500 4.0 / 2050 1.5		**28** M	0100 4.1 / 0722 1.4	1351 4.0 / 1954 1.5
14 M	0321 4.1 / 0919 1.4	1551 4.1 / 2143 1.4		**29** TU	0215 4.1 / 0829 1.3	1500 4.2 / 2100 1.3
15 TU	0411 4.1 / 1008 1.2	1635 4.3 / 2231 1.2		**30** W	0327 4.3 / 0933 1.1	1606 4.4 / 2203 1.0

JULY

Day	Time m	Time m		Day	Time m	Time m
1 TH	0435 4.4 / 1034 0.9	1706 4.6 / 2303 0.8		**16** F	0514 4.1 / 1106 1.3	1732 4.4 / 2330 1.2
2 F	0537 4.5 / 1131 0.8	1802 4.8 / ○2359 0.6		**17** SA	0558 4.2 / 1146 1.2	1814 4.5 ●
3 SA	0635 4.6 / 1225 0.6	1854 4.9		**18** SU	0009 1.1 / 0639 4.3	1225 1.1 / 1852 4.6
4 SU	0053 0.5 / 0728 4.7	1317 0.6 / 1943 5.0		**19** M	0047 1.1 / 0718 4.3	1301 1.1 / 1929 4.6
5 M	0143 0.4 / 0820 4.6	1404 0.6 / 2032 4.9		**20** TU	0122 1.0 / 0756 4.3	1334 1.1 / 2004 4.5
6 TU	0229 0.5 / 0908 4.5	1447 0.7 / 2117 4.8		**21** W	0155 1.0 / 0831 4.2	1407 1.1 / 2037 4.5
7 W	0314 0.6 / 0954 4.4	1529 0.9 / 2200 4.6		**22** TH	0228 1.0 / 0905 4.2	1438 1.2 / 2109 4.4
8 TH	0356 0.9 / 1037 4.2	1611 1.2 / 2242 4.4		**23** F	0301 1.1 / 0938 4.1	1512 1.2 / 2144 4.3
9 F	0438 1.2 / 1120 4.0	1655 1.5 / ◑2326 4.1		**24** SA	0336 1.2 / 1015 4.0	1551 1.4 / 2225 4.2
10 SA	0525 1.5 / 1208 3.8	1746 1.7		**25** SU	0420 1.4 / 1100 3.9	1641 1.6 / ◑2316 4.1
11 SU	0019 3.9 / 0618 1.7	1304 3.7 / 1847 1.9		**26** M	0517 1.5 / 1200 3.9	1750 1.7
12 M	0124 3.8 / 0721 1.8	1406 3.8 / 1954 1.8		**27** TU	0023 4.0 / 0635 1.7	1313 3.9 / 1919 1.7
13 TU	0230 3.8 / 0825 1.8	1506 3.9 / 2059 1.8		**28** W	0146 3.9 / 0800 1.6	1436 4.0 / 2040 1.5
14 W	0331 3.8 / 0926 1.7	1600 4.1 / 2158 1.6		**29** TH	0312 4.0 / 0916 1.4	1550 4.3 / 2152 1.2
15 TH	0426 4.0 / 1020 1.5	1649 4.3 / 2248 1.4		**30** F	0426 4.3 / 1024 1.1	1655 4.6 / 2256 0.9
				31 SA	0529 4.5 / 1123 0.8	1752 4.8 / ○2352 0.6

AUGUST

Day	Time m	Time m		Day	Time m	Time m
1 SU	0626 4.6 / 1216 0.6	1843 5.0		**16** M	0624 4.4 / 1208 1.0	1836 4.7
2 M	0044 0.4 / 0717 4.7	1306 0.4 / 1931 5.0		**17** TU	0031 0.9 / 0702 4.4	1245 0.9 / 1913 4.7
3 TU	0130 0.3 / 0805 4.7	1349 0.4 / 2015 5.0		**18** W	0106 0.8 / 0738 4.5	1319 0.8 / 1947 4.7
4 W	0213 0.3 / 0848 4.6	1428 0.5 / 2056 4.9		**19** TH	0138 0.7 / 0812 4.5	1349 0.8 / 2019 4.7
5 TH	0252 0.5 / 0926 4.5	1505 0.7 / 2132 4.7		**20** F	0209 0.8 / 0843 4.4	1419 0.9 / 2050 4.6
6 F	0327 0.7 / 0958 4.3	1539 1.0 / 2201 4.4		**21** SA	0238 0.9 / 0913 4.3	1450 1.0 / 2122 4.5
7 SA	0400 1.1 / 1026 4.1	1613 1.4 / ◑2230 4.1		**22** SU	0311 1.0 / 0946 4.2	1526 1.2 / 2159 4.3
8 SU	0433 1.5 / 1057 3.9	1650 1.7 / 2306 3.9		**23** M	0348 1.3 / 1028 4.0	1610 1.5 / ◑2248 4.0
9 M	0515 1.8 / 1141 3.7	1742 2.0		**24** TU	0438 1.7 / 1128 3.9	1715 1.9 / 2359 3.8
10 TU	0000 3.6 / 0613 2.1	1253 3.6 / 1856 2.2		**25** W	0558 2.0 / 1250 3.8	1902 2.0
11 W	0133 3.5 / 0728 2.1	1423 3.7 / 2017 2.1		**26** TH	0137 3.7 / 0751 1.9	1427 3.9 / 2039 1.7
12 TH	0300 3.6 / 0849 2.0	1531 3.9 / 2133 1.8		**27** F	0315 3.9 / 0906 1.6	1547 4.3 / 2152 1.3
13 F	0403 3.8 / 0956 1.7	1626 4.2 / 2229 1.5		**28** SA	0427 4.2 / 1020 1.1	1649 4.6 / 2250 0.8
14 SA	0455 4.1 / 1047 1.4	1713 4.4 / 2313 1.2		**29** SU	0524 4.5 / 1114 0.8	1741 4.9 / 2340 0.5
15 SU	0541 4.2 / 1129 1.2	1756 4.6 / 2353 1.0		**30** M	0614 4.7 / 1202 0.5	1828 5.1 ○
				31 TU	0026 0.2 / 0658 4.8	1247 0.3 / 1910 5.1

Chart Datum: 2·62 metres below Ordnance Datum (Newlyn)

ENGLAND - DARTMOUTH

YEAR 2004

LAT 50°21′N   LONG 3°34′W

TIMES AND HEIGHTS OF HIGH AND LOW WATERS

TIME ZONE (UT)
For Summer Time add ONE hour in **non-shaded areas**

SEPTEMBER

Day	Time	m	Time	m	Time	m	Time	m
1 W	0110	0.2	0739	4.8	1327	0.3	1950	5.0
16 TH	0041	0.6	0713	4.7	1255	0.6	1924	4.9
2 TH	0148	0.3	0815	4.7	1402	0.4	2024	4.9
17 F	0114	0.5	0746	4.7	1328	0.6	1957	4.8
3 F	0222	0.5	0847	4.6	1434	0.7	2053	4.7
18 SA	0145	0.6	0817	4.7	1358	0.7	2029	4.7
4 SA	0251	0.8	0911	4.4	1502	1.0	2118	4.4
19 SU	0216	0.8	0849	4.6	1430	0.9	2103	4.5
5 SU	0318	1.2	0935	4.2	1528	1.4	2143	4.1
20 M	0248	1.1	0924	4.4	1506	1.2	2142	4.3
6 M ◑	0343	1.6	1003	4.0	1557	1.8	2215	3.8
21 TU ◑	0326	1.4	1006	4.1	1551	1.6	2233	3.9
7 TU	0413	2.0	1044	3.8	1639	2.2	2303	3.5
22 W	0416	1.9	1108	3.9	1700	2.0	2350	3.6
8 W	0510	2.3	1144	3.6	1803	2.4		
23 TH	0546	2.2	1241	3.7	1906	2.1		
9 TH	0023	3.4	0643	2.4	1338	3.6	1941	2.3
24 F	0148	3.6	0758	2.1	1428	4.0	2042	1.7
10 F	0237	3.5	0817	2.2	1505	3.8	2109	2.0
25 SA	0321	4.0	0913	1.6	1543	4.4	2144	1.2
11 SA	0343	3.8	0932	1.8	1602	4.1	2203	1.5
26 SU	0423	4.3	1008	1.1	1637	4.7	2235	0.7
12 SU	0433	4.1	1021	1.4	1649	4.4	2247	1.2
27 M	0511	4.6	1057	0.7	1723	5.0	2320	0.4
13 M	0518	4.3	1104	1.1	1731	4.6	2326	0.9
28 TU ○	0554	4.8	1140	0.5	1805	5.1		
14 TU ●	0559	4.5	1143	0.9	1812	4.8		
29 W	0002	0.3	0633	4.9	1221	0.4	1845	5.1
15 W	0004	0.7	0638	4.6	1220	0.7	1850	4.9
30 TH	0042	0.3	0708	4.9	1259	0.4	1919	5.0

OCTOBER

Day	Time	m	Time	m	Time	m	Time	m
1 F	0117	0.4	0738	4.8	1331	0.6	1948	4.8
16 SA	0048	0.5	0720	4.9	1306	0.6	1936	4.9
2 SA	0147	0.7	0805	4.7	1400	0.8	2013	4.6
17 SU	0124	0.6	0755	4.9	1340	0.7	2012	4.8
3 SU	0213	1.0	0827	4.5	1425	1.1	2039	4.4
18 M	0158	0.8	0831	4.7	1417	0.9	2051	4.5
4 M	0235	1.3	0852	4.4	1447	1.5	2105	4.1
19 TU	0233	1.2	0910	4.5	1457	1.3	2135	4.2
5 TU	0255	1.7	0924	4.1	1508	1.8	2139	3.8
20 W ◑	0316	1.6	0957	4.3	1547	1.7	2231	3.9
6 W ◑	0315	2.0	1004	3.9	1538	2.2	2227	3.6
21 TH	0411	2.0	1059	2.0	1703	2.1	2356	3.6
7 TH	0352	2.4	1101	3.6	1713	2.5	2339	3.4
22 F	0548	2.3	1237	3.9	1904	2.0		
8 F	0600	2.6	1231	3.6	1904	2.4		
23 SA	0147	3.7	0745	2.1	1414	4.1	2024	1.6
9 SA	0203	3.4	0740	2.4	1427	3.8	2029	2.0
24 SU	0305	4.0	0852	1.6	1521	4.4	2120	1.2
10 SU	0312	3.8	0853	1.9	1527	4.1	2123	1.6
25 M	0400	4.4	0944	1.2	1614	4.7	2209	0.8
11 M	0401	4.1	0944	1.5	1615	4.4	2208	1.2
26 TU	0447	4.6	1031	0.9	1659	4.9	2253	0.6
12 TU	0446	4.4	1029	1.1	1659	4.7	2251	0.9
27 W	0526	4.8	1113	0.7	1740	4.9	2333	0.5
13 W	0527	4.6	1110	0.9	1741	4.8	2331	0.6
28 TH ○	0603	4.9	1152	0.6	1817	4.9		
14 TH ●	0607	4.7	1150	0.7	1822	4.9		
29 F	0010	0.6	0636	4.9	1228	0.6	1848	4.9
15 F	0010	0.5	0645	4.8	1228	0.6	1859	5.0
30 SA	0045	0.7	0703	4.8	1301	0.8	1916	4.7
31 SU	0113	0.9	0729	4.8	1329	1.0	1941	4.6

NOVEMBER

Day	Time	m	Time	m	Time	m	Time	m
1 M	0138	1.1	0755	4.6	1353	1.3	2008	4.4
16 TU	0148	0.9	0822	4.9	1413	0.9	2049	4.5
2 TU	0200	1.4	0823	4.5	1416	1.5	2039	4.1
17 W	0230	1.2	0906	4.7	1459	1.2	2137	4.3
3 W	0221	1.7	0856	4.2	1440	1.8	2116	3.9
18 TH	0317	1.5	0956	4.4	1552	1.5	2235	4.0
4 TH	0246	2.0	0938	4.0	1516	2.1	2205	3.6
19 F ◑	0414	1.9	1056	4.2	1701	1.8	2352	3.8
5 F ◑	0327	2.3	1032	3.8	1627	2.4	2311	3.5
20 SA	0532	2.1	1218	4.1	1831	1.8		
6 SA	0508	2.5	1143	3.7	1814	2.3		
21 SU	0115	3.8	0705	2.0	1339	4.1	1946	1.6
7 SU	0050	3.5	0650	2.4	1319	3.8	1934	2.0
22 M	0225	4.0	0813	1.7	1445	4.3	2045	1.4
8 M	0219	3.8	0801	2.0	1434	4.1	2033	1.6
23 TU	0322	4.2	0909	1.4	1540	4.4	2136	1.2
9 TU	0315	4.1	0857	1.6	1528	4.3	2123	1.3
24 W	0411	4.4	0959	1.2	1628	4.6	2221	1.0
10 W	0403	4.3	0947	1.3	1618	4.6	2211	1.0
25 TH	0454	4.6	1043	1.0	1711	4.7	2303	0.9
11 TH	0449	4.6	1035	1.0	1705	4.8	2257	0.8
26 F	0532	4.7	1123	0.9	1748	4.7	2340	0.9
12 F ●	0533	4.8	1120	0.8	1752	4.9	2341	0.6
27 SA	0606	4.8	1200	0.9	1822	4.6		
13 SA	0618	4.9	1203	0.6	1837	4.9		
28 SU	0014	1.0	0636	4.8	1234	1.0	1852	4.6
14 SU	0024	0.6	0658	5.0	1248	0.6	1920	4.9
29 M	0045	1.1	0705	4.7	1305	1.2	1922	4.5
15 M	0107	0.7	0739	5.0	1329	0.7	2004	4.8
30 TU	0113	1.3	0736	4.6	1332	1.3	1953	4.3

DECEMBER

Day	Time	m	Time	m	Time	m	Time	m
1 W	0140	1.4	0807	4.5	1401	1.5	2027	4.1
16 TH	0230	1.0	0905	4.9	1500	0.9	2138	4.4
2 TH	0208	1.6	0843	4.3	1431	1.7	2105	3.9
17 F	0317	1.2	0953	4.7	1548	1.1	2229	4.2
3 F	0239	1.8	0923	4.2	1509	1.9	2151	3.8
18 SA ◐	0406	1.4	1045	4.5	1640	1.4	2326	4.0
4 SA	0320	2.0	1009	4.0	1601	2.0	2245	3.7
19 SU	0500	1.7	1143	4.3	1741	1.6		
5 SU ◐	0420	2.2	1105	3.9	1715	2.1	2349	3.7
20 M	0605	1.8	1249	4.1	1849	1.7		
6 M	0544	2.2	1210	3.9	1834	2.0		
21 TU	0132	3.9	0718	1.9	1354	4.1	1955	1.7
7 TU	0100	3.8	0703	2.0	1321	4.0	1939	1.7
22 W	0233	4.0	0823	1.8	1455	4.1	2055	1.6
8 W	0210	4.0	0807	1.8	1429	4.2	2038	1.4
23 TH	0328	4.1	0922	1.6	1551	4.2	2148	1.5
9 TH	0311	4.2	0905	1.5	1532	4.4	2134	1.2
24 F	0419	4.3	1013	1.4	1641	4.3	2235	1.3
10 F	0409	4.4	1001	1.2	1631	4.6	2226	1.0
25 SA	0503	4.5	1059	1.3	1723	4.4	2315	1.2
11 SA	0503	4.7	1055	0.9	1727	4.7	2319	0.8
26 SU ○	0542	4.6	1139	1.2	1802	4.4	2352	1.2
12 SU ●	0555	4.8	1145	0.7	1821	4.8		
27 M	0618	4.7	1216	1.2	1838	4.4		
13 M	0008	0.7	0644	5.0	1236	0.6	1910	4.8
28 TU	0026	1.2	0653	4.7	1251	1.2	1912	4.4
14 TU	0058	0.7	0731	5.0	1325	0.6	1959	4.7
29 W	0100	1.2	0727	4.6	1323	1.2	1948	4.3
15 W	0144	0.8	0818	5.0	1413	0.7	2049	4.6
30 TH	0131	1.3	0802	4.5	1354	1.3	2023	4.2
31 F	0202	1.4	0837	4.4	1426	1.4	2059	4.1

Chart Datum: 2·62 metres below Ordnance Datum (Newlyn)

Chapter 5

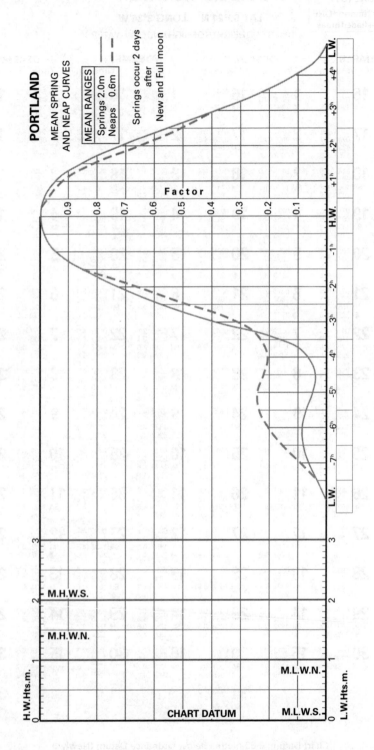

PORTLAND

MEAN SPRING
AND NEAP CURVES

MEAN RANGES
Springs 2.0m
Neaps 0.6m

Springs occur 2 days
after
New and Full moon

Factor

ENGLAND – PORTLAND

LAT 50°34'N   LONG 2°26'W

TIMES AND HEIGHTS OF HIGH AND LOW WATERS

Note - Double LWs occur at Portland. The predictions are for the first LW. The second LW occurs from 3 to 4 Hrs later and may, at Springs, on occasions be lower than the first.

JANUARY

Day	Time m	Time m	Time m	Time m		Day	Time m	Time m	Time m
1 TH	0051 1.4	0605 0.9	1257 1.4	1855 0.7		16 F	0516 0.6	1215 1.5	1804 0.5
2 F	0158 1.4	0717 0.8	1403 1.4	1952 0.6		17 SA	0109 1.5	0634 0.7	1331 1.5 · 1919 0.5
3 SA	0303 1.5	0823 0.8	1511 1.5	2044 0.6		18 SU	0236 1.5	0758 0.7	1501 1.6 · 2035 0.5
4 SU	0356 1.6	0919 0.7	1609 1.6	2133 0.5		19 M	0357 1.7	0924 0.6	1624 1.6 · 2144 0.5
5 M	0443 1.7	1008 0.6	1701 1.6	2219 0.5		20 TU	0504 1.8	1022 0.5	1735 1.8 · 2243 0.4
6 TU	0527 1.8	1053 0.5	1750 1.7	2303 0.4		21 W	0603 2.0	1117 0.4	1836 1.9 · ● 2335 0.3
7 W	0611 1.9	1134 0.5	1837 1.7	○ 2344 0.4		22 TH	0657 2.2	1207 0.3	1929 2.0
8 TH	0653 2.0	1213 0.4	1922 1.8			23 F	0022 0.2 · 0745 2.3	1253 0.2	2016 2.0
9 F	0023 0.4 · 0713 2.0	1249 0.4	2003 1.8			24 SA	0105 0.2 · 0829 2.3	1335 0.1	2057 2.0
10 SA	0100 0.4 · 0811 2.0	1323 0.4	2040 1.8			25 SU	0145 0.2 · 0908 2.2	1416 0.2	2132 1.9
11 SU	0136 0.4 · 0846 1.9	1357 0.4	2113 1.7			26 M	0222 0.3 · 0941 2.1	1454 0.2	2202 1.8
12 M	0210 0.4 · 0918 1.9	1433 0.4	2144 1.6			27 TU	0257 0.3 · 1009 1.9	1531 0.3	2228 1.6
13 TU	0246 0.4 · 0951 1.8	1512 0.4	2219 1.6			28 W	0331 0.5 · 1036 1.7	1607 0.4	2257 1.5
14 W	0325 0.5 · 1029 1.7	1558 0.4	2302 1.5			29 TH	0403 0.6 · 1107 1.5	1643 0.5	◐ 2333 1.4
15 TH	0413 0.5 · 1116 1.6	1655 0.5	◐ 2357 1.5			30 F	0440 0.7 · 1146 1.4	1727 0.6	
						31 SA	0023 1.3 · 0543 0.8	1243 1.3	1834 0.7

FEBRUARY

Day	Time m	Time m	Time m	Time m		Day	Time m	Time m	Time m
1 SU	0133 1.3 · 0726 0.8	1402 1.2	1953 0.7			16 M	0152 1.4 · 0742 0.7	1437 1.4	2026 0.6
2 M	0256 1.4 · 0852 0.8	1529 1.3	2102 0.6			17 TU	0339 1.5 · 0921 0.6	1625 1.5	2144 0.6
3 TU	0407 1.6 · 0951 0.7	1640 1.4	2158 0.5			18 W	0458 1.7 · 1025 0.5	1738 1.7	2241 0.4
4 W	0504 1.7 · 1038 0.5	1738 1.6	2246 0.4			19 TH	0558 2.0 · 1115 0.3	1834 1.9	2328 0.3
5 TH	0556 1.9 · 1120 0.4	1830 1.7	2330 0.3			20 F	0649 2.1 · 1158 0.1	● 1921 2.0	
6 F	0644 2.0 · 1159 0.3	1917 1.8 · ○	2002 2.1			21 SA	0010 0.2 · 0734 2.3	1239 0.0	2002 2.1
7 SA	0011 0.2 · 0728 2.1	1237 0.2	1959 1.9			22 SU	0050 0.1 · 0813 2.3	1317 0.0	2037 2.1
8 SU	0050 0.1 · 0808 2.1	1312 0.2	2036 1.9			23 M	0126 0.0 · 0847 2.2	1353 0.0	2107 2.0
9 M	0127 0.1 · 0844 2.1	1347 0.1	2108 1.9			24 TU	0200 0.1 · 0915 2.1	1427 0.0	2130 1.8
10 TU	0202 0.1 · 0915 2.0	1422 0.1	2136 1.8			25 W	0231 0.2 · 0938 1.9	1456 0.2	2151 1.7
11 W	0236 0.2 · 0945 1.9	1458 0.2	2204 1.7			26 TH	0257 0.3 · 1001 1.7	1519 0.3	2214 1.5
12 TH	0310 0.3 · 1017 1.8	1536 0.3	2238 1.6			27 F	0317 0.4 · 1025 1.5	1533 0.4	2240 1.4
13 F	0348 0.4 · 1055 1.6	1621 0.4	◐ 2321 1.3			28 SA	0338 0.5 · 1052 1.3	1555 0.5	2315 1.3
14 SA	0438 0.5 · 1144 1.5	1722 0.5				29 SU	0415 0.7 · 1133 1.2	1639 0.7	
15 SU	0022 1.4 · 0554 0.7	1253 1.4	1848 0.6						

MARCH

Day	Time m	Time m	Time m	Time m		Day	Time m	Time m	Time m
1 M	0016 1.3 · 0534 0.8	1302 1.1	1827 0.8			16 TU	0135 1.4 · 0755 0.7	1451 1.3	2028 0.7
2 TU	0154 1.3 · 0832 0.8	1500 1.2	2036 0.7			17 W	0334 1.5 · 0925 0.6	1632 1.5	2139 0.6
3 W	0332 1.4 · 0936 0.6	1627 1.3	2138 0.6			18 TH	0448 1.7 · 1017 0.4	1731 1.7	2228 0.4
4 TH	0442 1.6 · 1020 0.5	1727 1.5	2226 0.4			19 F	0543 2.0 · 1059 0.2	1819 1.9	2311 0.3
5 F	0538 1.8 · 1059 0.3	1817 1.7	2309 0.3			20 SA	0630 2.1 · 1138 0.1	1900 2.0	● 2349 0.1
6 SA	0628 2.0 · 1137 0.2	1902 1.9	○ 2350 0.1			21 SU	0712 2.2 · 1215 0.0	1938 2.1	
7 SU	0713 2.1 · 1214 0.1	1943 2.0				22 M	0026 0.0 · 0748 2.2	1252 -0.1	2009 2.1
8 M	0029 0.0 · 0752 2.2	1251 0.0	2018 2.0			23 TU	0102 0.0 · 0819 2.2	1326 -0.1	2036 2.0
9 TU	0107 0.0 · 0828 2.2	1328 -0.1	2050 2.0			24 W	0135 0.0 · 0844 2.0	1357 0.0	2057 1.9
10 W	0143 0.0 · 0900 2.1	1403 0.0	2118 1.9			25 TH	0204 0.1 · 0907 1.9	1422 0.1	2117 1.8
11 TH	0217 0.0 · 0930 2.0	1439 0.1	2146 1.8			26 F	0226 0.2 · 0929 1.7	1436 0.3	2137 1.6
12 F	0251 0.2 · 1001 1.8	1515 0.2	2218 1.7			27 SA	0242 0.4 · 0951 1.5	1447 0.4	2157 1.5
13 SA	0328 0.3 · 1038 1.6	1556 0.4	2258 1.5			28 SU	0302 0.5 · 1012 1.3	1508 0.5	◐ 2223 1.3
14 SU	0417 0.5 · 1126 1.4	1655 0.6	2357 1.4			29 M	0335 0.6 · 1046 1.2	1544 0.7	2314 1.3
15 M	0541 0.7 · 1240 1.3	1837 0.7				30 TU	0441 0.8 · 1213 1.1	1713 0.8	
						31 W	0050 1.3 · 0800 0.8	1435 1.1	2006 0.8

APRIL

Day	Time m	Time m	Time m	Time m		Day	Time m	Time m	Time m
1 TH	0249 1.4 · 0906 0.6	1607 1.3	2111 0.6			16 F	0423 1.8 · 0953 0.4	1705 1.7	2205 0.5
2 F	0410 1.6 · 0949 0.4	1703 1.6	2158 0.4			17 SA	0515 1.9 · 1032 0.2	1749 1.9	2244 0.3
3 SA	0508 1.8 · 1028 0.3	1751 1.8	2241 0.3			18 SU	0600 2.0 · 1109 0.1	1829 2.0	2321 0.2
4 SU	0559 2.0 · 1107 0.1	1834 2.0	2322 0.1			19 M	0641 2.1 · 1145 0.0	1905 2.1	● 2358 0.1
5 M	0645 2.1 · 1145 0.0	1915 2.1	○			20 TU	0717 2.1 · 1221 0.0	1936 2.1	
6 TU	0002 0.0 · 0726 2.2	1225 -0.1	1952 2.2			21 W	0034 0.1 · 0747 2.0	1255 0.0	2002 2.0
7 W	0041 -0.1 · 0804 2.2	1303 -0.1	2026 2.1			22 TH	0108 0.1 · 0813 1.9	1326 0.1	2024 1.9
8 TH	0119 0.0 · 0839 2.1	1341 0.0	2057 2.1			23 F	0138 0.2 · 0837 1.8	1350 0.2	2046 1.8
9 F	0156 0.0 · 0913 2.0	1418 0.1	2129 1.9			24 SA	0200 0.3 · 0902 1.6	1404 0.4	2107 1.7
10 SA	0234 0.2 · 0948 1.8	1457 0.3	2204 1.8			25 SU	0217 0.4 · 0925 1.5	1418 0.5	2126 1.6
11 SU	0317 0.4 · 1029 1.6	1542 0.5	2248 1.6			26 M	0239 0.5 · 0950 1.3	1441 0.6	2153 1.5
12 M	0414 0.6 · 1125 1.4	1648 0.7	◐ 2352 1.5			27 TU	0314 0.6 · 1029 1.2	1518 0.7	◐ 2239 1.4
13 TU	0548 0.7 · 1258 1.3	1834 0.8				28 W	0419 0.7 · 1149 1.1	1646 0.8	
14 W	0141 1.5 · 0757 0.7	1459 1.4	2017 0.8			29 TH	0001 1.3 · 0646 0.7	1357 1.2	1920 0.8
15 TH	0318 1.6 · 0908 0.5	1613 1.6	2119 0.6			30 F	0158 1.4 · 0815 0.6	1525 1.4	2032 0.7

Chapter 5

Chart Datum: 0·93 metres below Ordnance Datum (Newlyn)

TIME ZONE (UT)
For Summer Time add ONE hour in **non-shaded areas**

YEAR **2004**

ENGLAND – PORTLAND

LAT 50°34'N   LONG 2°26'W

TIMES AND HEIGHTS OF HIGH AND LOW WATERS

Note - Double LWs occur at Portland. The predictions are for the first LW. The second LW occurs from 3 to 4 Hrs later and may, at Springs, on occasions be lower than the first.

MAY

Day	Time	m	Time	m	Time	m	Time	m
1 SA	0324	1.6	0905	0.4	1623	1.6	2122	0.5
16 SU	0437	1.8	0956	0.3	1710	1.8	2211	0.5
2 SU	0428	1.8	0949	0.3	1713	1.8	2207	0.3
17 M	0523	1.8	1034	0.3	1751	1.9	2250	0.4
3 M	0522	1.9	1031	0.1	1759	2.0	2251	0.2
18 TU	0605	1.9	1111	0.2	1828	2.0	2328	0.3
4 TU	0612	2.1	1114	0.0	1842	2.1	2333	0.1 ○
19 W	0642	1.9	1149	0.2	1900 ●	2.0		
5 W	0658	2.2	1156	0.0	1923	2.2		
20 TH	0007	0.3	0714	1.9	1226	0.2	1929	2.0
6 TH	0015	0.0	0740	2.2	1238	0.0	2002	2.2
21 F	0043	0.3	0745	1.8	1259	0.3	1956	1.9
7 F	0057	0.0	0821	2.1	1320	0.1	2040	2.1
22 SA	0116	0.3	0815	1.7	1327	0.4	2023	1.9
8 SA	0139	0.1	0901	2.0	1402	0.2	2119	2.0
23 SU	0142	0.4	0844	1.6	1347	0.5	2048	1.8
9 SU	0224	0.3	0944	1.8	1447	0.4	2201	1.9
24 M	0204	0.4	0913	1.5	1409	0.5	2113	1.7
10 M	0314	0.4	1033	1.6	1538	0.6	2251	1.7
25 TU	0231	0.5	0943	1.4	1438	0.6	2142	1.6
11 TU	0417	0.6	1138	1.5	1644 ◐	0.7		
26 W	0309	0.6	1025	1.3	1521	0.7	2225	1.5
12 W	0000	1.6	0540	0.7	1307	1.4	1811	0.8
27 TH	0407	0.6	1129	1.3	1634 ◑	0.8	2330	1.4
13 TH	0129	1.6	0723	0.6	1431	1.5	1942	0.8
28 F	0533	0.6	1303	1.3	1816	0.8		
14 F	0244	1.6	0830	0.5	1535	1.6	2044	0.7
29 SA	0101	1.4	0703	0.6	1429	1.4	1937	0.7
15 SA	0345	1.7	0917	0.4	1626	1.7	2130	0.6
30 SU	0230	1.5	0810	0.5	1535	1.6	2038	0.6
31 M	0342	1.7	0905	0.3	1631	1.8	2130	0.4

JUNE

Day	Time	m	Time	m	Time	m	Time	m
1 TU	0443	1.8	0955	0.2	1723	1.9	2219	0.3
16 W	0525	1.7	1039	0.4	1750	1.8	2302	0.5
2 W	0539	2.0	1044	0.1	1812	2.1	2308	0.2
17 TH	0607	1.7	1121	0.4	1827	1.9	2344 ●	0.4
3 TH	0632	2.0	1133	0.1	1900	2.2	2355 ○	0.2
18 F	0648	1.7	1202	0.4	1903	1.9		
4 F	0723	2.1	1220	0.1	1946	2.2		
19 SA	0024	0.4	0725	1.7	1240	0.4	1938	1.9
5 SA	0043	0.2	0811	2.1	1308	0.2	2031	2.2
20 SU	0101	0.4	0802	1.7	1315	0.4	2012	1.9
6 SU	0131	0.2	0858	2.0	1354	0.3	2116	2.1
21 M	0133	0.4	0838	1.7	1345	0.4	2043	1.8
7 M	0220	0.3	0947	1.9	1442	0.4	2203	2.0
22 TU	0201	0.4	0911	1.6	1414	0.5	2113	1.7
8 TU	0312	0.4	1038	1.7	1531	0.5	2253	1.8
23 W	0231	0.4	0944	1.5	1445	0.5	2144	1.7
9 W	0408	0.5	1134	1.6	1626	0.7	2348	1.7
24 TH	0307	0.4	1020	1.5	1524	0.6	2221	1.6
10 TH	0511	0.5	1236	1.5	1730	0.7		
25 F	0352	0.5	1106	1.4	1614	0.6	2309 ◐	1.5
11 F	0049	1.6	0622	0.6	1342	1.5	1840	0.8
26 SA	0451	0.5	1207	1.4	1721	0.7		
12 SA	0154	1.6	0730	0.6	1444	1.5	1948	0.8
27 SU	0012	1.5	0601	0.5	1323	1.4	1837	0.7
13 SU	0255	1.5	0825	0.5	1539	1.6	2045	0.7
28 M	0130	1.5	0714	0.5	1441	1.5	1949	0.6
14 M	0350	1.6	0912	0.5	1627	1.7	2133	0.6
29 TU	0252	1.6	0823	0.4	1550	1.7	2056	0.5
15 TU	0439	1.6	0956	0.4	1710	1.8	2219	0.5
30 W	0407	1.7	0927	0.4	1653	1.8	2157	0.4

JULY

Day	Time	m	Time	m	Time	m	Time	m
1 TH	0515	1.8	1026	0.3	1751	2.0	2255	0.3
16 F	0542	1.6	1059	0.5	1803	1.8	2327	0.5
2 F	0617	1.9	1122	0.2	1846	2.1	2349 ○	0.3
17 SA	0630	1.7	1143	0.4	1847 ●	1.9		
3 SA	0715	2.0	1213	0.2	1938	2.2		
18 SU	0009	0.4	0715	1.7	1225	0.4	1928	2.0
4 SU	0039	0.2	0807	2.0	1302	0.2	2026	2.3
19 M	0047	0.4	0757	1.8	1303	0.3	2007	2.0
5 M	0128	0.2	0856	2.0	1348	0.2	2112	2.2
20 TU	0122	0.3	0835	1.8	1337	0.3	2042	1.9
6 TU	0215	0.2	0942	2.0	1432	0.3	2155	2.1
21 W	0153	0.3	0908	1.7	1409	0.3	2113	1.9
7 W	0301	0.2	1024	1.8	1515	0.4	2236	2.0
22 TH	0224	0.3	0938	1.7	1440	0.4	2142	1.8
8 TH	0346	0.3	1105	1.7	1558	0.5	2315	1.8
23 F	0257	0.3	1007	1.6	1513	0.4	2213	1.7
9 F	0434	0.4	1146	1.6	1645	0.6	2354 ◐	1.6
24 SA	0333	0.3	1041	1.5	1550	0.5	2249	1.6
10 SA	0525	0.5	1231	1.5	1739	0.7		
25 SU	0418	0.4	1125	1.5	1640	0.6	2335 ◐	1.5
11 SU	0037	1.5	0621	0.6	1327	1.4	1843	0.8
26 M	0516	0.5	1224	1.4	1747	0.6		
12 M	0134	1.4	0723	0.6	1433	1.4	1953	0.8
27 TU	0039	1.5	0630	0.5	1345	1.4	1911	0.7
13 TU	0244	1.4	0825	0.6	1537	1.5	2059	0.7
28 W	0206	1.5	0755	0.6	1517	1.6	2039	0.7
14 W	0352	1.4	0922	0.6	1630	1.6	2155	0.7
29 TH	0345	1.5	0917	0.5	1635	1.7	2154	0.5
15 TH	0450	1.5	1013	0.5	1718	1.7	2243	0.6
30 F	0507	1.7	1023	0.4	1741	1.9	2255	0.4
31 SA	0614	1.8	1118	0.3	1839	2.1	2347 ○	0.3

AUGUST

Day	Time	m	Time	m	Time	m	Time	m
1 SU	0711	2.0	1207	0.2	1930	2.3		
16 M	0704	1.8	1203	0.3	1916	2.0		
2 M	0034	0.1	0800	2.1	1253	0.1	2016	2.3
17 TU	0025	0.3	0745	1.9	1242	0.2	1955	2.1
3 TU	0118	0.1	0844	2.1	1334	0.1	2058	2.3
18 W	0101	0.2	0821	1.9	1317	0.2	2030	2.1
4 W	0200	0.1	0923	2.0	1413	0.2	2134	2.2
19 TH	0134	0.1	0853	1.9	1350	0.2	2101	2.0
5 TH	0239	0.1	0956	1.9	1450	0.2	2206	2.0
20 F	0206	0.2	0920	1.8	1421	0.2	2128	1.9
6 F	0317	0.2	1025	1.8	1526	0.4	2234	1.8
21 SA	0238	0.2	0945	1.8	1452	0.3	2156	1.8
7 SA	0353	0.4	1052	1.6	1601	0.5	2300 ◐	1.6
22 SU	0311	0.3	1015	1.7	1525	0.4	2228	1.7
8 SU	0430	0.5	1122	1.4	1639	0.7	2332	1.4
23 M	0348	0.4	1053	1.6	1607	0.5	2309 ◐	1.5
9 M	0509	0.6	1204	1.4	1734	0.8		
24 TU	0439	0.5	1145	1.5	1714	0.7		
10 TU	0017	1.3	0608	0.7	1306	1.3	1903	0.9
25 W	0009	1.4	0602	0.7	1307	1.4	1900	0.8
11 W	0129	1.2	0736	0.8	1434	1.4	2037	0.8
26 TH	0147	1.4	0753	0.7	1503	1.5	2048	0.7
12 TH	0311	1.3	0855	0.7	1557	1.5	2141	0.7
27 F	0351	1.5	0921	0.6	1631	1.7	2159	0.6
13 F	0430	1.4	0952	0.6	1655	1.7	2227	0.6
28 SA	0512	1.7	1021	0.5	1734	2.0	2251	0.4
14 SA	0528	1.5	1039	0.5	1745	1.8	2309	0.5
29 SU	0610	1.9	1109	0.3	1828	2.2	2336	0.2
15 SU	0618	1.7	1122	0.4	1832	1.9	2348	0.4
30 M	0659	2.1	1153	0.2	1914 ○	2.3		
31 TU	0018	0.1	0742	2.2	1234	0.1	1956	2.4

Chart Datum: 0·93 metres below Ordnance Datum (Newlyn)

ENGLAND – PORTLAND

LAT 50°34′N   LONG 2°26′W

TIMES AND HEIGHTS OF HIGH AND LOW WATERS

Note - Double LWs occur at Portland. The predictions are for the first LW. The second LW occurs from 3 to 4 Hrs later and may, at Springs, on occasions be lower than the first.

SEPTEMBER

Day	Time m	Time m	Time m	Time m
1 W	0058 0.0	0820 2.2	1312 0.1	2033 2.3
2 TH	0135 0.0	0853 2.1	1358 0.1	2104 2.2
3 F	0210 0.1	0921 2.0	1421 0.2	2130 2.0
4 SA	0242 0.2	0942 1.8	1451 0.3	2152 1.8
5 SU	0309 0.4	1003 1.6	1517 0.5	2214 1.6
6 M ◑	0327 0.5	1027 1.5	1536 0.7	2237 1.4
7 TU	0339 0.7	1058 1.4	1605 0.8	2308 1.2
8 W	0409 0.8	1152 1.3	1807 0.9	
9 TH	0028 1.1	0626 0.9	1328 1.3	2024 0.9
10 F	0254 1.2	0832 0.8	1523 1.5	2123 0.7
11 SA	0423 1.4	0930 0.7	1630 1.7	2204 0.6
12 SU	0513 1.6	1015 0.5	1721 1.8	2242 0.4
13 M	0558 1.8	1056 0.4	1808 2.0	2319 0.3
14 TU ●	0641 1.9	1135 0.2	1851 2.1	2355 0.2
15 W	0720 2.0	1213 0.2	1931 2.2	
16 TH	0031 0.1	0756 2.1	1249 0.1	2007 2.2
17 F	0106 0.1	0827 2.1	1324 0.1	2038 2.1
18 SA	0140 0.1	0855 2.0	1356 0.2	2107 2.0
19 SU	0213 0.2	0921 1.9	1429 0.3	2136 1.8
20 M	0245 0.3	0951 1.8	1503 0.4	2209 1.7
21 TU ◑	0321 0.5	1028 1.6	1548 0.6	2253 1.5
22 W	0413 0.7	1122 1.5	1710 0.8	
23 TH	0001 1.4	0558 0.9	1255 1.5	1919 0.8
24 F	0216 1.4	0803 0.8	1505 1.4	2054 0.7
25 SA	0406 1.5	0917 0.7	1621 1.6	2150 0.5
26 SU	0504 1.8	1008 0.5	1716 1.8	2233 0.3
27 M	0552 2.0	1050 0.4	1804 2.2	2313 0.2
28 TU ○	0635 2.1	1130 0.2	1848 2.3	2352 0.1
29 W	0714 2.2	1208 0.1	1927 2.3	
30 TH	0028 0.0	0748 2.2	1244 0.1	2001 2.3

OCTOBER

Day	Time m	Time m	Time m	Time m
1 F	0104 0.0	0818 2.2	1318 0.2	2029 2.1
2 SA	0136 0.1	0841 2.1	1350 0.2	2052 1.9
3 SU	0204 0.3	0900 1.9	1417 0.4	2112 1.7
4 M	0223 0.4	0919 1.7	1435 0.5	2133 1.5
5 TU	0230 0.6	0937 1.6	1449 0.7	2151 1.4
6 W ◑	0242 0.7	0959 1.5	1515 0.8	2215 1.2
7 TH	0305 0.8	1045 1.4	1625 0.9	2337 1.1
8 F	0403 1.0	1220 1.4	1954 0.9	
9 SA	0243 1.2	0858 0.8	1432 1.4	2050 0.7
10 SU	0402 1.4	0859 0.8	1551 1.6	2130 0.6
11 M	0445 1.6	0944 0.6	1645 1.8	2207 0.4
12 TU	0526 1.9	1024 0.4	1733 2.0	2244 0.2
13 W ○	0608 2.0	1102 0.3	1818 2.1	2320 0.1
14 TH	0647 2.1	1140 0.2	1859 2.2	2357 0.1
15 F	0724 2.2	1217 0.1	1938 2.2	
16 SA	0034 0.1	0757 2.2	1254 0.1	2012 2.1
17 SU	0111 0.1	0828 2.1	1330 0.2	2045 2.0
18 M	0147 0.3	0859 2.0	1407 0.3	2119 1.9
19 TU	0223 0.4	0933 1.9	1449 0.5	2158 1.7
20 W ◑	0305 0.6	1014 1.7	1547 0.7	2250 1.5
21 TH	0408 0.8	1115 1.6	1723 0.8	
22 F	0018 1.4	0559 1.0	1305 1.5	1923 0.8
23 SA	0235 1.5	0752 0.9	1450 1.7	2037 0.7
24 SU	0348 1.7	0858 0.6	1555 1.8	2125 0.5
25 M	0438 1.8	0944 0.6	1646 2.0	2205 0.3
26 TU	0521 2.0	1024 0.5	1733 2.1	2243 0.2
27 W	0602 2.1	1101 0.2	1815 2.2	2319 0.2
28 TH	0639 2.2	1138 0.3	1853 2.2	2355 0.1
29 F	0712 2.2	1214 0.3	1926 2.1	
30 SA	0030 0.2	0739 2.1	1249 0.3	1953 2.0
31 SU	0102 0.3	0802 2.0	1321 0.4	2017 1.9

NOVEMBER

Day	Time m	Time m	Time m	Time m
1 M	0128 0.4	0823 2.0	1348 0.5	2040 1.7
2 TU	0145 0.5	0845 1.8	1406 0.6	2103 1.5
3 W	0155 0.6	0904 1.7	1423 0.7	2125 1.4
4 TH ◐	0212 0.7	0927 1.6	1453 0.8	2158 1.3
5 F ◑	0238 0.8	1009 1.5	1557 0.9	2312 1.2
6 SA	0335 1.0	1124 1.4	1854 0.9	
7 SU	0135 1.2	0706 1.0	1328 1.5	1959 0.7
8 M	0310 1.4	0817 0.8	1459 1.6	2044 0.6
9 TU	0402 1.6	0904 0.7	1601 1.8	2124 0.4
10 W	0447 1.9	0946 0.5	1653 1.9	2204 0.3
11 TH	0530 2.0	1027 0.4	1741 2.1	2244 0.2
12 F ●	0612 2.2	1107 0.3	1827 2.1	2324 0.1
13 SA	0653 2.2	1148 0.2	1910 2.0	
14 SU	0005 0.1	0731 2.3	1229 0.2	1951 2.0
15 M	0047 0.2	0809 2.2	1311 0.3	2031 2.0
16 TU	0129 0.3	0847 2.1	1356 0.4	2113 1.9
17 W	0213 0.5	0928 2.0	1448 0.5	2200 1.7
18 TH	0303 0.7	1017 1.8	1552 0.7	2301 1.6
19 F	0407 0.8	1122 1.7	1714 0.7	
20 SA	0029 1.5	0532 0.9	1252 1.7	1846 0.7
21 SU	0200 1.5	0708 0.9	1414 1.7	1956 0.6
22 M	0308 1.6	0819 0.8	1517 1.8	2046 0.5
23 TU	0400 1.8	0909 0.7	1609 1.8	2128 0.4
24 W	0444 1.9	0951 0.6	1656 1.9	2207 0.4
25 TH	0525 2.0	1030 0.5	1739 1.9	2245 0.3
26 F	0602 2.0	1108 0.5	1818 1.9	2323 0.3
27 SA	0636 2.1	1147 0.4	1852 1.9	
28 SU	0000 0.4	0705 2.1	1225 0.4	1923 1.9
29 M	0035 0.4	0733 2.0	1300 0.4	1952 1.8
30 TU	0105 0.5	0800 2.0	1331 0.5	2022 1.7

DECEMBER

Day	Time m	Time m	Time m	Time m
1 W	0129 0.5	0827 1.9	1355 0.6	2052 1.6
2 TH	0148 0.6	0852 1.9	1418 0.6	2121 1.5
3 F	0212 0.7	0920 1.7	1450 0.7	2158 1.4
4 SA ◐	0246 0.8	0958 1.6	1540 0.7	2253 1.3
5 SU ◑	0342 0.9	1054 1.5	1701 0.7	
6 M	0021 1.3	0523 0.9	1218 1.5	1833 0.7
7 TU	0157 1.4	0703 0.8	1354 1.5	1939 0.6
8 W	0307 1.6	0809 0.7	1510 1.6	2033 0.5
9 TH	0403 1.7	0902 0.6	1612 1.8	2123 0.4
10 F	0454 1.9	0951 0.5	1708 1.9	2211 0.3
11 SA	0542 2.1	1039 0.4	1801 2.0	2259 0.2
12 SU ●	0629 2.2	1127 0.3	1852 2.0	2347 0.2
13 M	0715 2.3	1216 0.3	1941 2.0	
14 TU	0035 0.3	0801 2.3	1305 0.3	2029 2.0
15 W	0123 0.3	0847 2.2	1355 0.3	2117 1.9
16 TH	0210 0.4	0933 2.1	1447 0.4	2207 1.8
17 F	0259 0.5	1022 2.0	1542 0.5	2259 1.7
18 SA ◑	0352 0.7	1114 1.8	1643 0.6	2356 1.6
19 SU	0451 0.8	1212 1.7	1748 0.6	
20 M	0100 1.5	0559 0.8	1316 1.6	1853 0.6
21 TU	0208 1.5	0712 0.8	1422 1.6	1952 0.6
22 W	0309 1.6	0819 0.8	1522 1.6	2043 0.6
23 TH	0402 1.7	0914 0.7	1616 1.6	2130 0.5
24 F	0447 1.8	1001 0.7	1704 1.7	2215 0.5
25 SA	0528 1.9	1045 0.6	1747 1.7	2258 0.5
26 SU ○	0606 1.9	1128 0.5	1828 1.7	2339 0.4
27 M	0642 2.0	1209 0.5	1907 1.8	
28 TU	0019 0.4	0717 2.0	1249 0.4	1944 1.7
29 W	0056 0.4	0752 2.0	1324 0.4	2019 1.7
30 TH	0128 0.5	0825 1.9	1353 0.4	2053 1.6
31 F	0155 0.5	0856 1.8	1419 0.5	2125 1.6

Chart Datum: 0·93 metres below Ordnance Datum (Newlyn)
Register for your **FREE** weekly weather email service from Reeds Almanacs
at www.nauticaldata.com – **NOW!**
weekend weather reports sent to your email address, every Thursday

Chapter 5

231

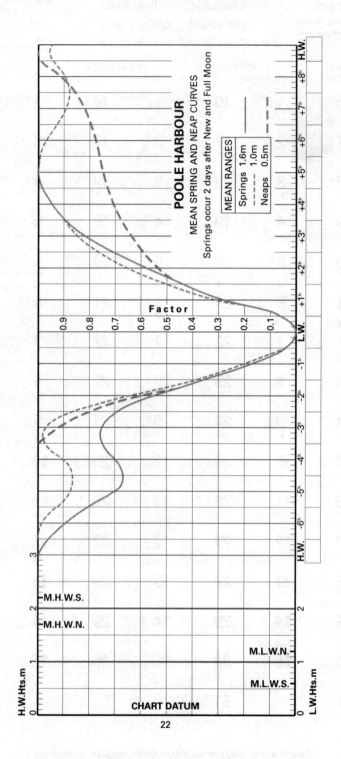

POOLE HARBOUR

MEAN SPRING AND NEAP CURVES

Springs occur 2 days after New and Full Moon

MEAN RANGES
Springs 1.6m
1.0m
Neaps 0.5m

ENGLAND – POOLE HARBOUR

LAT 50°42′N   LONG 1°59′W

TIMES AND HEIGHTS OF HIGH AND LOW WATERS

Note - HW times are not shown because they cannot be predicted with reasonable accuracy. Approximate times can be gained using LW times and the Tidal Curves at the start of this section.

Chart Datum: 1·40 metres below Ordnance Datum (Newlyn)

Symbols: ○ = Full Moon, ● = New Moon, ◑ = Quarter Moon

JANUARY

Day	Time m	Time m
1 TH	1139 (1.9, 1.2), 2357 (1.2)	—
16 F	1035 (1.9, 1.1), 2303 (1.0)	—
2 F	1243 (1.8, 1.2), (1.6)	—
17 SA	1150 (1.9, 1.1), (1.8)	—
3 SA	0059 (1.2), 1337 (1.2), (1.8)	—
18 SU	0019 (1.0, 2.0), 1307 (1.0, 1.9)	—
4 SU	0153 (1.2), 1424 (1.0), (1.8)	—
19 M	0133 (1.0, 1.9), 1415 (0.9, 2.0)	—
5 M	0240 (1.0), 1507 (1.0), (1.9)	—
20 TU	0238 (0.9, 2.1), 1514 (0.8, 2.1)	—
6 TU	0323 (1.0, 2.0), 1547 (0.9), (2.0)	—
21 W	0335 (0.8, 2.2), 1608 (0.7) ●, (2.2)	—
7 W	0403 (1.0, 2.0), 1626 (0.8) ○	—
22 TH	0427 (0.7, 2.3), 1658 (0.6)	—
8 TH	0441 (0.9, 2.1), 1703 (0.8)	—
23 F	0515 (0.7, 2.3), 1744 (0.6)	—
9 F	0517 (2.1, 0.9), 1738 (0.8)	—
24 SA	0601 (0.7, 2.2), 1827 (0.6)	—
10 SA	0552 (2.1, 0.9), 1812 (0.7)	—
25 SU	0644 (0.7, 2.3), 1907 (0.6)	—
11 SU	0627 (2.1, 0.9), 1848 (0.7)	—
26 M	0724 (0.8, 2.2), 1945 (0.7)	—
12 M	0705 (2.1, 0.9), 1927 (0.8)	—
27 TU	0804 (0.9, 2.1), 2022 (0.8)	—
13 TU	0747 (2.0, 0.9), 2010 (0.8)	—
28 W	0844 (1.1, 2.0), 2101 (0.9)	—
14 W	0835 (2.0, 0.9), 2059 (0.9)	—
29 TH	0929 (1.1, 1.9), 2146 (1.1) ◑	—
15 TH	0930 (2.0, 1.0), 2156 (0.9) ◑	—
30 F	1025 (1.2, 1.8), 2246 (1.3)	—
31 SA	1139 (1.3, 1.7), (1.6)	—

FEBRUARY

Day	Time m	Time m
1 SU	0005 (1.3, 1.7), 1255 (1.3), (1.6)	—
16 M	0003 (1.2, 1.8), 1258 (1.1, 1.8)	—
2 M	0119 (1.3, 1.8), 1356 (1.2), (1.7)	—
17 TU	0131 (1.1, 1.9), 1413 (0.9, 1.9)	—
3 TU	0217 (1.2, 1.8), 1445 (1.0), (1.9)	—
18 W	0240 (0.9, 2.0), 1512 (0.8, 2.1)	—
4 W	0305 (1.0, 1.9), 1528 (0.9), (2.0)	—
19 TH	0335 (0.8, 2.1), 1603 (0.7, 2.2)	—
5 TH	0347 (0.9, 2.0), 1608 (0.8), (2.0)	—
20 F	0422 (0.7, 2.1), 1648 (0.6) ●, (2.3)	—
6 F	0426 (0.8, 2.0), 1647 (0.7) ○, (2.1)	—
21 SA	0506 (0.6, 2.2), 1730 (0.5)	—
7 SA	0503 (0.8, 2.0), 1724 (0.6)	—
22 SU	0545 (2.3, 0.6), 1807 (2.1)	—
8 SU	0538 (2.1, 0.7), 1759 (0.6)	—
23 M	0622 (2.2, 0.6), 1841 (2.1, 0.6)	—
9 M	0613 (2.1, 0.7), 1834 (0.6)	—
24 TU	0656 (2.1, 0.6), 1912 (2.1, 0.6)	—
10 TU	0649 (2.1, 0.7), 1910 (0.6)	—
25 W	0727 (2.1, 0.7), 1942 (2.0, 0.8)	—
11 W	0728 (2.1, 0.8), 1948 (0.7)	—
26 TH	0757 (2.0, 0.9), 2012 (1.9, 1.0)	—
12 TH	0809 (2.1, 0.8), 2032 (0.8)	—
27 F	0830 (1.9, 1.0), 2048 (1.8, 1.1)	—
13 F	0858 (2.0, 0.9), 2124 (0.9) ◑	—
28 SA	0912 (1.2, 1.6), 2139 (1.3) ◑	—
14 SA	1000 (1.9, 1.0), 2233 (1.1)	—
29 SU	1019 (1.6, 1.3), 2311 (1.4)	—
15 SU	1124 (1.8, 1.2), (1.7)	—

MARCH

Day	Time m	Time m
1 M	1212 (1.6, 1.4), (1.5)	—
16 TU	0002 (1.2, 1.7), 1254 (1.1, 1.8)	—
2 TU	0052 (1.4, 1.6), 1329 (1.3), (1.7)	—
17 W	0133 (1.1, 1.8), 1408 (0.9, 1.9)	—
3 W	0159 (1.2, 1.7), 1422 (1.0), (1.8)	—
18 TH	0237 (0.9, 1.9), 1503 (0.8, 2.1)	—
4 TH	0247 (1.0, 1.9), 1506 (1.0), (2.0)	—
19 F	0326 (0.8, 2.0), 1548 (0.6, 2.2)	—
5 F	0328 (0.9, 2.0), 1546 (0.7), (2.1)	—
20 SA	0408 (0.6, 2.1), 1629 (0.5) ●, (2.2)	—
6 SA	0406 (0.7, 2.1), 1624 (0.6) ○, (2.1)	—
21 SU	0447 (0.6, 2.1), 1706 (0.5)	—
7 SU	0442 (0.6, 2.1), 1701 (0.5)	—
22 M	0523 (2.2, 0.5), 1740 (2.1, 0.5)	—
8 M	0518 (0.6, 2.1), 1737 (0.4)	—
23 TU	0555 (2.2, 0.5), 1811 (2.1, 0.6)	—
9 TU	0553 (2.2, 0.5), 1813 (0.4)	—
24 W	0625 (2.1, 0.6), 1839 (2.1, 0.6)	—
10 W	0629 (2.2, 0.5), 1849 (0.5)	—
25 TH	0652 (2.1, 0.7), 1906 (2.0, 0.8)	—
11 TH	0707 (2.1, 0.6), 1927 (0.6)	—
26 F	0719 (2.0, 0.8), 1934 (1.9, 0.9)	—
12 F	0747 (2.1, 0.7), 2010 (0.8)	—
27 SA	0748 (1.9, 0.9), 2007 (1.8, 1.1)	—
13 SA	0834 (2.0, 0.8), 2103 (0.9) ◑	—
28 SU	0825 (1.8, 1.1), 2053 (1.7, 1.3) ◑	—
14 SU	0937 (1.8, 1.0), 2219 (1.2)	—
29 M	0920 (1.6, 1.3), 2219 (1.6, 1.4)	—
15 M	1112 (1.9, 1.2), (1.7)	—
30 TU	1120 (1.5, 1.4), (1.6)	—
31 W	0021 (1.4, 1.5), 1256 (1.3, 1.7)	—

APRIL

Day	Time m	Time m
1 TH	0131 (1.3, 1.6), 1352 (1.1), (1.8)	—
16 F	0218 (0.9, 1.9), 1440 (0.8), (2.1)	—
2 F	0219 (1.0, 1.8), 1436 (0.9), (2.0)	—
17 SA	0304 (0.8, 2.0), 1522 (0.7), (2.1)	—
3 SA	0300 (0.8, 2.1), 1516 (0.7), (2.1)	—
18 SU	0344 (0.7, 2.1), 1601 (0.6), (2.2)	—
4 SU	0337 (0.7, 2.1), 1554 (0.6), (2.1)	—
19 M	0421 (0.6, 2.1), 1636 (0.6) ●, (2.2)	—
5 M	0414 (0.6, 2.2), 1632 (0.5) ○, (2.2)	—
20 TU	0455 (0.6, 2.1), 1710 (0.6)	—
6 TU	0452 (0.4, 2.2), 1710 (0.4)	—
21 W	0527 (2.1, 0.6), 1740 (0.6)	—
7 W	0529 (2.3, 0.4), 1749 (0.4)	—
22 TH	0556 (2.1, 0.7), 1809 (0.7)	—
8 TH	0608 (2.3, 0.4), 1828 (0.5)	—
23 F	0623 (2.1, 0.7), 1837 (2.0, 0.8)	—
9 F	0648 (2.2, 0.5), 1910 (0.6)	—
24 SA	0650 (2.0, 0.8), 1906 (0.9)	—
10 SA	0732 (2.1, 0.6), 1957 (0.8)	—
25 SU	0720 (1.9, 0.9), 1941 (1.1)	—
11 SU	0823 (2.0, 0.8), 2056 (1.0)	—
26 M	0758 (1.8, 1.0), 2027 (1.3)	—
12 M	0931 (1.8, 1.0), 2217 (1.2) ◑	—
27 TU	0851 (1.7, 1.2), 2139 (1.4) ◑	—
13 TU	1106 (1.8, 1.1), 2354 (1.2)	—
28 W	1018 (1.6, 1.3), 2325 (1.4)	—
14 W	1240 (1.6, 1.1), (1.7)	—
29 TH	1201 (1.6, 1.2), (1.7)	—
15 TH	0119 (1.1, 1.8), 1349 (0.9), (2.0)	—
30 F	0043 (1.3, 1.6), 1306 (1.1), (1.9)	—

Chapter 5

TIME ZONE (UT)
For Summer Time add ONE hour in **non-shaded areas**

YEAR **2004**

ENGLAND – POOLE HARBOUR

LAT 50°42′N LONG 1°59′W

TIMES AND HEIGHTS OF HIGH AND LOW WATERS

Note - HW times are not shown because they cannot be predicted with reasonable accuracy. Approximate times can be gained using LW times and the Tidal Curves at the start of this section.

MAY

Day	Time	m	Day	Time	m
1 SA	0137 1354 	1.0 1.8 0.9 2.0	16 SU	0231 1449 	0.8 1.9 0.8 2.1
2 SU	0220 1436 	0.9 1.9 0.7 2.1	17 M	0312 1527 	0.8 2.0 0.7 2.1
3 M	0300 1518 	0.7 2.0 0.6 2.2	18 TU	0350 1604 	0.7 2.0 0.7 2.1
4 TU	0341 1600 ○	0.6 2.1 0.5 2.3	19 W	0426 1639 ●	0.7 2.0 0.7 2.1
5 W	0423 1643 	0.4 2.2 0.5 2.3	20 TH	0500 1713	0.7 2.0 0.7
6 TH	0506 1727	0.4 2.3 0.5	21 F	 0531 1745	2.1 0.7 2.0 0.8
7 F	 0550 1811	2.3 0.4 2.3 0.6	22 SA	 0601 1816	2.1 0.8 2.0 0.9
8 SA	 0636 1859	2.3 0.5 2.2 0.7	23 SU	 0631 1848	2.0 0.8 2.0 0.9
9 SU	 0725 1951	2.1 0.7 2.1 0.8	24 M	 0703 1924	1.9 0.9 1.9 1.0
10 M	 0821 2053	2.0 0.8 2.0 1.0	25 TU	 0742 2009	1.9 1.0 1.8 1.2
11 TU	 0928 ◑ 2206	1.9 0.9 1.9 1.1	26 W	 0832 2107	1.8 1.1 1.8 1.3
12 W	 1047 2328	1.8 1.0 1.9 1.2	27 TH	 0935 ◐ 2219	1.7 1.2 1.8 1.3
13 TH	 1207 	1.7 1.0 1.9	28 F	 1049 2333	1.7 1.1 1.8 1.2
14 F	0044 1314 	1.0 1.8 0.9 2.0	29 SA	 1159 	1.7 1.0 1.9
15 SA	0144 1405 	0.9 1.9 0.8 2.0	30 SU	0038 1300 	1.0 1.8 0.9 2.0
			31 M	0133 1352 	0.9 1.9 0.8 2.1

JUNE

Day	Time	m	Day	Time	m
1 TU	0223 1442 	0.8 2.0 0.7 2.2	16 W	0319 1534 	0.8 1.9 0.9 2.0
2 W	0311 1531 	0.6 2.1 0.6 2.3	17 TH	0358 1613 ●	0.8 2.0 0.8 2.0
3 TH	0400 1621 ○	0.6 2.2 0.6 2.3	18 F	0436 1650 	0.8 2.0 0.8 2.0
4 F	0450 1711	0.5 2.3 0.6	19 SA	0512 1727	0.8 2.0 0.9
5 SA	 0539 1801	2.3 0.5 2.3 0.6	20 SU	 0545 1801	2.0 0.8 2.0 0.9
6 SU	 0630 1852	2.3 0.6 2.2 0.7	21 M	 0618 1835	2.0 0.8 2.0 0.9
7 M	 0721 1945	2.1 0.6 2.1 0.8	22 TU	 0652 1911	2.0 0.8 2.0 1.0
8 TU	 0815 2041	2.0 0.7 2.1 0.9	23 W	 0729 1952	1.9 0.9 1.9 1.0
9 W	 0912 ◑ 2142	1.9 0.8 2.0 1.0	24 TH	 0812 2039	1.9 0.9 1.9 1.0
10 TH	 1014 2249	1.8 0.9 1.9 1.0	25 F	 0901 ◐ 2134	1.8 0.9 1.9 1.1
11 F	 1120 2357	1.8 1.0 1.9 1.0	26 SA	 0959 2236	1.8 1.0 1.9 1.1
12 SA	 1224 	1.8 1.0 1.9	27 SU	 1102 2344	1.8 1.0 1.9 1.0
13 SU	0100 1320 	1.0 1.8 1.0 1.9	28 M	 1209 	1.8 1.0 2.0
14 M	0152 1409 	1.0 1.8 0.9 2.0	29 TU	0051 1315 	0.9 1.9 0.9 2.0
15 TU	0237 1453 	0.9 1.9 0.9 2.0	30 W	0154 1416 	0.8 2.0 0.8 2.1

JULY

Day	Time	m	Day	Time	m
1 TH	0252 1514 	0.7 2.1 0.7 2.2	16 F	0335 1552 	0.9 1.9 0.9 2.0
2 F	0347 1609 ○	0.6 2.2 0.7 2.3	17 SA	0415 1632 ●	0.8 2.0 0.9 2.0
3 SA	0441 1702	0.6 2.3 0.7	18 SU	0453 1710	0.8 2.0 0.8
4 SU	 0532 1753	2.3 0.5 2.3 0.6	19 M	 0529 1745	2.0 0.7 2.0 0.8
5 M	 0622 1843	2.2 0.5 2.3 0.7	20 TU	 0604 1819	2.0 0.7 2.0 0.8
6 TU	 0711 1931	2.1 0.6 2.2 0.7	21 W	 0637 1854	2.0 0.7 2.0 0.8
7 W	 0758 2020	2.1 0.6 2.1 0.8	22 TH	 0711 1930	2.0 0.7 2.0 0.8
8 TH	 0845 2109	2.0 0.8 2.1 0.9	23 F	 0748 2011	1.9 0.8 2.0 0.9
9 F	 0933 ◑ 2202	1.9 0.9 2.0 1.0	24 SA	 0831 2059	1.9 0.8 2.0 0.9
10 SA	 1025 2301	1.8 1.0 1.9 1.1	25 SU	 0921 ◐ 2155	1.9 0.9 1.9 1.0
11 SU	 1125 	1.7 1.1 1.8	26 M	 1022 2304	1.8 1.0 1.9 1.0
12 M	0007 1230 	1.2 1.6 1.2 1.8	27 TU	 1135 	1.8 1.0 1.9
13 TU	0110 1330 	1.1 1.7 1.2 1.8	28 W	0025 1256 	1.0 1.8 1.0 1.9
14 W	0205 1423 	1.0 1.8 1.1 1.9	29 TH	0142 1408 	0.9 1.9 1.0 2.0
15 TH	0252 1509 	1.0 1.9 1.0 1.9	30 F	0246 1510 	0.8 2.0 0.8 2.1
			31 SA	0343 1605 ○	0.7 2.1 0.7 2.2

AUGUST

Day	Time	m	Day	Time	m
1 SU	0435 1655 	0.6 2.3 0.7 2.3	16 M	0433 1651 ●	0.7 2.1 0.8 2.0
2 M	0524 1743	0.5 2.3 0.6	17 TU	0509 1726	0.7 2.1 0.7
3 TU	 0609 1827	2.2 0.4 2.3 0.6	18 W	 0543 1758	2.0 0.6 2.1 0.7
4 W	 0651 1909	2.2 0.5 2.3 0.7	19 TH	 0615 1831	2.0 0.6 2.1 0.7
5 TH	 0731 1949	2.1 0.6 2.2 0.7	20 F	 0648 1906	2.0 0.6 2.1 0.7
6 F	 0809 2029	2.0 0.7 2.1 0.8	21 SA	 0723 1944	2.0 0.7 2.1 0.8
7 SA	 0846 ◑ 2111	1.9 0.9 2.0 1.0	22 SU	 0802 2028	2.0 0.8 2.0 0.9
8 SU	 0929 2201	1.8 1.0 1.9 1.2	23 M	 0850 ◐ 2123	1.9 0.9 1.9 1.0
9 M	 1025 2310	1.6 1.2 1.8 1.3	24 TU	 0952 2239	1.8 1.1 1.8 1.2
10 TU	 1140 	1.6 1.3 1.7	25 W	 1120 	1.7 1.2 1.8
11 W	0030 1259 	1.3 1.6 1.3 1.7	26 TH	0018 1256 	1.2 1.8 1.2 1.9
12 TH	0138 1402 	1.2 1.7 1.2 1.8	27 F	0142 1410 	1.0 1.9 1.0 2.0
13 F	0231 1451 	1.0 1.9 1.1 1.9	28 SA	0245 1508 	0.8 2.1 0.9 2.1
14 SA	0315 1534 	0.9 2.0 1.0 2.0	29 SU	0337 1557 	0.7 2.2 0.7 2.2
15 SU	0355 1614 	0.8 2.0 0.9 2.0	30 M	0424 1643 ○	0.5 2.3 0.6 2.3
			31 TU	0507 1725	0.4 2.3 0.6

Chart Datum: 1·40 metres below Ordnance Datum (Newlyn)

ENGLAND – POOLE HARBOUR

LAT 50°42'N   LONG 1°59'W

TIMES AND HEIGHTS OF HIGH AND LOW WATERS

Note - HW times are not shown because they cannot be predicted with reasonable accuracy. Approximate times can be gained using LW times and the Tidal Curves at the start of this section.

SEPTEMBER

Day		Time	m	m	Time	m	m
1	W	0547	2.3	0.4	1804	2.3	0.6
2	TH	0624	2.2	0.5	1840	2.3	0.6
3	F	0657	2.1	0.6	1913	2.2	0.7
4	SA	0728	2.0	0.7	1945	2.1	0.8
5	SU	0800	1.9	0.9	2020	2.0	1.0
6	M	0836	1.8	1.1	2101	1.8	1.2 ◑
7	TU	0927	1.7	1.3	2207	1.7	1.3
8	W	1057	1.6	1.4	2354	1.6	1.4
9	TH	1236	1.6	1.4			
10	F	0115	1.3	1.7	1343	1.3	1.8
11	SA	0209	1.1	1.9	1432	1.1	1.9
12	SU	0252	0.9	2.0	1512	0.9	2.0
13	M	0331	0.8	2.1	1549	0.8	2.1
14	TU	0407	0.7	2.1	1624	0.7	2.1 ●
15	W	0442	0.6	2.1	1658	0.7	2.1
16	TH	0516	0.6	2.1	1732	0.6	
17	F	0549	0.6	2.1	1805	0.6	
18	SA	0622	0.6	2.1	1840	0.6	
19	SU	0658	0.7	2.1	1919	0.7	
20	M	0738	0.8	2.0	2003	0.9	
21	TU	0828	0.9	1.9	2102	1.0 ◐	
22	W	0940	1.2	1.8	2230	1.2	
23	TH	1123	1.3	1.7			
24	F	0018	1.2	1.8	1258	1.2	1.8
25	SA	0139	1.0	2.0	1406	1.0	2.0
26	SU	0236	0.8	2.1	1457	0.8	2.1
27	M	0322	0.7	2.2	1541	0.7	2.2
28	TU	0404	0.6	2.3	1622	0.6	2.3 ○
29	W	0443	0.5	2.3	1700	0.6	2.3
30	TH	0519	0.5	2.3	1735	0.6	

OCTOBER

Day		Time	m	m	Time	m	m
1	F	0552	2.2	0.6	1807	2.3	0.6
2	SA	0622	2.1	0.7	1837	2.1	0.7
3	SU	0651	2.1	0.8	1906	2.1	0.9
4	M	0720	2.0	0.9	1937	2.0	1.0
5	TU	0755	1.9	1.2	2015	1.9	1.2
6	W	0842	1.8	1.4	2113	1.7	1.4 ◑
7	TH	1014	1.6	1.5	2309	1.6	1.4
8	F	1206	1.6	1.5			
9	SA	0041	1.3	1.7	1315	1.3	1.7
10	SU	0138	1.2	1.9	1402	1.2	2.0
11	M	0221	1.0	2.0	1441	1.0	2.0
12	TU	0258	0.8	2.1	1517	0.8	2.1
13	W	0334	0.7	2.2	1552	0.7	2.1
14	TH	0409	0.6	2.2	1627	0.6	2.2 ●
15	F	0445	0.6	2.3	1703	0.6	
16	SA	0520	0.6	2.3	1739	0.6	
17	SU	0558	0.6	2.2	1819	0.6	
18	M	0639	0.7	2.1	1902	0.7	
19	TU	0725	0.9	2.1	1951	0.9	
20	W	0822	1.0	2.0	2057	1.0 ◐	
21	TH	0942	1.2	1.9	2226	1.2	
22	F	1117	1.3	1.9			
23	SA	0002	1.2	1.9	1243	1.2	1.9
24	SU	0118	1.0	2.0	1346	1.0	2.0
25	M	0213	0.9	2.1	1435	0.8	2.1
26	TU	0257	0.7	2.3	1517	0.7	2.1
27	W	0337	0.6	2.3	1555	0.7	2.2
28	TH	0413	0.6	2.3	1632	0.6	2.2 ○
29	F	0448	0.6	2.3	1706	0.6	
30	SA	0520	2.2	0.6	1738	2.2	0.7
31	SU	0551	2.1	0.8	1808	2.1	0.8

NOVEMBER

Day		Time	m	m	Time	m	m
1	M	0621	2.1	0.9	1837	0.9	
2	TU	0652	2.0	1.0	1908	1.0	
3	W	0727	1.9	1.2	1946	1.2	
4	TH	0812	1.8	1.3	2038	1.3	
5	F	0925	1.7	1.5	2202	1.4 ◑	
6	SA	1109	1.5	1.6	2341	1.4	
7	SU	1225	1.4	1.7			
8	M	0047	1.2	1.9	1318	1.2	1.8
9	TU	0135	1.0	2.0	1359	1.0	1.9
10	W	0216	0.9	2.1	1438	0.9	2.0
11	TH	0254	0.8	2.1	1516	0.7	2.1
12	F	0333	0.7	2.2	1556	0.6	2.2 ●
13	SA	0414	0.6	2.3	1637	0.6	2.3
14	SU	0456	0.6	2.3	1721	0.6	
15	M	0541	0.7	2.3	1806	0.6	
16	TU	0628	2.3	0.8	1855	2.2	0.7
17	W	0721	2.1	0.9	1950	0.8	
18	TH	0822	2.0	1.0	2054	1.0	
19	F	0933	2.0	1.2	2208	1.0 ◐	
20	SA	1053	1.9	1.2	2327	1.1	
21	SU	1210	2.0	1.2			
22	M	0039	1.0	2.0	1313	1.0	1.9
23	TU	0137	0.9	2.1	1404	0.9	2.0
24	W	0224	0.9	2.1	1448	0.8	2.0
25	TH	0305	0.8	2.2	1528	0.8	2.1
26	F	0343	0.8	2.2	1605	0.8	2.1 ○
27	SA	0419	0.8	2.2	1641	0.8	2.1
28	SU	0454	0.8	2.3	1715	0.8	
29	M	0528	2.1	0.8	1747	0.8	
30	TU	0600	2.1	0.9	1819	0.9	

DECEMBER

Day		Time	m	m	Time	m	m
1	W	0633	2.0	1.0	1851	1.0	
2	TH	0708	2.0	1.2	1928	1.2	
3	F	0750	1.9	1.2	2012	1.2	
4	SA	0843	1.8	1.3	2108	1.2	
5	SU	0950	1.8	1.4	2216	1.2 ◑	
6	M	1104	1.8	1.3	2327	1.2	
7	TU	1211	1.9	1.2			
8	W	0030	1.1	2.0	1307	1.1	1.9
9	TH	0125	1.0	2.1	1357	0.9	2.0
10	F	0215	0.8	2.1	1445	0.8	2.1
11	SA	0303	0.8	2.3	1532	0.7	2.2
12	SU	0352	0.7	2.3	1622	0.6	2.3 ●
13	M	0442	0.7	2.3	1712	0.6	
14	TU	0532	0.8	2.3	1802	0.6	
15	W	0624	2.3	0.7	1853	2.2	0.6
16	TH	0717	2.2	0.8	1946	2.1	0.7
17	F	0812	2.1	0.9	2041	0.8	
18	SA	0912	2.1	1.0	2139	0.9 ◐	
19	SU	1016	2.0	1.1	2241	1.0	
20	M	1123	2.0	1.1	2346	1.0	
21	TU	1230	2.0	1.1			
22	W	0050	1.0	2.0	1328	1.0	1.8
23	TH	0146	1.0	2.0	1418	1.0	1.9
24	F	0234	1.0	2.0	1502	0.9	1.9
25	SA	0317	0.9	2.0	1543	0.9	2.0
26	SU	0357	0.9	2.1	1622	0.9	2.0 ○
27	M	0436	0.9	2.1	1659	0.9	2.1
28	TU	0512	0.9	2.1	1734	0.8	
29	W	0547	0.9	2.0	1807	0.9	
30	TH	0620	2.0	1.0	1839	0.8	
31	F	0653	2.0	1.0	1912	1.9	0.9

Chart Datum: 1·40 metres below Ordnance Datum (Newlyn)

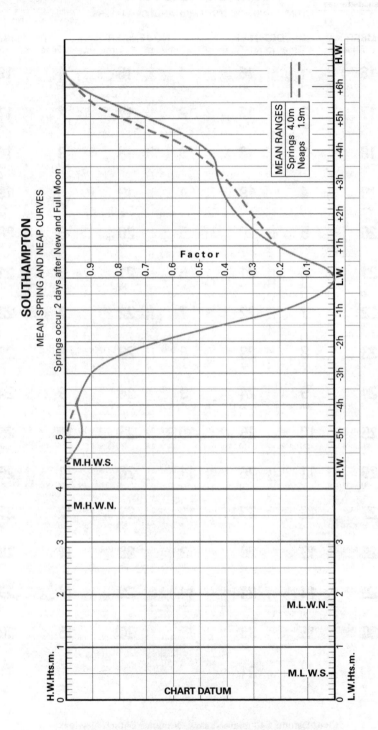

SOUTHAMPTON

MEAN SPRING AND NEAP CURVES

Springs occur 2 days after New and Full Moon

MEAN RANGES	
Springs	4.0m
Neaps	1.9m

Factor

H.W.Hts.m.

L.W.Hts.m.

M.H.W.S.
M.H.W.N.
M.L.W.N.
M.L.W.S.
CHART DATUM

ENGLAND – SOUTHAMPTON

LAT 50°54'N   LONG 1°24'W

TIMES AND HEIGHTS OF HIGH AND LOW WATERS

For Summer Time add ONE hour in **non-shaded areas**

YEAR 2004

Note - Double HWs occur at Southampton. The predictions are for the first HW.

JANUARY

Day	Time m		Day	Time m	
1 TH	0543 3.9 / 1140 1.9 / 1807 3.7		**16** F	0442 4.0 / 1038 1.6 / 1707 3.9 / 2308 1.5	
2 F	0001 1.8 / 0646 3.9 / 1243 1.8 / 1914 3.7		**17** SA	0551 4.0 / 1152 1.6 / 1822 3.9	
3 SA	0102 1.8 / 0744 3.9 / 1339 1.7 / 2013 3.8		**18** SU	0024 1.5 / 0703 4.1 / 1307 1.4 / 1937 4.0	
4 SU	0156 1.7 / 0834 4.0 / 1427 1.5 / 2102 4.0		**19** M	0137 1.4 / 0810 4.2 / 1416 1.2 / 2045 4.2	
5 M	0244 1.5 / 0917 4.2 / 1511 1.3 / 2144 4.1		**20** TU	0242 1.2 / 0911 4.4 / 1517 1.0 / 2144 4.3	
6 TU	0328 1.3 / 0956 4.3 / 1552 1.1 / 2221 4.2		**21** W	0341 1.0 / 1005 4.5 / 1612 0.7 / 2237 4.5	
7 W	0408 1.2 / 1033 4.3 / 1631 1.0 / 2257 4.3		**22** TH	0434 0.8 / 1055 4.6 / 1702 0.5 / 2325 4.6	
8 TH	0447 1.1 / 1108 4.4 / 1708 0.9 / 2332 4.3		**23** F	0523 0.7 / 1141 4.6 / 1749 0.4	
9 F	0523 1.1 / 1143 4.4 / 1743 0.9		**24** SA	0011 4.6 / 0608 0.7 / 1226 4.6 / 1831 0.4	
10 SA	0007 4.3 / 0558 1.1 / 1219 4.4 / 1817 0.9		**25** SU	0054 4.6 / 0650 0.7 / 1308 4.5 / 1911 0.5	
11 SU	0044 4.3 / 0633 1.1 / 1256 4.3 / 1852 0.9		**26** M	0135 4.5 / 0730 0.9 / 1348 4.4 / 1947 0.7	
12 M	0122 4.3 / 0710 1.2 / 1335 4.2 / 1930 1.0		**27** TU	0216 4.3 / 0808 1.1 / 1428 4.2 / 2023 1.0	
13 TU	0203 4.2 / 0751 1.2 / 1417 4.2 / 2012 1.1		**28** W	0256 4.1 / 0846 1.3 / 1509 4.0 / 2100 1.3	
14 W	0248 4.2 / 0838 1.4 / 1504 4.1 / 2101 1.3		**29** TH	0339 3.9 / 0929 1.6 / 1555 3.7 / 2145 1.6	
15 TH	0341 4.1 / 0933 1.5 / 1601 4.0 / 2159 1.4		**30** F	0429 3.8 / 1024 1.8 / 1653 3.6 / 2246 1.9	
			31 SA	0533 3.6 / 1137 2.0 / 1810 3.5	

FEBRUARY

Day	Time m		Day	Time m	
1 SU	0006 2.0 / 0650 3.6 / 1255 1.9 / 1935 3.5		**16** M	0000 1.7 / 0639 3.8 / 1252 1.6 / 1926 3.8	
2 M	0123 2.0 / 0802 3.8 / 1400 1.7 / 2041 3.7		**17** TU	0130 1.6 / 0803 4.0 / 1411 1.4 / 2043 4.0	
3 TU	0223 1.7 / 0857 3.9 / 1452 1.5 / 2129 4.0		**18** W	0241 1.3 / 0908 4.2 / 1514 1.0 / 2142 4.3	
4 W	0311 1.5 / 0940 4.1 / 1535 1.2 / 2208 4.1		**19** TH	0339 1.0 / 1001 4.4 / 1606 0.7 / 2231 4.5	
5 TH	0353 1.2 / 1018 4.3 / 1615 0.9 / 2242 4.3		**20** F	0428 0.7 / 1047 4.5 / 1652 0.4 / 2314 4.6	
6 F	0432 1.0 / 1052 4.3 / 1653 0.7 / 2316 4.4		**21** SA	0512 0.5 / 1128 4.6 / 1734 0.3 / 2353 4.6	
7 SA	0509 0.9 / 1126 4.4 / 1730 0.6 / 2349 4.4		**22** SU	0553 0.4 / 1206 4.6 / 1812 0.2	
8 SU	0545 0.7 / 1201 4.4 / 1805 0.6		**23** M	0030 4.6 / 0629 0.4 / 1242 4.5 / 1845 0.3	
9 M	0024 4.4 / 0619 0.7 / 1237 4.4 / 1838 0.6		**24** TU	0105 4.5 / 0702 0.6 / 1317 4.4 / 1916 0.5	
10 TU	0101 4.4 / 0654 0.7 / 1314 4.4 / 1913 0.6		**25** W	0139 4.4 / 0733 0.8 / 1351 4.2 / 1944 0.8	
11 W	0139 4.4 / 0731 0.8 / 1353 4.3 / 1950 0.8		**26** TH	0212 4.2 / 0802 1.1 / 1426 4.0 / 2013 1.2	
12 TH	0219 4.3 / 0811 1.0 / 1436 4.2 / 2032 1.0		**27** F	0247 4.0 / 0834 1.4 / 1504 3.8 / 2047 1.6	
13 F	0306 4.2 / 0859 1.2 / 1526 4.0 / 2123 1.3		**28** SA	0327 3.8 / 0915 1.7 / 1551 3.6 / 2135 1.9	
14 SA	0402 4.0 / 0959 1.5 / 1631 3.8 / 2231 1.6		**29** SU	0421 3.5 / 1021 2.0 / 1703 3.4 / 2302 2.2	
15 SU	0513 3.8 / 1119 1.6 / 1753 3.7				

MARCH

Day	Time m		Day	Time m	
1 M	0544 3.4 / 1205 2.1 / 1851 3.4		**16** TU	0633 3.7 / 1247 1.7 / 1929 3.7	
2 TU	0051 2.2 / 0725 3.5 / 1332 1.9 / 2016 3.6		**17** W	0131 1.7 / 0802 3.9 / 1407 1.4 / 2042 4.0	
3 W	0202 1.9 / 0832 3.7 / 1429 1.6 / 2107 3.9		**18** TH	0239 1.3 / 0903 4.1 / 1505 1.0 / 2134 4.3	
4 TH	0252 1.6 / 0918 4.0 / 1513 1.2 / 2145 4.1		**19** F	0330 1.0 / 0951 4.3 / 1551 0.7 / 2217 4.5	
5 F	0333 1.2 / 0955 4.2 / 1553 0.9 / 2219 4.3		**20** SA	0413 0.7 / 1031 4.5 / 1632 0.4 / 2255 4.6	
6 SA	0411 0.9 / 1029 4.3 / 1632 0.6 / 2251 4.4		**21** SU	0453 0.4 / 1107 4.5 / 1710 0.3 / 2329 4.6	
7 SU	0448 0.6 / 1103 4.4 / 1708 0.4 / 2325 4.5		**22** M	0529 0.3 / 1141 4.5 / 1745 0.2	
8 M	0524 0.5 / 1138 4.5 / 1744 0.3		**23** TU	0001 4.5 / 0602 0.4 / 1214 4.4 / 1816 0.4	
9 TU	0000 4.6 / 0559 0.4 / 1214 4.6 / 1818 0.3		**24** W	0033 4.5 / 0632 0.5 / 1246 4.3 / 1844 0.6	
10 W	0036 4.6 / 0634 0.4 / 1251 4.6 / 1853 0.4		**25** TH	0103 4.3 / 0659 0.7 / 1318 4.2 / 1909 0.9	
11 TH	0114 4.5 / 0710 0.5 / 1331 4.5 / 1929 0.6		**26** F	0134 4.2 / 0724 1.0 / 1350 4.1 / 1934 1.2	
12 F	0154 4.4 / 0749 0.8 / 1413 4.3 / 2010 0.9		**27** SA	0206 4.0 / 0752 1.3 / 1426 3.9 / 2005 1.6	
13 SA	0239 4.2 / 0835 1.1 / 1504 4.0 / 2100 1.3		**28** SU	0241 3.8 / 0828 1.6 / 1509 3.6 / 2048 1.9	
14 SU	0335 3.9 / 0934 1.5 / 1610 3.8 / 2211 1.7		**29** M	0327 3.6 / 0922 1.9 / 1614 3.4 / 2203 2.3	
15 M	0451 3.7 / 1102 1.7 / 1745 3.6 / 2355 1.9		**30** TU	0443 3.4 / 1102 2.1 / 1757 3.4	
			31 W	0008 2.3 / 0629 3.4 / 1247 2.0 / 1932 3.6	

APRIL

Day	Time m		Day	Time m	
1 TH	0128 2.0 / 0750 3.6 / 1351 1.6 / 2028 3.9		**16** F	0221 1.3 / 0845 4.1 / 1441 1.0 / 2112 4.3	
2 F	0219 1.6 / 0841 3.9 / 1439 1.2 / 2109 4.1		**17** SA	0308 1.0 / 0929 4.3 / 1524 0.8 / 2152 4.5	
3 SA	0302 1.2 / 0921 4.1 / 1521 0.8 / 2145 4.4		**18** SU	0348 0.7 / 1007 4.3 / 1603 0.6 / 2227 4.5	
4 SU	0341 0.8 / 0958 4.4 / 1601 0.5 / 2220 4.5		**19** M	0425 0.5 / 1042 4.4 / 1640 0.5 / 2259 4.5	
5 M	0420 0.5 / 1034 4.5 / 1640 0.3 / 2256 4.6		**20** TU	0500 0.5 / 1114 4.3 / 1714 0.5 / 2330 4.4	
6 TU	0459 0.3 / 1112 4.6 / 1718 0.2 / 2334 4.7		**21** W	0533 0.5 / 1145 4.3 / 1745 0.6	
7 W	0536 0.2 / 1151 4.7 / 1756 0.2		**22** TH	0000 4.4 / 0602 0.6 / 1217 4.3 / 1813 0.8	
8 TH	0012 4.7 / 0614 0.3 / 1231 4.7 / 1833 0.4		**23** F	0031 4.3 / 0628 0.8 / 1250 4.2 / 1839 1.0	
9 F	0053 4.6 / 0653 0.4 / 1314 4.5 / 1912 0.6		**24** SA	0102 4.2 / 0654 1.0 / 1324 4.1 / 1906 1.3	
10 SA	0136 4.5 / 0734 0.7 / 1400 4.3 / 1957 1.0		**25** SU	0135 4.0 / 0723 1.2 / 1400 3.9 / 1939 1.6	
11 SU	0224 4.2 / 0822 1.1 / 1455 4.0 / 2051 1.4		**26** M	0211 3.9 / 0800 1.5 / 1444 3.8 / 2022 1.9	
12 M	0324 3.9 / 0926 1.5 / 1609 3.8 / 2210 1.8		**27** TU	0256 3.7 / 0850 1.8 / 1545 3.6 / 2130 2.2	
13 TU	0447 3.7 / 1057 1.7 / 1749 3.7 / 2355 1.8		**28** W	0403 3.5 / 1009 2.0 / 1709 3.6 / 2312 2.2	
14 W	0629 3.7 / 1236 1.6 / 1922 3.9		**29** TH	0532 3.5 / 1146 1.9 / 1834 3.7	
15 TH	0121 1.7 / 0749 3.9 / 1349 1.4 / 2025 4.1		**30** F	0035 2.0 / 0653 3.6 / 1258 1.6 / 1936 3.9	

Chart Datum: 2·74 metres below Ordnance Datum (Newlyn)

Chapter 5

ENGLAND – SOUTHAMPTON

Note - Double HWs occur at Southampton. The predictions are for the first HW.

TIME ZONE (UT)
For Summer Time add ONE hour in **non-shaded areas**

LAT 50°54'N   LONG 1°24'W

TIMES AND HEIGHTS OF HIGH AND LOW WATERS

YEAR **2004**

MAY

Time	m		Time	m
1 0133	1.6	**16** 0234	1.1
0753	3.9	0859	4.1
SA 1352	1.3	SU 1448	1.0
2024	4.2	2121	4.3
2 0221	1.2	**17** 0315	0.9
0840	4.1	0938	4.2
SU 1440	0.9	M 1528	0.9
2106	4.4	2156	4.3
3 0305	0.8	**18** 0353	0.8
0923	4.3	1014	4.2
M 1524	0.6	TU 1606	0.8
2147	4.6	2229	4.3
4 0348	0.5	**19** 0429	0.7
1005	4.5	1047	4.2
TU 1608	0.4	W 1642	0.8
○ 2227	4.7	● 2300	4.3
5 0431	0.3	**20** 0503	0.7
1047	4.6	1120	4.2
W 1651	0.3	TH 1716	0.9
2309	4.8	2332	4.3
6 0514	0.3	**21** 0535	0.8
1131	4.7	1154	4.2
TH 1734	0.4	F 1748	1.0
2352	4.8		
7 0557	0.3	**22** 0005	4.2
1216	4.6	0604	0.9
F 1817	0.5	SA 1229	4.1
		1817	1.2
8 0037	4.7	**23** 0040	4.1
0640	0.5	0634	1.1
SA 1304	4.5	SU 1305	4.1
1902	0.8	1849	1.4
9 0125	4.5	**24** 0115	4.0
0726	0.8	0706	1.2
SU 1356	4.3	M 1344	4.0
1952	1.1	1924	1.6
10 0219	4.2	**25** 0154	3.9
0819	1.1	0743	1.4
M 1457	4.1	TU 1429	3.9
2052	1.5	2009	1.8
11 0323	4.0	**26** 0239	3.8
0924	1.4	0831	1.6
TU 1613	3.9	W 1523	3.8
◗ 2209	1.7	2108	1.9
12 0442	3.8	**27** 0336	3.7
1044	1.6	0934	1.7
W 1738	3.9	TH 1628	3.8
2336	1.8	◗ 2221	2.0
13 0607	3.8	**28** 0446	3.6
1206	1.6	1048	1.7
TH 1855	4.0	F 1739	3.9
		2336	1.8
14 0051	1.6	**29** 0558	3.7
0718	3.9	1159	1.6
F 1313	1.4	SA 1843	4.0
1953	4.2		
15 0148	1.4	**30** 0040	1.6
0814	4.0	0703	3.9
SA 1405	1.2	SU 1301	1.3
2040	4.3	1938	4.2
		31 0136	1.3
		0759	4.1
		M 1356	1.0
		2028	4.4

JUNE

Time	m		Time	m
1 0228	1.0	**16** 0321	1.1
0850	4.3	0949	4.0
TU 1448	0.8	W 1535	1.2
2116	4.6	2203	4.2
2 0318	0.7	**17** 0400	1.0
0939	4.4	1027	4.1
W 1539	0.7	TH 1615	1.2
2203	4.7	● 2238	4.2
3 0407	0.5	**18** 0438	1.0
1028	4.6	1102	4.1
TH 1628	0.6	F 1653	1.1
○ 2250	4.7	2313	4.2
4 0456	0.4	**19** 0514	1.0
1117	4.6	1138	4.1
F 1717	0.6	SA 1730	1.2
2338	4.7	2348	4.2
5 0545	0.4	**20** 0548	1.0
1207	4.6	1214	4.2
SA 1806	0.7	SU 1805	1.2
6 0028	4.6	**21** 0024	4.2
0633	0.5	0621	1.0
SU 1300	4.5	M 1251	4.1
1856	0.9	1838	1.3
7 0120	4.5	**22** 0101	4.1
0722	0.7	0654	1.1
M 1355	4.4	TU 1329	4.1
1949	1.1	1914	1.4
8 0214	4.3	**23** 0140	4.0
0815	1.0	0731	1.2
TU 1454	4.2	W 1411	4.1
2046	1.4	1955	1.5
9 0314	4.1	**24** 0221	3.9
0912	1.2	0813	1.3
W 1558	4.1	TH 1457	4.0
◗ 2150	1.6	2043	1.6
10 0418	3.9	**25** 0309	3.9
1015	1.4	0903	1.4
TH 1705	4.0	F 1549	4.0
2259	1.7	◗ 2139	1.7
11 0527	3.8	**26** 0405	3.8
1121	1.5	1001	1.5
F 1811	4.0	SA 1649	4.0
		2243	1.7
12 0005	1.6	**27** 0509	3.8
0632	3.8	1107	1.5
SA 1224	1.5	SU 1753	4.0
1910	4.0	2349	1.6
13 0103	1.6	**28** 0617	3.9
0732	3.8	1214	1.4
SU 1320	1.5	M 1856	4.2
2001	4.1		
14 0154	1.4	**29** 0054	1.4
0824	3.9	0722	4.0
M 1409	1.4	TU 1319	1.3
2046	4.1	1956	4.3
15 0239	1.3	**30** 0157	1.2
0909	4.0	0824	4.2
TU 1453	1.3	W 1421	1.1
2126	4.2	2052	4.4

JULY

Time	m		Time	m
1 0256	0.9	**16** 0340	1.3
0922	4.3	1013	4.0
TH 1519	1.0	F 1558	1.4
2146	4.6	2224	4.2
2 0352	0.7	**17** 0421	1.1
1017	4.5	1050	4.1
F 1616	0.8	SA 1638	1.2
○ 2239	4.6	● 2300	4.2
3 0446	0.6	**18** 0459	1.0
1110	4.5	1124	4.2
SA 1709	0.8	SU 1716	1.2
2330	4.6	2334	4.2
4 0538	0.5	**19** 0535	0.9
1202	4.6	1158	4.2
SU 1801	0.8	M 1752	1.1
5 0020	4.6	**20** 0008	4.2
0627	0.5	0609	0.9
M 1254	4.6	TU 1233	4.2
1850	0.8	1826	1.1
6 0110	4.5	**21** 0044	4.2
0715	0.6	0642	0.9
TU 1344	4.5	W 1309	4.2
1939	1.0	1859	1.2
7 0200	4.4	**22** 0120	4.2
0801	0.8	0715	1.0
W 1434	4.4	TH 1346	4.2
2027	1.1	1935	1.2
8 0249	4.2	**23** 0158	4.1
0847	1.0	0751	1.1
TH 1525	4.2	F 1426	4.2
2117	1.4	2015	1.3
9 0340	4.0	**24** 0239	4.1
0935	1.3	0833	1.2
F 1618	4.1	SA 1511	4.1
◗ 2210	1.6	2101	1.4
10 0435	3.8	**25** 0327	4.0
1027	1.5	0922	1.4
SA 1715	3.9	SU 1604	4.0
2308	1.7	◗ 2158	1.5
11 0536	3.7	**26** 0426	3.9
1127	1.7	1023	1.5
SU 1815	3.9	M 1708	4.0
		2306	1.6
12 0011	1.8	**27** 0537	3.8
0642	3.7	1136	1.6
M 1231	1.8	TU 1820	4.0
1917	3.9		
13 0113	1.7	**28** 0024	1.6
0748	3.7	0655	3.9
TU 1332	1.8	W 1256	1.6
2014	3.9	1933	4.1
14 0208	1.6	**29** 0140	1.4
0845	3.8	0811	4.0
W 1426	1.7	TH 1410	1.4
2103	4.0	2041	4.3
15 0256	1.4	**30** 0248	1.1
0932	3.9	0916	4.2
TH 1514	1.5	F 1514	1.2
2146	4.1	2140	4.4
		31 0347	0.9
		1013	4.4
		SA 1612	0.9
		○ 2233	4.6

AUGUST

Time	m		Time	m
1 0441	0.6	**16** 0442	0.9
1104	4.6	1105	4.3
SU 1705	0.8	M 1659	1.0
2322	4.6	● 2314	4.3
2 0531	0.4	**17** 0517	0.8
1152	4.6	1136	4.3
M 1753	0.6	TU 1734	0.9
		2346	4.4
3 0008	4.7	**18** 0551	0.7
0616	0.4	1208	4.4
TU 1238	4.6	W 1807	0.8
1837	0.6		
4 0052	4.6	**19** 0020	4.4
0658	0.4	0623	0.7
W 1321	4.6	TH 1242	4.4
1919	0.7	1838	0.9
5 0134	4.5	**20** 0055	4.4
0736	0.6	0654	0.8
TH 1403	4.5	F 1318	4.4
1958	0.9	1911	0.9
6 0215	4.3	**21** 0131	4.3
0813	0.9	0727	0.9
F 1444	4.3	SA 1355	4.3
2036	1.2	1947	1.1
7 0257	4.1	**22** 0210	4.2
0849	1.2	0805	1.1
SA 1526	4.1	SU 1437	4.2
◗ 2116	1.5	2030	1.3
8 0341	3.8	**23** 0256	4.1
0930	1.5	0851	1.2
SU 1613	3.9	M 1528	4.1
2205	1.8	◗ 2123	1.5
9 0435	3.6	**24** 0354	3.9
1024	1.9	0950	1.7
M 1711	3.7	TU 1633	3.9
2311	2.0	2235	1.7
10 0546	3.5	**25** 0512	3.6
1139	2.1	1115	1.9
TU 1827	3.6	W 1758	3.8
11 0033	2.0	**26** 0010	1.8
0715	3.5	0646	3.8
W 1303	2.1	TH 1252	1.8
1946	3.7	1927	4.0
12 0145	1.9	**27** 0139	1.6
0828	3.7	0811	4.0
TH 1410	1.9	F 1412	1.6
2046	3.9	2040	4.2
13 0239	1.6	**28** 0247	1.2
0919	3.9	0915	4.3
F 1500	1.7	SA 1515	1.2
2131	4.1	2136	4.4
14 0324	1.4	**29** 0343	0.8
0959	4.1	1007	4.5
SA 1543	1.4	SU 1607	0.9
2209	4.2	2224	4.6
15 0404	1.1	**30** 0431	0.5
1033	4.2	1053	4.7
SU 1622	1.2	M 1654	0.6
2242	4.3	○ 2307	4.7
		31 0515	0.3
		1134	4.7
		TU 1736	0.5
		2347	4.7

Chart Datum: 2·74 metres below Ordnance Datum (Newlyn)

ENGLAND – SOUTHAMPTON

TIME ZONE (UT)
For Summer Time add ONE hour in **non-shaded areas**

LAT 50°54'N   LONG 1°24'W

TIMES AND HEIGHTS OF HIGH AND LOW WATERS

Note - Double HWs occur at Southampton. The predictions are for the first HW.

YEAR 2004

SEPTEMBER

Time m	Time m
1 0555 0.3 / 1213 4.7 / W 1816 0.5	**16** 0526 0.5 / 1139 4.6 / TH 1742 0.6 / 2352 4.6
2 0026 4.6 / 0632 0.4 / TH 1251 4.6 / 1851 0.6	**17** 0558 0.5 / 1214 4.6 / F 1815 0.6
3 0103 4.5 / 0705 0.6 / F 1326 4.5 / 1924 0.8	**18** 0028 4.6 / 0631 0.6 / SA 1251 4.5 / 1848 0.7
4 0138 4.3 / 0735 0.9 / SA 1401 4.3 / 1954 1.1	**19** 0106 4.5 / 0705 0.8 / SU 1329 4.5 / 1925 0.9
5 0214 4.1 / 0805 1.2 / SU 1436 4.1 / 2026 1.4	**20** 0147 4.4 / 0743 1.1 / M 1412 4.3 / 2007 1.2
6 0252 3.9 / 0837 1.6 / M 1515 3.9 / ◑ 2105 1.6	**21** 0234 4.2 / 0830 1.5 / TU 1504 4.1 / ● 2102 1.6
7 0339 3.6 / 0923 2.0 / TU 1607 3.6 / 2206 2.1	**22** 0337 3.9 / 0935 1.8 / W 1616 3.9 / 2224 1.9
8 0450 3.5 / 1045 2.3 / W 1730 3.5 / 2350 2.3	**23** 0507 3.7 / 1115 2.0 / TH 1755 3.8
9 0639 3.5 / 1238 2.4 / TH 1914 3.6	**24** 0012 1.9 / 0652 3.8 / F 1258 1.9 / 1929 4.0
10 0120 2.1 / 0806 3.7 / F 1353 2.1 / 2022 3.8	**25** 0138 1.6 / 0811 4.1 / SA 1411 1.6 / 2035 4.2
11 0218 1.8 / 0856 4.0 / SA 1441 1.8 / 2108 4.0	**26** 0239 1.2 / 0907 4.4 / SU 1505 1.2 / 2125 4.5
12 0301 1.4 / 0933 4.2 / SU 1521 1.4 / 2143 4.2	**27** 0327 0.8 / 0952 4.6 / M 1551 0.8 / 2208 4.6
13 0339 1.1 / 1006 4.3 / M 1558 1.1 / 2215 4.4	**28** 0410 0.5 / 1032 4.7 / TU 1633 0.6 / ○ 2246 4.7
14 0416 0.8 / 1036 4.4 / TU 1633 0.9 / 2246 4.5	**29** 0450 0.4 / 1109 4.7 / W 1711 0.5 / 2322 4.6
15 0451 0.6 / 1107 4.5 / W 1708 0.7 / 2319 4.5	**30** 0527 0.4 / 1143 4.7 / TH 1747 0.5 / 2356 4.6

OCTOBER

Time m	Time m
1 0601 0.5 / 1216 4.6 / F 1820 0.6	**16** 0532 0.5 / 1148 4.7 / SA 1751 0.6
2 0029 4.5 / 0631 0.7 / SA 1249 4.5 / 1848 0.8	**17** 0005 4.7 / 0608 0.6 / SU 1228 4.7 / 1828 0.7
3 0103 4.3 / 0658 1.0 / SU 1321 4.3 / 1915 1.1	**18** 0047 4.6 / 0647 0.9 / M 1310 4.6 / 1909 0.9
4 0137 4.2 / 0725 1.3 / M 1354 4.1 / 1944 1.5	**19** 0132 4.4 / 0730 1.2 / TU 1357 4.3 / 1956 1.3
5 0213 4.0 / 0755 1.7 / TU 1430 3.9 / 2019 1.8	**20** 0226 4.2 / 0823 1.6 / W 1455 4.1 / ◑ 2057 1.6
6 0258 3.7 / 0837 2.1 / W 1518 3.7 / ◑ 2112 2.1	**21** 0337 3.9 / 0937 1.9 / TH 1614 3.9 / 2224 1.9
7 0404 3.5 / 0953 2.4 / TH 1634 3.5 / 2253 2.3	**22** 0513 3.8 / 1118 2.0 / F 1753 3.8
8 0548 3.5 / 1158 2.5 / F 1821 3.5	**23** 0004 1.8 / 0647 4.0 / SA 1248 1.8 / 1917 4.0
9 0038 2.2 / 0722 3.7 / SA 1317 2.2 / 1940 3.7	**24** 0120 1.5 / 0755 4.2 / SU 1352 1.5 / 2017 4.3
10 0139 1.8 / 0816 4.0 / SU 1406 1.8 / 2029 4.0	**25** 0216 1.2 / 0845 4.5 / M 1442 1.2 / 2104 4.4
11 0224 1.5 / 0855 4.2 / M 1446 1.5 / 2106 4.2	**26** 0301 0.9 / 0928 4.6 / TU 1525 0.9 / 2144 4.5
12 0304 1.1 / 0928 4.4 / TU 1524 1.1 / 2141 4.4	**27** 0341 0.7 / 1005 4.7 / W 1604 0.7 / 2220 4.5
13 0342 0.8 / 1001 4.6 / W 1601 0.8 / 2215 4.5	**28** 0419 0.6 / 1039 4.6 / TH 1641 0.6 / ○ 2254 4.5
14 0419 0.6 / 1035 4.7 / TH 1637 0.6 / ● 2250 4.6	**29** 0455 0.6 / 1112 4.6 / F 1716 0.7 / 2327 4.5
15 0455 0.5 / 1111 4.7 / F 1714 0.5 / 2327 4.7	**30** 0528 0.7 / 1144 4.5 / SA 1748 0.8
	31 0000 4.4 / 0558 0.9 / SU 1216 4.4 / 1816 1.0

NOVEMBER

Time m	Time m
1 0034 4.3 / 0627 1.2 / M 1249 4.3 / 1844 1.2	**16** 0036 4.6 / 0635 0.9 / TU 1259 4.6 / 1901 0.9
2 0109 4.2 / 0655 1.5 / TU 1323 4.1 / 1914 1.4	**17** 0128 4.5 / 0724 1.2 / W 1351 4.4 / 1953 1.2
3 0147 4.0 / 0728 1.8 / W 1400 4.0 / 1949 1.7	**18** 0226 4.3 / 0822 1.5 / TH 1453 4.2 / 2055 1.5
4 0232 3.9 / 0811 2.1 / TH 1447 3.8 / 2039 2.0	**19** 0337 4.1 / 0935 1.8 / F 1608 4.0 / ◑ 2212 1.7
5 0331 3.7 / 0916 2.3 / F 1551 3.6 / ◑ 2155 2.2	**20** 0500 4.0 / 1059 1.9 / SA 1730 3.9 / 2334 1.7
6 0452 3.7 / 1055 2.4 / SA 1717 3.6 / 2331 2.1	**21** 0619 4.1 / 1216 1.8 / SU 1845 4.0
7 0617 3.8 / 1218 2.2 / SU 1838 3.7	**22** 0044 1.5 / 0723 4.2 / M 1318 1.5 / 1945 4.1
8 0042 1.9 / 0719 4.0 / M 1315 1.9 / 1937 3.9	**23** 0140 1.3 / 0814 4.4 / TU 1409 1.3 / 2034 4.3
9 0135 1.5 / 0807 4.2 / TU 1401 1.5 / 2023 4.2	**24** 0226 1.2 / 0857 4.5 / W 1452 1.1 / 2116 4.3
10 0220 1.2 / 0847 4.4 / W 1444 1.2 / 2104 4.4	**25** 0308 1.0 / 0936 4.5 / TH 1532 1.0 / 2154 4.3
11 0303 0.9 / 0926 4.6 / TH 1525 0.9 / 2144 4.6	**26** 0347 1.0 / 1011 4.5 / F 1610 0.9 / ○ 2230 4.3
12 0344 0.7 / 1005 4.7 / F 1607 0.7 / ● 2224 4.7	**27** 0424 1.0 / 1045 4.4 / SA 1646 0.9 / 2304 4.3
13 0426 0.6 / 1045 4.7 / SA 1649 0.6 / 2306 4.7	**28** 0500 1.0 / 1118 4.4 / SU 1721 0.9 / 2339 4.3
14 0508 0.6 / 1127 4.8 / SU 1732 0.6 / 2350 4.7	**29** 0533 1.1 / 1151 4.4 / M 1753 1.0
15 0551 0.7 / 1211 4.7 / M 1815 0.7	**30** 0014 4.3 / 0605 1.3 / TU 1227 4.3 / 1823 1.2

DECEMBER

Time m	Time m
1 0051 4.2 / 0637 1.4 / W 1303 4.2 / 1855 1.3	**16** 0125 4.5 / 0721 1.1 / TH 1345 4.5 / 1948 0.9
2 0130 4.1 / 0712 1.6 / TH 1342 4.0 / 1931 1.5	**17** 0221 4.4 / 0815 1.3 / F 1441 4.3 / 2043 1.1
3 0212 4.0 / 0753 1.8 / F 1425 3.9 / 2014 1.7	**18** 0321 4.2 / 0915 1.5 / SA 1542 4.1 / ◑ 2142 1.4
4 0302 3.9 / 0845 2.0 / SA 1517 3.8 / 2110 1.8	**19** 0425 4.1 / 1020 1.6 / SU 1648 4.0 / 2247 1.5
5 0403 3.8 / 0952 2.1 / SU 1620 3.7 / ◑ 2220 1.9	**20** 0532 4.1 / 1127 1.7 / M 1756 3.9 / 2352 1.6
6 0511 3.9 / 1107 2.0 / M 1731 3.7 / 2333 1.8	**21** 0637 4.1 / 1231 1.7 / TU 1901 3.9
7 0617 4.0 / 1214 1.8 / TU 1838 3.9	**22** 0053 1.6 / 0734 4.1 / W 1329 1.5 / 1959 4.0
8 0037 1.6 / 0715 4.2 / W 1311 1.6 / 1937 4.0	**23** 0148 1.5 / 0825 4.2 / TH 1419 1.4 / 2050 4.0
9 0134 1.4 / 0806 4.4 / TH 1404 1.3 / 2029 4.2	**24** 0236 1.4 / 0910 4.2 / F 1504 1.3 / 2135 4.1
10 0225 1.1 / 0854 4.5 / F 1453 1.0 / 2118 4.4	**25** 0320 1.3 / 0950 4.3 / SA 1546 1.1 / 2214 4.2
11 0314 0.9 / 0940 4.7 / SA 1542 0.8 / 2205 4.6	**26** 0401 1.2 / 1027 4.3 / SU 1625 1.0 / ○ 2251 4.2
12 0403 0.8 / 1027 4.8 / SU 1631 0.6 / ● 2253 4.7	**27** 0440 1.2 / 1102 4.3 / M 1702 1.0 / 2326 4.3
13 0451 0.7 / 1114 4.8 / M 1720 0.6 / 2342 4.7	**28** 0518 1.1 / 1137 4.3 / TU 1738 1.0
14 0540 0.8 / 1202 4.7 / TU 1808 0.6	**29** 0001 4.3 / 0552 1.2 / W 1212 4.3 / 1810 1.0
15 0032 4.6 / 0629 0.9 / W 1253 4.6 / 1857 0.7	**30** 0037 4.3 / 0626 1.3 / TH 1248 4.2 / 1842 1.1
	31 0113 4.2 / 0659 1.4 / F 1324 4.1 / 1915 1.2

Chapter 5

TIDAL CURVES -
CHRISTCHURCH TO FRESHWATER

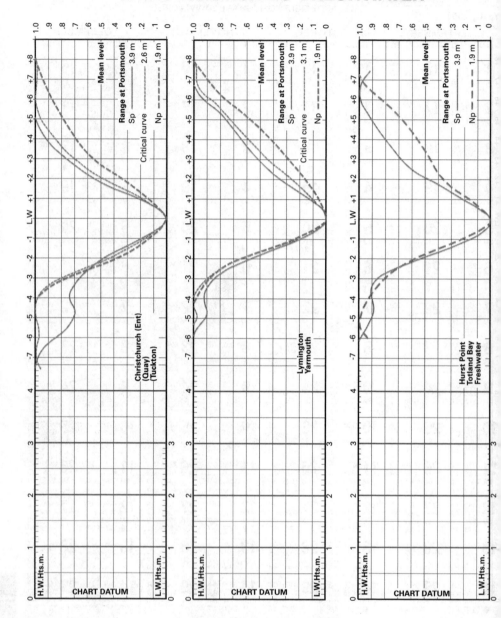

TIDAL CURVES -
BUCKLERS HARD TO SELSEY BILL

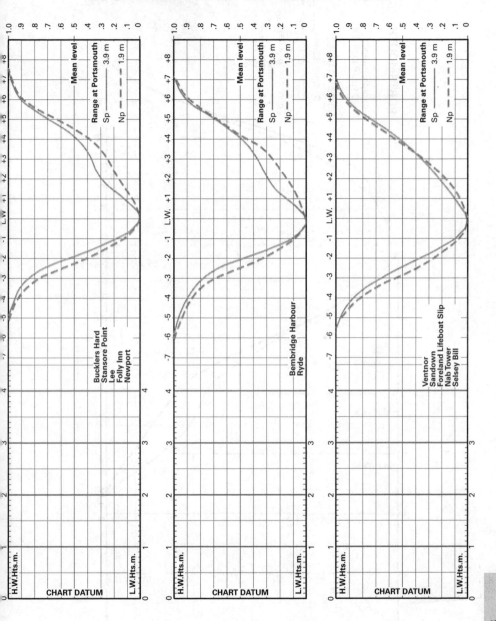

Register for your **FREE** weekly weather email service from Reeds Almanacs
at www.nauticaldata.com – **NOW!**
weekend weather reports sent to your email address, every Thursday

Chapter 5

241

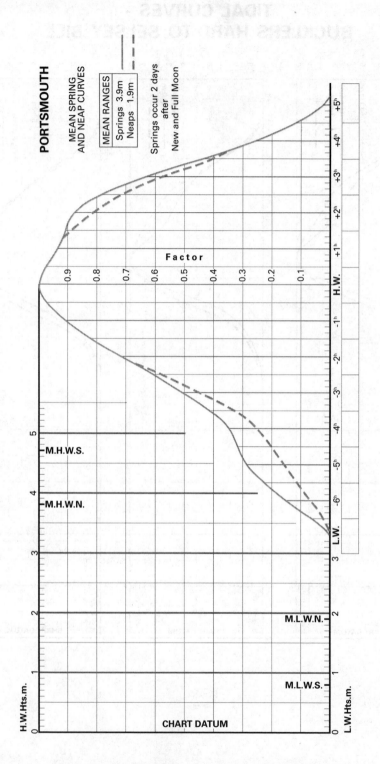

PORTSMOUTH

MEAN SPRING AND NEAP CURVES

MEAN RANGES	
Springs	3.9m
Neaps	1.9m

Springs occur 2 days after New and Full Moon

Factor: 0.9 0.8 0.7 0.6 0.5 0.4 0.3 0.2 0.1

H.W. -1ʰ -2ʰ -3ʰ -4ʰ -5ʰ -6ʰ L.W.

+5ʰ +4ʰ +3ʰ +2ʰ +1ʰ H.W.

M.H.W.S.
M.H.W.N.
M.L.W.N.
M.L.W.S.

H.W.Hts.m.
L.W.Hts.m.

CHART DATUM

TIME ZONE (UT)
For Summer Time add ONE hour in **non-shaded areas**

ENGLAND – PORTSMOUTH
LAT 50°48'N   LONG 1°07'W
TIMES AND HEIGHTS OF HIGH AND LOW WATERS

YEAR 2004

JANUARY

Day	Time	m	Time	m	Day	Time	m	Time	m
1 TH	0613	4.1	1154	1.9	**16** F	0514	4.2	1050	1.7
	1831	3.7				1732	4.0	2318	1.5
2 F	0012	1.9	0713	4.0	**17** SA	0623	4.2	1205	1.7
	1258	1.9	1937	3.7		1849	4.0		
3 SA	0114	1.8	0809	4.1	**18** SU	0034	1.6	0735	4.3
	1352	1.8	2038	3.9		1322	1.5	2007	4.1
4 SU	0208	1.8	0859	4.2	**19** M	0148	1.5	0842	4.4
	1439	1.6	2128	4.0		1430	1.3	2117	4.3
5 M	0255	1.6	0943	4.3	**20** TU	0253	1.3	0942	4.6
	1522	1.5	2211	4.2		1529	1.1	2219	4.5
6 TU	0338	1.5	1022	4.4	**21** W	0350	1.1	1037	4.7
	1602	1.3	2250	4.3		1623	0.9	2313	4.7
7 W	0418	1.4	1100	4.4	**22** TH	0442	1.0	1127	4.8
	1641	1.2	2328	4.4		1713	0.7		
8 TH	0456	1.3	1136	4.5	**23** F	0004	4.8	0530	0.9
	1718	1.1				1216	4.8	1759	0.7
9 F	0005	4.5	0532	1.3	**24** SA	0051	4.8	0616	0.9
	1212	4.4	1753	1.1		1302	4.7	1842	0.7
10 SA	0042	4.5	0607	1.3	**25** SU	0136	4.8	0659	1.0
	1248	4.4	1827	1.0		1345	4.6	1922	0.8
11 SU	0119	4.5	0642	1.3	**26** M	0218	4.7	0739	1.1
	1325	4.4	1903	1.0		1426	4.4	2000	0.9
12 M	0158	4.5	0720	1.3	**27** TU	0257	4.5	0819	1.3
	1404	4.3	1942	1.1		1505	4.2	2037	1.2
13 TU	0239	4.4	0802	1.4	**28** W	0336	4.3	0859	1.5
	1446	4.3	2025	1.1		1545	4.0	2116	1.4
14 W	0324	4.3	0850	1.4	**29** TH	0415	4.1	0944	1.8
	1533	4.2	2114	1.3		1627	3.8	2201	1.7
15 TH	0415	4.3	0945	1.6	**30** F	0500	4.0	1040	1.9
	1628	4.1	2211	1.4		1718	3.7	2301	2.0
					31 SA	0557	3.8	1154	2.1
						1827	3.6		

FEBRUARY

Day	Time	m	Time	m	Day	Time	m	Time	m
1 SU	0020	2.1	0708	3.8	**16** M	0018	1.8	0711	4.0
	1310	2.0	1951	3.6		1313	1.7	2000	3.9
2 M	0134	2.0	0820	3.9	**17** TU	0146	1.7	0833	4.1
	1411	1.8	2101	3.8		1428	1.4	2118	4.2
3 TU	0232	1.8	0917	4.0	**18** W	0255	1.4	0938	4.4
	1500	1.6	2152	4.1		1527	1.1	2217	4.5
4 W	0320	1.6	1002	4.2	**19** TH	0350	1.2	1032	4.5
	1543	1.3	2234	4.3		1618	0.9	2307	4.7
5 TH	0402	1.4	1043	4.3	**20** F	0437	0.9	1120	4.6
	1623	1.1	2312	4.4		1703	0.7	2353	4.8
6 F	0441	1.2	1121	4.4	**21** SA	0521	0.8	1203	4.7
	1702	1.0	2349	4.5		1745	0.6		
7 SA	0518	1.1	1157	4.4	**22** SU	0034	4.8	0600	0.7
	1739	0.8				1245	4.6	1822	0.6
8 SU	0025	4.5	0553	1.0	**23** M	0112	4.7	0637	0.7
	1234	4.5	1814	0.7		1322	4.6	1856	0.7
9 M	0102	4.6	0628	0.9	**24** TU	0146	4.6	0711	0.8
	1311	4.5	1849	0.6		1357	4.5	1927	0.8
10 TU	0139	4.6	0704	0.9	**25** W	0218	4.5	0742	1.0
	1349	4.5	1925	0.7		1430	4.3	1957	1.1
11 W	0216	4.5	0743	0.9	**26** TH	0249	4.4	0812	1.3
	1429	4.4	2003	0.9		1504	4.1	2027	1.3
12 TH	0257	4.5	0824	1.1	**27** F	0322	4.2	0845	1.5
	1512	4.3	2047	1.1		1542	3.9	2103	1.7
13 F	0341	4.3	0913	1.3	**28** SA	0401	3.9	0927	1.8
	1602	4.1	2139	1.4		1627	3.7	2154	2.0
14 SA	0435	4.1	1034	1.6	**29** SU	0452	3.7	1034	2.1
	1704	3.9	2248	1.7		1732	3.6	2326	2.2
15 SU	0545	4.0	1139	1.8					
	1826	3.8							

MARCH

Day	Time	m	Time	m	Day	Time	m	Time	m
1 M	0608	3.6	1227	2.2	**16** TU	0017	1.9	0701	3.8
	1907	3.5				1309	1.7	2003	3.9
2 TU	0107	2.2	0741	3.6	**17** W	0148	1.7	0831	4.0
	1344	2.0	2036	3.8		1423	1.4	2115	4.2
3 W	0214	1.9	0853	3.8	**18** TH	0252	1.4	0933	4.2
	1437	1.6	2131	4.0		1518	1.1	2208	4.5
4 TH	0302	1.6	0942	4.1	**19** F	0341	1.1	1022	4.4
	1521	1.3	2213	4.3		1603	0.8	2252	4.7
5 F	0343	1.3	1023	4.2	**20** SA	0423	0.8	1105	4.6
	1601	1.0	2250	4.4		1645	0.6	2333	4.7
6 SA	0421	1.0	1100	4.4	**21** SU	0502	0.7	1145	4.6
	1639	0.8	2326	4.5		1721	0.6		
7 SU	0457	0.8	1138	4.5	**22** M	0009	4.7	0538	0.6
	1716	0.6				1221	4.6	1755	0.6
8 M	0002	4.6	0533	0.7	**23** TU	0042	4.7	0610	0.6
	1216	4.5	1752	0.5		1255	4.6	1826	0.7
9 TU	0039	4.7	0608	0.6	**24** W	0112	4.6	0640	0.8
	1254	4.6	1828	0.5		1327	4.5	1854	0.8
10 W	0115	4.7	0644	0.6	**25** TH	0141	4.5	0707	0.9
	1332	4.6	1904	0.6		1358	4.4	1921	1.1
11 TH	0153	4.6	0722	0.7	**26** F	0210	4.4	0734	1.1
	1413	4.5	1942	0.8		1431	4.2	1949	1.3
12 F	0232	4.5	0802	0.9	**27** SA	0240	4.2	0803	1.4
	1456	4.4	2025	1.1		1507	4.0	2022	1.7
13 SA	0315	4.3	0849	1.2	**28** SU	0315	4.0	0840	1.7
	1546	4.1	2118	1.4		1550	3.8	2108	2.0
14 SU	0409	4.0	0952	1.6	**29** M	0402	3.7	0935	2.2
	1651	3.9	2234	1.8		1654	3.6	2234	2.3
15 M	0521	3.8	1127	1.8	**30** TU	0515	3.5	1135	2.2
	1821	3.8				1825	3.6		
					31 W	0036	2.3	0653	3.5
						1311	2.0	1959	3.8

APRIL

Day	Time	m	Time	m	Day	Time	m	Time	m
1 TH	0146	2.0	0816	3.7	**16** F	0233	1.4	0914	4.2
	1407	1.7	2056	4.0		1455	1.1	2145	4.5
2 F	0234	1.6	0909	4.0	**17** SA	0319	1.1	1001	4.4
	1451	1.3	2139	4.3		1537	0.9	2227	4.6
3 SA	0315	1.2	0951	4.2	**18** SU	0359	0.9	1042	4.5
	1531	1.0	2218	4.5		1616	0.8	2305	4.7
4 SU	0352	0.9	1031	4.4	**19** M	0436	0.7	1119	4.5
	1609	0.7	2255	4.6		1651	0.7	2339	4.7
5 M	0429	0.7	1111	4.5	**20** TU	0510	0.7	1154	4.5
	1647	0.6	2333	4.7		1725	0.7		
6 TU	0507	0.5	1151	4.6	**21** W	0010	4.6	0542	0.7
	1725	0.5				1227	4.5	1755	0.8
7 W	0012	4.8	0544	0.4	**22** TH	0039	4.6	0611	0.8
	1233	4.7	1804	0.5		1258	4.5	1824	1.0
8 TH	0052	4.8	0623	0.5	**23** F	0108	4.5	0638	1.0
	1315	4.7	1843	0.6		1331	4.4	1852	1.2
9 F	0132	4.7	0703	0.6	**24** SA	0138	4.4	0705	1.2
	1359	4.6	1925	0.8		1404	4.3	1921	1.4
10 SA	0213	4.6	0747	0.8	**25** SU	0209	4.2	0735	1.4
	1446	4.4	2012	1.1		1441	4.1	1956	1.7
11 SU	0300	4.3	0838	1.2	**26** M	0243	4.0	0813	1.6
	1541	4.2	2111	1.5		1525	3.9	2042	2.0
12 M	0356	4.0	0946	1.5	**27** TU	0329	3.8	0900	1.9
	1650	3.9	2232	1.8		1625	3.7	2154	2.2
13 TU	0513	3.8	1121	1.7	**28** W	0435	3.6	1033	2.1
	1824	3.9				1743	3.7	2340	2.2
14 W	0009	1.9	0655	3.7	**29** TH	0559	3.6	1216	1.8
	1255	1.7	1953	4.1		1906	3.8		
15 TH	0134	1.7	0817	4.0	**30** F	0058	2.0	0720	3.7
	1404	1.4	2056	4.3		1321	1.7	2008	4.1

Chapter 5

TIME ZONE (UT)
For Summer Time add ONE hour in **non-shaded areas**

ENGLAND – PORTSMOUTH
LAT 50°48′N   LONG 1°07′W
TIMES AND HEIGHTS OF HIGH AND LOW WATERS

YEAR 2004

MAY

Day	Time m	Time m	Day	Time m	Time m
1 SA	0152 1.6 / 0821 4.0	1409 1.3 / 2056 4.3	**16** SU	0246 1.2 / 0931 4.2	1504 1.1 / 2155 4.5
2 SU	0235 1.3 / 0910 4.2	1451 1.0 / 2139 4.5	**17** M	0327 1.1 / 1013 4.3	1542 1.0 / 2233 4.5
3 M	0315 1.0 / 0955 4.4	1533 0.8 / 2222 4.7	**18** TU	0405 1.0 / 1051 4.3	1619 1.0 / 2307 4.5
4 TU ○	0356 0.7 / 1041 4.6	1615 0.6 / 2304 4.8	**19** W ●	0441 0.9 / 1126 4.4	1654 1.0 / 2338 4.5
5 W	0438 0.5 / 1127 4.7	1658 0.6 / 2348 4.8	**20** TH	0515 0.9 / 1200 4.4	1728 1.0
6 TH	0521 0.5 / 1214 4.8	1742 0.6	**21** F	0009 4.5 / 0546 1.0	1234 4.4 / 1800 1.1
7 F	0031 4.8 / 0605 0.5	1301 4.8 / 1826 0.7	**22** SA	0041 4.5 / 0616 1.1	1308 4.4 / 1831 1.3
8 SA	0116 4.8 / 0651 0.6	1350 4.7 / 1914 0.9	**23** SU	0113 4.4 / 0646 1.2	1344 4.3 / 1903 1.4
9 SU	0202 4.6 / 0740 0.9	1441 4.5 / 2006 1.2	**24** M	0147 4.2 / 0718 1.4	1423 4.2 / 1939 1.6
10 M	0253 4.3 / 0836 1.1	1540 4.3 / 2108 1.5	**25** TU	0223 4.1 / 0757 1.5	1507 4.0 / 2024 1.8
11 TU ◑	0353 4.1 / 0943 1.4	1650 4.1 / 2221 1.7	**26** W	0308 3.9 / 0847 1.7	1559 3.9 / 2122 2.0
12 W	0507 3.9 / 1102 1.6	1810 4.1 / 2343 1.8	**27** TH ◐	0404 3.8 / 0950 1.8	1702 3.9 / 2234 2.0
13 TH	0634 3.8 / 1222 1.6	1924 4.2	**28** F	0511 3.8 / 1104 1.7	1810 4.0 / 2348 1.9
14 F	0059 1.6 / 0746 4.0	1329 1.4 / 2023 4.3	**29** SA	0623 3.8 / 1214 1.6	1915 4.1
15 SA	0159 1.4 / 0843 4.1	1420 1.2 / 2112 4.4	**30** SU	0053 1.6 / 0729 4.0	1315 1.4 / 2010 4.3
			31 M	0148 1.3 / 0828 4.2	1407 1.1 / 2101 4.5

JUNE

Day	Time m	Time m	Day	Time m	Time m
1 TU	0238 1.1 / 0922 4.4	1457 0.9 / 2151 4.7	**16** W	0334 1.2 / 1023 4.2	1549 1.3 / 2236 4.4
2 W	0326 0.8 / 1015 4.6	1546 0.8 / 2239 4.8	**17** TH	0413 1.2 / 1101 4.3	1628 1.2 / 2311 4.4
3 TH ○	0415 0.7 / 1108 4.7	1636 0.7 / 2328 4.9	**18** F	0451 1.1 / 1138 4.3	1705 1.2 / 2345 4.4
4 F	0505 0.6 / 1159 4.8	1726 0.7	**19** SA	0527 1.1 / 1213 4.4	1742 1.3
5 SA	0016 4.8 / 0554 0.6	1251 4.8 / 1816 0.8	**20** SU	0019 4.4 / 0554 1.1	1250 4.4 / 1816 1.3
6 SU	0105 4.8 / 0645 0.7	1343 4.7 / 1907 0.9	**21** M	0054 4.3 / 0633 1.2	1327 4.4 / 1850 1.4
7 M	0155 4.6 / 0736 0.8	1437 4.6 / 2000 1.1	**22** TU	0130 4.3 / 0707 1.2	1406 4.3 / 1926 1.5
8 TU	0248 4.4 / 0830 1.0	1534 4.5 / 2056 1.3	**23** W	0207 4.2 / 0744 1.3	1447 4.2 / 2007 1.5
9 W	0345 4.2 / 0927 1.2	1634 4.3 / 2157 1.5	**24** TH	0249 4.1 / 0827 1.4	1532 4.2 / 2054 1.6
10 TH	0447 4.0 / 1029 1.4	1737 4.2 / 2304 1.6	**25** F ◑	0336 4.0 / 0916 1.4	1623 4.1 / 2149 1.7
11 F	0554 3.9 / 1135 1.5	1840 4.2	**26** SA	0431 4.0 / 1014 1.5	1720 4.1 / 2251 1.7
12 SA	0012 1.6 / 0700 3.9	1239 1.5 / 1938 4.2	**27** SU	0534 3.9 / 1117 1.5	1823 4.2 / 2359 1.6
13 SU	0115 1.6 / 0801 3.9	1335 1.5 / 2031 4.2	**28** M	0643 4.0 / 1224 1.5	1928 4.3
14 M	0207 1.5 / 0854 4.0	1424 1.4 / 2118 4.3	**29** TU	0106 1.4 / 0753 4.1	1330 1.3 / 2029 4.4
15 TU	0252 1.3 / 0941 4.1	1508 1.4 / 2159 4.3	**30** W	0209 1.2 / 0858 4.3	1431 1.2 / 2126 4.6

JULY

Day	Time m	Time m	Day	Time m	Time m
1 TH	0307 1.0 / 0958 4.5	1529 1.0 / 2221 4.7	**16** F	0350 1.3 / 1042 4.2	1607 1.4 / 2249 4.3
2 F ○	0402 0.8 / 1055 4.7	1624 0.9 / 2313 4.8	**17** SA	0430 1.2 / 1121 4.3	1647 1.3 / 2326 4.3
3 SA	0456 0.7 / 1150 4.8	1717 0.9	**18** SU	0508 1.1 / 1157 4.4	1725 1.2
4 SU	0004 4.8 / 0547 0.6	1243 4.8 / 1808 0.8	**19** M	0001 4.4 / 0544 1.0	1234 4.4 / 1800 1.2
5 M	0055 4.7 / 0637 0.6	1335 4.8 / 1858 0.9	**20** TU	0037 4.3 / 0619 1.0	1310 4.4 / 1834 1.2
6 TU	0145 4.6 / 0726 0.7	1426 4.7 / 1946 1.0	**21** W	0113 4.3 / 0652 1.0	1346 4.4 / 1909 1.2
7 W	0235 4.5 / 0813 0.8	1515 4.6 / 2035 1.1	**22** TH	0149 4.3 / 0726 1.0	1423 4.4 / 1945 1.2
8 TH	0324 4.3 / 0900 1.1	1603 4.5 / 2124 1.3	**23** F	0228 4.2 / 0803 1.1	1502 4.4 / 2026 1.3
9 F ◑	0413 4.1 / 0948 1.3	1652 4.3 / 2217 1.5	**24** SA	0310 4.2 / 0846 1.2	1545 4.3 / 2114 1.4
10 SA	0504 3.9 / 1040 1.5	1743 4.1 / 2316 1.7	**25** SU	0358 4.1 / 0936 1.3	1635 4.2 / 2210 1.5
11 SU	0601 3.8 / 1140 1.6	1840 4.0	**26** M	0456 4.0 / 1037 1.5	1737 4.1 / 2319 1.6
12 M	0022 1.8 / 0707 3.7	1245 1.7 / 1940 4.0	**27** TU	0608 3.9 / 1150 1.6	1851 4.1
13 TU	0125 1.7 / 0814 3.8	1345 1.6 / 2038 4.0	**28** W	0040 1.6 / 0730 3.9	1311 1.6 / 2006 4.2
14 W	0220 1.6 / 0913 3.9	1438 1.7 / 2128 4.1	**29** TH	0157 1.4 / 0846 4.1	1423 1.5 / 2112 4.4
15 TH	0307 1.5 / 1001 4.1	1524 1.6 / 2211 4.2	**30** F	0301 1.2 / 0952 4.4	1525 1.2 / 2210 4.6
			31 SA ○	0358 0.9 / 1049 4.6	1620 1.0 / 2303 4.7

AUGUST

Day	Time m	Time m	Day	Time m	Time m
1 SU	0450 0.7 / 1142 4.8	1710 0.9 / 2353 4.8	**16** M	0448 1.0 / 1138 4.5	1706 1.1 / ● 2342 4.4
2 M	0539 0.6 / 1232 4.9	1758 0.8	**17** TU	0524 0.9 / 1212 4.5	1741 1.0
3 TU	0041 4.7 / 0624 0.5	1319 4.9 / 1842 0.8	**18** W	0017 4.4 / 0558 0.8	1247 4.5 / 1813 1.0
4 W	0127 4.7 / 0706 0.6	1402 4.8 / 1924 0.9	**19** TH	0052 4.4 / 0630 0.8	1321 4.5 / 1846 0.9
5 TH	0210 4.5 / 0746 0.8	1443 4.7 / 2004 1.0	**20** F	0128 4.4 / 0703 0.8	1356 4.5 / 1921 1.0
6 F	0251 4.4 / 0824 1.0	1522 4.5 / 2044 1.2	**21** SA	0205 4.4 / 0738 0.9	1432 4.5 / 1959 1.0
7 SA ◑	0331 4.2 / 0901 1.3	1559 4.3 / 2126 1.5	**22** SU	0244 4.3 / 0817 1.1	1512 4.4 / 2043 1.3
8 SU	0412 3.9 / 0944 1.6	1640 4.1 / 2216 1.8	**23** M	0330 4.2 / 0905 1.4	1600 4.2 / 2138 1.5
9 M	0501 3.7 / 1040 1.9	1731 3.9 / 2325 1.9	**24** TU	0428 4.0 / 1007 1.7	1702 4.0 / 2254 1.7
10 TU	0606 3.6 / 1155 2.1	1841 3.8	**25** W	0546 3.8 / 1135 1.9	1826 4.0
11 W	0045 2.0 / 0735 3.6	1314 2.1 / 2001 3.8	**26** TH	0033 1.8 / 0723 3.8	1311 1.9 / 1956 4.1
12 TH	0153 1.9 / 0852 3.8	1417 1.9 / 2105 4.0	**27** F	0157 1.6 / 0848 4.2	1425 1.6 / 2108 4.3
13 F	0246 1.7 / 0944 4.1	1506 1.7 / 2152 4.1	**28** SA	0300 1.2 / 0950 4.5	1523 1.3 / 2205 4.6
14 SA	0330 1.4 / 1026 4.3	1549 1.5 / 2231 4.3	**29** SU	0352 0.9 / 1042 4.7	1612 1.0 / 2254 4.7
15 SU	0410 1.1 / 1103 4.4	1629 1.3 / 2307 4.3	**30** M ○	0439 0.6 / 1129 4.8	1658 0.8 / 2339 4.8
			31 TU	0522 0.5 / 1212 4.9	1740 0.7

ENGLAND – PORTSMOUTH

LAT 50°48′N   LONG 1°07′W

TIMES AND HEIGHTS OF HIGH AND LOW WATERS

YEAR **2004**

SEPTEMBER

Day	Time m	Time m	Time m	Time m
1 W	0021 4.8	0602 0.5	1253 4.9	1819 0.7
16 TH	0531 0.7	1218 4.6	1747 0.8	
2 TH	0101 4.7	0639 0.6	1331 4.8	1855 0.8
17 F	0027 4.6	0604 0.7	1253 4.7	1820 0.8
3 F	0138 4.6	0712 0.8	1405 4.6	1928 1.0
18 SA	0105 4.6	0637 0.8	1328 4.6	1855 0.8
4 SA	0213 4.4	0743 1.0	1437 4.5	2000 1.2
19 SU	0143 4.6	0713 0.9	1405 4.6	1934 1.0
5 SU	0248 4.2	0815 1.3	1509 4.3	2035 1.5
20 M	0224 4.4	0753 1.2	1446 4.4	2018 1.3
6 M	0326 4.0	0851 1.7	1545 4.0	◑ 2116 1.8
21 TU	0312 4.2	0843 1.5	1535 4.2	● 2117 1.6
7 TU	0411 3.8	0942 2.1	1633 3.8	2222 2.1
22 W	0414 4.0	0955 1.9	1642 3.9	2245 1.9
8 W	0516 3.6	1112 2.3	1743 3.6	
23 TH	0541 3.8	1138 2.1	1817 3.8	
9 TH	0009 2.2	0657 3.6	1251 2.3	1927 3.7
24 F	0033 1.9	0728 3.9	1313 1.9	1957 4.0
10 F	0130 2.0	0832 3.8	1358 2.1	2044 3.9
25 SA	0154 1.6	0845 4.3	1421 1.6	2103 4.3
11 SA	0224 1.7	0923 4.1	1447 1.7	2131 4.1
26 SU	0251 1.2	0940 4.6	1512 1.2	2154 4.6
12 SU	0307 1.4	1002 4.3	1527 1.4	2208 4.3
27 M	0337 0.9	1025 4.8	1556 1.0	2237 4.7
13 M	0346 1.1	1037 4.5	1604 1.2	2243 4.4
28 TU	0419 0.7	1107 4.9	1637 0.8	○ 2318 4.8
14 TU	0422 0.9	1110 4.5	1639 1.0	● 2317 4.5
29 W	0458 0.6	1146 4.9	1715 0.7	2356 4.8
15 W	0457 0.7	1144 4.6	1713 0.9	2352 4.5
30 TH	0534 0.6	1222 4.8	1750 0.7	

OCTOBER

Day	Time m	Time m	Time m	Time m
1 F	0032 4.7	0607 0.7	1255 4.8	1822 0.8
16 SA	0003 4.7	0535 0.7	1226 4.8	1754 0.7
2 SA	0106 4.6	0637 0.9	1325 4.6	1852 1.0
17 SU	0044 4.8	0613 0.8	1304 4.7	1834 0.8
3 SU	0138 4.5	0706 1.1	1355 4.5	1921 1.3
18 M	0126 4.7	0654 1.0	1345 4.6	1917 1.0
4 M	0212 4.3	0735 1.4	1426 4.3	1952 1.5
19 TU	0212 4.5	0740 1.3	1430 4.4	2006 1.3
5 TU	0248 4.1	0810 1.8	1501 4.1	2030 1.9
20 W	0305 4.3	0837 1.6	1524 4.1	◑ 2112 1.6
6 W	0332 3.9	0857 2.2	1547 3.8	◑ 2128 2.2
21 TH	0413 4.1	0957 1.9	1636 3.9	2241 1.9
7 TH	0436 3.7	1029 2.4	1655 3.6	2324 2.3
22 F	0544 4.0	1132 2.0	1814 3.9	
8 F	0611 3.6	1221 2.4	1837 3.6	
23 SA	0017 1.8	0719 4.1	1258 1.8	1944 4.1
9 SA	0056 2.1	0752 3.8	1330 2.1	2007 3.8
24 SU	0133 1.6	0825 4.4	1401 1.5	2045 4.3
10 SU	0153 1.8	0846 4.1	1417 1.8	2056 4.1
25 M	0228 1.3	0916 4.6	1450 1.2	2133 4.5
11 M	0236 1.5	0925 4.3	1456 1.5	2134 4.3
26 TU	0312 1.0	1000 4.8	1532 1.0	2215 4.6
12 TU	0313 1.2	1000 4.5	1532 1.2	2210 4.4
27 W	0352 0.8	1040 4.8	1610 0.9	2254 4.7
13 W	0349 0.9	1035 4.6	1607 1.0	2246 4.6
28 TH	0428 0.8	1117 4.8	1647 0.8	○ 2330 4.7
14 TH	0424 0.8	1111 4.7	1642 0.8	● 2324 4.7
29 F	0503 0.8	1150 4.8	1721 0.9	
15 F	0500 0.7	1147 4.8	1718 0.7	
30 SA	0004 4.7	0535 0.9	1221 4.7	1753 1.0
31 SU	0037 4.6	0606 1.1	1251 4.6	1823 1.1

NOVEMBER

Day	Time m	Time m	Time m	Time m
1 M	0110 4.5	0636 1.3	1321 4.5	1852 1.3
16 TU	0117 4.8	0643 1.1	1333 4.7	1910 1.0
2 TU	0144 4.4	0707 1.5	1353 4.3	1923 1.5
17 W	0208 4.6	0736 1.3	1423 4.5	2005 1.2
3 W	0221 4.2	0742 1.8	1428 4.1	2001 1.8
18 TH	0306 4.4	0837 1.6	1521 4.2	2109 1.5
4 TH	0305 4.0	0827 2.1	1512 3.9	2053 2.1
19 F	0413 4.3	0948 1.8	1631 4.0	◑ 2223 1.6
5 F	0404 3.8	0940 2.4	1614 3.7	◑ 2217 2.2
20 SA	0532 4.2	1108 1.9	1754 4.0	2342 1.7
6 SA	0522 3.8	1124 2.4	1735 3.6	2356 2.2
21 SU	0649 4.3	1225 1.8	1911 4.0	
7 SU	0647 3.9	1240 2.2	1900 3.8	
22 M	0054 1.6	0752 4.4	1328 1.6	2013 4.2
8 M	0102 1.9	0750 4.1	1333 1.9	2001 4.0
23 TU	0152 1.4	0844 4.5	1419 1.4	2104 4.3
9 TU	0150 1.6	0837 4.3	1414 1.6	2049 4.2
24 W	0239 1.3	0930 4.6	1503 1.2	2149 4.4
10 W	0231 1.3	0918 4.5	1453 1.3	2132 4.4
25 TH	0320 1.2	1010 4.7	1543 1.1	2229 4.5
11 TH	0309 1.1	0958 4.7	1531 1.0	2215 4.6
26 F	0358 1.1	1047 4.7	1620 1.1	○ 2306 4.5
12 F	0348 0.9	1039 4.8	1611 0.8	● 2259 4.7
27 SA	0434 1.1	1120 4.7	1656 1.1	2341 4.5
13 SA	0429 0.8	1121 4.9	1652 0.7	2344 4.8
28 SU	0509 1.2	1152 4.6	1730 1.1	
14 SU	0511 0.7	1203 4.9	1736 0.7	
29 M	0014 4.5	0543 1.3	1224 4.6	1802 1.2
15 M	0029 4.8	0556 0.9	1247 4.8	1821 0.8
30 TU	0049 4.5	0615 1.4	1256 4.5	1834 1.3

DECEMBER

Day	Time m	Time m	Time m	Time m
1 W	0124 4.4	0648 1.6	1330 4.3	1906 1.6
16 TH	0206 4.7	0732 1.2	1418 4.5	2001 1.0
2 TH	0202 4.3	0723 1.8	1406 4.2	1943 1.6
17 F	0301 4.7	0827 1.3	1514 4.4	2056 1.2
3 F	0245 4.2	0805 2.0	1447 4.0	2027 1.8
18 SA	0400 4.5	0927 1.5	1613 4.2	◑ 2154 1.4
4 SA	0335 4.0	0858 2.1	1538 3.9	2123 1.9
19 SU	0501 4.4	1031 1.7	1716 4.0	2256 1.5
5 SU	0435 4.0	1005 2.2	1640 3.8	◑ 2231 1.9
20 M	0604 4.3	1138 1.7	1823 3.9	
6 M	0542 4.0	1119 2.1	1749 3.8	2342 1.9
21 TU	0001 1.6	0706 4.3	1245 1.7	1928 3.9
7 TU	0647 4.1	1226 1.9	1859 3.9	
22 W	0105 1.6	0803 4.3	1343 1.6	2029 4.0
8 W	0045 1.7	0745 4.3	1322 1.7	2000 4.1
23 TH	0201 1.6	0855 4.3	1433 1.5	2122 4.1
9 TH	0140 1.5	0837 4.5	1412 1.4	2056 4.3
24 F	0249 1.5	0941 4.4	1517 1.4	2208 4.2
10 F	0230 1.2	0925 4.6	1500 1.1	2149 4.5
25 SA	0332 1.4	1021 4.4	1558 1.3	2248 4.3
11 SA	0318 1.1	1013 4.8	1547 0.9	2240 4.7
26 SU	0412 1.4	1057 4.5	1637 1.2	○ 2324 4.4
12 SU	0407 1.0	1100 4.9	1637 0.8	● 2358 4.8
27 M	0451 1.3	1130 4.5	1714 1.2	2358 4.4
13 M	0457 0.9	1148 4.9	1727 0.7	
28 TU	0527 1.3	1204 4.5	1749 1.2	
14 TU	0021 4.8	0547 0.9	1236 4.8	1817 0.8
29 W	0033 4.4	0602 1.4	1239 4.4	1822 1.2
15 W	0113 4.8	0639 1.0	1326 4.7	1908 0.8
30 TH	0109 4.4	0635 1.5	1314 4.3	1854 1.2
31 F	0146 4.4	0708 1.5	1349 4.2	1927 1.3

Chapter 5

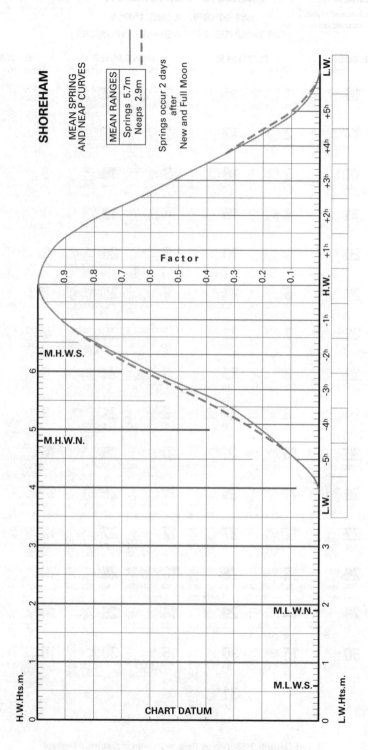

SHOREHAM

MEAN SPRING
AND NEAP CURVES

MEAN RANGES
Springs 5.7m
Neaps 2.9m

Springs occur 2 days
after
New and Full Moon

Factor

0.9 0.8 0.7 0.6 0.5 0.4 0.3 0.2 0.1

H.W.

M.H.W.S.

M.H.W.N.

L.W.

M.L.W.N.

M.L.W.S.

CHART DATUM

H.W.Hts.m.

L.W.Hts.m.

TIME ZONE (UT)
For Summer Time add ONE hour in **non-shaded areas**

ENGLAND – SHOREHAM

LAT 50°50'N   LONG 0°15'W

TIMES AND HEIGHTS OF HIGH AND LOW WATERS

YEAR 2004

JANUARY

Day	Time m	Time m	Day	Time m	Time m
1 TH	0602 5.1 / 1231 2.0	1831 4.8	**16** F	0502 5.4 / 1127 1.6	1731 5.2 / 2356 1.6
2 F	0055 1.9 / 0703 5.1	1335 1.9 / 1937 4.9	**17** SA	0616 5.3 / 1243 1.6	1851 5.1
3 SA	0158 1.9 / 0805 5.1	1431 1.8 / 2037 5.0	**18** SU	0114 1.6 / 0731 5.4	1357 1.5 / 2008 5.3
4 SU	0253 1.8 / 0857 5.1	1520 1.6 / 2127 5.2	**19** M	0227 1.5 / 0840 5.6	1502 1.2 / 2116 5.6
5 M	0340 1.6 / 0942 5.5	1603 1.4 / 2210 5.5	**20** TU	0330 1.2 / 0941 5.9	1600 1.0 / 2217 5.9
6 TU	0422 1.4 / 1021 5.7	1643 1.2 / 2249 5.7	**21** W	0425 1.0 / 1037 6.1	1653 0.7 / ● 2311 6.2
7 W	0501 1.3 / 1057 5.9	1721 1.1 / ○ 2326 5.8	**22** TH	0516 0.8 / 1128 6.3	1742 0.6
8 TH	0537 1.2 / 1133 5.9	1757 1.1	**23** F	0002 6.3 / 0603 0.8	1217 6.3 / 1829 0.6
9 F	0001 5.9 / 0612 1.2	1208 5.9 / 1832 1.0	**24** SA	0049 6.4 / 0649 0.8	1303 6.3 / 1914 0.6
10 SA	0036 5.9 / 0646 1.2	1243 5.9 / 1906 1.0	**25** SU	0132 6.4 / 0733 0.8	1348 6.1 / 1956 0.7
11 SU	0111 5.9 / 0720 1.2	1319 5.8 / 1940 1.1	**26** M	0213 6.2 / 0815 1.0	1425 5.9 / 2036 0.9
12 M	0146 5.9 / 0756 1.2	1357 5.8 / 2017 1.1	**27** TU	0251 6.0 / 0855 1.2	1503 5.7 / 2114 1.2
13 TU	0225 5.8 / 0837 1.3	1438 5.7 / 2059 1.2	**28** W	0328 5.7 / 0935 1.4	1543 5.3 / 2153 1.5
14 W	0309 5.7 / 0924 1.4	1526 5.5 / 2147 1.3	**29** TH	0409 5.4 / 1018 1.7	1629 5.0 / ◐ 2239 1.8
15 TH	0401 5.7 / 1020 1.5	1622 5.3 / ◐ 2245 1.5	**30** F	0458 5.0 / 1111 2.0	1727 4.7 / 2335 2.1
			31 SA	0558 4.8 / 1218 2.1	1834 4.6

FEBRUARY

Day	Time m	Time m	Day	Time m	Time m
1 SU	0052 2.2 / 0706 4.7	1346 2.1 / 1946 4.6	**16** M	0055 1.9 / 0710 5.0	1344 1.7 / 1959 5.0
2 M	0218 2.1 / 0814 4.9	1453 1.9 / 2054 4.9	**17** TU	0221 1.7 / 0834 5.3	1457 1.4 / 2117 5.4
3 TU	0317 1.9 / 0913 5.2	1542 1.6 / 2147 5.2	**18** W	0326 1.4 / 0941 5.6	1555 1.0 / 2217 5.8
4 W	0403 1.6 / 0959 5.4	1624 1.3 / 2230 5.6	**19** TH	0420 1.0 / 1035 6.0	1645 0.8 / 2307 6.2
5 TH	0443 1.4 / 1039 5.7	1702 1.1 / 2309 5.8	**20** F	0507 0.8 / 1123 6.2	1730 0.6 / ● 2352 6.4
6 F	0519 1.2 / 1116 5.9	1739 0.9 / ○ 2345 6.0	**21** SA	0551 0.7 / 1207 6.3	1813 0.5
7 SA	0555 1.0 / 1152 6.0	1815 0.8	**22** SU	0033 6.5 / 0632 0.6	1247 6.3 / 1852 0.5
8 SU	0020 6.1 / 0630 0.9	1228 6.1 / 1849 0.8	**23** M	0111 6.4 / 0710 0.7	1323 6.2 / 1928 0.6
9 M	0054 6.2 / 0704 0.9	1304 6.1 / 1923 0.7	**24** TU	0144 6.3 / 0745 0.8	1356 6.0 / 2001 0.8
10 TU	0128 6.2 / 0738 0.8	1340 6.1 / 1957 0.7	**25** W	0215 6.1 / 0817 1.0	1425 5.8 / 2033 1.0
11 W	0205 6.1 / 0815 0.9	1418 6.0 / 2035 0.8	**26** TH	0242 5.8 / 0850 1.2	1454 5.5 / 2107 1.3
12 TH	0244 6.0 / 0857 1.0	1500 5.8 / 2118 1.1	**27** F	0309 5.4 / 0926 1.5	1528 5.1 / 2145 1.7
13 F	0329 5.7 / 0946 1.3	1550 5.5 / ◐ 2211 1.4	**28** SA	0345 5.0 / 1011 1.9	1616 4.7 / ◐ 2235 2.1
14 SA	0424 5.4 / 1049 1.6	1655 5.1 / 2321 1.7	**29** SU	0442 4.7 / 1112 2.2	1740 4.4 / 2348 2.4
15 SU	0539 5.1 / 1214 1.8	1824 4.9			

MARCH

Day	Time m	Time m	Day	Time m	Time m
1 M	0615 4.4 / 1238 2.3	1905 4.4	**16** TU	0050 2.0 / 0704 4.7	1340 1.8 / 2002 4.9
2 TU	0135 2.4 / 0735 4.5	1421 2.1 / 2022 4.7	**17** W	0218 1.8 / 0835 5.1	1450 1.4 / 2116 5.4
3 W	0253 2.0 / 0845 4.9	1517 1.7 / 2123 5.1	**18** TH	0320 1.4 / 0937 5.5	1544 1.0 / 2208 5.9
4 TH	0340 1.6 / 0936 5.3	1559 1.3 / 2207 5.5	**19** F	0409 1.0 / 1026 5.9	1630 0.7 / 2252 6.2
5 F	0419 1.3 / 1018 5.6	1637 1.0 / 2246 5.9	**20** SA	0451 0.7 / 1109 6.2	1711 0.6 / ● 2332 6.4
6 SA	0456 1.0 / 1055 5.9	1714 0.8 / ● 2322 6.1	**21** SU	0531 0.6 / 1148 6.3	1749 0.5
7 SU	0532 0.8 / 1132 6.1	1750 0.6 / 2357 6.3	**22** M	0009 6.4 / 0607 0.6	1225 6.3 / 1824 0.5
8 M	0607 0.7 / 1208 6.3	1826 0.5	**23** TU	0043 6.4 / 0641 0.6	1257 6.2 / 1857 0.6
9 TU	0031 6.4 / 0642 0.6	1246 6.3 / 1900 0.5	**24** W	0113 6.2 / 0713 0.7	1325 6.0 / 1927 0.8
10 W	0107 6.4 / 0718 0.5	1321 6.3 / 1936 0.5	**25** TH	0137 6.0 / 0742 0.9	1350 5.8 / 1957 1.0
11 TH	0143 6.4 / 0755 0.6	1359 6.2 / 2014 0.7	**26** F	0159 5.8 / 0812 1.1	1416 5.6 / 2028 1.3
12 F	0221 6.1 / 0836 0.8	1440 5.9 / 2057 1.0	**27** SA	0224 5.5 / 0845 1.4	1446 5.2 / 2103 1.6
13 SA	0305 5.8 / 0924 1.2	1530 5.5 / ◐ 2150 1.4	**28** SU	0258 5.1 / 0925 1.7	1527 4.8 / ◐ 2150 2.0
14 SU	0359 5.3 / 1027 1.6	1638 5.0 / 2306 1.9	**29** M	0345 4.7 / 1022 2.1	1641 4.5 / 2302 2.4
15 M	0520 4.8 / 1200 1.9	1817 4.7	**30** TU	0519 4.3 / 1146 2.3	1826 4.4
			31 W	0043 2.4 / 0656 4.4	1333 2.1 / 1943 4.7

APRIL

Day	Time m	Time m	Day	Time m	Time m
1 TH	0216 2.1 / 0808 4.7	1440 1.7 / 2046 5.1	**16** F	0302 1.3 / 0918 5.5	1524 1.1 / 2145 5.9
2 F	0307 1.6 / 0903 5.2	1525 1.3 / 2133 5.6	**17** SA	0348 1.0 / 1004 5.8	1606 0.8 / 2227 6.1
3 SA	0347 1.2 / 0947 5.6	1605 1.0 / 2213 5.9	**18** SU	0428 0.8 / 1045 6.0	1645 0.7 / 2305 6.2
4 SU	0425 0.9 / 1027 6.0	1642 0.7 / 2251 6.2	**19** M	0505 0.7 / 1123 6.1	1721 0.7 / ● 2340 6.3
5 M	0502 0.6 / 1106 6.2	1720 0.5 / ○ 2329 6.4	**20** TU	0540 0.7 / 1158 6.1	1755 0.7
6 TU	0540 0.5 / 1145 6.4	1758 0.4	**21** W	0012 6.2 / 0612 0.7	1229 6.0 / 1827 0.8
7 W	0007 6.5 / 0618 0.4	1224 6.4 / 1836 0.4	**22** TH	0039 6.1 / 0643 0.8	1256 5.9 / 1858 0.9
8 TH	0044 6.5 / 0658 0.4	1303 6.4 / 1916 0.5	**23** F	0103 5.9 / 0713 0.9	1322 5.8 / 1928 1.1
9 F	0123 6.4 / 0739 0.5	1344 6.2 / 1959 0.7	**24** SA	0127 5.7 / 0744 1.1	1349 5.6 / 2000 1.3
10 SA	0203 6.1 / 0823 0.8	1429 5.9 / 2046 1.1	**25** SU	0155 5.5 / 0817 1.3	1421 5.3 / 2037 1.6
11 SU	0250 5.7 / 0915 1.2	1524 5.4 / 2144 1.5	**26** M	0229 5.1 / 0857 1.6	1502 5.0 / 2123 1.9
12 M	0351 5.2 / 1022 1.6	1639 5.0 / ◐ 2304 1.9	**27** TU	0315 4.8 / 0950 1.9	1606 4.7 / ◐ 2229 2.2
13 TU	0517 1.9 / 1155 1.9	1815 4.8	**28** W	0404 4.4 / 1104 2.1	1744 4.6 / 2354 2.3
14 W	0045 2.0 / 0658 4.7	1327 1.7 / 1952 5.0	**29** TH	0614 4.4 / 1232 2.0	1859 4.8
15 TH	0205 1.7 / 0822 5.1	1433 1.4 / 2056 5.5	**30** F	0121 2.0 / 0724 4.7	1349 1.7 / 2000 5.2

Chapter 5

Chart Datum: 3·27 metres below Ordnance Datum (Newlyn)

TIDES

ENGLAND – SHOREHAM YEAR 2004

LAT 50°50'N   LONG 0°15'W

TIMES AND HEIGHTS OF HIGH AND LOW WATERS

TIME ZONE (UT)
For Summer Time add ONE hour in **non-shaded areas**

MAY

Day	Time	m		Day	Time	m
1 SA	0222	1.6		**16** SU	0318	1.1
	0822	5.2			0934	5.6
	1441	1.4			1536	1.0
	2051	5.6			2155	5.9
2 SU	0307	1.2		**17** M	0358	1.0
	0910	5.6			1016	5.7
	1525	1.0			1615	1.0
	2136	6.0			2234	6.0
3 M	0349	0.9		**18** TU	0436	0.9
	0955	5.9			1054	5.8
	1607	0.7			1653	0.9
	2218	6.3			2309	6.0
4 TU	0430	0.6		**19** W	0512	0.9
	1038	6.2			1129	5.8
	1648	0.6			1729	0.9
	O 2300	6.4			● 2340	5.9
5 W	0512	0.4		**20** TH	0547	0.9
	1122	6.3			1201	5.8
	1732	0.5			1803	1.0
	2342	6.5				
6 TH	0556	0.4		**21** F	0009	5.9
	1205	6.4			0619	0.9
	1816	0.5			1232	5.8
					1835	1.1
7 F	0024	6.5		**22** SA	0037	5.7
	0640	0.4			0652	1.0
	1250	6.3			1302	5.7
	1902	0.6			1908	1.2
8 SA	0108	6.3		**23** SU	0105	5.6
	0727	0.5			0725	1.1
	1337	6.2			1333	5.6
	1950	0.8			1942	1.4
9 SU	0155	6.0		**24** M	0137	5.4
	0817	0.8			0800	1.3
	1428	5.9			1407	5.4
	2042	1.1			2020	1.6
10 M	0248	5.6		**25** TU	0213	5.2
	0912	1.1			0839	1.5
	1528	5.5			1448	5.2
	2143	1.5			2105	1.8
11 TU	0352	5.2		**26** W	0259	5.0
	1018	1.5			0928	1.7
	1638	5.2			1542	5.0
	◑ 2258	1.7			2201	1.9
12 W	0509	4.9		**27** TH	0400	4.8
	1140	1.6			1028	1.8
	1759	5.1			1653	4.9
					◑ 2309	2.0
13 TH	0025	1.8		**28** F	0520	4.7
	0634	4.9			1138	1.8
	1259	1.6			1807	5.0
	1919	5.2				
14 F	0136	1.6		**29** SA	0022	1.8
	0750	5.1			0634	4.9
	1401	1.4			1248	1.7
	2022	5.4			1911	5.2
15 SA	0232	1.3		**30** SU	0127	1.6
	0847	5.3			0736	5.2
	1452	1.2			1350	1.4
	2112	5.7			2007	5.6
				31 M	0223	1.2
					0831	5.5
					1444	1.1
					2058	5.9

JUNE

Day	Time	m		Day	Time	m
1 TU	0313	0.9		**16** W	0409	1.2
	0922	5.8			1025	5.5
	1534	0.9			1628	1.2
	2146	6.1			2237	5.7
2 W	0401	0.7		**17** TH	0448	1.1
	1012	6.1			1102	5.6
	1622	0.7			1706	1.2
	2234	6.3			● 2312	5.7
3 TH	0449	0.5		**18** F	0526	1.0
	1102	6.2			1137	5.7
	1712	0.6			1743	1.2
	O 2322	6.4			2345	5.7
4 F	0538	0.5		**19** SA	0602	1.0
	1152	6.3			1212	5.7
	1801	0.6			1819	1.2
5 SA	0011	6.4		**20** SU	0017	5.7
	0627	0.5			0637	1.1
	1244	6.3			1247	5.7
	1851	0.7			1854	1.2
6 SU	0101	6.2		**21** M	0051	5.6
	0718	0.6			0711	1.1
	1336	6.2			1320	5.6
	1943	0.8			1928	1.3
7 M	0152	6.0		**22** TU	0124	5.5
	0810	0.8			0746	1.2
	1429	6.0			1354	5.6
	2036	1.1			2004	1.4
8 TU	0246	5.7		**23** W	0201	5.4
	0906	1.0			0823	1.3
	1524	5.8			1432	5.5
	2134	1.3			2045	1.5
9 W	0344	5.4		**24** TH	0242	5.3
	1005	1.2			0904	1.4
	1622	5.5			1516	5.4
	◑ 2238	1.5			2132	1.6
10 TH	0446	5.2		**25** F	0331	5.2
	1110	1.4			0953	1.5
	1724	5.3			1608	5.3
	2347	1.6			◑ 2227	1.6
11 F	0552	5.0		**26** SA	0428	5.1
	1216	1.5			1050	1.6
	1830	5.3			1709	5.2
					2330	1.6
12 SA	0053	1.6		**27** SU	0536	5.0
	0701	5.0			1155	1.6
	1318	1.5			1816	5.3
	1934	5.3				
13 SU	0151	1.5		**28** M	0038	1.5
	0804	5.1			0647	5.1
	1413	1.5			1304	1.5
	2030	5.4			1923	5.5
14 M	0242	1.4		**29** TU	0144	1.3
	0857	5.2			0754	5.4
	1502	1.4			1410	1.3
	2118	5.5			2024	5.7
15 TU	0327	1.3		**30** W	0244	1.1
	0943	5.4			0856	5.6
	1546	1.3			1510	1.1
	2200	5.6			2122	5.9

JULY

Day	Time	m		Day	Time	m
1 TH	0341	0.9		**16** F	0429	1.3
	0954	5.9			1041	5.5
	1606	0.9			1649	1.4
	2217	6.1			2250	5.6
2 F	0434	0.7		**17** SA	0508	1.1
	1051	6.1			1119	5.7
	1700	0.8			1727	1.2
	O 2311	6.2			● 2326	5.7
3 SA	0527	0.6		**18** SU	0545	1.1
	1146	6.2			1155	5.8
	1752	0.7			1803	1.2
4 SU	0004	6.3		**19** M	0001	5.7
	0618	0.5			0621	1.0
	1239	6.3			1230	5.8
	1843	0.7			1838	1.2
5 M	0056	6.2		**20** TU	0035	5.7
	0709	0.6			0656	1.0
	1330	6.3			1303	5.8
	1933	0.8			1912	1.2
6 TU	0146	6.1		**21** W	0109	5.7
	0759	0.7			0729	1.0
	1419	6.2			1335	5.8
	2023	0.9			1945	1.2
7 W	0234	5.9		**22** TH	0143	5.7
	0849	0.8			0801	1.1
	1506	6.0			1410	5.8
	2114	1.1			2020	1.2
8 TH	0322	5.7		**23** F	0220	5.7
	0938	1.0			0837	1.1
	1552	5.8			1448	5.7
	2205	1.3			2100	1.3
9 F	0411	5.4		**24** SA	0302	5.5
	1028	1.3			0919	1.2
	1640	5.5			1532	5.6
	◑ 2259	1.5			2148	1.4
10 SA	0502	5.1		**25** SU	0350	5.4
	1122	1.5			1009	1.4
	1731	5.3			1624	5.4
	2358	1.7			◑ 2246	1.5
11 SU	0559	4.9		**26** M	0449	5.2
	1222	1.8			1111	1.6
	1829	5.1			1729	5.3
					2357	1.6
12 M	0102	1.8		**27** TU	0605	5.0
	0702	4.8			1228	1.7
	1328	1.8			1847	5.2
	1932	5.0				
13 TU	0205	1.8		**28** W	0116	1.6
	0811	4.8			0728	5.1
	1429	1.8			1349	1.6
	2035	5.1			2003	5.4
14 W	0259	1.6		**29** TH	0229	1.4
	0911	5.0			0844	5.4
	1522	1.7			1500	1.4
	2127	5.3			2111	5.7
15 TH	0347	1.4		**30** F	0332	1.1
	0959	5.3			0950	5.7
	1607	1.5			1559	1.1
	2211	5.4			2211	5.9
				31 SA	0427	0.8
					1048	6.1
					1653	0.9
					O 2306	6.2

AUGUST

Day	Time	m		Day	Time	m
1 SU	0518	0.6		**16** M	0524	1.0
	1140	6.3			1135	5.9
	1743	0.7			1742	1.1
	2357	6.3			● 2341	5.9
2 M	0607	0.5		**17** TU	0600	0.9
	1229	6.5			1208	6.0
	1831	0.7			1817	1.0
3 TU	0045	6.3		**18** W	0014	6.0
	0653	0.5			0633	0.8
	1315	6.5			1240	6.1
	1916	0.7			1849	1.0
4 W	0130	6.3		**19** TH	0047	6.0
	0738	0.6			0705	0.8
	1358	6.4			1311	6.1
	2000	0.8			1921	0.9
5 TH	0211	6.1		**20** F	0121	6.0
	0820	0.7			0735	0.8
	1437	6.2			1344	6.1
	2042	1.0			1954	1.0
6 F	0250	5.8		**21** SA	0156	6.0
	0900	1.0			0809	0.9
	1514	5.9			1420	6.0
	2122	1.2			2031	1.1
7 SA	0329	5.5		**22** SU	0234	5.8
	0939	1.3			0848	1.1
	1553	5.6			1500	5.8
	◑ 2203	1.5			2115	1.3
8 SU	0412	5.2		**23** M	0319	5.5
	1021	1.6			0936	1.2
	1637	5.2			1549	5.5
	2250	1.8			◑ 2211	1.6
9 M	0505	4.8		**24** TU	0416	5.2
	1113	2.0			1039	1.7
	1732	4.9			1655	5.1
	2353	2.1			2328	1.8
10 TU	0610	4.6		**25** W	0541	4.9
	1225	2.2			1209	2.0
	1839	4.7			1828	4.9
11 W	0122	2.1		**26** TH	0104	1.9
	0724	4.6			0722	4.9
	1358	2.2			1346	1.9
	1953	4.8			1959	5.1
12 TH	0235	1.9		**27** F	0227	1.6
	0843	4.8			0847	5.3
	1501	2.0			1459	1.5
	2102	5.0			2113	5.5
13 F	0327	1.6		**28** SA	0339	1.2
	0940	5.2			0950	5.8
	1549	1.7			1555	1.1
	2152	5.3			2210	5.9
14 SA	0410	1.4		**29** SU	0420	0.8
	1023	5.5			1042	6.2
	1630	1.4			1643	0.8
	2232	5.6			2259	6.2
15 SU	0448	1.1		**30** M	0506	0.6
	1100	5.8			1129	6.5
	1707	1.2			1728	0.6
	2307	5.8			O 2345	6.4
				31 TU	0549	0.5
					1212	6.6
					1811	0.6

Chart Datum: 3·27 metres below Ordnance Datum (Newlyn)

TIME ZONE (UT)	ENGLAND – SHOREHAM	YEAR 2004
For Summer Time add ONE hour in **non-shaded areas**	LAT 50°50'N LONG 0°15'W	

TIMES AND HEIGHTS OF HIGH AND LOW WATERS

SEPTEMBER

Day	Time m	Day	Time m
1 W	0027 6.4 / 0630 0.5 / 1252 6.6 / 1851 0.6	**16** TH	0605 0.7 / 1211 6.3 / 1822 0.8
2 TH	0106 6.3 / 0709 0.6 / 1328 6.5 / 1929 0.7	**17** F	0023 6.3 / 0637 0.7 / 1244 6.3 / 1855 0.8
3 F	0142 6.2 / 0745 0.8 / 1402 6.2 / 2003 0.9	**18** SA	0057 6.3 / 0709 0.7 / 1318 6.3 / 1929 0.8
4 SA	0214 5.9 / 0818 1.0 / 1432 5.9 / 2037 1.2	**19** SU	0132 6.2 / 0745 0.9 / 1354 6.1 / 2008 1.0
5 SU	0245 5.6 / 0851 1.3 / 1501 5.6 / 2112 1.5	**20** M	0211 5.9 / 0826 1.1 / 1435 5.8 / 2053 1.3
6 M	0320 5.2 / 0929 1.7 / 1536 5.1 / ◗ 2155 1.9	**21** TU	0257 5.5 / 0916 1.5 / 1525 5.4 / ◗ 2152 1.7
7 TU	0409 4.8 / 1018 2.1 / 1632 4.7 / 2253 2.2	**22** W	0359 5.1 / 1026 1.9 / 1640 4.9 / 2317 2.0
8 W	0525 4.5 / 1128 2.4 / 1756 4.5	**23** TH	0540 4.7 / 1208 2.2 / 1826 4.8
9 TH	0020 2.4 / 0647 4.4 / 1324 2.5 / 1918 4.5	**24** F	0104 2.0 / 0726 4.9 / 1346 2.0 / 2002 5.1
10 F	0208 2.2 / 0814 4.7 / 1439 2.1 / 2037 4.9	**25** SA	0223 1.6 / 0846 5.4 / 1453 1.5 / 2109 5.6
11 SA	0303 1.8 / 0916 5.2 / 1526 1.7 / 2129 5.3	**26** SU	0319 1.2 / 0941 5.9 / 1543 1.1 / 2200 6.0
12 SU	0345 1.4 / 0957 5.6 / 1605 1.4 / 2207 5.6	**27** M	0405 0.8 / 1026 6.3 / 1627 0.8 / 2244 6.3
13 M	0422 1.1 / 1033 5.9 / 1640 1.1 / 2242 5.9	**28** TU	0447 0.6 / 1108 6.5 / 1707 0.6 / ○ 2325 6.4
14 TU	0457 0.9 / 1106 6.1 / 1715 1.0 / ● 2315 6.1	**29** W	0526 0.5 / 1146 6.6 / 1746 0.6
15 W	0532 0.9 / 1139 6.2 / 1749 0.8 / 2349 6.2	**30** TH	0003 6.4 / 0603 0.6 / 1223 6.5 / 1822 0.7

OCTOBER

Day	Time m	Day	Time m
1 F	0038 6.3 / 0637 0.7 / 1255 6.4 / 1855 0.8	**16** SA	0610 0.7 / 1217 6.5 / 1831 0.7
2 SA	0110 6.2 / 0710 0.9 / 1323 6.2 / 1927 1.0	**17** SU	0035 6.4 / 0648 0.7 / 1255 6.4 / 1911 0.8
3 SU	0138 5.9 / 0740 1.1 / 1348 5.9 / 1958 1.2	**18** M	0115 6.2 / 0729 0.9 / 1334 6.2 / 1954 1.0
4 M	0205 5.6 / 0813 1.4 / 1414 5.5 / 2032 1.5	**19** TU	0158 5.9 / 0815 1.2 / 1419 5.8 / 2044 1.3
5 TU	0236 5.3 / 0849 1.8 / 1446 5.2 / 2113 1.9	**20** W	0250 5.5 / 0911 1.6 / 1517 5.3 / ◗ 2148 1.7
6 W	0318 4.9 / 0937 2.2 / 1533 4.7 / ◗ 2209 2.2	**21** TH	0404 5.1 / 1027 2.0 / 1643 4.9 / 2315 2.0
7 TH	0440 4.5 / 1047 2.5 / 1712 4.4 / 2331 2.5	**22** F	0541 4.9 / 1206 2.1 / 1823 4.8
8 F	0611 4.5 / 1229 2.6 / 1841 4.4	**23** SA	0053 1.9 / 0717 5.1 / 1333 1.9 / 1949 5.2
9 SA	0123 2.3 / 0731 4.7 / 1404 2.2 / 1957 4.8	**24** SU	0205 1.6 / 0826 5.5 / 1435 1.4 / 2050 5.6
10 F	0228 1.9 / 0835 5.2 / 1453 1.8 / 2052 5.2	**25** M	0258 1.2 / 0917 6.0 / 1522 1.1 / 2138 5.9
11 M	0311 1.5 / 0919 5.6 / 1532 1.4 / 2132 5.6	**26** TU	0342 0.9 / 1001 6.3 / 1604 0.8 / 2220 6.2
12 TU	0349 1.2 / 0956 6.0 / 1608 1.1 / 2209 6.0	**27** W	0422 0.8 / 1041 6.4 / 1642 0.7 / 2300 6.3
13 W	0424 0.9 / 1031 6.2 / 1643 0.9 / 2245 6.2	**28** TH	0459 0.7 / 1117 6.4 / 1719 0.7 / ○ 2336 6.3
14 TH	0459 0.8 / 1106 6.4 / 1718 0.7 / ● 2322 6.3	**29** F	0535 0.8 / 1151 6.4 / 1754 0.7
15 F	0534 0.7 / 1141 6.5 / 1754 0.7 / 2358 6.4	**30** SA	0009 6.2 / 0609 0.8 / 1222 6.2 / 1826 0.9
		31 SU	0040 6.1 / 0640 1.0 / 1248 6.0 / 1857 1.0

NOVEMBER

Day	Time m	Day	Time m
1 M	0108 5.9 / 0712 1.2 / 1314 5.8 / 1929 1.2	**16** TU	0106 6.2 / 0720 1.0 / 1325 6.1 / 1948 1.0
2 TU	0137 5.7 / 0745 1.5 / 1342 5.5 / 2004 1.5	**17** W	0157 6.0 / 0812 1.2 / 1416 5.8 / 2042 1.2
3 W	0209 5.4 / 0823 1.8 / 1416 5.2 / 2045 1.8	**18** TH	0255 5.7 / 0911 1.6 / 1519 5.4 / 2146 1.5
4 TH	0249 5.1 / 0910 2.1 / 1501 4.8 / 2137 2.1	**19** F	0406 5.4 / 1022 1.8 / 1636 5.1 / ◗ 2302 1.7
5 F	0355 4.8 / 1014 2.4 / 1618 4.5 / ◗ 2248 2.3	**20** SA	0525 5.2 / 1146 1.9 / 1759 5.0
6 SA	0527 4.6 / 1135 2.4 / 1756 4.5	**21** SU	0023 1.8 / 0644 5.3 / 1303 1.7 / 1916 5.2
7 SU	0013 2.3 / 0640 4.8 / 1302 2.2 / 1906 4.7	**22** M	0131 1.6 / 0751 5.5 / 1403 1.6 / 2018 5.4
8 M	0131 2.0 / 0742 5.2 / 1404 1.9 / 2003 5.1	**23** TU	0226 1.4 / 0844 5.8 / 1453 1.3 / 2108 5.7
9 TU	0225 1.7 / 0831 5.6 / 1449 1.5 / 2050 5.5	**24** W	0313 1.2 / 0930 6.0 / 1536 1.1 / 2153 5.8
10 W	0307 1.3 / 0914 5.9 / 1529 1.1 / 2133 5.9	**25** TH	0355 1.1 / 1011 6.1 / 1616 1.0 / 2233 6.0
11 TH	0347 1.1 / 0954 6.2 / 1608 0.9 / 2214 6.2	**26** F	0434 1.0 / 1048 6.1 / 1654 0.9 / ○ 2310 6.0
12 F	0426 0.9 / 1034 6.4 / 1648 0.7 / ● 2255 6.3	**27** SA	0511 1.0 / 1121 6.1 / 1731 1.0 / 2344 6.0
13 SA	0506 0.8 / 1114 6.5 / 1730 0.6 / 2337 6.4	**28** SU	0547 1.1 / 1152 6.0 / 1805 1.0
14 SU	0549 0.7 / 1155 6.5 / 1813 0.6	**29** M	0016 5.9 / 0620 1.2 / 1223 5.9 / 1838 1.1
15 M	0020 6.4 / 0633 0.8 / 1239 6.4 / 1859 0.7	**30** TU	0049 5.8 / 0653 1.3 / 1253 5.7 / 1911 1.3

DECEMBER

Day	Time m	Day	Time m
1 W	0121 5.7 / 0728 1.5 / 1324 5.5 / 1947 1.4	**16** TH	0158 6.2 / 0807 1.1 / 1416 6.0 / 2037 1.0
2 TH	0154 5.5 / 0805 1.7 / 1358 5.3 / 2026 1.6	**17** F	0253 6.0 / 0903 1.3 / 1513 5.7 / 2133 1.2
3 F	0231 5.3 / 0848 1.9 / 1440 5.1 / 2111 1.8	**18** SA	0351 5.8 / 1004 1.5 / 1613 5.4 / ◖ 2234 1.4
4 SA	0319 5.1 / 0940 2.1 / 1534 4.9 / 2206 2.0	**19** SU	0451 5.6 / 1110 1.6 / 1717 5.2 / 2339 1.6
5 SU	0424 4.9 / 1043 2.2 / 1647 4.7 / ◖ 2310 2.1	**20** M	0555 5.4 / 1218 1.7 / 1825 5.1
6 M	0539 5.0 / 1153 2.1 / 1806 4.8	**21** TU	0044 1.6 / 0700 5.4 / 1321 1.7 / 1932 5.1
7 TU	0019 2.0 / 0644 5.1 / 1300 1.9 / 1910 5.0	**22** W	0145 1.6 / 0801 5.4 / 1418 1.6 / 2032 5.2
8 W	0124 1.8 / 0742 5.4 / 1358 1.6 / 2006 5.4	**23** TH	0240 1.6 / 0855 5.5 / 1508 1.4 / 2123 5.4
9 TH	0220 1.5 / 0833 5.8 / 1449 1.3 / 2057 5.7	**24** F	0329 1.5 / 0941 5.6 / 1553 1.3 / 2209 5.6
10 F	0310 1.2 / 0921 6.1 / 1537 1.0 / 2146 6.0	**25** SA	0413 1.4 / 1022 5.8 / 1635 1.2 / 2248 5.7
11 SA	0358 1.0 / 1007 6.3 / 1625 0.8 / 2235 6.2	**26** SU	0453 1.3 / 1058 5.8 / 1714 1.1 / ○ 2325 5.8
12 SU	0446 0.9 / 1054 6.4 / 1713 0.7 / ● 2324 6.3	**27** M	0531 1.2 / 1133 5.8 / 1750 1.1
13 M	0535 0.8 / 1142 6.4 / 1802 0.6	**28** TU	0000 5.8 / 0606 1.2 / 1206 5.8 / 1825 1.1
14 TU	0014 6.4 / 0624 0.8 / 1232 6.4 / 1852 0.7	**29** W	0034 5.8 / 0640 1.3 / 1238 5.8 / 1859 1.2
15 W	0106 6.3 / 0715 0.9 / 1322 6.2 / 1943 0.8	**30** TH	0107 5.7 / 0714 1.4 / 1310 5.7 / 1933 1.2
		31 F	0138 5.7 / 0748 1.4 / 1343 5.6 / 2007 1.3

Chart Datum: 3·27 metres below Ordnance Datum (Newlyn)

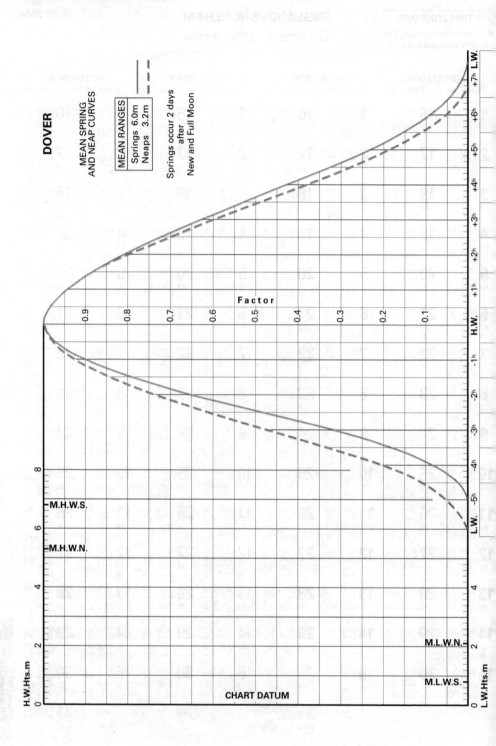

DOVER

MEAN SPRING
AND NEAP CURVES

MEAN RANGES
Springs 6.0m
Neaps 3.2m

Springs occur 2 days
after
New and Full Moon

TIME ZONE (UT)
For Summer Time add ONE hour in **non-shaded areas**

ENGLAND – DOVER

LAT 51°07'N   LONG 1°19'E

TIMES AND HEIGHTS OF HIGH AND LOW WATERS

YEAR 2004

JANUARY

Day	Time m	Time m	Time m	Time m
1 TH	0032 2.2	0552 5.6	1309 2.0	1842 5.3
16 F	0452 5.9	1209 1.7	1731 5.6	
2 F	0133 2.3	0700 5.5	1407 2.0	1944 5.4
17 SA	0035 2.0	0606 5.8	1320 1.8	1854 5.6
3 SA	0235 2.2	0802 5.6	1506 1.9	2039 5.5
18 SU	0152 2.0	0723 5.8	1432 1.7	2007 5.7
4 SU	0334 2.0	0856 5.6	1559 1.8	2126 5.7
19 M	0307 1.8	0833 6.0	1545 1.5	2110 6.0
5 M	0425 1.8	0941 5.9	1646 1.6	2208 6.0
20 TU	0419 1.5	0937 6.2	1657 1.3	2208 6.2
6 TU	0509 1.6	1021 6.0	1726 1.5	2245 6.1
21 W	0526 1.2	1034 6.4	1801 1.1	● 2259 6.5
7 W	0547 1.4	1057 6.1	1805 1.4	○ 2320 6.2
22 TH	0625 1.0	1126 6.6	1856 1.0	2345 6.7
8 TH	0625 1.3	1132 6.2	1842 1.4	2353 6.3
23 F	0719 0.8	1212 6.6	1945 0.9	
9 F	0703 1.3	1206 6.2	1920 1.4	
24 SA	0028 6.8	0807 0.8	1255 6.5	2028 0.9
10 SA	0025 6.4	0741 1.2	1239 6.2	1957 1.4
25 SU	0110 6.8	0851 0.8	1336 6.4	2106 1.0
11 SU	0058 6.4	0820 1.3	1312 6.2	2033 1.4
26 M	0151 6.7	0930 0.9	1416 6.2	2140 1.2
12 M	0133 6.4	0859 1.3	1348 6.2	2110 1.5
27 TU	0232 6.5	1005 1.1	1458 6.0	2211 1.5
13 TU	0212 6.4	0938 1.4	1430 6.1	2149 1.5
28 W	0314 6.2	1038 1.4	1542 5.7	2241 1.7
14 W	0257 6.3	1020 1.4	1518 6.0	2233 1.7
29 TH	0358 5.9	1113 1.7	1634 5.4	◑ 2318 2.0
15 TH	0349 6.1	1109 1.6	1617 5.8	◑ 2327 1.9
30 F	0450 5.6	1158 2.0	1736 5.2	
31 SA	0012 2.3	0556 5.3	1300 2.3	1846 5.1

FEBRUARY

Day	Time m	Time m	Time m	Time m
1 SU	0131 2.4	0709 5.2	1411 2.3	1956 5.2
16 M	0125 2.2	0710 5.5	1412 2.0	1958 5.4
2 M	0246 2.3	0818 5.3	1517 2.1	2056 5.4
17 TU	0251 2.0	0836 5.7	1537 1.8	2111 5.7
3 TU	0350 2.0	0915 5.6	1614 1.8	2145 5.7
18 W	0415 1.6	0946 6.0	1659 1.5	2209 6.1
4 W	0442 1.7	1000 5.8	1703 1.6	2225 6.0
19 TH	0527 1.2	1042 6.3	1801 1.1	2256 6.4
5 TH	0527 1.4	1038 6.0	1747 1.4	2300 6.2
20 F	0625 0.9	1126 6.5	1851 0.9	● 2337 6.7
6 F	0609 1.2	1114 6.2	1829 1.3	○ 2334 6.4
21 SA	0713 0.7	1205 6.6	1934 0.8	
7 SA	0650 1.1	1149 6.3	1909 1.2	
22 SU	0014 6.8	0755 0.6	1240 6.6	2009 0.8
8 SU	0007 6.5	0731 1.0	1223 6.4	1947 1.1
23 M	0052 6.8	0831 0.6	1313 6.5	2040 0.9
9 M	0041 6.6	0810 0.9	1255 6.5	2022 1.1
24 TU	0127 6.7	0901 0.8	1347 6.4	2106 1.1
10 TU	0115 6.7	0846 0.9	1330 6.5	2056 1.1
25 W	0201 6.6	0927 1.0	1420 6.2	2128 1.3
11 W	0152 6.7	0921 1.0	1407 6.4	2131 1.2
26 TH	0233 6.3	0950 1.3	1454 5.9	2151 1.5
12 TH	0232 6.6	0958 1.1	1451 6.3	2210 1.4
27 F	0305 6.0	1015 1.6	1532 5.6	2222 1.9
13 F	0319 6.3	1040 1.4	1542 5.9	◑ 2257 1.7
28 SA	0345 5.6	1050 2.0	1628 5.2	◑ 2306 2.2
14 SA	0416 6.0	1134 1.7	1650 5.5	
29 SU	0452 5.2	1144 2.4	1753 4.9	
15 SU	0000 2.0	0533 5.6	1248 2.0	1828 5.3

MARCH

Day	Time m	Time m	Time m	Time m
1 M	0018 2.5	0622 5.0	1321 2.5	1914 5.0
16 TU	0113 2.3	0710 5.3	1405 2.2	1953 5.3
2 TU	0204 2.5	0742 5.1	1444 2.3	2024 5.2
17 W	0249 2.0	0843 5.5	1541 1.9	2107 5.7
3 W	0317 2.2	0848 5.4	1547 2.0	2118 5.6
18 TH	0420 1.6	0948 5.9	1657 1.4	2200 6.1
4 TH	0414 1.7	0936 5.7	1640 1.6	2158 6.0
19 F	0523 1.1	1035 6.3	1750 1.1	2242 6.5
5 F	0503 1.4	1015 6.0	1727 1.4	2234 6.3
20 SA	0613 0.8	1113 6.5	1834 0.9	● 2319 6.7
6 SA	0548 1.1	1051 6.3	1811 1.2	○ 2308 6.5
21 SU	0656 0.6	1145 6.6	1911 0.9	2354 6.8
7 SU	0632 0.9	1126 6.5	1851 1.0	2342 6.7
22 M	0732 0.6	1216 6.6	1942 0.8	
8 M	0713 0.8	1159 6.6	1929 0.9	
23 TU	0028 6.8	0801 0.7	1247 6.5	2007 0.9
9 TU	0017 6.8	0751 0.7	1233 6.7	2003 0.8
24 W	0101 6.7	0826 0.9	1318 6.4	2029 1.0
10 W	0052 6.9	0826 0.7	1307 6.7	2037 0.8
25 TH	0130 6.5	0846 1.1	1346 6.3	2048 1.2
11 TH	0129 6.9	0900 0.8	1346 6.6	2111 1.0
26 F	0154 6.3	0905 1.3	1411 6.0	2113 1.4
12 F	0209 6.7	0936 1.0	1429 6.4	2150 1.2
27 SA	0218 6.0	0932 1.6	1437 5.7	2145 1.8
13 SA	0256 6.4	1018 1.4	1521 5.9	◑ 2237 1.6
28 SU	0251 5.7	1007 1.9	1516 5.4	◑ 2226 2.1
14 SU	0355 5.9	1111 1.9	1634 5.4	2342 2.1
29 M	0345 5.2	1054 2.3	1700 5.0	2326 2.5
15 M	0523 5.4	1230 2.2	1817 5.2	
30 TU	0544 4.9	1221 2.6	1832 4.9	
31 W	0121 2.6	0706 5.0	1409 2.5	1944 5.2

APRIL

Day	Time m	Time m	Time m	Time m
1 TH	0242 2.2	0813 5.3	1515 2.1	2040 5.6
16 F	0405 1.4	0931 5.9	1633 1.4	2137 6.2
2 F	0341 1.7	0903 5.7	1609 1.7	2123 6.0
17 SA	0502 1.0	1013 6.2	1722 1.1	2217 6.4
3 SA	0431 1.3	0944 6.1	1658 1.3	2201 6.3
18 SU	0549 0.8	1047 6.4	1804 1.0	2254 6.6
4 SU	0519 1.0	1021 6.4	1742 1.1	2237 6.6
19 M	0628 0.8	1118 6.5	1838 0.9	● 2329 6.7
5 M	0605 0.8	1057 6.6	1824 0.9	○ 2314 6.8
20 TU	0700 0.8	1149 6.5	1908 1.0	
6 TU	0648 0.6	1132 6.7	1904 0.8	2350 7.0
21 W	0002 6.6	0726 0.9	1220 6.5	1932 1.0
7 W	0728 0.6	1208 6.8	1941 0.7	
22 TH	0034 6.5	0748 1.1	1251 6.4	1953 1.1
8 TH	0028 7.0	0804 0.6	1246 6.8	2017 0.8
23 F	0101 6.4	0808 1.2	1318 6.3	2017 1.3
9 F	0108 6.9	0841 0.7	1328 6.7	2055 0.9
24 SA	0122 6.2	0832 1.4	1340 6.1	2045 1.4
10 SA	0152 6.7	0919 1.0	1415 6.3	2137 1.2
25 SU	0146 6.0	0902 1.6	1406 5.8	2119 1.7
11 SU	0244 6.2	1004 1.5	1514 5.9	2228 1.7
26 M	0220 5.7	0939 1.9	1446 5.5	2201 2.0
12 M	0353 5.7	1102 1.9	1632 5.5	◑ 2339 2.1
27 TU	0312 5.3	1025 2.2	1603 5.2	◑ 2258 2.3
13 TU	0523 5.3	1228 2.3	1803 5.2	
28 W	0507 5.0	1133 2.5	1744 5.1	
14 W	0113 2.2	0709 5.3	1402 2.2	1938 5.4
29 TH	0034 2.4	0627 5.1	1325 2.4	1857 5.2
15 TH	0247 1.9	0835 5.6	1528 1.8	2048 5.8
30 F	0200 2.1	0732 5.4	1435 2.1	1955 5.6

Chapter 5

TIDES

TIME ZONE (UT)
For Summer Time add ONE hour in **non-shaded areas**

ENGLAND – DOVER

LAT 51°07′N   LONG 1°19′E

TIMES AND HEIGHTS OF HIGH AND LOW WATERS

YEAR 2004

MAY

Time	m	Time	m
1 0300	1.7	**16** 0426	1.2
0824	5.7	0939	6.0
SA 1530	1.7	SU 1642	1.3
2042	6.0	2146	6.2
2 0353	1.3	**17** 0513	1.1
0908	6.1	1014	6.2
SU 1620	1.4	M 1725	1.2
2124	6.4	2225	6.4
3 0443	1.0	**18** 0552	1.1
0947	6.4	1048	6.3
M 1708	1.1	TU 1802	1.2
2204	6.7	2302	6.4
4 0533	0.8	**19** 0623	1.1
1026	6.6	1121	6.3
TU 1754	0.9	W 1833	1.2
○ 2244	6.9	● 2336	6.4
5 0620	0.7	**20** 0650	1.2
1105	6.8	1155	6.3
W 1838	0.8	TH 1900	1.2
2324	7.0		
6 0704	0.6	**21** 0009	6.3
1146	6.8	0714	1.3
TH 1920	0.7	F 1228	6.3
		1926	1.2
7 0007	7.0	**22** 0038	6.2
0746	0.7	0740	1.3
F 1230	6.8	SA 1258	6.2
2001	0.8	1955	1.3
8 0053	6.8	**23** 0104	6.0
0827	0.8	0810	1.5
SA 1318	6.6	SU 1325	6.1
2045	1.0	2028	1.5
9 0143	6.5	**24** 0131	5.9
0911	1.1	0843	1.6
SU 1412	6.3	M 1354	5.9
2134	1.3	2104	1.7
10 0243	6.1	**25** 0207	5.7
1002	1.5	0922	1.8
M 1513	6.0	TU 1436	5.7
2231	1.6	2147	1.9
11 0353	5.7	**26** 0258	5.5
1105	1.9	1007	2.0
TU 1622	5.7	W 1533	5.5
◑ 2343	1.8	2239	2.0
12 0514	5.4	**27** 0416	5.3
1223	2.1	1104	2.2
W 1738	5.5	TH 1647	5.4
		◐ 2350	2.1
13 0103	1.9	**28** 0538	5.3
0648	5.4	1225	2.2
TH 1340	2.0	F 1800	5.4
1904	5.5		
14 0220	1.7	**29** 0109	1.9
0804	5.6	0644	5.4
F 1450	1.8	SA 1342	2.1
2013	5.8	1903	5.7
15 0328	1.4	**30** 0214	1.7
0857	5.8	0740	5.7
SA 1551	1.5	SU 1443	1.8
2104	6.0	1957	6.0
		31 0310	1.4
		0828	6.0
		M 1539	1.5
		2045	6.3

JUNE

Time	m	Time	m
1 0406	1.1	**16** 0509	1.4
0914	6.3	1019	6.0
TU 1633	1.2	W 1726	1.4
2132	6.6	2236	6.1
2 0501	0.9	**17** 0546	1.4
0958	6.5	1057	6.1
W 1726	1.0	TH 1802	1.4
2218	6.7	● 2314	6.1
3 0555	0.8	**18** 0618	1.4
1045	6.6	1134	6.2
TH 1817	0.9	F 1835	1.3
○ 2306	6.8	2348	6.1
4 0646	0.8	**19** 0650	1.4
1132	6.7	1209	6.2
F 1906	0.9	SA 1908	1.3
2355	6.8		
5 0736	0.8	**20** 0021	6.1
1222	6.7	0722	1.4
SA 1956	0.8	SU 1242	6.2
		1942	1.4
6 0046	6.6	**21** 0053	6.0
0824	0.9	0757	1.5
SU 1314	6.6	M 1313	6.1
2046	0.9	2018	1.4
7 0142	6.4	**22** 0124	5.9
0914	1.1	0833	1.6
M 1407	6.4	TU 1344	6.1
2139	1.1	2057	1.5
8 0241	6.2	**23** 0158	5.9
1006	1.4	0912	1.6
TU 1503	6.2	W 1421	6.0
2234	1.3	2137	1.6
9 0343	5.9	**24** 0238	5.7
1101	1.6	0952	1.8
W 1601	6.0	TH 1505	5.9
2333	1.5	2222	1.7
10 0449	5.6	**25** 0328	5.7
1159	1.8	1208	1.9
TH 1703	5.8	F 1558	5.8
		◑ 2314	1.7
11 0034	1.6	**26** 0429	5.6
0602	5.5	1133	2.0
F 1300	1.9	SA 1700	5.7
1812	5.7		
12 0135	1.6	**27** 0016	1.8
0712	5.5	0541	5.6
SA 1400	1.9	SU 1242	2.0
1922	5.7	1807	5.8
13 0235	1.6	**28** 0124	1.7
0810	5.6	0651	5.7
SU 1459	1.8	M 1353	1.9
2021	5.8	1913	5.9
14 0334	1.6	**29** 0229	1.5
0857	5.7	0752	5.8
M 1555	1.7	TU 1500	1.7
2111	5.9	2013	6.1
15 0426	1.5	**30** 0333	1.4
0940	5.9	0849	6.1
TU 1644	1.5	W 1604	1.5
2156	6.0	2110	6.3

JULY

Time	m	Time	m
1 0437	1.2	**16** 0514	1.6
0943	6.3	1037	6.0
TH 1706	1.2	F 1737	1.5
2206	6.5	2255	6.0
2 0539	1.0	**17** 0554	1.5
1037	6.5	1115	6.2
F 1805	1.0	SA 1815	1.4
○ 2301	6.6	● 2330	6.1
3 0638	0.9	**18** 0632	1.4
1129	6.6	1149	6.3
SA 1901	0.9	SU 1853	1.3
2355	6.6		
4 0734	0.9	**19** 0003	6.1
1219	6.7	0709	1.4
SU 1956	0.8	M 1222	6.3
		1930	1.3
5 0046	6.6	**20** 0036	6.1
0825	0.9	0747	1.4
M 1307	6.7	TU 1254	6.3
2047	0.8	2009	1.2
6 0138	6.4	**21** 0107	6.1
0912	1.0	0823	1.4
TU 1355	6.6	W 1325	6.3
2135	0.8	2046	1.3
7 0228	6.3	**22** 0137	6.1
0956	1.1	0859	1.4
W 1443	6.5	TH 1358	6.3
2221	1.0	2123	1.3
8 0318	6.0	**23** 0212	6.1
1038	1.3	0934	1.5
TH 1532	6.3	F 1437	6.3
2305	1.2	2159	1.4
9 0410	5.8	**24** 0253	6.0
1121	1.6	1011	1.6
F 1623	6.0	SA 1521	6.2
◑ 2351	1.5	2241	1.5
10 0505	5.6	**25** 0342	5.9
1208	1.9	1056	1.7
SA 1720	5.7	SU 1615	6.0
		◑ 2331	1.7
11 0042	1.7	**26** 0444	5.7
0607	5.4	1153	1.9
SU 1303	2.0	M 1722	5.8
1823	5.6		
12 0138	1.9	**27** 0037	1.8
0713	5.3	0606	5.5
M 1404	2.1	TU 1310	2.1
1932	5.5	1840	5.7
13 0238	2.0	**28** 0155	1.8
0814	5.4	0730	5.6
TU 1507	2.0	W 1431	2.0
2035	5.6	1958	5.8
14 0337	1.9	**29** 0311	1.7
0908	5.6	0841	5.8
W 1606	1.9	TH 1547	1.7
2130	5.7	2109	6.0
15 0430	1.7	**30** 0425	1.5
0956	5.8	0943	6.1
TH 1655	1.6	F 1657	1.4
2216	5.9	2212	6.3
		31 0534	1.2
		1038	6.4
		SA 1801	1.1
		○ 2308	6.5

AUGUST

Time	m	Time	m
1 0635	1.0	**16** 0615	1.4
1126	6.6	1125	6.4
SU 1859	0.8	M 1836	1.2
2357	6.6	● 2340	6.2
2 0729	0.9	**17** 0654	1.3
1211	6.8	1156	6.5
M 1951	0.6	TU 1915	1.1
3 0041	6.6	**18** 0011	6.3
0815	0.8	0730	1.2
TU 1254	6.8	W 1228	6.5
2037	0.6	1952	1.1
4 0123	6.5	**19** 0041	6.4
0855	0.8	0805	1.2
W 1335	6.8	TH 1259	6.6
2117	0.7	2027	1.0
5 0203	6.4	**20** 0111	6.4
0930	1.0	0838	1.2
TH 1417	6.7	F 1332	6.6
2153	0.9	2100	1.1
6 0243	6.2	**21** 0144	6.4
1002	1.2	0910	1.3
F 1458	6.4	SA 1408	6.6
2226	1.2	2133	1.2
7 0326	5.9	**22** 0223	6.3
1033	1.5	0944	1.4
SA 1542	6.1	SU 1450	6.4
◑ 2300	1.5	2210	1.4
8 0414	5.6	**23** 0309	6.0
1107	1.9	1026	1.7
SU 1631	5.8	M 1541	6.1
2341	1.9	◑ 2257	1.8
9 0512	5.3	**24** 0409	5.7
1154	2.2	1121	2.0
M 1731	5.4	TU 1651	5.7
10 0037	2.2	**25** 0003	2.1
0620	5.2	0543	5.3
TU 1307	2.4	W 1242	2.3
1843	5.2	1830	5.4
11 0150	2.4	**26** 0136	2.2
0734	5.2	0725	5.4
W 1426	2.4	TH 1418	2.1
2001	5.3	2002	5.6
12 0300	2.2	**27** 0305	2.0
0842	5.4	0841	5.7
TH 1534	2.1	F 1543	1.8
2110	5.5	2118	5.9
13 0400	2.0	**28** 0426	1.6
0936	5.7	0943	6.1
F 1629	1.8	SA 1657	1.4
2159	5.8	2218	6.3
14 0451	1.7	**29** 0532	1.2
1018	6.0	1032	6.5
SA 1715	1.5	SU 1758	1.0
2236	6.0	2306	6.6
15 0535	1.5	**30** 0627	1.0
1052	6.2	1115	6.8
SU 1756	1.3	M 1850	0.7
2308	6.2	○ 2346	6.7
		31 0713	0.8
		1155	6.9
		TU 1935	0.5

Chart Datum: 3·67 metres below Ordnance Datum (Newlyn)
Register for your **FREE** weekly weather email service from Reeds Almanacs
at www.nauticaldata.com – **NOW!**
weekend weather reports sent to your email address, every Thursday

TIME ZONE (UT)
For Summer Time add ONE hour in **non-shaded areas**

ENGLAND – DOVER

LAT 51°07′N   LONG 1°19′E

TIMES AND HEIGHTS OF HIGH AND LOW WATERS

YEAR 2004

SEPTEMBER

Day	Time m	Time m	Time m	Time m
1 W	0023 6.7	0752 0.8	1233 7.0	2014 0.6
2 TH	0057 6.6	0826 0.8	1310 6.9	2047 0.7
3 F	0131 6.5	0855 1.0	1346 6.7	2115 0.9
4 SA	0206 6.3	0920 1.2	1422 6.5	2140 1.3
5 SU	0243 6.0	0942 1.5	1458 6.1	2203 1.6
6 M	0325 5.7	1009 1.9	1542 5.7	◑ 2233 2.1
7 TU	0422 5.3	1048 2.3	1645 5.3	2321 2.5
8 W	0536 5.1	1154 2.6	1804 5.0	
9 TH	0101 2.7	0656 5.0	1349 2.6	1927 5.1
10 F	0230 2.5	0813 5.2	1506 2.3	2045 5.4
11 SA	0335 2.1	0910 5.7	1603 1.9	2133 5.7
12 SU	0427 1.8	0949 6.0	1649 1.5	2207 6.1
13 M	0512 1.5	1022 6.3	1732 1.3	2238 6.3
14 TU	0552 1.2	1054 6.5	1812 1.1	2310 6.4
15 W	0630 1.2	1126 6.7	1851 1.0	2341 6.5
16 TH	0706 1.1	1157 6.8	1928 0.9	
17 F	0012 6.6	0740 1.1	1230 6.8	2002 0.9
18 SA	0043 6.7	0812 1.1	1304 6.8	2034 1.0
19 SU	0118 6.6	0845 1.2	1341 6.7	2107 1.2
20 M	0158 6.4	0922 1.4	1424 6.4	2146 1.5
21 TU	0246 6.1	1005 1.7	1519 5.9	◐ 2234 1.9
22 W	0352 5.6	1103 2.2	1645 5.5	2345 2.4
23 TH	0542 5.2	1233 2.4	1835 5.3	
24 F	0132 2.4	0719 5.3	1418 2.2	2008 5.6
25 SA	0309 2.1	0836 5.8	1546 1.7	2118 6.0
26 SU	0424 1.6	0932 6.2	1652 1.2	2209 6.4
27 M	0520 1.2	1018 6.6	1745 0.9	2250 6.6
28 TU	0606 1.0	1055 6.8	1830 0.7	○ 2324 6.7
29 W	0647 0.9	1132 7.0	1910 0.6	2356 6.7
30 TH	0721 0.9	1207 7.0	1943 0.7	

OCTOBER

Day	Time m	Time m	Time m	Time m
1 F	0028 6.7	0750 1.0	1242 6.9	2010 0.9
2 SA	0100 6.6	0815 1.1	1315 6.7	2032 1.2
3 SU	0132 6.4	0836 1.3	1345 6.4	2052 1.4
4 M	0203 6.1	0858 1.6	1415 6.1	2115 1.7
5 TU	0235 5.8	0928 1.9	1450 5.7	2148 2.1
6 W	0305 5.4	1008 2.3	1602 5.2	◑ 2232 2.5
7 TH	0455 5.1	1104 2.6	1731 5.0	2348 2.8
8 F	0616 5.0	1302 2.8	1851 5.0	
9 SA	0154 2.7	0731 5.2	1429 2.4	2002 5.3
10 SU	0303 2.3	0828 5.6	1527 1.9	2051 5.7
11 M	0355 1.9	0909 6.0	1614 1.5	2129 6.1
12 TU	0439 1.6	0944 6.3	1658 1.2	2203 6.4
13 W	0520 1.3	1018 6.6	1741 1.0	2236 6.6
14 TH	0600 1.2	1051 6.8	● 2309 6.7	
15 F	0637 1.1	1126 6.9	1859 0.9	2342 6.8
16 SA	0713 1.0	1201 7.0	1936 0.9	
17 SU	0018 6.8	0749 1.0	1239 6.9	2011 1.0
18 M	0057 6.7	0826 1.2	1321 6.7	2048 1.3
19 TU	0142 6.4	0907 1.4	1410 6.3	2130 1.4
20 W	0238 6.0	0955 1.8	1517 5.8	◐ 2224 2.1
21 TH	0357 5.6	1100 2.2	1652 5.4	2344 2.4
22 F	0531 5.4	1236 2.3	1831 5.4	
23 SA	0129 2.4	0703 5.5	1414 2.0	1959 6.0
24 SU	0256 2.0	0816 5.9	1531 1.6	2101 6.0
25 M	0401 1.6	0909 6.3	1631 1.2	2146 6.3
26 TU	0453 1.3	0951 6.6	1720 0.9	2224 6.5
27 W	0536 1.1	1029 6.7	1802 0.8	2256 6.6
28 TH	0614 1.0	1106 6.8	1837 0.9	2327 6.6
29 F	0646 1.0	1141 6.8	1907 1.0	
30 SA	0000 6.6	0714 1.1	1215 6.7	1931 1.2
31 SU	0033 6.5	0738 1.3	1246 6.5	1952 1.3

NOVEMBER

Day	Time m	Time m	Time m	Time m
1 M	0104 6.4	0801 1.4	1314 6.3	2014 1.5
2 TU	0133 6.2	0828 1.6	1341 6.0	2043 1.8
3 W	0201 5.9	0902 1.9	1414 5.7	2119 2.1
4 TH	0239 5.6	0943 2.2	1515 5.3	2204 2.4
5 F	0403 5.3	1036 2.5	1653 5.0	◑ 2304 2.7
6 SA	0527 5.1	1202 2.6	1808 5.1	
7 SU	0055 2.7	0638 5.3	1337 2.4	1913 5.3
8 M	0214 2.4	0736 5.6	1439 2.0	2005 5.7
9 TU	0310 2.0	0822 5.9	1531 1.6	2048 6.0
10 W	0359 1.7	0902 6.3	1620 1.3	2125 6.3
11 TH	0444 1.4	0940 6.6	1706 1.1	2202 6.6
12 F	0528 1.2	1018 6.8	1751 0.9	● 2239 6.7
13 SA	0610 1.1	1057 6.9	1834 0.9	2318 6.8
14 SU	0651 1.0	1138 7.0	1915 0.9	
15 M	0000 6.8	0732 1.0	1223 6.8	1955 1.1
16 TU	0046 6.7	0816 1.1	1311 6.6	2039 1.3
17 W	0138 6.5	0903 1.4	1409 6.2	2128 1.6
18 TH	0240 6.1	0959 1.7	1521 5.9	2227 2.0
19 F	0350 5.9	1108 1.9	1643 5.6	◐ 2343 2.2
20 SA	0506 5.7	1227 2.0	1810 5.5	
21 SU	0103 2.2	0627 5.7	1345 1.8	1927 5.6
22 M	0216 2.0	0739 5.9	1455 1.6	2027 5.9
23 TU	0320 1.7	0834 6.1	1555 1.3	2113 6.1
24 W	0414 1.5	0920 6.3	1646 1.2	2152 6.2
25 TH	0500 1.4	1001 6.5	1728 1.2	2227 6.3
26 F	0540 1.3	1040 6.5	1803 1.2	○ 2301 6.3
27 SA	0614 1.3	1116 6.5	1832 1.3	2336 6.5
28 SU	0645 1.3	1151 6.4	1859 1.4	
29 M	0011 6.4	0712 1.4	1225 6.3	1924 1.5
30 TU	0045 6.3	0740 1.5	1256 6.1	1952 1.6

DECEMBER

Day	Time m	Time m	Time m	Time m
1 W	0116 6.2	0811 1.6	1325 5.9	2025 1.7
2 TH	0145 6.0	0847 1.8	1358 5.7	2102 1.9
3 F	0220 5.8	0928 1.9	1442 5.5	2145 2.1
4 SA	0308 5.6	1016 2.1	1547 5.3	2235 2.3
5 SU	0415 5.4	1117 2.2	1708 5.2	◑ 2341 2.4
6 M	0529 5.4	1233 2.2	1817 5.3	
7 TU	0105 2.4	0635 5.6	1343 2.0	1915 5.6
8 W	0214 2.1	0731 5.8	1443 1.7	2004 5.8
9 TH	0313 1.8	0819 6.2	1539 1.4	2049 6.1
10 F	0407 1.6	0905 6.5	1633 1.2	2133 6.4
11 SA	0459 1.3	0951 6.7	1726 1.0	2218 6.6
12 SU	0549 1.1	1038 6.8	1815 0.9	● 2305 6.7
13 M	0638 1.0	1126 6.8	1904 1.0	2353 6.8
14 TU	0727 1.0	1217 6.7	1953 1.0	
15 W	0043 6.7	0818 1.0	1310 6.5	2043 1.2
16 TH	0137 6.6	0911 1.1	1408 6.3	2134 1.4
17 F	0232 6.4	1005 1.3	1510 6.1	2227 1.6
18 SA	0330 6.2	1101 1.4	1615 5.8	◐ 2322 1.8
19 SU	0431 6.0	1159 1.6	1724 5.6	
20 M	0021 1.9	0537 5.8	1259 1.7	1834 5.5
21 TU	0122 2.0	0647 5.8	1400 1.7	1937 5.6
22 W	0225 2.0	0751 5.8	1502 1.7	2032 5.7
23 TH	0326 1.9	0846 5.9	1601 1.6	2119 5.8
24 F	0422 1.7	0935 6.0	1651 1.6	2202 6.0
25 SA	0508 1.6	1019 6.1	1730 1.5	2241 6.2
26 SU	0548 1.5	1058 6.2	1805 1.5	○ 2319 6.3
27 M	0622 1.4	1135 6.2	1836 1.5	2355 6.3
28 TU	0655 1.4	1209 6.2	1908 1.5	
29 W	0029 6.3	0727 1.4	1242 6.1	1940 1.5
30 TH	0100 6.3	0802 1.5	1312 6.0	2015 1.6
31 F	0129 6.2	0839 1.5	1342 5.9	2051 1.7

Chart Datum: 3·67 metres below Ordnance Datum (Newlyn)

Chapter 5

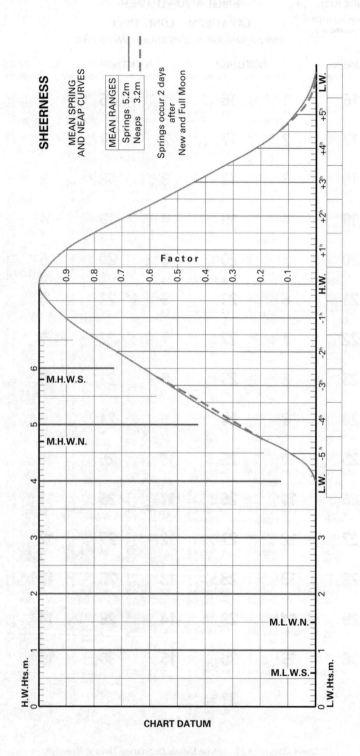

SHEERNESS

MEAN SPRING
AND NEAP CURVES

MEAN RANGES
Springs 5.2m
Neaps 3.2m

Springs occur 2 days
after
New and Full Moon

Factor

0.9 0.8 0.7 0.6 0.5 0.4 0.3 0.2 0.1

M.H.W.S.

M.H.W.N.

M.L.W.N.

M.L.W.S.

H.W.Hts.m.

L.W.Hts.m.

CHART DATUM

ENGLAND – SHEERNESS

LAT 51°27′N   LONG 0°45′E

TIMES AND HEIGHTS OF HIGH AND LOW WATERS

YEAR **2004**

JANUARY

Day	Time m	Day	Time m
1 TH	0040 1.7 / 0709 4.8 / 1339 1.3 / 1958 4.7	16 F	0607 5.1 / 1222 1.0 / 1901 5.0
2 F	0148 1.7 / 0814 4.7 / 1440 1.3 / 2101 4.8	17 SA	0041 1.4 / 0716 5.0 / 1335 1.1 / 2011 4.9
3 SA	0255 1.6 / 0919 4.8 / 1536 1.3 / 2158 4.9	18 SU	0201 1.4 / 0834 5.0 / 1458 1.1 / 2123 5.0
4 SU	0355 1.4 / 1016 4.9 / 1626 1.2 / 2247 5.0	19 M	0324 1.3 / 0948 5.2 / 1614 1.0 / 2229 5.2
5 M	0447 1.3 / 1106 5.1 / 1711 1.2 / 2330 5.2	20 TU	0441 1.1 / 1056 5.4 / 1720 0.9 / 2329 5.3
6 TU	0533 1.1 / 1150 5.2 / 1750 1.1	21 W	0551 0.8 / 1157 5.6 / 1817 0.8 ●
7 W	0009 5.3 / 0614 1.0 / 1229 5.3 / 1826 1.1	22 TH	0022 5.5 / 0651 0.6 / 1251 5.8 / 1906 0.8
8 TH	0046 5.4 / 0653 0.9 / 1307 5.4 / 1901 1.0	23 F	0112 5.6 / 0744 0.4 / 1341 5.8 / 1952 0.8
9 F	0121 5.4 / 0732 0.8 / 1343 5.4 / 1937 1.0	24 SA	0157 5.6 / 0832 0.4 / 1428 5.8 / 2033 0.8
10 SA	0156 5.4 / 0811 0.7 / 1420 5.5 / 2014 0.9	25 SU	0239 5.6 / 0915 0.4 / 1511 5.7 / 2110 0.9
11 SU	0231 5.4 / 0852 0.7 / 1458 5.5 / 2052 1.0	26 M	0320 5.5 / 0953 0.5 / 1553 5.5 / 2143 1.1
12 M	0307 5.4 / 0931 0.7 / 1538 5.4 / 2129 1.1	27 TU	0358 5.4 / 1026 0.7 / 1634 5.3 / 2215 1.2
13 TU	0345 5.3 / 1009 0.8 / 1620 5.3 / 2206 1.1	28 W	0437 5.3 / 1055 0.9 / 1714 5.1 / 2250 1.3
14 W	0425 5.2 / 1046 0.9 / 1706 5.2 / 2247 1.2	29 TH	0518 5.0 / 1127 1.1 / 1758 4.8 / 2333 1.5 ◐
15 TH	0512 5.2 / 1128 0.9 / 1758 5.1 / 2337 1.3 ◑	30 F	0606 4.8 / 1213 1.3 / 1850 4.6
		31 SA	0031 1.7 / 0707 4.6 / 1321 1.5 / 1953 4.5

FEBRUARY

Day	Time m	Day	Time m
1 SU	0152 1.7 / 0821 4.4 / 1442 1.6 / 2104 4.5	16 M	0132 1.5 / 0813 4.8 / 1438 1.4 / 2101 4.7
2 M	0314 1.6 / 0938 4.6 / 1550 1.5 / 2210 4.7	17 TU	0315 1.3 / 0940 4.9 / 1604 1.3 / 2218 4.9
3 TU	0419 1.4 / 1041 4.8 / 1645 1.3 / 2305 4.9	18 W	0443 1.1 / 1055 5.2 / 1715 1.1 / 2323 5.2
4 W	0514 1.2 / 1131 5.0 / 1731 1.2 / 2350 5.2	19 TH	0554 0.7 / 1156 5.5 / 1811 0.9
5 TH	0600 1.0 / 1213 5.3 / 1811 1.1	20 F	0015 5.4 / 0649 0.5 / 1246 5.7 / 1856 0.8 ●
6 F	0030 5.3 / 0641 0.8 / 1252 5.4 / 1847 1.0	21 SA	0101 5.6 / 0735 0.3 / 1330 5.8 / 1937 0.7 ○
7 SA	0107 5.4 / 0721 0.7 / 1329 5.5 / 1925 0.8	22 SU	0141 5.7 / 0816 0.3 / 1411 5.8 / 2013 0.7
8 SU	0143 5.6 / 0802 0.5 / 1406 5.6 / 2003 0.8	23 M	0219 5.7 / 0852 0.3 / 1448 5.7 / 2046 0.8
9 M	0217 5.6 / 0842 0.4 / 1443 5.7 / 2040 0.6	24 TU	0254 5.7 / 0923 0.4 / 1523 5.6 / 2116 0.9
10 TU	0251 5.6 / 0919 0.5 / 1520 5.6 / 2114 0.8	25 W	0326 5.6 / 0948 0.6 / 1556 5.4 / 2142 1.0
11 W	0326 5.6 / 0953 0.5 / 1558 5.5 / 2145 0.9	26 TH	0359 5.4 / 1010 0.8 / 1628 5.1 / 2209 1.1
12 TH	0403 5.5 / 1022 0.7 / 1639 5.3 / 2219 1.0	27 F	0433 5.2 / 1035 1.0 / 1703 4.9 / 2243 1.3
13 F	0445 5.4 / 1055 0.8 / 1726 5.1 / 2303 1.1 ◐	28 SA	0513 4.9 / 1112 1.3 / 1745 4.6 / 2330 1.5
14 SA	0537 5.2 / 1142 1.0 / 1825 4.9	29 SU	0606 4.5 / 1207 1.6 / 1844 4.3
15 SU	0004 1.3 / 0645 4.9 / 1256 1.3 / 1939 4.7		

MARCH

Day	Time m	Day	Time m
1 M	0040 1.7 / 0721 4.3 / 1339 1.8 / 2005 4.2	16 TU	0130 1.4 / 0808 4.7 / 1432 1.6 / 2050 4.6
2 TU	0229 1.7 / 0855 4.3 / 1515 1.7 / 2131 4.4	17 W	0321 1.2 / 0941 5.0 / 1559 1.4 / 2211 4.9
3 W	0351 1.5 / 1012 4.6 / 1620 1.5 / 2236 4.8	18 TH	0446 0.9 / 1052 5.3 / 1707 1.1 / 2312 5.2
4 TH	0451 1.2 / 1107 5.0 / 1710 1.2 / 2325 5.1	19 F	0548 0.6 / 1147 5.6 / 1757 0.9
5 F	0540 0.9 / 1151 5.3 / 1752 1.0	20 SA	0001 5.4 / 0635 0.4 / 1232 5.8 / 1837 0.8 ●
6 SA	0007 5.3 / 0622 0.7 / 1230 5.5 / 1830 0.9	21 SU	0042 5.6 / 0714 0.3 / 1311 5.8 / 1913 0.7 ○
7 SU	0045 5.6 / 0703 0.5 / 1308 5.7 / 1908 0.7	22 M	0118 5.7 / 0749 0.3 / 1346 5.8 / 1947 0.6
8 M	0120 5.6 / 0743 0.4 / 1344 5.8 / 1946 0.6	23 TU	0152 5.7 / 0820 0.4 / 1419 5.7 / 2019 0.7
9 TU	0155 5.7 / 0822 0.3 / 1421 5.8 / 2022 0.6	24 W	0224 5.7 / 0847 0.5 / 1449 5.6 / 2048 0.7
10 W	0229 5.8 / 0859 0.3 / 1457 5.7 / 2056 0.7	25 TH	0255 5.6 / 0911 0.7 / 1517 5.4 / 2114 0.9
11 TH	0305 5.8 / 0930 0.4 / 1534 5.6 / 2126 0.7	26 F	0325 5.4 / 0932 0.8 / 1546 5.2 / 2138 1.0
12 F	0343 5.7 / 0958 0.6 / 1614 5.4 / 2200 0.9	27 SA	0358 5.2 / 0956 1.1 / 1618 5.0 / 2207 1.2
13 SA	0426 5.5 / 1032 0.9 / 1700 5.1 / 2245 1.0 ◑	28 SU	0436 4.9 / 1029 1.3 / 1656 4.7 / 2248 1.4 ◐
14 SU	0520 5.2 / 1122 1.2 / 1758 4.8 / 2348 1.3	29 M	0523 4.6 / 1118 1.7 / 1744 4.4 / 2350 1.6
15 M	0634 4.8 / 1243 1.5 / 1918 4.5	30 TU	0631 4.3 / 1237 1.9 / 1907 4.2
		31 W	0133 1.7 / 0805 4.3 / 1430 1.9 / 2044 4.3

APRIL

Day	Time m	Day	Time m
1 TH	0313 1.5 / 0931 4.6 / 1543 1.6 / 2157 4.7	16 F	0432 0.7 / 1035 5.4 / 1645 1.1 / 2251 5.2
2 F	0416 1.1 / 1031 5.0 / 1637 1.3 / 2250 5.1	17 SA	0527 0.5 / 1126 5.6 / 1732 1.0 / 2337 5.4
3 SA	0508 0.8 / 1118 5.4 / 1722 1.0 / 2334 5.4	18 SU	0609 0.5 / 1208 5.7 / 1810 0.8
4 SU	0554 0.6 / 1200 5.6 / 1803 0.9	19 M	0016 5.5 / 0643 0.5 / 1244 5.7 / 1843 0.7 ●
5 M	0013 5.6 / 0637 0.5 / 1240 5.8 / 1843 0.7 ○	20 TU	0051 5.6 / 0714 0.5 / 1317 5.7 / 1917 0.7
6 TU	0051 5.7 / 0718 0.3 / 1318 5.9 / 1923 0.6	21 W	0123 5.7 / 0743 0.5 / 1347 5.6 / 1950 0.6
7 W	0128 5.9 / 0757 0.3 / 1355 5.9 / 2002 0.6	22 TH	0155 5.6 / 0811 0.6 / 1416 5.6 / 2021 0.7
8 TH	0206 5.9 / 0834 0.3 / 1433 5.8 / 2038 0.6	23 F	0226 5.6 / 0837 0.8 / 1444 5.5 / 2049 0.8
9 F	0245 5.9 / 0908 0.5 / 1512 5.7 / 2114 0.7	24 SA	0258 5.4 / 0901 1.0 / 1512 5.3 / 2115 1.0
10 SA	0327 5.7 / 0941 0.7 / 1554 5.4 / 2153 0.8	25 SU	0332 5.2 / 0927 1.2 / 1544 5.1 / 2144 1.1
11 SU	0416 5.5 / 1021 1.0 / 1642 5.1 / 2243 1.0	26 M	0410 5.0 / 1000 1.4 / 1622 4.8 / 2224 1.3
12 M	0516 5.1 / 1117 1.4 / 1745 4.7 / 2355 1.2 ◐	27 TU	0456 4.7 / 1046 1.6 / 1711 4.6 / 2321 1.5 ◐
13 TU	0634 4.9 / 1242 1.6 / 1908 4.6	28 W	0557 4.5 / 1155 1.8 / 1821 4.4
14 W	0142 1.2 / 0805 4.8 / 1421 1.6 / 2037 4.6	29 TH	0046 1.5 / 0717 4.5 / 1331 1.8 / 1951 4.4
15 TH	0318 1.0 / 0930 5.1 / 1542 1.4 / 2153 4.9	30 F	0222 1.4 / 0840 4.7 / 1451 1.6 / 2107 4.7

Chapter 5

Chart Datum: 2·90 metres below Ordnance Datum (Newlyn)

TIME ZONE (UT)
For Summer Time add ONE hour in **non-shaded areas**

ENGLAND – SHEERNESS
LAT 51°27'N LONG 0°45'E
TIMES AND HEIGHTS OF HIGH AND LOW WATERS

YEAR 2004

MAY

Day	Time	m	Day	Time	m
1 SA	0330 / 0945 / 1550 / 2205	1.1 / 5.1 / 1.3 / 5.1	**16** SU	0452 / 1055 / 1655 / 2305	0.7 / 5.5 / 1.1 / 5.3
2 SU	0426 / 1038 / 1641 / 2254	0.8 / 5.4 / 1.1 / 5.4	**17** M	0533 / 1138 / 1735 / 2346	0.7 / 5.5 / 1.0 / 5.4
3 M	0517 / 1125 / 1728 / 2338	0.6 / 5.6 / 0.9 / 5.6	**18** TU	0606 / 1214 / 1813	0.7 / 5.5 / 0.8
4 TU	0605 / 1208 / 1814 ○	0.5 / 5.8 / 0.8	**19** W	0022 / 0637 / 1247 / 1849 ●	5.5 / 0.7 / 5.5 / 0.8
5 W	0020 / 0650 / 1250 / 1859	5.8 / 0.4 / 5.9 / 0.6	**20** TH	0057 / 0707 / 1318 / 1924	5.5 / 0.8 / 5.5 / 0.7
6 TH	0103 / 0732 / 1331 / 1944	5.9 / 0.4 / 5.9 / 0.6	**21** F	0131 / 0738 / 1347 / 1958	5.5 / 0.8 / 5.5 / 0.8
7 F	0146 / 0812 / 1412 / 2027	6.0 / 0.5 / 5.8 / 0.5	**22** SA	0204 / 0808 / 1417 / 2029	5.4 / 0.9 / 5.4 / 0.8
8 SA	0231 / 0852 / 1455 / 2111	5.9 / 0.6 / 5.6 / 0.6	**23** SU	0238 / 0837 / 1448 / 2100	5.3 / 1.0 / 5.3 / 0.9
9 SU	0319 / 0932 / 1541 / 2158	5.8 / 0.9 / 5.4 / 0.7	**24** M	0314 / 0908 / 1522 / 2134	5.2 / 1.2 / 5.1 / 1.0
10 M	0414 / 1018 / 1634 / 2254	5.5 / 1.1 / 5.1 / 0.9	**25** TU	0353 / 0943 / 1601 / 2215	5.0 / 1.3 / 5.0 / 1.2
11 TU	0517 / 1116 / 1738 ◐	5.2 / 1.4 / 4.9	**26** W	0439 / 1028 / 1648 / 2307	4.9 / 1.5 / 4.8 / 1.2
12 W	0009 / 0629 / 1232 / 1853	1.0 / 5.1 / 1.6 / 4.8	**27** TH	0533 / 1126 / 1748 ◐	4.8 / 1.6 / 4.7
13 TH	0136 / 0748 / 1354 / 2011	1.0 / 5.0 / 1.6 / 4.8	**28** F	0012 / 0638 / 1237 / 1859	1.3 / 4.7 / 1.7 / 4.7
14 F	0254 / 0902 / 1506 / 2121	0.9 / 5.2 / 1.4 / 5.0	**29** SA	0128 / 0749 / 1352 / 2012	1.2 / 4.9 / 1.6 / 4.8
15 SA	0400 / 1004 / 1606 / 2218	0.7 / 5.4 / 1.2 / 5.2	**30** SU	0237 / 0857 / 1458 / 2117	1.0 / 5.1 / 1.4 / 5.1
			31 M	0339 / 0957 / 1557 / 2214	0.8 / 5.3 / 1.2 / 5.3

JUNE

Day	Time	m	Day	Time	m
1 TU	0437 / 1050 / 1653 / 2305	0.7 / 5.6 / 1.0 / 5.6	**16** W	0528 / 1145 / 1745 / 2359	1.0 / 5.3 / 1.0 / 5.3
2 W	0532 / 1139 / 1748 / 2355	0.6 / 5.7 / 0.8 / 5.8	**17** TH	0604 / 1221 / 1826 ●	1.0 / 5.4 / 0.9
3 TH	0623 / 1226 / 1841 ○	0.5 / 5.8 / 0.7	**18** F	0037 / 0638 / 1255 / 1904	5.3 / 1.0 / 5.4 / 0.8
4 F	0044 / 0710 / 1312 / 1933	5.9 / 0.5 / 5.8 / 0.6	**19** SA	0114 / 0712 / 1328 / 1940	5.4 / 1.0 / 5.4 / 0.8
5 SA	0134 / 0757 / 1358 / 2023	5.9 / 0.6 / 5.7 / 0.5	**20** SU	0150 / 0745 / 1401 / 2016	5.4 / 1.0 / 5.4 / 0.8
6 SU	0224 / 0841 / 1445 / 2114	5.9 / 0.7 / 5.6 / 0.5	**21** M	0225 / 0820 / 1434 / 2053	5.3 / 1.0 / 5.3 / 0.8
7 M	0316 / 0926 / 1534 / 2205	5.8 / 0.9 / 5.4 / 0.6	**22** TU	0302 / 0855 / 1510 / 2131	5.3 / 1.1 / 5.2 / 0.9
8 TU	0411 / 1013 / 1627 / 2300	5.6 / 1.1 / 5.3 / 0.7	**23** W	0341 / 0933 / 1548 / 2211	5.2 / 1.2 / 5.1 / 0.9
9 W	0509 / 1105 / 1724 ◐	5.4 / 1.3 / 5.1	**24** TH	0423 / 1013 / 1630 / 2253	5.1 / 1.3 / 5.0 / 1.0
10 TH	0001 / 0610 / 1206 / 1826	0.8 / 5.2 / 1.5 / 5.0	**25** F	0510 / 1058 / 1718 / 2341 ◐	5.1 / 1.4 / 5.0 / 1.0
11 F	0107 / 0715 / 1312 / 1932	0.8 / 5.1 / 1.5 / 5.0	**26** SA	0603 / 1151 / 1814	5.0 / 1.5 / 4.9
12 SA	0211 / 0821 / 1417 / 2038	0.9 / 5.1 / 1.5 / 5.0	**27** SU	0037 / 0705 / 1255 / 1920	1.1 / 5.0 / 1.5 / 4.9
13 SU	0311 / 0923 / 1518 / 2138	0.9 / 5.1 / 1.4 / 5.1	**28** M	0144 / 0812 / 1406 / 2031	1.0 / 5.0 / 1.4 / 5.1
14 M	0404 / 1018 / 1612 / 2231	0.9 / 5.2 / 1.4 / 5.1	**29** TU	0255 / 0918 / 1517 / 2138	1.0 / 5.2 / 1.3 / 5.2
15 TU	0449 / 1104 / 1701 / 2318	1.0 / 5.3 / 1.1 / 5.2	**30** W	0403 / 1020 / 1625 / 2240	0.9 / 5.3 / 1.1 / 5.4

JULY

Day	Time	m	Day	Time	m
1 TH	0506 / 1117 / 1731 / 2339	0.8 / 5.5 / 0.9 / 5.6	**16** F	0540 / 1201 / 1809	1.2 / 5.2 / 1.0
2 F	0604 / 1210 / 1832 ○	0.7 / 5.6 / 0.7	**17** SA	0023 / 0618 / 1239 / 1849 ●	5.3 / 1.1 / 5.3 / 0.9
3 SA	0034 / 0657 / 1301 / 1929	5.8 / 0.7 / 5.7 / 0.5	**18** SU	0102 / 0654 / 1315 / 1927	5.3 / 1.1 / 5.4 / 0.8
4 SU	0128 / 0747 / 1349 / 2023	5.9 / 0.7 / 5.7 / 0.4	**19** M	0137 / 0729 / 1349 / 2005	5.4 / 1.0 / 5.4 / 0.7
5 M	0220 / 0833 / 1437 / 2114	5.9 / 0.8 / 5.6 / 0.3	**20** TU	0213 / 0806 / 1423 / 2044	5.5 / 1.0 / 5.4 / 0.7
6 TU	0310 / 0918 / 1524 / 2202	5.9 / 0.9 / 5.6 / 0.4	**21** W	0249 / 0843 / 1457 / 2122	5.5 / 1.0 / 5.4 / 0.7
7 W	0359 / 1000 / 1611 / 2247	5.7 / 1.0 / 5.5 / 0.5	**22** TH	0325 / 0920 / 1532 / 2159	5.4 / 1.0 / 5.4 / 0.7
8 TH	0449 / 1042 / 1658 / 2332	5.5 / 1.2 / 5.3 / 0.7	**23** F	0403 / 0954 / 1608 / 2233	5.4 / 1.1 / 5.3 / 0.8
9 F	0539 / 1127 / 1749 ◐	5.3 / 1.3 / 5.2	**24** SA	0444 / 1029 / 1648 / 2307	5.3 / 1.2 / 5.2 / 0.9
10 SA	0019 / 0632 / 1219 / 1844	0.9 / 5.1 / 1.5 / 5.0	**25** SU	0530 / 1110 / 1736 / 2350 ◐	5.1 / 1.3 / 5.1 / 1.0
11 SU	0112 / 0730 / 1305 / 1946	1.1 / 4.9 / 1.6 / 4.9	**26** M	0625 / 1205 / 1837	5.0 / 1.4 / 5.0
12 M	0211 / 0832 / 1427 / 2052	1.2 / 4.8 / 1.5 / 4.9	**27** TU	0051 / 0731 / 1319 / 1953	1.1 / 4.9 / 1.5 / 5.0
13 TU	0311 / 0934 / 1532 / 2157	1.3 / 4.9 / 1.4 / 4.9	**28** W	0218 / 0846 / 1449 / 2113	1.2 / 4.9 / 1.4 / 5.1
14 W	0407 / 1030 / 1631 / 2253	1.3 / 5.0 / 1.3 / 5.0	**29** TH	0341 / 0957 / 1612 / 2227	1.2 / 5.1 / 1.2 / 5.3
15 TH	0456 / 1119 / 1723 / 2342	1.2 / 5.1 / 1.1 / 5.1	**30** F	0452 / 1103 / 1726 / 2333	1.1 / 5.3 / 0.9 / 5.5
			31 SA	0555 / 1200 / 1831 ○	0.9 / 5.5 / 0.6

AUGUST

Day	Time	m	Day	Time	m
1 SU	0031 / 0649 / 1252 / 1927	5.8 / 0.8 / 5.6 / 0.4	**16** M	0044 / 0638 / 1257 / 1911 ●	5.4 / 1.1 / 5.5 / 0.7
2 M	0123 / 0737 / 1339 / 2016	5.9 / 0.8 / 5.7 / 0.3	**17** TU	0119 / 0713 / 1331 / 1949	5.5 / 1.0 / 5.6 / 0.6
3 TU	0210 / 0821 / 1423 / 2101	6.0 / 0.8 / 5.8 / 0.2	**18** W	0153 / 0749 / 1404 / 2027	5.6 / 0.9 / 5.6 / 0.5
4 W	0255 / 0900 / 1504 / 2142	5.9 / 0.8 / 5.7 / 0.3	**19** TH	0228 / 0826 / 1436 / 2104	5.7 / 0.9 / 5.6 / 0.5
5 TH	0338 / 0937 / 1544 / 2218	5.8 / 0.9 / 5.6 / 0.5	**20** F	0303 / 0900 / 1509 / 2137	5.6 / 0.9 / 5.6 / 0.6
6 F	0419 / 1010 / 1623 / 2250	5.6 / 1.1 / 5.5 / 0.7	**21** SA	0338 / 0931 / 1543 / 2205	5.5 / 0.9 / 5.5 / 0.6
7 SA	0459 / 1044 / 1704 / 2320 ◑	5.3 / 1.2 / 5.3 / 1.0	**22** SU	0415 / 1000 / 1621 / 2233	5.4 / 1.0 / 5.4 / 0.9
8 SU	0542 / 1122 / 1750 / 2359	5.0 / 1.4 / 5.0 / 1.2	**23** M	0458 / 1037 / 1707 / 2311 ◑	5.2 / 1.2 / 5.2 / 1.1
9 M	0630 / 1214 / 1847	4.8 / 1.6 / 4.7	**24** TU	0549 / 1130 / 1808	5.0 / 1.4 / 5.0
10 TU	0058 / 0730 / 1330 / 2000	1.5 / 4.6 / 1.7 / 4.5	**25** W	0015 / 0658 / 1251 / 1931	1.4 / 4.7 / 1.6 / 4.8
11 W	0218 / 0843 / 1455 / 2122	1.6 / 4.5 / 1.7 / 4.6	**26** TH	0159 / 0822 / 1441 / 2104	1.5 / 4.7 / 1.5 / 4.9
12 TH	0332 / 0956 / 1607 / 2231	1.6 / 4.7 / 1.4 / 4.8	**27** F	0332 / 0945 / 1613 / 2226	1.4 / 4.9 / 1.2 / 5.2
13 F	0432 / 1054 / 1706 / 2324	1.5 / 5.0 / 1.2 / 5.1	**28** SA	0447 / 1055 / 1728 / 2331	1.2 / 5.2 / 0.8 / 5.5
14 SA	0521 / 1140 / 1753	1.3 / 5.2 / 1.0	**29** SU	0548 / 1151 / 1827	1.0 / 5.5 / 0.5
15 SU	0006 / 0602 / 1221 / 1834	5.3 / 1.2 / 5.4 / 0.9	**30** M	0024 / 0637 / 1239 / 1915 ○	5.8 / 0.9 / 5.7 / 0.3
			31 TU	0110 / 0720 / 1321 / 1958	6.0 / 0.8 / 5.8 / 0.2

Chart Datum: 2·90 metres below Ordnance Datum (Newlyn)

ENGLAND – SHEERNESS

YEAR **2004**

LAT 51°27'N LONG 0°45'E

TIMES AND HEIGHTS OF HIGH AND LOW WATERS

SEPTEMBER

Time	m	Time	m
1 0152	6.0	**16** 0127	5.8
0758	0.7	0726	0.8
W 1400	5.9	TH 1336	5.8
2037	0.3	2001	0.5
2 0231	5.9	**17** 0201	5.8
0834	0.8	0802	0.8
TH 1437	5.8	F 1409	5.8
2111	0.4	2037	0.5
3 0307	5.8	**18** 0236	5.8
0907	0.9	0836	0.9
F 1512	5.7	SA 1443	5.8
2139	0.6	2109	0.6
4 0342	5.5	**19** 0311	5.7
0936	1.0	0906	1.0
SA 1546	5.6	SU 1519	5.7
2203	0.8	2137	0.8
5 0415	5.3	**20** 0348	5.5
1003	1.2	0937	1.1
SU 1621	5.3	M 1600	5.5
2227	1.1	2206	1.0
6 0449	5.0	**21** 0430	5.2
1034	1.4	1017	1.2
M 1701	5.0	TU 1649	5.3
◑ 2259	1.4	◑ 2250	1.3
7 0530	4.7	**22** 0524	4.9
1117	1.6	1115	1.4
TU 1752	4.6	W 1756	4.9
2350	1.7		
8 0625	4.5	**23** 0002	1.6
1224	1.8	0637	4.6
W 1906	4.4	TH 1251	1.6
		1927	4.8
9 0117	2.0	**24** 0154	1.7
0746	4.3	0810	4.6
TH 1417	1.8	F 1447	1.4
2042	4.4	2104	4.9
10 0259	1.9	**25** 0326	1.5
0916	4.5	0937	4.9
F 1541	1.5	SA 1615	1.0
2202	4.7	2222	5.4
11 0406	1.6	**26** 0437	1.3
1023	4.8	1043	5.3
SA 1641	1.2	SU 1721	0.7
2257	5.1	2320	5.7
12 0457	1.4	**27** 0532	1.0
1112	5.2	1135	5.5
SU 1729	1.0	M 1812	0.5
2339	5.4		
13 0539	1.2	**28** 0008	5.9
1152	5.4	0616	0.9
M 1809	0.8	TU 1218	5.7
		○ 1853	0.4
14 0016	5.6	**29** 0049	5.9
0614	1.0	0654	0.9
TU 1229	5.6	W 1256	5.8
● 1847	0.7	1930	0.4
15 0052	5.7	**30** 0126	5.9
0650	0.9	0729	0.8
W 1303	5.7	TH 1332	5.9
1924	0.6	2003	0.4

OCTOBER

Time	m	Time	m
1 0201	5.8	**16** 0132	5.9
0803	0.8	0737	0.8
F 1406	5.8	SA 1343	5.9
2032	0.6	2008	0.6
2 0233	5.7	**17** 0209	5.8
0835	0.8	0814	0.8
SA 1439	5.7	SU 1421	5.9
2058	0.8	2042	0.7
3 0303	5.5	**18** 0246	5.7
0903	1.0	0849	0.9
SU 1511	5.6	M 1502	5.8
2120	1.0	2115	0.9
4 0332	5.3	**19** 0327	5.5
0928	1.1	0927	1.0
M 1545	5.3	TU 1548	5.5
2143	1.2	2152	1.2
5 0403	5.1	**20** 0412	5.2
0955	1.3	1015	1.1
TU 1623	5.0	W 1644	5.2
2213	1.5	◑ 2245	1.5
6 0440	4.8	**21** 0510	4.9
1033	1.5	1122	1.3
W 1710	4.7	TH 1757	5.0
◑ 2300	1.8		
7 0529	4.5	**22** 0002	1.7
1133	1.8	0628	4.6
TH 1816	4.4	F 1305	1.4
		1926	4.9
8 0014	2.1	**23** 0143	1.8
0646	4.3	0758	4.7
F 1319	1.9	SA 1443	1.2
1949	4.3	2053	5.1
9 0210	2.1	**24** 0306	1.6
0825	4.4	0917	5.0
SA 1502	1.6	SU 1600	0.9
2116	4.6	2203	5.4
10 0327	1.8	**25** 0413	1.3
0939	4.7	1020	5.3
SU 1603	1.2	M 1659	0.6
2215	5.0	2258	5.7
11 0420	1.5	**26** 0504	1.1
1032	5.1	1109	5.5
M 1652	1.0	TU 1745	0.6
2301	5.4	2343	5.8
12 0503	1.2	**27** 0546	1.0
1115	5.4	1151	5.7
TU 1735	0.8	W 1823	0.6
2341	5.6		
13 0542	1.0	**28** 0022	5.8
1154	5.6	0622	0.9
W 1815	0.6	TH 1228	5.7
		○ 1854	0.6
14 0019	5.8	**29** 0057	5.8
0620	0.8	0657	0.8
TH 1230	5.8	F 1303	5.8
● 1853	0.6	1924	0.7
15 0056	5.9	**30** 0129	5.7
0658	0.9	0732	0.8
F 1306	5.9	SA 1337	5.7
1932	0.5	1953	0.8
		31 0159	5.6
		0805	0.8
		SU 1410	5.7
		2019	0.9

NOVEMBER

Time	m	Time	m
1 0228	5.5	**16** 0229	5.7
0834	1.0	0844	0.8
M 1444	5.5	TU 1453	5.8
2044	1.1	2104	1.0
2 0257	5.3	**17** 0314	5.5
0900	1.1	0931	0.8
TU 1518	5.3	W 1545	5.6
2109	1.3	2149	1.2
3 0328	5.1	**18** 0404	5.2
0928	1.3	1026	1.0
W 1556	5.0	TH 1645	5.3
2141	1.5	2243	1.5
4 0404	4.9	**19** 0504	5.0
1006	1.4	1135	1.1
TH 1641	4.7	F 1754	5.1
2225	1.7	◑ 2353	1.6
5 0450	4.6	**20** 0616	4.9
1100	1.6	1259	1.1
F 1739	4.5	SA 1910	5.1
◑ 2328	2.0		
6 0556	4.4	**21** 0114	1.7
1219	1.7	0732	4.9
SA 1855	4.4	SU 1418	1.0
		2025	5.2
7 0057	2.0	**22** 0228	1.6
0723	4.4	0844	5.0
SU 1358	1.6	M 1526	0.9
2015	4.6	2131	5.3
8 0224	1.7	**23** 0332	1.4
0841	4.7	0946	5.2
M 1509	1.3	TU 1624	0.8
2121	5.0	2227	5.5
9 0326	1.6	**24** 0426	1.2
0941	5.0	1038	5.4
TU 1603	1.0	W 1709	0.8
2215	5.3	2313	5.5
10 0417	1.3	**25** 0511	1.1
1031	5.3	1122	5.5
W 1652	0.8	TH 1745	0.8
2302	5.6	2353	5.5
11 0503	1.1	**26** 0551	1.0
1115	5.6	1202	5.5
TH 1737	0.7	F 1817	0.9
2345	5.7	○	
12 0547	1.0	**27** 0028	5.6
1157	5.7	0628	0.9
F 1821	0.6	SA 1239	5.6
●		1847	0.9
13 0026	5.8	**28** 0101	5.6
0631	0.9	0706	0.8
SA 1239	5.9	SU 1315	5.6
1902	0.6	1918	0.9
14 0107	5.8	**29** 0132	5.5
0715	0.8	0741	0.9
SU 1322	5.9	M 1350	5.5
1943	0.7	1948	1.0
15 0147	5.8	**30** 0202	5.4
0759	0.7	0813	0.9
M 1406	5.9	TU 1425	5.4
2023	0.8	2017	1.1

DECEMBER

Time	m	Time	m
1 0233	5.3	**16** 0307	5.5
0843	1.0	0939	0.6
W 1500	5.2	TH 1543	5.7
2047	1.3	2145	1.1
2 0305	5.2	**17** 0358	5.4
0915	1.1	1032	0.7
TH 1538	5.1	F 1639	5.5
2121	1.4	2234	1.3
3 0342	5.0	**18** 0452	5.2
0954	1.2	1128	0.8
F 1621	4.9	SA 1737	5.3
2203	1.5	◑ 2329	1.4
4 0426	4.8	**19** 0551	5.1
1041	1.3	1229	0.9
SA 1710	4.8	SU 1840	5.2
2254	1.7		
5 0519	4.7	**20** 0031	1.5
1139	1.4	0654	5.0
SU 1809	4.7	M 1333	1.0
◑ 2357	1.8	1944	5.1
6 0624	4.6	**21** 0137	1.6
1248	1.4	0800	5.0
M 1916	4.7	TU 1436	1.0
		2049	5.0
7 0110	1.8	**22** 0242	1.5
0736	4.7	0905	5.0
TU 1401	1.3	W 1534	1.1
2024	4.9	2148	5.1
8 0222	1.6	**23** 0343	1.4
0844	4.9	1004	5.1
W 1507	1.1	TH 1625	1.1
2127	5.1	2241	5.2
9 0325	1.4	**24** 0437	1.2
0945	5.2	1056	5.2
TH 1606	0.9	F 1708	1.1
2222	5.4	2326	5.3
10 0423	1.2	**25** 0525	1.1
1039	5.4	1142	5.3
F 1701	0.8	SA 1746	1.1
2313	5.6		
11 0518	1.0	**26** 0006	5.3
1130	5.6	0608	1.0
SA 1752	0.8	SU 1224	5.3
		○ 1821	1.1
12 0001	5.7	**27** 0042	5.3
0611	0.9	0648	0.9
SU 1220	5.8	M 1302	5.4
● 1840	0.7	1854	1.1
13 0047	5.7	**28** 0115	5.4
0703	0.7	0725	0.9
M 1309	5.9	TU 1338	5.4
1927	0.7	1927	1.1
14 0133	5.7	**29** 0147	5.3
0755	0.6	0800	0.9
TU 1359	5.9	W 1413	5.3
2013	0.8	1959	1.1
15 0219	5.6	**30** 0219	5.3
0847	0.6	0834	0.9
W 1450	5.8	TH 1448	5.3
2059	0.9	2033	1.1
		31 0253	5.3
		0909	0.9
		F 1524	5.2
		2109	1.2

Chapter 5

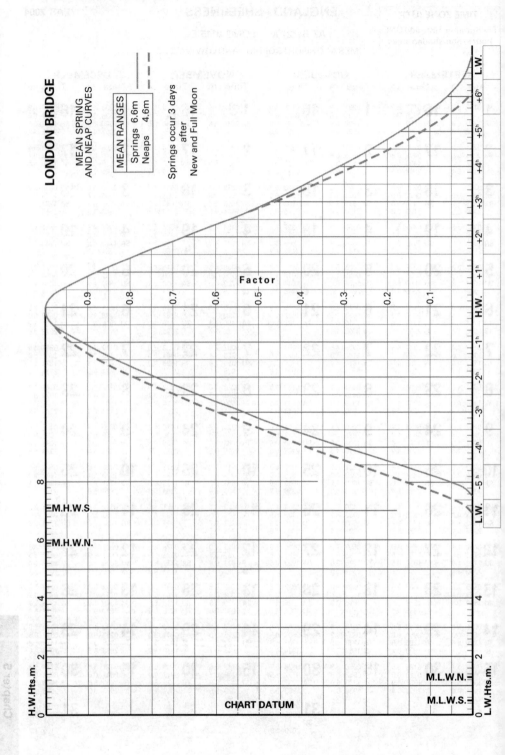

LONDON BRIDGE

MEAN SPRING
AND NEAP CURVES

MEAN RANGES	
Springs	6.6m
Neaps	4.6m

Springs occur 3 days
after
New and Full Moon

Factor

0.9 0.8 0.7 0.6 0.5 0.4 0.3 0.2 0.1

L.W.

+6ʰ +5ʰ +4ʰ +3ʰ +2ʰ +1ʰ H.W. -1ʰ -2ʰ -3ʰ -4ʰ -5ʰ L.W.

M.H.W.S.

M.H.W.N.

H.W.Hts.m.

M.L.W.N.

M.L.W.S.

L.W.Hts.m.

CHART DATUM

Register for your **FREE** weekly weather email service from Reeds Almanacs
at www.nauticaldata.com – **NOW!**
weekend weather reports sent to your email address, every Thursday

258

ENGLAND – LONDON BRIDGE

LAT 51°30′N   LONG 0°05′W

TIMES AND HEIGHTS OF HIGH AND LOW WATERS

YEAR 2004

JANUARY

Day					Day				
1 TH	0159 1.7	0827 5.8	1447 1.4	2116 5.9	**16** F	0110 1.3	0726 6.2	1357 1.2	2020 6.1
2 F	0259 1.8	0934 5.8	1545 1.4	2214 5.9	**17** SA	0211 1.5	0832 6.0	1512 1.4	2130 5.9
3 SA	0402 1.7	1035 5.9	1645 1.4	2308 6.0	**18** SU	0333 1.7	0951 6.0	1639 1.4	2243 6.0
4 SU	0504 1.5	1130 6.1	1742 1.3	2356 6.2	**19** M	0504 1.6	1107 6.2	1754 1.2	2348 6.2
5 M	0604 1.3	1219 6.3	1833 1.2		**20** TU	0627 1.3	1213 6.5	1859 1.0	
6 TU	0041 6.3	0657 1.1	1305 6.4	1920 1.1	**21** W ●	0046 6.5	0736 0.9	1313 6.8	1957 0.8
7 W ○	0122 6.4	0748 1.0	1347 6.5	2003 1.1	**22** TH	0139 6.7	0836 0.6	1408 7.0	2049 0.7
8 TH	0201 6.5	0833 0.9	1427 6.5	2042 1.1	**23** F	0229 6.9	0927 0.3	1512 7.2	2135 0.7
9 F	0238 6.4	0915 0.9	1505 6.5	2116 1.1	**24** SA	0315 6.9	1013 0.2	1546 7.2	2217 0.7
10 SA	0314 6.4	0952 0.9	1543 6.6	2149 1.1	**25** SU	0357 6.9	1054 0.3	1630 7.1	2254 0.8
11 SU	0349 6.5	1027 0.8	1622 6.6	2223 1.1	**26** M	0436 6.8	1130 0.5	1711 6.9	2327 1.0
12 M	0425 6.5	1101 0.9	1702 6.7	2259 1.0	**27** TU	0512 6.7	1200 0.7	1750 6.6	2356 1.1
13 TU	0503 6.5	1136 0.8	1744 6.6	2338 1.0	**28** W	0549 6.5	1228 0.9	1828 6.3	
14 W	0545 6.5	1215 0.9	1830 6.5		**29** TH ◐	0026 1.3	0629 6.3	1300 1.1	1908 6.0
15 TH ◐	0021 1.1	0631 6.4	1921 6.3		**30** F	0103 1.4	0716 6.0	1341 1.3	1955 5.8
					31 SA	0153 1.6	0816 5.7	1436 1.5	2056 5.6

FEBRUARY

Day					Day				
1 SU	0256 1.7	0932 5.5	1539 1.7	2208 5.6	**16** M	0250 1.8	0926 5.7	1605 1.8	2221 5.6
2 M	0403 1.7	1047 5.6	1644 1.6	2313 5.7	**17** TU	0445 1.8	1057 5.8	1742 1.6	2334 5.9
3 TU	0508 1.5	1148 5.9	1747 1.5		**18** W	0629 1.3	1209 6.2	1850 1.2	
4 W	0009 6.0	0613 1.2	1241 6.2	1845 1.3	**19** TH	0035 6.3	0733 0.8	1309 6.7	1946 0.9
5 TH	0059 6.2	0721 1.0	1329 6.4	1941 1.2	**20** F ●	0129 6.6	0827 0.4	1401 7.1	2035 0.6
6 F	0145 6.4	0820 0.8	1412 6.6	2030 1.1	**21** SA ○	0217 6.9	0915 0.1	1448 7.2	2120 0.5
7 SA	0226 6.5	0908 0.7	1452 6.7	2111 1.1	**22** SU	0259 7.0	0957 0.1	1530 7.2	2201 0.6
8 SU	0304 6.6	0949 0.6	1530 6.8	2147 1.0	**23** M	0337 7.0	1034 0.2	1607 7.1	2236 0.7
9 M	0338 6.6	1025 0.6	1606 6.9	2220 1.0	**24** TU	0411 6.9	1105 0.4	1640 6.9	2305 0.9
10 TU	0411 6.7	1056 0.6	1643 6.9	2251 0.9	**25** W	0442 6.8	1128 0.7	1710 6.7	2326 1.0
11 W	0446 6.8	1123 0.7	1722 6.8	2323 0.9	**26** TH	0514 6.7	1146 0.8	1742 6.5	2345 1.0
12 TH	0524 6.8	1152 0.7	1804 6.6	2358 0.9	**27** F	0550 6.5	1206 1.0	1817 6.2	
13 F ◐	0607 6.6	1227 0.9	1850 6.3		**28** SA ◐	0014 1.1	0632 6.1	1238 1.2	1859 5.9
14 SA	0039 1.1	0657 6.3	1314 1.2	1944 5.9	**29** SU	0055 1.3	0723 5.8	1326 1.5	1950 5.6
15 SU	0132 1.5	0800 5.9	1420 1.6	2055 5.6					

MARCH

Day					Day				
1 M	0158 1.6	0826 5.4	1441 1.8	2056 5.4	**16** TU	0231 1.8	0921 5.5	1546 2.0	2207 5.4
2 TU	0320 1.7	0952 5.4	1601 1.8	2226 5.4	**17** W	0504 1.7	1055 5.8	1732 1.7	2322 5.8
3 W	0433 1.6	1116 5.6	1713 1.6	2339 5.8	**18** TH	0622 1.1	1202 6.3	1834 1.2	
4 TH	0544 1.3	1216 6.1	1820 1.4		**19** F	0021 6.3	0717 0.5	1258 6.8	1926 0.8
5 F	0035 6.1	0701 1.0	1306 6.4	1921 1.2	**20** SA ●	0113 6.7	0806 0.2	1346 7.2	2013 0.5
6 SA	0123 6.4	0802 0.7	1350 6.7	2013 1.0	**21** SU	0158 7.0	0851 0.0	1429 7.3	2057 0.4
7 SU	0205 6.6	0851 0.5	1431 6.9	2058 0.9	**22** M	0237 7.0	0931 0.0	1507 7.2	2137 0.4
8 M	0243 6.7	0933 0.4	1509 7.0	2136 0.9	**23** TU	0312 7.0	1005 0.2	1539 7.0	2212 0.6
9 TU	0317 6.8	1010 0.4	1545 7.1	2210 0.8	**24** W	0343 6.9	1034 0.5	1606 6.8	2239 0.7
10 W	0351 7.0	1040 0.5	1621 7.0	2239 0.8	**25** TH	0413 6.8	1054 0.7	1633 6.7	2256 0.9
11 TH	0427 7.0	1105 0.6	1659 6.9	2307 0.7	**26** F	0444 6.7	1105 0.8	1702 6.6	2310 0.9
12 F	0505 7.0	1130 0.7	1738 6.6	2339 0.8	**27** SA	0519 6.5	1123 0.9	1737 6.4	2337 0.9
13 SA ◐	0548 6.7	1202 0.9	1822 6.2		**28** SU ◐	0600 6.2	1153 1.1	1819 6.0	
14 SU	0017 1.1	0639 6.3	1247 1.3	1914 5.7	**29** M	0014 1.1	0648 5.8	1235 1.4	1908 5.7
15 M	0110 1.5	0745 5.8	1353 1.8	2029 5.3	**30** TU	0109 1.5	0747 5.5	1341 1.8	2009 5.4
					31 W	0243 1.7	0900 5.4	1520 2.0	2132 5.4

APRIL

Day					Day				
1 TH	0404 1.5	1036 5.6	1641 1.6	2302 5.6	**16** F	0556 0.8	1142 6.5	1806 1.1	2358 6.4
2 F	0518 1.2	1143 6.0	1750 1.4		**17** SA	0648 0.4	1235 6.9	1858 0.7	
3 SA	0002 6.1	0630 0.9	1235 6.5	1850 1.2	**18** SU	0047 6.8	0735 0.2	1322 7.2	1945 0.5
4 SU	0051 6.4	0731 0.6	1320 6.8	1944 1.0	**19** M ●	0132 7.0	0818 0.1	1403 7.2	2029 0.4
5 M ○	0134 6.7	0822 0.5	1402 7.0	2032 0.8	**20** TU	0211 7.0	0858 0.2	1439 7.1	2110 0.4
6 TU	0213 6.8	0906 0.4	1442 7.1	2114 0.7	**21** W	0246 6.9	0933 0.4	1508 6.9	2145 0.6
7 W	0252 7.0	0945 0.4	1520 7.1	2152 0.7	**22** TH	0317 6.8	1001 0.7	1534 6.7	2212 0.7
8 TH	0330 7.1	1018 0.4	1559 7.1	2226 0.6	**23** F	0347 6.7	1020 0.9	1600 6.6	2228 0.8
9 F	0410 7.1	1046 0.5	1638 6.9	2256 0.6	**24** SA	0419 6.6	1031 0.9	1630 6.5	2244 0.8
10 SA	0452 7.0	1114 0.7	1718 6.5	2329 0.8	**25** SU	0455 6.4	1052 0.9	1706 6.3	2312 0.9
11 SU	0539 6.7	1149 1.0	1803 6.1		**26** M	0536 6.2	1125 1.1	1748 6.1	2349 1.1
12 M ◑	0010 1.1	0634 6.2	1237 1.4	1858 5.7	**27** TU ◐	0624 5.9	1207 1.4	1838 5.8	
13 TU	0108 1.4	0749 5.7	1346 1.9	2023 5.4	**28** W	0042 1.3	0721 5.7	1306 1.7	1937 5.5
14 W	0240 1.7	0924 5.7	1534 2.0	2152 5.5	**29** TH	0209 1.5	0826 5.6	1435 1.9	2048 5.5
15 TH	0451 1.4	1041 6.0	1706 1.6	2301 5.9	**30** F	0333 1.4	0945 5.7	1601 1.7	2211 5.7

Chapter 5

TIME ZONE (UT)
For Summer Time add ONE hour in **non-shaded areas**

ENGLAND – LONDON BRIDGE
LAT 51°30′N   LONG 0°05′W
TIMES AND HEIGHTS OF HIGH AND LOW WATERS

YEAR 2004

MAY

Day	Time	m	Day	Time	m
1 SA	0444 / 1059 / SA 1710 / 2317	1.1 / 6.1 / 1.4 / 6.1	16 SU	0610 / 1205 / SU 1823	0.5 / 6.8 / 0.8
2 SU	0551 / 1156 / SU 1811	0.8 / 6.5 / 1.2	17 M	0016 / 0657 / M 1251 / 1912	6.7 / 0.4 / 7.0 / 0.6
3 M	0010 / 0651 / M 1245 / 1907	6.4 / 0.6 / 6.8 / 0.9	18 TU	0102 / 0741 / TU 1333 / 1958	6.8 / 0.4 / 7.0 / 0.5
4 TU	0057 / 0745 / TU 1330 / ○ 2000	6.7 / 0.5 / 7.1 / 0.8	19 W	0143 / 0822 / W 1408 / ● 2040	6.8 / 0.5 / 6.9 / 0.6
5 W	0142 / 0834 / W 1414 / 2049	6.9 / 0.4 / 7.1 / 0.6	20 TH	0221 / 0858 / TH 1439 / 2116	6.7 / 0.7 / 6.7 / 0.7
6 TH	0227 / 0917 / TH 1457 / 2133	7.1 / 0.4 / 7.1 / 0.5	21 F	0255 / 0928 / F 1506 / 2146	6.6 / 0.8 / 6.6 / 0.8
7 F	0312 / 0956 / F 1539 / 2214	7.2 / 0.4 / 7.0 / 0.5	22 SA	0327 / 0949 / SA 1534 / 2207	6.5 / 1.0 / 6.5 / 0.9
8 SA	0358 / 1031 / SA 1622 / 2252	7.2 / 0.5 / 6.8 / 0.5	23 SU	0400 / 1007 / SU 1607 / 2229	6.4 / 1.0 / 6.4 / 0.9
9 SU	0446 / 1106 / SU 1706 / 2332	7.0 / 0.7 / 6.5 / 0.7	24 M	0438 / 1033 / M 1644 / 2300	6.3 / 1.0 / 6.3 / 0.9
10 M	0538 / 1145 / M 1755	6.7 / 1.0 / 6.2	25 TU	0519 / 1108 / TU 1726 / 2339	6.2 / 1.1 / 6.1 / 1.0
11 TU	0019 / 0638 / TU 1236 / ◐ 1855	0.9 / 6.3 / 1.4 / 5.8	26 W	0607 / 1152 / W 1815	6.1 / 1.3 / 5.9
12 W	0121 / 0750 / W 1343 / 2013	1.2 / 6.0 / 1.7 / 5.7	27 TH	0031 / 0659 / TH 1246 / ◐ 1910	1.1 / 6.0 / 1.5 / 5.8
13 TH	0243 / 0906 / TH 1507 / 2126	1.3 / 6.0 / 1.8 / 5.8	28 F	0139 / 0758 / F 1355 / 2012	1.2 / 5.9 / 1.7 / 5.8
14 F	0415 / 1014 / F 1628 / 2229	1.1 / 6.2 / 1.5 / 6.1	29 SA	0254 / 0904 / SA 1515 / 2121	1.2 / 6.0 / 1.6 / 5.9
15 SA	0518 / 1113 / SA 1730 / 2326	0.8 / 6.6 / 1.1 / 6.4	30 SU	0404 / 1014 / SU 1628 / 2229	1.0 / 6.2 / 1.4 / 6.1
			31 M	0511 / 1117 / M 1732 / 2330	0.8 / 6.5 / 1.2 / 6.4

JUNE

Day	Time	m	Day	Time	m
1 TU	0613 / 1211 / TU 1833	0.7 / 6.8 / 1.0	16 W	0031 / 0700 / W 1300 / 1923	6.6 / 0.8 / 6.7 / 0.8
2 W	0024 / 0710 / W 1302 / 1931	6.7 / 0.5 / 7.0 / 0.8	17 TH	0116 / 0744 / TH 1339 / ● 2009	6.6 / 0.8 / 6.7 / 0.8
3 TH	0117 / 0804 / TH 1350 / ○ 2028	6.9 / 0.5 / 7.1 / 0.6	18 F	0158 / 0824 / F 1414 / 2049	6.6 / 0.9 / 6.6 / 0.8
4 F	0208 / 0853 / F 1437 / 2119	7.1 / 0.4 / 7.1 / 0.5	19 SA	0237 / 0858 / SA 1446 / 2125	6.5 / 1.0 / 6.5 / 0.8
5 SA	0259 / 0939 / SA 1524 / 2207	7.2 / 0.4 / 7.0 / 0.4	20 SU	0313 / 0926 / SU 1518 / 2155	6.4 / 1.1 / 6.4 / 0.9
6 SU	0350 / 1020 / SU 1610 / 2253	7.2 / 0.6 / 6.9 / 0.4	21 M	0349 / 0952 / M 1553 / 2225	6.3 / 1.1 / 6.3 / 0.9
7 M	0441 / 1101 / M 1657 / 2338	7.1 / 0.7 / 6.7 / 0.5	22 TU	0426 / 1023 / TU 1629 / 2257	6.3 / 1.1 / 6.3 / 0.9
8 TU	0534 / 1143 / TU 1747	6.9 / 1.0 / 6.4	23 W	0506 / 1059 / W 1709 / 2335	6.3 / 1.1 / 6.3 / 0.9
9 W	0025 / 0630 / W 1231 / ◐ 1843	0.6 / 6.6 / 1.2 / 6.2	24 TH	0549 / 1140 / TH 1753	6.3 / 1.2 / 6.2
10 TH	0118 / 0732 / TH 1326 / 1945	0.8 / 6.4 / 1.4 / 6.1	25 F	0018 / 0636 / F 1227 / ◐ 1841	0.9 / 6.3 / 1.3 / 6.1
11 F	0216 / 0836 / F 1429 / 2050	0.9 / 6.2 / 1.6 / 6.0	26 SA	0109 / 0728 / SA 1322 / 1936	1.0 / 6.2 / 1.4 / 6.1
12 SA	0321 / 0938 / SA 1536 / 2151	1.0 / 6.2 / 1.5 / 6.1	27 SU	0209 / 0827 / SU 1428 / 2038	1.0 / 6.1 / 1.5 / 6.1
13 SU	0426 / 1036 / SU 1642 / 2249	1.0 / 6.3 / 1.4 / 6.3	28 M	0318 / 0934 / M 1543 / 2147	1.0 / 6.1 / 1.5 / 6.1
14 M	0523 / 1129 / M 1741 / 2342	0.9 / 6.5 / 1.1 / 6.4	29 TU	0432 / 1042 / TU 1656 / 2256	1.0 / 6.3 / 1.4 / 6.3
15 TU	0613 / 1216 / TU 1834	0.8 / 6.6 / 0.9	30 W	0541 / 1143 / W 1805 / 2359	0.9 / 6.5 / 1.2 / 6.5

JULY

Day	Time	m	Day	Time	m
1 TH	0644 / 1238 / TH 1913	0.8 / 6.7 / 0.9	16 F	0052 / 0707 / F 1313 / 1939	6.3 / 1.1 / 6.5 / 0.9
2 F	0058 / 0743 / F 1331 / ○ 2016	6.8 / 0.6 / 6.9 / 0.7	17 SA	0139 / 0755 / SA 1355 / ● 2028	6.4 / 1.0 / 6.5 / 0.8
3 SA	0155 / 0838 / SA 1422 / 2113	7.0 / 0.5 / 7.0 / 0.4	18 SU	0222 / 0837 / SU 1433 / 2112	6.5 / 1.0 / 6.5 / 0.8
4 SU	0249 / 0927 / SU 1511 / 2204	7.2 / 0.5 / 7.0 / 0.2	19 M	0301 / 0914 / M 1509 / 2150	6.5 / 1.1 / 6.4 / 0.8
5 M	0341 / 1013 / M 1558 / 2251	7.2 / 0.5 / 7.0 / 0.2	20 TU	0337 / 0945 / TU 1543 / 2224	6.5 / 1.1 / 6.4 / 0.8
6 TU	0431 / 1054 / TU 1644 / 2334	7.2 / 0.7 / 6.9 / 0.2	21 W	0412 / 1016 / W 1616 / 2255	6.5 / 1.1 / 6.4 / 0.8
7 W	0520 / 1135 / W 1729	7.1 / 0.8 / 6.7	22 TH	0448 / 1049 / TH 1650 / 2325	6.6 / 1.1 / 6.5 / 0.8
8 TH	0015 / 0608 / TH 1215 / 1815	0.4 / 6.8 / 1.0 / 6.6	23 F	0527 / 1125 / F 1728 / 2358	6.6 / 1.1 / 6.5 / 0.8
9 F	0054 / 0659 / F 1258 / ◐ 1905	0.6 / 6.5 / 1.2 / 6.4	24 SA	0608 / 1204 / SA 1811	6.5 / 1.1 / 6.4
10 SA	0135 / 0753 / SA 1345 / 2001	0.8 / 6.2 / 1.4 / 6.1	25 SU	0035 / 0655 / SU 1249 / ◐ 1900	0.8 / 6.3 / 1.3 / 6.3
11 SU	0221 / 0852 / SU 1438 / 2104	1.0 / 6.0 / 1.5 / 6.0	26 M	0121 / 0749 / M 1344 / 1959	1.0 / 6.1 / 1.5 / 6.1
12 M	0315 / 0952 / M 1537 / 2207	1.2 / 5.9 / 1.6 / 6.0	27 TU	0223 / 0855 / TU 1459 / 2110	1.3 / 5.9 / 1.7 / 5.9
13 TU	0415 / 1048 / TU 1639 / 2307	1.3 / 6.0 / 1.5 / 6.1	28 W	0351 / 1011 / W 1625 / 2229	1.4 / 5.8 / 1.6 / 6.0
14 W	0517 / 1141 / W 1742	1.3 / 6.2 / 1.3	29 TH	0517 / 1121 / TH 1750 / 2343	1.3 / 6.1 / 1.4 / 6.2
15 TH	0001 / 0614 / TH 1229 / 1842	6.2 / 1.2 / 6.4 / 1.1	30 F	0630 / 1222 / F 1908	1.1 / 6.3 / 1.0
			31 SA	0048 / 0732 / SA 1318 / ○ 2012	6.6 / 0.8 / 6.7 / 0.6

AUGUST

Day	Time	m	Day	Time	m
1 SU	0147 / 0828 / SU 1410 / 2107	7.0 / 0.6 / 7.0 / 0.2	16 M	0203 / 0822 / M 1417 / ● 2058	6.6 / 1.0 / 6.6 / 0.7
2 M	0241 / 0917 / M 1457 / 2156	7.2 / 0.5 / 7.1 / 0.0	17 TU	0243 / 0903 / TU 1454 / 2139	6.7 / 1.0 / 6.6 / 0.7
3 TU	0329 / 1001 / TU 1541 / 2239	7.3 / 0.5 / 7.1 / 0.0	18 W	0318 / 0938 / W 1526 / 2214	6.7 / 1.0 / 6.6 / 0.7
4 W	0414 / 1041 / W 1622 / 2318	7.3 / 0.5 / 7.1 / 0.1	19 TH	0352 / 1008 / TH 1556 / 2243	6.8 / 1.0 / 6.6 / 0.7
5 TH	0456 / 1117 / TH 1701 / 2351	7.2 / 0.7 / 7.0 / 0.3	20 F	0425 / 1037 / F 1626 / 2307	6.8 / 1.0 / 6.7 / 0.7
6 F	0536 / 1150 / F 1739	6.9 / 0.9 / 6.8	21 SA	0500 / 1106 / SA 1701 / 2331	6.8 / 1.0 / 6.7 / 0.8
7 SA	0019 / 0615 / SA 1223 / ◑ 1817	0.6 / 6.5 / 1.1 / 6.5	22 SU	0538 / 1138 / SU 1742	6.6 / 1.0 / 6.6
8 SU	0049 / 0655 / SU 1258 / 1902	0.8 / 6.2 / 1.3 / 6.2	23 M	0000 / 0620 / M 1216 / ◑ 1830	0.9 / 6.3 / 1.2 / 6.4
9 M	0125 / 0741 / M 1343 / 1958	1.1 / 5.8 / 1.5 / 5.9	24 TU	0040 / 0711 / TU 1305 / 1928	1.1 / 5.9 / 1.5 / 6.0
10 TU	0214 / 0843 / TU 1442 / 2112	1.4 / 5.6 / 1.6 / 5.6	25 W	0135 / 0816 / W 1419 / 2043	1.5 / 5.5 / 1.8 / 5.7
11 W	0315 / 0959 / W 1546 / 2229	1.6 / 5.5 / 1.7 / 5.7	26 TH	0311 / 0945 / TH 1609 / 2217	1.8 / 5.5 / 1.9 / 5.7
12 TH	0423 / 1104 / TH 1652 / 2334	1.6 / 5.7 / 1.5 / 5.9	27 F	0507 / 1107 / F 1756 / 2339	1.7 / 5.8 / 1.4 / 6.1
13 F	0531 / 1200 / F 1803	1.5 / 6.0 / 1.3	28 SA	0622 / 1211 / SA 1905	1.3 / 6.3 / 0.8
14 SA	0029 / 0637 / SA 1251 / 1915	6.2 / 1.3 / 6.3 / 1.0	29 SU	0043 / 0721 / SU 1306 / 2001	6.6 / 0.8 / 6.7 / 0.4
15 SU	0119 / 0734 / SU 1336 / 2011	6.4 / 1.1 / 6.5 / 0.8	30 M	0139 / 0812 / M 1355 / ○ 2052	7.0 / 0.5 / 7.0 / 0.0
			31 TU	0227 / 0859 / TU 1439 / 2137	7.3 / 0.4 / 7.2 / -0.1

Chart Datum: 2·90 metres below Ordnance Datum (Newlyn)

ENGLAND – LONDON BRIDGE

LAT 51°30'N   LONG 0°05'W

TIMES AND HEIGHTS OF HIGH AND LOW WATERS

YEAR **2004**

SEPTEMBER				OCTOBER				NOVEMBER				DECEMBER			
Time	**m**	**Time**	**m**	**Time**	**m**	**Time**	**m**	**Time**	**m**	**Time**	**m**	**Time**	**m**	**Time**	**m**
1 0311 W 0942 1519 2217	7.4 0.3 7.2 0.0	**16** 0251 TH 0919 1459 2151	6.9 0.9 6.7 0.6	**1** 0322 F 0954 1526 2218	7.2 0.4 7.1 0.4	**16** 0256 SA 0928 1504 2153	7.0 0.8 7.0 0.7	**1** 0342 M 1022 1602 2221	6.7 0.9 6.6 1.1	**16** 0354 TU 1029 1619 2240	6.8 0.7 7.0 0.9	**1** 0346 W 1018 1620 2215	6.4 1.1 6.3 1.2	**16** 0430 TH 1118 1706 2320	6.8 0.5 7.0 1.0
2 0350 TH 1020 1555 2251	7.3 0.4 7.2 0.2	**17** 0325 F 0951 1529 2221	6.9 0.9 6.8 0.7	**2** 0351 SA 1027 1557 2243	7.0 0.6 7.0 0.7	**17** 0333 SU 1002 1543 2220	7.0 0.8 7.0 0.8	**2** 0410 TU 1036 1637 2236	6.6 1.0 6.4 1.1	**17** 0438 W 1110 1710 2319	6.6 0.8 6.7 1.1	**2** 0421 TH 1043 1700 2247	6.3 1.1 6.2 1.2	**17** 0518 F 1205 1759	6.6 0.7 6.8
3 0426 F 1054 1628 2318	7.1 0.6 7.0 0.5	**18** 0358 SA 1020 1602 2243	6.9 0.9 6.9 0.8	**3** 0417 SU 1051 1628 2259	6.8 0.8 6.8 0.9	**18** 0410 M 1034 1625 2247	6.8 0.9 6.9 0.9	**3** 0443 W 1058 1717 2305	6.4 1.1 6.1 1.2	**18** 0524 TH 1157 1807	6.3 1.0 6.4	**3** 0500 F 1119 1744 2327	6.2 1.2 6.1 1.3	**18** 0005 SA 0608 1256 1856	1.2 6.4 0.8 6.5
4 0457 SA 1121 1701 2340	6.8 0.8 6.9 0.7	**19** 0433 SU 1047 1639 2304	6.8 0.9 6.9 0.8	**4** 0444 M 1107 1702 2311	6.6 1.0 6.5 1.0	**19** 0449 TU 1106 1711 2320	6.6 1.0 6.6 1.1	**4** 0522 TH 1133 1804 2344	6.1 1.3 5.9 1.5	**19** 0005 F 0617 1300 1913	1.4 6.0 1.2 6.1	**4** 0544 SA 1205 1834	6.0 1.3 6.0	**19** 0055 0706 SU 1352 1958	1.4 6.2 1.0 6.3
5 0527 SU 1144 1736 2359	6.6 1.0 6.6 0.9	**20** 0510 M 1116 1721 2333	6.6 1.0 6.7 1.0	**5** 0516 TU 1127 1742 2336	6.4 1.1 6.2 1.2	**20** 0531 W 1145 1805	6.2 1.2 6.2	**5** 0608 F 1223 1859	5.8 1.5 5.6	**20** 0106 SA 0731 1420 2028	1.7 5.7 1.3 6.0	**5** 0014 SU 0635 1307 1928	1.5 5.8 1.4 5.9	**20** 0152 0812 1453 2102	1.6 6.0 1.1 6.2
6 0559 M 1209 1816 ◐	6.3 1.2 6.3	**21** 0551 TU 1152 1810 ◐	6.3 1.2 6.3	**6** 0554 W 1201 1830 ◐	6.1 1.3 5.8	**21** 0003 TH 0621 1243 1912	1.4 5.8 1.5 5.8	**6** 0035 SA 0705 1350 2002	1.8 5.5 1.7 5.5	**21** 0228 SU 0852 1544 2139	1.9 5.8 1.2 6.1	**6** 0113 M 0734 1420 2028	1.7 5.7 1.4 5.9	**21** 0257 TU 0919 1556 2203	1.6 6.0 1.1 6.2
7 0025 TU 0637 1248 1905	1.2 5.9 1.4 5.4	**22** 0013 W 0639 1242 1911	1.3 5.8 1.6 5.8	**7** 0013 TH 0640 1257 1928	1.5 5.7 1.7 5.3	**22** 0105 F 0735 1421 2042	1.9 5.4 1.7 5.6	**7** 0153 SU 0817 1512 2118	2.1 5.4 1.6 5.6	**22** 0352 M 1000 1648 2242	1.7 6.0 0.9 6.4	**7** 0225 TU 0842 1530 2134	1.8 5.7 1.3 6.0	**22** 0405 W 1021 1655 2300	1.6 6.2 1.1 6.3
8 0107 W 0726 1351 2009	1.5 5.6 1.7 5.4	**23** 0110 TH 0745 1404 2036	1.8 5.4 1.9 5.5	**8** 0113 F 0741 1432 2045	1.9 5.3 1.8 5.3	**23** 0249 SA 0920 1616 2207	2.1 5.4 1.5 5.9	**8** 0328 TU 0949 1621 2233	2.0 5.5 1.3 6.3	**23** 0500 W 1059 1742 2337	1.4 6.4 0.6 6.7	**8** 0344 W 0955 1636 2241	1.7 5.9 1.1 6.2	**23** 0512 TH 1118 1749 2351	1.4 6.3 1.0 6.4
9 0218 TH 0838 1507 2144	1.9 5.3 1.8 5.4	**24** 0253 F 0932 1623 2218	2.1 5.3 1.8 5.7	**9** 0254 SA 0924 1550 2224	2.2 5.2 1.7 5.5	**24** 0432 SU 1033 1725 2313	1.8 5.9 0.9 6.4	**9** 0441 TU 1057 1723 2331	1.7 5.9 0.9 6.3	**24** 0556 W 1151 1831	1.4 6.7 0.6	**9** 0454 TH 1100 1737 2340	1.5 6.2 0.9 6.5	**24** 0611 F 1209 1838	1.4 6.5 1.0
10 0341 F 1025 1620 2305	2.0 5.4 1.6 5.6	**25** 0458 SA 1056 1750 2333	1.9 5.7 1.2 6.2	**10** 0420 SU 1054 1703 2327	2.0 5.6 1.3 6.0	**25** 0537 M 1132 1819	1.3 6.4 0.5	**10** 0542 TH 1148 1820	1.4 6.3 0.8	**25** 0025 TH 0647 1238 1916	6.9 1.0 6.9 0.5	**10** 0557 F 1156 1835	1.3 6.5 0.8	**25** 0038 SA 0703 1257 1923	6.5 1.0 6.6 1.0
11 0458 SA 1132 1734	1.8 5.8 1.3	**26** 0606 SU 1157 1848	1.3 6.0 0.6	**11** 0532 M 1149 1810	1.6 6.0 1.0	**26** 0008 TU 0630 1222 1907	6.9 0.8 6.8 0.2	**11** 0019 TH 0637 1234 1913	6.7 1.2 6.6 0.7	**26** 0110 F 0735 1321 1959	7.0 0.6 7.0 0.6	**11** 0032 SA 0657 1249 1931	6.7 1.0 6.8 0.8	**26** 0120 SU 0751 1341 2006	6.6 0.9 6.6 1.0
12 0003 SU 0611 1225 1849	6.1 1.4 6.2 1.0	**27** 0031 M 0659 1248 1939	6.8 0.8 6.8 0.2	**12** 0017 TU 0631 1235 1906	6.4 1.3 6.4 0.7	**27** 0057 W 0719 1307 1952	7.2 0.5 7.1 0.1	**12** 0105 F 0730 1317 2003	6.9 0.8 6.8 0.7	**27** 0148 SA 0819 1401 2038	6.9 0.6 6.9 0.7	**12** 0122 SU 0756 1340 2024	6.9 0.7 7.0 0.7	**27** 0158 M 0835 1421 2044	6.5 0.9 6.5 1.1
13 0053 M 0710 1311 1945	6.4 1.2 6.5 0.7	**28** 0122 TU 0749 1333 2025	7.2 0.5 7.1 0.0	**13** 0101 W 0721 1315 1956	6.7 1.1 6.6 0.6	**28** 0140 TH 0805 1348 2034	7.3 0.4 7.2 0.2	**13** 0148 SA 0820 1400 2048	7.0 0.8 7.0 0.6	**28** 0222 SU 0859 1437 2112	6.8 0.7 6.7 0.9	**13** 0210 M 0852 1432 2112	7.0 0.7 7.1 0.7	**28** 0231 TU 0914 1458 2115	6.5 0.9 6.5 1.2
14 0137 TU 0759 1351 ● 2033	6.6 1.0 6.6 0.4	**29** 0207 W 0834 1414 2108	7.4 0.3 7.2 0.0	**14** 0141 TH 0808 1352 2041	6.9 0.9 6.8 0.6	**29** 0218 F 0848 1425 2112	7.2 0.4 7.1 0.4	**14** 0230 SU 0906 1445 2128	7.0 0.7 7.1 0.7	**29** 0250 M 0933 1511 2137	6.6 0.8 6.6 1.1	**14** 0257 TU 0943 1523 2157	7.0 0.5 7.2 0.7	**29** 0302 W 0946 1533 2137	6.4 1.0 6.4 1.3
15 0215 W 0841 1427 2115	6.8 0.9 6.7 0.6	**30** 0247 TH 0916 1452 2146	7.4 0.3 7.2 0.1	**15** 0219 F 0850 1428 2120	7.0 0.9 6.9 0.6	**30** 0251 SA 0927 1459 2144	7.0 0.5 7.0 0.7	**15** 0312 M 0949 1531 2205	7.0 0.7 7.1 0.7	**30** 0316 TU 0958 1544 2153	6.5 1.0 6.4 1.2	**15** 0344 W 1031 1614 2239	6.9 0.5 7.1 0.8	**30** 0334 TH 1012 1608 2203	6.3 1.1 6.4 1.3
						31 0318 SU 0959 1530 2208	6.8 0.7 6.8 0.9							**31** 0408 F 1039 1645 2236	6.3 1.1 6.4 1.2

Chart Datum: 2·90 metres below Ordnance Datum (Newlyn)

Chapter 5

261

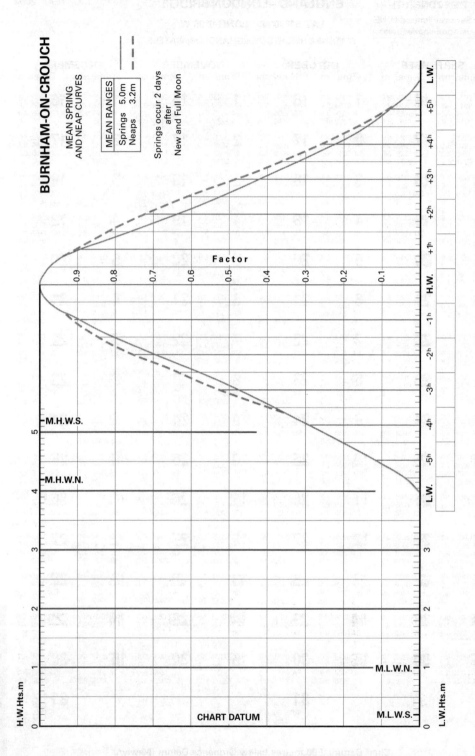

BURNHAM-ON-CROUCH

MEAN SPRING
AND NEAP CURVES

MEAN RANGES	
Springs	5.0m
Neaps	3.2m

Springs occur 2 days
after
New and Full Moon

Factor

0.9 0.8 0.7 0.6 0.5 0.4 0.3 0.2 0.1

H.W.Hts.m

M.H.W.S.

M.H.W.N.

CHART DATUM

L.W.Hts.m

M.L.W.N.

M.L.W.S.

TIME ZONE (UT)
For Summer Time add ONE hour in **non-shaded areas**

ENGLAND – BURNHAM-ON-CROUCH

LAT 51°37′N   LONG 0°48′E

TIMES AND HEIGHTS OF HIGH AND LOW WATERS

YEAR 2004

JANUARY

Time m	Time m
1 0051 1.3 / 0652 4.3 / TH 1353 0.8 / 1942 4.2	**16** 0559 4.5 / 1247 0.7 / F 1849 4.3
2 0200 1.3 / 0800 4.2 / F 1457 0.9 / 2045 4.2	**17** 0055 1.0 / 0709 4.5 / SA 1403 0.7 / 2000 4.3
3 0316 1.2 / 0904 4.3 / SA 1553 0.9 / 2144 4.3	**18** 0219 1.0 / 0826 4.5 / SU 1523 0.7 / 2112 4.5
4 0418 1.0 / 1003 4.5 / SU 1644 0.9 / 2235 4.5	**19** 0344 0.9 / 0938 4.6 / M 1632 0.7 / 2217 4.6
5 0511 0.9 / 1054 4.6 / M 1730 0.8 / 2322 4.7	**20** 0458 0.7 / 1044 4.8 / TU 1733 0.5 / 2319 4.7
6 0559 0.7 / 1142 4.7 / TU 1812 0.8 ●	**21** 0605 0.4 / 1147 5.1 / W 1828 0.5
7 0005 4.7 / 0638 0.5 / W 1224 4.7 / 1847 0.8 ○	**22** 0016 4.8 / 0700 0.2 / TH 1245 5.2 / 1913 0.5
8 0043 4.8 / 0712 0.5 / TH 1303 4.8 / 1919 0.8	**23** 0106 5.0 / 0747 0.1 / F 1334 5.3 / 1954 0.6
9 0116 4.8 / 0745 0.4 / F 1336 4.8 / 1950 0.8	**24** 0152 5.1 / 0831 0.1 / SA 1418 5.2 / 2032 0.7
10 0149 4.8 / 0819 0.4 / SA 1410 4.8 / 2022 0.8	**25** 0231 5.1 / 0912 0.1 / SU 1459 5.2 / 2108 0.8
11 0221 4.8 / 0854 0.4 / SU 1445 4.8 / 2055 0.8	**26** 0309 5.1 / 0951 0.2 / M 1539 5.0 / 2143 0.8
12 0255 4.8 / 0930 0.4 / M 1524 4.8 / 2130 0.8	**27** 0346 5.0 / 1028 0.3 / TU 1618 4.7 / 2219 0.9
13 0331 4.7 / 1010 0.4 / TU 1607 4.7 / 2210 0.8	**28** 0422 4.8 / 1105 0.4 / W 1656 4.6 / 2257 1.0
14 0412 4.7 / 1054 0.4 / W 1654 4.6 / 2256 0.9	**29** 0503 4.6 / 1145 0.7 / TH 1739 4.3 / 2341 1.1 ◑
15 0500 4.6 / 1143 0.5 / TH 1747 4.5 / 2347 1.0 ◑	**30** 0551 4.3 / 1238 0.9 / F 1828 4.1
	31 0041 1.2 / 0653 4.1 / SA 1342 1.0 / 1936 4.0

FEBRUARY

Time m	Time m
1 0200 1.2 / 0811 4.1 / SU 1455 1.1 / 2051 4.1	**16** 0148 1.0 / 0805 4.2 / M 1502 1.0 / 2049 4.1
2 0328 1.1 / 0926 4.2 / M 1603 1.1 / 2157 4.2	**17** 0334 0.9 / 0931 4.5 / TU 1623 0.9 / 2208 4.3
3 0439 1.0 / 1028 4.3 / TU 1700 1.0 / 2253 4.5	**18** 0459 0.7 / 1045 4.7 / W 1727 0.8 / 2313 4.6
4 0536 0.8 / 1122 4.6 / W 1749 0.9 / 2343 4.7	**19** 0606 0.3 / 1148 5.0 / TH 1821 0.7
5 0622 0.5 / 1209 4.7 / TH 1831 0.8	**20** 0010 4.8 / 0657 0.1 / F 1241 5.2 / 1902 0.5 ●
6 0026 4.8 / 0659 0.4 / F 1250 4.8 / 1904 0.8 ○	**21** 0058 5.1 / 0738 0.0 / SA 1326 5.3 / 1939 0.5
7 0104 4.8 / 0732 0.3 / SA 1325 5.0 / 1936 0.7	**22** 0137 5.2 / 0816 0.0 / SU 1403 5.2 / 2014 0.5
8 0138 5.0 / 0805 0.3 / SU 1358 5.1 / 2007 0.7	**23** 0213 5.2 / 0850 0.1 / M 1437 5.1 / 2045 0.5
9 0210 5.0 / 0839 0.2 / M 1431 5.1 / 2039 0.5	**24** 0244 5.1 / 0920 0.1 / TU 1509 5.0 / 2116 0.5
10 0240 5.0 / 0911 0.2 / TU 1506 5.1 / 2112 0.5	**25** 0315 5.1 / 0948 0.3 / W 1540 4.8 / 2144 0.7
11 0313 5.1 / 0945 0.2 / W 1544 5.0 / 2148 0.5	**26** 0346 5.0 / 1018 0.4 / TH 1611 4.6 / 2216 0.7
12 0350 5.0 / 1022 0.3 / TH 1627 4.7 / 2229 0.7	**27** 0421 4.7 / 1051 0.7 / F 1645 4.3 / 2254 0.9
13 0432 4.8 / 1106 0.4 / F 1715 4.5 / 2315 0.8	**28** 0503 4.5 / 1134 0.9 / SA 1728 4.2 / 2344 1.0 ◑
14 0526 4.6 / 1202 0.7 / SA 1813 4.2	**29** 0557 4.1 / 1240 1.1 / SU 1825 4.0
15 0018 0.9 / 0636 4.3 / SU 1325 0.9 / 1928 4.1	

MARCH

Time m	Time m
1 0100 1.2 / 0711 4.0 / M 1401 1.2 / 1946 3.8	**16** 0145 1.0 / 0803 4.1 / TU 1453 1.2 / 2039 4.0
2 0232 1.2 / 0845 4.0 / TU 1522 1.2 / 2116 4.0	**17** 0341 0.8 / 0934 4.3 / W 1618 1.0 / 2200 4.2
3 0400 1.0 / 1002 4.2 / W 1632 1.1 / 2223 4.3	**18** 0459 0.5 / 1043 4.7 / TH 1717 0.8 / 2302 4.6
4 0507 0.8 / 1059 4.6 / TH 1726 0.9 / 2317 4.6	**19** 0558 0.2 / 1140 5.1 / F 1806 0.7 / 2354 4.8
5 0557 0.5 / 1148 4.8 / F 1810 0.8	**20** 0643 0.1 / 1227 5.2 / SA 1845 0.5 ●
6 0002 4.7 / 0637 0.4 / SA 1229 5.0 / 1844 0.7 ○	**21** 0040 5.1 / 0719 0.0 / SU 1307 5.2 / 1919 0.4
7 0043 5.0 / 0713 0.2 / SU 1305 5.1 / 1917 0.5	**22** 0117 5.1 / 0752 0.1 / M 1342 5.2 / 1951 0.4
8 0118 5.1 / 0746 0.1 / M 1339 5.2 / 1948 0.4	**23** 0150 5.1 / 0821 0.1 / TU 1412 5.1 / 2021 0.4
9 0151 5.2 / 0818 0.1 / TU 1412 5.2 / 2020 0.3	**24** 0217 5.1 / 0847 0.2 / W 1438 4.8 / 2048 0.4
10 0222 5.2 / 0850 0.0 / W 1446 5.2 / 2054 0.3	**25** 0245 5.0 / 0912 0.3 / TH 1503 4.8 / 2115 0.4
11 0255 5.2 / 0922 0.1 / TH 1523 5.1 / 2129 0.3	**26** 0315 4.8 / 0937 0.5 / F 1531 4.7 / 2143 0.5
12 0331 5.2 / 0957 0.2 / F 1602 4.8 / 2208 0.4	**27** 0349 4.7 / 1007 0.7 / SA 1605 4.5 / 2220 0.7
13 0414 5.0 / 1039 0.5 / SA 1649 4.5 / 2255 0.7 ◑	**28** 0429 4.5 / 1047 0.9 / SU 1648 4.2 / 2311 0.9
14 0509 4.6 / 1134 0.9 / SU 1747 4.1 / 2359 0.9	**29** 0521 4.1 / 1149 1.2 / M 1744 4.0
15 0625 4.2 / 1306 1.1 / M 1905 3.8	**30** 0024 1.1 / 0625 4.0 / TU 1316 1.3 / 1855 3.8
	31 0149 1.1 / 0757 4.0 / W 1440 1.3 / 2027 3.8

APRIL

Time m	Time m
1 0316 1.0 / 0924 4.2 / TH 1555 1.1 / 2143 4.2	**16** 0442 0.3 / 1024 4.8 / F 1655 0.9 / 2238 4.6
2 0426 0.8 / 1025 4.5 / F 1652 1.0 / 2239 4.5	**17** 0534 0.1 / 1118 5.0 / SA 1741 0.7 / 2328 4.8
3 0521 0.4 / 1115 4.8 / SA 1737 0.8 / 2327 4.7	**18** 0619 0.1 / 1202 5.1 / SU 1822 0.5
4 0606 0.3 / 1158 5.1 / SU 1817 0.7	**19** 0013 5.0 / 0652 0.1 / M 1243 5.1 / 1856 0.4 ●
5 0011 5.0 / 0646 0.1 / M 1239 5.2 / 1851 0.4 ○	**20** 0051 5.0 / 0722 0.2 / TU 1316 5.0 / 1928 0.4
6 0050 5.1 / 0720 0.0 / TU 1315 5.3 / 1926 0.3	**21** 0123 5.0 / 0750 0.3 / W 1344 4.8 / 1957 0.4
7 0127 5.3 / 0755 0.0 / W 1351 5.3 / 2001 0.2	**22** 0152 5.0 / 0815 0.4 / TH 1409 4.8 / 2024 0.4
8 0202 5.3 / 0828 0.0 / TH 1426 5.2 / 2038 0.2	**23** 0219 4.8 / 0841 0.4 / F 1433 4.7 / 2051 0.4
9 0238 5.3 / 0903 0.1 / F 1503 5.1 / 2115 0.2	**24** 0249 4.7 / 0907 0.5 / SA 1501 4.7 / 2121 0.5
10 0319 5.2 / 0940 0.3 / SA 1544 4.7 / 2156 0.3	**25** 0324 4.6 / 0936 0.8 / SU 1536 4.6 / 2158 0.7
11 0407 4.8 / 1024 0.7 / SU 1632 4.3 / 2249 0.5	**26** 0405 4.5 / 1014 1.0 / M 1620 4.3 / 2249 0.8
12 0508 4.5 / 1126 1.0 / M 1735 4.1 ◐	**27** 0455 4.2 / 1113 1.2 / TU 1715 4.1 / 2357 0.9 ◑
13 0007 0.8 / 0628 4.2 / TU 1258 1.2 / 1856 3.8	**28** 0557 4.1 / 1234 1.3 / W 1822 4.0
14 0156 0.8 / 0759 4.2 / W 1439 1.2 / 2022 4.0	**29** 0115 0.9 / 0711 4.0 / TH 1353 1.3 / 1938 4.0
15 0334 0.7 / 0920 4.5 / TH 1558 1.1 / 2137 4.2	**30** 0231 0.8 / 0832 4.2 / F 1505 1.2 / 2052 4.1

Chart Datum: 2·35 metres below Ordnance Datum (Newlyn)

Chapter 5

TIME ZONE (UT)
For Summer Time add ONE hour in **non-shaded areas**

ENGLAND – BURNHAM-ON-CROUCH
LAT 51°37′N   LONG 0°48′E
TIMES AND HEIGHTS OF HIGH AND LOW WATERS

YEAR **2004**

MAY

Day	Time	m	Day	Time	m
1 SA	0339 / 0939 / 1605 / 2152	0.7 / 4.5 / 1.0 / 4.5	16 SU	0501 / 1043 / 1709 / 2253	0.2 / 4.8 / 0.8 / 4.7
2 SU	0438 / 1033 / 1655 / 2244	0.4 / 4.7 / 0.8 / 4.7	17 M	0544 / 1130 / 1753 / 2340	0.2 / 5.0 / 0.5 / 4.8
3 M	0528 / 1121 / 1741 / 2332	0.2 / 5.0 / 0.7 / 5.0	18 TU	0622 / 1212 / 1832	0.3 / 4.8 / 0.5
4 TU	0616 / 1206 / 1825 ○	0.1 / 5.1 / 0.4	19 W	0021 / 0652 / 1248 / 1906 ●	4.8 / 0.4 / 4.8 / 0.4
5 W	0018 / 0655 / 1249 / 1906	5.2 / 0.0 / 5.2 / 0.3	20 TH	0057 / 0721 / 1318 / 1937	4.8 / 0.4 / 4.7 / 0.4
6 TH	0102 / 0733 / 1329 / 1946	5.3 / 0.0 / 5.2 / 0.2	21 F	0129 / 0748 / 1344 / 2006	4.7 / 0.5 / 4.7 / 0.4
7 F	0143 / 0811 / 1408 / 2027	5.3 / 0.1 / 5.2 / 0.1	22 SA	0158 / 0816 / 1410 / 2035	4.7 / 0.5 / 4.7 / 0.4
8 SA	0226 / 0849 / 1449 / 2108	5.3 / 0.2 / 5.0 / 0.2	23 SU	0230 / 0844 / 1440 / 2108	4.7 / 0.7 / 4.7 / 0.5
9 SU	0312 / 0930 / 1534 / 2157	5.2 / 0.5 / 4.7 / 0.3	24 M	0305 / 0915 / 1517 / 2146	4.6 / 0.8 / 4.6 / 0.5
10 M	0407 / 1019 / 1627 / 2259	4.8 / 0.8 / 4.5 / 0.4	25 TU	0347 / 0952 / 1600 / 2234	4.5 / 1.0 / 4.3 / 0.7
11 TU	0512 / 1124 / 1731 ◐	4.6 / 1.1 / 4.2	26 W	0435 / 1045 / 1653 / 2332	4.3 / 1.1 / 4.2 / 0.8
12 W	0017 / 0623 / 1242 / 1839	0.5 / 4.5 / 1.2 / 4.1	27 TH	0531 / 1148 / 1751 ◑	4.2 / 1.2 / 4.1
13 TH	0145 / 0737 / 1407 / 1951	0.5 / 4.6 / 1.2 / 4.2	28 F	0038 / 0632 / 1259 / 1855	0.8 / 4.2 / 1.2 / 4.1
14 F	0307 / 0848 / 1522 / 2100	0.4 / 4.6 / 1.1 / 4.3	29 SA	0145 / 0741 / 1409 / 2002	0.7 / 4.3 / 1.1 / 4.2
15 SA	0411 / 0951 / 1621 / 2201	0.3 / 4.7 / 0.9 / 4.6	30 SU	0253 / 0848 / 1514 / 2104	0.5 / 4.5 / 1.0 / 4.5
			31 M	0355 / 0948 / 1612 / 2202	0.4 / 4.7 / 0.9 / 4.7

JUNE

Day	Time	m	Day	Time	m
1 TU	0452 / 1042 / 1708 / 2256	0.2 / 4.8 / 0.7 / 5.0	16 W	0546 / 1139 / 1810 / 2353	0.5 / 4.7 / 0.7 / 4.7
2 W	0544 / 1133 / 1801 / 2349	0.2 / 5.0 / 0.4 / 5.1	17 TH	0624 / 1220 / 1848 ●	0.7 / 4.7 / 0.5
3 TH	0633 / 1223 / 1850 ○	0.1 / 5.1 / 0.3	18 F	0036 / 0657 / 1256 / 1922	4.7 / 0.7 / 4.7 / 0.5
4 F	0041 / 0716 / 1309 / 1936	5.2 / 0.2 / 5.1 / 0.2	19 SA	0111 / 0728 / 1328 / 1953	4.7 / 0.7 / 4.7 / 0.4
5 SA	0130 / 0758 / 1355 / 2022	5.3 / 0.3 / 5.1 / 0.1	20 SU	0145 / 0758 / 1357 / 2025	4.7 / 0.7 / 4.7 / 0.4
6 SU	0218 / 0841 / 1440 / 2110	5.3 / 0.4 / 5.0 / 0.1	21 M	0217 / 0828 / 1428 / 2058	4.6 / 0.8 / 4.7 / 0.4
7 M	0309 / 0924 / 1528 / 2202	5.2 / 0.7 / 4.8 / 0.2	22 TU	0252 / 0901 / 1502 / 2135	4.6 / 0.8 / 4.6 / 0.5
8 TU	0404 / 1013 / 1621 / 2301	5.0 / 0.9 / 4.7 / 0.3	23 W	0330 / 0937 / 1543 / 2217	4.6 / 0.9 / 4.5 / 0.5
9 W	0501 / 1109 / 1716 ◐	4.8 / 1.0 / 4.6	24 TH	0414 / 1019 / 1627 / 2303 ◐	4.5 / 1.0 / 4.5 / 0.5
10 TH	0003 / 0600 / 1210 / 1812	0.3 / 4.6 / 1.1 / 4.5	25 F	0503 / 1109 / 1718 / 2354 ◑	4.5 / 1.1 / 4.3 / 0.5
11 F	0112 / 0700 / 1321 / 1913	0.4 / 4.6 / 1.2 / 4.3	26 SA	0557 / 1206 / 1812	4.3 / 1.1 / 4.3
12 SA	0222 / 0806 / 1433 / 2016	0.4 / 4.5 / 1.1 / 4.3	27 SU	0057 / 0657 / 1313 / 1915	0.5 / 4.3 / 1.1 / 4.3
13 SU	0326 / 0908 / 1538 / 2119	0.5 / 4.5 / 1.0 / 4.5	28 M	0206 / 0804 / 1425 / 2021	0.5 / 4.5 / 1.0 / 4.5
14 M	0420 / 1004 / 1634 / 2215	0.5 / 4.6 / 0.9 / 4.6	29 TU	0316 / 0909 / 1536 / 2126	0.5 / 4.6 / 0.9 / 4.7
15 TU	0506 / 1053 / 1724 / 2306	0.5 / 4.7 / 0.8 / 4.6	30 W	0421 / 1010 / 1641 / 2227	0.4 / 4.7 / 0.8 / 4.8

JULY

Day	Time	m	Day	Time	m
1 TH	0520 / 1107 / 1744 / 2328	0.3 / 4.8 / 0.5 / 5.0	16 F	0559 / 1156 / 1835	0.8 / 4.7 / 0.7
2 F	0616 / 1204 / 1841 ○	0.3 / 5.0 / 0.4	17 SA	0019 / 0637 / 1239 / 1911 ●	4.7 / 0.8 / 4.8 / 0.5
3 SA	0027 / 0704 / 1258 / 1933	5.2 / 0.3 / 5.1 / 0.2	18 SU	0100 / 0711 / 1315 / 1943	4.7 / 0.8 / 4.8 / 0.4
4 SU	0122 / 0747 / 1346 / 2021	5.3 / 0.4 / 5.1 / 0.1	19 M	0134 / 0743 / 1347 / 2014	4.7 / 0.8 / 4.8 / 0.4
5 M	0213 / 0830 / 1432 / 2108	5.3 / 0.5 / 5.1 / 0.1	20 TU	0206 / 0814 / 1417 / 2045	4.8 / 0.8 / 4.8 / 0.4
6 TU	0301 / 0913 / 1517 / 2155	5.3 / 0.7 / 5.1 / 0.1	21 W	0237 / 0844 / 1448 / 2118	4.8 / 0.8 / 4.7 / 0.4
7 W	0350 / 0956 / 1602 / 2243	5.2 / 0.8 / 5.0 / 0.1	22 TH	0312 / 0918 / 1521 / 2152	4.8 / 0.8 / 4.7 / 0.4
8 TH	0438 / 1042 / 1648 / 2330	5.0 / 0.9 / 4.8 / 0.3	23 F	0350 / 0954 / 1558 / 2231	4.7 / 0.8 / 4.7 / 0.4
9 F	0527 / 1129 / 1736 ◐	4.7 / 1.0 / 4.7	24 SA	0432 / 1036 / 1640 / 2313	4.7 / 0.9 / 4.7 / 0.4
10 SA	0022 / 0618 / 1226 / 1827	0.4 / 4.5 / 1.1 / 4.5	25 SU	0522 / 1124 / 1731 ◐	4.6 / 1.0 / 4.6
11 SU	0121 / 0716 / 1335 / 1929	0.7 / 4.3 / 1.2 / 4.3	26 M	0005 / 0618 / 1224 / 1831	0.5 / 4.3 / 1.1 / 4.5
12 M	0224 / 0819 / 1448 / 2034	0.8 / 4.3 / 1.2 / 4.3	27 TU	0116 / 0725 / 1342 / 1946	0.7 / 4.3 / 1.1 / 4.5
13 TU	0328 / 0921 / 1556 / 2139	0.9 / 4.3 / 1.0 / 4.3	28 W	0241 / 0837 / 1509 / 2101	0.8 / 4.3 / 1.0 / 4.5
14 W	0424 / 1017 / 1656 / 2238	0.9 / 4.5 / 0.9 / 4.5	29 TH	0358 / 0947 / 1628 / 2214	0.8 / 4.5 / 0.9 / 4.7
15 TH	0513 / 1108 / 1749 / 2331	0.9 / 4.6 / 0.8 / 4.6	30 F	0506 / 1052 / 1740 / 2322	0.7 / 4.7 / 0.5 / 5.0
			31 SA	0605 / 1154 / 1841 ○	0.5 / 5.0 / 0.3

AUGUST

Day	Time	m	Day	Time	m
1 SU	0024 / 0653 / 1249 / 1931	5.2 / 0.5 / 5.1 / 0.1	16 M	0044 / 0654 / 1257 / 1926 ●	5.0 / 0.8 / 5.0 / 0.4
2 M	0117 / 0736 / 1336 / 2015	5.3 / 0.5 / 5.2 / 0.0	17 TU	0118 / 0725 / 1330 / 1956	5.0 / 0.8 / 5.0 / 0.4
3 TU	0203 / 0816 / 1417 / 2056	5.5 / 0.5 / 5.3 / 0.0	18 W	0149 / 0755 / 1358 / 2025	5.0 / 0.8 / 5.0 / 0.3
4 W	0245 / 0855 / 1457 / 2135	5.3 / 0.7 / 5.2 / 0.0	19 TH	0217 / 0825 / 1427 / 2056	5.1 / 0.7 / 5.0 / 0.3
5 TH	0326 / 0931 / 1535 / 2212	5.2 / 0.7 / 5.2 / 0.1	20 F	0249 / 0856 / 1457 / 2126	5.1 / 0.7 / 5.0 / 0.3
6 F	0406 / 1008 / 1612 / 2247	5.0 / 0.8 / 5.0 / 0.3	21 SA	0324 / 0930 / 1529 / 2158	5.0 / 0.7 / 5.0 / 0.3
7 SA	0445 / 1047 / 1652 / 2326 ◐	4.7 / 0.9 / 4.8 / 0.5	22 SU	0402 / 1008 / 1608 / 2236	4.8 / 0.7 / 4.8 / 0.4
8 SU	0527 / 1132 / 1738	4.5 / 1.1 / 4.6	23 M	0447 / 1052 / 1656 / 2323 ◑	4.6 / 0.9 / 4.7 / 0.7
9 M	0011 / 0616 / 1231 / 1833	0.9 / 4.2 / 1.2 / 4.2	24 TU	0542 / 1149 / 1800	4.3 / 1.1 / 4.5
10 TU	0114 / 0720 / 1348 / 1948	1.1 / 4.1 / 1.2 / 4.1	25 W	0034 / 0651 / 1315 / 1923	1.0 / 4.1 / 1.2 / 4.2
11 W	0228 / 0835 / 1515 / 2105	1.2 / 4.1 / 1.2 / 4.1	26 TH	0216 / 0816 / 1501 / 2054	1.1 / 4.1 / 1.1 / 4.3
12 TH	0342 / 0944 / 1628 / 2214	1.2 / 4.3 / 1.0 / 4.3	27 F	0348 / 0938 / 1630 / 2215	1.0 / 4.3 / 0.8 / 4.6
13 F	0444 / 1042 / 1729 / 2311	1.1 / 4.6 / 0.8 / 4.6	28 SA	0458 / 1046 / 1741 / 2322	0.9 / 4.7 / 0.5 / 5.0
14 SA	0537 / 1133 / 1818	1.0 / 4.7 / 0.7	29 SU	0555 / 1145 / 1836	0.8 / 5.0 / 0.2
15 SU	0001 / 0621 / 1218 / 1854	4.7 / 0.9 / 4.8 / 0.5	30 M	0019 / 0641 / 1236 / 1920 ○	5.2 / 0.7 / 5.2 / 0.1
			31 TU	0106 / 0719 / 1319 / 1959	5.5 / 0.5 / 5.3 / 0.4

Chart Datum: 2·35 metres below Ordnance Datum (Newlyn)

ENGLAND – BURNHAM-ON-CROUCH

LAT 51°37′N   LONG 0°48′E

TIMES AND HEIGHTS OF HIGH AND LOW WATERS

YEAR 2004

SEPTEMBER

Day	Time	m	Time	m	Time	m	Time	m
1 W	0147	5.5	0756	0.5	1357		2034	0.0
2 TH	0223	5.3	0830	0.5	1431	5.3	2106	0.1
3 F	0257	5.2	0904	0.7	1502	5.2	2134	0.3
4 SA	0328	5.0	0935	0.7	1534	5.1	2204	0.4
5 SU	0359	4.7	1008	0.8	1609	4.8	2235	0.7
6 M	0432	4.5	1047	1.0	1650	4.6	2315 ◑	1.0
7 TU	0514	4.3	1139	1.1	1743	4.2		
8 W	0013	1.2	0611	4.1	1257	1.3	1857	4.0
9 TH	0135	1.5	0739	4.0	1429	1.2	2031	4.0
10 F	0301	1.5	0906	4.2	1555	1.1	2147	4.2
11 SA	0416	1.2	1011	4.5	1659	0.9	2246	4.6
12 SU	0511	1.1	1103	4.7	1748	0.7	2335	4.8
13 M	0556	0.9	1149	5.0	1827	0.5		
14 TU	0017	5.0	0631	0.9	1227	5.2	1900 ●	0.4
15 W	0053	5.1	0702	0.8	1303	5.1	1931	0.3
16 TH	0124	5.2	0732	0.7	1333	5.1	2000	0.2
17 F	0154	5.2	0803	0.5	1402	5.2	2030	0.2
18 SA	0225	5.2	0835	0.5	1433	5.2	2100	0.2
19 SU	0258	5.1	0909	0.5	1507	5.0	2131	0.3
20 M	0335	5.0			1547	5.0	2208	0.5
21 TU	0417	4.6	1032	0.9	1637	4.7	2256 ◑	0.9
22 W	0513	4.2	1134	1.0	1747	4.3		
23 TH	0011	1.2	0628	4.0	1315	1.1	1922	4.2
24 F	0205	1.3	0806	4.1	1506	1.0	2058	4.3
25 SA	0340	1.2	0929	4.3	1628	0.7	2213	4.7
26 SU	0446	1.0	1033	4.7	1730	0.3	2312	5.1
27 M	0538	0.8	1127	5.1	1820	0.1		
28 TU	0002	5.3	0622	0.7	1214	5.2	1859 ○	0.1
29 W	0047	5.5	0658	0.6	1256	5.3	1933	0.1
30 TH	0123	5.3	0732	0.5	1331	5.3	2004	0.2

OCTOBER

Day	Time	m	Time	m	Time	m	Time	m
1 F	0156	5.2	0805	0.5	1401	5.2	2032	0.3
2 SA	0224	5.1	0837	0.5	1431	5.1	2058	0.4
3 SU	0251	5.0	0906	0.7	1500	5.0	2124	0.5
4 M	0317	4.8	0936	0.8	1534	4.8	2152	0.8
5 TU	0348	4.6	1012	0.9	1613	4.5	2228	1.0
6 W	0427	4.3	1104	1.1	1704	4.2	2323 ◑	1.3
7 TH	0522	4.1	1220	1.2	1811	4.0		
8 F	0048	1.6	0638	4.0	1345	1.2	1944	4.0
9 SA	0214	1.6	0816	4.1	1509	1.1	2107	4.2
10 SU	0335	1.3	0928	4.3	1616	0.9	2209	4.5
11 M	0435	1.2	1022	4.6	1706	0.7	2258	4.8
12 TU	0518	1.0	1108	4.8	1748	0.4	2340	5.1
13 W	0558	0.9	1149	5.0	1827	0.3		
14 TH	0018	5.2	0634	0.7	1227	5.1	1901 ●	0.3
15 F	0054	5.3	0706	0.5	1304	5.2	1934	0.2
16 SA	0128	5.3	0741	0.4	1338	5.3	2006	0.2
17 SU	0201	5.3	0816	0.4	1414	5.3	2039	0.3
18 M	0236	5.1	0854	0.4	1452	5.2	2113	0.5
19 TU	0315	5.0	0934	0.5	1537	5.0	2152	0.8
20 W	0359	4.6	1026	0.8	1634	4.6	2247 ◑	1.1
21 TH	0457	4.2	1141	0.9	1751	4.3		
22 F	0008	1.5	0621	4.1	1322	1.0	1921	4.3
23 SA	0148	1.5	0750	4.1	1458	0.8	2044	4.5
24 SU	0319	1.3	0905	4.5	1610	0.4	2153	4.8
25 M	0422	1.0	1007	4.7	1706	0.2	2248	5.1
26 TU	0512	0.8	1059	5.0	1753	0.2	2335	5.2
27 W	0556	0.7	1145	5.1	1832	0.2		
28 TH	0018	5.2	0635	0.5	1226	5.2	1904 ○	0.3
29 F	0056	5.2	0709	0.5	1303	5.1	1933	0.4
30 SA	0127	5.1	0742	0.5	1333	5.1	2000	0.5
31 SU	0154	5.0	0813	0.5	1403	5.0	2027	0.7

NOVEMBER

Day	Time	m	Time	m	Time	m	Time	m
1 M	0217	4.8	0842	0.5	1434	4.8	2053	0.8
2 TU	0244	4.8	0912	0.7	1508	4.7	2120	0.9
3 W	0315	4.7	0948	0.8	1548	4.5	2154	1.1
4 TH	0355	4.5	1040	1.0	1636	4.2	2245	1.3
5 F	0448	4.2	1147	1.1	1736	4.1	2359 ◑	1.5
6 SA	0556	4.1	1301	1.1	1847	4.1		
7 SU	0120	1.6	0716	4.1	1413	1.0	2007	4.2
8 M	0236	1.5	0830	4.2	1519	0.8	2115	4.5
9 TU	0340	1.2	0930	4.5	1614	0.7	2209	4.7
10 W	0432	1.0	1020	4.7	1704	0.4	2256	5.0
11 TH	0517	0.9			1749	0.3	2340	5.1
12 F	0602	0.7	1151	5.1	1832 ●	0.3		
13 SA	0022	5.2	0644	0.5	1236	5.3	1910	0.3
14 SU	0103	5.2	0723	0.4	1318	5.3	1947	0.3
15 M	0142	5.2	0804	0.3	1359	5.3	2025	0.4
16 TU	0221	5.1	0846	0.3	1444	5.2	2104	0.7
17 W	0303	4.8	0933	0.4	1536	5.0	2149	0.9
18 TH	0352	4.6	1033	0.6	1637	4.7	2246	1.1
19 F	0454	4.3	1145	0.7	1747	4.5	2354 ◑	1.3
20 SA	0606	4.2	1309	0.7	1859	4.5		
21 SU	0117	1.5	0719	4.3	1429	0.5	2012	4.6
22 M	0239	1.3	0829	4.5	1537	0.4	2118	4.7
23 TU	0346	1.1	0931	4.7	1633	0.3	2214	4.8
24 W	0440	0.8	1025	4.8	1720	0.3	2302	5.0
25 TH	0527	0.7	1113	5.0	1800	0.2	2346	5.0
26 F	0612	0.5	1157	5.0	1835 ○	0.5		
27 SA	0025	5.0	0649	0.5	1237	5.0	1905	0.5
28 SU	0100	4.8	0723	0.5	1312	4.8	1934	0.7
29 M	0129	4.8	0755	0.5	1344	4.8	2002	0.8
30 TU	0155	4.8	0826	0.5	1416	4.7	2030	0.8

DECEMBER

Day	Time	m	Time	m	Time	m	Time	m
1 W	0222	4.7	0856	0.7	1450	4.6	2059	0.9
2 TH	0255	4.7	0933	0.7	1528	4.5	2133	1.0
3 F	0334	4.6	1019	0.8	1612	4.3	2217	1.2
4 SA	0422	4.3	1114	0.9	1703	4.3	2313	1.3
5 SU	0519	4.2	1212	0.9	1801 ◑	4.2		
6 M	0017	1.3	0621	4.1	1316	0.9	1904	4.2
7 TU	0127	1.3	0730	4.2	1422	0.8	2013	4.3
8 W	0237	1.2	0835	4.3	1524	0.7	2117	4.6
9 TH	0340	1.0	0935	4.6	1622	0.5	2212	4.7
10 F	0438	0.9	1028	4.8	1714	0.4	2304	5.0
11 SA	0532	0.7	1121	5.1	1806	0.4	2354	5.1
12 SU	0625	0.5	1213	5.2	1851 ●	0.4		
13 M	0042	5.1	0712	0.3	1304	5.3	1934	0.4
14 TU	0128	5.1	0759	0.2	1352	5.3	2016	0.5
15 W	0212	5.1	0846	0.2	1441	5.2	2059	0.7
16 TH	0258	5.0	0937	0.2	1533	5.1	2143	0.9
17 F	0347	4.8	1032	0.3	1629	5.0	2233	1.0
18 SA	0440	4.7	1131	0.3	1725	4.7	2329 ◐	1.1
19 SU	0538	4.6	1236	0.4	1824	4.6		
20 M	0032	1.2	0637	4.5	1344	0.4	1929	4.5
21 TU	0145	1.2	0744	4.5	1452	0.4	2033	4.5
22 W	0300	1.1	0849	4.5	1551	0.7	2134	4.5
23 TH	0404	1.0	0950	4.6	1642	0.7	2226	4.6
24 F	0459	0.8	1044	4.7	1727	0.7	2314	4.7
25 SA	0549	0.7	1133	4.7	1808	0.8	2359	4.7
26 SU	0634	0.5	1218	4.7	1843 ○	0.8		
27 M	0039	4.7	0711	0.5	1259	4.7	1915	0.8
28 TU	0112	4.7	0744	0.4	1333	4.7	1945	0.8
29 W	0142	4.7	0814	0.5	1404	4.7	2014	0.8
30 TH	0211	4.7	0844	0.5	1435	4.7	2043	0.9
31 F	0242	4.7	0918	0.5	1510	4.6	2116	0.9

Chart Datum: 2·35 metres below Ordnance Datum (Newlyn)

Chapter 5

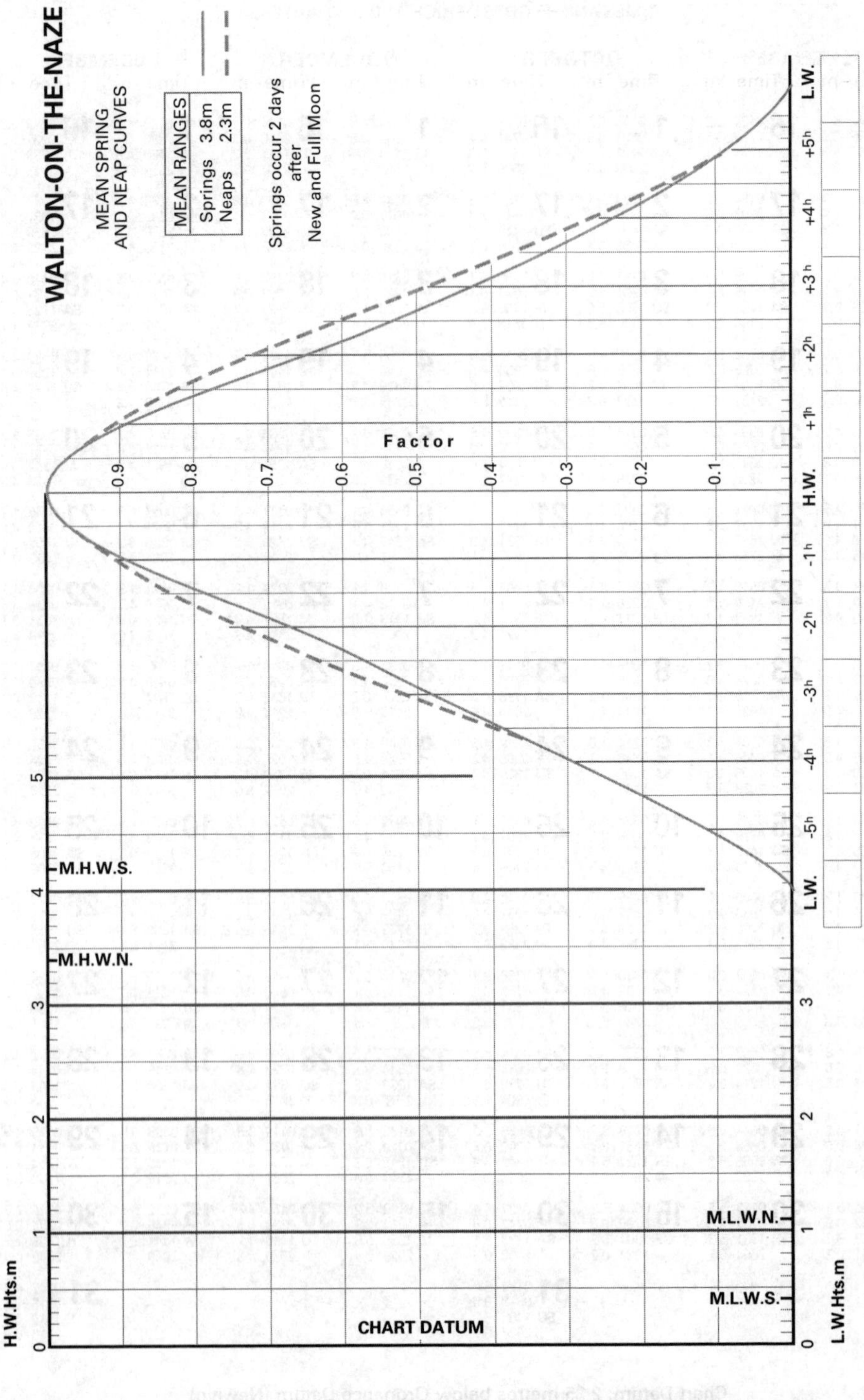

WALTON-ON-THE-NAZE

MEAN SPRING
AND NEAP CURVES

MEAN RANGES	
Springs	3.8m
Neaps	2.3m

Springs occur 2 days
after
New and Full Moon

Factor

0.9 0.8 0.7 0.6 0.5 0.4 0.3 0.2 0.1

L.W. +5ʰ +4ʰ +3ʰ +2ʰ +1ʰ H.W. -1ʰ -2ʰ -3ʰ -4ʰ -5ʰ L.W.

M.H.W.S.

M.H.W.N.

M.L.W.N.

M.L.W.S.

H.W.Hts.m

L.W.Hts.m

CHART DATUM

ENGLAND – WALTON-ON-THE-NAZE

LAT 51°51′N   LONG 1°17′E

YEAR **2004**

TIMES AND HEIGHTS OF HIGH AND LOW WATERS

JANUARY

Day	Time m	Time m	Time m	Time m
1 TH	0616 3.5	1255 0.9	1904 3.4	
16 F	0522 3.6	1153 0.8	1813 3.5	
2 F	0102 1.4	0721 3.4	1354 1.0	2005 3.4
17 SA	0001 1.1	0632 3.6	1305 0.8	1921 3.5
3 SA	0212 1.3	0823 3.5	1447 1.0	2101 3.5
18 SU	0119 1.1	0746 3.6	1419 0.8	2030 3.6
4 SU	0310 1.1	0919 3.6	1535 1.0	2150 3.6
19 M	0238 1.0	0855 3.7	1523 0.8	2133 3.7
5 M	0400 1.0	1009 3.7	1618 0.9	2235 3.8
20 TU	0348 0.8	0959 3.8	1621 0.7	2232 3.8
6 TU	0445 3.8	1054 3.8	1657 0.9	2316 3.8
21 W	0451 0.6	1059 4.1	1714 0.7	● 2327 3.9
7 W	0525 0.7	1135 3.8	1734 0.9	○ 2353 3.9
22 TH	0548 0.4	1155 4.2	1802 0.7	
8 TH	0601 0.7	1213 3.9	1809 0.9	
23 F	0017 4.0	0639 0.3	1246 4.3	1846 0.7
9 F	0027 3.9	0636 0.6	1248 3.9	1842 0.9
24 SA	0104 4.1	0726 0.3	1332 4.2	1927 0.8
10 SA	0101 3.9	0713 0.6	1323 3.9	1916 0.9
25 SU	0145 4.1	0810 0.3	1415 4.2	2006 0.8
11 SU	0135 3.9	0750 0.6	1400 3.9	1951 0.9
26 M	0225 4.1	0852 0.4	1456 4.0	2044 0.9
12 M	0210 3.9	0830 0.6	1440 3.9	2029 0.9
27 TU	0303 4.0	0932 0.5	1537 3.8	2123 1.0
13 TU	0248 3.8	0913 0.6	1525 3.8	2113 0.9
28 W	0341 3.9	1012 0.6	1617 3.7	2203 1.1
14 W	0331 3.8	1000 0.6	1614 3.7	2202 1.0
29 TH	0424 3.7	1055 0.8	1701 3.5	◑ 2250 1.2
15 TH	0421 3.7	1053 0.7	1710 3.6	◐ 2257 1.1
30 F	0514 3.5	1145 1.0	1753 3.3	2348 1.3
31 SA	0617 3.3	1245 1.1	1858 3.2	

FEBRUARY

Day	Time m	Time m	Time m	Time m
1 SU	0102 1.3	0732 3.3	1353 1.2	2010 3.3
16 M	0051 1.1	0726 3.4	1359 1.1	2009 3.3
2 M	0223 1.2	0844 3.4	1456 1.2	2114 3.4
17 TU	0229 1.0	0849 3.6	1515 1.0	2124 3.5
3 TU	0330 1.1	0944 3.5	1550 1.1	2208 3.6
18 W	0349 0.8	1000 3.8	1615 0.9	2227 3.7
4 W	0423 0.9	1035 3.7	1636 1.0	2255 3.8
19 TH	0452 0.5	1100 4.0	1706 0.8	2321 3.9
5 TH	0508 0.7	1120 3.8	1717 0.9	2337 3.9
20 F	0545 0.3	1151 4.2	● 1750 0.7	
6 F	0547 0.6	1200 3.9	○ 1753 0.9	
21 SA	0008 4.1	0629 0.2	1237 4.3	1830 0.7
7 SA	0015 3.9	0623 0.5	1236 4.0	1827 0.8
22 SU	0049 4.2	0710 0.2	1316 4.2	1907 0.7
8 SU	0050 4.0	0658 0.5	1311 4.1	1900 0.8
23 M	0126 4.2	0746 0.3	1352 4.1	1941 0.7
9 M	0123 4.0	0734 0.4	1345 4.1	1934 0.7
24 TU	0159 4.1	0819 0.3	1425 4.0	2014 0.7
10 TU	0155 4.0	0809 0.4	1422 4.1	2010 0.7
25 W	0231 4.1	0849 0.5	1457 3.9	2045 0.8
11 W	0229 4.1	0846 0.4	1501 4.0	2049 0.7
26 TH	0303 4.0	0921 0.6	1529 3.7	2119 0.8
12 TH	0307 4.0	0926 0.5	1546 3.8	2133 0.8
27 F	0340 3.8	0957 0.8	1605 3.5	2200 1.0
13 F	0352 3.9	1013 0.6	1636 3.6	2223 0.9
28 SA	0424 3.6	1043 1.0	1650 3.3	2254 1.1
14 SA	0448 3.7	1111 0.8	1737 3.4	2326 1.0
29 SU	0520 3.3	1147 1.2	1749 3.2	
15 SU	0601 3.5	1229 1.0	1850 3.3	

MARCH

Day	Time m	Time m	Time m	Time m
1 M	0006 1.3	0634 3.2	1303 1.3	1908 3.1
16 TU	0048 1.1	0724 3.3	1351 1.3	1959 3.2
2 TU	0131 1.3	0805 3.2	1418 1.3	2034 3.2
17 W	0236 0.9	0851 3.5	1510 1.1	2116 3.4
3 W	0253 1.1	0918 3.4	1523 1.2	2139 3.5
18 TH	0349 0.7	0958 3.8	1606 0.9	2216 3.7
4 TH	0356 0.9	1013 3.7	1614 1.0	2230 3.7
19 F	0444 0.4	1052 4.1	1652 0.8	2306 3.9
5 F	0443 0.7	1100 3.9	1655 0.9	2314 3.8
20 SA	0530 0.3	1138 4.2	1732 0.7	● 2350 4.1
6 SA	0524 0.6	1140 4.0	1731 0.8	○ 2353 4.0
21 SU	0609 0.2	1218 4.2	1809 0.6	
7 SU	0602 0.4	1216 4.1	1806 0.7	
22 M	0028 4.1	0644 0.3	1254 4.2	1843 0.6
8 M	0029 4.1	0637 0.3	1252 4.2	1840 0.6
23 TU	0102 4.1	0715 0.3	1325 4.1	1915 0.6
9 TU	0103 4.2	0712 0.3	1325 4.2	1914 0.5
24 W	0131 4.1	0743 0.4	1353 3.9	1944 0.6
10 W	0136 4.2	0746 0.2	1401 4.2	1950 0.5
25 TH	0200 4.0	0810 0.5	1419 3.9	2013 0.6
11 TH	0210 4.2	0821 0.3	1439 4.1	2028 0.5
26 F	0231 3.9	0837 0.7	1448 3.8	2044 0.7
12 F	0248 4.2	0859 0.4	1520 3.9	2111 0.6
27 SA	0306 3.8	0910 0.8	1523 3.6	2124 0.8
13 SA	0333 4.0	0944 0.7	1609 3.6	◐ 2201 0.8
28 SU	0348 3.6	0953 1.0	1608 3.4	◑ 2218 1.0
14 SU	0430 3.7	1043 1.0	1709 3.3	2308 1.0
29 M	0442 3.3	1059 1.3	1706 3.2	2332 1.2
15 M	0549 3.4	1211 1.2	1829 3.1	
30 TU	0550 3.2	1221 1.4	1819 3.1	
31 W	0052 1.2	0718 3.2	1339 1.4	1947 3.1

APRIL

Day	Time m	Time m	Time m	Time m
1 TH	0212 1.1	0842 3.4	1449 1.2	2100 3.4
16 F	0333 0.5	0940 3.9	1545 1.0	2153 3.7
2 F	0318 0.9	0941 3.6	1542 1.1	2154 3.6
17 SA	0422 0.3	1031 4.0	1628 0.8	2241 3.9
3 SA	0409 0.6	1029 3.9	1624 0.9	2240 3.8
18 SU	0504 0.3	1114 4.1	1707 0.7	2324 4.0
4 SU	0452 0.5	1110 4.1	1702 0.8	2322 4.0
19 M	0540 0.3	1153 4.1	1744 0.6 ●	
5 M	0533 0.3	1149 4.2	1739 0.6 ○	
20 TU	0001 4.0	0612 0.4	1227 4.0	1818 0.6
6 TU	0000 4.1	0610 0.2	1226 4.3	1816 0.5
21 W	0034 4.0	0642 0.5	1256 3.9	1849 0.6
7 W	0038 4.3	0647 0.2	1303 4.3	1854 0.4
22 TH	0104 4.0	0709 0.6	1322 3.9	1918 0.6
8 TH	0115 4.3	0723 0.2	1340 4.2	1933 0.4
23 F	0133 3.9	0736 0.6	1347 3.8	1947 0.6
9 F	0153 4.3	0800 0.3	1419 4.1	2013 0.4
24 SA	0204 3.8	0804 0.7	1417 3.8	2020 0.7
10 SA	0235 4.2	0840 0.5	1501 3.8	2058 0.5
25 SU	0240 3.7	0836 0.9	1453 3.7	2100 0.8
11 SU	0325 3.9	0928 0.8	1552 3.5	2155 0.7
26 M	0323 3.6	0917 1.1	1539 3.5	2155 0.9
12 M	0429 3.6	1034 1.1	1657 3.3	◑ 2316 0.9
27 TU	0416 3.4	1020 1.3	1636 3.3	◑ 2307 1.0
13 TU	0553 3.4	1204 1.3	1820 3.1	
28 W	0520 3.3	1141 1.4	1746 3.2	
14 W	0058 0.9	0720 3.4	1338 1.3	1943 3.2
29 TH	0020 1.0	0634 3.2	1255 1.4	1900 3.2
15 TH	0229 0.8	0838 3.6	1452 1.2	2054 3.4
30 F	0130 0.9	0752 3.4	1402 1.3	2011 3.3

Chart Datum: 2·16 metres below Ordnance Datum (Newlyn)

Chapter 5

ENGLAND – WALTON-ON-THE-NAZE

YEAR 2004

LAT 51°51′N   LONG 1°17′E

TIMES AND HEIGHTS OF HIGH AND LOW WATERS

TIME ZONE (UT)
For Summer Time add ONE hour in **non-shaded areas**

MAY

Time	m		Time	m
1 0234	0.8	**16**	0351	0.4
0856	3.6		0958	3.9
SA 1458	1.1	SU	1558	0.9
2109	3.6		2208	3.8
2 0329	0.6	**17**	0431	0.4
0948	3.8		1043	4.0
SU 1545	0.9	M	1639	0.7
2159	3.8		2252	3.9
3 0416	0.4	**18**	0507	0.5
1034	4.0		1123	3.9
M 1628	0.8	TU	1718	0.7
2245	4.2		2332	3.9
4 0501	0.3	**19**	0540	0.6
1117	4.1		1158	3.9
TU 1711	0.6	W	1755	0.6
○ 2329	4.2	●		
5 0543	0.2	**20**	0007	3.9
1159	4.2		0611	0.6
W 1755	0.5	TH	1229	3.8
			1828	0.6
6 0012	4.3	**21**	0040	3.8
0624	0.2		0640	0.7
TH 1240	4.2	F	1256	3.8
1837	0.4		1859	0.6
7 0055	4.3	**22**	0111	3.8
0704	0.3		0710	0.7
F 1321	4.2	SA	1323	3.8
1921	0.3		1930	0.6
8 0140	4.3	**23**	0144	3.8
0745	0.4		0740	0.8
SA 1404	4.0	SU	1355	3.8
2006	0.4		2005	0.7
9 0228	4.2	**24**	0221	3.7
0830	0.7		0813	0.9
SU 1451	3.8	M	1433	3.7
2059	0.5		2047	0.7
10 0325	3.9	**25**	0304	3.6
0923	0.9		0854	1.1
M 1546	3.6	TU	1518	3.5
2205	0.6		2139	0.8
11 0433	3.7	**26**	0355	3.5
1032	1.2		0950	1.2
TU 1653	3.4	W	1613	3.4
◑ 2325	0.7		2241	0.9
12 0547	3.6	**27**	0453	3.4
1149	1.3		1058	1.3
W 1804	3.3	TH	1714	3.3
		◐	2345	0.9
13 0048	0.7	**28**	0557	3.4
0659	3.6		1205	1.3
TH 1308	1.3	F	1819	3.3
1913	3.4			
14 0204	0.6	**29**	0048	0.8
0808	3.7		0703	3.6
F 1418	1.2	SA	1310	1.2
2019	3.5		1923	3.4
15 0304	0.5	**30**	0151	0.7
0908	3.8		0808	3.6
SA 1513	1.0	SU	1410	1.1
2117	3.7		2023	3.6
		31	0249	0.6
			0905	3.8
		M	1505	1.0
			2118	3.8

JUNE

Time	m		Time	m
1 0342	0.4	**16**	0433	0.7
0957	3.9		1051	3.8
TU 1557	0.8	W	1655	0.8
2210	4.0		2305	3.8
2 0431	0.4	**17**	0510	0.8
1046	4.0		1131	3.8
W 1647	0.6	TH	1735	0.7
2301	4.1	●	2346	3.8
3 0519	0.3	**18**	0545	0.8
1134	4.1		1206	3.8
TH 1737	0.5	F	1812	0.7
○ 2351	4.2			
4 0605	0.4	**19**	0022	3.8
1220	4.1		0618	0.8
F 1827	0.4	SA	1239	3.8
			1845	0.6
5 0041	4.3	**20**	0057	3.8
0650	0.5		0650	0.8
SA 1307	4.1	SU	1309	3.8
1916	0.3		1919	0.6
6 0132	4.3	**21**	0131	3.7
0736	0.6		0723	0.9
SU 1355	4.0	M	1342	3.8
2008	0.3		1955	0.6
7 0225	4.2	**22**	0207	3.7
0823	0.8		0758	0.9
M 1445	3.9	TU	1418	3.7
2104	0.4		2035	0.7
8 0322	4.0	**23**	0247	3.7
0916	1.0		0837	1.0
TU 1540	3.8	W	1500	3.6
2207	0.5		2120	0.7
9 0422	3.9	**24**	0333	3.6
1016	1.1		0923	1.1
W 1637	3.7	TH	1546	3.6
◑ 2312	0.5		2210	0.7
10 0523	3.7	**25**	0424	3.6
1119	1.2		1017	1.2
TH 1736	3.6	F	1639	3.5
		◐	2304	0.7
11 0017	0.6	**26**	0520	3.5
0624	3.7		1115	1.2
F 1225	1.3	SA	1736	3.5
1836	3.5			
12 0122	0.6	**27**	0003	0.7
0727	3.6		0621	3.5
SA 1332	1.2	SU	1218	1.2
1937	3.5		1838	3.5
13 0222	0.7	**28**	0107	0.7
0827	3.6		0725	3.6
SU 1433	1.1	M	1325	1.1
2037	3.6		1942	3.6
14 0312	0.7	**29**	0212	0.7
0920	3.7		0828	3.7
M 1525	1.0	TU	1431	1.0
2131	3.7		2044	3.8
15 0355	0.7	**30**	0313	0.6
1008	3.8		0926	3.8
TU 1612	0.9	W	1532	0.9
2220	3.7		2143	3.9

JULY

Time	m		Time	m
1 0408	0.5	**16**	0445	0.9
1021	3.9		1108	3.8
TH 1631	0.7	F	1721	0.8
2241	4.0		2330	3.8
2 0501	0.5	**17**	0524	0.9
1115	4.0		1149	3.9
F 1728	0.6	SA	1800	0.7
○ 2338	4.2			
3 0552	0.5	**18**	0010	3.8
1208	4.1		0600	0.9
SA 1824	0.4	SU	1226	3.9
			1834	0.6
4 0033	4.3	**19**	0046	3.8
0639	0.6		0634	0.9
SU 1258	4.1	M	1259	3.9
1915	0.3		1907	0.6
5 0126	4.3	**20**	0119	3.9
0725	0.7		0707	0.9
M 1346	4.1	TU	1331	3.9
2006	0.3		1941	0.6
6 0217	4.3	**21**	0152	3.9
0811	0.8		0740	0.9
TU 1433	4.1	W	1403	3.8
2057	0.3		2016	0.6
7 0307	4.2	**22**	0228	3.9
0858	0.9		0816	0.9
W 1520	4.0	TH	1437	3.8
2148	0.3		2054	0.6
8 0358	4.0	**23**	0307	3.8
0947	1.0		0856	1.0
TH 1608	3.9	F	1516	3.8
2239	0.5		2135	0.6
9 0449	3.8	**24**	0352	3.8
1038	1.1		0941	1.0
F 1658	3.8	SA	1600	3.8
◑ 2330	0.6		2220	0.6
10 0542	3.6	**25**	0443	3.7
1134	1.2		1032	1.1
SA 1752	3.6	SU	1653	3.7
		◐	2314	0.7
11 0025	0.8	**26**	0542	3.5
0639	3.5		1132	1.2
SU 1238	1.3	M	1756	3.6
1851	3.5			
12 0124	0.9	**27**	0021	0.8
0740	3.5		0648	3.5
M 1346	1.3	TU	1245	1.2
1954	3.5		1908	3.6
13 0223	1.0	**28**	0140	0.9
0839	3.5		0757	3.6
TU 1450	1.1	W	1406	1.1
2056	3.5		2020	3.6
14 0316	1.0	**29**	0252	0.9
0933	3.6		0904	3.6
W 1546	1.0	TH	1520	1.0
2153	3.6		2130	3.8
15 0402	1.0	**30**	0355	0.8
1022	3.7		1007	3.8
TH 1636	0.9	F	1627	0.7
2244	3.7		2235	4.0
		31	0451	0.7
			1106	4.0
		SA	1728	0.5
		○	2335	4.2

AUGUST

Time	m		Time	m
1 0541	0.7	**16**	0542	0.9
1159	4.1		1207	4.0
SU 1821	0.3	M	1816	0.6
●				
2 0028	4.3	**17**	0029	4.0
0627	0.7		0615	0.9
M 1248	4.2	TU	1241	4.0
1909	0.2		1848	0.6
3 0116	4.4	**18**	0101	4.0
0710	0.7		0647	0.9
TU 1331	4.3	W	1311	4.0
1953	0.2		1919	0.5
4 0200	4.3	**19**	0131	4.1
0751	0.8		0719	0.8
W 1412	4.2	TH	1341	4.0
2035	0.2		1952	0.5
5 0242	4.2	**20**	0204	4.1
0831	0.8		0753	0.8
TH 1452	4.2	F	1412	4.0
2115	0.3		2025	0.5
6 0324	4.0	**21**	0240	4.0
0911	0.9		0830	0.8
F 1531	4.0	SA	1446	4.0
2153	0.5		2100	0.5
7 0405	3.8	**22**	0320	4.0
0953	1.0		0911	0.9
SA 1612	3.9	SU	1526	3.9
◔ 2234	0.7		2141	0.6
8 0449	3.6	**23**	0407	3.7
1041	1.2		0958	1.0
SU 1700	3.7	M	1617	3.8
2320	1.0	◐	2231	0.8
9 0540	3.4	**24**	0504	3.5
1138	1.3		1059	1.2
M 1758	3.4	TU	1723	3.6
			2341	1.1
10 0019	1.2	**25**	0615	3.3
0643	3.3		1220	1.3
TU 1251	1.3	W	1846	3.4
1910	3.3			
11 0128	1.3	**26**	0117	1.2
0755	3.3		0737	3.3
W 1411	1.3	TH	1358	1.2
2024	3.3		2013	3.5
12 0237	1.3	**27**	0242	1.1
0901	3.5		0855	3.5
TH 1520	1.1	F	1522	0.9
2130	3.5		2131	3.7
13 0335	1.2	**28**	0348	1.0
0957	3.7		1001	3.8
F 1617	0.9	SA	1628	0.7
2225	3.7		2235	4.0
14 0424	1.1	**29**	0441	0.9
1046	3.8		1057	4.0
SA 1703	0.8	SU	1723	0.4
2313	3.8		2330	4.2
15 0506	1.0	**30**	0528	0.8
1129	3.9		1146	4.2
SU 1742	0.7	M	1810	0.3
2354	4.0	○		
		31	0017	4.4
			0609	0.7
		TU	1230	4.3
			1851	0.2

Chart Datum: 2·16 metres below Ordnance Datum (Newlyn)

ENGLAND – WALTON-ON-THE-NAZE

YEAR 2004

LAT 51°51'N LONG 1°17'E

TIMES AND HEIGHTS OF HIGH AND LOW WATERS

SEPTEMBER

Time m   Time m

1 0059 4.4   **16** 0035 4.2
0648 0.7   0622 0.8
W 1309 4.3   TH 1244 4.1
1929 0.2   1853 0.4

2 0137 4.3   **17** 0106 4.2
0725 0.4   0656 0.7
TH 1345 4.3   F 1315 4.2
2003 0.3   1925 0.4

3 0212 4.2   **18** 0139 4.2
0801 0.8   0730 0.7
F 1418 4.2   SA 1347 4.2
2034 0.5   1957 0.4

4 0245 4.0   **19** 0213 4.1
0835 0.8   0807 0.7
SA 1451 4.1   SU 1423 4.2
2106 0.6   2031 0.5

5 0317 3.8   **20** 0252 4.0
0911 0.9   0847 0.6
SU 1527 3.9   M 1504 4.0
2140 0.8   2111 0.7

6 0352 3.6   **21** 0336 3.5
0953 1.1   0936 1.0
M 1610 3.7   TU 1557 3.8
2222 1.1   2202 1.0

7 0435 3.5   **22** 0434 3.4
1048 1.2   1043 1.1
TU 1705 3.4   W 1709 3.5
2322 1.3   2320 1.3

8 0535 3.3   **23** 0553 3.2
1203 1.4   1220 1.2
W 1821 3.2   TH 1845 3.4

9 0038 1.5   **24** 0106 1.4
0701 3.2   0727 3.3
TH 1329 1.3   F 1403 1.1
1951 3.2   2017 3.5

10 0158 1.5   **25** 0235 1.3
0825 3.4   0847 3.5
F 1449 1.2   SA 1520 0.8
2104 3.4   2129 3.8

11 0308 1.3   **26** 0337 1.1
0927 3.6   0948 3.8
SA 1549 1.0   SU 1618 0.5
2201 3.7   2226 4.1

12 0400 1.2   **27** 0425 0.9
1017 3.8   1040 4.1
SU 1635 0.8   M 1705 0.3
2248 3.9   2314 4.3

13 0442 1.0   **28** 0507 0.8
1101 4.0   1125 4.2
M 1713 0.7   TU 1747 0.3
2328 4.0   O 2357 4.4

14 0517 1.0   **29** 0546 0.7
1138 4.0   1206 4.3
TU 1748 0.6   W 1824 0.3
●

15 0003 4.1   **30** 0034 4.3
0550 0.9   0623 0.7
W 1213 4.1   TH 1242 4.3
1821 0.4   1857 0.4

OCTOBER

Time m   Time m

1 0108 4.2   **16** 0039 4.3
0658 0.7   0632 0.6
F 1314 4.2   SA 1250 4.3
1927 0.5   1859 0.4

2 0138 4.1   **17** 0114 4.3
0732 0.7   0710 0.6
SA 1345 4.1   SU 1327 4.3
1955 0.6   1934 0.5

3 0206 4.0   **18** 0151 4.1
0803 0.8   0750 0.6
SU 1416 4.0   M 1407 4.2
2023 0.7   2011 0.7

4 0233 3.9   **19** 0231 4.0
0836 0.9   0834 0.7
M 1451 3.9   TU 1454 4.0
2054 0.9   2054 0.9

5 0305 3.7   **20** 0317 3.7
0915 1.0   0930 0.9
TU 1532 3.6   W 1554 3.7
2132 1.1   ◑ 2152 1.2

6 0346 3.5   **21** 0418 3.4
1011 1.2   1050 1.0
W 1625 3.4   TH 1714 3.5
◑ 2231 1.4   2317 1.5

7 0443 3.3   **22** 0545 3.3
1128 1.3   1226 1.1
TH 1735 3.2   F 1844 3.5
2354 1.6

8 0603 3.2   **23** 0051 1.5
1248 1.3   0712 3.3
F 1906 3.2   SA 1355 0.9
2004 3.6

9 0115 1.6   **24** 0215 1.4
0707 3.3   0824 3.6
SA 1406 1.2   SU 1503 0.6
2026 3.4   2110 3.9

10 0230 1.4   **25** 0314 1.1
0846 3.5   0923 3.8
SU 1508 1.0   M 1555 0.4
2125 3.6   2203 4.1

11 0326 1.3   **26** 0401 0.9
0938 3.7   1013 4.0
M 1555 0.8   TU 1639 0.4
2212 3.9   2248 4.2

12 0407 1.1   **27** 0442 0.8
1022 3.9   1057 4.1
TU 1635 0.6   W 1718 0.4
2252 4.1   2329 4.2

13 0444 1.0   **28** 0521 0.7
1101 4.0   1137 4.2
W 1713 0.5   TH 1753 0.5
2329 4.2   O

14 0520 0.8   **29** 0006 4.2
1138 4.1   0558 0.7
TH 1749 0.5   F 1213 4.1
●   1824 0.6

15 0004 4.3   **30** 0038 4.1
0555 0.7   0633 0.7
F 1214 4.2   SA 1245 4.1
1825 0.4   1853 0.7

31 0106 4.0
0706 0.7
SU 1316 4.0
1921 0.8

NOVEMBER

Time m   Time m

1 0131 3.9   **16** 0135 4.1
0737 0.7   0742 0.5
M 1348 3.9   TU 1359 4.2
1949 0.9   2001 0.8

2 0159 3.9   **17** 0219 3.9
0810 0.8   0833 0.6
TU 1424 3.8   W 1453 4.0
2019 1.0   2050 1.0

3 0231 3.8   **18** 0309 3.7
0849 0.9   0937 0.7
W 1505 3.6   TH 1557 3.8
2056 1.2   2151 1.2

4 0313 3.6   **19** 0414 3.5
0945 1.1   1055 0.8
TH 1556 3.4   F 1710 3.6
2150 1.4   ◑ 2304 1.4

5 0408 3.4   **20** 0530 3.4
1057 1.2   1214 0.8
F 1658 3.3   SA 1823 3.6
◑ 2308 1.5

6 0519 3.3   **21** 0022 1.5
1207 1.2   0642 3.5
SA 1811 3.3   SU 1329 0.7
1933 3.7

7 0024 1.6   **22** 0138 1.4
0639 3.3   0749 3.6
SU 1314 1.1   M 1432 0.6
1928 3.4   2036 3.8

8 0135 1.5   **23** 0240 1.2
0750 3.4   0849 3.8
M 1415 0.9   TU 1524 0.5
2033 3.6   2130 3.9

9 0235 1.3   **24** 0331 1.0
0848 3.6   0941 3.9
TU 1507 0.8   W 1608 0.5
2125 3.8   2216 4.0

10 0323 1.1   **25** 0415 0.8
0936 3.8   1027 4.0
W 1553 0.6   TH 1646 0.6
2210 4.0   2258 4.0

11 0406 1.0   **26** 0457 0.7
1021 4.0   1109 4.0
TH 1636 0.5   F 1721 0.7
2252 4.1   O 2336 4.0

12 0448 0.8   **27** 0536 0.7
1103 4.1   1147 4.0
F 1718 0.5   SA 1754 0.7
● 2333 4.2

13 0531 0.7   **28** 0010 3.9
1146 4.1   0613 0.7
SA 1759 0.5   SU 1223 3.9
1825 0.8

14 0013 4.2   **29** 0040 3.9
0613 0.6   0647 0.7
SU 1229 4.3   M 1256 3.9
1839 0.5   1855 0.9

15 0054 4.2   **30** 0107 3.9
0657 0.5   0720 0.7
M 1312 4.3   TU 1329 3.8
1919 0.4   1925 0.9

DECEMBER

Time m   Time m

1 0136 3.8   **16** 0213 4.0
0753 0.8   0837 0.6
W 1405 3.7   TH 1450 4.1
1956 1.0   2044 1.0

2 0210 3.8   **17** 0304 3.9
0833 0.8   0936 0.5
TH 1445 3.6   F 1548 4.0
2033 1.1   2138 1.1

3 0251 3.7   **18** 0400 3.8
0922 0.9   1040 0.5
F 1531 3.5   SA 1647 3.8
2120 1.3   ◑ 2237 1.2

4 0341 3.5   **19** 0500 3.7
1021 1.0   1143 0.6
SA 1624 3.5   SU 1748 3.7
2220 1.4   2339 1.3

5 0440 3.4   **20** 0602 3.6
1121 1.0   1247 0.7
SU 1724 3.4   M 1851 3.6
◑ 2325 1.4

6 0545 3.3   **21** 0048 1.3
1221 1.0   0706 3.6
M 1828 3.4   TU 1350 0.7
1953 3.6

7 0031 1.4   **22** 0157 1.2
0652 3.4   0809 3.6
TU 1322 0.9   W 1445 0.8
1934 3.5   2051 3.6

8 0136 1.3   **23** 0257 1.1
0755 3.5   0907 3.7
W 1420 0.8   TH 1533 0.8
2035 3.7   2142 3.7

9 0235 1.1   **24** 0349 0.9
0852 3.7   0959 3.8
TH 1514 0.7   F 1615 0.8
2128 3.8   2228 3.8

10 0329 1.0   **25** 0436 0.8
0944 3.9   1046 3.8
F 1603 0.6   SA 1653 0.9
2218 4.0   2311 3.8

11 0420 0.8   **26** 0520 0.7
1034 4.1   1129 3.8
SA 1652 0.6   SU 1730 0.9
2306 4.1   O 2349 3.8

12 0511 0.7   **27** 0600 0.7
1124 4.2   1209 3.8
SU 1739 0.6   M 1804 0.9
● 2352 4.1

13 0601 0.5   **28** 0023 3.8
1214 4.3   0635 0.6
M 1825 0.6   TU 1244 3.8
1836 0.9

14 0039 4.1   **29** 0054 3.8
0651 0.4   0708 0.7
TU 1304 4.3   W 1317 3.8
1910 0.7   1907 0.9

15 0125 4.1   **30** 0124 3.8
0742 0.4   0740 0.7
W 1356 4.2   TH 1350 3.8
1956 0.8   1939 1.0

31 0157 3.8
0816 0.7
F 1426 3.7
2014 1.0

Chapter 5

Chart Datum: 2·16 metres below Ordnance Datum (Newlyn)

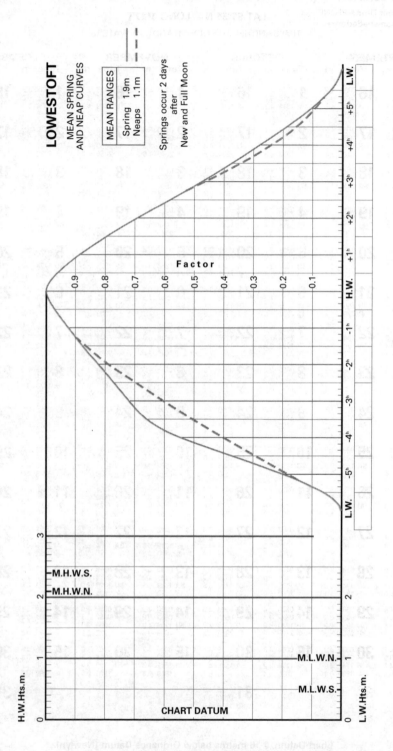

LOWESTOFT
MEAN SPRING
AND NEAP CURVES

MEAN RANGES
Spring 1.9m
Neaps 1.1m

Springs occur 2 days
after
New and Full Moon

ENGLAND – LOWESTOFT

LAT 52°28'N   LONG 1°45'E

TIMES AND HEIGHTS OF HIGH AND LOW WATERS

YEAR 2004

TIME ZONE (UT)
For Summer Time add ONE hour in **non-shaded areas**

JANUARY

Day	Time m	Day	Time m
1 TH	0348 2.3 / 1052 0.8 / 1741 2.1 / 2255 1.4	**16** F	0256 2.4 / 0949 0.7 / 1630 2.1 / 2141 1.2
2 F	0457 2.2 / 1149 0.9 / 1835 2.1	**17** SA	0403 2.4 / 1059 0.7 / 1738 2.1 / 2306 1.1
3 SA	0006 1.3 / 0600 2.2 / 1239 0.9 / 1921 2.2	**18** SU	0525 2.3 / 1206 0.7 / 1833 2.2
4 SU	0102 1.2 / 0700 2.2 / 1323 0.9 / 1958 2.3	**19** M	0026 1.0 / 0634 2.4 / 1306 0.8 / 1924 2.3
5 M	0148 1.1 / 0756 2.2 / 1401 1.0 / 2030 2.3	**20** TU	0134 0.9 / 0740 2.4 / 1403 0.8 / 2012 2.4
6 TU	0230 1.0 / 0844 2.2 / 1435 1.0 / 2058 2.4	**21** W	0237 0.7 / 0844 2.5 / 1457 0.8 / ● 2100 2.5
7 W	0308 0.9 / 0924 2.2 / 1508 0.9 / ○ 2128 2.4	**22** TH	0334 0.5 / 0942 2.5 / 1547 0.8 / 2146 2.5
8 TH	0347 0.8 / 1001 2.3 / 1543 0.9 / 2202 2.5	**23** F	0425 0.3 / 1034 2.5 / 1632 0.8 / 2231 2.6
9 F	0426 0.7 / 1037 2.3 / 1620 0.9 / 2239 2.5	**24** SA	0512 0.3 / 1122 2.4 / 1713 0.8 / 2315 2.6
10 SA	0507 0.7 / 1115 2.3 / 1658 0.9 / 2317 2.5	**25** SU	0556 0.3 / 1208 2.3 / 1751 0.9 / 2358 2.6
11 SU	0548 0.6 / 1153 2.2 / 1737 0.9 / 2357 2.5	**26** M	0639 0.3 / 1253 2.2 / 1826 0.9
12 M	0629 0.6 / 1233 2.2 / 1817 1.0	**27** TU	0039 2.5 / 0720 0.5 / 1340 2.1 / 1901 1.0
13 TU	0037 2.5 / 0711 0.6 / 1316 2.2 / 1858 1.0	**28** W	0120 2.5 / 0802 0.6 / 1431 2.0 / 1940 1.1
14 W	0119 2.4 / 0755 0.6 / 1404 2.1 / 1944 1.1	**29** TH	0204 2.3 / 0849 0.8 / 1534 2.1 / ◐ 2026 1.2
15 TH	0204 2.4 / 0847 0.7 / 1503 2.1 / ◑ 2037 1.1	**30** F	0256 2.2 / 0948 0.9 / 1639 2.0 / 2128 1.3
		31 SA	0408 2.1 / 1101 1.0 / 1737 2.0 / 2314 1.3

FEBRUARY

Day	Time m	Day	Time m
1 SU	0527 2.1 / 1204 1.1 / 1833 2.1	**16** M	0519 2.2 / 1151 1.0 / 1805 2.1
2 M	0031 1.2 / 0642 2.1 / 1256 1.1 / 1923 2.2	**17** TU	0020 0.9 / 0639 2.3 / 1300 1.0 / 1903 2.2
3 TU	0126 1.0 / 0753 2.1 / 1340 1.1 / 2003 2.2	**18** W	0133 0.7 / 0754 2.3 / 1401 0.9 / 1958 2.3
4 W	0212 0.9 / 0841 2.2 / 1418 1.0 / 2037 2.3	**19** TH	0235 0.5 / 0852 2.4 / 1453 0.9 / 2046 2.4
5 TH	0253 0.8 / 0917 2.2 / 1454 1.0 / 2110 2.4	**20** F	0327 0.4 / 0939 2.4 / 1537 0.8 / ● 2131 2.5
6 F	0333 0.7 / 0950 2.3 / 1531 0.9 / ○ 2145 2.4	**21** SA	0412 0.3 / 1021 2.4 / 1617 0.7 / 2213 2.6
7 SA	0413 0.6 / 1023 2.3 / 1609 0.8 / 2222 2.5	**22** SU	0453 0.2 / 1101 2.4 / 1652 0.7 / 2254 2.6
8 SU	0453 0.5 / 1058 2.3 / 1647 0.8 / 2259 2.5	**23** M	0532 0.3 / 1139 2.3 / 1726 0.7 / 2333 2.6
9 M	0532 0.4 / 1133 2.3 / 1724 0.8 / 2336 2.5	**24** TU	0608 0.4 / 1215 2.2 / 1757 0.8
10 TU	0609 0.4 / 1210 2.3 / 1759 0.8	**25** W	0010 2.5 / 0641 0.5 / 1250 2.1 / 1829 0.8
11 W	0013 2.5 / 0646 0.5 / 1249 2.2 / 1835 0.9	**26** TH	0048 2.4 / 0714 0.7 / 1324 2.1 / 1904 0.9
12 TH	0053 2.5 / 0725 0.5 / 1331 2.1 / 1916 0.9	**27** F	0129 2.3 / 0749 0.8 / 1404 2.0 / 1946 1.0
13 F	0137 2.5 / 0810 0.6 / 1421 2.1 / ◑ 2006 1.0	**28** SA	0218 2.2 / 0831 1.0 / 1456 2.0 / ◐ 2040 1.2
14 SA	0230 2.4 / 0907 0.8 / 1530 2.0 / 2109 1.0	**29** SU	0327 2.0 / 0935 1.2 / 1618 2.0 / 2209 1.2
15 SU	0344 2.3 / 1028 0.9 / 1659 2.0 / 2246 1.1		

MARCH

Day	Time m	Day	Time m
1 M	0504 2.0 / 1130 1.3 / 1732 2.0	**16** TU	0533 2.2 / 1146 1.1 / 1738 2.1
2 TU	0001 1.1 / 0628 2.0 / 1236 1.2 / 1834 2.1	**17** W	0019 0.8 / 0658 2.2 / 1258 1.1 / 1844 2.1
3 W	0100 1.0 / 0739 2.1 / 1324 1.2 / 1927 2.1	**18** TH	0128 0.6 / 0803 2.3 / 1356 1.0 / 1942 2.2
4 TH	0147 0.8 / 0823 2.2 / 1402 1.1 / 2008 2.2	**19** F	0224 0.4 / 0847 2.4 / 1442 0.9 / 2029 2.4
5 F	0230 0.7 / 0857 2.2 / 1438 0.9 / 2045 2.3	**20** SA	0310 0.3 / 0925 2.4 / 1520 0.8 / ● 2110 2.5
6 SA	0310 0.6 / 0928 2.3 / 1515 0.8 / ○ 2121 2.4	**21** SU	0350 0.3 / 1000 2.3 / 1555 0.7 / 2150 2.5
7 SU	0349 0.4 / 1000 2.3 / 1552 0.7 / 2157 2.5	**22** M	0427 0.3 / 1034 2.3 / 1628 0.6 / 2229 2.5
8 M	0429 0.3 / 1033 2.4 / 1629 0.6 / 2234 2.6	**23** TU	0501 0.3 / 1107 2.3 / 1659 0.6 / 2307 2.5
9 TU	0507 0.3 / 1108 2.3 / 1705 0.6 / 2312 2.6	**24** W	0533 0.4 / 1138 2.2 / 1730 0.7 / 2343 2.4
10 W	0544 0.3 / 1144 2.3 / 1740 0.7 / 2350 2.6	**25** TH	0602 0.6 / 1209 2.2 / 1801 0.7
11 TH	0620 0.4 / 1222 2.3 / 1816 0.7	**26** F	0019 2.3 / 0629 0.7 / 1241 2.2 / 1834 0.8
12 F	0032 2.5 / 0657 0.5 / 1304 2.2 / 1858 0.8	**27** SA	0100 2.2 / 0659 0.9 / 1318 2.1 / 1915 0.9
13 SA	0120 2.4 / 0741 0.7 / 1349 2.1 / ◑ 1949 0.8	**28** SU	0148 2.1 / 0736 1.1 / 1404 2.0 / ◐ 2006 1.0
14 SU	0220 2.3 / 0837 0.9 / 1454 2.0 / 2058 0.9	**29** M	0255 2.0 / 0827 1.3 / 1503 2.0 / 2122 1.1
15 M	0353 2.2 / 1009 1.1 / 1621 2.0 / 2252 0.9	**30** TU	0445 2.0 / 0959 1.4 / 1628 2.0 / 2323 1.0
		31 W	0603 2.0 / 1207 1.3 / 1744 2.0

APRIL

Day	Time m	Day	Time m
1 TH	0023 0.9 / 0706 2.1 / 1254 1.2 / 1842 2.1	**16** F	0109 0.5 / 0749 2.3 / 1336 1.0 / 1918 2.2
2 F	0111 0.8 / 0751 2.2 / 1333 1.1 / 1929 2.2	**17** SA	0201 0.4 / 0829 2.3 / 1419 0.9 / 2005 2.3
3 SA	0155 0.6 / 0826 2.3 / 1410 0.9 / 2010 2.3	**18** SU	0244 0.4 / 0902 2.3 / 1455 0.9 / 2046 2.4
4 SU	0237 0.5 / 0858 2.3 / 1448 0.8 / 2048 2.4	**19** M	0321 0.4 / 0934 2.3 / 1529 0.7 / ● 2126 2.4
5 M	0319 0.4 / 0931 2.4 / 1527 0.7 / ○ 2127 2.5	**20** TU	0356 0.4 / 1005 2.3 / 1602 0.6 / 2204 2.4
6 TU	0359 0.2 / 1006 2.4 / 1606 0.6 / 2207 2.6	**21** W	0428 0.5 / 1036 2.3 / 1635 0.6 / 2242 2.4
7 W	0438 0.2 / 1042 2.4 / 1644 0.5 / 2248 2.6	**22** TH	0457 0.6 / 1105 2.3 / 1706 0.7 / 2318 2.3
8 TH	0517 0.3 / 1119 2.4 / 1723 0.5 / 2331 2.6	**23** F	0523 0.7 / 1135 2.2 / 1738 0.7 / 2355 2.2
9 F	0555 0.4 / 1159 2.3 / 1804 0.6	**24** SA	0549 0.8 / 1207 2.3 / 1812 0.8
10 SA	0018 2.5 / 0635 0.6 / 1242 2.2 / 1850 0.6	**25** SU	0036 2.1 / 0620 1.0 / 1245 2.1 / 1852 0.8
11 SU	0114 2.4 / 0721 0.9 / 1331 2.2 / 1948 0.7	**26** M	0123 2.1 / 0659 1.1 / 1329 2.1 / 1943 0.9
12 M	0228 2.2 / 0821 1.1 / 1434 2.1 / ◑ 2111 0.8	**27** TU	0226 2.0 / 0748 1.3 / 1423 2.1 / ◐ 2052 1.0
13 TU	0414 2.2 / 0959 1.2 / 1553 2.1 / 2251 0.7	**28** W	0416 2.4 / 0854 1.4 / 1528 2.0 / 2230 0.9
14 W	0541 2.2 / 1134 1.2 / 1711 2.0 / 2337 0.8	**29** TH	0528 2.0 / 1047 1.4 / 1647 2.0 / 2337 0.8
15 TH	0005 0.6 / 0656 2.3 / 1242 1.1 / 1820 2.1	**30** F	0624 2.1 / 1159 1.2 / 1752 2.1

Chart Datum: 1·50 metres below Ordnance Datum (Newlyn)

Chapter 5

TIME ZONE (UT)
For Summer Time add ONE hour in **non-shaded areas**

ENGLAND – LOWESTOFT
LAT 52°28′N   LONG 1°45′E
TIMES AND HEIGHTS OF HIGH AND LOW WATERS

YEAR 2004

MAY

Time	m		Time	m
1 0027	0.7		**16** 0129	0.5
0711	2.2		0802	2.3
SA 1248	1.1		SU 1348	1.0
1844	2.2		1938	2.3
2 0115	0.5		**17** 0212	0.5
0750	2.3		0837	2.3
SU 1332	1.0		M 1427	0.9
1930	2.3		2022	2.3
3 0201	0.4		**18** 0249	0.6
0826	2.3		0908	2.3
M 1416	0.8		TU 1504	0.8
2014	2.4		2103	2.3
4 0245	0.3		**19** 0323	0.6
0902	2.4		0938	2.3
TU 1459	0.7		W 1539	0.7
○ 2058	2.5		● 2143	2.3
5 0329	0.3		**20** 0354	0.7
0939	2.4		1007	2.4
W 1543	0.6		TH 1613	0.7
2143	2.6		2222	2.3
6 0411	0.3		**21** 0422	0.7
1017	2.4		1036	2.4
TH 1627	0.5		F 1647	0.7
2230	2.6		2300	2.2
7 0453	0.4		**22** 0449	0.8
1058	2.4		1107	2.4
F 1712	0.5		SA 1721	0.7
2319	2.6		2338	2.2
8 0536	0.6		**23** 0519	0.9
1140	2.4		1141	2.3
SA 1759	0.5		SU 1758	0.7
9 0014	2.4		**24** 0018	2.1
0620	0.8		0553	1.0
SU 1226	2.3		M 1220	2.3
1852	0.5		1839	0.8
10 0118	2.3		**25** 0104	2.1
0709	1.0		0634	1.1
M 1318	2.3		TU 1305	2.2
1956	0.5		1928	0.8
11 0241	2.2		**26** 0158	2.0
0809	1.2		0723	1.2
TU 1419	2.2		W 1354	2.2
◑ 2114	0.6		2028	0.8
12 0411	2.2		**27** 0314	2.0
0933	1.3		0820	1.3
W 1529	2.2		TH 1449	2.1
2232	0.5		◑ 2138	0.8
13 0526	2.2		**28** 0442	2.0
1100	1.3		0930	1.3
TH 1642	2.2		F 1549	2.1
2338	0.5		2246	0.7
14 0631	2.1		**29** 0539	2.1
1207	1.2		1050	1.3
F 1749	2.2		SA 1657	2.2
			2343	0.6
15 0037	0.5		**30** 0628	2.2
0722	2.3		1157	1.2
SA 1303	1.1		SU 1759	2.2
1848	2.2			
			31 0036	0.5
			0712	2.2
			M 1253	1.0
			1852	2.3

JUNE

Time	m		Time	m
1 0126	0.5		**16** 0218	0.8
0753	2.3		0844	2.3
TU 1344	0.9		W 1443	0.9
1944	2.4		2049	2.2
2 0215	0.4		**17** 0253	0.8
0834	2.4		0914	2.3
W 1435	0.7		TH 1521	0.8
2034	2.5		● 2132	2.2
3 0303	0.4		**18** 0325	0.9
0914	2.4		0943	2.4
TH 1525	0.6		F 1558	0.7
○ 2126	2.6		2211	2.2
4 0350	0.4		**19** 0355	0.9
0957	2.5		1013	2.4
F 1615	0.5		SA 1634	0.7
2220	2.6		2249	2.2
5 0436	0.5		**20** 0426	0.9
1040	2.5		1046	2.4
SA 1706	0.4		SU 1711	0.7
2316	2.5		2326	2.2
6 0522	0.7		**21** 0500	0.9
1126	2.5		1123	2.4
SU 1759	0.3		M 1750	0.7
7 0014	2.4		**22** 0004	2.2
0609	0.8		0537	1.0
M 1215	2.4		TU 1203	2.4
1853	0.3		1830	0.7
8 0118	2.3		**23** 0045	2.1
0657	1.0		0618	1.0
TU 1306	2.4		W 1244	2.4
1952	0.4		1914	0.7
9 0232	2.2		**24** 0129	2.1
0750	1.1		0702	1.1
W 1400	2.4		TH 1328	2.3
○ 2055	0.4		2002	0.7
10 0348	2.2		**25** 0218	2.1
0851	1.2		0751	1.1
TH 1500	2.3		F 1414	2.3
2201	0.5		◑ 2055	0.7
11 0454	2.2		**26** 0323	2.0
1006	1.3		0846	1.2
F 1606	2.2		SA 1504	2.3
2304	0.6		2156	0.7
12 0555	2.2		**27** 0447	2.1
1119	1.2		0950	1.2
SA 1713	2.2		SU 1605	2.3
			2300	0.7
13 0001	0.6		**28** 0546	2.1
0648	2.2		1106	1.2
SU 1222	1.2		M 1718	2.3
1814	2.2			
14 0053	0.7		**29** 0001	0.6
0733	2.2		0636	2.2
M 1315	1.1		TU 1218	1.1
1910	2.4		1822	2.3
15 0138	0.7		**30** 0057	0.6
0811	2.3		0724	2.3
TU 1401	1.0		W 1300	0.9
2002	2.2		1922	2.4

JULY

Time	m		Time	m
1 0151	0.6		**16** 0230	1.0
0809	2.4		0852	2.3
TH 1418	0.8		F 1508	0.8
2021	2.5		2128	2.2
2 0243	0.6		**17** 0304	1.0
0854	2.4		0922	2.4
F 1515	0.6		SA 1546	0.7
○ 2120	2.5		● 2204	2.2
3 0335	0.6		**18** 0337	1.0
0940	2.5		0954	2.4
SA 1610	0.4		SU 1622	0.7
2218	2.5		2237	2.2
4 0424	0.7		**19** 0411	0.9
1026	2.5		1029	2.5
SU 1702	0.3		M 1659	0.6
2313	2.5		2310	2.2
5 0511	0.8		**20** 0447	0.9
1113	2.6		1106	2.5
M 1753	0.2		TU 1737	0.6
			2344	2.2
6 0007	2.4		**21** 0524	0.9
0555	0.8		1143	2.5
TU 1200	2.6		W 1815	0.6
1842	0.2			
7 0102	2.3		**22** 0020	2.2
0638	0.9		0601	0.9
W 1247	2.5		TH 1221	2.5
1931	0.3		1852	0.6
8 0201	2.2		**23** 0059	2.2
0721	1.0		0640	1.0
TH 1334	2.5		F 1300	2.5
2023	0.4		1931	0.6
9 0307	2.1		**24** 0140	2.1
0806	1.1		0721	1.0
F 1424	2.4		SA 1341	2.4
◑ 2119	0.6		2015	0.6
10 0412	2.1		**25** 0229	2.1
0900	1.2		0809	1.1
SA 1523	2.3		SU 1428	2.4
2220	0.7		○ 2108	0.7
11 0510	2.1		**26** 0336	2.1
1014	1.3		0906	1.2
SU 1632	2.2		M 1526	2.3
2321	0.7		2216	0.8
12 0606	2.1		**27** 0501	2.1
1138	1.2		1022	1.2
M 1741	2.2		TU 1648	2.3
			2331	0.8
13 0017	0.9		**28** 0603	2.2
0658	2.2		1154	1.1
TU 1245	1.1		W 1806	2.3
1849	2.1			
14 0108	1.0		**29** 0036	0.8
0743	2.2		0656	2.3
W 1340	1.0		TH 1306	0.9
1955	2.1		1914	2.4
15 0152	1.0		**30** 0136	0.8
0820	2.3		0747	2.3
TH 1427	0.9		F 1410	0.7
2047	2.1		2022	2.4
			31 0233	0.8
			0836	2.4
			SA 1510	0.5
			○ 2122	2.5

AUGUST

Time	m		Time	m
1 0326	0.8		**16** 0322	1.0
0924	2.5		0932	2.5
SU 1604	0.3		M 1602	0.6
2214	2.5		● 2214	2.3
2 0413	0.8		**17** 0356	0.9
1010	2.6		1006	2.6
M 1652	0.2		TU 1638	0.5
2301	2.5		2245	2.3
3 0456	0.8		**18** 0431	0.8
1055	2.7		1042	2.6
TU 1737	0.2		W 1714	0.5
2347	2.4		2318	2.3
4 0535	0.8		**19** 0506	0.8
1138	2.7		1118	2.6
W 1820	0.2		TH 1749	0.5
			2352	2.3
5 0032	2.3		**20** 0541	0.8
0612	0.9		1154	2.6
TH 1221	2.6		F 1824	0.5
1901	0.3			
6 0117	2.2		**21** 0028	2.3
0648	0.9		0615	0.9
F 1303	2.6		SA 1232	2.6
1942	0.5		1859	0.6
7 0205	2.1		**22** 0108	2.2
0727	1.0		0654	0.9
SA 1347	2.4		SU 1312	2.6
◑ 2026	0.7		1939	0.7
8 0303	2.1		**23** 0153	2.2
0811	1.1		0740	1.0
SU 1439	2.3		M 1401	2.4
2119	0.9		◑ 2028	0.9
9 0409	2.0		**24** 0249	2.1
0910	1.2		0837	1.1
M 1550	2.2		TU 1506	2.3
2232	1.1		2136	1.0
10 0510	2.1		**25** 0411	2.1
1051	1.3		1000	1.1
TU 1714	2.1		W 1641	2.3
2344	1.2		2311	1.1
11 0609	2.1		**26** 0529	2.2
1219	1.2		1146	1.0
W 1837	2.1		TH 1808	2.3
12 0044	1.2		**27** 0026	1.1
0705	2.2		0630	2.3
TH 1320	1.0		F 1301	0.8
1951	2.1		1925	2.4
13 0135	1.2		**28** 0130	1.0
0750	2.3		0727	2.4
F 1409	0.9		SA 1406	0.6
2039	2.2		2028	2.4
14 0215	1.1		**29** 0226	1.0
0826	2.3		0818	2.5
SA 1449	0.8		SU 1502	0.4
2114	2.2		2117	2.5
15 0249	1.1		**30** 0314	0.9
0858	2.4		0905	2.6
SU 1526	0.7		M 1549	0.3
2145	2.3		○ 2159	2.5
			31 0355	0.6
			0949	2.7
			TU 1632	0.2
			2239	2.5

Chart Datum: 1·50 metres below Ordnance Datum (Newlyn)

ENGLAND – LOWESTOFT

LAT 52°28'N   LONG 1°45'E

TIMES AND HEIGHTS OF HIGH AND LOW WATERS

YEAR **2004**

SEPTEMBER

Day	Time m	Time m	Time m	Time m
1 W	0433 0.8	1031 2.7	1712 0.2	2318 2.4
16 TH	0408 0.8	1013 2.7	1644 0.4	2248 2.4
2 TH	0509 0.8	1112 2.7	1749 0.3	2356 2.3
17 F	0443 0.8	1050 2.7	1719 0.4	2323 2.4
3 F	0543 0.8	1152 2.7	1824 0.5	
18 SA	0518 0.8	1127 2.7	1754 0.5	2359 2.4
4 SA	0033 2.3	0617 0.9	1232 2.5	1858 0.7
19 SU	0554 0.8	1207 2.6	1829 0.6	
5 SU	0109 2.2	0653 1.0	1314 2.4	1933 0.9
20 M	0039 2.3	0633 0.9	1252 2.5	1909 0.8
6 M	0148 2.1	0735 1.1	1403 2.3	2013 1.1
21 TU	0124 2.3	0722 0.9	1348 2.4	○ 2000 1.0
7 TU	0238 2.1	0829 1.2	1515 2.1	2110 1.3
22 W	0220 2.2	0826 1.0	1507 2.3	2111 1.2
8 W	0351 2.1	1000 1.3	1654 2.1	2313 1.4
23 TH	0335 2.2	1008 1.0	1655 2.3	2302 1.3
9 TH	0508 2.1	1152 1.2	1821 2.1	
24 F	0457 2.2	1143 0.9	1822 2.3	
10 F	0025 1.3	0611 2.2	1252 1.0	1930 2.2
25 SA	0019 1.2	0605 2.3	1253 0.7	1932 2.4
11 SA	0116 1.3	0706 2.3	1338 0.9	2014 2.3
26 SU	0122 1.1	0705 2.4	1353 0.5	2021 2.5
12 SU	0154 1.2	0749 2.3	1418 0.8	2047 2.3
27 M	0212 1.0	0756 2.5	1443 0.4	2101 2.5
13 M	0226 1.1	0826 2.4	1455 0.6	2116 2.4
28 TU	0254 0.9	0841 2.6	1526 0.3	○ 2136 2.5
14 TU	0258 1.0	0901 2.5	1532 0.5	● 2145 2.4
29 W	0331 0.8	0924 2.7	1605 0.3	2212 2.5
15 W	0332 0.9	0937 2.6	1608 0.4	2215 2.4
30 TH	0407 0.8	1005 2.7	1641 0.4	2247 2.4

OCTOBER

Day	Time m	Time m	Time m	Time m
1 F	0442 0.7	1046 2.7	1714 0.5	2321 2.4
16 SA	0419 0.7	1023 2.7	1650 0.5	2255 2.5
2 SA	0515 0.8	1124 2.6	1745 0.7	2353 2.4
17 SU	0458 0.7	1105 2.7	1727 0.6	2334 2.5
3 SU	0549 0.9	1203 2.5	1814 0.8	
18 M	0539 0.7	1150 2.6	1806 0.7	
4 M	0025 2.3	0624 0.9	1245 2.3	1844 1.0
19 TU	0015 2.4	0624 0.8	1243 2.5	1850 0.9
5 TU	0102 2.3	0704 1.0	1334 2.2	1919 1.2
20 W	0103 2.3	0720 0.8	1349 2.3	● 1944 1.2
6 W	0147 2.2	0756 1.1	1446 2.1	○ 2006 1.4
21 TH	0200 2.3	0834 0.9	1527 2.3	2059 1.3
7 TH	0244 2.2	0915 1.2	1634 2.1	2121 1.5
22 F	0311 2.2	1012 0.8	1704 2.3	2246 1.4
8 F	0402 2.1	1114 1.1	1750 2.1	2353 1.5
23 SA	0429 2.3	1129 0.7	1819 2.4	
9 SA	0519 2.2	1211 1.0	1852 2.2	
24 SU	0000 1.3	0539 2.3	1233 0.6	1918 2.4
10 SU	0040 1.4	0617 2.3	1257 0.9	1937 2.3
25 M	0059 1.2	0639 2.4	1329 0.5	2002 2.4
11 M	0116 1.2	0705 2.3	1338 0.7	2011 2.4
26 TU	0147 1.1	0730 2.5	1416 0.5	2037 2.4
12 TU	0150 1.1	0746 2.4	1417 0.6	2041 2.4
27 W	0228 1.0	0816 2.6	1457 0.5	2110 2.5
13 W	0225 1.0	0825 2.5	1456 0.5	2112 2.5
28 TH	0305 0.9	0859 2.6	1533 0.5	○ 2143 2.5
14 TH	0303 0.9	0904 2.6	1534 0.4	● 2144 2.5
29 F	0341 0.9	0941 2.6	1607 0.6	2216 2.5
15 F	0341 0.8	0943 2.7	1612 0.4	2219 2.5
30 SA	0417 0.8	1021 2.6	1639 0.7	2248 2.5
31 SU	0452 0.8	1101 2.6	1707 0.8	2318 2.4

NOVEMBER

Day	Time m	Time m	Time m	Time m
1 M	0526 0.8	1139 2.4	1734 1.0	2350 2.4
16 TU	0533 0.6	1144 2.6	1751 0.9	2358 2.5
2 TU	0601 0.9	1221 2.3	1803 1.1	
17 W	0626 0.6	1244 2.4	1839 1.0	
3 W	0026 2.4	0641 1.0	1309 2.2	1839 1.2
18 TH	0048 2.4	0726 0.7	1357 2.3	1934 1.2
4 TH	0110 2.3	0731 1.0	1415 2.1	1926 1.4
19 F	0146 2.4	0838 0.7	1531 2.3	○ 2042 1.4
5 F	0203 2.2	0839 1.1	1600 2.1	○ 2026 1.5
20 SA	0250 2.3	0955 0.7	1650 2.3	2209 1.4
6 SA	0305 2.2	1014 1.1	1709 2.1	2153 1.5
21 SU	0401 2.3	1103 0.6	1756 2.3	2322 1.3
7 SU	0418 2.2	1120 1.0	1805 2.2	2331 1.4
22 M	0510 2.4	1204 0.6	1851 2.3	
8 M	0525 2.3	1209 0.8	1852 2.3	
23 TU	0023 1.2	0611 2.4	1259 0.6	1935 2.4
9 TU	0022 1.3	0618 2.3	1253 0.7	1930 2.3
24 W	0116 1.1	0705 2.4	1346 0.6	2012 2.4
10 W	0106 1.2	0705 2.4	1336 0.6	2005 2.4
25 TH	0201 1.0	0753 2.5	1426 0.7	2045 2.4
11 TH	0149 1.0	0749 2.5	1419 0.5	2039 2.5
26 F	0241 0.9	0839 2.5	1502 0.7	○ 2117 2.5
12 F	0232 0.9	0832 2.6	1501 0.5	● 2115 2.5
27 SA	0320 0.8	0923 2.4	1536 0.8	2149 2.5
13 SA	0316 0.8	0916 2.7	1543 0.5	2152 2.5
28 SU	0358 0.8	1005 2.4	1606 0.9	2219 2.5
14 SU	0400 0.7	1002 2.7	1625 0.5	2232 2.5
29 M	0434 0.8	1045 2.3	1634 0.9	2249 2.5
15 M	0445 0.6	1051 2.6	1707 0.7	2313 2.5
30 TU	0510 0.7	1124 2.3	1702 1.0	2322 2.5

DECEMBER

Day	Time m	Time m	Time m	Time m
1 W	0547 0.8	1204 2.2	1735 1.1	
16 TH	0627 0.4	1243 2.4	1830 1.0	
2 TH	0000 2.4	0627 0.9	1249 2.1	1814 1.2
17 F	0036 2.5	0723 0.4	1348 2.3	1918 1.1
3 F	0044 2.4	0713 0.9	1339 2.1	1859 1.3
18 SA	0128 2.5	0822 0.5	1506 2.3	◐ 2012 1.2
4 SA	0132 2.3	0807 0.9	1442 2.0	1952 1.3
19 SU	0224 2.4	0925 0.6	1619 2.2	2114 1.3
5 SU	0224 2.3	0910 0.9	1613 2.1	○ 2052 1.4
20 M	0326 2.4	1029 0.6	1721 2.2	2230 1.3
6 M	0320 2.3	1017 0.9	1714 2.1	2204 1.4
21 TU	0437 2.6	1130 0.7	1816 2.2	2342 1.3
7 TU	0424 2.3	1117 0.8	1804 2.2	2320 1.3
22 W	0543 2.3	1225 0.8	1906 2.2	
8 W	0530 2.3	1209 0.7	1849 2.3	
23 TH	0044 1.2	0643 2.3	1315 0.8	1947 2.3
9 TH	0022 1.3	0626 2.4	1259 0.6	1930 2.3
24 F	0138 1.0	0740 2.3	1359 0.9	2024 2.3
10 F	0116 1.1	0717 2.5	1347 0.6	2010 2.4
25 SA	0225 0.9	0832 2.3	1437 1.0	2057 2.4
11 SA	0207 0.9	0807 2.5	1434 0.6	2049 2.5
26 SU	0308 0.8	0919 2.3	1511 1.0	○ 2128 2.4
12 SU	0257 0.8	0859 2.6	1521 0.6	● 2131 2.5
27 M	0347 0.8	1001 2.3	1543 1.0	2158 2.5
13 M	0348 0.6	0952 2.6	1608 0.7	2214 2.5
28 TU	0425 0.8	1038 2.2	1612 1.0	2230 2.5
14 TU	0440 0.5	1047 2.6	1655 0.8	2259 2.6
29 W	0501 0.7	1114 2.2	1644 1.0	2305 2.5
15 W	0533 0.4	1144 2.5	1742 0.9	2346 2.6
30 TH	0537 0.7	1149 2.2	1719 1.0	2343 2.5
31 F	0615 0.7	1226 2.2	1757 1.0	

Chart Datum: 1·50 metres below Ordnance Datum (Newlyn)

Chapter 5

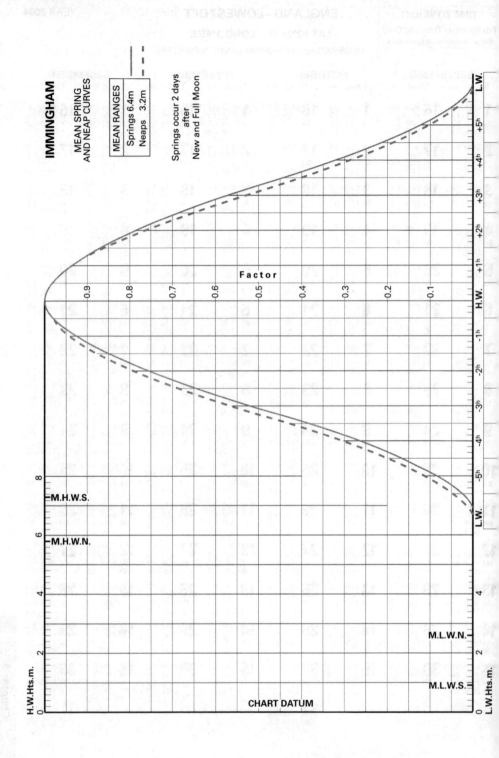

IMMINGHAM
MEAN SPRING
AND NEAP CURVES

MEAN RANGES
Springs 6.4m
Neaps 3.2m

Springs occur 2 days
after
New and Full Moon

Factor
0.9
0.8
0.7
0.6
0.5
0.4
0.3
0.2
0.1

L.W.
+5h
+4h
+3h
+2h
+1h
H.W.
-1h
-2h
-3h
-4h
-5h
L.W.

8
M.H.W.S.
6
M.H.W.N.
4
2
H.W.Hts.m.
0

M.L.W.N.
4
2
M.L.W.S.
L.W.Hts.m.

CHART DATUM

ENGLAND – IMMINGHAM

LAT 53°38′N   LONG 0°11′W

TIMES AND HEIGHTS OF HIGH AND LOW WATERS

YEAR **2004**

JANUARY

Day	Time	m	Time	m	Time	m	Time	m
1 TH	0019	6.0	0653	2.3	1325	5.7	1904	2.9
2 F	0125	5.9	0753	2.4	1422	5.8	2015	2.8
3 SA	0229	6.0	0851	2.4	1516	5.9	2119	2.6
4 SU	0327	6.1	0942	2.2	1603	6.2	2212	2.3
5 M	0417	6.2	1027	2.1	1643	6.4	2257	2.0
6 TU	0500	6.4	1109	1.9	1720	6.7	2339	1.8
7 W O	0540	6.5	1149	1.8	1756	6.8		
8 TH	0020	1.6	0618	6.6	1226	1.8	1831	6.9
9 F	0100	1.5	0657	6.7	1302	1.8	1906	6.9
10 SA	0138	1.5	0735	6.7	1337	1.8	1940	6.9
11 SU	0214	1.5	0814	6.6	1412	1.8	2014	6.9
12 M	0251	1.5	0852	6.5	1449	1.9	2050	6.8
13 TU	0330	1.6	0933	6.4	1530	2.0	2130	6.8
14 W	0412	1.7	1019	6.3	1615	2.2	2218	6.6
15 TH ◑	0501	1.8	1112	6.1	1708	2.3	2314	6.5
16 F	0600	2.0	1217	6.0	1813	2.5		
17 SA	0022	6.3	0709	2.1	1332	5.9	1931	2.5
18 SU	0144	6.3	0825	2.1	1443	6.1	2053	2.3
19 M	0304	6.4	1004	1.9	1547	6.4	2206	1.9
20 TU	0414	6.6	1035	1.7	1643	6.7	2309	1.5
21 W ●	0517	6.9	1130	1.5	1734	7.0		
22 TH	0005	1.1	0613	7.1	1221	1.4	1820	7.2
23 F	0058	0.9	0704	7.2	1308	1.3	1904	7.4
24 SA	0145	0.7	0751	7.1	1352	1.3	1946	7.4
25 SU	0229	0.8	0834	7.0	1432	1.5	2026	7.3
26 M	0309	1.0	0913	6.7	1509	1.7	2105	7.1
27 TU	0345	1.3	0950	6.4	1543	1.9	2143	6.8
28 W	0419	1.7	1027	6.1	1618	2.2	2225	6.4
29 TH ◐	0455	2.1	1109	5.8	1659	2.5	2314	6.0
30 F	0539	2.4	1203	5.6	1751	2.8		
31 SA	0018	5.7	0635	2.7	1312	5.5	1859	3.0

FEBRUARY

Day	Time	m	Time	m	Time	m	Time	m
1 SU	0136	5.6	0745	2.8	1423	5.6	2022	2.9
2 M	0251	5.6	0858	2.7	1526	5.8	2141	2.6
3 TU	0354	5.9	0959	2.4	1617	6.2	2237	2.2
4 W	0444	6.2	1048	2.2	1700	6.5	2324	1.8
5 TH	0526	6.4	1132	1.9	1738	6.7		
6 F ●	0007	1.6	0605	6.6	1213	1.8	1814	6.9
7 SA	0049	1.3	0644	6.8	1250	1.7	1850	7.0
8 SU	0128	1.2	0721	6.8	1326	1.6	1924	7.1
9 M	0204	1.1	0756	6.9	1400	1.5	1957	7.2
10 TU	0238	1.1	0832	6.8	1435	1.5	2032	7.2
11 W	0311	1.2	0908	6.7	1512	1.6	2110	7.1
12 TH	0345	1.3	0947	6.5	1551	1.8	2153	6.9
13 F ◑	0428	1.6	1032	6.2	1637	2.0	2245	6.6
14 SA	0520	2.0	1129	5.9	1736	2.4	2352	6.2
15 SU	0631	2.4	1249	5.7	1900	2.6		
16 M	0126	5.9	0801	2.5	1419	5.8	2042	2.5
17 TU	0304	6.0	0924	2.3	1534	6.1	2205	2.0
18 W	0422	6.4	1029	2.0	1635	6.5	2307	1.5
19 TH	0523	6.7	1123	1.7	1725	6.9		
20 F ●	0000	1.0	0613	7.0	1211	1.4	1808	7.2
21 SA	0048	0.7	0655	7.1	1255	1.2	1849	7.4
22 SU	0130	0.6	0733	7.1	1334	1.2	1927	7.5
23 M	0208	0.7	0808	7.0	1410	1.2	2003	7.4
24 TU	0241	0.9	0838	6.8	1441	1.4	2037	7.2
25 W	0309	1.2	0905	6.6	1509	1.6	2109	6.9
26 TH	0335	1.6	0931	6.3	1538	1.9	2141	6.5
27 F	0403	2.0	1002	6.0	1611	2.3	2218	6.1
28 SA	0441	2.4	1042	5.7	1657	2.6	2311	5.6
29 SU	0534	2.8	1150	5.4	1803	2.9		

MARCH

Day	Time	m	Time	m	Time	m	Time	m
1 M	0045	5.3	0648	3.1	1334	5.3	1927	3.0
2 TU	0220	5.4	0814	3.0	1451	5.6	2109	2.7
3 W	0332	5.7	0934	2.7	1550	6.0	2216	2.2
4 TH	0425	6.1	1030	2.3	1635	6.3	2304	1.8
5 F	0508	6.4	1114	2.0	1715	6.7	2347	1.4
6 SA O	0547	6.7	1154	1.7	1751	7.0		
7 SU	0028	1.1	0623	6.9	1232	1.5	1825	7.2
8 M	0107	0.9	0658	7.0	1308	1.3	1900	7.4
9 TU	0142	0.8	0732	7.1	1343	1.2	1935	7.5
10 W	0216	0.8	0805	7.1	1419	1.2	2011	7.5
11 TH	0249	0.9	0840	6.9	1454	1.3	2051	7.3
12 F	0323	1.2	0918	6.7	1532	1.5	2135	6.9
13 SA ◑	0402	1.7	1002	6.3	1616	1.9	2228	6.4
14 SU	0453	2.2	1058	5.9	1718	2.3	2343	5.9
15 M	0609	2.7	1224	5.6	1855	2.6		
16 TU	0138	5.7	0752	2.8	1405	5.7	2048	2.4
17 W	0315	5.9	0918	2.5	1523	6.1	2202	1.8
18 TH	0426	6.4	1019	2.1	1622	6.5	2257	1.3
19 F	0517	6.8	1109	1.6	1708	6.9	2344	0.9
20 SA ●	0558	7.0	1205	1.3	1749	7.2		
21 SU	0026	0.7	0633	7.1	1234	1.1	1827	7.3
22 M	0105	0.7	0705	7.1	1311	1.1	1903	7.4
23 TU	0139	0.8	0735	7.0	1344	1.1	1937	7.3
24 W	0208	1.0	0800	6.8	1412	1.3	2008	7.1
25 TH	0233	1.3	0824	6.7	1438	1.5	2036	6.8
26 F	0256	1.6	0847	6.4	1505	1.8	2105	6.4
27 SA	0323	2.0	0915	6.2	1536	2.1	2139	6.0
28 SU ◐	0356	2.4	0951	5.8	1618	2.5	2225	5.6
29 M	0444	2.8	1042	5.5	1724	2.8	2351	5.2
30 TU	0600	3.2	1236	5.2	1851	2.9		
31 W	0148	5.3	0732	3.2	1413	5.4	2025	2.7

APRIL

Day	Time	m	Time	m	Time	m	Time	m
1 TH	0303	5.6	0858	2.8	1514	5.8	2141	2.2
2 F	0357	6.1	0958	2.4	1601	6.3	2232	1.7
3 SA	0441	6.5	1044	2.0	1641	6.7	2316	1.2
4 SU	0519	6.8	1125	1.6	1719	7.0	2358	0.9
5 M O	0555	7.0	1205	1.3	1755	7.3		
6 TU	0037	0.7	0629	7.2	1244	1.1	1833	7.5
7 W	0116	0.6	0704	7.3	1323	0.9	1912	7.6
8 TH	0152	0.7	0740	7.2	1402	0.9	1953	7.5
9 F	0228	0.9	0817	7.1	1440	1.1	2037	7.2
10 SA	0305	1.3	0857	6.8	1522	1.4	2125	6.8
11 SU	0347	1.8	0943	6.4	1612	1.8	2226	6.2
12 M ◑	0442	2.4	1044	5.9	1724	2.2		
13 TU	0000	5.7	0603	2.8	1216	5.7	1906	2.4
14 W	0146	5.7	0742	2.9	1350	5.8	2038	2.0
15 TH	0309	6.0	0859	2.5	1502	6.1	2142	1.6
16 F	0410	6.4	0956	2.1	1558	6.5	2233	1.2
17 SA	0455	6.7	1044	1.7	1643	6.9	2317	1.0
18 SU	0532	6.9	1127	1.4	1724	7.1	2357	0.9
19 M ●	0604	6.9	1207	1.2	1801	7.1		
20 TU	0033	0.9	0633	6.9	1243	1.2	1836	7.1
21 W	0105	1.1	0701	6.6	1316	1.2	1910	7.0
22 TH	0133	1.3	0726	6.8	1345	1.3	1941	6.8
23 F	0159	1.5	0750	6.7	1412	1.5	2010	6.6
24 SA	0225	1.7	0816	6.5	1441	1.7	2040	6.3
25 SU	0253	2.0	0845	6.3	1513	2.0	2116	6.0
26 M	0325	2.4	0921	6.0	1555	2.3	2203	5.6
27 TU ◐	0411	2.7	1009	5.6	1658	2.6	2317	5.3
28 W	0519	3.1	1129	5.4	1819	2.7		
29 TH	0103	5.3	0646	3.1	1316	5.5	1941	2.5
30 F	0220	5.6	0807	2.9	1424	5.8	2052	2.0

Chapter 5

TIME ZONE (UT)
For Summer Time add ONE hour in **non-shaded areas**

ENGLAND – IMMINGHAM

LAT 53°38′N   LONG 0°11′W

TIMES AND HEIGHTS OF HIGH AND LOW WATERS

YEAR 2004

MAY

Time m	Time m
1 0317 6.0 / 0911 2.5 / SA 1516 6.2 / 2149 1.6	**16** 0421 6.5 / 1013 1.8 / SU 1614 6.7 / 2242 1.3
2 0404 6.5 / 1004 2.0 / SU 1601 6.7 / 2238 1.2	**17** 0458 6.6 / 1057 1.6 / M 1656 6.8 / 2322 1.3
3 0444 6.8 / 1051 1.6 / M 1644 7.1 / 2323 0.9	**18** 0531 6.7 / 1138 1.4 / TU 1735 6.8 / 2358 1.3
4 0523 7.1 / 1136 1.2 / TU 1726 7.3 O	**19** 0601 6.8 / 1215 1.4 / W 1812 6.8 ●
5 0006 0.7 / 0600 7.2 / W 1220 1.0 / 1810 7.5	**20** 0031 1.4 / 0629 6.8 / TH 1250 1.4 / 1846 6.7
6 0049 0.7 / 0639 7.3 / TH 1304 0.8 / 1855 7.5	**21** 0103 1.5 / 0658 6.8 / F 1322 1.5 / 1919 6.6
7 0130 0.8 / 0719 7.3 / F 1348 0.8 / 1941 7.4	**22** 0132 1.7 / 0726 6.7 / SA 1354 1.6 / 1952 6.5
8 0211 1.0 / 0800 7.1 / SA 1433 1.0 / 2031 7.1	**23** 0202 1.8 / 0757 6.6 / SU 1426 1.7 / 2027 6.3
9 0254 1.4 / 0844 6.8 / SU 1522 1.3 / 2127 6.6	**24** 0232 2.0 / 0829 6.4 / M 1501 1.9 / 2106 6.1
10 0342 1.9 / 0935 6.5 / M 1620 1.6 / 2237 6.1	**25** 0308 2.3 / 0906 6.1 / TU 1544 2.1 / 2154 5.8
11 0440 2.4 / 1039 6.1 / TU 1732 1.9 ◐	**26** 0352 2.5 / 0952 5.9 / W 1640 2.3 / 2254 5.6
12 0009 5.9 / 0554 2.7 / W 1204 5.9 / 1855 2.0	**27** 0449 2.8 / 1055 5.7 / TH 1747 2.3 ◐
13 0129 5.9 / 0714 2.7 / TH 1323 6.0 / 2008 1.8	**28** 0010 5.6 / 0558 2.8 / F 1213 5.7 / 1857 2.2
14 0239 6.1 / 0825 2.5 / F 1430 6.2 / 2108 1.6	**29** 0125 5.7 / 0712 2.7 / SA 1325 5.9 / 2004 1.9
15 0337 6.3 / 0923 2.2 / SA 1526 6.5 / 2158 1.4	**30** 0227 6.0 / 0821 2.4 / SU 1426 6.3 / 2105 1.6
	31 0321 6.4 / 0923 2.1 / M 1522 6.6 / 2200 1.3

JUNE

Time m	Time m
1 0409 6.7 / 1018 1.7 / TU 1614 7.0 / 2251 1.1	**16** 0458 6.4 / 1110 1.8 / W 1712 6.4 / 2326 1.7
2 0454 7.0 / 1110 1.3 / W 1704 7.2 / 2339 0.9	**17** 0532 6.6 / 1151 1.6 / TH 1751 6.5 ●
3 0537 7.1 / 1200 1.0 / TH 1755 7.4 O	**18** 0003 1.7 / 0604 6.7 / F 1230 1.6 / 1827 6.5
4 0026 0.9 / 0620 7.3 / F 1250 0.9 / 1846 7.4	**19** 0039 1.7 / 0637 6.7 / SA 1307 1.6 / 1904 6.5
5 0113 1.0 / 0705 7.3 / SA 1340 0.8 / 1939 7.2	**20** 0113 1.8 / 0711 6.7 / SU 1343 1.6 / 1941 6.4
6 0200 1.2 / 0750 7.2 / SU 1431 0.9 / 2034 7.0	**21** 0146 1.9 / 0746 6.6 / M 1419 1.7 / 2018 6.4
7 0247 1.5 / 0838 7.0 / M 1524 1.1 / 2133 6.7	**22** 0219 2.0 / 0821 6.5 / TU 1456 1.7 / 2058 6.3
8 0336 1.8 / 0930 6.7 / TU 1620 1.3 / 2239 6.3	**23** 0255 2.1 / 0857 6.4 / W 1535 1.8 / 2140 6.1
9 0429 2.2 / 1029 6.4 / W 1720 1.5 ◑ 2347 6.1	**24** 0335 2.2 / 0937 6.3 / TH 1620 1.9 / 2229 6.0
10 0529 2.4 / 1136 6.2 / TH 1823 1.7	**25** 0422 2.4 / 1026 6.2 / F 1712 1.9 ◑ 2326 5.9
11 0052 6.0 / 0633 2.6 / F 1244 6.1 / 1926 1.8	**26** 0518 2.5 / 1125 6.1 / SA 1811 2.0
12 0153 6.0 / 0740 2.5 / SA 1348 6.1 / 2024 1.9	**27** 0031 5.9 / 0622 2.5 / SU 1232 6.2 / 1916 1.9
13 0250 6.0 / 0842 2.4 / SU 1448 6.2 / 2117 1.8	**28** 0138 6.0 / 0733 2.4 / M 1342 6.3 / 2023 1.8
14 0339 6.1 / 0937 2.2 / M 1541 6.3 / 2204 1.8	**29** 0241 6.2 / 0845 2.2 / TU 1450 6.5 / 2127 1.6
15 0421 6.3 / 1026 1.9 / TU 1629 6.4 / 2246 1.8	**30** 0339 6.5 / 0951 1.9 / W 1553 6.7 / 2225 1.4

JULY

Time m	Time m
1 0432 6.7 / 1051 1.5 / TH 1653 7.0 / 2320 1.3	**16** 0508 6.5 / 1133 1.8 / F 1734 6.3 / 2343 1.9
2 0521 7.0 / 1148 1.1 / F 1751 7.1 O	**17** 0545 6.6 / 1215 1.6 / SA 1813 6.4 ●
3 0012 1.2 / 0609 7.2 / SA 1244 0.9 / 1847 7.2	**18** 0023 1.8 / 0621 6.8 / SU 1256 1.5 / 1850 6.5
4 0103 1.2 / 0657 7.3 / SU 1337 0.7 / 1942 7.2	**19** 0100 1.8 / 0657 6.8 / M 1335 1.4 / 1928 6.6
5 0151 1.2 / 0743 7.3 / M 1428 0.7 / 2035 7.1	**20** 0135 1.8 / 0733 6.8 / TU 1412 1.4 / 2005 6.6
6 0237 1.4 / 0830 7.2 / TU 1516 0.8 / 2126 6.8	**21** 0207 1.8 / 0807 6.8 / W 1446 1.4 / 2042 6.5
7 0322 1.6 / 0917 7.0 / W 1604 1.0 / 2217 6.6	**22** 0241 1.8 / 0841 6.8 / TH 1520 1.5 / 2119 6.5
8 0407 1.9 / 1006 6.8 / TH 1651 1.3 / 2308 6.2	**23** 0316 1.9 / 0917 6.7 / F 1555 1.6 / 2158 6.3
9 0453 2.2 / 1059 6.5 / F 1739 1.7 ◑	**24** 0356 2.0 / 0958 6.6 / SA 1636 1.7 / 2244 6.2
10 0001 6.0 / 0542 2.4 / SA 1157 6.2 / 1830 2.0	**25** 0442 2.2 / 1048 6.4 / SU 1727 1.9 ◑ 2340 6.0
11 0057 5.8 / 0640 2.6 / SU 1259 6.0 / 1927 2.3	**26** 0540 2.4 / 1150 6.3 / M 1831 2.1
12 0154 5.7 / 0749 2.7 / M 1404 5.9 / 2028 2.4	**27** 0051 5.9 / 0651 2.5 / TU 1307 6.1 / 1948 2.2
13 0251 5.8 / 0859 2.6 / TU 1507 5.9 / 2125 2.3	**28** 0208 5.9 / 0816 2.4 / W 1432 6.2 / 2104 2.1
14 0343 6.0 / 0958 2.3 / W 1604 6.0 / 2215 2.2	**29** 0317 6.2 / 0937 2.1 / TH 1548 6.4 / 2211 1.9
15 0428 6.2 / 1048 2.0 / TH 1652 6.2 / 2300 2.1	**30** 0418 6.5 / 1045 1.6 / F 1655 6.7 / 2310 1.6
	31 0512 6.9 / 1145 1.1 / SA 1755 7.0 O

AUGUST

Time m	Time m
1 0003 1.4 / 0601 7.2 / SU 1240 0.8 / 1848 7.2	**16** 0007 1.8 / 0602 6.9 / M 1241 1.3 / ● 1832 6.7
2 0053 1.2 / 0647 7.4 / M 1329 0.5 / 1937 7.3	**17** 0044 1.7 / 0637 7.0 / TU 1319 1.2 / 1908 6.8
3 0138 1.1 / 0731 7.5 / TU 1415 0.5 / 2021 7.2	**18** 0118 1.6 / 0712 7.1 / W 1354 1.2 / 1943 6.8
4 0220 1.2 / 0813 7.5 / W 1457 0.6 / 2101 7.0	**19** 0150 1.6 / 0745 7.1 / TH 1426 1.2 / 2016 6.8
5 0259 1.4 / 0854 7.3 / TH 1536 0.9 / 2139 6.7	**20** 0222 1.6 / 0817 7.1 / F 1456 1.2 / 2050 6.7
6 0336 1.6 / 0934 7.0 / F 1612 1.4 / 2217 6.3	**21** 0255 1.6 / 0852 7.0 / SA 1527 1.4 / 2125 6.6
7 0411 2.0 / 1016 6.6 / SA 1646 1.8 / ◐ 2257 6.0	**22** 0330 1.8 / 0932 6.8 / SU 1602 1.7 / 2206 6.3
8 0448 2.3 / 1105 6.2 / SU 1725 2.3 / 2346 5.7	**23** 0412 2.0 / 1019 6.5 / M 1648 2.0 / ◐ 2257 6.0
9 0535 2.7 / 1206 5.8 / M 1817 2.7	**24** 0506 2.4 / 1121 6.2 / TU 1753 2.4
10 0050 5.5 / 0639 2.9 / TU 1320 5.6 / 1926 2.9	**25** 0011 5.7 / 0624 2.6 / W 1253 5.9 / 1925 2.6
11 0201 5.5 / 0811 2.9 / W 1436 5.6 / 2047 2.8	**26** 0146 5.8 / 0808 2.6 / TH 1434 5.9 / 2056 2.5
12 0306 5.8 / 0937 2.6 / TH 1542 5.8 / 2152 2.6	**27** 0306 6.1 / 0939 2.1 / F 1556 6.3 / 2206 2.1
13 0401 6.1 / 1031 2.2 / F 1635 6.1 / 2242 2.3	**28** 0410 6.5 / 1042 1.5 / SA 1700 6.7 / 2302 1.7
14 0446 6.4 / 1117 1.8 / SA 1718 6.4 / 2327 2.0	**29** 0502 7.0 / 1139 1.0 / SU 1752 7.1 / 2351 1.4
15 0525 6.7 / 1159 1.5 / SU 1756 6.6	**30** 0547 7.3 / 1227 0.6 / M 1837 7.3 O
	31 0036 1.1 / 0629 7.5 / TU 1312 0.4 / 1916 7.3

Chart Datum: 3·90 metres below Ordnance Datum (Newlyn)

ENGLAND – IMMINGHAM

YEAR 2004

LAT 53°38'N   LONG 0°11'W

TIMES AND HEIGHTS OF HIGH AND LOW WATERS

SEPTEMBER

Day	Time m	Time m	Time m	Time m
1 W	0118 1.0	0709 7.6	1952 7.2	
16 TH	0053 1.4	0643 7.3	1326 1.0	1914 7.1
2 TH	0156 1.1	0747 7.6	1428 0.7	2025 7.0
17 F	0126 1.4	0717 7.4	1358 1.0	1946 7.1
3 F	0230 1.3	0824 7.4	1459 1.1	2055 6.7
18 SA	0159 1.4	0751 7.4	1429 1.1	2019 7.0
4 SA	0301 1.5	0859 7.0	1526 1.5	2123 6.4
19 SU	0233 1.4	0829 7.2	1459 1.4	2054 6.7
5 SU	0329 1.9	0934 6.6	1552 2.0	2153 6.1
20 M	0309 1.6	0910 6.9	1535 1.8	2135 6.4
6 M	0400 2.2	1014 6.1	1625 2.4	◐ 2231 5.8
21 TU	0351 2.0	1001 6.5	1620 2.3	◐ 2226 6.0
7 TU	0443 2.6	1111 5.6	1714 2.9	2341 5.4
22 W	0448 2.4	1112 5.9	1730 2.8	2347 5.7
8 W	0546 3.0	1241 5.3	1827 3.2	
23 TH	0620 2.7	1305 5.7	1918 3.0	
9 TH	0117 5.4	0715 3.1	1408 5.4	2008 3.2
24 F	0133 5.7	0817 2.5	1442 5.9	2051 2.7
10 F	0234 5.6	0916 2.7	1519 5.7	2132 2.8
25 SA	0254 6.1	0937 1.9	1556 6.4	2155 2.2
11 SA	0334 6.0	1010 2.2	1613 6.1	2223 2.4
26 SU	0354 6.6	1031 1.3	1650 6.9	2246 1.7
12 SU	0420 6.4	1054 1.8	1655 6.5	2305 2.0
27 M	0441 7.1	1121 0.9	1734 7.1	2331 1.4
13 M	0459 6.8	1135 1.4	1732 6.7	2343 1.8
28 TU	0525 7.4	1204 0.6	1812 7.3	O
14 TU	0535 7.0	1214 1.2	1808 6.9	●
29 W	0012 1.1	0604 7.6	1244 0.6	1845 7.3
15 W	0019 1.6	0609 7.2	1251 1.0	1841 7.0
30 TH	0052 1.1	0642 7.6	1321 0.7	1917 7.2

OCTOBER

Day	Time m	Time m	Time m	Time m
1 F	0127 1.1	0719 7.5	1352 1.0	1946 7.0
16 SA	0101 1.2	0650 7.5	1328 1.0	1917 7.2
2 SA	0159 1.3	0753 7.2	1419 1.3	2012 6.8
17 SU	0138 1.2	0729 7.5	1402 1.2	1952 7.1
3 SU	0226 1.5	0825 6.9	1443 1.7	2036 6.6
18 M	0215 1.3	0812 7.2	1438 1.5	2031 6.9
4 M	0253 1.8	0857 6.5	1508 2.1	2102 6.3
19 TU	0256 1.6	0859 6.8	1518 1.9	2114 6.5
5 TU	0324 2.2	0931 6.1	1540 2.5	2136 6.0
20 W	0344 1.9	0957 6.3	1608 2.5	◐ 2211 6.1
6 W	0405 2.6	1021 5.6	1625 2.9	◐ 2227 5.6
21 TH	0451 2.3	1123 5.8	1724 2.9	2336 5.8
7 TH	0508 2.9	1201 5.3	1737 3.3	
22 F	0630 2.5	1310 5.8	1906 3.0	
8 F	0029 5.4	0636 3.1	1337 5.3	1916 3.3
23 SA	0115 5.9	0807 2.2	1432 6.1	2029 2.7
9 SA	0157 5.6	0829 2.8	1447 5.7	2054 3.0
24 SU	0230 6.3	0915 1.7	1538 6.5	2129 2.2
10 SU	0258 6.0	0933 2.3	1541 6.1	2149 2.5
25 M	0328 6.7	1007 1.3	1627 6.8	2219 1.8
11 M	0346 6.4	1018 1.8	1624 6.5	2231 2.1
26 TU	0416 7.0	1052 1.0	1706 7.0	2303 1.5
12 TU	0425 6.8	1059 1.4	1702 6.8	2309 1.8
27 W	0458 7.2	1133 0.9	1740 7.1	2344 1.3
13 W	0501 7.1	1139 1.1	1736 7.1	2346 1.5
28 TH	0538 7.4	1211 1.0	1812 7.1	O
14 TH	0537 7.3	1217 0.9	1809 7.2	●
29 F	0023 1.2	0615 7.3	1245 1.1	1842 7.1
15 F	0023 1.3	0612 7.5	1253 0.9	1842 7.3
30 SA	0058 1.3	0652 7.2	1315 1.3	1910 7.0
31 SU	0129 1.4	0726 7.0	1342 1.6	1936 6.9

NOVEMBER

Day	Time m	Time m	Time m	Time m
1 M	0157 1.6	0758 6.8	1408 1.8	2002 6.7
16 TU	0206 1.2	0804 7.2	1424 1.6	2017 7.0
2 TU	0226 1.8	0830 6.4	1435 2.1	2031 6.5
17 W	0254 1.4	0858 6.8	1510 2.0	2105 6.7
3 W	0259 2.1	0906 6.1	1508 2.5	2106 6.2
18 TH	0349 1.7	1004 6.3	1605 2.4	2204 6.4
4 TH	0340 2.4	0954 5.7	1550 2.8	2152 5.8
19 F	0457 2.0	1128 6.0	1714 2.8	◐ 2321 6.2
5 F	0439 2.7	1111 5.4	1652 3.2	◐ 2312 5.5
20 SA	0618 2.1	1250 6.0	1835 2.9	
6 SA	0600 2.8	1247 5.4	1819 3.3	
21 SU	0043 6.1	0734 1.9	1401 6.1	1950 2.7
7 SU	0057 5.6	0723 2.7	1400 5.7	1944 3.1
22 M	0154 6.3	0838 1.7	1502 6.3	2053 2.4
8 M	0205 5.9	0834 2.3	1457 6.0	2052 2.7
23 TU	0254 6.6	0931 1.5	1552 6.6	2146 2.1
9 TU	0257 6.3	0929 1.9	1544 6.4	2144 2.3
24 W	0346 6.6	1018 1.4	1633 6.7	2233 1.8
10 W	0342 6.7	1016 1.5	1624 6.8	2229 1.9
25 TH	0431 6.6	1059 1.4	1708 6.8	2316 1.6
11 TH	0423 7.0	1100 1.2	1702 7.0	2312 1.6
26 F	0513 7.0	1137 1.4	1742 6.9	O 2356 1.5
12 F	0504 7.3	1141 1.0	1738 7.2	● 2355 1.3
27 SA	0553 7.0	1211 1.5	1813 6.9	
13 SA	0546 7.5	1222 1.0	1816 7.3	
28 SU	0032 1.5	0630 6.9	1244 1.6	1843 6.9
14 SU	0037 1.1	0630 7.5	1302 1.0	1854 7.3
29 M	0106 1.5	0706 6.8	1313 1.6	1913 6.9
15 M	0121 1.1	0716 7.4	1343 1.2	1934 7.2
30 TU	0138 1.6	0740 6.6	1343 1.9	1943 6.8

DECEMBER

Day	Time m	Time m	Time m	Time m
1 W	0210 1.8	0815 6.4	1413 2.1	2015 6.6
16 TH	0255 1.1	0902 6.9	1505 1.8	2059 7.1
2 TH	0245 2.0	0853 6.2	1447 2.3	2050 6.4
17 F	0348 1.3	1002 6.6	1556 2.1	2153 6.8
3 F	0325 2.2	0937 5.9	1527 2.6	2132 6.1
18 SA	0445 1.5	1107 6.3	1651 2.4	◐ 2254 6.6
4 SA	0415 2.4	1032 5.7	1618 2.8	2226 5.9
19 SU	0546 1.7	1212 6.1	1752 2.6	
5 SU	0517 2.5	1141 5.6	1721 3.0	◐ 2337 5.8
20 M	0002 6.4	0648 1.9	1314 6.0	1858 2.7
6 M	0626 2.5	1254 5.7	1834 3.0	
21 TU	0109 6.3	0750 2.0	1413 6.0	2007 2.6
7 TU	0052 5.9	0733 2.3	1359 5.9	1946 2.8
22 W	0213 6.2	0848 2.0	1508 6.1	2110 2.4
8 W	0158 6.2	0836 2.0	1455 6.2	2052 2.5
23 TH	0313 6.3	0940 2.0	1556 6.3	2204 2.2
9 TH	0255 6.5	0932 1.7	1545 6.5	2149 2.1
24 F	0407 6.4	1025 2.0	1638 6.5	2252 1.9
10 F	0348 6.8	1022 1.5	1630 6.8	2241 1.7
25 SA	0454 6.5	1106 1.9	1716 6.6	2335 1.8
11 SA	0439 7.1	1110 1.3	1713 7.1	2332 1.4
26 SU	0537 6.6	1145 1.9	1751 6.8	O
12 SU	0529 7.3	1157 1.2	1756 7.3	●
27 M	0015 1.6	0615 6.6	1221 1.8	1825 6.9
13 M	0022 1.1	0620 7.3	1244 1.2	1839 7.3
28 TU	0053 1.6	0652 6.6	1255 1.8	1858 6.9
14 TU	0112 1.0	0712 7.3	1330 1.3	1924 7.3
29 W	0129 1.6	0728 6.5	1328 1.9	1932 6.9
15 W	0203 1.0	0805 7.1	1417 1.5	2010 7.2
30 TH	0203 1.7	0803 6.5	1359 2.0	2005 6.8
31 F	0237 1.7	0840 6.4	1432 2.1	2038 6.6

Chapter 5

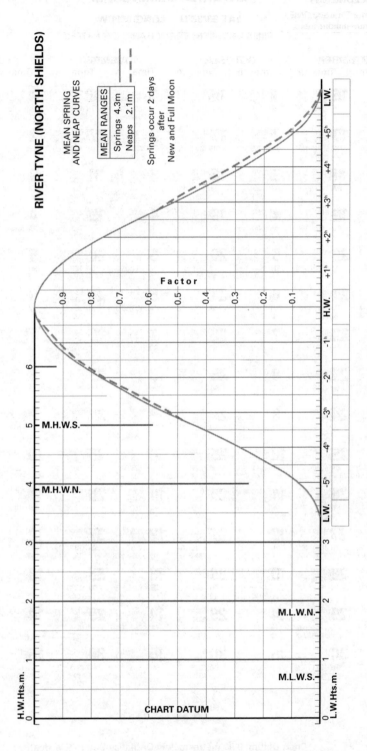

RIVER TYNE (NORTH SHIELDS)

MEAN SPRING
AND NEAP CURVES

MEAN RANGES
Springs 4.3m
Neaps 2.1m

Springs occur 2 days
after
New and Full Moon

Factor

ENGLAND – NORTH SHIELDS

LAT 55°01'N   LONG 1°26'W

TIMES AND HEIGHTS OF HIGH AND LOW WATERS

YEAR **2004**

JANUARY

Day	Time m	Day	Time m
1 TH	0439 1.7 / 1057 4.0 / 1700 2.2 / 2304 4.2	**16** F	0335 1.4 / 0949 4.2 / 1549 1.9 / 2201 4.4
2 F	0542 1.8 / 1157 4.1 / 1807 2.1	**17** SA	0444 1.4 / 1058 4.2 / 1708 1.8 / 2317 4.4
3 SA	0008 4.2 / 0638 1.8 / 1251 4.2 / 1903 1.9	**18** SU	0557 1.4 / 1207 4.3 / 1827 1.7
4 SU	0105 4.3 / 0726 1.7 / 1338 4.4 / 1951 1.7	**19** M	0032 4.6 / 0705 1.4 / 1310 4.5 / 1936 1.4
5 M	0153 4.4 / 0808 1.6 / 1418 4.5 / 2034 1.5	**20** TU	0140 4.7 / 0806 1.2 / 1406 4.8 / 2037 1.1
6 TU	0236 4.5 / 0846 1.5 / 1455 4.6 / 2113 1.4	**21** W	0239 4.9 / 0900 1.1 / 1455 5.0 / ● 2131 0.8
7 W	0315 4.6 / 0922 1.4 / 1529 4.7 / ○ 2150 1.2	**22** TH	0333 5.1 / 0949 1.0 / 1541 5.1 / 2221 0.6
8 TH	0352 4.6 / 0956 1.4 / 1602 4.8 / 2226 1.1	**23** F	0422 5.1 / 1034 1.0 / 1625 5.2 / 2307 0.5
9 F	0427 4.7 / 1030 1.4 / 1635 4.9 / 2302 1.0	**24** SA	0508 5.0 / 1115 1.1 / 1708 5.2 / 2351 0.5
10 SA	0504 4.7 / 1104 1.4 / 1709 4.9 / 2339 1.0	**25** SU	0552 4.9 / 1154 1.2 / 1750 5.1
11 SU	0541 4.7 / 1140 1.4 / 1744 4.8	**26** M	0032 0.7 / 0634 4.7 / 1232 1.3 / 1832 5.0
12 M	0018 1.0 / 0620 4.6 / 1218 1.5 / 1823 4.8	**27** TU	0111 0.9 / 0717 4.6 / 1309 1.5 / 1915 4.7
13 TU	0100 1.1 / 0703 4.5 / 1258 1.6 / 1906 4.7	**28** W	0151 1.2 / 0801 4.4 / 1349 1.7 / 2002 4.5
14 W	0145 1.2 / 0751 4.4 / 1344 1.7 / 1956 4.6	**29** TH	0234 1.5 / 0850 4.0 / 1438 2.0 / ◐ 2056 4.2
15 TH	0236 1.3 / 0846 4.3 / 1440 1.8 / ◑ 2054 4.5	**30** F	0325 1.8 / 0947 3.9 / 1543 2.2 / 2200 4.0
		31 SA	0431 2.0 / 1055 3.8 / 1707 2.2 / 2317 3.9

FEBRUARY

Day	Time m	Day	Time m
1 SU	0548 2.1 / 1206 3.9 / 1828 2.1	**16** M	0541 1.8 / 1148 4.1 / 1821 1.7
2 M	0033 3.9 / 0656 2.0 / 1309 4.1 / 1930 1.9	**17** TU	0033 4.3 / 0701 1.6 / 1302 4.3 / 1937 1.3
3 TU	0135 4.1 / 0749 1.8 / 1358 4.3 / 2018 1.6	**18** W	0145 4.5 / 0804 1.4 / 1400 4.6 / 2036 1.0
4 W	0223 4.3 / 0832 1.7 / 1438 4.5 / 2059 1.3	**19** TH	0241 4.8 / 0855 1.2 / 1449 4.9 / 2126 0.6
5 TH	0302 4.5 / 0909 1.5 / 1513 4.7 / 2136 1.1	**20** F	0328 4.9 / 0939 1.0 / 1531 5.1 / ● 2211 0.4
6 F	0338 4.6 / 0944 1.3 / 1546 4.8 / ○ 2212 0.9	**21** SA	0410 5.0 / 1018 0.9 / 1611 5.2 / 2250 0.4
7 SA	0412 4.8 / 1017 1.2 / 1618 5.0 / 2247 0.7	**22** SU	0449 5.0 / 1054 0.9 / 1648 5.2 / 2327 0.4
8 SU	0446 4.8 / 1051 1.1 / 1650 5.0 / 2323 0.6	**23** M	0525 4.9 / 1127 0.9 / 1725 5.1
9 M	0521 4.8 / 1124 1.0 / 1725 5.1 / 2359 0.6	**24** TU	0000 0.6 / 0600 4.7 / 1200 1.1 / 1801 5.0
10 TU	0558 4.8 / 1158 1.1 / 1801 5.0	**25** W	0032 0.9 / 0635 4.5 / 1231 1.2 / 1838 4.8
11 W	0036 0.7 / 0636 4.7 / 1235 1.2 / 1841 5.0	**26** TH	0103 1.2 / 0711 4.3 / 1305 1.5 / 1918 4.5
12 TH	0116 0.9 / 0719 4.5 / 1316 1.3 / 1927 4.8	**27** F	0138 1.5 / 0751 4.1 / 1345 1.7 / 2005 4.2
13 F	0201 1.3 / 0809 4.3 / 1405 1.6 / ◐ 2023 4.6	**28** SA	0220 1.8 / 0841 3.9 / 1440 2.0 / ◐ 2105 3.9
14 SA	0257 1.4 / 0910 4.2 / 1511 1.8 / 2134 4.3	**29** SU	0320 2.1 / 0946 3.7 / 1602 2.2 / 2224 3.7
15 SU	0411 1.7 / 1025 4.0 / 1642 1.9 / 2303 4.2		

MARCH

Day	Time m	Day	Time m
1 M	0451 2.3 / 1111 3.7 / 1748 2.2	**16** TU	0539 2.0 / 1138 4.0 / 1823 1.5
2 TU	0000 3.7 / 0627 2.2 / 1235 3.8 / 1905 1.9	**17** W	0038 4.2 / 0659 1.8 / 1255 4.3 / 1934 1.2
3 W	0114 3.9 / 0729 2.0 / 1332 4.1 / 1956 1.6	**18** TH	0144 4.5 / 0756 1.5 / 1351 4.6 / 2028 0.8
4 TH	0202 4.2 / 0813 1.7 / 1414 4.4 / 2037 1.2	**19** F	0233 4.7 / 0842 1.2 / 1436 4.8 / 2112 0.6
5 F	0241 4.5 / 0850 1.4 / 1449 4.6 / 2113 0.9	**20** SA	0313 4.9 / 0921 1.0 / ● 1514 5.0 / 2150 0.4
6 SA	0315 4.7 / 0923 1.2 / 1521 4.9 / ○ 2148 0.7	**21** SU	0349 4.9 / 0956 0.9 / 1549 5.1 / 2225 0.4
7 SU	0348 4.9 / 0956 1.0 / 1553 5.1 / 2223 0.5	**22** M	0422 4.9 / 1028 0.8 / 1623 5.1 / 2256 0.5
8 M	0421 5.0 / 1029 0.8 / 1625 5.2 / 2259 0.4	**23** TU	0454 4.8 / 1059 0.8 / 1657 5.1 / 2325 0.7
9 TU	0455 5.0 / 1103 0.8 / 1700 5.2 / 2334 0.4	**24** W	0525 4.7 / 1129 0.9 / 1731 4.9 / 2353 0.9
10 W	0531 5.0 / 1137 0.8 / 1738 5.2	**25** TH	0556 4.6 / 1200 1.1 / 1807 4.7
11 TH	0011 0.5 / 0609 4.8 / 1214 0.9 / 1819 5.1	**26** F	0021 1.2 / 0629 4.4 / 1232 1.3 / 1845 4.4
12 F	0050 0.8 / 0651 4.6 / 1255 1.1 / 1908 4.8	**27** SA	0053 1.5 / 0705 4.2 / 1310 1.6 / 1930 4.1
13 SA	0134 1.2 / 0740 4.4 / 1346 1.4 / ◐ 2008 4.5	**28** SU	0130 1.8 / 0750 4.0 / 1359 1.9 / ◐ 2026 3.8
14 SU	0232 1.6 / 0842 4.1 / 1517 1.7 / 2128 4.1	**29** M	0224 2.2 / 0850 3.7 / 1513 2.1 / 2141 3.6
15 M	0356 1.9 / 1005 3.9 / 1642 1.8 / 2308 4.0	**30** TU	0354 2.4 / 1012 3.6 / 1657 2.1 / 2316 3.6
		31 W	0548 2.3 / 1145 3.7 / 1825 1.8

APRIL

Day	Time m	Day	Time m
1 TH	0036 3.9 / 0656 2.0 / 1252 4.0 / 1920 1.5	**16** F	0127 4.4 / 0736 1.5 / 1331 4.5 / 2007 0.8
2 F	0128 4.2 / 0742 1.7 / 1337 4.3 / 2003 1.1	**17** SA	0211 4.6 / 0819 1.2 / 1414 4.7 / 2047 0.7
3 SA	0207 4.5 / 0819 1.4 / 1414 4.6 / 2041 0.8	**18** SU	0248 4.7 / 0855 1.0 / 1450 4.9 / 2122 0.6
4 SU	0242 4.7 / 0853 1.1 / 1448 4.9 / 2117 0.5	**19** M	0321 4.8 / 0929 0.9 / 1524 5.0 / ● 2153 0.6
5 M	0317 4.9 / 0928 0.8 / 1522 5.1 / ○ 2154 0.3	**20** TU	0352 4.8 / 1001 0.8 / 1558 4.9 / 2222 0.7
6 TU	0351 5.1 / 1003 0.7 / 1558 5.3 / 2231 0.2	**21** W	0423 4.8 / 1033 0.9 / 1631 4.9 / 2251 0.9
7 W	0427 5.1 / 1040 0.6 / 1637 5.3 / 2309 0.3	**22** TH	0453 4.7 / 1104 0.9 / 1706 4.7 / 2319 1.0
8 TH	0505 5.0 / 1117 0.6 / 1719 5.2 / 2348 0.6	**23** F	0524 4.6 / 1135 1.1 / 1742 4.6 / 2348 1.3
9 F	0545 4.9 / 1158 0.7 / 1806 5.0	**24** SA	0557 4.5 / 1209 1.2 / 1821 4.3
10 SA	0029 0.9 / 0630 4.7 / 1245 1.0 / 1901 4.7	**25** SU	0019 1.5 / 0633 4.3 / 1248 1.5 / 1906 4.1
11 SU	0119 1.3 / 0722 4.4 / 1344 1.3 / 2008 4.3	**26** M	0057 1.8 / 0716 4.1 / 1337 1.7 / 2000 3.9
12 M	0223 1.7 / 0828 4.1 / 1504 1.5 / ◐ 2134 4.1	**27** TU	0148 2.1 / 0812 3.9 / 1442 1.9 / ◐ 2107 3.7
13 TU	0353 2.0 / 0954 4.0 / 1645 1.5 / 2309 4.0	**28** W	0306 2.3 / 0923 3.7 / 1607 1.9 / 2228 3.7
14 W	0530 2.0 / 1124 4.0 / 1814 1.3	**29** TH	0448 2.3 / 1046 3.8 / 1730 1.7 / 2343 3.9
15 TH	0028 4.2 / 0643 1.8 / 1237 4.3 / 1918 1.0	**30** F	0605 2.0 / 1156 4.0 / 1831 1.4

Chart Datum: 2·60 metres below Ordnance Datum (Newlyn)

Chapter 5

ENGLAND – NORTH SHIELDS

YEAR 2004

LAT 55°01'N   LONG 1°26'W

TIMES AND HEIGHTS OF HIGH AND LOW WATERS

TIME ZONE (UT)
For Summer Time add ONE hour in **non-shaded areas**

MAY

Day	Time m	Time m	Time m	Time m		Day	Time m	Time m	Time m	Time m
1 SA	0040 4.2	0656 1.7	1248 4.3	1919 1.1		**16** SU	0140 4.5	0747 1.4	1344 4.6	2015 0.9
2 SU	0125 4.5	0738 1.4	1331 4.6	2002 0.7		**17** M	0218 4.6	0826 1.2	1423 4.7	2049 0.9
3 M	0205 4.7	0818 1.1	1411 4.9	2043 0.5		**18** TU	0252 4.7	0902 1.1	1500 4.7	2121 0.9
4 TU	0243 4.9	0857 0.8	1451 5.1	○ 2124 0.4		**19** W	0324 4.7	0936 1.0	1535 4.7	● 2151 1.0
5 W	0321 5.1	0938 0.6	1533 5.3	2205 0.3		**20** TH	0356 4.7	1010 1.0	1611 4.7	2222 1.1
6 TH	0401 5.1	1020 0.5	1618 5.3	2247 0.5		**21** F	0427 4.7	1044 1.0	1647 4.6	2253 1.2
7 F	0443 5.1	1104 0.5	1707 5.2	2331 0.7		**22** SA	0459 4.6	1118 1.1	1725 4.5	2324 1.4
8 SA	0527 4.9	1152 0.7	1802 4.9			**23** SU	0533 4.5	1154 1.2	1804 4.3	2358 1.6
9 SU	0018 1.1	0616 4.7	1246 0.8	1902 4.6		**24** M	0610 4.4	1234 1.3	1848 4.2	
10 M	0112 1.4	0712 4.5	1350 1.1	2011 4.3		**25** TU	0037 1.7	0653 4.2	1321 1.5	1937 4.0
11 TU	0219 1.8	0819 4.3	1506 1.2	◑ 2129 4.1		**26** W	0125 1.9	0743 4.1	1417 1.6	2035 3.9
12 W	0339 2.0	0937 4.2	1630 1.3	2249 4.1		**27** TH	0228 2.1	0843 4.0	1523 1.7	◐ 2141 3.9
13 TH	0502 1.9	1057 4.2	1746 1.2	2359 4.2		**28** F	0344 2.1	0950 4.0	1633 1.5	2248 4.0
14 F	0610 1.8	1205 4.3	1847 1.1			**29** SA	0459 1.9	1057 4.1	1736 1.3	2348 4.2
15 SA	0055 4.3	0703 1.6	1300 4.5	1935 1.0		**30** SU	0601 1.7	1156 4.3	1832 1.1	
						31 M	0041 4.4	0654 1.5	1249 4.6	1922 0.8

JUNE

Day	Time m	Time m	Time m	Time m		Day	Time m	Time m	Time m	Time m
1 TU	0128 4.7	0742 1.2	1338 4.9	2010 0.7		**16** W	0225 4.5	0839 1.3	1439 4.5	2053 1.3
2 W	0213 4.9	0830 0.9	1427 5.1	2058 0.6		**17** TH	0301 4.6	0917 1.2	1519 4.5	● 2128 1.3
3 TH	0256 5.0	0918 0.7	1517 5.2	○ 2145 0.6		**18** F	0335 4.7	0954 1.1	1556 4.5	2201 1.3
4 F	0341 5.1	1007 0.6	1609 5.2	2232 0.7		**19** SA	0408 4.7	1030 1.1	1633 4.5	2234 1.3
5 SA	0427 5.1	1058 0.5	1703 5.1	2321 0.9		**20** SU	0441 4.7	1105 1.0	1710 4.5	2308 1.4
6 SU	0515 5.0	1151 0.5	1800 4.9			**21** M	0516 4.6	1142 1.1	1749 4.4	2343 1.5
7 M	0011 1.1	0606 4.9	1247 0.6	1858 4.7		**22** TU	0552 4.6	1222 1.1	1829 4.3	
8 TU	0104 1.4	0701 4.7	1346 0.8	2000 4.4		**23** W	0021 1.6	0631 4.5	1304 1.2	1913 4.2
9 W	0202 1.6	0802 4.5	1449 1.0	◐ 2105 4.2		**24** TH	0104 1.7	0715 4.4	1351 1.3	2002 4.1
10 TH	0306 1.8	0908 4.4	1556 1.2	2211 4.1		**25** F	0153 1.8	0806 4.3	1444 1.3	◑ 2056 4.1
11 F	0415 1.9	1017 4.3	1703 1.3	2315 4.1		**26** SA	0251 1.8	0902 4.3	1542 1.3	2157 4.1
12 SA	0523 1.8	1123 4.3	1804 1.3			**27** SU	0357 1.8	1004 4.3	1645 1.3	2259 4.2
13 SU	0013 4.2	0622 1.7	1222 4.3	1855 1.3		**28** M	0506 1.7	1109 4.4	1748 1.2	
14 M	0103 4.3	0713 1.6	1313 4.4	1939 1.3		**29** TU	0000 4.3	0612 1.6	1214 4.5	1849 1.1
15 TU	0146 4.4	0758 1.4	1358 4.4	2017 1.3		**30** W	0057 4.5	0715 1.3	1316 4.7	1947 1.0

JULY

Day	Time m	Time m	Time m	Time m		Day	Time m	Time m	Time m	Time m
1 TH	0150 4.7	0813 1.0	1414 4.9	2041 0.9		**16** F	0242 4.5	0902 1.3	1506 4.4	2111 1.4
2 F	0239 4.9	0909 0.8	1511 5.0	○ 2133 0.8		**17** SA	0318 4.6	0940 1.1	1544 4.5	● 2146 1.4
3 SA	0328 5.0	1003 0.5	1605 5.1	2223 0.9		**18** SU	0352 4.7	1016 1.0	1619 4.6	2220 1.3
4 SU	0416 5.1	1055 0.4	1659 5.1	2312 0.9		**19** M	0424 4.8	1052 0.9	1654 4.6	2254 1.3
5 M	0504 5.1	1146 0.4	1751 5.0	2358 1.1		**20** TU	0458 4.8	1127 0.9	1729 4.6	2328 1.3
6 TU	0552 5.1	1236 0.5	1843 4.8			**21** W	0532 4.8	1204 0.9	1806 4.5	
7 W	0044 1.2	0642 4.9	1326 0.6	1934 4.5		**22** TH	0003 1.3	0607 4.8	1242 0.9	1844 4.5
8 TH	0132 1.4	0734 4.8	1416 0.9	2028 4.3		**23** F	0040 1.4	0646 4.7	1321 1.0	1927 4.4
9 F	0222 1.6	0829 4.5	1509 1.2	◑ 2124 4.1		**24** SA	0121 1.5	0730 4.6	1406 1.1	2015 4.3
10 SA	0319 1.8	0929 4.3	1606 1.4	2223 4.0		**25** SU	0209 1.6	0821 4.5	1458 1.3	◑ 2111 4.2
11 SU	0424 1.9	1033 4.2	1708 1.6	2324 4.0		**26** M	0309 1.7	0923 4.4	1601 1.4	2216 4.2
12 M	0535 1.9	1140 4.1	1810 1.7			**27** TU	0423 1.8	1036 4.3	1714 1.5	2327 4.2
13 TU	0023 4.1	0639 1.8	1243 4.1	1905 1.7		**28** W	0546 1.7	1155 4.4	1830 1.3	
14 W	0116 4.2	0734 1.7	1338 4.2	1952 1.6		**29** TH	0036 4.4	0703 1.4	1310 4.6	1936 1.3
15 TH	0202 4.4	0821 1.5	1425 4.3	2033 1.5		**30** F	0137 4.6	0808 1.1	1414 4.8	2034 1.1
						31 SA	0230 4.9	0905 0.7	1509 5.0	○ 2126 1.0

AUGUST

Day	Time m	Time m	Time m	Time m		Day	Time m	Time m	Time m	Time m
1 SU	0318 5.1	0957 0.4	1600 5.1	2213 0.9		**16** M	0332 4.8	0957 0.9	1559 4.5	● 2202 1.2
2 M	0404 5.2	1046 0.3	1647 5.1	2256 0.9		**17** TU	0403 4.9	1031 0.7	1631 4.8	2234 1.1
3 TU	0448 5.3	1131 0.2	1732 5.0	2337 0.9		**18** W	0434 5.0	1105 0.6	1704 4.8	2306 1.0
4 W	0531 5.2	1213 0.4	1816 4.8			**19** TH	0506 5.1	1139 0.6	1738 4.8	2339 1.1
5 TH	0016 1.1	0614 5.1	1254 0.6	1858 4.6		**20** F	0540 5.0	1213 0.7	1813 4.7	
6 F	0055 1.3	0658 4.9	1334 0.9	1942 4.4		**21** SA	0013 1.2	0616 4.9	1250 0.9	1852 4.6
7 SA	0135 1.5	0745 4.6	1416 1.3	◑ 2030 4.2		**22** SU	0051 1.3	0659 4.6	1331 1.1	1938 4.4
8 SU	0222 1.7	0838 4.3	1504 1.6	2124 4.0		**23** M	0136 1.5	0751 4.6	1421 1.4	◐ 2034 4.3
9 M	0322 2.0	0940 4.0	1605 1.9	2229 3.9		**24** TU	0236 1.7	0857 4.3	1529 1.7	2144 4.1
10 TU	0442 2.1	1056 3.9	1722 2.1	2341 3.9		**25** W	0359 1.8	1022 4.2	1657 1.8	2307 4.1
11 W	0608 2.0	1216 3.9	1837 2.0			**26** TH	0540 1.7	1156 4.3	1826 1.7	
12 TH	0048 4.0	0715 1.8	1322 4.1	1934 1.9		**27** F	0026 4.3	0703 1.4	1315 4.5	1934 1.5
13 F	0142 4.3	0805 1.6	1412 4.3	2018 1.7		**28** SA	0130 4.6	0807 1.0	1414 4.8	2028 1.3
14 SA	0224 4.5	0846 1.3	1451 4.4	2056 1.5		**29** SU	0221 4.9	0859 0.6	1503 5.0	2114 1.0
15 SU	0300 4.7	0923 1.1	1526 4.6	2130 1.3		**30** M	0306 5.2	0945 0.4	1546 5.1	○ 2155 0.9
						31 TU	0346 5.3	1027 0.2	1626 5.1	2233 0.8

Chart Datum: 2·60 metres below Ordnance Datum (Newlyn)

ENGLAND – NORTH SHIELDS

LAT 55°01'N   LONG 1°26'W

TIMES AND HEIGHTS OF HIGH AND LOW WATERS

YEAR 2004

SEPTEMBER

Day	Time m				Day	Time m			
1 W	0425 5.4	1106 0.3	1704 5.1	2309 0.9	**16** TH	0405 5.2	1036 0.5	1634 5.0	2240 0.9
2 TH	0504 5.3	1142 0.5	1741 4.9	2343 1.0	**17** F	0437 5.3	1110 0.5	1707 5.0	2314 0.9
3 F	0542 5.2	1215 0.7	1818 4.7		**18** SA	0512 5.2	1144 0.6	1743 4.9	2349 1.0
4 SA	0017 1.2	1248 1.1	1855 4.5		**19** SU	0552 5.1	1221 0.9	1823 4.8	
5 SU	0053 1.4	0703 4.6	1322 1.5	1935 4.2	**20** M	0028 1.2	0638 4.9	1303 1.2	1909 4.5
6 M	0134 1.7	0751 4.3	1403 1.8	2024 4.0	**21** TU	0117 1.4	0735 4.5	1356 1.6	2007 4.3
7 TU	0228 2.0	0852 3.9	1501 2.2	2129 3.8	**22** W	0223 1.7	0850 4.1	1514 2.0	2125 4.1
8 W	0349 2.2	1012 3.7	1631 2.4	2253 3.8	**23** TH	0401 1.8	1028 4.1	1657 2.1	2258 4.1
9 TH	0535 2.2	1148 3.8	1811 2.3		**24** F	0546 1.6	1203 4.3	1824 1.9	
10 F	0017 3.9	0652 1.9	1302 4.0	1914 2.1	**25** SA	0019 4.3	0701 1.3	1313 4.6	1925 1.6
11 SA	0116 4.2	0742 1.6	1350 4.3	1958 1.8	**26** SU	0120 4.7	0758 0.9	1405 4.8	2014 1.3
12 SU	0158 4.5	0822 1.3	1427 4.5	2034 1.5	**27** M	0207 5.0	0844 0.6	1447 5.0	2055 1.1
13 M	0233 4.7	0857 1.0	1500 4.7	2106 1.3	**28** TU	0247 5.2	0925 0.4	1525 5.1	2132 0.9
14 TU ●	0304 4.9	0930 0.8	1531 4.9	2137 1.1	**29** W	0324 5.3	1001 0.4	1559 5.1	2207 0.9
15 W	0334 5.1	1003 0.6	1602 5.0	2208 0.9	**30** TH	0400 5.3	1035 0.5	1633 5.1	2240 0.9

OCTOBER

Day	Time m				Day	Time m			
1 F	0435 5.3	1106 0.7	1705 4.9	2313 1.0	**16** SA	0411 5.4	1042 0.5	1638 5.2	2251 0.8
2 SA	0512 5.1	1136 1.0	1738 4.8	2345 1.2	**17** SU	0451 5.3	1119 0.7	1717 5.0	2331 0.9
3 SU	0549 4.8	1205 1.3	1812 4.6		**18** M	0536 5.1	1159 1.0	1800 4.9	
4 M	0019 1.4	0629 4.5	1236 1.6	1849 4.4	**19** TU	0017 1.1	0629 4.8	1246 1.4	1850 4.6
5 TU	0058 1.7	0716 4.2	1313 2.0	1935 4.1	**20** W ◑	0113 1.4	0734 4.5	1346 1.8	1953 4.3
6 W	0149 2.0	0814 3.9	1406 2.3	2035 3.9	**21** TH	0229 1.6	0856 4.2	1511 2.1	2114 4.2
7 TH	0304 2.2	0930 3.7	1536 2.5	2157 3.8	**22** F	0406 1.7	1030 4.2	1650 2.2	2246 4.2
8 F	0448 2.2	1105 3.7	1731 2.5	2329 3.9	**23** SA	0537 1.5	1154 4.3	1808 1.9	
9 SA	0613 1.9	1224 4.0	1840 2.2		**24** SU	0002 4.5	0645 1.2	1257 4.6	1905 1.7
10 SU	0035 4.1	0705 1.6	1314 4.3	1924 1.9	**25** M	0100 4.7	0738 0.9	1344 4.8	1951 1.4
11 M	0121 4.4	0746 1.3	1352 4.5	2001 1.6	**26** TU	0146 5.0	0821 0.8	1423 4.9	2030 1.2
12 TU	0156 4.7	0822 1.0	1425 4.8	2034 1.3	**27** W	0225 5.1	0858 0.7	1458 5.0	2106 1.1
13 W	0229 5.0	0856 0.8	1457 5.0	2106 1.1	**28** TH	0300 5.2	0931 0.7	1531 5.0	2140 1.0
14 TH ●	0301 5.2	0931 0.6	1531 5.1	2140 0.9	**29** F	0336 5.2	1002 0.8	1602 5.0	2214 1.0
15 F	0334 5.3	1006 0.5	1603 5.2	2215 0.8	**30** SA	0411 5.1	1032 1.0	1634 4.9	2247 1.1
					31 SU	0447 4.9	1101 1.2	1706 4.8	2321 1.2

NOVEMBER

Day	Time m				Day	Time m			
1 M	0525 4.7	1131 1.4	1739 4.7	2355 1.4	**16** TU	0532 5.1	1148 1.2	1746 5.0	
2 TU	0605 4.5	1202 1.7	1816 4.5		**17** W	0017 1.0	0630 4.8	1240 1.5	1840 4.7
3 W	0034 1.6	0650 4.2	1239 2.0	1859 4.3	**18** TH	0119 1.2	0736 4.5	1343 1.9	1943 4.5
4 TH	0123 1.8	0744 4.0	1328 2.3	1954 4.1	**19** F ◐	0231 1.3	0852 4.3	1459 2.1	2058 4.4
5 F ◐	0228 2.0	0851 3.8	1442 2.5	2105 3.9	**20** SA	0351 1.4	1012 4.2	1621 2.1	2218 4.4
6 SA	0350 2.1	1010 3.8	1623 2.5	2226 3.9	**21** SU	0510 1.4	1125 4.3	1734 2.0	2330 4.5
7 SU	0512 1.9	1126 4.0	1744 2.3	2337 4.1	**22** M	0615 1.2	1225 4.5	1833 1.8	
8 M	0614 1.6	1223 4.2	1837 2.0		**23** TU	0030 4.6	0708 1.1	1314 4.6	1922 1.6
9 TU	0029 4.4	0700 1.3	1307 4.5	1918 1.7	**24** W	0119 4.8	0752 1.1	1355 4.7	2004 1.4
10 W	0112 4.7	0741 1.0	1346 4.8	1957 1.4	**25** TH	0201 4.9	0829 1.1	1432 4.8	2042 1.3
11 TH	0151 4.9	0820 0.8	1422 5.0	2035 1.1	**26** F ○	0240 4.9	0902 1.1	1505 4.9	2119 1.2
12 F ●	0229 5.2	0859 0.7	1459 5.1	2113 1.0	**27** SA	0317 4.9	0934 1.2	1538 4.9	2155 1.1
13 SA	0309 5.3	0939 0.6	1536 5.2	2154 0.8	**28** SU	0354 4.8	1006 1.3	1610 4.9	2230 1.2
14 SU	0352 5.3	1019 0.7	1616 5.2	2238 0.8	**29** M	0431 4.8	1037 1.4	1643 4.8	2305 1.2
15 M	0439 5.3	1102 0.9	1659 5.1	2325 0.9	**30** TU	0509 4.6	1108 1.5	1717 4.7	2341 1.3

DECEMBER

Day	Time m				Day	Time m			
1 W	0549 4.5	1141 1.7	1753 4.6		**16** TH	0019 0.7	0627 4.9	1234 1.4	1830 5.0
2 TH	0020 1.5	0631 4.3	1219 1.9	1834 4.4	**17** F	0116 0.9	0727 4.7	1328 1.7	1927 4.8
3 F	0105 1.6	0718 4.1	1302 2.1	1922 4.3	**18** SA	0215 1.0	0829 4.4	1428 1.9	2030 4.6 ◑
4 SA	0157 1.7	0813 4.0	1358 2.2	2018 4.2	**19** SU	0319 1.2	0935 4.3	1534 2.0	2138 4.5
5 SU ◐	0258 1.8	0914 3.9	1508 2.3	2122 4.1	**20** M	0426 1.4	1041 4.2	1644 2.0	2247 4.4
6 M	0405 1.8	1020 4.0	1625 2.2	2228 4.2	**21** TU	0532 1.5	1143 4.2	1751 1.9	2352 4.4
7 TU	0510 1.6	1123 4.1	1733 2.1	2329 4.3	**22** W	0631 1.5	1238 4.3	1850 1.8	
8 W	0608 1.4	1217 4.4	1829 1.8		**23** TH	0050 4.5	0720 1.5	1327 4.4	1941 1.6
9 TH	0024 4.6	0659 1.2	1306 4.6	1919 1.6	**24** F	0141 4.5	0803 1.5	1409 4.6	2025 1.5
10 F	0115 4.8	0747 1.0	1351 4.8	2007 1.3	**25** SA	0226 4.6	0840 1.5	1447 4.7	2105 1.4
11 SA	0204 5.0	0833 0.9	1434 5.0	2054 1.0	**26** SU ○	0306 4.6	0915 1.5	1522 4.8	2143 1.3
12 SU ●	0253 5.2	0920 0.9	1517 5.1	2143 0.8	**27** M	0345 4.6	0949 1.4	1556 4.8	2219 1.2
13 M	0344 5.2	1006 0.9	1602 5.2	2233 0.7	**28** TU	0421 4.6	1022 1.5	1628 4.8	2254 1.2
14 TU	0436 5.2	1054 1.0	1648 5.2	2325 0.7	**29** W	0457 4.6	1054 1.5	1701 4.8	2329 1.2
15 W	0531 5.1	1143 1.2	1738 5.1		**30** TH	0534 4.5	1127 1.6	1736 4.7	
					31 F	0006 1.2	0611 4.5	1203 1.6	1812 4.7

Chart Datum: 2·60 metres below Ordnance Datum (Newlyn)

Chapter 5

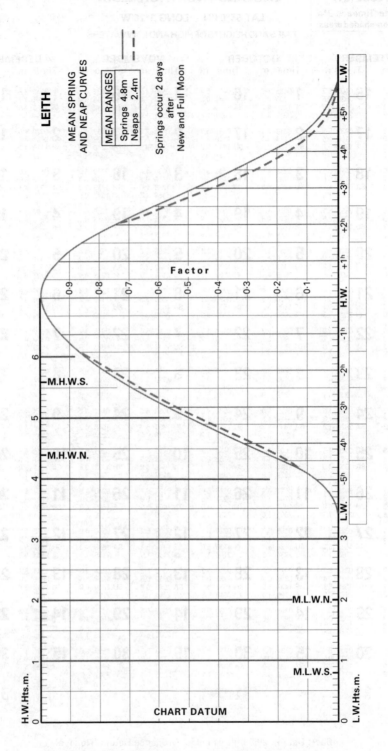

LEITH

MEAN SPRING AND NEAP CURVES

MEAN RANGES	
Springs	4.8m
Neaps	2.4m

Springs occur 2 days after New and Full Moon

Factor

CHART DATUM

M.H.W.S.

M.H.W.N.

M.L.W.N.

M.L.W.S.

H.W.Hts.m.

L.W.Hts.m.

SCOTLAND – LEITH

TIME ZONE (UT)
For Summer Time add ONE hour in **non-shaded areas**

LAT 55°59′N   LONG 3°11′W

TIMES AND HEIGHTS OF HIGH AND LOW WATERS

YEAR 2004

JANUARY

Day	Time	m	Time	m	Time	m	Time	m
1 TH	0329	1.9	0955	4.4	1539	2.3	2215	4.6
16 F	0204	1.5	0850	4.7	1423	2.0	2110	4.8
2 F	0433	2.0	1055	4.4	1645	2.2	2315	4.5
17 SA	0320	1.6	0958	4.7	1553	2.0	2227	4.8
3 SA	0526	1.9	1154	4.5	1742	2.0		
18 SU	0444	1.6	1107	4.8	1714	1.8	2340	5.0
4 SU	0013	4.6	0609	1.8	1246	4.7	1830	1.8
19 M	0557	1.5	1211	5.0	1825	1.5		
5 M	0104	4.7	0648	1.7	1329	4.9	1913	1.6
20 TU	0045	5.2	0659	1.3	1309	5.2	1929	1.1
6 TU	0147	4.9	0724	1.6	1406	5.0	1952	1.4
21 W ●	0144	5.4	0755	1.2	1401	5.4	2027	0.8
7 W	0225	5.0	0800	1.5	1441	5.1	2030	1.2
22 TH	0236	5.6	0845	1.1	1449	5.6	2118	0.5
8 TH	0301	5.1	0836	1.4	1515	5.2	2107	1.1
23 F	0325	5.7	0930	1.0	1536	5.7	2204	0.4
9 F	0336	5.2	0912	1.2	1549	5.2	2146	1.1
24 SA	0412	5.6	1011	1.0	1622	5.6	2247	0.5
10 SA	0412	5.2	0949	1.4	1624	5.2	2225	1.0
25 SU	0458	5.5	1048	1.1	1707	5.4	2325	0.7
11 SU	0449	5.2	1024	1.4	1659	5.2	2303	1.1
26 M	0542	5.2	1118	1.3	1751	5.4	2355	1.0
12 M	0529	5.1	1057	1.5	1737	5.2	2342	1.2
27 TU	0627	5.0	1143	1.5	1836	5.1		
13 TU	0611	5.0	1130	1.7	1818	5.1		
28 W	0019	1.3	0711	4.7	1217	1.8	1922	4.8
14 W	0021	1.3	0657	4.9	1211	1.8	1905	5.0
29 TH	0052	1.7	0759	4.5	1303	2.1	2015	4.6
15 TH ◑	0107	1.4	0750	4.8	1307	1.9	2000	4.9
30 F	0139	2.0	0852	4.3	1412	2.3	2114	4.3
31 SA	0254	2.2	0950	4.2	1552	2.4	2219	4.2

FEBRUARY

Day	Time	m	Time	m	Time	m	Time	m
1 SU	0431	2.3	1056	4.2	1711	2.2	2331	4.3
16 M	0430	2.0	1044	4.5	1712	1.8	2333	4.7
2 M	0538	2.1	1207	4.4	1811	2.0		
17 TU	0555	1.8	1200	4.7	1832	1.5		
3 TU	0039	4.4	0628	2.0	1305	4.6	1859	1.7
18 W	0046	5.0	0657	1.6	1304	5.0	1933	1.0
4 W	0129	4.7	0710	1.8	1348	4.9	1941	1.4
19 TH	0143	5.3	0749	1.3	1355	5.3	2024	0.7
5 TH	0209	4.9	0748	1.6	1425	5.1	2019	1.2
20 F ●	0230	5.5	0833	1.0	1440	5.5	2108	0.4
6 F ○	0244	5.1	0825	1.4	1500	5.2	2058	0.9
21 SA	0313	5.6	0913	0.9	1521	5.7	2148	0.3
7 SA	0319	5.2	0902	1.2	1533	5.4	2136	0.8
22 SU	0353	5.5	0949	0.8	1601	5.7	2223	0.4
8 SU	0353	5.3	0938	1.1	1605	5.4	2213	0.7
23 M	0432	5.4	1020	0.9	1640	5.6	2252	0.6
9 M	0429	5.4	1012	1.1	1639	5.5	2249	0.7
24 TU	0510	5.2	1044	1.0	1718	5.4	2313	0.9
10 TU	0506	5.3	1042	1.1	1715	5.4	2322	0.8
25 W	0547	5.0	1105	1.2	1756	5.1	2330	1.2
11 W	0546	5.2	1109	1.2	1754	5.3	2353	1.0
26 TH	0626	4.7	1132	1.5	1836	4.8	2357	1.5
12 TH	0629	5.1	1141	1.4	1839	5.2		
27 F	0707	4.5	1207	1.8	1923	4.5		
13 F ◑	0027	1.2	0717	4.8	1227	1.6	1931	4.9
28 SA	0036	1.9	0756	4.3	1301	2.2	2020	4.2
14 SA	0118	1.5	0813	4.6	1334	1.9	2040	4.7
29 SU	0136	2.3	0855	4.1	1440	2.4	2127	4.1
15 SU	0236	1.9	0925	4.5	1522	2.0	2209	4.6

MARCH

Day	Time	m	Time	m	Time	m	Time	m
1 M	0335	2.5	1003	4.0	1643	2.3	2244	4.0
16 TU	0433	2.2	1034	4.4	1722	1.7	2334	4.6
2 TU	0514	2.4	1122	4.2	1753	2.0		
17 W	0551	1.9	1155	4.6	1834	1.3		
3 W	0008	4.3	0612	2.1	1235	4.4	1844	1.7
18 TH	0044	5.0	0648	1.6	1257	5.0	1927	0.9
4 TH	0105	4.6	0655	1.8	1323	4.8	1926	1.4
19 F	0136	5.2	0733	1.3	1343	5.3	2010	0.6
5 F	0146	4.9	0733	1.5	1402	5.1	2004	1.0
20 SA ●	0217	5.4	0812	1.0	1423	5.5	2048	0.5
6 SA ○	0221	5.2	0809	1.2	1436	5.3	2040	0.7
21 SU	0254	5.5	0848	0.8	1501	5.6	2122	0.4
7 SU	0255	5.4	0844	1.0	1508	5.5	2117	0.5
22 M	0329	5.4	0921	0.7	1537	5.6	2152	0.5
8 M	0328	5.5	0919	0.8	1540	5.6	2153	0.4
23 TU	0403	5.3	0950	0.8	1612	5.5	2216	0.7
9 TU	0404	5.6	0953	0.7	1615	5.7	2227	0.4
24 W	0437	5.2	1014	0.9	1648	5.3	2232	0.9
10 W	0441	5.5	1023	0.8	1653	5.6	2259	0.6
25 TH	0511	5.0	1035	1.1	1724	5.1	2249	1.2
11 TH	0521	5.4	1049	0.9	1734	5.5	2326	0.9
26 F	0546	4.8	1057	1.4	1803	4.8	2312	1.5
12 F	0603	5.1	1121	1.2	1821	5.2	2359	1.3
27 SA	0625	4.6	1128	1.6	1847	4.5	2345	1.9
13 SA	0650	4.9	1207	1.5	1917	4.9		
28 SU ◑	0711	4.3	1213	2.0	1940	4.2		
14 SU	0051	1.7	0747	4.6	1318	1.8	2032	4.6
29 M	0036	2.3	0808	4.1	1337	2.3	2044	4.0
15 M	0228	2.1	0905	4.3	1533	2.0	2205	4.4
30 TU	0230	2.6	0918	4.0	1604	2.3	2158	4.0
31 W	0443	2.5	1036	4.1	1724	2.0	2319	4.2

APRIL

Day	Time	m	Time	m	Time	m	Time	m
1 TH	0543	2.2	1152	4.4	1815	1.6		
16 F	0028	4.9	0623	1.6	1237	5.0	1906	0.9
2 F	0025	4.6	0627	1.8	1246	4.7	1856	1.3
17 SA	0116	5.1	0706	1.3	1322	5.2	1946	0.8
3 SA	0111	4.9	0705	1.5	1327	5.1	1934	0.9
18 SU	0155	5.2	0743	1.1	1401	5.4	2020	0.7
4 SU	0148	5.2	0741	1.1	1403	5.4	2012	0.6
19 M ●	0229	5.3	0818	0.9	1437	5.4	2049	0.7
5 M ○	0224	5.5	0817	0.8	1437	5.6	2049	0.3
20 TU	0302	5.3	0851	0.8	1512	5.4	2115	0.7
6 TU	0259	5.6	0854	0.6	1513	5.7	2126	0.2
21 W	0335	5.2	0922	0.8	1547	5.3	2138	0.9
7 W	0337	5.7	0930	0.5	1551	5.8	2203	0.3
22 TH	0407	5.1	0949	0.9	1622	5.1	2157	1.1
8 TH	0416	5.6	1005	0.6	1634	5.7	2237	0.6
23 F	0440	5.0	1013	1.1	1658	5.0	2217	1.3
9 F	0457	5.4	1039	0.8	1720	5.5	2311	1.0
24 SA	0514	4.8	1037	1.3	1737	4.8	2241	1.6
10 SA	0542	5.2	1117	1.0	1812	5.2	2351	1.5
25 SU	0552	4.6	1108	1.6	1821	4.5	2313	1.9
11 SU	0632	4.9	1211	1.4	1914	4.8		
26 M	0635	4.4	1154	1.8	1910	4.3		
12 M ◑	0055	1.9	0734	4.5	1342	1.7	2034	4.5
27 TU ◑	0002	2.3	0728	4.2	1307	2.1	2008	4.2
13 TU	0243	2.3	0859	4.4	1549	1.7	2201	4.5
28 W	0143	2.5	0835	4.1	1452	2.1	2116	4.1
14 W	0423	2.2	1025	4.5	1715	1.5	2324	4.7
29 TH	0344	2.5	0950	4.2	1631	1.9	2228	4.3
15 TH	0531	1.9	1139	4.7	1818	1.2		
30 F	0454	2.2	1100	4.4	1727	1.6	2333	4.6

Chart Datum: 2·90 metres below Ordnance Datum (Newlyn)

Chapter 5

SCOTLAND – LEITH

TIME ZONE (UT)
For Summer Time add ONE hour in **non-shaded areas**

LAT 55°59′N   LONG 3°11′W

TIMES AND HEIGHTS OF HIGH AND LOW WATERS

YEAR 2004

MAY

Day	Time m	Time m	Time m	Time m
1 SA	0543 1.8	1158 4.7	1813 1.2	
2 SU	0026 4.9	0624 1.5	1245 5.1	1854 0.9
3 M	0110 5.2	0705 1.1	1326 5.4	1936 0.6
4 TU ○	0151 5.5	0745 0.8	1406 5.6	2017 0.4
5 W	0230 5.6	0827 0.6	1448 5.8	2059 0.4
6 TH	0311 5.7	0910 0.5	1532 5.8	2141 0.5
7 F	0353 5.6	0955 0.5	1620 5.7	2224 0.8
8 SA	0438 5.4	1042 0.7	1711 5.5	2309 1.2
9 SU	0527 5.2	1133 0.9	1808 5.2	
10 M	0000 1.6	0622 4.9	1236 1.2	1914 4.9
11 TU ◐	0106 2.0	0730 4.7	1359 1.5	2028 4.7
12 W	0232 2.2	0849 4.6	1533 1.5	2143 4.6
13 TH	0351 2.1	1003 4.6	1646 1.4	2255 4.7
14 F	0453 1.9	1110 4.8	1747 1.2	2357 4.8
15 SA	0545 1.7	1207 4.9	1835 1.1	
16 SU	0046 4.9	0629 1.5	1255 5.1	1913 1.1
17 M	0127 5.0	0709 1.2	1336 5.1	1944 1.0
18 TU	0203 5.1	0747 1.1	1414 5.2	2011 1.0
19 W ●	0236 5.1	0823 1.0	1449 5.1	2038 1.0
20 TH	0309 5.1	0857 1.0	1525 5.1	2105 1.1
21 F	0341 5.1	0928 1.0	1601 5.0	2132 1.3
22 SA	0414 5.0	0958 1.1	1638 4.9	2159 1.4
23 SU	0449 4.9	1029 1.3	1717 4.8	2229 1.6
24 M	0527 4.7	1105 1.4	1758 4.6	2304 1.9
25 TU	0609 4.6	1150 1.6	1844 4.5	2352 2.1
26 W	0657 4.4	1248 1.8	1936 4.4	
27 TH ◐	0106 2.3	0754 4.4	1400 1.8	2036 4.4
28 F	0235 2.3	0901 4.4	1520 1.7	2141 4.5
29 SA	0352 2.1	1008 4.5	1628 1.5	2244 4.6
30 SU	0451 1.9	1108 4.8	1723 1.2	2341 4.9
31 M	0541 1.5	1202 5.0	1812 1.0	

JUNE

Day	Time m	Time m	Time m	Time m
1 TU	0032 5.2	0628 1.2	1252 5.3	1900 0.8
2 W	0120 5.4	0717 0.9	1341 5.5	1949 0.6
3 TH ○	0205 5.5	0808 0.7	1429 5.7	2039 0.6
4 F	0250 5.6	0900 0.5	1519 5.7	2129 0.7
5 SA	0336 5.6	0953 0.5	1611 5.7	2218 0.9
6 SU	0425 5.5	1046 0.6	1705 5.5	2307 1.2
7 M	0517 5.3	1139 0.7	1802 5.3	2357 1.5
8 TU	0615 5.1	1237 1.0	1904 5.0	
9 W ◐	0052 1.8	0719 5.0	1342 1.2	2007 4.8
10 TH	0155 2.0	0826 4.8	1453 1.4	2111 4.6
11 F	0302 2.0	0930 4.8	1601 1.5	2214 4.6
12 SA	0404 2.0	1032 4.7	1701 1.5	2315 4.6
13 SU	0501 1.9	1131 4.7	1752 1.5	
14 M	0009 4.7	0551 1.7	1224 4.8	1830 1.5
15 TU	0057 4.8	0637 1.5	1311 4.8	1903 1.4
16 W	0137 4.9	0719 1.3	1353 4.9	1935 1.3
17 TH ●	0213 5.0	0759 1.2	1431 4.9	2008 1.3
18 F	0248 5.0	0836 1.1	1507 5.0	2041 1.3
19 SA	0321 5.1	0911 1.1	1543 5.0	2115 1.4
20 SU	0355 5.0	0946 1.1	1620 5.0	2149 1.4
21 M	0431 5.0	1023 1.1	1657 4.9	2224 1.5
22 TU	0508 4.9	1101 1.2	1737 4.8	2300 1.7
23 W	0547 4.8	1142 1.3	1819 4.7	2340 1.8
24 TH ◐	0629 4.8	1228 1.4	1906 4.7	
25 F ◐	0028 1.9	0716 4.7	1320 1.5	1958 4.6
26 SA	0131 2.0	0811 4.6	1419 1.5	2056 4.6
27 SU	0244 2.0	0915 4.7	1526 1.5	2159 4.7
28 M	0356 1.9	1023 4.8	1634 1.4	2301 4.8
29 TU	0501 1.7	1127 4.9	1737 1.2	
30 W	0000 5.0	0601 1.4	1228 5.2	1836 1.1

JULY

Day	Time m	Time m	Time m	Time m
1 TH	0055 5.2	0701 1.1	1325 5.4	1934 1.0
2 F ○	0146 5.4	0800 0.8	1419 5.6	2029 0.9
3 SA	0236 5.5	0858 0.5	1511 5.7	2121 0.9
4 SU	0325 5.6	0951 0.4	1603 5.7	2209 0.9
5 M	0414 5.6	1042 0.4	1654 5.6	2255 1.1
6 TU	0505 5.5	1131 0.5	1747 5.4	2339 1.3
7 W	0558 5.4	1218 0.7	1840 5.1	
8 TH	0020 1.5	0652 5.2	1304 1.1	1934 4.9
9 F ◐	0103 1.7	0749 5.0	1352 1.4	2028 4.6
10 SA	0156 1.9	0847 4.8	1449 1.7	2125 4.5
11 SU	0303 2.1	0946 4.6	1555 1.8	2223 4.4
12 M	0415 2.1	1047 4.5	1656 1.9	2324 4.4
13 TU	0518 1.9	1150 4.5	1748 1.7	
14 W	0023 4.6	0613 1.8	1248 4.6	1831 1.8
15 TH	0113 4.7	0700 1.6	1336 4.7	1910 1.6
16 F	0154 4.9	0742 1.4	1416 4.9	1947 1.5
17 SA ●	0231 5.0	0820 1.2	1452 5.0	2024 1.4
18 SU	0305 5.1	0857 1.0	1526 5.1	2101 1.3
19 M	0339 5.2	0935 0.9	1601 5.1	2138 1.3
20 TU	0413 5.2	1012 0.9	1637 5.1	2213 1.3
21 W	0447 5.2	1050 0.9	1714 5.1	2247 1.4
22 TH	0523 5.1	1126 1.0	1753 5.0	2317 1.5
23 F	0600 5.1	1201 1.1	1836 4.9	2350 1.6
24 SA ◐	0642 5.0	1239 1.3	1923 4.8	
25 SU ◐	0034 1.8	0731 4.9	1326 1.4	2016 4.7
26 M	0137 1.9	0824 4.7	1430 1.6	2119 4.6
27 TU	0302 2.0	0946 4.7	1556 1.7	2228 4.7
28 W	0435 1.8	1104 4.8	1720 1.6	2336 4.8
29 TH	0553 1.5	1215 5.0	1829 1.4	
30 F	0039 5.1	0700 1.1	1318 5.3	1928 1.2
31 SA ○	0136 5.3	0801 0.6	1413 5.6	2021 1.0

AUGUST

Day	Time m	Time m	Time m	Time m
1 SU	0226 5.6	0855 0.4	1502 5.7	2109 0.9
2 M	0313 5.7	0943 0.2	1550 5.7	2153 0.8
3 TU	0359 5.8	1028 0.2	1636 5.6	2233 0.9
4 W	0445 5.7	1109 0.4	1721 5.4	2309 1.0
5 TH	0531 5.5	1145 0.7	1807 5.2	2339 1.3
6 F	0617 5.3	1214 1.1	1853 4.9	
7 SA ◐	0008 1.6	0704 5.0	1241 1.4	1940 4.6
8 SU	0049 1.8	0757 4.7	1321 1.8	2032 4.4
9 M	0151 2.1	0855 4.4	1427 2.1	2129 4.3
10 TU	0327 2.3	1000 4.3	1605 2.3	2233 4.3
11 W	0453 2.2	1113 4.2	1719 2.2	2346 4.4
12 TH	0558 1.9	1226 4.4	1812 2.0	
13 F	0048 4.6	0648 1.7	1319 4.6	1855 1.8
14 SA	0135 4.8	0730 1.4	1359 4.9	1933 1.6
15 SU	0212 5.1	0808 1.2	1433 5.1	2010 1.4
16 M ●	0246 5.2	0843 0.9	1505 5.2	2045 1.2
17 TU	0318 5.3	0919 0.7	1538 5.3	2121 1.1
18 W	0350 5.4	0955 0.6	1612 5.3	2154 1.0
19 TH	0422 5.5	1029 0.6	1647 5.3	2225 1.1
20 F	0456 5.4	1101 0.7	1725 5.3	2250 1.2
21 SA	0533 5.3	1129 0.9	1806 5.1	2317 1.4
22 SU	0615 5.2	1158 1.2	1850 4.9	2356 1.6
23 M ◐	0704 5.0	1241 1.5	1942 4.7	
24 TU	0055 1.8	0805 4.7	1350 1.8	2046 4.6
25 W	0233 2.0	0928 4.6	1546 2.0	2206 4.5
26 TH	0437 1.9	1056 4.7	1721 1.6	2325 4.7
27 F	0600 1.5	1214 5.0	1828 1.6	
28 SA	0033 5.0	0704 1.1	1316 5.3	1921 1.3
29 SU	0127 5.4	0757 0.7	1405 5.6	2008 1.1
30 M ○	0213 5.6	0844 0.4	1448 5.7	2050 0.8
31 TU	0255 5.8	0926 0.2	1530 5.7	2129 0.7

Chart Datum: 2·90 metres below Ordnance Datum (Newlyn)

SCOTLAND – LEITH

LAT 55°59'N   LONG 3°11'W

TIMES AND HEIGHTS OF HIGH AND LOW WATERS

YEAR **2004**

SEPTEMBER

Day	Time m	Time m	Time m	Time m	Day	Time m	Time m	Time m	Time m
1 W	0337 5.9	1004 0.2	1610 5.6	2204 0.8	**16** TH	0321 5.6	0929 0.5	1543 5.6	2129 0.9
2 TH	0418 5.8	1038 0.4	1650 5.4	2235 0.9	**17** F	0354 5.7	1002 0.5	1619 5.5	2158 0.9
3 F	0459 5.6	1104 0.8	1730 5.2	2258 1.2	**18** SA	0430 5.6	1031 0.7	1657 5.4	2224 1.0
4 SA	0539 5.3	1121 1.1	1810 4.9	2322 1.5	**19** SU	0510 5.5	1057 0.9	1738 5.3	2254 1.2
5 SU	0622 5.0	1143 1.5	1852 4.7	2356 1.8	**20** M	0555 5.3	1126 1.3	1823 5.0	2336 1.5
6 M ◐	0711 4.6	1218 1.9	1942 4.4		**21** TU	0648 5.0	1213 1.8	1917 4.7	
7 TU	0048 2.1	0808 4.3	1317 2.3	2040 4.2	**22** W	0042 1.9	0756 4.7	1343 2.2	2028 4.5
8 W	0229 2.4	0915 4.1	1515 2.6	2147 4.2	**23** TH	0250 2.1	0927 4.5	1555 2.3	2157 4.5
9 TH	0434 2.3	1031 4.1	1659 2.5	2305 4.3	**24** F	0449 1.8	1056 4.7	1718 2.1	2318 4.8
10 F	0544 2.0	1157 4.3	1757 2.2		**25** SA	0601 1.4	1211 5.0	1817 1.7	
11 SA	0018 4.5	0634 1.7	1254 4.6	1840 1.9	**26** SU	0023 5.1	0657 1.0	1306 5.4	1904 1.4
12 SU	0107 4.9	0713 1.4	1333 4.9	1916 1.6	**27** M	0113 5.5	0743 0.6	1350 5.6	1945 1.1
13 M	0145 5.1	0748 1.1	1406 5.1	1949 1.3	**28** TU	0155 5.7	0823 0.4	1428 5.7	O 2024 0.9
14 TU ●	0218 5.4	0821 0.8	1438 5.4	2023 1.1	**29** W	0234 5.8	0900 0.4	1505 5.7	2100 0.8
15 W	0250 5.5	0855 0.6	1510 5.5	2056 0.9	**30** TH	0312 5.8	0933 0.5	1541 5.6	2133 0.8

OCTOBER

Day	Time m	Time m	Time m	Time m	Day	Time m	Time m	Time m	Time m
1 F	0350 5.7	1000 0.7	1618 5.6	2202 0.9	**16** SA	0328 5.8	0932 0.5	1551 5.7	2136 0.8
2 SA	0428 5.5	1020 1.0	1654 5.2	2224 1.2	**17** SU	0408 5.7	1005 0.6	1631 5.5	2210 0.9
3 SU	0507 5.2	1034 1.3	1730 5.0	2246 1.4	**18** M	0453 5.6	1037 1.1	1715 5.3	2248 1.2
4 M	0548 4.9	1056 1.6	1810 4.7	2316 1.7	**19** TU	0544 5.3	1115 1.6	1803 5.1	2341 1.5
5 TU	0634 4.6	1128 2.0	1857 4.5		**20** W ◐	0642 5.0	1217 2.0	1902 4.8	
6 W	0003 2.1	0728 4.3	1219 2.4	1954 4.3	**21** TH	0107 1.8	0757 4.7	1401 2.4	2021 4.6
7 TH	0129 2.4	0833 4.1	1411 2.8	2105 4.2	**22** F	0309 1.9	0924 4.6	1546 2.3	2149 4.6
8 F	0403 2.4	0945 4.1	1628 2.6	2220 4.3	**23** SA	0440 1.6	1046 4.8	1657 2.1	2304 4.9
9 SA	0515 2.1	1105 4.3	1728 2.3	2333 4.5	**24** SU	0545 1.3	1155 5.1	1752 1.8	
10 SU	0603 1.7	1210 4.6	1810 2.0		**25** M	0004 5.2	0637 1.0	1247 5.3	1837 1.5
11 M	0027 4.8	0641 1.4	1254 5.0	1845 1.6	**26** TU	0052 5.4	0720 0.8	1328 5.4	1917 1.2
12 TU	0108 5.2	0715 1.1	1330 5.3	1919 1.3	**27** W	0133 5.6	0756 0.7	1405 5.5	1955 1.0
13 W	0143 5.4	0749 0.8	1404 5.5	1953 1.1	**28** TH	0211 5.6	0828 0.7	1439 5.5	O 2031 0.9
14 TH ●	0216 5.6	0823 0.6	1439 5.6	2027 0.9	**29** F	0249 5.6	0857 0.8	1514 5.5	2105 0.9
15 F	0251 5.8	0858 0.5	1514 5.6	2102 0.8	**30** SA	0326 5.5	0921 1.0	1548 5.3	2134 1.0
					31 SU	0403 5.3	0940 1.2	1622 5.2	2200 1.2

NOVEMBER

Day	Time m	Time m	Time m	Time m	Day	Time m	Time m	Time m	Time m
1 M	0442 5.1	1000 1.5	1657 5.0	2225 1.4	**16** TU	0444 5.6	1037 1.3	1659 5.4	2305 1.1
2 TU	0522 4.9	1025 1.8	1735 4.8	2257 1.7	**17** W	0538 5.4	1129 1.7	1751 5.2	
3 W	0606 4.6	1058 2.1	1819 4.6	2342 2.0	**18** TH	0006 1.3	0639 5.1	1232 2.0	1854 4.9
4 TH	0656 4.4	1145 2.4	1913 4.4		**19** F	0122 1.5	0752 4.8	1351 2.3	◑ 2012 4.4
5 F ◑	0051 2.2	0753 4.3	1314 2.7	2020 4.3	**20** SA	0252 1.6	0907 4.8	1512 2.3	2128 4.8
6 SA	0234 2.3	0859 4.2	1518 2.7	2132 4.3	**21** SU	0411 1.5	1020 4.8	1620 2.1	2236 4.9
7 SU	0419 2.1	1008 4.4	1635 2.4	2239 4.5	**22** M	0515 1.4	1124 4.9	1716 1.9	2336 5.1
8 M	0513 1.8	1112 4.6	1724 2.1	2336 4.8	**23** TU	0608 1.3	1218 5.1	1805 1.7	
9 TU	0555 1.5	1205 4.9	1805 1.8		**24** W	0027 5.4	0650 1.2	1303 5.2	1847 1.5
10 W	0023 5.1	0634 1.2	1249 5.2	1843 1.4	**25** TH	0111 5.3	0724 1.2	1341 5.3	1927 1.3
11 TH	0105 5.4	0711 0.9	1329 5.5	1921 1.2	**26** F	0152 5.3	0753 1.2	1417 5.3	O 2006 1.2
12 F ●	0144 5.6	0749 0.7	1408 5.6	2000 0.9	**27** SA	0230 5.3	0821 1.2	1451 5.3	2041 1.1
13 SA	0225 5.8	0828 0.7	1447 5.7	2041 0.8	**28** SU	0308 5.2	0848 1.3	1525 5.3	2114 1.2
14 SU	0308 5.8	0909 0.7	1528 5.7	2125 0.8	**29** M	0345 5.2	0915 1.4	1558 5.2	2145 1.3
15 M	0354 5.8	0952 1.0	1611 5.6	2212 0.9	**30** TU	0422 5.0	0943 1.6	1632 5.1	2216 1.4

DECEMBER

Day	Time m	Time m	Time m	Time m	Day	Time m	Time m	Time m	Time m
1 W	0501 4.9	1013 1.8	1709 4.9	2251 1.6	**16** TH	0532 5.5	1129 1.5	1742 5.4	
2 TH	0542 4.8	1047 2.0	1751 4.8	2333 1.7	**17** F	0007 1.0	0629 5.2	1220 1.7	1841 5.2
3 F	0626 4.6	1130 2.2	1837 4.6		**18** SA ◑	0107 1.2	0732 5.0	1316 2.0	1947 5.0
4 SA	0025 1.9	0716 4.5	1229 2.4	1932 4.5	**19** SU	0212 1.4	0836 4.8	1420 2.1	2055 4.9
5 SU ◑	0130 2.0	0812 4.4	1351 2.5	2036 4.5	**20** M	0322 1.6	0940 4.7	1528 2.1	2159 4.9
6 M	0246 2.0	0915 4.4	1516 2.4	2141 4.5	**21** TU	0429 1.7	1043 4.9	1631 2.1	2301 4.9
7 TU	0400 1.8	1017 4.6	1624 2.2	2242 4.7	**22** W	0528 1.4	1142 4.7	1729 1.9	2359 4.9
8 W	0458 1.6	1116 4.8	1717 1.9	2338 5.0	**23** TH	0615 1.7	1234 4.8	1822 1.7	
9 TH	0548 1.4	1209 5.1	1806 1.6		**24** F	0051 4.9	0651 1.6	1320 5.0	1907 1.4
10 F	0029 5.2	0635 1.1	1257 5.3	1852 1.3	**25** SA	0137 5.0	0723 1.6	1400 5.1	1948 1.4
11 SA	0118 5.4	0722 1.0	1342 5.5	1941 1.0	**26** SU	0218 5.0	0755 1.5	1436 5.1	O 2026 1.3
12 SU ●	0206 5.6	0810 0.9	1426 5.6	2032 0.8	**27** M	0256 5.1	0827 1.5	1509 5.2	2101 1.3
13 M	0255 5.8	0859 0.9	1512 5.7	2126 0.7	**28** TU	0331 5.1	0900 1.5	1542 5.2	2134 1.2
14 TU	0345 5.8	0949 1.1	1559 5.6	2219 0.7	**29** W	0406 5.1	0933 1.6	1616 5.1	2209 1.2
15 W	0437 5.7	1039 1.2	1648 5.5	2313 0.8	**30** TH	0441 5.0	1007 1.6	1651 5.1	2244 1.3
					31 F	0519 4.9	1040 1.7	1728 5.0	2321 1.4

Chapter 5

Chart Datum: 2·90 metres below Ordnance Datum (Newlyn)

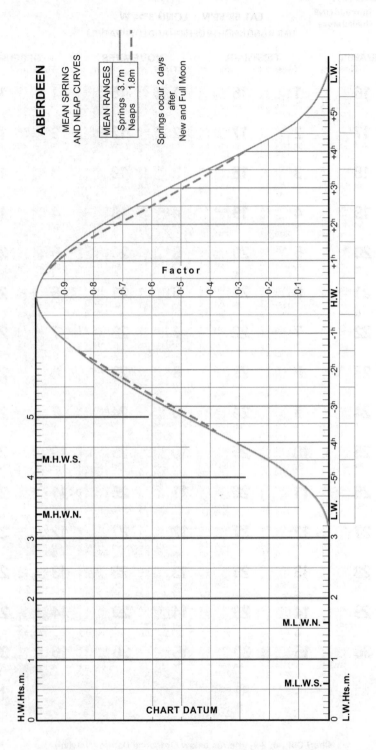

ABERDEEN

MEAN SPRING
AND NEAP CURVES

MEAN RANGES
Springs 3.7m
Neaps 1.8m

Springs occur 2 days
after
New and Full Moon

Factor

0·9 0·8 0·7 0·6 0·5 0·4 0·3 0·2 0·1

L.W.
+5ʰ +4ʰ +3ʰ +2ʰ +1ʰ H.W. -1ʰ -2ʰ -3ʰ -4ʰ -5ʰ L.W.

M.H.W.S.

M.H.W.N.

M.L.W.N.

M.L.W.S.

H.W.Hts.m.

L.W.Hts.m.

CHART DATUM

<table>
<tr><td>TIME ZONE (UT)
For Summer Time add ONE hour in non-shaded areas</td><td><h1>SCOTLAND – ABERDEEN</h1>LAT 57°09′N   LONG 2°05′W
TIMES AND HEIGHTS OF HIGH AND LOW WATERS</td><td>YEAR 2004</td></tr>
</table>

JANUARY

Day	Time m	Day	Time m
1 TH	0217 1.5 / 0853 3.4 / 1438 1.9 / 2059 3.6	**16** F	0114 1.2 / 0744 3.6 / 1333 1.7 / 1956 3.8
2 F	0323 1.6 / 0954 3.5 / 1548 1.9 / 2203 3.6	**17** SA	0222 1.3 / 0853 3.6 / 1449 1.7 / 2112 3.8
3 SA	0422 1.6 / 1046 3.6 / 1646 1.7 / 2258 3.6	**18** SU	0333 1.3 / 1001 3.7 / 1605 1.5 / 2227 3.9
4 SU	0509 1.5 / 1130 3.7 / 1733 1.6 / 2346 3.7	**19** M	0444 1.3 / 1103 3.9 / 1715 1.3 / 2334 4.1
5 M	0550 1.5 / 1210 3.9 / 1814 1.4	**20** TU	0545 1.2 / 1158 4.1 / 1814 1.0
6 TU	0029 3.8 / 0626 1.4 / 1246 4.0 / 1852 1.3	**21** W	0033 4.2 / 0637 1.1 / 1248 4.3 / ● 1905 0.7
7 W	0108 3.9 / 0701 1.4 / 1320 4.1 / ○ 1927 1.1	**22** TH	0126 4.3 / 0724 1.0 / 1334 4.4 / 1954 0.6
8 TH	0145 3.9 / 0734 1.3 / 1353 4.1 / 2003 1.0	**23** F	0216 4.3 / 0808 1.0 / 1418 4.5 / 2040 0.5
9 F	0221 4.0 / 0808 1.3 / 1427 4.2 / 2038 1.0	**24** SA	0302 4.3 / 0850 1.0 / 1501 4.5 / 2124 0.5
10 SA	0258 4.0 / 0843 1.3 / 1501 4.2 / 2115 0.9	**25** SU	0347 4.2 / 0929 1.1 / 1544 4.4 / 2206 0.6
11 SU	0336 3.9 / 0918 1.3 / 1537 4.1 / 2154 0.9	**26** M	0430 4.0 / 1008 1.2 / 1627 4.2 / 2247 0.9
12 M	0416 3.9 / 0956 1.3 / 1616 4.1 / 2235 1.0	**27** TU	0513 3.8 / 1047 1.4 / 1710 4.0 / 2328 1.1
13 TU	0459 3.8 / 1037 1.4 / 1659 4.0 / 2320 1.1	**28** W	0557 3.6 / 1130 1.6 / 1757 3.8
14 W	0547 3.7 / 1124 1.5 / 1749 3.9	**29** TH	0013 1.4 / 0645 3.4 / 1222 1.8 / ◐ 1850 3.6
15 TH	0013 1.2 / 0642 3.6 / 1223 1.6 / ◑ 1848 3.8	**30** F	0106 1.6 / 0742 3.3 / 1328 1.9 / 1954 3.4
		31 SA	0211 1.8 / 0850 3.3 / 1449 2.0 / 2112 3.3

FEBRUARY

Day	Time m	Day	Time m
1 SU	0331 1.9 / 1001 3.3 / 1615 1.9 / 2228 3.4	**16** M	0317 1.6 / 0940 3.5 / 1600 1.5 / 2227 3.7
2 M	0442 1.8 / 1101 3.5 / 1714 1.7 / 2328 3.5	**17** TU	0441 1.5 / 1053 3.7 / 1716 1.2 / 2338 3.9
3 TU	0532 1.7 / 1149 3.7 / 1759 1.5	**18** W	0542 1.3 / 1152 3.9 / 1812 0.9
4 W	0015 3.6 / 0611 1.5 / 1229 3.8 / 1836 1.2	**19** TH	0034 4.1 / 0631 1.1 / 1241 4.2 / 1900 0.6
5 TH	0055 3.8 / 0646 1.4 / 1304 4.0 / 1912 1.0	**20** F	0122 4.2 / 0714 1.0 / 1323 4.3 / ● 1943 0.4
6 F	0131 3.9 / 0720 1.2 / 1337 4.1 / ○ 1946 0.8	**21** SA	0203 4.3 / 0753 0.9 / 1403 4.4 / 2023 0.4
7 SA	0205 4.0 / 0753 1.1 / 1410 4.2 / 2022 0.7	**22** SU	0242 4.2 / 0829 0.8 / 1441 4.4 / 2100 0.4
8 SU	0240 4.1 / 0827 1.0 / 1443 4.3 / 2057 0.6	**23** M	0318 4.1 / 0903 0.9 / 1517 4.4 / 2134 0.6
9 M	0315 4.1 / 0901 1.0 / 1517 4.3 / 2133 0.6	**24** TU	0354 4.0 / 0936 1.0 / 1554 4.2 / 2207 0.8
10 TU	0351 4.0 / 0935 1.0 / 1554 4.3 / 2210 0.7	**25** W	0429 3.8 / 1009 1.1 / 1631 4.0 / 2240 1.1
11 W	0430 4.0 / 1012 1.1 / 1634 4.2 / 2251 0.8	**26** TH	0505 3.6 / 1043 1.3 / 1712 3.8 / 2315 1.4
12 TH	0513 3.8 / 1054 1.2 / 1721 4.1 / 2338 1.0	**27** F	0546 3.5 / 1125 1.6 / 1800 3.5 / 2359 1.6
13 F	0604 3.7 / 1146 1.4 / ◑ 1818 3.9	**28** SA	0637 3.3 / 1222 1.8 / 1901 3.3
14 SA	0036 1.3 / 0705 3.5 / 1256 1.6 / 1930 3.7	**29** SU	0101 1.9 / 0742 3.2 / 1347 2.0 / 2020 3.1
15 SU	0150 1.5 / 0819 3.5 / 1423 1.7 / 2058 3.6		

MARCH

Day	Time m	Day	Time m
1 M	0233 2.0 / 0906 3.2 / 1538 1.9 / 2155 3.2	**16** TU	0317 1.8 / 0929 3.4 / 1605 1.4 / 2233 3.6
2 TU	0416 2.0 / 1026 3.3 / 1651 1.7 / 2307 3.3	**17** W	0439 1.6 / 1046 3.6 / 1712 1.1 / 2338 3.8
3 W	0512 1.8 / 1122 3.5 / 1737 1.4 / 2355 3.6	**18** TH	0534 1.4 / 1142 3.9 / 1803 0.8
4 TH	0552 1.5 / 1204 3.7 / 1814 1.1	**19** F	0026 4.0 / 0617 1.1 / 1227 4.1 / 1845 0.6
5 F	0033 3.8 / 0626 1.3 / 1240 3.9 / 1848 0.9	**20** SA	0106 4.1 / 0655 0.9 / 1305 4.2 / ● 1923 0.4
6 SA	0108 3.9 / 0658 1.1 / 1313 4.1 / ○ 1922 0.6	**21** SU	0141 4.1 / 0730 0.8 / 1341 4.3 / 1958 0.4
7 SU	0141 4.1 / 0731 0.9 / 1346 4.3 / 1957 0.4	**22** M	0214 4.1 / 0803 0.7 / 1415 4.3 / 2030 0.5
8 M	0214 4.2 / 0804 0.8 / 1419 4.4 / 2032 0.4	**23** TU	0246 4.1 / 0835 0.8 / 1449 4.3 / 2100 0.6
9 TU	0248 4.2 / 0838 0.7 / 1454 4.4 / 2108 0.4	**24** W	0317 4.0 / 0906 0.9 / 1523 4.1 / 2129 0.8
10 W	0324 4.2 / 0912 0.7 / 1532 4.4 / 2144 0.5	**25** TH	0348 3.8 / 0936 1.0 / 1559 3.9 / 2158 1.1
11 TH	0402 4.1 / 0949 0.8 / 1614 4.3 / 2224 0.7	**26** F	0421 3.7 / 1009 1.2 / 1638 3.7 / 2229 1.4
12 F	0444 3.9 / 1032 1.0 / 1703 4.0 / 2311 1.1	**27** SA	0458 3.5 / 1048 1.4 / 1724 3.5 / 2308 1.6
13 SA	0534 1.3 / 1125 1.3 / 1804 3.8 / ◑	**28** SU	0545 3.3 / 1138 1.6 / 1823 3.2 / ◑
14 SU	0012 1.4 / 0637 3.5 / 1240 1.5 / 1924 3.5	**29** M	0003 1.9 / 0647 3.2 / 1256 1.8 / 1939 3.1
15 M	0135 1.7 / 0758 3.3 / 1421 1.6 / 2101 3.4	**30** TU	0136 2.1 / 0808 3.1 / 1444 1.8 / 2111 3.1
		31 W	0334 2.0 / 0937 3.2 / 1612 1.6 / 2231 3.3

APRIL

Day	Time m	Day	Time m
1 TH	0440 1.8 / 1043 3.4 / 1702 1.3 / 2322 3.5	**16** F	0513 1.3 / 1122 3.8 / 1743 0.8
2 F	0521 1.5 / 1129 3.6 / 1741 1.0	**17** SA	0005 3.9 / 0554 1.1 / 1205 4.0 / 1821 0.6
3 SA	0001 3.7 / 0555 1.2 / 1206 3.9 / 1816 0.7	**18** SU	0042 4.0 / 0631 0.9 / 1242 4.1 / 1856 0.6
4 SU	0036 4.0 / 0629 1.0 / 1241 4.1 / 1851 0.5	**19** M	0114 4.0 / 0705 0.8 / 1316 4.2 / ● 1928 0.6
5 M	0110 4.1 / 0703 0.8 / 1316 4.3 / ○ 1928 0.3	**20** TU	0144 4.0 / 0737 0.8 / 1350 4.2 / 1958 0.7
6 TU	0145 4.3 / 0738 0.6 / 1353 4.4 / 2004 0.2	**21** W	0214 4.0 / 0809 0.8 / 1424 4.1 / 2027 0.8
7 W	0220 4.3 / 0814 0.5 / 1432 4.5 / 2042 0.3	**22** TH	0244 4.0 / 0840 0.9 / 1458 4.0 / 2056 1.0
8 TH	0258 4.2 / 0852 0.6 / 1514 4.4 / 2121 0.5	**23** F	0315 3.9 / 0912 1.0 / 1534 3.8 / 2125 1.2
9 F	0338 4.1 / 0933 0.7 / 1601 4.2 / 2204 0.8	**24** SA	0347 3.7 / 0946 1.1 / 1614 3.6 / 2157 1.4
10 SA	0422 3.9 / 1021 0.9 / 1656 4.0 / 2255 1.2	**25** SU	0424 3.6 / 1025 1.3 / 1701 3.4 / 2236 1.6
11 SU	0515 3.7 / 1122 1.1 / 1805 3.7	**26** M	0508 3.4 / 1115 1.5 / 1758 3.2 / 2328 1.9
12 M	0002 1.6 / 0622 3.5 / 1244 1.3 / ◐ 1928 3.4	**27** TU	0607 3.2 / 1222 1.6 / 1906 3.1 / ◐
13 TU	0131 1.8 / 0745 3.4 / 1425 1.4 / 2104 3.4	**28** W	0047 2.0 / 0720 3.2 / 1350 1.6 / 2022 3.1
14 W	0310 1.8 / 0915 3.4 / 1555 1.2 / 2225 3.6	**29** TH	0229 2.0 / 0838 3.2 / 1512 1.5 / 2138 3.3
15 TH	0422 1.6 / 1029 3.6 / 1656 0.9 / 2322 3.7	**30** F	0345 1.8 / 0949 3.3 / 1611 1.2 / 2236 3.5

Chart Datum: 2·25 metres below Ordnance Datum (Newlyn)

Chapter 5

SCOTLAND – ABERDEEN

YEAR 2004

TIME ZONE (UT)
For Summer Time add ONE hour in **non-shaded areas**

LAT 57°09'N   LONG 2°05'W

TIMES AND HEIGHTS OF HIGH AND LOW WATERS

MAY

Time	m		Time	m
1 SA 0435	1.5		**16 SU** 0525	1.2
1042	3.6		1137	3.8
1657	0.9		1752	0.8
2320	3.7			
2 SU 0516	1.2		**17 M** 0011	3.8
1126	3.8		0603	1.1
1738	0.7		1216	3.9
2359	4.0		1826	0.8
3 M 0555	1.0		**18 TU** 0045	3.9
1206	4.1		0640	1.0
1818	0.5		1252	3.9
			1859	0.8
4 TU 0037	4.1		**19** 0116	3.9
0633	0.7		0715	0.9
1247	4.3		1328	3.9
○1858	0.3		●1930	0.9
5 W 0116	4.3		**20 TH** 0147	4.0
0713	0.6		0749	0.9
1329	4.4		1404	3.9
1939	0.3		2001	1.0
6 TH 0155	4.3		**21 F** 0218	3.9
0754	0.5		0822	0.9
1414	4.4		1440	3.8
2021	0.4		2031	1.1
7 F 0236	4.3		**22 SA** 0250	3.9
0838	0.5		0856	1.0
1502	4.3		1518	3.7
2105	0.7		2103	1.3
8 SA 0319	4.1		**23 SU** 0324	3.8
0927	0.6		0932	1.1
1556	4.1		1558	3.6
2154	1.0		2138	1.4
9 SU 0408	4.0		**24 M** 0401	3.7
1022	0.8		1012	1.2
1657	3.9		1643	3.5
2249	1.3		2218	1.5
10 M 0505	3.8		**25 TU** 0445	3.5
1127	0.9		1059	1.3
1807	3.7		1735	3.3
2357	1.6		2307	1.7
11 TU 0614	3.6		**26 W** 0537	3.4
1245	1.1		1156	1.4
1924	3.5		1834	3.3
◐				
12 W 0117	1.7		**27 TH** 0009	1.8
0729	3.5		0639	3.3
1409	1.1		1303	1.4
2045	3.5		◑1936	3.3
13 TH 0240	1.7		**28 F** 0127	1.8
0848	3.5		0744	3.3
1526	1.1		1412	1.3
2157	3.5		2041	3.3
14 F 0348	1.6		**29 SA** 0240	1.7
0958	3.6		0849	3.4
1626	1.0		1514	1.2
2252	3.6		2143	3.5
15 SA 0442	1.4		**30 SU** 0340	1.5
1052	3.7		0950	3.6
1713	0.9		1609	1.0
2335	3.7		2237	3.7
			31 M 0433	1.3
			1045	3.8
			1659	0.8
			2323	3.9

JUNE

Time	m		Time	m
1 TU 0521	1.1		**16 W** 0018	3.8
1134	4.0		0619	1.1
1747	0.6		1233	3.7
			1834	1.1
2 W 0007	4.1		**17 TH** 0053	3.9
0607	0.8		0657	1.1
1223	4.2		1312	3.8
1833	0.5		●1908	1.1
3 TH 0051	4.2		**18 F** 0127	3.9
0654	0.6		0733	1.0
1313	4.3		1350	3.8
○1920	0.5		1942	1.2
4 F 0134	4.3		**19 SA** 0200	3.9
0742	0.5		0808	1.0
1404	4.4		1428	3.8
2007	0.6		2015	1.2
5 SA 0219	4.3		**20 SU** 0233	3.9
0833	0.5		0844	1.0
1457	4.3		1505	3.7
2056	0.8		2048	1.3
6 SU 0307	4.2		**21 M** 0308	3.9
0925	0.5		0920	1.0
1555	4.1		1544	3.7
2147	1.0		2124	1.3
7 M 0359	4.1		**22 TU** 0345	3.8
1022	0.6		0959	1.0
1655	3.9		1625	3.6
2241	1.3		2202	1.4
8 TU 0456	3.9		**23 W** 0424	3.7
1122	0.7		1041	1.1
1756	3.7		1710	3.5
2340	1.5		2245	1.5
9 W 0557	3.8		**24 TH** 0509	3.7
1227	0.9		1128	1.1
1900	3.6		1759	3.5
◐			2334	1.6
10 TH 0045	1.6		**25 F** 0600	3.6
0701	3.7		1221	1.2
1334	1.0		1853	3.4
2007	3.5		◐	
11 F 0153	1.7		**26 SA** 0034	1.6
0809	3.6		0657	3.6
1441	1.1		1321	1.2
2113	3.4		1952	3.4
12 SA 0300	1.6		**27 SU** 0141	1.6
0917	3.6		0759	3.6
1544	1.2		1424	1.1
2211	3.5		2054	3.5
13 SU 0402	1.5		**28 M** 0248	1.6
1016	3.6		0905	3.7
1636	1.2		1526	1.1
2259	3.6		2155	3.6
14 M 0454	1.4		**29 TU** 0353	1.4
1107	3.6		1011	3.8
1720	1.2		1627	1.0
2340	3.7		2252	3.8
15 TU 0538	1.3		**30 W** 0454	1.2
1152	3.7		1112	4.0
1758	1.1		1725	0.9
			2344	4.0

JULY

Time	m		Time	m
1 TH 0551	0.9		**16 F** 0034	3.8
1210	4.1		0642	1.2
1819	0.8		1301	3.7
			1852	1.3
2 F 0033	4.1		**17 SA** 0111	3.9
0645	0.7		0719	1.0
1306	4.2		1339	3.8
○1910	0.8		●1926	1.3
3 SA 0121	4.2		**18 SU** 0144	4.0
0737	0.5		0754	0.9
1400	4.3		1414	3.8
1959	0.8		2000	1.2
4 SU 0208	4.3		**19 M** 0218	4.0
0829	0.4		0829	0.8
1454	4.3		1449	3.9
2047	0.9		2033	1.2
5 M 0257	4.3		**20 TU** 0251	4.0
0920	0.3		0904	0.8
1547	4.2		1525	3.8
2134	1.0		2107	1.2
6 TU 0346	4.3		**21 W** 0325	4.0
1011	0.4		0940	0.8
1639	4.0		1601	3.8
2222	1.1		2142	1.2
7 W 0437	4.2		**22 TH** 0401	4.0
1102	0.6		1017	0.8
1730	3.8		1640	3.7
2310	1.3		2219	1.3
8 TH 0529	4.0		**23 F** 0440	3.9
1154	0.8		1057	0.9
1823	3.6		1723	3.7
			2300	1.3
9 F 0002	1.5		**24 SA** 0524	3.9
0623	3.8		1143	1.0
1248	1.1		1812	3.6
◐1918	3.5		2350	1.5
10 SA 0100	1.6		**25 SU** 0616	3.8
0722	3.6		1237	1.1
1345	1.3		1908	3.5
2018	3.4		◐	
11 SU 0204	1.7		**26 M** 0053	1.6
0827	3.5		0719	3.7
1448	1.4		1341	1.2
2121	3.4		2012	3.5
12 M 0315	1.7		**27 TU** 0207	1.6
0936	3.4		0832	3.6
1554	1.5		1452	1.3
2220	3.4		2122	3.6
13 TU 0424	1.6		**28 W** 0326	1.5
1039	3.5		0951	3.7
1650	1.5		1608	1.3
2311	3.5		2230	3.7
14 W 0518	1.5		**29 TH** 0443	1.3
1133	3.5		1105	3.9
1736	1.5		1716	1.2
2355	3.7		2330	3.9
15 TH 0603	1.3		**30 F** 0547	1.0
1220	3.6		1208	4.1
1816	1.4		1813	1.1
			31 SA 0022	4.1
			0642	0.7
			1304	4.2
			○1903	0.9

AUGUST

Time	m		Time	m
1 SU 0111	4.3		**16 M** 0124	4.1
0732	0.4		0734	0.8
1355	4.3		1354	4.0
1949	0.9		●1940	1.1
2 M 0157	4.4		**17 TU** 0156	4.2
0820	0.3		0807	0.7
1442	4.3		1426	4.0
2032	0.8		2012	1.0
3 TU 0241	4.5		**18 W** 0228	4.2
0905	0.3		0839	0.6
1527	4.2		1459	4.1
2113	0.9		2044	1.0
4 W 0325	4.4		**19 TH** 0300	4.3
0948	0.4		0914	0.6
1611	4.1		1532	4.0
2153	1.0		2116	1.0
5 TH 0409	4.3		**20 F** 0334	4.2
1030	0.6		0948	0.7
1654	3.9		1608	4.0
2233	1.1		2151	1.1
6 F 0453	4.1		**21 SA** 0412	4.2
1111	0.9		1025	0.8
1738	3.7		1648	3.9
2315	1.4		2229	1.2
7 SA 0540	3.9		**22 SU** 0455	4.0
1155	1.2		1107	1.0
1825	3.5		1734	3.7
◐			2316	1.4
8 SU 0005	1.6		**23 M** 0547	3.9
0633	3.6		1200	1.2
1245	1.5		1831	3.6
1919	3.3		◑	
9 M 0107	1.8		**24 TU** 0019	1.5
0735	3.4		0654	3.7
1346	1.7		1310	1.5
2024	3.3		1940	3.5
10 TU 0226	1.9		**25 W** 0144	1.6
0853	3.3		0819	3.6
1506	1.8		1435	1.6
2137	3.3		2101	3.5
11 W 0358	1.8		**26 TH** 0321	1.6
1013	3.3		0951	3.6
1626	1.8		1606	1.6
2242	3.4		2219	3.7
12 TH 0501	1.6		**27 F** 0445	1.3
1117	3.4		1109	3.8
1719	1.7		1714	1.4
2333	3.6		2322	3.9
13 F 0548	1.4		**28 SA** 0546	0.9
1206	3.6		1208	4.1
1800	1.6		1806	1.2
14 SA 0015	3.8		**29 SU** 0014	4.2
0626	1.2		0635	0.6
1246	3.7		1258	4.2
1835	1.4		1851	1.0
15 SU 0052	3.9		**30 M** 0058	4.4
0701	1.0		0720	0.4
1321	3.9		1341	4.3
1908	1.2		○1931	0.8
			31 TU 0139	4.5
			0801	0.3
			1421	4.3
			2009	0.8

Chart Datum: 2·25 metres below Ordnance Datum (Newlyn)

SCOTLAND – ABERDEEN

YEAR **2004**

LAT 57°09'N   LONG 2°05'W

TIMES AND HEIGHTS OF HIGH AND LOW WATERS

SEPTEMBER

Day	Time m	Time m	Time m	Time m
1 W	0219 4.6	0840 0.3	1459 4.3	2045 0.8
16 TH	0159 4.4	0811 0.5	1428 4.2	2017 0.8
2 TH	0258 4.5	0916 0.4	1535 4.1	2120 0.9
17 F	0233 4.4	0845 0.5	1502 4.2	2050 0.8
3 F	0336 4.4	0951 0.7	1612 3.9	2155 1.1
18 SA	0309 4.4	0919 0.6	1538 4.2	2125 0.9
4 SA	0416 4.1	1025 1.0	1650 3.8	2232 1.3
19 SU	0349 4.3	0956 0.8	1618 4.0	2205 1.1
5 SU	0458 3.9	1101 1.3	1731 3.6	2314 1.5
20 M	0435 4.1	1039 1.1	1704 3.8	2255 1.3
6 M	0547 3.6	1144 1.7	1821 3.4	◐
21 TU	0532 3.9	1135 1.5	1803 3.6	◐
7 TU	0012 1.8	0649 3.3	1244 1.9	1926 3.3
22 W	0005 1.5	0648 3.6	1254 1.8	1921 3.5
8 W	0137 2.0	0809 3.2	1415 2.1	2047 3.3
23 TH	0142 1.6	0822 3.5	1436 1.9	2049 3.5
9 TH	0329 1.9	0944 3.2	1602 2.0	2208 3.4
24 F	0328 1.5	0959 3.6	1606 1.7	2211 3.7
10 F	0440 1.7	1056 3.4	1659 1.9	2306 3.6
25 SA	0443 1.2	1108 3.9	1706 1.5	2312 4.0
11 SA	0525 1.4	1144 3.6	1739 1.6	2349 3.8
26 SU	0536 0.8	1159 4.1	1752 1.2	2359 4.2
12 SU	0602 1.2	1221 3.8	1812 1.4	
27 M	0621 0.6	1241 4.2	1832 1.0	
13 M	0024 4.0	0634 0.9	1254 4.0	1843 1.2
28 TU	0039 4.4	0700 0.4	1318 4.3	1908 0.9
14 TU	0057 4.2	0706 0.7	1329 4.1	● 1914 1.0
29 W	0117 4.5	0736 0.4	1353 4.3	1943 0.8
15 W	0128 4.3	0738 0.6	1356 4.2	1945 0.9
30 TH	0153 4.5	0810 0.5	1426 4.3	2017 0.8

OCTOBER

Day	Time m	Time m	Time m	Time m
1 F	0229 4.5	0842 0.7	1458 4.2	2049 0.9
16 SA	0208 4.5	0816 0.5	1433 4.4	2027 0.8
2 SA	0305 4.3	0912 0.9	1531 4.0	2122 1.1
17 SU	0248 4.5	0854 0.7	1512 4.3	2107 0.9
3 SU	0343 4.1	0942 1.2	1605 3.9	2157 1.3
18 M	0333 4.3	0935 1.0	1554 4.1	2153 1.0
4 M	0424 3.8	1014 1.5	1643 3.7	2237 1.5
19 TU	0426 4.1	1023 1.3	1644 3.9	2251 1.3
5 TU	0511 3.6	1053 1.8	1730 3.5	2329 1.8
20 W	0531 3.8	1125 1.7	1748 3.7	◐
6 W	0613 3.3	1147 2.1	1834 3.3	◐
21 TH	0009 1.5	0653 3.6	1251 1.9	1909 3.6
7 TH	0049 1.9	0729 3.2	1321 2.3	1953 3.3
22 F	0147 1.5	0825 3.6	1429 2.0	2036 3.6
8 F	0238 1.9	0900 3.2	1519 2.2	2120 3.3
23 SA	0319 1.3	0951 3.7	1548 1.8	2154 3.8
9 SA	0402 1.7	1018 3.4	1625 2.0	2226 3.5
24 SU	0426 1.1	1052 3.9	1644 1.5	2252 4.0
10 SU	0450 1.4	1108 3.6	1706 1.7	2312 3.8
25 M	0516 0.9	1139 4.1	1729 1.3	2337 4.2
11 M	0527 1.2	1145 3.8	1739 1.4	2349 4.0
26 TU	0557 0.7	1217 4.2	1808 1.1	
12 TU	0600 0.9	1219 4.0	1811 1.2	
27 W	0016 4.3	0634 0.7	1251 4.2	1843 1.0
13 W	0022 4.3	0632 0.7	1251 4.2	1843 1.0
28 TH	0053 4.4	0707 0.7	1323 4.3	1918 0.9
14 TH	0056 4.4	0706 0.6	1324 4.3	● 1916 0.8
29 F	0129 4.4	0739 0.8	1355 4.2	1951 0.9
15 F	0131 4.5	0741 0.6	1358 4.4	1951 0.8
30 SA	0204 4.3	0810 1.0	1426 4.2	2025 1.0
31 SU	0241 4.2	0839 1.1	1458 4.1	2058 1.1

NOVEMBER

Day	Time m	Time m	Time m	Time m
1 M	0319 4.0	0909 1.3	1531 4.0	2133 1.3
16 TU	0327 4.3	0924 1.1	1539 4.2	2153 0.9
2 TU	0359 3.8	0942 1.6	1608 3.8	2213 1.5
17 W	0426 4.1	1017 1.4	1633 4.0	2255 1.1
3 W	0446 3.6	1020 1.8	1652 3.6	2303 1.7
18 TH	0534 3.9	1121 1.7	1738 3.9	
4 TH	0544 3.4	1110 2.0	1751 3.5	
19 F	0009 1.2	0647 3.7	1238 1.9	◐ 1852 3.8
5 F	0009 1.8	0650 3.3	1226 2.2	◐ 1902 3.4
20 SA	0131 1.3	0806 3.6	1359 1.9	2009 3.7
6 SA	0135 1.8	0805 3.3	1405 2.2	2018 3.4
21 SU	0249 1.2	0922 3.7	1512 1.8	2123 3.8
7 SU	0256 1.7	0920 3.4	1524 2.0	2129 3.5
22 M	0355 1.2	1022 3.8	1612 1.6	2223 3.9
8 M	0355 1.5	1018 3.6	1616 1.8	2223 3.7
23 TU	0447 1.1	1110 3.9	1700 1.5	2311 4.1
9 TU	0440 1.2	1102 3.8	1657 1.5	2306 4.0
24 W	0530 1.0	1149 4.0	1743 1.3	2353 4.1
10 W	0519 1.0	1141 4.0	1735 1.3	2346 4.2
25 TH	0607 1.0	1224 4.1	1821 1.2	
11 TH	0557 0.8	1217 4.2	1812 1.1	○ 1858 1.1
26 F	0032 4.2	0641 1.0	1258 4.1	1858 1.1
12 F	0025 4.4	0635 0.7	1254 4.4	● 1850 0.9
27 SA	0110 4.2	0713 1.1	1330 4.1	1934 1.1
13 SA	0106 4.5	0714 0.6	1331 4.4	1930 0.8
28 SU	0148 4.1	0745 1.2	1402 4.2	2009 1.1
14 SU	0149 4.5	0754 0.7	1410 4.4	2013 0.8
29 M	0225 4.0	0817 1.2	1435 4.1	2043 1.2
15 M	0236 4.5	0838 0.9	1453 4.4	2100 0.8
30 TU	0303 3.9	0849 1.4	1508 4.0	2119 1.2

DECEMBER

Day	Time m	Time m	Time m	Time m
1 W	0343 3.8	0922 1.6	1545 3.9	2159 1.3
16 TH	0423 4.2	1010 1.3	1624 4.2	2251 0.8
2 TH	0427 3.7	1000 1.7	1626 3.8	2243 1.5
17 F	0523 4.0	1106 1.5	1722 4.1	2352 1.0
3 F	0516 3.5	1045 1.9	1715 3.7	2335 1.6
18 SA	0625 3.8	1207 1.7	1825 4.0	◐
4 SA	0612 3.4	1140 2.0	1814 3.6	
19 SU	0056 1.1	0729 3.6	1313 1.8	1930 3.8
5 SU	0038 1.6	0711 3.4	1251 2.1	◑ 1917 3.5
20 M	0203 1.3	0836 3.6	1421 1.8	2040 3.8
6 M	0145 1.6	0814 3.4	1407 2.0	2021 3.6
21 TU	0309 1.4	0940 3.6	1529 1.8	2147 3.8
7 TU	0248 1.5	0918 3.6	1512 1.9	2124 3.7
22 W	0410 1.4	1035 3.7	1630 1.6	2245 3.8
8 W	0345 1.3	1013 3.7	1608 1.7	2220 3.9
23 TH	0501 1.4	1122 3.8	1721 1.5	2335 3.8
9 TH	0435 1.1	1101 3.9	1657 1.4	2312 4.1
24 F	0543 1.4	1202 3.9	1805 1.4	
10 F	0523 1.0	1145 4.1	1745 1.2	
25 SA	0019 3.9	0620 1.4	1240 4.0	1845 1.3
11 SA	0000 4.3	0609 0.9	1228 4.3	○ 1831 1.0
26 SU	0100 3.9	0656 1.4	1314 4.1	○ 1922 1.2
12 SU	0049 4.4	0655 0.8	1311 4.4	● 1919 0.8
27 M	0139 3.9	0730 1.4	1348 4.1	1958 1.1
13 M	0139 4.5	0742 0.9	1355 4.4	2008 0.7
28 TU	0216 3.9	0802 1.4	1420 4.1	2032 1.1
14 TU	0231 4.5	0830 1.0	1441 4.4	2059 0.6
29 W	0252 3.9	0835 1.4	1453 4.1	2107 1.1
15 W	0326 4.3	0919 1.1	1530 4.4	2153 0.7
30 TH	0328 3.8	0908 1.4	1528 4.0	2143 1.1
31 F	0406 3.8	0943 1.5	1605 4.0	2222 1.2

Chapter 5

Chart Datum: 2·25 metres below Ordnance Datum (Newlyn)
Register for your **FREE** weekly weather email service from Reeds Almanacs
》 at www.nauticaldata.com – **NOW!**
weekend weather reports sent to your email address, every Thursday 《

289

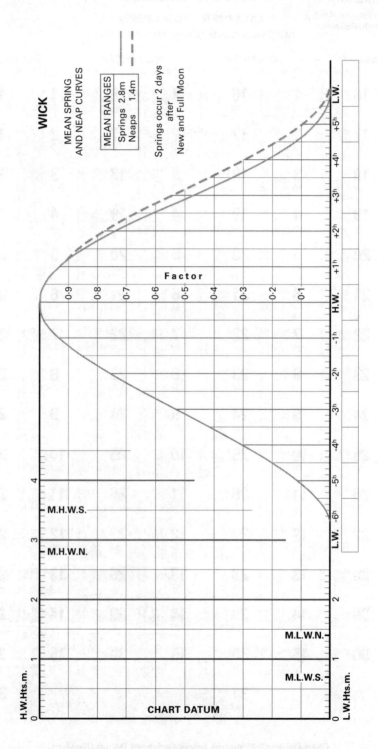

WICK

MEAN SPRING
AND NEAP CURVES

MEAN RANGES	
Springs	2.8m
Neaps	1.4m

Springs occur 2 days
after
New and Full Moon

Factor

SCOTLAND – WICK

YEAR 2004

LAT 58°26'N   LONG 3°05'W

TIMES AND HEIGHTS OF HIGH AND LOW WATERS

JANUARY

Day	Time m	Time m	Time m	Time m		Day	Time m	Time m	Time m
1 TH	0017 1.3	0637 2.8	1228 1.7	1841 2.9		16 F	0532 2.9	1114 1.5	1746 3.1
2 F	0120 1.3	0739 2.8	1340 1.6	1946 2.9		17 SA	0020 1.1	0639 2.9	1242 1.5 · 1900 3.1
3 SA	0213 1.3	0834 2.9	1438 1.5	2045 3.0		18 SU	0131 1.1	0747 3.0	1400 1.3 · 2016 3.1
4 SU	0258 1.3	0921 3.1	1524 1.4	2135 3.0		19 M	0237 1.1	0852 3.2	1507 1.1 · 2127 3.3
5 M	0338 1.3	1001 3.2	1605 1.2	2218 3.1		20 TU	0334 1.0	0950 3.3	1605 0.9 · 2227 3.4
6 TU	0414 1.2	1038 3.3	1643 1.1	2258 3.2		21 W	0425 1.0	1042 3.5	1656 0.7 · ● 2321 3.5
7 W	0448 1.2	1113 3.3	1718 1.0	○ 2335 3.2		22 TH	0511 0.9	1130 3.6	1744 0.5
8 TH	0521 1.2	1147 3.4	1753 0.9			23 F	0010 3.5	0554 0.9	1216 3.7 · 1829 0.5
9 F	0012 3.2	0552 1.2	1222 3.4	1827 0.9		24 SA	0057 3.6	0635 0.9	1259 3.7 · 1913 0.5
10 SA	0049 3.2	0625 1.1	1256 3.4	1903 0.9		25 SU	0141 3.4	0713 1.0	1342 3.6 · 1954 0.6
11 SU	0126 3.2	0700 1.2	1332 3.4	1940 0.9		26 M	0223 3.2	0750 1.1	1423 3.5 · 2034 0.8
12 M	0205 3.1	0737 1.2	1409 3.3	2020 0.9		27 TU	0305 3.0	0826 1.2	1505 3.3 · 2114 1.0
13 TU	0247 3.0	0816 1.2	1451 3.3	2105 0.9		28 W	0348 2.9	0904 1.4	1550 3.1 · 2158 1.2
14 W	0335 3.0	0901 1.3	1539 3.2	2159 1.0		29 TH	0435 2.7	0952 1.5	1641 2.9 · ◗ 2254 1.4
15 TH	0430 2.9	0956 1.4	1637 3.1	◗ 2307 1.1		30 F	0530 2.7	1108 1.6	1743 2.8
						31 SA	0005 1.5	0635 2.7	1245 1.7 · 1855 2.7

FEBRUARY

Day	Time m	Time m	Time m	Time m		Day	Time m	Time m	Time m
1 SU	0126 1.6	0747 2.7	1411 1.6	2013 2.7		16 M	0116 1.3	0723 2.8	1359 1.3 · 2016 2.9
2 M	0233 1.5	0849 2.9	1508 1.4	2115 2.8		17 TU	0234 1.3	0840 3.0	1511 1.0 · 2130 3.1
3 TU	0321 1.4	0937 3.0	1552 1.2	2202 2.9		18 W	0333 1.2	0942 3.2	1605 0.8 · 2226 3.3
4 W	0400 1.3	1018 3.1	1630 1.1	2243 3.1		19 TH	0420 1.0	1033 3.4	1651 0.6 · 2314 3.4
5 TH	0435 1.2	1055 3.3	1704 0.9	2320 3.2		20 F	0500 0.9	1119 3.6	1732 0.4 · ● 2358 3.4
6 F	0507 1.1	1130 3.4	1737 0.8	○ 2357 3.2		21 SA	0538 0.8	1201 3.7	1811 0.4
7 SA	0539 1.0	1205 3.5	1811 0.6			22 SU	0037 3.4	0613 0.8	1240 3.7 · 1847 0.4
8 SU	0032 3.3	0610 0.9	1240 3.5	1844 0.6		23 M	0115 3.3	0646 0.8	1317 3.6 · 1920 0.5
9 M	0109 3.3	0644 0.9	1315 3.5	1919 0.6		24 TU	0150 3.2	0718 0.9	1352 3.5 · 1952 0.7
10 TU	0145 3.2	0718 0.9	1351 3.5	1956 0.6		25 W	0223 3.1	0749 1.0	1427 3.3 · 2022 0.9
11 W	0223 3.2	0755 1.0	1430 3.4	2035 0.7		26 TH	0257 2.9	0822 1.1	1504 3.1 · 2054 1.2
12 TH	0305 3.1	0834 1.1	1514 3.3	2121 0.9		27 F	0335 2.8	0900 1.3	1548 2.9 · 2134 1.4
13 F	0353 2.9	0921 1.2	1609 3.1	◗ 2221 1.1		28 SA	0422 2.7	0955 1.5	1646 2.7 · ◗ 2240 1.6
14 SA	0452 2.8	1030 1.4	1720 3.0	2347 1.3		29 SU	0527 2.6	1146 1.6	1805 2.5
15 SU	0604 2.8	1220 1.4	1846 2.9						

MARCH

Day	Time m	Time m	Time m	Time m		Day	Time m	Time m	Time m
1 M	0029 1.7	0649 2.6	1339 1.6	1940 2.5		16 TU	0114 1.5	0709 2.7	1403 1.1 · 2023 2.8
2 TU	0206 1.6	0810 2.7	1445 1.4	2053 2.7		17 W	0232 1.4	0831 2.9	1507 0.9 · 2127 3.0
3 W	0301 1.5	0908 2.8	1530 1.1	2142 2.8		18 TH	0325 1.2	0931 3.1	1555 0.6 · 2216 3.2
4 TH	0341 1.3	0952 3.0	1607 0.9	2222 3.0		19 F	0406 1.0	1019 3.3	1635 0.5 · 2258 3.3
5 F	0415 1.1	1031 3.2	1640 0.7	2259 3.2		20 SA	0441 0.8	1101 3.5	1711 0.4 · ● 2336 3.3
6 SA	0446 1.0	1107 3.3	1713 0.6	○ 2334 3.3		21 SU	0515 0.7	1140 3.6	1744 0.4
7 SU	0517 0.8	1142 3.5	1746 0.4			22 M	0011 3.3	0547 0.7	1216 3.5 · 1815 0.4
8 M	0009 3.4	0549 0.7	1218 3.6	1819 0.3		23 TU	0044 3.3	0619 0.7	1250 3.5 · 1845 0.6
9 TU	0045 3.4	0622 0.6	1254 3.6	1854 0.4		24 W	0115 3.2	0649 0.7	1322 3.3 · 1913 0.7
10 W	0121 3.3	0657 0.6	1331 3.6	1931 0.5		25 TH	0144 3.1	0720 0.8	1354 3.2 · 1941 0.9
11 TH	0158 3.3	0734 0.7	1411 3.4	2009 0.7		26 F	0213 3.0	0751 1.0	1429 3.0 · 2009 1.1
12 F	0238 3.1	0814 0.9	1457 3.2	2053 0.9		27 SA	0247 2.8	0826 1.2	1509 2.8 · 2042 1.4
13 SA	0325 3.0	0902 1.1	1555 3.0	◗ 2152 1.2		28 SU	0328 2.7	0914 1.4	1603 2.6 · ◗ 2130 1.6
14 SU	0423 2.8	1019 1.3	1712 2.8	2332 1.4		29 M	0424 2.6	1055 1.5	1720 2.4 · 2329 1.7
15 M	0540 2.7	1226 1.3	1850 2.7			30 TU	0548 2.5	1252 1.5	1858 2.4
						31 W	0124 1.7	0718 2.5	1407 1.3 · 2019 2.6

APRIL

Day	Time m	Time m	Time m	Time m		Day	Time m	Time m	Time m
1 TH	0228 1.5	0827 2.7	1455 1.0	2110 2.8		16 F	0304 1.2	0909 3.1	1534 0.6 · 2154 3.1
2 F	0310 1.3	0916 2.9	1533 0.8	2151 3.0		17 SA	0343 1.0	0956 3.2	1610 0.5 · 2233 3.2
3 SA	0344 1.1	0957 3.1	1608 0.6	2228 3.1		18 SU	0417 0.8	1037 3.3	1643 0.5 · 2309 3.2
4 SU	0416 0.9	1036 3.3	1642 0.4	2305 3.3		19 M	0449 0.7	1114 3.4	1713 0.5 · ● 2342 3.2
5 M	0449 0.7	1114 3.5	1716 0.3	○ 2342 3.4		20 TU	0521 0.7	1149 3.4	1743 0.6
6 TU	0524 0.5	1152 3.6	1752 0.2			21 W	0012 3.2	0553 0.7	1222 3.3 · 1812 0.7
7 W	0019 3.4	0600 0.5	1232 3.6	1829 0.3		22 TH	0042 3.2	0625 0.7	1255 3.2 · 1841 0.8
8 TH	0056 3.4	0638 0.5	1313 3.5	1908 0.5		23 F	0111 3.1	0657 0.8	1328 3.0 · 1908 1.0
9 F	0135 3.3	0718 0.6	1358 3.4	1949 0.7		24 SA	0141 3.0	0729 0.9	1403 2.9 · 1937 1.2
10 SA	0217 3.2	0803 0.8	1449 3.1	2037 1.0		25 SU	0214 2.9	0806 1.1	1444 2.7 · 2010 1.3
11 SU	0306 3.0	0902 1.0	1554 2.9	2145 1.3		26 M	0253 2.8	0855 1.2	1535 2.5 · 2056 1.5
12 M	0407 2.8	1043 1.1	1717 2.7	◗ 2329 1.5		27 TU	0344 2.6	1017 1.3	1644 2.4 · ◗ 2225 1.7
13 TU	0527 2.7	1228 1.1	1852 2.7			28 W	0456 2.5	1157 1.3	1809 2.4
14 W	0105 1.5	0654 2.7	1352 0.9	2013 2.8		29 TH	0021 1.6	0620 2.5	1312 1.2 · 1926 2.5
15 TH	0216 1.3	0811 2.9	1450 0.7	2110 3.0		30 F	0134 1.5	0732 2.7	1407 1.0 · 2024 2.7

Chapter 5

Chart Datum: 1·71 metres below Ordnance Datum (Newlyn)
Register for your **FREE** weekly weather email service from Reeds Almanacs
at www.nauticaldata.com – **NOW!**
》 weekend weather reports sent to your email address, every Thursday 《

291

TIME ZONE (UT)
For Summer Time add ONE hour in **non-shaded areas**

SCOTLAND – WICK

LAT 58°26'N   LONG 3°05'W

TIMES AND HEIGHTS OF HIGH AND LOW WATERS

YEAR 2004

MAY

#	Time	m	#	Time	m
1 SA	0224 / 0828 / 1451 / 2111	1.3 / 2.8 / 0.7 / 2.9	**16** SU	0314 / 0927 / 1540 / 2203	1.0 / 3.1 / 0.7 / 3.0
2 SU	0305 / 0916 / 1530 / 2153	1.0 / 3.1 / 0.5 / 3.1	**17** M	0350 / 1009 / 1612 / 2239	0.9 / 3.1 / 0.7 / 3.1
3 M	0342 / 1001 / 1608 / 2233	0.8 / 3.3 / 0.4 / 3.3	**18** TU	0425 / 1048 / 1643 / 2313	0.8 / 3.2 / 0.7 / 3.2
4 TU ○	0420 / 1044 / 1647 / 2313	0.6 / 3.4 / 0.3 / 3.4	**19** W ●	0500 / 1124 / 1715 / 2344	0.8 / 3.2 / 0.8 / 3.2
5 W	0500 / 1128 / 1727 / 2353	0.5 / 3.5 / 0.3 / 3.4	**20** TH	0535 / 1159 / 1746	0.7 / 3.1 / 0.9
6 TH	0541 / 1213 / 1808	0.4 / 3.6 / 0.4	**21** F	0015 / 0608 / 1234 / 1816	3.2 / 0.8 / 3.0 / 0.9
7 F	0034 / 0625 / 1301 / 1851	3.4 / 0.4 / 3.5 / 0.6	**22** SA	0046 / 0643 / 1309 / 1846	3.1 / 0.8 / 3.0 / 1.1
8 SA	0117 / 0712 / 1352 / 1938	3.3 / 0.5 / 3.3 / 0.9	**23** SU	0118 / 0718 / 1346 / 1917	3.1 / 0.9 / 2.8 / 1.2
9 SU	0203 / 0807 / 1449 / 2032	3.2 / 0.7 / 3.1 / 1.1	**24** M	0152 / 0757 / 1427 / 1954	3.0 / 1.0 / 2.7 / 1.3
10 M	0255 / 0919 / 1556 / 2145	3.1 / 0.8 / 2.9 / 1.4	**25** TU	0231 / 0844 / 1514 / 2039	2.9 / 1.1 / 2.6 / 1.4
11 TU ○	0359 / 1046 / 1713 / 2311	2.9 / 0.9 / 2.7 / 1.5	**26** W	0318 / 0946 / 1612 / 2143	2.7 / 1.1 / 2.5 / 1.5
12 W	0513 / 1210 / 1832	2.8 / 0.9 / 2.7	**27** TH ●	0417 / 1103 / 1721 / 2313	2.7 / 1.1 / 2.5 / 1.5
13 TH	0033 / 0628 / 1324 / 1943	1.4 / 2.8 / 0.8 / 2.8	**28** F	0527 / 1213 / 1829	2.7 / 1.0 / 2.6
14 F	0142 / 0739 / 1420 / 2038	1.3 / 2.9 / 0.8 / 2.9	**29** SA	0030 / 0635 / 1313 / 1931	1.4 / 2.7 / 0.9 / 2.7
15 SA	0233 / 0838 / 1504 / 2123	1.2 / 3.0 / 0.7 / 2.9	**30** SU	0131 / 0737 / 1405 / 2026	1.3 / 2.9 / 0.8 / 2.9
			31 M	0222 / 0834 / 1453 / 2115	1.1 / 3.0 / 0.6 / 3.1

JUNE

#	Time	m	#	Time	m
1 TU	0309 / 0928 / 1538 / 2202	0.9 / 3.2 / 0.5 / 3.2	**16** W	0407 / 1025 / 1619 / 2247	1.0 / 3.0 / 1.0 / 3.1
2 W	0355 / 1019 / 1622 / 2247	0.7 / 3.4 / 0.5 / 3.4	**17** TH ●	0445 / 1105 / 1654 / 2322	0.9 / 3.0 / 1.0 / 3.2
3 TH ○	0442 / 1110 / 1708 / 2332	0.6 / 3.5 / 0.5 / 3.4	**18** F	0522 / 1142 / 1727 / 2355	0.8 / 3.0 / 1.0 / 3.2
4 F	0530 / 1201 / 1755	0.5 / 3.5 / 0.6	**19** SA	0558 / 1218 / 1800	0.8 / 3.0 / 1.0
5 SA	0017 / 0620 / 1254 / 1842	3.5 / 0.4 / 3.4 / 0.8	**20** SU	0028 / 0633 / 1255 / 1832	3.2 / 0.8 / 3.0 / 1.1
6 SU	0104 / 0714 / 1348 / 1932	3.4 / 0.4 / 3.3 / 0.9	**21** M	0102 / 0709 / 1332 / 1905	3.1 / 0.8 / 2.9 / 1.1
7 M	0153 / 0812 / 1446 / 2026	3.3 / 0.5 / 3.1 / 1.1	**22** TU	0137 / 0747 / 1411 / 1941	3.1 / 0.8 / 2.8 / 1.2
8 TU	0246 / 0917 / 1547 / 2126	3.2 / 0.6 / 2.9 / 1.3	**23** W	0214 / 0828 / 1453 / 2022	3.0 / 0.9 / 2.8 / 1.2
9 W ○	0345 / 1025 / 1649 / 2233	3.1 / 0.7 / 2.8 / 1.4	**24** TH	0256 / 0914 / 1541 / 2109	2.9 / 0.9 / 2.7 / 1.3
10 TH	0448 / 1133 / 1753 / 2343	3.0 / 0.8 / 2.7 / 1.4	**25** F ●	0344 / 1011 / 1637 / 2208	2.9 / 1.0 / 2.7 / 1.4
11 F	0553 / 1239 / 1857	2.9 / 0.9 / 2.7	**26** SA	0441 / 1116 / 1738 / 2325	2.8 / 1.0 / 2.7 / 1.4
12 SA	0051 / 0657 / 1339 / 1955	1.4 / 2.9 / 0.9 / 2.7	**27** SU	0546 / 1221 / 1841	2.8 / 0.9 / 2.7
13 SU	0153 / 0759 / 1427 / 2046	1.3 / 2.9 / 0.9 / 2.8	**28** M	0039 / 0652 / 1323 / 1942	1.3 / 2.9 / 0.9 / 2.9
14 M	0243 / 0854 / 1508 / 2131	1.2 / 2.9 / 0.9 / 2.9	**29** TU	0145 / 0759 / 1421 / 2041	1.2 / 3.0 / 0.8 / 3.0
15 TU	0327 / 0942 / 1544 / 2210	1.1 / 3.0 / 0.9 / 3.0	**30** W	0245 / 0904 / 1515 / 2136	1.0 / 3.1 / 0.7 / 3.2

JULY

#	Time	m	#	Time	m
1 TH	0341 / 1004 / 1607 / 2227	0.8 / 3.3 / 0.7 / 3.3	**16** F	0434 / 1050 / 1639 / 2303	1.0 / 2.9 / 1.1 / 3.2
2 F ○	0435 / 1101 / 1658 / 2317	0.6 / 3.4 / 0.7 / 3.4	**17** SA ●	0511 / 1128 / 1713 / 2338	0.9 / 3.0 / 1.1 / 3.2
3 SA	0527 / 1155 / 1746	0.5 / 3.4 / 0.7	**18** SU	0546 / 1204 / 1746	0.8 / 3.0 / 1.0
4 SU	0005 / 0619 / 1249 / 1833	3.5 / 0.3 / 3.4 / 0.8	**19** M	0012 / 0619 / 1240 / 1817	3.3 / 0.7 / 3.0 / 1.0
5 M	0054 / 0710 / 1340 / 1920	3.5 / 0.3 / 3.3 / 0.9	**20** TU	0046 / 0653 / 1315 / 1849	3.3 / 0.7 / 3.0 / 1.0
6 TU	0142 / 0802 / 1431 / 2005	3.5 / 0.4 / 3.2 / 1.0	**21** W	0120 / 0727 / 1351 / 1923	3.3 / 0.7 / 3.0 / 1.0
7 W	0231 / 0854 / 1522 / 2051	3.4 / 0.5 / 3.0 / 1.1	**22** TH	0155 / 0803 / 1429 / 1959	3.2 / 0.7 / 2.9 / 1.1
8 TH	0321 / 0947 / 1613 / 2141	3.3 / 0.7 / 2.8 / 1.3	**23** F	0232 / 0842 / 1510 / 2038	3.2 / 0.8 / 2.9 / 1.1
9 F ○	0413 / 1042 / 1706 / 2241	3.1 / 0.9 / 2.7 / 1.4	**24** SA	0314 / 0926 / 1558 / 2124	3.1 / 0.9 / 2.8 / 1.2
10 SA	0510 / 1141 / 1803 / 2351	2.9 / 1.1 / 2.6 / 1.4	**25** SU ●	0404 / 1023 / 1654 / 2226	3.0 / 1.0 / 2.8 / 1.3
11 SU	0611 / 1244 / 1904	2.8 / 1.2 / 2.7	**26** M	0506 / 1135 / 1758 / 2355	2.9 / 1.1 / 2.8 / 1.4
12 M	0107 / 0716 / 1346 / 2005	1.4 / 2.7 / 1.2 / 2.7	**27** TU	0620 / 1250 / 1907	2.9 / 1.1 / 2.8
13 TU	0216 / 0823 / 1438 / 2059	1.3 / 2.7 / 1.2 / 2.8	**28** W	0122 / 0738 / 1403 / 2016	1.3 / 2.9 / 1.1 / 2.9
14 W	0310 / 0920 / 1523 / 2145	1.2 / 2.8 / 1.2 / 3.0	**29** TH	0238 / 0855 / 1507 / 2120	1.1 / 3.0 / 1.0 / 3.1
15 TH	0354 / 1008 / 1603 / 2226	1.1 / 2.9 / 1.2 / 3.1	**30** F	0340 / 1001 / 1602 / 2216	0.8 / 3.2 / 0.9 / 3.3
			31 SA ○	0434 / 1058 / 1650 / 2306	0.6 / 3.4 / 0.9 / 3.5

AUGUST

#	Time	m	#	Time	m
1 SU	0523 / 1149 / 1735 / 2354	0.4 / 3.4 / 0.8 / 3.6	**16** M ●	0525 / 1145 / 1726 / 2351	0.7 / 3.1 / 1.0 / 3.4
2 M	0610 / 1237 / 1817	0.3 / 3.5 / 0.8	**17** TU	0557 / 1219 / 1756	0.6 / 3.2 / 0.9
3 TU	0039 / 0654 / 1322 / 1857	3.7 / 0.3 / 3.4 / 0.8	**18** W	0025 / 0628 / 1253 / 1827	3.4 / 0.5 / 3.2 / 0.8
4 W	0123 / 0736 / 1405 / 1935	3.6 / 0.3 / 3.2 / 0.9	**19** TH	0058 / 0701 / 1326 / 1859	3.4 / 0.5 / 3.2 / 0.8
5 TH	0206 / 0817 / 1447 / 2012	3.5 / 0.5 / 3.1 / 1.0	**20** F	0132 / 0734 / 1402 / 1933	3.4 / 0.6 / 3.1 / 0.9
6 F	0248 / 0857 / 1529 / 2051	3.4 / 0.8 / 2.9 / 1.2	**21** SA	0207 / 0810 / 1440 / 2010	3.3 / 0.7 / 3.1 / 1.0
7 SA ○	0333 / 0939 / 1614 / 2137	3.1 / 1.0 / 2.8 / 1.3	**22** SU	0248 / 0850 / 1523 / 2053	3.2 / 0.9 / 3.0 / 1.2
8 SU	0422 / 1030 / 1706 / 2246	2.9 / 1.2 / 2.7 / 1.5	**23** M ●	0337 / 0941 / 1617 / 2150	3.1 / 1.0 / 2.9 / 1.3
9 M	0522 / 1137 / 1808	2.7 / 1.4 / 2.6	**24** TU	0442 / 1059 / 1724 / 2336	2.9 / 1.3 / 2.8 / 1.4
10 TU	0021 / 0634 / 1300 / 1920	1.5 / 2.6 / 1.5 / 2.7	**25** W	0605 / 1235 / 1843	2.8 / 1.4 / 2.8
11 W	0154 / 0755 / 1415 / 2028	1.5 / 2.6 / 1.5 / 2.8	**26** TH	0123 / 0738 / 1401 / 2003	1.3 / 2.9 / 1.3 / 2.9
12 TH	0255 / 0902 / 1507 / 2121	1.3 / 2.7 / 1.4 / 2.9	**27** F	0242 / 0900 / 1506 / 2111	1.1 / 3.0 / 1.2 / 3.1
13 F	0340 / 0952 / 1548 / 2204	1.1 / 2.8 / 1.3 / 3.1	**28** SA	0340 / 1000 / 1556 / 2206	0.8 / 3.2 / 1.0 / 3.4
14 SA	0418 / 1033 / 1623 / 2242	1.0 / 3.0 / 1.2 / 3.2	**29** SU	0427 / 1050 / 1638 / 2254	0.5 / 3.4 / 0.9 / 3.6
15 SU	0453 / 1110 / 1655 / 2318	0.9 / 3.1 / 1.1 / 3.3	**30** M ○	0510 / 1135 / 1717 / 2337	0.3 / 3.5 / 0.8 / 3.7
			31 TU	0550 / 1217 / 1753	0.3 / 3.5 / 0.7

Chart Datum: 1·71 metres below Ordnance Datum (Newlyn)

SCOTLAND – WICK

YEAR **2004**

LAT 58°26'N   LONG 3°05'W

TIMES AND HEIGHTS OF HIGH AND LOW WATERS

SEPTEMBER

Time m	Time m
1 0019 3.8 / 0627 0.3 / W 1256 3.4 / 1828 0.7	**16** 0559 0.4 / 1224 3.4 / TH 1802 0.7
2 0058 3.7 / 0702 0.4 / TH 1332 3.3 / 1902 0.8	**17** 0032 3.6 / 0631 0.5 / F 1259 3.4 / 1835 0.7
3 0135 3.6 / 0736 0.6 / F 1407 3.2 / 1936 0.9	**18** 0107 3.6 / 0705 0.6 / SA 1334 3.3 / 1910 0.8
4 0212 3.4 / 0807 0.9 / SA 1442 3.0 / 2009 1.1	**19** 0145 3.5 / 0742 0.7 / SU 1412 3.2 / 1948 1.0
5 0251 3.1 / 0839 1.1 / SU 1520 2.9 / 2048 1.3	**20** 0229 3.3 / 0822 1.0 / M 1455 3.1 / 2033 1.1
6 0335 2.9 / 0917 1.4 / M 1607 2.7 / ◗ 2145 1.5	**21** 0322 3.1 / 0914 1.3 / TU 1550 2.9 / ◗ 2140 1.3
7 0434 2.7 / 1019 1.6 / TU 1710 2.6 / 2339 1.6	**22** 0435 2.9 / 1046 1.5 / W 1703 2.8 / 2349 1.4
8 0553 2.5 / 1210 1.7 / W 1831 2.6	**23** 0610 2.8 / 1235 1.6 / TH 1831 2.8
9 0128 1.5 / 0729 2.6 / TH 1351 1.7 / 1953 2.7	**24** 0129 1.2 / 0748 2.9 / F 1400 1.5 / 1954 3.0
10 0233 1.3 / 0843 2.7 / F 1447 1.5 / 2052 2.9	**25** 0239 0.9 / 0858 3.1 / SA 1457 1.3 / 2059 3.2
11 0317 1.1 / 0931 2.9 / SA 1526 1.4 / 2137 3.1	**26** 0329 0.7 / 0950 3.3 / SU 1541 1.1 / 2151 3.4
12 0353 0.9 / 1009 3.0 / SU 1559 1.2 / 2215 3.2	**27** 0411 0.5 / 1033 3.4 / M 1618 0.9 / 2235 3.6
13 0425 0.8 / 1044 3.2 / M 1630 1.1 / 2250 3.4	**28** 0448 0.4 / 1113 3.6 / TU 1653 0.8 / ○ 2315 3.7
14 0457 0.7 / 1118 3.3 / TU 1659 0.9 / ● 2324 3.6	**29** 0522 0.4 / 1150 3.5 / W 1727 0.7 / 2353 3.7
15 0527 0.5 / 1151 3.4 / W 1730 0.8 / 2358 3.6	**30** 0555 0.5 / 1224 3.4 / TH 1800 0.7

OCTOBER

Time m	Time m
1 0029 3.6 / 0627 0.6 / F 1257 3.4 / 1833 0.8	**16** 0007 3.7 / 0603 0.5 / SA 1231 3.5 / 1813 0.7
2 0104 3.5 / 0656 0.8 / SA 1328 3.3 / 1905 0.9	**17** 0047 3.6 / 0640 0.7 / SU 1309 3.5 / 1853 0.8
3 0139 3.3 / 0725 1.0 / SU 1359 3.1 / 1938 1.1	**18** 0130 3.5 / 0720 0.9 / M 1350 3.3 / 1937 0.9
4 0215 3.1 / 0754 1.3 / M 1433 3.0 / 2015 1.3	**19** 0220 3.3 / 0805 1.2 / TU 1436 3.2 / 2031 1.1
5 0257 2.9 / 0826 1.5 / TU 1515 2.9 / 2107 1.5	**20** 0321 3.1 / 0905 1.5 / W 1535 3.0 / ◗ 2202 1.3
6 0353 2.7 / 0913 1.7 / W 1613 2.7 / ◗ 2255 1.6	**21** 0441 2.9 / 1047 1.7 / TH 1652 2.9 / 2353 1.2
7 0513 2.5 / 1113 1.9 / TH 1737 2.6	**22** 0614 2.8 / 1226 1.7 / F 1818 2.9
8 0044 1.6 / 0650 2.5 / F 1309 1.8 / 1904 2.7	**23** 0118 1.1 / 0739 3.0 / SA 1343 1.5 / 1936 3.1
9 0156 1.4 / 0808 2.7 / SA 1413 1.6 / 2011 2.9	**24** 0221 0.9 / 0841 3.1 / SU 1436 1.3 / 2038 3.3
10 0241 1.2 / 0857 2.9 / SU 1453 1.4 / 2059 3.0	**25** 0308 0.7 / 0928 3.3 / M 1518 1.2 / 2128 3.4
11 0318 1.0 / 0935 3.1 / M 1527 1.2 / 2139 3.2	**26** 0347 0.6 / 1009 3.4 / TU 1554 1.0 / 2211 3.5
12 0351 0.8 / 1011 3.2 / TU 1558 1.1 / 2216 3.4	**27** 0421 0.6 / 1046 3.4 / W 1628 0.9 / 2251 3.6
13 0423 0.6 / 1045 3.4 / W 1629 0.9 / 2252 3.6	**28** 0453 0.6 / 1120 3.5 / TH 1702 0.8 / ○ 2328 3.6
14 0455 0.5 / 1120 3.5 / TH 1702 0.8 / ● 2329 3.7	**29** 0524 0.7 / 1153 3.4 / F 1736 0.8
15 0528 0.5 / 1155 3.5 / F 1737 0.7	**30** 0003 3.5 / 0554 0.8 / SA 1225 3.4 / 1809 0.9
	31 0038 3.4 / 0624 1.0 / SU 1255 3.3 / 1843 1.0

NOVEMBER

Time m	Time m
1 0112 3.2 / 0653 1.2 / M 1326 3.2 / 1918 1.1	**16** 0124 3.5 / 0709 1.0 / TU 1335 3.5 / 1938 0.9
2 0149 3.1 / 0721 1.4 / TU 1359 3.1 / 1956 1.3	**17** 0219 3.3 / 0800 1.3 / W 1426 3.3 / 2044 1.0
3 0231 2.9 / 0754 1.6 / W 1439 3.0 / 2046 1.4	**18** 0323 3.1 / 0904 1.5 / TH 1526 3.2 / 2209 1.1
4 0322 2.7 / 0839 1.7 / TH 1530 2.8 / 2207 1.5	**19** 0438 3.0 / 1030 1.7 / F 1638 3.1 / ◗ 2333 1.1
5 0432 2.6 / 0958 1.9 / F 1641 2.7 / ◗ 2343 1.5	**20** 0555 2.9 / 1153 1.7 / SA 1753 3.1
6 0555 2.6 / 1157 1.9 / SA 1803 2.7	**21** 0049 1.0 / 0708 3.0 / SU 1306 1.6 / 1904 3.1
7 0057 1.4 / 0710 2.7 / SU 1314 1.7 / 1913 2.9	**22** 0151 1.0 / 0808 3.0 / M 1404 1.4 / 2007 3.2
8 0152 1.2 / 0807 2.9 / M 1405 1.5 / 2009 3.0	**23** 0240 0.9 / 0858 3.2 / TU 1450 1.3 / 2100 3.3
9 0234 1.0 / 0852 3.0 / TU 1446 1.3 / 2055 3.2	**24** 0319 0.9 / 0940 3.2 / W 1530 1.2 / 2146 3.4
10 0312 0.8 / 0932 3.2 / W 1522 1.1 / 2138 3.4	**25** 0354 0.9 / 1018 3.3 / TH 1607 1.1 / 2228 3.4
11 0347 0.7 / 1011 3.4 / TH 1558 1.0 / 2220 3.6	**26** 0426 0.9 / 1054 3.4 / F 1643 1.0 / ○ 2306 3.4
12 0424 0.6 / 1049 3.5 / F 1636 0.8 / ● 2303 3.7	**27** 0458 1.0 / 1127 3.4 / SA 1720 1.0 / 2343 3.3
13 0502 0.6 / 1128 3.6 / SA 1717 0.7 / 2347 3.7	**28** 0530 1.1 / 1200 3.4 / SU 1756 1.0
14 0542 0.7 / 1208 3.6 / SU 1800 0.7	**29** 0019 3.3 / 0601 1.2 / M 1232 3.4 / 1831 1.0
15 0033 3.6 / 0623 0.8 / M 1250 3.6 / 1846 0.7	**30** 0055 3.2 / 0632 1.3 / TU 1304 3.3 / 1907 1.1

DECEMBER

Time m	Time m
1 0132 3.1 / 0703 1.4 / W 1337 3.2 / 1945 1.2	**16** 0216 3.4 / 0754 1.2 / TH 1418 3.5 / 2043 0.8
2 0212 2.9 / 0737 1.5 / TH 1415 3.1 / 2029 1.3	**17** 0315 3.2 / 0849 1.4 / F 1514 3.4 / 2149 0.9
3 0257 2.8 / 0818 1.6 / F 1459 3.0 / 2124 1.3	**18** 0416 3.0 / 0951 1.5 / SA 1614 3.3 / ◗ 2256 1.0
4 0351 2.7 / 0911 1.7 / SA 1553 2.9 / 2235 1.4	**19** 0518 2.9 / 1101 1.6 / SU 1718 3.2
5 0456 2.7 / 1028 1.8 / SU 1659 2.9 / ◗ 2347 1.3	**20** 0004 1.1 / 0621 2.9 / M 1213 1.6 / 1823 3.1
6 0603 2.7 / 1156 1.9 / M 1808 2.9	**21** 0109 1.1 / 0724 2.9 / TU 1322 1.5 / 1929 3.1
7 0049 1.2 / 0705 2.8 / TU 1304 1.6 / 1910 3.0	**22** 0205 1.2 / 0821 3.0 / W 1421 1.4 / 2030 3.1
8 0143 1.1 / 0801 3.0 / W 1358 1.4 / 2008 3.1	**23** 0251 1.2 / 0910 3.1 / TH 1511 1.3 / 2123 3.1
9 0230 1.0 / 0851 3.2 / TH 1447 1.3 / 2102 3.3	**24** 0330 1.2 / 0953 3.2 / F 1554 1.2 / 2210 3.2
10 0315 0.9 / 0937 3.4 / F 1533 1.1 / 2154 3.5	**25** 0406 1.2 / 1032 3.3 / SA 1633 1.1 / 2252 3.2
11 0358 0.8 / 1022 3.5 / SA 1619 0.9 / 2245 3.6	**26** 0441 1.2 / 1109 3.4 / SU 1711 1.0 / ○ 2330 3.2
12 0443 0.8 / 1107 3.6 / SU 1706 0.7 / ● 2336 3.6	**27** 0515 1.2 / 1143 3.4 / M 1748 1.0
13 0529 0.8 / 1152 3.7 / M 1756 0.7	**28** 0007 3.2 / 0548 1.2 / TU 1217 3.4 / 1822 1.0
14 0027 3.6 / 0615 0.9 / TU 1239 3.7 / 1847 0.6	**29** 0043 3.2 / 0619 1.3 / W 1249 3.4 / 1857 1.0
15 0121 3.5 / 0704 1.1 / W 1327 3.6 / 1942 0.7	**30** 0118 3.1 / 0651 1.3 / TH 1322 3.3 / 1932 1.0
	31 0154 3.0 / 0723 1.3 / F 1356 3.3 / 2008 1.1

Chart Datum: 1·71 metres below Ordnance Datum (Newlyn)

Chapter 5

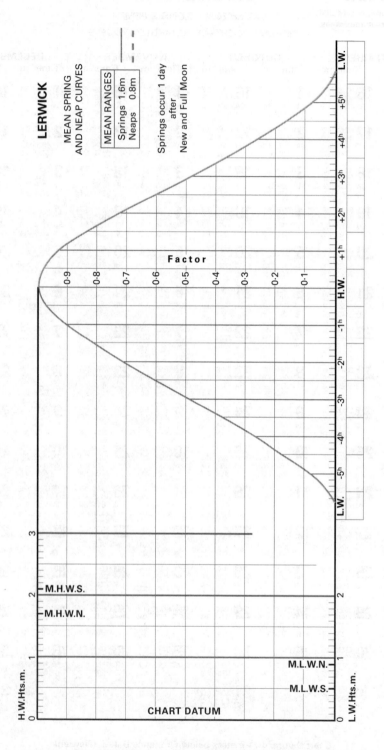

LERWICK

MEAN SPRING AND NEAP CURVES

MEAN RANGES
Springs 1.6m
Neaps 0.8m

Springs occur 1 day after New and Full Moon

Factor

0·9 0·8 0·7 0·6 0·5 0·4 0·3 0·2 0·1

L.W. +5ʰ +4ʰ +3ʰ +2ʰ +1ʰ H.W. -1ʰ -2ʰ -3ʰ -4ʰ -5ʰ L.W.

H.W.Hts.m.

M.H.W.S.
M.H.W.N.

M.L.W.N.
M.L.W.S.

L.W.Hts.m.

CHART DATUM

SCOTLAND – LERWICK

LAT 60°09′N   LONG 1°08′W

TIMES AND HEIGHTS OF HIGH AND LOW WATERS

JANUARY

Day	Time	m	Time	m	Time	m	Time	m
1 TH	0002	0.9	0612	1.7	1220	1.1	1823	1.8
2 F	0105	0.9	0713	1.7	1328	1.1	1928	1.8
3 SA	0157	0.9	0806	1.8	1422	1.0	2024	1.8
4 SU	0240	0.9	0852	1.9	1508	0.9	2113	1.9
5 M	0319	0.9	0933	2.0	1547	0.9	2156	1.9
6 TU	0355	0.9	1011	2.1	1624	0.8	2236	2.0
7 W	0429	0.9	1046	2.1	1659	0.7	○ 2314	2.0
8 TH	0503	0.9	1120	2.2	1735	0.7	2351	2.0
9 F	0538	0.9	1155	2.2	1811	0.6		
10 SA	0028	2.0	0613	0.8	1230	2.2	1848	0.6
11 SU	0106	2.0	0649	0.8	1307	2.1	1927	0.6
12 M	0146	1.9	0727	0.9	1345	2.1	2009	0.6
13 TU	0228	1.9	0809	0.9	1428	2.0	2054	0.6
14 W	0316	1.8	0856	0.9	1518	2.0	2145	0.7
15 TH	0410	1.8	0952	1.0	1617	1.9	◑ 2246	0.8
16 F	0511	1.8	1104	1.0	1727	1.9		
17 SA	0001	0.8	0620	1.8	1234	1.0	1845	1.9
18 SU	0114	0.8	0729	1.9	1349	0.9	2000	1.9
19 M	0218	0.8	0830	2.0	1451	0.8	2107	2.0
20 TU	0314	0.7	0926	2.1	1546	0.6	2207	2.1
21 W	0405	0.7	1017	2.2	1636	0.5	● 2302	2.2
22 TH	0452	0.7	1106	2.3	1723	0.4	2351	2.2
23 F	0536	0.7	1151	2.3	1808	0.3		
24 SA	0037	2.2	0618	0.7	1236	2.3	1852	0.3
25 SU	0120	2.1	0659	0.7	1318	2.3	1935	0.4
26 M	0201	2.0	0739	0.8	1400	2.2	2017	0.5
27 TU	0240	1.9	0818	0.8	1440	2.1	2059	0.7
28 W	0321	1.8	0858	0.9	1523	1.9	2143	0.8
29 TH	0404	1.7	0948	1.0	1610	1.8	◐ 2238	0.9
30 F	0458	1.6	1104	1.1	1711	1.7	2352	1.0
31 SA	0611	1.6	1239	1.1	1841	1.6		

FEBRUARY

Day	Time	m	Time	m	Time	m	Time	m
1 SU	0109	1.1	0726	1.7	1355	1.0	1957	1.7
2 M	0213	1.0	0825	1.8	1451	0.9	2055	1.7
3 TU	0302	1.0	0912	1.9	1534	0.8	2142	1.8
4 W	0341	0.9	0953	2.0	1611	0.7	2222	1.9
5 TH	0417	0.9	1030	2.1	1645	0.6	2259	2.0
6 F	0450	0.8	1105	2.1	1719	0.5	○ 2335	2.0
7 SA	0524	0.7	1140	2.2	1754	0.4		
8 SU	0011	2.0	0558	0.7	1215	2.2	1828	0.4
9 M	0047	2.0	0632	0.6	1250	2.2	1905	0.4
10 TU	0123	2.0	0708	0.6	1326	2.2	1943	0.4
11 W	0201	1.9	0746	0.7	1405	2.1	2025	0.5
12 TH	0242	1.9	0829	0.7	1451	2.0	2112	0.6
13 F	0331	1.8	0921	0.8	1548	1.9	◑ 2209	0.8
14 SA	0430	1.7	1029	0.9	1700	1.8	2327	0.9
15 SU	0542	1.7	1213	0.9	1831	1.7		
16 M	0100	0.9	0707	1.7	1344	0.9	2002	1.8
17 TU	0213	0.9	0821	1.9	1451	0.7	2112	1.9
18 W	0311	0.8	0921	2.0	1544	0.5	2208	2.0
19 TH	0359	0.7	1011	2.1	1629	0.4	2255	2.1
20 F	0440	0.6	1056	2.2	1711	0.3	● 2337	2.1
21 SA	0519	0.6	1137	2.3	1750	0.2		
22 SU	0015	2.1	0556	0.5	1217	2.3	1827	0.3
23 M	0052	2.0	0632	0.5	1253	2.2	1903	0.3
24 TU	0126	2.0	0707	0.6	1328	2.1	1938	0.5
25 W	0158	1.9	0741	0.7	1403	2.0	2011	0.6
26 TH	0231	1.8	0815	0.8	1440	1.9	2045	0.8
27 F	0308	1.7	0856	0.9	1522	1.7	2126	0.9
28 SA	0352	1.6	0957	1.0	1615	1.6	◐ 2230	1.1
29 SU	0449	1.6	1145	1.1	1730	1.5		

MARCH

Day	Time	m	Time	m	Time	m	Time	m
1 M	0018	1.1	0627	1.6	1320	1.0	1933	1.5
2 TU	0144	1.1	0755	1.6	1426	0.9	2038	1.6
3 W	0242	1.0	0848	1.7	1510	0.8	2123	1.7
4 TH	0322	0.9	0929	1.9	1546	0.6	2200	1.8
5 F	0356	0.8	1006	2.0	1620	0.5	2236	1.9
6 SA	0429	0.6	1041	2.1	1653	0.3	○ 2311	2.0
7 SU	0502	0.5	1117	2.2	1728	0.2	2346	2.0
8 M	0536	0.5	1152	2.2	1803	0.2		
9 TU	0021	2.1	0610	0.4	1228	2.2	1839	0.2
10 W	0056	2.0	0647	0.4	1305	2.2	1917	0.3
11 TH	0132	2.0	0726	0.5	1346	2.1	1959	0.4
12 F	0211	1.9	0810	0.6	1434	2.0	2045	0.6
13 SA	0258	1.8	0903	0.7	1534	1.8	◑ 2143	0.8
14 SU	0358	1.7	1016	0.8	1652	1.7	2311	1.0
15 M	0515	1.6	1216	0.8	1838	1.6		
16 TU	0057	1.0	0654	1.7	1344	0.7	2009	1.7
17 W	0210	0.9	0813	1.8	1446	0.5	2110	1.8
18 TH	0303	0.8	0910	1.9	1534	0.4	2156	1.9
19 F	0345	0.7	0957	2.0	1613	0.3	2237	2.0
20 SA	0422	0.5	1038	2.1	1649	0.2	● 2313	2.0
21 SU	0457	0.5	1116	2.2	1724	0.2	2347	2.0
22 M	0532	0.4	1151	2.2	1757	0.2		
23 TU	0018	2.0	0605	0.4	1225	2.1	1829	0.4
24 W	0048	1.9	0637	0.5	1257	2.0	1900	0.5
25 TH	0117	1.9	0709	0.6	1329	1.8	1929	0.6
26 F	0146	1.8	0743	0.7	1404	1.7	1959	0.8
27 SA	0220	1.7	0823	0.8	1446	1.7	2034	0.9
28 SU	0301	1.6	0917	0.9	1539	1.5	◐ 2123	1.1
29 M	0355	1.0	1056	1.0	1646	1.4	2328	1.1
30 TU	0505	1.5	1232	0.9	1857	1.4		
31 W	0104	1.1	0707	1.5	1342	0.8	2007	1.5

APRIL

Day	Time	m	Time	m	Time	m	Time	m
1 TH	0207	1.0	0811	1.6	1431	0.7	2050	1.6
2 F	0249	0.8	0854	1.7	1510	0.5	2127	1.8
3 SA	0325	0.7	0932	1.9	1546	0.4	2203	1.9
4 SU	0400	0.5	1010	2.0	1622	0.2	2239	2.0
5 M	0435	0.4	1048	2.1	1658	0.1	○ 2316	2.1
6 TU	0511	0.3	1126	2.2	1736	0.1	2352	2.1
7 W	0548	0.3	1205	2.2	1814	0.2		
8 TH	0028	2.1	0627	0.3	1247	2.2	1854	0.3
9 F	0106	2.0	0710	0.4	1334	2.0	1938	0.5
10 SA	0147	1.9	0759	0.5	1429	1.9	2027	0.7
11 SU	0237	1.8	0858	0.6	1535	1.7	2129	0.9
12 M	0339	1.7	1023	0.7	1656	1.6	◑ 2309	1.0
13 TU	0500	1.6	1212	0.7	1841	1.6		
14 W	0045	1.0	0639	1.6	1330	0.6	1957	1.6
15 TH	0152	0.9	0753	1.7	1428	0.5	2049	1.7
16 F	0242	0.7	0848	1.8	1512	0.4	2132	1.8
17 SA	0322	0.6	0934	1.9	1549	0.3	2209	1.9
18 SU	0358	0.5	1013	2.0	1622	0.3	2243	1.9
19 M	0432	0.4	1050	2.0	1655	0.3	● 2314	1.9
20 TU	0506	0.4	1124	2.0	1726	0.4	2344	1.9
21 W	0539	0.4	1157	2.0	1756	0.4		
22 TH	0013	1.9	0611	0.5	1229	1.9	1825	0.6
23 F	0041	1.9	0644	0.5	1302	1.8	1854	0.7
24 SA	0111	1.8	0720	0.6	1339	1.7	1925	0.8
25 SU	0145	1.8	0802	0.7	1422	1.6	2001	0.9
26 M	0226	1.7	0855	0.8	1515	1.5	2049	1.0
27 TU	0318	1.6	1011	0.8	1617	1.4	◐ 2218	1.1
28 W	0423	1.5	1141	0.8	1738	1.4		
29 TH	0013	1.0	0543	1.5	1249	0.7	1914	1.5
30 F	0118	0.9	0713	1.6	1342	0.6	2005	1.6

Chapter 5

TIME ZONE (UT)
For Summer Time add ONE hour in **non-shaded areas**

SCOTLAND – LERWICK

LAT 60°09′N   LONG 1°08′W

TIMES AND HEIGHTS OF HIGH AND LOW WATERS

YEAR 2004

MAY

Day	Time m	Time m	Time m	Time m	Day	Time m	Time m	Time m	Time m
1 SA	0206 0.8	0808 1.7	1427 0.5	2046 1.7	16 SU	0255 0.6	0903 1.8	1520 0.4	2135 1.8
2 SU	0248 0.7	0853 1.8	1508 0.3	2126 1.9	17 M	0333 0.6	0945 1.9	1553 0.4	2210 1.9
3 M	0327 0.5	0936 2.0	1549 0.2	2205 2.0	18 TU	0409 0.5	1023 1.9	1626 0.5	2243 1.9
4 TU	0406 0.4	1019 2.1	1629 0.2	○2245 2.1	19 W	0443 0.5	1059 1.9	1657 0.5	●2315 1.9
5 W	0447 0.3	1102 2.2	1710 0.2	2324 2.1	20 TH	0517 0.5	1134 1.9	1728 0.6	2345 1.9
6 TH	0529 0.3	1148 2.2	1752 0.3		21 F	0552 0.5	1209 1.8	1758 0.7	
7 F	0004 2.1	0612 0.3	1237 2.1	1836 0.4	22 SA	0015 1.9	0627 0.5	1245 1.8	1830 0.7
8 SA	0047 2.0	0701 0.3	1331 2.0	1924 0.6	23 SU	0047 1.9	0705 0.6	1323 1.7	1905 0.8
9 SU	0134 2.0	0755 0.4	1430 1.8	2017 0.8	24 M	0123 1.8	0748 0.6	1407 1.6	1944 0.9
10 M	0228 1.9	0859 0.5	1535 1.7	2123 0.9	25 TU	0205 1.7	0837 0.7	1456 1.5	2031 0.9
11 TU	0332 1.8	1023 0.5	1650 1.6	◐2249 1.0	26 W	0254 1.7	0935 0.7	1551 1.5	2134 1.0
12 W	0445 1.7	1150 0.6	1815 1.6		27 TH	0353 1.6	1044 0.7	1653 1.5	◐2259 1.0
13 TH	0013 0.9	0609 1.7	1302 0.5	1922 1.6	28 F	0458 1.6	1152 0.7	1804 1.5	
14 F	0120 0.8	0720 1.7	1358 0.5	2014 1.7	29 SA	0019 0.9	0609 1.6	1251 0.6	1910 1.6
15 SA	0212 0.7	0816 1.8	1442 0.5	2057 1.7	30 SU	0118 0.8	0718 1.7	1343 0.5	2002 1.7
					31 M	0208 0.7	0814 1.8	1432 0.4	2049 1.9

JUNE

Day	Time m	Time m	Time m	Time m	Day	Time m	Time m	Time m	Time m
1 TU	0255 0.6	0905 1.9	1518 0.3	2134 2.0	16 W	0349 0.6	1001 1.8	1601 0.7	2217 1.9
2 W	0341 0.4	0955 2.0	1604 0.3	2218 2.1	17 TH	0427 0.6	1041 1.8	1635 0.7	●2252 1.9
3 TH	0427 0.3	1045 2.1	1650 0.3	○2302 2.1	18 F	0503 0.6	1119 1.8	1708 0.7	2326 1.9
4 F	0515 0.3	1138 2.1	1737 0.4	2347 2.1	19 SA	0539 0.5	1156 1.8	1741 0.7	2359 1.9
5 SA	0604 0.2	1233 2.1	1825 0.5		20 SU	0615 0.5	1232 1.8	1816 0.8	
6 SU	0035 2.1	0655 0.3	1329 2.0	1914 0.6	21 M	0033 1.9	0653 0.5	1311 1.7	1852 0.8
7 M	0127 2.0	0751 0.3	1426 1.9	2007 0.8	22 TU	0109 1.9	0733 0.6	1351 1.7	1930 0.8
8 TU	0222 2.0	0851 0.4	1523 1.7	2105 0.8	23 W	0149 1.8	0816 0.6	1434 1.6	2013 0.8
9 W	0319 1.9	0958 0.5	1623 1.6	◐2210 0.9	24 TH	0233 1.8	0902 0.6	1522 1.6	2101 0.9
10 TH	0421 1.8	1111 0.5	1729 1.6	2324 0.9	25 F	0323 1.7	0953 0.6	1615 1.6	◐2158 0.9
11 F	0529 1.7	1220 0.6	1833 1.6		26 SA	0420 1.7	1053 0.6	1714 1.6	2309 0.9
12 SA	0035 0.9	0638 1.7	1319 0.6	1928 1.6	27 SU	0523 1.7	1159 0.6	1818 1.6	
13 SU	0136 0.8	0739 1.7	1408 0.6	2017 1.7	28 M	0027 0.8	0633 1.7	1303 0.6	1921 1.7
14 M	0226 0.7	0831 1.7	1449 0.6	2100 1.7	29 TU	0133 0.8	0741 1.7	1401 0.5	2017 1.7
15 TU	0309 0.7	0918 1.7	1526 0.6	2140 1.8	30 W	0230 0.6	0843 1.9	1456 0.5	2109 1.9

JULY

Day	Time m	Time m	Time m	Time m	Day	Time m	Time m	Time m	Time m
1 TH	0324 0.5	0941 2.0	1548 0.5	2159 2.0	16 F	0415 0.7	1027 1.8	1621 0.8	2235 1.9
2 F	0416 0.4	1038 2.1	1638 0.5	○2248 2.1	17 SA	0451 0.6	1106 1.8	1655 0.8	●2311 2.0
3 SA	0507 0.3	1135 2.1	1726 0.5	2338 2.2	18 SU	0526 0.5	1143 1.9	1729 0.7	2345 2.0
4 SU	0557 0.2	1228 2.1	1814 0.6		19 M	0601 0.5	1218 1.9	1802 0.7	
5 M	0028 2.2	0647 0.2	1320 2.0	1900 0.6	20 TU	0019 2.0	0635 0.5	1254 1.8	1836 0.7
6 TU	0118 2.2	0737 0.2	1409 1.9	1947 0.7	21 W	0054 2.0	0712 0.5	1330 1.8	1911 0.7
7 W	0207 2.1	0828 0.3	1457 1.8	2035 0.7	22 TH	0130 2.0	0749 0.5	1407 1.8	1949 0.7
8 TH	0256 2.0	0921 0.5	1545 1.7	2125 0.8	23 F	0208 1.9	0829 0.5	1449 1.7	2031 0.8
9 F	0347 1.9	1018 0.6	1637 1.6	◐2224 0.9	24 SA	0252 1.9	0914 0.6	1536 1.7	2120 0.8
10 SA	0443 1.7	1122 0.7	1735 1.6	2339 0.9	25 SU	0344 1.8	1007 0.6	1631 1.7	◐2221 0.9
11 SU	0549 1.7	1229 0.8	1838 1.6		26 M	0447 1.8	1114 0.7	1735 1.7	2343 0.9
12 M	0056 0.9	0659 1.6	1329 0.8	1937 1.6	27 TU	0601 1.7	1231 0.7	1846 1.7	
13 TU	0200 0.8	0802 1.6	1420 0.8	2029 1.7	28 W	0109 0.8	0722 1.8	1343 0.7	1954 1.8
14 W	0251 0.8	0857 1.7	1505 0.8	2116 1.8	29 TH	0219 0.7	0835 1.9	1445 0.7	2054 1.9
15 TH	0336 0.7	0945 1.7	1544 0.8	2157 1.9	30 F	0318 0.5	0939 2.0	1540 0.7	2149 2.1
					31 SA	0411 0.4	1037 2.1	1629 0.6	○2240 2.2

AUGUST

Day	Time m	Time m	Time m	Time m	Day	Time m	Time m	Time m	Time m
1 SU	0500 0.3	1128 2.1	1715 0.6	2329 2.2	16 M	0505 0.5	1122 1.9	1710 0.7	●2325 2.1
2 M	0546 0.2	1216 2.1	1758 0.5		17 TU	0538 0.4	1155 2.0	1742 0.6	2358 2.1
3 TU	0014 2.3	0630 0.2	1300 2.0	1839 0.5	18 W	0611 0.4	1228 2.0	1814 0.6	
4 W	0059 2.3	0713 0.2	1341 2.0	1919 0.6	19 TH	0031 2.1	0645 0.4	1302 1.9	1848 0.6
5 TH	0142 2.2	0755 0.4	1422 1.9	2000 0.7	20 F	0105 2.1	0720 0.4	1336 1.9	1924 0.6
6 F	0224 2.1	0838 0.5	1502 1.8	2042 0.8	21 SA	0142 2.1	0759 0.5	1414 1.9	2004 0.7
7 SA	0307 1.9	0922 0.7	1544 1.7	◑2130 0.9	22 SU	0224 2.0	0842 0.6	1459 1.8	2051 0.8
8 SU	0354 1.8	1013 0.9	1632 1.6	2238 1.0	23 M	0316 1.9	0933 0.7	1553 1.8	◑2152 0.9
9 M	0452 1.6	1123 1.0	1737 1.6		24 TU	0423 1.8	1041 0.9	1659 1.7	2323 0.9
10 TU	0015 1.0	0615 1.6	1246 1.0	1857 1.6	25 W	0547 1.7	1216 0.9	1821 1.7	
11 W	0137 1.0	0739 1.6	1356 1.0	2003 1.7	26 TH	0107 0.9	0724 1.8	1339 0.9	1944 1.8
12 TH	0236 0.9	0842 1.6	1449 1.0	2055 1.8	27 F	0219 0.7	0841 1.9	1442 0.8	2048 2.0
13 F	0322 0.8	0931 1.7	1530 0.9	2139 1.9	28 SA	0316 0.5	0940 2.0	1533 0.7	2142 2.1
14 SA	0359 0.7	1011 1.8	1606 0.8	2217 2.0	29 SU	0404 0.4	1029 2.1	1617 0.6	2229 2.2
15 SU	0433 0.6	1048 1.9	1638 0.8	2252 2.1	30 M	0446 0.2	1113 2.1	1657 0.6	○2313 2.3
					31 TU	0526 0.2	1153 2.1	1735 0.5	2354 2.3

Chart Datum: 1·22 metres below Ordnance Datum (Local)

SCOTLAND – LERWICK

LAT 60°09′N   LONG 1°08′W

TIMES AND HEIGHTS OF HIGH AND LOW WATERS

YEAR **2004**

SEPTEMBER

Time	m	Time	m
1 0605	0.2	**16** 0542	0.3
1231	2.1	1158	2.1
W 1812	0.5	TH 1749	0.5
2 0033	2.3	**17** 0005	2.3
0642	0.3	0616	0.3
TH 1307	2.0	F 1232	2.1
1849	0.5	1824	0.5
3 0111	2.2	**18** 0041	2.2
0719	0.4	0652	0.4
F 1341	1.9	SA 1305	2.1
1925	0.6	1901	0.6
4 0148	2.1	**19** 0119	2.2
0754	0.6	0731	0.5
SA 1415	1.9	SU 1342	2.0
2002	0.8	1944	0.7
5 0226	1.9	**20** 0204	2.1
0829	0.8	0815	0.7
SU 1452	1.8	M 1426	1.9
2045	1.0	2034	0.8
6 0310	1.8	**21** 0301	1.9
0909	1.0	0908	0.9
M 1535	1.7	TU 1523	1.8
◑ 2146	1.0	◑ 2141	0.9
7 0403	1.6	**22** 0416	1.8
1010	1.1	1024	1.1
TU 1631	1.6	W 1636	1.8
2334	1.1	2332	0.9
8 0520	1.5	**23** 0553	1.7
1202	1.2	1218	1.1
W 1803	1.6	TH 1810	1.8
9 0108	1.0	**24** 0109	0.8
0721	1.6	0734	1.8
TH 1330	1.2	F 1337	1.0
1937	1.7	1937	1.9
10 0213	0.9	**25** 0215	0.7
0826	1.7	0839	1.9
F 1428	1.1	SA 1434	0.9
2032	1.8	2038	2.0
11 0257	0.8	**26** 0306	0.5
0910	1.8	0928	2.0
SA 1508	1.0	SU 1518	0.8
2114	1.9	2128	2.2
12 0333	0.7	**27** 0348	0.4
0946	1.9	1011	2.1
SU 1541	0.9	M 1557	0.7
2150	2.0	2211	2.3
13 0404	0.6	**28** 0425	0.3
1020	2.0	1049	2.1
M 1612	0.7	TU 1634	0.6
2224	2.1	○ 2251	2.3
14 0436	0.4	**29** 0501	0.3
1053	2.0	1124	2.1
TU 1643	0.6	W 1710	0.5
● 2258	2.2	2328	2.3
15 0508	0.4	**30** 0536	0.3
1125	2.1	1157	2.1
W 1716	0.6	TH 1745	0.5
2331	2.2		

OCTOBER

Time	m	Time	m
1 0004	2.3	**16** 0549	0.4
0610	0.4	1202	2.2
F 1229	2.1	SA 1803	0.5
1820	0.6		
2 0039	2.2	**17** 0020	2.3
0642	0.6	0628	0.5
SA 1300	2.0	SU 1239	2.2
1854	0.7	1845	0.6
3 0114	2.1	**18** 0105	2.2
0713	0.8	0710	0.7
SU 1331	2.0	M 1319	2.1
1930	0.8	1932	0.7
4 0151	1.9	**19** 0157	2.1
0744	0.9	0757	0.9
M 1405	1.9	TU 1406	2.0
2012	0.9	2028	0.8
5 0234	1.8	**20** 0303	1.9
0818	1.1	0855	1.0
TU 1447	1.8	W 1507	1.9
2109	1.0	◑ 2144	0.9
6 0328	1.7	**21** 0420	1.8
0908	1.2	1021	1.2
W 1541	1.7	TH 1624	1.8
◑ 2251	1.1	2335	0.8
7 0436	1.6	**22** 0558	1.7
1115	1.3	1208	1.2
TH 1653	1.7	F 1758	1.8
8 0023	1.0	**23** 0057	0.7
0649	1.6	0723	1.8
F 1250	1.2	SA 1319	1.1
1855	1.7	1919	1.9
9 0131	0.9	**24** 0158	0.6
0755	1.7	0819	1.9
SA 1351	1.1	SU 1413	0.9
1956	1.8	2017	2.0
10 0218	0.8	**25** 0246	0.5
0837	1.8	0904	2.0
SU 1433	1.0	M 1456	0.8
2039	1.9	2106	2.1
11 0255	0.7	**26** 0325	0.5
0912	1.9	0944	2.1
M 1508	0.9	TU 1534	0.7
2115	2.0	2148	2.2
12 0328	0.6	**27** 0400	0.5
0945	2.0	1020	2.1
TU 1540	0.7	W 1610	0.6
2151	2.1	2226	2.2
13 0402	0.4	**28** 0434	0.5
1018	2.1	1053	2.2
W 1614	0.6	TH 1646	0.6
2226	2.2	○ 2303	2.2
14 0436	0.4	**29** 0507	0.5
1053	2.2	1124	2.2
TH 1649	0.6	F 1721	0.6
● 2303	2.3	2338	2.2
15 0512	0.4	**30** 0539	0.6
1127	2.2	1155	2.2
F 1725	0.5	SA 1756	0.6
2341	2.3		
		31 0013	2.1
		0609	0.8
		SU 1231	2.1
		1831	0.7

NOVEMBER

Time	m	Time	m
1 0048	2.0	**16** 0102	2.2
0639	0.9	0656	0.8
M 1257	2.1	TU 1306	2.2
1908	0.8	1927	0.6
2 0126	1.9	**17** 0201	2.1
0710	1.0	0748	0.9
TU 1331	2.0	W 1359	2.1
1950	0.9	2028	0.7
3 0210	1.8	**18** 0305	1.9
0745	1.1	0848	1.1
W 1412	1.9	TH 1501	2.0
2044	1.0	2142	0.7
4 0302	1.7	**19** 0414	1.8
0832	1.2	1004	1.2
TH 1505	1.8	F 1612	1.9
2202	1.0	◑ 2312	0.8
5 0403	1.6	**20** 0534	1.8
1002	1.3	1133	1.1
F 1609	1.7	SA 1731	1.9
◑ 2327	1.0		
6 0523	1.6	**21** 0028	0.7
1153	1.3	0648	1.8
SA 1727	1.7	SU 1246	1.1
		1847	2.0
7 0033	0.9	**22** 0130	0.7
0700	1.7	0748	1.9
SU 1259	1.2	M 1344	1.0
1858	1.8	1947	2.0
8 0127	0.8	**23** 0219	0.7
0749	1.8	0832	1.9
M 1348	1.0	TU 1431	0.9
1951	1.9	2038	2.1
9 0210	0.7	**24** 0259	0.7
0829	1.9	0913	2.0
TU 1429	0.9	W 1512	0.8
2034	2.0	2123	2.1
10 0249	0.6	**25** 0335	0.7
0906	2.0	0950	2.1
W 1506	0.8	TH 1550	0.7
2115	2.1	2204	2.1
11 0327	0.5	**26** 0409	0.7
0943	2.1	1025	2.1
TH 1544	0.7	F 1627	0.7
2156	2.2	○ 2243	2.1
12 0406	0.5	**27** 0442	0.7
1021	2.2	1058	2.2
F 1624	0.6	SA 1704	0.7
● 2238	2.3	2320	2.1
13 0446	0.5	**28** 0514	0.8
1100	2.3	1131	2.2
SA 1705	0.5	SU 1740	0.6
2322	2.3	2356	2.1
14 0527	0.6	**29** 0546	0.9
1139	2.2	1203	2.2
SU 1748	0.5	M 1816	0.7
15 0009	2.3	**30** 0033	2.0
0610	0.6	0617	1.0
M 1220	2.3	TU 1236	2.1
1835	0.5	1854	0.8

DECEMBER

Time	m	Time	m
1 0111	1.9	**16** 0158	2.1
0651	1.0	0739	0.9
W 1311	2.1	TH 1354	2.2
1936	0.8	2020	0.5
2 0153	1.8	**17** 0253	2.0
0728	1.1	0832	1.0
TH 1350	2.0	F 1450	2.1
2023	0.9	2121	0.6
3 0239	1.8	**18** 0351	1.9
0812	1.1	0930	1.0
F 1437	1.9	SA 1549	2.1
2117	0.9	◑ 2230	0.7
4 0331	1.7	**19** 0452	1.8
0908	1.2	1039	1.1
SA 1532	1.8	SU 1653	2.0
2221	0.9	2344	0.8
5 0429	1.7	**20** 0558	1.8
1023	1.2	1158	1.1
SU 1633	1.8	M 1805	1.9
◑ 2329	0.9		
6 0536	1.7	**21** 0051	0.8
1151	1.2	0700	1.8
M 1741	1.8	TU 1308	1.0
		1911	1.9
7 0030	0.9	**22** 0147	0.8
0644	1.8	0754	1.9
TU 1255	1.1	W 1406	0.9
1851	1.9	2010	1.9
8 0122	0.8	**23** 0233	0.9
0739	1.9	0842	1.9
W 1347	1.0	TH 1454	0.9
1950	2.0	2102	1.9
9 0210	0.7	**24** 0313	0.9
0827	2.0	0925	2.0
TH 1434	0.9	F 1537	0.8
2042	2.1	2148	2.0
10 0256	0.6	**25** 0350	0.9
0911	2.1	1005	2.1
F 1519	0.7	SA 1617	0.8
2132	2.2	2230	2.0
11 0341	0.6	**26** 0426	0.9
0955	2.2	1042	2.1
SA 1605	0.6	SU 1655	0.7
2222	2.1	○ 2310	2.0
12 0427	0.6	**27** 0500	0.9
1039	2.3	1117	2.2
SU 1652	0.5	M 1731	0.7
2313	2.3	2347	2.0
13 0513	0.6	**28** 0533	0.9
1124	2.3	1150	2.2
M 1741	0.5	TU 1807	0.7
14 0007	2.3	**29** 0023	2.0
0600	0.7	0605	0.9
TU 1211	2.3	W 1223	2.1
1831	0.4	1842	0.7
15 0103	2.2	**30** 0058	1.9
0648	0.8	0638	0.9
W 1301	2.3	TH 1257	2.1
1924	0.5	1919	0.7
		31 0135	1.9
		0713	1.0
		F 1333	2.1
		1958	0.7

Chapter 5

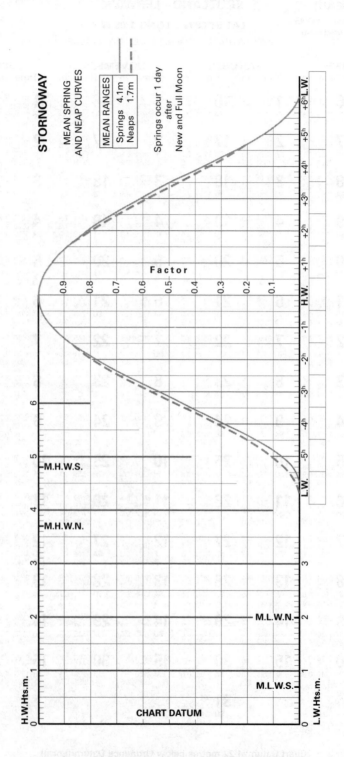

STORNOWAY

MEAN SPRING
AND NEAP CURVES

MEAN RANGES
Springs 4.1m
Neaps 1.7m

Springs occur 1 day
after
New and Full Moon

SCOTLAND – STORNOWAY

LAT 58°12'N   LONG 6°23'W

YEAR 2004

TIMES AND HEIGHTS OF HIGH AND LOW WATERS

JANUARY

Day	Time m	Time m	Time m	Time m
1 TH	0232 3.5	0812 2.1	1436 1.1	2050 1.9
16 F	0117 3.7	0702 1.7	1331 3.9	1959 1.5
2 F	0335 3.6	0922 2.1	1538 3.8	2151 1.8
17 SA	0225 3.8	0816 1.8	1444 4.0	2110 1.5
3 SA	0425 3.8	1021 1.9	1630 3.8	2241 1.7
18 SU	0331 4.0	0934 1.7	1555 4.1	2220 1.4
4 SU	0505 3.9	1111 1.6	1714 3.9	2324 1.6
19 M	0431 4.2	1047 1.4	1659 4.4	2321 1.2
5 M	0540 4.1	1155 1.6	1753 4.0	
20 TU	0525 4.5	1149 1.2	1755 4.4	
6 TU	0003 1.5	0612 4.2	1236 1.4	1829 4.1
21 W	0014 1.0	0614 4.7	1244 0.9	● 1845 4.5
7 W	0040 1.4	0644 4.4	1313 1.3	○ 1904 4.1
22 TH	0102 0.9	0700 4.9	1333 0.7	1930 4.6
8 TH	0115 1.2	0715 4.5	1349 1.1	1938 4.2
23 F	0146 0.8	0743 5.1	1418 0.6	2012 4.6
9 F	0149 1.1	0747 4.5	1424 1.1	2013 4.2
24 SA	0227 0.8	0825 5.1	1459 0.6	2052 4.4
10 SA	0224 1.1	0820 4.5	1501 1.0	2050 4.1
25 SU	0307 0.8	0905 4.9	1539 0.7	2132 4.3
11 SU	0259 1.1	0855 4.4	1538 1.0	2129 4.0
26 M	0346 1.0	0946 4.7	1619 0.9	2212 4.0
12 M	0336 1.2	0933 4.2	1619 1.1	2213 3.9
27 TU	0427 1.3	1029 4.4	1700 1.2	2256 3.7
13 TU	0417 1.3	1018 4.2	1704 1.2	2306 3.8
28 W	0510 1.6	1118 4.1	1743 1.5	2352 3.5
14 W	0504 1.5	1113 4.1	1755 1.3	☾
29 TH	0558 1.9	1218 3.8	1832 1.8	☾
15 TH	0009 3.7	0558 1.6	1220 4.0	◗ 1853 1.4
30 F	0115 3.4	0658 2.1	1334 3.6	1932 2.0
31 SA	0244 3.4	0821 2.2	1458 3.5	2055 2.1

FEBRUARY

Day	Time m	Time m	Time m	Time m
1 SU	0352 3.5	0950 2.1	1606 3.5	2212 2.0
16 M	0315 3.7	0929 1.8	1556 3.8	2217 1.6
2 M	0443 3.7	1054 1.9	1659 3.6	2306 1.8
17 TU	0424 4.0	1053 1.5	1703 4.0	2320 1.4
3 TU	0525 3.9	1143 1.7	1742 3.8	2350 1.6
18 W	0520 4.3	1152 1.1	1755 4.2	
4 W	0601 4.1	1224 1.4	1819 4.0	
19 TH	0010 1.1	0606 4.7	1241 0.8	1838 4.4
5 TH	0028 1.4	0632 4.3	1300 1.2	1852 4.2
20 F	0054 0.8	0648 4.9	1323 0.5	● 1915 4.5
6 F	0103 1.1	0701 4.5	1334 0.9	○ 1923 4.3
21 SA	0133 0.7	0725 5.1	1400 0.4	1949 4.6
7 SA	0136 0.9	0731 4.6	1408 0.7	1955 4.4
22 SU	0209 0.6	0800 5.1	1436 0.4	2022 4.5
8 SU	0209 0.8	0800 4.7	1441 0.6	2027 4.4
23 M	0245 0.6	0833 5.0	1510 0.5	2053 4.4
9 M	0243 0.7	0831 4.7	1516 0.6	2100 4.4
24 TU	0319 0.8	0907 4.7	1543 0.8	2124 4.2
10 TU	0317 0.8	0905 4.6	1553 0.7	2137 4.2
25 W	0354 1.0	0942 4.4	1617 1.1	2158 3.9
11 W	0354 0.9	0945 4.4	1633 0.8	2221 4.0
26 TH	0431 1.4	1022 4.1	1653 1.4	2237 3.7
12 TH	0435 1.1	1033 4.2	1718 1.1	2318 3.8
27 F	0511 1.7	1112 3.7	1734 1.8	2334 3.4
13 F	0523 1.4	1138 4.0	1811 1.4	◗
28 SA	0601 2.0	1222 3.4	1824 2.1	◗
14 SA	0033 3.6	0622 1.6	1303 3.8	1918 1.6
29 SU	0117 3.3	0710 2.3	1416 3.3	1938 2.3
15 SU	0156 3.6	0743 1.8	1433 3.7	2047 1.7

MARCH

Day	Time m	Time m	Time m	Time m
1 M	0313 3.4	0918 2.3	1542 3.3	2142 2.3
16 TU	0308 3.7	0942 1.7	1603 3.7	2216 1.8
2 TU	0416 3.5	1037 2.0	1640 3.5	2247 2.0
17 W	0417 4.0	1055 1.4	1703 3.9	2312 1.4
3 W	0502 3.8	1125 1.7	1723 3.8	2331 1.7
18 TH	0511 4.3	1145 1.0	1748 4.2	2357 1.1
4 TH	0538 4.1	1204 1.4	1758 4.0	
19 F	0553 4.6	1226 0.7	1823 4.4	
5 F	0008 1.4	0608 4.4	1238 1.0	1829 4.3
20 SA	0036 0.9	0629 4.9	1302 0.5	● 1854 4.5
6 SA	0042 1.1	0637 4.6	1310 0.7	○ 1859 4.5
21 SU	0112 0.7	0702 5.0	1335 0.4	1922 4.6
7 SU	0114 0.8	0706 4.8	1342 0.4	1929 4.7
22 M	0146 0.6	0732 5.0	1407 0.5	1950 4.5
8 M	0147 0.6	0736 5.0	1415 0.3	2000 4.7
23 TU	0219 0.6	0802 4.8	1437 0.6	2017 4.4
9 TU	0220 0.5	0807 5.0	1449 0.3	2032 4.7
24 W	0251 0.8	0832 4.6	1508 0.8	2045 4.3
10 W	0255 0.5	0841 4.9	1525 0.4	2108 4.5
25 TH	0324 1.0	0905 4.3	1539 1.1	2116 4.1
11 TH	0331 0.6	0920 4.6	1604 0.7	2149 4.2
26 F	0358 1.3	0941 4.0	1612 1.4	2151 3.8
12 F	0412 0.9	1009 4.3	1647 1.1	2245 3.9
27 SA	0436 1.7	1028 3.7	1649 1.8	2240 3.6
13 SA	0459 1.3	1118 3.9	1739 1.5	◗
28 SU	0521 2.0	1138 3.4	1735 2.1	◗
14 SU	0009 3.7	0559 1.6	1300 3.6	1850 1.9
29 M	0006 3.4	0624 2.3	1325 3.2	1841 2.4
15 M	0143 3.6	0738 1.9	1439 3.5	2045 2.0
30 TU	0210 3.3	0826 2.3	1507 3.3	2052 2.4
31 W	0333 3.5	1006 2.1	1609 3.5	2214 2.2

APRIL

Day	Time m	Time m	Time m	Time m
1 TH	0424 3.8	1054 1.7	1652 3.8	2259 1.8
16 F	0452 4.3	1124 1.0	1731 4.1	2334 1.2
2 F	0502 4.1	1131 1.3	1727 4.1	2335 1.5
17 SA	0532 4.5	1201 0.8	1802 4.3	
3 SA	0535 4.4	1205 1.0	1759 4.5	
18 SU	0011 1.0	0605 4.7	1235 0.7	1829 4.4
4 SU	0010 1.1	0606 4.7	1238 0.6	1830 4.7
19 M	0047 0.8	0636 4.7	1306 0.7	● 1855 4.5
5 M	0045 0.8	0638 5.0	1312 0.4	○ 1902 4.9
20 TU	0121 0.8	0705 4.7	1336 0.7	1921 4.5
6 TU	0120 0.5	0710 5.1	1347 0.2	1934 5.0
21 W	0153 0.8	0734 4.6	1406 0.8	1947 4.5
7 W	0156 0.4	0745 5.1	1423 0.3	2009 4.9
22 TH	0225 0.9	0805 4.4	1435 1.0	2016 4.3
8 TH	0233 0.4	0823 4.9	1500 0.5	2047 4.7
23 F	0258 1.1	0838 4.2	1506 1.2	2048 4.2
9 F	0313 0.6	0907 4.6	1540 0.8	2132 4.4
24 SA	0333 1.4	0917 3.9	1539 1.5	2126 3.9
10 SA	0357 0.9	1002 4.2	1624 1.2	2235 4.1
25 SU	0411 1.6	1007 3.6	1616 1.8	2216 3.7
11 SU	0448 1.3	1126 3.8	1718 1.7	
26 M	0457 1.9	1117 3.4	1701 2.1	2335 3.5
12 M	0005 3.8	0558 1.7	1306 3.5	◗ 1840 2.0
27 TU	0558 2.1	1243 3.3	1805 2.3	◗
13 TU	0134 3.8	0752 1.8	1439 3.5	2039 2.1
28 W	0102 3.5	0726 2.2	1412 3.3	1939 2.4
14 W	0254 3.9	0935 1.6	1558 3.7	2159 1.8
29 TH	0225 3.6	0905 2.0	1521 3.5	2114 2.2
15 TH	0401 4.1	1039 1.3	1653 3.9	2251 1.5
30 F	0328 3.8	1004 1.7	1610 3.8	2209 1.9

Chapter 5

Chart Datum: 2·71 metres below Ordnance Datum (Newlyn)
Register for your **FREE** weekly weather email service from Reeds Almanacs
》 at www.nauticaldata.com – **NOW!** 《
weekend weather reports sent to your email address, every Thursday

299

TIDES

TIME ZONE (UT)
For Summer Time add ONE hour in **non-shaded areas**

SCOTLAND – STORNOWAY
LAT 58°12′N   LONG 6°23′W
TIMES AND HEIGHTS OF HIGH AND LOW WATERS

YEAR 2004

MAY

Day	Time m	Time m	Time m	Time m
1 SA	0415 4.1	1046 1.3	1649 4.2	2252 1.5
2 SU	0455 4.4	1125 1.0	1725 4.5	2332 1.2
3 M	0532 4.7	1203 0.7	1800 4.8	
4 TU	0011 0.9	0609 4.9	1241 0.4	○ 1835 5.0
5 W	0052 0.6	0647 5.1	1320 0.4	1912 5.0
6 TH	0134 0.5	0728 5.0	1400 0.4	1951 5.0
7 F	0216 0.6	0813 4.8	1440 0.6	2036 4.8
8 SA	0302 0.7	0905 4.5	1524 1.0	2128 4.5
9 SU	0352 1.0	1010 4.1	1612 1.4	2237 4.3
10 M	0451 1.3	1132 3.8	1711 1.8	2356 4.1
11 TU	0607 1.5	1255 3.6	1833 2.0 ◐	
12 W	0113 4.0	0736 1.6	1418 3.6	2007 2.0
13 TH	0226 4.0	0900 1.5	1534 3.7	2123 1.9
14 F	0331 4.1	1004 1.4	1628 3.8	2218 1.6
15 SA	0423 4.2	1050 1.2	1706 4.0	2303 1.4
16 SU	0505 4.3	1129 1.1	1737 4.1	2343 1.2
17 M	0540 4.4	1204 1.0	1804 4.2	
18 TU	0020 1.1	0612 4.4	1237 1.0	1830 4.3
19 W	0057 1.1	0643 4.4	1308 1.0	● 1858 4.4
20 TH	0131 1.0	0714 4.3	1339 1.0	1926 4.4
21 F	0205 1.1	0748 4.2	1410 1.1	1958 4.3
22 SA	0240 1.2	0825 4.0	1443 1.3	2034 4.2
23 SU	0317 1.4	0908 3.8	1517 1.5	2115 4.0
24 M	0357 1.5	0958 3.6	1555 1.7	2205 3.8
25 TU	0443 1.7	1058 3.5	1640 1.9	2308 3.7
26 W	0538 1.8	1206 3.4	1738 2.1	
27 TH	0016 3.6	0644 1.8	1314 3.4	◑ 1850 2.2
28 F	0122 3.7	0754 1.7	1420 3.6	2004 2.1
29 SA	0225 3.9	0859 1.5	1517 3.8	2109 1.9
30 SU	0322 4.0	0954 1.3	1606 4.1	2203 1.6
31 M	0412 4.3	1043 1.0	1649 4.4	2253 1.3

JUNE

Day	Time m	Time m	Time m	Time m
1 TU	0459 4.5	1129 0.8	1730 4.6	2341 1.0
2 W	0545 4.7	1214 0.7	1812 4.8	
3 TH	0030 0.8	0632 4.8	1259 0.6	○ 1855 4.9
4 F	0119 0.7	0721 4.8	1344 0.7	1941 5.0
5 SA	0208 0.7	0813 4.7	1429 0.8	2030 4.9
6 SU	0259 0.7	0908 4.4	1515 1.0	2125 4.7
7 M	0352 0.9	1009 4.2	1605 1.3	2226 4.5
8 TU	0450 1.1	1115 3.9	1702 1.6	2332 4.3
9 W	0552 1.3	1224 3.7	1807 1.8 ◐	
10 TH	0039 4.1	0658 1.4	1337 3.6	1920 1.9
11 F	0146 4.0	0808 1.5	1450 3.6	2033 1.9
12 SA	0251 4.0	0913 1.5	1550 3.6	2136 1.8
13 SU	0348 4.0	1008 1.5	1635 3.8	2229 1.7
14 M	0436 4.0	1054 1.4	1711 3.9	2316 1.5
15 TU	0517 4.0	1135 1.4	1743 4.0	2358 1.4
16 W	0555 4.0	1212 1.3	1814 4.2	
17 TH	0038 1.3	0630 4.0	1248 1.2	● 1844 4.3
18 F	0116 1.2	0705 4.0	1321 1.2	1916 4.3
19 SA	0153 1.2	0741 4.0	1355 1.2	1949 4.3
20 SU	0229 1.2	0819 4.0	1429 1.2	2025 4.2
21 M	0305 1.2	0857 3.9	1504 1.3	2103 4.1
22 TU	0344 1.3	0942 3.8	1541 1.5	2144 4.0
23 W	0426 1.4	1031 3.7	1622 1.6	2232 3.9
24 TH	0513 1.4	1125 3.6	1710 1.8	2328 3.8
25 F	0605 1.5	1223 3.6	1807 1.8 ◐	
26 SA	0029 3.8	0701 1.5	1324 3.6	1909 1.9
27 SU	0131 3.9	0802 1.4	1425 3.7	2014 1.8
28 M	0234 4.0	0905 1.4	1523 3.9	2119 1.6
29 TU	0336 4.1	1006 1.2	1617 4.2	2222 1.4
30 W	0435 4.3	1103 1.1	1708 4.4	2322 1.2

JULY

Day	Time m	Time m	Time m	Time m
1 TH	0532 4.4	1156 1.0	1757 4.7	
2 F	0019 1.0	0626 4.5	1247 0.9	○ 1845 4.9
3 SA	0114 0.8	0719 4.6	1336 0.8	1933 5.0
4 SU	0206 0.6	0810 4.6	1422 0.8	2021 5.0
5 M	0255 0.6	0859 4.5	1507 0.9	2110 4.9
6 TU	0343 0.6	0949 4.3	1552 1.1	2200 4.7
7 W	0431 0.8	1041 4.0	1640 1.3	2255 4.5
8 TH	0520 1.1	1138 3.8	1731 1.6	2354 4.2
9 F	0612 1.3	1242 3.6	1829 1.8 ◐	
10 SA	0058 4.0	0709 1.6	1354 3.5	1935 2.0
11 SU	0206 3.8	0813 1.8	1504 3.5	2050 2.0
12 M	0312 3.7	0921 1.8	1602 3.6	2158 1.9
13 TU	0411 3.7	1021 1.8	1648 3.7	2255 1.8
14 W	0501 3.7	1111 1.7	1727 3.9	2343 1.6
15 TH	0544 3.8	1154 1.5	1802 4.1	
16 F	0026 1.4	0623 3.9	1234 1.4	1835 4.2
17 SA	0106 1.3	0658 4.0	1309 1.3	● 1906 4.3
18 SU	0141 1.1	0732 4.0	1343 1.2	1937 4.4
19 M	0215 1.0	0806 4.1	1416 1.1	2008 4.4
20 TU	0249 1.0	0840 4.1	1449 1.1	2040 4.4
21 W	0324 0.9	0916 4.0	1522 1.2	2113 4.3
22 TH	0400 1.0	0954 3.9	1559 1.3	2151 4.2
23 F	0440 1.1	1039 3.8	1639 1.4	2237 4.0
24 SA	0525 1.2	1133 3.7	1727 1.6	2337 3.9
25 SU	0616 1.3	1235 3.7	1823 1.7 ◐	
26 M	0047 3.8	0715 1.5	1342 3.7	1930 1.8
27 TU	0201 3.8	0824 1.5	1451 3.8	2048 1.7
28 W	0318 3.9	0941 1.5	1557 4.0	2210 1.6
29 TH	0429 4.0	1052 1.4	1656 4.3	2320 1.3
30 F	0531 4.2	1150 1.2	1749 4.6	
31 SA	0019 1.0	0624 4.4	1242 1.0	○ 1836 4.9

AUGUST

Day	Time m	Time m	Time m	Time m
1 SU	0110 0.7	0712 4.6	1327 0.8	1921 5.1
2 M	0157 0.5	0756 4.6	1410 0.7	2003 5.2
3 TU	0239 0.4	0837 4.6	1450 0.7	2044 5.1
4 W	0320 0.5	0917 4.4	1529 0.9	2126 4.9
5 TH	0400 0.7	0958 4.2	1609 1.1	2209 4.6
6 F	0441 1.0	1043 3.9	1651 1.4	2259 4.2
7 SA	0523 1.4	1137 3.7	1738 1.8 ◐	
8 SU	0000 3.9	0609 1.7	1252 3.5	1835 2.0
9 M	0119 3.6	0705 2.0	1418 3.4	1957 2.2
10 TU	0241 3.5	0827 2.2	1531 3.5	2135 2.2
11 W	0351 3.5	0954 2.1	1627 3.7	2243 2.0
12 TH	0448 3.6	1054 2.0	1711 3.9	2333 1.8
13 F	0532 3.7	1139 1.7	1747 4.1	
14 SA	0013 1.5	0609 3.9	1219 1.5	1819 4.3
15 SU	0049 1.2	0642 4.1	1253 1.3	1848 4.5
16 M	0121 1.0	0712 4.3	1325 1.1	● 1916 4.6
17 TU	0152 0.8	0742 4.4	1355 0.9	1943 4.7
18 W	0223 0.7	0812 4.4	1426 0.9	2012 4.7
19 TH	0256 0.7	0843 4.4	1458 0.9	2041 4.6
20 F	0330 0.7	0917 4.3	1532 1.0	2116 4.5
21 SA	0407 0.9	0956 4.2	1610 1.2	2158 4.3
22 SU	0448 1.1	1046 3.9	1654 1.4	2255 4.0
23 M	0536 1.4	1156 3.7	1748 1.7 ◐	
24 TU	0020 3.8	0636 1.7	1316 3.7	1859 1.9
25 W	0154 3.7	0758 1.9	1436 3.8	2045 1.9
26 TH	0322 3.8	0940 1.8	1550 4.0	2221 1.6
27 F	0435 4.0	1052 1.6	1651 4.4	2324 1.2
28 SA	0531 4.2	1145 1.3	1741 4.7	
29 SU	0014 0.9	0617 4.5	1231 1.0	1823 5.0
30 M	0058 0.6	0657 4.7	1312 0.8	○ 1903 5.2
31 TU	0138 0.4	0733 4.7	1350 0.7	1939 5.3

Chart Datum: 2·71 metres below Ordnance Datum (Newlyn)

SCOTLAND – STORNOWAY

LAT 58°12′N   LONG 6°23′W

TIMES AND HEIGHTS OF HIGH AND LOW WATERS

YEAR 2004

SEPTEMBER

Time	m	Time	m	Time	m	Time	m
1 W	0214 0.4 / 0807 4.7 / 1426 0.7 / 2014 5.2	**16** TH	0153 0.5 / 0742 4.8 / 1359 0.7 / 1943 5.0				
2 TH	0250 0.5 / 0840 4.6 / 1501 0.8 / 2049 4.9	**17** F	0225 0.5 / 0812 4.8 / 1432 0.7 / 2014 4.9				
3 F	0324 0.7 / 0913 4.3 / 1537 1.1 / 2125 4.6	**18** SA	0259 0.6 / 0845 4.6 / 1507 0.9 / 2050 4.7				
4 SA	0359 1.1 / 0948 4.1 / 1614 1.4 / 2205 4.2	**19** SU	0336 0.8 / 0924 4.4 / 1545 1.1 / 2134 4.4				
5 SU	0435 1.5 / 1030 3.8 / 1655 1.8 / 2258 3.8	**20** M	0417 1.2 / 1015 4.1 / 1630 1.4 / 2237 4.0				
6 M ☾	0515 1.9 / 1132 3.6 / 1745 2.2	**21** TU ☾	0505 1.6 / 1136 3.9 / 1726 1.8				
7 TU	0023 3.5 / 0604 2.2 / 1325 3.5 / 1858 2.4	**22** W	0023 3.7 / 0609 2.0 / 1307 3.8 / 1853 2.0				
8 W	0211 3.4 / 0717 2.4 / 1455 3.5 / 2118 2.4	**23** TH	0203 3.6 / 0758 2.2 / 1431 3.9 / 2106 1.9				
9 TH	0329 3.4 / 0931 2.4 / 1559 3.7 / 2230 2.1	**24** F	0330 3.8 / 0944 2.0 / 1545 4.1 / 2225 1.5				
10 F	0428 3.6 / 1035 2.2 / 1646 3.9 / 2314 1.8	**25** SA	0435 4.0 / 1044 1.6 / 1642 4.5 / 2316 1.2				
11 SA	0511 3.8 / 1118 1.9 / 1723 4.2 / 2350 1.5	**26** SU	0523 4.3 / 1131 1.3 / 1727 4.8 / 2359 0.8				
12 SU	0546 4.1 / 1154 1.6 / 1754 4.4	**27** M	0602 4.5 / 1212 1.0 / 1806 5.1				
13 M	0022 1.2 / 0615 4.3 / 1227 1.3 / 1821 4.9	**28** TU ○	0036 0.6 / 0635 4.7 / 1250 0.9 / 1840 5.2				
14 TU ●	0052 0.9 / 0644 4.6 / 1257 1.1 / 1848 4.9	**29** W	0111 0.5 / 0706 4.8 / 1325 0.8 / 1912 5.2				
15 W	0122 0.7 / 0713 4.7 / 1328 0.9 / 1915 5.0	**30** TH	0144 0.6 / 0735 4.8 / 1359 0.8 / 1944 5.1				

OCTOBER

Time	m	Time	m
1 F	0216 0.7 / 0804 4.7 / 1433 0.9 / 2015 4.8	**16** SA	0157 0.5 / 0746 5.0 / 1409 0.7 / 1955 5.0
2 SA	0248 0.9 / 0833 4.5 / 1506 1.2 / 2047 4.5	**17** SU	0233 0.7 / 0823 4.9 / 1447 0.9 / 2036 4.8
3 SU	0320 1.3 / 0904 4.3 / 1542 1.5 / 2124 4.2	**18** M	0312 1.0 / 0906 4.6 / 1530 1.1 / 2128 4.4
4 M	0354 1.6 / 0942 4.0 / 1621 1.9 / 2213 3.8	**19** TU	0355 1.4 / 1005 4.3 / 1619 1.5 / 2248 4.0
5 TU	0431 2.0 / 1037 3.8 / 1708 2.2 / 2335 3.5	**20** W ☾	0446 1.8 / 1133 4.1 / 1724 1.8
6 W ☾	0518 2.3 / 1217 3.6 / 1815 2.5	**21** TH	0032 3.7 / 0600 2.2 / 1259 4.0 / 1910 2.0
7 TH	0129 3.4 / 0625 2.6 / 1404 3.6 / 2040 2.5	**22** F	0202 3.7 / 0757 2.3 / 1418 4.1 / 2100 1.8
8 F	0254 3.4 / 0849 2.6 / 1517 3.7 / 2159 2.2	**23** SA	0323 3.9 / 0927 2.0 / 1528 4.3 / 2208 1.5
9 SA	0355 3.7 / 1002 2.3 / 1609 4.0 / 2241 1.9	**24** SU	0423 4.1 / 1023 1.7 / 1624 4.5 / 2255 1.2
10 SU	0439 3.9 / 1045 2.0 / 1648 4.2 / 2315 1.5	**25** M	0507 4.3 / 1108 1.4 / 1707 4.7 / 2334 1.0
11 M	0513 4.2 / 1120 1.7 / 1720 4.5 / 2346 1.2	**26** TU	0541 4.5 / 1147 1.2 / 1744 4.9
12 TU	0543 4.5 / 1152 1.4 / 1749 4.8	**27** W	0009 0.9 / 0611 4.6 / 1225 1.1 / 1816 4.9
13 W	0017 0.9 / 0612 4.8 / 1224 1.1 / 1817 5.0	**28** TH	0042 0.8 / 0639 4.7 / 1300 1.0 / 1847 4.9
14 TH ●	0049 0.7 / 0642 5.0 / 1258 0.9 / 1847 5.0	**29** F	0114 0.9 / 0707 4.7 / 1334 1.0 / 1917 4.8
15 F	0122 0.5 / 0713 5.0 / 1332 0.7 / 1920 5.2	**30** SA	0145 1.0 / 0734 4.7 / 1408 1.1 / 1948 4.6
		31 SU	0216 1.2 / 0804 4.5 / 1442 1.3 / 2022 4.4

NOVEMBER

Time	m	Time	m
1 M	0248 1.4 / 0836 4.4 / 1518 1.6 / 2101 4.1	**16** TU	0257 1.1 / 0902 4.8 / 1525 1.1 / 2137 4.4
2 TU	0322 1.7 / 0916 4.1 / 1557 1.8 / 2152 3.8	**17** W	0344 1.4 / 1006 4.5 / 1621 1.4 / 2256 4.0
3 W	0400 2.0 / 1011 3.9 / 1644 2.1 / 2306 3.6	**18** TH	0439 1.8 / 1122 4.3 / 1732 1.6
4 TH	0445 2.3 / 1131 3.7 / 1746 2.3	**19** F ☾	0018 3.8 / 0553 2.1 / 1238 4.2 / 1855 1.7
5 F ☾	0034 3.5 / 0549 2.5 / 1255 3.7 / 1914 2.4	**20** SA	0138 3.8 / 0725 2.2 / 1350 4.2 / 2021 1.7
6 SA	0157 3.5 / 0722 2.6 / 1411 3.8 / 2054 2.2	**21** SU	0255 3.8 / 0847 2.0 / 1458 4.3 / 2131 1.5
7 SU	0305 3.7 / 0859 2.4 / 1512 3.9 / 2148 1.9	**22** M	0357 4.0 / 0949 1.8 / 1556 4.4 / 2222 1.4
8 M	0354 3.9 / 0953 2.1 / 1559 4.2 / 2228 1.6	**23** TU	0442 4.1 / 1038 1.6 / 1642 4.5 / 2304 1.3
9 TU	0432 4.2 / 1034 1.8 / 1637 4.4 / 2304 1.3	**24** W	0518 4.3 / 1121 1.4 / 1721 4.5 / 2340 1.3
10 W	0506 4.5 / 1111 1.5 / 1713 4.7 / 2339 1.0	**25** TH	0548 4.4 / 1200 1.3 / 1756 4.6
11 TH	0540 4.8 / 1149 1.2 / 1748 4.9	**26** F	0015 1.2 / 0617 4.5 / 1238 1.2 / 1828 4.5
12 F ●	0016 0.8 / 0613 5.0 / 1229 1.0 / 1824 5.1	**27** SA	0048 1.2 / 0646 4.5 / 1315 1.2 / 1901 4.4
13 SA	0054 0.7 / 0649 5.1 / 1310 0.8 / 1903 5.1	**28** SU	0121 1.2 / 0716 4.6 / 1351 1.3 / 1935 4.3
14 SU	0134 0.7 / 0728 5.1 / 1352 0.8 / 1947 4.9	**29** M	0154 1.3 / 0749 4.5 / 1427 1.3 / 2011 4.2
15 M	0214 0.8 / 0811 5.0 / 1437 0.9 / 2036 4.7	**30** TU	0227 1.4 / 0824 4.4 / 1504 1.5 / 2052 4.0

DECEMBER

Time	m	Time	m
1 W	0302 1.6 / 0905 4.2 / 1544 1.6 / 2140 3.8	**16** TH	0339 1.3 / 0955 4.8 / 1620 1.0 / 2238 4.2
2 TH	0341 1.8 / 0953 4.1 / 1628 1.8 / 2237 3.7	**17** F	0431 1.5 / 1057 4.6 / 1718 1.3 / 2344 3.9
3 F	0424 2.0 / 1052 3.9 / 1720 1.9 / 2342 3.6	**18** SA	0531 1.8 / 1202 4.4 / 1820 1.4 ☾
4 SA	0519 2.2 / 1155 3.8 / 1821 2.0	**19** SU	0055 3.7 / 0638 1.9 / 1309 4.2 / 1926 1.6
5 SU ☾	0049 3.5 / 0625 2.3 / 1259 3.8 / 1927 2.0	**20** M	0208 3.7 / 0751 2.0 / 1416 4.1 / 2035 1.6
6 M	0155 3.6 / 0736 2.3 / 1359 3.9 / 2032 1.8	**21** TU	0317 3.7 / 0903 1.9 / 1520 4.1 / 2138 1.6
7 TU	0253 3.6 / 0842 2.1 / 1457 4.0 / 2129 1.6	**22** W	0411 3.8 / 1005 1.8 / 1615 4.1 / 2231 1.6
8 W	0343 4.1 / 0939 1.9 / 1549 4.2 / 2218 1.4	**23** TH	0454 4.0 / 1057 1.7 / 1702 4.1 / 2315 1.5
9 TH	0427 4.3 / 1030 1.6 / 1636 4.5 / 2304 1.2	**24** F	0531 4.1 / 1143 1.6 / 1742 4.1 / 2354 1.4
10 F	0509 4.6 / 1119 1.4 / 1723 4.7 / 2349 1.0	**25** SA	0605 4.3 / 1225 1.4 / 1820 4.1
11 SA	0551 4.8 / 1207 1.1 / 1809 4.8	**26** SU ○	0032 1.4 / 0637 4.4 / 1305 1.3 / 1855 4.1
12 SU ●	0034 0.9 / 0633 5.0 / 1256 0.9 / 1857 4.8	**27** M	0108 1.3 / 0710 4.4 / 1343 1.2 / 1930 4.1
13 M	0119 0.8 / 0719 5.1 / 1346 0.8 / 1947 4.8	**28** TU	0142 1.2 / 0742 4.5 / 1419 1.2 / 2005 4.1
14 TU	0204 0.9 / 0807 5.0 / 1435 0.8 / 2040 4.6	**29** W	0216 1.2 / 0816 4.4 / 1454 1.2 / 2041 4.1
15 W	0250 1.0 / 0858 4.9 / 1526 0.9 / 2136 4.4	**30** TH	0251 1.3 / 0851 4.3 / 1530 1.3 / 2120 4.0
		31 F	0326 1.4 / 0928 4.2 / 1608 1.4 / 2202 3.8

Chapter 5

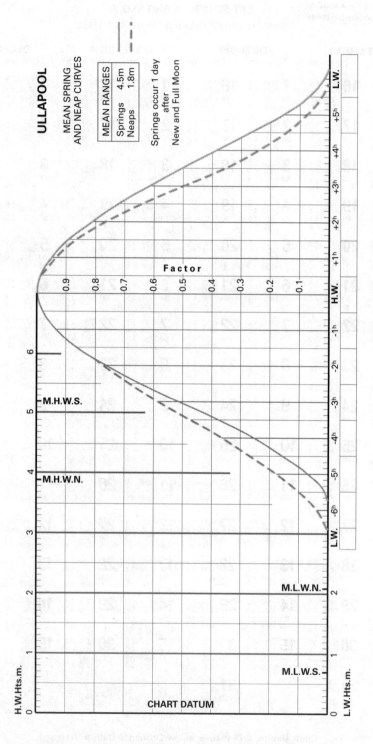

ULLAPOOL

MEAN SPRING AND NEAP CURVES

MEAN RANGES	
Springs	4.5m
Neaps	1.8m

Springs occur 1 day after New and Full Moon

Factor

0.9 0.8 0.7 0.6 0.5 0.4 0.3 0.2 0.1

H.W.Hts.m.

M.H.W.S.

M.H.W.N.

CHART DATUM

L.W.Hts.m.

L.W.

H.W.

L.W.

M.L.W.N.

M.L.W.S.

TIME ZONE (UT)
For Summer Time add ONE hour in **non-shaded areas**

LAT 57°54'N   LONG 5°10'W

TIMES AND HEIGHTS OF HIGH AND LOW WATERS

JANUARY

Time m	Time m
1 TH 0235 4.0 / 0820 2.4 / 1444 4.2 / 2054 2.1	**16** F 0122 4.2 / 0711 2.1 / 1333 4.4 / 2003 1.8
2 F 0339 4.0 / 0931 4.2 / 1545 4.2 / 2157 2.1	**17** SA 0232 4.3 / 0828 2.1 / 1449 4.4 / 2119 1.8
3 SA 0430 4.2 / 1032 2.2 / 1637 4.3 / 2250 2.0	**18** SU 0340 4.4 / 0946 2.0 / 1603 4.5 / 2230 1.7
4 SU 0512 4.4 / 1121 2.0 / 1722 4.4 / 2334 1.9	**19** M 0441 4.7 / 1056 1.7 / 1709 4.7 / 2330 1.5
5 M 0548 4.6 / 1204 1.8 / 1801 4.5	**20** TU 0535 5.0 / 1156 1.4 / 1806 4.9
6 TU 0012 1.7 / 0620 4.7 / 1243 1.7 / 1838 4.7	**21** W 0022 1.3 / 0622 5.3 / 1249 1.1 / ● 1855 5.1
7 W 0049 1.6 / 0651 4.9 / 1319 1.5 / 1912 4.7	**22** TH 0110 1.1 / 0707 5.5 / 1338 0.8 / 1940 5.2
8 TH 0123 1.5 / 0721 5.0 / 1355 1.4 / 1946 4.8	**23** F 0155 1.0 / 0749 5.6 / 1423 0.7 / 2022 5.2
9 F 0157 1.5 / 0752 5.0 / 1430 1.4 / 2021 4.8	**24** SA 0237 1.0 / 0831 5.5 / 1506 0.7 / 2103 5.0
10 SA 0231 1.4 / 0825 5.0 / 1505 1.3 / 2057 4.8	**25** SU 0318 1.1 / 0912 5.4 / 1547 0.9 / 2143 4.8
11 SU 0307 1.4 / 0900 5.0 / 1542 1.3 / 2136 4.7	**26** M 0358 1.2 / 0953 5.1 / 1626 1.1 / 2223 4.5
12 M 0344 1.5 / 0939 4.9 / 1621 1.4 / 2220 4.5	**27** TU 0438 1.5 / 1036 4.8 / 1706 1.4 / 2307 4.2
13 TU 0425 1.6 / 1023 4.8 / 1705 1.5 / 2311 4.4	**28** W 0520 1.8 / 1124 4.5 / 1748 1.7
14 W 0512 1.8 / 1115 4.6 / 1754 1.6	**29** TH 0002 4.0 / 0607 2.1 / 1225 4.2 / ◑ 1835 2.0
15 TH 0013 4.3 / 0606 1.9 / 1219 4.5 / ◐ 1853 1.8	**30** F 0115 3.8 / 0706 2.4 / 1339 3.9 / 1936 2.3
	31 SA 0238 3.8 / 0828 2.5 / 1459 3.9 / 2058 2.4

FEBRUARY

Time m	Time m
1 SU 0354 3.9 / 0958 2.4 / 1611 3.9 / 2218 2.3	**16** M 0324 4.2 / 0936 2.1 / 1607 4.2 / 2225 2.0
2 M 0450 4.1 / 1103 2.2 / 1706 4.1 / 2314 2.1	**17** TU 0435 4.5 / 1058 1.7 / 1716 4.5 / 2328 1.7
3 TU 0532 4.3 / 1150 2.0 / 1750 4.3 / 2358 1.9	**18** W 0531 4.8 / 1157 1.3 / 1807 4.8
4 W 0607 4.6 / 1230 1.7 / 1826 4.5	**19** TH 0018 1.3 / 0615 5.1 / 1246 1.0 / 1848 5.0
5 TH 0035 1.7 / 0638 4.8 / 1307 1.4 / 1859 4.7	**20** F 0102 1.1 / 0655 5.4 / 1329 0.7 / ● 1925 5.1
6 F 0110 1.4 / 0707 5.0 / 1341 1.2 / ○ 1930 4.9	**21** SA 0142 0.9 / 0732 5.5 / 1408 0.6 / 2000 5.1
7 SA 0144 1.2 / 0736 5.1 / 1415 1.0 / 2002 5.0	**22** SU 0219 0.8 / 0807 5.5 / 1444 0.6 / 2033 5.1
8 SU 0218 1.1 / 0807 5.2 / 1448 0.9 / 2035 5.0	**23** M 0255 0.8 / 0842 5.4 / 1518 0.7 / 2104 4.9
9 M 0251 1.0 / 0840 5.2 / 1522 0.9 / 2111 4.9	**24** TU 0329 1.0 / 0915 5.1 / 1551 0.9 / 2135 4.6
10 TU 0326 1.0 / 0916 5.2 / 1558 0.9 / 2150 4.8	**25** W 0403 1.2 / 0950 4.8 / 1624 1.2 / 2208 4.4
11 W 0404 1.2 / 0955 5.0 / 1636 1.1 / 2234 4.6	**26** TH 0439 1.5 / 1027 4.4 / 1658 1.6 / 2245 4.1
12 TH 0445 1.4 / 1042 4.8 / 1720 1.3 / 2329 4.4	**27** F 0517 1.9 / 1114 4.1 / 1737 1.9 / 2338 3.8
13 F 0534 1.6 / 1140 4.5 / 1812 1.7 / ◑	**28** SA 0604 2.2 / 1231 3.8 / 1825 2.3 / ◐
14 SA 0040 4.2 / 0633 1.9 / 1302 4.2 / 1921 2.0	**29** SU 0120 3.7 / 0716 2.5 / 1409 3.6 / 1943 2.5
15 SU 0202 4.1 / 0755 2.1 / 1436 4.1 / 2056 2.1	

MARCH

Time m	Time m
1 M 0304 3.7 / 0920 2.5 / 1541 3.7 / 2146 2.5	**16** TU 0315 4.1 / 0943 2.0 / 1614 4.1 / 2224 2.0
2 TU 0420 3.9 / 1044 2.3 / 1645 3.9 / 2255 2.2	**17** W 0427 4.4 / 1058 1.6 / 1714 4.4 / 2321 1.6
3 W 0508 4.1 / 1132 1.9 / 1730 4.2 / 2339 1.9	**18** TH 0519 4.7 / 1149 1.2 / 1757 4.7
4 TH 0544 4.4 / 1210 1.6 / 1805 4.5	**19** F 0006 1.3 / 0600 5.0 / 1232 0.9 / 1832 4.9
5 F 0015 1.6 / 0613 4.7 / 1244 1.2 / 1835 4.7	**20** SA 0045 1.0 / 0636 5.2 / 1309 0.6 / 1903 5.0
6 SA 0050 1.2 / 0642 5.0 / 1317 0.9 / ○ 1905 5.0	**21** SU 0129 0.5 / 0709 5.3 / 1343 0.5 / 1932 5.1
7 SU 0123 1.0 / 0711 5.2 / 1350 0.6 / 1936 5.1	**22** M 0156 0.7 / 0740 5.3 / 1415 0.5 / 2000 5.0
8 M 0156 0.7 / 0742 5.4 / 1423 0.5 / 2009 5.2	**23** TU 0228 0.7 / 0811 5.2 / 1445 0.6 / 2028 4.9
9 TU 0230 0.6 / 0815 5.4 / 1457 0.5 / 2043 5.2	**24** W 0300 0.9 / 0842 5.0 / 1515 0.9 / 2056 4.7
10 W 0305 0.7 / 0851 5.3 / 1532 0.6 / 2121 5.0	**25** TH 0332 1.1 / 0914 4.7 / 1546 1.1 / 2124 4.5
11 TH 0342 0.8 / 0931 5.1 / 1610 0.9 / 2205 4.7	**26** F 0404 1.4 / 0949 4.3 / 1617 1.5 / 2157 4.2
12 F 0423 1.1 / 1019 4.7 / 1652 1.2 / 2258 4.4	**27** SA 0440 1.7 / 1033 4.0 / 1652 1.9 / 2239 3.9
13 SA 0511 1.5 / 1123 4.3 / 1743 1.7 / ◑	**28** SU 0523 2.1 / 1143 3.7 / 1735 2.2 / ◐ 2358 3.7
14 SU 0014 4.1 / 0611 1.9 / 1259 4.0 / 1856 2.1	**29** M 0624 2.4 / 1325 3.5 / 1840 2.5
15 M 0145 4.0 / 0746 2.1 / 1443 3.9 / 2052 2.3	**30** TU 0201 3.6 / 0828 2.5 / 1458 3.6 / 2058 2.6
	31 W 0331 3.7 / 1009 2.2 / 1610 3.8 / 2222 2.3

APRIL

Time m	Time m
1 TH 0428 4.0 / 1059 1.8 / 1656 4.1 / 2307 1.9	**16** F 0458 4.6 / 1126 1.1 / 1735 4.5 / 2342 1.3
2 F 0507 4.3 / 1136 1.4 / 1732 4.4 / 2344 1.5	**17** SA 0538 4.8 / 1206 0.9 / 1808 4.7
3 SA 0539 4.6 / 1211 1.0 / 1803 4.7	**18** SU 0021 1.0 / 0611 5.0 / 1242 0.7 / 1836 4.8
4 SU 0019 1.1 / 0609 5.0 / 1245 0.7 / 1834 5.0	**19** M 0057 0.8 / 0643 5.0 / 1314 0.7 / ● 1904 4.9
5 M 0054 0.8 / 0640 5.2 / 1320 0.4 / ○ 1907 5.2	**20** TU 0130 0.8 / 0713 5.0 / 1344 0.7 / 1931 4.9
6 TU 0129 0.5 / 0714 5.4 / 1354 0.3 / 1941 5.3	**21** W 0202 0.8 / 0744 4.9 / 1414 0.8 / 1957 4.8
7 W 0205 0.4 / 0751 5.4 / 1430 0.3 / 2018 5.3	**22** TH 0233 1.0 / 0815 4.7 / 1443 1.0 / 2025 4.7
8 TH 0243 0.5 / 0831 5.3 / 1508 0.5 / 2058 5.1	**23** F 0305 1.1 / 0849 4.5 / 1514 1.2 / 2055 4.5
9 F 0323 0.7 / 0917 4.9 / 1548 0.9 / 2145 4.8	**24** SA 0338 1.4 / 0927 4.2 / 1546 1.5 / 2129 4.3
10 SA 0407 1.0 / 1013 4.5 / 1632 1.3 / 2244 4.4	**25** SU 0415 1.7 / 1015 4.0 / 1621 1.8 / 2212 4.0
11 SU 0459 1.4 / 1132 4.1 / 1727 1.8	**26** M 0458 1.9 / 1122 3.7 / 1704 2.1 / 2321 3.8
12 M 0006 4.1 / 0608 1.8 / 1308 3.9 / ◑ 1850 2.2	**27** TU 0556 2.2 / 1247 3.6 / 1805 2.4 / ◐
13 TU 0135 4.0 / 0752 2.0 / 1443 3.9 / 2046 2.2	**28** W 0103 3.7 / 0730 2.3 / 1407 3.6 / 1951 2.5
14 W 0301 4.1 / 0935 1.8 / 1602 4.0 / 2207 1.9	**29** TH 0227 3.7 / 0909 2.1 / 1517 3.7 / 2126 2.2
15 TH 0409 4.3 / 1040 1.4 / 1656 4.3 / 2259 1.6	**30** F 0331 3.9 / 1008 1.7 / 1610 4.0 / 2220 1.9

Chapter 5

SCOTLAND – ULLAPOOL

YEAR 200(4)

LAT 57°54'N LONG 5°10'W

TIMES AND HEIGHTS OF HIGH AND LOW WATERS

TIME ZONE (UT)
For Summer Time add ONE hour in **non-shaded areas**

MAY

Day	Time m	Time m	Time m	Time m
1 SA	0418 4.2	1052 1.4	2303 1.5	
2 SU	0457 4.6	1131 1.0	1728 4.7	2343 1.1
3 M	0533 4.9	1209 0.6	1803 5.0	
4 TU ○	0022 0.8	0610 5.2	1248 0.4	1839 5.2
5 W	0102 0.5	0650 5.3	1327 0.3	1917 5.3
6 TH	0143 0.4	0733 5.3	1407 0.4	1958 5.3
7 F	0225 0.5	0820 5.1	1449 0.6	2044 5.1
8 SA	0311 0.7	0914 4.8	1533 1.0	2136 4.8
9 SU	0400 1.0	1021 4.4	1623 1.4	2242 4.5
10 M	0458 1.3	1140 4.1	1723 1.8	2358 4.3
11 TU ☽	0611 1.6	1300 3.9	1844 2.1	
12 W	0117 4.2	0739 1.7	1422 3.9	2016 2.1
13 TH	0233 4.2	0902 1.6	1543 4.0	2130 1.9
14 F	0338 4.3	1004 1.4	1626 4.2	2226 1.6
15 SA	0429 4.4	1053 1.3	1747 4.3	2312 1.4
16 SU	0510 4.5	1134 1.1	1741 4.5	2353 1.2
17 M	0546 4.6	1210 1.0	1811 4.6	
18 TU	0030 1.1	0619 4.7	1244 1.0	1839 4.7
19 W ●	0106 1.1	0652 4.7	1316 1.0	1907 4.7
20 TH	0139 1.1	0725 4.6	1347 1.1	1936 4.7
21 F	0212 1.1	0759 4.5	1418 1.2	2005 4.6
22 SA	0246 1.2	0836 4.4	1450 1.4	2038 4.5
23 SU	0321 1.4	0917 4.2	1524 1.6	2115 4.3
24 M	0359 1.6	1005 4.0	1602 1.8	2201 4.2
25 TU	0443 1.8	1102 3.8	1645 2.0	2259 4.0
26 W	0536 1.9	1208 3.7	1742 2.1	
27 TH ◐	0013 3.9	0644 2.0	1316 3.7	1856 2.2
28 F	0127 3.9	0800 1.9	1421 3.8	2018 2.1
29 SA	0231 4.0	0907 1.7	1519 4.0	2124 1.9
30 SU	0326 4.2	1002 1.4	1608 4.3	2218 1.6
31 M	0415 4.5	1050 1.1	1653 4.6	2306 1.2

JUNE

Day	Time m	Time m	Time m	Time m
1 TU	0501 4.8	1136 0.8	1735 4.9	2353 0.9
2 W	0548 5.0	1221 0.7	1817 5.1	
3 TH ○	0039 0.7	0635 5.1	1306 0.6	1900 5.2
4 F ●	0127 0.6	0725 5.1	1351 0.6	1946 5.2
5 SA	0215 0.6	0819 5.0	1437 0.8	2036 5.1
6 SU	0305 0.7	0917 4.8	1525 1.1	2131 5.0
7 M	0358 0.9	1020 4.5	1617 1.4	2232 4.7
8 TU	0455 1.1	1125 4.3	1715 1.6	2338 4.5
9 W ☽	0557 1.4	1233 4.1	1820 1.9	
10 TH	0046 4.3	0703 1.5	1343 3.9	1930 1.9
11 F	0154 4.2	0811 1.6	1451 3.9	2041 1.9
12 SA	0259 4.2	0916 1.6	1549 4.0	2144 1.8
13 SU	0355 4.2	1011 1.6	1636 4.1	2239 1.7
14 M	0442 4.2	1059 1.5	1715 4.3	2326 1.6
15 TU	0524 4.3	1141 1.4	1750 4.4	
16 W	0008 1.5	0602 4.4	1219 1.4	1822 4.5
17 TH ●	0047 1.4	0639 4.4	1254 1.3	1853 4.6
18 F	0123 1.3	0715 4.5	1328 1.3	1924 4.6
19 SA	0159 1.3	0751 4.4	1402 1.4	1955 4.6
20 SU	0234 1.3	0828 4.4	1435 1.4	2029 4.6
21 M	0310 1.3	0906 4.3	1511 1.5	2105 4.5
22 TU	0347 1.4	0947 4.2	1548 1.6	2146 4.4
23 W	0428 1.5	1033 4.1	1630 1.7	2233 4.3
24 TH ◐	0513 1.6	1126 4.0	1717 1.8	2327 4.2
25 F ◐	0604 1.6	1226 3.9	1814 1.9	
26 SA	0030 4.1	0703 1.7	1330 4.0	1919 1.9
27 SU	0136 4.1	0808 1.6	1431 4.1	2029 1.9
28 M	0240 4.2	0913 1.5	1530 4.3	2135 1.7
29 TU	0341 4.4	1014 1.4	1624 4.5	2237 1.5
30 W	0441 4.6	1111 1.2	1715 4.8	2333 1.2

JULY

Day	Time m	Time m	Time m	Time m
1 TH	0537 4.8	1203 1.0	1804 5.0	
2 F	0027 0.9	0631 4.9	1253 0.9	1851 5.2
3 SA ○	0120 0.7	0724 5.0	1342 0.8	1939 5.3
4 SU	0211 0.6	0816 5.0	1430 0.9	2028 5.3
5 M	0300 0.6	0907 4.9	1517 1.0	2117 5.2
6 TU	0349 0.7	0959 4.7	1604 1.1	2209 5.0
7 W	0438 0.9	1052 4.4	1652 1.4	2303 4.7
8 TH	0527 1.2	1149 4.2	1743 1.6	
9 F ☽	0002 4.4	0617 1.4	1250 4.0	1839 1.8
10 SA	0106 4.2	0713 1.5	1357 3.9	1944 2.0
11 SU	0212 4.0	0815 1.9	1505 3.9	2056 2.1
12 M	0318 3.9	0923 1.9	1604 3.9	2206 2.0
13 TU	0417 4.0	1025 1.9	1653 4.1	2304 1.9
14 W	0508 4.1	1117 1.7	1734 4.3	2352 1.7
15 TH	0551 4.2	1200 1.5	1810 4.4	
16 F	0033 1.6	0630 4.3	1239 1.6	1842 4.6
17 SA ●	0112 1.4	0705 4.5	1315 1.5	1913 4.7
18 SU	0148 1.3	0739 4.5	1349 1.4	1943 4.8
19 M	0222 1.2	0812 4.6	1423 1.3	2014 4.8
20 TU	0256 1.1	0846 4.6	1457 1.3	2047 4.8
21 W	0330 1.1	0921 4.5	1531 1.3	2122 4.7
22 TH ◐	0406 1.2	1000 4.4	1609 1.4	2201 4.6
23 F	0444 1.2	1044 4.3	1650 1.5	2246 4.5
24 SA	0527 1.4	1138 4.2	1737 1.7	2341 4.3
25 SU ◐	0617 1.5	1242 4.1	1834 1.8	
26 M	0050 4.2	0718 1.7	1352 4.1	1943 1.9
27 TU	0207 4.1	0832 1.8	1501 4.2	2104 1.9
28 W	0325 4.2	0951 1.7	1608 4.4	2222 1.7
29 TH	0439 4.5	1100 1.5	1707 4.7	2328 1.4
30 F	0541 4.6	1157 1.3	1758 5.0	
31 SA ○	0025 1.0	0632 4.9	1248 1.1	1844 5.3

AUGUST

Day	Time m	Time m	Time m	Time m
1 SU	0116 0.7	0719 5.0	1334 0.9	1928 5.4
2 M	0203 0.5	0802 5.1	1418 0.8	2010 5.5
3 TU	0247 0.4	0844 5.0	1500 0.8	2052 5.4
4 W	0328 0.5	0925 4.8	1540 0.9	2135 5.1
5 TH	0408 0.7	1007 4.6	1621 1.2	2219 4.8
6 F	0448 1.1	1052 4.3	1703 1.5	2308 4.5
7 SA ☽	0529 1.4	1145 4.0	1749 1.8	
8 SU	0007 4.1	0613 1.8	1254 3.8	1845 2.1
9 M	0120 3.9	0709 2.1	1414 3.7	2002 2.3
10 TU	0240 3.7	0827 2.3	1532 3.8	2137 2.3
11 W	0355 3.8	0957 2.3	1632 4.0	2249 2.1
12 TH	0454 3.9	1100 2.1	1718 4.2	2339 1.9
13 F	0539 4.1	1146 1.9	1754 4.4	
14 SA	0020 1.6	0615 4.4	1224 1.7	1825 4.6
15 SU	0056 1.4	0647 4.6	1259 1.4	1854 4.8
16 M ●	0129 1.1	0717 4.7	1332 1.2	1922 5.0
17 TU	0202 1.0	0747 4.8	1404 1.1	1950 5.1
18 W	0233 0.8	0818 4.9	1436 1.0	2020 5.1
19 TH	0305 0.8	0850 4.8	1509 1.0	2053 5.0
20 F	0337 0.9	0925 4.7	1543 1.1	2129 4.9
21 SA	0413 1.0	1006 4.5	1622 1.3	2211 4.7
22 SU ◐	0452 1.2	1056 4.4	1706 1.5	2304 4.4
23 M	0539 1.6	1202 4.2	1800 1.6	
24 TU	0020 4.1	0639 1.9	1324 4.1	1913 2.0
25 W	0157 4.0	0807 2.1	1447 4.1	2054 2.1
26 TH	0331 4.1	0948 2.0	1602 4.3	2226 1.8
27 F	0447 4.3	1100 1.7	1702 4.7	2330 1.4
28 SA	0542 4.6	1153 1.4	1750 5.0	
29 SU	0020 1.1	0625 4.9	1238 1.1	1831 5.3
30 M ○	0105 0.8	0703 5.1	1319 0.8	1909 5.5
31 TU	0145 0.6	0739 5.2	1358 0.7	1946 5.6

Chart Datum: 2·75 metres below Ordnance Datum (Newlyn)

SCOTLAND – ULLAPOOL

LAT 57°54′N   LONG 5°10′W

TIMES AND HEIGHTS OF HIGH AND LOW WATERS

YEAR 2004

SEPTEMBER

Time m	Time m
1 0223 0.4 / 0813 5.1 / W 1435 0.7 / 2022 5.4	**16** 0203 0.6 / 0747 5.2 / TH 1409 0.8 / 1952 5.4
2 0259 0.5 / 0846 5.0 / TH 1511 0.8 / 2057 5.2	**17** 0235 0.6 / 0819 5.1 / F 1443 0.8 / 2025 5.3
3 0333 0.8 / 0919 5.0 / F 1547 1.1 / 2134 4.8	**18** 0308 0.7 / 0854 5.0 / SA 1518 0.9 / 2103 5.1
4 0407 1.1 / 0953 4.9 / SA 1624 1.4 / 2213 4.5	**19** 0344 0.9 / 0934 4.8 / SU 1558 1.2 / 2147 4.8
5 0442 1.5 / 1032 4.1 / SU 1704 1.8 / 2304 4.1	**20** 0424 1.3 / 1024 4.5 / M 1643 1.5 / 2245 4.4
6 0520 1.9 / 1129 3.9 / M 1752 2.2 ☽	**21** 0511 1.7 / 1136 4.2 / TU 1740 1.9 ●
7 0027 3.8 / 0607 2.3 / TU 1314 3.7 / 1905 2.6	**22** 0021 4.0 / 0615 2.2 / W 1311 4.1 / 1905 2.2
8 0203 3.6 / 0724 2.6 / W 1453 3.7 / 2111 2.5	**23** 0207 3.9 / 0806 2.4 / TH 1440 4.2 / 2105 2.1
9 0330 3.7 / 0931 2.6 / TH 1605 3.9 / 2233 2.2	**24** 0340 4.1 / 0951 2.2 / F 1556 4.4 / 2228 1.7
10 0433 3.9 / 1042 2.3 / F 1654 4.2 / 2320 1.9	**25** 0445 4.4 / 1053 1.8 / SA 1651 4.8 / 2321 1.3
11 0517 4.2 / 1125 2.0 / SA 1729 4.4 / 2356 1.6	**26** 0531 4.7 / 1139 1.4 / SU 1734 5.1
12 0551 4.4 / 1201 1.7 / SU 1759 4.7	**27** 0005 0.9 / 0608 5.0 / M 1220 1.1 / 1811 5.4
13 0029 1.3 / 0620 4.7 / M 1234 1.4 / 1826 5.0	**28** 0044 0.7 / 0641 5.2 / TU 1258 0.8 / ○ 1846 5.5
14 0101 1.0 / 0648 4.9 / TU 1306 1.1 / ● 1853 5.2	**29** 0120 0.5 / 0711 5.2 / W 1334 0.7 / 1919 5.5
15 0132 0.8 / 0717 5.1 / W 1337 0.9 / 1921 5.3	**30** 0154 0.5 / 0741 5.2 / TH 1408 0.8 / 1951 5.4

OCTOBER

Time m	Time m
1 0226 0.7 / 0810 5.1 / F 1442 0.9 / 2023 5.1	**16** 0206 0.6 / 0752 5.4 / SA 1419 0.7 / 2003 5.4
2 0257 0.9 / 0839 4.9 / SA 1515 1.2 / 2057 4.8	**17** 0242 0.7 / 0830 5.2 / SU 1458 0.9 / 2046 5.1
3 0329 1.2 / 0908 4.6 / SU 1550 1.5 / 2133 4.4	**18** 0321 1.0 / 0914 5.0 / M 1541 1.2 / 2138 4.7
4 0402 1.6 / 0941 4.3 / M 1628 1.9 / 2220 4.1	**19** 0404 1.5 / 1009 4.7 / TU 1631 1.6 / 2253 4.3
5 0437 2.0 / 1025 4.0 / TU 1713 2.2 / 2340 3.8	**20** 0456 1.9 / 1129 4.4 / W 1735 1.9 ●
6 0521 2.4 / 1159 3.8 / W 1819 2.5 ☽	**21** 0032 4.1 / 0610 2.3 / TH 1302 4.2 / 1912 2.1
7 0121 3.6 / 0627 2.7 / TH 1358 3.7 / 2027 2.6	**22** 0207 4.0 / 0804 2.4 / F 1427 4.3 / 2059 2.0
8 0251 3.7 / 0847 2.7 / F 1522 3.9 / 2159 2.3	**23** 0330 4.2 / 0933 2.2 / SA 1538 4.5 / 2209 1.6
9 0358 3.9 / 1008 2.4 / SA 1616 4.1 / 2245 2.0	**24** 0428 4.5 / 1030 1.8 / SU 1631 4.8 / 2259 1.3
10 0443 4.2 / 1052 2.1 / SU 1653 4.4 / 2321 1.6	**25** 0511 4.7 / 1116 1.5 / M 1713 5.0 / 2340 1.0
11 0517 4.5 / 1127 1.7 / M 1723 4.7 / 2354 1.3	**26** 0546 4.9 / 1156 1.2 / TU 1749 5.2
12 0547 4.8 / 1201 1.4 / TU 1752 5.0	**27** 0017 0.9 / 0616 5.1 / W 1234 1.0 / 1822 5.3
13 0026 0.9 / 0616 5.1 / W 1234 1.1 / 1821 5.3	**28** 0052 0.8 / 0645 5.2 / TH 1309 1.0 / ○ 1854 5.3
14 0059 0.7 / 0646 5.3 / TH 1308 0.8 / ● 1852 5.4	**29** 0124 0.9 / 0713 5.1 / F 1343 1.0 / 1926 5.2
15 0132 0.6 / 0718 5.4 / F 1342 0.7 / 1926 5.5	**30** 0155 1.0 / 0741 5.1 / SA 1416 1.2 / 1959 5.0
	31 0226 1.2 / 0810 4.9 / SU 1450 1.4 / 2033 4.7

NOVEMBER

Time m	Time m
1 0258 1.4 / 0840 4.7 / M 1524 1.6 / 2112 4.4	**16** 0307 1.2 / 0906 5.1 / TU 1534 1.2 / 2145 4.8
2 0331 1.7 / 0914 4.5 / TU 1602 1.9 / 2200 4.2	**17** 0355 1.6 / 1006 4.9 / W 1629 1.5 / 2301 4.4
3 0407 2.1 / 0957 4.2 / W 1647 2.2 / 2307 3.9	**18** 0452 1.9 / 1121 4.6 / TH 1737 1.8
4 0449 2.4 / 1104 4.0 / TH 1746 2.4	**19** 0022 4.2 / 0605 2.2 / F 1241 4.5 / ☽ 1900 1.9
5 0033 3.8 / 0549 2.6 / F 1250 3.9 / ☽ 1919 2.5	**20** 0144 4.2 / 0734 2.3 / SA 1358 4.5 / 2024 1.9
6 0153 3.8 / 0731 2.7 / SA 1415 3.9 / 2054 2.3	**21** 0300 4.2 / 0854 2.2 / SU 1507 4.6 / 2133 1.7
7 0303 3.9 / 0906 2.5 / SU 1518 4.1 / 2153 2.0	**22** 0359 4.4 / 0956 1.9 / M 1603 4.7 / 2226 1.5
8 0356 4.2 / 1002 2.2 / M 1604 4.4 / 2235 1.7	**23** 0445 4.6 / 1046 1.7 / TU 1649 4.8 / 2311 1.4
9 0436 4.5 / 1044 1.8 / TU 1641 4.7 / 2313 1.4	**24** 0522 4.8 / 1130 1.5 / W 1728 4.9 / 2350 1.3
10 0511 4.8 / 1123 1.5 / W 1715 5.0 / 2349 1.1	**25** 0555 4.9 / 1210 1.4 / TH 1803 5.0
11 0544 5.1 / 1200 1.2 / TH 1750 5.2	**26** 0025 1.2 / 0625 5.0 / F 1248 1.3 / ○ 1837 5.0
12 0026 0.8 / 0618 5.3 / F 1239 1.0 / ● 1827 5.4	**27** 0059 1.2 / 0654 5.0 / SA 1324 1.3 / 1911 4.9
13 0104 0.7 / 0654 5.5 / SA 1319 0.8 / 1908 5.4	**28** 0132 1.3 / 0724 5.0 / SU 1359 1.4 / 1946 4.8
14 0142 0.7 / 0733 5.5 / SU 1401 0.8 / 1953 5.3	**29** 0204 1.4 / 0754 4.9 / M 1433 1.5 / 2023 4.7
15 0223 0.9 / 0816 5.4 / M 1445 0.9 / 2044 5.1	**30** 0237 1.6 / 0826 4.8 / TU 1509 1.6 / 2102 4.5

DECEMBER

Time m	Time m
1 0311 1.8 / 0901 4.7 / W 1547 1.8 / 2146 4.3	**16** 0350 1.4 / 0958 5.2 / TH 1626 1.2 / 2246 4.6
2 0347 2.0 / 0943 4.5 / TH 1629 2.0 / 2238 4.1	**17** 0444 1.7 / 1059 4.9 / F 1724 1.4 / 2351 4.4
3 0429 2.2 / 1034 4.3 / F 1719 2.1 / 2339 4.0	**18** 0543 1.9 / 1206 4.7 / SA 1827 1.7 ☽
4 0520 2.4 / 1141 4.2 / SA 1821 2.2	**19** 0101 4.2 / 0649 2.1 / SU 1316 4.5 / 1933 1.8
5 0048 3.9 / 0626 2.5 / SU 1258 4.1 / ☽ 1932 2.2	**20** 0213 4.2 / 0801 2.2 / M 1425 4.4 / 2041 1.9
6 0156 4.0 / 0745 2.4 / M 1406 4.2 / 2041 2.1	**21** 0321 4.2 / 0911 2.1 / TU 1529 4.4 / 2144 1.9
7 0257 4.1 / 0856 2.3 / TU 1504 4.3 / 2139 1.8	**22** 0416 4.3 / 1014 2.0 / W 1624 4.5 / 2239 1.8
8 0349 4.4 / 0954 2.0 / W 1554 4.6 / 2228 1.6	**23** 0501 4.5 / 1108 1.9 / TH 1711 4.5 / 2325 1.7
9 0434 4.7 / 1044 1.7 / TH 1641 4.8 / 2314 1.3	**24** 0540 4.6 / 1154 1.8 / F 1752 4.6
10 0516 5.0 / 1131 1.4 / F 1727 5.1 / 2358 1.1	**25** 0005 1.7 / 0614 4.8 / SA 1235 1.6 / 1830 4.7
11 0557 5.2 / 1217 1.2 / SA 1813 5.2	**26** 0043 1.6 / 0646 4.9 / SU 1313 1.6 / ○ 1906 4.7
12 0042 1.0 / 0639 5.4 / SU 1304 1.0 / ● 1901 5.3	**27** 0118 1.6 / 0716 4.9 / M 1349 1.5 / 1941 4.7
13 0127 0.9 / 0723 5.5 / M 1352 0.9 / 1953 5.3	**28** 0151 1.6 / 0747 5.0 / TU 1424 1.5 / 2015 4.7
14 0213 1.0 / 0811 5.5 / TU 1441 0.9 / 2047 5.1	**29** 0225 1.6 / 0818 4.9 / W 1459 1.5 / 2050 4.6
15 0300 1.2 / 0902 5.4 / W 1532 1.0 / 2144 4.9	**30** 0258 1.6 / 0850 4.9 / TH 1534 1.6 / 2126 4.5
	31 0333 1.7 / 0926 4.8 / F 1611 1.6 / 2205 4.4

Chart Datum: 2·75 metres below Ordnance Datum (Newlyn)

Chapter 5

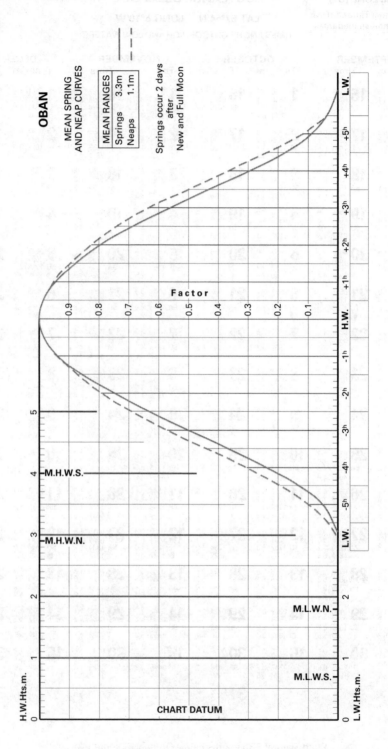

OBAN

MEAN SPRING
AND NEAP CURVES

MEAN RANGES	
Springs	3.3m
Neaps	1.1m

Springs occur 2 days
after
New and Full Moon

TIME ZONE (UT)
For Summer Time add ONE hour in **non-shaded areas**

SCOTLAND – OBAN

YEAR 2004

LAT 56°25′N   LONG 5°29′W

TIMES AND HEIGHTS OF HIGH AND LOW WATERS

JANUARY

Day	Time m	Time m	Day	Time m	Time m
1 TH	0021 2.9	0643 1.7	16 F	0545 1.5	1155 3.3
	1329 3.1	1927 1.9		1848 1.8	
2 F	0139 2.9	0758 1.8	17 SA	0046 3.1	0659 1.5
	1431 3.2	2027 1.9		1330 3.3	2004 1.7
3 SA	0237 3.0	0910 1.8	18 SU	0222 3.2	0816 1.4
	1518 3.3	2119 1.7		1455 3.3	2112 1.5
4 SU	0324 3.2	1005 1.7	19 M	0333 3.4	0930 1.3
	1559 3.4	2203 1.6		1600 3.5	2211 1.3
5 M	0407 3.4	1049 1.6	20 TU	0428 3.7	1035 1.1
	1638 3.5	2244 1.4		1652 3.7	2303 1.0
6 TU	0448 3.6	1126 1.6	21 W	0515 3.9	1132 0.9
	1717 3.7	2324 1.3		1737 3.8	● 2351 0.8
7 W	0527 3.7	1201 1.5	22 TH	0558 4.1	1221 0.8
	1756 3.7	O		1819 3.8	
8 TH	0002 1.2	0604 3.8	23 F	0035 0.7	0640 4.2
	1238 1.4	1833 3.8		1308 0.8	1857 3.8
9 F	0039 1.1	0640 3.8	24 SA	0119 0.7	0720 4.2
	1314 1.4	1907 3.7		1351 0.9	1934 3.8
10 SA	0114 1.1	0714 3.8	25 SU	0201 0.7	0759 4.1
	1349 1.4	1939 3.7		1431 1.0	2009 3.6
11 SU	0148 1.1	0747 3.8	26 M	0241 0.8	0837 3.9
	1422 1.5	2011 3.6		1510 1.2	2042 3.5
12 M	0223 1.1	0822 3.7	27 TU	0320 1.0	0914 3.7
	1455 1.5	2047 3.4		1549 1.4	2115 3.3
13 TU	0302 1.2	0901 3.7	28 W	0400 1.3	0954 3.4
	1534 1.6	2129 3.3		1630 1.6	2151 3.1
14 W	0347 1.3	0947 3.5	29 TH	0444 1.5	1038 3.2
	1625 1.7	2218 3.2		1718 1.8	◐ 2236 3.0
15 TH	0440 1.4	1043 3.4	30 F	0534 1.8	1139 3.0
	1731 1.7	◐ 2321 3.1		1815 1.9	2341 2.8
			31 SA	0635 2.0	1324 2.9
				1921 2.0	

FEBRUARY

Day	Time m	Time m	Day	Time m	Time m
1 SU	0138 2.8	0758 2.0	16 M	0217 3.0	0805 1.6
	1502 3.0	2033 1.9		1511 3.1	2100 1.6
2 M	0301 3.0	1003 1.9	17 TU	0339 3.3	0934 1.4
	1555 3.1	2139 1.7		1620 3.3	2208 1.3
3 TU	0356 3.2	1052 1.7	18 W	0432 3.6	1041 1.1
	1635 3.3	2229 1.5		1705 3.5	2259 1.0
4 W	0440 3.4	1128 1.6	19 TH	0514 3.9	1131 0.9
	1712 3.5	2310 1.3		1740 3.7	2343 0.8
5 TH	0519 3.6	1159 1.4	20 F	0552 4.1	1214 0.8
	1749 3.7	2347 1.1		1812 3.8	●
6 F	0556 3.8	1230 1.2	21 SA	0024 0.6	0627 4.2
	1824 3.8	O		1253 0.7	1843 3.9
7 SA	0021 0.9	0629 3.9	22 SU	0104 0.5	0702 4.2
	1302 1.1	1855 3.8		1329 0.7	1913 3.8
8 SU	0055 0.8	0701 4.0	23 M	0141 0.6	0735 4.1
	1333 1.0	1922 3.8		1403 0.8	1942 3.8
9 M	0128 0.7	0731 4.0	24 TU	0215 0.7	0806 3.9
	1402 1.0	1950 3.7		1436 1.0	2009 3.7
10 TU	0202 0.7	0803 3.9	25 W	0248 0.9	0837 3.7
	1431 1.1	2022 3.6		1508 1.2	2037 3.5
11 W	0239 0.8	0838 3.8	26 TH	0321 1.2	0909 3.5
	1506 1.2	2100 3.5		1544 1.5	2108 3.3
12 TH	0322 0.9	0919 3.6	27 F	0358 1.5	0943 3.2
	1550 1.4	2144 3.3		1628 1.7	2144 3.1
13 F	0412 1.2	1007 3.4	28 SA	0443 1.8	1024 2.9
	1647 1.6	◐ 2239 3.1		1725 1.9	◐ 2230 2.9
14 SA	0516 1.4	1113 3.1	29 SU	0545 2.1	1153 2.7
	1806 1.7			1834 2.0	
15 SU	0004 3.0	0636 1.5			
	1309 2.9	1935 1.7			

MARCH

Day	Time m	Time m	Day	Time m	Time m
1 M	0005 2.7	0710 2.2	16 TU	0219 3.0	0810 1.6
	1456 2.7	1953 2.0		1527 2.9	2053 1.5
2 TU	0253 2.8	1008 2.0	17 W	0333 3.3	0943 1.3
	1549 3.0	2115 1.8		1622 3.1	2159 1.2
3 W	0349 3.0	1045 1.7	18 TH	0421 3.6	1038 1.1
	1624 3.2	2210 1.5		1657 3.4	2246 0.9
4 TH	0427 3.3	1114 1.4	19 F	0458 3.8	1118 0.9
	1657 3.4	2250 1.2		1723 3.6	2327 0.7
5 F	0502 3.6	1141 1.2	20 SA	0532 4.0	1154 0.7
	1730 3.6	2325 0.9		1750 3.7	●
6 SA	0536 3.8	1209 0.9	21 SU	0005 0.5	0606 4.1
	1802 3.8	O 2358 0.7		1228 0.7	1817 3.9
7 SU	0609 4.0	1238 0.8	22 M	0041 0.5	0635 4.1
	1831 3.9			1300 0.7	1845 3.9
8 M	0030 0.5	0638 4.1	23 TU	0115 0.6	0705 4.1
	1307 0.7	1856 3.9		1331 0.8	1911 3.9
9 TU	0105 0.4	0708 4.1	24 W	0147 0.7	0734 3.9
	1336 0.7	1924 3.9		1401 0.9	1937 3.8
10 W	0141 0.4	0740 4.0	25 TH	0216 1.0	0803 3.7
	1407 0.8	1957 3.8		1432 1.1	2005 3.6
11 TH	0220 0.5	0815 3.8	26 F	0246 1.3	0832 3.4
	1443 0.9	2035 3.6		1506 1.4	2035 3.4
12 F	0304 0.8	0855 3.5	27 SA	0319 1.6	0902 3.2
	1527 1.2	2118 3.4		1547 1.6	2110 3.2
13 SA	0356 1.1	0941 3.2	28 SU	0400 1.9	0936 2.9
	1625 1.4	◐ 2214 3.1		1643 1.8	◐ 2152 2.9
14 SU	0504 1.4	1049 2.9	29 M	0509 2.1	1035 2.6
	1746 1.6	2351 2.9		1755 2.0	2302 2.6
15 M	0630 1.6	1332 2.7	30 TU	0647 2.2	1425 2.6
	1919 1.7			1914 2.0	
			31 W	0228 2.8	0947 2.0
				1519 2.9	2034 1.8

APRIL

Day	Time m	Time m	Day	Time m	Time m
1 TH	0322 3.0	1014 1.7	16 F	0355 3.5	1016 1.1
	1556 3.1	2133 1.5		1630 3.3	2222 0.9
2 F	0358 3.3	1039 1.4	17 SA	0431 3.7	1053 0.9
	1629 3.4	2215 1.1		1652 3.5	2303 0.8
3 SA	0433 3.6	1107 1.0	18 SU	0503 3.9	1126 0.8
	1701 3.6	2251 0.8		1719 3.7	2340 0.7
4 SU	0506 3.9	1136 0.8	19 M	0535 4.0	1156 0.8
	1731 3.8	2327 0.5		1747 3.8	●
5 M	0539 4.0	1206 0.6	20 TU	0014 0.7	0605 4.0
	1759 3.9	O		1227 0.8	1814 3.9
6 TU	0003 0.3	0610 4.1	21 W	0048 0.8	0635 3.9
	1237 0.5	1827 4.0		1258 0.8	1841 3.9
7 W	0041 0.2	0643 4.1	22 TH	0118 0.9	0705 3.8
	1310 0.5	1859 3.9		1329 1.0	1910 3.8
8 TH	0122 0.3	0718 4.0	23 F	0148 1.2	0735 3.6
	1346 0.6	1936 3.8		1401 1.1	1940 3.7
9 F	0205 0.5	0756 3.8	24 SA	0219 1.4	0806 3.4
	1427 0.8	2017 3.6		1436 1.4	2012 3.5
10 SA	0254 0.7	0839 3.4	25 SU	0251 1.7	0837 3.2
	1515 1.1	2105 3.4		1516 1.6	2048 3.3
11 SU	0351 1.1	0930 3.0	26 M	0330 1.9	0916 2.9
	1616 1.3	2207 3.1		1607 1.8	2132 3.0
12 M	0502 1.4	1050 2.7	27 TU	0445 2.1	1020 2.7
	1733 1.5	◐		1714 1.9	◐ 2238 2.8
13 TU	0002 2.9	0627 1.5	28 W	0622 2.1	1332 2.6
	1342 2.6	1904 1.6		1826 1.9	
14 W	0205 3.0	0814 1.5	29 TH	0106 2.8	0817 2.0
	1515 2.8	2035 1.4		1433 2.8	1937 1.7
15 TH	0311 3.3	0929 1.3	30 F	0230 3.0	0913 1.7
	1603 3.1	2136 1.2		1515 3.0	2038 1.5

Chart Datum: 2·10 metres below Ordnance Datum (Newlyn)

TIME ZONE (UT)
For Summer Time add ONE hour in **non-shaded areas**

SCOTLAND – OBAN

LAT 56°25′N   LONG 5°29′W

YEAR 2004

TIMES AND HEIGHTS OF HIGH AND LOW WATERS

MAY

Day	Time m	Day	Time m
1 SA	0314 3.3 / 0951 1.4 / 1551 3.3 / 2128 1.1	**16** SU	0359 3.5 / 1019 1.1 / 1615 3.3 / 2235 1.0
2 SU	0353 3.6 / 1025 1.1 / 1624 3.5 / 2211 0.8	**17** M	0433 3.6 / 1052 1.1 / 1645 3.5 / 2312 1.0
3 M	0430 3.8 / 1058 0.8 / 1655 3.7 / 2254 0.5	**18** TU	0505 3.7 / 1123 1.0 / 1715 3.7 / 2348 1.0
4 TU	0506 4.0 / 1132 0.6 / 1727 3.9 / ○ 2336 0.4	**19** W	0538 3.7 / 1155 1.0 / ● 1746 3.8
5 W	0543 4.1 / 1208 0.5 / 1802 4.0	**20** TH	0021 1.1 / 0610 3.7 / 1229 1.0 / 1817 3.8
6 TH	0021 0.3 / 0621 4.1 / 1247 0.5 / 1840 4.0	**21** F	0054 1.2 / 0643 3.7 / 1303 1.1 / 1850 3.7
7 F	0107 0.4 / 0702 3.9 / 1329 0.6 / 1922 3.9	**22** SA	0128 1.4 / 0718 3.5 / 1339 1.2 / 1924 3.6
8 SA	0156 0.5 / 0745 3.6 / 1416 0.8 / 2009 3.7	**23** SU	0203 1.5 / 0753 3.4 / 1415 1.3 / 1959 3.5
9 SU	0249 0.8 / 0833 3.3 / 1508 1.0 / 2102 3.4	**24** M	0239 1.7 / 0830 3.2 / 1454 1.5 / 2037 3.3
10 M	0348 1.1 / 0930 3.0 / 1607 1.2 / 2208 3.2	**25** TU	0322 1.9 / 0913 3.0 / 1538 1.6 / 2122 3.2
11 TU	0457 1.3 / 1057 2.7 / 1717 1.4 / ◑ 2353 3.1	**26** W	0423 2.0 / 1009 2.8 / 1632 1.7 / 2218 3.1
12 W	0618 1.5 / 1312 2.7 / 1839 1.5	**27** TH	0540 2.0 / 1136 2.8 / 1733 1.7 / ◑ 2333 3.0
13 TH	0131 3.1 / 0747 1.5 / 1436 2.8 / 2000 1.4	**28** F	0659 1.9 / 1325 2.8 / 1837 1.6
14 F	0236 3.2 / 0855 1.4 / 1524 3.0 / 2103 1.2	**29** SA	0105 3.1 / 0805 1.7 / 1421 3.0 / 1939 1.5
15 SA	0322 3.4 / 0942 1.2 / 1549 3.1 / 2152 1.1	**30** SU	0215 3.3 / 0857 1.4 / 1504 3.2 / 2038 1.2
		31 M	0308 3.5 / 0941 1.2 / 1544 3.4 / 2133 1.0

JUNE

Day	Time m	Day	Time m
1 TU	0355 3.7 / 1022 0.9 / 1623 3.7 / 2225 0.7	**16** W	0440 3.4 / 1053 1.2 / 1650 3.5 / 2326 1.3
2 W	0439 3.9 / 1104 0.8 / 1704 3.8 / 2316 0.6	**17** TH	0517 3.5 / 1129 1.2 / ● 1727 3.6
3 TH	0524 4.0 / 1147 0.6 / ○ 1746 4.0	**18** F	0002 1.3 / 0555 3.6 / 1207 1.1 / 1803 3.7
4 F	0007 0.5 / 0608 3.9 / 1232 0.6 / 1831 4.0	**19** SA	0039 1.4 / 0633 3.6 / 1245 1.1 / 1839 3.7
5 SA	0058 0.5 / 0654 3.8 / 1318 0.6 / 1917 3.9	**20** SU	0116 1.4 / 0710 3.5 / 1322 1.2 / 1916 3.7
6 SU	0150 0.6 / 0741 3.6 / 1407 0.7 / 2006 3.8	**21** M	0155 1.5 / 0747 3.4 / 1358 1.2 / 1952 3.6
7 M	0244 0.8 / 0831 3.3 / 1458 0.9 / 2100 3.6	**22** TU	0232 1.6 / 0823 3.3 / 1433 1.3 / 2028 3.5
8 TU	0340 1.1 / 0927 3.1 / 1553 1.1 / 2200 3.4	**23** W	0310 1.6 / 0901 3.2 / 1511 1.4 / 2107 3.4
9 W	0441 1.3 / 1035 2.9 / 1653 1.2 / ◑ 2314 3.2	**24** TH	0351 1.7 / 0944 3.1 / 1555 1.5 / 2152 3.3
10 TH	0548 1.4 / 1206 2.8 / 1759 1.4	**25** F	0444 1.7 / 1035 3.0 / 1646 1.5 / ◑ 2247 3.3
11 F	0038 3.1 / 0658 1.5 / 1324 2.8 / 1910 1.4	**26** SA	0549 1.7 / 1138 2.9 / 1745 1.5 / 2353 3.2
12 SA	0148 3.1 / 0804 1.5 / 1419 2.9 / 2019 1.4	**27** SU	0658 1.7 / 1256 3.0 / 1851 1.4
13 SU	0242 3.2 / 0857 1.5 / 1500 3.0 / 2117 1.4	**28** M	0112 3.3 / 0803 1.5 / 1412 3.1 / 1958 1.3
14 M	0325 3.3 / 0940 1.4 / 1537 3.2 / 2206 1.4	**29** TU	0228 3.4 / 0902 1.4 / 1513 3.3 / 2105 1.2
15 TU	0404 3.3 / 1017 1.3 / 1614 3.3 / 2248 1.3	**30** W	0331 3.5 / 0956 1.1 / 1605 3.6 / 2208 1.0

JULY

Day	Time m	Day	Time m
1 TH	0426 3.7 / 1047 0.9 / 1655 3.8 / 2306 0.8	**16** F	0509 3.4 / 1113 1.3 / 1717 3.5 / 2357 1.4
2 F	0517 3.8 / 1135 0.8 / ○ 1742 3.9	**17** SA	0548 3.5 / 1152 1.1 / ● 1756 3.6
3 SA	0001 0.7 / 0605 3.8 / 1223 0.6 / 1829 4.0	**18** SU	0032 1.4 / 0626 3.6 / 1230 1.0 / 1832 3.7
4 SU	0054 0.6 / 0652 3.7 / 1310 0.6 / 1915 4.0	**19** M	0108 1.3 / 0703 3.6 / 1305 1.0 / 1907 3.8
5 M	0145 0.7 / 0738 3.6 / 1357 0.6 / 2001 3.9	**20** TU	0143 1.3 / 0736 3.6 / 1338 1.0 / 1939 3.7
6 TU	0234 0.8 / 0823 3.5 / 1444 0.7 / 2048 3.8	**21** W	0217 1.3 / 0806 3.5 / 1410 1.0 / 2011 3.7
7 W	0323 1.0 / 0907 3.3 / 1532 0.9 / 2135 3.6	**22** TH	0246 1.3 / 0836 3.4 / 1444 1.1 / 2044 3.6
8 TH	0412 1.2 / 0954 3.1 / 1620 1.1 / 2225 3.3	**23** F	0316 1.4 / 0911 3.3 / 1523 1.2 / 2122 3.5
9 F	0502 1.4 / 1045 2.9 / 1711 1.3 / ◑ 2322 3.1	**24** SA	0356 1.5 / 0953 3.2 / 1610 1.3 / 2208 3.4
10 SA	0555 1.6 / 1149 2.8 / 1808 1.5	**25** SU	0450 1.6 / 1046 3.0 / 1706 1.4 / ◑ 2306 3.3
11 SU	0034 3.0 / 0653 1.7 / 1305 2.8 / 1912 1.7	**26** M	0602 1.7 / 1158 3.0 / 1816 1.5
12 M	0151 2.9 / 0755 1.7 / 1411 2.9 / 2031 1.7	**27** TU	0027 3.1 / 0722 1.6 / 1341 3.0 / 1933 1.5
13 TU	0255 3.0 / 0855 1.7 / 1506 3.0 / 2145 1.7	**28** W	0210 3.2 / 0838 1.5 / 1508 3.2 / 2052 1.4
14 W	0345 3.1 / 0947 1.6 / 1553 3.2 / 2239 1.6	**29** TH	0333 3.3 / 0945 1.3 / 1610 3.5 / 2205 1.2
15 TH	0428 3.2 / 1032 1.4 / 1636 3.4 / 2321 1.5	**30** F	0434 3.5 / 1041 1.0 / 1659 3.8 / 2307 0.9
		31 SA	0524 3.6 / 1131 0.8 / ○ 1744 4.0

AUGUST

Day	Time m	Day	Time m
1 SU	0000 0.7 / 0607 3.7 / 1217 0.6 / 1825 4.2	**16** M	0020 1.2 / 0612 3.7 / 1212 0.9 / ● 1817 3.9
2 M	0048 0.6 / 0646 3.8 / 1301 0.5 / 1906 4.2	**17** TU	0051 1.1 / 0645 3.8 / 1244 0.8 / 1849 3.9
3 TU	0132 0.6 / 0724 3.7 / 1343 0.5 / 1945 4.1	**18** W	0121 1.0 / 0713 3.8 / 1314 0.7 / 1917 4.0
4 W	0214 0.7 / 0800 3.6 / 1424 0.6 / 2023 4.0	**19** TH	0150 1.0 / 0738 3.7 / 1345 0.8 / 1946 3.9
5 TH	0254 0.9 / 0835 3.5 / 1504 0.8 / 2100 3.7	**20** F	0216 1.1 / 0805 3.6 / 1418 0.8 / 2016 3.8
6 F	0333 1.1 / 0907 3.3 / 1543 1.1 / 2137 3.4	**21** SA	0244 1.2 / 0838 3.5 / 1456 1.0 / 2052 3.7
7 SA	0413 1.4 / 0941 3.1 / 1625 1.4 / ◑ 2217 3.2	**22** SU	0321 1.3 / 0918 3.3 / 1542 1.2 / 2134 3.4
8 SU	0459 1.6 / 1021 3.0 / 1712 1.6 / 2309 2.9	**23** M	0412 1.5 / 1008 3.1 / 1640 1.4 / ◑ 2229 3.2
9 M	0553 1.8 / 1123 2.8 / 1811 1.9	**24** TU	0527 1.7 / 1123 2.9 / 1758 1.6
10 TU	0039 2.8 / 0658 1.9 / 1324 2.8 / 1929 2.0	**25** W	0003 2.9 / 0700 1.7 / 1354 3.0 / 1927 1.6
11 W	0244 2.8 / 0814 1.8 / 1452 2.9 / 2151 1.9	**26** TH	0235 2.9 / 0829 1.6 / 1518 3.1 / 2059 1.5
12 TH	0348 3.0 / 0928 1.7 / 1548 3.1 / 2243 1.8	**27** F	0354 3.2 / 0942 1.3 / 1613 3.6 / 2214 1.2
13 F	0426 3.2 / 1021 1.5 / 1630 3.3 / 2320 1.6	**28** SA	0444 3.4 / 1036 1.0 / 1656 3.9 / 2307 0.9
14 SA	0501 3.4 / 1102 1.2 / 1708 3.5 / 2351 1.4	**29** SU	0523 3.6 / 1122 0.7 / 1734 4.1 / 2351 0.7
15 SU	0537 3.6 / 1138 1.0 / 1744 3.7	**30** M	0556 3.8 / 1203 0.5 / 1810 4.3 / ○
		31 TU	0031 0.6 / 0628 3.9 / 1244 0.4 / 1844 4.3

Chart Datum: 2·10 metres below Ordnance Datum (Newlyn)

SCOTLAND – OBAN

TIME ZONE (UT)
For Summer Time add ONE hour in **non-shaded areas**

YEAR 2004

LAT 56°25′N   LONG 5°29′W

TIMES AND HEIGHTS OF HIGH AND LOW WATERS

SEPTEMBER

Day	Time m	Time m	Time m	Time m		Day	Time m	Time m	Time m	Time m
1 W	0109 0.6	0659 3.9	1918 4.2			**16** TH	0050 0.8	0641 3.9	1246 0.6	1848 4.1
2 TH	0144 0.7	0729 3.8	1358 0.6	1949 4.0		**17** F	0117 0.8	0705 3.9	1319 0.6	1917 4.1
3 F	0218 0.9	0757 3.7	1432 0.8	2020 3.8		**18** SA	0146 0.8	0735 3.8	1355 0.7	1949 3.9
4 SA	0252 1.1	0824 3.5	1506 1.2	2051 3.5		**19** SU	0218 1.0	0810 3.6	1436 0.9	2026 3.7
5 SU	0329 1.4	0854 3.2	1544 1.5	2125 3.2		**20** M	0258 1.2	0851 3.4	1525 1.2	2108 3.3
6 M	0413 1.6	0930 3.1	1629 1.8	◑ 2204 2.9		**21** TU	0351 1.5	0944 3.2	1630 1.5	◑ 2205 3.0
7 TU	0508 1.8	1018 2.9	1731 2.1	2321 2.7		**22** W	0511 1.7	1113 3.0	1756 1.7	
8 W	0618 2.0	1241 2.7	1859 2.2			**23** TH	0028 2.7	0647 1.8	1400 3.1	1933 1.7
9 TH	0242 2.7	0741 1.9	1458 2.9	2158 2.0		**24** F	0251 2.9	0822 1.6	1509 3.4	2111 1.5
10 F	0338 2.9	1544 3.1	2234 1.8			**25** SA	0352 3.2	0931 1.3	1558 3.7	2210 1.2
11 SA	0411 3.2	1002 1.5	1616 3.4	2302 1.5		**26** SU	0433 3.4	1021 1.0	1637 4.0	2253 0.9
12 SU	0442 3.4	1040 1.2	1648 3.6	2327 1.3		**27** M	0503 3.6	1103 0.7	1711 4.2	2330 0.8
13 M	0514 3.6	1114 1.0	1721 3.9	2354 1.0		**28** TU	0531 3.8	1142 0.6	1744 4.3	O
14 TU	0546 3.8	1145 0.8	1752 4.0	●		**29** W	0005 0.7	0558 3.9	1220 0.5	1815 4.3
15 W	0022 0.9	0616 3.9	1215 0.6	1821 4.1		**30** TH	0038 0.7	0627 4.0	1256 0.6	1845 4.2

OCTOBER

Day	Time m	Time m	Time m	Time m		Day	Time m	Time m	Time m	Time m
1 F	0110 0.8	0654 4.0	1329 0.8	1914 4.1		**16** SA	0046 0.7	0636 4.0	1257 0.6	1851 4.1
2 SA	0142 0.9	0721 3.9	1401 1.0	1944 3.8		**17** SU	0121 0.8	0711 3.9	1338 0.7	1928 3.9
3 SU	0215 1.1	0749 3.7	1433 1.4	2013 3.6		**18** M	0200 0.9	0751 3.8	1425 1.0	2008 3.6
4 M	0251 1.4	0820 3.5	1509 1.7	2045 3.3		**19** TU	0246 1.2	0837 3.5	1520 1.3	2056 3.3
5 TU	0335 1.6	0857 3.3	1556 2.0	2120 3.0		**20** W	0344 1.4	0937 3.3	1630 1.6	◑ 2203 2.9
6 W	0431 1.9	0944 3.0	1704 2.3	◑ 2221 2.7		**21** TH	0501 1.6	1128 3.1	1755 1.7	
7 TH	0542 2.0	1121 2.8	1951 2.3			**22** F	0058 2.7	0630 1.7	1343 3.2	1936 1.7
8 F	0213 2.7	0704 2.0	1436 3.0	2137 2.1		**23** SA	0238 2.9	0801 1.5	1447 3.5	2058 1.5
9 SA	0306 2.9	0828 1.8	1517 3.2	2204 1.8		**24** SU	0332 3.1	0908 1.3	1533 3.7	2148 1.3
10 SU	0341 3.2	0924 1.6	1547 3.5	2227 1.5		**25** M	0407 3.4	0957 1.1	1610 3.9	2227 1.1
11 M	0412 3.4	1004 1.3	1617 3.7	2251 1.2		**26** TU	0433 3.6	1039 0.9	1643 4.1	2301 1.0
12 TU	0443 3.6	1038 1.0	1648 4.0	2318 1.0		**27** W	0458 3.8	1118 0.8	1714 4.2	2333 0.9
13 W	0514 3.8	1110 0.8	1719 4.1	2346 0.8		**28** TH	0527 3.9	1154 0.8	1745 4.2	O
14 TH	0541 4.0	1143 0.6	1749 4.1			**29** F	0005 0.9	0555 4.0	1230 0.9	1814 4.1
15 F	0015 0.7	0607 4.0	1219 0.5	1819 4.2		**30** SA	0037 0.9	0624 4.0	1302 1.1	1844 4.0
						31 SU	0110 1.1	0653 4.0	1334 1.3	1915 3.8

NOVEMBER

Day	Time m	Time m	Time m	Time m		Day	Time m	Time m	Time m	Time m
1 M	0145 1.2	0724 3.8	1408 1.6	1948 3.6		**16** TU	0148 0.9	0743 3.9	1420 1.0	2002 3.6
2 TU	0223 1.4	0758 3.6	1445 1.9	2022 3.3		**17** W	0238 1.1	0834 3.7	1518 1.3	2055 3.2
3 W	0306 1.7	0837 3.4	1534 2.1	2101 3.1		**18** TH	0336 1.3	0938 3.4	1624 1.5	2203 2.9
4 TH	0358 1.9	0925 3.2	1642 2.3	2204 2.8		**19** F	0444 1.5	1003 3.3	1741 1.7	◑
5 F	0502 2.0	1038 3.0	1816 2.3	◑		**20** SA	0014 2.8	0601 1.6	1305 3.3	1907 1.7
6 SA	0117 2.8	0612 2.0	1334 3.0	2025 2.2		**21** SU	0156 2.9	0723 1.5	1412 3.5	2021 1.6
7 SU	0219 2.9	0725 1.9	1504 3.2	2106 1.9		**22** M	0255 3.1	0833 1.4	1502 3.6	2114 1.5
8 M	0300 3.1	0826 1.7	1504 3.5	2137 1.6		**23** TU	0330 3.3	0927 1.3	1541 3.7	2155 1.3
9 TU	0335 3.4	0913 1.4	1538 3.7	2208 1.4		**24** W	0356 3.6	1013 1.2	1615 3.8	2229 1.3
10 W	0407 3.6	1611 3.9	2239 1.1			**25** TH	0426 3.6	1054 1.1	1647 3.9	2302 1.2
11 TH	0437 3.8	1645 4.1	2310 0.9			**26** F	0457 3.8	1131 1.2	1719 3.9	2335 1.1
12 F	0507 4.0	1113 0.7	1720 4.2	● 2344 0.8		**27** SA	0530 3.9	1207 1.2	1751 3.9	
13 SA	0540 4.1	1156 0.6	1756 4.2			**28** SU	0010 1.1	0602 4.0	1242 1.4	1825 3.9
14 SU	0021 0.7	0616 4.1	1241 0.7	1834 4.1		**29** M	0047 1.2	0636 3.9	1317 1.5	1900 3.7
15 M	0103 0.8	0657 4.0	1328 0.8	1916 3.9		**30** TU	0124 1.3	0711 3.8	1353 1.7	1936 3.6

DECEMBER

Day	Time m	Time m	Time m	Time m		Day	Time m	Time m	Time m	Time m
1 W	0203 1.4	0748 3.7	1433 1.9	2014 3.4		**16** TH	0230 0.9	0833 3.9	1510 1.1	2050 3.4
2 TH	0243 1.6	0827 3.5	1518 2.0	2055 3.2		**17** F	0323 1.1	0929 3.7	1608 1.3	2146 3.1
3 F	0326 1.7	0910 3.4	1613 2.2	2145 3.0		**18** SA	0420 1.2	1035 3.5	1709 1.5	◑ 2255 3.0
4 SA	0415 1.9	1003 3.3	1721 2.2	2253 2.9		**19** SU	0523 1.4	1200 3.3	1815 1.7	
5 SU	0511 1.9	1111 3.2	1835 2.2	◑		**20** M	0025 2.9	0632 1.5	1320 3.3	1923 1.7
6 M	0046 2.9	0612 1.9	1243 3.2	1941 2.0		**21** TU	0141 2.9	0745 1.6	1423 3.3	2025 1.7
7 TU	0158 3.0	0713 1.8	1357 3.4	2034 1.8		**22** W	0236 3.1	0853 1.5	1513 3.4	2115 1.6
8 W	0245 3.2	0813 1.6	1449 3.6	2118 1.6		**23** TH	0319 3.2	0949 1.5	1553 3.5	2157 1.5
9 TH	0325 3.4	0908 1.3	1534 3.8	2159 1.3		**24** F	0358 3.4	1037 1.5	1629 3.6	2236 1.4
10 F	0403 3.7	1001 1.1	1617 3.9	2240 1.1		**25** SA	0436 3.6	1119 1.5	1705 3.6	2314 1.3
11 SA	0443 3.9	1051 0.9	1700 4.0	2322 0.9		**26** SU	0514 3.7	1157 1.5	1741 3.7	O 2352 1.3
12 SU	0525 4.0	1142 0.8	1744 4.1	●		**27** M	0552 3.8	1233 1.5	1818 3.8	
13 M	0006 0.8	0608 4.1	1232 0.8	1827 4.0		**28** TU	0031 1.4	0628 3.9	1309 1.5	1854 3.7
14 TU	0052 0.8	0654 4.1	1323 0.8	1913 3.8		**29** W	0110 1.2	0705 3.8	1346 1.6	1931 3.7
15 W	0140 0.8	0742 4.0	1416 0.9	2000 3.6		**30** TH	0146 1.3	0740 3.8	1422 1.7	2006 3.6
						31 F	0221 1.4	0815 3.7	1457 1.7	2040 3.4

Chart Datum: 2·10 metres below Ordnance Datum (Newlyn)

Chapter 5

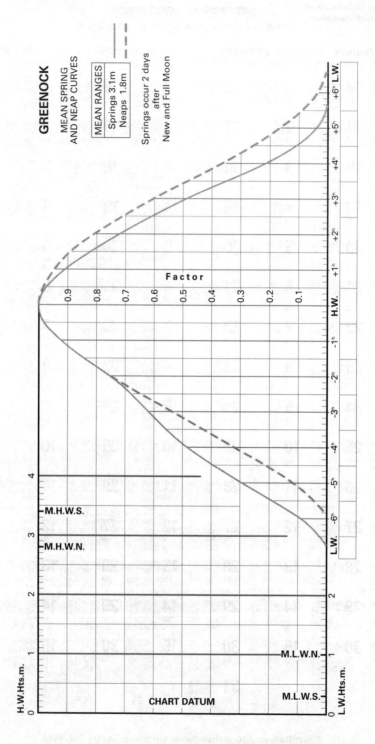

GREENOCK

MEAN SPRING
AND NEAP CURVES

MEAN RANGES
Springs 3.1m
Neaps 1.8m

Springs occur 2 days
after
New and Full Moon

TIME ZONE (UT)
For Summer Time add ONE hour in **non-shaded areas**

SCOTLAND – GREENOCK

LAT 55°57'N   LONG 4°46'W

TIMES AND HEIGHTS OF HIGH AND LOW WATERS

YEAR **2004**

JANUARY

Time m	Time m
1 TH 0057 0.9 / 0715 3.0 / 1315 1.3 / 1936 3.1	**16** F 0630 2.9 / 1223 0.9 / 1835 3.2
2 F 0156 0.9 / 0817 3.0 / 1421 1.3 / 2054 3.0	**17** SA 0049 0.6 / 0734 2.8 / 1330 0.9 / 1943 3.1
3 SA 0251 0.9 / 0928 3.0 / 1520 1.1 / 2205 3.0	**18** SU 0155 0.7 / 0903 2.9 / 1440 0.9 / 2112 3.1
4 SU 0341 0.9 / 1026 3.1 / 1609 1.0 / 2259 3.0	**19** M 0300 0.7 / 1018 3.0 / 1546 0.9 / 2229 3.2
5 M 0425 0.9 / 1112 3.2 / 1651 0.9 / 2344 3.1	**20** TU 0401 0.7 / 1115 3.3 / 1643 0.5 / 2332 3.3
6 TU 0506 0.8 / 1152 3.4 / 1727 0.8	**21** W 0457 0.6 / 1204 3.5 / 1733 0.3 ●
7 W 0024 3.1 / 0542 0.8 / 1227 3.4 / 1759 0.7 ○	**22** TH 0028 3.3 / 0547 0.6 / 1251 3.6 / 1819 0.2
8 TH 0100 3.1 / 0617 0.8 / 1259 3.5 / 1831 0.6	**23** F 0122 3.3 / 0635 0.6 / 1336 3.7 / 1905 0.1
9 F 0135 3.0 / 0652 0.7 / 1333 3.5 / 1905 0.6	**24** SA 0210 3.3 / 0721 0.6 / 1419 3.8 / 1949 0.2
10 SA 0211 3.0 / 0729 0.7 / 1408 3.6 / 1942 0.5	**25** SU 0254 3.3 / 0805 0.7 / 1500 3.8 / 2034 0.3
11 SU 0249 3.0 / 0809 0.7 / 1446 3.6 / 2022 0.4	**26** M 0335 3.3 / 0848 0.7 / 1540 3.7 / 2118 0.4
12 M 0329 3.0 / 0851 0.7 / 1525 3.5 / 2106 0.4	**27** TU 0413 3.3 / 0931 0.8 / 1620 3.6 / 2205 0.6
13 TU 0410 3.0 / 0936 0.7 / 1606 3.5 / 2154 0.4	**28** W 0451 3.2 / 1015 0.9 / 1700 3.4 / 2257 0.8
14 W 0452 3.0 / 1026 0.8 / 1649 3.4 / 2248 0.5	**29** TH 0531 3.1 / 1104 1.1 / 1743 3.2 / 2358 0.9 ☽
15 TH 0538 2.9 / 1122 0.9 / 1738 3.3 / 2347 0.6 ☽	**30** F 0614 3.0 / 1204 1.2 / 1830 3.0
	31 SA 0108 1.1 / 0702 2.9 / 1326 1.3 / 1927 2.8

FEBRUARY

Time m	Time m
1 SU 0216 1.1 / 0804 2.8 / 1448 1.2 / 2059 2.7	**16** M 0129 0.9 / 0814 2.7 / 1427 0.9 / 2054 2.8
2 M 0315 1.0 / 0937 2.9 / 1547 1.1 / 2240 2.8	**17** TU 0250 0.9 / 1007 2.9 / 1542 0.7 / 2233 2.9
3 TU 0406 0.9 / 1045 3.0 / 1633 0.9 / 2330 2.9	**18** W 0359 0.8 / 1105 3.2 / 1638 0.4 / 2335 3.1
4 W 0449 0.8 / 1130 3.2 / 1711 0.7	**19** TH 0453 0.7 / 1154 3.4 / 1724 0.2
5 TH 0012 2.9 / 0526 0.7 / 1207 3.3 / 1745 0.6	**20** F 0027 3.2 / 0539 0.6 / 1240 3.5 / 1806 0.1 ●
6 F 0051 3.0 / 0601 0.6 / 1240 3.4 / 1816 0.5 ○	**21** SA 0115 3.2 / 0621 0.5 / 1323 3.6 / 1847 0.1
7 SA 0126 3.0 / 0634 0.6 / 1314 3.4 / 1848 0.3	**22** SU 0157 3.2 / 0700 0.5 / 1404 3.7 / 1926 0.1
8 SU 0200 3.0 / 0709 0.5 / 1351 3.5 / 1923 0.3	**23** M 0233 3.3 / 0738 0.5 / 1441 3.7 / 2004 0.2
9 M 0233 3.0 / 0746 0.4 / 1428 3.6 / 2000 0.2	**24** TU 0305 3.3 / 0815 0.5 / 1516 3.7 / 2042 0.3
10 TU 0307 3.1 / 0825 0.4 / 1506 3.6 / 2041 0.4	**25** W 0337 3.3 / 0851 0.6 / 1550 3.6 / 2121 0.5
11 W 0341 3.1 / 0908 0.4 / 1545 3.6 / 2126 0.4	**26** TH 0410 3.3 / 0928 0.7 / 1625 3.4 / 2202 0.7
12 TH 0417 3.1 / 0954 0.4 / 1625 3.5 / 2215 0.4	**27** F 0444 3.2 / 1009 0.8 / 1702 3.2 / 2248 0.9
13 F 0455 3.0 / 1046 0.7 / 1709 3.3 / 2311 0.6	**28** SA 0523 3.0 / 1056 1.0 / 1745 2.9 / 2350 1.2 ☽
14 SA 0540 2.9 / 1148 0.8 / 1800 3.1	**29** SU 0610 2.9 / 1159 1.2 / 1838 2.7
15 SU 0015 0.7 / 0637 2.8 / 1302 0.9 / 1902 2.9	

MARCH

Time m	Time m
1 M 0132 1.3 / 0708 2.7 / 1409 1.3 / 1949 2.5	**16** TU 0117 1.1 / 0750 2.6 / 1426 0.8 / 2118 2.6
2 TU 0248 1.2 / 0825 2.7 / 1520 1.1 / 2222 2.6	**17** W 0251 1.1 / 0956 2.9 / 1534 0.5 / 2236 2.8
3 W 0343 1.0 / 1010 2.8 / 1607 0.9 / 2312 2.8	**18** TH 0356 0.9 / 1052 3.1 / 1625 0.3 / 2329 3.0
4 TH 0426 0.8 / 1102 3.0 / 1646 0.6 / 2353 2.9	**19** F 0444 0.7 / 1139 3.4 / 1709 0.1
5 F 0503 0.6 / 1139 3.2 / 1720 0.4	**20** SA 0015 3.1 / 0524 0.5 / 1223 3.5 / 1747 0.1 ●
6 SA 0030 3.0 / 0536 0.5 / 1215 3.3 / 1751 0.3 ○	**21** SU 0056 3.2 / 0601 0.4 / 1304 3.5 / 1823 0.1
7 SU 0105 3.0 / 0608 0.4 / 1251 3.4 / 1822 0.1	**22** M 0132 3.2 / 0635 0.4 / 1342 3.5 / 1858 0.2
8 M 0137 3.0 / 0642 0.3 / 1329 3.5 / 1857 0.0	**23** TU 0202 3.2 / 0708 0.4 / 1417 3.5 / 1932 0.3
9 TU 0208 3.1 / 0719 0.2 / 1407 3.6 / 1934 0.0	**24** W 0231 3.3 / 0741 0.4 / 1449 3.5 / 2006 0.4
10 W 0239 3.2 / 0758 0.2 / 1446 3.6 / 2015 0.0	**25** TH 0301 3.3 / 0814 0.4 / 1521 3.4 / 2042 0.5
11 TH 0311 3.2 / 0840 0.2 / 1524 3.6 / 2059 0.1	**26** F 0332 3.3 / 0850 0.5 / 1554 3.2 / 2119 0.7
12 F 0345 3.2 / 0926 0.3 / 1603 3.5 / 2147 0.3	**27** SA 0405 3.2 / 0928 0.7 / 1630 3.0 / 2201 0.9
13 SA 0423 3.1 / 1019 0.5 / 1646 3.3 / 2242 0.6 ☽	**28** SU 0442 3.1 / 1013 0.9 / 1713 2.8 / 2253 1.1
14 SU 0507 2.9 / 1124 0.7 / 1737 3.0 / 2349 0.9	**29** M 0527 2.9 / 1110 1.1 / 1808 2.6
15 M 0605 2.7 / 1249 0.9 / 1843 2.7	**30** TU 0007 1.3 / 0626 2.7 / 1235 1.2 / 1919 2.4
	31 W 0205 1.3 / 0739 2.6 / 1437 1.1 / 2130 2.5

APRIL

Time m	Time m
1 TH 0307 1.1 / 0910 2.7 / 1529 0.8 / 2239 2.7	**16** F 0338 0.9 / 1029 3.2 / 1603 0.2 / 2309 3.0
2 F 0353 0.8 / 1018 2.9 / 1610 0.5 / 2320 2.9	**17** SA 0424 0.7 / 1116 3.3 / 1645 0.1 / 2350 3.1
3 SA 0431 0.6 / 1102 3.1 / 1645 0.3 / 2357 3.0	**18** SU 0503 0.5 / 1158 3.4 / 1722 0.1
4 SU 0505 0.4 / 1141 3.3 / 1718 0.1	**19** M 0027 3.1 / 0538 0.4 / 1239 3.4 / 1757 0.2 ●
5 M 0032 3.0 / 0539 0.2 / 1222 3.4 / 1752 0.0 ○	**20** TU 0100 3.2 / 0609 0.4 / 1316 3.3 / 1830 0.3
6 TU 0106 3.1 / 0615 0.1 / 1303 3.5 / 1829 -0.1	**21** W 0130 3.2 / 0640 0.3 / 1350 3.3 / 1902 0.4
7 W 0139 3.2 / 0653 0.0 / 1345 3.6 / 1910 -0.1	**22** TH 0159 3.3 / 0711 0.3 / 1422 3.2 / 1936 0.5
8 TH 0212 3.3 / 0734 0.0 / 1425 3.6 / 1953 0.0	**23** F 0229 3.3 / 0744 0.4 / 1454 3.2 / 2011 0.6
9 F 0245 3.3 / 0818 0.1 / 1506 3.5 / 2038 0.2	**24** SA 0259 3.3 / 0820 0.4 / 1528 3.1 / 2050 0.7
10 SA 0321 3.3 / 0907 0.2 / 1548 3.4 / 2128 0.5	**25** SU 0332 3.3 / 0859 0.6 / 1606 2.9 / 2134 0.8
11 SU 0401 3.2 / 1004 0.4 / 1634 3.1 / 2226 0.8	**26** M 0409 3.1 / 0945 0.7 / 1651 2.7 / 2224 1.0
12 M 0447 3.0 / 1116 0.7 / 1731 2.8 / 2340 1.1 ☽	**27** TU 0452 2.9 / 1042 0.9 / 1748 2.6 / 2328 1.2 ☽
13 TU 0551 2.8 / 1250 0.7 / 1900 2.6	**28** W 0550 2.8 / 1156 1.0 / 1858 2.5
14 W 0113 1.2 / 0802 2.7 / 1412 0.6 / 2117 2.7	**29** TH 0050 1.2 / 0701 2.7 / 1328 0.9 / 2020 2.5
15 TH 0236 1.1 / 0934 2.9 / 1513 0.4 / 2221 2.9	**30** F 0209 1.1 / 0818 2.7 / 1435 0.7 / 2142 2.7

Chart Datum: 1·62 metres below Ordnance Datum (Newlyn)

Chapter 5

TIME ZONE (UT)
For Summer Time add ONE hour in **non-shaded areas**

SCOTLAND – GREENOCK
LAT 55°57′N   LONG 4°46′W
TIMES AND HEIGHTS OF HIGH AND LOW WATERS

YEAR 2004

MAY

Day	Time	m	Day	Time	m
1 SA	0306 / 0927 / 1523 / 2235	0.9 / 2.9 / 0.4 / 2.8	16 SU	0357 / 1047 / 1617 / 2316	0.7 / 3.2 / 0.2 / 3.0
2 SU	0351 / 1021 / 1605 / 2318	0.6 / 3.1 / 0.2 / 3.0	17 M	0439 / 1130 / 1656 / 2353	0.5 / 3.2 / 0.3 / 3.1
3 M	0431 / 1107 / 1644 / 2357	0.4 / 3.3 / 0.0 / 3.1	18 TU	0515 / 1211 / 1732	0.5 / 3.2 / 0.3
4 TU	0511 / 1152 / 1724 / O	0.2 / 3.4 / 0.0	19 W	0027 / 0547 / 1249 / ● 1805	3.1 / 0.4 / 3.1 / 0.4
5 W	0035 / 0550 / 1238 / 1805	3.2 / 0.1 / 3.5 / 0.0	20 TH	0100 / 0618 / 1324 / 1839	3.2 / 0.4 / 3.1 / 0.5
6 TH	0113 / 0632 / 1324 / 1849	3.3 / 0.0 / 3.5 / 0.0	21 F	0131 / 0649 / 1357 / 1914	3.3 / 0.4 / 3.0 / 0.6
7 F	0150 / 0716 / 1409 / 1936	3.4 / 0.0 / 3.5 / 0.2	22 SA	0202 / 0722 / 1431 / 1951	3.3 / 0.4 / 3.0 / 0.6
8 SA	0227 / 0805 / 1455 / 2026	3.4 / 0.1 / 3.4 / 0.4	23 SU	0234 / 0759 / 1508 / 2032	3.3 / 0.5 / 2.9 / 0.7
9 SU	0307 / 0858 / 1542 / 2121	3.4 / 0.2 / 3.2 / 0.6	24 M	0308 / 0840 / 1549 / 2117	3.3 / 0.5 / 2.8 / 0.8
10 M	0350 / 0959 / 1636 / 2221	3.3 / 0.4 / 3.0 / 0.9	25 TU	0345 / 0927 / 1636 / 2206	3.2 / 0.6 / 2.7 / 0.9
11 TU	0442 / 1114 / 1745 / ◑ 2333	3.1 / 0.5 / 2.8 / 1.0	26 W	0427 / 1022 / 1732 / 2302	3.0 / 0.7 / 2.6 / 1.0
12 W	0553 / 1234 / 1917	2.9 / 0.5 / 2.7	27 TH	0520 / 1127 / 1833 / ◐	2.9 / 0.7 / 2.6
13 TH	0050 / 0736 / 1344 / 2046	1.1 / 2.9 / 0.5 / 2.7	28 F	0004 / 0623 / 1235 / 1936	1.0 / 2.8 / 0.7 / 2.6
14 F	0204 / 0900 / 1443 / 2147	1.1 / 3.0 / 0.4 / 2.9	29 SA	0109 / 0731 / 1339 / 2042	0.9 / 2.8 / 0.5 / 2.7
15 SA	0306 / 0958 / 1533 / 2235	0.9 / 3.1 / 0.3 / 3.0	30 SU	0212 / 0840 / 1435 / 2145	0.8 / 2.9 / 0.4 / 2.8
			31 M	0309 / 0942 / 1526 / 2238	0.6 / 3.1 / 0.2 / 2.9

JUNE

Day	Time	m	Day	Time	m
1 TU	0359 / 1036 / 1613 / 2325	0.4 / 3.2 / 0.1 / 3.1	16 W	0456 / 1147 / 1711 / 2359	0.6 / 3.0 / 0.5 / 3.1
2 W	0445 / 1127 / 1659	0.2 / 3.3 / 0.1	17 TH	0532 / 1227 / 1749 / ●	0.5 / 3.0 / 0.6
3 TH	0009 / 0530 / 1217 / O 1746	3.2 / 0.1 / 3.4 / 0.1	18 F	0035 / 0605 / 1304 / 1824	3.2 / 0.5 / 2.9 / 0.6
4 F	0053 / 0617 / 1308 / 1835	3.3 / 0.0 / 3.4 / 0.2	19 SA	0108 / 0636 / 1339 / 1900	3.2 / 0.5 / 2.9 / 0.6
5 SA	0135 / 0705 / 1400 / 1926	3.4 / 0.0 / 3.4 / 0.3	20 SU	0140 / 0710 / 1415 / 1938	3.3 / 0.5 / 2.9 / 0.6
6 SU	0217 / 0757 / 1452 / 2020	3.5 / 0.0 / 3.3 / 0.5	21 M	0213 / 0746 / 1454 / 2019	3.3 / 0.4 / 2.8 / 0.6
7 M	0301 / 0852 / 1545 / 2114	3.5 / 0.1 / 3.2 / 0.6	22 TU	0249 / 0826 / 1536 / 2101	3.3 / 0.4 / 2.8 / 0.6
8 TU	0348 / 0951 / 1643 / 2211	3.4 / 0.3 / 3.0 / 0.8	23 W	0327 / 0910 / 1621 / 2146	3.2 / 0.5 / 2.8 / 0.7
9 W	0440 / 1056 / 1744 / ◑ 2311	3.3 / 0.4 / 2.9 / 0.9	24 TH	0407 / 0959 / 1709 / 2234	3.2 / 0.5 / 2.7 / 0.7
10 TH	0543 / 1204 / 1847	3.1 / 0.4 / 2.8	25 F	0453 / 1055 / 1759 / ◐ 2327	3.1 / 0.5 / 2.7 / 0.8
11 F	0015 / 0655 / 1309 / 1950	1.0 / 3.0 / 0.4 / 2.8	26 SA	0546 / 1155 / 1851	3.0 / 0.5 / 2.7
12 SA	0123 / 0813 / 1407 / 2053	1.0 / 3.0 / 0.4 / 2.8	27 SU	0025 / 0646 / 1256 / 1948	0.8 / 3.0 / 0.4 / 2.7
13 SU	0228 / 0920 / 1500 / 2149	0.9 / 3.0 / 0.4 / 2.9	28 M	0127 / 0753 / 1354 / 2055	0.8 / 3.0 / 0.4 / 2.7
14 M	0326 / 1015 / 1548 / 2238	0.8 / 3.0 / 0.4 / 2.9	29 TU	0230 / 0905 / 1452 / 2203	0.7 / 3.0 / 0.4 / 2.8
15 TU	0415 / 1103 / 1631 / 2321	0.7 / 3.0 / 0.5 / 3.0	30 W	0331 / 1010 / 1548 / 2301	0.5 / 3.1 / 0.3 / 3.0

JULY

Day	Time	m	Day	Time	m
1 TH	0427 / 1109 / 1641 / 2351	0.3 / 3.2 / 0.3 / 3.2	16 F	0521 / 1214 / 1736	0.6 / 2.9 / 0.6
2 F	0518 / 1205 / 1733 / O	0.2 / 3.3 / 0.3	17 SA	0015 / 0555 / 1254 / ● 1812	3.2 / 0.5 / 2.9 / 0.6
3 SA	0039 / 0608 / 1301 / 1825	3.3 / 0.0 / 3.3 / 0.4	18 SU	0050 / 0627 / 1330 / 1847	3.2 / 0.5 / 2.8 / 0.6
4 SU	0125 / 0657 / 1357 / 1917	3.5 / 0.0 / 3.3 / 0.4	19 M	0121 / 0658 / 1406 / 1922	3.3 / 0.4 / 2.8 / 0.6
5 M	0211 / 0747 / 1451 / 2008	3.6 / 0.0 / 3.2 / 0.5	20 TU	0155 / 0730 / 1441 / 1958	3.3 / 0.4 / 2.8 / 0.5
6 TU	0255 / 0837 / 1541 / 2058	3.6 / 0.1 / 3.2 / 0.6	21 W	0230 / 0806 / 1518 / 2037	3.3 / 0.3 / 2.9 / 0.5
7 W	0340 / 0929 / 1630 / 2147	3.6 / 0.2 / 3.1 / 0.7	22 TH	0308 / 0846 / 1556 / 2118	3.3 / 0.3 / 2.9 / 0.5
8 TH	0427 / 1025 / 1717 / 2238	3.5 / 0.3 / 3.1 / 0.8	23 F	0346 / 0930 / 1635 / 2202	3.3 / 0.3 / 2.9 / 0.5
9 F	0516 / 1126 / 1803 / ◑ 2333	3.3 / 0.5 / 3.0 / 0.9	24 SA	0427 / 1020 / 1716 / 2251	3.3 / 0.4 / 2.8 / 0.6
10 SA	0609 / 1230 / 1849	3.1 / 0.6 / 2.9	25 SU	0512 / 1116 / 1801 / ◐ 2347	3.2 / 0.4 / 2.8 / 0.7
11 SU	0036 / 0708 / 1331 / 1939	1.0 / 3.0 / 0.7 / 2.8	26 M	0604 / 1217 / 1853	3.0 / 0.5 / 2.7
12 M	0146 / 0822 / 1428 / 2043	1.0 / 2.8 / 0.7 / 2.8	27 TU	0049 / 0708 / 1321 / 2003	0.8 / 2.9 / 0.6 / 2.7
13 TU	0255 / 0942 / 1522 / 2156	1.0 / 2.8 / 0.7 / 2.8	28 W	0159 / 0831 / 1426 / 2138	0.8 / 2.9 / 0.6 / 2.8
14 W	0353 / 1042 / 1611 / 2252	0.8 / 2.8 / 0.7 / 3.0	29 TH	0314 / 0957 / 1533 / 2246	0.7 / 3.0 / 0.6 / 3.0
15 TH	0441 / 1131 / 1655 / 2337	0.7 / 2.9 / 0.7 / 3.1	30 F	0418 / 1104 / 1633 / 2340	0.4 / 3.1 / 0.6 / 3.2
			31 SA	0512 / 1203 / 1726 / O	0.2 / 3.2 / 0.5

AUGUST

Day	Time	m	Day	Time	m
1 SU	0029 / 0559 / 1259 / 1815	3.4 / 0.1 / 3.2 / 0.5	16 M	0029 / 0607 / 1317 / ● 1824	3.3 / 0.4 / 3.0 / 0.6
2 M	0116 / 0645 / 1352 / 1902	3.5 / 0.0 / 3.2 / 0.5	17 TU	0101 / 0636 / 1349 / 1856	3.3 / 0.3 / 2.9 / 0.5
3 TU	0200 / 0729 / 1439 / 1947	3.6 / 0.0 / 3.2 / 0.5	18 W	0133 / 0706 / 1420 / 1929	3.4 / 0.3 / 3.0 / 0.5
4 W	0242 / 0814 / 1522 / 2031	3.7 / 0.1 / 3.2 / 0.5	19 TH	0209 / 0739 / 1451 / 2006	3.4 / 0.2 / 3.0 / 0.5
5 TH	0323 / 0859 / 1600 / 2114	3.7 / 0.2 / 3.2 / 0.6	20 F	0246 / 0816 / 1524 / 2046	3.5 / 0.2 / 3.0 / 0.4
6 F	0402 / 0945 / 1637 / 2157	3.6 / 0.4 / 3.2 / 0.7	21 SA	0322 / 0857 / 1557 / 2129	3.5 / 0.2 / 3.0 / 0.5
7 SA	0442 / 1037 / 1714 / ◑ 2243	3.4 / 0.6 / 3.1 / 0.8	22 SU	0400 / 0944 / 1633 / 2217	3.4 / 0.4 / 3.0 / 0.6
8 SU	0523 / 1139 / 1754 / 2337	3.2 / 0.8 / 3.0 / 1.0	23 M	0441 / 1038 / 1714 / ◐ 2314	3.4 / 0.6 / 2.9 / 0.7
9 M	0610 / 1251 / 1839	2.9 / 1.0 / 2.9	24 TU	0530 / 1141 / 1805	3.1 / 0.8 / 2.8
10 TU	0053 / 0706 / 1359 / 1933	1.2 / 2.7 / 1.0 / 2.8	25 W	0021 / 0632 / 1254 / 1917	0.9 / 2.8 / 0.9 / 2.7
11 W	0227 / 0843 / 1459 / 2054	1.2 / 2.6 / 1.0 / 2.8	26 TH	0143 / 0812 / 1415 / 2128	0.9 / 2.7 / 1.0 / 2.8
12 TH	0333 / 1032 / 1552 / 2226	1.0 / 2.7 / 0.9 / 2.9	27 F	0312 / 1005 / 1531 / 2238	0.7 / 2.9 / 0.9 / 3.1
13 F	0422 / 1121 / 1638 / 2317	0.8 / 2.8 / 0.8 / 3.1	28 SA	0414 / 1110 / 1629 / 2330	0.5 / 3.1 / 0.8 / 3.3
14 SA	0503 / 1202 / 1717 / 2356	0.6 / 2.9 / 0.7 / 3.2	29 SU	0503 / 1203 / 1717	0.2 / 3.2 / 0.6
15 SU	0537 / 1241 / 1752	0.5 / 2.9 / 0.6	30 M	0016 / 0545 / 1252 / O 1759	3.5 / 0.1 / 3.3 / 0.5
			31 TU	0101 / 0625 / 1336 / 1840	3.6 / 0.0 / 3.3 / 0.5

Chart Datum: 1·62 metres below Ordnance Datum (Newlyn)

SCOTLAND – GREENOCK

LAT 55°57′N   LONG 4°46′W

TIMES AND HEIGHTS OF HIGH AND LOW WATERS

YEAR 2004

SEPTEMBER

Day	Time	m	Time	m	Time	m	Time	m
1 W	0143	3.7	0705	0.1	1415	3.3	1919	0.5
2 TH	0222	3.7	0743	0.2	1449	3.3	1957	0.5
3 F	0258	3.7	0822	0.3	1521	3.3	2035	0.6
4 SA	0332	3.6	0901	0.5	1554	3.3	2113	0.7
5 SU	0407	3.4	0943	0.8	1628	3.3	2153	0.8
6 M ◑	0444	3.2	1031	1.0	1707	3.2	2238	1.1
7 TU	0526	2.9	1143	1.3	1751	3.0	2340	1.3
8 W	0620	2.7	1328	1.4	1846	2.9		
9 TH	0156	1.3	0736	2.5	1434	1.4	1956	2.8
10 F	0306	1.1	1020	2.7	1528	1.1	2152	2.9
11 SA	0355	0.9	1103	2.9	1613	0.9	2249	3.1
12 SU	0434	0.7	1141	3.0	1650	0.8	2328	3.2
13 M O	0508	0.5	1217	3.1	1723	0.7		
14 TU	0000	3.3	0537	0.4	1251	3.1	1753	0.6
15 W	0033	3.4	0605	0.3	1321	3.1	1824	0.5
16 TH	0108	3.5	0635	0.2	1350	3.2	1858	0.4
17 F	0145	3.5	0709	0.2	1419	3.2	1935	0.4
18 SA	0222	3.6	0747	0.2	1450	3.3	2015	0.4
19 SU	0259	3.6	0828	0.3	1523	3.3	2059	0.5
20 M	0337	3.5	0914	0.5	1559	3.2	2149	0.6
21 TU	0418	3.3	1008	0.8	1641	3.1	2250	0.8
22 W	0506	3.0	1115	1.1	1734	2.9		
23 TH	0007	1.0	0613	2.8	1242	1.3	1855	2.8
24 F	0148	1.0	0842	2.7	1417	1.3	2120	2.9
25 SA	0307	0.7	1012	2.9	1527	1.1	2224	3.2
26 SU	0401	0.4	1105	3.2	1618	0.9	2313	3.5
27 M	0446	0.2	1150	3.3	1701	0.7	2358	3.6
28 TU ●	0525	0.1	1232	3.4	1739	0.6		
29 W	0040	3.7	0601	0.1	1309	3.4	1814	0.5
30 TH	0120	3.7	0636	0.2	1342	3.4	1849	0.5

OCTOBER

Day	Time	m	Time	m	Time	m	Time	m
1 F	0156	3.7	0711	0.4	1413	3.5	1923	0.6
2 SA	0230	3.6	0746	0.5	1444	3.5	1958	0.6
3 SU	0302	3.5	0822	0.7	1516	3.5	2034	0.7
4 M	0336	3.4	0900	0.9	1549	3.5	2113	0.8
5 TU	0412	3.2	0942	1.2	1627	3.3	2157	1.1
6 W	0454	2.9	1036	1.4	1711	3.1	2254	1.3
7 TH	0550	2.7	1231	1.6	1807	3.0		
8 F	0050	1.4	0707	2.6	1357	1.5	1916	2.9
9 SA	0225	1.2	0944	2.7	1453	1.3	2047	2.9
10 SU	0316	1.0	1030	2.9	1538	1.1	2203	3.1
11 M	0356	0.7	1108	3.1	1616	0.9	2247	3.3
12 TU	0431	0.5	1143	3.2	1649	0.7	2324	3.4
13 W	0502	0.4	1216	3.2	1721	0.6		
14 TH ●	0001	3.5	0532	0.3	1247	3.3	1754	0.5
15 F	0040	3.6	0605	0.2	1318	3.4	1830	0.4
16 SA	0120	3.6	0642	0.2	1350	3.4	1909	0.4
17 SU	0200	3.7	0723	0.3	1423	3.5	1952	0.4
18 M	0240	3.6	0807	0.5	1459	3.5	2040	0.5
19 TU	0321	3.5	0856	0.7	1537	3.4	2134	0.7
20 W	0405	3.3	0952	1.0	1622	3.3	2241	0.9
21 TH	0459	3.0	1105	1.3	1721	3.1		
22 F	0008	1.0	0627	2.8	1238	1.4	1902	2.9
23 SA	0139	0.9	0847	2.8	1403	1.4	2058	3.1
24 SU	0245	0.7	0955	3.1	1507	1.2	2200	3.4
25 M	0337	0.5	1044	3.2	1557	0.9	2249	3.5
26 TU	0421	0.3	1125	3.4	1639	0.6	2333	3.6
27 W	0500	0.3	1203	3.4	1716	0.7		
28 TH O	0015	3.6	0535	0.3	1238	3.5	1750	0.6
29 F	0054	3.6	0609	0.5	1309	3.5	1822	0.6
30 SA	0130	3.5	0643	0.6	1340	3.6	1855	0.6
31 SU	0203	3.5	0717	0.7	1412	3.6	1929	0.7

NOVEMBER

Day	Time	m	Time	m	Time	m	Time	m
1 M	0236	3.4	0753	0.9	1445	3.6	2005	0.7
2 TU	0311	3.3	0831	1.0	1518	3.6	2045	0.9
3 W	0348	3.1	0914	1.2	1555	3.4	2130	1.0
4 TH	0432	2.9	1006	1.4	1638	3.3	2225	1.2
5 F	0530	2.8	1117	1.5	1732	3.1	2340	1.3
6 SA	0642	2.7	1248	1.5	1838	3.0		
7 SU	0115	1.2	0808	2.7	1348	1.4	1950	3.0
8 M	0220	1.0	0932	2.9	1450	1.2	2101	3.1
9 TU	0307	0.8	1022	3.1	1534	1.0	2159	3.3
10 W	0347	0.6	1102	3.2	1613	0.8	2246	3.4
11 TH ●	0424	0.4	1139	3.3	1650	0.6	2330	3.5
12 F ●	0502	0.3	1214	3.4	1729	0.5		
13 SA	0014	3.6	0540	0.3	1251	3.5	1808	0.4
14 SU	0059	3.6	0622	0.4	1328	3.6	1851	0.4
15 M	0144	3.6	0707	0.5	1405	3.7	1939	0.4
16 TU	0229	3.6	0756	0.7	1445	3.7	2030	0.5
17 W	0315	3.4	0849	0.9	1527	3.6	2129	0.6
18 TH	0407	3.2	0949	1.1	1617	3.4	2237	0.8
19 F	0512	3.0	1059	1.3	1721	3.3	2355	0.8
20 SA	0639	2.9	1216	1.4	1849	3.2		
21 SU	0109	0.8	0812	2.9	1330	1.3	2020	3.2
22 M	0212	0.7	0919	3.1	1435	1.2	2127	3.4
23 TU	0306	0.6	1010	3.2	1530	1.0	2220	3.5
24 W	0353	0.5	1053	3.3	1615	0.9	2307	3.5
25 TH	0434	0.5	1131	3.4	1655	0.7	2351	3.5
26 F O	0513	0.6	1207	3.5	1731	0.6		
27 SA	0031	3.4	0548	0.7	1241	3.6	1804	0.7
28 SU	0108	3.4	0623	0.8	1314	3.6	1836	0.7
29 M	0143	3.3	0658	0.8	1347	3.6	1911	0.7
30 TU	0217	3.2	0735	0.9	1420	3.7	1947	0.7

DECEMBER

Day	Time	m	Time	m	Time	m	Time	m
1 W	0253	3.2	0815	1.0	1455	3.6	2027	0.8
2 TH	0332	3.1	0858	1.1	1532	3.5	2112	0.9
3 F	0417	3.0	0946	1.2	1613	3.4	2202	1.0
4 SA	0510	2.9	1041	1.3	1701	3.2	2301	1.0
5 SU ○	0609	2.8	1143	1.4	1757	3.1		
6 M	0007	1.0	0711	2.8	1248	1.3	1857	3.1
7 TU	0112	0.9	0817	2.9	1350	1.2	2003	3.1
8 W	0210	0.8	0923	3.0	1446	1.1	2110	3.2
9 TH	0301	0.6	1018	3.1	1537	0.9	2210	3.3
10 F	0349	0.5	1105	3.3	1623	0.7	2303	3.4
11 SA	0435	0.5	1148	3.4	1708	0.5	2354	3.5
12 SU ●	0521	0.4	1230	3.5	1754	0.4		
13 M	0044	3.5	0608	0.5	1313	3.7	1841	0.3
14 TU	0135	3.6	0658	0.6	1356	3.7	1931	0.3
15 W	0226	3.5	0750	0.7	1440	3.8	2024	0.3
16 TH	0318	3.4	0843	0.8	1526	3.7	2120	0.4
17 F	0412	3.3	0939	1.0	1616	3.6	2220	0.5
18 SA ◐	0510	3.2	1038	1.1	1712	3.5	2325	0.6
19 SU	0611	3.1	1142	1.2	1816	3.4		
20 M	0032	0.7	0713	3.0	1250	1.2	1927	3.3
21 TU	0135	0.7	0819	3.0	1358	1.2	2042	3.2
22 W	0233	0.7	0922	3.1	1500	1.1	2148	3.2
23 TH	0325	0.7	1016	3.2	1553	0.9	2244	3.2
24 F	0412	0.7	1102	3.3	1639	0.8	2332	3.2
25 SA	0456	0.7	1142	3.4	1719	0.7		
26 SU O	0016	3.2	0535	0.8	1221	3.5	1755	0.7
27 M	0056	3.1	0612	0.8	1256	3.5	1828	0.7
28 TU	0132	3.1	0648	0.8	1329	3.6	1901	0.7
29 W	0207	3.1	0724	0.8	1402	3.6	1935	0.7
30 TH	0242	3.1	0801	0.9	1437	3.6	2012	0.7
31 F	0319	3.0	0840	0.9	1513	3.5	2051	0.7

Chart Datum: 1·62 metres below Ordnance Datum (Newlyn)

Chapter 5

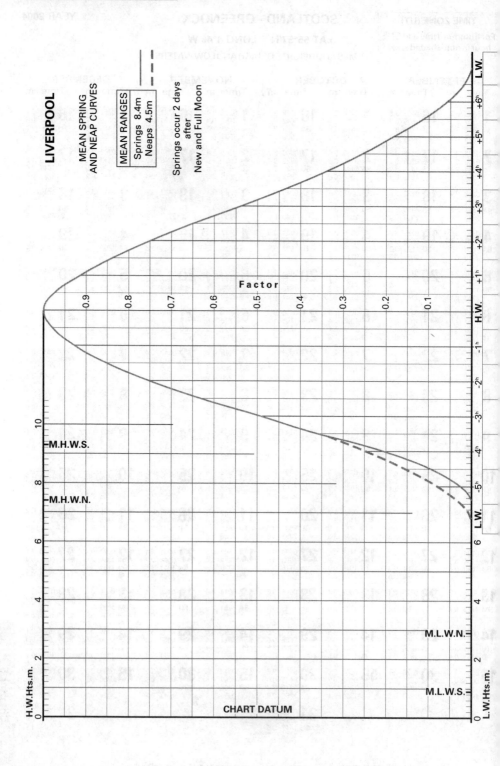

LIVERPOOL

MEAN SPRING
AND NEAP CURVES

MEAN RANGES
Springs 8.4m
Neaps 4.5m

Springs occur 2 days
after
New and Full Moon

Factor

0.9 0.8 0.7 0.6 0.5 0.4 0.3 0.2 0.1

L.W. +6h +5h +4h +3h +2h +1h H.W. -1h -2h -3h -4h -5h L.W.

M.H.W.S.

M.H.W.N.

M.L.W.N.

M.L.W.S.

CHART DATUM

H.W.Hts.m.

L.W.Hts.m.

ENGLAND – LIVERPOOL (ALFRED DK)

TIME ZONE (UT)
For Summer Time add ONE hour in **non-shaded areas**

LAT 53°24'N   LONG 3°01'W

TIMES AND HEIGHTS OF HIGH AND LOW WATERS

YEAR 2004

JANUARY

Day	Time m	Time m	Day	Time m	Time m
1 TH	0014 2.8	0612 7.3	**16** F	0514 7.9	1137 2.8
	1238 3.2	1836 7.7		1741 8.2	
2 F	0113 2.9	0718 7.4	**17** SA	0029 2.6	0624 7.8
	1343 3.2	1940 7.7		1252 2.8	1851 8.1
3 SA	0214 2.9	0817 7.6	**18** SU	0148 2.5	0737 8.0
	1446 2.9	2037 7.9		1413 2.6	2004 8.3
4 SU	0309 2.7	0906 8.0	**19**	0301 2.2	0845 8.4
	1539 2.6	2126 8.1		1528 2.2	2113 8.6
5 M	0354 2.4	0949 8.3	**20** TU	0404 1.8	0944 8.9
	1624 2.3	2209 8.3		1632 1.7	2213 9.0
6 TU	0434 2.2	1028 8.6	**21** W	0500 1.4	1037 9.3
	1704 2.1	2248 8.5		1729 1.2	2306 9.2
7 W	0512 2.0	1104 8.9	**22** TH	0550 1.2	1126 9.6
	1744 1.9	O 2324 8.6		1821 0.9	2355 9.4
8 TH	0549 1.9	1140 8.9	**23** F	0637 1.1	1213 9.8
	1823 1.8			1909 0.8	
9 F	0001 8.7	0626 1.8	**24** SA	0041 9.4	0722 1.1
	1217 8.9	1901 1.8		1258 9.8	1953 0.8
10 SA	0038 8.7	0704 1.8	**25** SU	0124 9.2	0803 1.3
	1254 9.0	1940 1.8		1341 9.6	2034 1.0
11 SU	0116 8.7	0741 1.8	**26** M	0205 9.0	0843 1.6
	1332 9.0	2018 1.8		1422 9.3	2113 1.4
12 M	0155 8.7	0820 2.0	**27** TU	0244 8.6	0921 1.9
	1412 8.9	2056 1.9		1502 8.9	2149 1.8
13 TU	0236 8.6	0900 2.1	**28** W	0323 8.2	0959 2.4
	1455 8.8	2137 2.0		1543 8.4	2227 2.4
14 W	0322 8.4	0943 2.3	**29** TH	0406 7.7	1041 2.8
	1542 8.6	2223 2.3		1629 7.9	◐ 2310 2.8
15 TH	0413 8.1	1035 2.6	**30** F	0458 7.3	1135 3.2
	1637 8.4	◑ 2319 2.5		1727 7.4	
			31 SA	0005 3.2	0605 7.1
				1241 3.4	1839 7.2

FEBRUARY

Day	Time m	Time m	Day	Time m	Time m
1 SU	0111 3.4	0725 7.1	**16** M	0120 3.0	0716 7.6
	1354 3.4	1958 7.3		1359 2.9	1957 7.7
2 M	0219 3.2	0835 7.5	**17** TU	0251 2.7	0837 8.0
	1503 3.1	2101 7.6		1527 2.4	2113 8.2
3 TU	0321 2.9	0927 7.9	**18** W	0400 2.1	0939 8.6
	1600 2.6	2151 8.0		1632 1.7	2211 8.7
4 W	0412 2.5	1011 8.4	**19** TH	0455 1.6	1030 9.2
	1647 2.2	2233 8.4		1725 1.1	2300 9.1
5 TH	0456 2.1	1050 8.7	**20** F	0542 1.2	1116 9.6
	1730 1.8	2311 8.6		1812 0.7	● 2343 9.3
6 F	0537 1.8	1126 9.0	**21** SA	0626 0.9	1158 9.8
	1811 1.6	O 2347 8.8		1854 0.6	
7 SA	0616 1.6	1202 9.1	**22** SU	0023 9.4	0705 0.9
	1850 1.3			1238 9.8	1932 0.6
8 SU	0023 9.0	0653 1.5	**23** M	0101 9.3	0742 1.0
	1238 9.3	1927 1.2		1316 9.6	2007 0.8
9 M	0100 9.1	0729 1.4	**24** TU	0135 9.1	0816 1.2
	1315 9.4	2002 1.2		1351 9.4	2039 1.2
10 TU	0137 9.1	0804 1.4	**25** W	0209 8.8	0847 1.6
	1353 9.4	2036 1.3		1426 9.0	2106 1.7
11 W	0215 9.0	0840 1.5	**26** TH	0242 8.4	0915 2.1
	1432 9.2	2110 1.5		1501 8.5	2132 2.3
12 TH	0255 8.8	0918 1.8	**27** F	0317 8.0	0946 2.6
	1516 8.9	2149 1.8		1540 7.9	2206 2.8
13 F	0341 8.4	1002 2.2	**28** SA	0359 7.5	1033 3.1
	1606 8.5	2238 2.4		1630 7.3	◑ 2258 3.3
14 SA	0438 7.9	1101 2.7	**29** SU	0457 7.0	1143 3.5
	1709 8.0	2347 2.9		1740 6.8	
15 SU	0550 7.6	1220 3.0			
	1827 7.6				

MARCH

Day	Time m	Time m	Day	Time m	Time m
1 M	0013 3.7	0625 6.8	**16** TU	0109 3.3	0708 7.4
	1308 3.6	1917 6.8		1402 2.9	2000 7.5
2 TU	0136 3.6	0801 7.1	**17** W	0247 2.8	0830 7.9
	1429 3.3	2036 7.2		1526 2.2	2110 8.1
3 W	0251 3.2	0902 7.6	**18** TH	0353 2.2	0929 8.6
	1536 2.7	2129 7.8		1624 1.5	2201 8.6
4 TH	0351 2.7	0948 8.2	**19** F	0443 1.5	1016 9.1
	1627 2.1	2211 8.3		1711 0.9	2244 9.1
5 F	0438 2.1	1027 8.7	**20** SA	0526 1.1	1058 9.5
	1710 1.6	2249 8.7		1753 0.6	● 2323 9.3
6 SA	0519 1.7	1104 9.0	**21** SU	0606 0.9	1137 9.6
	1750 1.2	2325 9.0		1830 0.6	2359 9.3
7 SU	0558 1.3	1139 9.3	**22** M	0643 0.8	1213 9.6
	1828 0.9			1904 0.7	
8 M	0001 9.2	0635 1.0	**23** TU	0031 9.2	0716 0.9
	1216 9.5	1904 0.7		1248 9.4	1934 1.0
9 TU	0037 9.4	0710 0.9	**24** W	0103 9.0	0746 1.2
	1253 9.7	1939 0.7		1320 9.2	1959 1.3
10 W	0114 9.4	0745 0.9	**25** TH	0134 8.8	0811 1.5
	1331 9.6	2011 0.9		1352 8.8	2020 1.7
11 TH	0152 9.3	0820 1.0	**26** F	0205 8.5	0835 1.9
	1411 9.4	2044 1.3		1425 8.4	2044 2.2
12 F	0232 9.0	0857 1.4	**27** SA	0237 8.1	0906 2.4
	1454 8.9	2123 1.8		1502 7.9	2118 2.7
13 SA	0316 8.5	0942 2.0	**28** SU	0316 7.7	0949 3.0
	1544 8.3	◑ 2212 2.5		1547 7.3	◑ 2208 3.3
14 SU	0412 7.9	1041 2.6	**29** M	0407 7.1	1057 3.4
	1650 7.6	2324 3.1		1651 6.8	2324 3.7
15 M	0531 7.4	1209 3.0	**30** TU	0525 6.7	1226 3.6
	1822 7.2			1832 6.6	
			31 W	0052 3.7	0715 6.9
				1350 3.2	2000 7.0

APRIL

Day	Time m	Time m	Day	Time m	Time m
1 TH	0212 3.3	0825 7.4	**16** F	0332 2.1	0906 8.5
	1500 2.6	2056 7.7		1603 1.4	2138 8.5
2 F	0317 2.7	0913 8.1	**17** SA	0420 1.6	0953 9.0
	1553 2.0	2139 8.3		1647 1.0	2219 8.9
3 SA	0406 2.1	0954 8.6	**18** SU	0502 1.2	1034 9.2
	1638 1.4	2218 8.8		1725 0.9	2256 9.0
4 SU	0450 1.5	1032 9.1	**19**	0539 1.0	1111 9.3
	1720 0.9	2255 9.2		1759 0.9	● 2330 9.1
5 M	0531 1.1	1110 9.4	**20** TU	0614 1.0	1146 9.2
	1759 0.6	O 2332 9.4		1830 1.0	
6 TU	0610 0.7	1149 9.7	**21** W	0001 9.0	0646 1.1
	1837 0.5			1219 9.1	1856 1.2
7 W	0010 9.6	0647 0.6	**22** TH	0032 8.9	0714 1.3
	1229 9.8	1912 0.5		1250 8.9	1918 1.5
8 TH	0050 9.6	0725 0.6	**23** F	0102 8.7	0739 1.6
	1310 9.6	1947 0.8		1322 8.6	1942 1.8
9 F	0131 9.4	0803 0.8	**24** SA	0133 8.5	0806 1.9
	1353 9.3	2024 1.2		1356 8.3	2011 2.2
10 SA	0213 9.0	0844 1.3	**25** SU	0207 8.2	0839 2.3
	1440 8.8	2106 1.8		1433 7.9	2047 2.7
11 SU	0301 8.5	0934 1.9	**26** M	0246 7.8	0923 2.8
	1534 8.1	2200 2.6		1518 7.4	2135 3.2
12 M	0402 7.9	1040 2.5	**27** TU	0335 7.3	1026 3.2
	1647 7.4	◑ 2318 3.1		1617 6.9	◑ 2245 3.6
13 TU	0525 7.4	1214 2.8	**28** W	0443 7.0	1146 3.3
	1822 7.2			1739 6.8	
14 W	0104 3.2	0657 7.5	**29** TH	0008 3.6	0612 7.0
	1356 2.5	1947 7.5		1304 3.0	1908 7.0
15 TH	0231 2.7	0810 8.0	**30** F	0124 3.2	0731 7.4
	1509 2.0	2049 8.0		1412 2.5	2009 7.6

Chart Datum: 4·93 metres below Ordnance Datum (Newlyn)

Chapter 5

TIDES

ENGLAND – LIVERPOOL (ALFRED DK)

YEAR **2004**

LAT 53°24'N   LONG 3°01'W

TIMES AND HEIGHTS OF HIGH AND LOW WATERS

MAY

Day	Time	m	Day	Time	m
1 SA	0229 / 0826 / 1510 / 2057	2.7 / 8.0 / 1.9 / 8.2	16 SU	0348 / 0922 / 1614 / 2148	1.9 / 8.6 / 1.5 / 8.5
2 SU	0324 / 0912 / 1600 / 2140	2.1 / 8.6 / 1.3 / 8.8	17 M	0430 / 1005 / 1651 / 2226	1.6 / 8.8 / 1.4 / 8.7
3 M	0413 / 0956 / 1645 / 2221	1.5 / 9.1 / 0.9 / 9.2	18 TU	0508 / 1044 / 1724 / 2300	1.4 / 8.8 / 1.4 / 8.8
4 TU	0459 / 1039 / 1727 / 2303 ○	1.0 / 9.5 / 0.6 / 9.5	19 W	0543 / 1119 / 1753 / 2332 ●	1.4 / 8.8 / 1.5 / 8.8
5 W	0543 / 1122 / 1808 / 2345	0.7 / 9.7 / 0.5 / 9.6	20 TH	0615 / 1152 / 1820	1.5 / 8.7 / 1.6
6 TH	0626 / 1207 / 1849	0.5 / 9.7 / 0.6	21 F	0003 / 0645 / 1225 / 1846	8.7 / 1.6 / 8.6 / 1.7
7 F	0028 / 0708 / 1254 / 1928	9.6 / 0.6 / 9.5 / 0.9	22 SA	0036 / 0715 / 1259 / 1915	8.6 / 1.8 / 8.4 / 1.9
8 SA	0114 / 0753 / 1342 / 2011	9.4 / 0.8 / 9.1 / 1.3	23 SU	0110 / 0747 / 1335 / 1949	8.5 / 2.0 / 8.2 / 2.2
9 SU	0202 / 0841 / 1433 / 2059	9.0 / 1.2 / 8.6 / 1.9	24 M	0146 / 0824 / 1414 / 2028	8.3 / 2.2 / 8.0 / 2.5
10 M	0255 / 0937 / 1532 / 2158	8.6 / 1.7 / 8.0 / 2.5	25 TU	0227 / 0908 / 1458 / 2115	8.0 / 2.5 / 7.7 / 2.9
11 TU	0359 / 1045 / 1644 / 2313 ◐	8.1 / 2.2 / 7.6 / 2.9	26 W	0314 / 1003 / 1551 / 2214	7.7 / 2.8 / 7.4 / 3.2
12 W	0514 / 1206 / 1803	7.8 / 2.4 / 7.4	27 TH	0412 / 1108 / 1655 / 2324 ◐	7.5 / 2.9 / 7.2 / 3.2
13 TH	0039 / 0630 / 1327 / 1916	3.0 / 7.8 / 2.3 / 7.6	28 F	0520 / 1216 / 1808	7.4 / 2.7 / 7.3
14 F	0157 / 0737 / 1436 / 2016	2.7 / 8.0 / 2.0 / 7.9	29 SA	0033 / 0629 / 1321 / 1914	3.0 / 7.7 / 2.4 / 7.7
15 SA	0258 / 0833 / 1530 / 2105	2.3 / 8.3 / 1.7 / 8.3	30 SU	0139 / 0733 / 1423 / 2011	2.6 / 8.1 / 2.0 / 8.2
			31 M	0240 / 0829 / 1520 / 2102	2.1 / 8.6 / 1.5 / 8.7

JUNE

Day	Time	m	Day	Time	m
1 TU	0336 / 0921 / 1611 / 2150	1.6 / 9.0 / 1.1 / 9.1	16 W	0436 / 1018 / 1647 / 2234	2.0 / 8.4 / 1.9 / 8.5
2 W	0429 / 1011 / 1659 / 2237	1.2 / 9.3 / 0.9 / 9.4	17 TH	0513 / 1056 / 1720 / 2309 ●	1.8 / 8.4 / 1.9 / 8.6
3 TH	0519 / 1101 / 1745 / 2324 ○	0.9 / 9.5 / 0.8 / 9.5	18 F	0549 / 1132 / 1752 / 2343	1.8 / 8.4 / 1.9 / 8.6
4 F	0609 / 1151 / 1831	0.7 / 9.5 / 0.8	19 SA	0625 / 1207 / 1824	1.8 / 8.4 / 1.9
5 SA	0012 / 0659 / 1243 / 1917	9.5 / 0.7 / 9.3 / 1.1	20 SU	0017 / 0700 / 1243 / 1858	8.6 / 1.9 / 8.4 / 2.0
6 SU	0103 / 0750 / 1335 / 2005	9.4 / 0.8 / 9.1 / 1.4	21 M	0054 / 0737 / 1320 / 1935	8.5 / 1.9 / 8.3 / 2.1
7 M	0154 / 0842 / 1428 / 2055	9.2 / 1.1 / 8.7 / 1.8	22 TU	0131 / 0815 / 1358 / 2015	8.4 / 2.0 / 8.2 / 2.3
8 TU	0248 / 0937 / 1523 / 2151	8.6 / 1.4 / 8.3 / 2.2	23 W	0211 / 0856 / 1440 / 2058	8.3 / 2.2 / 8.1 / 2.5
9 W	0346 / 1035 / 1623 / 2251 ◐	8.5 / 1.8 / 7.9 / 2.5	24 TH	0255 / 0941 / 1525 / 2146	8.2 / 2.3 / 7.9 / 2.6
10 TH	0448 / 1135 / 1728 / 2357	8.2 / 2.1 / 7.6 / 2.7	25 F	0344 / 1031 / 1618 / 2242 ◐	8.1 / 2.4 / 7.7 / 2.8
11 F	0553 / 1239 / 1834	8.0 / 2.2 / 7.5	26 SA	0440 / 1128 / 1718 / 2344	8.0 / 2.5 / 7.7 / 2.8
12 SA	0105 / 0656 / 1345 / 1935	2.8 / 7.9 / 2.3 / 7.6	27 SU	0541 / 1231 / 1823	8.0 / 2.4 / 7.8
13 SU	0211 / 0755 / 1444 / 2028	2.6 / 8.0 / 2.3 / 7.9	28 M	0051 / 0645 / 1339 / 1928	2.7 / 8.1 / 2.2 / 8.1
14 M	0307 / 0848 / 1532 / 2115	2.4 / 8.1 / 2.1 / 8.1	29 TU	0200 / 0750 / 1444 / 2029	2.4 / 8.4 / 1.9 / 8.4
15 TU	0354 / 0935 / 1612 / 2156	2.2 / 8.3 / 2.0 / 8.3	30 W	0306 / 0853 / 1545 / 2126	2.0 / 8.7 / 1.6 / 8.9

JULY

Day	Time	m	Day	Time	m
1 TH	0408 / 0952 / 1639 / 2219	1.5 / 8.9 / 1.3 / 9.2	16 F	0451 / 1039 / 1656 / 2252	2.2 / 8.2 / 2.2 / 8.5
2 F	0506 / 1048 / 1731 / 2310 ○	1.2 / 9.2 / 1.1 / 9.5	17 SA	0532 / 1117 / 1734 / 2328 ●	2.0 / 8.3 / 2.0 / 8.7
3 SA	0601 / 1142 / 1821	0.9 / 9.3 / 1.1	18 SU	0611 / 1154 / 1811	1.8 / 8.4 / 1.9
4 SU	0001 / 0654 / 1235 / 1910	9.6 / 0.7 / 9.3 / 1.1	19 M	0004 / 0649 / 1229 / 1847	8.7 / 1.7 / 8.5 / 1.9
5 M	0052 / 0746 / 1325 / 1958	9.6 / 0.7 / 9.2 / 1.3	20 TU	0040 / 0726 / 1305 / 1923	8.8 / 1.7 / 8.5 / 1.9
6 TU	0142 / 0836 / 1414 / 2045	9.5 / 0.8 / 8.9 / 1.5	21 W	0115 / 0803 / 1341 / 2000	8.8 / 1.7 / 8.5 / 1.9
7 W	0231 / 0923 / 1502 / 2131	9.2 / 1.1 / 8.6 / 1.9	22 TH	0152 / 0839 / 1418 / 2038	8.8 / 1.7 / 8.5 / 2.0
8 TH	0320 / 1008 / 1550 / 2219	8.9 / 1.5 / 8.2 / 2.2	23 F	0232 / 0915 / 1458 / 2118	8.7 / 1.9 / 8.4 / 2.2
9 F	0410 / 1055 / 1641 / 2310	8.5 / 1.9 / 7.8 / 2.6	24 SA	0315 / 0955 / 1543 / 2203	8.6 / 2.1 / 8.2 / 2.4
10 SA	0504 / 1144 / 1739	8.0 / 2.4 / 7.5	25 SU	0404 / 1042 / 1636 / 2259 ◐	8.3 / 2.3 / 7.9 / 2.7
11 SU	0007 / 0605 / 1240 / 1843	2.9 / 7.7 / 2.7 / 7.3	26 M	0502 / 1141 / 1741	8.1 / 2.6 / 7.8
12 M	0111 / 0710 / 1340 / 1947	3.0 / 7.5 / 2.8 / 7.4	27 TU	0010 / 0609 / 1300 / 1853	2.8 / 7.9 / 2.6 / 7.8
13 TU	0217 / 0813 / 1440 / 2043	2.9 / 7.6 / 2.9 / 7.7	28 W	0130 / 0724 / 1419 / 2007	2.7 / 7.9 / 2.5 / 8.1
14 W	0317 / 0908 / 1532 / 2131	2.7 / 7.8 / 2.6 / 8.0	29 TH	0250 / 0839 / 1530 / 2113	2.3 / 8.2 / 2.1 / 8.6
15 TH	0407 / 0956 / 1616 / 2214	2.4 / 8.0 / 2.4 / 8.3	30 F	0400 / 0945 / 1630 / 2210	1.7 / 8.6 / 1.7 / 9.1
			31 SA	0502 / 1042 / 1724 / 2301 ○	1.3 / 9.0 / 1.3 / 9.5

AUGUST

Day	Time	m	Day	Time	m
1 SU	0557 / 1134 / 1814 / 2350	0.8 / 9.2 / 1.1 / 9.7	16 M	0556 / 1136 / 1757 / 2346 ●	1.6 / 8.6 / 1.8 / 9.0
2 M	0648 / 1222 / 1901	0.6 / 9.3 / 1.0	17 TU	0633 / 1210 / 1833	1.4 / 8.7 / 1.6
3 TU	0037 / 0734 / 1308 / 1944	9.8 / 0.5 / 9.3 / 1.0	18 W	0019 / 0708 / 1244 / 1907	9.1 / 1.3 / 8.8 / 1.5
4 W	0122 / 0817 / 1350 / 2024	9.7 / 0.6 / 9.1 / 1.2	19 TH	0053 / 0742 / 1317 / 1941	9.1 / 1.3 / 8.9 / 1.5
5 TH	0204 / 0856 / 1430 / 2103	9.4 / 0.9 / 8.8 / 1.6	20 F	0128 / 0814 / 1352 / 2015	9.1 / 1.3 / 8.8 / 1.6
6 F	0245 / 0934 / 1509 / 2141	9.0 / 1.4 / 8.4 / 2.1	21 SA	0205 / 0846 / 1429 / 2051	9.1 / 1.5 / 8.7 / 1.8
7 SA	0327 / 1011 / 1549 / 2223 ◑	8.5 / 2.0 / 7.9 / 2.6	22 SU	0246 / 0921 / 1511 / 2131	8.8 / 1.9 / 8.4 / 2.2
8 SU	0411 / 1051 / 1636 / 2314	8.0 / 2.6 / 7.5 / 3.0	23 M	0333 / 1004 / 1602 / 2224 ◑	8.4 / 2.3 / 8.0 / 2.6
9 M	0505 / 1142 / 1737	7.5 / 3.1 / 7.1	24 TU	0432 / 1105 / 1708 / 2340	7.9 / 2.8 / 7.6 / 3.0
10 TU	0019 / 0616 / 1245 / 1858	3.3 / 7.1 / 3.3 / 7.1	25 W	0546 / 1233 / 1832	7.6 / 3.1 / 7.5
11 W	0133 / 0738 / 1354 / 2014	3.4 / 7.1 / 3.3 / 7.3	26 TH	0118 / 0716 / 1410 / 1959	3.0 / 7.5 / 2.9 / 7.8
12 TH	0246 / 0845 / 1501 / 2111	3.1 / 7.4 / 3.1 / 7.8	27 F	0251 / 0841 / 1527 / 2108	2.5 / 7.9 / 2.4 / 8.5
13 F	0347 / 0938 / 1556 / 2156	2.7 / 7.8 / 2.7 / 8.2	28 SA	0401 / 0944 / 1626 / 2203	1.8 / 8.5 / 1.8 / 9.1
14 SA	0435 / 1022 / 1640 / 2236	2.2 / 8.1 / 2.3 / 8.6	29 SU	0457 / 1035 / 1716 / 2250	1.1 / 9.0 / 1.3 / 9.6
15 SU	0517 / 1100 / 1720 / 2312	1.9 / 8.4 / 2.0 / 8.8	30 M	0546 / 1121 / 1801 / 2334 ○	0.6 / 9.3 / 0.9 / 9.8
			31 TU	0631 / 1203 / 1843	0.4 / 9.4 / 0.7

Chart Datum: 4·93 metres below Ordnance Datum (Newlyn)

ENGLAND – LIVERPOOL (ALFRED DK)

LAT 53°24′N   LONG 3°01′W

TIMES AND HEIGHTS OF HIGH AND LOW WATERS

SEPTEMBER

Day	Time m	Time m	Time m	Time m
1 W	0016 9.9	0711 0.4	1243 9.3	1921 0.9
16 TH	0642 1.0	1215 9.1	1846 1.2	
2 TH	0055 9.7	0748 0.6	1319 9.2	1957 1.1
17 F	0026 9.4	0715 1.0	1250 9.2	1919 1.1
3 F	0133 9.4	0822 1.0	1354 8.9	2030 1.5
18 SA	0103 9.4	0747 1.1	1325 9.1	1953 1.3
4 SA	0208 9.0	0853 1.6	1427 8.5	2101 2.0
19 SU	0141 9.2	0819 1.4	1403 8.9	2029 1.6
5 SU	0244 8.5	0921 2.1	1502 8.1	2133 2.5
20 M	0222 8.9	0855 1.9	1446 8.5	2111 2.1
6 M ◑	0323 7.9	0953 2.8	1542 7.6	2218 3.1
21 TU ◐	0311 8.3	0940 2.5	1539 8.0	2206 2.7
7 TU	0411 7.3	1041 3.3	1636 7.1	2329 3.6
22 W	0414 7.6	1045 3.1	1650 7.5	2332 3.1
8 W	0521 6.8	1154 3.7	1804 6.8	
23 TH	0541 7.2	1227 3.4	1827 7.4	
9 TH	0055 3.6	0706 6.7	1317 3.7	1945 7.1
24 F	0124 3.0	0724 7.4	1410 3.0	1956 7.8
10 F	0219 3.3	0823 7.2	1435 3.3	2047 7.6
25 SA	0253 2.3	0839 8.0	1521 2.4	2059 8.6
11 SA	0325 2.7	0915 7.7	1535 2.8	2133 8.2
26 SU	0354 1.6	0934 8.6	1614 1.7	2149 9.2
12 SU	0413 2.1	0958 8.2	1621 2.3	2211 8.6
27 M	0443 0.9	1019 9.1	1700 1.2	2232 9.6
13 M	0453 1.7	1035 8.6	1700 1.9	2246 9.0
28 TU ○	0527 0.6	1100 9.3	1741 0.9	2313 9.8
14 TU ●	0531 1.3	1109 8.8	1736 1.5	2319 9.2
29 W	0606 0.5	1137 9.4	1819 0.8	2350 9.7
15 W	0607 1.1	1142 9.0	1811 1.3	2352 9.3
30 TH	0642 0.6	1212 9.3	1854 0.9	

OCTOBER

Day	Time m	Time m	Time m	Time m
1 F	0026 9.6	0715 0.9	1245 9.1	1926 1.2
16 SA	0000 9.6	0647 0.9	1223 9.4	1858 1.0
2 SA	0100 9.3	0743 1.3	1317 8.9	1955 1.6
17 SU	0040 9.5	0722 1.1	1302 9.3	1936 1.1
3 SU	0133 8.9	0801 1.8	1348 8.6	2022 2.0
18 M	0122 9.2	0758 1.5	1344 9.0	2016 1.5
4 M	0206 8.4	0833 2.3	1421 8.2	2052 2.5
19 TU	0208 8.8	0839 2.0	1432 8.6	2104 2.0
5 TU	0244 7.9	0904 2.9	1500 7.7	2134 3.1
20 W ◐	0302 8.2	0930 2.6	1529 8.0	2207 2.6
6 W ◑	0330 7.3	0950 3.4	1550 7.2	2243 3.6
21 TH ◑	0411 7.5	1043 3.2	1646 7.6	2338 2.9
7 TH	0434 6.6	1105 3.9	1706 6.8	
22 F	0544 7.2	1224 3.3	1820 7.6	
8 F	0015 3.7	0625 6.6	1236 3.9	1904 6.9
23 SA	0119 2.7	0714 7.5	1355 2.9	1937 8.0
9 SA	0140 3.4	0749 7.0	1357 3.6	2011 7.5
24 SU	0237 2.1	0820 8.1	1500 2.3	2037 8.6
10 SU	0247 2.7	0842 7.7	1500 2.9	2058 8.1
25 M	0334 1.5	0911 8.6	1552 1.7	2126 9.1
11 M	0337 2.1	0924 8.2	1547 2.3	2137 8.6
26 TU	0420 1.1	0955 9.0	1636 1.3	2209 9.4
12 TU	0418 1.6	1001 8.7	1628 1.8	2212 9.0
27 W	0500 0.9	1034 9.2	1715 1.1	2248 9.5
13 W ○	0457 1.2	1035 9.0	1706 1.4	2247 9.3
28 TH	0537 0.9	1109 9.2	1752 1.1	2324 9.4
14 TH	0535 0.9	1110 9.3	1744 1.1	2322 9.6
29 F	0609 1.0	1142 9.2	1826 1.2	2358 9.3
15 F	0612 0.8	1145 9.4	1822 1.0	
30 SA	0639 1.3	1213 9.0	1857 1.4	
31 SU	0030 9.0	0705 1.6	1244 8.9	1925 1.7

NOVEMBER

Day	Time m	Time m	Time m	Time m
1 M	0103 8.7	0730 2.0	1317 8.6	1953 2.1
16 TU	0112 9.2	0747 1.5	1334 9.2	2015 1.4
2 TU	0137 8.4	0757 2.4	1352 8.3	2025 2.5
17 W	0203 8.8	0834 2.0	1427 8.8	2109 1.8
3 W	0216 7.9	0831 2.8	1431 7.9	2107 3.0
18 TH	0300 8.3	0930 2.5	1526 8.4	2213 2.2
4 TH	0301 7.4	0917 3.3	1519 7.5	2209 3.4
19 F ◐	0408 7.8	1039 2.9	1637 8.1	2330 2.5
5 F ◑	0359 7.0	1024 3.7	1623 7.1	2329 3.5
20 SA	0527 7.5	1200 3.1	1754 8.0	
6 SA	0520 6.8	1147 3.8	1750 7.1	
21 SU	0050 2.4	0643 7.6	1320 2.9	1904 8.1
7 SU	0046 3.3	0653 7.0	1303 3.6	1912 7.4
22 M	0203 2.2	0748 8.0	1427 2.5	2005 8.5
8 M	0153 2.8	0754 7.6	1407 3.0	2007 8.0
23 TU	0302 1.8	0841 8.3	1521 2.1	2057 8.8
9 TU	0249 2.2	0840 8.1	1502 2.4	2052 8.5
24 W	0350 1.6	0927 8.7	1607 1.8	2143 9.0
10 W	0337 1.7	0921 8.7	1550 1.9	2133 9.0
25 TH	0430 1.5	1007 8.9	1648 1.6	2223 9.0
11 TH ○	0421 1.3	0959 9.1	1634 1.4	2213 9.3
26 F	0505 1.5	1043 9.0	1725 1.5	2300 9.0
12 F ●	0503 1.0	1039 9.4	1717 1.1	2255 9.6
27 SA	0537 1.5	1116 9.0	1759 1.6	2334 8.9
13 SA	0544 0.9	1119 9.6	1800 1.0	2338 9.6
28 SU	0607 1.7	1148 8.9	1832 1.7	
14 SU	0624 0.9	1201 9.6	1843 0.9	
29 M	0007 8.8	0635 1.9	1222 8.8	1904 1.9
15 M	0023 9.5	0704 1.1	1247 9.5	1927 1.1
30 TU	0042 8.6	0704 2.1	1256 8.7	1937 2.1

DECEMBER

Day	Time m	Time m	Time m	Time m
1 W	0118 8.4	0736 2.3	1333 8.5	2012 2.4
16 TH	0159 9.0	0833 1.7	1420 9.3	2110 1.4
2 TH	0157 8.1	0813 2.7	1413 8.2	2053 2.7
17 F	0253 8.6	0925 2.1	1515 9.0	2205 1.7
3 F	0240 7.8	0857 3.0	1457 7.9	2144 2.9
18 SA ◑	0349 8.2	1020 2.4	1612 8.6	2302 2.0
4 SA	0329 7.5	0951 3.3	1550 7.7	2244 3.1
19 SU	0451 7.9	1120 2.7	1715 8.3	
5 SU	0429 7.2	1056 3.4	1651 7.5	2350 3.1
20 M	0003 2.3	0558 7.7	1226 2.9	1820 8.1
6 M ◑	0538 7.2	1204 3.4	1759 7.6	
21 TU	0109 2.5	0705 7.7	1336 2.8	1926 8.1
7 TU	0055 2.8	0647 7.5	1310 3.1	1903 7.9
22 W	0215 2.5	0805 7.9	1441 2.7	2025 8.2
8 W	0158 2.5	0747 7.9	1413 2.7	2001 8.3
23 TH	0311 2.4	0857 8.1	1536 2.4	2117 8.3
9 TH	0255 2.0	0839 8.5	1511 2.2	2054 8.8
24 F	0357 2.2	0942 8.4	1622 2.2	2202 8.5
10 F	0347 1.6	0927 8.9	1605 1.7	2145 9.2
25 SA	0436 2.1	1022 8.6	1702 2.0	2243 8.6
11 SA ○	0436 1.3	1013 9.3	1655 1.3	2234 9.4
26 SU	0511 2.0	1059 8.8	1740 1.9	2319 8.6
12 SU ●	0522 1.1	1100 9.5	1745 1.1	2324 9.5
27 M	0545 2.0	1133 8.8	1817 1.9	2354 8.6
13 M	0609 1.1	1148 9.7	1835 1.0	
28 TU	0618 2.0	1208 8.9	1853 1.9	
14 TU	0014 9.5	0655 1.2	1237 9.6	1926 1.0
29 W	0029 8.6	0651 2.0	1244 8.8	1928 2.0
15 W	0106 9.3	0743 1.4	1328 9.5	2017 1.1
30 TH	0105 8.5	0724 2.1	1320 8.7	2003 2.1
31 F	0142 8.4	0800 2.3	1357 8.6	2040 2.2

Chart Datum: 4·93 metres below Ordnance Datum (Newlyn)

Chapter 5

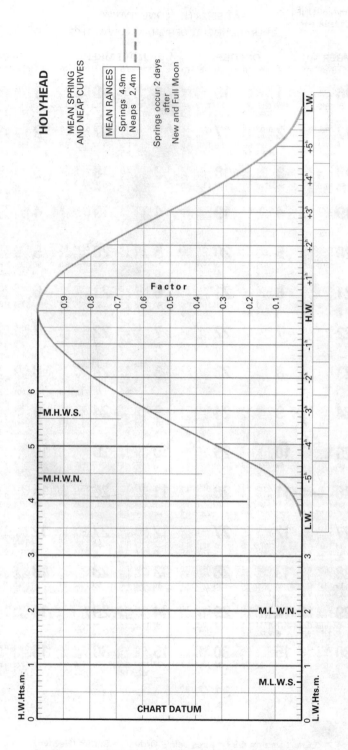

HOLYHEAD

MEAN SPRING
AND NEAP CURVES

MEAN RANGES	
Springs	4.9m
Neaps	2.4m

Springs occur 2 days
after
New and Full Moon

WALES–HOLYHEAD

LAT 53°19′N LONG 4°37′W

YEAR **2004**

TIMES AND HEIGHTS OF HIGH AND LOW WATERS

JANUARY

Day	Time m	Time m	Time m	Time m		Day	Time m	Time m	Time m	Time m
1 TH	0542 4.4	1139 2.2	1750 4.7			16 F	0427 4.7	1029 1.8	1648 4.9	2317 1.6
2 F	0015 2.0	0645 4.5	1244 2.2	1854 4.7		17 SA	0540 4.7	1142 1.8	1803 4.9	
3 SA	0112 1.9	0739 4.6	1341 2.0	1950 4.7		18 SU	0028 1.5	0650 4.8	1255 1.7	1917 5.0
4 SU	0202 1.8	0825 4.8	1430 1.9	2037 4.8		19 M	0134 1.4	0754 5.1	1401 1.4	2023 5.2
5 M	0245 1.7	0904 5.0	1513 1.7	2119 5.0		20 TU	0234 1.2	0850 5.4	1501 1.1	2121 5.4
6 TU	0323 1.6	0940 5.2	1550 1.5	2156 5.1		21 W	0327 1.1	0941 5.6	1555 0.8 ●	2213 5.5
7 W	0357 1.5	1013 5.3	1626 1.4	2232 5.1 ○		22 TH	0416 0.9	1028 5.8	1645 0.6	2301 5.6
8 TH	0431 1.4	1046 5.4	1701 1.3	2307 5.2		23 F	0502 0.8	1114 5.9	1731 0.6	2346 5.5
9 F	0506 1.3	1120 5.4	1736 1.2	2343 5.2		24 SA	0545 0.9	1158 5.9	1815 0.6	
10 SA	0541 1.3	1156 5.4	1813 1.2			25 SU	0030 5.4	0627 1.0	1242 5.8	1858 0.8
11 SU	0020 5.1	0618 1.3	1234 5.4	1851 1.2		26 M	0112 5.2	0709 1.1	1324 5.6	1941 1.0
12 M	0100 5.1	0657 1.4	1313 5.4	1932 1.2		27 TU	0154 5.0	0752 1.4	1405 5.3	2024 1.3
13 TU	0142 5.0	0740 1.5	1356 5.3	2017 1.3		28 W	0236 4.7	0836 1.7	1449 5.0	2110 1.7
14 W	0229 4.9	0828 1.6	1444 5.1	2109 1.4		29 TH	0323 4.5	0928 2.0	1540 4.7	2203 2.0 ☽
15 TH	0323 4.7	0923 1.7	1540 5.0	2209 1.5 ☽		30 F	0422 4.3	1032 2.2	1643 4.4	2309 2.2
						31 SA	0535 4.2	1148 2.4	1800 4.3	

FEBRUARY

Day	Time m	Time m	Time m	Time m		Day	Time m	Time m	Time m	Time m
1 SU	0022 2.2	0653 4.3	1305 2.3	1918 4.4		16 M	0008 1.8	0631 4.6	1245 1.8	1916 4.7
2 M	0130 2.2	0757 4.5	1408 2.0	2020 4.5		17 TU	0127 1.7	0746 4.9	1401 1.5	2027 5.0
3 TU	0225 2.0	0845 4.8	1457 1.8	2107 4.7		18 W	0232 1.4	0846 5.2	1501 1.1	2122 5.2
4 W	0307 1.7	0924 5.0	1536 1.5	2144 4.9		19 TH	0323 1.2	0934 5.5	1551 0.8	2208 5.4
5 TH	0343 1.5	0958 5.2	1611 1.2	2218 5.1		20 F	0407 0.9	1018 5.7	1634 0.6 ●	2249 5.5
6 F	0416 1.3	1030 5.4	1644 1.0	2251 5.2 ○		21 SA	0447 0.7	1058 5.9	1714 0.5	2327 5.5
7 SA	0450 1.1	1103 5.5	1718 0.8	2325 5.3		22 SU	0525 0.7	1137 5.9	1751 0.5	
8 SU	0524 0.9	1138 5.6	1753 0.8			23 M	0003 5.4	0602 0.7	1215 5.8	1827 0.7
9 M	0000 5.4	0558 0.9	1214 5.6	1828 0.7		24 TU	0039 5.3	0638 0.9	1251 5.6	1902 0.9
10 TU	0037 5.3	0635 0.9	1251 5.6	1905 0.8		25 W	0112 5.1	0714 1.1	1327 5.3	1937 1.2
11 W	0116 5.2	0714 1.0	1330 5.5	1946 1.0		26 TH	0146 4.9	0751 1.5	1403 5.0	2015 1.6
12 TH	0157 5.1	0758 1.2	1414 5.3	2033 1.2		27 F	0224 4.6	0834 1.8	1445 4.6	2059 1.9
13 F	0245 4.9	0849 1.5	1506 5.1	2130 1.5		28 SA	0310 4.4	0928 2.2	1543 4.3	2157 2.3 ☽
14 SA	0345 4.7	0954 1.7	1614 4.8	2244 1.8		29 SU	0419 4.2	1046 2.4	1703 4.1	2322 2.5
15 SU	0504 4.5	1117 1.9	1745 4.6							

MARCH

Day	Time m	Time m	Time m	Time m		Day	Time m	Time m	Time m	Time m
1 M	0554 4.1	1223 2.4	1845 4.1			16 TU	0002 2.1	0623 4.5	1245 1.7	1923 4.6
2 TU	0054 2.4	0722 4.3	1340 2.1	2000 4.3		17 W	0124 1.8	0740 4.8	1400 1.4	2028 4.9
3 W	0200 2.1	0819 4.6	1433 1.7	2048 4.6		18 TH	0225 1.5	0837 5.2	1454 1.0	2115 5.1
4 TH	0245 1.8	0900 4.9	1512 1.4	2124 4.9		19 F	0312 1.0	0921 5.5	1537 0.7	2154 5.3
5 F	0321 1.4	0934 5.2	1546 1.0	2156 5.1		20 SA	0351 0.9	1000 5.6	1615 0.6 ●	2228 5.4
6 SA	0354 1.1	1006 5.4	1619 0.8	2227 5.3 ○		21 SU	0427 0.7	1036 5.7	1649 0.5	2301 5.4
7 SU	0426 0.8	1038 5.6	1652 0.5	2300 5.5		22 M	0501 0.6	1112 5.7	1722 0.6	2333 5.4
8 M	0459 0.6	1113 5.8	1726 0.4	2335 5.6		23 TU	0534 0.7	1146 5.6	1754 0.7	
9 TU	0534 0.5	1149 5.8	1801 0.4			24 W	0005 5.3	0607 0.8	1220 5.5	1825 0.9
10 W	0011 5.5	0610 0.6	1227 5.8	1838 0.6		25 TH	0036 5.2	0640 1.1	1253 5.2	1857 1.2
11 TH	0049 5.4	0650 0.7	1307 5.6	1919 0.8		26 F	0107 5.0	0716 1.4	1327 4.9	1932 1.5
12 F	0131 5.3	0734 1.0	1352 5.3	2006 1.2		27 SA	0141 4.8	0755 1.7	1405 4.6	2011 1.9
13 SA	0218 5.0	0827 1.3	1446 5.0	2105 1.6		28 SU	0222 4.5	0845 2.0	1456 4.3	2104 2.3
14 SU	0319 4.7	0937 1.7	1602 4.6	2226 2.0		29 M	0320 4.2	0955 2.3	1614 4.0	2226 2.5 ☽
15 M	0445 4.5	1111 1.9	1749 4.4			30 TU	0453 4.1	1134 2.3	1803 4.0	
						31 W	0006 2.5	0631 4.2	1259 2.1	1925 4.2

APRIL

Day	Time m	Time m	Time m	Time m		Day	Time m	Time m	Time m	Time m
1 TH	0121 2.2	0738 4.5	1355 1.7	2014 4.6		16 F	0206 1.5	0817 5.1	1434 1.0	2056 5.1
2 F	0209 1.8	0822 4.8	1436 1.3	2051 4.9		17 SA	0251 1.2	0859 5.3	1514 0.8	2131 5.2
3 SA	0247 1.4	0859 5.1	1512 0.9	2124 5.2		18 SU	0328 1.0	0936 5.5	1549 0.7	2202 5.3
4 SU	0322 1.0	0933 5.4	1546 0.6	2157 5.4		19 M	0403 0.8	1011 5.5	1621 0.7 ●	2233 5.4
5 M	0356 0.7	1008 5.7	1621 0.4	2231 5.6 ○		20 TU	0435 0.8	1045 5.5	1652 0.8	2304 5.4
6 TU	0431 0.5	1045 5.8	1657 0.3	2308 5.7		21 W	0508 0.8	1118 5.4	1723 0.9	2335 5.3
7 W	0509 0.4	1124 5.9	1735 0.3	2346 5.7		22 TH	0541 1.0	1151 5.3	1754 1.1	
8 TH	0549 0.4	1205 5.8	1815 0.5			23 F	0005 5.2	0614 1.1	1225 5.1	1825 1.3
9 F	0027 5.6	0632 0.6	1250 5.6	1859 0.9		24 SA	0038 5.0	0650 1.4	1300 4.8	1900 1.6
10 SA	0112 5.3	0721 0.9	1340 5.2	1950 1.3		25 SU	0113 4.9	0730 1.6	1340 4.6	1940 1.9
11 SU	0203 5.0	0820 1.3	1442 4.8	2054 1.7		26 M	0154 4.6	0818 1.9	1429 4.3	2031 2.2
12 M	0309 4.7	0937 1.6	1609 4.5	2220 2.1 ☽		27 TU	0247 4.4	0922 2.1	1538 4.1	2140 2.4
13 TU	0438 4.6	1110 1.7	1753 4.4	2352 2.1		28 W	0403 4.3	1044 2.1	1713 4.1	2309 2.4
14 W	0611 4.6	1236 1.6	1916 4.6			29 TH	0533 4.3	1204 1.9	1832 4.3	
15 TH	0109 1.8	0723 4.9	1344 1.3	2013 4.9		30 F	0026 2.2	0643 4.5	1304 1.6	1927 4.6

Chart Datum: 3·05 metres below Ordnance Datum (Newlyn)

Chapter 5

TIME ZONE (UT)
For Summer Time add ONE hour in **non-shaded** areas

WALES – HOLYHEAD
LAT 53°19'N   LONG 4°37'W
TIMES AND HEIGHTS OF HIGH AND LOW WATERS

YEAR 2004

MAY

Day	Time m	Time m	Time m	Time m	Day	Time m	Time m	Time m	Time m
1 SA	0121 1.8	0735 4.8		2010 4.9	16 SU	0222 1.4	0830 5.1	1445 1.1	2102 5.0
2 SU	0205 1.4	0818 5.1	1432 0.9	2048 5.2	17 M	0302 1.2	0909 5.2	1520 1.0	2135 5.1
3 M	0245 1.0	0858 5.4	1511 0.6	2125 5.4	18 TU	0338 1.1	0945 5.2	1553 1.0	2207 5.2
4 TU	0324 0.7	0938 5.7	1550 0.4	○ 2203 5.6	19 W	0412 1.0	1020 5.2	1625 1.1	● 2238 5.2
5 W	0405 0.5	1019 5.8	1630 0.3	2243 5.7	20 TH	0446 1.1	1054 5.2	1656 1.1	2310 5.2
6 TH	0447 0.4	1103 5.8	1713 0.4	2326 5.7	21 F	0520 1.1	1129 5.1	1729 1.2	2343 5.2
7 F	0533 0.4	1150 5.7	1758 0.6		22 SA	0555 1.2	1204 4.9	1803 1.4	
8 SA	0011 5.6	0622 0.6	1241 5.4	1847 1.0	23 SU	0017 5.1	0632 1.4	1241 4.8	1839 1.6
9 SU	0101 5.4	0717 0.9	1338 5.1	1943 1.4	24 M	0054 4.9	0713 1.6	1323 4.6	1920 1.8
10 M	0157 5.2	0821 1.2	1445 4.8	2049 1.7	25 TU	0135 4.8	0800 1.7	1410 4.4	2008 2.0
11 TU	0304 4.9	0935 1.4	1609 4.5	◑ 2207 2.0	26 W	0225 4.6	0855 1.8	1509 4.3	2108 2.1
12 W	0424 4.8	1056 1.5	1735 4.5	2328 2.0	27 TH	0326 4.5	1000 1.8	1621 4.2	◐ 2217 2.2
13 TH	0544 4.8	1210 1.4	1847 4.6		28 F	0437 4.6	1108 1.7	1733 4.3	2327 2.0
14 F	0038 1.8	0652 4.9	1313 1.3	1943 4.8	29 SA	0546 4.6	1210 1.5	1834 4.6	
15 SA	0135 1.6	0746 5.0	1404 1.2	2026 4.9	30 SU	0028 1.8	0644 4.8	1304 1.2	1925 4.8
					31 M	0122 1.5	0736 5.0	1353 1.0	2011 5.1

JUNE

Day	Time m	Time m	Time m	Time m	Day	Time m	Time m	Time m	Time m
1 TU	0210 1.1	0824 5.3	1439 0.8	2055 5.3	16 W	0317 1.4	0923 4.9	1529 1.3	2145 5.1
2 W	0257 0.9	0912 5.5	1524 0.6	2139 5.5	17 TH	0355 1.3	1001 5.0	1604 1.3	● 2219 5.1
3 TH	0344 0.6	1000 5.6	1610 0.6	○ 2224 5.7	18 F	0431 1.3	1037 5.0	1637 1.3	2252 5.2
4 F	0433 0.5	1050 5.7	1658 0.6	2312 5.7	19 SA	0506 1.2	1113 5.0	1711 1.3	2326 5.2
5 SA	0524 0.5	1142 5.6	1748 0.8		20 SU	0542 1.2	1149 4.9	1746 1.4	
6 SU	0001 5.7	0617 0.6	1237 5.4	1839 1.0	21 M	0001 5.1	0619 1.3	1227 4.9	1823 1.5
7 M	0054 5.5	0714 0.8	1335 5.1	1935 1.3	22 TU	0039 5.1	0658 1.3	1306 4.8	1903 1.6
8 TU	0150 5.4	0814 1.0	1437 4.8	2035 1.5	23 W	0119 5.0	0740 1.4	1350 4.7	1946 1.7
9 W	0250 5.1	0918 1.2	1545 4.6	◑ 2140 1.8	24 TH	0202 4.9	0826 1.5	1438 4.5	2035 1.8
10 TH	0356 5.0	1025 1.4	1655 4.5	2249 1.9	25 F	0251 4.8	0918 1.5	1533 4.5	◑ 2132 1.8
11 F	0504 4.8	1131 1.5	1803 4.5	2355 1.9	26 SA	0347 4.7	1016 1.5	1636 4.5	2234 1.8
12 SA	0609 4.8	1231 1.5	1902 4.6		27 SU	0451 4.8	1118 1.5	1741 4.6	2339 1.7
13 SU	0055 1.8	0707 4.8	1326 1.5	1950 4.7	28 M	0556 4.8	1220 1.4	1843 4.7	
14 M	0149 1.6	0758 4.8	1412 1.4	2032 4.8	29 TU	0042 1.6	0700 5.0	1319 1.2	1940 5.0
15 TU	0235 1.5	0843 4.9	1453 1.4	2110 5.0	30 W	0142 1.3	0800 5.1	1415 1.0	2032 5.2

JULY

Day	Time m	Time m	Time m	Time m	Day	Time m	Time m	Time m	Time m
1 TH	0238 1.0	0857 5.3	1507 0.9	2123 5.4	16 F	0342 1.5	0948 4.8	1548 1.5	2203 5.1
2 F	0333 0.8	0951 5.5	1559 0.8	○ 2213 5.6	17 SA	0418 1.3	1024 4.9	1622 1.4	● 2237 5.2
3 SA	0426 0.6	1044 5.5	1649 0.8	2302 5.7	18 SU	0452 1.2	1058 5.0	1656 1.3	2310 5.3
4 SU	0519 0.5	1136 5.5	1738 0.8	2352 5.6	19 M	0526 1.1	1132 5.0	1730 1.2	2344 5.3
5 M	0610 0.5	1228 5.4	1828 0.9		20 TU	0601 1.1	1207 5.0	1805 1.2	
6 TU	0041 5.7	0701 0.6	1320 5.2	1917 1.1	21 W	0019 5.3	0636 1.1	1245 5.0	1841 1.3
7 W	0132 5.6	0753 0.8	1412 5.0	2008 1.3	22 TH	0057 5.3	0714 1.1	1323 4.9	1919 1.3
8 TH	0223 5.4	0846 1.1	1505 4.7	2102 1.6	23 F	0135 5.2	0753 1.2	1404 4.8	2002 1.4
9 F	0317 5.1	0941 1.3	1603 4.5	◑ 2201 1.8	24 SA	0217 5.1	0838 1.3	1451 4.7	2051 1.6
10 SA	0415 4.8	1041 1.6	1705 4.4	2305 1.9	25 SU	0306 5.0	0931 1.4	1546 4.6	◑ 2150 1.7
11 SU	0518 4.6	1142 1.8	1810 4.4		26 M	0405 4.8	1034 1.5	1654 4.6	2300 1.8
12 M	0012 2.0	0624 4.5	1243 1.9	1911 4.5	27 TU	0519 4.7	1146 1.6	1809 4.6	
13 TU	0116 1.9	0727 4.5	1340 1.8	2004 4.6	28 W	0016 1.7	0638 4.8	1258 1.5	1919 4.8
14 W	0213 1.7	0822 4.6	1429 1.7	2049 4.8	29 TH	0128 1.5	0751 4.9	1403 1.4	2021 5.1
15 TH	0301 1.6	0908 4.7	1511 1.6	2128 5.0	30 F	0233 1.2	0854 5.2	1500 1.1	2115 5.4
					31 SA	0329 0.9	0948 5.4	1552 0.9	○ 2204 5.7

AUGUST

Day	Time m	Time m	Time m	Time m	Day	Time m	Time m	Time m	Time m
1 SU	0421 0.6	1038 5.5	1639 0.8	2251 5.8	16 M	0432 1.1	1038 5.1	1635 1.2	● 2248 5.4
2 M	0508 0.4	1124 5.5	1724 0.7	2336 5.9	17 TU	0503 0.9	1109 5.2	1707 1.0	2320 5.5
3 TU	0554 0.4	1209 5.5	1807 0.8		18 W	0535 0.8	1142 5.3	1740 1.0	2354 5.6
4 W	0021 5.9	0638 0.5	1253 5.3	1850 0.9	19 TH	0609 0.8	1217 5.3	1814 1.0	
5 TH	0105 5.7	0721 0.8	1335 5.1	1933 1.1	20 F	0029 5.5	0643 0.9	1253 5.1	1850 1.1
6 F	0148 5.4	0805 1.1	1418 4.8	2018 1.4	21 SA	0106 5.4	0720 1.0	1332 5.1	1931 1.2
7 SA	0233 5.1	0850 1.4	1504 4.6	◑ 2109 1.8	22 SU	0146 5.3	0803 1.2	1415 4.9	2018 1.5
8 SU	0322 4.6	0941 1.8	1559 4.4	2210 2.1	23 M	0233 5.1	0854 1.5	1509 4.7	◑ 2117 1.7
9 M	0422 4.5	1044 2.1	1708 4.3	2325 2.3	24 TU	0334 4.8	1001 1.8	1621 4.6	2236 1.9
10 TU	0537 4.3	1157 2.2	1828 4.3		25 W	0501 4.6	1126 1.9	1751 4.6	
11 W	0044 2.2	0700 4.3	1311 2.2	1938 4.5	26 TH	0007 1.9	0638 4.6	1251 1.8	1912 4.8
12 TH	0154 2.0	0807 4.4	1410 2.0	2031 4.7	27 F	0128 1.6	0756 4.9	1400 1.5	2015 5.2
13 F	0245 1.8	0856 4.6	1455 1.8	2111 4.9	28 SA	0232 1.2	0855 5.2	1455 1.3	2107 5.5
14 SA	0326 1.6	0934 4.8	1532 1.6	2145 5.1	29 SU	0324 0.8	0943 5.5	1542 1.0	2152 5.8
15 SU	0400 1.5	1007 5.0	1604 1.3	2217 5.3	30 M	0409 0.5	1025 5.7	1623 0.8	○ 2234 5.9
					31 TU	0450 0.4	1104 5.6	1703 0.7	2314 5.9

WALES – HOLYHEAD

LAT 53°19'N   LONG 4°37'W

TIMES AND HEIGHTS OF HIGH AND LOW WATERS

SEPTEMBER

Day	Time m	Day	Time m
1 W	0529 0.4 / 1142 5.5 / 1741 0.7 / 2354 5.9	16 TH	0505 0.6 / 1113 5.5 / 1712 0.8 / 2325 5.8
2 TH	0607 0.6 / 1219 5.4 / 1819 0.9	17 F	0538 0.6 / 1147 5.5 / 1746 0.8
3 F	0032 5.7 / 0644 0.8 / 1256 5.2 / 1857 1.1	18 SA	0001 5.7 / 0612 0.7 / 1224 5.5 / 1824 0.9
4 SA	0111 5.4 / 0721 1.2 / 1332 5.0 / 1936 1.4	19 SU	0040 5.6 / 0651 1.0 / 1304 5.3 / 1906 1.1
5 SU	0149 5.1 / 0759 1.6 / 1410 4.7 / 2020 1.8	20 M	0122 5.4 / 0735 1.3 / 1349 5.1 / 1956 1.4
6 M	0231 4.7 / 0843 2.0 / 1457 4.5 / 2116 2.2 ◑	21 TU	0213 5.0 / 0829 1.7 / 1446 4.8 / 2102 1.8 ◑
7 TU	0327 4.3 / 0940 2.3 / 1603 4.3 / 2234 2.4	22 W	0323 4.7 / 0944 2.0 / 1606 4.6 / 2232 2.0
8 W	0449 4.1 / 1105 2.6 / 1737 4.2	23 TH	0508 4.5 / 1121 2.2 / 1745 4.6
9 TH	0011 2.4 / 0634 4.1 / 1239 2.5 / 1907 4.4	24 F	0009 1.9 / 0647 4.6 / 1248 2.0 / 1906 4.9
10 F	0129 2.2 / 0749 4.4 / 1346 2.2 / 2004 4.7	25 SA	0127 1.5 / 0757 4.9 / 1354 1.7 / 2006 5.3
11 SA	0221 1.8 / 0836 4.6 / 1431 1.9 / 2045 5.0	26 SU	0225 1.1 / 0848 5.2 / 1443 1.3 / 2053 5.6
12 SU	0259 1.5 / 0911 4.9 / 1506 1.6 / 2118 5.2	27 M	0311 0.8 / 0928 5.4 / 1525 1.0 / 2134 5.8
13 M	0332 1.2 / 0941 5.1 / 1537 1.3 / 2148 5.4	28 TU	0350 0.6 / 1004 5.5 / 1602 0.8 / 2211 5.9 ○
14 TU	0402 0.9 / 1010 5.3 / 1607 1.0 / 2219 5.6 ●	29 W	0426 0.5 / 1039 5.6 / 1638 0.7 / 2248 5.9
15 W	0433 0.7 / 1041 5.4 / 1639 0.9 / 2251 5.7	30 TH	0501 0.6 / 1112 5.6 / 1713 0.8 / 2325 5.8

OCTOBER

Day	Time m	Day	Time m
1 F	0534 0.8 / 1146 5.5 / 1748 0.9	16 SA	0509 0.6 / 1121 5.7 / 1723 0.7 / 2338 5.8
2 SA	0001 5.6 / 0607 1.0 / 1219 5.3 / 1824 1.2	17 SU	0548 0.8 / 1200 5.7 / 1805 0.9
3 SU	0036 5.3 / 0640 1.3 / 1252 5.1 / 1901 1.5	18 M	0021 5.6 / 0630 1.0 / 1244 5.5 / 1852 1.1
4 M	0112 5.0 / 0718 1.4 / 1328 4.9 / 1942 1.9	19 TU	0109 5.3 / 0718 1.4 / 1334 5.2 / 1949 1.5
5 TU	0151 4.7 / 0756 2.1 / 1410 4.6 / 2034 2.2	20 W	0209 4.9 / 0819 1.9 / 1436 4.9 / 2102 1.8 ◑
6 W	0243 4.4 / 0849 2.4 / 1509 4.4 / 2147 2.5	21 TH	0330 4.6 / 0941 2.2 / 1601 4.8 / 2234 1.9
7 TH	0404 4.1 / 1008 2.7 / 1641 4.2 / 2327 2.5	22 F	0515 4.5 / 1114 2.2 / 1735 4.8
8 F	0554 4.1 / 1152 2.7 / 1818 4.4	23 SA	0002 1.7 / 0641 4.7 / 1234 2.0 / 1849 5.1
9 SA	0047 2.2 / 0713 4.4 / 1306 2.4 / 1922 4.7	24 SU	0112 1.4 / 0743 5.0 / 1335 1.7 / 1946 5.3
10 SU	0141 1.8 / 0801 4.7 / 1354 2.0 / 2006 5.0	25 M	0206 1.1 / 0829 5.2 / 1423 1.4 / 2032 5.6
11 M	0221 1.5 / 0836 5.0 / 1430 1.6 / 2041 5.3	26 TU	0249 0.9 / 0906 5.4 / 1503 1.2 / 2111 5.7
12 TU	0255 1.1 / 0907 5.2 / 1503 1.3 / 2114 5.5	27 W	0326 0.8 / 0940 5.5 / 1539 1.0 / 2147 5.8
13 W	0327 0.9 / 0938 5.4 / 1535 1.0 / 2147 5.7	28 TH	0359 0.8 / 1012 5.5 / 1614 0.9 / 2223 5.7 ○
14 TH	0400 0.7 / 1010 5.6 / 1609 0.8 / 2221 5.9	29 F	0432 0.9 / 1045 5.5 / 1649 1.0 / 2259 5.6
15 F	0433 0.6 / 1044 5.7 / 1644 0.7 / 2258 5.9	30 SA	0504 1.0 / 1117 5.5 / 1723 1.1 / 2334 5.4
		31 SU	0536 1.2 / 1149 5.4 / 1759 1.3

NOVEMBER

Day	Time m	Day	Time m
1 M	0008 5.2 / 0609 1.5 / 1223 5.2 / 1835 1.6	16 TU	0012 5.6 / 0618 1.1 / 1233 5.6 / 1848 1.1
2 TU	0044 5.0 / 0644 1.8 / 1258 5.0 / 1917 1.8	17 W	0107 5.3 / 0712 1.5 / 1328 5.4 / 1950 1.3
3 W	0124 4.7 / 0724 2.1 / 1339 4.8 / 2006 2.1	18 TH	0211 5.0 / 0815 1.8 / 1432 5.2 / 2101 1.5
4 TH	0214 4.4 / 0814 2.4 / 1432 4.6 / 2109 2.3	19 F	0330 4.7 / 0930 2.1 / 1548 5.0 / 2220 1.6 ◑
5 F	0323 4.2 / 0922 2.6 / 1547 4.4 / 2230 2.3 ◑	20 SA	0456 4.6 / 1050 2.1 / 1708 5.0 / 2336 1.6
6 SA	0456 4.2 / 1048 2.6 / 1714 4.4 / 2349 2.2	21 SU	0613 4.7 / 1202 2.0 / 1819 5.1
7 SU	0615 4.4 / 1206 2.4 / 1824 4.6	22 M	0042 1.5 / 0713 4.9 / 1304 1.8 / 1917 5.2
8 M	0048 1.9 / 0710 4.6 / 1302 2.1 / 1916 4.9	23 TU	0136 1.3 / 0801 5.1 / 1355 1.6 / 2005 5.3
9 TU	0134 1.5 / 0753 4.9 / 1346 1.7 / 1959 5.2	24 W	0221 1.2 / 0840 5.2 / 1439 1.4 / 2047 5.4
10 W	0213 1.2 / 0829 5.2 / 1425 1.4 / 2037 5.5	25 TH	0300 1.2 / 0916 5.3 / 1518 1.3 / 2126 5.4
11 TH	0251 1.0 / 0905 5.5 / 1503 1.1 / 2116 5.7	26 F	0335 1.2 / 0949 5.4 / 1555 1.2 / 2203 5.4 ○
12 F	0328 0.8 / 0941 5.7 / 1542 0.9 / 2155 5.8 ●	27 SA	0409 1.2 / 1023 5.5 / 1631 1.2 / 2239 5.4
13 SA	0406 0.7 / 1019 5.8 / 1623 0.7 / 2237 5.9	28 SU	0441 1.3 / 1056 5.4 / 1707 1.3 / 2314 5.3
14 SU	0447 0.7 / 1100 5.8 / 1707 0.7 / 2323 5.8	29 M	0514 1.4 / 1129 5.4 / 1742 1.4 / 2350 5.1
15 M	0531 0.9 / 1144 5.8 / 1755 0.9	30 TU	0548 1.6 / 1202 5.3 / 1820 1.5

DECEMBER

Day	Time m	Day	Time m
1 W	0026 5.0 / 0624 1.7 / 1239 5.2 / 1859 1.7	16 TH	0105 5.4 / 0705 1.3 / 1320 5.7 / 1943 1.0
2 TH	0107 4.8 / 0704 1.9 / 1319 5.0 / 1944 1.8	17 F	0203 5.1 / 0802 1.5 / 1418 5.5 / 2044 1.2
3 F	0152 4.6 / 0749 2.1 / 1406 4.8 / 2036 2.0	18 SA	0307 4.9 / 0904 1.8 / 1520 5.3 / 2149 1.4 ◑
4 SA	0247 4.4 / 0844 2.3 / 1502 4.7 / 2136 2.0	19 SU	0416 4.7 / 1010 1.9 / 1627 5.1 / 2255 1.6
5 SU	0354 4.4 / 0948 2.4 / 1609 4.6 / 2242 2.0 ◑	20 M	0526 4.6 / 1119 2.0 / 1735 5.0
6 M	0506 4.4 / 1058 2.3 / 1718 4.7 / 2345 1.9	21 TU	0000 1.6 / 0630 4.7 / 1225 2.0 / 1839 4.9
7 TU	0610 4.6 / 1202 2.1 / 1820 4.8	22 W	0100 1.7 / 0727 4.8 / 1324 1.8 / 1937 5.0
8 W	0041 1.6 / 0703 4.8 / 1258 1.9 / 1913 5.1	23 TH	0152 1.6 / 0814 4.9 / 1417 1.7 / 2026 5.0
9 TH	0131 1.4 / 0751 5.1 / 1348 1.6 / 2003 5.3	24 F	0237 1.6 / 0856 5.1 / 1503 1.6 / 2110 5.1
10 F	0217 1.1 / 0835 5.3 / 1435 1.3 / 2050 5.5	25 SA	0317 1.5 / 0933 5.2 / 1544 1.5 / 2150 5.1
11 SA	0302 1.0 / 0918 5.6 / 1522 1.0 / 2137 5.7	26 SU	0353 1.5 / 1008 5.3 / 1621 1.4 / 2227 5.1 ○
12 SU	0347 0.8 / 1002 5.8 / 1610 0.8 / 2226 5.7 ●	27 M	0427 1.4 / 1042 5.4 / 1657 1.3 / 2302 5.1
13 M	0434 0.8 / 1048 5.9 / 1700 0.7 / 2316 5.7	28 TU	0500 1.4 / 1115 5.4 / 1731 1.3 / 2337 5.1
14 TU	0522 0.9 / 1136 5.9 / 1752 0.7	29 W	0534 1.5 / 1148 5.4 / 1806 1.3
15 W	0009 5.6 / 0612 1.1 / 1227 5.8 / 1846 0.8	30 TH	0012 5.0 / 0608 1.5 / 1224 5.3 / 1843 1.4
		31 F	0049 4.9 / 0645 1.6 / 1301 5.2 / 1921 1.5

Chapter 5

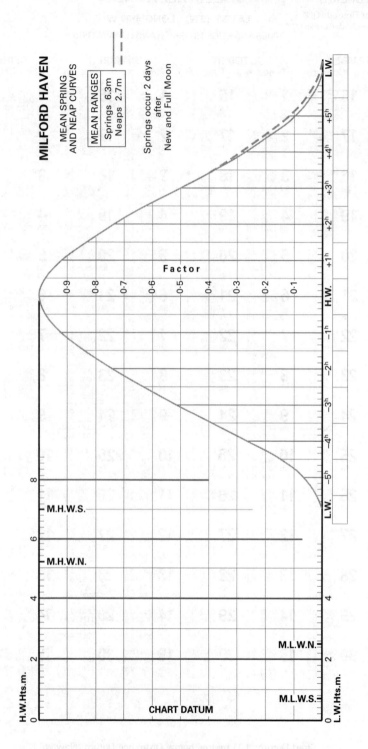

MILFORD HAVEN
MEAN SPRING
AND NEAP CURVES

MEAN RANGES
Springs 6.3m
Neaps 2.7m

Springs occur 2 days
after
New and Full Moon

Factor
0·9 0·8 0·7 0·6 0·5 0·4 0·3 0·2 0·1

H.W.
+1ʰ +2ʰ +3ʰ +4ʰ +5ʰ L.W.
−1ʰ −2ʰ −3ʰ −4ʰ −5ʰ

M.H.W.S.
M.H.W.N.
M.L.W.N.
M.L.W.S.

CHART DATUM

H.W.Hts.m.
L.W.Hts.m.

WALES – MILFORD HAVEN

LAT 51°42'N   LONG 5°03'W

TIMES AND HEIGHTS OF HIGH AND LOW WATERS

YEAR **2004**

JANUARY

Day	Time m	Time m	Time m		Day	Time m	Time m	Time m
1 TH	0055 5.3	0718 2.5	1954 2.4		**16** F	0613 2.1	1226 5.8	1856 2.1
2 F	0203 5.3	0827 2.5	1431 5.5 / 2057 2.3		**17** SA	0107 5.6	0728 2.1	1340 5.8 / 2013 2.1
3 SA	0305 5.4	0928 2.3	1530 5.6 / 2151 2.1		**18** SU	0223 5.7	0847 2.0	1456 5.9 / 2129 1.9
4 SU	0359 5.7	1019 2.1	1621 5.8 / 2238 1.9		**19**	0334 6.0	1000 1.7	1606 6.1 / 2234 1.5
5 M	0445 5.9	1104 1.9	1705 6.0 / 2319 1.7		**20** TU	0437 6.4	1103 1.3	1708 6.5 / 2330 1.2
6 TU	0525 6.2	1144 1.7	1745 6.2 / 2357 1.7		**21** W	0534 6.8	1158 1.0	1803 6.7
7 W	0602 6.4	1221 1.5	1823 6.3		**22** TH	0021 1.0	0625 7.1	1250 0.7 / 1851 6.9
8 TH	0033 1.4	0637 6.5	1257 1.4 / 1858 6.4		**23** F	0109 0.8	0712 7.2	1336 0.6 / 1937 6.9
9	0108 1.4	0712 6.6	1332 1.3 / 1933 6.4		**24** SA	0153 0.8	0756 7.2	1420 0.7 / 2019 6.8
10 SA	0143 1.3	0747 6.6	1408 1.2 / 2009 6.4		**25** SU	0234 0.9	0838 7.1	1500 0.8 / 2058 6.6
11 SU	0219 1.3	0824 6.6	1445 1.2 / 2047 6.3		**26**	0313 1.1	0917 6.8	1538 1.1 / 2136 6.3
12 M	0257 1.4	0902 6.5	1524 1.4 / 2126 6.2		**27** TU	0350 1.4	0956 6.5	1615 1.5 / 2214 6.0
13 TU	0337 1.5	0944 6.4	1605 1.6 / 2210 6.0		**28** W	0427 1.8	1036 6.1	1652 1.9 / 2253 5.6
14 W	0420 1.7	1030 6.2	1652 1.9 / 2259 5.8		**29** TH	0507 2.2	1119 5.7	1736 2.3 / 2340 5.3
15 TH	0511 1.9	1123 6.0	1747 1.9 / 2357 5.6		**30** F	0558 2.5	1213 5.3	1834 2.6
					31 SA	0044 5.0	0709 2.7	1326 5.1 / 1950 2.7

FEBRUARY

Day	Time m	Time m	Time m		Day	Time m	Time m	Time m
1 SU	0209 5.0	0837 2.7	1447 5.1 / 2110 2.6		**16** M	0159 5.4	0832 2.2	1444 5.4 / 2119 2.2
2 M	0325 5.2	0951 2.5	1555 5.3 / 2212 2.3		**17** TU	0325 5.7	0956 1.9	1605 5.8 / 2230 1.7
3 TU	0423 5.6	1045 2.1	1648 5.7 / 2300 1.9		**18** W	0434 6.2	1101 1.4	1707 6.2 / 2326 1.3
4 W	0508 5.9	1129 1.8	1730 6.0 / 2341 1.6		**19** TH	0529 6.7	1154 0.9	1757 6.6
5 TH	0547 6.3	1207 1.4	1808 6.3		**20** F	0014 0.9	0615 7.0	1240 0.6 / 1840 6.9
6 F	0018 1.3	0622 6.5	1244 1.2 / 1843 6.5		**21** SA	0057 0.7	0658 7.2	1320 0.5 / 1919 7.0
7 SA	0054 1.1	0657 6.7	1318 1.0 / 1918 6.6		**22** SU	0135 0.6	0736 7.3	1357 0.5 / 1955 7.0
8 SU	0129 0.9	0733 6.8	1353 0.9 / 1953 6.7		**23** M	0210 0.6	0813 7.2	1431 0.7 / 2029 6.8
9 M	0205 0.9	0808 6.9	1428 0.8 / 2029 6.7		**24** TU	0243 0.8	0847 6.9	1503 0.9 / 2101 6.5
10 TU	0240 0.9	0845 6.9	1504 0.9 / 2106 6.6		**25** W	0314 1.1	0919 6.6	1532 1.3 / 2132 6.2
11 W	0317 1.0	0923 6.7	1541 1.1 / 2144 6.4		**26** TH	0343 1.5	0951 6.2	1602 1.7 / 2204 5.8
12 TH	0356 1.3	1004 6.5	1621 1.4 / 2227 6.1		**27** F	0414 1.9	1026 5.7	1635 2.1 / 2241 5.4
13 F	0440 1.6	1051 6.1	1709 1.8 / 2320 5.7		**28** SA	0452 2.4	1109 5.2	1719 2.5 / 2330 5.0
14 SA	0535 2.0	1150 5.7	1813 2.2		**29** SU	0553 2.8	1211 4.8	1835 2.9
15 SU	0030 5.4	0653 2.3	1311 5.4 / 1945 2.4					

MARCH

Day	Time m	Time m	Time m		Day	Time m	Time m	Time m
1 M	0053 4.7	0737 2.9	1359 4.7 / 2024 2.9		**16** TU	0150 5.3	0832 2.3	1444 5.2 / 2116 2.3
2 TU	0248 4.9	0921 2.7	1530 5.0 / 2145 2.5		**17** W	0322 5.6	0955 1.8	1603 5.7 / 2225 1.7
3 W	0357 5.3	1022 2.2	1626 5.4 / 2237 2.0		**18** TH	0427 6.2	1054 1.3	1657 6.2 / 2316 1.2
4 TH	0444 5.8	1107 1.7	1708 5.9 / 2319 1.6		**19** F	0516 6.7	1141 0.9	1741 6.6 / 2358 0.9
5 F	0523 6.3	1145 1.3	1745 6.3 / 2356 1.2		**20** SA	0558 7.0	1220 0.6	1820 6.9
6 SA	0559 6.6	1220 0.9	1820 6.7		**21** SU	0035 0.7	0636 7.2	1256 0.5 / 1854 7.0
7 SU	0032 0.8	0634 7.0	1256 0.6 / 1855 6.9		**22** M	0110 0.6	0710 7.2	1328 0.5 / 1927 6.9
8 M	0108 0.5	0710 7.2	1331 0.5 / 1930 7.1		**23** TU	0141 0.6	0743 7.1	1358 0.7 / 1957 6.8
9 TU	0144 0.5	0746 7.2	1406 0.5 / 2006 7.1		**24** W	0211 0.8	0814 6.9	1427 0.9 / 2026 6.6
10 W	0219 0.5	0822 7.2	1441 0.6 / 2042 6.9		**25** TH	0240 1.1	0843 6.5	1454 1.2 / 2054 6.3
11 TH	0256 0.7	0900 6.9	1517 0.9 / 2120 6.6		**26** F	0307 1.4	0913 6.1	1521 1.6 / 2124 6.0
12 F	0334 1.0	0941 6.6	1556 1.3 / 2202 6.2		**27** SA	0336 1.8	0945 5.7	1551 2.0 / 2157 5.5
13 SA	0417 1.5	1027 6.0	1642 1.8 / 2255 5.7		**28** SU	0411 2.3	1023 5.2	1629 2.5 / 2241 5.1
14 SU	0514 2.0	1128 5.5	1748 2.3		**29** M	0502 2.7	1118 4.8	1731 2.9 / 2351 4.8
15 M	0009 5.3	0641 2.4	1258 5.1 / 1936 2.5		**30** TU	0641 2.9	1256 4.5	1931 3.0
					31 W	0154 4.8	0836 2.7	1451 4.8 / 2104 2.6

APRIL

Day	Time m	Time m	Time m		Day	Time m	Time m	Time m
1 TH	0318 5.2	0945 2.2	1551 5.3 / 2202 2.1		**16** F	0405 6.2	1033 1.3	1635 6.2 / 2253 1.3
2 F	0408 5.7	1032 1.7	1634 5.9 / 2246 1.6		**17** SA	0452 6.6	1115 1.0	1716 6.5 / 2332 1.0
3 SA	0449 6.3	1112 1.2	1713 6.4 / 2325 1.1		**18** SU	0532 6.8	1152 0.8	1752 6.7
4 SU	0527 6.7	1149 0.8	1749 6.8		**19**	0008 0.8	0608 6.9	1225 0.8 / 1825 6.8
5 M	0003 0.7	0604 7.1	1227 0.5 / 1826 7.1		**20** TU	0041 0.8	0641 6.9	1256 0.9 / 1856 6.8
6 TU	0042 0.4	0642 7.3	1304 0.3 / 1903 7.2		**21** W	0112 0.6	0712 6.8	1326 0.9 / 1925 6.7
7 W	0120 0.3	0721 7.4	1342 0.3 / 1941 7.2		**22** TH	0141 1.0	0743 6.6	1355 1.1 / 1954 6.5
8 TH	0158 0.4	0800 7.2	1419 0.5 / 2020 7.0		**23** F	0210 1.2	0813 6.4	1423 1.3 / 2023 6.3
9 F	0237 0.6	0841 6.9	1458 0.9 / 2101 6.7		**24** SA	0239 1.5	0843 6.1	1451 1.6 / 2054 6.0
10 SA	0319 1.0	0925 6.5	1540 1.4 / 2147 6.3		**25** SU	0310 1.8	0916 5.7	1523 2.0 / 2128 5.7
11 SU	0407 1.5	1016 5.9	1630 1.9 / 2245 5.8		**26** M	0347 2.2	0955 5.3	1602 2.4 / 2212 5.3
12 M	0510 2.0	1123 5.4	1744 2.4		**27** TU	0437 2.5	1048 4.9	1659 2.7 / 2316 5.0
13 TU	0004 5.4	0644 2.3	1256 5.1 / 1932 2.5		**28** W	0557 2.7	1208 4.7	1836 2.8
14 W	0143 5.4	0825 2.1	1435 5.3 / 2102 2.2		**29** TH	0048 4.9	0738 2.6	1350 4.9 / 2009 2.6
15 TH	0306 5.8	0939 1.7	1545 5.7 / 2205 1.7		**30** F	0219 5.2	0851 2.2	1500 5.3 / 2113 2.1

Chapter 5

Chart Datum: 3·71 metres below Ordnance Datum (Newlyn)

WALES – MILFORD HAVEN

YEAR 2004

TIME ZONE (UT)
For Summer Time add ONE hour in **non-shaded areas**

LAT 51°42′N   LONG 5°03′W

TIMES AND HEIGHTS OF HIGH AND LOW WATERS

MAY

Day	Time	m	Day	Time	m
1 SA	0319 / 0945 / 1550 / 2203	5.7 / 1.7 / 5.8 / 1.6	16 SU	0419 / 1041 / 1643 / 2300	6.3 / 1.3 / 6.2 / 1.3
2 SU	0406 / 1031 / 1633 / 2248	6.2 / 1.2 / 6.3 / 1.1	17 M	0500 / 1118 / 1721 / 2337	6.4 / 1.2 / 6.4 / 1.2
3 M	0450 / 1114 / 1715 / 2331	6.7 / 0.8 / 6.8 / 0.8	18 TU	0538 / 1153 / 1755	6.5 / 1.1 / 6.5
4 TU	0532 / 1156 / 1756 O	7.0 / 0.5 / 7.1	19 W	0011 / 0642 / 1226 / 1827 ●	1.2 / 6.5 / 1.1 / 6.5
5 W	0013 / 0615 / 1238 / 1837	0.5 / 7.3 / 0.4 / 7.2	20 TH	0044 / 0645 / 1258 / 1859	1.2 / 6.5 / 1.2 / 6.5
6 TH	0057 / 0658 / 1320 / 1920	0.4 / 7.3 / 0.4 / 7.2	21 F	0117 / 0718 / 1329 / 1930	1.2 / 6.4 / 1.3 / 6.4
7 F	0140 / 0742 / 1402 / 2004	0.4 / 7.1 / 0.7 / 7.0	22 SA	0148 / 0750 / 1400 / 2002	1.4 / 6.2 / 1.4 / 6.3
8 SA	0225 / 0828 / 1446 / 2050	0.7 / 6.8 / 1.0 / 6.7	23 SU	0221 / 0823 / 1432 / 2035	1.6 / 6.0 / 1.7 / 6.0
9 SU	0313 / 0918 / 1533 / 2142	1.0 / 6.3 / 1.5 / 6.3	24 M	0255 / 0858 / 1507 / 2112	1.8 / 5.7 / 1.9 / 5.8
10 M	0407 / 1013 / 1629 / 2243	1.5 / 5.9 / 1.9 / 5.9	25	0335 / 0939 / 1548 / 2157	2.0 / 5.4 / 2.2 / 5.6
11 TU	0514 / 1120 / 1744 / 2356 ◑	1.9 / 5.4 / 2.2 / 5.6	26	0423 / 1030 / 1641 / 2254	2.2 / 5.2 / 2.4 / 5.4
12 W	0636 / 1241 / 1912	2.1 / 5.2 / 2.3	27 TH	0525 / 1133 / 1751 ◐	2.4 / 5.1 / 2.5
13 TH	0118 / 0757 / 1403 / 2030	5.6 / 2.0 / 5.4 / 2.1	28 F	0002 / 0641 / 1248 / 1910	5.3 / 2.3 / 5.1 / 2.4
14 F	0232 / 0905 / 1509 / 2131	5.8 / 1.8 / 5.7 / 1.8	29 SA	0117 / 0752 / 1400 / 2018	5.4 / 2.1 / 5.4 / 2.1
15 SA	0331 / 0957 / 1601 / 2219	6.1 / 1.5 / 6.0 / 1.5	30 SU	0224 / 0853 / 1500 / 2116	5.7 / 1.8 / 5.8 / 1.7
			31 M	0321 / 0948 / 1552 / 2210	6.1 / 1.4 / 6.2 / 1.3

JUNE

Day	Time	m	Day	Time	m
1 TU	0413 / 1039 / 1641 / 2300	6.5 / 1.0 / 6.6 / 1.0	16 W	0509 / 1124 / 1729 / 2347	6.1 / 1.5 / 6.2 / 1.5
2 W	0503 / 1128 / 1729 / 2350	6.8 / 0.8 / 6.9 / 0.7	17 TH	0548 / 1200 / 1805 ●	6.2 / 1.4 / 6.3
3 TH	0553 / 1215 / 1817 O	7.0 / 0.7 / 7.1	18 F	0023 / 0625 / 1236 / 1840	1.4 / 6.2 / 1.4 / 6.3
4 F	0039 / 0642 / 1303 / 1905	0.6 / 7.0 / 0.7 / 7.1	19 SA	0059 / 0700 / 1310 / 1914	1.4 / 6.2 / 1.4 / 6.3
5 SA	0129 / 0731 / 1351 / 1954	0.6 / 6.9 / 0.8 / 7.0	20 SU	0133 / 0735 / 1344 / 1948	1.4 / 6.1 / 1.5 / 6.3
6 SU	0219 / 0822 / 1439 / 2045	0.7 / 6.7 / 1.0 / 6.8	21 M	0208 / 0810 / 1419 / 2023	1.5 / 6.0 / 1.5 / 6.2
7 M	0310 / 0913 / 1529 / 2137	1.0 / 6.4 / 1.3 / 6.5	22 TU	0244 / 0847 / 1455 / 2101	1.6 / 5.9 / 1.7 / 6.1
8 TU	0404 / 1007 / 1624 / 2233	1.3 / 6.0 / 1.7 / 6.2	23 W	0323 / 0926 / 1535 / 2143	1.7 / 5.8 / 1.8 / 5.9
9 W	0503 / 1104 / 1726 / 2334 ◑	1.6 / 5.7 / 1.9 / 5.9	24 TH	0406 / 1010 / 1621 / 2230	1.8 / 5.6 / 2.0 / 5.8
10 TH	0607 / 1208 / 1834	1.8 / 5.5 / 2.1	25 F	0454 / 1101 / 1713 / 2324	1.9 / 5.5 / 2.1 / 5.7
11 F	0039 / 0712 / 1316 / 1942	5.8 / 1.9 / 5.4 / 2.1	26 SA	0551 / 1159 / 1816	2.0 / 5.4 / 2.1
12 SA	0146 / 0816 / 1421 / 2044	5.7 / 1.9 / 5.5 / 2.0	27 SU	0026 / 0656 / 1306 / 1924	5.7 / 2.0 / 5.5 / 2.1
13 SU	0246 / 0913 / 1518 / 2139	5.8 / 1.9 / 5.6 / 1.9	28 M	0134 / 0804 / 1413 / 2032	5.8 / 1.9 / 5.7 / 1.9
14 M	0340 / 1002 / 1607 / 2226	5.9 / 1.7 / 5.8 / 1.7	29 TU	0241 / 0910 / 1516 / 2137	6.0 / 1.6 / 6.0 / 1.6
15 TU	0427 / 1045 / 1650 / 2308	6.0 / 1.6 / 6.0 / 1.6	30 W	0343 / 1011 / 1615 / 2238	6.2 / 1.4 / 6.3 / 1.2

JULY

Day	Time	m	Day	Time	m
1 TH	0443 / 1108 / 1711 / 2335	6.5 / 1.1 / 6.7 / 0.9	16 F	0532 / 1142 / 1749	5.9 / 1.6 / 6.1
2 F	0539 / 1201 / 1805 O	6.7 / 0.9 / 6.9	17 SA	0009 / 0610 / 1220 / 1826 ●	1.6 / 6.1 / 1.5 / 6.3
3 SA	0029 / 0633 / 1253 / 1856	0.7 / 6.8 / 0.8 / 7.1	18 SU	0046 / 0646 / 1255 / 1900	1.4 / 6.2 / 1.4 / 6.4
4 SU	0122 / 0724 / 1342 / 1946	0.6 / 6.9 / 0.8 / 7.1	19 M	0120 / 0721 / 1330 / 1935	1.3 / 6.2 / 1.3 / 6.5
5 M	0212 / 0814 / 1431 / 2035	0.6 / 6.8 / 0.9 / 7.0	20 TU	0154 / 0756 / 1404 / 2009	1.3 / 6.3 / 1.3 / 6.5
6 TU	0301 / 0901 / 1518 / 2123	0.8 / 6.6 / 1.1 / 6.8	21 W	0229 / 0830 / 1440 / 2045	1.3 / 6.2 / 1.3 / 6.4
7 W	0349 / 0948 / 1605 / 2211	1.0 / 6.3 / 1.4 / 6.5	22 TH	0305 / 0907 / 1517 / 2122	1.3 / 6.2 / 1.4 / 6.3
8 TH	0436 / 1035 / 1653 / 2259	1.3 / 5.9 / 1.7 / 6.1	23 F	0342 / 0945 / 1556 / 2203	1.4 / 6.0 / 1.6 / 6.2
9 F	0524 / 1124 / 1744 / 2352 ◑	1.7 / 5.6 / 2.0 / 5.8	24 SA	0423 / 1028 / 1639 / 2249	1.6 / 5.8 / 1.7 / 6.0
10 SA	0617 / 1220 / 1842	2.0 / 5.4 / 2.2	25 SU	0509 / 1118 / 1731 / 2344 ◑	1.8 / 5.7 / 2.0 / 5.8
11 SU	0051 / 0715 / 1324 / 1947	5.5 / 2.2 / 5.2 / 2.3	26 M	0607 / 1220 / 1838	2.0 / 5.5 / 2.1
12 M	0155 / 0819 / 1430 / 2055	5.4 / 2.3 / 5.3 / 2.3	27 TU	0052 / 0721 / 1336 / 1959	5.6 / 2.1 / 5.5 / 2.1
13 TU	0259 / 0921 / 1532 / 2155	5.4 / 2.2 / 5.4 / 2.2	28 W	0211 / 0843 / 1453 / 2119	5.6 / 2.0 / 5.7 / 1.9
14 W	0358 / 1015 / 1624 / 2245	5.6 / 2.0 / 5.7 / 2.0	29 TH	0327 / 0957 / 1602 / 2229	5.8 / 1.7 / 6.1 / 1.5
15 TH	0448 / 1101 / 1710 / 2329	5.7 / 1.8 / 5.9 / 1.8	30 F	0435 / 1059 / 1704 / 2329	6.2 / 1.4 / 6.5 / 1.1
			31 SA	0535 / 1154 / 1758 O	6.5 / 1.0 / 6.9

AUGUST

Day	Time	m	Day	Time	m
1 SU	0023 / 0627 / 1245 / 1848	0.7 / 6.8 / 0.8 / 7.2	16 M	0028 / 0628 / 1237 / 1841 ●	1.3 / 6.4 / 1.2 / 6.6
2 M	0113 / 0714 / 1331 / 1934	0.5 / 6.9 / 0.6 / 7.3	17 TU	0101 / 0701 / 1311 / 1915	1.1 / 6.5 / 1.0 / 6.8
3 TU	0159 / 0758 / 1414 / 2017	0.5 / 6.9 / 0.7 / 7.2	18 W	0134 / 0734 / 1344 / 1948	1.0 / 6.6 / 0.9 / 6.8
4 W	0241 / 0839 / 1455 / 2059	0.6 / 6.8 / 0.8 / 7.0	19 TH	0207 / 0808 / 1418 / 2022	1.0 / 6.6 / 0.9 / 6.8
5 TH	0320 / 0918 / 1533 / 2139	0.9 / 6.5 / 1.1 / 6.7	20 F	0241 / 0842 / 1453 / 2057	1.0 / 6.6 / 1.1 / 6.7
6 F	0358 / 0956 / 1611 / 2218	1.2 / 6.2 / 1.5 / 6.2	21 SA	0316 / 0917 / 1529 / 2135	1.1 / 6.4 / 1.3 / 6.5
7 SA	0435 / 1035 / 1650 / 2300 ◑	1.7 / 5.8 / 1.9 / 5.8	22 SU	0352 / 0957 / 1609 / 2217	1.4 / 6.1 / 1.6 / 6.1
8 SU	0516 / 1119 / 1736 / 2349	2.1 / 5.4 / 2.3 / 5.4	23 M	0434 / 1044 / 1658 / 2311 ◑	1.8 / 5.8 / 2.0 / 5.7
9 M	0607 / 1216 / 1841	2.4 / 5.1 / 2.6	24 TU	0530 / 1146 / 1807	2.2 / 5.5 / 2.3
10 TU	0056 / 0718 / 1338 / 2008	5.1 / 2.7 / 5.0 / 2.7	25 W	0024 / 0654 / 1313 / 1946	5.4 / 2.4 / 5.3 / 2.4
11 W	0221 / 0843 / 1502 / 2131	5.0 / 2.6 / 5.1 / 2.5	26 TH	0159 / 0837 / 1446 / 2119	5.3 / 2.3 / 5.5 / 2.1
12 TH	0336 / 0952 / 1606 / 2229	5.2 / 2.4 / 5.5 / 2.2	27 F	0329 / 0956 / 1602 / 2230	5.6 / 1.9 / 6.0 / 1.5
13 F	0432 / 1043 / 1653 / 2314	5.5 / 2.0 / 5.9 / 1.8	28 SA	0437 / 1056 / 1700 / 2326	6.1 / 1.4 / 6.5 / 1.0
14 SA	0516 / 1125 / 1733 / 2353	5.9 / 1.7 / 6.2 / 1.5	29 SU	0530 / 1147 / 1749	6.6 / 1.0 / 7.0
15 SU	0554 / 1202 / 1808	6.1 / 1.4 / 6.4	30 M	0013 / 0615 / 1232 / 1833 O	0.6 / 6.9 / 0.7 / 7.3
			31 TU	0057 / 0656 / 1312 / 1914	0.4 / 7.1 / 0.5 / 7.4

Chart Datum: 3·71 metres below Ordnance Datum (Newlyn)

WALES – MILFORD HAVEN

LAT 51°42′N   LONG 5°03′W

TIMES AND HEIGHTS OF HIGH AND LOW WATERS

YEAR **2004**

SEPTEMBER

Day	Time m	Time m	Time m	Time m		Day	Time m	Time m	Time m	Time m
1 W	0136 0.4	0734 7.1	1952 7.3			16 TH	0108 0.7	0707 7.0	1320 0.7	1922 7.2
2 TH	0212 0.6	0810 6.9	1425 0.8	2028 7.1		17 F	0142 0.7	0741 7.0	1354 0.7	1957 7.1
3 F	0245 0.9	0843 6.7	1457 1.1	2102 6.7		18 SA	0216 0.8	0815 6.9	1429 0.9	2032 6.9
4 SA	0317 1.2	0915 6.3	1529 1.5	2135 6.3		19 SU	0250 1.1	0852 6.6	1506 1.2	2111 6.6
5 SU	0347 1.7	0948 5.9	1600 1.9	2210 5.8		20 M	0327 1.4	0932 6.3	1547 1.6	2154 6.1
6 M	0419 2.1	1025 5.5	1637 2.4	2252 5.3		21 TU	0410 1.9	1021 5.8	1640 2.1	2251 5.6
7 TU	0501 2.6	1113 5.1	1736 2.8	2352 4.8		22 W	0510 2.4	1130 5.4	1800 2.5	
8 W	0613 2.9	1234 4.8	1922 3.0			23 TH	0015 5.2	0651 2.7	1309 5.3	1954 2.5
9 TH	0141 4.7	0806 3.0	1434 4.9	2108 2.8		24 F	0205 5.2	0840 2.4	1448 5.6	2122 2.0
10 F	0316 5.0	0930 2.6	1544 5.4	2209 2.3		25 SA	0331 5.7	0953 1.9	1557 6.2	2225 1.4
11 SA	0412 5.4	1022 2.2	1630 5.8	2252 1.8		26 SU	0429 6.2	1047 1.4	1648 6.7	2313 1.0
12 SU	0453 5.9	1102 1.7	1708 6.3	2328 1.4		27 M	0515 6.7	1131 1.0	1737 7.1	2355 0.7
13 M	0529 6.3	1138 1.3	1742 6.6			28 TU	0555 7.0	1211 0.7	1812 7.3	O
14 TU	0002 1.1	0602 6.6	1212 1.0	1815 6.9		29 W	0032 0.5	0631 7.1	1247 0.6	1848 7.3
15 W	0035 0.9	0634 6.6	1246 0.8	1848 7.1		30 TH	0107 0.6	0705 7.1	1321 0.7	1922 7.2

OCTOBER

Day	Time m	Time m	Time m	Time m		Day	Time m	Time m	Time m	Time m
1 F	0139 0.7	0737 7.0	1353 0.9	1955 7.0		16 SA	0116 0.6	0715 7.2	1332 0.7	1933 7.2
2 SA	0209 1.0	0808 6.7	1423 1.2	2026 6.6		17 SU	0153 0.8	0753 7.1	1410 0.9	2013 7.0
3 SU	0238 1.3	0838 6.4	1452 1.6	2057 6.2		18 M	0231 1.1	0833 6.8	1452 1.2	2056 6.6
4 M	0306 1.8	0908 6.0	1521 2.0	2130 5.8		19 TU	0312 1.5	0918 6.4	1539 1.7	2145 6.0
5 TU	0335 2.2	0942 5.6	1556 2.4	2208 5.3		20 W	0401 2.0	1014 5.9	1639 2.1	2249 5.5
6 W	0413 2.6	1027 5.2	1648 2.9	2304 4.8		21 TH	0509 2.5	1129 5.5	1810 2.4	
7 TH	0516 3.0	1139 4.8	1834 3.1			22 F	0018 5.2	0656 2.7	1306 5.5	1951 2.3
8 F	0047 4.6	0719 3.1	1348 4.9	2029 2.9		23 SA	0200 5.3	0830 2.4	1434 5.8	2109 1.9
9 SA	0241 4.9	0852 2.6	1507 5.3	2134 2.4		24 SU	0315 5.8	0936 1.9	1537 6.3	2205 1.5
10 SU	0338 5.4	0947 2.3	1554 5.8	2217 1.9		25 M	0408 6.3	1026 1.4	1626 6.7	2250 1.1
11 M	0419 5.9	1029 1.8	1633 6.3	2255 1.4		26 TU	0451 6.6	1108 1.1	1708 7.0	2329 0.9
12 TU	0455 6.4	1106 1.3	1709 6.7	2330 1.1		27 W	0530 6.8	1145 0.9	1746 7.1	
13 W	0530 6.7	1142 1.0	1744 7.0			28 TH	0004 0.9	0604 6.9	1220 0.9	1821 7.1
14 TH	0004 0.8	0604 7.0	1218 0.8	1819 7.2		29 F	0037 0.9	0637 6.9	1253 1.0	1854 7.0
15 F	0040 0.6	0639 7.2	1255 0.6	1856 7.3		30 SA	0108 1.0	0708 6.8	1324 1.1	1926 6.8
						31 SU	0138 1.2	0738 6.7	1355 1.4	1957 6.5

NOVEMBER

Day	Time m	Time m	Time m	Time m		Day	Time m	Time m	Time m	Time m
1 M	0207 1.5	0809 6.4	1425 1.7	2029 6.2		16 TU	0220 1.2	0824 6.9	1447 1.2	2051 6.5
2 TU	0236 1.8	0840 6.1	1457 2.0	2102 5.8		17 W	0307 1.5	0915 6.5	1540 1.6	2146 6.1
3 W	0308 2.2	0915 5.8	1534 2.4	2141 5.4		18 TH	0402 2.0	1015 6.2	1644 1.9	2250 5.7
4 TH	0346 2.6	0959 5.4	1623 2.7	2234 5.0		19 F	0512 2.3	1124 5.9	1804 2.1	
5 F	0443 2.9	1102 5.1	1744 2.9	2352 4.8		20 SA	0006 5.4	0637 2.4	1244 5.8	1925 2.1
6 SA	0619 3.0	1233 5.0	1925 2.8			21 SU	0129 5.5	0757 2.3	1400 5.9	2035 1.9
7 SU	0134 4.9	0752 2.8	1405 5.3	2037 2.5		22 M	0239 5.7	0903 2.0	1503 6.2	2132 1.7
8 M	0245 5.4	0856 2.4	1503 5.7	2129 2.0		23 TU	0335 6.1	0955 1.7	1555 6.4	2219 1.5
9 TU	0333 5.8	0945 1.9	1548 6.2	2213 1.6		24 W	0421 6.3	1040 1.5	1640 6.6	2259 1.3
10 W	0414 6.3	1028 1.5	1630 6.6	2253 1.2		25 TH	0502 6.5	1119 1.4	1720 6.7	2336 1.3
11 TH	0454 6.7	1109 1.1	1710 7.0	2333 0.9		26 F	0538 6.6	1155 1.3	1756 6.7	O
12 F	0533 7.0	1150 0.9	1752 7.2	●		27 SA	0010 1.3	0612 6.7	1230 1.3	1831 6.6
13 SA	0013 0.7	0613 7.2	1232 0.7	1833 7.3		28 SU	0043 1.5	0645 6.6	1304 1.4	1905 6.5
14 SU	0055 0.7	0655 7.2	1315 0.7	1917 7.2		29 M	0116 1.4	0718 6.6	1337 1.5	1938 6.3
15 M	0137 0.9	0738 7.1	1400 0.9	2002 6.9		30 TU	0147 1.6	0750 6.4	1409 1.7	2012 6.1

DECEMBER

Day	Time m	Time m	Time m	Time m		Day	Time m	Time m	Time m	Time m
1 W	0219 1.8	0824 6.2	1443 1.9	2047 5.9		16 TH	0305 1.3	0913 6.8	1539 1.2	2141 6.3
2 TH	0253 2.0	0901 6.0	1521 2.1	2126 5.6		17 F	0358 1.6	1007 6.6	1635 1.5	2236 6.0
3 F	0332 2.3	0943 5.7	1606 2.4	2213 5.3		18 SA	0456 1.9	1104 6.3	1736 1.8	◐ 2335 5.7
4 SA	0421 2.5	1034 5.5	1703 2.5	2310 5.1		19 SU	0600 2.1	1206 6.0	1840 2.0	
5 SU	0524 2.7	1137 5.4	1815 2.6	O		20 M	0041 5.6	0708 2.2	1313 5.9	1945 2.1
6 M	0018 5.1	0641 2.7	1248 5.4	1927 2.4		21 TU	0149 5.5	0815 2.2	1418 5.8	2048 2.1
7 TU	0132 5.3	0753 2.5	1358 5.6	2031 2.2		22 W	0252 5.7	0917 2.1	1518 5.9	2143 2.0
8 W	0236 5.6	0853 2.1	1458 6.0	2127 1.8		23 TH	0348 5.8	1010 1.9	1611 6.0	2230 1.8
9 TH	0330 6.0	0948 1.7	1551 6.3	2217 1.5		24 F	0436 6.1	1056 1.8	1657 6.1	2312 1.7
10 F	0419 6.5	1038 1.4	1641 6.7	2306 1.2		25 SA	0518 6.2	1137 1.7	1739 6.2	2351 1.6
11 SA	0507 6.8	1128 1.1	1730 6.9	2353 1.0		26 SU	0557 6.4	1215 1.6	1817 6.3	O
12 SU	0554 7.1	1217 0.8	1819 7.1	●		27 M	0027 1.5	0632 6.5	1252 1.5	1853 6.3
13 M	0040 0.9	0642 7.2	1306 0.8	1908 7.1		28 TU	0102 1.5	0707 6.5	1326 1.5	1927 6.3
14 TU	0128 0.9	0731 7.2	1356 0.8	1958 6.9		29 W	0135 1.5	0740 6.5	1359 1.5	2001 6.2
15 W	0216 1.0	0821 7.1	1446 1.0	2049 6.7		30 TH	0208 1.6	0814 6.4	1433 1.6	2035 6.1
						31 F	0242 1.7	0848 6.3	1508 1.7	2110 5.9

Chart Datum: 3·71 metres below Ordnance Datum (Newlyn)

Chapter 5

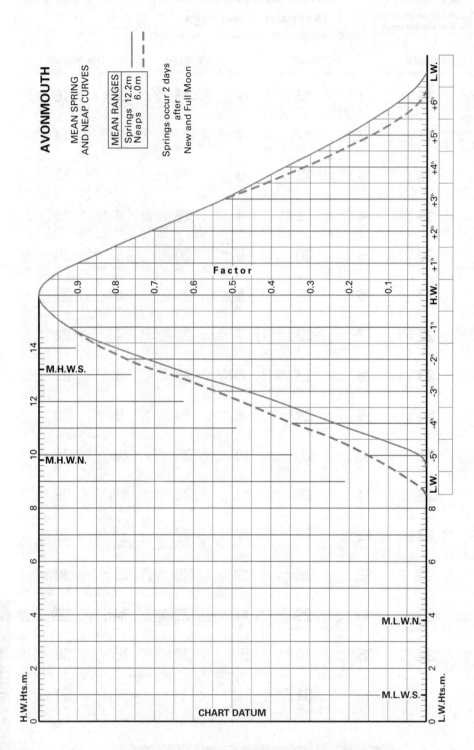

AVONMOUTH

MEAN SPRING
AND NEAP CURVES

MEAN RANGES
Springs 12.2m
Neaps 6.0m

Springs occur 2 days
after
New and Full Moon

ENGLAND – AVONMOUTH

YEAR 2004

LAT 51°30′N   LONG 2°44′W

TIMES AND HEIGHTS OF HIGH AND LOW WATERS

Time m

JANUARY

1 TH — 0133 10.1 / 0733 3.8 / 1415 10.1 / 2010 3.6
2 F — 0241 10.0 / 0838 3.9 / 1516 10.3 / 2117 3.6
3 SA — 0342 10.3 / 0955 3.7 / 1613 10.6 / 2229 3.2
4 SU — 0437 10.8 / 1103 3.1 / 1705 11.0 / 2330 2.7
5 M — 0526 11.3 / 1157 2.6 / 1752 11.5
6 TU — 0020 2.2 / 0610 11.8 / 1246 2.2 / 1835 11.8
7 W ○ — 0107 1.9 / 0651 12.2 / 1916 12.0
8 TH — 0151 1.8 / 0731 12.3 / 1415 2.1 / 1956 12.0
9 F — 0233 1.9 / 0810 12.3 / 1455 2.2 / 2035 12.0
10 SA — 0310 2.0 / 0846 12.3 / 1531 2.3 / 2111 12.0
11 SU — 0342 2.1 / 0922 12.2 / 1602 2.3 / 2146 11.9
12 M — 0413 2.2 / 0958 12.1 / 1634 2.3 / 2222 11.8
13 TU — 0446 2.2 / 1037 12.0 / 1709 2.3 / 2302 11.6
14 W — 0525 2.3 / 1120 11.7 / 1749 2.5 / 2347 11.3
15 TH ◐ — 0609 2.6 / 1211 11.4 / 1836 2.8

16 F — 0040 10.9 / 0701 3.0 / 1312 11.0 / 1932 3.2
17 SA — 0148 10.5 / 0810 3.4 / 1428 10.7 / 2053 3.5
18 SU — 0313 10.5 / 0949 3.4 / 1551 10.9 / 2238 3.3
19 M — 0432 11.1 / 1112 2.9 / 1703 11.5 / 2349 2.6
20 TU — 0536 11.9 / 1218 2.2 / 1804 12.2
21 W ● — 0050 2.0 / 0631 12.6 / 1318 1.7 / 1859 12.7
22 TH — 0147 1.5 / 0722 13.2 / 1413 1.3 / 1950 13.1
23 F — 0239 1.2 / 0811 13.5 / 1504 1.0 / 2037 13.3
24 SA — 0325 1.1 / 0856 13.5 / 1549 1.0 / 2121 13.2
25 SU — 0405 1.3 / 0938 13.3 / 1626 1.3 / 2159 12.8
26 M — 0436 1.6 / 1015 12.9 / 1654 1.7 / 2234 12.3
27 TU — 0459 2.0 / 1049 12.3 / 1718 2.1 / 2304 11.7
28 W — 0523 2.4 / 1122 11.6 / 1745 2.5 / 2336 11.1
29 TH ◑ — 0553 2.8 / 1159 10.8 / 1820 2.9
30 F — 0015 10.4 / 0633 3.3 / 1248 10.1 / 1905 3.5
31 SA — 0110 9.8 / 0727 3.9 / 1356 9.6 / 2008 3.9

FEBRUARY

1 SU — 0228 9.6 / 0842 4.1 / 1518 9.6 / 2126 3.9
2 M — 0350 9.9 / 1006 3.8 / 1629 10.1 / 2245 3.4
3 TU — 0455 10.6 / 1120 3.2 / 1726 10.8 / 2349 2.7
4 W — 0547 11.3 / 1219 2.5 / 1815 11.5
5 TH — 0022 2.2 / 0633 12.0 / 1312 2.1 / 1859 12.0
6 F ○ — 0135 1.9 / 0715 12.4 / 1403 1.9 / 1942 12.3
7 SA — 0223 1.8 / 0756 12.6 / 1450 1.8 / 2021 12.5
8 SU — 0306 1.7 / 0834 12.8 / 1530 1.8 / 2058 12.6
9 M — 0341 1.7 / 0910 12.8 / 1602 1.8 / 2133 12.6
10 TU — 0410 1.7 / 0945 12.8 / 1628 1.8 / 2206 12.6
11 W — 0437 1.7 / 1020 12.7 / 1654 1.8 / 2242 12.3
12 TH — 0507 1.8 / 1059 12.4 / 1725 2.0 / 2321 11.9
13 F ◐ — 0543 2.2 / 1143 11.7 / 1803 2.5
14 SA — 0007 11.1 / 0626 2.8 / 1237 10.9 / 1850 3.2
15 SU — 0108 10.4 / 0725 3.5 / 1352 10.2 / 1959 3.9

16 M — 0241 9.9 / 0918 4.0 / 1533 10.1 / 2221 3.9
17 TU — 0418 10.4 / 1102 3.3 / 1656 10.8 / 2339 3.0
18 W — 0529 11.4 / 1210 2.4 / 1759 11.4
19 TH — 0041 2.1 / 0625 12.4 / 1309 1.6 / 1852 12.6
20 F ● — 0136 1.4 / 0714 13.2 / 1403 1.0 / 1939 13.2
21 SA — 0227 0.9 / 0758 13.7 / 1451 0.6 / 2022 13.5
22 SU — 0311 0.7 / 0840 13.8 / 1532 0.6 / 2101 13.4
23 M — 0348 0.8 / 0916 13.6 / 1606 0.9 / 2134 13.1
24 TU — 0416 1.3 / 0948 13.1 / 1629 1.4 / 2202 12.7
25 W — 0433 1.7 / 1015 12.5 / 1645 1.8 / 2226 12.1
26 TH — 0448 2.0 / 1042 11.8 / 1705 2.1 / 2252 11.5
27 F — 0511 2.4 / 1110 11.1 / 1731 2.6 / 2323 10.8
28 SA ◑ — 0542 2.9 / 1145 10.2 / 1807 3.3
29 SU — 0002 10.0 / 0626 3.7 / 1239 9.4 / 1903 4.0

MARCH

1 M — 0110 9.3 / 0741 4.3 / 1416 9.0 / 2035 4.4
2 TU — 0302 9.2 / 0920 4.3 / 1555 9.4 / 2207 3.9
3 W — 0425 10.0 / 1050 3.5 / 1702 10.4 / 2323 3.1
4 TH — 0523 11.0 / 1158 2.7 / 1753 11.3
5 F — 0023 2.3 / 0611 11.9 / 1255 2.1 / 1838 12.1
6 SA ○ — 0117 1.9 / 0654 12.5 / 1347 1.7 / 1920 12.6
7 SU — 0206 1.6 / 0735 13.0 / 1434 1.5 / 2000 13.0
8 M — 0250 1.4 / 0814 13.2 / 1515 1.3 / 2037 13.1
9 TU — 0327 1.3 / 0850 13.4 / 1547 1.3 / 2111 13.2
10 W — 0356 1.2 / 0925 13.4 / 1612 1.4 / 2145 13.1
11 TH — 0421 1.3 / 1001 13.1 / 1634 1.6 / 2220 12.7
12 F — 0447 1.5 / 1039 12.6 / 1700 1.9 / 2258 12.1
13 SA ◑ — 0519 2.0 / 1120 11.7 / 1734 2.5 / 2342 11.1
14 SU — 0559 2.8 / 1213 10.6 / 1819 3.5
15 M — 0042 10.0 / 0658 3.8 / 1335 9.6 / 1931 4.4

16 TU — 0235 9.5 / 0922 4.2 / 1531 9.7 / 2218 4.1
17 W — 0412 10.2 / 1055 3.3 / 1650 10.6 / 2328 2.9
18 TH — 0519 11.4 / 1157 2.2 / 1748 11.8
19 F — 0024 1.9 / 0611 12.5 / 1251 1.3 / 1836 12.7
20 SA ● — 0115 1.1 / 0656 13.3 / 1340 0.7 / 1919 13.3
21 SU — 0203 0.7 / 0737 13.7 / 1425 0.5 / 1958 13.5
22 M — 0245 0.5 / 0815 13.7 / 1505 0.5 / 2033 13.4
23 TU — 0321 0.8 / 0849 13.4 / 1537 0.9 / 2103 13.1
24 W — 0348 1.2 / 0917 12.9 / 1558 1.4 / 2128 12.6
25 TH — 0403 1.7 / 0942 12.4 / 1611 1.8 / 2151 12.1
26 F — 0414 1.9 / 1005 11.8 / 1626 2.0 / 2214 11.6
27 SA — 0434 2.2 / 1030 11.1 / 1650 2.4 / 2240 11.0
28 SU ◑ — 0502 2.7 / 1101 10.3 / 1721 3.1 / 2316 10.2
29 M — 0540 3.4 / 1147 9.5 / 1808 3.9
30 TU — 0013 9.4 / 0643 4.2 / 1310 8.8 / 1938 4.6
31 W — 0205 9.0 / 0837 4.4 / 1517 9.1 / 2130 4.2

APRIL

1 TH — 0349 9.7 / 1015 3.7 / 1630 10.2 / 2252 3.3
2 F — 0451 10.8 / 1130 2.8 / 1724 11.3 / 2355 2.5
3 SA — 0541 11.8 / 1227 2.1 / 1810 12.2
4 SU — 0048 1.8 / 0625 12.6 / 1319 1.6 / 1851 12.9
5 M ○ — 0139 1.4 / 0707 13.2 / 1406 1.2 / 1932 13.3
6 TU — 0223 1.1 / 0747 13.5 / 1447 1.1 / 2010 13.5
7 W — 0302 0.9 / 0826 13.7 / 1522 1.0 / 2047 13.6
8 TH — 0335 0.9 / 0905 13.6 / 1550 1.2 / 2124 13.4
9 F — 0403 1.1 / 0943 13.2 / 1615 1.5 / 2201 12.8
10 SA — 0432 1.5 / 1023 12.5 / 1642 2.0 / 2241 12.0
11 SU — 0505 2.1 / 1107 11.4 / 1717 2.8 / 2328 10.9
12 M ◑ — 0548 3.0 / 1203 10.3 / 1805 3.8
13 TU — 0037 9.9 / 0659 3.9 / 1341 9.5 / 1954 4.5
14 W — 0236 9.7 / 0917 3.9 / 1520 9.8 / 2200 3.8
15 TH — 0354 10.4 / 1032 3.0 / 1628 10.8 / 2303 2.7

16 F — 0455 11.5 / 1129 2.0 / 1723 11.8 / 2355 1.8
17 SA — 0545 12.4 / 1220 1.2 / 1809 12.6
18 SU — 0043 1.1 / 0629 13.0 / 1307 0.8 / 1850 13.0
19 M ● — 0130 0.8 / 0708 13.3 / 1351 0.7 / 1927 13.2
20 TU — 0212 0.8 / 0745 13.2 / 1430 0.8 / 2000 13.0
21 W — 0248 1.0 / 0817 12.9 / 1503 1.2 / 2029 12.7
22 TH — 0317 1.5 / 0846 12.5 / 1526 1.6 / 2055 12.4
23 F — 0334 1.8 / 0912 12.0 / 1540 1.9 / 2119 12.0
24 SA — 0346 2.0 / 0936 11.6 / 1557 2.1 / 2143 11.5
25 SU — 0407 2.2 / 1002 11.0 / 1621 2.4 / 2212 11.0
26 M — 0437 2.6 / 1035 10.4 / 1654 2.9 / 2250 10.4
27 TU ◑ — 0515 3.2 / 1122 9.8 / 1738 3.6 / 2345 9.7
28 W — 0612 3.8 / 1232 9.2 / 1852 4.2
29 TH — 0109 9.3 / 0750 4.1 / 1419 9.3 / 2042 4.2
30 F — 0258 9.6 / 0925 3.7 / 1544 10.1 / 2206 3.4

Chart Datum: 6·50 metres below Ordnance Datum (Newlyn)

Chapter 5

TIME ZONE (UT)
For Summer Time add ONE hour in **non-shaded areas**

ENGLAND – AVONMOUTH

LAT 51°30'N   LONG 2°44'W

TIMES AND HEIGHTS OF HIGH AND LOW WATERS

YEAR 2004

MAY

Time m	Time m
1 SA 0408 10.7 / 1043 2.9 / 1644 11.1 / 2313 2.6	**16** SU 0510 12.0 / 1141 1.7 / 1734 12.1
2 SU 0503 11.7 / 1147 2.2 / 1734 12.1	**17** M 0006 1.6 / 0554 12.4 / 1229 1.4 / 1815 12.4
3 M 0010 1.9 / 0551 12.6 / 1241 1.6 / 1818 12.9	**18** TU 0052 1.3 / 0635 12.6 / 1313 1.3 / 1852 12.6
4 TU 0102 1.4 / 0636 13.2 / 1331 1.2 / ○ 1901 13.4	**19** W 0135 1.3 / 0712 12.5 / 1354 1.3 / ● 1927 12.5
5 W 0150 1.0 / 0720 13.6 / 1415 1.0 / 1943 13.6	**20** TH 0213 1.5 / 0747 12.3 / 1429 1.5 / 1959 12.4
6 TH 0234 0.8 / 0803 13.7 / 1455 1.1 / 2025 13.6	**21** F 0245 1.8 / 0819 12.0 / 1457 1.8 / 2029 12.1
7 F 0313 0.8 / 0847 13.5 / 1531 1.1 / 2106 13.4	**22** SA 0309 2.0 / 0849 11.7 / 1519 2.0 / 2057 11.8
8 SA 0350 1.0 / 0930 13.1 / 1603 1.5 / 2149 12.8	**23** SU 0329 2.2 / 0918 11.4 / 1540 2.2 / 2126 11.5
9 SU 0425 1.5 / 1015 12.3 / 1637 2.0 / 2234 11.9	**24** M 0354 2.3 / 0949 11.0 / 1608 2.4 / 2158 11.1
10 M 0505 2.2 / 1104 11.3 / 1716 2.9 / 2327 11.0	**25** TU 0426 2.6 / 1025 10.7 / 1643 2.7 / 2238 10.7
11 TU 0555 3.0 / 1205 10.4 / 1812 3.7 / ◑	**26** W 0506 2.9 / 1111 10.2 / 1727 3.2 / 2330 10.3
12 W 0044 10.2 / 0709 3.5 / 1332 9.9 / 1952 4.0	**27** TH 0600 3.3 / 1210 9.9 / 1829 3.6 / ◑
13 TH 0214 10.2 / 0843 3.4 / 1450 10.2 / 2123 3.6	**28** F 0037 10.0 / 0711 3.5 / 1324 9.9 / 1949 3.7
14 F 0322 10.7 / 0953 2.9 / 1553 10.8 / 2224 2.8	**29** SA 0158 10.2 / 0831 3.3 / 1444 10.3 / 2112 3.3
15 SA 0419 11.4 / 1050 2.2 / 1647 11.5 / 2318 2.1	**30** SU 0313 10.8 / 0949 2.9 / 1555 11.0 / 2225 2.7
	31 M 0418 11.5 / 1101 2.4 / 1654 11.8 / 2330 2.1

JUNE

Time m	Time m
1 TU 0515 12.3 / 1203 1.9 / 1746 12.6	**16** W 0013 2.1 / 0601 11.7 / 1235 1.9 / 1819 11.9
2 W 0027 1.6 / 0607 12.9 / 1257 1.4 / 1834 13.1	**17** TH 0059 1.9 / 0642 11.8 / 1319 1.8 / ● 1858 12.1
3 TH 0120 1.2 / 0657 13.2 / 1348 1.2 / ○ 1921 13.4	**18** F 0141 1.9 / 0721 11.8 / 1359 1.8 / 1936 12.1
4 F 0210 0.9 / 0745 13.4 / 1435 1.1 / 2008 13.5	**19** SA 0220 2.0 / 0759 11.7 / 1436 1.9 / 2012 12.0
5 SA 0258 0.9 / 0834 13.2 / 1519 1.2 / 2055 13.3	**20** SU 0254 2.2 / 0835 11.6 / 1507 2.1 / 2046 11.8
6 SU 0343 1.1 / 0923 12.9 / 1600 1.5 / 2142 12.8	**21** M 0324 2.3 / 0910 11.4 / 1535 2.3 / 2119 11.6
7 M 0426 1.4 / 1011 12.4 / 1640 2.0 / 2231 12.2	**22** TU 0353 2.4 / 0944 11.2 / 1605 2.4 / 2153 11.4
8 TU 0509 1.9 / 1100 11.7 / 1722 2.5 / 2324 11.5	**23** W 0425 2.5 / 1020 11.1 / 1639 2.5 / 2231 11.2
9 W 0556 2.4 / 1155 11.0 / 1811 3.1 / ◑	**24** TH 0503 2.6 / 1100 10.9 / 1720 2.7 / 2316 11.0
10 TH 0026 11.0 / 0649 2.8 / 1259 10.6 / 1910 3.4	**25** F 0548 2.7 / 1148 10.7 / 1809 2.9 / ◐
11 F 0136 10.7 / 0750 3.0 / 1406 10.4 / 2020 3.5	**26** SA 0009 10.8 / 0640 2.9 / 1245 10.6 / 1907 3.1
12 SA 0239 10.7 / 0854 3.0 / 1506 10.5 / 2129 3.2	**27** SU 0113 10.7 / 0741 3.0 / 1351 10.5 / 2018 3.2
13 SU 0336 10.9 / 0957 2.8 / 1602 10.8 / 2231 2.9	**28** M 0224 10.8 / 0854 3.1 / 1505 10.8 / 2140 3.0
14 M 0429 11.2 / 1055 2.5 / 1653 11.3 / 2325 2.4	**29** TU 0337 11.2 / 1020 2.8 / 1617 11.3 / 2256 2.5
15 TU 0517 11.5 / 1147 2.2 / 1738 11.7	**30** W 0445 11.7 / 1132 2.4 / 1720 12.0

JULY

Time m	Time m
1 TH 0001 2.0 / 0545 12.2 / 1233 1.9 / 1814 12.6	**16** F 0027 2.4 / 0618 11.4 / 1249 2.1 / 1837 11.8
2 F 0100 1.5 / 0641 12.7 / 1330 1.5 / ○ 1907 13.1	**17** SA 0116 2.1 / 0702 11.6 / 1337 1.9 / ● 1919 12.1
3 SA 0157 1.2 / 0734 13.0 / 1424 1.3 / 1958 13.3	**18** SU 0203 2.1 / 0744 11.8 / 1422 1.9 / 1958 12.1
4 SU 0251 1.0 / 0826 13.1 / 1514 1.2 / 2047 13.4	**19** M 0247 2.1 / 0824 11.8 / 1503 2.0 / 2036 12.1
5 M 0340 1.0 / 0916 13.0 / 1600 1.3 / 2135 13.2	**20** TU 0326 2.2 / 0901 11.8 / 1537 2.2 / 2111 12.0
6 TU 0425 1.1 / 1002 12.8 / 1640 1.6 / 2221 12.8	**21** W 0358 2.3 / 0935 11.7 / 1606 2.2 / 2144 11.9
7 W 0505 1.4 / 1046 12.3 / 1716 2.0 / 2306 12.3	**22** TH 0425 2.3 / 1008 11.7 / 1634 2.2 / 2218 11.9
8 TH 0541 1.9 / 1129 11.7 / 1750 2.4 / 2352 11.6	**23** F 0454 2.3 / 1043 11.6 / 1707 2.3 / 2257 11.7
9 F 0616 2.3 / 1214 11.1 / 1827 2.9 / ◑	**24** SA 0529 2.3 / 1123 11.4 / 1745 2.4 / 2341 11.4
10 SA 0043 11.0 / 0655 2.8 / 1305 10.5 / 1911 3.3	**25** SU 0609 2.5 / 1210 11.0 / 1831 2.8 / ◐
11 SU 0141 10.5 / 0743 3.1 / 1405 10.2 / 2007 3.6	**26** M 0035 11.0 / 0658 2.9 / 1309 10.6 / 1929 3.3
12 M 0243 10.3 / 0841 3.4 / 1508 10.1 / 2118 3.7	**27** TU 0143 10.6 / 0802 3.4 / 1424 10.4 / 2056 3.5
13 TU 0344 10.3 / 0952 3.4 / 1609 10.4 / 2234 3.3	**28** W 0305 10.6 / 0945 3.5 / 1550 10.6 / 2234 3.2
14 W 0440 10.6 / 1101 3.0 / 1704 10.9 / 2336 2.8	**29** TH 0426 11.0 / 1114 3.0 / 1704 11.4 / 2348 2.5
15 TH 0532 11.0 / 1158 2.5 / 1753 11.4	**30** F 0534 11.7 / 1221 2.3 / 1805 12.2
	31 SA 0051 1.8 / 0633 12.4 / 1322 1.7 / ○ 1859 13.0

AUGUST

Time m	Time m
1 SU 0151 1.2 / 0727 12.9 / 1418 1.2 / 1949 13.5	**16** M 0149 1.9 / 0726 12.1 / 1409 1.8 / ● 1942 12.5
2 M 0245 0.8 / 0817 13.3 / 1509 0.9 / 2037 13.7	**17** TU 0237 1.8 / 0806 12.2 / 1454 1.8 / 2019 12.6
3 TU 0333 0.6 / 0903 13.4 / 1552 0.9 / 2121 13.7	**18** W 0318 1.9 / 0842 12.3 / 1531 1.9 / 2054 12.5
4 W 0415 0.7 / 0944 13.2 / 1629 1.1 / 2201 13.3	**19** TH 0352 2.0 / 0916 12.3 / 1559 2.0 / 2126 12.5
5 TH 0448 1.1 / 1021 12.7 / 1657 1.6 / 2237 12.7	**20** F 0416 2.1 / 0947 12.2 / 1621 2.0 / 2158 12.4
6 F 0514 1.6 / 1054 12.1 / 1718 2.1 / 2311 11.9	**21** SA 0436 2.1 / 1020 12.1 / 1647 2.0 / 2234 12.2
7 SA 0537 2.1 / 1126 11.4 / 1743 2.6 / ◑ 2345 11.1	**22** SU 0503 2.2 / 1056 11.7 / 1718 2.3 / 2314 11.7
8 SU 0606 2.7 / 1201 10.7 / 1817 3.2	**23** M 0536 2.5 / 1139 11.2 / 1757 2.8
9 M 0028 10.3 / 0645 3.3 / 1250 10.0 / 1904 3.8	**24** TU 0004 10.9 / 0618 3.1 / 1234 10.4 / 1849 3.6
10 TU 0132 9.6 / 0741 3.8 / 1404 9.5 / 2014 4.2	**25** W 0111 10.1 / 0718 3.9 / 1356 9.8 / 2024 4.2
11 W 0256 9.4 / 0856 4.0 / 1528 9.7 / 2142 4.1	**26** TH 0251 9.8 / 0938 4.2 / 1542 10.1 / 2232 3.6
12 TH 0409 9.8 / 1021 3.6 / 1636 10.3 / 2306 3.4	**27** F 0423 10.5 / 1111 3.3 / 1659 11.1 / 2345 2.6
13 F 0509 10.5 / 1131 2.9 / 1731 11.1	**28** SA 0531 11.5 / 1215 2.3 / 1759 12.3
14 SA 0006 2.6 / 0559 11.2 / 1228 2.3 / 1818 11.8	**29** SU 0044 1.6 / 0626 12.5 / 1313 1.5 / 1850 13.2
15 SU 0059 2.1 / 0644 11.8 / 1320 2.0 / 1901 12.3	**30** M 0140 0.9 / 0715 13.2 / 1405 0.9 / ○ 1936 13.8
	31 TU 0230 0.7 / 0800 13.6 / 1452 0.5 / 2019 14.0

Chart Datum: 6·50 metres below Ordnance Datum (Newlyn)

TIME ZONE (UT)
For Summer Time add ONE hour in **non-shaded areas**

ENGLAND – AVONMOUTH

LAT 51°30'N   LONG 2°44'W

TIMES AND HEIGHTS OF HIGH AND LOW WATERS

SEPTEMBER

Time m	Time m
1 0315 0.3 / 0841 13.6 / W 1533 0.6 / 2058 13.9	**16** 0257 1.6 / 0816 12.8 / TH 1510 1.6 / 2029 13.1
2 0352 0.6 / 0918 13.4 / TH 1606 1.0 / 2133 13.5	**17** 0331 1.7 / 0850 12.8 / F 1540 1.7 / 2102 13.0
3 0421 1.1 / 0949 12.9 / F 1628 1.6 / 2203 12.8	**18** 0355 1.8 / 0922 12.7 / SA 1602 1.8 / 2136 12.8
4 0440 1.7 / 1016 12.2 / SA 1642 2.1 / 2229 12.0	**19** 0413 2.0 / 0956 12.4 / SU 1625 2.0 / 2212 12.4
5 0455 2.2 / 1041 11.5 / SU 1700 2.5 / 2256 11.1	**20** 0437 2.2 / 1032 11.9 / M 1655 2.3 / 2252 11.6
6 0518 2.7 / 1109 10.8 / M 1726 3.1 / ◑ 2328 10.2	**21** 0508 2.7 / 1115 11.1 / TU 1731 3.0 / ◑ 2341 10.6
7 0549 3.4 / 1147 9.9 / TU 1805 3.9	**22** 0549 3.5 / 1211 10.1 / W 1824 4.0
8 0018 9.3 / 0639 4.1 / W 1254 9.2 / 1914 4.6	**23** 0055 9.6 / 0651 4.4 / TH 1355 9.5 / 2046 4.5
9 0207 8.8 / 0810 4.6 / TH 1455 9.1 / 2104 4.6	**24** 0258 9.5 / 0950 4.3 / F 1542 10.1 / 2231 3.5
10 0344 9.3 / 0951 4.2 / F 1612 10.0 / 2248 3.8	**25** 0420 10.5 / 1103 3.1 / SA 1651 11.3 / 2333 2.3
11 0447 10.2 / 1111 3.2 / SA 1708 11.0 / 2348 2.8	**26** 0521 11.7 / 1159 2.0 / SU 1745 12.5
12 0537 11.2 / 1208 2.4 / SU 1756 11.9	**27** 0026 1.3 / 0610 12.7 / M 1251 1.1 / 1831 13.5
13 0039 2.1 / 0620 12.0 / M 1300 1.9 / 1837 12.5	**28** 0116 0.6 / 0654 13.4 / TU 1340 0.6 / ○ 1914 14.0
14 0129 1.7 / 0701 12.5 / TU 1348 1.7 / ● 1917 12.9	**29** 0203 0.3 / 0735 13.7 / W 1424 0.5 / 1954 14.0
15 0215 1.6 / 0740 12.7 / W 1433 1.6 / 1954 13.0	**30** 0245 0.4 / 0812 13.6 / TH 1504 0.7 / 2030 13.7

OCTOBER

Time m	Time m
1 0321 0.8 / 0845 13.3 / F 1535 1.2 / 2101 13.2	**16** 0300 1.5 / 0822 13.2 / SA 1513 1.4 / 2039 13.3
2 0347 1.4 / 0913 12.8 / SA 1556 1.8 / 2128 12.5	**17** 0329 1.6 / 0859 13.1 / SU 1542 1.6 / 2117 13.0
3 0403 2.0 / 0938 12.2 / SU 1606 2.3 / 2152 11.8	**18** 0354 1.9 / 0936 12.7 / M 1610 1.9 / 2157 12.4
4 0416 2.3 / 1001 11.6 / M 1622 2.6 / 2216 11.1	**19** 0420 2.3 / 1016 12.0 / TU 1642 2.4 / 2240 11.5
5 0436 2.7 / 1026 10.8 / TU 1646 3.1 / 2243 10.2	**20** 0453 2.9 / 1102 11.0 / W 1723 3.2 / ◑ 2333 10.4
6 0504 3.3 / 1059 10.0 / W 1720 3.8 / ◑ 2323 9.3	**21** 0538 3.8 / 1206 10.1 / TH 1826 4.1
7 0544 4.1 / 1152 9.2 / TH 1816 4.6	**22** 0100 9.6 / 0700 4.6 / F 1404 9.8 / 2049 4.2
8 0054 8.6 / 0710 4.9 / F 1416 8.9 / 2020 4.9	**23** 0251 9.8 / 0933 4.1 / SA 1526 10.5 / 2208 3.2
9 0311 9.0 / 0915 4.6 / SA 1540 9.7 / 2214 4.1	**24** 0400 10.7 / 1037 2.9 / SU 1628 11.6 / 2305 2.2
10 0416 10.1 / 1041 3.6 / SU 1637 10.8 / 2320 3.0	**25** 0457 11.8 / 1131 1.9 / M 1719 12.6 / 2356 1.3
11 0506 11.1 / 1139 2.6 / M 1724 11.8	**26** 0544 12.6 / 1220 1.2 / TU 1805 13.3
12 0010 2.2 / 0550 12.0 / TU 1229 2.0 / 1807 12.6	**27** 0044 0.8 / 0626 13.2 / W 1307 0.9 / 1846 13.6
13 0058 1.7 / 0630 12.7 / W 1317 1.7 / 1847 13.0	**28** 0129 0.7 / 0704 13.4 / TH 1350 0.8 / ○ 1924 13.6
14 0144 1.5 / 0709 13.0 / TH 1401 1.5 / ● 1925 13.3	**29** 0210 0.8 / 0740 13.3 / F 1430 1.1 / 1959 13.2
15 0225 1.4 / 0746 13.2 / F 1440 1.4 / 2002 13.4	**30** 0246 1.2 / 0812 13.0 / SA 1502 1.5 / 2031 12.8
	31 0313 1.7 / 0841 12.5 / SU 1524 2.1 / 2058 12.2

NOVEMBER

Time m	Time m
1 0331 2.1 / 0907 12.0 / M 1537 2.4 / 2123 11.6	**16** 0343 1.8 / 0925 12.9 / TU 1605 1.8 / 2150 12.5
2 0346 2.4 / 0931 11.5 / TU 1555 2.6 / 2149 11.0	**17** 0417 2.2 / 1010 12.2 / W 1645 2.3 / 2238 11.6
3 0408 2.7 / 0958 11.0 / W 1622 3.0 / 2218 10.4	**18** 0457 2.9 / 1102 11.4 / TH 1733 3.0 / 2335 10.8
4 0437 3.2 / 1033 10.3 / TH 1657 3.5 / 2300 9.7	**19** 0548 3.6 / 1210 10.6 / F 1840 3.6 / ◑
5 0518 3.8 / 1123 9.6 / F 1748 4.2 / ◑	**20** 0053 10.2 / 0712 4.0 / SA 1341 10.5 / 2011 3.6
6 0006 9.0 / 0622 4.5 / SA 1251 9.2 / 1922 4.6	**21** 0219 10.2 / 0851 3.8 / SU 1453 10.9 / 2126 3.1
7 0206 9.0 / 0814 4.6 / SU 1448 9.6 / 2104 4.2	**22** 0325 10.8 / 0957 3.1 / M 1553 11.5 / 2225 2.5
8 0328 9.6 / 0942 3.9 / M 1552 10.5 / 2225 3.4	**23** 0421 11.4 / 1053 2.4 / TU 1645 12.1 / 2318 2.0
9 0424 10.8 / 1050 3.1 / TU 1644 11.5 / 2326 2.6	**24** 0510 12.0 / 1143 1.9 / W 1732 12.5
10 0512 11.8 / 1146 2.3 / W 1730 12.3	**25** 0007 1.6 / 0553 12.5 / TH 1231 1.6 / 1815 12.8
11 0017 2.0 / 0556 12.5 / TH 1237 1.8 / 1814 12.9	**26** 0053 1.4 / 0633 12.7 / F 1315 1.5 / ○ 1855 12.8
12 0106 1.6 / 0637 13.1 / F 1324 1.5 / ● 1856 13.3	**27** 0135 1.4 / 0710 12.7 / SA 1356 1.6 / 1932 12.6
13 0150 1.4 / 0718 13.4 / SA 1408 1.3 / 1939 13.5	**28** 0212 1.6 / 0745 12.6 / SU 1431 1.9 / 2006 12.3
14 0231 1.3 / 0800 13.5 / SU 1449 1.3 / 2022 13.4	**29** 0244 1.9 / 0817 12.3 / M 1459 2.2 / 2038 11.9
15 0308 1.5 / 0842 13.3 / M 1528 1.4 / 2105 13.1	**30** 0309 2.2 / 0847 12.0 / TU 1521 2.5 / 2108 11.5

DECEMBER

Time m	Time m
1 0330 2.4 / 0917 11.6 / W 1543 2.7 / 2138 11.1	**16** 0422 1.9 / 1008 12.8 / TH 1651 1.8 / 2236 12.2
2 0356 2.6 / 0947 11.2 / TH 1613 2.9 / 2211 10.7	**17** 0504 2.3 / 1058 12.2 / F 1736 2.2 / 2326 11.6
3 0427 2.9 / 1023 10.8 / F 1650 3.2 / 2250 10.3	**18** 0549 2.8 / 1154 11.6 / SA 1824 2.7 / ◑
4 0508 3.3 / 1108 10.3 / SA 1737 3.5 / 2342 9.9	**19** 0023 11.0 / 0640 3.2 / SU 1300 11.1 / 1918 3.0
5 0601 3.7 / 1208 10.0 / SU 1839 3.8 / ◑	**20** 0130 10.6 / 0742 3.5 / M 1407 10.9 / 2020 3.2
6 0049 9.7 / 0710 4.0 / M 1324 10.0 / 1954 3.9	**21** 0236 10.5 / 0853 3.5 / TU 1509 10.9 / 2127 3.2
7 0209 9.9 / 0833 3.9 / TU 1443 10.4 / 2115 3.6	**22** 0336 10.7 / 1003 3.3 / W 1605 11.1 / 2227 2.8
8 0325 10.5 / 0951 3.4 / W 1551 11.1 / 2231 3.1	**23** 0431 11.0 / 1103 2.9 / TH 1658 11.4 / 2327 2.6
9 0427 11.3 / 1100 2.8 / TH 1651 11.8 / 2335 2.4	**24** 0521 11.5 / 1154 2.5 / F 1746 11.7
10 0521 12.1 / 1159 2.2 / F 1743 12.5	**25** 0016 2.2 / 0605 11.9 / SA 1242 2.2 / 1830 11.9
11 0030 1.9 / 0610 12.8 / SA 1253 1.7 / 1832 13.0	**26** 0102 2.0 / 0646 12.1 / SU 1326 2.1 / ○ 1911 12.0
12 0121 1.5 / 0657 13.2 / SU 1344 1.4 / ● 1921 13.3	**27** 0145 1.9 / 0725 12.2 / M 1408 2.1 / 1949 12.0
13 0210 1.4 / 0744 13.5 / M 1433 1.2 / 2010 13.3	**28** 0224 2.0 / 0802 12.2 / TU 1445 2.3 / 2026 11.8
14 0256 1.4 / 0831 13.4 / TU 1521 1.3 / 2059 13.1	**29** 0258 2.1 / 0837 12.0 / W 1517 2.5 / 2100 11.7
15 0340 1.6 / 0919 13.2 / W 1606 1.5 / 2147 12.8	**30** 0327 2.3 / 0910 11.8 / TH 1544 2.6 / 2133 11.5
	31 0353 2.5 / 0942 11.6 / F 1612 2.7 / 2204 11.3

Chart Datum: 6·50 metres below Ordnance Datum (Newlyn)

Chapter 5

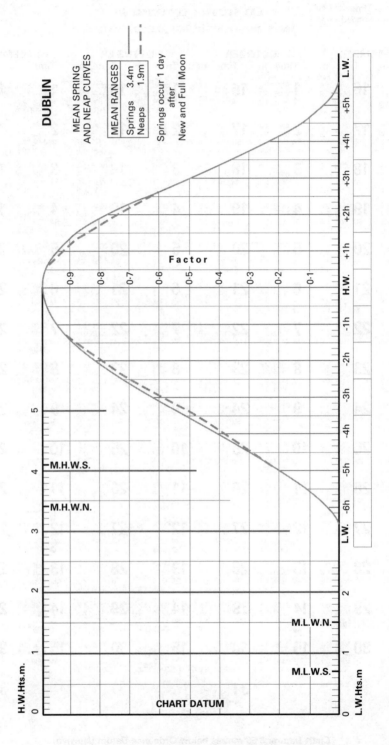

DUBLIN

MEAN SPRING
AND NEAP CURVES

MEAN RANGES	
Springs	3.4m
Neaps	1.9m

Springs occur 1 day
after
New and Full Moon

Factor

0·9 0·8 0·7 0·6 0·5 0·4 0·3 0·2 0·1

H.W.Hts.m.

M.H.W.S.

M.H.W.N.

CHART DATUM

M.L.W.N.

M.L.W.S.

L.W.Hts.m

IRELAND – DUBLIN (NORTH WALL)

LAT 53°21′N LONG 6°13′W

TIMES AND HEIGHTS OF HIGH AND LOW WATERS

YEAR **2004**

JANUARY

Day	Time m	Time m	Time m	Time m		Day	Time m	Time m	Time m
1 TH	0008 1.3	0705 3.4	1913 3.6		16 F	0552 3.5	1128 1.4	1811 3.7
2 F	0115 1.4	0802 3.5	1338 1.6	2012 3.5	17 SA	0015 1.1	0658 3.5	1241 1.4 · 1920 3.7
3 SA	0217 1.4	0854 3.5	1439 1.5	2107 3.5	18 SU	0126 1.1	0805 3.6	1353 1.3 · 2033 3.7
4 SU	0309 1.4	0940 3.7	1530 1.4	2155 3.6	19 M	0232 1.0	0908 3.8	1459 1.1 · 2140 3.8
5 M	0350 1.3	1021 3.8	1612 1.3	2237 3.6	20 TU	0332 0.9	1004 4.0	1558 0.9 · 2239 3.9
6 TU	0426 1.3	1057 3.8	1649 1.2	2315 3.6	21 W	0423 0.8	1055 4.1	● 2331 4.0
7 W	0457 1.2	1131 3.9	1723 1.1	○ 2349 3.7	22 TH	0508 0.7	1142 4.2	1737 0.5
8 TH	0526 1.2	1203 3.9	1754 1.0		23 F	0019 4.0	0550 0.7	1226 4.3 · 1821 0.4
9 F	0023 3.7	0555 1.1	1236 4.0	1826 0.9	24 SA	0104 3.9	0631 0.7	1310 4.2 · 1905 0.5
10 SA	0059 3.7	0628 1.1	1313 4.0	1902 0.9	25 SU	0148 3.8	0713 0.8	1353 4.2 · 1950 0.6
11 SU	0138 3.7	0705 1.1	1354 4.0	1942 0.8	26 M	0232 3.7	0757 0.9	1438 4.0 · 2035 0.8
12 M	0221 3.7	0748 1.1	1438 3.9	2027 0.8	27 TU	0317 3.6	0845 1.1	1525 3.9 · 2123 0.9
13 TU	0307 3.7	0835 1.1	1524 3.9	2116 0.8	28 W	0406 3.4	0937 1.2	1616 3.7 · 2212 1.2
14 W	0357 3.6	0927 1.2	1614 3.8	2210 0.9	29 TH	0501 3.3	1034 1.4	1713 3.5 · ◐ 2307 1.4
15 TH	0452 3.6	1024 1.3	1708 3.8	◑ 2309 1.0	30 F	0603 3.2	1136 1.6	1820 3.3
					31 SA	0009 1.6	0707 3.2	1246 1.6 · 1928 3.3

FEBRUARY

Day	Time m	Time m	Time m	Time m		Day	Time m	Time m	Time m
1 SU	0123 1.6	0809 3.3	1404 1.6	2032 3.3	16 M	0104 1.3	0746 3.5	1343 1.3 · 2030 3.5
2 M	0240 1.6	0905 3.4	1509 1.5	2129 3.4	17 TU	0225 1.3	0858 3.6	1459 1.1 · 2142 3.6
3 TU	0331 1.5	0953 3.6	1555 1.3	2217 3.5	18 W	0329 1.1	0959 3.8	1558 0.8 · 2240 3.8
4 W	0408 1.3	1035 3.7	1631 1.1	2256 3.6	19 TH	0418 0.9	1050 4.0	1646 0.6 · 2329 3.9
5 TH	0439 1.2	1110 3.8	1702 0.9	2331 3.7	20 F	0500 0.7	1134 4.1	● 1727 0.4
6 F	0507 1.0	1142 3.9	1731 0.8	○	21 SA	0010 3.9	0537 0.6	1213 4.2 · 1806 0.4
7 SA	0002 3.7	0535 0.9	1214 4.0	1802 0.7	22 SU	0045 3.8	0613 0.6	1249 4.2 · 1843 0.4
8 SU	0035 3.8	0606 0.8	1836 0.6		23 M	0118 3.8	0649 0.6	1325 4.1 · 1920 0.5
9 M	0111 3.9	0641 0.7	1327 4.1	1915 0.5	24 TU	0152 3.7	0727 0.7	1404 4.0 · 1958 0.7
10 TU	0151 3.9	0721 0.7	1409 4.1	1957 0.5	25 W	0229 3.6	0809 0.9	1444 3.8 · 2038 0.9
11 W	0234 3.8	0805 0.8	1454 4.0	2044 0.6	26 TH	0309 3.5	0855 1.0	1528 3.6 · 2121 1.1
12 TH	0321 3.7	0854 0.9	1543 3.9	2135 0.8	27 F	0354 3.3	0946 1.2	1618 3.4 · 2209 1.4
13 F	0413 3.6	0949 1.1	1637 3.8	2232 1.0	28 SA	0450 3.2	1047 1.5	1722 3.2 · 2310 1.6
14 SA	0513 3.5	1054 1.2	1743 3.6	2341 1.2	29 SU	0609 3.1	1158 1.6	1846 3.0
15 SU	0626 3.4	1215 1.4	1906 3.5					

MARCH

Day	Time m	Time m	Time m	Time m		Day	Time m	Time m	Time m
1 M	0025 1.8	0726 3.1	2001 3.1		16 TU	0052 1.5	0735 3.4	1342 1.2 · 2032 3.4
2 TU	0202 1.7	0832 3.3	1441 1.4	2104 3.2	17 W	0219 1.4	0850 3.6	1455 1.0 · 2142 3.6
3 W	0308 1.5	0926 3.4	1529 1.2	2155 3.4	18 TH	0320 1.1	0952 3.8	1549 0.7 · 2236 3.7
4 TH	0346 1.3	1009 3.6	1604 1.0	2234 3.5	19 F	0405 0.9	1042 3.9	1632 0.5 · 2319 3.8
5 F	0415 1.1	1045 3.8	1634 0.7	2306 3.7	20 SA	0444 0.7	1123 4.0	● 1710 0.4 · 2355 3.8
6 SA	0442 0.9	1116 3.9	1703 0.5	2335 3.8	21 SU	0519 0.6	1156 4.1	1745 0.4
7 SU	0510 0.7	1147 4.1	1734 0.3		22 M	0022 3.7	0552 0.6	1227 4.0 · 1817 0.4
8 M	0006 3.9	0541 0.5	1221 4.1	1808 0.3	23 TU	0047 3.7	0625 0.6	1258 4.0 · 1850 0.6
9 TU	0041 4.0	0616 0.4	1300 4.2	1847 0.3	24 W	0116 3.7	0700 0.6	1334 3.9 · 1922 0.7
10 W	0120 4.0	0655 0.4	1342 4.1	1929 0.4	25 TH	0150 3.6	0738 0.7	1412 3.7 · 1957 0.9
11 TH	0202 3.9	0740 0.5	1428 4.0	2016 0.6	26 F	0227 3.6	0820 0.9	1454 3.6 · 2035 1.1
12 F	0248 3.8	0830 0.7	1519 3.9	2108 0.8	27 SA	0308 3.4	0907 1.1	1540 3.3 · 2118 1.4
13 SA	0342 3.7	0928 0.9	1617 3.7	2208 1.1	28 SU	0356 3.3	1007 1.3	1637 3.1 · ◐ 2217 1.6
14 SU	0444 3.5	1039 1.2	1734 3.4	2322 1.4	29 M	0501 3.1	1119 1.5	1803 3.0 · 2340 1.8
15 M	0605 3.4	1208 1.3	1906 3.3		30 TU	0640 3.0	1237 1.5	1929 3.0
					31 W	0108 1.8	0755 3.1	1355 1.4 · 2034 3.1

APRIL

Day	Time m	Time m	Time m	Time m		Day	Time m	Time m	Time m
1 TH	0226 1.6	0852 3.3	1449 1.1	2125 3.4	16 F	0257 1.2	0935 3.8	1527 0.7 · 2218 3.7
2 F	0309 1.3	0936 3.6	1527 0.8	2203 3.6	17 SA	0342 1.0	1024 3.9	1609 0.6 · 2259 3.7
3 SA	0341 1.0	1012 3.8	1600 0.5	2235 3.7	18 SU	0422 0.8	1104 3.9	1647 0.5 · 2332 3.7
4 SU	0410 0.7	1045 4.0	1631 0.3	2304 3.9	19 M	0457 0.7	1137 3.9	● 1721 0.6 · 2357 3.7
5 M	0441 0.5	1118 4.1	1705 0.2	○ 2336 4.0	20 TU	0531 0.6	1205 3.9	1752 0.6
6 TU	0515 0.3	1155 4.2	1742 0.1		21 W	0019 3.7	0604 0.6	1236 3.8 · 1822 0.7
7 W	0012 4.1	0552 0.3	1236 4.2	1821 0.2	22 TH	0048 3.7	0639 0.7	1310 3.7 · 1852 0.8
8 TH	0052 4.1	0634 0.3	1321 4.1	1905 0.4	23 F	0121 3.7	0715 0.8	1348 3.6 · 1925 1.0
9 F	0137 4.0	0721 0.4	1411 4.0	1954 0.6	24 SA	0158 3.6	0755 0.9	1430 3.5 · 2002 1.2
10 SA	0227 3.9	0817 0.6	1507 3.8	2050 0.9	25 SU	0239 3.5	0842 1.1	1515 3.3 · 2046 1.4
11 SU	0323 3.7	0922 0.9	1612 3.6	2155 1.2	26 M	0327 3.4	0938 1.3	1610 3.2 · 2142 1.6
12 M	0430 3.5	1038 1.1	1736 3.4	◐ 2310 1.5	27 TU	0424 3.2	1046 1.4	1721 3.0 · ◐ 2300 1.7
13 TU	0556 3.4	1204 1.2	1905 3.3		28 W	0542 3.1	1157 1.4	1844 3.0
14 W	0037 1.5	0722 3.5	1330 1.1	2024 3.4	29 TH	0019 1.7	0703 3.2	1304 1.2 · 1951 3.2
15 TH	0158 1.4	0835 3.6	1437 0.9	2127 3.6	30 F	0127 1.5	0804 3.3	1359 1.0 · 2042 3.4

Chart Datum: 0·20 metres above Ordnance Datum (Dublin)
Register for your **FREE** weekly weather email service from Reeds Almanacs
at www.nauticaldata.com – **NOW!**
weekend weather reports sent to your email address, every Thursday

Chapter 5

331

IRELAND – DUBLIN (NORTH WALL)

TIME ZONE (UT)
For Summer Time add ONE hour in **non-shaded areas**

LAT 53°21'N   LONG 6°13'W

TIMES AND HEIGHTS OF HIGH AND LOW WATERS

YEAR 2004

MAY

#	Time	m	#	Time	m
1 SA	0218 / 0851 / 1444 / 2122	1.3 / 3.6 / 0.7 / 3.6	**16** SU	0313 / 0956 / 1542 / 2230	1.1 / 3.8 / 0.8 / 3.7
2 SU	0258 / 0932 / 1522 / 2157	1.0 / 3.8 / 0.5 / 3.8	**17** M	0356 / 1039 / 1621 / 2304	1.0 / 3.8 / 0.8 / 3.7
3 M	0335 / 1011 / 1600 / 2232	0.7 / 4.0 / 0.3 / 3.9	**18** TU	0434 / 1114 / 1656 / 2330	0.9 / 3.8 / 0.8 / 3.7
4 TU ○	0412 / 1051 / 1638 / 2309	0.5 / 4.1 / 0.2 / 4.1	**19** W ●	0511 / 1144 / 1728 / 2356	0.8 / 3.7 / 0.9 / 3.7
5 W	0451 / 1133 / 1718 / 2348	0.3 / 4.2 / 0.2 / 4.1	**20** TH	0546 / 1216 / 1758	0.8 / 3.7 / 0.9
6 TH	0533 / 1219 / 1801	0.3 / 4.2 / 0.3	**21** F	0025 / 0621 / 1251 / 1828	3.7 / 0.9 / 3.6 / 1.0
7 F	0032 / 0619 / 1309 / 1848	4.1 / 0.3 / 4.1 / 0.5	**22** SA	0059 / 0658 / 1329 / 1901	3.7 / 0.9 / 3.6 / 1.1
8 SA	0121 / 0713 / 1404 / 1940	4.1 / 0.5 / 3.9 / 0.8	**23** SU	0137 / 0738 / 1410 / 1938	3.7 / 1.0 / 3.5 / 1.2
9 SU	0214 / 0813 / 1505 / 2039	4.0 / 0.6 / 3.7 / 1.0	**24** M	0219 / 0822 / 1455 / 2023	3.6 / 1.1 / 3.4 / 1.3
10 M	0314 / 0921 / 1614 / 2143	3.8 / 0.8 / 3.6 / 1.3	**25** TU	0306 / 0914 / 1546 / 2115	3.5 / 1.2 / 3.3 / 1.5
11 TU ◐	0424 / 1032 / 1731 / 2254	3.7 / 0.9 / 3.4 / 1.4	**26** W	0358 / 1011 / 1644 / 2218	3.4 / 1.2 / 3.2 / 1.6
12 W	0543 / 1148 / 1848	3.6 / 1.0 / 3.4	**27** TH ◐	0458 / 1113 / 1748 / 2325	3.4 / 1.2 / 3.2 / 1.6
13 TH	0009 / 0659 / 1302 / 1958	1.5 / 3.6 / 1.0 / 3.5	**28** F	0603 / 1213 / 1852	3.4 / 1.1 / 3.3
14 F	0122 / 0807 / 1406 / 2059	1.4 / 3.7 / 0.9 / 3.5	**29** SA	0029 / 0705 / 1309 / 1947	1.5 / 3.5 / 1.0 / 3.4
15 SA	0223 / 0906 / 1458 / 2149	1.3 / 3.8 / 0.8 / 3.6	**30** SU	0125 / 0801 / 1400 / 2036	1.3 / 3.6 / 0.8 / 3.6
			31 M	0214 / 0852 / 1447 / 2120	1.1 / 3.8 / 0.6 / 3.8

JUNE

#	Time	m	#	Time	m
1 TU	0300 / 0941 / 1532 / 2204	0.8 / 4.0 / 0.5 / 4.0	**16** W	0413 / 1049 / 1632 / 2304	1.1 / 3.7 / 1.1 / 3.7
2 W	0346 / 1030 / 1616 / 2248	0.6 / 4.1 / 0.4 / 4.1	**17** TH ●	0453 / 1124 / 1706 / 2335	1.1 / 3.6 / 1.1 / 3.8
3 TH ○	0433 / 1119 / 1701 / 2333	0.5 / 4.1 / 0.4 / 4.2	**18** F	0530 / 1158 / 1737	1.0 / 3.6 / 1.1
4 F	0521 / 1210 / 1747	0.4 / 4.1 / 0.5	**19** SA	0007 / 0606 / 1233 / 1808	3.8 / 1.0 / 3.6 / 1.1
5 SA	0020 / 0612 / 1303 / 1835	4.2 / 0.4 / 4.0 / 0.6	**20** SU	0041 / 0641 / 1310 / 1840	3.8 / 1.0 / 3.6 / 1.1
6 SU	0111 / 0708 / 1400 / 1928	4.1 / 0.5 / 3.9 / 0.8	**21** M	0118 / 0718 / 1349 / 1917	3.8 / 1.0 / 3.6 / 1.2
7 M	0205 / 0807 / 1500 / 2024	4.1 / 0.6 / 3.8 / 1.0	**22** TU	0158 / 0758 / 1432 / 1958	3.8 / 1.0 / 3.5 / 1.2
8 TU	0305 / 0910 / 1603 / 2124	4.0 / 0.7 / 3.6 / 1.2	**23** W	0243 / 0843 / 1518 / 2045	3.7 / 1.0 / 3.5 / 1.3
9 W ◐	0410 / 1014 / 1709 / 2227	3.9 / 0.8 / 3.5 / 1.3	**24** TH	0330 / 0933 / 1607 / 2137	3.7 / 1.0 / 3.4 / 1.3
10 TH	0518 / 1119 / 1815 / 2332	3.8 / 0.9 / 3.4 / 1.4	**25** F ◐	0421 / 1026 / 1701 / 2233	3.6 / 1.0 / 3.4 / 1.4
11 F	0626 / 1225 / 1920	3.7 / 1.0 / 3.4	**26** SA	0516 / 1123 / 1758 / 2333	3.6 / 1.0 / 3.4 / 1.4
12 SA	0039 / 0730 / 1327 / 2018	1.4 / 3.7 / 1.0 / 3.5	**27** SU	0616 / 1221 / 1858	3.6 / 1.0 / 3.5
13 SU	0143 / 0829 / 1424 / 2110	1.4 / 3.7 / 1.1 / 3.5	**28** M	0035 / 0717 / 1320 / 1956	1.3 / 3.7 / 0.9 / 3.6
14 M	0240 / 0923 / 1512 / 2154	1.3 / 3.7 / 1.1 / 3.6	**29** TU	0135 / 0820 / 1416 / 2051	1.2 / 3.8 / 0.8 / 3.7
15 TU	0329 / 1009 / 1555 / 2232	1.2 / 3.7 / 1.1 / 3.7	**30** W	0234 / 0920 / 1510 / 2144	1.0 / 3.9 / 0.7 / 3.9

JULY

#	Time	m	#	Time	m
1 TH	0330 / 1017 / 1601 / 2234	0.8 / 4.0 / 0.7 / 4.0	**16** F	0438 / 1105 / 1647 / 2315	1.2 / 3.6 / 1.2 / 3.8
2 F ○	0423 / 1111 / 1650 / 2322	0.6 / 4.0 / 0.6 / 4.2	**17** SA ●	0514 / 1140 / 1718 / 2347	1.1 / 3.6 / 1.2 / 3.9
3 SA	0515 / 1203 / 1737	0.5 / 4.1 / 0.6	**18** SU	0547 / 1214 / 1747	1.0 / 3.6 / 1.1
4 SU	0010 / 0606 / 1255 / 1823	4.2 / 0.4 / 4.0 / 0.7	**19** M	0019 / 0618 / 1248 / 1817	3.9 / 0.9 / 3.6 / 1.1
5 M	0059 / 0659 / 1348 / 1911	4.2 / 0.4 / 3.9 / 0.8	**20** TU	0054 / 0650 / 1324 / 1851	3.9 / 0.9 / 3.7 / 1.0
6 TU	0150 / 0753 / 1441 / 2002	4.2 / 0.5 / 3.8 / 0.9	**21** W	0132 / 0726 / 1403 / 1929	3.9 / 0.8 / 3.7 / 1.0
7 W	0244 / 0848 / 1536 / 2056	4.1 / 0.6 / 3.6 / 1.1	**22** TH	0214 / 0808 / 1446 / 2012	3.9 / 0.8 / 3.7 / 1.0
8 TH	0340 / 0944 / 1632 / 2152	4.0 / 0.8 / 3.5 / 1.2	**23** F	0258 / 0854 / 1531 / 2059	3.9 / 0.8 / 3.6 / 1.1
9 F ◐	0440 / 1041 / 1731 / 2250	3.8 / 1.0 / 3.4 / 1.4	**24** SA	0345 / 0944 / 1620 / 2150	3.8 / 0.9 / 3.6 / 1.2
10 SA	0543 / 1139 / 1831 / 2352	3.7 / 1.1 / 3.4 / 1.5	**25** SU ◐	0437 / 1038 / 1715 / 2248	3.7 / 1.0 / 3.5 / 1.3
11 SU	0647 / 1240 / 1930	3.6 / 1.3 / 3.4	**26** M	0537 / 1139 / 1817 / 2355	3.6 / 1.1 / 3.5 / 1.3
12 M	0059 / 0749 / 1344 / 2026	1.5 / 3.5 / 1.4 / 3.4	**27** TU	0646 / 1247 / 1926	3.6 / 1.1 / 3.5
13 TU	0207 / 0847 / 1443 / 2116	1.5 / 3.5 / 1.4 / 3.5	**28** W	0109 / 0801 / 1356 / 2032	1.3 / 3.6 / 1.1 / 3.6
14 W	0307 / 0940 / 1531 / 2201	1.4 / 3.5 / 1.3 / 3.6	**29** TH	0221 / 0911 / 1459 / 2132	1.2 / 3.7 / 1.0 / 3.8
15 TH	0357 / 1025 / 1612 / 2240	1.3 / 3.5 / 1.3 / 3.7	**30** F	0326 / 1013 / 1554 / 2225	0.9 / 3.9 / 0.9 / 4.0
			31 SA ○	0422 / 1107 / 1642 / 2313	0.7 / 4.0 / 0.8 / 4.2

AUGUST

#	Time	m	#	Time	m
1 SU	0511 / 1156 / 1726 / 2357	0.5 / 4.0 / 0.7 / 4.3	**16** M ●	0521 / 1151 / 1723 / 2354	0.8 / 3.7 / 1.0 / 4.0
2 M	0558 / 1242 / 1808	0.4 / 4.0 / 0.7	**17** TU	0549 / 1221 / 1751	0.7 / 3.8 / 0.9
3 TU	0041 / 0642 / 1327 / 1850	4.3 / 0.4 / 3.9 / 0.7	**18** W	0026 / 0618 / 1254 / 1822	4.0 / 0.6 / 3.8 / 0.8
4 W	0125 / 0728 / 1411 / 1934	4.2 / 0.4 / 3.8 / 0.8	**19** TH	0102 / 0653 / 1331 / 1859	4.1 / 0.6 / 3.8 / 0.8
5 TH	0211 / 0816 / 1456 / 2021	4.1 / 0.6 / 3.6 / 1.0	**20** F	0142 / 0733 / 1411 / 1940	4.1 / 0.6 / 3.8 / 0.8
6 F	0259 / 0904 / 1543 / 2112	4.0 / 0.8 / 3.5 / 1.1	**21** SA	0225 / 0817 / 1455 / 2025	4.0 / 0.7 / 3.8 / 0.9
7 SA	0351 / 0954 / 1635 / 2207	3.8 / 1.0 / 3.4 / 1.3	**22** SU ◐	0312 / 0907 / 1544 / 2116	3.9 / 0.8 / 3.7 / 1.1
8 SU	0449 / 1047 / 1734 / 2307	3.6 / 1.3 / 3.3 / 1.5	**23** M	0404 / 1002 / 1638 / 2217	3.8 / 1.0 / 3.5 / 1.2
9 M	0558 / 1146 / 1839	3.4 / 1.5 / 3.3	**24** TU	0507 / 1108 / 1745 / 2332	3.6 / 1.3 / 3.4 / 1.4
10 TU	0015 / 0709 / 1256 / 1943	1.6 / 3.3 / 1.6 / 3.3	**25** W	0630 / 1226 / 1906	3.5 / 1.4 / 3.5
11 W	0135 / 0816 / 1414 / 2042	1.6 / 3.3 / 1.6 / 3.4	**26** TH	0101 / 0758 / 1347 / 2022	1.4 / 3.5 / 1.4 / 3.6
12 TH	0250 / 0916 / 1512 / 2134	1.5 / 3.4 / 1.5 / 3.6	**27** F	0224 / 0913 / 1456 / 2125	1.2 / 3.6 / 1.2 / 3.8
13 F	0342 / 1006 / 1554 / 2217	1.3 / 3.5 / 1.4 / 3.7	**28** SA	0329 / 1013 / 1549 / 2218	0.9 / 3.8 / 1.0 / 4.0
14 SA	0420 / 1046 / 1627 / 2253	1.1 / 3.6 / 1.2 / 3.9	**29** SU	0419 / 1103 / 1633 / 2303	0.6 / 3.9 / 0.8 / 4.2
15 SU	0452 / 1120 / 1656 / 2325	1.0 / 3.6 / 1.1 / 3.9	**30** M ○	0503 / 1146 / 1712 / 2342	0.4 / 4.0 / 0.7 / 4.3
			31 TU	0542 / 1224 / 1749	0.3 / 3.9 / 0.6

Chart Datum: 0·20 metres above Ordnance Datum (Dublin)

IRELAND – DUBLIN (NORTH WALL)

YEAR 2004

LAT 53°21'N   LONG 6°13'W

TIMES AND HEIGHTS OF HIGH AND LOW WATERS

SEPTEMBER

Day	Time m	Time m		Day	Time m	Time m
1 W	0019 4.3 / 0620 0.3	1300 3.9 / 1825 0.6		16 TH	0547 0.4	1222 4.0 / 1755 0.6
2 TH	0057 4.2 / 0659 0.5	1335 3.8 / 1904 0.7		17 F	0032 4.2 / 0622 0.4	1258 4.0 / 1830 0.6
3 F	0137 4.1 / 0738 0.6	1412 3.7 / 1946 0.9		18 SA	0112 4.2 / 0701 0.5	1339 4.0 / 1912 0.7
4 SA	0219 3.9 / 0820 0.9	1453 3.6 / 2033 1.0		19 SU	0156 4.1 / 0746 0.7	1424 3.9 / 1959 0.8
5 SU	0305 3.7 / 0906 1.1	1538 3.4 / 2126 1.3		20 M	0246 3.9 / 0837 0.9	1514 3.7 / 2054 1.0
6 M	0358 3.5 / 0957 1.4	1633 3.3 / 2227 1.5		21 TU	0343 3.7 / 0937 1.2	1612 3.6 / ◑ 2202 1.3
7 TU	0506 3.2 / 1058 1.6	1747 3.2 / 2337 1.6		22 W	0454 3.5 / 1050 1.5	1725 3.5 / 2328 1.4
8 W	0632 3.1 / 1210 1.8	1905 3.2		23 TH	0632 3.4 / 1217 1.6	1855 3.5
9 TH	0102 1.6 / 0749 3.1	1342 1.8 / 2012 3.4		24 F	0104 1.3 / 0801 3.5	1342 1.5 / 2014 3.7
10 F	0229 1.5 / 0854 3.3	1450 1.6 / 2108 3.5		25 SA	0224 1.1 / 0913 3.6	1447 1.3 / 2117 3.9
11 SA	0319 1.2 / 0945 3.5	1531 1.4 / 2152 3.7		26 SU	0321 0.8 / 1008 3.8	1536 1.0 / 2209 4.1
12 SU	0354 1.0 / 1024 3.6	1602 1.2 / 2228 3.7		27 M	0406 0.6 / 1053 3.9	1617 0.8 / 2251 4.2
13 M	0423 0.8 / 1056 3.7	1629 1.0 / 2258 4.0		28 TU	0446 0.4 / 1132 3.9	1654 0.7 / ○ 2327 4.2
14 TU	0450 0.6 / 1124 3.8	● 1655 0.8 / 2326 4.1		29 W	0522 0.4 / 1204 3.9	1729 0.6 / 2359 4.2
15 W	0517 0.5 / 1151 3.9	1723 0.7 / 2357 4.2		30 TH	0556 0.4 / 1232 3.9	1803 0.6

OCTOBER

Day	Time m	Time m		Day	Time m	Time m
1 F	0032 4.1 / 0629 0.6	1302 3.8 / 1839 0.7		16 SA	0007 4.2 / 0555 0.4	1231 4.1 / 1808 0.5
2 SA	0109 4.0 / 0704 0.8	1337 3.8 / 1919 0.8		17 SU	0050 4.2 / 0636 0.5	1314 4.1 / 1853 0.6
3 SU	0149 3.9 / 0741 1.0	1415 3.7 / 2002 1.0		18 M	0138 4.1 / 0722 0.8	1402 4.0 / 1944 0.8
4 M	0233 3.7 / 0822 1.2	1457 3.6 / 2053 1.2		19 TU	0233 3.9 / 0817 1.1	1456 3.8 / 2046 1.0
5 TU	0322 3.4 / 0912 1.5	1546 3.4 / 2154 1.4		20 W	0337 3.6 / 0923 1.4	1559 3.7 / ◑ 2201 1.2
6 W	0425 3.2 / 1016 1.7	1654 3.3 / ◑ 2304 1.6		21 TH	0459 3.5 / 1040 1.6	1717 3.6 / 2326 1.3
7 TH	0555 3.1 / 1132 1.9	1823 3.2		22 F	0631 3.4 / 1204 1.6	1843 3.6
8 F	0024 1.6 / 0717 3.1	1258 1.9 / 1936 3.3		23 SA	0054 1.2 / 0752 3.5	1323 1.5 / 1957 3.8
9 SA	0148 1.5 / 0824 3.3	1412 1.7 / 2034 3.5		24 SU	0206 1.0 / 0858 3.7	1425 1.3 / 2100 3.9
10 SU	0241 1.2 / 0914 3.5	1455 1.4 / 2120 3.7		25 M	0301 0.8 / 0950 3.8	1514 1.1 / 2152 4.1
11 M	0317 1.0 / 0953 3.7	1528 1.2 / 2156 3.9		26 TU	0345 0.6 / 1034 3.9	1556 0.9 / 2235 4.1
12 TU	0348 0.7 / 1025 3.8	1556 1.0 / 2227 4.0		27 W	0424 0.6 / 1111 3.9	1634 0.8 / 2311 4.1
13 W	0416 0.5 / 1052 3.9	● 1624 0.8 / 2257 4.1		28 TH	0500 0.6 / 1142 3.9	1710 0.8 / ○ 2342 4.1
14 TH	0446 0.4 / 1120 4.0	● 1655 0.6 / 2329 4.2		29 F	0533 0.7 / 1208 3.9	1746 0.8
15 F	0519 0.3 / 1153 4.1	1730 0.5		30 SA	0013 4.0 / 0604 0.8	1237 3.9 / 1821 0.8
				31 SU	0049 3.9 / 0636 0.9	1311 3.9 / 1900 0.9

NOVEMBER

Day	Time m	Time m		Day	Time m	Time m
1 M	0128 3.8 / 0711 1.1	1348 3.8 / 1942 1.1		16 TU	0131 4.0 / 0709 0.9	1349 4.1 / 1940 0.8
2 TU	0211 3.6 / 0750 1.3	1430 3.7 / 2030 1.2		17 W	0231 3.9 / 0806 1.1	1447 4.0 / 2045 0.9
3 W	0258 3.4 / 0836 1.5	1517 3.6 / 2126 1.4		18 TH	0339 3.7 / 0911 1.4	1552 3.9 / 2155 1.0
4 TH	0356 3.3 / 0938 1.7	1614 3.4 / 2231 1.5		19 F	0455 3.6 / 1023 1.5	1705 3.8 / ◑ 2311 1.1
5 F	0512 3.1 / 1053 1.9	1729 3.3 / ◑ 2340 1.5		20 SA	0613 3.5 / 1138 1.6	1820 3.8
6 SA	0633 3.1 / 1208 1.9	1845 3.3		21 SU	0027 1.1 / 0725 3.6	1250 1.5 / 1929 3.8
7 SU	0049 1.4 / 0739 3.3	1315 1.7 / 1946 3.5		22 M	0135 1.0 / 0828 3.7	1353 1.4 / 2031 3.9
8 M	0146 1.2 / 0831 3.5	1405 1.5 / 2034 3.6		23 TU	0232 0.9 / 0922 3.8	1447 1.2 / 2126 4.0
9 TU	0230 1.0 / 0912 3.7	1445 1.3 / 2114 3.8		24 W	0320 0.9 / 1008 3.9	1534 1.1 / 2214 4.0
10 W	0307 0.8 / 0946 3.8	1520 1.0 / 2151 4.0		25 TH	0402 0.9 / 1047 3.9	1616 1.0 / 2253 3.9
11 TH	0342 0.6 / 1018 4.0	1554 0.8 / 2228 4.1		26 F	0439 0.9 / 1120 3.9	1655 1.0 / ○ 2327 3.9
12 F	0417 0.5 / 1052 4.1	1631 0.6 / ● 2308 4.2		27 SA	0513 0.9 / 1148 3.9	1732 1.0
13 SA	0455 0.4 / 1129 4.2	1711 0.5 / 2351 4.2		28 SU	0000 3.8 / 0545 1.0	1219 3.9 / 1809 1.0
14 SU	0535 0.5 / 1211 4.2	1755 0.5		29 M	0035 3.8 / 0616 1.1	1252 3.9 / 1847 1.0
15 M	0038 4.2 / 0619 0.7	1257 4.2 / 1844 0.6		30 TU	0112 3.7 / 0650 1.2	1329 3.9 / 1926 1.1

DECEMBER

Day	Time m	Time m		Day	Time m	Time m
1 W	0153 3.6 / 0726 1.3	1409 3.8 / 2009 1.2		16 TH	0227 3.9 / 0753 1.1	1437 4.2 / 2034 0.7
2 TH	0237 3.5 / 0809 1.5	1453 3.7 / 2056 1.3		17 F	0328 3.8 / 0852 1.2	1537 4.1 / 2137 0.8
3 F	0327 3.4 / 0859 1.6	1542 3.6 / 2149 1.3		18 SA	0434 3.6 / 0955 1.4	1641 4.0 / ◐ 2241 1.0
4 SA	0425 3.3 / 1000 1.7	1637 3.5 / 2248 1.4		19 SU	0540 3.6 / 1101 1.5	1747 3.9 / 2347 1.1
5 SU	0529 3.3 / 1107 1.8	1737 3.4 / ◑ 2348 1.3		20 M	0646 3.5 / 1209 1.5	1853 3.8
6 M	0634 3.3 / 1211 1.7	1838 3.5		21 TU	0055 1.2 / 0748 3.6	1316 1.5 / 1956 3.7
7 TU	0045 1.2 / 0731 3.4	1307 1.6 / 1935 3.6		22 W	0159 1.2 / 0845 3.6	1418 1.4 / 2056 3.7
8 W	0138 1.1 / 0820 3.6	1357 1.4 / 2027 3.7		23 TH	0254 1.2 / 0936 3.7	1513 1.3 / 2149 3.7
9 TH	0226 0.9 / 0904 3.8	1443 1.2 / 2117 3.9		24 F	0341 1.2 / 1020 3.8	1601 1.2 / 2235 3.7
10 F	0310 0.8 / 0947 4.0	1528 0.9 / 2206 4.0		25 SA	0422 1.2 / 1058 3.9	1643 1.1 / 2313 3.7
11 SA	0354 0.7 / 1029 4.1	1613 0.7 / 2254 4.1		26 SU	0458 1.2 / 1131 3.9	1722 1.1 / ○ 2347 3.7
12 SU	0438 0.6 / 1113 4.2	1700 0.6 / ● 2343 4.2		27 M	0530 1.2 / 1203 3.9	1758 1.0
13 M	0522 0.6 / 1159 4.3	1748 0.5		28 TU	0021 3.7 / 0601 1.2	1236 3.9 / 1833 1.0
14 TU	0034 4.1 / 0608 0.7	1248 4.3 / 1840 0.5		29 W	0056 3.7 / 0631 1.2	1310 3.9 / 1907 1.0
15 W	0129 4.0 / 0658 0.9	1340 4.2 / 1935 0.6		30 TH	0132 3.6 / 0704 1.2	1346 3.9 / 1943 1.0
				31 F	0211 3.6 / 0740 1.3	1426 3.8 / 2021 1.0

Chart Datum: 0·20 metres above Ordnance Datum (Dublin)

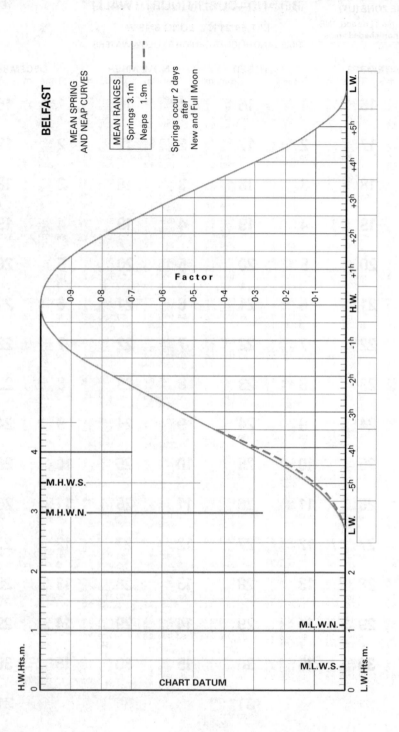

BELFAST

MEAN SPRING
AND NEAP CURVES

MEAN RANGES
Springs 3.1m
Neaps 1.9m

Springs occur 2 days
after
New and Full Moon

NORTHERN IRELAND – BELFAST

LAT 54°36'N   LONG 5°55'W

TIMES AND HEIGHTS OF HIGH AND LOW WATERS

YEAR **2004**

JANUARY

Day	Time m	Time m		Day	Time m	Time m
1 TH	0000 0.9 / 0615 2.9	1210 1.2 / 1826 3.1		**16** F	0507 2.9 / 1114 1.1	1734 3.3 / 2354 0.8
2 F	0059 1.0 / 0713 2.9	1314 1.2 / 1931 3.0		**17** SA	0614 2.9 / 1229 1.1	1844 3.2
3 SA	0156 1.0 / 0809 3.0	1415 1.2 / 2032 3.0		**18** SU	0104 0.8 / 0724 3.0	1345 1.0 / 1953 3.3
4 SU	0246 1.0 / 0900 3.1	1507 1.1 / 2124 3.1		**19** M	0209 0.8 / 0831 3.2	1450 0.8 / 2059 3.3
5 M	0328 1.0 / 0945 3.2	1550 1.0 / 2208 3.1		**20** TU	0307 0.7 / 0931 3.3	1547 0.7 / 2158 3.4
6 TU	0406 0.9 / 1026 3.4	1627 0.9 / 2247 3.2		**21** W	0359 0.7 / 1025 3.5	1640 0.5 / ● 2252 3.4
7 W	0442 0.9 / 1104 3.4	1702 0.8 / 2323 3.2		**22** TH	0449 0.7 / 1115 3.6	1731 0.4 / 2344 3.3
8 TH	0518 0.9 / 1140 3.5	1738 0.8 / 2356 3.2		**23** F	0538 0.7 / 1204 3.6	1820 0.4
9 F	0554 0.9 / 1214 3.5	1814 0.7		**24** SA	0034 3.3 / 0625 0.7	1252 3.7 / 1906 0.4
10 SA	0025 3.1 / 0630 0.9	1246 3.5 / 1850 0.7		**25** SU	0123 3.2 / 0710 0.7	1337 3.7 / 1951 0.4
11 SU	0058 3.1 / 0708 0.8	1321 3.5 / 1928 0.6		**26** M	0210 3.2 / 0753 0.8	1421 3.6 / 2034 0.5
12 M	0136 3.1 / 0747 0.8	1359 3.5 / 2009 0.6		**27** TU	0254 3.1 / 0835 0.8	1503 3.5 / 2117 0.6
13 TU	0220 3.1 / 0829 0.9	1443 3.5 / 2054 0.6		**28** W	0338 3.0 / 0918 0.9	1547 3.3 / 2203 0.8
14 W	0309 3.0 / 0916 0.9	1532 3.4 / 2147 0.7		**29** TH	0423 2.9 / 1007 1.0	1635 3.1 / ◐ 2258 0.9
15 TH	0405 2.9 / 1010 1.0	1629 3.3 / ◑ 2247 0.8		**30** F	0513 2.9 / 1106 1.2	1730 2.9
				31 SA	0003 1.1 / 0611 2.8	1220 1.2 / 1837 2.8

FEBRUARY

Day	Time m	Time m		Day	Time m	Time m
1 SU	0109 1.1 / 0720 2.8	1333 1.2 / 2000 2.8		**16** M	0048 1.0 / 0701 2.9	1339 1.0 / 1944 3.0
2 M	0209 1.1 / 0829 3.0	1435 1.1 / 2106 2.9		**17** TU	0204 0.9 / 0822 3.0	1447 0.8 / 2058 3.1
3 TU	0259 1.0 / 0923 3.1	1525 1.0 / 2154 3.0		**18** W	0304 0.8 / 0926 3.2	1545 0.6 / 2156 3.2
4 W	0343 0.9 / 1007 3.2	1607 0.8 / 2234 3.0		**19** TH	0356 0.7 / 1017 3.4	1636 0.4 / 2246 3.2
5 TH	0423 0.8 / 1046 3.3	1645 0.7 / 2309 3.1		**20** F	0443 0.7 / 1104 3.5	1723 0.3 / ● 2332 3.2
6 F	0501 0.8 / 1119 3.4	1721 0.6 / ○ 2338 3.1		**21** SA	0527 0.6 / 1149 3.6	1806 0.3
7 SA	0537 0.7 / 1149 3.5	1757 0.5		**22** SU	0016 3.2 / 0607 0.6	1232 3.6 / 1844 0.3
8 SU	0003 3.1 / 0612 0.7	1220 3.5 / 1831 0.4		**23** M	0058 3.2 / 0645 0.6	1313 3.6 / 1919 0.4
9 M	0034 3.1 / 0647 0.6	1255 3.6 / 1906 0.4		**24** TU	0137 3.1 / 0720 0.6	1351 3.5 / 1953 0.5
10 TU	0111 3.1 / 0722 0.6	1334 3.6 / 1944 0.4		**25** W	0214 3.1 / 0756 0.7	1428 3.4 / 2028 0.6
11 W	0152 3.1 / 0801 0.6	1417 3.6 / 2025 0.4		**26** TH	0251 3.1 / 0835 0.8	1507 3.2 / 2108 0.8
12 TH	0237 3.1 / 0845 0.7	1505 3.5 / 2113 0.6		**27** F	0332 3.0 / 0918 0.9	1550 3.0 / 2156 1.0
13 F	0328 3.0 / 0936 0.8	1600 3.3 / ◐ 2211 0.8		**28** SA	0419 2.9 / 1012 1.1	1642 2.8 / ◑ 2303 1.2
14 SA	0427 2.9 / 1040 1.0	1706 3.2 / 2321 0.9		**29** SU	0515 2.8 / 1131 1.2	1746 2.7
15 SU	0538 2.9 / 1210 1.1	1822 3.0				

MARCH

Day	Time m	Time m		Day	Time m	Time m
1 M	0026 1.2 / 0622 2.8	1256 1.2 / 1919 2.6		**16** TU	0041 1.1 / 0650 2.8	1335 0.8 / 1948 2.9
2 TU	0135 1.2 / 0749 2.8	1403 1.1 / 2047 2.7		**17** W	0159 1.0 / 0817 3.0	1443 0.6 / 2057 3.0
3 W	0232 1.1 / 0855 3.0	1457 0.9 / 2135 2.9		**18** TH	0259 0.9 / 0916 3.2	1539 0.4 / 2148 3.1
4 TH	0319 0.9 / 0940 3.1	1542 0.7 / 2212 3.0		**19** F	0349 0.7 / 1004 3.4	1625 0.3 / 2232 3.2
5 F	0401 0.8 / 1015 3.2	1621 0.5 / 2244 3.0		**20** SA	0433 0.6 / 1050 3.5	1707 0.3 / ● 2313 3.2
6 SA	0439 0.7 / 1045 3.3	1658 0.4 / ○ 2309 3.1		**21** SU	0511 0.6 / 1127 3.5	1744 0.3 / 2351 3.2
7 SU	0515 0.6 / 1115 3.4	1732 0.3 / 2335 3.1		**22** M	0546 0.6 / 1206 3.5	1816 0.4
8 M	0549 0.5 / 1150 3.5	1806 0.3		**23** TU	0027 3.2 / 0617 0.6	1243 3.4 / 1845 0.5
9 TU	0008 3.2 / 0622 0.5	1229 3.6 / 1840 0.2		**24** W	0101 3.2 / 0649 0.6	1318 3.4 / 1915 0.6
10 W	0046 3.2 / 0657 0.4	1311 3.6 / 1917 0.3		**25** TH	0134 3.2 / 0722 0.6	1352 3.3 / 1948 0.7
11 TH	0126 3.2 / 0736 0.5	1356 3.6 / 1959 0.4		**26** F	0210 3.2 / 0759 0.7	1430 3.1 / 2025 0.9
12 F	0210 3.2 / 0820 0.5	1445 3.4 / 2047 0.6		**27** SA	0250 3.1 / 0841 0.8	1513 3.0 / 2109 1.0
13 SA	0300 3.1 / 0912 0.7	1543 3.2 / ◐ 2143 0.8		**28** SU	0336 3.0 / 0932 1.0	◐ 2209 1.2
14 SU	0359 2.9 / 1021 0.9	1652 3.0 / 2258 1.1		**29** M	0431 2.9 / 1046 1.1	1708 2.6 / 2344 1.3
15 M	0515 2.8 / 1209 1.0	1814 2.8		**30** TU	0535 2.8 / 1221 1.1	1822 2.5
				31 W	0100 1.3 / 0647 2.8	1329 1.0 / 2011 2.6

APRIL

Day	Time m	Time m		Day	Time m	Time m
1 TH	0201 1.1 / 0801 2.9	1425 0.8 / 2059 2.8		**16** F	0245 0.9 / 0855 3.2	1521 0.4 / 2127 3.1
2 F	0251 0.9 / 0852 3.0	1511 0.6 / 2134 2.9		**17** SA	0334 0.8 / 0941 3.4	1605 0.3 / 2209 3.1
3 SA	0334 0.8 / 0930 3.2	1551 0.4 / 2203 3.0		**18** SU	0415 0.7 / 1023 3.4	1643 0.4 / 2247 3.2
4 SU	0412 0.6 / 1005 3.3	1627 0.3 / 2232 3.1		**19** M	0451 0.6 / 1102 3.4	1716 0.4 / ● 2323 3.2
5 M	0448 0.5 / 1042 3.3	1701 0.2 / ○ 2305 3.2		**20** TU	0523 0.6 / 1138 3.4	1746 0.6 / 2355 3.2
6 TU	0521 0.5 / 1122 3.5	1736 0.2 / 2343 3.3		**21** W	0552 0.7 / 1212 3.3	1814 0.7
7 W	0556 0.4 / 1205 3.6	1814 0.2		**22** TH	0028 3.3 / 0621 0.7	1246 3.3 / 1843 0.8
8 TH	0024 3.3 / 0634 0.4	1252 3.6 / 1854 0.3		**23** F	0102 3.3 / 0654 0.7	1321 3.2 / 1916 0.8
9 F	0108 3.4 / 0717 0.4	1341 3.5 / 1939 0.5		**24** SA	0139 3.3 / 0731 0.7	1359 3.1 / 1954 0.9
10 SA	0154 3.3 / 0805 0.5	1435 3.3 / 2029 0.7		**25** SU	0218 3.2 / 0813 0.8	1442 2.9 / 2039 1.1
11 SU	0245 3.2 / 0903 0.7	1536 3.1 / 2129 1.0		**26** M	0302 3.1 / 0903 0.9	1535 2.8 / 2134 1.2
12 M	0346 3.0 / 1024 0.8	1648 2.9 / 2250 1.2		**27** TU	0354 3.0 / 1007 1.0	1637 2.6 / ◐ 2249 1.3
13 TU	0504 2.9 / 1203 0.8	1816 2.8		**28** W	0456 2.9 / 1135 1.0	1744 2.6
14 W	0028 1.2 / 0640 2.9	1323 0.7 / 1940 2.8		**29** TH	0015 1.3 / 0601 2.8	1247 0.9 / 1853 2.7
15 TH	0144 1.1 / 0758 3.0	1429 0.5 / 2040 3.0		**30** F	0120 1.2 / 0704 2.9	1344 0.9 / 1954 2.8

Chart Datum: 2·01 metres below Ordnance Datum (Belfast)

Chapter 5

335

NORTHERN IRELAND – BELFAST

YEAR 2004

LAT 54°36'N   LONG 5°55'W

TIMES AND HEIGHTS OF HIGH AND LOW WATERS

TIME ZONE (UT)
For Summer Time add ONE hour in **non-shaded areas**

MAY

Day	Time m	Time m	Time m	Time m
1 SA	0213 1.0	0800 3.1	2040 3.0	
2 SU	0258 0.8	0847 3.2	1512 0.4	2120 3.1
3 M	0338 0.7	0930 3.4	1550 0.3	2159 3.2
4 TU ○	0416 0.6	1014 3.5	1628 0.3	2239 3.3
5 W	0454 0.5	1100 3.6	1708 0.3	2323 3.4
6 TH	0535 0.4	1148 3.6	1751 0.3	
7 F	0009 3.5	0619 0.4	1240 3.5	1837 0.5
8 SA	0057 3.5	0707 0.4	1334 3.4	1927 0.6
9 SU	0147 3.4	0801 0.5	1431 3.3	2022 0.8
10 M	0240 3.3	0907 0.6	1534 3.1	2126 1.0
11 TU ◔	0342 3.2	1027 0.6	1645 2.9	2243 1.1
12 W	0455 1.0	1145 3.0	1804 2.8	
13 TH	0001 1.1	0617 3.0	1257 0.6	1913 2.9
14 F	0112 1.1	0727 3.1	1400 0.5	2010 2.9
15 SA	0215 1.0	0825 3.2	1453 0.5	2057 3.0
16 SU	0307 0.8	0913 3.3	1536 0.5	2140 3.1
17 M	0351 0.8	0956 3.3	1614 0.6	2218 3.2
18 TU	0429 0.7	1035 3.3	1648 0.6	2253 3.2
19 W ●	0502 0.7	1111 3.3	1718 0.7	2327 3.3
20 TH	0531 0.8	1145 3.2	1747 0.8	
21 F	0002 3.4	0601 0.8	1220 3.2	1818 0.9
22 SA	0038 3.4	0634 0.8	1256 3.1	1853 0.9
23 SU	0115 3.4	0711 0.8	1334 3.0	1933 1.0
24 M	0154 3.3	0752 0.8	1416 2.9	2018 1.0
25 TU	0234 3.2	0840 0.9	1506 2.8	2108 1.1
26 W	0321 3.1	0935 0.9	1605 2.8	2205 1.2
27 TH ◑	0416 3.0	1039 0.9	1707 2.7	2309 1.2
28 F	0517 3.0	1146 0.8	1807 2.8	
29 SA	0015 1.1	0618 3.1	1248 0.7	1903 2.9
30 SU	0118 1.0	0717 3.2	1342 0.6	1955 3.0
31 M	0212 0.9	0811 3.3	1430 0.5	2043 3.2

JUNE

Day	Time m	Time m	Time m	Time m
1 TU	0300 0.8	0902 3.4	1515 0.4	2130 3.3
2 W	0346 0.6	0952 3.5	1600 0.4	2218 3.4
3 TH ○	0433 0.5	1043 3.5	1646 0.4	2307 3.5
4 F	0521 0.4	1136 3.5	1735 0.5	2358 3.5
5 SA	0611 0.4	1231 3.5	1827 0.6	
6 SU	0049 3.5	0705 0.4	1327 3.3	1920 0.7
7 M	0141 3.5	0802 0.4	1425 3.2	2017 0.8
8 TU	0234 3.4	0905 0.4	1526 3.1	2117 0.9
9 W ◑	0332 3.3	1011 0.5	1630 3.0	2221 1.0
10 TH	0435 3.2	1115 0.5	1734 2.9	2325 1.0
11 F	0541 3.1	1219 0.6	1835 2.9	
12 SA	0029 1.1	0646 3.1	1320 0.6	1930 2.9
13 SU	0133 1.0	0747 3.1	1415 0.7	2020 3.0
14 M	0231 1.0	0842 3.1	1502 0.7	2106 3.1
15 TU	0322 0.9	0930 3.2	1543 0.8	2148 3.3
16 W	0405 0.9	1012 3.2	1619 0.8	2227 3.3
17 TH ●	0442 0.8	1050 3.2	1653 0.9	2304 3.3
18 F	0514 0.8	1126 3.1	1725 0.9	2341 3.4
19 SA	0546 0.8	1200 3.1	1800 0.9	
20 SU	0017 3.4	0619 0.8	1236 3.1	1836 0.9
21 M	0054 3.4	0655 0.8	1311 3.0	1915 0.9
22 TU	0129 3.4	0734 0.7	1349 3.0	1956 0.9
23 W	0207 3.4	0816 0.7	1433 2.9	2040 1.0
24 TH	0248 3.3	0902 0.7	1524 2.9	2128 1.0
25 F ◑	0336 3.2	0955 0.7	1621 2.9	2221 1.0
26 SA	0432 3.2	1054 0.7	1719 2.9	2320 1.1
27 SU	0534 3.2	1156 0.7	1818 2.9	
28 M	0024 1.0	0637 3.2	1258 0.7	1915 3.0
29 TU	0131 0.9	0740 3.3	1356 0.6	2012 3.1
30 W	0233 0.8	0840 3.4	1450 0.6	2107 3.3

JULY

Day	Time m	Time m	Time m	Time m
1 TH	0329 0.7	0937 3.4	1542 0.6	2201 3.4
2 F ○	0422 0.5	1032 3.4	1633 0.6	2254 3.5
3 SA	0514 0.4	1126 3.4	1724 0.6	2346 3.5
4 SU	0607 0.4	1221 3.3	1817 0.7	
5 M	0038 3.6	0700 0.3	1316 3.3	1909 0.7
6 TU	0130 3.6	0753 0.3	1411 3.2	2002 0.8
7 W	0220 3.5	0846 0.3	1506 3.1	2054 0.8
8 TH	0311 3.5	0941 0.4	1600 3.0	2146 0.9
9 F ◑	0403 3.3	1036 0.6	1653 2.9	2241 1.0
10 SA	0458 3.2	1134 0.7	1746 2.9	2341 1.1
11 SU	0557 3.0	1233 0.8	1841 2.9	
12 M	0045 1.1	0703 2.9	1332 0.9	1938 2.9
13 TU	0151 1.1	0810 2.9	1426 0.9	2032 3.0
14 W	0251 1.0	0907 3.0	1512 0.9	2121 3.1
15 TH	0341 0.9	0954 3.0	1553 0.9	2205 3.3
16 F	0421 0.9	1034 3.1	1629 0.9	2244 3.3
17 SA ●	0456 0.8	1111 3.1	1705 0.9	2321 3.4
18 SU	0529 0.7	1144 3.1	1741 0.9	2355 3.4
19 M	0603 0.7	1214 3.0	1817 0.8	
20 TU	0027 3.4	0636 0.6	1244 3.0	1853 0.8
21 W	0100 3.5	0711 0.6	1318 3.0	1930 0.8
22 TH	0136 3.5	0748 0.6	1358 3.0	2009 0.8
23 F	0217 3.4	0829 0.6	1443 3.0	2052 0.8
24 SA	0302 3.4	0916 0.6	1534 3.0	2140 0.9
25 SU ◑	0354 3.3	1010 0.7	1631 2.9	2237 1.0
26 M	0455 3.2	1113 0.8	1734 2.9	2345 1.1
27 TU	0604 3.1	1223 0.8	1840 3.0	
28 W	0107 1.0	0716 3.1	1336 0.8	1948 3.1
29 TH	0221 0.9	0826 3.2	1438 0.8	2052 3.2
30 F	0322 0.7	0929 3.3	1533 0.7	2149 3.4
31 SA ○	0417 0.5	1024 3.3	1625 0.7	2242 3.5

AUGUST

Day	Time m	Time m	Time m	Time m
1 SU	0509 0.4	1117 3.3	1715 0.7	2332 3.6
2 M	0559 0.3	1208 3.3	1803 0.7	
3 TU	0022 3.6	0646 0.3	1258 3.2	1849 0.7
4 W	0110 3.6	0731 0.3	1347 3.2	1934 0.7
5 TH	0156 3.6	0814 0.4	1433 3.1	2017 0.8
6 F	0240 3.5	0857 0.5	1517 3.1	2101 0.8
7 SA	0325 3.4	0942 0.7	1602 3.0	2148 0.9
8 SU	0412 3.2	1034 0.9	1649 2.9	2245 1.1
9 M	0505 3.0	1138 1.1	1743 2.9	2356 1.2
10 TU	0610 2.8	1246 1.2	1848 2.9	
11 W	0110 1.2	0739 2.7	1349 1.2	1959 3.0
12 TH	0219 1.1	0850 2.8	1442 1.1	2058 3.1
13 F	0314 1.0	0939 2.9	1527 1.0	2144 3.2
14 SA	0357 0.8	1019 3.0	1606 0.9	2222 3.3
15 SU	0433 0.7	1054 3.0	1643 0.8	2256 3.4
16 M ●	0507 0.6	1124 3.1	1719 0.8	2325 3.4
17 TU	0540 0.6	1147 3.5	1753 0.8	2354 3.5
18 W	0612 0.5	1213 3.1	1827 0.7	
19 TH	0028 3.5	0644 0.5	1247 3.1	1900 0.7
20 F	0106 3.5	0718 0.4	1325 3.1	1936 0.7
21 SA	0147 3.5	0756 0.5	1408 3.1	2017 0.7
22 SU	0232 3.5	0841 0.6	1456 3.1	2105 0.8
23 M ◑	0324 3.3	0933 0.8	1551 3.0	2202 1.0
24 TU	0426 3.2	1036 1.0	1658 2.9	2318 1.1
25 W	0542 3.0	1157 1.1	1815 2.9	
26 TH	0101 1.1	0704 3.0	1329 1.1	1936 3.0
27 F	0218 0.9	0825 3.1	1435 1.0	2046 3.2
28 SA	0319 0.6	0927 3.2	1529 0.8	2141 3.4
29 SU	0412 0.4	1018 3.3	1617 0.8	2230 3.5
30 M ○	0459 0.3	1104 3.3	1702 0.7	2316 3.4
31 TU	0543 0.3	1149 3.3	1743 0.7	

Chart Datum: 2·01 metres below Ordnance Datum (Belfast)

NORTHERN IRELAND – BELFAST

YEAR **2004**

LAT 54°36′N   LONG 5°55′W

TIMES AND HEIGHTS OF HIGH AND LOW WATERS

SEPTEMBER

Day	Time	m	Time	m	Time	m	Time	m
1 W	0000	3.6	0623	0.3	1233	3.2	1822	0.7
2 TH	0044	3.6	0659	0.4	1314	3.2	1900	0.7
3 F	0125	3.5	0733	0.5	1353	3.2	1938	0.8
4 SA	0204	3.4	0808	0.7	1431	3.2	2017	0.8
5 SU	0244	3.3	0846	0.8	1512	3.1	2100	0.9
6 M	0328	3.1	0932	1.0	1558	3.0	) 2153	1.1
7 TU	0419	2.9	1035	1.2	1652	2.9	2308	1.2
8 W	0522	2.7	1200	1.4	1756	2.9		
9 TH	0033	1.3	0659	2.6	1313	1.3	1916	2.9
10 F	0144	1.1	0831	2.7	1412	1.2	2028	3.0
11 SA	0241	1.0	0919	2.9	1501	1.1	2115	3.2
12 SU	0326	0.8	0956	3.0	1542	0.9	2152	3.3
13 M	0404	0.6	1028	3.1	1619	0.8	2221	3.4
14 TU	0439	0.5	1053	3.1	1654	0.7	2250	3.5
15 W	0512	0.5	1114	3.2	1726	0.7	2322	3.5
16 TH	0542	0.4	1143	3.2	1757	0.7	2358	3.6
17 F	0613	0.4	1218	3.3	1831	0.6		
18 SA	0038	3.6	0648	0.4	1257	3.3	1908	0.6
19 SU	0122	3.6	0728	0.5	1339	3.3	1950	0.7
20 M	0209	3.5	0813	0.7	1426	3.2	2039	0.8
21 TU	0304	3.3	0906	0.9	1523	3.1	) 2141	1.0
22 W	0412	3.1	1011	1.2	1634	3.0	2313	1.1
23 TH	0534	2.9	1146	1.3	1802	2.9		
24 F	0059	1.0	0706	2.9	1324	1.2	1932	3.0
25 SA	0213	0.8	0825	3.0	1429	1.1	2039	3.3
26 SU	0311	0.6	0919	3.2	1521	0.9	2130	3.4
27 M	0400	0.4	1004	3.3	1605	0.8	2214	3.6
28 TU	0442	0.4	1045	3.3	1645	0.7	O 2256	3.6
29 W	0520	0.4	1125	3.3	1721	0.7	2336	3.6
30 TH	0554	0.5	1203	3.3	1754	0.7		

OCTOBER

Day	Time	m	Time	m	Time	m	Time	m
1 F	0015	3.5	0624	0.6	1239	3.3	1827	0.8
2 SA	0053	3.5	0654	0.7	1314	3.3	1902	0.8
3 SU	0130	3.4	0727	0.9	1351	3.3	1941	0.9
4 M	0209	3.2	0804	1.0	1432	3.3	2023	1.0
5 TU	0252	3.1	0848	1.2	1518	3.2	2114	1.1
6 W	0344	2.9	0945	1.3	1611	3.0	) 2224	1.2
7 TH	0446	2.7	1114	1.5	1713	2.9	2355	1.3
8 F	0601	2.6	1235	1.4	1823	2.9		
9 SA	0105	1.1	0754	2.7	1338	1.3	1936	3.0
10 SU	0203	1.0	0843	2.9	1429	1.1	2030	3.1
11 M	0250	0.8	0919	3.0	1512	1.0	2109	3.3
12 TU	0330	0.6	0948	3.1	1550	0.9	2143	3.4
13 W	0405	0.5	1015	3.2	1624	0.6	2217	3.5
14 TH	0437	0.5	1044	3.3	1656	0.7	● 2254	3.6
15 F	0509	0.5	1118	3.4	1729	0.6	2335	3.7
16 SA	0544	0.5	1155	3.5	1806	0.6		
17 SU	0019	3.7	0623	0.5	1237	3.5	1847	0.6
18 M	0107	3.6	0710	0.6	1322	3.4	1933	0.7
19 TU	0159	3.4	0755	0.9	1412	3.3	2027	1.0
20 W	0259	3.2	0851	1.1	1510	3.2	) 2137	1.0
21 TH	0410	3.0	1002	1.3	1625	3.0	2318	1.0
22 F	0533	2.9	1140	1.4	1754	3.0		
23 SA	0045	1.2	0702	2.9	1307	1.3	1918	3.1
24 SU	0156	0.7	0808	3.0	1412	1.1	2020	3.3
25 M	0252	0.6	0859	3.2	1504	1.0	2110	3.5
26 TU	0339	0.5	0942	3.3	1547	0.9	2154	3.5
27 W	0418	0.5	1022	3.3	1625	0.8	2234	3.6
28 TH	0453	0.6	1059	3.4	1659	0.6	O 2313	3.5
29 F	0524	0.7	1135	3.4	1730	0.8	2349	3.5
30 SA	0553	0.8	1209	3.5	1802	0.8		
31 SU	0025	3.4	0623	0.9	1245	3.5	1836	0.9

NOVEMBER

Day	Time	m	Time	m	Time	m	Time	m
1 M	0102	3.3	0657	1.0	1323	3.5	1914	0.9
2 TU	0141	3.2	0735	1.1	1403	3.4	1957	1.0
3 W	0224	3.1	0819	1.2	1447	3.3	2046	1.1
4 TH	0315	2.9	0913	1.4	1537	3.2	2147	1.2
5 F	0416	2.8	1021	1.4	1635	3.1	) 2303	1.2
6 SA	0522	2.7	1143	1.5	1739	3.0		
7 SU	0016	1.1	0633	2.8	1251	1.4	1842	3.0
8 M	0116	1.0	0738	2.9	1346	1.2	1938	3.1
9 TU	0205	0.9	0825	3.0	1431	1.1	2026	3.3
10 W	0247	0.7	0905	3.2	1513	0.9	2109	3.4
11 TH	0325	0.6	0942	3.3	1551	0.8	2151	3.6
12 F	0402	0.5	1019	3.4	1628	0.7	● 2234	3.6
13 SA	0440	0.5	1059	3.5	1708	0.6	2320	3.7
14 SU	0522	0.6	1143	3.6	1751	0.6		
15 M	0009	3.6	0607	0.7	1229	3.6	1837	0.6
16 TU	0102	3.5	0655	0.8	1318	3.5	1929	0.6
17 W	0158	3.4	0749	1.0	1410	3.5	2029	0.7
18 TH	0300	3.2	0848	1.1	1508	3.3	2142	0.8
19 F	0408	3.0	0958	1.2	1618	3.2	) 2302	0.8
20 SA	0524	2.9	1117	1.3	1736	3.2		
21 SU	0017	0.8	0636	3.0	1232	1.3	1849	3.2
22 M	0124	0.7	0738	3.0	1339	1.2	1951	3.3
23 TU	0222	0.7	0830	3.1	1435	1.0	2044	3.4
24 W	0310	0.7	0915	3.3	1523	0.9	2131	3.4
25 TH	0351	0.7	0957	3.3	1604	0.9	2214	3.4
26 F	0427	0.8	1036	3.4	1641	0.9	O 2253	3.4
27 SA	0500	0.9	1112	3.5	1714	0.9	2330	3.4
28 SU	0531	1.0	1148	3.5	1746	0.9		
29 M	0005	3.3	0602	1.0	1225	3.6	1820	0.9
30 TU	0042	3.2	0637	1.1	1303	3.6	1857	0.9

DECEMBER

Day	Time	m	Time	m	Time	m	Time	m
1 W	0120	3.2	0716	1.1	1341	3.5	1938	0.9
2 TH	0201	3.1	0759	1.2	1421	3.4	2022	1.0
3 F	0247	3.0	0846	1.2	1504	3.3	2113	1.0
4 SA	0341	2.9	0939	1.3	1555	3.2	2210	1.0
5 SU	0441	2.8	1038	1.3	1652	3.1	) 2312	1.0
6 M	0542	2.8	1141	1.3	1752	3.1		
7 TU	0014	1.0	0640	2.9	1245	1.3	1850	3.2
8 W	0111	0.9	0735	3.0	1343	1.2	1946	3.3
9 TH	0203	0.8	0825	3.2	1435	1.0	2038	3.4
10 F	0250	0.7	0912	3.3	1523	0.9	2129	3.5
11 SA	0335	0.6	0958	3.4	1609	0.7	2219	3.6
12 SU	0421	0.6	1046	3.5	1656	0.6	● 2311	3.6
13 M	0509	0.7	1135	3.6	1745	0.5		
14 TU	0004	3.5	0558	0.7	1225	3.6	1836	0.5
15 W	0059	3.4	0650	0.8	1315	3.6	1930	0.5
16 TH	0155	3.3	0744	0.9	1407	3.6	2028	0.5
17 F	0254	3.2	0841	1.0	1502	3.5	2130	0.6
18 SA	0355	3.1	0940	1.0	1602	3.4	) 2235	0.6
19 SU	0458	3.0	1044	1.1	1706	3.3	2340	0.7
20 M	0600	3.0	1150	1.1	1811	3.2		
21 TU	0043	0.8	0659	3.0	1256	1.2	1915	3.2
22 W	0144	0.8	0755	3.0	1400	1.1	2016	3.2
23 TH	0238	0.9	0847	3.1	1457	1.0	2110	3.2
24 F	0324	0.9	0934	3.3	1546	1.0	2157	3.2
25 SA	0404	0.9	1016	3.4	1627	0.9	2239	3.2
26 SU	0440	0.9	1056	3.5	1703	0.9	O 2317	3.2
27 M	0514	1.0	1133	3.5	1736	0.9	2352	3.2
28 TU	0547	1.0	1209	3.6	1808	0.9		
29 W	0027	3.1	0622	1.0	1246	3.6	1843	0.8
30 TH	0101	3.1	0659	1.0	1320	3.5	1919	0.8
31 F	0135	3.0	0737	1.0	1354	3.5	1958	0.8

Chart Datum: 2·01 metres below Ordnance Datum (Belfast)

Chapter 5

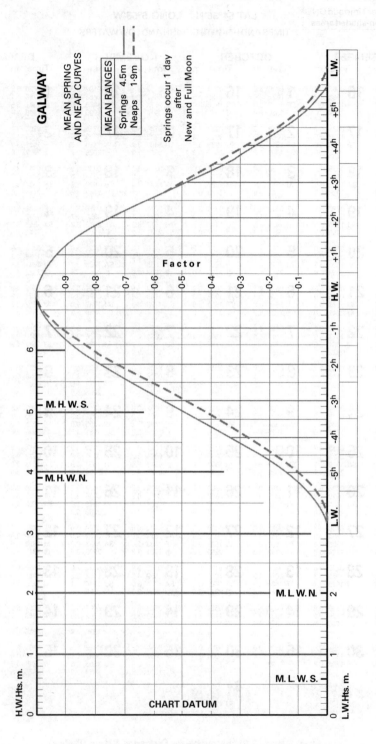

GALWAY

MEAN SPRING
AND NEAP CURVES

MEAN RANGES	
Springs	4.5m
Neaps	1.9m

Springs occur 1 day
after
New and Full Moon

TIME ZONE (UT)
For Summer Time add ONE hour in **non-shaded areas**

IRELAND – GALWAY

LAT 53°16'N   LONG 9°03'W

TIMES AND HEIGHTS OF HIGH AND LOW WATERS

YEAR **2004**

JANUARY

Time	m		Time	m
1 0013	3.9	**16**	0503	1.8
0608	2.1		1128	4.2
TH 1227	3.9	F	1735	1.6
1832	1.9			
2 0115	4.0	**17**	0021	4.2
0712	2.0		0616	1.8
F 1332	3.9	SA	1240	4.2
1938	1.9		1858	1.6
3 0213	4.1	**18**	0129	4.3
0810	1.9		0735	1.6
SA 1431	4.0	SU	1358	4.3
2030	1.8		2013	1.5
4 0301	4.2	**19**	0234	4.5
0858	1.7		0840	1.3
SU 1520	4.1	M	1505	4.5
2112	1.7		2110	1.2
5 0342	4.3	**20**	0330	4.8
0941	1.5		0935	1.0
M 1602	4.2	TU	1601	4.7
2149	1.5		2159	1.0
6 0419	4.5	**21**	0421	5.0
1021	1.4		1025	0.7
TU 1642	4.4	W	1652	4.9
2226	1.4		2246	0.8
7 0457	4.6	**22**	0511	5.2
1100	1.2		1112	0.5
W 1721	4.5	TH	1741	5.0
O 2303	1.3		2331	0.7
8 0535	4.6	**23**	0559	5.2
1137	1.1		1157	0.4
TH 1800	4.5	F	1827	5.0
2340	1.2			
9 0613	4.7	**24**	0014	0.7
1212	1.0		0644	5.2
F 1839	4.6	SA	1239	0.4
			1911	4.9
10 0017	1.2	**25**	0057	0.8
0650	4.7		0727	5.1
SA 1247	0.9	SU	1319	0.5
1917	4.6		1954	4.7
11 0055	1.2	**26**	0138	0.9
0726	4.7		0810	4.9
SU 1323	0.9	M	1358	0.7
1956	4.5		2038	4.5
12 0134	1.3	**27**	0220	1.2
0803	4.7		0853	4.6
M 1401	1.0	TU	1439	1.1
2037	4.4		2124	4.2
13 0216	1.4	**28**	0305	1.5
0842	4.6		0939	4.3
TU 1443	1.2	W	1523	1.4
2124	4.3		2214	4.0
14 0304	1.6	**29**	0359	1.8
0929	4.5		1027	4.0
W 1532	1.3	TH	1614	1.7
2219	4.2		☽ 2308	3.8
15 0359	1.7	**30**	0506	2.0
1025	4.3		1121	3.7
TH 1628	1.5	F	1718	2.0
☽ 2317	4.2			
		31	0009	3.7
			0622	2.1
		SA	1229	3.6
			1840	2.1

FEBRUARY

Time	m		Time	m
1 0126	3.7	**16**	0110	4.0
0737	2.1		0721	1.7
SU 1355	3.6	M	1352	4.0
2000	2.0		2010	1.7
2 0240	3.8	**17**	0227	4.2
0840	1.9		0839	1.4
M 1504	3.7	TU	1505	4.2
2056	1.8		2109	1.4
3 0330	4.0	**18**	0326	4.5
0928	1.6		0934	1.1
TU 1552	4.0	W	1559	4.5
2138	1.6		2155	1.1
4 0410	4.2	**19**	0416	4.8
1009	1.3		1020	0.7
W 1632	4.2	TH	1646	4.7
2216	1.3		2237	0.8
5 0447	4.4	**20**	0502	5.0
1046	1.0		1101	0.4
TH 1710	4.4	F	1729	4.9
2253	1.1		● 2318	0.6
6 0523	4.6	**21**	0546	5.2
1122	0.8		1141	0.3
F 1746	4.6	SA	1811	5.0
O 2330	0.9		2357	0.5
7 0559	4.8	**22**	0627	5.2
1157	0.6		1217	0.3
SA 1823	4.7	SU	1850	4.9
8 0005	0.8	**23**	0034	0.5
0634	4.9		0706	5.1
SU 1230	0.5	M	1253	0.4
1857	4.8		1927	4.8
9 0040	0.7	**24**	0111	0.7
0708	4.9		0744	4.9
M 1303	0.5	TU	1328	0.6
1932	4.7		2004	4.6
10 0116	0.8	**25**	0148	0.9
0742	4.9		0821	4.6
TU 1338	0.6	W	1402	0.9
2008	4.6		2041	4.3
11 0154	0.9	**26**	0225	1.2
0816	4.7		0858	4.3
W 1417	0.8	TH	1438	1.3
2047	4.5		2120	4.0
12 0237	1.1	**27**	0307	1.6
0857	4.5		0938	4.0
TH 1501	1.1	F	1517	1.7
2136	4.3		2205	3.8
13 0327	1.4	**28**	0402	2.0
0950	4.3		1027	3.7
F 1553	1.5	SA	1607	2.1
☽ 2238	4.1		☽ 2300	3.6
14 0428	1.7	**29**	0537	2.2
1059	4.1		1127	3.4
SA 1658	1.8	SU	1750	2.3
2349	4.0			
15 0544	1.8			
1220	3.9			
SU 1833	1.9			

MARCH

Time	m		Time	m
1 0014	3.4	**16**	0102	3.9
0705	2.2		0721	1.7
M 1320	3.3	TU	1356	3.9
1933	2.2		2008	1.8
2 0228	3.6	**17**	0221	4.2
0817	1.9		0836	1.4
TU 1457	3.6	W	1501	4.2
2036	1.9		2100	1.4
3 0319	3.8	**18**	0316	4.5
0907	1.6		0928	1.1
W 1540	3.9	TH	1548	4.5
2119	1.6		2141	1.1
4 0356	4.1	**19**	0402	4.8
0946	1.2		1004	0.7
TH 1616	4.2	F	1630	4.8
2157	1.2		2220	0.8
5 0430	4.4	**20**	0445	5.0
1023	0.8		1041	0.5
F 1651	4.5	SA	1709	4.9
2233	0.9		● 2257	0.5
6 0504	4.6	**21**	0526	5.1
1058	0.5		1117	0.4
SA 1725	4.7	SU	1747	5.0
O 2308	0.6		2334	0.5
7 0539	4.9	**22**	0605	5.1
1131	0.3		1151	0.4
SU 1759	4.9	M	1824	5.0
2343	0.4			
8 0613	5.0	**23**	0010	0.5
1204	0.2		0641	5.1
M 1832	5.0	TU	1225	0.4
			1858	4.9
9 0017	0.3	**24**	0044	0.6
0646	5.1		0717	4.9
TU 1238	0.2	W	1255	0.7
1905	5.0		1931	4.7
10 0053	0.4	**25**	0118	0.9
0719	5.0		0751	4.6
W 1313	0.4	TH	1327	1.0
1938	4.8		2004	4.4
11 0131	0.6	**26**	0152	1.2
0754	4.8		0826	4.3
TH 1351	0.7	F	1359	1.4
2015	4.6		2039	4.2
12 0213	0.9	**27**	0228	1.6
0834	4.6		0904	4.0
F 1433	1.1	SA	1433	1.7
2101	4.3		2122	3.9
13 0302	1.2	**28**	0312	1.9
0928	4.2		0953	3.7
SA 1524	1.5	SU	1514	2.1
☽ 2205	4.0		☽ 2215	3.6
14 0404	1.6	**29**	0459	2.2
1043	3.9		1052	3.4
SU 1634	1.9	M	1627	2.4
	2327	3.8		2320	3.4
15 0530	1.8	**30**	0633	2.1
1216	3.7		1217	3.3
M 1838	2.0	TU	1900	2.3
		31	0152	3.5
			0740	1.9
		W	1431	3.6
			2002	2.0

APRIL

Time	m		Time	m
1 0248	3.8	**16**	0255	4.5
0832	1.6		0902	1.0
TH 1512	3.9	F	1527	4.6
2048	1.6		2119	1.1
2 0326	4.1	**17**	0340	4.8
0913	1.2		0940	0.8
F 1547	4.3	SA	1606	4.8
2127	1.2		2156	0.8
3 0400	4.4	**18**	0421	4.9
0951	0.8		1016	0.7
SA 1620	4.6	SU	1644	4.9
2204	0.8		2233	0.7
4 0434	4.7	**19**	0501	5.0
1027	0.5		1050	0.6
SU 1653	4.9	M	1720	4.9
2240	0.5		● 2310	0.6
5 0509	4.9	**20**	0539	5.0
1101	0.2		1123	0.7
M 1727	5.1	TU	1755	4.9
O 2316	0.3		2345	0.7
6 0544	5.1	**21**	0615	4.9
1136	0.2		1153	0.8
TU 1802	5.2	W	1828	4.8
2352	0.2			
7 0621	5.2	**22**	0018	0.8
1211	0.2		0650	4.7
W 1837	5.2	TH	1224	1.0
			1901	4.7
8 0030	0.3	**23**	0051	1.0
0658	5.1		0725	4.5
TH 1248	0.4	F	1255	1.2
1913	5.0		1935	4.5
9 0111	0.4	**24**	0126	1.3
0738	4.9		0801	4.3
F 1328	0.7	SA	1328	1.5
1954	4.8		2011	4.2
10 0155	0.8	**25**	0203	1.6
0823	4.6		0841	4.0
SA 1413	1.2	SU	1404	1.8
2042	4.4		2053	4.0
11 0247	1.2	**26**	0246	1.9
0921	4.2		0930	3.7
SU 1507	1.7	M	1446	2.1
2149	4.1		2146	3.8
12 0353	1.6	**27**	0403	2.1
1040	3.9		1027	3.6
M 1628	2.0	TU	1550	2.4
☽ 2319	3.9		☽ 2247	3.6
13 0528	1.7	**28**	0554	2.1
1214	3.8		1135	3.5
TU 1831	2.0	W	1818	2.3
			2355	3.6
14 0050	4.0	**29**	0656	1.9
0707	1.6		1319	3.6
W 1343	4.0	TH	1919	2.1
1949	1.8			
15 0202	4.2	**30**	0142	3.8
0816	1.3		0748	1.6
TH 1442	4.3	F	1423	4.0
2039	1.4		2008	1.7

Chart Datum: 0·20 metres above Ordnance Datum (Dublin)
Register for your **FREE** weekly weather email service from Reeds Almanacs
at www.nauticaldata.com – **NOW!**
weekend weather reports sent to your email address, every Thursday

Chapter 5

TIME ZONE (UT)
For Summer Time add ONE hour in **non-shaded areas**

IRELAND – GALWAY

LAT 53°16′N   LONG 9°03′W

TIMES AND HEIGHTS OF HIGH AND LOW WATERS

YEAR **2004**

MAY

Time	m		Time	m
1 0236	4.1	**16**	0313	4.6
0834	1.2		0911	1.1
SA 1504	4.3	SU	1539	4.6
2051	1.3		2131	1.1
2 0317	4.4	**17**	0355	4.7
0915	0.9		0948	1.0
SU 1540	4.7	M	1616	4.7
2131	0.9		2209	1.0
3 0355	4.7	**18**	0434	4.7
0953	0.6		1022	1.0
M 1615	5.0	TU	1651	4.8
2209	0.6		2246	0.9
4 0434	5.0	**19**	0512	4.7
1030	0.4		1055	1.0
TU 1652	5.2	W	1725	4.8
O 2248	0.3	●	2322	1.0
5 0515	5.1	**20**	0550	4.6
1108	0.3		1126	1.1
W 1732	5.3	TH	1759	4.7
2328	0.2		2357	1.1
6 0558	5.2	**21**	0627	4.5
1147	0.4		1157	1.2
TH 1813	5.3	F	1835	4.6
7 0011	0.3	**22**	0032	1.2
0641	5.1		0704	4.4
F 1229	0.5	SA	1231	1.4
1855	5.1		1911	4.5
8 0056	0.4	**23**	0109	1.3
0727	4.9		0742	4.3
SA 1313	0.9	SU	1307	1.6
1941	4.9		1949	4.3
9 0144	0.7	**24**	0148	1.5
0817	4.6		0823	4.1
SU 1401	1.4	M	1346	1.8
2034	4.5		2032	4.1
10 0239	1.1	**25**	0232	1.7
0917	4.2		0909	3.9
M 1459	1.7	TU	1431	2.0
2142	4.2		2121	4.0
11 0346	1.4	**26**	0327	1.8
1032	4.0		1002	3.8
TU 1623	2.0	W	1529	2.1
◑ 2305	4.1		2217	3.9
12 0513	1.5	**27**	0448	1.8
1154	3.9		1100	3.8
W 1802	2.0	TH	1700	2.2
		◑	2315	3.9
13 0023	4.1	**28**	0600	1.7
0635	1.5		1201	3.9
TH 1312	4.0	F	1824	2.0
1915	1.8			
14 0131	4.2	**29**	0016	3.9
0741	1.4		0658	1.6
F 1412	4.3	SA	1307	4.0
2009	1.5		1922	1.7
15 0226	4.4	**30**	0124	4.1
0831	1.2		0750	1.3
SA 1459	4.5	SU	1407	4.3
2052	1.3		2012	1.4
		31	0225	4.4
			0837	1.1
		M	1455	4.6
			2057	1.0

JUNE

Time	m		Time	m
1 0316	4.6	**16**	0409	4.3
0920	0.8		0957	1.4
TU 1539	4.9	W	1624	4.5
2140	0.7		2226	1.2
2 0404	4.9	**17**	0449	4.4
1002	0.6		1031	1.3
W 1623	5.1	TH	1700	4.5
2224	0.5	●	2304	1.1
3 0452	5.0	**18**	0529	4.4
1045	0.6		1106	1.3
TH 1708	5.3	F	1737	4.5
O 2310	0.4		2343	1.1
4 0541	5.1	**19**	0608	4.4
1129	0.6		1141	1.3
F 1755	5.3	SA	1815	4.5
2357	0.3			
5 0630	5.0	**20**	0020	1.1
1215	0.7		0647	4.4
SA 1843	5.2	SU	1218	1.4
			1853	4.5
6 0046	0.4	**21**	0057	1.2
0718	4.9		0726	4.3
SU 1303	0.9	M	1255	1.4
1932	5.0		1931	4.4
7 0136	0.6	**22**	0134	1.2
0809	4.6		0805	4.2
M 1352	1.2	TU	1334	1.5
2026	4.7		2011	4.3
8 0228	0.9	**23**	0214	1.3
0906	4.4		0847	4.1
TU 1448	1.5	W	1416	1.6
2129	4.4		2055	4.2
9 0328	1.1	**24**	0257	1.4
1011	4.1		0933	4.1
W 1557	1.7	TH	1504	1.8
◑ 2239	4.2		2144	4.1
10 0438	1.4	**25**	0347	1.5
1119	4.0		1023	4.0
TH 1718	1.8	F	1602	1.8
2346	4.1	◑	2238	4.1
11 0549	1.5	**26**	0444	1.5
1226	4.0		1117	4.0
F 1831	1.8	SA	1709	1.8
			2335	4.1
12 0050	4.1	**27**	0547	1.5
0655	1.5		1214	4.1
SA 1330	4.1	SU	1822	1.7
1932	1.7			
13 0149	4.2	**28**	0036	4.1
0752	1.5		0655	1.5
SU 1425	4.2	M	1317	4.3
2022	1.5		1929	1.5
14 0242	4.2	**29**	0144	4.3
0839	1.5		0758	1.3
M 1509	4.3	TU	1418	4.5
2106	1.4		2027	1.2
15 0327	4.3	**30**	0248	4.5
0920	1.4		0853	1.1
TU 1548	4.4	W	1512	4.8
2146	1.2		2119	0.9

JULY

Time	m		Time	m
1 0344	4.7	**16**	0434	4.1
0942	0.9		1015	1.4
TH 1603	5.0	F	1645	4.4
2209	0.6		2250	1.1
2 0438	4.8	**17**	0514	4.3
1030	0.8		1053	1.3
F 1653	5.1	SA	1722	4.5
O 2258	0.4	●	2328	1.0
3 0530	4.9	**18**	0554	4.4
1118	0.7		1130	1.2
SA 1743	5.2	SU	1800	4.5
2348	0.3			
4 0620	4.9	**19**	0005	0.9
1205	0.7		0631	4.4
SU 1833	5.2	M	1206	1.1
			1836	4.6
5 0035	0.3	**20**	0040	0.8
0708	4.9		0708	4.5
M 1252	0.8	TU	1241	1.1
1921	5.0		1912	4.6
6 0122	0.4	**21**	0113	0.8
0756	4.7		0744	4.5
TU 1338	0.9	W	1316	1.1
2011	4.8		1947	4.5
7 0209	0.6	**22**	0148	0.9
0845	4.5		0821	4.4
W 1425	1.2	TH	1354	1.2
2104	4.6		2024	4.4
8 0258	0.9	**23**	0226	1.0
0938	4.3		0859	4.3
TH 1519	1.5	F	1436	1.4
2202	4.3		2105	4.3
9 0352	1.2	**24**	0309	1.2
1035	4.1		0943	4.2
F 1623	1.7	SA	1525	1.5
◑ 2302	4.1		2157	4.2
10 0452	1.5	**25**	0359	1.4
1134	3.9		1035	4.1
SA 1736	1.8	SU	1623	1.7
		◑	2258	4.1
11 0002	3.9	**26**	0457	1.6
0557	1.7		1133	4.1
SU 1237	3.8	M	1732	1.7
1848	1.9			
12 0105	3.8	**27**	0004	4.0
0704	1.8		0606	1.7
M 1343	3.9	TU	1241	4.1
1952	1.8		1854	1.7
13 0209	3.8	**28**	0120	4.1
0805	1.8		0731	1.6
TU 1442	4.0	W	1354	4.3
2045	1.6		2011	1.4
14 0304	3.9	**29**	0234	4.2
0854	1.7		0839	1.4
W 1528	4.1	TH	1459	4.6
2129	1.4		2110	1.0
15 0351	4.0	**30**	0336	4.5
0936	1.6		0933	1.0
TH 1607	4.3	F	1554	4.8
2210	1.3		2202	0.7
		31	0430	4.7
			1022	0.9
		SA	1644	5.0
		O	2250	0.4

AUGUST

Time	m		Time	m
1 0520	4.9	**16**	0536	4.5
1108	0.7		1112	1.0
SU 1733	5.2	M	1743	4.7
2336	0.2	●	2340	0.6
2 0607	4.9	**17**	0611	4.6
1152	0.6		1146	0.8
M 1820	5.2	TU	1817	4.8
3 0019	0.2	**18**	0013	0.5
0651	4.9		0645	4.7
TU 1234	0.6	W	1220	0.7
1904	5.1		1848	4.8
4 0101	0.3	**19**	0046	0.5
0734	4.8		0717	4.7
W 1315	0.7	TH	1253	0.8
1948	5.0		1919	4.8
5 0141	0.5	**20**	0119	0.6
0817	4.6		0749	4.6
TH 1356	0.9	F	1328	0.9
2033	4.7		1950	4.7
6 0222	0.8	**21**	0155	0.8
0900	4.4		0821	4.5
F 1439	1.3	SA	1407	1.1
2120	4.3		2026	4.5
7 0306	1.2	**22**	0236	1.1
0946	4.1		0900	4.3
SA 1529	1.6	SU	1452	1.4
◑ 2212	4.0		2116	4.2
8 0356	1.6	**23**	0323	1.4
1036	3.9		0952	4.2
SU 1635	1.9	M	1548	1.6
2309	3.7	◑	2226	4.0
9 0458	1.9	**24**	0423	1.8
1134	3.7		1058	4.0
M 1801	2.0	TU	1700	1.8
			2344	3.9
10 0016	3.6	**25**	0541	1.9
0615	2.1		1216	4.0
TU 1253	3.6	W	1841	1.8
1923	2.0			
11 0140	3.5	**26**	0113	3.9
0733	2.1		0728	1.9
W 1424	3.7	TH	1346	4.1
2029	1.8		2012	1.5
12 0252	3.7	**27**	0235	4.1
0833	1.9		0836	1.6
TH 1518	3.9	F	1456	4.5
2116	1.5		2109	1.1
13 0341	3.9	**28**	0333	4.5
0919	1.7		0926	1.2
F 1558	4.2	SA	1548	4.8
2154	1.2		2154	0.7
14 0422	4.1	**29**	0421	4.7
0959	1.4		1010	0.9
SA 1634	4.4	SU	1634	5.1
2230	1.0		2236	0.4
15 0459	4.4	**30**	0505	4.9
1036	1.2		1052	0.6
SU 1709	4.5	M	1718	5.3
2306	0.7	O	2317	0.2
		31	0548	5.0
			1132	0.5
		TU	1801	5.3
			2356	0.6

Chart Datum: 0·20 metres above Ordnance Datum (Dublin)

TIME ZONE (UT)
For Summer Time add ONE hour in **non-shaded areas**

IRELAND – GALWAY
LAT 53°16′N   LONG 9°03′W
TIMES AND HEIGHTS OF HIGH AND LOW WATERS

SEPTEMBER
Time m	Time m
1 0629 5.0 / 1210 0.5 / W 1842 5.2	**16** 0614 4.9 / 1152 0.5 / TH 1820 5.0
2 0033 0.3 / 0707 4.9 / TH 1244 0.4 / 1921 5.0	**17** 0015 0.4 / 0645 5.0 / F 1226 0.6 / 1850 5.0
3 0110 0.5 / 0744 4.8 / F 1325 0.8 / 1959 4.7	**18** 0049 0.6 / 0716 4.9 / SA 1302 0.7 / 1923 4.8
4 0146 0.9 / 0821 4.5 / SA 1402 1.2 / 2039 4.4	**19** 0125 0.8 / 0748 4.7 / SU 1342 0.9 / 2001 4.6
5 0223 1.3 / 0858 4.2 / SU 1442 1.6 / 2123 4.0	**20** 0206 1.2 / 0827 4.5 / M 1427 1.3 / 2052 4.3
6 0304 1.7 / 0941 3.9 / M 1535 2.0 / ☽ 2217 3.7	**21** 0255 1.6 / 0921 4.2 / TU 1523 1.7 / ● 2210 4.0
7 0401 2.1 / 1032 3.7 / TU 1721 2.4 / 2326 3.4	**22** 0359 2.0 / 1036 4.0 / W 1641 1.9 / 2339 3.8
8 0543 2.3 / 1141 3.5 / W 1855 2.2	**23** 0545 2.2 / 1208 3.9 / TH 1852 1.9
9 0120 3.4 / 0707 2.3 / TH 1412 3.6 / 2008 1.9	**24** 0117 3.9 / 0727 2.0 / F 1344 4.2 / 2009 1.5
10 0242 3.7 / 0810 2.0 / F 1504 3.9 / 2054 1.6	**25** 0231 4.3 / 0825 1.6 / SA 1446 4.6 / 2058 1.1
11 0325 4.0 / 0856 1.7 / SA 1541 4.2 / 2128 1.2	**26** 0321 4.6 / 0911 1.2 / SU 1534 4.9 / 2138 0.7
12 0401 4.2 / 0935 1.4 / SU 1614 4.4 / 2202 1.0	**27** 0403 4.9 / 0951 0.6 / M 1617 5.2 / 2215 0.5
13 0435 4.5 / 1011 1.1 / M 1646 4.7 / 2237 0.6	**28** 0444 5.1 / 1030 0.7 / TU 1658 5.3 / ○ 2252 0.4
14 0509 4.7 / 1046 0.8 / TU 1718 4.9 / 2310 0.5	**29** 0523 5.1 / 1108 0.5 / W 1738 5.3 / 2328 0.4
15 0542 4.9 / 1120 0.6 / W 1749 5.0 / 2343 0.4	**30** 0601 5.1 / 1145 0.6 / TH 1816 5.2

OCTOBER
Time m	Time m
1 0003 0.6 / 0637 5.0 / F 1221 0.7 / 1852 5.0	**16** 0613 5.2 / 1201 0.5 / SA 1827 5.2
2 0037 0.8 / 0712 4.8 / SA 1255 1.0 / 1929 4.8	**17** 0021 0.7 / 0648 5.1 / SU 1241 0.6 / 1906 5.0
3 0110 1.1 / 0746 4.6 / SU 1329 1.3 / 2006 4.4	**18** 0101 0.9 / 0727 4.9 / M 1323 0.9 / 1951 4.7
4 0144 1.5 / 0821 4.3 / M 1406 1.7 / 2048 4.1	**19** 0146 1.3 / 0811 4.7 / TU 1411 1.3 / 2048 4.3
5 0221 1.9 / 0902 4.0 / TU 1449 2.0 / 2140 3.7	**20** 0238 1.8 / 0909 4.3 / W 1510 1.7 / ☽ 2206 4.0
6 0308 2.3 / 0952 3.8 / W 1642 2.3 / ☽ 2247 3.5	**21** 0350 2.2 / 1028 4.1 / TH 1636 1.9 / 2336 3.9
7 0517 2.5 / 1055 3.6 / TH 1820 2.3	**22** 0551 2.2 / 1201 4.1 / F 1840 1.8
8 0047 3.5 / 0637 2.4 / F 1333 3.6 / 1926 2.0	**23** 0106 4.1 / 0709 2.0 / SA 1325 4.3 / 1949 1.5
9 0213 3.7 / 0736 2.2 / SA 1431 3.9 / 2015 1.7	**24** 0212 4.4 / 0804 1.6 / SU 1425 4.7 / 2036 1.2
10 0254 4.1 / 0823 1.8 / SU 1509 4.2 / 2053 1.3	**25** 0259 4.7 / 0849 1.3 / M 1512 4.9 / 2115 0.9
11 0329 4.4 / 0904 1.4 / M 1542 4.5 / 2129 1.0	**26** 0340 5.0 / 0929 1.0 / TU 1554 5.1 / 2151 0.8
12 0402 4.6 / 0941 1.1 / TU 1613 4.8 / 2204 0.7	**27** 0418 5.1 / 1007 0.9 / W 1634 5.2 / 2227 0.7
13 0434 4.9 / 1016 0.8 / W 1644 5.0 / 2238 0.5	**28** 0456 5.1 / 1045 0.8 / TH 1712 5.2 / ○ 2301 0.8
14 0506 5.1 / 1050 0.6 / TH 1716 5.1 / ● 2311 0.4	**29** 0532 5.1 / 1121 0.8 / F 1750 5.1 / 2333 1.0
15 0539 5.2 / 1125 0.5 / F 1750 5.2 / 2345 0.5	**30** 0607 5.0 / 1156 1.0 / SA 1827 4.9
	31 0005 1.2 / 0642 4.9 / SU 1230 1.2 / 1903 4.7

NOVEMBER
Time m	Time m
1 0039 1.4 / 0717 4.7 / M 1305 1.4 / 1941 4.4	**16** 0047 1.0 / 0715 5.1 / TU 1313 0.8 / 1947 4.8
2 0114 1.7 / 0754 4.4 / TU 1343 1.7 / 2024 4.1	**17** 0135 1.4 / 0805 4.8 / W 1404 1.1 / 2045 4.4
3 0152 2.0 / 0835 4.2 / W 1426 2.0 / 2115 3.9	**18** 0231 1.8 / 0904 4.5 / TH 1503 1.5 / 2158 4.2
4 0239 2.4 / 0924 4.0 / TH 1535 2.2 / 2216 3.7	**19** 0344 2.0 / 1018 4.3 / F 1622 1.7 / ☽ 2318 4.1
5 0419 2.6 / 1022 3.8 / F 1732 2.2 / ☽ 2331 3.7	**20** 0523 2.1 / 1138 4.3 / SA 1802 1.7
6 0556 2.5 / 1126 3.8 / SA 1835 2.1	**21** 0035 4.2 / 0637 1.9 / SU 1252 4.4 / 1915 1.5
7 0104 3.8 / 0653 2.3 / SU 1306 3.9 / 1928 1.8	**22** 0140 4.4 / 0735 1.7 / M 1354 4.6 / 2008 1.4
8 0203 4.1 / 0743 2.0 / M 1414 4.1 / 2013 1.5	**23** 0231 4.6 / 0824 1.5 / TU 1446 4.7 / 2050 1.2
9 0243 4.4 / 0824 1.6 / TU 1455 4.4 / 2053 1.2	**24** 0314 4.6 / 0906 1.3 / W 1530 4.8 / 2127 1.2
10 0319 4.7 / 0907 1.3 / W 1530 4.7 / 2130 0.9	**25** 0353 4.9 / 0946 1.2 / TH 1610 4.9 / 2203 1.2
11 0353 5.0 / 0945 1.0 / TH 1607 5.0 / 2205 0.7	**26** 0429 4.9 / 1024 1.1 / F 1649 4.9 / ○ 2236 1.2
12 0429 5.2 / 1022 0.7 / F 1645 5.2 / ● 2241 0.6	**27** 0505 4.9 / 1102 1.1 / SA 1727 4.8 / 2309 1.3
13 0507 5.3 / 1101 0.6 / SA 1727 5.2 / 2320 0.6	**28** 0542 4.9 / 1138 1.2 / SU 1805 4.7 / 2342 1.4
14 0548 5.3 / 1142 0.5 / SU 1811 5.2	**29** 0619 4.8 / 1215 1.3 / M 1844 4.6
15 0002 0.8 / 0630 5.3 / M 1227 0.6 / 1857 5.0	**30** 0018 1.6 / 0656 4.7 / TU 1252 1.4 / 1923 4.4

DECEMBER
Time m	Time m
1 0057 1.7 / 0735 4.5 / W 1330 1.6 / 2005 4.2	**16** 0129 1.2 / 0759 5.0 / TH 1356 0.8 / 2036 4.6
2 0137 1.9 / 0815 4.4 / TH 1412 1.7 / 2052 4.1	**17** 0221 1.4 / 0854 4.8 / F 1449 1.1 / 2138 4.4
3 0222 2.1 / 0859 4.2 / F 1500 1.9 / 2145 3.9	**18** 0322 1.7 / 0957 4.5 / SA 1551 1.4 / ☽ 2245 4.2
4 0318 2.3 / 0949 4.1 / SA 1604 2.0 / 2243 3.9	**19** 0436 1.9 / 1103 4.3 / SU 1705 1.6 / 2352 4.2
5 0438 2.3 / 1043 4.0 / SU 1723 2.0 / ☽ 2343 3.9	**20** 0552 1.9 / 1209 4.3 / M 1824 1.7
6 0553 2.2 / 1139 4.0 / M 1828 1.9	**21** 0057 4.2 / 0657 1.9 / TU 1315 4.2 / 1931 1.7
7 0043 4.1 / 0652 2.1 / TU 1241 4.1 / 1924 1.7	**22** 0158 4.3 / 0755 1.8 / W 1415 4.3 / 2023 1.6
8 0142 4.3 / 0745 1.8 / W 1348 4.3 / 2012 1.4	**23** 0248 4.4 / 0845 1.6 / TH 1506 4.4 / 2105 1.6
9 0231 4.6 / 0832 1.5 / TH 1446 4.6 / 2056 1.2	**24** 0331 4.5 / 0929 1.5 / F 1551 4.4 / 2144 1.5
10 0316 4.9 / 0916 1.1 / F 1536 4.8 / 2138 1.0	**25** 0410 4.6 / 1010 1.4 / SA 1632 4.5 / 2220 1.5
11 0359 5.1 / 1000 0.9 / SA 1623 5.0 / 2220 1.0	**26** 0448 4.6 / 1050 1.3 / SU 1712 4.5 / ○ 2256 1.4
12 0445 5.3 / 1045 0.6 / SU 1712 5.1 / ● 2305 0.8	**27** 0526 4.7 / 1129 1.2 / M 1751 4.5 / 2332 1.4
13 0532 5.3 / 1131 0.5 / M 1802 5.1 / 2351 0.8	**28** 0604 4.7 / 1206 1.2 / TU 1830 4.5
14 0620 5.3 / 1219 0.5 / TU 1851 5.0	**29** 0009 1.4 / 0642 4.7 / W 1242 1.2 / 1909 4.5
15 0039 0.9 / 0708 5.2 / W 1307 0.6 / 1941 4.7	**30** 0046 1.5 / 0719 4.6 / TH 1317 1.2 / 1948 4.4
	31 0124 1.6 / 0756 4.5 / F 1353 1.3 / 2028 4.3

Chapter 5

Chart Datum: 0·20 metres above Ordnance Datum (Dublin)
Register for your **FREE** weekly weather email service from Reeds Almanacs
》》 at www.nauticaldata.com **– NOW!**
weekend weather reports sent to your email address, every Thursday 《《

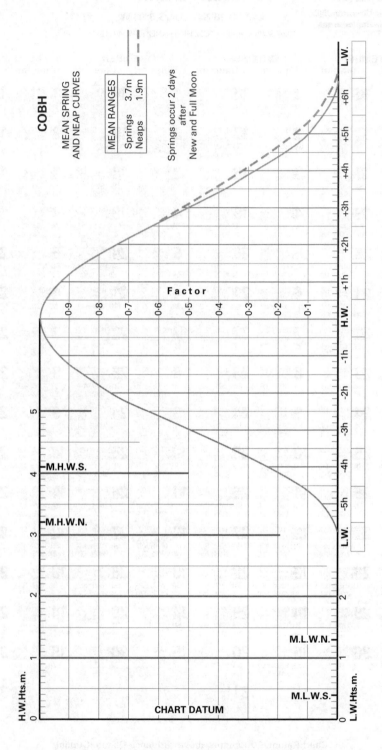

COBH

MEAN SPRING
AND NEAP CURVES

MEAN RANGES	
Springs	3.7m
Neaps	1.9m

Springs occur 2 days
after
New and Full Moon

Factor

0·9 0·8 0·7 0·6 0·5 0·4 0·3 0·2 0·1

H.W.Hts.m.

M.H.W.S.

M.H.W.N.

CHART DATUM

L.W. +6h +5h +4h +3h +2h +1h H.W. -1h -2h -3h -4h -5h L.W.

M.L.W.N.

M.L.W.S.

L.W.Hts.m.

Register for your **FREE** weekly weather email service from Reeds Almanacs
at www.nauticaldata.com **– NOW!**
weekend weather reports sent to your email address, every Thursday

342

IRELAND – COBH

YEAR 2004

TIME ZONE (UT)
For Summer Time add ONE hour in **non-shaded areas**

LAT 51°51′N   LONG 8°18′W
TIMES AND HEIGHTS OF HIGH AND LOW WATERS

JANUARY

Day	Time	m	Day	Time	m
1 TH	0644 / 1236 / 1912	1.2 / 3.4 / 1.3	**16** F	0541 / 1141 / 1817	1.2 / 3.6 / 1.3
2 F	0101 / 0744 / 1336 / 2009	3.3 / 1.2 / 3.4 / 1.3	**17** SA	0010 / 0650 / 1248 / 1929	3.6 / 1.2 / 3.6 / 1.2
3 SA	0203 / 0839 / 1432 / 2103	3.4 / 1.2 / 3.5 / 1.2	**18** SU	0120 / 0803 / 1400 / 2042	3.6 / 1.1 / 3.6 / 1.1
4 SU	0259 / 0932 / 1524 / 2152	3.5 / 1.1 / 3.6 / 1.1	**19** M	0233 / 0917 / 1510 / 2150	3.7 / 1.0 / 3.7 / 0.9
5 M	0350 / 1019 / 1611 / 2236	3.7 / 1.1 / 3.7 / 1.0	**20** TU	0343 / 1024 / 1615 / 2250	3.9 / 0.8 / 3.8 / 0.7
6 TU	0435 / 1101 / 1654 / 2315	3.8 / 1.0 / 3.8 / 0.9	**21** W	0445 / 1120 / 1711 / ●2342	4.0 / 0.6 / 4.0 / 0.5
7 W	0516 / 1139 / 1732 / ○2350	3.9 / 0.9 / 3.9 / 0.8	**22** TH	0537 / 1210 / 1759	4.2 / 0.5 / 4.1
8 TH	0553 / 1214 / 1807	4.0 / 0.9 / 3.9	**23** F	0029 / 0623 / 1256 / 1843	0.4 / 4.3 / 0.4 / 4.1
9 F	0024 / 0628 / 1249 / 1840	0.8 / 4.0 / 0.9 / 3.9	**24** SA	0114 / 0707 / 1338 / 1924	0.3 / 4.2 / 0.4 / 4.0
10 SA	0059 / 0703 / 1326 / 1915	0.8 / 4.0 / 0.9 / 3.9	**25** SU	0156 / 0749 / 1420 / 2004	0.4 / 4.1 / 0.6 / 3.9
11 SU	0137 / 0739 / 1404 / 1953	0.8 / 4.0 / 0.9 / 3.9	**26** M	0239 / 0830 / 1500 / 2043	0.5 / 4.0 / 0.7 / 3.8
12 M	0218 / 0819 / 1445 / 2034	0.9 / 3.9 / 1.0 / 3.8	**27** TU	0320 / 0911 / 1540 / 2122	0.7 / 3.8 / 0.9 / 3.6
13 TU	0301 / 0902 / 1529 / 2119	0.9 / 3.9 / 1.0 / 3.8	**28** W	0402 / 0952 / 1622 / 2203	0.9 / 3.7 / 1.1 / 3.5
14 W	0349 / 0949 / 1617 / 2209	1.0 / 3.8 / 1.1 / 3.7	**29** TH	0447 / 1036 / 1708 / ◐2249	1.1 / 3.5 / 1.2 / 3.4
15 TH	0441 / 1041 / 1712 / ◐2305	1.1 / 3.7 / 1.4 / 3.6	**30** F	0539 / 1127 / 1803 / 2347	1.3 / 3.3 / 1.4 / 3.2
			31 SA	0639 / 1231 / 1907	1.4 / 3.2 / 1.4

FEBRUARY

Day	Time	m	Day	Time	m
1 SU	0100 / 0745 / 1345 / 2015	3.2 / 1.4 / 3.2 / 1.4	**16** M	0052 / 0739 / 1340 / 2023	3.4 / 1.3 / 3.3 / 1.2
2 M	0218 / 0851 / 1453 / 2119	3.3 / 1.3 / 3.3 / 1.3	**17** TU	0222 / 0908 / 1504 / 2142	3.4 / 1.1 / 3.4 / 1.0
3 TU	0323 / 0952 / 1550 / 2215	3.5 / 1.2 / 3.5 / 1.1	**18** W	0340 / 1020 / 1611 / 2244	3.7 / 0.8 / 3.7 / 0.7
4 W	0416 / 1042 / 1638 / 2259	3.7 / 1.0 / 3.7 / 0.9	**19** TH	0439 / 1114 / 1703 / 2333	3.9 / 0.5 / 3.9 / 0.4
5 TH	0500 / 1124 / 1719 / 2336	3.8 / 0.8 / 3.8 / 0.7	**20** F	0527 / 1159 / 1748 / ●	4.1 / 0.4 / 4.0
6 F	0538 / 1200 / 1755 / ○	4.0 / 0.7 / 3.9	**21** SA	0016 / 0608 / 1240 / 1827	0.3 / 4.2 / 0.3 / 4.1
7 SA	0009 / 0613 / 1235 / 1828	0.6 / 4.0 / 0.6 / 4.0	**22** SU	0056 / 0647 / 1317 / 1903	0.2 / 4.2 / 0.3 / 4.1
8 SU	0043 / 0647 / 1309 / 1901	0.6 / 4.1 / 0.6 / 4.0	**23** M	0132 / 0723 / 1352 / 1937	0.3 / 4.1 / 0.4 / 4.0
9 M	0119 / 0721 / 1345 / 1935	0.6 / 4.1 / 0.6 / 4.0	**24** TU	0208 / 0758 / 1425 / 2009	0.4 / 4.0 / 0.6 / 3.9
10 TU	0157 / 0757 / 1422 / 2012	0.6 / 4.0 / 0.7 / 3.9	**25** W	0242 / 0833 / 1458 / 2042	0.6 / 3.9 / 0.7 / 3.8
11 W	0237 / 0836 / 1501 / 2052	0.6 / 4.0 / 0.8 / 3.9	**26** TH	0317 / 0907 / 1532 / 2118	0.8 / 3.7 / 0.9 / 3.6
12 TH	0320 / 0919 / 1543 / 2137	0.8 / 3.9 / 0.9 / 3.8	**27** F	0355 / 0944 / 1609 / 2158	1.0 / 3.5 / 1.1 / 3.4
13 F	0408 / 1006 / 1633 / ◐2229	0.9 / 3.7 / 1.1 / 3.6	**28** SA	0440 / 1027 / 1658 / 2249	1.2 / 3.3 / 1.4 / 3.2
14 SA	0504 / 1104 / 1735 / 2333	1.1 / 3.5 / 1.2 / 3.5	**29** SU	0541 / 1124 / 1808 / 2358	1.4 / 3.1 / 1.5 / 3.1
15 SU	0615 / 1215 / 1855	1.2 / 3.3 / 1.3			

MARCH

Day	Time	m	Day	Time	m
1 M	0656 / 1249 / 1929	1.5 / 3.0 / 1.5	**16** TU	0041 / 0727 / 1335 / 2015	3.2 / 1.3 / 3.1 / 1.2
2 TU	0137 / 0812 / 1423 / 2045	3.1 / 1.4 / 3.1 / 1.4	**17** W	0221 / 0906 / 1501 / 2137	3.3 / 1.0 / 3.3 / 0.9
3 W	0258 / 0923 / 1528 / 2149	3.3 / 1.2 / 3.3 / 1.1	**18** TH	0333 / 1012 / 1602 / 2234	3.6 / 0.7 / 3.6 / 0.6
4 TH	0353 / 1018 / 1617 / 2236	3.5 / 0.9 / 3.6 / 0.8	**19** F	0426 / 1101 / 1649 / 2319	3.9 / 0.4 / 3.9 / 0.3
5 F	0436 / 1101 / 1657 / 2313	3.8 / 0.7 / 3.8 / 0.6	**20** SA	0509 / 1142 / 1730 / ●2358	4.1 / 0.3 / 4.0 / 0.2
6 SA	0514 / 1137 / 1733 / ○2347	3.9 / 0.5 / 3.9 / 0.5	**21** SU	0548 / 1218 / 1806	4.2 / 0.2 / 4.1
7 SU	0548 / 1211 / 1806	4.1 / 0.4 / 4.0	**22** M	0033 / 0622 / 1251 / 1838	0.2 / 4.2 / 0.3 / 4.0
8 M	0020 / 0622 / 1245 / 1838	0.4 / 4.1 / 0.4 / 4.0	**23** TU	0105 / 0655 / 1321 / 1907	0.3 / 4.1 / 0.4 / 4.0
9 TU	0056 / 0656 / 1320 / 1912	0.3 / 4.1 / 0.4 / 4.1	**24** W	0136 / 0725 / 1350 / 1936	0.4 / 4.0 / 0.5 / 3.9
10 W	0133 / 0732 / 1357 / 1948	0.3 / 4.1 / 0.4 / 4.0	**25** TH	0206 / 0756 / 1419 / 2007	0.6 / 3.8 / 0.7 / 3.8
11 TH	0213 / 0811 / 1436 / 2028	0.4 / 4.0 / 0.6 / 3.9	**26** F	0238 / 0828 / 1450 / 2041	0.8 / 3.7 / 0.9 / 3.6
12 F	0256 / 0853 / 1518 / 2112	0.6 / 3.8 / 0.7 / 3.8	**27** SA	0312 / 0902 / 1524 / 2120	1.0 / 3.5 / 1.1 / 3.5
13 SA	0344 / 0940 / 1608 / 2204	0.8 / 3.6 / 1.0 / 3.6	**28** SU	0355 / 0943 / 1610 / ◐2207	1.2 / 3.3 / 1.3 / 3.2
14 SU	0441 / 1038 / 1711 / 2310	1.0 / 3.3 / 1.2 / 3.3	**29** M	0454 / 1036 / 1718 / 2311	1.4 / 3.1 / 1.5 / 3.0
15 M	0554 / 1156 / 1836	1.2 / 3.1 / 1.3	**30** TU	0612 / 1152 / 1845	1.5 / 2.9 / 1.5
			31 W	0045 / 0732 / 1341 / 2004	3.0 / 1.4 / 3.0 / 1.4

APRIL

Day	Time	m	Day	Time	m
1 TH	0220 / 0843 / 1454 / 2109	3.2 / 1.2 / 3.2 / 1.1	**16** F	0312 / 0950 / 1540 / 2212	3.6 / 0.7 / 3.6 / 0.5
2 F	0317 / 0940 / 1543 / 2158	3.4 / 0.9 / 3.5 / 0.8	**17** SA	0402 / 1037 / 1625 / 2256	3.8 / 0.5 / 3.8 / 0.4
3 SA	0401 / 1025 / 1624 / 2239	3.7 / 0.6 / 3.7 / 0.5	**18** SU	0444 / 1116 / 1705 / 2333	4.0 / 0.4 / 3.9 / 0.3
4 SU	0440 / 1105 / 1701 / 2316	3.9 / 0.4 / 3.9 / 0.4	**19** M	0522 / 1151 / 1740 / ●	4.0 / 0.3 / 4.0
5 M	0517 / 1142 / 1736 / ○2353	4.0 / 0.3 / 4.0 / 0.2	**20** TU	0006 / 0555 / 1222 / 1810	0.3 / 4.0 / 0.4 / 4.0
6 TU	0553 / 1219 / 1812	4.1 / 0.2 / 4.1	**21** W	0037 / 0626 / 1251 / 1839	0.4 / 4.0 / 0.5 / 3.9
7 W	0032 / 0630 / 1257 / 1849	0.2 / 4.1 / 0.2 / 4.1	**22** TH	0105 / 0655 / 1318 / 1907	0.5 / 3.9 / 0.6 / 3.9
8 TH	0112 / 0710 / 1337 / 1928	0.2 / 4.1 / 0.3 / 4.1	**23** F	0134 / 0724 / 1347 / 1938	0.7 / 3.8 / 0.8 / 3.8
9 F	0155 / 0751 / 1419 / 2011	0.3 / 4.0 / 0.5 / 4.0	**24** SA	0205 / 0756 / 1418 / 2013	0.8 / 3.7 / 0.9 / 3.6
10 SA	0241 / 0837 / 1505 / 2058	0.5 / 3.8 / 0.7 / 3.8	**25** SU	0241 / 0831 / 1454 / 2052	1.0 / 3.5 / 1.1 / 3.5
11 SU	0333 / 0927 / 1559 / 2153	0.7 / 3.5 / 0.9 / 3.5	**26** M	0325 / 0913 / 1541 / 2139	1.2 / 3.3 / 1.2 / 3.3
12 M	0433 / 1029 / 1706 / ◐2305	1.0 / 3.2 / 1.1 / 3.3	**27** TU	0422 / 1005 / 1644 / ◐2239	1.3 / 3.2 / 1.4 / 3.1
13 TU	0548 / 1151 / 1832	1.2 / 3.0 / 1.2	**28** W	0534 / 1114 / 1803 / 2357	1.4 / 3.0 / 1.4 / 3.1
14 W	0040 / 0724 / 1328 / 2007	3.2 / 1.1 / 3.1 / 1.1	**29** TH	0650 / 1240 / 1918	1.4 / 3.0 / 1.3
15 TH	0209 / 0850 / 1444 / 2119	3.4 / 0.9 / 3.3 / 0.8	**30** F	0121 / 0757 / 1358 / 2020	3.2 / 1.2 / 3.2 / 1.1

Chapter 5

Chart Datum: 0·13 metres above Ordnance Datum (Dublin)

TIME ZONE (UT)
For Summer Time add ONE hour in **non-shaded areas**

IRELAND – COBH

LAT 51°51′N   LONG 8°18′W

TIMES AND HEIGHTS OF HIGH AND LOW WATERS

YEAR 2004

MAY

Day	Time m	Day	Time m
1 SA	0225 3.4 / 0854 0.9 / 1453 3.5 / 2113 0.8	**16** SU	0328 3.7 / 1003 0.6 / 1553 3.7 / 2224 0.5
2 SU	0315 3.7 / 0944 0.7 / 1540 3.7 / 2200 0.6	**17** M	0412 3.8 / 1044 0.6 / 1634 3.8 / 2303 0.5
3 M	0400 3.9 / 1029 0.5 / 1624 3.9 / 2245 0.4	**18** TU	0451 3.9 / 1121 0.6 / 1711 3.8 / 2338 0.6
4 TU	0443 4.0 / 1113 0.3 / 1706 4.1 / ○2329 0.2	**19** W	0527 3.9 / 1153 0.6 / 1744 3.9 ●
5 W	0526 4.1 / 1156 0.2 / 1748 4.2	**20** TH	0008 0.6 / 0559 3.8 / 1223 0.7 / 1814 3.8
6 TH	0012 0.2 / 0609 4.1 / 1240 0.2 / 1831 4.2	**21** F	0038 0.7 / 0629 3.8 / 1252 0.7 / 1844 3.8
7 F	0058 0.2 / 0654 4.0 / 1324 0.3 / 1915 4.1	**22** SA	0108 0.8 / 0700 3.7 / 1323 0.8 / 1917 3.7
8 SA	0145 0.3 / 0740 3.9 / 1412 0.4 / 2002 4.0	**23** SU	0142 0.9 / 0733 3.6 / 1357 0.9 / 1953 3.7
9 SU	0235 0.5 / 0830 3.7 / 1503 0.6 / 2054 3.8	**24** M	0221 1.0 / 0811 3.5 / 1437 1.0 / 2034 3.6
10 M	0330 0.7 / 0924 3.5 / 1600 0.8 / 2153 3.5	**25** TU	0306 1.1 / 0854 3.4 / 1524 1.1 / 2121 3.5
11 TU	0432 0.9 / 1027 3.3 / 1706 0.9 / ◑2303 3.4	**26** W	0358 1.2 / 0945 3.3 / 1619 1.2 / 2215 3.4
12 W	0545 1.0 / 1142 3.2 / 1824 1.0	**27** TH	0500 1.3 / 1044 3.3 / 1724 1.2 / ◐2319 3.3
13 TH	0025 3.3 / 0707 1.0 / 1303 3.2 / 1942 0.9	**28** F	0607 1.2 / 1152 3.3 / 1831 1.2
14 F	0140 3.4 / 0818 0.9 / 1411 3.4 / 2047 0.7	**29** SA	0027 3.4 / 0711 1.1 / 1300 3.4 / 1934 1.0
15 SA	0239 3.6 / 0915 0.8 / 1506 3.5 / 2139 0.6	**30** SU	0132 3.5 / 0809 0.9 / 1401 3.6 / 2031 0.8
		31 M	0228 3.7 / 0904 0.8 / 1456 3.7 / 2125 0.6

JUNE

Day	Time m	Day	Time m
1 TU	0322 3.8 / 0957 0.6 / 1548 3.9 / 2218 0.5	**16** W	0419 3.7 / 1049 0.8 / 1642 3.7 / 2309 0.8
2 W	0414 4.0 / 1049 0.4 / 1640 4.0 / 2309 0.3	**17** TH	0500 3.7 / 1126 0.8 / 1720 3.8 / ●2343 0.8
3 TH	0505 4.0 / 1139 0.3 / 1730 4.1 / ○	**18** F	0537 3.7 / 1200 0.8 / 1756 3.8
4 F	0000 0.3 / 0554 4.0 / 1228 0.3 / 1818 4.1	**19** SA	0016 0.8 / 0611 3.7 / 1232 0.8 / 1829 3.8
5 SA	0050 0.3 / 0644 4.0 / 1317 0.3 / 1908 4.1	**20** SU	0050 0.8 / 0645 3.7 / 1306 0.8 / 1903 3.8
6 SU	0140 0.3 / 0733 3.9 / 1408 0.4 / 1958 4.0	**21** M	0126 0.9 / 0719 3.7 / 1342 0.9 / 1940 3.7
7 M	0232 0.4 / 0825 3.8 / 1500 0.5 / 2051 3.8	**22** TU	0205 0.9 / 0757 3.6 / 1422 0.9 / 2019 3.7
8 TU	0326 0.6 / 0918 3.6 / 1555 0.6 / 2147 3.7	**23** W	0248 1.0 / 0839 3.6 / 1505 1.0 / 2103 3.6
9 W	0424 0.8 / 1015 3.4 / 1654 0.8 / 2247 3.5	**24** TH	0334 1.1 / 0925 3.5 / 1553 1.0 / 2151 3.6
10 TH	0526 0.9 / 1116 3.3 / 1759 0.9 / 2351 3.4	**25** F	0424 1.1 / 1016 3.5 / 1646 1.1 / ◐2244 3.6
11 F	0632 0.9 / 1221 3.3 / 1904 0.9	**26** SA	0521 1.1 / 1112 3.5 / 1745 1.1 / 2342 3.6
12 SA	0056 3.4 / 0734 0.9 / 1325 3.3 / 2004 0.9	**27** SU	0623 1.1 / 1213 3.5 / 1848 1.0
13 SU	0155 3.5 / 0830 0.9 / 1422 3.4 / 2057 0.8	**28** M	0045 3.6 / 0726 1.0 / 1316 3.6 / 1952 0.9
14 M	0247 3.5 / 0921 0.8 / 1513 3.5 / 2146 0.8	**29** TU	0148 3.6 / 0829 0.8 / 1419 3.7 / 2055 0.8
15 TU	0335 3.6 / 1007 0.8 / 1559 3.6 / 2230 0.8	**30** W	0250 3.7 / 0931 0.8 / 1521 3.8 / 2157 0.7

JULY

Day	Time m	Day	Time m
1 TH	0351 3.8 / 1031 0.6 / 1621 3.9 / 2256 0.5	**16** F	0438 3.6 / 1105 0.9 / 1701 3.7 / 2324 0.8
2 F	0450 3.9 / 1126 0.4 / 1718 4.1 / ○2351 0.4	**17** SA	0520 3.7 / 1142 0.8 / 1740 3.8 / ●2359 0.8
3 SA	0544 4.0 / 1218 0.3 / 1810 4.1	**18** SU	0557 3.8 / 1215 0.7 / 1816 3.8
4 SU	0042 0.3 / 0635 4.0 / 1308 0.3 / 1859 4.1	**19** M	0033 0.8 / 0631 3.8 / 1248 0.7 / 1849 3.9
5 M	0132 0.3 / 0724 3.9 / 1357 0.3 / 1948 4.1	**20** TU	0108 0.8 / 0705 3.8 / 1323 0.7 / 1923 3.8
6 TU	0221 0.4 / 0812 3.9 / 1446 0.4 / 2036 3.9	**21** W	0145 0.8 / 0740 3.7 / 1401 0.8 / 1959 3.8
7 W	0310 0.5 / 0900 3.7 / 1536 0.5 / 2125 3.8	**22** TH	0224 0.8 / 0818 3.7 / 1441 0.8 / 2038 3.8
8 TH	0400 0.7 / 0948 3.6 / 1625 0.7 / 2214 3.6	**23** F	0305 0.9 / 0859 3.7 / 1523 0.9 / 2121 3.8
9 F	0450 0.8 / 1037 3.5 / 1718 0.8 / 2306 3.5	**24** SA	0348 1.0 / 0943 3.7 / 1609 0.9 / 2208 3.7
10 SA	0544 1.0 / 1130 3.3 / 1813 1.0	**25** SU	0436 1.0 / 1033 3.6 / 1702 1.0 / ◐2302 3.6
11 SU	0002 3.4 / 0640 1.1 / 1229 3.3 / 1910 1.1	**26** M	0534 1.1 / 1132 3.5 / 1805 1.1
12 M	0103 3.3 / 0738 1.1 / 1331 3.3 / 2008 1.1	**27** TU	0005 3.5 / 0644 1.2 / 1240 3.5 / 1917 1.1
13 TU	0203 3.3 / 0835 1.1 / 1431 3.3 / 2105 1.1	**28** W	0116 3.5 / 0800 1.1 / 1353 3.5 / 2033 1.0
14 W	0259 3.4 / 0931 1.1 / 1527 3.5 / 2158 1.0	**29** TH	0230 3.5 / 0913 0.9 / 1506 3.7 / 2145 0.8
15 TH	0351 3.5 / 1022 1.0 / 1617 3.6 / 2244 0.9	**30** F	0340 3.7 / 1019 0.7 / 1613 3.9 / 2248 0.6
		31 SA	0441 3.8 / 1117 0.5 / 1710 4.0 / ○2342 0.4

AUGUST

Day	Time m	Day	Time m
1 SU	0534 4.0 / 1207 0.3 / 1800 4.2	**16** M	0539 3.8 / 1155 0.6 / 1756 3.9 ●
2 M	0030 0.3 / 0622 4.0 / 1254 0.2 / 1845 4.2	**17** TU	0012 0.6 / 0612 3.8 / 1226 0.6 / 1828 4.0
3 TU	0116 0.3 / 0706 4.0 / 1338 0.2 / 1928 4.1	**18** W	0045 0.6 / 0643 3.9 / 1258 0.6 / 1859 4.0
4 W	0159 0.3 / 0749 3.9 / 1422 0.3 / 2010 4.0	**19** TH	0120 0.6 / 0716 3.9 / 1334 0.6 / 1933 4.0
5 TH	0241 0.5 / 0830 3.8 / 1504 0.5 / 2052 3.9	**20** F	0156 0.7 / 0750 3.8 / 1412 0.6 / 2009 3.9
6 F	0323 0.6 / 0910 3.7 / 1545 0.6 / 2133 3.7	**21** SA	0233 0.8 / 0828 3.8 / 1452 0.7 / 2049 3.9
7 SA	0405 0.8 / 0951 3.5 / 1628 0.9 / ○2215 3.5	**22** SU	0314 0.9 / 0910 3.7 / 1536 0.9 / ◐2133 3.7
8 SU	0449 1.0 / 1035 3.4 / 1715 1.1 / 2303 3.3	**23** M	0400 1.0 / 0959 3.6 / 1628 1.0 / ◐2226 3.5
9 M	0540 1.2 / 1127 3.2 / 1812 1.2	**24** TU	0457 1.2 / 1058 3.5 / 1732 1.2 / 2333 3.4
10 TU	0002 3.2 / 0642 1.3 / 1237 3.1 / 1917 1.3	**25** W	0613 1.3 / 1214 3.3 / 1853 1.3
11 W	0117 3.1 / 0751 1.3 / 1356 3.2 / 2026 1.3	**26** TH	0056 3.3 / 0741 1.2 / 1342 3.4 / 2022 1.2
12 TH	0229 3.2 / 0859 1.2 / 1504 3.3 / 2130 1.2	**27** F	0223 3.4 / 0905 1.0 / 1504 3.6 / 2141 0.9
13 F	0329 3.4 / 0959 1.1 / 1558 3.5 / 2223 1.0	**28** SA	0336 3.6 / 1012 0.7 / 1608 3.9 / 2242 0.6
14 SA	0419 3.6 / 1046 0.9 / 1643 3.7 / 2305 0.8	**29** SU	0434 3.8 / 1106 0.4 / 1700 4.1 / 2331 0.4
15 SU	0502 3.7 / 1123 0.7 / 1722 3.9 / 2340 0.7	**30** M	0521 4.0 / 1152 0.2 / 1744 4.2 / ○
		31 TU	0013 0.2 / 0603 4.1 / 1234 0.2 / 1824 4.3

Chart Datum: 0·13 metres above Ordnance Datum (Dublin)

TIME ZONE (UT)
For Summer Time add ONE hour in **non-shaded areas**

YEAR **2004**

LAT 51°51′N   LONG 8°18′W

TIMES AND HEIGHTS OF HIGH AND LOW WATERS

SEPTEMBER

Day	Time	m	Day	Time	m
1 W	0053 / 0643 / 1313 / 1902	0.2 / 4.1 / 0.2 / 4.2	**16** TH	0018 / 0615 / 1231 / 1831	0.5 / 4.0 / 0.4 / 4.1
2 TH	0130 / 0720 / 1350 / 1938	0.3 / 4.0 / 0.3 / 4.1	**17** F	0052 / 0648 / 1306 / 1904	0.5 / 4.0 / 0.5 / 4.1
3 F	0206 / 0755 / 1426 / 2013	0.5 / 3.9 / 0.5 / 3.9	**18** SA	0128 / 0722 / 1345 / 1941	0.6 / 4.0 / 0.5 / 4.0
4 SA	0242 / 0829 / 1502 / 2049	0.7 / 3.7 / 0.7 / 3.7	**19** SU	0206 / 0800 / 1427 / 2021	0.7 / 3.9 / 0.7 / 3.9
5 SU	0317 / 0905 / 1539 / 2126	0.9 / 3.6 / 0.9 / 3.5	**20** M	0248 / 0844 / 1513 / 2107	0.8 / 3.8 / 0.9 / 3.7
6 M	0356 / 0945 / 1621 / 2207	1.1 / 3.4 / 1.2 / 3.3	**21** TU	0337 / 0935 / 1607 / 2203	1.0 / 3.6 / 1.1 / 3.4
7 TU	0443 / 1034 / 1717 / 2301	1.4 / 3.2 / 1.4 / 3.1	**22** W	0438 / 1039 / 1716 / 2316	1.2 / 3.4 / 1.3 / 3.2
8 W	0549 / 1142 / 1830	1.5 / 3.0 / 1.5	**23** TH	0600 / 1205 / 1844	1.3 / 3.2 / 1.4
9 TH	0024 / 0710 / 1326 / 1949	3.0 / 1.5 / 3.0 / 1.5	**24** F	0051 / 0736 / 1346 / 2022	3.1 / 1.3 / 3.3 / 1.2
10 F	0203 / 0828 / 1443 / 2102	3.1 / 1.4 / 3.2 / 1.3	**25** SA	0224 / 0901 / 1502 / 2136	3.3 / 1.0 / 3.6 / 0.9
11 SA	0308 / 0933 / 1536 / 2157	3.3 / 1.1 / 3.5 / 1.0	**26** SU	0329 / 1002 / 1557 / 2229	3.6 / 0.6 / 3.9 / 0.6
12 SU	0356 / 1020 / 1619 / 2239	3.6 / 0.7 / 3.7 / 0.8	**27** M	0420 / 1051 / 1643 / 2313	3.9 / 0.4 / 4.1 / 0.4
13 M	0437 / 1056 / 1656 / 2313	3.8 / 0.7 / 3.9 / 0.6	**28** TU	0503 / 1133 / 1723 / 2351	4.1 / 0.2 / 4.3 / 0.3
14 TU	0512 / 1127 / 1729 / 2345	3.9 / 0.5 / 4.0 / 0.5	**29** W	0542 / 1210 / 1800	4.2 / 0.2 / 4.3
15 W	0545 / 1157 / 1800	4.0 / 0.5 / 4.1	**30** TH	0026 / 0617 / 1245 / 1833	0.3 / 4.1 / 0.3 / 4.2

OCTOBER

Day	Time	m	Day	Time	m
1 F	0059 / 0649 / 1318 / 1905	0.4 / 4.0 / 0.4 / 4.0	**16** SA	0027 / 0623 / 1245 / 1841	0.5 / 4.1 / 0.4 / 4.1
2 SA	0130 / 0720 / 1350 / 1937	0.6 / 3.9 / 0.6 / 3.9	**17** SU	0106 / 0701 / 1326 / 1921	0.5 / 4.1 / 0.5 / 4.0
3 SU	0202 / 0752 / 1422 / 2009	0.8 / 3.8 / 0.8 / 3.7	**18** M	0148 / 0743 / 1412 / 2005	0.6 / 4.0 / 0.7 / 3.9
4 M	0233 / 0826 / 1456 / 2043	1.0 / 3.6 / 1.1 / 3.6	**19** TU	0235 / 0831 / 1502 / 2055	0.8 / 3.8 / 0.9 / 3.6
5 TU	0309 / 0906 / 1537 / 2123	1.2 / 3.4 / 1.3 / 3.4	**20** W	0329 / 0927 / 1601 / 2155	1.0 / 3.6 / 1.1 / 3.4
6 W	0355 / 0953 / 1633 / 2214	1.4 / 3.2 / 1.5 / 3.1	**21** TH	0436 / 1037 / 1713 / 2312	1.2 / 3.4 / 1.3 / 3.2
7 TH	0502 / 1057 / 1749 / 2329	1.6 / 3.0 / 1.6 / 3.0	**22** F	0559 / 1207 / 1844	1.3 / 3.3 / 1.3
8 F	0629 / 1239 / 1911	1.6 / 3.0 / 1.6	**23** SA	0048 / 0732 / 1338 / 2014	3.2 / 1.2 / 3.5 / 1.1
9 SA	0122 / 0749 / 1410 / 2023	3.0 / 1.4 / 3.2 / 1.4	**24** SU	0211 / 0847 / 1444 / 2118	3.4 / 0.9 / 3.7 / 0.8
10 SU	0234 / 0853 / 1503 / 2118	3.3 / 1.2 / 3.5 / 1.1	**25** M	0310 / 0943 / 1536 / 2207	3.7 / 0.6 / 4.0 / 0.6
11 M	0322 / 0940 / 1544 / 2202	3.6 / 0.9 / 3.7 / 0.8	**26** TU	0358 / 1029 / 1620 / 2249	3.9 / 0.5 / 4.1 / 0.5
12 TU	0402 / 1019 / 1621 / 2240	3.8 / 0.7 / 3.9 / 0.6	**27** W	0440 / 1109 / 1659 / 2325	4.1 / 0.4 / 4.2 / 0.5
13 W	0438 / 1054 / 1655 / 2315	4.0 / 0.5 / 4.1 / 0.5	**28** TH	0517 / 1145 / 1734 / 2359	4.1 / 0.4 / 4.2 / 0.5
14 TH	0513 / 1129 / 1729 / 2351	4.1 / 0.4 / 4.2 / 0.5	**29** F	0551 / 1218 / 1806	4.1 / 0.5 / 4.1
15 F	0547 / 1205 / 1804	4.1 / 0.4 / 4.2	**30** SA	0029 / 0622 / 1249 / 1836	0.6 / 4.0 / 0.7 / 4.0
			31 SU	0059 / 0652 / 1319 / 1905	0.7 / 3.9 / 0.8 / 3.9

NOVEMBER

Day	Time	m	Day	Time	m
1 M	0128 / 0723 / 1349 / 1937	0.9 / 3.8 / 1.0 / 3.8	**16** TU	0142 / 0738 / 1408 / 1959	0.6 / 4.1 / 0.7 / 3.9
2 TU	0158 / 0758 / 1424 / 2011	1.0 / 3.7 / 1.2 / 3.6	**17** W	0233 / 0830 / 1501 / 2053	0.8 / 3.9 / 0.9 / 3.7
3 W	0234 / 0838 / 1506 / 2052	1.2 / 3.5 / 1.4 / 3.4	**18** TH	0330 / 0928 / 1601 / 2154	0.9 / 3.7 / 1.0 / 3.5
4 TH	0321 / 0925 / 1600 / 2143	1.4 / 3.4 / 1.5 / 3.3	**19** F	0435 / 1036 / 1710 / 2305	1.1 / 3.5 / 1.2 / 3.3
5 F	0424 / 1024 / 1710 / 2248	1.5 / 3.2 / 1.6 / 3.1	**20** SA	0550 / 1153 / 1831	1.1 / 3.5 / 1.2
6 SA	0543 / 1140 / 1827	1.6 / 3.2 / 1.6	**21** SU	0025 / 0710 / 1309 / 1946	3.3 / 1.1 / 3.6 / 1.1
7 SU	0014 / 0659 / 1307 / 1936	3.1 / 1.5 / 3.3 / 1.4	**22** M	0139 / 0817 / 1412 / 2046	3.5 / 0.9 / 3.7 / 0.9
8 M	0136 / 0802 / 1409 / 2032	3.3 / 1.2 / 3.5 / 1.2	**23** TU	0238 / 0913 / 1504 / 2136	3.6 / 0.8 / 3.8 / 0.8
9 TU	0232 / 0854 / 1457 / 2121	3.6 / 1.0 / 3.7 / 0.9	**24** W	0328 / 1001 / 1550 / 2220	3.6 / 0.7 / 3.9 / 0.7
10 W	0318 / 0940 / 1539 / 2205	3.8 / 0.8 / 3.9 / 0.7	**25** TH	0412 / 1043 / 1631 / 2259	3.9 / 0.7 / 4.0 / 0.7
11 TH	0400 / 1023 / 1620 / 2247	4.0 / 0.6 / 4.1 / 0.6	**26** F	0452 / 1121 / 1708 / 2333	4.0 / 0.7 / 4.0 / 0.7
12 F	0442 / 1105 / 1701 / 2329	4.1 / 0.5 / 4.2 / 0.5	**27** SA	0528 / 1155 / 1742	4.0 / 0.8 / 4.0
13 SA	0523 / 1148 / 1743	4.2 / 0.5 / 4.2	**28** SU	0005 / 0600 / 1226 / 1813	0.8 / 4.0 / 0.9 / 3.9
14 SU	0011 / 0606 / 1232 / 1826	0.5 / 4.2 / 0.5 / 4.2	**29** M	0035 / 0632 / 1256 / 1844	0.9 / 4.0 / 1.0 / 3.9
15 M	0055 / 0650 / 1318 / 1911	0.5 / 4.2 / 0.5 / 4.1	**30** TU	0105 / 0705 / 1328 / 1916	0.9 / 3.9 / 1.1 / 3.8

DECEMBER

Day	Time	m	Day	Time	m
1 W	0137 / 0740 / 1405 / 1951	1.0 / 3.8 / 1.2 / 3.7	**16** TH	0230 / 0827 / 1458 / 2048	0.6 / 4.0 / 0.7 / 3.8
2 TH	0215 / 0820 / 1447 / 2032	1.2 / 3.7 / 1.3 / 3.6	**17** F	0324 / 0922 / 1553 / 2142	0.7 / 3.9 / 0.9 / 3.6
3 F	0300 / 0905 / 1536 / 2120	1.3 / 3.6 / 1.4 / 3.5	**18** SA	0421 / 1018 / 1652 / 2240	0.9 / 3.7 / 1.0 / 3.5
4 SA	0354 / 0956 / 1633 / 2216	1.4 / 3.5 / 1.5 / 3.4	**19** SU	0524 / 1119 / 1756 / 2343	1.0 / 3.6 / 1.2 / 3.4
5 SU	0457 / 1055 / 1738 / 2321	1.4 / 3.4 / 1.5 / 3.4	**20** M	0630 / 1223 / 1902	1.0 / 3.6 / 1.1
6 M	0604 / 1201 / 1844	1.4 / 3.5 / 1.4	**21** TU	0050 / 0735 / 1326 / 2003	3.4 / 1.1 / 3.6 / 1.1
7 TU	0029 / 0709 / 1305 / 1945	3.4 / 1.3 / 3.6 / 1.3	**22** W	0154 / 0834 / 1424 / 2058	3.5 / 1.0 / 3.6 / 1.1
8 W	0134 / 0808 / 1404 / 2040	3.6 / 1.1 / 3.7 / 1.1	**23** TH	0251 / 0928 / 1516 / 2149	3.6 / 1.0 / 3.7 / 1.0
9 TH	0231 / 0903 / 1457 / 2133	3.8 / 1.0 / 3.9 / 0.9	**24** F	0342 / 1017 / 1603 / 2234	3.7 / 1.0 / 3.8 / 1.0
10 F	0324 / 0956 / 1549 / 2225	3.9 / 0.8 / 4.0 / 0.7	**25** SA	0428 / 1059 / 1646 / 2313	3.8 / 0.9 / 3.8 / 0.9
11 SA	0416 / 1048 / 1640 / 2314	4.1 / 0.6 / 4.1 / 0.6	**26** SU	0509 / 1136 / 1725 / 2347	3.9 / 0.9 / 3.9 / 0.9
12 SU	0507 / 1138 / 1730	4.2 / 0.5 / 4.1	**27** M	0547 / 1209 / 1800	4.0 / 0.9 / 3.9
13 M	0002 / 0556 / 1227 / 1818	0.5 / 4.3 / 0.5 / 4.1	**28** TU	0019 / 0621 / 1241 / 1832	0.9 / 3.9 / 1.0 / 3.9
14 TU	0050 / 0645 / 1316 / 1906	0.5 / 4.2 / 0.5 / 4.1	**29** W	0050 / 0654 / 1314 / 1904	0.9 / 3.9 / 1.0 / 3.8
15 W	0139 / 0735 / 1406 / 1956	0.5 / 4.2 / 0.6 / 4.0	**30** TH	0123 / 0728 / 1350 / 1938	0.9 / 3.9 / 1.1 / 3.8
			31 F	0200 / 0805 / 1428 / 2016	1.0 / 3.8 / 1.1 / 3.7

Chart Datum: 0·13 metres above Ordnance Datum (Dublin)

Chapter 5

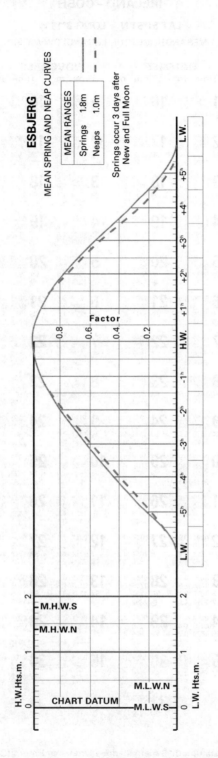

ESBJERG

MEAN SPRING AND NEAP CURVES

MEAN RANGES	
Springs	1.8m
Neaps	1.0m

Springs occur 3 days after
New and Full Moon

TIME ZONE -0100
(Danish Standard Time)
Subtract 1 hour for UT
For Danish Summer Time add
ONE hour in **non-shaded areas**

DENMARK – ESBJERG

LAT 55°28′N   LONG 8°27′E

TIMES AND HEIGHTS OF HIGH AND LOW WATERS

YEAR 2004

JANUARY

Day	Time m	Time m	Time m	Time m		Day	Time m	Time m	Time m	Time m
1 TH	0303 0.5	0940 1.9	1559 0.4	2225 1.6		16 F	0216 0.3	0833 1.9	1501 0.3	2114 1.6
2 F	0408 0.5	1044 1.8	1659 0.4	2324 1.7		17 SA	0317 0.3	0939 1.8	1604 0.3	2222 1.6
3 SA	0514 0.5	1146 1.8	1757 0.4			18 SU	0426 0.3	1054 1.8	1711 0.4	2337 1.6
4 SU	0020 1.7	0615 0.4	1244 1.8	1849 0.4		19 M	0540 0.3	1214 1.7	1818 0.4	
5 M	0112 1.6	0711 0.4	1337 1.8	1935 0.4		20 TU	0048 1.7	0650 0.3	1328 1.7	1919 0.3
6 TU	0201 1.8	0800 0.4	1424 1.8	2016 0.4		21 W	0151 1.7	0752 0.2	● 1431 1.7	2013 0.3
7 W	0244 1.8	0844 0.3	1506 1.7	○ 2054 0.4		22 TH	0248 1.8	0848 0.1	1526 1.7	2103 0.3
8 TH	0321 1.8	0938 0.3	1543 1.7	2127 0.4		23 F	0338 1.9	0938 0.1	1616 1.7	2150 0.2
9 F	0353 1.9	0957 0.3	1615 1.7	2201 0.3		24 SA	0422 1.9	1024 0.1	1700 1.7	2233 0.3
10 SA	0422 1.9	1030 0.3	1647 1.7	2236 0.3		25 SU	0504 1.9	1109 0.1	1739 1.6	2314 0.2
11 SU	0452 1.9	1106 0.2	1719 1.7	2311 0.3		26 M	0545 1.8	1154 0.1	1816 1.6	2357 0.2
12 M	0524 1.9	1146 0.2	1756 1.7	2352 0.2		27 TU	0623 1.9	1237 0.2	1854 1.6	
13 TU	0602 2.0	1227 0.2	1837 1.7			28 W	0041 0.2	0705 1.9	1319 0.3	1934 1.5
14 W	0036 0.2	0646 2.0	1313 0.2	1922 1.7		29 TH	0125 0.3	0751 1.8	1406 0.3	◐ 2020 1.5
15 TH	0123 0.2	0737 1.9	1404 0.2	◑ 2014 1.6		30 F	0214 0.3	0843 1.7	1458 0.4	2116 1.5
						31 SA	0312 0.4	0944 1.7	1558 0.5	2221 1.5

FEBRUARY

Day	Time m	Time m	Time m	Time m		Day	Time m	Time m	Time m	Time m
1 SU	0421 0.4	1051 1.6	1704 0.5	2329 1.6		16 M	0402 0.3	1040 1.6	1647 0.4	2312 1.5
2 M	0537 0.4	1159 1.6	1808 0.4			17 TU	0524 0.3	1209 1.5	1802 0.4	
3 TU	0032 1.6	0643 0.4	1300 1.6	1903 0.4		18 W	0035 1.6	0642 0.2	1324 1.6	1906 0.3
4 W	0127 1.7	0736 0.3	1355 1.6	1951 0.3		19 TH	0142 1.7	0745 0.1	1425 1.6	2001 0.2
5 TH	0215 1.7	0821 0.3	1443 1.6	2030 0.3		20 F	0238 1.8	0837 0.0	● 1518 1.6	2050 0.1
6 F	0258 1.8	0901 0.2	1524 1.6	○ 2107 0.2		21 SA	0326 1.8	0923 -0.1	1603 1.6	2133 0.1
7 SA	0335 1.8	0937 0.1	1601 1.7	2144 0.2		22 SU	0409 1.9	1007 -0.1	1640 1.6	2213 0.0
8 SU	0406 1.8	1012 0.1	1634 1.6	2217 0.1		23 M	0448 1.9	1049 0.0	1712 1.6	2253 0.0
9 M	0438 1.9	1049 0.0	1705 1.7	2255 0.1		24 TU	0521 1.8	1124 0.0	1743 1.6	2331 0.0
10 TU	0510 1.9	1125 0.0	1740 1.6	2334 0.1		25 W	0555 1.8	1202 0.1	1811 1.5	
11 W	0548 1.9	1205 0.0	1815 1.6			26 TH	0007 0.1	0627 1.7	1238 0.2	1844 1.5
12 TH	0014 0.0	0629 1.9	1249 0.0	1856 1.6		27 F	0047 0.1	0705 1.7	1314 0.3	1921 1.5
13 F	0100 0.1	0715 1.8	1337 0.1	◑ 1944 1.6		28 SA	0129 0.2	0750 1.6	1357 0.3	◐ 2009 1.5
14 SA	0151 0.1	0810 1.8	1424 0.1	2040 1.5		29 SU	0218 0.3	0842 1.5	1447 0.4	2109 1.5
15 SU	0250 0.2	0917 1.7	1532 0.3	2148 1.5						

MARCH

Day	Time m	Time m	Time m	Time m		Day	Time m	Time m	Time m	Time m
1 M	0320 0.4	0949 1.4	1554 0.5	2220 1.5		16 TU	0352 0.2	1043 1.4	1629 0.4	2300 1.4
2 TU	0446 0.4	1109 1.4	1717 0.5	2339 1.5		17 W	0519 0.2	1208 1.4	1749 0.4	
3 W	0606 0.4	1224 1.4	1826 0.4			18 TH	0023 1.5	0633 0.1	1316 1.5	1853 0.2
4 TH	0045 1.6	0705 0.2	1324 1.5	1917 0.3		19 F	0128 1.7	0730 0.2	1413 1.5	1945 0.1
5 F	0141 1.6	0753 0.1	1414 1.6	2002 0.2		20 SA	0222 1.7	0820 -0.1	● 1501 1.6	2029 0.0
6 SA	0228 1.7	0833 0.0	1459 1.6	○ 2042 0.1		21 SU	0309 1.8	0905 -0.1	1541 1.6	2112 -0.1
7 SU	0307 1.6	0911 0.0	1538 1.6	2118 0.0		22 M	0351 1.8	0945 -0.1	1614 1.6	2152 -0.1
8 M	0344 1.8	0949 -0.1	1612 1.6	2156 0.0		23 TU	0425 1.8	1020 -0.1	1644 1.6	2228 -0.1
9 TU	0418 1.8	1023 -0.1	1646 1.6	2234 -0.1		24 W	0456 1.7	1055 0.0	1708 1.5	2303 -0.1
10 W	0454 1.8	1102 -0.1	1717 1.6	2312 -0.1		25 TH	0523 1.7	1125 0.1	1733 1.5	2338 0.0
11 TH	0531 1.8	1143 -0.1	1753 1.6	2354 -0.1		26 F	0552 1.6	1157 0.1	1800 1.5	
12 F	0611 1.8	1223 0.0	1832 1.6			27 SA	0011 0.0	0623 1.5	1229 0.2	1836 1.5
13 SA	0041 -0.1	0659 1.7	1309 0.1	◑ 1916 1.5		28 SU	0050 0.1	0704 1.5	1305 0.2	◐ 1918 1.5
14 SU	0131 0.0	0756 1.6	1402 0.2	2012 1.5		29 M	0134 0.2	0755 1.4	1351 0.3	2012 1.5
15 M	0233 0.1	0908 1.5	1507 0.4	2126 1.4		30 TU	0229 0.3	0857 1.3	1451 0.4	2118 1.4
						31 W	0350 0.3	1017 1.3	1614 0.4	2237 1.4

APRIL

Day	Time m	Time m	Time m	Time m		Day	Time m	Time m	Time m	Time m
1 TH	0519 0.3	1139 1.3	1738 0.4	2354 1.5		16 F	0004 1.6	0616 0.0	1258 1.4	1829 0.2
2 F	0624 0.2	1246 1.4	1839 0.2			17 SA	0106 1.7	0711 -0.1	1350 1.5	1920 0.0
3 SA	0057 1.6	1341 1.5	1926 0.1			18 SU	0200 1.7	0759 -0.2	1434 1.6	2007 -0.1
4 SU	0150 1.7	0800 -0.1	1427 1.6	2009 0.0		19 M	0247 1.8	0841 -0.2	1513 1.6	● 2051 -0.1
5 M	0236 1.7	0841 -0.1	1508 1.6	○ 2052 -0.1		20 TU	0326 1.7	0917 -0.1	1548 1.6	2127 -0.1
6 TU	0316 1.8	0918 -0.2	1546 1.6	2131 -0.1		21 W	0402 1.7	0954 -0.1	1615 1.6	2204 -0.1
7 W	0356 1.8	0958 -0.2	1620 1.6	2210 -0.2		22 TH	0430 1.6	1023 0.0	1640 1.5	2239 -0.1
8 TH	0435 1.8	1038 -0.2	1655 1.6	2253 -0.2		23 F	0456 1.5	1053 0.1	1701 1.5	2310 0.0
9 F	0514 1.7	1117 -0.1	1731 1.6	2337 -0.2		24 SA	0520 1.5	1121 0.1	1727 1.5	2344 0.0
10 SA	0559 1.6	1201 0.0	1810 1.5			25 SU	0551 1.4	1152 0.1	1801 1.5	
11 SU	0023 -0.1	0650 1.5	1248 0.1	1858 1.5		26 M	0019 0.1	0629 1.4	1229 0.2	1843 1.5
12 M	0117 0.0	0751 1.4	1343 0.3	◑ 1959 1.4		27 TU	0103 0.1	0717 1.3	1313 0.2	◐ 1933 1.5
13 TU	0224 0.1	0912 1.3	1451 0.4	2119 1.4		28 W	0158 0.2	0816 1.3	1410 0.3	2033 1.5
14 W	0348 0.1	1042 1.3	1612 0.4	2250 1.5		29 TH	0306 0.2	0928 1.3	1522 0.3	2144 1.5
15 TH	0510 0.1	1156 1.4	1728 0.3			30 F	0426 0.2	1049 1.3	1644 0.3	2300 1.5

Chart Datum: 0·69 metres below Dansk Normal Null

Chapter 5

DENMARK – ESBJERG

TIME ZONE -0100
(Danish Standard Time)
Subtract 1 hour for UT
For Danish Summer Time add ONE hour in **non-shaded areas**

LAT 55°28′N   LONG 8°27′E

TIMES AND HEIGHTS OF HIGH AND LOW WATERS

YEAR **2004**

MAY

Day	Time m	Time m	Time m	Time m		Day	Time m	Time m	Time m	Time m
1 SA	0537 0.1	1200 1.4	1751 0.2			16 SU	0039 1.7	0644 -0.1	1317 1.5	1855 0.0
2 SU	0009 1.6	0634 0.0	1300 1.5	1848 0.1		17 M	0132 1.7	0729 -0.1	1403 1.6	1943 0.0
3 M	0109 1.6	0722 -0.1	1351 1.5	1937 0.0		18 TU	0219 1.7	0813 -0.1	1445 1.6	2025 -0.1
4 TU	0201 1.7	0807 -0.2	1437 1.6	2021 -0.1		19 W	0302 1.7	0853 -0.1	1520 1.6	2107 -0.1
5 W	0249 1.7	0852 -0.2	1517 1.6	2106 -0.2		20 TH	0339 1.6	0925 0.0	1551 1.6	2145 0.0
6 TH	0334 1.7	0933 -0.2	1557 1.6	2151 -0.2		21 F	0408 1.5	0958 0.1	1616 1.6	2217 0.0
7 F	0418 1.7	1014 -0.1	1635 1.6	2236 -0.2		22 SA	0434 1.4	1026 0.1	1639 1.6	2251 0.1
8 SA	0503 1.6	1058 0.0	1714 1.6	2322 -0.2		23 SU	0459 1.4	1055 0.1	1704 1.6	2323 0.1
9 SU	0552 1.5	1143 0.1	1758 1.6			24 M	0528 1.4	1127 0.1	1737 1.6	
10 M	0013 -0.1	0646 1.4	1232 0.2	1850 1.5		25 TU	0000 0.1	0605 1.4	1204 0.2	1816 1.6
11 TU	0111 0.0	0751 1.3	1327 0.3	1952 1.5 ◑		26 W	0043 0.1	0652 1.4	1250 0.2	1904 1.6
12 W	0217 0.1	0907 1.3	1434 0.3	2109 1.5		27 TH	0133 0.1	0747 1.3	1343 0.2	1959 1.6 ◐
13 TH	0334 0.1	1023 1.3	1549 0.3	2230 1.5		28 F	0233 0.1	0850 1.3	1445 0.2	2102 1.6
14 F	0449 0.0	1129 1.4	1700 0.2	2339 1.6		29 SA	0340 0.1	1000 1.4	1554 0.2	2211 1.6
15 SA	0551 0.0	1226 1.4	1801 0.1			30 SU	0448 0.1	1111 1.4	1703 0.2	2322 1.6
						31 M	0550 0.0	1216 1.4	1806 0.1	

JUNE

Day	Time m	Time m	Time m	Time m		Day	Time m	Time m	Time m	Time m
1 TU	0029 1.6	0646 0.0	1313 1.5	1903 0.0		16 W	0150 1.7	0747 0.1	1413 1.6	2005 0.0
2 W	0130 1.7	0737 -0.1	1405 1.6	1956 -0.1		17 TH	0236 1.6	0826 0.1	1455 1.6	2050 0.1 ●
3 TH	0225 1.7	0824 -0.1	1453 1.6	2047 -0.1 ○		18 F	0316 1.6	0903 0.1	1531 1.6	2127 0.1
4 F	0317 1.6	0910 0.0	1538 1.6	2136 -0.1		19 SA	0351 1.5	0937 0.2	1600 1.6	2203 0.1
5 SA	0408 1.6	0956 0.0	1620 1.6	2223 -0.1		20 SU	0419 1.4	1006 0.2	1625 1.6	2236 0.1
6 SU	0458 1.5	1043 0.0	1705 1.6	2313 -0.1		21 M	0446 1.4	1038 0.2	1651 1.6	2308 0.1
7 M	0549 1.5	1128 0.1	1752 1.6			22 TU	0514 1.4	1109 0.2	1720 1.7	2345 0.1
8 TU	0006 -0.1	0642 1.4	1216 0.2	1843 1.6		23 W	0550 1.4	1148 0.1	1758 1.7	
9 W	0102 0.0	0740 1.3	1310 0.2	1942 1.6 ◑		24 TH	0025 0.1	0631 1.4	1232 0.1	1842 1.7
10 TH	0203 0.0	0843 1.3	1409 0.2	2047 1.6		25 F	0110 0.1	0719 1.5	1319 0.1	1931 1.7 ◐
11 F	0307 0.1	0947 1.3	1514 0.2	2155 1.6		26 SA	0202 0.1	0813 1.4	1412 0.2	2027 1.7
12 SA	0412 0.1	1048 1.4	1621 0.2	2301 1.7		27 SU	0259 0.1	0914 1.4	1513 0.2	2130 1.7
13 SU	0514 0.1	1146 1.5	1725 0.2			28 M	0402 0.1	1020 1.4	1620 0.2	2241 1.7
14 M	0003 1.7	0610 0.1	1240 1.5	1823 0.1		29 TU	0507 0.1	1130 1.5	1730 0.2	2354 1.6
15 TU	0059 1.7	0701 0.0	1329 1.6	1917 0.1		30 W	0610 0.1	1237 1.5	1836 0.1	

JULY

Day	Time m	Time m	Time m	Time m		Day	Time m	Time m	Time m	Time m
1 TH	0105 1.6	0709 0.1	1339 1.6	1937 0.1		16 F	0209 1.6	0803 0.2	1430 1.7	2031 0.2
2 F	0210 1.6	0804 0.1	1434 1.6	2032 0.0 ○		17 SA	0255 1.6	0843 0.2	1509 1.7	2112 0.2 ●
3 SA	0309 1.6	0855 0.1	1524 1.7	2124 -0.1		18 SU	0334 1.6	0917 0.2	1544 1.7	2148 0.2
4 SU	0403 1.6	0943 0.1	1612 1.7	2215 -0.1		19 M	0406 1.5	0950 0.2	1612 1.7	2219 0.2
5 M	0454 1.6	1028 0.1	1658 1.8	2305 -0.1		20 TU	0435 1.5	1021 0.2	1639 1.8	2253 0.1
6 TU	0540 1.5	1113 0.1	1744 1.8	2354 0.0		21 W	0504 1.5	1055 0.2	1707 1.8	2327 0.1
7 W	0626 1.5	1200 0.1	1830 1.8			22 TH	0536 1.6	1133 0.1	1742 1.8	
8 TH	0044 0.0	0713 1.4	1249 0.2	1919 1.8		23 F	0004 0.1	0611 1.6	1211 0.1	1821 1.9
9 F	0134 0.1	0802 1.4	1340 0.2	2014 1.7 ◑		24 SA	0047 0.1	0653 1.6	1255 0.1	1906 1.9
10 SA	0227 0.2	0856 1.4	1436 0.2	2113 1.7		25 SU	0133 0.1	0740 1.6	1345 0.1	1958 1.8 ◐
11 SU	0325 0.2	0954 1.5	1538 0.3	2217 1.7		26 M	0224 0.2	0834 1.6	1441 0.2	2058 1.7
12 M	0427 0.3	1055 1.5	1646 0.3	2322 1.7		27 TU	0323 0.3	0936 1.5	1545 0.3	2209 1.7
13 TU	0529 0.3	1155 1.5	1752 0.3			28 W	0431 0.3	1049 1.5	1659 0.3	2333 1.6
14 W	0023 1.6	0627 0.3	1251 1.6	1853 0.2		29 TH	0543 0.4	1208 1.6	1815 0.3	
15 TH	0118 1.6	0717 0.3	1344 1.7	1946 0.2		30 F	0054 1.6	0651 0.3	1320 1.6	1923 0.2
						31 SA	0204 1.6	0750 0.3	1421 1.7	2022 0.1 ○

AUGUST

Day	Time m	Time m	Time m	Time m		Day	Time m	Time m	Time m	Time m
1 SU	0304 1.7	0842 0.2	1515 1.8	2115 0.0		16 M	0311 1.7	0856 0.3	1522 1.9	2124 0.2 ●
2 M	0357 1.7	0927 0.2	1603 1.9	2204 0.0		17 TU	0348 1.7	0929 0.3	1554 1.9	2158 0.2
3 TU	0442 1.7	1012 0.1	1647 1.9	2250 0.0		18 W	0418 1.7	1002 0.2	1622 1.9	2230 0.1
4 W	0521 1.6	1056 0.1	1727 1.9	2332 0.0		19 TH	0448 1.7	1037 0.2	1652 1.9	2304 0.1
5 TH	0559 1.6	1138 0.1	1808 1.9			20 F	0516 1.7	1111 0.1	1724 2.0	2342 0.1
6 F	0014 0.1	0636 1.6	1219 0.1	1849 1.9		21 SA	0550 1.7	1151 0.1	1801 2.0	
7 SA	0059 0.2	0715 1.6	1304 0.2	1933 1.8 ◑		22 SU	0020 0.1	0627 1.7	1234 0.1	1846 1.9
8 SU	0144 0.3	0759 1.6	1354 0.2	2024 1.7		23 M	0104 0.2	0708 1.7	1319 0.2	1936 1.9 ◐
9 M	0232 0.4	0851 1.6	1450 0.4	2123 1.7		24 TU	0154 0.3	0759 1.7	1413 0.3	2036 1.7
10 TU	0330 0.5	0953 1.6	1557 0.4	2232 1.6		25 W	0251 0.4	0901 1.6	1520 0.4	2153 1.7
11 W	0439 0.5	1102 1.6	1715 0.4	2341 1.6		26 TH	0401 0.5	1021 1.6	1644 0.4	2329 1.6
12 TH	0549 0.5	1208 1.6	1826 0.4			27 F	0523 0.6	1152 1.6	1808 0.4	
13 F	0045 1.6	0649 0.5	1308 1.7	1923 0.3		28 SA	0052 1.6	0637 0.5	1308 1.8	1915 0.2
14 SA	0141 1.6	0738 0.4	1400 1.8	2010 0.3		29 SU	0159 1.7	0735 0.4	1410 1.9	2012 0.1
15 SU	0230 1.7	0818 0.3	1445 1.8	2051 0.2		30 M	0255 1.7	0824 0.3	1503 2.0	2102 0.1 ○
						31 TU	0341 1.8	0910 0.2	1549 2.0	2146 0.1

Chart Datum: 0·69 metres below Dansk Normal Null

TIME ZONE -0100
(Danish Standard Time)
Subtract 1 hour for UT
For Danish Summer Time add ONE hour in **non-shaded areas**

DENMARK – ESBJERG

LAT 55°28'N   LONG 8°27'E

TIMES AND HEIGHTS OF HIGH AND LOW WATERS

YEAR **2004**

SEPTEMBER

Day	Time m	Day	Time m
1 W	0420 1.8 / 0953 0.1 / 1628 2.1 / 2225 0.1	**16** TH	0354 1.9 / 0938 0.2 / 1600 2.0 / 2204 0.1
2 TH	0456 1.8 / 1033 0.1 / 1706 2.0 / 2305 0.1	**17** F	0424 1.9 / 1012 0.2 / 1633 2.0 / 2240 0.1
3 F	0526 1.8 / 1111 0.1 / 1741 2.0 / 2344 0.2	**18** SA	0455 1.9 / 1051 0.1 / 1706 2.0 / 2316 0.2
4 SA	0557 1.7 / 1151 0.2 / 1814 1.9	**19** SU	0527 1.8 / 1131 0.1 / 1746 2.0 / 2356 0.2
5 SU	0019 0.3 / 0628 1.7 / 1231 0.2 / 1852 1.8	**20** M	0602 1.8 / 1212 0.2 / 1830 1.9
6 M	0058 0.4 / 0705 1.7 / 1312 0.3 / 1933 1.8	**21** TU	0041 0.3 / 0645 1.8 / 1300 0.3 / 1920 1.8
7 TU	0139 0.5 / 0750 1.7 / 1402 0.4 / 2024 1.7	**22** W	0129 0.5 / 0736 1.8 / 1358 0.4 / 2025 1.7
8 W	0226 0.6 / 0846 1.7 / 1504 0.5 / 2130 1.6	**23** TH	0227 0.6 / 0841 1.7 / 1509 0.5 / 2155 1.6
9 TH	0331 0.7 / 0957 1.7 / 1630 0.6 / 2251 1.6	**24** F	0344 0.7 / 1010 1.7 / 1640 0.5 / 2332 1.6
10 F	0457 0.7 / 1111 1.7 / 1752 0.6	**25** SA	0509 0.7 / 1143 1.8 / 1801 0.4
11 SA	0005 1.6 / 0609 0.6 / 1228 1.7 / 1852 0.5	**26** SU	0046 1.7 / 0619 0.6 / 1255 1.9 / 1903 0.3
12 SU	0106 1.7 / 0703 0.5 / 1324 1.8 / 1939 0.4	**27** M	0146 1.8 / 0715 0.4 / 1354 2.0 / 1956 0.2
13 M	0158 1.7 / 0748 0.4 / 1410 1.9 / 2018 0.3	**28** TU	0235 1.8 / 0805 0.3 / 1445 2.1 / 2041 0.1
14 TU ●	0243 1.8 / 0825 0.4 / 1452 2.0 / 2056 0.2	**29** W	0317 1.9 / 0850 0.2 / 1528 2.1 / 2121 0.1
15 W	0320 1.8 / 0902 0.3 / 1527 2.0 / 2129 0.2	**30** TH	0355 1.9 / 0930 0.2 / 1607 2.1 / 2201 0.2

OCTOBER

Day	Time m	Day	Time m
1 F	0426 1.9 / 1009 0.2 / 1641 2.1 / 2236 0.3	**16** SA	0400 1.9 / 0950 0.2 / 1612 2.1 / 2213 0.2
2 SA	0455 1.9 / 1047 0.2 / 1711 2.0 / 2309 0.3	**17** SU	0433 1.9 / 1030 0.2 / 1652 2.0 / 2254 0.3
3 SU	0520 1.9 / 1122 0.3 / 1741 1.9 / 2343 0.4	**18** M	0507 1.9 / 1111 0.2 / 1734 2.0 / 2336 0.3
4 M	0548 1.9 / 1159 0.3 / 1812 1.8	**19** TU	0546 1.9 / 1158 0.2 / 1820 1.9
5 TU	0014 0.5 / 0620 1.9 / 1238 0.4 / 1851 1.8	**20** W ◑	0019 0.5 / 0630 1.9 / 1250 0.3 / 1917 1.8
6 W	0051 0.6 / 0702 1.8 / 1321 0.5 / 1937 1.7	**21** TH	0110 0.6 / 0723 1.8 / 1352 0.4 / 2029 1.7
7 TH	0133 0.6 / 0754 1.8 / 1416 0.6 / 2036 1.6	**22** F	0212 0.7 / 0835 1.8 / 1507 0.5 / 2200 1.6
8 F	0228 0.7 / 0857 1.8 / 1533 0.7 / 2155 1.6	**23** SA	0330 0.7 / 1004 1.8 / 1631 0.5 / 2320 1.7
9 SA	0349 0.8 / 1014 1.8 / 1701 0.6 / 2318 1.6	**24** SU	0450 0.7 / 1129 1.9 / 1744 0.4
10 SU	0515 0.7 / 1133 1.8 / 1807 0.5	**25** M	0025 1.8 / 0557 0.6 / 1235 2.0 / 1842 0.3
11 M	0025 1.7 / 0617 0.6 / 1237 1.9 / 1858 0.4	**26** TU	0120 1.8 / 0653 0.4 / 1331 2.1 / 1929 0.2
12 TU	0119 1.8 / 0707 0.5 / 1330 2.0 / 1942 0.3	**27** W	0208 1.9 / 0742 0.3 / 1420 2.1 / 2015 0.2
13 W	0206 1.9 / 0752 0.4 / 1415 2.0 / 2020 0.2	**28** TH	0251 1.9 / 0825 0.2 / 1505 2.1 / 2057 0.2
14 TH ●	0249 1.9 / 0831 0.3 / 1456 2.1 / 2059 0.2	**29** F	0327 2.0 / 0908 0.2 / 1545 2.1 / 2133 0.3
15 F	0325 1.9 / 0910 0.2 / 1535 2.1 / 2137 0.2	**30** SA	0400 2.0 / 0948 0.2 / 1617 2.0 / 2208 0.3
		31 SU	0427 1.9 / 1023 0.3 / 1647 1.9 / 2241 0.4

NOVEMBER

Day	Time m	Day	Time m
1 M	0451 1.9 / 1059 0.3 / 1712 1.9 / 2309 0.5	**16** TU	0454 1.9 / 1100 0.2 / 1728 1.9 / 2318 0.4
2 TU	0516 1.9 / 1134 0.4 / 1741 1.8 / 2341 0.5	**17** W	0536 1.9 / 1151 0.3 / 1820 1.8
3 W	0548 1.9 / 1210 0.5 / 1816 1.7	**18** TH	0006 0.5 / 0624 1.9 / 1246 0.3 / 1920 1.7
4 TH	0014 0.6 / 0626 1.9 / 1252 0.5 / 1901 1.7	**19** F ◑	0059 0.6 / 0721 1.9 / 1348 0.4 / 2031 1.7
5 F ◑	0057 0.6 / 0714 1.9 / 1342 0.6 / 1957 1.7	**20** SA	0200 0.6 / 0831 1.9 / 1458 0.4 / 2145 1.6
6 SA	0149 0.7 / 0811 1.9 / 1446 0.6 / 2104 1.6	**21** SU ◐	0309 0.6 / 0949 1.9 / 1610 0.4 / 2254 1.7
7 SU	0255 0.7 / 0917 1.9 / 1600 0.6 / 2220 1.7	**22** M	0420 0.6 / 1101 1.9 / 1715 0.4 / 2354 1.8
8 M	0412 0.7 / 1030 1.9 / 1710 0.5 / 2333 1.7	**23** TU	0526 0.5 / 1205 2.0 / 1812 0.3
9 TU	0523 0.6 / 1141 1.9 / 1808 0.4	**24** W	0049 1.8 / 0623 0.4 / 1303 2.1 / 1904 0.3
10 W	0034 1.8 / 0621 0.5 / 1243 2.0 / 1859 0.3	**25** TH	0137 1.9 / 0716 0.3 / 1355 2.1 / 1951 0.3
11 TH	0126 1.9 / 0712 0.4 / 1337 2.0 / 1946 0.3	**26** F ○	0221 1.9 / 0805 0.3 / 1442 2.0 / 2030 0.3
12 F ●	0213 1.9 / 0800 0.3 / 1426 2.0 / 2027 0.2	**27** SA	0301 2.0 / 0850 0.2 / 1522 2.0 / 2109 0.3
13 SA	0256 1.9 / 0845 0.3 / 1511 2.0 / 2109 0.2	**28** SU	0337 1.9 / 0928 0.3 / 1558 1.9 / 2145 0.4
14 SU	0336 1.9 / 0929 0.2 / 1557 2.0 / 2153 0.3	**29** M	0406 1.9 / 1007 0.3 / 1627 1.8 / 2215 0.5
15 M	0413 1.9 / 1013 0.2 / 1642 1.9 / 2235 0.3	**30** TU	0431 1.9 / 1043 0.4 / 1653 1.7 / 2246 0.5

DECEMBER

Day	Time m	Day	Time m
1 W	0456 1.9 / 1114 0.4 / 1718 1.7 / 2315 0.5	**16** TH	0532 2.0 / 1144 0.2 / 1818 1.7 / 2355 0.4
2 TH	0524 1.9 / 1151 0.4 / 1753 1.7 / 2351 0.5	**17** F	0620 2.0 / 1237 0.2 / 1913 1.7
3 F	0601 1.9 / 1230 0.5 / 1833 1.7	**18** SA ☽	0046 0.4 / 0714 2.0 / 1332 0.3 / 2010 1.6
4 SA	0033 0.5 / 0646 1.9 / 1314 0.5 / 1922 1.7	**19** SU	0141 0.5 / 0815 2.0 / 1432 0.3 / 2111 1.6
5 SU	0120 0.5 / 0736 1.9 / 1408 0.5 / 2020 1.7	**20** M	0241 0.5 / 0921 1.9 / 1536 0.4 / 2213 1.7
6 M	0216 0.6 / 0833 1.9 / 1508 0.5 / 2124 1.7	**21** TU	0346 0.5 / 1029 1.9 / 1639 0.4 / 2313 1.7
7 TU	0321 0.6 / 0938 1.9 / 1613 0.4 / 2234 1.7	**22** W	0452 0.4 / 1133 1.9 / 1739 0.4
8 W	0430 0.5 / 1047 1.9 / 1717 0.4 / 2342 1.7	**23** TH	0009 1.8 / 0555 0.4 / 1233 1.9 / 1833 0.3
9 TH	0536 0.5 / 1156 1.9 / 1816 0.4	**24** F	0103 1.8 / 0653 0.3 / 1327 1.9 / 1922 0.3
10 F	0043 1.8 / 0636 0.4 / 1300 1.9 / 1910 0.3	**25** SA	0152 1.9 / 0746 0.3 / 1417 1.9 / 2008 0.3
11 SA	0139 1.8 / 0731 0.3 / 1400 1.9 / 2000 0.3	**26** SU ○	0238 1.9 / 0832 0.3 / 1502 1.8 / 2050 0.4
12 SU ●	0229 1.9 / 0822 0.3 / 1455 1.9 / 2049 0.3	**27** M	0316 1.9 / 0915 0.3 / 1541 1.7 / 2124 0.4
13 M	0316 1.9 / 0913 0.2 / 1548 1.9 / 2135 0.3	**28** TU	0351 1.9 / 0955 0.3 / 1613 1.7 / 2158 0.4
14 TU	0401 1.9 / 1003 0.2 / 1638 1.8 / 2219 0.3	**29** W	0418 1.9 / 1027 0.4 / 1640 1.6 / 2228 0.4
15 W	0446 1.9 / 1053 0.2 / 1727 1.8 / 2306 0.4	**30** TH	0443 1.9 / 1100 0.4 / 1705 1.6 / 2259 0.4
		31 F	0509 1.9 / 1113 0.3 / 1735 1.6 / 2334 0.4

Chart Datum: 0·69 metres below Dansk Normal Null

Chapter 5

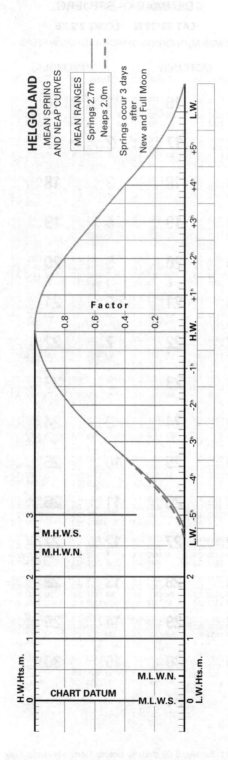

HELGOLAND
MEAN SPRING
AND NEAP CURVES

MEAN RANGES
Springs 2.7m
Neaps 2.0m

Springs occur 3 days
after
New and Full Moon

Factor
0.8
0.6
0.4
0.2

H.W.

L.W.

+5ʰ +4ʰ +3ʰ +2ʰ +1ʰ

-1ʰ -2ʰ -3ʰ -4ʰ -5ʰ

L.W.

3

M.H.W.S.
M.H.W.N.

2

2

1

1

H.W.Hts.m.

M.L.W.N.

L.W.Hts.m.

0

CHART DATUM

M.L.W.S.

0

TIME ZONE -0100
(German Standard Time)
Subtract 1 hour for UT
For German Summer Time add
ONE hour in **non-shaded areas**

GERMANY – HELGOLAND

LAT 54°11'N   LONG 7°53'E

TIMES AND HEIGHTS OF HIGH AND LOW WATERS

YEAR **2004**

JANUARY

Day	Time	m		Day	Time	m
1 TH	0027 / 0621 / 1310 / 1900	0.5 / 2.6 / 0.4 / 2.3		**16** F	0523 / 1215 / 1803	2.7 / 0.2 / 2.4
2 F	0132 / 0726 / 1415 / 2006	0.6 / 2.5 / 0.5 / 2.3		**17** SA	0040 / 0625 / 1320 / 1908	0.4 / 2.6 / 0.3 / 2.4
3 SA	0245 / 0835 / 1520 / 2111	0.6 / 2.5 / 0.6 / 2.4		**18** SU	0155 / 0741 / 1437 / 2024	0.4 / 2.6 / 0.3 / 2.4
4 SU	0353 / 0938 / 1617 / 2207	0.5 / 2.6 / 0.5 / 2.6		**19** M	0316 / 0901 / 1553 / 2138	0.3 / 2.6 / 0.3 / 2.5
5 M	0449 / 1030 / 1705 / 2253	0.4 / 2.6 / 0.4 / 2.7		**20** TU	0431 / 1014 / 1702 / 2244	0.1 / 2.6 / 0.2 / 2.7
6 TU	0535 / 1114 / 1749 / 2333	0.4 / 2.6 / 0.4 / 2.7		**21** W	0539 / 1118 / 1802 / ● 2340	0.0 / 2.7 / 0.2 / 2.8
7 W	0615 / 1154 / 1828 ○	0.3 / 2.7 / 0.3		**22** TH	0636 / 1212 / 1854	0.0 / 2.7 / 0.1
8 TH	0009 / 0653 / 1231 / 1905	2.8 / 0.2 / 2.6 / 0.3		**23** F	0029 / 0727 / 1302 / 1942	2.8 / -0.1 / 2.7 / 0.1
9 F	0045 / 0732 / 1308 / 1942	2.8 / 0.2 / 2.6 / 0.3		**24** SA	0115 / 0816 / 1351 / 2028	2.9 / 0.0 / 2.6 / 0.1
10 SA	0122 / 0810 / 1345 / 2018	2.8 / 0.2 / 2.6 / 0.2		**25** SU	0201 / 0903 / 1436 / 2109	2.9 / 0.0 / 2.6 / 0.1
11 SU	0157 / 0847 / 1421 / 2052	2.8 / 0.1 / 2.5 / 0.1		**26** M	0245 / 0943 / 1515 / 2145	2.9 / 0.1 / 2.6 / 0.1
12 M	0231 / 0923 / 1459 / 2131	2.8 / 0.1 / 2.5 / 0.1		**27** TU	0324 / 1017 / 1550 / 2219	2.9 / 0.2 / 2.5 / 0.2
13 TU	0308 / 1004 / 1542 / 2213	2.7 / 0.0 / 2.4 / 0.1		**28** W	0402 / 1050 / 1626 / 2254	2.9 / 0.3 / 2.5 / 0.3
14 W	0351 / 1045 / 1627 / 2256	2.7 / 0.0 / 2.4 / 0.2		**29** TH	0440 / 1123 / 1703 / ◐ 2332	2.8 / 0.4 / 2.4 / 0.4
15 TH	0435 / 1126 / 1712 / ◐ 2340	2.7 / 0.1 / 2.4 / 0.3		**30** F	0523 / 1201 / 1748	2.6 / 0.5 / 2.3
				31 SA	0023 / 0618 / 1257 / 1850	0.5 / 2.5 / 0.6 / 2.3

FEBRUARY

Day	Time	m		Day	Time	m
1 SU	0135 / 0729 / 1412 / 2007	0.6 / 2.4 / 0.6 / 2.4		**16** M	0125 / 0714 / 1409 / 1957	0.3 / 2.4 / 0.4 / 2.4
2 M	0257 / 0847 / 1528 / 2122	0.5 / 2.4 / 0.6 / 2.5		**17** TU	0259 / 0847 / 1539 / 2125	0.2 / 2.4 / 0.3 / 2.5
3 TU	0411 / 0956 / 1633 / 2223	0.4 / 2.4 / 0.5 / 2.6		**18** W	0426 / 1010 / 1655 / 2237	0.1 / 2.5 / 0.3 / 2.6
4 W	0510 / 1051 / 1727 / 2311	0.4 / 2.5 / 0.4 / 2.7		**19** TH	0536 / 1116 / 1756 / 2333	0.0 / 2.5 / 0.2 / 2.8
5 TH	0557 / 1136 / 1813 / 2351	0.3 / 2.6 / 0.3 / 2.8		**20** F	0633 / 1208 / 1847 ●	-0.1 / 2.6 / 0.1
6 F	0640 / 1217 / 1854 ○	0.2 / 2.6 / 0.2		**21** SA	0020 / 0720 / 1252 / 1931	2.8 / -0.1 / 2.6 / 0.0
7 SA	0029 / 0720 / 1254 / 1932	2.8 / 0.1 / 2.6 / 0.1		**22** SU	0102 / 0802 / 1333 / 2011	2.9 / -0.1 / 2.6 / 0.0
8 SU	0106 / 0759 / 1330 / 2008	2.8 / 0.0 / 2.6 / 0.0		**23** M	0142 / 0841 / 1411 / 2047	2.9 / 0.0 / 2.6 / 0.0
9 M	0142 / 0835 / 1406 / 2042	2.8 / -0.0 / 2.6 / -0.1		**24** TU	0220 / 0915 / 1445 / 2119	2.9 / 0.1 / 2.6 / 0.0
10 TU	0215 / 0910 / 1442 / 2119	2.8 / -0.1 / 2.5 / -0.1		**25** W	0255 / 0943 / 1515 / 2148	2.9 / 0.1 / 2.6 / 0.1
11 W	0251 / 0947 / 1522 / 2158	2.7 / -0.1 / 2.5 / 0.0		**26** TH	0327 / 1009 / 1544 / 2217	2.8 / 0.2 / 2.6 / 0.1
12 TH	0331 / 1025 / 1601 / 2236	2.8 / -0.1 / 2.5 / 0.0		**27** F	0358 / 1034 / 1612 / 2246	2.7 / 0.3 / 2.5 / 0.3
13 F	0410 / 1059 / 1639 / ◐ 2312	2.7 / 0.0 / 2.5 / 0.1		**28** SA	0432 / 1102 / 1647 / 2324	2.5 / 0.4 / 2.4 / 0.4
14 SA	0452 / 1139 / 1724	2.6 / 0.2 / 2.4		**29** SU	0517 / 1149 / 1742	2.4 / 0.5 / 2.3
15 SU	0005 / 0551 / 1242 / 1831	0.2 / 2.5 / 0.3 / 2.4				

MARCH

Day	Time	m		Day	Time	m
1 M	0029 / 0626 / 1306 / 1903	0.5 / 2.2 / 0.6 / 2.3		**16** TU	0115 / 0706 / 1358 / 1946	0.2 / 2.3 / 0.4 / 2.4
2 TU	0159 / 0754 / 1438 / 2033	0.5 / 2.2 / 0.6 / 2.4		**17** W	0257 / 0844 / 1534 / 2117	0.1 / 2.3 / 0.3 / 2.5
3 W	0330 / 0919 / 1600 / 2149	0.4 / 2.3 / 0.5 / 2.5		**18** TH	0426 / 1008 / 1650 / 2228	0.0 / 2.3 / 0.2 / 2.6
4 TH	0442 / 1025 / 1702 / 2245	0.3 / 2.4 / 0.4 / 2.7		**19** F	0531 / 1108 / 1745 / 2319	-0.1 / 2.4 / 0.1 / 2.7
5 F	0536 / 1114 / 1753 / 2327	0.2 / 2.5 / 0.2 / 2.7		**20** SA	0620 / 1153 / 1831 ●	-0.2 / 2.5 / 0.0
6 SA	0621 / 1155 / 1836 ○	0.0 / 2.6 / 0.1		**21** SU	0003 / 0703 / 1233 / 1912	2.8 / -0.2 / 2.5 / -0.1
7 SU	0006 / 0700 / 1233 / 1913	2.8 / -0.1 / 2.6 / 0.0		**22** M	0044 / 0741 / 1309 / 1948	2.8 / -0.1 / 2.6 / -0.1
8 M	0043 / 0737 / 1308 / 1949	2.8 / -0.2 / 2.6 / -0.1		**23** TU	0119 / 0813 / 1341 / 2021	2.8 / 0.0 / 2.6 / -0.1
9 TU	0118 / 0813 / 1343 / 2024	2.8 / -0.2 / 2.6 / -0.2		**24** W	0151 / 0841 / 1410 / 2050	2.8 / 0.0 / 2.6 / 0.0
10 W	0153 / 0849 / 1419 / 2100	2.8 / -0.2 / 2.6 / -0.2		**25** TH	0222 / 0905 / 1437 / 2117	2.8 / 0.1 / 2.6 / 0.0
11 TH	0230 / 0925 / 1455 / 2137	2.8 / -0.2 / 2.5 / -0.2		**26** F	0252 / 0929 / 1505 / 2144	2.7 / 0.1 / 2.6 / 0.0
12 F	0309 / 1000 / 1532 / 2215	2.7 / -0.1 / 2.5 / -0.1		**27** SA	0322 / 0953 / 1532 / 2210	2.6 / 0.2 / 2.5 / 0.2
13 SA	0350 / 1035 / 1612 / ◐ 2254	2.7 / 0.1 / 2.5 / 0.0		**28** SU	0354 / 1019 / 1603 / ◐ 2243	2.5 / 0.3 / 2.5 / 0.3
14 SU	0435 / 1117 / 1701 / 2350	2.5 / 0.2 / 2.4 / 0.1		**29** M	0435 / 1101 / 1652 / 2341	2.3 / 0.5 / 2.4 / 0.4
15 M	0538 / 1225 / 1813	2.4 / 0.3 / 2.3		**30** TU	0538 / 1212 / 1809	2.2 / 0.6 / 2.3
				31 W	0108 / 0705 / 1348 / 1942	0.5 / 2.1 / 0.6 / 2.4

APRIL

Day	Time	m		Day	Time	m
1 TH	0245 / 0836 / 1519 / 2107	0.4 / 2.2 / 0.5 / 2.5		**16** F	0416 / 0954 / 1634 / 2209	-0.1 / 2.3 / 0.1 / 2.6
2 F	0406 / 0949 / 1628 / 2209	0.2 / 2.4 / 0.3 / 2.6		**17** SA	0513 / 1048 / 1723 / 2256	-0.2 / 2.3 / 0.0 / 2.7
3 SA	0505 / 1042 / 1721 / 2255	0.0 / 2.5 / 0.2 / 2.7		**18** SU	0555 / 1128 / 1804 / 2338	-0.2 / 2.4 / -0.1 / 2.7
4 SU	0551 / 1125 / 1807 / 2335	-0.1 / 2.6 / 0.1 / 2.8		**19** M	0634 / 1206 / 1845 ●	-0.1 / 2.5 / -0.1
5 M	0632 / 1204 / 1846 ○	-0.2 / 2.6 / -0.1		**20** TU	0019 / 0711 / 1241 / 1922	2.7 / -0.1 / 2.6 / -0.1
6 TU	0013 / 0709 / 1239 / 1923	2.8 / -0.2 / 2.7 / -0.1		**21** W	0054 / 0740 / 1310 / 1953	2.7 / 0.0 / 2.7 / -0.1
7 W	0049 / 0745 / 1314 / 1959	2.8 / -0.2 / 2.7 / -0.2		**22** TH	0123 / 0805 / 1336 / 2020	2.7 / 0.0 / 2.7 / -0.1
8 TH	0127 / 0823 / 1350 / 2038	2.8 / -0.2 / 2.6 / -0.2		**23** F	0151 / 0830 / 1403 / 2048	2.7 / 0.0 / 2.7 / 0.0
9 F	0208 / 0900 / 1429 / 2118	2.8 / -0.1 / 2.6 / -0.2		**24** SA	0222 / 0855 / 1433 / 2116	2.6 / 0.1 / 2.6 / 0.0
10 SA	0252 / 0938 / 1510 / 2201	2.7 / 0.0 / 2.6 / -0.1		**25** SU	0254 / 0923 / 1504 / 2146	2.5 / 0.2 / 2.6 / 0.1
11 SU	0339 / 1020 / 1557 / 2250	2.6 / 0.1 / 2.6 / 0.2		**26** M	0330 / 0954 / 1539 / 2223	2.4 / 0.3 / 2.5 / 0.2
12 M	0433 / 1111 / 1654 / ◐ 2352	2.4 / 0.3 / 2.5 / 0.1		**27** TU	0411 / 1035 / 1624 / ◐ 2314	2.3 / 0.4 / 2.4 / 0.3
13 TU	0540 / 1221 / 1808	2.3 / 0.3 / 2.4		**28** W	0507 / 1136 / 1729	2.2 / 0.5 / 2.4
14 W	0115 / 0705 / 1351 / 1936	0.1 / 2.2 / 0.3 / 2.4		**29** TH	0028 / 0623 / 1301 / 1852	0.3 / 2.2 / 0.5 / 2.4
15 TH	0252 / 0837 / 1523 / 2103	0.0 / 0.2 / 0.2 / 2.5		**30** F	0157 / 0747 / 1430 / 2015	0.3 / 2.2 / 0.4 / 2.5

Chart Datum: 1·68 metres below Normal Null (German reference level)

TIME ZONE -0100
(German Standard Time)
Subtract 1 hour for UT
For German Summer Time add
ONE hour in non-shaded areas

GERMANY – HELGOLAND
LAT 54°11'N   LONG 7°53'E
TIMES AND HEIGHTS OF HIGH AND LOW WATERS

YEAR 2004

Moon phase key: ○ = Full Moon, ● = New Moon, ◐ = First Quarter, ◑ = Last Quarter

MAY

Day				
1 SA	0318 0.1	0903 2.3	1543 0.3	2123 2.6
2 SU	0421 0.0	1000 2.5	1640 0.2	2215 2.7
3 M	0511 -0.1	1046 2.6	1729 0.1	2300 2.8
4 TU ○	0557 -0.2	1128 2.7	1814 0.0	2341 2.8
5 W	0637 -0.2	1206 2.7	1854 -0.1	
6 TH	0020 2.8	0716 -0.2	1244 2.7	1934 -0.2
7 F	0103 2.8	0757 -0.1	1325 2.7	2019 -0.2
8 SA	0152 2.7	0840 -0.1	1411 2.7	2107 -0.2
9 SU	0243 2.6	0925 0.0	1459 2.7	2157 -0.2
10 M	0337 2.5	1014 0.1	1550 2.6	2252 -0.1
11 TU ◑	0434 2.4	1109 0.2	1650 2.6	2355 0.0
12 W	0539 2.2	1215 0.3	1759 2.5	
13 TH	0108 0.0	0654 2.2	1333 0.3	1917 2.5
14 F	0230 0.0	0813 2.2	1453 0.2	2034 2.6
15 SA	0345 -0.1	0923 2.2	1600 0.1	2138 2.6
16 SU	0440 -0.1	1014 2.3	1650 0.0	2226 2.6
17 M	0520 -0.1	1055 2.4	1732 0.0	2308 2.6
18 TU	0558 -0.1	1133 2.5	1815 0.0	2350 2.7
19 W ●	0636 0.0	1210 2.6	1854 0.0	
20 TH	0027 2.7	0708 0.1	1241 2.7	1926 0.0
21 F	0058 2.6	0734 0.1	1309 2.7	1955 0.0
22 SA	0127 2.6	0802 0.1	1339 2.7	2026 0.0
23 SU	0201 2.5	0832 0.1	1412 2.7	2058 0.1
24 M	0237 2.5	0905 0.2	1448 2.7	2134 0.1
25 TU	0315 2.4	0941 0.3	1526 2.6	2214 0.1
26 W	0357 2.3	1023 0.3	1609 2.6	2301 0.1
27 TH ◐	0447 2.3	1114 0.3	1702 2.5	2359 0.1
28 F	0548 2.2	1221 0.3	1808 2.5	
29 SA	0109 0.1	0658 2.3	1338 0.4	1921 2.5
30 SU	0223 0.1	0809 2.4	1450 0.3	2030 2.6
31 M	0329 0.0	0910 2.5	1552 0.2	2130 2.7

JUNE

Day				
1 TU	0426 -0.1	1002 2.6	1649 0.1	2223 2.8
2 W	0519 -0.1	1051 2.7	1741 0.0	2311 2.8
3 TH ○	0606 -0.1	1137 2.7	1829 -0.1	2358 2.8
4 F	0651 -0.1	1221 2.8	1917 -0.2	
5 SA	0048 2.7	0738 -0.1	1310 2.8	2010 -0.2
6 SU	0144 2.7	0829 0.0	1402 2.8	2105 -0.2
7 M	0240 2.5	0919 0.0	1453 2.8	2157 -0.2
8 TU	0333 2.4	1008 0.1	1544 2.7	2249 -0.1
9 W ◑	0426 2.4	1059 0.2	1639 2.7	2345 0.0
10 TH	0524 2.3	1156 0.2	1739 2.7	
11 F	0044 0.0	0626 2.2	1258 0.2	1844 2.6
12 SA	0148 0.1	0731 2.2	1405 0.2	1951 2.6
13 SU	0253 0.1	0835 2.3	1513 0.2	2056 2.6
14 M	0352 0.1	0930 2.4	1611 0.1	2151 2.6
15 TU	0439 0.1	1018 2.5	1701 0.1	2238 2.6
16 W	0521 0.1	1101 2.6	1745 0.1	2322 2.6
17 TH ●	0603 0.1	1142 2.7	1827 0.1	
18 F	0002 2.6	0640 0.2	1217 2.7	1903 0.1
19 SA	0038 2.6	0712 0.2	1250 2.8	1938 0.1
20 SU	0112 2.6	0745 0.2	1324 2.8	2013 0.1
21 M	0147 2.6	0819 0.2	1359 2.8	2048 0.1
22 TU	0223 2.5	0854 0.1	1434 2.7	2125 0.1
23 W	0301 2.4	0931 0.2	1512 2.7	2205 0.0
24 TH	0343 2.4	1013 0.2	1554 2.6	2249 0.0
25 F ◐	0429 2.3	1058 0.2	1640 2.6	2333 0.0
26 SA	0518 2.3	1148 0.2	1730 2.6	
27 SU	0025 0.1	0611 2.3	1248 0.1	1830 2.6
28 M	0127 0.1	0713 2.4	1357 0.3	1937 2.6
29 TU	0236 0.1	0818 2.5	1506 0.2	2046 2.7
30 W	0342 0.1	0921 2.5	1613 0.1	2151 2.7

JULY

Day				
1 TH	0445 0.1	1022 2.6	1717 0.0	2252 2.7
2 F ○	0544 0.1	1118 2.7	1816 -0.1	2348 2.7
3 SA	0638 0.0	1211 2.8	1910 -0.2	
4 SU	0043 2.7	0730 0.0	1302 2.9	2006 -0.2
5 M	0139 2.6	0822 0.0	1354 2.9	2100 -0.2
6 TU	0232 2.6	0910 0.0	1444 2.9	2149 -0.1
7 W	0320 2.5	0954 0.0	1531 2.9	2234 -0.1
8 TH	0406 2.4	1038 0.1	1618 2.8	2319 0.1
9 F ◑	0453 2.4	1124 0.2	1707 2.8	
10 SA	0003 0.2	0543 2.4	1212 0.3	1759 2.7
11 SU	0050 0.2	0635 2.3	1308 0.3	1857 2.6
12 M	0147 0.3	0735 2.4	1416 0.4	2003 2.5
13 TU	0253 0.4	0839 2.4	1527 0.3	2110 2.5
14 W	0355 0.4	0940 2.5	1629 0.3	2209 2.5
15 TH	0449 0.3	1033 2.6	1720 0.2	2258 2.6
16 F	0536 0.3	1118 2.7	1805 0.2	2342 2.6
17 SA ●	0619 0.3	1159 2.8	1846 0.2	
18 SU	0022 2.6	0658 0.2	1236 2.8	1925 0.1
19 M	0059 2.6	0730 0.2	1312 2.9	2003 0.1
20 TU	0134 2.6	0809 0.1	1345 2.8	2037 0.0
21 W	0208 2.6	0842 0.1	1418 2.8	2111 0.0
22 TH	0243 2.5	0918 0.0	1453 2.7	2149 0.0
23 F	0323 2.5	0959 0.0	1534 2.7	2229 0.0
24 SA ◐	0406 2.4	1039 0.1	1615 2.7	2306 0.0
25 SU	0446 2.4	1117 0.1	1656 2.7	2345 0.1
26 M	0528 2.4	1204 0.2	1746 2.6	
27 TU	0038 0.2	0623 2.4	1310 0.3	1855 2.6
28 W	0150 0.3	0736 2.4	1431 0.2	2015 2.6
29 TH	0310 0.3	0854 2.5	1552 0.1	2135 2.6
30 F	0426 0.3	1007 2.7	1706 0.0	2246 2.7
31 SA ○	0534 0.2	1110 2.8	1811 0.0	2347 2.7

AUGUST

Day				
1 SU	0632 0.1	1205 2.9	1907 -0.1	
2 M	0040 2.7	0723 0.1	1254 2.9	1958 -0.1
3 TU	0129 2.7	0811 0.0	1341 3.0	2047 -0.1
4 W	0216 2.6	0854 0.0	1426 3.0	2130 0.0
5 TH	0257 2.6	0932 0.0	1508 3.0	2206 0.1
6 F	0335 2.6	1008 0.1	1548 2.9	2240 0.2
7 SA ◑	0413 2.5	1046 0.2	1628 2.8	2313 0.3
8 SU	0452 2.5	1124 0.3	1710 2.7	2348 0.4
9 M	0535 2.5	1210 0.5	1800 2.5	
10 TU	0038 0.6	0630 2.4	1315 0.6	1906 2.4
11 W	0149 0.6	0743 2.5	1437 0.6	2026 2.4
12 TH	0309 0.6	0901 2.5	1556 0.5	2140 2.5
13 F	0420 0.5	1007 2.7	1658 0.4	2238 2.6
14 SA	0515 0.4	1058 2.7	1747 0.3	2324 2.6
15 SU	0601 0.3	1139 2.8	1829 0.2	
16 M ●	0004 2.7	0642 0.3	1217 2.8	1909 0.1
17 TU	0041 2.7	0720 0.2	1253 2.9	1945 0.0
18 W	0115 2.7	0753 0.1	1326 2.9	2018 0.0
19 TH	0148 2.7	0825 0.0	1356 2.8	2051 0.0
20 F	0221 2.6	0859 0.0	1429 2.8	2125 0.0
21 SA	0257 2.6	0936 0.0	1507 2.8	2202 0.0
22 SU	0336 2.6	1014 0.1	1547 2.8	2235 0.1
23 M ◐	0412 2.5	1048 0.2	1626 2.7	2310 0.2
24 TU	0452 2.5	1131 0.2	1717 2.6	
25 W	0003 0.4	0550 2.4	1242 0.3	1832 2.5
26 TH	0124 0.5	0713 2.5	1415 0.3	2005 2.5
27 F	0258 0.5	0844 2.6	1549 0.2	2134 2.5
28 SA	0422 0.4	1003 2.7	1705 0.1	2246 2.6
29 SU	0529 0.3	1104 2.8	1806 0.0	2342 2.7
30 M ○	0624 0.2	1155 2.9	1857 -0.1	
31 TU	0030 2.7	0711 0.1	1240 3.0	1943 0.0

Chart Datum: 1·68 metres below Normal Null (German reference level)

TIME ZONE -0100
(German Standard Time)
Subtract 1 hour for UT
For German Summer Time add
ONE hour in **non-shaded areas**

GERMANY – HELGOLAND

LAT 54°11′N   LONG 7°53′E

TIMES AND HEIGHTS OF HIGH AND LOW WATERS

YEAR **2004**

SEPTEMBER

Day	Time m	Time m	Day	Time m	Time m
1 W	0113 2.7 / 0752 0.1	1322 3.0 / 2023 0.0	**16** TH	0049 2.7 / 0729 0.1	1259 2.9 / 1952 0.0
2 TH	0151 2.7 / 0830 0.1	1402 3.1 / 2059 0.1	**17** F	0122 2.7 / 0802 0.1	1331 2.9 / 2024 0.0
3 F	0226 2.7 / 0904 0.1	1439 3.0 / 2129 0.2	**18** SA	0154 2.7 / 0835 0.1	1403 2.9 / 2057 0.1
4 SA	0257 2.7 / 0935 0.1	1513 2.9 / 2156 0.3	**19** SU	0228 2.7 / 0909 0.1	1440 2.8 / 2131 0.2
5 SU	0329 2.7 / 1007 0.2	1546 2.8 / 2223 0.4	**20** M	0304 2.7 / 0947 0.1	1521 2.8 / 2206 0.3
6 M	0401 2.6 / 1039 0.4	1612 2.6 / ◑ 2252 0.6	**21** TU	0343 2.6 / 1026 0.2	1607 2.6 / ◑ 2246 0.4
7 TU	0439 2.5 / 1118 0.5	1708 2.4 / 2336 0.7	**22** W	0430 2.6 / 1117 0.3	1707 2.5 / 2347 0.6
8 W	0531 2.5 / 1218 0.7	1813 2.3	**23** TH	0537 2.5 / 1234 0.4	1829 2.4
9 TH	0048 0.8 / 0648 2.4	1344 0.7 / 1939 2.3	**24** F	0115 0.6 / 0706 2.5	1414 0.4 / 2006 2.4
10 F	0220 0.8 / 0817 2.5	1517 0.6 / 2106 2.4	**25** SA	0255 0.6 / 0840 2.6	1550 0.2 / 2136 2.5
11 SA	0346 0.7 / 0936 2.6	1632 0.5 / 2214 2.5	**26** SU	0419 0.5 / 0957 2.7	1702 0.1 / 2241 2.5
12 SU	0450 0.5 / 1033 2.8	1724 0.3 / 2301 2.6	**27** M	0519 0.3 / 1053 2.8	1753 0.0 / 2329 2.6
13 M	0538 0.4 / 1114 2.8	1805 0.2 / 2339 2.7	**28** TU	0606 0.2 / 1137 2.9	1838 0.0 / O
14 TU	0619 0.3 / 1150 2.9	1843 0.1 / ●	**29** W	0010 2.7 / 0649 0.1	1220 2.9 / 1918 0.1
15 W	0015 2.7 / 0656 0.2	1226 2.9 / 1918 0.0	**30** TH	0049 2.7 / 0728 0.1	1259 3.0 / 1953 0.2

OCTOBER

Day	Time m	Time m	Day	Time m	Time m
1 F	0122 2.8 / 0802 0.1	1334 3.0 / 2023 0.2	**16** SA	0050 2.8 / 0733 0.2	1304 3.0 / 1955 0.1
2 SA	0152 2.8 / 0834 0.2	1406 2.9 / 2049 0.3	**17** SU	0125 2.8 / 0810 0.1	1341 2.9 / 2031 0.2
3 SU	0220 2.8 / 0902 0.2	1438 2.8 / 2114 0.3	**18** M	0202 2.8 / 0848 0.1	1422 2.8 / 2107 0.3
4 M	0249 2.7 / 0931 0.3	1510 2.7 / 2140 0.4	**19** TU	0242 2.8 / 0930 0.2	1508 2.7 / 2148 0.4
5 TU	0320 2.7 / 1001 0.4	1546 2.6 / 2209 0.6	**20** W	0327 2.7 / 1018 0.3	1602 2.6 / ◑ 2237 0.5
6 W	0356 2.6 / 1038 0.6	1629 2.4 / 2250 0.8	**21** TH	0422 2.7 / 1117 0.3	1707 2.4 / 2343 0.6
7 TH	0445 2.5 / 1133 0.7	1730 2.3 / 2357 0.9	**22** F	0533 2.6 / 1235 0.4	1828 2.3
8 F	0558 2.5 / 1254 0.8	1852 2.3	**23** SA	0109 0.7 / 0658 2.6	1409 0.3 / 2001 2.3
9 SA	0128 0.9 / 0727 2.5	1429 0.7 / 2022 2.4	**24** SU	0243 0.6 / 0827 2.7	1539 0.2 / 2124 2.4
10 SU	0301 0.8 / 0852 2.6	1551 0.5 / 2137 2.5	**25** M	0402 0.4 / 0941 2.7	1645 0.1 / 2224 2.5
11 M	0412 0.6 / 0955 2.8	1649 0.3 / 2228 2.6	**26** TU	0457 0.3 / 1033 2.8	1730 0.0 / 2306 2.6
12 TU	0503 0.5 / 1040 2.8	1731 0.2 / 2307 2.7	**27** W	0540 0.2 / 1115 2.8	1809 0.1 / 2344 2.7
13 W	0545 0.3 / 1117 2.9	1809 0.1 / 2343 2.8	**28** TH	0621 0.2 / 1156 2.9	1847 0.2 / O
14 TH	0624 0.2 / 1154 2.9	1845 0.1 / ●	**29** F	0021 2.8 / 0700 0.2	1234 2.9 / 1920 0.2
15 F	0017 2.8 / 0659 0.2	1229 3.0 / 1920 0.1	**30** SA	0053 2.8 / 0734 0.2	1307 2.9 / 1947 0.3
			31 SU	0121 2.9 / 0804 0.2	1337 2.8 / 2013 0.3

NOVEMBER

Day	Time m	Time m	Day	Time m	Time m
1 M	0149 2.8 / 0833 0.3	1409 2.7 / 2040 0.4	**16** TU	0146 2.9 / 0839 0.1	1417 2.8 / 2057 0.3
2 TU	0219 2.8 / 0903 0.3	1444 2.6 / 2108 0.5	**17** W	0233 2.8 / 0927 0.1	1508 2.7 / 2142 0.4
3 W	0252 2.8 / 0935 0.4	1521 2.5 / 2141 0.6	**18** TH	0322 2.8 / 1020 0.2	1601 2.5 / 2234 0.5
4 TH	0328 2.7 / 1012 0.5	1603 2.4 / 2221 0.7	**19** F	0418 2.8 / 1119 0.3	1703 2.4 / ◑ 2336 0.6
5 F	0414 2.6 / 1101 0.6	1656 2.3 / ◑ 2317 0.8	**20** SA	0524 2.7 / 1228 0.3	1816 2.3
6 SA	0515 2.5 / 1209 0.7	1806 2.3	**21** SU	0050 0.5 / 0640 2.6	1347 0.3 / 1936 2.3
7 SU	0035 0.9 / 0633 2.5	1332 0.6 / 1927 2.3	**22** M	0211 0.5 / 0759 2.7	1506 0.2 / 2051 2.3
8 M	0203 0.8 / 0755 2.6	1454 0.5 / 2044 2.5	**23** TU	0326 0.4 / 0910 2.7	1610 0.2 / 2151 2.4
9 TU	0319 0.7 / 0905 2.7	1558 0.4 / 2142 2.6	**24** W	0424 0.3 / 1005 2.7	1656 0.2 / 2235 2.5
10 W	0416 0.6 / 0957 2.8	1647 0.3 / 2226 2.7	**25** TH	0510 0.3 / 1050 2.8	1735 0.2 / 2315 2.7
11 TH	0504 0.4 / 1040 2.8	1729 0.2 / 2306 2.8	**26** F	0553 0.3 / 1132 2.8	1814 0.3 / O 2353 2.8
12 F	0548 0.3 / 1120 2.9	1810 0.2 / ● 2343 2.8	**27** SA	0634 0.3 / 1211 2.8	1849 0.4
13 SA	0628 0.2 / 1158 2.9	1848 0.2	**28** SU	0027 2.9 / 0709 0.3	1245 2.8 / 1918 0.4
14 SU	0020 2.8 / 0707 0.2	1240 2.9 / 1929 0.2	**29** M	0057 2.9 / 0741 0.3	1317 2.7 / 1947 0.4
15 M	0101 2.9 / 0751 0.1	1327 2.9 / 2013 0.3	**30** TU	0129 2.9 / 0813 0.3	1351 2.7 / 2018 0.4

DECEMBER

Day	Time m	Time m	Day	Time m	Time m
1 W	0202 2.9 / 0846 0.3	1427 2.6 / 2050 0.4	**16** TH	0230 2.9 / 0930 0.0	1508 2.6 / 2140 0.3
2 TH	0236 2.8 / 0920 0.4	1503 2.5 / 2124 0.5	**17** F	0318 2.9 / 1019 0.1	1556 2.5 / 2226 0.3
3 F	0311 2.8 / 0957 0.4	1543 2.5 / 2203 0.6	**18** SA	0409 2.9 / 1111 0.2	1648 2.4 / ◑ 2318 0.4
4 SA	0351 2.7 / 1040 0.4	1629 2.4 / 2250 0.6	**19** SU	0505 2.8 / 1206 0.3	1747 2.3
5 SU	0440 2.6 / 1131 0.5	1724 2.3 / 2348 0.7	**20** M	0016 0.4 / 0607 2.7	1306 0.3 / 1852 2.3
6 M	0541 2.5 / 1235 0.5	1829 2.3	**21** TU	0122 0.4 / 0714 2.7	1412 0.3 / 1959 2.3
7 TU	0100 0.7 / 0652 2.6	1347 0.5 / 1940 2.4	**22** W	0234 0.4 / 0824 2.6	1518 0.4 / 2103 2.4
8 W	0215 0.7 / 0803 2.7	1456 0.4 / 2044 2.5	**23** TH	0343 0.4 / 0928 2.6	1615 0.4 / 2159 2.5
9 TH	0321 0.6 / 0906 2.8	1555 0.3 / 2138 2.6	**24** F	0441 0.3 / 1023 2.6	1703 0.4 / 2247 2.7
10 F	0419 0.4 / 0959 2.8	1648 0.3 / 2227 2.7	**25** SA	0529 0.3 / 1110 2.7	1746 0.4 / 2330 2.8
11 SA	0513 0.3 / 1049 2.9	1737 0.2 / 2313 2.8	**26** SU	0612 0.3 / 1153 2.7	1825 0.4 / O
12 SU	0603 0.2 / 1136 2.9	1823 0.2 / ● 2359 2.8	**27** M	0008 2.8 / 0650 0.3	1230 2.7 / 1900 0.4
13 M	0651 0.1 / 1226 2.8	1912 0.2	**28** TU	0042 2.9 / 0726 0.3	1304 2.7 / 1933 0.4
14 TU	0047 2.9 / 0743 0.1	1322 2.8 / 2004 0.2	**29** W	0116 2.9 / 0802 0.2	1338 2.6 / 2007 0.3
15 W	0138 2.9 / 0838 0.0	1417 2.7 / 2054 0.2	**30** TH	0151 2.9 / 0836 0.3	1412 2.6 / 2040 0.3
			31 F	0223 2.8 / 0909 0.2	1446 2.5 / 2113 0.3

Chart Datum: 1·68 metres below Normal Null (German reference level)

Chapter 5

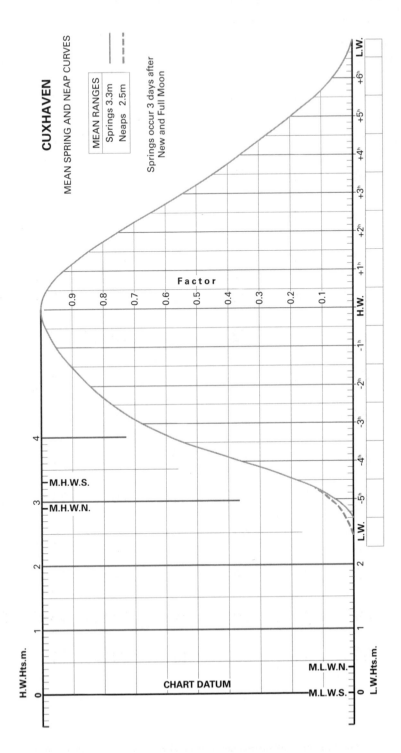

CUXHAVEN

MEAN SPRING AND NEAP CURVES

MEAN RANGES
Springs 3.3m
Neaps 2.5m

Springs occur 3 days after
New and Full Moon

Factor

0.9 0.8 0.7 0.6 0.5 0.4 0.3 0.2 0.1

H.W. +1ʰ +2ʰ +3ʰ +4ʰ +5ʰ +6ʰ L.W.

-1ʰ -2ʰ -3ʰ -4ʰ -5ʰ L.W.

H.W.Hts.m.

M.H.W.S.
M.H.W.N.

CHART DATUM

L.W.Hts.m.
M.L.W.N.
M.L.W.S.

TIME ZONE -0100
(German Standard Time)
Subtract 1 hour for UT
For German Summer Time add ONE hour in **non-shaded areas**

GERMANY – CUXHAVEN

LAT 53°52′N   LONG 8°43′E

TIMES AND HEIGHTS OF HIGH AND LOW WATERS

YEAR **2004**

JANUARY

Day	Time m				Day	Time m			
1 TH	0144 0.5	0730 3.1	1428 3.0	2009 2.7	16 F	0100 0.3	0635 3.2	1334 0.2	1916 2.9
2 F	0248 0.6	0835 3.0	1532 0.5	2115 2.8	17 SA	0156 0.4	0736 3.1	1437 0.3	2023 2.9
3 SA	0402 0.6	0944 3.0	1639 0.6	2220 3.0	18 SU	0310 0.4	0851 3.1	1554 0.4	2138 3.0
4 SU	0513 0.5	1047 3.1	1740 0.5	2317 3.1	19 M	0431 0.3	1011 3.1	1713 0.3	2251 3.1
5 M	0611 0.4	1140 3.1	1831 0.4		20 TU	0550 0.1	1126 3.1	1826 0.2	2356 3.2
6 TU	0004 3.2	0658 0.4	1225 3.2	1916 0.4	21 W ●	0700 0.0	1232 3.2	1929 0.2	
7 W ○	0044 3.3	0740 0.3	1306 3.2	1955 0.3	22 TH	0052 3.3	0758 0.0	1328 3.2	2022 0.1
8 TH	0120 3.4	0819 0.3	1345 3.2	2032 0.3	23 F	0141 3.4	0850 -0.1	1419 3.2	2110 0.1
9 F	0157 3.4	0859 0.2	1423 3.2	2110 0.3	24 SA	0228 3.4	0940 0.0	1508 3.2	2157 0.1
10 SA	0233 3.4	0938 0.2	1500 3.2	2146 0.2	25 SU	0313 3.5	1028 0.0	1552 3.2	2238 0.1
11 SU	0308 3.4	1014 0.1	1536 3.1	2220 0.1	26 M	0356 3.5	1109 0.1	1630 3.1	2312 0.1
12 M	0342 3.3	1047 0.1	1614 3.0	2256 0.1	27 TU	0434 3.5	1143 0.1	1705 3.0	2343 0.2
13 TU	0421 3.3	1124 0.0	1656 2.9	2336 0.2	28 W	0512 3.4	1215 0.2	1738 3.0	
14 W	0504 3.3	1206 0.1	1739 2.9		29 TH ◑	0014 0.3	0549 3.3	1245 0.3	1814 2.9
15 TH ◐	0017 0.2	0547 3.2	1248 0.1	1824 2.9	30 F	0049 0.4	0631 3.1	1319 0.5	1858 2.8
					31 SA	0136 0.5	0725 2.9	1411 0.6	2000 2.8

FEBRUARY

Day	Time m				Day	Time m			
1 SU	0245 0.6	0837 2.9	1525 0.7	2116 2.9	16 M	0234 0.3	0824 2.9	1522 0.4	2109 2.9
2 M	0410 0.6	0956 2.9	1645 0.6	2231 3.0	17 TU	0409 0.2	0958 2.9	1656 0.3	2235 3.0
3 TU	0529 0.5	1106 2.9	1755 0.5	2333 3.1	18 W	0540 0.1	1122 3.0	1818 0.2	2347 3.2
4 W	0631 0.4	1202 3.1	1851 0.4		19 TH	0654 0.0	1230 3.1	1923 0.1	
5 TH	0021 3.3	0720 0.3	1249 3.2	1938 0.3	20 F ●	0044 3.3	0753 -0.1	1323 3.1	2015 0.0
6 F ○	0103 3.4	0804 0.2	1331 3.2	2019 0.2	21 SA	0132 3.4	0841 -0.1	1409 3.2	2058 0.0
7 SA	0141 3.4	0846 0.1	1410 3.2	2059 0.1	22 SU	0215 3.4	0926 -0.1	1450 3.2	2138 0.0
8 SU	0218 3.4	0925 0.0	1446 3.2	2136 0.0	23 M	0255 3.5	1007 0.0	1527 3.2	2214 0.0
9 M	0252 3.4	1000 -0.1	1520 3.1	2209 -0.1	24 TU	0331 3.6	1041 0.0	1559 3.2	2244 0.0
10 TU	0326 3.4	1033 -0.1	1555 3.0	2243 -0.1	25 W	0405 3.5	1110 0.1	1627 3.1	2311 0.0
11 W	0403 3.3	1109 -0.1	1634 3.0	2321 -0.1	26 TH	0437 3.4	1135 0.2	1655 3.1	2337 0.1
12 TH	0444 3.3	1147 0.0	1713 3.0	2357 0.0	27 F	0508 3.3	1157 0.3	1722 3.0	
13 F ◐	0523 3.3	1221 0.1	1751 3.0		28 SA	0001 0.3	0541 3.1	1220 0.4	1756 2.9
14 SA	0031 0.1	0604 3.2	1258 0.2	1836 2.9	29 SU	0035 0.4	0626 2.9	1301 0.6	1852 2.8
15 SU	0118 0.2	0702 3.0	1356 0.3	1943 2.8					

MARCH

Day	Time m				Day	Time m			
1 M	0136 0.5	0735 2.7	1415 0.7	2013 2.8	16 TU	0221 0.2	0818 2.8	1508 0.4	2056 2.9
2 TU	0307 0.6	0903 2.7	1549 0.6	2142 2.9	17 W	0403 0.1	0956 2.8	1649 0.3	2227 3.0
3 W	0444 0.5	1029 2.8	1717 0.5	2258 3.1	18 TH	0537 0.0	1120 2.9	1811 0.2	2339 3.2
4 TH	0602 0.3	1136 3.0	1824 0.4	2354 3.2	19 F	0647 -0.1	1222 3.0	1910 0.0	
5 F	0658 0.2	1227 3.1	1916 0.2		20 SA ●	0031 3.3	0739 -0.2	1308 3.1	1956 -0.1
6 SA ○	0039 3.3	0743 0.0	1310 3.2	2000 0.1	21 SU	0115 3.4	0823 -0.2	1349 3.1	2037 -0.1
7 SU	0118 3.4	0823 -0.1	1348 3.2	2039 0.0	22 M	0155 3.4	0903 -0.1	1425 3.2	2113 -0.1
8 M	0155 3.4	0901 -0.2	1423 3.2	2115 -0.1	23 TU	0231 3.5	0938 -0.1	1456 3.2	2145 0.0
9 TU	0229 3.4	0937 -0.2	1456 3.2	2150 -0.2	24 W	0303 3.5	1007 0.0	1522 3.3	2213 0.0
10 W	0303 3.4	1012 -0.2	1530 3.1	2223 -0.2	25 TH	0333 3.4	1032 0.0	1548 3.2	2238 0.0
11 TH	0340 3.4	1047 -0.2	1607 3.1	2259 -0.2	26 F	0402 3.3	1054 0.1	1614 3.2	2302 0.0
12 F	0422 3.4	1122 -0.1	1645 3.1	2334 -0.1	27 SA	0432 3.2	1116 0.2	1641 3.1	2326 0.2
13 SA ◑	0503 3.3	1156 0.1	1724 3.0		28 SU	0503 3.0	1138 0.4	1713 3.0	2355 0.3
14 SU	0010 0.0	0548 3.1	1224 0.2	1812 2.9	29 M	0544 2.8	1213 0.5	1803 2.9	
15 M	0101 0.1	0651 2.9	1336 0.3	1924 2.8	30 TU	0048 0.4	0647 2.7	1321 0.6	1919 2.8
					31 W	0214 0.5	0815 2.7	1456 0.6	2052 2.9

APRIL

Day	Time m				Day	Time m			
1 TH	0356 0.4	0947 2.8	1632 0.5	2215 3.1	16 F	0526 -0.1	1107 2.8	1752 0.1	2321 3.2
2 F	0522 0.2	1101 2.9	1747 0.3	2318 3.2	17 SA	0628 -0.2	1202 2.9	1845 -0.1	
3 SA	0624 0.0	1156 3.1	1843 0.2		18 SU	0009 3.3	0713 -0.2	1242 3.0	1927 -0.1
4 SU	0005 3.3	0710 -0.1	1240 3.2	1930 0.0	19 M ●	0050 3.3	0753 -0.2	1320 3.1	2009 -0.1
5 M ○	0046 3.4	0752 -0.2	1319 3.3	2011 -0.1	20 TU	0130 3.4	0832 -0.1	1355 3.2	2046 -0.1
6 TU	0124 3.5	0830 -0.3	1354 3.3	2047 -0.2	21 W	0205 3.4	0905 0.0	1423 3.3	2115 -0.1
7 W	0200 3.5	0906 -0.3	1427 3.3	2123 -0.2	22 TH	0235 3.4	0931 0.0	1448 3.3	2141 0.0
8 TH	0238 3.5	0944 -0.2	1502 3.3	2159 -0.3	23 F	0303 3.3	0955 0.0	1513 3.3	2207 0.0
9 F	0319 3.4	1022 -0.2	1541 3.2	2237 -0.2	24 SA	0332 3.2	1019 0.1	1542 3.2	2234 0.0
10 SA	0405 3.3	1059 0.0	1623 3.2	2318 -0.1	25 SU	0405 3.1	1045 0.2	1614 3.2	2304 0.1
11 SU	0453 3.2	1138 0.1	1709 3.1		26 M	0440 3.0	1113 0.3	1648 3.1	2337 0.2
12 M	0004 0.0	0547 3.0	1225 0.3	1805 3.0	27 TU ◑	0521 2.8	1150 0.4	1734 3.0	
13 TU	0101 0.1	0653 2.8	1330 0.3	1918 2.9	28 W	0025 0.3	0618 2.7	1247 0.5	1841 2.9
14 W	0221 0.1	0818 2.7	1459 0.3	2047 3.0	29 TH	0137 0.3	0734 2.7	1410 0.5	2004 3.0
15 TH	0357 0.0	0950 2.7	1635 0.2	2214 3.1	30 F	0306 0.3	0900 2.8	1541 0.5	2126 3.1

Chart Datum: 1·66 metres below Normal Null (German reference level)

Chapter 5

GERMANY – CUXHAVEN

YEAR 2004

LAT 53°52′N   LONG 8°43′E

TIMES AND HEIGHTS OF HIGH AND LOW WATERS

TIME ZONE -0100
(German Standard Time)
Subtract 1 hour for UT
For German Summer Time add
ONE hour in **non-shaded areas**

MAY

Date	Time	m	Date	Time	m
1 SA	0431 / 1016 / 1659 / 2232	0.1 / 2.9 / 0.3 / 3.2	**16** SU	0555 / 1128 / 1811 / 2339	-0.1 / 2.9 / 0.0 / 3.3
2 SU	0537 / 1115 / 1759 / 2325	0.0 / 3.1 / 0.2 / 3.4	**17** M	0637 / 1209 / 1854	-0.1 / 3.0 / 0.0
3 M	0629 / 1202 / 1851	-0.1 / 3.2 / 0.1	**18** TU	0020 / 0718 / 1247 / 1937	3.3 / -0.1 / 3.2 / 0.0
4 TU	0010 / 0715 / 1244 / 1936	3.5 / -0.2 / 3.3 / -0.1 ○	**19** W	0102 / 0758 / 1323 / 2017	3.3 / 0.0 / 3.3 / 0.0 ●
5 W	0052 / 0756 / 1322 / 2016	3.5 / -0.2 / 3.4 / -0.2	**20** TH	0139 / 0832 / 1353 / 2048	3.3 / 0.0 / 3.4 / 0.0
6 TH	0133 / 0835 / 1358 / 2056	3.5 / -0.2 / 3.4 / -0.2	**21** F	0210 / 0859 / 1420 / 2115	3.3 / 0.1 / 3.4 / 0.0
7 F	0217 / 0916 / 1439 / 2139	3.5 / -0.2 / 3.4 / -0.2	**22** SA	0240 / 0926 / 1449 / 2146	3.2 / 0.1 / 3.4 / 0.0
8 SA	0306 / 1001 / 1524 / 2225	3.4 / -0.1 / 3.3 / -0.2	**23** SU	0312 / 0955 / 1522 / 2218	3.2 / 0.1 / 3.3 / 0.1
9 SU	0358 / 1046 / 1612 / 2314	3.2 / 0.0 / 3.3 / -0.2	**24** M	0348 / 1026 / 1557 / 2253	3.1 / 0.2 / 3.3 / 0.1
10 M	0452 / 1132 / 1704	3.1 / 0.1 / 3.3	**25** TU	0427 / 1101 / 1636 / 2332	3.0 / 0.3 / 3.2 / 0.1
11 TU	0006 / 0549 / 1223 / 1801	0.0 / 3.0 / 0.3 / 3.2 ◑	**26** W	0510 / 1140 / 1720	2.9 / 0.3 / 3.1
12 W	0105 / 0653 / 1326 / 1910	0.0 / 2.8 / 0.3 / 3.1	**27** TH	0016 / 0600 / 1229 / 1815	0.1 / 2.8 / 0.3 / 3.1 ◑
13 TH	0216 / 0808 / 1443 / 2029	0.0 / 2.7 / 0.3 / 3.1	**28** F	0111 / 0701 / 1333 / 1922	0.1 / 2.8 / 0.4 / 3.0
14 F	0338 / 0928 / 1606 / 2147	0.0 / 2.7 / 0.0 / 3.2	**29** SA	0220 / 0813 / 1449 / 2034	0.1 / 2.9 / 0.4 / 3.1
15 SA	0456 / 1037 / 1718 / 2251	-0.1 / 2.8 / 0.1 / 3.2	**30** SU	0335 / 0925 / 1604 / 2141	0.1 / 3.0 / 0.3 / 3.3
			31 M	0444 / 1027 / 1709 / 2240	0.0 / 3.1 / 0.2 / 3.4

JUNE

Date	Time	m	Date	Time	m
1 TU	0543 / 1120 / 1808 / 2334	0.0 / 3.2 / 0.1 / 3.4	**16** W	0642 / 1215 / 1907	0.1 / 3.2 / 0.1
2 W	0637 / 1208 / 1902	-0.1 / 3.3 / 0.0	**17** TH	0035 / 0725 / 1255 / 1948	3.3 / 0.1 / 3.3 / 0.1 ●
3 TH	0025 / 0726 / 1253 / 1950	3.5 / -0.1 / 3.4 / -0.1	**18** F	0116 / 0803 / 1330 / 2025	3.3 / 0.2 / 3.4 / 0.1
4 F	0114 / 0810 / 1337 / 2037	3.5 / -0.1 / 3.4 / -0.2	**19** SA	0152 / 0837 / 1402 / 2059	3.3 / 0.2 / 3.5 / 0.1
5 SA	0206 / 0858 / 1425 / 2128	3.4 / -0.1 / 3.5 / -0.2	**20** SU	0226 / 0910 / 1436 / 2135	3.2 / 0.2 / 3.5 / 0.1
6 SU	0301 / 0951 / 1516 / 2222	3.3 / 0.0 / 3.5 / -0.2	**21** M	0302 / 0943 / 1510 / 2210	3.2 / 0.2 / 3.5 / 0.1
7 M	0357 / 1041 / 1607 / 2314	3.2 / 0.0 / 3.5 / -0.1	**22** TU	0338 / 1016 / 1546 / 2245	3.1 / 0.2 / 3.4 / 0.1
8 TU	0450 / 1128 / 1658	3.1 / 0.1 / 3.4	**23** W	0416 / 1052 / 1625 / 2324	3.0 / 0.2 / 3.3 / 0.0
9 W	0006 / 0543 / 1217 / 1752	0.0 / 3.0 / 0.2 / 3.4 ◑	**24** TH	0458 / 1133 / 1708	3.0 / 0.2 / 3.3
10 TH	0100 / 0640 / 1310 / 1851	0.0 / 2.9 / 0.2 / 3.3	**25** F	0006 / 0544 / 1216 / 1754	0.0 / 2.9 / 0.2 / 3.2 ●
11 F	0157 / 0741 / 1411 / 1956	0.1 / 2.8 / 0.3 / 3.2	**26** SA	0050 / 0633 / 1303 / 1845	0.0 / 2.9 / 0.2 / 3.2
12 SA	0300 / 0845 / 1519 / 2104	0.1 / 2.8 / 0.3 / 3.2	**27** SU	0140 / 0728 / 1401 / 1945	0.1 / 2.9 / 0.3 / 3.2
13 SU	0406 / 0949 / 1629 / 2208	0.1 / 2.9 / 0.2 / 3.2	**28** M	0241 / 0832 / 1509 / 2051	0.1 / 3.0 / 0.3 / 3.2
14 M	0506 / 1045 / 1730 / 2303	0.1 / 3.0 / 0.1 / 3.2	**29** TU	0350 / 0937 / 1620 / 2159	0.2 / 3.1 / 0.2 / 3.3
15 TU	0557 / 1132 / 1821 / 2351	0.1 / 3.1 / 0.1 / 3.2	**30** W	0458 / 1040 / 1729 / 2305	0.1 / 3.2 / 0.1 / 3.3

JULY

Date	Time	m	Date	Time	m
1 TH	0604 / 1139 / 1835	0.1 / 3.3 / 0.0	**16** F	0013 / 0658 / 1233 / 1926	3.2 / 0.3 / 3.3 / 0.2
2 F	0008 / 0705 / 1234 / 1935	3.4 / 0.1 / 3.4 / -0.1 ○	**17** SA	0058 / 0742 / 1312 / 2009	3.3 / 0.3 / 3.4 / 0.2 ●
3 SA	0106 / 0800 / 1326 / 2030	3.4 / 0.0 / 3.5 / -0.1	**18** SU	0139 / 0822 / 1350 / 2049	3.3 / 0.2 / 3.5 / 0.1
4 SU	0202 / 0853 / 1417 / 2125	3.4 / 0.0 / 3.5 / -0.2	**19** M	0216 / 0859 / 1426 / 2127	3.3 / 0.2 / 3.5 / 0.1
5 M	0259 / 0946 / 1509 / 2220	3.3 / 0.0 / 3.6 / -0.1	**20** TU	0252 / 0935 / 1459 / 2201	3.3 / 0.2 / 3.5 / 0.1
6 TU	0352 / 1036 / 1558 / 2310	3.2 / 0.0 / 3.6 / -0.1	**21** W	0325 / 1007 / 1532 / 2233	3.2 / 0.1 / 3.4 / 0.0
7 W	0440 / 1119 / 1645 / 2354	3.1 / 0.0 / 3.5 / 0.0	**22** TH	0400 / 1040 / 1608 / 2309	3.1 / 0.1 / 3.4 / 0.0
8 TH	0525 / 1159 / 1731	3.1 / 0.1 / 3.5	**23** F	0440 / 1120 / 1650 / 2350	3.1 / 0.1 / 3.3 / 0.0
9 F	0038 / 0610 / 1243 / 1820	0.1 / 3.0 / 0.2 / 3.4 ◑	**24** SA	0522 / 1159 / 1731	3.0 / 0.1 / 3.3
10 SA	0121 / 0657 / 1329 / 1911	0.2 / 2.9 / 0.3 / 3.3	**25** SU	0028 / 0602 / 1236 / 1812	0.0 / 3.0 / 0.2 / 3.2 ◑
11 SU	0207 / 0748 / 1423 / 2010	0.3 / 2.9 / 0.4 / 3.2	**26** M	0105 / 0646 / 1319 / 1902	0.1 / 3.0 / 0.3 / 3.2
12 M	0302 / 0848 / 1529 / 2116	0.4 / 2.9 / 0.4 / 3.1	**27** TU	0155 / 0743 / 1422 / 2011	0.3 / 3.0 / 0.3 / 3.1
13 TU	0407 / 0953 / 1642 / 2224	0.4 / 3.0 / 0.4 / 3.1	**28** W	0305 / 0855 / 1542 / 2131	0.3 / 3.0 / 0.3 / 3.1
14 W	0512 / 1055 / 1747 / 2323	0.4 / 3.1 / 0.3 / 3.1	**29** TH	0427 / 1012 / 1706 / 2252	0.3 / 3.1 / 0.2 / 3.2
15 TH	0609 / 1148 / 1840	0.3 / 3.2 / 0.2	**30** F	0546 / 1123 / 1824	0.3 / 3.3 / 0.1
			31 SA	0004 / 0657 / 1225 / 1930	3.3 / 3.4 / 3.4 / 0.0 ○

AUGUST

Date	Time	m	Date	Time	m
1 SU	0105 / 0758 / 1320 / 2027	3.3 / 0.1 / 3.5 / -0.1	**16** M	0123 / 0807 / 1333 / 2034	3.3 / 0.3 / 3.5 / 0.1 ●
2 M	0200 / 0850 / 1410 / 2120	3.3 / 0.0 / 3.6 / -0.1	**17** TU	0201 / 0846 / 1409 / 2111	3.3 / 0.2 / 3.5 / 0.1
3 TU	0251 / 0938 / 1458 / 2210	3.3 / 0.0 / 3.7 / -0.1	**18** W	0235 / 0921 / 1441 / 2144	3.3 / 0.1 / 3.5 / 0.0
4 W	0338 / 1021 / 1542 / 2253	3.3 / 0.0 / 3.7 / 0.0	**19** TH	0306 / 0952 / 1511 / 2214	3.3 / 0.1 / 3.5 / 0.0
5 TH	0418 / 1058 / 1623 / 2330	3.2 / 0.0 / 3.6 / 0.1	**20** F	0338 / 1023 / 1545 / 2247	3.2 / 0.0 / 3.4 / 0.0
6 F	0454 / 1132 / 1702	3.2 / 0.1 / 3.5	**21** SA	0413 / 1059 / 1624 / 2324	3.1 / 0.0 / 3.4 / 0.0
7 SA	0004 / 0530 / 1207 / 1741	0.2 / 3.1 / 0.1 / 3.4 ◑	**22** SU	0452 / 1135 / 1704	3.1 / 0.1 / 3.4
8 SU	0036 / 0606 / 1242 / 1822	0.3 / 3.1 / 0.4 / 3.3	**23** M	0000 / 0529 / 1208 / 1743	0.1 / 3.1 / 0.2 / 3.2 ◑
9 M	0108 / 0647 / 1324 / 1913	0.4 / 3.0 / 0.5 / 3.1	**24** TU	0033 / 0609 / 1247 / 1833	0.3 / 3.0 / 0.3 / 3.1
10 TU	0153 / 0744 / 1425 / 2020	0.6 / 2.9 / 0.6 / 3.0	**25** W	0121 / 0708 / 1353 / 1949	0.4 / 2.9 / 0.3 / 3.0
11 W	0302 / 0858 / 1547 / 2140	0.7 / 3.0 / 0.6 / 3.0	**26** TH	0238 / 0831 / 1526 / 2122	0.5 / 3.0 / 0.3 / 3.0
12 TH	0424 / 1016 / 1711 / 2256	0.7 / 3.1 / 0.5 / 3.0	**27** F	0414 / 1000 / 1702 / 2252	0.5 / 3.1 / 0.2 / 3.1
13 F	0539 / 1123 / 1818 / 2355	0.5 / 3.2 / 0.4 / 3.1	**28** SA	0544 / 1118 / 1823	0.4 / 3.3 / 0.1
14 SA	0638 / 1213 / 1909	0.4 / 3.3 / 0.3	**29** SU	0005 / 0655 / 1220 / 1927	3.2 / 0.3 / 3.4 / 0.0
15 SU	0042 / 0725 / 1255 / 1953	3.2 / 0.3 / 3.4 / 0.2	**30** M	0102 / 0752 / 1311 / 2020	3.2 / 0.1 / 3.6 / -0.1 ○
			31 TU	0150 / 0840 / 1357 / 2106	3.3 / 0.0 / 3.6 / -0.1

Chart Datum: 1·66 metres below Normal Null (German reference level)

TIME ZONE -0100
(German Standard Time)
Subtract 1 hour for UT
For German Summer Time add
ONE hour in **non-shaded areas**

GERMANY – CUXHAVEN

LAT 53°52′N   LONG 8°43′E

YEAR **2004**

TIMES AND HEIGHTS OF HIGH AND LOW WATERS

SEPTEMBER

Day	Time	m	Time	m	Time	m	Time	m
1 W	0234	3.3	0921	0.1	1440	3.6	2149	0.0
16 TH	0209	3.3	0859	0.1	1415	3.5	2118	0.0
2 TH	0314	3.3	0958	0.1	1518	3.7	2227	0.1
17 F	0239	3.4	0931	0.1	1446	3.5	2150	0.0
3 F	0347	3.3	1031	0.1	1554	3.6	2257	0.2
18 SA	0310	3.3	1001	0.0	1519	3.5	2221	0.1
4 SA	0416	3.3	1100	0.1	1628	3.5	2323	0.3
19 SU	0343	3.2	1034	0.0	1557	3.4	2255	0.2
5 SU	0446	3.2	1128	0.2	1701	3.4	2348	0.4
20 M	0420	3.2	1109	0.1	1639	3.3	2330	0.3
6 M	0516	3.2	1157	0.4	1737	3.2	☾	
21 TU	0459	3.2	1146	0.2	1724	3.2	☾	
7 TU	0014	0.6	0551	3.0	1231	0.5	1821	3.0
22 W	0008	0.5	0546	3.1	1233	0.3	1822	3.0
8 W	0053	0.7	0644	2.9	1327	0.4	1927	2.8
23 TH	0104	0.6	0652	3.0	1345	0.4	1945	2.9
9 TH	0201	0.9	0802	2.9	1453	0.7	2053	2.8
24 F	0230	0.7	0821	3.0	1525	0.4	2123	2.9
10 F	0334	0.9	0932	2.9	1631	0.7	2222	2.9
25 SA	0412	0.6	0955	3.1	1705	0.3	2253	3.0
11 SA	0505	0.7	1051	3.2	1752	0.5	2331	3.1
26 SU	0542	0.5	1113	3.3	1822	0.1		
12 SU	0614	0.5	1148	3.3	1848	0.3		
27 M	0000	3.1	0646	0.3	1209	3.4	1916	0.0
13 M	0020	3.2	0704	0.4	1230	3.4	1930	0.2
28 TU	0049	3.1	0734	0.1	1254	3.5	○ 2002	0.0
14 TU	0059	3.3	0745	0.3	1307	3.4	● 2008	0.1
29 W	0131	3.2	0818	0.1	1336	3.5	2044	0.0
15 W	0136	3.3	0823	0.2	1342	3.5	2044	0.0
30 TH	0209	3.3	0857	0.1	1416	3.6	2122	0.1

OCTOBER

Day	Time	m	Time	m	Time	m	Time	m
1 F	0242	3.4	0931	0.2	1450	3.6	2154	0.2
16 SA	0208	3.4	0903	0.1	1418	3.6	2121	0.1
2 SA	0311	3.4	1001	0.2	1522	3.6	2220	0.3
17 SU	0240	3.4	0937	0.1	1456	3.5	2156	0.2
3 SU	0337	3.4	1027	0.2	1553	3.4	2243	0.3
18 M	0317	3.3	1013	0.1	1539	3.4	2232	0.3
4 M	0404	3.3	1053	0.3	1625	3.2	2306	0.5
19 TU	0357	3.3	1053	0.2	1627	3.3	2311	0.4
5 TU	0434	3.2	1120	0.4	1659	3.1	2332	0.6
20 W	0442	3.3	1138	0.3	1719	3.1	☾ 2358	0.6
6 W	0508	3.1	1153	0.6	1742	2.9	☾	
21 TH	0536	3.2	1233	0.4	1823	2.9		
7 TH	0009	0.8	0557	3.0	1244	0.7	1842	2.7
22 F	0100	0.7	0645	3.1	1348	0.4	1944	2.8
8 F	0112	0.9	0710	3.0	1404	0.8	2005	2.7
23 SA	0224	0.7	0811	3.1	1522	0.4	2116	2.8
9 SA	0243	1.0	0840	3.0	1543	0.7	2136	2.8
24 SU	0401	0.6	0942	3.2	1656	0.3	2240	2.9
10 SU	0420	0.9	1006	3.1	1711	0.5	2252	3.0
25 M	0526	0.4	1056	3.3	1807	0.1	2341	3.0
11 M	0536	0.6	1109	3.3	1812	0.3	2346	3.1
26 TU	0624	0.3	1149	3.4	1854	0.0		
12 TU	0630	0.5	1154	3.4	1855	0.2		
27 W	0024	3.1	0708	0.2	1230	3.4	1935	0.1
13 W	0026	3.3	0713	0.3	1232	3.4	1934	0.1
28 TH	0102	3.2	0750	0.2	1311	3.4	○ 2015	0.2
14 TH	0103	3.3	0752	0.2	1309	3.5	● 2011	0.1
29 F	0138	3.3	0830	0.2	1349	3.5	2050	0.3
15 F	0137	3.4	0829	0.2	1343	3.6	2046	0.1
30 SA	0209	3.4	0903	0.2	1422	3.5	2120	0.3
31 SU	0236	3.4	0931	0.3	1452	3.4	2145	0.4

NOVEMBER

Day	Time	m	Time	m	Time	m	Time	m
1 M	0303	3.4	0958	0.3	1524	3.3	2210	0.4
16 TU	0300	3.4	1004	0.1	1534	3.3	2223	0.3
2 TU	0332	3.3	1026	0.3	1557	3.1	2236	0.5
17 W	0347	3.4	1051	0.2	1625	3.2	2307	0.5
3 W	0404	3.3	1056	0.4	1634	3.0	2306	0.6
18 TH	0436	3.4	1141	0.3	1719	3.1	2355	0.6
4 TH	0440	3.2	1132	0.5	1715	2.9	2343	0.8
19 F	0531	3.3	1237	0.4	1820	2.9	☾	
5 F	0524	3.1	1218	0.6	1808	2.8	☾	
20 SA	0054	0.6	0635	3.2	1344	0.4	1931	2.8
6 SA	0036	0.9	0626	3.0	1323	0.7	1918	2.7
21 SU	0207	0.6	0751	3.1	1503	0.3	2050	2.7
7 SU	0153	0.9	0745	3.0	1447	0.7	2041	2.8
22 M	0330	0.5	0911	3.2	1624	0.3	2205	2.8
8 M	0322	0.9	0907	3.1	1613	0.6	2158	3.0
23 TU	0449	0.4	1023	3.2	1732	0.2	2305	2.9
9 TU	0442	0.7	1016	3.2	1720	0.4	2258	3.1
24 W	0551	0.3	1119	3.3	1821	0.2	2350	3.0
10 W	0542	0.5	1108	3.4	1811	0.3	2344	3.2
25 TH	0638	0.3	1203	3.3	1903	0.2		
11 TH	0632	0.4	1152	3.5	1855	0.2		
26 F	0030	3.2	0722	0.3	1245	3.3	○ 1944	0.3
12 F	0024	3.4	0716	0.3	1233	3.5	● 1936	0.2
27 SA	0107	3.3	0803	0.3	1324	3.3	2020	0.4
13 SA	0102	3.4	0756	0.2	1313	3.5	2014	0.2
28 SU	0140	3.4	0838	0.3	1358	3.3	2050	0.4
14 SU	0137	3.4	0835	0.2	1354	3.5	2054	0.2
29 M	0209	3.5	0908	0.3	1430	3.2	2119	0.4
15 M	0216	3.4	0918	0.1	1443	3.4	2139	0.3
30 TU	0239	3.5	0939	0.3	1504	3.2	2149	0.4

DECEMBER

Day	Time	m	Time	m	Time	m	Time	m
1 W	0312	3.4	1012	0.3	1539	3.1	2219	0.4
16 TH	0342	3.5	1055	0.1	1624	3.2	2307	0.3
2 TH	0346	3.4	1045	0.4	1616	3.0	2251	0.5
17 F	0430	3.5	1143	0.1	1714	3.1	2350	0.4
3 F	0421	3.3	1120	0.4	1656	2.9	2327	0.6
18 SA	0520	3.5	1233	0.2	1806	2.9	☾	
4 SA	0502	3.2	1200	0.4	1741	2.8		
19 SU	0039	0.4	0615	3.4	1326	0.3	1902	2.8
5 SU	0011	0.6	0551	3.1	1249	0.5	1836	2.8
20 M	0136	0.5	0717	3.2	1424	0.3	2004	2.7
6 M	0108	0.7	0652	3.0	1352	0.5	1942	2.8
21 TU	0242	0.5	0824	3.2	1530	0.3	2110	2.8
7 TU	0219	0.7	0803	3.1	1505	0.5	2053	2.9
22 W	0355	0.5	0935	3.2	1638	0.4	2214	2.9
8 W	0335	0.7	0912	3.2	1616	0.4	2159	3.0
23 TH	0506	0.4	1040	3.1	1738	0.4	2311	3.0
9 TH	0443	0.6	1015	3.3	1718	0.4	2255	3.2
24 F	0605	0.4	1135	3.1	1829	0.4		
10 F	0544	0.4	1110	3.4	1812	0.3	2344	3.3
25 SA	0000	3.2	0655	0.4	1222	3.2	1915	0.4
11 SA	0639	0.3	1202	3.4	1902	0.3		
26 SU	0042	3.3	0739	0.4	1304	3.2	○ 1956	0.4
12 SU	0030	3.4	0729	0.2	1251	3.4	● 1950	0.2
27 M	0119	3.4	0817	0.3	1342	3.2	2031	0.4
13 M	0115	3.4	0817	0.1	1343	3.4	2038	0.2
28 TU	0152	3.5	0853	0.3	1416	3.2	2104	0.4
14 TU	0202	3.5	0909	0.1	1438	3.3	2131	0.3
29 W	0226	3.5	0929	0.3	1451	3.2	2137	0.4
15 W	0252	3.5	1004	0.1	1533	3.3	2222	0.3
30 TH	0300	3.5	1004	0.3	1526	3.1	2209	0.3
31 F	0332	3.4	1031	0.3	1601	3.0	2240	0.3

Chart Datum: 1·66 metres below Normal Null (German reference level)

Chapter 5

357

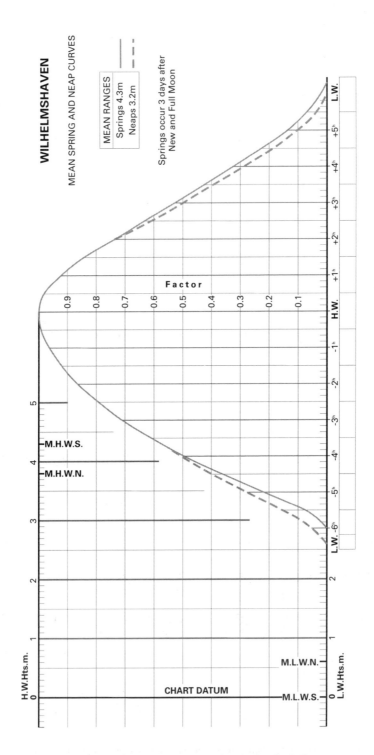

WILHELMSHAVEN

MEAN SPRING AND NEAP CURVES

MEAN RANGES
Springs 4.3m
Neaps 3.2m

Springs occur 3 days after
New and Full Moon

TIME ZONE -0100
(German Standard Time)
Subtract 1 hour for UT
For German Summer Time add ONE hour in **non-shaded areas**

GERMANY – WILHELMSHAVEN

LAT 53°31′N   LONG 8°09′E

TIMES AND HEIGHTS OF HIGH AND LOW WATERS

YEAR **2004**

JANUARY

Day	Time	m	Day	Time	m
1 TH	0044 / 0714 / 1329 / 1951	0.6 / 4.0 / 0.5 / 3.6	16 F	0002 / 0620 / 1233 / 1858	0.4 / 4.1 / 0.3 / 3.8
2 F	0147 / 0818 / 1432 / 2055	0.7 / 4.0 / 0.7 / 3.7	17 SA	0056 / 0721 / 1335 / 2004	0.5 / 4.0 / 0.4 / 3.8
3 SA	0301 / 0927 / 1539 / 2200	0.7 / 3.9 / 0.7 / 3.9	18 SU	0208 / 0836 / 1451 / 2120	0.5 / 4.0 / 0.4 / 3.9
4 SU	0412 / 1030 / 1641 / 2257	0.7 / 4.0 / 0.6 / 4.0	19 M	0329 / 0957 / 1612 / 2234	0.4 / 4.0 / 0.4 / 4.0
5 M	0513 / 1122 / 1734 / 2345	0.5 / 4.0 / 0.5 / 4.1	20 TU	0449 / 1113 / 1728 / 2340	0.2 / 4.1 / 0.3 / 4.1
6 TU	0603 / 1207 / 1820	0.5 / 4.1 / 0.4	21 W ●	0600 / 1219 / 1834	0.1 / 4.1 / 0.2
7 W ○	0027 / 0646 / 1249 / 1900	4.2 / 0.4 / 4.2 / 0.4	22 TH	0038 / 0701 / 1317 / 1928	4.3 / 0.0 / 4.2 / 0.2
8 TH	0105 / 0726 / 1330 / 1938	4.3 / 0.3 / 4.1 / 0.4	23 F	0129 / 0754 / 1409 / 2016	4.4 / 0.0 / 4.1 / 0.1
9 F	0143 / 0805 / 1409 / 2016	4.3 / 0.3 / 4.1 / 0.3	24 SA	0217 / 0845 / 1458 / 2103	4.4 / 0.0 / 4.1 / 0.3
10 SA	0220 / 0844 / 1446 / 2052	4.4 / 0.2 / 4.1 / 0.3	25 SU	0304 / 0934 / 1542 / 2144	4.5 / 0.0 / 4.1 / 0.1
11 SU	0255 / 0918 / 1522 / 2124	4.3 / 0.1 / 4.0 / 0.2	26 M	0347 / 1015 / 1620 / 2217	4.5 / 0.0 / 4.0 / 0.1
12 M	0330 / 0951 / 1600 / 2159	4.3 / 0.1 / 3.9 / 0.2	27 TU	0426 / 1050 / 1652 / 2248	4.5 / 0.1 / 4.0 / 0.2
13 TU	0409 / 1028 / 1643 / 2239	4.3 / 0.1 / 3.9 / 0.2	28 W	0502 / 1121 / 1724 / 2319	4.4 / 0.2 / 3.9 / 0.3
14 W	0451 / 1108 / 1725 / 2320	4.2 / 0.1 / 3.8 / 0.3	29 TH	0537 / 1150 / 1757 / 2352	4.2 / 0.4 / 3.8 / 0.5
15 TH ◑	0534 / 1148 / 1808	4.2 / 0.1 / 3.8	30 F	0615 / 1224 / 1840	4.0 / 0.5 / 3.7
			31 SA	0038 / 0708 / 1315 / 1940	0.6 / 3.8 / 0.7 / 3.7

FEBRUARY

Day	Time	m	Day	Time	m
1 SU	0146 / 0819 / 1427 / 2055	0.8 / 3.7 / 0.8 / 3.7	16 M	0132 / 0811 / 1419 / 2052	0.4 / 3.8 / 0.6 / 3.8
2 M	0310 / 0938 / 1546 / 2211	0.8 / 3.8 / 0.7 / 3.9	17 TU	0305 / 0944 / 1554 / 2219	0.4 / 3.8 / 0.5 / 3.9
3 TU	0429 / 1048 / 1656 / 2314	0.6 / 3.8 / 0.6 / 4.0	18 W	0437 / 1110 / 1719 / 2333	0.2 / 3.9 / 0.4 / 4.1
4 W	0533 / 1144 / 1754	0.5 / 4.0 / 0.5	19 TH	0554 / 1219 / 1827	0.1 / 4.0 / 0.2
5 TH	0004 / 0625 / 1233 / 1842	4.2 / 0.4 / 4.1 / 0.4	20 F ●	0032 / 0656 / 1314 / 1920	4.3 / 0.0 / 4.1 / 0.1
6 F ○	0048 / 0710 / 1317 / 1925	4.3 / 0.2 / 4.1 / 0.3	21 SA	0122 / 0747 / 1401 / 2005	4.4 / -0.1 / 4.1 / 0.0
7 SA	0129 / 0752 / 1358 / 2005	4.3 / 0.1 / 4.1 / 0.2	22 SU	0207 / 0832 / 1443 / 2045	4.4 / -0.1 / 4.1 / 0.0
8 SU	0208 / 0831 / 1435 / 2042	4.4 / 0.0 / 4.1 / 0.1	23 M	0248 / 0914 / 1519 / 2122	4.5 / 0.0 / 4.1 / 0.0
9 M	0244 / 0906 / 1510 / 2115	4.4 / -0.1 / 4.1 / -0.1	24 TU	0325 / 0950 / 1550 / 2152	4.5 / 0.0 / 4.1 / 0.0
10 TU	0318 / 0938 / 1547 / 2148	4.3 / -0.1 / 4.0 / -0.1	25 W	0358 / 1018 / 1617 / 2218	4.5 / 0.0 / 4.1 / 0.1
11 W	0356 / 1014 / 1626 / 2224	4.3 / -0.1 / 3.9 / 0.0	26 TH	0429 / 1042 / 1643 / 2243	4.3 / 0.1 / 4.0 / 0.1
12 TH	0435 / 1051 / 1703 / 2300	4.3 / 0.0 / 3.9 / 0.1	27 F	0457 / 1104 / 1708 / 2308	4.2 / 0.2 / 3.9 / 0.3
13 F ◑	0513 / 1124 / 1737 / 2333	4.3 / 0.1 / 3.9 / 0.2	28 SA ◑	0526 / 1127 / 1739 / 2340	4.0 / 0.4 / 3.8 / 0.5
14 SA	0552 / 1159 / 1819	4.1 / 0.2 / 3.8	29 SU	0608 / 1206 / 1833	3.7 / 0.7 / 3.7
15 SU	0019 / 0649 / 1255 / 1925	0.3 / 3.9 / 0.4 / 3.7			

MARCH

Day	Time	m	Day	Time	m
1 M	0038 / 0716 / 1317 / 1952	0.7 / 3.6 / 0.8 / 3.6	16 TU	0119 / 0806 / 1407 / 2042	0.3 / 3.7 / 0.6 / 3.8
2 TU	0207 / 0845 / 1449 / 2122	0.8 / 3.6 / 0.8 / 3.7	17 W	0259 / 0944 / 1547 / 2215	0.3 / 3.7 / 0.5 / 3.9
3 W	0342 / 1011 / 1617 / 2241	0.6 / 3.7 / 0.7 / 3.9	18 TH	0435 / 1110 / 1712 / 2328	0.1 / 3.8 / 0.3 / 4.1
4 TH	0502 / 1120 / 1726 / 2340	0.4 / 3.9 / 0.5 / 4.1	19 F	0548 / 1214 / 1813	-0.1 / 3.9 / 0.1
5 F	0601 / 1214 / 1820	0.2 / 4.0 / 0.3	20 SA ●	0022 / 0642 / 1302 / 1901	4.3 / -0.1 / 4.0 / 0.0
6 SA ○	0027 / 0648 / 1300 / 1906	4.3 / 0.1 / 4.1 / 0.2	21 SU	0109 / 0729 / 1344 / 1944	4.3 / -0.1 / 4.0 / -0.1
7 SU	0109 / 0730 / 1341 / 1947	4.3 / -0.1 / 4.1 / 0.0	22 M	0151 / 0810 / 1420 / 2021	4.4 / -0.1 / 4.1 / -0.1
8 M	0148 / 0808 / 1417 / 2024	4.4 / -0.2 / 4.2 / -0.1	23 TU	0227 / 0846 / 1450 / 2054	4.4 / -0.1 / 4.2 / -0.1
9 TU	0224 / 0845 / 1451 / 2058	4.4 / -0.3 / 4.1 / -0.2	24 W	0259 / 0916 / 1516 / 2121	4.4 / 0.0 / 4.2 / -0.1
10 W	0300 / 0919 / 1526 / 2130	4.4 / -0.3 / 4.1 / -0.2	25 TH	0328 / 0940 / 1540 / 2145	4.3 / 0.0 / 4.1 / 0.1
11 TH	0337 / 0953 / 1602 / 2204	4.4 / -0.2 / 4.0 / -0.2	26 F	0356 / 1001 / 1605 / 2209	4.2 / 0.1 / 4.1 / 0.0
12 F	0416 / 1028 / 1637 / 2238	4.3 / -0.1 / 4.0 / -0.1	27 SA	0423 / 1023 / 1628 / 2233	4.1 / 0.2 / 4.0 / 0.1
13 SA ◑	0455 / 1101 / 1712 / 2313	4.2 / 0.1 / 4.0 / 0.1	28 SU	0450 / 1045 / 1657 / 2301	3.9 / 0.4 / 3.9 / 0.3
14 SU	0538 / 1138 / 1758	4.0 / 0.3 / 3.8	29 M	0527 / 1119 / 1745 / 2351	3.6 / 0.5 / 3.7 / 0.5
15 M	0001 / 0639 / 1237 / 1909	0.2 / 3.8 / 0.5 / 3.8	30 TU	0630 / 1224 / 1901	3.5 / 0.7 / 3.6
			31 W	0115 / 0758 / 1358 / 2035	0.6 / 3.5 / 0.8 / 3.7

APRIL

Day	Time	m	Day	Time	m
1 TH	0254 / 0931 / 1533 / 2201	0.6 / 3.6 / 0.7 / 3.9	16 F	0425 / 1100 / 1653 / 2315	0.0 / 3.7 / 0.2 / 4.1
2 F	0422 / 1049 / 1650 / 2307	0.3 / 3.8 / 0.4 / 4.1	17 SA	0530 / 1156 / 1747	-0.2 / 3.8 / 0.0
3 SA	0526 / 1146 / 1748 / 2357	0.1 / 4.0 / 0.3 / 4.2	18 SU	0004 / 0617 / 1238 / 1832	4.2 / -0.2 / 3.9 / -0.1
4 SU	0616 / 1233 / 1837	-0.1 / 4.1 / 0.1	19 M ●	0047 / 0700 / 1316 / 1915	4.3 / -0.2 / 4.0 / -0.1
5 M ○	0041 / 0659 / 1315 / 1919	4.3 / -0.2 / 4.2 / -0.1	20 TU	0127 / 0740 / 1350 / 1954	4.3 / -0.1 / 4.1 / -0.1
6 TU	0121 / 0739 / 1351 / 1957	4.4 / -0.3 / 4.2 / -0.2	21 W	0202 / 0813 / 1418 / 2024	4.2 / -0.1 / 4.2 / -0.1
7 W	0159 / 0817 / 1425 / 2033	4.5 / -0.3 / 4.2 / -0.2	22 TH	0231 / 0839 / 1442 / 2050	4.3 / 0.0 / 4.2 / -0.1
8 TH	0237 / 0854 / 1500 / 2108	4.4 / -0.3 / 4.2 / -0.3	23 F	0258 / 0902 / 1507 / 2115	4.2 / 0.0 / 4.2 / -0.1
9 F	0318 / 0930 / 1537 / 2144	4.4 / -0.2 / 4.1 / -0.3	24 SA	0326 / 0925 / 1534 / 2142	4.1 / 0.0 / 4.1 / 0.0
10 SA	0402 / 1007 / 1617 / 2223	4.2 / 0.0 / 4.1 / -0.1	25 SU	0357 / 0951 / 1603 / 2211	4.0 / 0.1 / 4.1 / 0.1
11 SU	0447 / 1045 / 1700 / 2306	4.1 / 0.2 / 4.0 / 0.0	26 M	0428 / 1020 / 1635 / 2244	3.8 / 0.3 / 4.0 / 0.2
12 M ◑	0537 / 1131 / 1754	3.9 / 0.3 / 3.9	27 TU	0506 / 1056 / 1720 / 2329	3.7 / 0.5 / 3.9 / 0.3
13 TU	0002 / 0643 / 1233 / 1907	0.1 / 3.7 / 0.5 / 3.9	28 W	0602 / 1152 / 1826	3.5 / 0.6 / 3.8
14 W	0120 / 0808 / 1400 / 2037	0.2 / 3.6 / 0.5 / 3.9	29 TH	0039 / 0719 / 1314 / 1950	0.4 / 3.5 / 0.7 / 3.8
15 TH	0256 / 0941 / 1535 / 2206	0.2 / 3.6 / 0.4 / 4.0	30 F	0207 / 0848 / 1445 / 2114	0.4 / 3.6 / 0.6 / 3.9

Chapter 5

Chart Datum: 2·26 metres below Normal Null (German reference level)

TIME ZONE -0100
(German Standard Time)
Subtract 1 hour for UT
For German Summer Time add ONE hour in **non-shaded areas**

GERMANY – WILHELMSHAVEN
LAT 53°31'N   LONG 8°09'E
TIMES AND HEIGHTS OF HIGH AND LOW WATERS

YEAR 2004

MAY

Day	Time m	Time m	Time m	Time m
1 SA	0333 0.2	1007 3.8	1603 0.4	2223 4.1
2 SU	0440 0.0	1108 4.0	1706 0.2	2319 4.3
3 M	0535 -0.1	1158 4.1	1759 0.1	
4 TU	0007 4.4	0623 -0.2	1241 4.2	○ 1846 -0.1
5 W	0051 4.5	0707 -0.3	1320 4.3	1927 -0.2
6 TH	0133 4.5	0747 -0.3	1357 4.3	2006 -0.3
7 F	0217 4.4	0828 -0.2	1437 4.3	2048 -0.3
8 SA	0305 4.3	0911 -0.1	1521 4.2	2132 -0.3
9 SU	0356 4.1	0954 0.0	1607 4.2	2218 -0.2
10 M	0447 4.0	1039 0.2	1657 4.2	2309 0.0
11 TU	0541 3.8	1129 0.3	1754 4.1	◐
12 W	0007 0.1	0644 3.7	1230 0.4	1902 4.0
13 TH	0118 0.1	0759 3.6	1345 0.4	2022 4.0
14 F	0240 0.1	0919 3.6	1507 0.3	2141 4.1
15 SA	0358 0.1	1030 3.7	1619 0.1	2247 4.2
16 SU	0458 -0.1	1123 3.8	1713 0.0	2336 4.2
17 M	0542 -0.1	1204 4.0	1758 0.0	
18 TU	0017 4.2	0624 -0.1	1243 4.1	1844 0.0
19 W	0058 4.2	0706 0.0	1318 4.2	● 1925 0.0
20 TH	0134 4.2	0740 0.0	1348 4.3	1957 0.0
21 F	0205 4.2	0808 0.0	1415 4.3	2025 0.0
22 SA	0234 4.1	0834 0.0	1443 4.3	2054 0.0
23 SU	0306 4.0	0903 0.1	1515 4.2	2126 0.0
24 M	0340 3.9	0934 0.2	1548 4.2	2200 0.1
25 TU	0417 3.9	1008 0.3	1625 4.1	2238 0.1
26 W	0458 3.7	1047 0.3	1709 4.0	2321 0.2
27 TH	0547 3.6	1136 0.4	1803 3.9	◐
28 F	0015 0.2	0649 3.6	1239 0.5	1910 3.9
29 SA	0124 0.2	0802 3.7	1355 0.5	2024 4.0
30 SU	0239 0.2	0916 3.8	1510 0.4	2133 4.1
31 M	0348 0.0	1020 4.0	1616 0.2	2235 4.3

JUNE

Day	Time m	Time m	Time m	Time m
1 TU	0448 -0.1	1115 4.1	1716 0.1	2331 4.3
2 W	0545 -0.1	1204 4.2	1811 0.0	
3 TH	0023 4.4	0636 -0.2	1250 4.3	○ 1859 -0.2
4 F	0113 4.4	0722 -0.2	1334 4.4	1946 -0.2
5 SA	0204 4.3	0810 -0.1	1422 4.4	2036 -0.2
6 SU	0259 4.2	0901 -0.1	1512 4.4	2129 -0.3
7 M	0355 4.1	0949 0.0	1603 4.4	2220 -0.2
8 TU	0447 4.0	1035 0.1	1653 4.3	2311 -0.1
9 W	0537 3.9	1123 0.2	1747 4.3	◐
10 TH	0004 0.0	0632 3.7	1215 0.3	1845 4.2
11 F	0101 0.0	0731 3.7	1315 0.3	1949 4.1
12 SA	0204 0.1	0835 3.7	1422 0.2	2058 4.1
13 SU	0310 0.1	0940 3.7	1532 0.2	2203 4.1
14 M	0411 0.1	1037 3.9	1633 0.1	2259 4.1
15 TU	0503 0.1	1125 4.0	1726 0.1	2345 4.1
16 W	0549 0.1	1208 4.1	1814 0.1	
17 TH	0028 4.2	0634 0.1	1248 4.2	● 1858 0.1
18 F	0108 4.2	0713 0.1	1323 4.3	1936 0.1
19 SA	0145 4.2	0746 0.1	1356 4.4	2010 0.1
20 SU	0220 4.1	0819 0.1	1430 4.4	2045 0.1
21 M	0255 4.1	0853 0.1	1504 4.4	2119 0.1
22 TU	0330 4.0	0925 0.1	1539 4.3	2153 0.0
23 W	0407 3.9	1000 0.2	1617 4.2	2231 0.0
24 TH	0449 3.9	1041 0.2	1659 4.2	2313 0.0
25 F	0534 3.8	1124 0.2	1745 4.1	◐ 2357 0.0
26 SA	0622 3.7	1211 0.3	1835 4.1	
27 SU	0047 0.1	0717 3.8	1309 0.4	1935 4.1
28 M	0147 0.2	0821 3.9	1416 0.4	2042 4.1
29 TU	0255 0.1	0928 3.9	1526 0.3	2152 4.2
30 W	0403 0.1	1032 4.0	1636 0.1	2300 4.2

JULY

Day	Time m	Time m	Time m	Time m
1 TH	0511 0.1	1132 4.2	1743 0.0	
2 F	0004 4.3	0614 0.0	1228 4.3	○ 1843 -0.1
3 SA	0103 4.3	0711 0.0	1321 4.4	1938 -0.2
4 SU	0200 4.3	0804 0.0	1413 4.5	2033 -0.2
5 M	0256 4.2	0856 0.0	1505 4.5	2128 -0.2
6 TU	0349 4.1	0945 0.0	1555 4.5	2218 -0.2
7 W	0436 4.0	1027 0.0	1642 4.5	2303 -0.1
8 TH	0519 3.9	1107 0.1	1727 4.4	2346 0.0
9 F	0602 3.9	1149 0.2	1814 4.3	○
10 SA	0029 0.1	0646 3.8	1235 0.3	1903 4.2
11 SU	0114 0.2	0736 3.8	1328 0.4	2000 4.1
12 M	0209 0.4	0835 3.8	1434 0.5	2107 4.0
13 TU	0314 0.5	0940 3.9	1547 0.4	2215 4.0
14 W	0419 0.4	1043 4.0	1653 0.3	2313 4.0
15 TH	0517 0.3	1137 4.1	1749 0.3	
16 F	0002 4.1	0608 0.3	1222 4.2	1837 0.2
17 SA	0047 4.2	0653 0.3	1303 4.3	● 1920 0.2
18 SU	0130 4.2	0733 0.2	1342 4.4	2000 0.1
19 M	0209 4.2	0810 0.2	1419 4.5	2038 0.1
20 TU	0245 4.2	0846 0.1	1453 4.4	2111 0.0
21 W	0318 4.1	0917 0.1	1526 4.4	2142 0.0
22 TH	0353 4.0	0949 0.0	1602 4.3	2217 0.0
23 F	0432 4.0	1028 0.1	1643 4.3	2257 0.0
24 SA	0514 3.9	1108 0.1	1722 4.3	2335 0.0
25 SU	0551 3.9	1144 0.2	1802 4.2	◐
26 M	0012 0.1	0632 3.8	1227 0.3	1851 4.1
27 TU	0100 0.2	0729 3.8	1328 0.4	1958 4.0
28 W	0209 0.4	0842 3.9	1446 0.3	2120 4.0
29 TH	0331 0.4	1000 4.0	1611 0.2	2242 4.1
30 F	0453 0.3	1112 4.2	1730 0.1	2356 4.2
31 SA	0606 0.1	1216 4.3	1838 0.0	○

AUGUST

Day	Time m	Time m	Time m	Time m
1 SU	0100 4.2	0708 0.1	1313 4.4	1936 -0.1
2 M	0156 4.2	0800 0.0	1405 4.5	2029 -0.1
3 TU	0247 4.2	0849 0.0	1454 4.6	2120 -0.1
4 W	0333 4.2	0932 0.0	1539 4.7	2205 -0.1
5 TH	0413 4.1	1009 0.0	1619 4.6	2241 0.0
6 F	0447 4.1	1041 0.1	1657 4.5	2315 0.1
7 SA	0520 4.0	1115 0.2	1734 4.4	2346 0.3
8 SU	0553 3.9	1150 0.3	1811 4.2	
9 M	0018 0.4	0632 3.8	1231 0.5	1859 4.0
10 TU	0103 0.6	0726 3.8	1332 0.7	2005 3.8
11 W	0210 0.8	0839 3.8	1453 0.7	2125 3.8
12 TH	0331 0.8	0958 4.0	1617 0.6	2240 3.9
13 F	0447 0.6	1107 4.1	1726 0.4	2340 4.0
14 SA	0547 0.5	1159 4.2	1819 0.3	
15 SU	0028 4.1	0636 0.4	1243 4.3	1904 0.2
16 M	0112 4.2	0719 0.3	1323 4.4	● 1945 0.1
17 TU	0153 4.2	0757 0.2	1401 4.4	2022 0.0
18 W	0228 4.2	0833 0.1	1434 4.5	2055 0.0
19 TH	0259 4.2	0904 0.0	1506 4.4	2124 -0.1
20 F	0331 4.1	0933 0.0	1540 4.4	2156 -0.1
21 SA	0406 4.1	1007 0.0	1618 4.4	2233 0.0
22 SU	0443 4.0	1043 0.1	1655 4.3	2307 0.1
23 M	0516 4.0	1116 0.2	1731 4.2	◑ 2339 0.2
24 TU	0553 3.9	1153 0.3	1819 4.0	
25 W	0025 0.4	0651 3.8	1256 0.4	1933 3.9
26 TH	0142 0.6	0813 3.9	1427 0.4	2106 3.9
27 F	0318 0.6	0944 4.0	1604 0.3	2238 4.0
28 SA	0449 0.5	1104 4.2	1728 0.1	2354 4.1
29 SU	0603 0.3	1209 4.3	1835 0.0	
30 M	0054 4.2	0701 0.2	1303 4.5	○ 1930 -0.1
31 TU	0145 4.2	0749 0.1	1351 4.5	2017 -0.1

Chart Datum: 2·26 metres below Normal Null (German reference level)

TIME ZONE -0100
(German Standard Time)
Subtract 1 hour for UT
For German Summer Time add
ONE hour in **non-shaded areas**

GERMANY – WILHELMSHAVEN

LAT 53°31′N LONG 8°09′E

TIMES AND HEIGHTS OF HIGH AND LOW WATERS

YEAR **2004**

SEPTEMBER

Date	Day	Time	m	Time	m	Time	m	Time	m
1	W	0229	4.2	0832	0.0	1435	4.6	2101	0.0
16	TH	0201	4.2	0810	0.1	1407	4.5	2030	0.0
2	TH	0307	4.2	0911	0.0	1514	4.7	2139	0.0
17	F	0232	4.3	0842	0.1	1439	4.5	2101	0.0
3	F	0339	4.2	0943	0.1	1548	4.6	2209	0.1
18	SA	0303	4.2	0912	0.0	1513	4.5	2131	0.0
4	SA	0407	4.2	1010	0.1	1620	4.4	2234	0.2
19	SU	0335	4.2	0943	0.0	1550	4.4	2204	0.1
5	SU	0434	4.1	1037	0.2	1651	4.3	2259	0.4
20	M	0409	4.1	1017	0.1	1628	4.3	2238	0.3
6	M	0501	4.0	1105	0.4	1722	4.1	◐ 2324	0.6
21	TU	0445	4.1	1052	0.3	1710	4.1	◐ 2315	0.5
7	TU	0533	3.9	1139	0.6	1803	3.8		
22	W	0528	4.0	1136	0.4	1806	3.9		
8	W	0002	0.8	0623	3.8	1233	0.8	1906	3.7
23	TH	0008	0.7	0632	3.9	1246	0.5	1926	3.8
9	TH	0108	1.0	0738	3.8	1358	0.9	2033	3.6
24	F	0132	0.8	0802	3.9	1424	0.9	2105	3.8
10	F	0239	1.0	0909	3.9	1535	0.9	2202	3.8
25	SA	0314	0.8	0938	4.0	1605	0.4	2237	3.9
11	SA	0410	0.9	1031	4.0	1658	0.6	2313	3.9
26	SU	0445	0.6	1058	4.2	1725	0.1	2347	4.0
12	SU	0521	0.6	1131	4.2	1756	0.3		
27	M	0552	0.4	1157	4.3	1823	0.0		
13	M	0004	4.1	0613	0.4	1216	4.3	1840	0.2
28	TU	0038	4.1	0642	0.2	1245	4.4	○ 1911	0.0
14	TU	0047	4.2	0656	0.3	1258	4.4	● 1919	0.1
29	W	0122	4.1	0727	0.1	1330	4.5	1955	0.0
15	W	0126	4.2	0735	0.2	1333	4.4	1956	0.0
30	TH	0201	4.2	0807	0.1	1409	4.5	2033	0.1

OCTOBER

Date	Day	Time	m	Time	m	Time	m	Time	m
1	F	0233	4.3	0842	0.1	1443	4.5	2105	0.2
16	SA	0159	4.3	0815	0.1	1410	4.5	2033	0.1
2	SA	0300	4.3	0912	0.1	1513	4.5	2130	0.2
17	SU	0231	4.3	0848	0.1	1448	4.5	2107	0.2
3	SU	0325	4.3	0936	0.2	1542	4.3	2152	0.3
18	M	0306	4.3	0922	0.1	1530	4.3	2141	0.3
4	M	0350	4.2	1001	0.2	1612	4.1	2215	0.4
19	TU	0344	4.2	0959	0.2	1614	4.2	2218	0.5
5	TU	0417	4.1	1028	0.4	1642	3.9	2241	0.6
20	W	0427	4.2	1042	0.3	1704	4.0	◐ 2303	0.6
6	W	0448	4.0	1100	0.6	1720	3.7	2316	0.9
21	TH	0518	4.1	1135	0.5	1805	3.8		
7	TH	0534	3.8	1149	0.8	1818	3.5		
22	F	0003	0.8	0626	4.0	1248	0.5	1925	3.7
8	F	0017	1.1	0645	3.8	1307	0.9	1941	3.5
23	SA	0125	0.9	0753	4.0	1420	0.5	2057	3.7
9	SA	0146	1.2	0816	3.8	1445	0.9	2114	3.7
24	SU	0301	0.8	0925	4.1	1554	0.4	2223	3.8
10	SU	0323	1.0	0943	4.0	1614	0.7	2232	3.9
25	M	0426	0.6	1041	4.2	1708	0.2	2326	3.9
11	M	0441	0.8	1050	4.2	1718	0.4	2329	4.0
26	TU	0527	0.4	1136	4.3	1758	0.1		
12	TU	0537	0.5	1138	4.3	1804	0.2		
27	W	0011	4.0	0613	0.2	1220	4.4	1841	0.1
13	W	0012	4.2	0623	0.4	1220	4.4	1844	0.1
28	TH	0050	4.1	0657	0.2	1302	4.4	○ 1923	0.2
14	TH	0052	4.2	0704	0.3	1258	4.4	● 1923	0.1
29	F	0127	4.2	0738	0.2	1339	4.4	2000	0.3
15	F	0127	4.3	0740	0.2	1334	4.5	1959	0.0
30	SA	0157	4.3	0812	0.2	1411	4.4	2028	0.3
31	SU	0223	4.3	0840	0.2	1440	4.3	2053	0.3

NOVEMBER

Date	Day	Time	m	Time	m	Time	m	Time	m
1	M	0249	4.3	0906	0.3	1510	4.2	2117	0.4
16	TU	0248	4.4	0911	0.1	1523	4.2	2131	0.4
2	TU	0316	4.2	0933	0.3	1542	4.0	2143	0.5
17	W	0334	4.3	0956	0.2	1613	4.1	2213	0.5
3	W	0346	4.2	1003	0.4	1615	3.9	2212	0.6
18	TH	0421	4.3	1044	0.3	1705	3.9	2300	0.6
4	TH	0420	4.1	1037	0.6	1653	3.7	2249	0.8
19	F	0515	4.2	1139	0.4	1804	3.8	◐ 2356	0.7
5	F	0503	4.0	1121	0.7	1743	3.6	◑ 2340	1.0
20	SA	0619	4.1	1244	0.4	1914	3.6		
6	SA	0603	3.8	1224	0.8	1853	3.5		
21	SU	0107	0.7	0734	4.1	1402	0.4	2032	3.6
7	SU	0055	1.1	0722	3.8	1348	0.8	2017	3.6
22	M	0228	0.7	0855	4.1	1522	0.4	2147	3.7
8	M	0223	1.0	0845	4.0	1514	0.7	2137	3.8
23	TU	0347	0.6	1008	4.2	1631	0.3	2248	3.8
9	TU	0344	0.9	0956	4.1	1624	0.5	2240	4.0
24	W	0450	0.4	1105	4.2	1722	0.2	2335	4.0
10	W	0448	0.7	1051	4.3	1717	0.3	2329	4.1
25	TH	0539	0.3	1150	4.2	1806	0.3		
11	TH	0539	0.5	1148	4.4	1803	0.2		
26	F	0015	4.1	0626	0.3	1232	4.3	○ 1849	0.4
12	F	0011	4.2	0626	0.4	1221	4.4	● 1846	0.2
27	SA	0052	4.2	0709	0.3	1310	4.3	1927	0.4
13	SA	0049	4.3	0707	0.2	1302	4.5	1925	0.2
28	SU	0125	4.3	0745	0.3	1344	4.2	1957	0.4
14	SU	0126	4.3	0745	0.2	1345	4.5	2006	0.2
29	M	0155	4.4	0815	0.3	1415	4.2	2026	0.4
15	M	0205	4.4	0827	0.1	1432	4.4	2049	0.3
30	TU	0225	4.4	0847	0.3	1448	4.1	2055	0.4

DECEMBER

Date	Day	Time	m	Time	m	Time	m	Time	m
1	W	0256	4.3	0919	0.4	1523	4.0	2125	0.5
16	TH	0330	4.5	0958	0.1	1613	4.1	2212	0.3
2	TH	0329	4.3	0951	0.4	1558	3.9	2156	0.6
17	F	0418	4.4	1046	0.1	1701	4.0	2254	0.4
3	F	0404	4.2	1025	0.5	1635	3.8	2232	0.7
18	SA	0508	4.4	1135	0.2	1751	3.8	◐ 2341	0.5
4	SA	0443	4.1	1103	0.5	1719	3.7	2315	0.7
19	SU	0602	4.3	1227	0.3	1846	3.7		
5	SU	0532	4.0	1151	0.6	1813	3.6	◑	
20	M	0036	0.6	0702	4.2	1325	0.4	1947	3.6
6	M	0011	0.8	0632	3.9	1253	0.6	1920	3.6
21	TU	0140	0.6	0809	4.1	1430	0.5	2052	3.7
7	TU	0121	0.9	0742	4.0	1406	0.6	2032	3.8
22	W	0252	0.6	0920	4.1	1536	0.5	2156	3.8
8	W	0237	0.9	0853	4.1	1518	0.5	2140	3.9
23	TH	0402	0.5	1025	4.1	1637	0.5	2253	4.0
9	TH	0346	0.7	0957	4.2	1621	0.4	2238	4.1
24	F	0504	0.4	1119	4.1	1730	0.5	2342	4.1
10	F	0448	0.6	1055	4.3	1717	0.3	2328	4.2
25	SA	0557	0.4	1205	4.1	1818	0.5		
11	SA	0545	0.4	1148	4.4	1810	0.3		
26	SU	0024	4.2	0644	0.4	1247	4.2	○ 1901	0.5
12	SU	0015	4.3	0635	0.2	1239	4.4	● 1858	0.2
27	M	0102	4.3	0724	0.4	1325	4.2	1937	0.4
13	M	0101	4.4	0723	0.1	1331	4.3	1947	0.3
28	TU	0137	4.4	0800	0.4	1401	4.1	2010	0.4
14	TU	0149	4.4	0814	0.1	1427	4.3	2039	0.3
29	W	0212	4.4	0836	0.3	1436	4.1	2044	0.4
15	W	0240	4.4	0908	0.1	1522	4.2	2128	0.3
30	TH	0246	4.4	0910	0.3	1510	4.0	2115	0.3
31	F	0319	4.3	0941	0.3	1544	3.9	2145	0.3

Chart Datum: 2·26 metres below Normal Null (German reference level)

Chapter 5

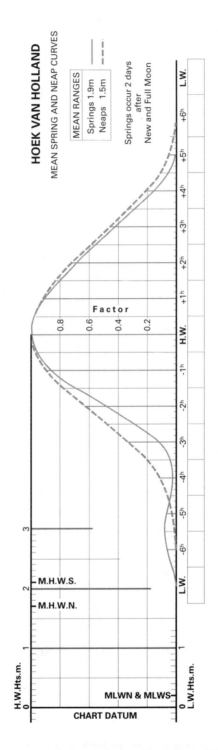

HOEK VAN HOLLAND
MEAN SPRING AND NEAP CURVES

MEAN RANGES
Springs 1.9m
Neaps 1.5m

Springs occur 2 days
after
New and Full Moon

Factor

TIME ZONE -0100
(Dutch Standard Time)
Subtract 1 hour for UT
For Dutch Summer Time add
ONE hour in **non-shaded areas**

NETHERLANDS – HOEK VAN HOLLAND

LAT 51°59′N   LONG 4°07′E

TIMES AND HEIGHTS OF HIGH AND LOW WATERS

YEAR 2004

Note - Double LWs often occur. The predictions are for the lower LW which is usually the first.

JANUARY

Day	Time m	Time m	Time m	Time m
1 TH	0340 0.5	0955 1.7	1554 0.2	2256 1.8
16 F	0245 0.5	0906 1.8	1425 0.1	2139 1.9
2 F	0429 0.5	1104 1.7	1655 0.2	2350 1.8
17 SA	0346 0.5	1016 1.8	1545 0.1	2250 1.9
3 SA	0524 0.4	1216 1.7	1800 0.3	
18 SU	0424 0.4	1120 1.8	1650 0.2	
4 SU	0046 1.8	0615 0.4	1254 1.8	1900 0.3
19 M	0000 1.9	0524 0.4	1226 1.9	1754 0.2
5 M	0124 1.8	0700 0.3	1345 1.8	1935 0.3
20 TU	0055 1.9	0625 0.3	1322 2.0	2107 0.3
6 TU	0216 1.9	0734 0.3	1425 1.9	2030 0.4
21 W	0155 1.9	0716 0.3	1411 2.1	● 2225 0.3
7 W	0249 1.9	0820 0.3	1454 2.0	○ 2130 0.4
22 TH	0245 1.9	0749 0.2	1458 2.2	2316 0.4
8 TH	0326 1.9	0850 0.2	1536 1.9	2227 0.4
23 F	0335 2.0	0831 0.1	1545 2.2	2354 0.4
9 F	0351 2.0	0915 0.2	1605 2.1	2330 0.4
24 SA	0415 2.0	0918 0.0	1630 2.0	
10 SA	0424 1.9	0934 0.2	1638 2.1	
25 SU	0055 0.4	0458 2.0	0954 0.0	1719 2.2
11 SU	0004 0.4	0505 1.9	1015 0.1	1715 2.1
26 M	0146 0.4	0545 2.0	1050 0.0	1805 2.1
12 M	0105 0.4	0539 1.9	1056 0.1	1755 2.1
27 TU	0225 0.4	0625 2.0	1145 0.0	1849 2.0
13 TU	0151 0.4	0615 1.8	1135 0.1	1839 2.1
28 W	0257 0.5	0715 1.9	1234 0.0	1939 1.9
14 W	0236 0.4	0755 1.8	1236 0.0	1935 2.0
29 TH	0140 0.4	0800 1.9	1350 0.1	◐ 2035 1.8
15 TH	0304 0.5	0755 1.8	1330 0.0	◐ 2036 2.0
30 F	0225 0.4	0855 1.8	1510 0.2	2125 1.7
31 SA	0355 0.4	1006 1.7	1615 0.2	2244 1.6

FEBRUARY

Day	Time m	Time m	Time m	Time m
1 SU	0444 0.4	1120 1.6	1725 0.3	
16 M	0405 0.3	1055 1.8	1644 0.2	2345 1.6
2 M	0005 1.6	0544 0.3	1223 1.7	1825 0.3
17 TU	0514 0.3	1216 1.8	1940 0.3	
3 TU	0110 1.7	0640 0.3	1325 1.7	1920 0.4
18 W	0055 1.7	0614 0.2	1315 2.0	2120 0.3
4 W	0155 1.7	0714 0.3	1404 1.8	2010 0.4
19 TH	0149 1.8	0945 0.2	1405 2.1	2215 0.3
5 TH	0234 1.8	0806 0.2	1445 1.9	2130 0.4
20 F	0239 1.9	1035 0.1	1451 2.2	● 2254 0.3
6 F	0303 1.9	0814 0.2	1515 2.0	2230 0.4
21 SA	0318 1.9	1114 0.0	1535 2.2	2334 0.4
7 SA	0339 1.9	0834 0.2	1549 2.1	2305 0.4
22 SU	0354 2.1	1210 0.0	1616 2.2	
8 SU	0409 1.9	0915 0.1	1626 2.1	
23 M	0036 0.4	0439 2.0	1305 0.0	1655 2.1
9 M	0000 0.3	0446 1.9	0946 0.1	1657 2.2
24 TU	0115 0.4	0516 2.0	1345 0.0	1735 2.1
10 TU	0035 0.3	0519 1.9	1026 0.0	1735 2.1
25 W	0155 0.4	0556 2.0	1105 0.0	1815 2.0
11 W	0125 0.3	0555 1.9	1106 0.0	1818 2.1
26 TH	0225 0.4	0632 2.0	1159 0.1	1855 1.9
12 TH	0154 0.4	0635 1.9	1145 0.0	1906 2.0
27 F	0025 0.3	0715 1.9	1255 0.1	1940 1.8
13 F	0230 0.4	0725 1.9	◐ 1959 1.9	
28 SA	0130 0.2	0806 1.8	◐ 2036 1.6	
14 SA	0214 0.4	0826 1.9	1415 0.1	2105 1.8
29 SU	0214 0.3	0859 1.7	1550 0.3	2124 1.5
15 SU	0304 0.3	0946 1.8	1534 0.1	2219 1.7

MARCH

Day	Time m	Time m	Time m	Time m
1 M	0430 0.3	1025 1.5	1704 0.3	2315 1.4
16 TU	0355 0.2	1056 1.7	1644 0.3	2335 1.5
2 TU	0530 0.2	1200 1.6	1804 0.3	
17 W	0504 0.2	1215 1.8	2000 0.3	
3 W	0046 1.5	0625 0.2	1259 1.7	1900 0.3
18 TH	0044 1.6	0820 0.1	1315 2.0	2120 0.2
4 TH	0136 1.6	0654 0.2	1356 1.8	2120 0.3
19 F	0134 1.7	0924 0.0	1359 2.1	2204 0.3
5 F	0216 1.7	0725 0.2	1419 2.0	2225 0.3
20 SA	0223 1.8	1005 0.0	1439 2.1	● 2224 0.3
6 SA	0234 1.8	0744 0.2	1449 2.1	○ 2237 0.3
21 SU	0306 1.9	1054 0.0	1516 2.1	2315 0.3
7 SU	0315 1.9	0809 0.1	1521 2.2	2255 0.3
22 M	0335 2.0	1134 0.0	1555 2.1	
8 M	0346 1.9	0839 0.0	1557 2.2	2346 0.3
23 TU	0000 0.3	0415 2.0	1225 0.0	1628 2.1
9 TU	0418 2.0	0915 0.0	1635 2.2	
24 W	0045 0.3	0448 2.1	1305 0.0	1705 2.0
10 W	0014 0.3	0458 2.0	0955 0.0	1712 2.2
25 TH	0126 0.3	0526 2.1	1327 0.1	1739 2.0
11 TH	0100 0.3	0535 2.0	1039 0.0	1755 2.1
26 F	0145 0.2	0555 2.0	1330 0.2	1815 1.9
12 F	0135 0.3	0616 2.0	1124 0.0	1839 2.0
27 SA	0000 0.2	0636 2.0	1300 0.2	1850 1.8
13 SA	0145 0.3	0702 2.0	◐ 1935 1.8	
28 SU	0024 0.1	0716 1.8	◐ 1936 1.6	
14 SU	0130 0.2	0755 1.9	1434 0.1	2034 1.6
29 M	0124 0.1	0815 1.7	1510 0.3	2025 1.5
15 M	0235 0.2	0915 1.8	1534 0.2	2216 1.5
30 TU	0357 0.2	0935 1.5	1646 0.3	2154 1.3
31 W	0454 0.2	1115 1.5	1746 0.3	

APRIL

Day	Time m	Time m	Time m	Time m
1 TH	0006 1.4	0555 0.2	1235 1.7	1850 0.3
16 F	0035 1.6	0757 0.0	1253 2.0	2057 0.2
2 F	0045 1.5	0635 0.2	1309 1.9	2106 0.3
17 SA	0125 1.7	0910 0.0	1339 2.1	2135 0.2
3 SA	0135 1.7	0645 0.2	1345 2.0	2206 0.2
18 SU	0205 1.8	0945 0.0	1419 2.1	2210 0.3
4 SU	0206 1.8	0710 0.1	1415 2.1	2227 0.3
19 M	0239 1.9	1030 0.1	1455 2.0	● 2245 0.3
5 M	0239 1.9	0740 0.0	1455 2.2	○ 2250 0.3
20 TU	0316 2.0	1100 0.1	1529 2.0	2331 0.2
6 TU	0316 2.0	0812 0.0	1529 2.2	2035 0.3
21 W	0350 2.0	1140 0.1	1606 2.0	
7 W	0351 2.1	0849 0.0	1607 2.2	2115 0.3
22 TH	0016 0.2	0418 2.0	1220 0.1	1634 1.9
8 TH	0429 2.1	0932 0.0	1649 2.1	2156 0.2
23 F	0045 0.2	0456 2.1	1250 0.1	1709 1.9
9 F	0508 2.1	1019 0.0	1732 2.0	2239 0.1
24 SA	0115 0.1	0530 2.0	1320 0.2	1742 1.8
10 SA	0556 2.1	1315 0.1	1819 1.9	2333 0.1
25 SU	0125 0.1	0602 1.9	1340 0.2	1816 1.8
11 SU	0639 0.1	1335 0.1	1916 1.7	
26 M	0010 0.2	0640 1.9	1400 0.3	1849 1.7
12 M	0120 0.1	0739 1.9	1430 0.1	◑ 2025 1.5
27 TU	0116 0.1	0725 1.7	1450 0.3	◑ 1944 1.5
13 TU	0224 0.1	0904 1.8	1525 0.3	2159 1.4
28 W	0204 0.1	0906 1.6	1615 0.3	2120 1.4
14 W	0344 0.1	1056 1.8	1815 0.3	2336 1.5
29 TH	0440 0.2	1019 1.6	1705 0.3	2244 1.4
15 TH	0500 0.1	1204 1.9	2000 0.2	
30 F	0536 0.1	1134 1.8	1820 0.3	2355 1.5

Chart Datum: 0·84 metres below NAP Datum

TIDES

NETHERLANDS – HOEK VAN HOLLAND

TIME ZONE -0100
(Dutch Standard Time)
Subtract 1 hour for UT
For Dutch Summer Time add
ONE hour in **non-shaded areas**

LAT 51°59'N   LONG 4°07'E

TIMES AND HEIGHTS OF HIGH AND LOW WATERS

YEAR 2004

Note - Double LWs often occur. The predictions are for the lower LW which is usually the first.

MAY

Day	Time m		Day	Time m
1 SA	0600 0.1 / 1223 1.9 / 2036 0.2		16 SU	0056 1.7 / 0825 0.0 / 1315 2.0 / 2114 0.2
2 SU	0050 1.7 / 0600 0.1 / 1310 2.1 / 2136 0.2		17 M	0135 1.8 / 0910 0.1 / 1356 2.0 / 2135 0.3
3 M	0125 1.8 / 0629 0.0 / 1346 2.1 / 2215 0.3		18 TU	0215 1.9 / 0910 0.1 / 1428 2.0 / 2207 0.3
4 TU	0206 1.9 / 0705 0.0 / 1426 2.2 / ○ 1935 0.3		19 W	0255 1.9 / 0937 0.2 / 1505 1.9 / ● 2254 0.2
5 W	0243 2.0 / 0746 0.0 / 1506 2.2 / 2009 0.2		20 TH	0321 2.0 / 1045 0.2 / 1545 1.9 / 2334 0.2
6 TH	0326 2.1 / 0825 0.0 / 1546 2.1 / 2049 0.1		21 F	0355 2.0 / 1136 0.2 / 1620 1.9
7 F	0405 2.2 / 0916 0.1 / 1628 2.1 / 2135 0.1		22 SA	0010 0.1 / 0431 2.0 / 1205 0.2 / 1649 1.8
8 SA	0449 2.2 / 1225 0.1 / 1715 1.9 / 2225 0.0		23 SU	0040 0.1 / 0508 2.0 / 1250 0.3 / 1714 1.8
9 SU	0536 2.1 / 1304 0.2 / 1805 1.8 / 2325 0.0		24 M	0115 0.1 / 0546 1.9 / 1324 0.3 / 1751 1.7
10 M	0625 2.1 / 1340 0.2 / 1905 1.6		25 TU	0000 0.1 / 0615 1.9 / 1357 0.3 / 1829 1.7
11 TU	0045 0.0 / 0746 1.9 / 1430 0.3 / ◑ 2019 1.5		26 W	0034 0.0 / 0654 1.8 / 1455 0.3 / 1936 1.6
12 W	0154 0.0 / 0905 1.8 / 1635 0.3 / 2144 1.5		27 TH	0135 0.0 / 0820 1.7 / 1537 0.3 / ◐ 2045 1.5
13 TH	0320 0.0 / 1024 1.8 / 1804 0.3 / 2305 1.5		28 F	0225 0.1 / 0941 1.8 / 1640 0.3 / 2200 1.5
14 F	0620 0.0 / 1146 1.9 / 1915 0.2		29 SA	0324 0.1 / 1034 1.8 / 1730 0.3 / 2305 1.6
15 SA	0005 1.6 / 0727 0.0 / 1229 2.0 / 2036 0.2		30 SU	0425 0.1 / 1140 2.0 / 1840 0.3
			31 M	0006 1.7 / 0516 1.9 / 1228 2.1 / 1804 0.3

JUNE

Day	Time m		Day	Time m
1 TU	0055 1.8 / 0554 0.0 / 1316 2.1 / 1835 0.3		16 W	0149 1.8 / 0740 0.2 / 1415 1.9 / 1945 0.2
2 W	0135 1.9 / 0646 0.0 / 1358 2.1 / 1916 0.2		17 TH	0229 1.9 / 0840 0.3 / 1456 1.8 / ● 2024 0.2
3 TH	0219 2.1 / 0728 0.1 / 1440 2.1 / ○ 1955 0.2		18 F	0305 1.9 / 0937 0.3 / 1529 1.8 / 2110 0.2
4 F	0305 2.1 / 0809 0.1 / 1527 2.0 / 2031 0.1		19 SA	0334 1.9 / 1050 0.3 / 1555 1.8 / 2140 0.1
5 SA	0347 2.2 / 0859 0.2 / 1617 2.0 / 2119 0.0		20 SU	0415 2.0 / 1135 0.3 / 1635 1.8 / 2359 0.1
6 SU	0436 2.2 / 1255 0.3 / 1705 1.9 / 2216 0.0		21 M	0444 2.0 / 1227 0.3 / 1703 1.8 / 2235 0.1
7 M	0525 2.1 / 1325 0.3 / 1755 1.8 / 2315 -0.1		22 TU	0526 1.9 / 1315 0.3 / 1745 1.7 / 2303 0.1
8 TU	0614 2.1 / 1425 0.3 / 1855 1.7 / 2354 0.0		23 W	0559 1.9 / 1355 0.3 / 1814 1.7 / 2354 0.0
9 W	0014 -0.1 / 0723 2.0 / 1536 0.3 / ◑ 2016 1.6		24 TH	0639 1.9 / 1440 0.3 / 1916 1.6
10 TH	0124 -0.1 / 0835 1.9 / 1625 0.3 / 2120 1.6		25 F	0050 0.0 / 0735 1.9 / 1525 0.4 / ◐ 2015 1.6
11 F	0234 0.0 / 0955 1.9 / 1725 0.3 / 2236 1.6		26 SA	0134 0.0 / 0834 1.9 / 1600 0.4 / 2115 1.6
12 SA	0400 0.0 / 1106 1.9 / 1825 0.3 / 2336 1.7		27 SU	0245 0.0 / 0949 1.9 / 1610 0.4 / 2226 1.7
13 SU	0645 0.0 / 1154 1.9 / 1937 0.3		28 M	0346 0.0 / 1052 2.0 / 1644 0.3 / 2319 1.7
14 M	0014 1.7 / 0600 0.1 / 1243 1.9 / 2040 0.3		29 TU	0440 0.0 / 1149 2.0 / 1729 0.3
15 TU	0105 1.8 / 0650 0.2 / 1336 1.9 / 1854 0.3		30 W	0020 1.9 / 0546 0.1 / 1245 2.0 / 1809 0.3

JULY

Day	Time m		Day	Time m
1 TH	0109 2.0 / 0624 0.1 / 1339 2.0 / 1900 0.2		16 F	0215 1.8 / 0804 0.3 / 1434 1.8 / 2005 0.2
2 F	0158 2.1 / 0720 0.2 / 1427 2.0 / ○ 1939 0.2		17 SA	0255 1.9 / 0900 0.4 / 1526 1.8 / ● 2035 0.2
3 SA	0247 2.1 / 0800 0.3 / 1516 1.9 / 2021 0.1		18 SU	0325 1.9 / 1010 0.4 / 1545 1.8 / 2104 0.2
4 SU	0335 2.2 / 1154 0.3 / 1605 1.9 / 2105 0.0		19 M	0354 2.0 / 1120 0.4 / 1614 1.9 / 2129 0.1
5 M	0422 2.2 / 1256 0.4 / 1656 1.9 / 2155 0.0		20 TU	0436 2.0 / 1205 0.4 / 1655 1.8 / 2154 0.1
6 TU	0515 2.2 / 1334 0.4 / 1746 1.8 / 2244 -0.1		21 W	0510 2.0 / 1255 0.4 / 1725 1.8 / 2235 0.1
7 W	0605 2.1 / 1436 0.4 / 1835 1.8 / 2344 -0.1		22 TH	0546 2.0 / 1335 0.4 / 1759 1.8 / 2305 0.1
8 TH	0706 2.0 / 1526 0.4 / 1923 1.8		23 F	0619 2.0 / 1415 0.4 / 1839 1.8 / 2353 0.0
9 F	0054 -0.1 / 0805 1.9 / 1616 0.4 / ◑ 2030 1.7		24 SA	0705 2.0 / 1444 0.4 / 1925 1.9
10 SA	0210 0.0 / 0904 1.9 / 1650 0.4 / 2130 1.7		25 SU	0055 0.0 / 0754 2.0 / 1500 0.4 / ◐ 2036 1.8
11 SU	0320 0.0 / 1015 1.8 / 1605 0.4 / 2245 1.7		26 M	0200 0.0 / 0906 2.0 / 1510 0.4 / 2136 1.8
12 M	0430 0.1 / 1126 1.8 / 1654 0.3 / 2339 1.7		27 TU	0315 0.1 / 1015 1.9 / 1616 0.4 / 2246 1.8
13 TU	0530 0.2 / 1220 1.8 / 1749 0.3		28 W	0414 0.1 / 1119 1.8 / 1705 0.3 / 2356 1.9
14 W	0040 1.7 / 0630 0.2 / 1316 1.8 / 1834 0.3		29 TH	0524 0.2 / 1224 1.8 / 1804 0.3
15 TH	0129 1.8 / 0726 0.3 / 1406 1.8 / 1925 0.2		30 F	0055 2.0 / 0624 0.3 / 1329 1.9 / 1845 0.2
			31 SA	0149 2.1 / 1006 0.3 / 1419 1.9 / ○ 1929 0.2

AUGUST

Day	Time m		Day	Time m
1 SU	0238 2.2 / 1055 0.4 / 1505 1.9 / 2016 0.1		16 M	0304 2.0 / 1030 0.5 / 1525 1.9 / ● 2035 0.2
2 M	0325 2.2 / 1140 0.4 / 1555 1.9 / 2049 0.0		17 TU	0335 2.1 / 1057 0.5 / 1555 1.9 / 2055 0.2
3 TU	0408 2.2 / 1224 0.4 / 1635 1.9 / 2135 0.0		18 W	0409 2.1 / 1135 0.5 / 1629 1.9 / 2136 0.1
4 W	0456 2.2 / 1314 0.4 / 1718 2.0 / 2219 0.0		19 TH	0441 2.2 / 1236 0.4 / 1706 1.9 / 2159 0.1
5 TH	0546 2.1 / 1416 0.4 / 1806 1.9 / 2315 0.0		20 F	0515 2.2 / 1304 0.4 / 1738 1.9 / 2234 0.1
6 F	0624 2.1 / 1455 0.4 / 1849 1.9 / 2314 0.0		21 SA	0555 2.1 / 1356 0.4 / 1815 1.9 / 2314 0.0
7 SA	0005 0.0 / 0715 2.0 / 1530 0.5 / 1934 1.9		22 SU	0638 2.1 / 1420 0.4 / 1855 1.9
8 SU	0124 0.1 / 0804 1.8 / 1405 0.4 / 2024 1.8		23 M	0015 0.1 / 0725 2.0 / 1234 0.4 / ◑ 1945 1.9
9 M	0237 0.1 / 0916 1.7 / 1520 0.4 / 2135 1.7		24 TU	0140 0.1 / 0825 1.9 / 1427 0.4 / 2055 1.8
10 TU	0355 0.2 / 1025 1.6 / 1625 0.3 / 2300 1.6		25 W	0254 0.2 / 0940 1.8 / 1540 0.4 / 2220 1.8
11 W	0516 0.3 / 1156 1.6 / 1724 0.3		26 TH	0414 0.3 / 1105 1.7 / 1700 0.4 / 2334 1.8
12 TH	0025 1.7 / 0604 0.3 / 1255 1.7 / 1813 0.3		27 F	0524 0.4 / 1226 1.7 / 1745 0.3
13 F	0120 1.8 / 0700 0.4 / 1356 1.7 / 1905 0.2		28 SA	0049 2.0 / 0855 0.4 / 1326 1.8 / 1835 0.2
14 SA	0205 1.9 / 0750 0.4 / 1430 1.8 / 1944 0.2		29 SU	0141 2.1 / 0950 0.4 / 1408 1.9 / 1915 0.2
15 SU	0234 1.9 / 0830 0.5 / 1455 1.8 / 2004 0.2		30 M	0229 2.2 / 1040 0.4 / 1455 1.9 / ○ 1956 0.1
			31 TU	0308 2.3 / 1120 0.5 / 1536 2.0 / 2024 0.1

Chart Datum: 0·84 metres below NAP Datum

TIME ZONE -0100
(Dutch Standard Time)
Subtract 1 hour for UT
For Dutch Summer Time add
ONE hour in **non-shaded areas**

NETHERLANDS – HOEK VAN HOLLAND

LAT 51°59'N   LONG 4°07'E

TIMES AND HEIGHTS OF HIGH AND LOW WATERS

YEAR **2004**

Note - Double LWs often occur. The predictions are for the lower LW which is usually the first.

SEPTEMBER

#	Time	m	#	Time	m
1 W	0347 / 1616 / 2109	2.3 / 2.0 / 0.1	16 TH	0342 / 1120 / 1559 / 2058	2.3 / 0.5 / 2.1 / 0.1
2 TH	0435 / 1255 / 1655 / 2156	2.2 / 0.5 / 2.1 / 0.1	17 F	0416 / 1154 / 1635 / 2129	2.3 / 0.5 / 2.1 / 0.1
3 F	0515 / 1334 / 1735 / 2235	2.1 / 0.5 / 2.1 / 0.1	18 SA	0451 / 1240 / 1712 / 2209	2.3 / 0.4 / 2.1 / 0.1
4 SA	0556 / 1425 / 1816 / 2324	2.1 / 0.5 / 2.1 / 0.2	19 SU	0528 / 1029 / 1747 / 2255	2.2 / 0.4 / 2.1 / 0.1
5 SU	0635 / 1154 / 1855	2.0 / 0.4 / 2.0	20 M	0611 / 1115 / 1832 / 2355	2.1 / 0.4 / 2.1 / 0.2
6 M	0035 / 0719 / 1255 / 1939 ☾	0.2 / 1.8 / 0.4 / 1.9	21 TU	0659 / 1215 / 1926 ○	2.0 / 0.4 / 2.0
7 TU	0157 / 0800 / 1410 / 2046	0.3 / 1.7 / 0.4 / 1.7	22 W	0216 / 0801 / 1404 / 2025	0.3 / 1.8 / 0.4 / 1.9
8 W	0330 / 0915 / 1615 / 2154	0.4 / 1.6 / 0.3 / 1.6	23 TH	0316 / 0920 / 1524 / 2216	0.3 / 1.6 / 0.4 / 1.8
9 TH	0435 / 1114 / 1716 / 2356	0.4 / 1.5 / 0.3 / 1.6	24 F	0415 / 1100 / 1650 / 2340	0.4 / 1.6 / 0.3 / 1.9
10 F	0534 / 1236 / 1755	0.4 / 1.6 / 0.3	25 SA	0715 / 1215 / 1937	0.4 / 1.7 / 0.3
11 SA	0056 / 0635 / 1315 / 1850	1.8 / 0.5 / 1.7 / 0.3	26 SU	0045 / 0856 / 1315 / 2054	2.0 / 0.4 / 1.8 / 0.2
12 SU	0135 / 0910 / 1400 / 1914	1.9 / 0.5 / 1.8 / 0.3	27 M	0128 / 0934 / 1354 / 2144	2.2 / 0.4 / 1.9 / 0.1
13 M	0215 / 1010 / 1435 / 1934	2.0 / 0.5 / 1.9 / 0.3	28 TU	0215 / 1014 / 1435 / 2235 ○	2.2 / 0.5 / 2.0 / 0.1
14 TU	0239 / 1040 / 1455 / 1955 ●	2.1 / 0.5 / 1.9 / 0.2	29 W	0248 / 1044 / 1515 / 2010	2.3 / 0.5 / 2.1 / 0.2
15 W	0305 / 1040 / 1525 / 2026	2.2 / 0.5 / 1.9 / 0.2	30 TH	0328 / 1135 / 1555 / 2046	2.2 / 0.5 / 2.1 / 0.2

OCTOBER

#	Time	m	#	Time	m
1 F	0409 / 1226 / 1626	2.2 / 0.5 / 2.2	16 SA	0347 / 0855 / 1605 / 2108	2.3 / 0.5 / 2.2 / 0.1
2 SA	0056 / 0446 / 1315 / 1706	0.2 / 2.1 / 0.4 / 2.2	17 SU	0425 / 0929 / 1646 / 2156	2.3 / 0.4 / 2.3 / 0.2
3 SU	0115 / 0525 / 1025 / 1739	0.3 / 2.0 / 0.4 / 2.1	18 M	0507 / 1008 / 1728 / 2245	2.2 / 0.3 / 2.2 / 0.3
4 M	0145 / 0559 / 1115 / 1815	0.3 / 2.0 / 0.3 / 2.1	19 TU	0551 / 1106 / 1812	2.1 / 0.3 / 2.2
5 TU	0000 / 0636 / 1205 / 1900	0.4 / 1.9 / 0.3 / 2.0	20 W	0115 / 0639 / 1204 / 1905 ☾	0.3 / 1.9 / 0.3 / 2.1
6 W	0140 / 0704 / 1304 / 1944 ☾	0.4 / 1.7 / 0.3 / 1.8	21 TH	0205 / 0745 / 1350 / 2014	0.4 / 1.7 / 0.3 / 1.9
7 TH	0310 / 0815 / 1556 / 2126	0.5 / 1.6 / 0.3 / 1.6	22 F	0255 / 0904 / 1455 / 2155	0.5 / 1.5 / 0.3 / 1.8
8 F	0420 / 0934 / 1656 / 2300	0.5 / 1.5 / 0.3 / 1.6	23 SA	0550 / 1044 / 1800 / 2335	0.5 / 1.5 / 0.3 / 2.0
9 SA	0514 / 1155 / 1734	0.5 / 1.5 / 0.3	24 SU	0720 / 1206 / 1924	0.4 / 1.7 / 0.2
10 SU	0025 / 0620 / 1246 / 1836	1.8 / 0.5 / 1.6 / 0.3	25 M	0024 / 0825 / 1255 / 2034	2.1 / 0.4 / 1.8 / 0.1
11 M	0100 / 0840 / 1326 / 1900	2.0 / 0.5 / 1.8 / 0.3	26 TU	0111 / 0920 / 1335 / 2115	2.2 / 0.4 / 1.9 / 0.1
12 TU	0136 / 0940 / 1349 / 1854	2.1 / 0.4 / 1.9 / 0.3	27 W	0151 / 0956 / 1416 / 2205	2.2 / 0.5 / 2.0 / 0.2
13 W	0205 / 1015 / 1426 / 1919	2.2 / 0.5 / 2.0 / 0.2	28 TH	0236 / 1015 / 1448 / 2234 ○	2.2 / 0.5 / 2.1 / 0.2
14 TH	0238 / 0744 / 1456 / 1955 ●	2.3 / 0.5 / 2.1 / 0.2	29 F	0309 / 1105 / 1525 / 2310	2.2 / 0.5 / 2.2 / 0.3
15 F	0311 / 0819 / 1528 / 2030	2.3 / 0.4 / 2.2 / 0.4	30 SA	0346 / 1150 / 1606	2.1 / 0.4 / 2.2
			31 SU	0000 / 0425 / 0919 / 1640	0.3 / 2.0 / 0.4 / 2.2

NOVEMBER

#	Time	m	#	Time	m
1 M	0040 / 0459 / 1005 / 1716	0.4 / 2.0 / 0.3 / 2.1	16 TU	0451 / 0954 / 1708	2.1 / 0.2 / 2.3
2 TU	0100 / 0524 / 1044 / 1749	0.4 / 1.9 / 0.3 / 2.1	17 W	0035 / 0537 / 1055 / 1757	0.4 / 2.0 / 0.2 / 2.2
3 W	0117 / 0559 / 1140 / 1823	0.5 / 1.9 / 0.3 / 2.0	18 TH	0120 / 0629 / 1205 / 1855	0.4 / 1.8 / 0.2 / 2.1
4 TH	0140 / 0635 / 1246 / 1915	0.5 / 1.8 / 0.3 / 1.8	19 F	0157 / 0733 / 1314 / 2025 ☾	0.5 / 1.7 / 0.2 / 2.0
5 F	0230 / 0724 / 1334 / 2046 ☾	0.5 / 1.7 / 0.3 / 1.7	20 SA	0414 / 0905 / 1424 / 2150	0.5 / 1.6 / 0.2 / 1.9
6 SA	0350 / 0844 / 1626 / 2200	0.5 / 1.5 / 0.3 / 1.7	21 SU	0546 / 1025 / 1755 / 2304	0.5 / 1.6 / 0.2 / 2.0
7 SU	0450 / 1014 / 1716 / 2326	0.5 / 1.5 / 0.3 / 1.8	22 M	0645 / 1129 / 1905	0.5 / 1.7 / 0.1
8 M	0550 / 1134 / 1800 / 2005	0.5 / 1.6 / 0.3 / 0.1	23 TU	0005 / 0800 / 1225 / 2005	2.0 / 0.4 / 1.8 / 0.1
9 TU	0015 / 0800 / 1230 / 1754	2.0 / 0.5 / 1.8 / 0.3	24 W	0049 / 0845 / 1309 / 2050	2.1 / 0.4 / 1.9 / 0.2
10 W	0055 / 0905 / 1310 / 1820	2.1 / 0.4 / 1.9 / 0.2	25 TH	0128 / 0936 / 1355 / 2100	2.1 / 0.5 / 2.0 / 0.3
11 TH	0130 / 0955 / 1348 / 1849	2.2 / 0.5 / 2.0 / 0.2	26 F	0216 / 0950 / 1424 / 2120 ○	2.1 / 0.5 / 2.1 / 0.3
12 F	0206 / 0726 / 1422 / 1925 ●	2.3 / 0.4 / 2.1 / 0.2	27 SA	0255 / 0804 / 1505 / 2210	2.1 / 0.4 / 2.1 / 0.3
13 SA	0245 / 0756 / 1506 / 2010	2.3 / 0.4 / 2.2 / 0.2	28 SU	0329 / 0844 / 1545 / 2300	2.0 / 0.3 / 2.1 / 0.4
14 SU	0325 / 0836 / 1546 / 2049	2.3 / 0.3 / 2.3 / 0.2	29 M	0408 / 1205 / 1619 / 2345	2.0 / 0.3 / 2.1 / 0.4
15 M	0407 / 0915 / 1627 / 2135	2.2 / 0.3 / 2.3 / 0.3	30 TU	0439 / 0954 / 1655	2.0 / 0.3 / 2.1

DECEMBER

#	Time	m	#	Time	m
1 W	0027 / 0515 / 1046 / 1736	0.5 / 1.9 / 0.2 / 2.0	16 TH	0057 / 0536 / 1039 / 1755	0.4 / 1.9 / 0.1 / 2.2
2 TH	0057 / 0546 / 1120 / 1806	0.5 / 1.9 / 0.2 / 2.0	17 F	0200 / 0621 / 1134 / 1855	0.5 / 1.9 / 0.1 / 2.1
3 F	0140 / 0619 / 1204 / 1845	0.5 / 1.8 / 0.2 / 1.9	18 SA	0254 / 0736 / 1244 / 1955 ☾	0.5 / 1.8 / 0.1 / 2.0
4 SA	0210 / 0716 / 1254 / 1934	0.5 / 1.7 / 0.2 / 1.8	19 SU	0400 / 0835 / 1355 / 2116	0.5 / 1.7 / 0.1 / 2.0
5 SU	0326 / 0804 / 1405 / 2105 ☾	0.5 / 1.6 / 0.2 / 1.8	20 M	0455 / 0935 / 1510 / 2225	0.5 / 1.7 / 0.1 / 1.9
6 M	0410 / 0925 / 1455 / 2205	0.5 / 1.6 / 0.2 / 1.9	21 TU	0610 / 1050 / 1836 / 2323	0.5 / 1.7 / 0.2 / 1.9
7 TU	0500 / 1035 / 1600 / 2305	0.5 / 1.7 / 0.2 / 2.0	22 W	0710 / 1145 / 1910	0.5 / 1.8 / 0.1
8 W	0540 / 1140 / 1643	0.5 / 1.8 / 0.1	23 TH	0019 / 0814 / 1245 / 1910	1.9 / 0.5 / 1.9 / 0.3
9 TH	0006 / 0545 / 1230 / 1740	2.1 / 0.5 / 1.9 / 0.2	24 F	0116 / 0916 / 1324 / 1927	1.9 / 0.4 / 1.9 / 0.3
10 F	0056 / 0619 / 1316 / 1826	2.2 / 0.4 / 2.0 / 0.2	25 SA	0159 / 0725 / 1415 / 2017	1.9 / 0.4 / 2.0 / 0.3
11 SA	0136 / 0653 / 1358 / 1910 ●	2.2 / 0.4 / 2.1 / 0.2	26 SU	0239 / 0816 / 1455 / 2120 ○	1.9 / 0.3 / 2.0 / 0.4
12 SU	0221 / 0736 / 1441 / 1956	2.2 / 0.3 / 2.2 / 0.3	27 M	0319 / 0845 / 1534 / 2205	1.9 / 0.3 / 2.1 / 0.4
13 M	0305 / 0818 / 1526 / 2040	2.2 / 0.2 / 2.3 / 0.3	28 TU	0354 / 0930 / 1605 / 2320	1.9 / 0.2 / 2.1 / 0.4
14 TU	0356 / 0859 / 1615 / 2130	2.1 / 0.2 / 2.3 / 0.4	29 W	0425 / 0950 / 1639	1.9 / 0.2 / 2.1
15 W	0438 / 0945 / 1657	2.0 / 0.1 / 2.3	30 TH	0014 / 0454 / 1014 / 1715	0.5 / 1.9 / 0.2 / 2.0
			31 F	0055 / 0535 / 1055 / 1749	0.5 / 1.8 / 0.2 / 2.0

Chart Datum: 0·84 metres below NAP Datum

Chapter 5

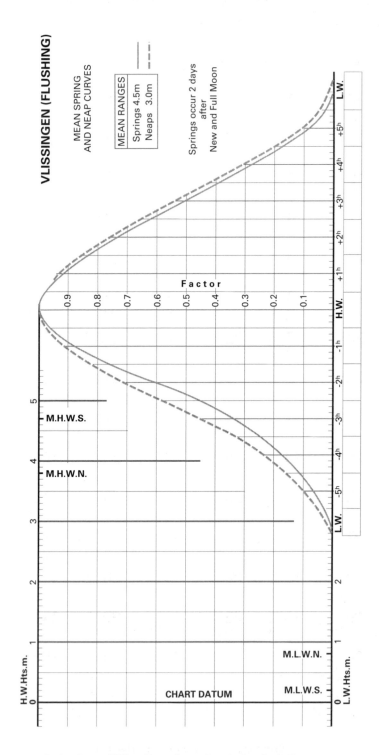

VLISSINGEN (FLUSHING)

MEAN SPRING
AND NEAP CURVES

MEAN RANGES
Springs 4.5m
Neaps 3.0m

Springs occur 2 days
after
New and Full Moon

Factor

TIME ZONE -0100
(Dutch Standard Time)
Subtract 1 hour for UT
For Dutch Summer Time add
ONE hour in **non-shaded areas**

NETHERLANDS – VLISSINGEN

LAT 51°27′N   LONG 3°36′E

TIMES AND HEIGHTS OF HIGH AND LOW WATERS

YEAR 2004

JANUARY

Day	Time m	Time m	Time m	Time m
1 TH	0249 1.1	0909 3.9	1535 0.8	2206 3.8
2 F	0405 1.1	1020 3.8	1650 0.8	2259 3.9
3 SA	0510 1.1	1120 3.9	1746 0.8	2355 4.0
4 SU	0554 1.0	1209 4.0	1831 0.8	
5 M	0039 4.1	0645 0.9	1255 4.1	1908 0.8
6 TU	0125 4.2	0729 0.7	1335 4.2	1946 0.7
7 W	0158 4.3	0804 0.6	1411 4.4	2022 0.7
8 TH	0231 4.4	0851 0.5	1445 4.5	2058 0.6
9 F	0305 4.4	0926 0.4	1518 4.6	2136 0.6
10 SA	0338 4.5	1005 0.4	1556 4.6	2210 0.6
11 SU	0415 4.5	1046 0.3	1631 4.6	2248 0.7
12 M	0451 4.4	1119 0.2	1709 4.5	2326 0.7
13 TU	0528 4.3	1206 0.4	1750 4.5	
14 W	0005 0.8	0615 4.2	1246 0.4	1846 4.3
15 TH ◐	0055 0.8	0710 4.1	1335 0.5	1945 4.2
16 F	0155 0.9	0816 4.1	1436 0.6	2052 4.1
17 SA	0300 1.0	0926 4.0	1539 0.6	2205 4.1
18 SU	0416 0.9	1036 4.1	1700 0.6	2316 4.1
19 M	0530 0.8	1138 4.3	1810 0.6	
20 TU	0015 4.3	0635 0.6	1237 4.5	1906 0.5
21 W ●	0112 4.4	0735 0.4	1335 4.7	1958 0.4
22 TH	0201 4.6	0828 0.2	1420 4.8	2046 0.4
23 F	0247 4.7	0915 0.1	1507 4.9	2130 0.5
24 SA	0332 4.7	1005 0.0	1556 4.9	2209 0.5
25 SU	0416 4.7	1045 0.0	1637 4.8	2249 0.6
26 M	0455 4.7	1125 0.1	1720 4.6	2330 0.7
27 TU	0542 4.5	1206 0.2	1808 4.4	
28 W	0010 0.8	0626 4.4	1246 0.4	1851 4.2
29 TH	0051 0.9	0710 4.2	1336 0.6	1946 3.9
30 F	0156 1.0	0805 3.9	1426 0.8	2034 3.7
31 SA	0306 1.1	0904 3.7	1525 1.0	2207 3.5

FEBRUARY

Day	Time m	Time m	Time m	Time m
1 SU	0410 1.2	1036 3.6	1645 1.0	2316 3.6
2 M	0520 1.1	1134 3.7	1755 1.0	
3 TU	0015 3.7	0619 0.9	1235 3.9	1846 0.9
4 W	0102 4.0	0716 0.8	1319 4.1	1925 0.8
5 TH	0145 4.1	0756 0.6	1355 4.3	2002 0.7
6 F	0216 4.3	0836 0.5	1428 4.5	2035 0.6
7 SA	0249 4.5	0910 0.3	1506 4.7	2116 0.5
8 SU	0321 4.6	0951 0.2	1537 4.8	2151 0.5
9 M	0357 4.6	1025 0.1	1612 4.8	2232 0.5
10 TU	0433 4.6	1105 0.1	1649 4.7	2310 0.5
11 W	0509 4.6	1145 0.1	1731 4.6	2351 0.6
12 TH	0542 4.5	1225 0.2	1815 4.5	
13 F	0036 0.6	0636 4.4	1310 0.4	1911 4.2
14 SA	0126 0.7	0738 4.2	1406 0.5	2015 4.0
15 SU	0230 0.9	0849 4.0	1516 0.7	2136 3.8
16 M	0344 0.9	1009 3.9	1640 0.8	2256 3.8
17 TU	0526 0.8	1130 4.1	1800 0.7	
18 W	0008 4.0	0636 0.5	1235 4.4	1901 0.6
19 TH	0102 4.3	0729 0.3	1329 4.6	1950 0.5
20 F ●	0150 4.5	0819 0.1	1415 4.8	2031 0.5
21 SA	0236 4.6	0906 0.0	1456 4.9	2111 0.5
22 SU	0316 4.7	0947 -0.1	1536 4.9	2149 0.5
23 M	0350 4.8	1026 0.0	1616 4.8	2226 0.5
24 TU	0429 4.7	1100 0.1	1650 4.6	2259 0.5
25 W	0506 4.6	1136 0.2	1730 4.5	2336 0.6
26 TH	0546 4.5	1159 0.4	1805 4.2	
27 F	0006 0.7	0621 4.3	1236 0.6	1848 4.0
28 SA ◐	0046 0.8	0705 4.0	1315 0.8	1929 3.7
29 SU	0135 1.0	0805 3.7	1414 1.1	2036 3.4

MARCH

Day	Time m	Time m	Time m	Time m
1 M	0325 1.2	0925 3.4	1606 1.2	2214 3.3
2 TU	0446 1.1	1105 3.5	1720 1.1	2346 3.5
3 W	0556 1.0	1209 3.8	1815 0.9	
4 TH	0036 3.8	0644 0.8	1255 4.1	1905 0.8
5 F	0118 4.1	0732 0.5	1335 4.4	1942 0.6
6 SA ●	0148 4.3	0810 0.3	1410 4.6	2021 0.5
7 SU	0226 4.5	0848 0.2	1441 4.8	2056 0.4
8 M	0257 4.7	0925 0.0	1513 4.9	2136 0.3
9 TU	0331 4.8	1003 0.0	1549 4.9	2212 0.3
10 W	0406 4.8	1042 0.0	1626 4.9	2252 0.3
11 TH	0446 4.8	1122 0.0	1706 4.7	2330 0.4
12 F	0527 4.7	1206 0.2	1756 4.5	
13 SA ◐	0016 0.4	0612 4.5	1234 0.4	1845 4.2
14 SU	0105 0.6	0709 4.2	1346 0.6	1952 3.8
15 M	0209 0.7	0836 3.9	1455 0.9	2116 3.6
16 TU	0347 0.8	0959 3.8	1630 0.9	2245 3.6
17 W	0516 0.7	1130 4.0	1756 0.8	2359 3.9
18 TH	0625 0.4	1228 4.4	1856 0.6	
19 F	0055 4.2	0726 0.2	1318 4.6	1935 0.5
20 SA ●	0136 4.4	0805 0.0	1401 4.8	2016 0.5
21 SU	0217 4.6	0847 0.0	1435 4.8	2051 0.4
22 M	0250 4.7	0921 0.0	1510 4.8	2126 0.4
23 TU	0325 4.7	0958 0.1	1547 4.7	2202 0.4
24 W	0359 4.7	1025 0.2	1621 4.6	2236 0.4
25 TH	0432 4.7	1101 0.3	1655 4.4	2302 0.5
26 F	0508 4.5	1127 0.5	1726 4.3	2324 0.5
27 SA	0542 4.3	1150 0.6	1759 4.1	
28 SU ◐	0006 0.6	0619 4.1	1225 0.8	1834 3.8
29 M	0046 0.8	0710 3.7	1313 1.0	1940 3.5
30 TU	0200 1.1	0836 3.4	1514 1.2	2104 3.3
31 W	0406 1.1	1026 3.4	1646 1.1	2300 3.4

APRIL

Day	Time m	Time m	Time m	Time m
1 TH	0526 0.9	1138 3.8	1746 0.9	
2 F	0000 3.8	0616 0.7	1228 4.2	1836 0.7
3 SA	0046 4.1	0706 0.4	1306 4.5	1911 0.6
4 SU	0117 4.4	0740 0.2	1338 4.7	1950 0.4
5 M ○	0150 4.6	0815 0.1	1411 4.9	2031 0.3
6 TU	0226 4.8	0856 0.0	1445 5.0	2108 0.2
7 W	0303 4.9	0936 -0.1	1525 5.0	2151 0.2
8 TH	0343 4.9	1017 -0.1	1606 4.9	2230 0.2
9 F	0423 4.9	1058 0.0	1647 4.7	2316 0.2
10 SA	0506 4.8	1139 0.2	1735 4.4	
11 SU	0000 0.4	0556 4.5	1231 0.4	1825 4.1
12 M ◐	0056 0.4	0655 4.2	1330 0.7	1934 3.8
13 TU	0205 0.6	0828 3.9	1456 0.9	2105 3.6
14 W	0346 0.7	1006 3.9	1630 1.0	2235 3.6
15 TH	0510 0.5	1120 4.1	1746 0.8	2346 3.9
16 F	0615 0.3	1220 4.4	1835 0.6	
17 SA	0035 4.2	0706 0.1	1305 4.6	1920 0.5
18 SU	0116 4.4	0745 0.0	1338 4.7	1955 0.5
19 M ●	0151 4.5	0819 0.1	1415 4.7	2030 0.4
20 TU	0226 4.6	0856 0.1	1449 4.6	2106 0.4
21 W	0259 4.7	0926 0.2	1521 4.6	2141 0.3
22 TH	0332 4.7	1000 0.3	1552 4.5	2210 0.4
23 F	0406 4.6	1031 0.4	1626 4.4	2240 0.4
24 SA	0437 4.5	1056 0.5	1656 4.3	2310 0.5
25 SU	0511 4.3	1126 0.7	1728 4.1	2335 0.6
26 M	0550 4.1	1201 0.8	1811 3.9	
27 TU ◐	0019 0.7	0636 3.8	1243 1.0	1911 3.6
28 W	0115 0.9	0755 3.6	1415 1.2	2036 3.4
29 TH	0326 0.9	0923 3.6	1555 1.1	2154 3.5
30 F	0424 0.8	1045 3.8	1706 0.9	2312 3.8

Chapter 5

Chart Datum: 2·32 metres below NAP Datum

TIDES

NETHERLANDS – VLISSINGEN YEAR 2004

TIME ZONE -0100
(Dutch Standard Time)
Subtract 1 hour for UT
For Dutch Summer Time add
ONE hour in **non-shaded areas**

LAT 51°27′N   LONG 3°36′E

TIMES AND HEIGHTS OF HIGH AND LOW WATERS

MAY

Day	Time m	Time m	Time m	Time m
1 SA	0524 0.6	1141 4.2	1756 0.7	
2 SU	0002 4.1	0620 0.4	1226 4.5	1841 0.5
3 M	0042 4.4	0706 0.2	1306 4.7	1920 0.4
4 TU	0116 4.6	0749 0.1	1341 4.9	○ 2002 0.3
5 W	0158 4.8	0828 0.0	1420 5.0	2046 0.2
6 TH	0235 4.9	0910 0.0	1501 4.9	2131 0.1
7 F	0321 5.0	0953 0.0	1545 4.8	2216 0.1
8 SA	0405 4.9	1038 0.2	1630 4.6	2302 0.1
9 SU	0453 4.8	1125 0.3	1709 4.4	2352 0.2
10 M	0547 4.5	1211 0.5	1822 4.1	
11 TU	0056 0.3	0655 4.2	1316 0.8	◑ 1935 3.9
12 W	0206 0.4	0820 4.1	1434 0.9	2056 3.7
13 TH	0314 0.4	0939 4.2	1610 0.9	2209 3.8
14 F	0451 0.4	1056 4.2	1714 0.8	2316 4.0
15 SA	0550 0.2	1149 4.4	1816 0.7	
16 SU	0008 4.2	0635 0.2	1235 4.5	1852 0.6
17 M	0049 4.3	0718 0.2	1315 4.5	1930 0.5
18 TU	0125 4.4	0752 0.2	1351 4.5	2001 0.4
19 W	0206 4.5	0825 0.3	1426 4.5	● 2046 0.4
20 TH	0238 4.5	0901 0.4	1457 4.5	2118 0.3
21 F	0309 4.5	0932 0.4	1532 4.4	2156 0.4
22 SA	0345 4.5	1006 0.5	1601 4.3	2225 0.4
23 SU	0417 4.4	1035 0.6	1636 4.2	2255 0.5
24 M	0451 4.3	1106 0.7	1709 4.1	2330 0.5
25 TU	0529 4.1	1139 0.8	1755 4.0	
26 W	0004 0.6	0616 4.0	1230 0.9	1845 3.8
27 TH	0104 0.7	0726 3.8	1335 1.0	◑ 1955 3.7
28 F	0230 0.7	0846 3.8	1505 1.0	2110 3.7
29 SA	0336 0.6	0956 4.0	1615 0.9	2220 3.8
30 SU	0446 0.5	1056 4.2	1716 0.8	2317 4.1
31 M	0535 0.3	1146 4.5	1806 0.6	

JUNE

Day	Time m	Time m	Time m	Time m
1 TU	0002 4.4	0631 0.2	1229 4.7	1848 0.4
2 W	0050 4.6	0715 0.1	1316 4.8	1938 0.3
3 TH	0133 4.8	0806 0.1	1359 4.8	○ 2026 0.2
4 F	0218 4.9	0850 0.1	1445 4.8	2116 0.1
5 SA	0305 4.9	0937 0.2	1532 4.7	2202 0.1
6 SU	0352 4.9	1022 0.3	1620 4.6	2252 0.0
7 M	0445 4.7	1110 0.5	1716 4.4	2345 0.1
8 TU	0541 4.6	1159 0.6	1811 4.2	
9 W	0042 0.1	0644 4.4	1254 0.8	◑ 1916 4.1
10 TH	0146 0.2	0755 4.2	1410 0.9	2026 4.0
11 F	0256 0.3	0906 4.1	1535 0.9	2132 3.9
12 SA	0415 0.4	1016 4.1	1634 0.9	2235 4.0
13 SU	0516 0.4	1116 4.2	1746 0.8	2331 4.1
14 M	0607 0.4	1205 4.2	1826 0.7	
15 TU	0022 4.2	0645 0.4	1249 4.3	1902 0.6
16 W	0106 4.3	0722 0.5	1329 4.3	1945 0.5
17 TH	0146 4.3	0755 0.5	1408 4.3	● 2020 0.5
18 F	0219 4.4	0836 0.5	1438 4.3	2055 0.4
19 SA	0255 4.4	0910 0.6	1512 4.4	2136 0.4
20 SU	0329 4.4	0945 0.6	1546 4.3	2215 0.4
21 M	0405 4.4	1020 0.7	1621 4.3	2256 0.4
22 TU	0435 4.3	1056 0.8	1656 4.2	2326 0.5
23 W	0515 4.3	1130 0.8	1736 4.1	
24 TH	0006 0.5	0555 4.2	1209 0.9	1825 4.0
25 F	0050 0.5	0649 4.1	1305 0.9	◑ 1920 3.9
26 SA	0145 0.5	0758 4.1	1359 0.9	2025 3.9
27 SU	0246 0.5	0906 4.1	1510 0.9	2136 4.0
28 M	0350 0.5	1006 4.2	1620 0.8	2235 4.1
29 TU	0456 0.4	1111 4.4	1726 0.7	2333 4.3
30 W	0601 0.4	1202 4.5	1827 0.5	

JULY

Day	Time m	Time m	Time m	Time m
1 TH	0027 4.5	0656 0.3	1257 4.6	1920 0.4
2 F	0117 4.7	0746 0.3	1345 4.6	○ 2012 0.2
3 SA	0206 4.8	0835 0.3	1436 4.7	2103 0.1
4 SU	0257 4.9	0922 0.4	1522 4.7	2152 0.0
5 M	0346 4.9	1008 0.5	1612 4.6	2246 0.0
6 TU	0435 4.8	1056 0.6	1658 4.6	2336 0.0
7 W	0529 4.7	1146 0.7	1751 4.5	
8 TH	0019 0.1	0626 4.5	1236 0.8	1841 4.3
9 F	0115 0.2	0719 4.3	1325 0.9	◑ 1939 4.2
10 SA	0205 0.4	0819 4.1	1423 0.9	2046 4.0
11 SU	0304 0.5	0925 4.0	1535 1.0	2150 3.9
12 M	0420 0.7	1035 3.9	1645 0.9	2255 3.9
13 TU	0526 0.7	1132 4.0	1756 0.8	2355 4.0
14 W	0609 0.7	1226 4.0	1835 0.8	
15 TH	0046 4.1	0655 0.7	1311 4.1	1926 0.7
16 F	0129 4.2	0735 0.7	1355 4.2	2005 0.6
17 SA	0210 4.3	0816 0.7	1425 4.3	● 2042 0.5
18 SU	0246 4.4	0850 0.7	1459 4.4	2119 0.4
19 M	0317 4.5	0925 0.7	1531 4.4	2155 0.4
20 TU	0349 4.5	1005 0.7	1608 4.4	2236 0.3
21 W	0421 4.5	1036 0.7	1642 4.4	2304 0.3
22 TH	0455 4.5	1116 0.7	1716 4.3	2345 0.3
23 F	0536 4.4	1150 0.8	1755 4.3	
24 SA	0026 0.4	0619 4.4	1229 0.8	1839 4.2
25 SU	0110 0.4	0716 4.3	1326 0.8	◑ 1941 4.1
26 M	0206 0.5	0821 4.2	1426 0.9	2048 4.1
27 TU	0316 0.6	0928 4.1	1540 0.9	2200 4.1
28 W	0425 0.6	1035 4.1	1656 0.8	2308 4.2
29 TH	0538 0.6	1145 4.2	1811 0.6	
30 F	0011 4.4	0640 0.5	1246 4.4	1909 0.4
31 SA	0109 4.6	0731 0.5	1337 4.5	○ 2006 0.2

AUGUST

Day	Time m	Time m	Time m	Time m
1 SU	0159 4.8	0821 0.4	1425 4.7	2055 0.0
2 M	0247 4.9	0908 0.5	1511 4.7	2146 0.0
3 TU	0332 4.9	0956 0.5	1553 4.8	2228 0.0
4 W	0417 4.9	1036 0.6	1635 4.7	2309 0.0
5 TH	0500 4.8	1115 0.7	1721 4.7	2352 0.1
6 F	0547 4.6	1156 0.7	1806 4.5	
7 SA	0036 0.3	0636 4.3	1234 0.8	◑ 1856 4.3
8 SU	0116 0.5	0726 4.1	1329 0.9	1946 4.1
9 M	0205 0.7	0819 3.8	1440 1.0	2050 3.8
10 TU	0316 0.9	0933 3.6	1544 1.1	2216 3.7
11 W	0436 1.0	1100 3.6	1710 1.0	2330 3.8
12 TH	0535 1.0	1206 3.8	1816 0.9	
13 F	0025 3.9	0630 0.9	1256 4.0	1905 0.8
14 SA	0116 4.1	0716 0.8	1335 4.2	1950 0.6
15 SU	0156 4.3	0756 0.8	1410 4.3	2025 0.5
16 M	0225 4.5	0830 0.7	1439 4.5	● 2100 0.4
17 TU	0258 4.6	0906 0.6	1508 4.6	2137 0.3
18 W	0325 4.7	0940 0.6	1540 4.6	2212 0.2
19 TH	0357 4.7	1016 0.6	1616 4.6	2245 0.2
20 F	0433 4.7	1056 0.6	1647 4.6	2326 0.2
21 SA	0507 4.7	1126 0.7	1726 4.5	
22 SU	0002 0.3	0549 4.5	1206 0.7	1807 4.4
23 M	0042 0.4	0640 4.4	1256 0.8	◑ 1859 4.3
24 TU	0136 0.6	0740 4.1	1356 0.9	2010 4.1
25 W	0235 0.8	0855 3.9	1516 0.9	2136 4.0
26 TH	0354 0.9	1015 3.8	1645 0.9	2258 4.1
27 F	0526 0.8	1136 4.0	1806 0.6	
28 SA	0005 4.4	0636 0.7	1238 4.3	1905 0.4
29 SU	0105 4.7	0726 0.6	1326 4.5	1956 0.1
30 M	0151 4.9	0809 0.5	1411 4.7	○ 2041 0.0
31 TU	0232 5.0	0856 0.5	1450 4.8	2125 0.0

Chart Datum: 2·32 metres below NAP Datum

TIME ZONE -0100
(Dutch Standard Time)
Subtract 1 hour for UT
For Dutch Summer Time add
ONE hour in **non-shaded areas**

NETHERLANDS – VLISSINGEN

YEAR 2004

LAT 51°27'N   LONG 3°36'E

TIMES AND HEIGHTS OF HIGH AND LOW WATERS

SEPTEMBER

Day	Time	m	Time	m	Time	m	Time	m
1 W	0316	5.0	0932	0.6	1547	4.8	2205	0.0
2 TH	0356	4.9	1008	0.6	1609	4.9	2242	0.1
3 F	0436	4.8	1046	0.6	1647	4.8	2316	0.3
4 SA	0512	4.6	1120	0.7	1725	4.6	2350	0.5
5 SU	0548	4.4	1201	0.8	1805	4.4		
6 M ◑	0025	0.7	0636	4.1	1246	0.9	1849	4.1
7 TU	0105	0.9	0720	3.8	1324	1.1	1956	3.8
8 W	0221	1.2	0820	3.5	1504	1.2	2115	3.5
9 TH	0356	1.3	1015	3.4	1636	1.2	2300	3.6
10 F	0516	1.2	1125	3.9	1746	1.0		
11 SA	0006	3.9	0606	1.1	1231	3.9	1840	0.8
12 SU	0050	4.2	0656	0.9	1308	4.2	1925	0.6
13 M	0128	4.4	0735	0.8	1339	4.4	1955	0.5
14 TU ●	0156	4.6	0806	0.7	1409	4.6	2036	0.3
15 W	0228	4.8	0835	0.6	1442	4.7	2105	0.2
16 TH	0257	4.9	0915	0.5	1516	4.8	2146	0.2
17 F	0331	4.9	0952	0.5	1546	4.8	2220	0.2
18 SA	0405	4.9	1031	0.5	1623	4.8	2301	0.2
19 SU	0446	4.8	1109	0.5	1701	4.8	2335	0.3
20 M	0525	4.6	1146	0.6	1742	4.6		
21 TU ◐	0015	0.5	0616	4.3	1235	0.7	1835	4.4
22 W	0116	0.7	0715	4.0	1340	0.9	1950	4.0
23 TH	0214	1.0	0835	3.7	1506	1.0	2126	3.9
24 F	0350	1.1	1005	3.7	1646	0.9	2255	4.1
25 SA	0514	1.0	1125	3.9	1806	0.6		
26 SU	0005	4.4	0626	0.8	1228	4.3	1856	0.3
27 M	0055	4.7	0717	0.5	1311	4.5	1942	0.1
28 TU ○	0135	4.9	0756	0.6	1351	4.7	2026	0.0
29 W	0215	4.9	0835	0.6	1427	4.8	2101	0.1
30 TH	0251	4.9	0910	0.5	1505	4.9	2138	0.2

OCTOBER

Day	Time	m	Time	m	Time	m	Time	m
1 F	0327	4.8	0946	0.6	1541	4.9	2216	0.3
2 SA	0403	4.7	1020	0.6	1617	4.8	2246	0.5
3 SU	0439	4.6	1049	0.6	1653	4.7	2316	0.6
4 M	0511	4.4	1126	0.7	1727	4.4	2340	0.8
5 TU	0550	4.1	1155	0.9	1811	4.1		
6 W ◑	0016	1.0	0630	3.9	1229	1.0	1855	3.8
7 TH	0105	1.3	0726	3.6	1425	1.2	2026	3.5
8 F	0316	1.4	0856	3.3	1556	1.2	2216	3.5
9 SA	0436	1.3	1057	3.5	1654	1.1	2328	3.8
10 SU	0529	1.1	1145	3.8	1806	0.8		
11 M	0016	4.2	0626	0.9	1230	4.1	1845	0.6
12 TU	0049	4.5	0700	0.8	1302	4.4	1926	0.4
13 W	0126	4.7	0732	0.6	1335	4.6	1958	0.3
14 TH ●	0156	4.9	0808	0.5	1408	4.8	2035	0.2
15 F	0226	5.0	0846	0.5	1443	4.9	2116	0.1
16 SA	0305	5.1	0925	0.4	1519	5.0	2156	0.2
17 SU	0343	5.0	1006	0.4	1558	5.0	2232	0.2
18 M	0423	4.8	1051	0.4	1639	4.9	2315	0.4
19 TU	0505	4.6	1136	0.5	1725	4.7		
20 W ◐	0000	0.6	0555	4.3	1226	0.6	1821	4.4
21 TH	0056	0.9	0659	3.9	1329	0.8	1946	4.0
22 F	0210	1.1	0828	3.7	1506	0.8	2116	3.9
23 SA	0335	1.2	0956	3.7	1625	0.7	2245	4.1
24 SU	0516	1.1	1115	4.0	1746	0.5	2344	4.4
25 M	0609	0.9	1206	4.3	1840	0.3		
26 TU	0036	4.6	0656	0.7	1248	4.5	1922	0.2
27 W	0116	4.8	0736	0.6	1329	4.7	1959	0.2
28 TH ○	0152	4.8	0810	0.6	1405	4.8	2035	0.4
29 F	0227	4.8	0847	0.5	1439	4.8	2109	0.3
30 SA	0306	4.7	0922	0.5	1516	4.8	2146	0.4
31 SU	0337	4.6	0958	0.5	1549	4.7	2217	0.6

NOVEMBER

Day	Time	m	Time	m	Time	m	Time	m
1 M	0411	4.5	1035	0.6	1627	4.6	2246	0.7
2 TU	0446	4.3	1100	0.7	1659	4.4	2310	0.9
3 W	0516	4.2	1124	0.8	1738	4.2	2339	1.0
4 TH	0558	4.0	1210	0.9	1825	3.9		
5 F ◑	0036	1.2	0650	3.7	1304	1.1	1936	3.6
6 SA	0150	1.4	0805	3.5	1506	1.1	2054	3.6
7 SU	0340	1.3	0936	3.5	1617	1.0	2230	3.8
8 M	0446	1.2	1049	3.8	1716	0.8	2326	4.1
9 TU	0536	1.0	1142	4.1	1759	0.6		
10 W	0010	4.5	0615	0.8	1221	4.4	1842	0.4
11 TH	0045	4.7	0658	0.6	1259	4.7	1922	0.3
12 F ●	0122	4.9	0738	0.5	1336	4.9	2005	0.2
13 SA	0159	5.0	0820	0.4	1416	5.0	2047	0.2
14 SU	0240	5.0	0906	0.3	1458	5.1	2128	0.2
15 M	0322	4.9	0946	0.3	1541	5.0	2212	0.3
16 TU	0406	4.8	1036	0.3	1625	4.9	2259	0.5
17 W	0453	4.5	1116	0.4	1716	4.7	2345	0.7
18 TH	0549	4.3	1220	0.5	1815	4.4		
19 F ◐	0046	0.9	0655	4.0	1325	0.6	1935	4.2
20 SA	0156	1.1	0804	3.9	1446	0.6	2100	4.1
21 SU	0314	1.2	0925	3.8	1610	0.6	2215	4.2
22 M	0450	1.1	1039	4.0	1726	0.5	2319	4.3
23 TU	0545	0.9	1138	4.2	1816	0.4		
24 W	0009	4.5	0636	0.8	1226	4.4	1858	0.3
25 TH	0056	4.6	0710	0.7	1306	4.5	1935	0.4
26 F ○	0135	4.6	0745	0.6	1346	4.6	2010	0.4
27 SA	0208	4.6	0826	0.5	1421	4.7	2045	0.5
28 SU	0246	4.6	0902	0.5	1455	4.7	2118	0.6
29 M	0317	4.5	0940	0.5	1536	4.6	2150	0.7
30 TU	0356	4.4	1016	0.6	1605	4.6	2226	0.8

DECEMBER

Day	Time	m	Time	m	Time	m	Time	m
1 W	0425	4.3	1056	0.6	1646	4.4	2250	0.9
2 TH	0500	4.2	1115	0.7	1715	4.2	2326	1.0
3 F	0535	4.1	1156	0.8	1759	4.1		
4 SA ◑	0006	1.1	0626	3.9	1246	0.8	1856	3.9
5 SU	0100	1.2	0726	3.8	1344	0.9	2010	3.8
6 M	0214	1.3	0835	3.7	1505	0.9	2120	3.9
7 TU	0346	1.2	0951	3.8	1605	0.8	2226	4.1
8 W	0433	1.0	1050	4.1	1705	0.6	2322	4.4
9 TH	0536	0.9	1139	4.3	1806	0.5		
10 F	0010	4.6	0626	0.7	1227	4.6	1856	0.4
11 SA	0056	4.7	0716	0.5	1313	4.8	1938	0.3
12 SU ●	0136	4.8	0800	0.4	1355	4.9	2025	0.3
13 M	0223	4.8	0851	0.3	1441	5.0	2110	0.3
14 TU	0306	4.8	0938	0.2	1528	5.0	2157	0.4
15 W	0356	4.7	1025	0.2	1617	4.9	2242	0.5
16 TH	0445	4.6	1116	0.2	1711	4.8	2332	0.7
17 F	0538	4.4	1209	0.2	1812	4.6		
18 SA ◐	0026	0.8	0639	4.3	1310	0.3	1918	4.4
19 SU	0126	1.0	0746	4.1	1405	0.4	2026	4.2
20 M	0235	1.1	0850	4.0	1525	0.6	2136	4.1
21 TU	0345	1.1	1000	4.0	1647	0.6	2242	4.1
22 W	0505	1.0	1105	4.1	1740	0.6	2340	4.2
23 TH	0600	0.9	1155	4.2	1828	0.6		
24 F	0025	4.2	0645	0.8	1245	4.3	1906	0.6
25 SA	0110	4.3	0726	0.7	1329	4.4	1946	0.6
26 SU ○	0155	4.4	0806	0.6	1409	4.5	2022	0.6
27 M	0228	4.4	0845	0.5	1445	4.5	2055	0.7
28 TU	0305	4.4	0926	0.5	1519	4.5	2132	0.7
29 W	0340	4.4	1006	0.5	1556	4.5	2205	0.7
30 TH	0408	4.4	1041	0.5	1626	4.4	2235	0.8
31 F	0446	4.3	1110	0.5	1702	4.4	2316	0.9

Chapter 5

Chart Datum: 2·32 metres below NAP Datum

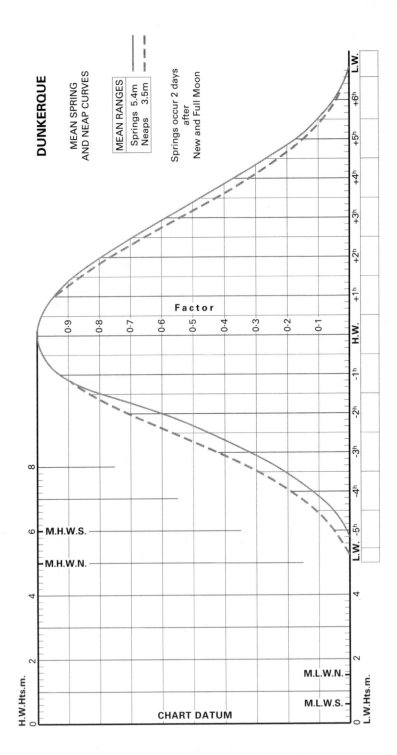

DUNKERQUE

MEAN SPRING
AND NEAP CURVES

MEAN RANGES
Springs 5.4m
Neaps 3.5m

Springs occur 2 days
after
New and Full Moon

Factor

0·9 0·8 0·7 0·6 0·5 0·4 0·3 0·2 0·1

H.W.

M.H.W.S.

M.H.W.N.

H.W.Hts.m.

L.W.

M.L.W.N.

M.L.W.S.

L.W.Hts.m.

CHART DATUM

Register for your **FREE** weekly weather email service from Reeds Almanacs
at www.nauticaldata.com – **NOW!**
weekend weather reports sent to your email address, every Thursday

370

TIME ZONE -0100
(French Standard Time)
Subtract 1 hour for UT
For French Summer Time add
ONE hour in **non-shaded areas**

FRANCE – DUNKERQUE

LAT 51°03′N   LONG 2°22′E

TIMES AND HEIGHTS OF HIGH AND LOW WATERS

YEAR 2004

JANUARY

Day	Time	m	Day	Time	m
1 TH	0207 / 1441 / 2034	1.7 / 1.5 / 4.9	**16** F	0101 / 0640 / 1340 / 1922	1.5 / 5.2 / 1.2 / 5.2
2 F	0309 / 0852 / 1543 / 2132	1.8 / 4.9 / 1.5 / 4.9	**17** SA	0212 / 0748 / 1455 / 2035	1.6 / 5.2 / 1.2 / 5.1
3 SA	0411 / 0950 / 1644 / 2226	1.7 / 5.0 / 1.5 / 5.0	**18** SU	0330 / 0902 / 1608 / 2153	1.5 / 5.2 / 1.2 / 5.2
4 SU	0509 / 1043 / 1738 / 2314	1.5 / 5.1 / 1.4 / 5.2	**19** M	0445 / 1017 / 1719 / 2301	1.4 / 5.4 / 1.1 / 5.4
5 M	0559 / 1130 / 1823 / 2357	1.4 / 5.3 / 1.3 / 5.3	**20** TU	0554 / 1121 / 1823 / 2359	1.1 / 5.7 / 0.9 / 5.6
6 TU	0641 / 1212 / 1900	1.2 / 5.4 / 1.2	**21** W	0653 / 1217 / 1917	0.8 / 5.9 / 0.8
7 W	0031 / 0719 / 1248 / 1936	5.5 / 1.1 / 5.6 / 1.1	**22** TH	0044 / 0744 / 1308 / 2005	5.8 / 0.6 / 6.1 / 0.7
8 TH	0104 / 0756 / 1321 / 2012	5.6 / 1.0 / 5.7 / 1.1	**23** F	0131 / 0831 / 1356 / 2050	5.9 / 0.5 / 6.1 / 0.7
9 F	0138 / 0833 / 1356 / 2048	5.7 / 0.9 / 5.7 / 1.0	**24** SA	0215 / 0915 / 1442 / 2132	5.9 / 0.4 / 6.1 / 0.8
10 SA	0214 / 0911 / 1433 / 2125	5.7 / 0.8 / 5.8 / 1.0	**25** SU	0257 / 0958 / 1526 / 2212	5.9 / 0.5 / 5.9 / 0.9
11 SU	0250 / 0948 / 1511 / 2202	5.7 / 0.8 / 5.7 / 1.1	**26** M	0336 / 1039 / 1607 / 2251	5.8 / 0.6 / 5.7 / 1.0
12 M	0326 / 1025 / 1550 / 2239	5.6 / 0.9 / 5.6 / 1.2	**27** TU	0415 / 1117 / 1646 / 2328	5.7 / 0.8 / 5.5 / 1.2
13 TU	0402 / 1104 / 1630 / 2319	5.5 / 0.9 / 5.5 / 1.2	**28** W	0455 / 1156 / 1727	5.5 / 1.0 / 5.3
14 W	0445 / 1147 / 1718	5.4 / 1.0 / 5.4	**29** TH	0010 / 0539 / 1239 / 1815	1.4 / 5.2 / 1.3 / 5.0
15 TH	0004 / 0538 / 1237 / 1816	1.3 / 5.3 / 1.1 / 5.3	**30** F	0058 / 0632 / 1333 / 1917	1.6 / 5.0 / 1.5 / 4.7
			31 SA	0201 / 0742 / 1438 / 2033	1.8 / 4.7 / 1.7 / 4.6

FEBRUARY

Day	Time	m	Day	Time	m
1 SU	0311 / 0901 / 1549 / 2145	1.9 / 4.6 / 1.8 / 4.6	**16** M	0303 / 0849 / 1550 / 2146	1.6 / 5.0 / 1.4 / 4.9
2 M	0425 / 1011 / 1703 / 2247	1.8 / 4.8 / 1.7 / 4.8	**17** TU	0433 / 1018 / 1714 / 2259	1.5 / 5.2 / 1.2 / 5.2
3 TU	0534 / 1109 / 1803 / 2338	1.6 / 5.0 / 1.5 / 5.1	**18** W	0551 / 1124 / 1819 / 2355	1.1 / 5.5 / 1.0 / 5.5
4 W	0624 / 1156 / 1846	1.3 / 5.3 / 1.3	**19** TH	0647 / 1217 / 1909	0.8 / 5.8 / 0.8
5 TH	0016 / 0704 / 1234 / 1922	5.3 / 1.1 / 5.5 / 1.1	**20** F	0037 / 0735 / 1302 / 1952	5.7 / 0.5 / 6.0 / 0.7
6 F	0050 / 0741 / 1308 / 1957	5.5 / 0.9 / 5.7 / 1.0	**21** SA	0118 / 0817 / 1344 / 2032	5.9 / 0.4 / 6.1 / 0.6
7 SA	0123 / 0818 / 1342 / 2033	5.7 / 0.7 / 5.8 / 0.8	**22** SU	0156 / 0857 / 1422 / 2110	6.0 / 0.3 / 6.0 / 0.7
8 SU	0157 / 0855 / 1417 / 2109	5.8 / 0.6 / 5.9 / 0.8	**23** M	0232 / 0935 / 1459 / 2145	6.0 / 0.4 / 6.0 / 0.7
9 M	0230 / 0932 / 1451 / 2145	5.8 / 0.5 / 5.9 / 0.8	**24** TU	0307 / 1009 / 1533 / 2218	5.9 / 0.5 / 5.8 / 0.8
10 TU	0303 / 1008 / 1526 / 2220	5.8 / 0.5 / 5.8 / 0.8	**25** W	0340 / 1041 / 1605 / 2250	5.8 / 0.7 / 5.6 / 1.0
11 W	0338 / 1045 / 1602 / 2256	5.8 / 0.6 / 5.7 / 0.9	**26** TH	0414 / 1112 / 1639 / 2323	5.6 / 0.9 / 5.4 / 1.2
12 TH	0418 / 1123 / 1646 / 2336	5.7 / 0.7 / 5.6 / 1.1	**27** F	0452 / 1146 / 1717	5.4 / 1.2 / 5.1
13 F	0506 / 1207 / 1741	5.6 / 0.9 / 5.3	**28** SA	0002 / 0537 / 1229 / 1808	1.5 / 5.0 / 1.5 / 4.7
14 SA	0027 / 0607 / 1305 / 1848	1.3 / 5.4 / 1.2 / 5.1	**29** SU	0053 / 0638 / 1332 / 1922	1.8 / 4.7 / 1.9 / 4.4
15 SU	0135 / 0720 / 1425 / 2010	1.5 / 5.1 / 1.4 / 4.9			

MARCH

Day	Time	m	Day	Time	m
1 M	0208 / 0805 / 1455 / 2057	2.0 / 4.4 / 2.0 / 4.3	**16** TU	0254 / 0851 / 1546 / 2142	1.6 / 4.9 / 1.5 / 4.8
2 TU	0336 / 0936 / 1625 / 2217	2.0 / 4.5 / 1.9 / 4.5	**17** W	0431 / 1017 / 1710 / 2251	1.4 / 5.2 / 1.3 / 5.1
3 W	0503 / 1045 / 1737 / 2314	1.7 / 4.8 / 1.6 / 4.9	**18** TH	0542 / 1118 / 1808 / 2344	1.0 / 5.5 / 1.0 / 5.4
4 TH	0600 / 1135 / 1824 / 2356	1.3 / 5.2 / 1.2 / 5.3	**19** F	0634 / 1207 / 1852	0.7 / 5.8 / 0.8
5 F	0642 / 1214 / 1900	1.0 / 5.5 / 1.0	**20** SA	0020 / 0717 / 1246 / 1931	5.7 / 0.5 / 5.9 / 0.7
6 SA	0029 / 0719 / 1247 / 1935	5.5 / 0.7 / 5.7 / 0.8	**21** SU	0056 / 0756 / 1321 / 2007	5.8 / 0.4 / 6.0 / 0.7
7 SU	0101 / 0756 / 1320 / 2010	5.8 / 0.5 / 5.9 / 0.7	**22** M	0130 / 0832 / 1355 / 2042	5.9 / 0.4 / 6.0 / 0.6
8 M	0132 / 0833 / 1353 / 2046	5.9 / 0.4 / 6.0 / 0.6	**23** TU	0204 / 0905 / 1428 / 2114	6.0 / 0.4 / 5.9 / 0.7
9 TU	0204 / 0910 / 1426 / 2122	6.0 / 0.3 / 6.0 / 0.6	**24** W	0236 / 0936 / 1459 / 2146	5.9 / 0.5 / 5.8 / 0.7
10 W	0238 / 0946 / 1500 / 2158	6.0 / 0.3 / 6.0 / 0.6	**25** TH	0307 / 1006 / 1527 / 2216	5.8 / 0.7 / 5.7 / 0.9
11 TH	0314 / 1023 / 1537 / 2234	6.0 / 0.4 / 5.9 / 0.7	**26** F	0339 / 1034 / 1558 / 2247	5.7 / 0.9 / 5.4 / 1.1
12 F	0355 / 1101 / 1622 / 2314	5.9 / 0.4 / 5.6 / 0.9	**27** SA	0413 / 1104 / 1633 / 2321	5.4 / 1.2 / 5.1 / 1.3
13 SA	0445 / 1145 / 1718	5.7 / 0.9 / 5.3	**28** SU	0453 / 1142 / 1719	5.1 / 1.5 / 4.7
14 SU	0003 / 0549 / 1245 / 1830	1.2 / 5.3 / 1.3 / 4.9	**29** M	0005 / 0551 / 1237 / 1832	1.7 / 4.7 / 1.9 / 4.4
15 M	0117 / 0709 / 1412 / 2003	1.5 / 5.0 / 1.5 / 4.6	**30** TU	0112 / 0717 / 1400 / 2003	1.9 / 4.4 / 2.1 / 4.2
			31 W	0243 / 0851 / 1542 / 2136	2.0 / 4.4 / 2.0 / 4.4

APRIL

Day	Time	m	Day	Time	m
1 TH	0419 / 1009 / 1659 / 2238	1.7 / 4.7 / 1.6 / 4.8	**16** F	0523 / 1100 / 1747 / 2321	0.9 / 5.5 / 1.0 / 5.4
2 F	0524 / 1102 / 1750 / 2324	1.3 / 5.2 / 1.2 / 5.2	**17** SA	0612 / 1145 / 1828 / 2359	0.7 / 5.7 / 0.9 / 5.6
3 SA	0609 / 1143 / 1830	0.9 / 5.5 / 0.9	**18** SU	0653 / 1221 / 1905	0.6 / 5.8 / 0.8
4 SU	0001 / 0649 / 1218 / 1906	5.5 / 0.6 / 5.8 / 0.7	**19** M	0029 / 0729 / 1253 / 1939	5.8 / 0.5 / 5.8 / 0.7
5 M	0029 / 0727 / 1250 / 1942	5.8 / 0.4 / 5.9 / 0.6	**20** TU	0102 / 0801 / 1325 / 2012	5.8 / 0.6 / 5.9 / 0.7
6 TU	0101 / 0805 / 1322 / 2019	6.0 / 0.3 / 6.0 / 0.5	**21** W	0134 / 0833 / 1357 / 2045	5.9 / 0.6 / 5.8 / 0.7
7 W	0135 / 0844 / 1358 / 2058	6.1 / 0.3 / 6.1 / 0.5	**22** TH	0206 / 0904 / 1427 / 2117	5.9 / 0.7 / 5.7 / 0.7
8 TH	0213 / 0923 / 1437 / 2136	6.1 / 0.3 / 6.0 / 0.5	**23** F	0238 / 0935 / 1456 / 2148	5.8 / 0.8 / 5.6 / 0.9
9 F	0254 / 1003 / 1519 / 2217	6.1 / 0.4 / 5.9 / 0.7	**24** SA	0310 / 1004 / 1528 / 2220	5.6 / 1.0 / 5.4 / 1.1
10 SA	0341 / 1044 / 1610 / 2301	6.0 / 0.7 / 5.6 / 0.9	**25** SU	0345 / 1035 / 1604 / 2254	5.4 / 1.3 / 5.1 / 1.3
11 SU	0438 / 1134 / 1712 / 2356	5.7 / 1.0 / 5.2 / 1.2	**26** M	0425 / 1114 / 1652 / 2337	5.1 / 1.5 / 4.8 / 1.5
12 M	0546 / 1241 / 1824	5.3 / 1.4 / 4.9	**27** TU	0524 / 1206 / 1802	4.8 / 1.8 / 4.5
13 TU	0116 / 0707 / 1411 / 1958	1.4 / 5.0 / 1.6 / 4.6	**28** W	0039 / 0642 / 1317 / 1919	1.7 / 4.5 / 2.0 / 4.4
14 W	0251 / 0848 / 1539 / 2128	1.5 / 4.9 / 1.5 / 4.8	**29** TH	0156 / 0801 / 1448 / 2040	1.8 / 4.5 / 1.9 / 4.5
15 TH	0418 / 1004 / 1653 / 2232	1.2 / 5.2 / 1.3 / 5.1	**30** F	0325 / 0919 / 1610 / 2151	1.6 / 4.8 / 1.6 / 4.8

Chart Datum: 2·69 metres below IGN Datum

Chapter 5

371

TIME ZONE -0100
(French Standard Time)
Subtract 1 hour for UT
For French Summer Time add
ONE hour in **non-shaded areas**

FRANCE – DUNKERQUE

LAT 51°03′N   LONG 2°22′E

TIMES AND HEIGHTS OF HIGH AND LOW WATERS

YEAR 2004

MAY

Time m	Time m
1 0436 1.2 / 1018 5.2 / SA 1706 1.2 / 2241 5.2	**16** 0542 0.8 / 1113 5.5 / SU 1758 1.0 / 2327 5.5
2 0529 0.9 / 1102 5.5 / SU 1752 1.0 / 2322 5.5	**17** 0623 0.8 / 1151 5.6 / M 1836 0.9
3 0614 0.6 / 1140 5.7 / M 1832 0.8 / 2357 5.8	**18** 0001 5.6 / 0658 0.8 / TU 1225 5.6 / 1911 0.9
4 0655 0.5 / 1215 5.9 / TU 1912 0.7 / O	**19** 0036 5.7 / 0731 0.8 / W 1259 5.7 / ● 1945 0.8
5 0030 6.0 / 0737 0.4 / W 1253 6.0 / 1953 0.6	**20** 0110 5.7 / 0804 0.8 / TH 1332 5.7 / 2019 0.8
6 0111 6.1 / 0819 0.3 / TH 1334 6.1 / 2036 0.5	**21** 0142 5.7 / 0838 0.9 / F 1403 5.6 / 2054 0.8
7 0155 6.2 / 0903 0.4 / F 1420 6.0 / 2120 0.5	**22** 0216 5.7 / 0911 1.0 / SA 1435 5.5 / 2128 0.9
8 0243 6.1 / 0948 0.5 / SA 1512 5.8 / 2206 0.6	**23** 0253 5.5 / 0944 1.1 / SU 1511 5.4 / 2203 1.0
9 0338 5.9 / 1037 0.8 / SU 1609 5.6 / 2257 0.8	**24** 0332 5.4 / 1018 1.3 / M 1552 5.2 / 2239 1.2
10 0437 5.7 / 1133 1.1 / M 1709 5.2 / 2357 1.0	**25** 0415 5.2 / 1058 1.5 / TU 1641 5.0 / 2321 1.3
11 0542 5.4 / 1241 1.4 / TU 1816 5.0 / ◐	**26** 0508 5.0 / 1146 1.6 / W 1738 4.8
12 0116 1.2 / 0659 5.1 / W 1359 1.5 / 1942 4.8	**27** 0016 1.4 / 0609 4.8 / TH 1244 1.7 / ◐ 1840 4.7
13 0236 1.2 / 0828 5.1 / TH 1514 1.5 / 2059 4.9	**28** 0119 1.5 / 0713 4.8 / F 1354 1.7 / 1945 4.7
14 0350 1.1 / 0935 5.2 / F 1621 1.3 / 2158 5.1	**29** 0232 1.4 / 0819 4.9 / SA 1512 1.5 / 2051 4.9
15 0452 0.9 / 1029 5.4 / SA 1715 1.1 / 2246 5.3	**30** 0344 1.2 / 0921 5.2 / SU 1617 1.3 / 2149 5.2
	31 0445 0.9 / 1014 5.4 / M 1710 1.1 / 2238 5.5

JUNE

Time m	Time m
1 0537 0.7 / 1101 5.7 / TU 1759 0.9 / 2323 5.7	**16** 0630 1.1 / 1202 5.4 / W 1848 1.0
2 0625 0.6 / 1145 5.8 / W 1846 0.8	**17** 0015 5.5 / 0706 1.1 / TH 1240 5.5 / ● 1925 1.0
3 0005 6.0 / 0713 0.5 / TH 1232 5.8 / O 1933 0.6	**18** 0053 5.5 / 0742 1.0 / F 1315 5.5 / 2001 0.9
4 0054 6.1 / 0801 0.5 / F 1321 5.9 / 2021 0.5	**19** 0127 5.6 / 0819 1.1 / SA 1348 5.5 / 2038 0.9
5 0145 6.1 / 0850 0.5 / SA 1414 5.9 / 2110 0.5	**20** 0203 5.6 / 0855 1.1 / SU 1422 5.5 / 2114 0.9
6 0240 6.1 / 0940 0.7 / SU 1510 5.8 / 2201 0.5	**21** 0241 5.6 / 0931 1.1 / M 1500 5.5 / 2150 0.9
7 0335 6.0 / 1032 0.8 / M 1604 5.6 / 2254 0.7	**22** 0320 5.5 / 1006 1.2 / TU 1540 5.3 / 2227 1.0
8 0431 5.7 / 1127 1.1 / TU 1658 5.4 / 2351 0.8	**23** 0401 5.4 / 1044 1.3 / W 1623 5.2 / 2306 1.1
9 0529 5.5 / 1226 1.3 / W 1757 5.2 / ◐	**24** 0444 5.2 / 1126 1.4 / TH 1708 5.1 / 2350 1.1
10 0058 1.0 / 0636 5.3 / TH 1329 1.4 / 1907 5.0	**25** 0533 5.2 / 1213 1.4 / F 1758 5.0 / ◐
11 0203 1.1 / 0750 5.1 / F 1433 1.4 / 2015 5.0	**26** 0045 1.2 / 0628 5.1 / SA 1309 1.5 / 1854 5.0
12 0307 1.1 / 0854 5.1 / SA 1534 1.4 / 2114 5.1	**27** 0145 1.2 / 0727 5.1 / SU 1416 1.5 / 1954 5.1
13 0408 1.1 / 0948 5.2 / SU 1632 1.3 / 2206 5.2	**28** 0255 1.2 / 0829 5.2 / M 1528 1.4 / 2058 5.2
14 0502 1.1 / 1036 5.3 / M 1723 1.2 / 2253 5.3	**29** 0402 1.0 / 0932 5.3 / TU 1632 1.2 / 2201 5.4
15 0549 1.1 / 1121 5.3 / TU 1808 1.1 / 2336 5.4	**30** 0505 0.9 / 1033 5.5 / W 1732 1.1 / 2301 5.6

JULY

Time m	Time m
1 0603 0.8 / 1129 5.6 / TH 1828 0.9 / 2357 5.9	**16** 0002 5.3 / 0651 1.2 / F 1227 5.3 / 1912 1.1
2 0658 0.7 / 1224 5.8 / F 1922 0.7 / O	**17** 0041 5.4 / 0728 1.2 / SA 1303 5.4 / ● 1948 1.0
3 0048 6.0 / 0751 0.7 / SA 1317 5.9 / 2013 0.5	**18** 0116 5.5 / 0804 1.1 / SU 1335 5.5 / 2023 0.9
4 0141 6.1 / 0842 0.6 / SU 1409 5.9 / 2104 0.4	**19** 0150 5.6 / 0840 1.0 / M 1408 5.6 / 2059 0.8
5 0234 6.1 / 0932 0.7 / M 1501 5.8 / 2153 0.4	**20** 0225 5.7 / 0916 1.0 / TU 1443 5.6 / 2135 0.7
6 0325 6.0 / 1020 0.8 / TU 1549 5.7 / 2242 0.5	**21** 0302 5.7 / 0951 1.0 / W 1519 5.6 / 2211 0.8
7 0416 5.8 / 1107 1.0 / W 1636 5.6 / 2331 0.6	**22** 0337 5.6 / 1026 1.1 / TH 1553 5.5 / 2247 0.8
8 0506 5.6 / 1155 1.1 / TH 1723 5.4	**23** 0412 5.5 / 1102 1.1 / F 1628 5.4 / 2325 0.9
9 0025 0.8 / 0558 5.4 / F 1245 1.3 / ● 1816 5.2	**24** 0453 5.4 / 1142 1.2 / SA 1709 5.3
10 0117 1.0 / 0657 5.1 / SA 1339 1.5 / 1917 5.1	**25** 0009 1.0 / 0543 5.3 / SU 1228 1.3 / ◐ 1804 5.2
11 0214 1.2 / 0800 5.0 / SU 1438 1.6 / 2022 5.0	**26** 0103 1.1 / 0644 5.2 / M 1328 1.5 / 1909 5.2
12 0313 1.4 / 0902 4.9 / M 1541 1.6 / 2124 4.9	**27** 0211 1.2 / 0750 5.1 / TU 1446 1.5 / 2021 5.1
13 0416 1.4 / 1000 4.9 / TU 1646 1.5 / 2223 5.0	**28** 0329 1.3 / 0905 5.1 / W 1604 1.4 / 2143 5.2
14 0517 1.4 / 1056 5.0 / W 1745 1.4 / 2317 5.2	**29** 0444 1.2 / 1023 5.3 / TH 1717 1.2 / 2257 5.5
15 0609 1.3 / 1145 5.2 / TH 1832 1.3	**30** 0555 1.0 / 1129 5.5 / F 1822 0.9 / 2357 5.8
	31 0654 0.8 / 1224 5.7 / SA 1917 0.6 / O

AUGUST

Time m	Time m
1 0045 6.0 / 0745 0.7 / SU 1312 5.9 / 2006 0.4	**16** 0100 5.6 / 0746 1.0 / M 1317 5.7 / ● 2004 0.7
2 0133 6.1 / 0832 0.7 / M 1357 5.9 / 2052 0.3	**17** 0131 5.8 / 0820 0.9 / TU 1347 5.8 / 2038 0.6
3 0220 6.2 / 0916 0.7 / TU 1441 5.9 / 2137 0.3	**18** 0202 5.9 / 0855 0.9 / W 1418 5.8 / 2113 0.6
4 0306 6.1 / 0958 0.8 / W 1522 5.9 / 2220 0.4	**19** 0234 5.9 / 0928 0.9 / TH 1448 5.8 / 2148 0.6
5 0350 5.9 / 1038 0.9 / TH 1601 5.8 / 2300 0.6	**20** 0305 5.8 / 1001 0.9 / F 1517 5.8 / 2222 0.6
6 0431 5.7 / 1116 1.1 / F 1641 5.6 / 2340 0.8	**21** 0338 5.8 / 1035 1.0 / SA 1549 5.7 / 2257 0.8
7 0512 5.5 / 1156 1.3 / SA 1723 5.4 / O	**22** 0417 5.7 / 1111 1.1 / SU 1630 5.6 / 2337 0.9
8 0024 1.1 / 0559 5.2 / SU 1243 1.5 / 1814 5.1	**23** 0506 5.5 / 1155 1.3 / M 1724 5.4 / ◐
9 0114 1.4 / 0656 4.9 / M 1340 1.7 / 1921 4.8	**24** 0028 1.2 / 0611 5.2 / TU 1253 1.5 / 1838 5.1
10 0217 1.7 / 0808 4.6 / TU 1449 1.8 / 2041 4.7	**25** 0140 1.5 / 0726 4.9 / W 1419 1.7 / 2006 5.0
11 0328 1.8 / 0924 4.6 / W 1608 1.8 / 2157 4.7	**26** 0310 1.6 / 0900 4.9 / TH 1551 1.6 / 2145 5.1
12 0449 1.7 / 1033 4.8 / TH 1724 1.6 / 2301 5.0	**27** 0441 1.4 / 1026 5.1 / F 1714 1.2 / 2257 5.5
13 0553 1.5 / 1128 5.0 / F 1817 1.3 / 2350 5.2	**28** 0554 1.1 / 1127 5.5 / SA 1818 0.8 / 2353 5.8
14 0637 1.3 / 1211 5.3 / SA 1856 1.1	**29** 0647 0.9 / 1216 5.7 / SU 1908 0.5
15 0027 5.5 / 0712 1.2 / SU 1246 5.5 / 1930 0.9	**30** 0036 6.1 / 0732 0.7 / M 1258 5.9 / O 1952 0.4
	31 0119 6.2 / 0813 0.7 / TU 1335 6.0 / 2033 0.3

Chart Datum: 2·69 metres below IGN Datum

TIME ZONE -0100
(French Standard Time)
Subtract 1 hour for UT
For French Summer Time add
ONE hour in **non-shaded areas**

LAT 51°03′N   LONG 2°22′E

TIMES AND HEIGHTS OF HIGH AND LOW WATERS

SEPTEMBER

Time	m		Time	m
1 0159	6.2	**16** 0132		6.0
0852	0.7	0827		0.8
W 1412	6.0	TH 1345		6.0
2113	0.3	2046		0.5
2 0239	6.1	**17** 0203		6.0
0929	0.8	0901		0.8
TH 1448	6.0	F 1414		6.0
2150	0.5	2121		0.5
3 0315	5.9	**18** 0235		6.0
1004	0.9	0935		0.8
F 1523	5.9	SA 1446		6.0
2225	0.7	2156		0.6
4 0350	5.8	**19** 0310		5.9
1037	1.0	1009		0.9
SA 1559	5.7	SU 1522		5.9
2258	0.9	2232		0.8
5 0426	5.5	**20** 0351		5.8
1112	1.2	1046		1.1
SU 1636	5.5	M 1605		5.7
2333	1.2	2312		1.0
6 0505	5.2	**21** 0443		5.4
1150	1.5	1131		1.3
M 1721	5.1	TU 1705		5.4
		◐		
7 0016	1.6	**22** 0004		1.4
0555	4.8	0553		5.1
TU 1242	1.8	W 1235		1.6
1822	4.7	1829		5.0
8 0117	2.0	**23** 0127		1.7
0708	4.6	0718		4.8
W 1355	2.1	TH 1411		1.8
1952	4.4	2010		4.9
9 0240	2.2	**24** 0310		1.8
0842	4.4	0903		4.8
TH 1527	2.1	F 1549		1.6
2128	4.5	2145		5.2
10 0419	2.0	**25** 0440		1.5
1005	4.6	1021		5.1
F 1655	1.8	SA 1708		1.1
2239	4.9	2251		5.6
11 0529	1.7	**26** 0544		1.1
1103	5.0	1116		5.5
SA 1751	1.4	SU 1805		0.7
2327	1.3	2342		5.9
12 0613	1.4	**27** 0631		0.9
1146	5.3	1200		5.8
SU 1831	1.0	M 1851		0.5
13 0004	5.5	**28** 0020		6.1
0648	1.1	0712		0.8
M 1221	5.6	TU 1235		6.0
1905	0.8	○ 1931		0.4
14 0035	5.8	**29** 0057		6.1
0720	1.0	0749		0.8
TU 1251	5.8	W 1307		6.0
● 1937	0.7	2008		0.4
15 0104	5.9	**30** 0132		6.1
0754	0.9	0824		0.8
W 1318	5.9	TH 1341		6.1
2011	0.6	2044		0.5

OCTOBER

Time	m		Time	m
1 0207	6.1	**16** 0133		6.2
0857	0.8	0834		0.8
F 1415	6.0	SA 1345		6.1
2117	0.6	2055		0.6
2 0240	5.9	**17** 0210		6.1
0930	0.9	0912		0.8
SA 1448	5.9	SU 1423		6.1
2149	0.8	2133		0.7
3 0312	5.8	**18** 0251		6.0
1002	1.0	0950		0.9
SU 1521	5.8	M 1505		6.0
2220	1.1	2213		0.9
4 0344	5.5	**19** 0337		5.7
1034	1.3	1032		1.1
M 1556	5.5	TU 1558		5.7
2252	1.4	2259		1.2
5 0420	5.2	**20** 0436		5.4
1110	1.5	1124		1.3
TU 1638	5.1	W 1708		5.4
2330	1.7	◐ 2359		1.6
6 0506	4.8	**21** 0548		5.0
1155	1.8	1236		1.6
W 1737	4.7	TH 1830		5.1
◐				
7 0025	2.1	**22** 0131		1.8
0619	4.5	0713		4.8
TH 1300	2.1	F 1411		1.7
1902	4.4	2009		5.0
8 0146	2.3	**23** 0305		1.8
0749	4.3	0852		4.9
F 1435	2.2	SA 1539		1.4
2043	4.4	2133		5.3
9 0333	2.2	**24** 0425		1.5
0922	4.5	1002		5.2
SA 1611	1.9	SU 1652		1.0
2202	4.8	2233		5.6
10 0449	1.8	**25** 0523		1.2
1025	4.9	1053		5.5
SU 1711	1.4	M 1745		0.7
2252	5.2	2322		5.8
11 0537	1.4	**26** 0608		1.0
1110	5.3	1133		5.7
M 1755	1.1	TU 1828		0.6
2331	5.6			
12 0615	1.2	**27** 0001		6.0
1146	5.6	0646		0.9
TU 1831	0.8	W 1206		5.9
		1906		0.6
13 0003	5.8	**28** 0031		6.0
0649	1.0	0721		0.9
W 1216	5.8	TH 1239		6.0
1906	0.6	○ 1941		0.7
14 0029	6.0	**29** 0105		6.0
0723	0.9	0755		0.9
TH 1242	6.0	F 1313		6.0
● 1941	0.6	2015		0.7
15 0100	6.1	**30** 0137		6.0
0758	0.8	0828		0.9
F 1311	6.1	SA 1346		6.0
2017	0.5	2047		0.9
		31 0208		5.9
		0902		0.9
		SU 1420		5.9
		2119		1.0

NOVEMBER

Time	m		Time	m
1 0240	5.7	**16** 0241		6.0
0935	1.1	0941		0.8
M 1453	5.7	TU 1503		6.0
2150	1.2	2205		1.0
2 0313	5.5	**17** 0335		5.7
1008	1.3	1031		1.0
TU 1529	5.5	W 1603		5.8
2223	1.5	2258		1.2
3 0350	5.2	**18** 0434		5.4
1042	1.5	1128		1.2
W 1611	5.2	TH 1709		5.5
2300	1.8			
4 0435	4.9	**19** 0001		1.5
1125	1.7	0538		5.1
TH 1707	4.8	F 1238		1.4
2349	2.0	◐ 1822		5.2
5 0542	4.6	**20** 0123		1.7
1221	1.9	0654		5.0
F 1820	4.6	SA 1357		1.4
◐		1952		5.1
6 0058	2.2	**21** 0241		1.7
0657	4.5	0822		5.0
SA 1334	2.0	SU 1513		1.3
1940	4.5	2105		5.3
7 0226	2.2	**22** 0352		1.5
0817	4.5	0927		5.2
SU 1508	1.9	M 1621		1.1
2103	4.8	2203		5.5
8 0351	1.9	**23** 0451		1.4
0930	4.8	1018		5.4
M 1618	1.5	TU 1717		0.9
2203	5.1	2253		5.6
9 0448	1.5	**24** 0539		1.2
1022	5.2	1101		5.6
TU 1709	1.1	W 1802		0.9
2247	5.5	2334		5.7
10 0533	1.3	**25** 0619		1.1
1101	5.5	1140		5.7
W 1752	0.9	TH 1841		0.9
2325	5.7			
11 0613	1.1	**26** 0007		5.8
1134	5.8	0656		1.1
TH 1832	0.7	F 1216		5.8
2358	5.9	○ 1916		0.9
12 0652	0.9	**27** 0042		5.8
1207	5.9	0730		1.0
F 1911	0.6	SA 1253		5.8
●		1950		1.0
13 0031	6.1	**28** 0115		5.8
0731	0.8	0806		1.0
SA 1244	6.1	SU 1328		5.8
1951	0.6	2023		1.0
14 0110	6.1	**29** 0147		5.7
0812	0.8	0841		1.0
SU 1325	6.2	M 1402		5.8
2034	0.6	2057		1.1
15 0154	6.1	**30** 0220		5.6
0855	0.8	0916		1.1
M 1411	6.2	TU 1437		5.6
2118	0.8	2131		1.3

DECEMBER

Time	m		Time	m
1 0256	5.5	**16** 0330		5.8
0951	1.2	1030		0.7
W 1514	5.5	TH 1600		5.9
2205	1.5	2254		1.1
2 0334	5.3	**17** 0422		5.6
1026	1.3	1124		0.9
TH 1556	5.3	F 1658		5.7
2241	1.6	2349		1.3
3 0417	5.1	**18** 0517		5.4
1105	1.5	1223		1.1
F 1645	5.1	SA 1802		5.4
2324	1.8	◐		
4 0508	4.9	**19** 0054		1.5
1152	1.6	0619		5.2
SA 1743	4.9	SU 1326		1.1
		1914		5.2
5 0019	1.9	**20** 0158		1.6
0609	4.8	0732		5.1
SU 1248	1.7	M 1431		1.2
◐ 1845	4.8	2022		5.1
6 0122	1.9	**21** 0302		1.6
0713	4.7	0839		5.1
M 1357	1.6	TU 1536		1.2
1951	4.9	2122		5.2
7 0237	1.9	**22** 0404		1.6
0817	4.9	0937		5.2
TU 1513	1.5	W 1638		1.2
2057	5.1	2217		5.2
8 0348	1.7	**23** 0503		1.5
0917	5.1	1030		5.3
W 1617	1.3	TH 1733		1.2
2154	5.3	2307		5.3
9 0446	1.4	**24** 0554		1.3
1010	5.4	1118		5.4
TH 1711	1.0	F 1819		1.2
2243	5.6	2351		5.4
10 0537	1.2	**25** 0637		1.2
1056	5.6	1202		5.5
F 1800	0.9	SA 1859		1.2
2329	5.7			
11 0624	1.0	**26** 0028		5.6
1141	5.9	0715		1.1
SA 1846	0.8	SU 1243		5.6
		○ 1935		1.1
12 0010	5.9	**27** 0103		5.6
0711	0.9	0752		1.0
SU 1228	6.1	M 1319		5.6
● 1933	0.7	2009		1.1
13 0058	6.0	**28** 0136		5.6
0759	0.7	0828		1.0
M 1317	6.2	TU 1353		5.7
2021	0.7	2043		1.1
14 0146	6.0	**29** 0208		5.6
0848	0.7	0904		1.0
TU 1409	6.2	W 1427		5.6
2111	0.8	2117		1.2
15 0238	5.9	**30** 0243		5.6
0938	0.7	0938		1.0
W 1505	6.1	TH 1502		5.6
2201	0.9	2151		1.3
		31 0319		5.5
		1012		1.0
		F 1540		5.5
		2225		1.3

Chart Datum: 2·69 metres below IGN Datum

Chapter 5

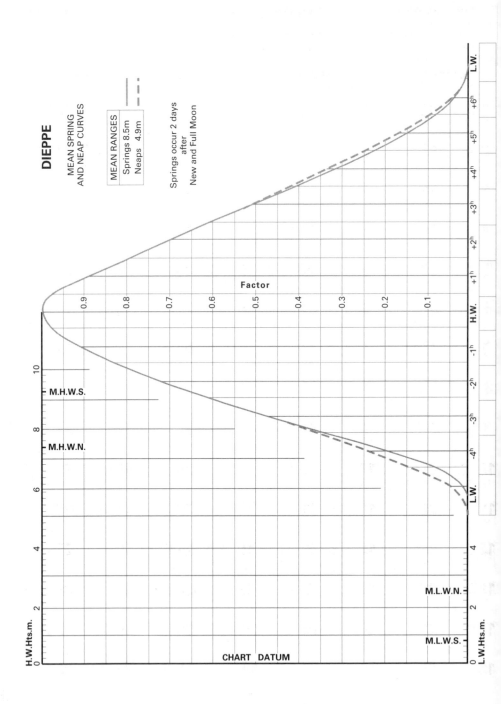

DIEPPE

MEAN SPRING
AND NEAP CURVES

MEAN RANGES
Springs 8.5m
Neaps 4.9m

Springs occur 2 days
after
New and Full Moon

Factor

0.9 0.8 0.7 0.6 0.5 0.4 0.3 0.2 0.1

H.W.Hts.m.

M.H.W.S.

M.H.W.N.

CHART DATUM

L.W.Hts.m.

M.L.W.N.

M.L.W.S.

L.W.

H.W.

L.W.

TIME ZONE -0100
(French Standard Time)
Subtract 1 hour for UT
For French Summer Time add
ONE hour in **non-shaded areas**

FRANCE – DIEPPE

YEAR **2004**

LAT 49°56'N   LONG 1°05'E

TIMES AND HEIGHTS OF HIGH AND LOW WATERS

JANUARY

Time	m	Time	m
1 0038	2.6	**16** 0530	7.8
0627	7.3	1220	2.3
TH 1316	2.8	F 1758	7.6
1857	7.1		
2 0140	2.7	**17** 0049	2.3
0734	7.3	0642	7.7
F 1421	2.7	SA 1332	2.3
2005	7.2	1916	7.6
3 0246	2.7	**18** 0207	2.3
0838	7.4	0800	7.8
SA 1525	2.5	SU 1452	2.1
2106	7.4	2032	7.8
4 0348	2.5	**19** 0327	2.1
0931	7.7	0910	8.2
SU 1620	2.2	M 1605	1.7
2156	7.7	2141	8.2
5 0440	2.2	**20** 0436	1.7
1016	8.0	1013	8.6
M 1708	1.9	TU 1709	1.3
2239	8.0	2242	8.6
6 0525	2.0	**21** 0538	1.4
1056	8.3	1110	9.0
TU 1750	1.7	W 1808	1.0
2318	8.2	● 2337	9.0
7 0606	1.8	**22** 0635	1.2
1134	8.5	1201	9.2
W 1829	1.6	TH 1903	0.7
○ 2355	8.4		
8 0643	1.7	**23** 0031	9.2
1210	8.6	0727	1.0
TH 1906	1.4	F 1249	9.4
		1953	0.8
9 0034	8.6	**24** 0116	9.3
0719	1.6	0814	1.0
F 1246	8.7	SA 1333	9.4
1943	1.4	2037	0.6
10 0110	8.6	**25** 0158	9.2
0756	1.6	0855	1.1
SA 1322	8.7	SU 1414	9.2
2020	1.4	2116	0.8
11 0147	8.6	**26** 0237	9.0
0833	1.6	0932	1.3
SU 1400	8.7	M 1453	8.9
2057	1.4	2150	1.2
12 0225	8.5	**27** 0314	8.6
0911	1.7	1004	1.6
M 1438	8.5	TU 1531	8.5
2134	1.5	2221	1.6
13 0304	8.4	**28** 0350	8.2
0950	1.8	1036	2.0
TU 1519	8.3	W 1609	8.0
2213	1.7	2252	2.0
14 0346	8.2	**29** 0428	7.8
1032	2.0	1113	2.4
W 1603	8.1	TH 1652	7.5
2256	1.9	◐ 2331	2.3
15 0433	8.0	**30** 0514	7.3
1121	2.2	1202	2.8
TH 1655	7.8	F 1746	6.9
◐ 2347	2.1		
		31 0023	2.9
		0618	6.9
		SA 1308	3.1
		1902	6.6

FEBRUARY

Time	m	Time	m
1 0137	3.2	**16** 0137	2.6
0742	6.8	0738	7.4
SU 1432	3.1	M 1431	2.4
2025	6.7	2022	7.4
2 0305	3.1	**17** 0313	2.4
0857	7.1	0904	7.7
M 1546	2.7	TU 1555	2.0
2130	7.2	2140	7.9
3 0413	2.7	**18** 0430	2.0
0953	7.5	1012	8.3
TU 1643	2.3	W 1705	1.4
2220	7.6	2242	8.5
4 0505	2.2	**19** 0536	1.5
1038	8.0	1107	8.8
W 1731	1.8	TH 1806	1.0
2302	8.1	2332	8.9
5 0550	1.9	**20** 0631	1.1
1119	8.4	1154	9.2
TH 1814	1.5	F 1856	0.7
2341	8.5	●	
6 0631	1.6	**21** 0019	9.2
1157	8.7	0718	0.9
F 1855	1.2	SA 1235	9.4
○		1940	0.5
7 0020	8.7	**22** 0058	9.4
0710	1.3	0758	0.8
SA 1234	8.9	SU 1314	9.5
1934	1.0	2017	0.5
8 0057	8.9	**23** 0134	9.3
0748	1.2	0832	0.9
SU 1310	9.1	M 1350	9.4
2011	0.9	2049	0.7
9 0133	9.0	**24** 0208	9.1
0825	1.1	0901	1.1
M 1346	9.1	TU 1423	9.1
2047	0.9	2116	1.0
10 0209	9.0	**25** 0239	8.9
0900	1.1	0927	1.4
TU 1423	9.1	W 1455	8.7
2121	0.9	2139	1.4
11 0245	8.9	**26** 0308	8.5
0935	1.2	0952	1.7
W 1500	8.9	TH 1525	8.2
2155	1.2	2204	1.9
12 0322	8.7	**27** 0336	8.0
1012	1.5	1021	2.2
TH 1539	8.5	F 1557	7.6
2231	1.5	2235	2.4
13 0402	8.4	**28** 0410	7.4
1054	1.8	1101	2.7
F 1625	8.1	SA 1638	7.0
◐ 2316	1.9	◐ 2319	3.0
14 0452	7.9	**29** 0500	6.8
1147	2.2	1157	3.2
SA 1724	7.6	SU 1748	6.4
15 0014	2.4		
0604	7.5		
SU 1258	2.4		
1849	7.2		

MARCH

Time	m	Time	m
1 0026	3.5	**16** 0128	2.9
0632	6.4	0735	7.1
M 1325	3.4	TU 1425	2.5
1941	6.3	2025	7.2
2 0215	3.5	**17** 0313	2.6
0822	6.5	0905	7.6
TU 1510	3.1	W 1554	2.0
2104	6.8	2139	7.9
3 0345	3.0	**18** 0432	1.9
0929	7.1	1007	8.3
W 1617	2.5	TH 1702	1.4
2157	7.5	2233	8.5
4 0442	2.3	**19** 0531	1.4
1017	7.8	1055	8.8
TH 1708	1.9	F 1755	0.9
2241	8.1	2317	9.0
5 0529	1.8	**20** 0618	1.0
1058	8.4	1137	9.2
F 1754	1.4	SA 1839	0.7
2320	8.6	● 2356	9.2
6 0612	1.4	**21** 0658	0.9
1137	8.8	1214	9.3
SA 1836	1.0	SU 1916	0.6
○ 2357	9.0		
7 0653	1.0	**22** 0033	9.3
1214	9.1	0732	0.8
SU 1915	0.7	M 1249	9.4
		1948	0.6
8 0036	9.2	**23** 0105	9.3
0731	0.8	0802	0.9
M 1250	9.4	TU 1321	9.3
1953	0.5	2016	0.8
9 0111	9.4	**24** 0135	9.1
0809	0.7	0829	1.0
TU 1326	9.5	W 1351	9.1
2028	0.5	2040	1.0
10 0147	9.4	**25** 0203	8.9
0844	0.7	0853	1.3
W 1402	9.4	TH 1420	8.7
2102	0.6	2102	1.4
11 0222	9.3	**26** 0230	8.5
0918	0.9	0916	1.6
TH 1439	9.2	F 1448	8.2
2135	0.9	2126	1.8
12 0258	9.0	**27** 0255	8.1
0953	1.2	0943	2.1
F 1519	8.7	SA 1517	7.7
2211	1.4	2155	2.4
13 0338	8.5	**28** 0326	7.5
1034	1.6	1018	2.6
SA 1604	8.1	SU 1554	7.1
◐ 2254	2.0	◐ 2235	3.0
14 0428	7.8	**29** 0410	6.9
1127	2.2	1108	3.1
SU 1705	7.4	M 1652	6.4
2354	2.6	2336	3.5
15 0545	7.2	**30** 0527	6.3
1243	2.6	1226	3.4
M 1841	7.0	TU 1848	6.2
		31 0119	3.6
		0735	6.3
		W 1420	3.2
		2026	6.7

APRIL

Time	m	Time	m
1 0303	3.1	**16** 0415	1.8
0852	7.0	0946	8.3
TH 1538	2.5	F 1641	1.4
2123	7.4	2210	8.5
2 0405	2.3	**17** 0508	1.4
0944	7.7	1032	8.7
F 1632	1.9	SA 1730	1.1
2209	8.1	2251	8.9
3 0455	1.7	**18** 0551	1.1
1028	8.4	1112	9.0
SA 1721	1.3	SU 1810	0.9
2249	8.7	2328	9.0
4 0542	1.2	**19** 0627	1.0
1108	8.9	1147	9.1
SU 1806	0.9	M 1844	0.9
2328	9.1	●	
5 0626	0.9	**20** 0002	9.1
1146	9.2	0659	1.0
M 1848	0.6	TU 1220	9.1
○		1913	0.9
6 0007	9.4	**21** 0033	9.0
0707	0.7	0729	1.0
TU 1225	9.5	W 1251	9.0
1928	0.4	1941	1.0
7 0045	9.5	**22** 0103	9.0
0746	0.5	0758	1.1
W 1303	9.6	TH 1321	8.8
2005	0.4	2008	1.2
8 0123	9.5	**23** 0132	8.8
0823	0.5	0824	1.3
TH 1342	9.5	F 1351	8.6
2041	0.6	2033	1.5
9 0200	9.4	**24** 0159	8.5
0900	0.7	0848	1.6
F 1421	9.2	SA 1421	8.2
2117	1.0	2058	1.9
10 0239	9.0	**25** 0227	8.1
0938	1.1	0916	2.0
SA 1504	8.7	SU 1451	7.7
2156	1.5	2129	2.4
11 0323	8.4	**26** 0300	7.6
1023	1.6	0951	2.4
SU 1554	8.0	M 1530	7.2
2244	2.1	2209	2.9
12 0419	7.7	**27** 0344	7.0
1120	2.1	1040	2.9
M 1703	7.3	TU 1625	6.7
◑ 2350	2.7	◑ 2308	3.2
13 0545	7.1	**28** 0453	6.6
1241	2.5	1150	3.2
TU 1841	7.1	W 1755	6.5
14 0130	2.8	**29** 0034	3.3
0728	7.1	0636	6.5
W 1420	2.3	TH 1324	3.0
2014	7.4	1931	6.8
15 0304	2.4	**30** 0208	3.0
0849	7.7	0800	7.0
TH 1539	1.8	F 1445	2.5
2120	8.0	2035	7.4

Chart Datum: 4·43 metres below IGN Datum

FRANCE – DIEPPE

TIME ZONE -0100
(French Standard Time)
Subtract 1 hour for UT
For French Summer Time add
ONE hour in **non-shaded areas**

LAT 49°56′N   LONG 1°05′E

TIMES AND HEIGHTS OF HIGH AND LOW WATERS

YEAR **2004**

MAY

Time	m		Time	m
1 SA 0316 / 0859 / 1546 / 2126	2.3 / 7.7 / 1.9 / 8.1	**16** SU 0429 / 1001 / 1651 / 2219	1.6 / 8.3 / 1.4 / 8.5
2 SU 0411 / 0948 / 1639 / 2211	1.7 / 8.3 / 1.3 / 8.6	**17** M 0513 / 1041 / 1732 / 2257	1.5 / 8.5 / 1.4 / 8.7
3 M 0503 / 1033 / 1729 / 2254	1.3 / 8.8 / 1.0 / 9.0	**18** TU 0551 / 1118 / 1806 / 2331	1.4 / 8.6 / 1.3 / 8.7
4 TU 0552 / 1116 / 1816 / ○ 2335	0.9 / 9.1 / 0.7 / 9.3	**19** W 0625 / 1151 / 1839 ●	1.3 / 8.7 / 1.3
5 W 0639 / 1158 / 1900	0.7 / 9.4 / 0.6	**20** TH 0003 / 0659 / 1224 / 1911	8.7 / 1.3 / 8.7 / 1.4
6 TH 0019 / 0722 / 1241 / 1942	9.5 / 0.6 / 9.5 / 0.6	**21** F 0035 / 0731 / 1257 / 1942	8.7 / 1.3 / 8.6 / 1.5
7 F 0101 / 0804 / 1324 / 2022	9.5 / 0.6 / 9.4 / 0.7	**22** SA 0106 / 0801 / 1329 / 2012	8.6 / 1.5 / 8.4 / 1.7
8 SA 0143 / 0846 / 1409 / 2104	9.3 / 0.7 / 9.1 / 1.1	**23** SU 0137 / 0830 / 1402 / 2041	8.4 / 1.7 / 8.2 / 2.0
9 SU 0228 / 0930 / 1457 / 2149	8.9 / 1.1 / 8.6 / 1.6	**24** M 0210 / 0901 / 1437 / 2115	8.1 / 1.9 / 7.8 / 2.3
10 M 0318 / 1019 / 1553 / 2243	8.4 / 1.5 / 8.0 / 2.1	**25** TU 0247 / 0938 / 1518 / 2156	7.7 / 2.2 / 7.5 / 2.6
11 TU 0420 / 1120 / 1703 / ◐ 2351	7.8 / 2.0 / 7.6 / 2.4	**26** W 0332 / 1025 / 1609 / 2250	7.3 / 2.5 / 7.2 / 2.8
12 W 0538 / 1235 / 1822	7.4 / 2.2 / 7.4	**27** TH 0430 / 1125 / 1715 / ◐ 2356	7.0 / 2.7 / 7.0 / 2.9
13 TH 0115 / 0700 / 1353 / 1939	2.5 / 7.4 / 2.1 / 7.5	**28** F 0543 / 1236 / 1830	7.0 / 2.6 / 7.1
14 F 0231 / 0814 / 1503 / 2045	2.3 / 7.6 / 1.9 / 7.9	**29** SA 0112 / 0659 / 1349 / 1938	2.7 / 7.2 / 2.4 / 7.5
15 SA 0336 / 0913 / 1602 / 2136	1.9 / 8.0 / 1.6 / 8.3	**30** SU 0222 / 0806 / 1455 / 2037	2.3 / 7.6 / 1.9 / 8.0
		31 M 0324 / 0904 / 1555 / 2130	1.8 / 8.1 / 1.5 / 8.5

JUNE

Time	m		Time	m
1 TU 0422 / 0957 / 1651 / 2219	1.4 / 8.6 / 1.2 / 8.9	**16** W 0516 / 1050 / 1733 / 2303	1.7 / 8.2 / 1.7 / 8.3
2 W 0518 / 1047 / 1744 / 2307	1.1 / 8.9 / 1.0 / 9.1	**17** TH 0556 / 1128 / 1811 / ● 2339	1.6 / 8.3 / 1.7 / 8.4
3 TH 0610 / 1135 / 1834 / ○ 2354	0.9 / 9.2 / 0.8 / 9.3	**18** F 0634 / 1204 / 1848	1.5 / 8.4 / 1.6
4 F 0701 / 1224 / 1922	0.7 / 9.3 / 0.8	**19** SA 0015 / 0711 / 1239 / 1924	8.4 / 1.5 / 8.4 / 1.7
5 SA 0045 / 0750 / 1313 / 2010	9.3 / 0.7 / 9.3 / 0.9	**20** SU 0049 / 0745 / 1315 / 1958	8.4 / 1.5 / 8.4 / 1.7
6 SU 0133 / 0838 / 1402 / 2058	9.2 / 0.7 / 9.1 / 1.1	**21** M 0124 / 0819 / 1351 / 2032	8.4 / 1.6 / 8.3 / 1.8
7 M 0223 / 0927 / 1454 / 2147	8.9 / 1.0 / 8.7 / 1.4	**22** TU 0200 / 0854 / 1428 / 2107	8.2 / 1.7 / 8.1 / 2.0
8 TU 0316 / 1018 / 1548 / 2240	8.5 / 1.3 / 8.3 / 1.8	**23** W 0238 / 0931 / 1507 / 2147	8.0 / 1.9 / 7.9 / 2.1
9 W 0412 / 1112 / 1645 / ◐ 2338	8.1 / 1.6 / 8.0 / 2.1	**24** TH 0320 / 1013 / 1550 / 2232	7.6 / 2.0 / 7.7 / 2.3
10 TH 0512 / 1210 / 1746	7.8 / 1.9 / 7.7	**25** F 0406 / 1100 / 1639 / ◐ 2324	7.6 / 2.2 / 7.6 / 2.4
11 F 0039 / 0617 / 1310 / 1850	2.3 / 7.5 / 2.1 / 7.6	**26** SA 0500 / 1154 / 1736	7.5 / 2.2 / 7.5
12 SA 0142 / 0724 / 1411 / 1955	2.3 / 7.5 / 2.1 / 7.6	**27** SU 0023 / 0603 / 1256 / 1841	2.4 / 7.5 / 2.2 / 7.6
13 SU 0243 / 0828 / 1510 / 2054	2.2 / 7.6 / 2.0 / 7.8	**28** M 0129 / 0713 / 1404 / 1949	2.2 / 7.6 / 2.1 / 7.9
14 M 0340 / 0923 / 1604 / 2143	2.0 / 7.8 / 1.9 / 8.0	**29** TU 0239 / 0823 / 1514 / 2053	2.0 / 7.9 / 1.8 / 8.2
15 TU 0431 / 1009 / 1651 / 2226	1.9 / 8.0 / 1.8 / 8.2	**30** W 0347 / 0926 / 1619 / 2151	1.7 / 8.3 / 1.5 / 8.6

JULY

Time	m		Time	m
1 TH 0450 / 1025 / 1718 / 2246	1.3 / 8.6 / 1.3 / 8.9	**16** F 0535 / 1111 / 1753 / 2322	1.8 / 8.0 / 1.9 / 8.2
2 F 0549 / 1121 / 1815 / ○ 2340	1.0 / 8.9 / 1.1 / 9.1	**17** SA 0618 / 1149 / 1833 / ● 2359	1.7 / 8.3 / 1.7 / 8.4
3 SA 0647 / 1214 / 1910	0.8 / 9.1 / 1.0	**18** SU 0657 / 1226 / 1911	1.5 / 8.4 / 1.6
4 SU 0036 / 0742 / 1306 / 2003	9.2 / 0.7 / 9.2 / 0.9	**19** M 0037 / 0734 / 1302 / 1947	8.5 / 1.4 / 8.5 / 1.6
5 M 0127 / 0834 / 1355 / 2053	9.2 / 0.7 / 9.2 / 1.0	**20** TU 0113 / 0811 / 1337 / 2022	8.6 / 1.4 / 8.6 / 1.5
6 TU 0215 / 0922 / 1443 / 2140	9.1 / 0.8 / 9.0 / 1.2	**21** W 0148 / 0846 / 1413 / 2057	8.6 / 1.4 / 8.5 / 1.6
7 W 0303 / 1006 / 1529 / 2224	8.9 / 1.0 / 8.7 / 1.4	**22** TH 0224 / 0920 / 1449 / 2133	8.5 / 1.4 / 8.4 / 1.7
8 TH 0349 / 1048 / 1614 / 2308	8.5 / 1.4 / 8.3 / 1.8	**23** F 0301 / 0955 / 1526 / 2211	8.4 / 1.6 / 8.3 / 1.8
9 F 0436 / 1130 / 1702 / ◐ 2354	8.1 / 1.8 / 7.9 / 2.1	**24** SA 0340 / 1033 / 1606 / 2253	8.2 / 1.7 / 8.1 / 2.0
10 SA 0527 / 1217 / 1755	7.7 / 2.1 / 7.6	**25** SU 0424 / 1116 / 1653 / ◐ 2343	8.0 / 2.0 / 7.9 / 2.2
11 SU 0045 / 0626 / 1311 / 1857	2.4 / 7.3 / 2.4 / 7.3	**26** M 0518 / 1211 / 1753	7.7 / 2.2 / 7.7
12 M 0147 / 0735 / 1415 / 2005	2.6 / 7.1 / 2.6 / 7.3	**27** TU 0046 / 0629 / 1321 / 1909	2.3 / 7.5 / 2.4 / 7.6
13 TU 0253 / 0844 / 1520 / 2107	2.5 / 7.2 / 2.5 / 7.5	**28** W 0204 / 0753 / 1444 / 2027	2.3 / 7.6 / 2.2 / 7.8
14 W 0356 / 0942 / 1619 / 2159	2.3 / 7.5 / 2.3 / 7.7	**29** TH 0324 / 0909 / 1559 / 2136	2.0 / 7.9 / 1.9 / 8.2
15 TH 0449 / 1029 / 1709 / 2243	2.1 / 7.8 / 2.1 / 8.0	**30** F 0434 / 1016 / 1704 / 2238	1.5 / 8.4 / 1.5 / 8.7
		31 SA 0539 / 1116 / 1806 / ○ 2334	1.2 / 8.8 / 1.2 / 9.0

AUGUST

Time	m		Time	m
1 SU 0641 / 1209 / 1903	0.8 / 9.2 / 0.9	**16** M 0642 / 1208 / 1856 ●	1.4 / 8.7 / 1.4
2 M 0029 / 0736 / 1256 / 1955	9.3 / 0.6 / 9.3 / 0.8	**17** TU 0020 / 0720 / 1243 / 1932	8.8 / 1.2 / 8.8 / 1.3
3 TU 0115 / 0823 / 1340 / 2040	9.4 / 0.5 / 9.4 / 0.8	**18** W 0055 / 0755 / 1317 / 2007	8.9 / 1.0 / 9.0 / 1.2
4 W 0158 / 0904 / 1421 / 2120	9.3 / 0.6 / 9.2 / 1.0	**19** TH 0129 / 0829 / 1351 / 2040	9.0 / 1.0 / 9.0 / 1.2
5 TH 0238 / 0940 / 1500 / 2155	9.1 / 0.9 / 9.0 / 1.3	**20** F 0203 / 0901 / 1424 / 2114	9.0 / 1.1 / 8.9 / 1.3
6 F 0317 / 1011 / 1537 / 2228	8.7 / 1.3 / 8.6 / 1.7	**21** SA 0238 / 0932 / 1459 / 2148	8.8 / 1.3 / 8.7 / 1.5
7 SA 0355 / 1042 / 1615 / ◐ 2302	8.3 / 1.8 / 8.1 / 2.1	**22** SU 0314 / 1005 / 1536 / 2226	8.5 / 1.6 / 8.4 / 1.8
8 SU 0435 / 1118 / 1658 / 2345	7.7 / 2.3 / 7.5 / 2.6	**23** M 0354 / 1045 / 1619 / ◐ 2313	8.2 / 1.9 / 8.0 / 2.1
9 M 0526 / 1207 / 1754	7.1 / 2.8 / 7.0	**24** TU 0446 / 1138 / 1718	7.7 / 2.4 / 7.6
10 TU 0046 / 0638 / 1318 / 1914	3.0 / 6.7 / 3.1 / 6.8	**25** W 0016 / 0603 / 1254 / 1846	2.5 / 7.3 / 2.7 / 7.3
11 W 0209 / 0807 / 1444 / 2037	3.1 / 6.7 / 3.1 / 6.9	**26** TH 0145 / 0743 / 1432 / 2020	2.6 / 7.3 / 2.6 / 7.5
12 TH 0328 / 0920 / 1556 / 2139	2.8 / 7.1 / 2.7 / 7.3	**27** F 0317 / 0910 / 1553 / 2136	2.2 / 7.7 / 2.1 / 8.1
13 F 0429 / 1012 / 1651 / 2226	2.4 / 7.6 / 2.3 / 7.8	**28** SA 0432 / 1017 / 1702 / 2237	1.6 / 8.4 / 1.6 / 8.7
14 SA 0519 / 1054 / 1737 / 2306	1.9 / 8.0 / 1.9 / 8.2	**29** SU 0537 / 1111 / 1802 / 2327	1.1 / 9.0 / 1.1 / 9.2
15 SU 0602 / 1132 / 1818 / 2343	1.6 / 8.4 / 1.6 / 8.5	**30** M 0634 / 1157 / 1853 ○	0.7 / 9.3 / 0.8
		31 TU 0014 / 0721 / 1238 / 1938	9.4 / 0.5 / 9.5 / 0.7

Chart Datum: 4·43 metres below IGN Datum

TIME ZONE -0100
(French Standard Time)
Subtract 1 hour for UT
For French Summer Time add ONE hour in **non-shaded areas**

FRANCE – DIEPPE

LAT 49°56'N LONG 1°05'E

YEAR 2004

TIMES AND HEIGHTS OF HIGH AND LOW WATERS

SEPTEMBER

Day	Time m	Time m	Time m	Time m
1 W	0055 9.5	0801 0.5	1317 9.5	2016 0.8
16 TH	0030 9.2	0731 0.8	1250 9.3	1944 0.9
2 TH	0133 9.5	0836 0.7	1352 9.3	2050 1.0
17 F	0104 9.3	0805 0.8	1324 9.3	2019 0.9
3 F	0208 9.2	0905 1.0	1425 9.1	2118 1.3
18 SA	0139 9.3	0837 0.9	1358 9.2	2052 1.1
4 SA	0241 8.8	0929 1.4	1457 8.6	2144 1.7
19 SU	0214 9.1	0908 1.2	1433 9.0	2126 1.3
5 SU	0312 8.3	0954 1.9	1528 8.1	2212 2.2
20 M	0251 8.7	0942 1.6	1511 8.5	2205 1.7
6 M ◑	0345 7.7	1025 2.4	1602 7.5	2249 2.7
21 TU ◑	0333 8.2	1023 2.1	1556 8.0	2253 2.2
7 TU	0426 7.0	1108 3.1	1649 6.9	2343 3.2
22 W	0429 7.5	1121 2.7	1701 7.3	
8 W	0535 6.4	1217 3.6	1817 6.4	
23 TH	0001 2.7	0558 7.0	1246 3.0	1845 7.1
9 TH	0116 3.5	0732 6.3	1410 3.6	2008 6.5
24 F	0144 2.7	0750 7.2	1434 2.7	2023 7.5
10 F	0301 3.2	0857 6.6	1534 3.0	2116 7.1
25 SA	0319 2.2	0911 7.9	1554 2.0	2133 8.2
11 SA	0406 2.5	0949 7.5	1629 2.4	2203 7.7
26 SU	0430 1.5	1008 8.6	1656 1.4	2225 8.8
12 SU	0455 2.0	1030 8.1	1713 1.8	2242 8.3
27 M	0528 1.0	1055 9.1	1749 1.0	2310 9.3
13 M	0538 1.5	1107 8.6	1754 1.5	2319 8.7
28 TU ○	0615 0.8	1136 9.4	1833 0.8	2350 9.5
14 TU ◐	0618 1.2	1143 8.9	1832 1.2	2354 9.0
29 W	0655 0.7	1213 9.5	1912 0.8	
15 W	0656 1.0	1217 9.1	1909 1.0	
30 TH	0029 9.5	0730 0.8	1247 9.4	1945 0.9

OCTOBER

Day	Time m	Time m	Time m	Time m
1 F	0103 9.4	0800 0.9	1319 9.3	2015 1.1
16 SA	0038 9.4	0738 0.8	1257 9.5	1956 0.8
2 SA	0135 9.1	0826 1.2	1350 9.0	2041 1.4
17 SU	0115 9.4	0813 1.0	1334 9.4	2032 1.0
3 SU	0206 8.8	0849 1.6	1419 8.6	2106 1.8
18 M	0154 9.2	0848 1.3	1412 9.0	2110 1.3
4 M	0235 8.3	0913 2.0	1447 8.1	2132 2.2
19 TU	0235 8.7	0927 1.7	1455 8.5	2153 1.7
5 TU	0305 7.7	0943 2.6	1517 7.5	2205 2.7
20 W ◑	0323 8.1	1014 2.3	1547 7.9	2246 2.2
6 W	0342 7.1	1023 3.2	1559 6.9	2253 3.3
21 TH	0427 7.5	1118 2.8	1702 7.3	
7 TH	0442 6.4	1126 3.7	1718 6.3	
22 F	0000 2.7	0605 7.1	1252 3.0	1843 7.2
8 F	0014 3.7	0642 6.2	1319 3.8	1923 6.3
23 SA	0144 2.6	0741 7.4	1428 2.5	2009 7.6
9 SA	0216 3.4	0816 6.7	1455 3.2	2037 7.0
24 SU	0307 2.1	0852 8.0	1539 1.9	2113 8.2
10 SU	0327 2.7	0911 7.5	1551 2.5	2127 7.7
25 M	0411 1.5	0945 8.6	1636 1.4	2203 8.8
11 M	0418 2.0	0954 8.1	1637 1.9	2208 8.3
26 TU	0503 1.2	1029 9.0	1724 1.1	2245 9.1
12 TU	0502 1.5	1033 8.7	1719 1.4	2246 8.8
27 W	0546 1.0	1109 9.2	1805 1.0	2324 9.2
13 W	0544 1.2	1110 9.0	1800 1.1	2323 9.1
28 TH	0622 1.0	1144 9.3	1841 1.0	2359 9.2
14 TH ◐	0624 0.9	1146 9.3	1840 0.9	
29 F	0654 1.1	1216 9.2	1912 1.1	
15 F	0000 9.3	0702 0.8	1221 9.4	1918 0.8
30 SA	0033 9.1	0724 1.2	1247 9.1	1942 1.2
31 SU	0105 8.9	0752 1.4	1318 8.9	2011 1.5

NOVEMBER

Day	Time m	Time m	Time m	Time m
1 M	0137 8.6	0819 1.8	1348 8.6	2038 1.8
16 TU	0142 9.1	0836 1.3	1401 9.1	2102 1.2
2 TU	0207 8.2	0845 2.2	1417 8.1	2105 2.2
17 W	0229 8.7	0921 1.7	1450 8.6	2150 1.6
3 W	0238 7.8	0916 2.6	1449 7.6	2137 2.6
18 TH	0324 8.2	1014 2.2	1548 8.0	2247 2.0
4 TH	0316 7.2	0955 3.1	1531 7.0	2222 3.1
19 F ◑	0431 7.7	1121 2.6	1700 7.6	2358 2.3
5 F	0410 6.8	1053 3.5	1637 6.6	2328 3.4
20 SA	0549 7.5	1242 2.6	1819 7.5	
6 SA	0539 6.5	1217 3.6	1815 6.5	
21 SU	0119 2.3	0707 7.6	1359 2.4	1934 7.7
7 SU	0105 3.3	0713 6.8	1350 3.2	1938 6.9
22 M	0232 2.1	0816 7.9	1505 2.0	2039 8.0
8 M	0228 2.8	0818 7.4	1457 2.6	2037 7.5
23 TU	0334 1.8	0912 8.3	1603 1.7	2132 8.4
9 TU	0327 2.2	0908 8.0	1550 2.0	2125 8.1
24 W	0427 1.6	0959 8.6	1652 1.5	2217 8.6
10 W	0418 1.7	0952 8.6	1639 1.5	2208 8.6
25 TH	0510 1.5	1039 8.8	1733 1.4	2257 8.7
11 TH	0505 1.3	1033 9.0	1725 1.2	2250 9.0
26 F ○	0547 1.5	1115 8.9	1809 1.4	2333 8.8
12 F ●	0549 1.1	1113 9.3	1810 1.0	2331 9.3
27 SA	0622 1.5	1149 8.9	1843 1.4	
13 SA	0632 1.0	1153 9.4	1853 0.8	
28 SU	0008 8.7	0655 1.5	1221 8.8	1916 1.4
14 SU	0014 9.4	0714 0.9	1234 9.5	1936 0.8
29 M	0043 8.6	0728 1.6	1254 8.7	1949 1.5
15 M	0057 9.4	0754 1.1	1316 9.4	2018 0.9
30 TU	0116 8.5	0759 1.9	1327 8.5	2020 1.8

DECEMBER

Day	Time m	Time m	Time m	Time m
1 W	0149 8.2	0829 2.1	1400 8.2	2050 2.0
16 TH	0229 8.9	0923 1.5	1448 8.9	2151 1.2
2 TH	0223 7.9	0901 2.4	1435 7.8	2123 2.3
17 F	0321 8.6	1015 1.7	1542 8.5	2243 1.5
3 F	0302 7.6	0940 2.7	1516 7.5	2204 2.6
18 SA ◑	0417 8.2	1111 2.0	1639 8.1	2337 1.9
4 SA	0348 7.3	1029 3.0	1607 7.1	2257 2.8
19 SU	0515 7.9	1209 2.3	1740 7.8	
5 SU ◑	0448 7.0	1130 3.1	1712 7.0	
20 M	0035 2.2	0618 7.7	1312 2.4	1845 7.6
6 M	0001 2.9	0559 7.0	1240 3.0	1825 7.0
21 TU	0138 2.3	0725 7.6	1417 2.3	1953 7.6
7 TU	0114 2.8	0711 7.3	1351 2.7	1934 7.4
22 W	0242 2.3	0830 7.8	1520 2.2	2055 7.7
8 W	0224 2.4	0814 7.8	1457 2.3	2035 7.8
23 TH	0342 2.2	0925 8.0	1616 2.0	2148 7.9
9 TH	0327 2.0	0908 8.3	1556 1.8	2128 8.3
24 F	0434 2.1	1012 8.2	1703 1.8	2234 8.1
10 F	0424 1.7	0957 8.7	1651 1.4	2218 8.7
25 SA	0519 1.9	1053 8.4	1745 1.7	2314 8.3
11 SA	0516 1.4	1045 9.0	1743 1.1	2307 9.0
26 SU ○	0559 1.8	1129 8.5	1823 1.6	2351 8.4
12 SU ●	0607 1.2	1131 9.3	1833 0.9	2355 9.2
27 M	0637 1.7	1204 8.6	1900 1.5	
13 M	0655 1.1	1219 9.4	1922 0.8	
28 TU	0028 8.5	0713 1.7	1239 8.6	1935 1.5
14 TU	0047 9.3	0744 1.1	1307 9.4	2011 0.8
29 W	0103 8.5	0747 1.8	1314 8.5	2009 1.6
15 W	0137 9.2	0833 1.2	1357 9.2	2101 0.9
30 TH	0137 8.4	0820 1.9	1349 8.4	2042 1.7
31 F	0212 8.3	0852 2.0	1423 8.3	2114 1.8

Chart Datum: 4·43 metres below IGN Datum

Chapter 5

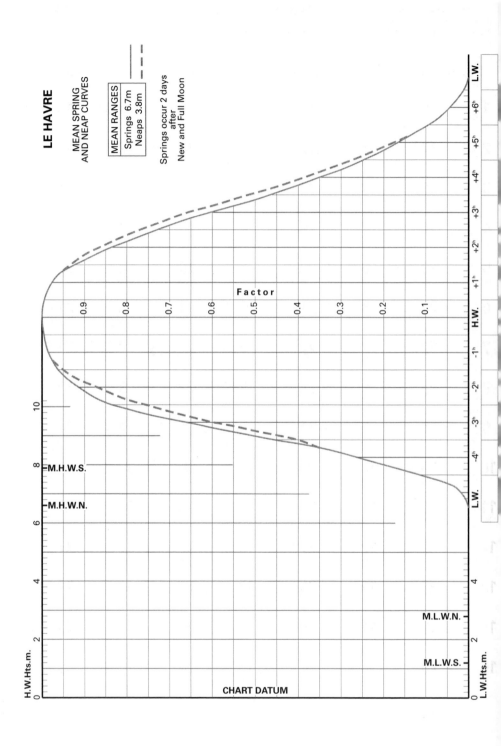

LE HAVRE

MEAN SPRING AND NEAP CURVES

MEAN RANGES
Springs 6.7m
Neaps 3.8m

Springs occur 2 days after New and Full Moon

Factor

0.9 0.8 0.7 0.6 0.5 0.4 0.3 0.2 0.1

L.W. +6ʰ +5ʰ +4ʰ +3ʰ +2ʰ +1ʰ H.W. -1ʰ -2ʰ -3ʰ -4ʰ L.W.

M.H.W.S.

M.H.W.N.

M.L.W.N.

M.L.W.S.

CHART DATUM

H.W.Hts.m.

L.W.Hts.m.

TIME ZONE -0100

TIME ZONE -0100
(French Standard Time)
Subtract 1 hour for UT
For French Summer Time add
ONE hour in **non-shaded areas**

FRANCE – LE HAVRE

YEAR 2004

LAT 49°29′N   LONG 0°07′E

TIMES AND HEIGHTS OF HIGH AND LOW WATERS

JANUARY

Time	m	Time	m
1 0539 6.6 / 1221 3.1 / TH 1804 6.5		**16** 0437 6.9 / 1127 2.7 / F 1701 6.8 / 2359 2.6	
2 0046 3.0 / 0644 6.6 / F 1328 3.1 / 1913 6.5		**17** 0550 6.9 / 1237 2.7 / SA 1823 6.8	
3 0154 3.0 / 0745 6.7 / SA 1434 2.9 / 2014 6.7		**18** 0117 2.6 / 0705 7.0 / SU 1403 2.5 / 1941 6.9	
4 0256 2.8 / 0836 6.9 / SU 1530 2.6 / 2103 6.9		**19** 0239 2.4 / 0814 7.2 / M 1517 2.1 / 2050 7.2	
5 0349 2.6 / 0918 7.1 / M 1618 2.3 / 2145 7.1		**20** 0347 2.1 / 0916 7.5 / TU 1622 1.7 / 2151 7.5	
6 0434 2.4 / 0956 7.3 / TU 1700 2.1 / 2223 7.2		**21** 0449 1.8 / 1011 7.7 / W 1723 1.4 / ● 2244 7.8	
7 0514 2.2 / 1032 7.4 / W 1739 1.9 / ○ 2259 7.3		**22** 0548 1.5 / 1101 7.9 / TH 1819 1.1 / 2333 7.9	
8 0552 2.1 / 1107 7.5 / TH 1816 1.8 / 2335 7.4		**23** 0641 1.4 / 1147 8.0 / F 1907 1.0	
9 0628 2.0 / 1142 7.6 / F 1852 1.7		**24** 0018 7.9 / 0726 1.3 / SA 1231 8.0 / 1950 1.0	
10 0011 7.4 / 0705 2.0 / SA 1218 7.6 / 1930 1.7		**25** 0100 7.8 / 0806 1.4 / SU 1312 7.8 / 2026 1.2	
11 0048 7.4 / 0743 2.0 / SU 1255 7.6 / 2007 1.7		**26** 0140 7.6 / 0842 1.7 / M 1351 7.6 / 2058 1.5	
12 0127 7.3 / 0821 2.0 / M 1336 7.4 / 2044 1.9		**27** 0218 7.4 / 0914 2.0 / TU 1429 7.4 / 2129 1.9	
13 0208 7.2 / 0900 2.2 / TU 1417 7.3 / 2123 2.0		**28** 0255 7.1 / 0945 2.4 / W 1508 7.0 / 2200 2.4	
14 0251 7.1 / 0942 2.4 / W 1502 7.1 / 2205 2.2		**29** 0334 6.8 / 1019 2.8 / TH 1553 6.5 / ◑ 2236 2.8	
15 0339 7.0 / 1030 2.5 / TH 1554 7.0 / ◐ 2256 2.4		**30** 0423 6.6 / 1104 3.1 / F 1651 6.3 / 2325 3.2	
		31 0529 6.3 / 1206 3.4 / SA 1811 6.2	

FEBRUARY

Time	m	Time	m
1 0036 3.4 / 0650 6.3 / SU 1335 3.4 / 1935 6.2		**16** 0046 2.9 / 0647 6.7 / M 1347 2.8 / 1935 6.7	
2 0211 3.3 / 0802 6.4 / M 1455 3.0 / 2040 6.5		**17** 0223 2.7 / 0808 6.9 / TU 1505 2.3 / 2051 7.1	
3 0321 3.0 / 0856 6.7 / TU 1553 2.6 / 2128 6.8		**18** 0341 2.3 / 0913 7.3 / W 1619 1.8 / 2149 7.4	
4 0415 2.6 / 0939 7.0 / W 1642 2.2 / 2208 7.1		**19** 0450 1.8 / 1005 7.6 / TH 1723 1.4 / 2236 7.7	
5 0501 2.2 / 1017 7.3 / TH 1726 1.9 / 2244 7.3		**20** 0547 1.4 / 1050 7.8 / F 1813 1.0 / ● 2319 7.8	
6 0543 1.9 / 1053 7.5 / F 1807 1.6 / ○ 2320 7.5		**21** 0633 1.2 / 1131 8.0 / SA 1854 0.9 / 2358 7.9	
7 0622 1.7 / 1129 7.7 / SA 1845 1.4 / 2356 7.6		**22** 0710 1.1 / 1210 8.0 / SU 1928 0.9	
8 0701 1.5 / 1205 7.8 / SU 1922 1.2		**23** 0034 7.9 / 0743 1.2 / M 1246 7.9 / 1958 1.1	
9 0033 7.7 / 0735 1.4 / M 1242 7.8 / 1957 1.2		**24** 0109 7.7 / 0812 1.4 / TU 1321 7.8 / 2024 1.4	
10 0110 7.7 / 0811 1.5 / TU 1320 7.7 / 2032 1.3		**25** 0141 7.5 / 0837 1.9 / W 1353 7.5 / 2049 1.6	
11 0148 7.6 / 0846 1.6 / W 1359 7.6 / 2106 1.6		**26** 0210 7.3 / 0901 2.1 / TH 1424 7.2 / 2111 2.2	
12 0226 7.4 / 0922 1.9 / TH 1438 7.4 / 2141 1.9		**27** 0239 7.0 / 0927 2.5 / F 1457 6.8 / 2139 2.7	
13 0307 7.2 / 1003 2.2 / F 1524 7.1 / ◑ 2225 2.3		**28** 0314 6.6 / 1002 3.0 / SA 1541 6.3 / ◑ 2222 3.2	
14 0358 7.0 / 1054 2.5 / SA 1628 6.8 / 2323 2.7		**29** 0408 6.2 / 1057 3.4 / SU 1700 5.9 / 2328 3.6	
15 0514 6.7 / 1203 2.8 / SU 1803 6.6			

MARCH

Time	m	Time	m
1 0546 6.0 / 1224 3.6 / M 1854 5.9		**16** 0035 3.2 / 0641 6.5 / TU 1332 2.8 / 1938 6.6	
2 0117 3.7 / 0725 6.1 / TU 1417 3.3 / 2012 6.2		**17** 0223 2.9 / 0804 6.8 / W 1506 2.3 / 2048 7.0	
3 0253 3.2 / 0830 6.4 / W 1527 2.7 / 2105 6.7		**18** 0345 2.3 / 0905 7.2 / TH 1620 1.8 / 2138 7.4	
4 0353 2.6 / 0917 6.9 / TH 1620 2.2 / 2145 7.1		**19** 0447 1.7 / 0951 7.5 / F 1713 1.3 / 2219 7.6	
5 0442 2.1 / 0956 7.2 / F 1707 1.7 / 2222 7.4		**20** 0535 1.4 / 1032 7.7 / SA 1755 1.1 / ● 2256 7.8	
6 0526 1.7 / 1033 7.6 / SA 1748 1.3 / ○ 2259 7.6		**21** 0612 1.2 / 1109 7.9 / SU 1829 1.0 / 2331 7.8	
7 0605 1.4 / 1109 7.8 / SU 1827 1.1 / 2335 7.8		**22** 0644 1.1 / 1144 7.9 / M 1858 1.0	
8 0642 1.1 / 1146 7.9 / M 1903 0.9		**23** 0004 7.8 / 0713 1.2 / TU 1217 7.9 / 1925 1.2	
9 0011 7.9 / 0718 1.0 / TU 1223 8.0 / 1938 0.9		**24** 0035 7.7 / 0739 1.3 / W 1249 7.7 / 1950 1.4	
10 0048 7.9 / 0753 1.0 / W 1301 8.0 / 2012 1.0		**25** 0105 7.6 / 0803 1.6 / TH 1320 7.5 / 2011 1.8	
11 0125 7.8 / 0828 1.2 / TH 1340 7.8 / 2045 1.3		**26** 0131 7.4 / 0824 2.0 / F 1348 7.1 / 2033 2.2	
12 0202 7.6 / 0903 1.6 / F 1420 7.4 / 2119 1.8		**27** 0156 7.1 / 0848 2.4 / SA 1418 6.8 / 2058 2.7	
13 0242 7.3 / 0941 2.0 / SA 1507 7.0 / ◑ 2201 2.4		**28** 0227 6.7 / 0920 2.8 / SU 1458 6.3 / ◑ 2137 3.2	
14 0334 6.9 / 1031 2.5 / SU 1616 6.6 / 2302 2.9		**29** 0314 6.2 / 1008 3.3 / M 1604 5.9 / 2238 3.7	
15 0456 6.5 / 1145 2.9 / M 1801 6.4		**30** 0438 5.9 / 1130 3.6 / TU 1809 5.8	
		31 0028 3.8 / 0641 5.9 / W 1330 3.4 / 1934 6.1	

APRIL

Time	m	Time	m
1 0214 3.3 / 0753 6.3 / TH 1447 2.8 / 2030 6.6		**16** 0328 2.2 / 0844 7.1 / F 1557 1.8 / 2115 7.3	
2 0317 2.6 / 0844 6.8 / F 1544 2.2 / 2114 7.1		**17** 0423 1.7 / 0928 7.4 / SA 1646 1.5 / 2153 7.5	
3 0408 2.1 / 0926 7.2 / SA 1633 1.7 / 2152 7.5		**18** 0506 1.5 / 1007 7.6 / SU 1724 1.3 / 2229 7.7	
4 0454 1.6 / 1004 7.6 / SU 1718 1.3 / 2230 7.7		**19** 0541 1.4 / 1042 7.7 / M 1755 1.3 / ● 2301 7.7	
5 0537 1.2 / 1043 7.8 / M 1759 1.0 / ○ 2307 7.9		**20** 0612 1.3 / 1116 7.7 / TU 1824 1.3 / 2332 7.7	
6 0617 1.0 / 1122 8.0 / TU 1838 0.8 / 2345 8.0		**21** 0641 1.3 / 1149 7.7 / W 1852 1.4	
7 0657 0.8 / 1202 8.1 / W 1915 0.8		**22** 0003 7.6 / 0708 1.5 / TH 1221 7.5 / 1917 1.7	
8 0024 8.0 / 0733 0.9 / TH 1242 8.0 / 1951 1.0		**23** 0032 7.5 / 0733 1.7 / F 1253 7.3 / 1941 1.9	
9 0103 7.9 / 0810 1.1 / F 1324 7.7 / 2027 1.4		**24** 0100 7.3 / 0757 2.0 / SA 1323 7.1 / 2005 2.3	
10 0144 7.6 / 0847 1.5 / SA 1409 7.4 / 2104 1.9		**25** 0127 7.1 / 0822 2.3 / SU 1355 6.7 / 2033 2.7	
11 0228 7.3 / 0928 1.9 / SU 1502 7.0 / 2149 2.5		**26** 0202 6.7 / 0854 2.7 / M 1437 6.4 / 2111 3.1	
12 0325 6.8 / 1022 2.5 / M 1619 6.5 / ◑ 2256 3.0		**27** 0249 6.4 / 0939 3.0 / TU 1537 6.1 / ◑ 2207 3.5	
13 0454 6.5 / 1142 2.8 / TU 1801 6.4		**28** 0359 6.0 / 1051 3.3 / W 1714 6.0 / 2344 3.6	
14 0039 3.1 / 0631 6.5 / W 1328 2.6 / 1927 6.7		**29** 0543 6.0 / 1238 3.2 / TH 1844 6.2	
15 0216 2.7 / 0748 6.7 / TH 1452 2.2 / 2029 7.0		**30** 0131 3.2 / 0703 6.3 / F 1355 2.7 / 1945 6.7	

Chart Datum: 4·38 metres below IGN Datum

TIME ZONE -0100
(French Standard Time)
Subtract 1 hour for UT
For French Summer Time add ONE hour in **non-shaded areas**

FRANCE – LE HAVRE
LAT 49°29'N   LONG 0°07'E
TIMES AND HEIGHTS OF HIGH AND LOW WATERS

YEAR **2004**

MAY

Day	Time m	Time m	Time m	Time m		Day	Time m	Time m	Time m	Time m
1 SA	0228 2.6	0800 6.8	1455 2.2	2033 7.1		**16** SU	0340 2.0	0859 7.2	1600 1.9	2122 7.4
2 SU	0322 2.1	0847 7.2	1549 1.7	2116 7.5		**17** M	0425 1.8	0939 7.3	1641 1.8	2158 7.5
3 M	0414 1.7	0931 7.5	1639 1.3	2157 7.7		**18** TU	0503 1.7	1016 7.4	1716 1.7	2231 7.5
4 TU	0503 1.3	1013 7.8	1726 1.1	○ 2238 7.9		**19** W	0537 1.6	1050 7.5	1749 1.7	● 2303 7.5
5 W	0549 1.0	1057 7.9	1810 0.9	2319 8.0		**20** TH	0610 1.6	1124 7.4	1821 1.8	2335 7.5
6 TH	0634 0.9	1141 8.0	1852 0.9			**21** F	0640 1.7	1159 7.3	1850 1.9	
7 F	0002 8.0	0715 0.9	1227 7.9	1934 1.1		**22** SA	0006 7.4	0709 1.8	1232 7.2	1918 2.1
8 SA	0045 7.9	0757 1.1	1313 7.7	2014 1.5		**23** SU	0038 7.3	0737 2.0	1306 7.0	1947 2.3
9 SU	0131 7.6	0839 1.4	1404 7.3	2057 2.0		**24** M	0110 7.1	0807 2.2	1342 6.8	2019 2.6
10 M	0221 7.3	0925 1.9	1502 7.0	2150 2.5		**25** TU	0148 6.9	0841 2.5	1425 6.6	2058 2.8
11 TU	0323 6.9	1024 2.3	1618 6.7	◑ 2302 2.8		**26** W	0235 6.6	0925 2.7	1517 6.4	2150 3.1
12 W	0443 6.6	1143 2.5	1740 6.6			**27** TH	0333 6.4	1026 2.9	1625 6.3	◑ 2305 3.2
13 TH	0026 2.8	0604 6.6	1301 2.4	1855 6.8		**28** F	0445 6.3	1145 2.9	1744 6.4	
14 F	0140 2.6	0715 6.8	1410 2.2	1956 7.0		**29** SA	0024 3.0	0603 6.5	1258 2.6	1850 6.7
15 SA	0245 2.3	0812 7.0	1510 2.0	2043 7.2		**30** SU	0132 2.7	0707 6.8	1402 2.3	1945 7.1
						31 M	0235 2.2	0803 7.1	1503 1.9	2035 7.4

JUNE

Day	Time m	Time m	Time m	Time m		Day	Time m	Time m	Time m	Time m
1 TU	0334 1.8	0855 7.4	1600 1.6	2123 7.6		**16** W	0426 2.1	0953 7.1	1640 2.0	2206 7.3
2 W	0430 1.5	0946 7.6	1654 1.4	2210 7.8		**17** TH	0506 1.9	1024 7.2	1720 2.1	● 2240 7.4
3 TH	0522 1.2	1036 7.8	1745 1.2	○ 2257 7.9		**18** F	0544 1.9	1107 7.2	1757 2.0	2314 7.4
4 F	0612 1.0	1126 7.8	1834 1.2	2345 7.9		**19** SA	0619 1.8	1142 7.2	1830 2.1	2348 7.3
5 SA	0701 1.0	1216 7.8	1921 1.3			**20** SU	0653 1.8	1217 7.2	1904 2.1	
6 SU	0034 7.8	0747 1.1	1307 7.7	2009 1.5		**21** M	0022 7.3	0726 1.9	1253 7.1	1938 2.2
7 M	0123 7.6	0834 1.3	1400 7.4	2059 1.9		**22** TU	0058 7.2	0801 2.0	1330 7.0	2014 2.3
8 TU	0216 7.4	0924 1.6	1456 7.1	2152 2.2		**23** W	0137 7.1	0837 2.1	1411 6.9	2053 2.5
9 W	0313 7.1	1018 2.0	1557 6.9	◑ 2250 2.5		**24** TH	0220 7.0	0918 2.3	1456 6.8	2138 2.6
10 TH	0415 6.8	1118 2.2	1701 6.8	2350 2.6		**25** F	0307 6.8	1004 2.4	1546 6.7	◑ 2231 2.7
11 F	0521 6.7	1217 2.4	1806 6.8			**26** SA	0400 6.7	1100 2.5	1645 6.7	2331 2.7
12 SA	0051 2.6	0627 6.7	1316 2.5	1908 6.8		**27** SU	0504 6.7	1203 2.5	1752 6.8	
13 SU	0151 2.5	0730 6.8	1414 2.4	2003 7.0		**28** M	0038 2.6	0615 6.8	1311 2.4	1858 7.0
14 M	0249 2.4	0825 6.9	1509 2.3	2049 7.1		**29** TU	0149 2.4	0723 6.9	1423 2.2	1959 7.2
15 TU	0340 2.2	0912 7.0	1557 2.2	2129 7.2		**30** W	0301 2.1	0828 7.2	1529 1.9	2056 7.4

JULY

Day	Time m	Time m	Time m	Time m		Day	Time m	Time m	Time m	Time m
1 TH	0403 1.7	0928 7.4	1629 1.7	2151 7.7		**16** F	0443 2.2	1016 7.1	1659 2.3	2224 7.2
2 F	0501 1.4	1024 7.6	1727 1.5	○ 2244 7.8		**17** SA	0525 2.0	1052 7.2	1741 2.1	● 2259 7.3
3 SA	0558 1.1	1118 7.8	1823 1.3	2335 7.9		**18** SU	0605 1.8	1128 7.3	1820 2.0	2334 7.4
4 SU	0653 1.0	1209 7.8	1917 1.3			**19** M	0643 1.7	1203 7.3	1856 1.9	
5 M	0025 7.9	0745 1.0	1259 7.8	2006 1.4		**20** TU	0009 7.5	0719 1.6	1238 7.3	1932 1.9
6 TU	0114 7.8	0832 1.1	1348 7.6	2052 1.6		**21** W	0044 7.5	0754 1.6	1314 7.3	2007 1.9
7 W	0201 7.6	0915 1.3	1435 7.4	2136 1.9		**22** TH	0121 7.4	0829 1.7	1351 7.3	2043 2.0
8 TH	0248 7.3	0955 1.7	1522 7.1	2218 2.2		**23** F	0200 7.3	0904 1.9	1430 7.2	2120 2.2
9 F	0337 7.0	1035 2.1	1611 6.9	◑ 2302 2.5		**24** SA	0240 7.2	0940 2.1	1512 7.0	2201 2.4
10 SA	0430 6.8	1122 2.5	1706 6.7	◑ 2354 2.8		**25** SU	0324 7.0	1023 2.3	1559 6.9	◑ 2250 2.5
11 SU	0531 6.6	1215 2.8	1808 6.6			**26** M	0418 6.8	1116 2.5	1700 6.8	2353 2.7
12 M	0055 2.9	0640 6.5	1320 2.9	1916 6.6		**27** TU	0533 6.7	1227 2.7	1819 6.8	
13 TU	0202 2.9	0751 6.5	1426 2.9	2016 6.8		**28** W	0113 2.6	0659 6.7	1353 2.6	1936 7.0
14 W	0303 2.7	0849 6.7	1523 2.7	2106 6.9		**29** TH	0241 2.3	0816 7.0	1509 2.3	2044 7.3
15 TH	0356 2.4	0936 6.9	1614 2.5	2147 7.1		**30** F	0345 1.9	0922 7.3	1615 1.9	2144 7.6
						31 SA	0450 1.5	1020 7.6	1719 1.6	○ 2237 7.8

AUGUST

Day	Time m	Time m	Time m	Time m		Day	Time m	Time m	Time m	Time m
1 SU	0553 1.1	1110 7.8	1819 1.3	2326 8.0		**16** M	0552 1.7	1108 7.4	1807 1.8	● 2316 7.6
2 M	0648 0.9	1158 7.9	1910 1.2			**17** TU	0629 1.5	1142 7.5	1844 1.6	2350 7.7
3 TU	0011 8.0	0734 0.8	1242 7.9	1953 1.2		**18** W	0704 1.3	1217 7.6	1917 1.5	
4 W	0055 7.9	0814 0.9	1324 7.8	2031 1.3		**19** TH	0025 7.7	0737 1.3	1251 7.6	1950 1.5
5 TH	0136 7.8	0848 1.2	1403 7.6	2104 1.7		**20** F	0100 7.7	0810 1.4	1327 7.6	2024 1.6
6 F	0215 7.5	0918 1.6	1441 7.3	2136 2.1		**21** SA	0137 7.6	0842 1.6	1403 7.4	2058 1.9
7 SA	0254 7.2	0950 2.1	1519 7.0	◑ 2208 2.5		**22** SU	0214 7.4	0916 1.9	1441 7.2	2135 2.2
8 SU	0337 6.8	1022 2.6	1603 6.7	2249 2.9		**23** M	0256 7.1	0953 2.3	1524 7.0	◑ 2220 2.5
9 M	0431 6.4	1107 3.1	1704 6.4	2348 3.3		**24** TU	0350 6.8	1044 2.7	1627 6.7	2322 2.8
10 TU	0548 6.2	1216 3.4	1825 6.3			**25** W	0515 6.5	1159 3.0	1802 6.6	
11 W	0115 3.3	0719 6.2	1349 3.4	1947 6.4		**26** TH	0053 2.9	0656 6.6	1341 2.9	1930 6.8
12 TH	0234 3.1	0830 6.4	1500 3.1	2046 6.7		**27** F	0227 2.5	0818 6.9	1504 2.5	2042 7.2
13 F	0334 2.6	0920 6.7	1557 2.7	2130 7.0		**28** SA	0341 1.9	0922 7.4	1614 1.9	2139 7.6
14 SA	0425 2.3	0959 7.0	1646 2.3	2207 7.2		**29** SU	0449 1.4	1012 7.7	1718 1.5	2226 7.9
15 SU	0511 1.9	1034 7.3	1729 2.0	2241 7.4		**30** M	0547 1.0	1056 7.9	1810 1.2	○ 2309 8.0
						31 TU	0633 0.8	1137 8.0	1852 1.1	2350 8.1

Chart Datum: 4·38 metres below IGN Datum

TIME ZONE -0100
(French Standard Time)
Subtract 1 hour for UT
For French Summer Time add
ONE hour in **non-shaded areas**

FRANCE – LE HAVRE

LAT 49°29′N   LONG 0°07′E

YEAR **2004**

TIMES AND HEIGHTS OF HIGH AND LOW WATERS

SEPTEMBER

Time	m		Time	m
1 0712	0.8		**16** 0640	1.1
1216	8.0		1150	7.9
W 1928	1.1		TH 1855	1.3
2 0029	8.0		**17** 0001	7.9
0744	1.0		0713	1.1
TH 1253	7.9		F 1225	7.9
1959	1.3		1929	1.3
3 0105	7.9		**18** 0037	7.9
0813	1.3		0747	1.2
F 1327	7.7		SA 1301	7.8
2027	1.6		2003	1.4
4 0140	7.6		**19** 0114	7.7
0839	1.7		0820	1.5
SA 1359	7.4		SU 1337	7.6
2052	2.1		2038	1.7
5 0214	7.2		**20** 0154	7.4
0902	2.2		0853	1.9
SU 1430	7.1		M 1416	7.3
2118	2.5		2114	2.1
6 0249	6.8		**21** 0238	7.1
0928	2.7		0931	2.4
M 1505	6.7		TU 1502	7.0
◗ 2151	3.0		◗ 2159	2.6
7 0335	6.3		**22** 0339	6.7
1008	3.3		1025	3.0
TU 1558	6.3		W 1613	6.6
2244	3.5		2306	3.0
8 0455	5.9		**23** 0519	6.4
1113	3.7		1151	3.3
W 1735	6.0		TH 1801	6.5
9 0020	3.7		**24** 0101	3.0
0646	5.9		0701	6.6
TH 1318	3.8		F 1345	3.0
1915	6.1		1929	6.8
10 0208	3.3		**25** 0228	2.4
0804	6.2		0817	7.0
F 1440	3.3		SA 1506	2.4
2021	6.5		2036	7.2
11 0312	2.8		**26** 0340	1.8
0855	6.7		0912	7.5
SA 1537	2.7		SU 1611	1.8
2106	6.9		2125	7.6
12 0403	2.2		**27** 0440	1.4
0934	7.1		0955	7.8
SU 1625	2.2		M 1704	1.4
2142	7.3		2208	7.9
13 0448	1.5		**28** 0528	1.1
1008	7.4		1034	7.9
M 1707	1.8		TU 1748	1.2
2217	7.8		○ 2247	8.0
14 0528	1.5		**29** 0607	1.0
1042	7.6		1111	8.0
TU 1745	1.6		W 1824	1.2
● 2251	7.8		2324	8.1
15 0605	1.3		**30** 0640	1.0
1116	7.8		1145	8.0
W 1820	1.4		TH 1856	1.2
2326	7.9		2359	8.0

OCTOBER

Time	m		Time	m
1 0709	1.2		**16** 0647	1.1
1218	7.9		1157	8.0
F 1925	1.4		SA 1906	1.2
2 0033	7.8		**17** 0015	7.9
0736	1.5		0724	1.3
SA 1250	7.7		SU 1235	7.9
1951	1.7		1944	1.3
3 0107	7.5		**18** 0056	7.7
0800	1.9		0800	1.6
SU 1319	7.4		M 1315	7.7
2014	2.1		2021	1.7
4 0138	7.2		**19** 0140	7.4
0822	2.4		0837	2.1
M 1347	7.1		TU 1400	7.3
2038	2.5		2101	2.1
5 0210	6.8		**20** 0232	7.0
0848	2.9		0920	2.6
TU 1417	6.7		W 1453	7.0
2109	3.0		◗ 2151	2.5
6 0250	6.3		**21** 0342	6.7
0925	3.4		1021	3.1
W 1504	6.3		TH 1614	6.6
2156	3.5		2305	2.9
7 0401	5.9		**22** 0524	6.5
1025	3.8		1200	3.3
TH 1634	5.9		F 1755	6.6
2323	3.8			
8 0605	5.9		**23** 0055	2.8
1226	4.0		0652	6.7
F 1832	5.9		SA 1341	2.9
			1914	6.8
9 0126	3.5		**24** 0217	2.3
0724	6.2		0800	7.2
SA 1405	3.4		SU 1451	2.3
1942	6.3		2016	7.2
10 0235	2.9		**25** 0321	1.8
0818	6.7		0850	7.5
SU 1502	2.8		M 1549	1.8
2030	6.8		2104	7.6
11 0326	2.3		**26** 0414	1.5
0859	7.2		0930	7.7
M 1549	2.2		TU 1637	1.5
2110	7.3		2144	7.8
12 0412	1.8		**27** 0457	1.4
0935	7.5		1007	7.9
TU 1632	1.8		W 1717	1.4
2146	7.6		2222	7.9
13 0454	1.5		**28** 0533	1.4
1010	7.8		1042	7.9
W 1712	1.5		TH 1752	1.4
2222	7.8		○ 2258	7.9
14 0533	1.3		**29** 0605	1.4
1045	7.9		1115	7.9
TH 1751	1.3		F 1823	1.5
● 2258	8.0		2332	7.8
15 0610	1.1		**30** 0634	1.6
1121	8.0		1146	7.8
F 1829	1.2		SA 1853	1.6
2336	8.0			
			31 0006	7.7
			0703	1.8
			SU 1217	7.6
			1921	1.8

NOVEMBER

Time	m		Time	m
1 0039	7.4		**16** 0045	7.7
0729	2.1		0747	1.7
M 1247	7.4		TU 1303	7.7
1946	2.1		2012	1.6
2 0112	7.1		**17** 0135	7.5
0754	2.5		0831	2.1
TU 1316	7.1		W 1352	7.4
2012	2.5		2058	1.9
3 0145	6.8		**18** 0231	7.1
0822	2.9		0922	2.5
W 1348	6.8		TH 1451	7.1
2043	2.9		2154	2.3
4 0225	6.4		**19** 0343	6.8
0859	3.3		1028	2.9
TH 1434	6.4		F 1607	6.8
2126	3.3		◗ 2309	2.6
5 0324	6.1		**20** 0505	6.7
0953	3.7		1152	2.9
F 1542	6.1		SA 1729	6.7
◗ 2236	3.5			
6 0504	6.0		**21** 0030	2.6
1127	3.8		0621	6.9
SA 1729	6.0		SU 1310	2.7
			1841	6.9
7 0021	3.5		**22** 0141	2.4
0629	6.3		0726	7.1
SU 1311	3.5		M 1416	2.4
1847	6.3		1944	7.1
8 0138	3.0		**23** 0243	2.1
0728	6.7		0818	7.3
M 1409	2.9		TU 1513	2.1
1942	6.7		2036	7.3
9 0236	2.5		**24** 0336	2.0
0814	7.1		0901	7.5
TU 1502	2.4		W 1602	1.9
2028	7.2		2119	7.5
10 0326	2.0		**25** 0420	1.9
0855	7.5		0940	7.6
W 1550	2.0		TH 1643	1.8
2110	7.5		2159	7.6
11 0413	1.7		**26** 0457	1.8
0934	7.7		1015	7.7
TH 1636	1.6		F 1719	1.7
2150	7.7		○ 2236	7.6
12 0458	1.4		**27** 0532	1.8
1013	7.9		1048	7.7
F 1722	1.4		SA 1754	1.7
● 2231	7.9		2311	7.6
13 0542	1.3		**28** 0605	1.9
1052	8.0		1121	7.6
SA 1806	1.2		SU 1827	1.8
2314	8.0		2346	7.5
14 0624	1.3		**29** 0637	2.0
1134	8.0		1153	7.5
SU 1848	1.2		M 1858	1.9
2359	7.9			
15 0706	1.4		**30** 0020	7.3
1217	7.9		0707	2.2
M 1930	1.3		TU 1225	7.4
			1928	2.1

DECEMBER

Time	m		Time	m
1 0054	7.1		**16** 0132	7.6
0738	2.5		0834	1.8
W 1257	7.2		TH 1348	7.6
1958	2.3		2100	1.6
2 0129	6.9		**17** 0227	7.4
0809	2.7		0926	2.1
TH 1332	7.0		F 1443	7.3
2030	2.6		2151	1.9
3 0208	6.7		**18** 0325	7.1
0845	3.0		1020	2.4
F 1415	6.7		SA 1542	7.1
2110	2.9		◗ 2245	2.2
4 0256	6.5		**19** 0427	6.9
0932	3.2		1117	2.6
SA 1508	6.5		SU 1646	6.9
2203	3.1		2344	2.5
5 0357	6.4		**20** 0531	6.9
1035	3.4		1219	2.8
SU 1613	6.4		M 1753	6.8
◗ 2312	3.1			
6 0513	6.4		**21** 0047	2.6
1149	3.3		0636	6.9
M 1731	6.4		TU 1324	2.8
			1901	6.8
7 0024	3.0		**22** 0151	2.6
0624	6.6		0738	7.0
TU 1259	3.1		W 1428	2.6
1840	6.7		2003	6.9
8 0131	2.7		**23** 0251	2.6
0721	6.9		0830	7.1
W 1404	2.7		TH 1524	2.4
1939	6.9		2056	7.0
9 0234	2.4		**24** 0342	2.4
0811	7.2		0915	7.2
TH 1507	2.3		F 1612	2.2
2031	7.2		2141	7.2
10 0332	2.0		**25** 0427	2.4
0858	7.5		0955	7.4
F 1603	1.9		SA 1653	2.1
2121	7.5		2221	7.3
11 0426	1.7		**26** 0507	2.2
0944	7.7		1030	7.4
SA 1655	1.5		SU 1732	1.9
2210	7.7		○ 2257	7.4
12 0517	1.5		**27** 0545	2.1
1030	7.9		1104	7.5
SU 1746	1.3		M 1809	1.9
● 2259	7.8		2332	7.4
13 0607	1.4		**28** 0622	2.1
1118	8.0		1138	7.5
M 1835	1.1		TU 1844	1.9
2349	7.9			
14 0655	1.4		**29** 0006	7.3
1207	7.9		0655	2.1
TU 1923	1.2		W 1211	7.4
			1917	1.9
15 0040	7.8		**30** 0040	7.3
0744	1.6		0709	2.2
W 1256	7.8		TH 1244	7.4
2011	1.3		1951	2.0
			31 0114	7.2
			0802	2.3
			F 1319	7.3
			2023	2.1

Chart Datum: 4·38 metres below IGN Datum

Chapter 5

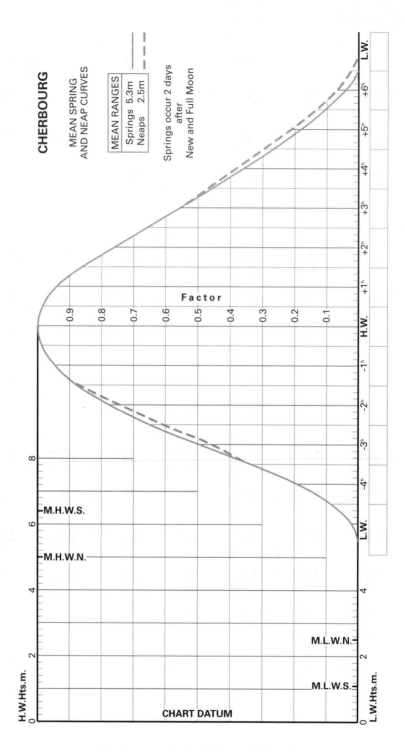

CHERBOURG

MEAN SPRING
AND NEAP CURVES

MEAN RANGES	
Springs	5.3m
Neaps	2.5m

Springs occur 2 days
after
New and Full Moon

TIME ZONE -0100
(French Standard Time)
Subtract 1 hour for UT
For French Summer Time add
ONE hour in **non-shaded areas**

FRANCE – CHERBOURG

LAT 49°39'N   LONG 1°38'W

TIMES AND HEIGHTS OF HIGH AND LOW WATERS

YEAR **2004**

JANUARY

#	Time m	Time m	Time m	Time m		#	Time m	Time m	Time m	Time m
1 TH	0336 5.0	1028 2.8	1559 5.0	2252 2.6		**16**	0237 5.2	0926 2.4	F 1458 5.3	2159 2.2
2 F	0441 5.0	1135 2.7	1706 5.0	2356 2.6		**17**	0349 5.2	1040 2.4	SA 1617 5.2	2315 2.2
3 SA	0543 5.1	1235 2.5	1808 5.1			**18**	0506 5.4	1157 2.2	SU 1738 5.4	
4 SU	0055 2.4	0635 5.3	1327 2.3	1901 5.3		**19**	0033 2.1	M 0616 5.6	1307 1.9	1849 5.6
5 M	0143 2.3	0721 5.5	1412 2.1	1946 5.5		**20**	0139 1.8	TU 0717 6.0	1409 1.5	1950 5.9
6 TU	0226 2.1	0800 5.7	1451 1.9	2026 5.7		**21**	0237 1.6	W 0812 6.2	1505 1.2	● 2046 6.2
7 W	0304 2.0	0837 5.9	1528 1.7	○ 2102 5.8		**22**	0330 1.4	TH 0904 6.4	1556 1.0	2136 6.3
8 TH	0341 1.9	0911 6.0	1604 1.6	2137 5.8		**23**	0418 1.3	F 0951 6.5	1643 0.9	2221 6.3
9 F	0417 1.8	0946 6.1	1640 1.5	2213 5.9		**24**	0503 1.3	SA 1035 6.5	1726 0.9	2303 6.2
10 SA	0453 1.8	1021 6.1	1716 1.5	2249 5.8		**25**	0544 1.3	SU 1116 6.4	1806 1.1	2342 6.1
11 SU	0529 1.8	1059 6.0	1753 1.5	2328 5.8		**26**	0623 1.5	M 1155 6.2	1843 1.4	
12 M	0607 1.8	1138 5.9	1831 1.6			**27**	0017 5.8	TU 0700 1.8	1231 5.9	1918 1.7
13 TU	0009 5.6	0647 1.9	1218 5.8	1912 1.7		**28**	0052 5.5	W 0737 2.1	1307 5.5	1954 2.1
14 W	0050 5.5	0732 2.1	1302 5.6	1958 1.9		**29**	0130 5.2	TH 0818 2.5	1349 5.1	◑ 2036 2.4
15 TH	0138 5.3	0824 2.2	1353 5.4	◑ 2053 2.1		**30**	0217 5.0	F 0910 2.7	1444 4.8	2132 2.8
						31	0323 4.8	SA 1022 2.9	1603 4.6	2250 2.9

FEBRUARY

#	Time m	Time m	Time m	Time m		#	Time m	Time m	Time m	Time m
1 SU	0448 4.7	1147 2.8	1733 4.7			**16**	0446 5.1	1140 2.4	M 1734 5.1	
2 M	0015 2.8	0603 4.9	1258 2.6	1840 4.9		**17**	0024 2.4	0609 5.4	TU 1302 2.0	1852 5.4
3 TU	0120 2.6	0659 5.2	1351 2.3	1929 5.2		**18**	0137 2.0	0715 5.7	W 1407 1.6	1952 5.8
4 W	0209 2.3	0743 5.5	1435 1.9	2011 5.5		**19**	0235 1.7	0810 6.1	TH 1501 1.2	2043 6.1
5 TH	0250 2.0	0823 5.8	1514 1.6	2049 5.8		**20**	0324 1.4	0858 6.4	F 1547 0.9	● 2126 6.3
6 F	0328 1.7	0900 6.0	1551 1.4	○ 2126 6.0		**21**	0407 1.2	0940 6.6	SA 1628 0.8	2205 6.4
7 SA	0405 1.5	0935 6.2	1627 1.2	2202 6.1		**22**	0446 1.1	1018 6.6	SU 1705 0.8	2240 6.3
8 SU	0441 1.4	1011 6.3	1703 1.1	2237 6.1		**23**	0521 1.1	1053 6.5	M 1738 0.9	2312 6.2
9 M	0517 1.3	1048 6.3	1738 1.0	2314 6.1		**24**	0553 1.3	1125 6.3	TU 1809 1.0	2342 6.0
10 TU	0552 1.3	1124 6.3	1814 1.1	2350 6.0		**25**	0624 1.5	1155 6.0	W 1837 1.5	
11 W	0629 1.4	1200 6.1	1851 1.3			**26**	0009 5.7	0654 1.9	TH 1223 5.6	1907 1.9
12 TH	0025 5.8	0709 1.6	1237 5.9	1931 1.6		**27**	0036 5.4	0727 2.2	F 1254 5.2	1940 2.4
13 F	0105 5.6	0754 1.9	1322 5.5	2020 2.0		**28**	0110 5.1	0807 2.6	SA 1335 4.8	2024 2.8
14 SA	0157 5.3	0851 2.3	1423 5.2	2123 2.4		**29**	0201 4.7	0907 2.9	SU 1449 4.4	2137 3.1
15 SU	0310 5.1	1007 2.4	1554 5.0	2249 2.5						

MARCH

#	Time m	Time m	Time m	Time m		#	Time m	Time m	Time m	Time m
1 M	0339 4.5	1047 3.0	1700 4.4	2330 3.1		**16**	0440 4.9	1138 2.4	TU 1743 5.0	
2 TU	0531 4.6	1226 2.8	1820 4.7			**17**	0026 2.5	0607 5.2	W 1300 2.0	1854 5.4
3 W	0056 2.8	0635 5.0	1327 2.4	1910 5.1		**18**	0135 2.1	0710 5.7	TH 1400 1.5	1945 5.8
4 TH	0148 2.3	0722 5.4	1412 1.9	1951 5.5		**19**	0227 1.6	0800 6.1	F 1448 1.2	2028 6.1
5 F	0230 1.9	0803 5.8	1452 1.5	2029 5.9		**20**	0310 1.3	0842 6.3	SA 1529 1.0	● 2106 6.3
6 SA	0308 1.6	0841 6.1	1529 1.2	○ 2106 6.1		**21**	0348 1.1	0919 6.5	SU 1605 0.9	2140 6.3
7 SU	0345 1.2	0918 6.4	1605 0.9	2142 6.3		**22**	0422 1.0	0953 6.5	M 1637 0.9	2211 6.3
8 M	0421 0.9	0954 6.5	1641 0.7	2218 6.4		**23**	0453 1.1	1025 6.4	TU 1706 1.0	2239 6.2
9 TU	0457 0.9	1030 6.6	1717 0.7	2253 6.4		**24**	0522 1.2	1054 6.2	W 1734 1.2	2306 6.0
10 W	0532 0.9	1105 6.5	1752 0.8	2328 6.3		**25**	0550 1.4	1121 5.9	TH 1801 1.6	2330 5.8
11 TH	0609 1.1	1141 6.3	1828 1.1			**26**	0618 1.7	1147 5.6	F 1828 1.9	2355 5.5
12 F	0003 6.0	0648 1.4	1218 5.9	1908 1.6		**27**	0649 2.1	1215 5.2	SA 1859 2.4	
13 SA	0041 5.7	0733 1.8	1303 5.5	◑ 1956 2.1		**28**	0025 5.1	0725 2.5	SU 1252 4.8	◑ 1939 2.8
14 SU	0132 5.3	0830 2.2	1407 5.0	2103 2.6		**29**	0109 4.8	0816 2.8	M 1355 4.4	2045 3.1
15 M	0250 5.0	0955 2.5	1556 4.8	2242 2.8		**30**	0232 4.4	0947 3.0	TU 1617 4.3	2240 3.2
						31	0445 4.5	1140 2.8	W 1749 4.6	

APRIL

#	Time m	Time m	Time m	Time m		#	Time m	Time m	Time m	Time m
1 TH	0018 2.8	0600 4.9	1249 2.4	1839 5.1		**16**	0116 2.0	0649 5.6	F 1339 1.6	1922 5.8
2 F	0113 2.4	0650 5.3	1337 1.9	1920 5.5		**17**	0205 1.7	0736 6.0	SA 1423 1.3	2002 6.0
3 SA	0157 1.9	0732 5.7	1419 1.4	2000 5.9		**18**	0245 1.4	0816 6.2	SU 1501 1.2	2037 6.2
4 SU	0238 1.6	0813 6.1	1458 1.1	2038 6.2		**19**	0321 1.3	0852 6.3	M 1535 1.1	● 2110 6.2
5 M	0317 1.1	0852 6.4	1537 0.8	○ 2116 6.4		**20**	0354 1.2	0925 6.3	TU 1605 1.1	2139 6.2
6 TU	0355 0.9	0930 6.6	1615 0.6	2153 6.6		**21**	0424 1.2	0956 6.2	W 1634 1.3	2207 6.1
7 W	0433 0.7	1008 6.6	1652 0.6	2229 6.6		**22**	0453 1.3	1025 6.0	TH 1703 1.4	2234 6.0
8 TH	0512 0.8	1046 6.5	1730 0.8	2306 6.4		**23**	0522 1.5	1053 5.8	F 1731 1.7	2300 5.8
9 F	0551 1.0	1125 6.3	1809 1.2	2344 6.1		**24**	0551 1.7	1121 5.5	SA 1800 2.0	2327 5.5
10 SA	0633 1.3	1207 5.9	1853 1.7			**25**	0622 2.0	1152 5.2	SU 1832 2.4	
11 SU	0026 5.7	0721 1.7	1258 5.4	1946 2.2		**26**	0000 5.2	0659 2.3	M 1232 4.9	1914 2.7
12 M	0122 5.3	0824 2.2	1410 4.9	2102 2.7		**27**	0046 4.9	0749 2.6	TU 1333 4.6	◑ 2017 3.0
13 TU	0246 4.9	0953 2.4	1604 4.8	2245 2.7		**28**	0157 4.6	0906 2.8	W 1519 4.4	2151 3.1
14 W	0433 4.9	1131 2.3	1736 5.0			**29**	0343 4.6	1042 2.7	TH 1655 4.7	2320 2.8
15 TH	0015 2.4	0552 5.3	1244 1.9	1836 5.4		**30**	0505 4.8	1156 2.3	F 1753 5.1	

Chapter 5

Chart Datum: 3·33 metres below IGN Datum

TIME ZONE -0100
(French Standard Time)
Subtract 1 hour for UT
For French Summer Time add
ONE hour in **non-shaded areas**

FRANCE – CHERBOURG

LAT 49°39'N   LONG 1°38'W

TIMES AND HEIGHTS OF HIGH AND LOW WATERS

YEAR 2004

MAY

	Time	m		Time	m
1 SA	0025 0603 1250 1839	2.3 5.2 1.9 5.5	**16** SU	0130 0701 1348 1928	1.9 5.7 1.6 5.8
2 SU	0115 0651 1338 1922	1.9 5.7 1.5 5.9	**17** M	0213 0744 1427 2005	1.7 5.8 1.5 5.9
3 M	0201 0736 1422 2003	1.5 6.0 1.1 6.2	**18** TU	0251 0823 1502 2039	1.5 5.9 1.5 6.0
4 TU	0245 0820 1506 2045	1.1 6.3 0.9 6.4	**19** W	0325 0858 1535 2110	1.5 5.9 1.5 6.0
5 W	0328 0904 1548 2126	0.9 6.5 0.8 6.6	**20** TH	0358 0931 1607 2140	1.5 5.9 1.6 6.0
6 TH	0411 0947 1630 2207	0.8 6.5 0.8 6.6	**21** F	0429 1002 1638 2209	1.5 5.8 1.7 5.9
7 F	0454 1030 1712 2248	0.8 6.4 1.0 6.4	**22** SA	0501 1033 1709 2239	1.6 5.7 1.9 5.7
8 SA	0538 1115 1757 2332	1.0 6.2 1.4 6.1	**23** SU	0533 1106 1741 2312	1.7 5.5 2.1 5.6
9 SU	0625 1203 1847	1.3 5.8 1.8	**24** M	0607 1142 1817 2350	1.9 5.3 2.3 5.3
10 M	0021 1259 1947	5.8 5.4 2.3	**25** TU	0646 1225 1901	2.1 5.0 2.5
11 TU	0120 0824 1414 2102	5.4 2.0 5.0 2.5	**26** W	0036 0734 1320 1958	5.1 2.3 4.8 2.7
12 W	0239 0944 1545 2227	5.1 2.2 4.9 2.6	**27** TH	0135 0837 1431 2109	4.9 2.4 4.7 2.8
13 TH	0405 1103 1702 2340	5.1 2.1 5.1 2.4	**28** F	0248 0948 1549 2224	4.8 2.4 4.9 2.6
14 F	0516 1208 1800	5.3 2.0 5.3	**29** SA	0401 1059 1654 2330	5.0 2.2 5.1 2.3
15 SA	0041 0613 1302 1847	2.1 5.5 1.8 5.6	**30** SU	0506 1200 1749	5.2 1.9 5.4
			31 M	0031 0603 1256 1840	2.0 5.5 1.6 5.8

JUNE

	Time	m		Time	m
1 TU	0124 0657 1347 1928	1.6 5.9 1.3 6.1	**16** W	0222 0757 1433 2011	1.9 5.5 1.9 5.7
2 W	0215 0750 1437 2015	1.3 6.1 1.1 6.3	**17** TH	0301 0837 1511 2047	1.7 5.6 1.8 5.8
3 TH	0304 0841 1525 2102	1.0 6.3 1.0 6.5	**18** F	0337 0913 1547 2121	1.7 5.7 1.8 5.8
4 F	0353 0931 1613 2149	0.9 6.3 1.1 6.5	**19** SA	0412 0947 1621 2154	1.6 5.7 1.8 5.8
5 SA	0441 1020 1701 2237	0.9 6.3 1.2 6.4	**20** SU	0447 1021 1655 2227	1.6 5.6 1.9 5.8
6 SU	0531 1110 1751 2326	1.0 6.1 1.4 6.2	**21** M	0521 1056 1730 2303	1.5 5.5 2.0 5.7
7 M	0621 1201 1844	1.2 5.8 1.7	**22** TU	0557 1133 1807 2342	1.7 5.4 2.1 5.6
8 TU	0017 0715 1256 1941	5.9 1.5 5.5 2.0	**23** W	0635 1214 1848	1.8 5.3 2.2
9 W	0113 0813 1357 2044	5.6 1.7 5.3 2.3	**24** TH	0023 0717 1300 1936	5.4 1.9 5.2 2.3
10 TH	0215 0914 1502 2149	5.4 2.0 5.1 2.4	**25** F	0110 0805 1351 2031	5.3 2.1 5.1 2.4
11 F	0320 1017 1608 2253	5.2 2.1 5.1 2.4	**26** SA	0203 0902 1450 2133	5.2 2.1 5.1 2.4
12 SA	0425 1119 1708 2354	5.2 2.1 5.2 2.3	**27** SU	0304 1006 1554 2241	5.1 2.1 5.1 2.3
13 SU	0526 1215 1802	5.2 2.1 5.3	**28** M	0411 1113 1700 2347	5.2 2.0 5.3 2.1
14 M	0050 0622 1306 1850	2.2 5.3 2.0 5.5	**29** TU	0521 1218 1802	5.4 1.9 5.6
15 TU	0138 0712 1352 1933	2.0 5.4 1.9 5.6	**30** W	0053 0628 1319 1900	1.8 5.6 1.6 5.9

JULY

	Time	m		Time	m
1 TH	0152 0730 1416 1955	1.5 5.9 1.4 6.1	**16** F	0242 0821 1454 2031	1.9 5.5 2.0 5.7
2 F	0248 0828 1510 2048	1.2 6.1 1.3 6.3	**17** SA	0322 0900 1532 2107	1.8 5.6 1.9 5.8
3 SA	0342 0923 1603 2140	1.0 6.2 1.2 6.4	**18** SU	0359 0935 1608 2141	1.6 5.8 1.8 5.9
4 SU	0434 1015 1654 2230	0.9 6.2 1.2 6.5	**19** M	0434 1009 1643 2215	1.5 5.7 1.7 6.0
5 M	0524 1105 1744 2319	0.9 6.2 1.3 6.4	**20** TU	0509 1043 1718 2251	1.5 5.8 1.7 6.0
6 TU	0612 1152 1832	1.0 6.0 1.5	**21** W	0543 1119 1753 2327	1.4 5.7 1.7 5.9
7 W	0006 0659 1238 1920	6.2 1.2 5.8 1.7	**22** TH	0617 1156 1830	1.5 5.7 1.8
8 TH	0052 0745 1323 2009	5.9 1.5 5.5 2.0	**23** F	0004 0654 1234 1910	5.8 1.6 5.5 1.9
9 F	0138 0831 1410 2100	5.6 1.9 5.3 2.3	**24** SA	0041 0734 1314 1955	5.6 1.8 5.4 2.1
10 SA	0229 0922 1503 2158	5.3 2.2 5.1 2.5	**25** SU	0125 0822 1401 2050	5.4 2.0 5.3 2.3
11 SU	0327 1020 1606 2302	5.0 2.4 5.0 2.6	**26** M	0219 0920 1502 2157	5.2 2.2 5.2 2.4
12 M	0435 1124 1713	4.9 2.5 5.0	**27** TU	0329 1033 1619 2315	5.1 2.3 5.2 2.3
13 TU	0007 0545 1228 1815	2.5 4.9 2.5 5.2	**28** W	0455 1151 1738	2.2 5.2 5.4
14 W	0108 0647 1324 1907	2.3 5.1 2.3 5.4	**29** TH	0033 0616 1303 1846	2.0 5.4 1.7 5.7
15 TH	0158 0738 1412 1951	2.1 5.3 2.2 5.5	**30** F	0140 0725 1406 1946	1.7 5.7 1.4 6.0
			31 SA	0240 0825 1504 2041	1.3 6.0 1.4 6.3

AUGUST

	Time	m		Time	m
1 SU	0335 0918 1556 2132	1.0 6.2 1.2 6.5	**16** M	0340 0917 1551 2125	1.5 5.9 1.6 6.1
2 M	0424 1007 1644 2219	0.8 6.3 1.1 6.6	**17** TU	0415 0951 1625 2158	1.3 6.0 1.5 6.2
3 TU	0510 1050 1728 2303	0.7 6.3 1.1 6.6	**18** W	0448 1024 1658 2232	1.2 6.1 1.4 6.3
4 W	0552 1130 1809 2343	0.8 6.2 1.3 6.4	**19** TH	0521 1058 1732 2305	1.1 6.1 1.4 6.2
5 TH	0630 1207 1847	1.1 6.0 1.5	**20** F	0554 1131 1806 2340	1.2 6.0 1.5 6.1
6 F	0020 0706 1241 1925	6.1 1.4 5.7 1.9	**21** SA	0627 1204 1842	1.4 5.9 1.7
7 SA	0056 0742 1316 2005	5.7 1.9 5.4 2.3	**22** SU	0013 0704 1239 1924	5.9 1.5 5.7 1.9
8 SU	0136 0822 1358 2055	5.3 2.3 5.1 2.6	**23** M	0053 0748 1322 2015	5.6 2.0 5.4 2.2
9 M	0226 0914 1456 2203	4.9 2.7 4.8 2.8	**24** TU	0147 0845 1424 2126	5.2 2.4 5.1 2.5
10 TU	0342 1029 1623 2326	4.6 2.9 4.7 2.8	**25** W	0306 1006 1557 2258	4.9 2.6 5.0 2.5
11 W	0517 1155 1748	4.6 2.9 4.9	**26** TH	0455 1143 1733	4.9 2.5 5.2
12 TH	0043 0631 1304 1848	2.6 4.9 2.7 5.1	**27** F	0029 0622 1301 1844	2.2 5.3 2.0 5.6
13 F	0140 0723 1356 1934	2.3 5.2 2.4 5.4	**28** SA	0137 0723 1404 1942	1.7 5.9 1.4 6.1
14 SA	0225 0805 1439 2013	2.0 5.5 2.1 5.7	**29** SU	0234 0820 1456 2033	1.3 6.4 0.9 6.4
15 SU	0304 0843 1516 2050	1.7 5.7 1.8 5.9	**30** M	0323 0907 1543 2119	0.9 6.6 0.6 6.6
			31 TU	0407 0948 1625 2200	0.7 6.5 1.0 6.7

Chart Datum: 3·33 metres below IGN Datum

TIME ZONE -0100
(French Standard Time)
Subtract 1 hour for UT
For French Summer Time add
ONE hour in **non-shaded areas**

FRANCE – CHERBOURG

YEAR 2004

LAT 49°39'N   LONG 1°38'W

TIMES AND HEIGHTS OF HIGH AND LOW WATERS

SEPTEMBER

Day	Time	m	Time	m	Day	Time	m	Time	m
1 W	0447 / 1025 / 1703 / 2237	0.7 / 6.4 / 1.0 / 6.7			**16** TH	0421 / 0958 / 1633 / 2207	1.0 / 6.3 / 1.1 / 6.5		
2 TH	0522 / 1059 / 1737 / 2312	0.9 / 6.3 / 1.2 / 6.4			**17** F	0454 / 1030 / 1707 / 2241	1.0 / 6.3 / 1.1 / 6.4		
3 F	0555 / 1129 / 1810 / 2344	1.1 / 6.1 / 1.5 / 6.1			**18** SA	0527 / 1103 / 1742 / 2315	1.1 / 6.3 / 1.3 / 6.3		
4 SA	0625 / 1157 / 1841	1.5 / 5.8 / 1.8			**19** SU	0601 / 1135 / 1818 / 2351	1.3 / 6.1 / 1.5 / 6.0		
5 SU	0013 / 0654 / 1225 / 1914	5.7 / 2.0 / 5.5 / 2.2			**20** M	0639 / 1211 / 1900	1.7 / 5.8 / 1.9		
6 M	0045 / 0727 / 1258 / ◐1955	5.3 / 2.4 / 5.1 / 2.6			**21** TU	0033 / 0723 / 1257 / ◑1954	5.6 / 2.2 / 5.4 / 2.3		
7 TU	0126 / 0811 / 1345 / 2057	4.8 / 2.9 / 4.8 / 3.0			**22** W	0132 / 0825 / 1405 / 2112	5.1 / 2.6 / 5.1 / 2.6		
8 W	0242 / 0927 / 1524 / 2243	4.4 / 3.2 / 4.5 / 3.1			**23** TH	0309 / 1001 / 1556 / 2258	4.8 / 2.9 / 4.9 / 2.6		
9 TH	0456 / 1126 / 1723	4.4 / 3.2 / 4.6			**24** F	0508 / 1147 / 1733	4.9 / 2.7 / 5.2		
10 F	0020 / 0615 / 1244 / 1826	2.8 / 4.8 / 2.8 / 5.0			**25** SA	0029 / 0625 / 1300 / 1839	2.1 / 5.4 / 2.2 / 5.7		
11 SA	0117 / 0702 / 1335 / 1910	2.4 / 5.2 / 2.4 / 5.4			**26** SU	0130 / 0719 / 1355 / 1931	1.6 / 5.8 / 1.7 / 6.1		
12 SU	0200 / 0740 / 1415 / 1949	2.0 / 5.5 / 2.0 / 5.8			**27** M	0220 / 0804 / 1441 / 2016	1.2 / 6.2 / 1.4 / 6.5		
13 M	0238 / 0816 / 1451 / 2025	1.6 / 5.8 / 1.7 / 6.1			**28** TU	0304 / 0844 / 1522 / ○2056	1.0 / 6.4 / 1.1 / 6.7		
14 TU	0313 / 0851 / ●1525 / 2100	1.3 / 6.1 / 1.4 / 6.3			**29** W	0342 / 0920 / 1559 / 2133	0.9 / 6.5 / 1.1 / 6.7		
15 W	0347 / 0925 / 1559 / 2134	1.1 / 6.2 / 1.2 / 6.4			**30** TH	0417 / 0953 / 1633 / 2207	0.9 / 6.5 / 1.1 / 6.6		

OCTOBER

Day	Time	m	Time	m	Day	Time	m	Time	m
1 F	0448 / 1023 / 1704 / 2238	1.1 / 6.3 / 1.3 / 6.3			**16** SA	0427 / 1002 / 1643 / 2217	1.0 / 6.5 / 1.0 / 6.5		
2 SA	0518 / 1050 / 1734 / 2307	1.3 / 6.2 / 1.5 / 6.0			**17** SU	0503 / 1037 / 1721 / 2256	1.1 / 6.4 / 1.2 / 6.3		
3 SU	0546 / 1116 / 1803 / 2335	1.7 / 5.9 / 1.9 / 5.7			**18** M	0541 / 1114 / 1802 / 2337	1.4 / 6.2 / 1.5 / 6.0		
4 M	0614 / 1141 / 1833	2.1 / 5.6 / 2.2			**19** TU	0622 / 1155 / 1848	1.8 / 5.9 / 1.9		
5 TU	0003 / 0645 / 1211 / 1910	5.2 / 2.5 / 5.2 / 2.6			**20** W	0026 / 0713 / 1248 / ◑1948	5.5 / 2.3 / 5.5 / 2.3		
6 W	0041 / 0725 / 1254 / ◑2003	4.8 / 3.0 / 4.8 / 3.0			**21** TH	0134 / 0824 / 1404 / 2113	5.1 / 2.8 / 5.1 / 2.5		
7 TH	0149 / 0833 / 1418 / 2144	4.5 / 3.3 / 4.5 / 3.2			**22** F	0321 / 1008 / 1554 / 2255	4.9 / 2.9 / 5.0 / 2.4		
8 F	0418 / 1042 / 1640 / 2337	4.4 / 3.3 / 4.6 / 2.9			**23** SA	0503 / 1140 / 1719	5.1 / 2.6 / 5.3		
9 SA	0541 / 1209 / 1749	4.7 / 3.0 / 4.9			**24** SU	0013 / 0607 / 1243 / 1818	2.1 / 5.5 / 2.2 / 5.7		
10 SU	0040 / 0627 / 1259 / 1834	2.5 / 5.1 / 2.5 / 5.3			**25** M	0110 / 0655 / 1334 / 1907	1.7 / 5.8 / 1.8 / 6.1		
11 M	0123 / 0705 / 1339 / 1913	2.0 / 5.6 / 2.1 / 5.8			**26** TU	0156 / 0737 / 1417 / 1950	1.4 / 6.1 / 1.5 / 6.3		
12 TU	0201 / 0742 / 1416 / 1951	1.6 / 5.9 / 1.7 / 6.1			**27** W	0236 / 0814 / 1456 / 2029	1.2 / 6.3 / 1.3 / 6.4		
13 W	0238 / 0817 / 1453 / 2028	1.3 / 6.2 / 1.4 / 6.4			**28** TH	0313 / 0849 / 1531 / ○2104	1.2 / 6.4 / 1.3 / 6.4		
14 TH	0314 / 0853 / 1530 / ●2104	1.1 / 6.4 / 1.1 / 6.5			**29** F	0345 / 0920 / 1604 / 2137	1.2 / 6.3 / 1.3 / 6.3		
15 F	0351 / 0927 / 1606 / 2140	0.9 / 6.5 / 1.0 / 6.6			**30** SA	0416 / 0948 / 1635 / 2207	1.4 / 6.3 / 1.4 / 6.1		
					31 SU	0446 / 1016 / 1705 / 2237	1.6 / 6.1 / 1.6 / 5.9		

NOVEMBER

Day	Time	m	Time	m	Day	Time	m	Time	m
1 M	0515 / 1043 / 1735 / 2306	1.9 / 5.9 / 1.9 / 5.6			**16** TU	0529 / 1102 / 1754 / 2333	1.5 / 6.3 / 1.4 / 6.0		
2 TU	0545 / 1111 / 1806 / 2338	2.2 / 5.6 / 2.2 / 5.3			**17** W	0617 / 1150 / 1847	1.9 / 6.0 / 1.7		
3 W	0618 / 1144 / 1843	2.6 / 5.3 / 2.5			**18** TH	0027 / 0714 / 1247 / 1949	5.6 / 2.3 / 5.6 / 2.1		
4 TH	0018 / 0658 / 1228 / ◐1931	4.9 / 2.9 / 5.0 / 2.8			**19** F	0136 / 0825 / 1401 / 2106	5.2 / 2.6 / 5.3 / 2.3		
5 F	0119 / 0758 / 1337 / ◐2047	4.6 / 3.2 / 4.7 / 3.0			**20** SA	0305 / 0951 / 1527 / 2228	5.1 / 2.7 / 5.2 / 2.3		
6 SA	0304 / 0933 / 1523 / 2227	4.5 / 3.3 / 4.6 / 2.9			**21** SU	0427 / 1109 / 1643 / 2337	5.2 / 2.5 / 5.3 / 2.1		
7 SU	0438 / 1106 / 1647 / 2340	4.7 / 3.0 / 4.9 / 2.6			**22** M	0530 / 1211 / 1743	5.4 / 2.3 / 5.6		
8 M	0535 / 1207 / 1742	5.1 / 2.6 / 5.2			**23** TU	0036 / 0620 / 1303 / 1835	1.9 / 5.7 / 2.0 / 5.8		
9 TU	0034 / 0619 / 1254 / 1828	2.2 / 5.5 / 2.2 / 5.6			**24** W	0124 / 0704 / 1349 / 1920	1.7 / 5.9 / 1.8 / 6.0		
10 W	0118 / 0700 / 1337 / 1911	1.8 / 5.9 / 1.8 / 6.0			**25** TH	0206 / 0743 / 1429 / 2001	1.6 / 6.0 / 1.6 / 6.0		
11 TH	0200 / 0739 / 1419 / 1953	1.4 / 6.2 / 1.4 / 6.3			**26** F	0243 / 0818 / 1506 / ○2038	1.6 / 6.1 / 1.6 / 6.1		
12 F	0241 / 0818 / 1501 / ●2035	1.2 / 6.4 / 1.2 / 6.5			**27** SA	0318 / 0852 / 1540 / 2113	1.6 / 6.1 / 1.6 / 6.0		
13 SA	0322 / 0857 / 1542 / 2117	1.1 / 6.6 / 1.0 / 6.5			**28** SU	0351 / 0923 / 1613 / 2146	1.7 / 6.1 / 1.6 / 5.9		
14 SU	0403 / 0937 / 1624 / 2200	1.1 / 6.6 / 1.0 / 6.5			**29** M	0424 / 0953 / 1645 / 2218	1.8 / 6.0 / 1.7 / 5.8		
15 M	0445 / 1018 / 1708 / 2245	1.2 / 6.5 / 1.1 / 6.3			**30** TU	0456 / 1024 / 1718 / 2250	2.0 / 5.9 / 1.9 / 5.6		

DECEMBER

Day	Time	m	Time	m	Day	Time	m	Time	m
1 W	0528 / 1056 / 1751 / 2325	2.2 / 5.7 / 2.1 / 5.4			**16** TH	0616 / 1148 / 1844	1.7 / 6.2 / 1.4		
2 TH	0603 / 1132 / 1828	2.4 / 5.5 / 2.3			**17** F	0025 / 0710 / 1242 / 1940	5.8 / 2.0 / 5.9 / 1.7		
3 F	0005 / 0643 / 1214 / 1911	5.1 / 2.7 / 5.2 / 2.5			**18** SA	0122 / 0809 / 1340 / ◐2039	5.5 / 2.2 / 5.6 / 2.0		
4 SA	0056 / 0733 / 1307 / 2006	4.9 / 2.8 / 5.0 / 2.6			**19** SU	0224 / 0912 / 1444 / 2142	5.3 / 2.4 / 5.4 / 2.2		
5 SU	0201 / 0837 / 1415 / ◐2114	4.8 / 2.9 / 4.9 / 2.7			**20** M	0330 / 1020 / 1550 / 2248	5.2 / 2.5 / 5.3 / 2.3		
6 M	0316 / 0951 / 1529 / 2227	4.8 / 2.9 / 4.9 / 2.6			**21** TU	0435 / 1126 / 1656 / 2350	5.2 / 2.5 / 5.2 / 2.3		
7 TU	0425 / 1102 / 1637 / 2332	5.0 / 2.7 / 5.1 / 2.3			**22** W	0535 / 1226 / 1758	5.3 / 2.3 / 5.3		
8 W	0522 / 1203 / 1736	5.3 / 2.3 / 5.4			**23** TH	0047 / 0628 / 1319 / 1852	2.2 / 5.5 / 2.2 / 5.5		
9 TH	0031 / 0613 / 1257 / 1830	2.0 / 5.7 / 2.0 / 5.7			**24** F	0137 / 0714 / 1405 / 1939	2.1 / 5.7 / 2.0 / 5.6		
10 F	0123 / 0701 / 1348 / 1921	1.7 / 6.0 / 1.6 / 6.0			**25** SA	0220 / 0756 / 1446 / 2021	2.0 / 5.8 / 1.9 / 5.7		
11 SA	0212 / 0748 / 1437 / 2011	1.4 / 6.3 / 1.3 / 6.3			**26** SU	0259 / 0833 / 1523 / ○2059	2.0 / 5.9 / 1.7 / 5.8		
12 SU	0300 / 0834 / 1525 / ●2101	1.3 / 6.5 / 1.1 / 6.4			**27** M	0336 / 0908 / 1559 / 2134	1.9 / 5.9 / 1.7 / 5.8		
13 M	0348 / 0920 / 1613 / 2150	1.2 / 6.6 / 1.0 / 6.4			**28** TU	0411 / 0940 / 1633 / 2207	1.9 / 6.0 / 1.7 / 5.8		
14 TU	0436 / 1008 / 1702 / 2240	1.3 / 6.5 / 1.0 / 6.3			**29** W	0445 / 1013 / 1707 / 2240	1.9 / 5.9 / 1.7 / 5.7		
15 W	0525 / 1057 / 1752 / 2332	1.5 / 6.4 / 1.2 / 6.1			**30** TH	0518 / 1046 / 1741 / 2314	2.0 / 5.9 / 1.8 / 5.6		
					31 F	0552 / 1122 / 1815 / 2351	2.1 / 5.7 / 1.9 / 5.5		

Chart Datum: 3·33 metres below IGN Datum

Chapter 5

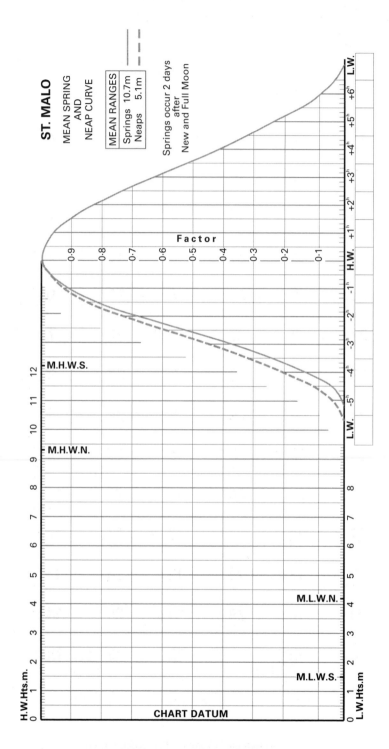

ST. MALO

MEAN SPRING
AND
NEAP CURVE

MEAN RANGES
Springs 10.7m
Neaps 5.1m

Springs occur 2 days
after
New and Full Moon

Factor

TIME ZONE -0100
(French Standard Time)
Subtract 1 hour for UT
For French Summer Time add
ONE hour in **non-shaded areas**

LAT 48°38'N   LONG 2°02'W

TIMES AND HEIGHTS OF HIGH AND LOW WATERS

JANUARY

Day	Time m	Time m	Time m	Time m
1 TH	0137 9.0	0823 4.6	1414 9.1	2054 4.4
2 F	0248 9.0	0931 4.5	1524 9.1	2159 4.3
3 SA	0353 9.3	1035 4.2	1624 9.4	2258 3.9
4 SU	0447 9.7	1130 3.8	1715 9.8	2350 3.6
5 M	0533 10.2	1218 3.4	1759 10.2	
6 TU	0037 3.2	0614 10.6	1301 3.0	1839 10.5
7 W ○	0118 2.9	0652 11.0	1341 2.7	1917 10.8
8 TH	0156 2.7	0728 11.2	1419 2.5	1953 11.0
9 F	0234 2.6	0803 11.4	1457 2.4	2028 11.0
10 SA	0311 2.5	0834 11.4	1535 2.3	2104 11.0
11 SU	0349 2.5	0915 11.4	1613 2.4	2140 10.9
12 M	0427 2.7	0953 11.2	1652 2.6	2218 10.6
13 TU	0506 2.9	1032 10.9	1731 2.9	2258 10.3
14 W	0547 3.2	1115 10.5	1814 3.2	2344 9.9
15 TH ◑	0634 3.6	1206 10.1	1905 3.6	
16 F	0042 9.6	0732 3.8	1310 9.7	2008 3.8
17 SA	0155 9.4	0846 3.9	1428 9.6	2124 3.7
18 SU	0317 9.6	1006 3.6	1550 9.8	2242 3.4
19 M	0433 10.2	1120 3.0	1704 10.4	2352 2.9
20 TU	0538 10.9	1227 2.4	1808 11.0	
21 W ●	0059 2.3	0634 11.5	1328 1.8	1904 11.5
22 TH	0156 1.9	0725 12.0	1424 1.5	1953 11.8
23 F	0246 1.6	0812 12.3	1512 1.2	2038 12.0
24 SA	0332 1.5	0855 12.3	1556 1.2	2119 11.9
25 SU	0412 1.7	0935 12.1	1636 1.5	2156 11.5
26 M	0449 2.1	1012 11.6	1711 2.0	2231 11.0
27 TU	0521 2.6	1048 11.0	1743 2.6	2305 10.4
28 W	0551 3.2	1122 10.3	1813 3.3	2340 9.8
29 TH ◐	0624 3.9	1200 9.5	1848 4.0	
30 F	0022 9.2	0707 4.4	1250 8.9	1937 4.5
31 SA	0122 8.7	0811 4.8	1408 8.4	2047 4.8

FEBRUARY

Day	Time m	Time m	Time m	Time m
1 SU	0250 8.6	0936 4.9	1540 8.5	2210 4.7
2 M	0410 8.9	1054 4.5	1650 9.0	2319 4.2
3 TU	0509 9.5	1153 3.8	1741 9.6	
4 W	0016 3.6	0556 10.2	1243 3.2	1825 10.2
5 TH	0103 3.1	0637 10.8	1328 2.7	1904 10.7
6 F ○	0146 2.6	0716 11.3	1410 2.2	1942 11.2
7 SA	0226 2.2	0754 11.7	1451 1.9	2019 11.5
8 SU	0306 1.9	0830 11.9	1530 1.6	2054 11.6
9 M	0344 1.7	0906 12.0	1607 1.6	2129 11.6
10 TU	0420 1.8	0942 11.9	1643 1.7	2204 11.4
11 W	0455 2.0	1018 11.6	1718 2.1	2239 11.0
12 TH	0531 2.5	1055 11.1	1753 2.6	2318 10.5
13 F ◑	0610 3.0	1138 10.4	1835 3.3	
14 SA	0004 9.9	0659 3.6	1234 9.7	1930 3.9
15 SU	0115 9.3	0811 4.1	1357 9.2	2051 4.2
16 M	0253 9.2	0943 4.0	1540 9.2	2225 4.0
17 TU	0426 9.7	1111 3.4	1704 9.9	2346 3.3
18 W	0535 10.5	1223 2.6	1807 10.7	
19 TH	0056 2.5	0630 11.3	1324 1.9	1858 11.4
20 F ●	0150 1.9	0717 12.0	1415 1.3	1942 11.9
21 SA	0237 1.4	0759 12.4	1459 1.0	2021 12.1
22 SU	0317 1.2	0837 12.5	1538 1.0	2057 12.1
23 M	0353 1.3	0912 12.3	1611 1.2	2130 11.9
24 TU	0423 1.6	0945 11.9	1640 1.6	2200 11.5
25 W	0449 2.1	1014 11.3	1705 2.3	2227 10.9
26 TH	0512 2.8	1041 10.6	1727 3.0	2254 10.3
27 F	0535 3.5	1108 9.8	1752 3.8	2323 9.5
28 SA ◐	0606 4.2	1142 9.0	1828 4.5	
29 SU	0004 8.8	0653 4.9	1241 8.2	1929 5.2

MARCH

Day	Time m	Time m	Time m	Time m
1 M	0132 8.2	0821 5.3	1450 8.0	2117 5.3
2 TU	0331 8.3	1017 5.0	1625 8.5	2251 4.8
3 W	0444 9.0	1129 4.2	1720 9.3	2352 3.9
4 TH	0534 9.9	1222 3.3	1804 10.1	
5 F	0044 3.1	0617 10.7	1309 2.6	1844 10.9
6 SA ○	0128 2.4	0657 11.4	1353 1.9	1923 11.5
7 SU	0211 1.8	0736 12.0	1435 1.4	2000 11.9
8 M	0251 1.4	0813 12.4	1514 1.1	2036 12.2
9 TU	0329 1.1	0849 12.6	1551 1.0	2110 12.3
10 W	0405 1.1	0924 12.5	1625 1.2	2144 12.0
11 TH	0439 1.5	1000 12.1	1658 1.7	2219 11.6
12 F	0513 2.1	1036 11.4	1732 2.5	2255 10.9
13 SA ◑	0550 2.9	1117 10.5	1810 3.4	2340 10.0
14 SU	0638 3.7	1213 9.5	1905 4.2	
15 M	0053 9.2	0751 4.3	1348 8.8	2036 4.7
16 TU	0248 8.9	0936 4.3	1543 9.0	2223 4.4
17 W	0423 9.6	1109 3.6	1701 9.8	2343 3.5
18 TH	0526 10.5	1217 2.6	1756 10.7	
19 F	0047 2.5	0616 11.4	1311 1.9	1841 11.5
20 SA ●	0135 1.9	0659 12.0	1356 1.4	1921 11.9
21 SU	0216 1.4	0737 12.3	1435 1.1	1956 12.2
22 M	0252 1.3	0812 12.4	1509 1.1	2028 12.2
23 TU	0324 1.3	0844 12.3	1539 1.3	2058 12.0
24 W	0351 1.6	0914 11.9	1604 1.7	2126 11.7
25 TH	0414 2.1	0940 11.4	1626 2.3	2151 11.2
26 F	0435 2.7	1005 10.7	1646 3.0	2215 10.5
27 SA	0457 3.3	1029 9.9	1710 3.7	2240 9.8
28 SU ◐	0524 4.1	1057 9.1	1741 4.5	2314 9.0
29 M	0604 4.8	1144 8.3	1831 5.2	
30 TU	0022 8.3	0714 5.3	1349 7.8	2013 5.6
31 W	0240 8.1	0927 5.2	1546 8.3	2213 5.1

APRIL

Day	Time m	Time m	Time m	Time m
1 TH	0405 8.8	1053 4.4	1647 9.2	2319 4.1
2 F	0500 9.8	1149 3.4	1733 10.1	
3 SA	0011 3.1	0546 10.7	1238 2.5	1814 11.0
4 SU	0059 2.3	0629 11.5	1325 1.8	1855 11.7
5 M ○	0144 1.6	0710 12.2	1408 1.2	1933 12.2
6 TU	0227 1.1	0749 12.7	1449 0.9	2010 12.5
7 W	0307 0.9	0827 12.8	1527 0.8	2047 12.6
8 TH	0345 1.0	0904 12.7	1603 1.1	2123 12.4
9 F	0421 1.4	0942 12.2	1638 1.8	2159 11.8
10 SA	0457 2.0	1021 11.4	1714 2.6	2239 11.0
11 SU	0537 2.9	1107 10.4	1756 3.6	2329 10.1
12 M ◑	0628 3.7	1210 9.4	1856 4.5	
13 TU	0051 9.2	0747 4.3	1350 8.9	2034 4.8
14 W	0241 9.1	0931 4.3	1533 9.2	2214 4.3
15 TH	0405 9.7	1054 3.5	1642 9.9	2325 3.5
16 F	0504 10.5	1155 2.8	1732 10.7	
17 SA	0022 2.7	0551 11.2	1244 2.1	1814 11.3
18 SU	0107 2.1	0632 11.7	1326 1.8	1851 11.7
19 M ●	0146 1.8	0709 11.9	1402 1.6	1925 11.9
20 TU	0220 1.7	0743 12.0	1434 1.6	1956 12.0
21 W	0250 1.8	0814 11.9	1502 1.8	2025 11.9
22 TH	0317 1.9	0842 11.6	1527 2.0	2052 11.6
23 F	0341 2.3	0909 11.2	1551 2.5	2118 11.2
24 SA	0405 2.7	0935 10.7	1615 3.1	2144 10.7
25 SU	0430 3.3	1002 10.0	1641 3.8	2212 10.0
26 M	0459 3.9	1034 9.3	1714 4.4	2248 9.3
27 TU ◐	0539 4.5	1121 8.6	1803 5.1	2348 8.6
28 W	0642 5.0	1255 8.2	1927 5.4	
29 TH	0140 8.4	0825 5.0	1447 8.4	2116 5.0
30 F	0310 8.9	1000 4.4	1557 9.1	2230 4.2

Chapter 5

Chart Datum: 6·29 metres below IGN Datum

Register for your **FREE** weekly weather email service from Reeds Almanacs
》 at www.nauticaldata.com – **NOW!** 《
weekend weather reports sent to your email address, every Thursday

387

FRANCE – ST MALO

YEAR 2004

LAT 48°38′N LONG 2°02′W

TIMES AND HEIGHTS OF HIGH AND LOW WATERS

TIME ZONE -0100
(French Standard Time)
Subtract 1 hour for UT
For French Summer Time add
ONE hour in **non-shaded areas**

MAY

Day	Time m	Day	Time m
1 SA	0413 9.7 / 1103 3.5 / 1650 10.0 / 2326 3.3	**16 SU**	0517 10.8 / 1205 2.7 / 1740 10.9
2 SU	0505 10.6 / 1158 2.6 / 1736 10.9	**17 M**	0029 2.7 / 0600 11.1 / 1247 2.5 / 1818 11.2
3 M	0021 2.4 / 0553 11.4 / 1248 1.9 / 1820 11.6	**18 TU**	0108 2.5 / 0637 11.3 / 1324 2.3 / 1852 11.4
4 TU	0111 1.7 / 0638 12.1 / 1336 1.4 / 1902 12.2 ○	**19 W**	0143 2.3 / 0712 11.3 / 1356 2.3 / 1924 11.5 ●
5 W	0158 1.3 / 0721 12.5 / 1421 1.1 / 1943 12.5	**20 TH**	0215 2.3 / 0745 11.3 / 1427 2.3 / 1955 11.5
6 TH	0243 1.0 / 0804 12.7 / 1503 1.1 / 2023 12.6	**21 F**	0245 2.4 / 0815 11.2 / 1456 2.5 / 2024 11.4
7 F	0325 1.1 / 0846 12.5 / 1543 1.4 / 2104 12.4	**22 SA**	0314 2.5 / 0845 10.9 / 1525 2.8 / 2054 11.1
8 SA	0405 1.5 / 0928 12.0 / 1622 2.0 / 2146 11.8	**23 SU**	0344 2.8 / 0915 10.6 / 1555 3.2 / 2124 10.7
9 SU	0447 2.1 / 1014 11.3 / 1703 2.8 / 2233 11.1	**24 M**	0414 3.2 / 0948 10.1 / 1627 3.7 / 2158 10.2
10 M	0532 2.8 / 1106 10.4 / 1752 3.6 / 2329 10.2	**25 TU**	0448 3.7 / 1026 9.6 / 1704 4.2 / 2239 9.7
11 TU	0628 3.6 / 1211 9.6 / 1856 4.3 ◑	**26 W**	0530 4.1 / 1114 9.1 / 1753 4.6 / 2334 9.2
12 W	0047 9.6 / 0741 4.1 / 1335 9.2 / 2022 4.5	**27 TH**	0626 4.4 / 1220 8.8 / 1859 4.8 ◑
13 TH	0215 9.5 / 0906 4.0 / 1500 9.4 / 2143 4.2	**28 F**	0050 9.0 / 0740 4.5 / 1342 8.8 / 2020 4.7
14 F	0331 9.8 / 1018 3.6 / 1606 9.9 / 2249 3.6	**29 SA**	0209 9.2 / 0901 4.2 / 1456 9.2 / 2135 4.1
15 SA	0429 10.3 / 1117 3.1 / 1657 10.4 / 2342 3.1	**30 SU**	0318 9.8 / 1011 3.6 / 1559 9.9 / 2239 3.4
		31 M	0419 10.4 / 1113 2.9 / 1653 10.6 / 2338 2.7

JUNE

Day	Time m	Day	Time m
1 TU	0514 11.1 / 1210 2.3 / 1744 11.4	**16 W**	0031 3.1 / 0608 10.5 / 1247 3.0 / 1823 10.9
2 W	0037 2.1 / 0606 11.7 / 1304 1.8 / 1833 11.9	**17 TH**	0111 2.9 / 0647 10.7 / 1325 2.9 / 1859 11.1 ●
3 TH	0130 1.6 / 0656 12.1 / 1354 1.5 / 1920 12.3 ○	**18 F**	0147 2.8 / 0723 10.8 / 1401 2.8 / 1933 11.2
4 F	0221 1.3 / 0746 12.2 / 1442 1.5 / 2006 12.4	**19 SA**	0222 2.7 / 0757 10.8 / 1435 2.8 / 2006 11.2
5 SA	0309 1.3 / 0834 12.1 / 1528 1.7 / 2053 12.3	**20 SU**	0257 2.7 / 0831 10.8 / 1509 2.9 / 2040 11.1
6 SU	0356 1.5 / 0922 11.8 / 1614 2.1 / 2140 11.9	**21 M**	0331 2.8 / 0905 10.6 / 1544 3.0 / 2114 10.9
7 M	0442 2.0 / 1011 11.3 / 1700 2.7 / 2230 11.3	**22 TU**	0407 3.0 / 0941 10.4 / 1620 3.3 / 2151 10.6
8 TU	0531 2.5 / 1102 10.7 / 1750 3.3 / 2324 10.7	**23 W**	0444 3.2 / 1019 10.1 / 1659 3.6 / 2231 10.3
9 W	0623 3.1 / 1157 10.1 / 1846 3.8 ◐	**24 TH**	0525 3.5 / 1101 9.8 / 1743 3.9 / 2316 10.0
10 TH	0025 10.1 / 0720 3.6 / 1259 9.6 / 1949 4.1	**25 F**	0611 3.7 / 1150 9.5 / 1834 4.1 ◐
11 F	0132 9.8 / 0823 3.8 / 1408 9.5 / 2055 4.1	**26 SA**	0010 9.7 / 0705 3.9 / 1248 9.3 / 1935 4.1
12 SA	0241 9.7 / 0926 3.8 / 1515 9.6 / 2158 3.9	**27 SU**	0115 9.6 / 0809 3.9 / 1357 9.4 / 2044 4.0
13 SU	0343 9.8 / 1025 3.7 / 1612 9.9 / 2255 3.6	**28 M**	0226 9.8 / 0920 3.7 / 1507 9.7 / 2155 3.6
14 M	0438 10.1 / 1118 3.4 / 1702 10.3 / 2345 3.3	**29 TU**	0335 10.1 / 1031 3.3 / 1614 10.3 / 2302 3.1
15 TU	0526 10.3 / 1205 3.2 / 1745 10.6	**30 W**	0442 10.6 / 1137 2.8 / 1716 10.9

JULY

Day	Time m	Day	Time m
1 TH	0007 2.5 / 0544 11.1 / 1213 2.3 / 1813 11.5	**16 F**	0048 3.3 / 0629 10.3 / 1304 3.2 / 1842 10.7
2 F	0109 2.0 / 0642 11.5 / 1336 2.0 / 1907 12.0 ○	**17 SA**	0130 3.0 / 0709 10.6 / 1345 3.0 / 1919 11.0 ●
3 SA	0206 1.6 / 0737 11.8 / 1430 1.7 / 1958 12.2	**18 SU**	0209 2.8 / 0746 10.8 / 1424 2.8 / 1955 11.2
4 SU	0300 1.4 / 0829 12.0 / 1521 1.7 / 2047 12.3	**19 M**	0247 2.6 / 0821 10.9 / 1501 2.7 / 2030 11.3
5 M	0351 1.4 / 0917 11.9 / 1609 1.8 / 2134 12.1	**20 TU**	0325 2.4 / 0856 11.0 / 1538 2.6 / 2104 11.4
6 TU	0438 1.6 / 1003 11.6 / 1654 2.2 / 2220 11.7	**21 W**	0401 2.4 / 0930 11.0 / 1614 2.6 / 2139 11.3
7 W	0522 2.0 / 1047 11.1 / 1738 2.7 / 2304 11.2	**22 TH**	0437 2.5 / 1005 10.8 / 1650 2.8 / 2215 11.0
8 TH	0604 2.6 / 1130 10.6 / 1821 3.2 / 2350 10.6	**23 F**	0513 2.7 / 1041 10.5 / 1727 3.1 / 2254 10.7
9 F	0646 3.2 / 1215 10.0 / 1906 3.8 ◐	**24 SA**	0551 3.1 / 1120 10.2 / 1808 3.4 / 2336 10.3
10 SA	0041 9.9 / 0731 3.7 / 1307 9.6 / 1958 4.2	**25 SU**	0633 3.4 / 1206 9.8 / 1857 3.8 ◐
11 SU	0139 9.5 / 0824 4.1 / 1410 9.3 / 2100 4.4	**26 M**	0031 9.9 / 0726 3.8 / 1307 9.5 / 2000 4.0
12 M	0248 9.2 / 0927 4.3 / 1520 9.3 / 2206 4.3	**27 TU**	0142 9.6 / 0836 4.0 / 1425 9.5 / 2119 4.0
13 TU	0356 9.3 / 1031 4.2 / 1625 9.6 / 2307 4.0	**28 W**	0305 9.6 / 0958 3.8 / 1549 9.8 / 2239 3.5
14 W	0456 9.5 / 1129 3.9 / 1718 10.0	**29 TH**	0426 10.0 / 1116 3.4 / 1704 10.5 / 2351 2.8
15 TH	0000 3.6 / 0546 9.9 / 1220 3.5 / 1803 10.4	**30 F**	0538 10.6 / 1226 2.7 / 1807 11.2
		31 SA	0100 2.2 / 0639 11.3 / 1328 2.2 / 1902 11.9 ○

AUGUST

Day	Time m	Day	Time m
1 SU	0200 1.6 / 0732 11.8 / 1424 1.7 / 1951 12.4	**16 M**	0157 2.5 / 0730 11.1 / 1414 2.7 / 1940 11.6 ●
2 M	0254 1.2 / 0820 12.1 / 1514 1.4 / 2037 12.6	**17 TU**	0236 2.2 / 0805 11.4 / 1450 2.2 / 2015 11.8
3 TU	0341 1.1 / 0903 12.2 / 1558 1.4 / 2119 12.5	**18 W**	0313 1.9 / 0839 11.6 / 1526 2.0 / 2049 12.0
4 W	0423 1.2 / 0943 12.0 / 1638 1.7 / 2158 12.2	**19 TH**	0348 1.8 / 0912 11.6 / 1600 1.8 / 2122 11.9
5 TH	0500 1.6 / 1020 11.6 / 1713 2.2 / 2235 11.6	**20 F**	0422 1.9 / 0944 11.5 / 1634 2.2 / 2155 11.7
6 F	0533 2.3 / 1055 11.0 / 1745 2.9 / 2310 10.8	**21 SA**	0454 2.2 / 1017 11.2 / 1707 2.6 / 2229 11.2
7 SA	0603 3.0 / 1129 10.3 / 1817 3.6 / 2348 10.0	**22 SU**	0526 2.7 / 1051 10.7 / 1743 3.1 / 2307 10.6
8 SU	0635 3.7 / 1207 9.7 / 1856 4.3	**23 M**	0602 3.3 / 1132 10.1 / 1826 3.7 / 2355 9.9 ◐
9 M	0035 9.2 / 0719 4.4 / 1300 9.1 / 1953 4.8	**24 TU**	0651 4.0 / 1229 9.5 / 1928 4.3
10 TU	0145 8.7 / 0824 4.9 / 1422 8.7 / 2116 5.0	**25 W**	0112 9.3 / 0803 4.4 / 1401 9.2 / 2058 4.4
11 W	0318 8.6 / 0950 4.9 / 1554 8.9 / 2237 4.7	**26 TH**	0257 9.2 / 0944 4.4 / 1546 9.5 / 2232 3.9
12 TH	0436 9.0 / 1105 4.5 / 1659 9.5 / 2340 4.1	**27 F**	0430 9.7 / 1113 3.9 / 1704 10.3 / 2348 3.0
13 F	0530 9.6 / 1202 3.9 / 1746 10.1	**28 SA**	0539 10.6 / 1224 2.9 / 1803 11.3
14 SA	0032 3.5 / 0614 10.2 / 1250 3.4 / 1827 10.7	**29 SU**	0057 2.1 / 0633 11.4 / 1323 2.1 / 1853 12.1
15 SU	0116 2.9 / 0653 10.7 / 1333 2.9 / 1904 11.2	**30 M**	0152 1.4 / 0720 12.0 / 1413 1.5 / 1937 12.6 ○
		31 TU	0239 1.0 / 0802 12.4 / 1458 1.2 / 2018 12.8

Chart Datum: 6·29 metres below IGN Datum

TIME ZONE -0100
(French Standard Time)
Subtract 1 hour for UT
For French Summer Time add
ONE hour in **non-shaded areas**

FRANCE – ST MALO

LAT 48°38'N   LONG 2°02'W

TIMES AND HEIGHTS OF HIGH AND LOW WATERS

YEAR 2004

SEPTEMBER

Day	Time m	Time m	Time m	Time m
1 W	0321 0.9	0840 12.4	1553 1.0	2055 12.7
2 TH	0357 1.1	0915 12.2	1610 1.5	2129 12.3
3 F	0427 1.6	0946 11.8	1640 2.1	2200 11.7
4 SA	0453 2.3	1016 11.3	1705 2.8	2230 10.9
5 SU	0516 3.1	1043 10.6	1728 3.6	2259 10.0
6 M	0540 3.9	1112 9.8	1756 4.4	2332 9.1
7 TU	0615 4.7	1153 9.0	1842 5.1	
8 W	0033 8.3	0713 5.4	1317 8.3	2013 5.5
9 TH	0243 8.1	0909 5.6	1524 8.4	2212 5.2
10 F	0416 8.6	1045 5.0	1637 9.1	2320 4.4
11 SA	0509 9.4	1143 4.1	1723 10.0	
12 SU	0010 3.5	0551 10.2	1229 3.3	1803 10.7
13 M	0054 2.8	0629 10.9	1311 2.7	1841 11.4
14 TU ●	0135 2.2	0705 11.5	1349 2.1	1917 11.9
15 W	0214 1.8	0741 11.8	1428 1.8	1952 12.3
16 TH	0251 1.5	0814 12.1	1505 1.6	2026 12.4
17 F	0326 1.5	0847 12.1	1540 1.6	2059 12.4
18 SA	0359 1.6	0919 12.0	1613 1.8	2132 12.1
19 SU	0431 2.1	0951 11.6	1646 2.3	2207 11.5
20 M	0502 2.7	1026 11.0	1722 3.0	2245 10.7
21 TU ◑	0537 3.5	1107 10.3	1805 3.8	2335 9.7
22 W	0627 4.3	1209 9.4	1911 4.5	
23 TH	0106 9.0	0749 4.9	1402 9.0	2054 4.6
24 F	0306 9.0	0948 4.7	1547 9.5	2233 3.9
25 SA	0430 9.8	1114 3.8	1657 10.5	2344 2.9
26 SU	0529 10.8	1216 2.7	1749 11.5	
27 M	0044 2.0	0616 11.6	1307 1.9	1834 12.2
28 TU ○	0132 1.4	0658 12.1	1352 1.5	1915 12.6
29 W	0214 1.2	0736 12.4	1432 1.3	1952 12.7
30 TH	0251 1.2	0810 12.4	1507 1.4	2026 12.6

OCTOBER

Day	Time m	Time m	Time m	Time m
1 F	0322 1.4	0841 12.3	1537 1.7	2057 12.2
2 SA	0349 1.9	0910 11.9	1603 2.2	2125 11.6
3 SU	0412 2.5	0936 11.4	1625 2.8	2151 10.9
4 M	0433 3.2	1001 10.7	1646 3.6	2216 10.0
5 TU	0456 4.0	1026 9.9	1712 4.3	2245 9.2
6 W	0526 4.8	1100 9.1	1751 5.1	2330 8.3
7 TH	0616 5.5	1207 8.3	1904 5.7	
8 F	0152 7.9	0805 5.9	1437 8.2	2127 5.5
9 SA	0339 8.4	1009 5.3	1557 8.9	2245 4.6
10 SU	0435 9.3	1108 4.4	1647 9.8	2334 3.7
11 M	0517 10.2	1143 3.4	1729 10.7	
12 TU	0021 2.8	0556 11.0	1237 2.6	1809 11.5
13 W	0103 2.0	0633 11.6	1319 2.0	1847 12.1
14 TH ●	0144 1.7	0710 12.1	1400 1.6	1924 12.5
15 F	0223 1.4	0745 12.4	1439 1.4	2000 12.6
16 SA	0300 1.4	0820 12.5	1517 1.4	2036 12.5
17 SU	0335 1.6	0854 12.3	1553 1.7	2112 12.2
18 M	0409 2.1	0930 11.9	1630 2.3	2150 11.5
19 TU	0444 2.8	1010 11.2	1709 3.0	2234 10.6
20 W ◑	0524 3.7	1057 10.3	1758 3.8	2333 9.6
21 TH	0620 4.5	1211 9.4	1910 4.5	
22 F	0112 9.0	0753 5.0	1401 9.2	2053 4.5
23 SA	0258 9.2	0943 4.6	1532 9.7	2221 3.8
24 SU	0413 10.0	1057 3.7	1636 10.6	2324 2.9
25 M	0506 10.8	1153 2.8	1725 11.4	
26 TU	0019 2.2	0550 11.5	1241 2.2	1809 11.9
27 W	0103 1.8	0630 11.9	1323 1.8	1848 12.2
28 TH ○	0142 1.7	0705 12.1	1400 1.7	1923 12.2
29 F	0215 1.7	0738 12.1	1433 1.8	1956 12.0
30 SA	0245 1.9	0808 12.0	1502 2.1	2026 11.7
31 SU	0311 2.2	0836 11.7	1528 2.4	2054 11.3

NOVEMBER

Day	Time m	Time m	Time m	Time m
1 M	0336 2.7	0903 11.3	1553 2.9	2121 10.7
2 TU	0401 3.3	0929 10.7	1618 3.5	2148 10.1
3 W	0427 4.0	0957 10.1	1647 4.2	2219 9.3
4 TH	0458 4.7	1032 9.3	1724 4.8	2303 8.6
5 F ◐	0545 5.3	1129 8.6	1824 5.3	
6 SA	0037 8.1	0706 5.7	1318 8.3	2005 5.0
7 SU	0232 8.3	0858 5.4	1454 8.7	2142 4.8
8 M	0341 9.0	1013 4.6	1556 9.5	2243 3.9
9 TU	0431 9.9	1107 3.6	1645 10.4	2334 3.1
10 W	0515 10.7	1156 2.8	1730 11.2	
11 TH	0024 2.3	0556 11.4	1243 2.2	1813 11.8
12 F ●	0110 1.8	0637 12.0	1329 1.7	1855 12.3
13 SA	0153 1.5	0716 12.4	1413 1.4	1936 12.5
14 SU	0235 1.5	0756 12.5	1456 1.4	2017 12.4
15 M	0315 1.7	0836 12.4	1538 1.7	2059 12.0
16 TU	0355 2.2	0919 12.0	1621 2.1	2144 11.4
17 W	0436 2.8	1005 11.3	1706 2.8	2235 10.6
18 TH	0523 3.6	1100 10.5	1800 3.5	2337 9.8
19 F ◑	0624 4.3	1210 9.8	1909 4.0	
20 SA	0059 9.3	0746 4.6	1336 9.6	2030 4.1
21 SU	0225 9.4	0911 4.3	1458 9.8	2146 3.8
22 M	0337 9.8	1021 3.8	1602 10.3	2249 3.3
23 TU	0432 10.4	1118 3.2	1653 10.8	2341 2.8
24 W	0518 10.9	1207 2.8	1739 11.2	
25 TH	0027 2.5	0558 11.3	1249 2.5	1819 11.4
26 F ○	0106 2.4	0635 11.5	1327 2.4	1856 11.4
27 SA	0140 2.3	0709 11.6	1401 2.3	1930 11.4
28 SU	0212 2.4	0740 11.6	1432 2.4	2002 11.2
29 M	0243 2.6	0811 11.4	1503 2.6	2032 11.0
30 TU	0312 2.9	0840 11.2	1532 2.9	2103 10.6

DECEMBER

Day	Time m	Time m	Time m	Time m
1 W	0342 3.2	0911 10.8	1602 3.3	2134 10.2
2 TH	0413 3.7	0944 10.3	1635 3.8	2209 9.7
3 F	0448 4.2	1021 9.8	1713 4.2	2251 9.2
4 SA	0531 4.6	1109 9.3	1803 4.5	2348 8.7
5 SU ◐	0630 4.9	1213 8.9	1908 4.7	
6 M	0107 8.6	0745 4.9	1333 8.9	2026 4.6
7 TU	0207 8.9	0903 4.5	1449 9.3	2139 4.1
8 W	0333 9.5	1011 3.9	1552 9.9	2243 3.4
9 TH	0428 10.2	1111 3.2	1648 10.6	2340 2.8
10 F	0519 11.0	1207 2.5	1740 11.2	
11 SA	0037 2.2	0607 11.6	1301 2.0	1830 11.7
12 SU ●	0127 1.9	0654 12.1	1352 1.6	1919 12.0
13 M	0216 1.7	0741 12.3	1442 1.4	2007 12.1
14 TU	0304 1.7	0828 12.3	1531 1.5	2056 11.9
15 W	0350 2.0	0916 12.1	1619 1.8	2144 11.5
16 TH	0438 2.4	1005 11.6	1708 2.2	2234 11.0
17 F	0526 3.0	1057 11.0	1759 2.8	2327 10.4
18 SA ◑	0619 3.5	1152 10.4	1853 3.3	
19 SU	0026 9.9	0717 3.9	1255 9.9	1951 3.7
20 M	0131 9.5	0821 4.1	1404 9.7	2054 3.9
21 TU	0241 9.4	0928 4.1	1514 9.7	2157 3.8
22 W	0346 9.7	1032 3.9	1615 9.9	2256 3.6
23 TH	0442 10.0	1128 3.5	1709 10.1	2348 3.3
24 F	0529 10.4	1216 3.2	1755 10.4	
25 SA	0034 3.1	0611 10.7	1259 2.9	1836 10.6
26 SU ○	0114 2.9	0648 11.0	1337 2.7	1913 10.8
27 M	0151 2.8	0723 11.1	1413 2.6	1948 10.8
28 TU	0226 2.7	0757 11.2	1448 2.6	2021 10.8
29 W	0300 2.8	0830 11.2	1522 2.7	2054 10.7
30 TH	0333 2.9	0902 11.0	1555 2.8	2127 10.5
31 F	0407 3.1	0936 10.8	1629 3.1	2200 10.2

Chart Datum: 6·29 metres below IGN Datum

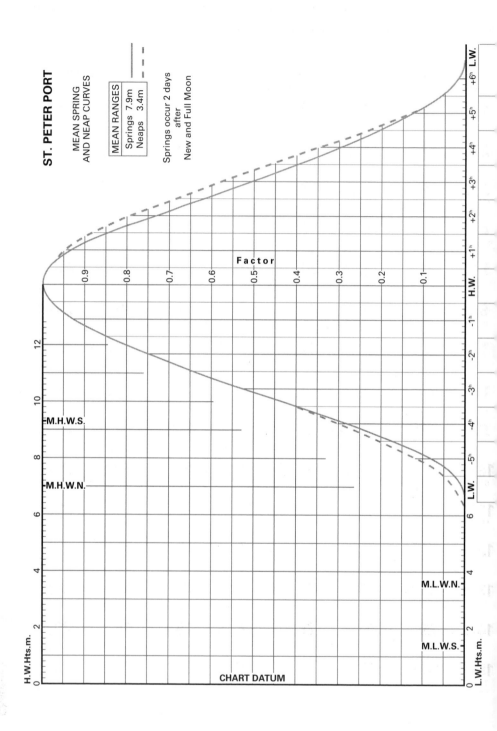

ST. PETER PORT

MEAN SPRING
AND NEAP CURVES

MEAN RANGES
Springs 7.9m
Neaps 3.4m

Springs occur 2 days
after
New and Full Moon

Factor

CHANNEL ISLES – ST PETER PORT

YEAR 2004

LAT 49°27'N   LONG 2°31'W

TIMES AND HEIGHTS OF HIGH AND LOW WATERS

JANUARY

Time	m	Time	m
1 0106 / 0735 / TH 1338 / 2005	6.9 / 3.7 / 7.0 / 3.5	**16** 0010 / 0632 / F 1241 / 1908	7.5 / 3.1 / 7.6 / 3.0
2 0215 / 0845 / F 1444 / 2108	6.9 / 3.7 / 7.0 / 3.5	**17** 0122 / 0750 / SA 1357 / 2028	7.4 / 3.2 / 7.5 / 3.0
3 0316 / 0945 / SA 1542 / 2203	7.1 / 3.5 / 7.2 / 3.3	**18** 0242 / 0913 / SU 1516 / 2148	7.5 / 3.0 / 7.6 / 2.8
4 0408 / 1034 / SU 1632 / 2250	7.4 / 3.1 / 7.4 / 3.0	**19** 0355 / 1026 / M 1627 / 2256	7.9 / 2.5 / 7.9 / 2.4
5 0453 / 1118 / M 1717 / 2332	7.8 / 2.8 / 7.7 / 2.7	**20** 0459 / 1130 / TU 1730 / 2355	8.4 / 2.0 / 8.3 / 2.0
6 0535 / 1159 / TU 1759 ●	8.1 / 2.5 / 8.0	**21** 0555 / 1226 / W 1825	8.9 / 1.5 / 8.7
7 0012 / 0614 / W 1238 / 1839 ○	2.4 / 8.4 / 2.3 / 8.2	**22** 0049 / 0646 / TH 1318 / 1915	1.6 / 9.3 / 1.1 / 9.0
8 0051 / 0652 / TH 1317 / 1918	2.2 / 8.5 / 2.1 / 8.3	**23** 0138 / 0733 / F 1406 / 2000	1.3 / 9.5 / 0.9 / 9.2
9 0128 / 0729 / F 1354 / 1955	2.1 / 8.6 / 2.0 / 8.4	**24** 0222 / 0817 / SA 1449 / 2042	1.2 / 9.5 / 0.9 / 9.1
10 0205 / 0804 / SA 1431 / 2030	2.1 / 8.6 / 2.0 / 8.3	**25** 0303 / 0858 / SU 1528 / 2121	1.3 / 9.4 / 1.1 / 8.9
11 0241 / 0840 / SU 1507 / 2105	2.2 / 8.6 / 2.1 / 8.2	**26** 0341 / 0935 / M 1605 / 2156	1.6 / 9.0 / 1.6 / 8.4
12 0318 / 0917 / M 1545 / 2143	2.3 / 8.5 / 2.2 / 8.1	**27** 0415 / 1011 / TU 1639 / 2230	2.1 / 8.4 / 2.1 / 7.9
13 0357 / 0958 / TU 1625 / 2225	2.5 / 8.3 / 2.4 / 7.9	**28** 0449 / 1047 / W 1713 / 2306	2.6 / 7.8 / 2.7 / 7.4
14 0440 / 1044 / W 1709 / 2313	2.7 / 8.0 / 2.6 / 7.7	**29** 0526 / 1127 / TH 1752 / 2348	3.2 / 7.3 / 3.3 / 7.0
15 0531 / 1137 / TH 1802 ○	2.9 / 7.8 / 2.9	**30** 0613 / 1218 / F 1843	3.6 / 6.8 / 3.7
		31 0047 / 0719 / SA 1331 / 1952	6.6 / 3.9 / 6.5 / 3.9

FEBRUARY

Time	m	Time	m
1 0208 / 0838 / SU 1453 / 2107	6.5 / 3.9 / 6.5 / 3.8	**16** 0219 / 0857 / M 1508 / 2138	7.1 / 3.3 / 7.1 / 3.3
2 0326 / 0954 / M 1603 / 2215	6.8 / 3.6 / 6.8 / 3.5	**17** 0349 / 1023 / TU 1628 / 2253	7.4 / 2.8 / 7.5 / 2.8
3 0427 / 1054 / TU 1658 / 2310	7.2 / 3.2 / 7.3 / 3.0	**18** 0455 / 1127 / W 1729 / 2351	8.1 / 2.1 / 8.1 / 2.1
4 0516 / 1142 / W 1745 / 2356	7.7 / 2.7 / 7.7 / 2.6	**19** 0549 / 1220 / TH 1819	8.7 / 1.5 / 8.7
5 0600 / 1225 / TH 1828	8.2 / 2.2 / 8.1	**20** 0041 / 0636 / F 1308 / 1903 ●	1.5 / 9.2 / 1.0 / 9.1
6 0038 / 0640 / F 1306 / 1907 ○	2.1 / 8.6 / 1.8 / 8.5	**21** 0125 / 0719 / SA 1350 / 1943	1.1 / 9.6 / 0.7 / 9.3
7 0118 / 0718 / SA 1344 / 1944	1.8 / 8.9 / 1.5 / 8.7	**22** 0205 / 0758 / SU 1428 / 2020	0.9 / 9.7 / 0.7 / 9.3
8 0155 / 0754 / SU 1420 / 2018	1.5 / 9.0 / 1.3 / 8.8	**23** 0241 / 0834 / M 1502 / 2053	1.0 / 9.5 / 0.9 / 9.1
9 0231 / 0829 / M 1455 / 2052	1.5 / 9.1 / 1.3 / 8.8	**24** 0313 / 0906 / TU 1532 / 2122	1.2 / 9.2 / 1.3 / 8.7
10 0306 / 0904 / TU 1529 / 2126	1.5 / 9.0 / 1.5 / 8.7	**25** 0340 / 0936 / W 1559 / 2150	1.7 / 8.6 / 1.9 / 8.3
11 0341 / 0940 / W 1604 / 2202	1.7 / 8.8 / 1.8 / 8.4	**26** 0406 / 1005 / TH 1623 / 2217	2.3 / 8.0 / 2.5 / 7.7
12 0418 / 1020 / TH 1642 / 2243	2.1 / 8.4 / 2.2 / 8.0	**27** 0433 / 1035 / F 1650 / 2248	2.9 / 7.4 / 3.1 / 7.2
13 0501 / 1106 / F 1728 / 2333	2.5 / 7.9 / 2.7 / 7.5	**28** 0505 / 1113 / SA 1727 / 2329	3.4 / 6.8 / 3.7 / 6.7
14 0556 / 1205 / SA 1828	3.0 / 7.4 / 3.2	**29** 0559 / 1213 / SU 1835	3.9 / 6.3 / 4.1
15 0042 / 0713 / SU 1329 / 1956	7.1 / 3.4 / 7.0 / 3.5		

MARCH

Time	m	Time	m
1 0046 / 0740 / M 1402 / 2017	6.3 / 4.2 / 6.1 / 4.2	**16** 0213 / 0900 / TU 1514 / 2140	6.8 / 3.4 / 6.8 / 3.5
2 0242 / 0916 / TU 1540 / 2143	6.4 / 3.9 / 6.5 / 3.8	**17** 0346 / 1021 / W 1626 / 2248	7.3 / 2.8 / 7.5 / 2.8
3 0403 / 1031 / W 1640 / 2248	6.9 / 3.3 / 7.1 / 3.2	**18** 0446 / 1117 / TH 1718 / 2339	8.0 / 2.1 / 8.1 / 2.1
4 0456 / 1123 / TH 1727 / 2337	7.5 / 2.7 / 7.7 / 2.5	**19** 0535 / 1204 / F 1802	8.7 / 1.4 / 8.7
5 0540 / 1206 / F 1809	8.1 / 2.0 / 8.2	**20** 0023 / 0617 / SA 1246 / 1841 ●	1.5 / 9.2 / 1.0 / 9.1
6 0020 / 0620 / SA 1247 / 1847 ○	1.9 / 8.7 / 1.5 / 8.7	**21** 0103 / 0656 / SU 1324 / 1918	1.1 / 9.5 / 0.7 / 9.4
7 0100 / 0659 / SU 1325 / 1923	1.4 / 9.1 / 1.0 / 9.1	**22** 0140 / 0733 / M 1359 / 1951	0.9 / 9.6 / 0.7 / 9.4
8 0137 / 0735 / M 1400 / 1958	1.0 / 9.4 / 0.8 / 9.3	**23** 0212 / 0805 / TU 1429 / 2021	0.9 / 9.4 / 0.9 / 9.2
9 0213 / 0810 / TU 1435 / 2031	0.9 / 9.5 / 0.8 / 9.3	**24** 0240 / 0835 / W 1456 / 2048	1.2 / 9.1 / 1.3 / 8.9
10 0248 / 0845 / W 1508 / 2104	0.9 / 9.4 / 1.0 / 9.1	**25** 0306 / 0902 / TH 1520 / 2113	1.6 / 8.6 / 1.8 / 8.4
11 0322 / 0920 / TH 1541 / 2139	1.2 / 9.1 / 1.4 / 8.7	**26** 0329 / 0929 / F 1542 / 2138	2.1 / 8.1 / 2.4 / 7.9
12 0358 / 0958 / F 1618 / 2218	1.7 / 8.6 / 2.0 / 8.2	**27** 0353 / 0956 / SA 1606 / 2205	2.7 / 7.5 / 3.0 / 7.4
13 0438 / 1042 / SA 1701 / 2306	2.3 / 7.8 / 2.7 / 7.5	**28** 0421 / 1030 / SU 1638 / 2241	3.3 / 6.9 / 3.6 / 6.8
14 0533 / 1142 / SU 1803	3.0 / 7.1 / 3.4	**29** 0504 / 1122 / M 1734 / 2345	3.8 / 6.3 / 4.1 / 6.4
15 0017 / 0657 / M 1318 / 1945	6.9 / 3.5 / 6.6 / 3.8	**30** 0645 / 1308 / TU 1932	4.2 / 6.0 / 4.3
		31 0145 / 0838 / W 1506 / 2107	6.3 / 4.0 / 6.4 / 3.9

APRIL

Time	m	Time	m
1 0326 / 0956 / TH 1610 / 2215	6.7 / 3.4 / 7.0 / 3.3	**16** 0423 / 1052 / F 1652 / 2313	8.0 / 2.1 / 8.1 / 2.1
2 0423 / 1050 / F 1657 / 2306	7.4 / 2.6 / 7.7 / 2.5	**17** 0509 / 1136 / SA 1734 / 2355	8.6 / 1.6 / 8.6 / 1.6
3 0509 / 1135 / SA 1738 / 2350	8.1 / 1.9 / 8.3 / 1.8	**18** 0550 / 1216 / SU 1812	9.0 / 1.2 / 9.0
4 0551 / 1216 / SU 1818	8.8 / 1.3 / 8.9	**19** 0033 / 0628 / M 1253 / 1847 ●	1.3 / 9.2 / 1.1 / 9.2
5 0032 / 0631 / M 1256 / 1855 ○	1.2 / 9.3 / 0.8 / 9.3	**20** 0109 / 0703 / TU 1326 / 1919	1.2 / 9.2 / 1.1 / 9.2
6 0112 / 0709 / TU 1334 / 1931	0.8 / 9.6 / 0.6 / 9.6	**21** 0140 / 0735 / W 1355 / 1948	1.2 / 9.2 / 1.3 / 9.1
7 0150 / 0747 / W 1411 / 2007	0.6 / 9.7 / 0.6 / 9.6	**22** 0208 / 0805 / TH 1422 / 2016	1.4 / 8.9 / 1.6 / 8.8
8 0227 / 0824 / TH 1446 / 2043	0.7 / 9.6 / 0.8 / 9.4	**23** 0234 / 0833 / F 1447 / 2042	1.7 / 8.5 / 2.0 / 8.4
9 0304 / 0902 / F 1522 / 2120	1.0 / 9.2 / 1.4 / 8.9	**24** 0300 / 0901 / SA 1512 / 2108	2.2 / 8.0 / 2.5 / 8.0
10 0342 / 0943 / SA 1601 / 2201	1.6 / 8.5 / 2.1 / 8.3	**25** 0326 / 0930 / SU 1538 / 2137	2.7 / 7.5 / 3.0 / 7.5
11 0427 / 1030 / SU 1648 / 2253	2.3 / 7.7 / 2.9 / 7.5	**26** 0356 / 1005 / M 1613 / 2216	3.2 / 7.0 / 3.6 / 7.0
12 0526 / 1136 / M 1756 ○	3.0 / 7.0 / 3.6	**27** 0440 / 1058 / TU 1707 / 2316 ◐	3.7 / 6.5 / 4.0 / 6.6
13 0010 / 0659 / TU 1321 / 1946	7.0 / 3.5 / 6.6 / 3.8	**28** 0602 / 1223 / W 1843	4.0 / 6.4 / 4.2
14 0205 / 0851 / W 1503 / 2126	6.9 / 3.3 / 7.0 / 3.4	**29** 0048 / 0752 / TH 1408 / 2021	6.5 / 3.8 / 6.5 / 3.9
15 0327 / 1001 / TH 1605 / 2226	7.4 / 2.7 / 7.6 / 2.7	**30** 0226 / 0908 / F 1521 / 2130	6.8 / 3.3 / 7.0 / 3.3

Chapter 5

Chart Datum: 5·06 metres below Ordnance Datum (Local)

TIME ZONE (UT)
For Summer Time add ONE
hour in **non-shaded areas**

CHANNEL ISLES – ST PETER PORT

YEAR **2004**

LAT 49°27′N   LONG 2°31′W

TIMES AND HEIGHTS OF HIGH AND LOW WATERS

MAY

Day	Time	m	Day	Time	m
1 SA	0334	7.4	**16** SU	0435	8.2
	1005	2.6		1101	2.0
	1613	7.7		1659	8.3
	2225	2.5		2322	2.0
2 SU	0427	8.1	**17** M	0518	8.4
	1055	2.0		1141	1.8
	1659	8.3		1738	8.6
	2314	1.9			
3 M	0514	8.7	**18** TU	0000	1.8
	1140	1.4		0556	8.6
	1742	8.9		1219	1.7
				1814	8.7
4 TU	0000	1.3	**19** W	0036	1.7
	0558	9.2		0632	8.7
	1225	1.0		1252	1.7
○	1823	9.3	●	1847	8.8
5 W	0044	0.9	**20** TH	0108	1.7
	0642	9.5		0707	8.6
	1307	0.7		1323	1.8
	1904	9.6		1919	8.8
6 TH	0127	0.7	**21** F	0139	1.8
	0724	9.6		0739	8.5
	1348	0.7		1353	2.0
	1945	9.6		1949	8.6
7 F	0209	0.7	**22** SA	0209	2.0
	0807	9.4		0811	8.2
	1429	1.0		1422	2.2
	2026	9.4		2019	8.3
8 SA	0251	1.0	**23** SU	0239	2.3
	0850	9.0		0842	7.9
	1510	1.5		1452	2.6
	2108	9.0		2049	8.0
9 SU	0335	1.5	**24** M	0310	2.7
	0936	8.4		0915	7.5
	1554	2.1		1524	3.0
	2155	8.4		2123	7.7
10 M	0426	2.2	**25** TU	0346	3.0
	1029	7.8		0955	7.2
	1647	2.8		1603	3.4
	2250	7.7		2204	7.3
11 TU	0529	2.8	**26** W	0432	3.3
	1135	7.2		1045	6.9
	1756	3.4		1654	3.6
◐				2259	7.1
12 W	0003	7.3	**27** TH	0535	3.5
	0650	3.1		1149	6.7
	1304	6.9		1803	3.8
	1928	3.6	◑		
13 TH	0135	7.2	**28** F	0008	7.0
	0819	3.0		0656	3.5
	1427	7.1		1304	6.8
	2052	3.3		1925	3.6
14 F	0251	7.4	**29** SA	0124	7.1
	0925	2.7		0812	3.1
	1528	7.5		1418	7.2
	2152	2.8		2038	3.2
15 SA	0348	7.8	**30** SU	0236	7.5
	1017	2.3		0916	2.7
	1617	7.9		1520	7.7
	2240	2.4		2140	2.6
			31 M	0339	8.0
				1012	2.2
				1615	8.2
				2236	2.1

JUNE

Day	Time	m	Day	Time	m
1 TU	0435	8.4	**16** W	0526	8.0
	1104	1.7		1145	2.3
	1706	8.7		1743	8.2
	2328	1.5			
2 W	0528	8.9	**17** TH	0005	2.2
	1155	1.4		0606	8.1
	1755	9.1		1223	2.2
			●	1820	8.4
3 TH	0019	1.2	**18** F	0042	2.1
	0618	9.1		0644	8.2
	1244	1.1		1258	2.2
○	1842	9.4		1856	8.4
4 F	0108	0.9	**19** SA	0117	2.1
	0707	9.3		0721	8.2
	1331	1.1		1332	2.2
	1928	9.5		1931	8.4
5 SA	0157	0.9	**20** SU	0152	2.1
	0756	9.2		0756	8.1
	1418	1.2		1406	2.3
	2015	9.4		2004	8.3
6 SU	0245	1.0	**21** M	0227	2.3
	0844	9.0		0831	8.0
	1505	1.5		1441	2.5
	2102	9.1		2038	8.2
7 M	0334	1.4	**22** TU	0302	2.4
	0933	8.6		0906	7.8
	1553	2.0		1517	2.7
	2151	8.6		2114	8.0
8 TU	0425	1.9	**23** W	0340	2.6
	1025	8.1		0944	7.6
	1645	2.5		1555	2.9
	2244	8.1		2154	7.8
9 W	0521	2.3	**24** TH	0421	2.8
	1122	7.6		1027	7.4
	1742	2.9		1639	3.1
○	2343	7.7		2240	7.6
10 TH	0623	2.7	**25** F	0510	3.0
	1226	7.3		1117	7.3
	1849	3.2		1731	3.2
			◑	2334	7.5
11 F	0051	7.4	**26** SA	0607	3.0
	0731	2.9		1215	7.2
	1336	7.2		1832	3.2
	2001	3.3			
12 SA	0202	7.3	**27** SU	0036	7.5
	0836	2.9		0713	3.0
	1440	7.3		1321	7.3
	2106	3.1		1943	3.1
13 SU	0304	7.4	**28** M	0146	7.5
	0933	2.8		0824	2.8
	1534	7.5		1431	7.6
	2200	2.9		2056	2.8
14 M	0357	7.6	**29** TU	0257	7.8
	1022	2.7		0932	2.6
	1621	7.8		1537	7.9
	2246	2.7		2203	2.4
15 TU	0443	7.8	**30** W	0404	8.1
	1105	2.5		1035	2.2
	1704	8.0		1638	8.4
	2327	2.4		2304	1.9

JULY

Day	Time	m	Day	Time	m
1 TH	0506	8.4	**16** F	0547	7.7
	1134	1.9		1200	2.6
	1735	8.8		1802	8.1
2 F	0002	1.5	**17** SA	0024	2.4
	0603	8.7		0629	8.0
	1230	1.5		1241	2.4
○	1828	9.1	●	1841	8.3
3 SA	0058	1.2	**18** SU	0103	2.2
	0658	9.0		0708	8.2
	1322	1.3		1319	2.2
	1919	9.4		1918	8.5
4 SU	0150	0.9	**19** M	0141	2.0
	0749	9.1		0746	8.3
	1412	1.2		1355	2.1
	2008	9.5		1954	8.5
5 M	0240	0.9	**20** TU	0217	2.0
	0838	9.1		0821	8.3
	1459	1.3		1431	2.1
	2055	9.3		2028	8.5
6 TU	0327	1.1	**21** W	0252	2.0
	0925	8.9		0854	8.2
	1545	1.6		1506	2.2
	2140	9.0		2101	8.4
7 W	0413	1.4	**22** TH	0327	2.1
	1010	8.5		0928	8.1
	1629	2.0		1541	2.3
	2225	8.6		2137	8.3
8 TH	0458	1.9	**23** F	0403	2.3
	1055	8.0		1004	7.9
	1714	2.5		1618	2.5
	2311	8.0		2217	8.1
9 F	0544	2.5	**24** SA	0442	2.5
	1142	7.6		1046	7.7
	1801	3.0		1700	2.8
○				2302	7.9
10 SA	0001	7.5	**25** SU	0528	2.6
	0634	2.9		1135	7.5
	1235	7.2		1751	3.0
	1856	3.4	◑	2357	7.6
11 SU	0100	7.1	**26** M	0625	3.0
	0732	3.3		1236	7.3
	1337	7.0		1857	3.2
	2000	3.6			
12 M	0208	6.9	**27** TU	0106	7.4
	0835	3.4		0739	3.2
	1442	7.0		1353	7.3
	2108	3.5		2020	3.1
13 TU	0314	7.0	**28** W	0229	7.4
	0937	3.4		0904	3.1
	1542	7.2		1514	7.6
	2208	3.3		2144	2.8
14 W	0412	7.2	**29** TH	0350	7.6
	1031	3.1		1020	2.7
	1633	7.5		1625	8.0
	2258	3.0		2255	2.3
15 TH	0502	7.4	**30** F	0459	8.1
	1118	2.9		1126	2.2
	1719	7.8		1727	8.6
	2343	2.7		2357	1.7
			31 SA	0559	8.6
				1223	1.7
				1822	9.1
			○		

AUGUST

Day	Time	m	Day	Time	m
1 SU	0052	1.2	**16** M	0050	2.0
	0652	9.0		0653	8.4
	1316	1.3		1304	1.9
	1911	9.5	●	1903	8.8
2 M	0142	0.8	**17** TU	0127	1.7
	0740	9.3		0729	8.6
	1403	1.0		1340	1.7
	1957	9.7		1938	9.0
3 TU	0227	0.7	**18** W	0201	1.5
	0824	9.4		0803	8.8
	1446	1.0		1415	1.6
	2039	9.7		2011	9.0
4 W	0309	0.8	**19** TH	0234	1.5
	0905	9.2		0834	8.7
	1525	1.2		1448	1.6
	2118	9.3		2043	9.0
5 TH	0348	1.2	**20** F	0306	1.6
	0942	8.8		0905	8.6
	1602	1.6		1520	1.8
	2155	8.8		2116	8.8
6 F	0424	1.7	**21** SA	0339	1.9
	1018	8.3		0938	8.4
	1636	2.2		1554	2.1
	2231	8.2		2151	8.5
7 SA	0459	2.4	**22** SU	0413	2.2
	1053	7.7		1015	8.1
	1711	2.8		1631	2.5
◑	2308	7.5		2232	8.0
8 SU	0536	3.1	**23** M	0454	2.7
	1133	7.2		1100	7.6
	1752	3.4		1718	3.0
	2353	6.9	○	2324	7.5
9 M	0624	3.6	**24** TU	0549	3.2
	1225	6.7		1201	7.2
	1850	3.9		1825	3.4
10 TU	0100	6.5	**25** W	0038	7.1
	0700	4.0		0711	3.6
	1342	6.5		1331	7.0
	2008	4.0		2005	3.5
11 W	0230	6.4	**26** TH	0223	7.0
	0849	4.0		0859	3.5
	1506	6.7		1510	7.3
	2134	3.8		2145	3.1
12 TH	0350	6.7	**27** F	0355	7.4
	1004	3.7		1022	3.0
	1612	7.1		1625	7.9
	2240	3.4		2255	2.4
13 F	0446	7.2	**28** SA	0500	8.0
	1100	3.2		1123	2.3
	1703	7.6		1722	8.6
	2329	2.9		2351	1.7
14 SA	0532	7.6	**29** SU	0553	8.7
	1146	2.7		1215	1.6
	1746	8.0		1812	9.3
15 SU	0011	2.4	**30** M	0040	1.1
	0614	8.1		0639	9.2
	1227	2.3		1302	1.1
	1826	8.4	○	1856	9.7
			31 TU	0128	0.7
				0722	9.6
				1344	0.8
				1937	9.9

Chart Datum: 5·06 metres below Ordnance Datum (Local)

CHANNEL ISLES – ST PETER PORT

YEAR 2004

LAT 49°27′N LONG 2°31′W

TIMES AND HEIGHTS OF HIGH AND LOW WATERS

SEPTEMBER

Day	Time m	Time m	Day	Time m	Time m
1 W	0205 0.6	0801 9.6	16 TH	0137 1.2	0736 9.2
	1423 0.8	2015 9.8		1352 1.2	1947 9.4
2 TH	0242 0.7	0836 9.4	17 F	0210 1.1	0808 9.2
	1457 1.1	2049 9.5		1425 1.2	2020 9.4
3 F	0315 1.2	0908 9.0	18 SA	0242 1.3	0839 9.1
	1528 1.5	2120 8.9		1458 1.4	2053 9.1
4 SA	0344 1.8	0937 8.5	19 SU	0314 1.7	0912 8.8
	1555 2.1	2149 8.3		1531 1.9	2129 8.7
5 SU	0411 2.5	1005 7.9	20 M	0348 2.2	0949 8.3
	1622 2.8	2219 7.6		1609 2.4	2209 8.0
6 M	0437 3.2	1036 7.3	21 TU	0429 2.9	1035 7.7
	1652 3.5	☾ 2254 6.9		1657 3.1	☾ 2304 7.3
7 TU	0512 3.8	1117 6.7	22 W	0527 3.6	1141 7.1
	1739 4.1	2350 6.3		1813 3.7	
8 W	0623 4.3	1234 6.3	23 TH	0029 6.8	0706 4.0
	1918 4.4			1329 6.9	2014 3.7
9 TH	0146 6.1	0809 4.4	24 F	0237 6.9	0908 3.7
	1434 6.4	2106 4.2		1513 7.3	2148 3.1
10 F	0335 6.5	0943 4.0	25 SA	0357 7.5	1019 3.0
	1553 6.9	2224 3.6		1618 8.1	2248 2.3
11 SA	0429 7.1	1112 3.4	26 SU	0451 8.3	1112 2.2
	1643 7.5	2310 2.9		1708 8.8	2336 1.6
12 SU	0512 7.7	1125 2.7	27 M	0536 8.9	1157 1.6
	1725 8.1	2350 2.3		1752 9.4	
13 M	0551 8.3	1204 2.2	28 TU	0019 1.1	0617 9.3
	1803 8.6			1240 1.1	○ 1833 9.7
14 TU	0027 1.8	0628 8.7	29 W	0100 0.8	0655 9.6
	1242 1.7	● 1840 9.1		1318 0.9	1911 9.8
15 W	0103 1.4	0703 9.0	30 TH	0137 0.8	0731 9.6
	1318 1.4	1914 9.3		1354 0.9	1946 9.7

OCTOBER

Day	Time m	Time m	Day	Time m	Time m
1 F	0210 1.0	0803 9.4	16 SA	0144 1.0	0741 9.5
	1425 1.2	2018 9.3		1403 1.1	1958 9.5
2 SA	0239 1.4	0832 9.1	17 SU	0219 1.2	0816 9.3
	1453 1.7	2046 8.9		1439 1.3	2034 9.2
3 SU	0304 2.0	0858 8.6	18 M	0254 1.7	0853 9.0
	1518 2.2	2113 8.3		1516 1.8	2114 8.7
4 M	0327 2.6	0924 8.0	19 TU	0332 2.3	0934 8.4
	1541 2.9	2140 7.6		1559 2.4	2159 8.0
5 TU	0350 3.3	0952 7.4	20 W	0418 3.0	1025 7.8
	1608 3.5	2212 7.0		1654 3.1	☾ 2300 7.3
6 W	0420 3.9	1028 6.9	21 TH	0524 3.7	1138 7.2
	1647 4.1	☾ 2301 6.4		1818 3.6	
7 TH	0515 4.5	1135 6.4	22 F	0034 6.8	0712 4.0
	1827 4.5			1327 7.1	2012 3.5
8 F	0054 6.1	0729 4.6	23 SA	0230 7.1	0857 3.6
	1345 6.3	2027 4.3		1456 7.5	2131 2.9
9 SA	0303 6.5	0907 4.2	24 SU	0337 7.7	1000 2.9
	1518 6.8	2147 3.7		1555 8.1	2225 2.3
10 SU	0358 7.1	1008 3.5	25 M	0427 8.3	1048 2.2
	1609 7.5	2235 3.0		1643 8.7	2310 1.8
11 M	0440 7.8	1052 2.8	26 TU	0510 8.8	1132 1.7
	1651 8.1	2316 2.3		1726 9.1	2351 1.4
12 TU	0519 8.4	1132 2.1	27 W	0549 9.2	1212 1.4
	1731 8.7	2354 1.7		1806 9.4	
13 W	0556 8.9	1211 1.6	28 TH	0029 1.2	0625 9.4
	1809 9.2			1250 1.3	○ 1842 9.4
14 TH	0032 1.3	0631 9.2	29 F	0105 1.3	0659 9.4
	1249 1.2	1845 9.5		1324 1.3	1916 9.3
15 F	0108 1.1	0706 9.5	30 SA	0137 1.5	0730 9.2
	1326 1.0	1922 9.6		1354 1.6	1948 9.0
			31 SU	0205 1.8	0759 8.9
				1422 1.9	2017 8.6

NOVEMBER

Day	Time m	Time m	Day	Time m	Time m
1 M	0231 2.3	0827 8.6	16 TU	0243 1.7	0843 9.1
	1448 2.4	2045 8.2		1511 1.7	2109 8.7
2 TU	0256 2.8	0854 8.1	17 W	0328 2.3	0930 8.6
	1515 2.9	2115 7.6		1601 2.2	2200 8.1
3 W	0322 3.3	0924 7.6	18 TH	0420 2.9	1025 8.1
	1544 3.4	2149 7.1		1700 2.8	2302 7.5
4 TH	0355 3.8	1002 7.1	19 F	0527 3.4	1135 7.6
	1625 3.9	2238 6.6 ☾		1815 3.2	●
5 F	0447 4.3	1103 6.7	20 SA	0023 7.2	0655 3.6
	1740 4.3	○		1300 7.4	1941 3.2
6 SA	0001 6.3	0630 4.5	21 SU	0153 7.3	0823 3.4
	1237 6.5	1931 4.2		1419 7.6	2054 2.9
7 SU	0152 6.5	0810 4.2	22 M	0301 7.6	0926 3.0
	1413 6.8	2049 3.7		1520 7.9	2151 2.6
8 M	0304 7.0	0917 3.6	23 TU	0353 8.0	1017 2.6
	1516 7.4	2146 3.1		1611 8.3	2238 2.3
9 TU	0354 7.6	1008 3.0	24 W	0437 8.4	1102 2.2
	1606 8.0	2233 2.5		1656 8.5	2320 2.0
10 W	0437 8.2	1054 2.3	25 TH	0518 8.7	1143 2.0
	1651 8.5	2316 1.9		1737 8.7	2359 1.9
11 TH	0518 8.8	1137 1.8	26 F	0555 8.9	1221 1.9
	1734 9.0	2359 1.5		1815 8.8	○
12 F	0558 9.2	1220 1.4	27 SA	0035 1.9	0630 8.9
	1817 9.3	●		1256 1.9	1851 8.7
13 SA	0040 1.2	0638 9.5	28 SU	0108 2.0	0703 8.9
	1303 1.4	1858 9.5		1329 2.0	1925 8.6
14 SU	0121 1.2	0718 9.6	29 M	0138 2.2	0735 8.7
	1345 1.1	1940 9.4		1359 2.2	1957 8.4
15 M	0202 1.3	0800 9.4	30 TU	0208 2.4	0806 8.5
	1427 1.3	2023 9.1		1430 2.5	2029 8.1

DECEMBER

Day	Time m	Time m	Day	Time m	Time m
1 W	0238 2.8	0837 8.2	16 TH	0329 1.9	0928 9.0
	1501 2.8	2102 7.7		1602 1.7	2158 8.5
2 TH	0309 3.1	0911 7.8	17 F	0419 2.3	1020 8.6
	1536 3.2	2139 7.3		1654 2.1	2251 8.0
3 F	0346 3.5	0950 7.4	18 SA	0514 2.8	1116 8.1
	1617 3.5	2223 7.0		1751 2.6	☾ 2350 7.6
4 SA	0433 3.8	1041 7.1	19 SU	0617 3.2	1219 7.7
	1711 3.7	2320 6.8		1854 2.9	
5 SU	0536 4.0	1144 7.0	20 M	0058 7.3	0729 3.3
	1822 3.8	○		1328 7.5	2002 3.1
6 M	0031 6.8	0657 4.0	21 TU	0208 7.3	0840 3.3
	1257 7.0	1939 3.6		1436 7.4	2106 3.1
7 TU	0148 7.0	0814 3.6	22 W	0310 7.4	0940 3.1
	1410 7.3	2047 3.2		1535 7.3	2201 3.0
8 W	0254 7.4	0917 3.1	23 TH	0403 7.7	1032 2.9
	1513 7.7	2145 2.8		1626 7.7	2249 2.8
9 TH	0349 8.0	1013 2.6	24 F	0448 8.0	1117 2.7
	1610 8.2	2238 2.3		1712 7.9	2332 2.6
10 F	0440 8.5	1105 2.1	25 SA	0530 8.2	1158 2.4
	1702 8.6	2329 1.9		1754 8.1	
11 SA	0529 8.9	1155 1.6	26 SU	0011 2.4	0609 8.4
	1753 8.9	○		1237 2.3	1833 8.2
12 SU	0018 1.6	0617 9.3	27 M	0048 2.3	0646 8.5
	1246 1.3	● 1842 9.2		1312 2.2	1911 8.3
13 M	0106 1.4	0704 9.5	28 TU	0122 2.3	0721 8.6
	1335 1.1	1931 9.2		1347 2.2	1946 8.2
14 TU	0153 1.4	0751 9.5	29 W	0155 2.3	0755 8.5
	1423 1.1	2020 9.1		1421 2.3	2020 8.1
15 W	0241 1.6	0839 9.3	30 TH	0228 2.5	0829 8.3
	1512 1.3	2108 8.9		1454 2.4	2054 8.0
			31 F	0302 2.7	0902 8.1
				1528 2.6	2127 7.8

Chapter 5

Chart Datum: 5·06 metres below Ordnance Datum (Local)

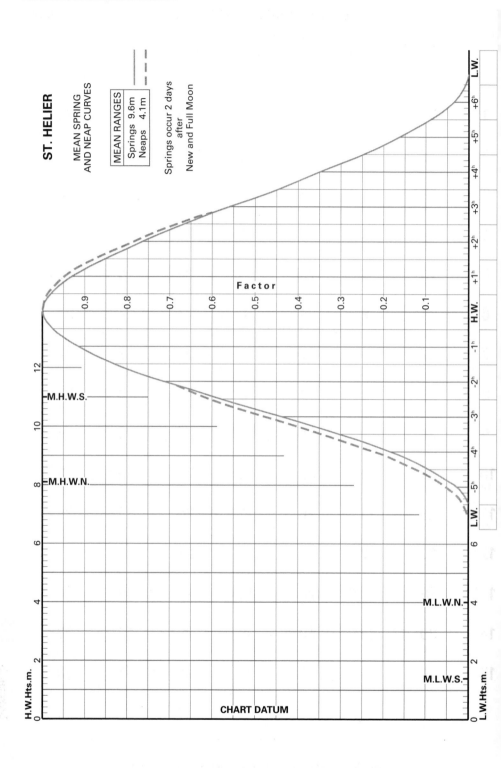

ST. HELIER

MEAN SPRING
AND NEAP CURVES

MEAN RANGES	
Springs	9.6m
Neaps	4.1m

Springs occur 2 days
after
New and Full Moon

TIME ZONE (UT)
For Summer Time add ONE hour in **non-shaded areas**

CHANNEL ISLES – ST HELIER

LAT 49°11'N   LONG 2°07'W

TIMES AND HEIGHTS OF HIGH AND LOW WATERS

YEAR 2004

JANUARY

Time	m	Time	m
1 TH	0055 8.2 / 0735 4.1 / 1328 8.2 / 2009 3.9	**16** F	0001 8.7 / 0635 3.5 / 1227 8.8 / 1911 3.5
2 F	0203 8.1 / 0842 4.1 / 1437 8.2 / 2112 3.8	**17** SA	0112 8.6 / 0750 3.6 / 1343 8.7 / 2030 3.5
3 SA	0307 8.4 / 0945 3.8 / 1538 8.5 / 2209 3.5	**18** SU	0231 8.7 / 0911 3.3 / 1505 8.9 / 2149 3.2
4 SU	0402 8.7 / 1039 3.4 / 1630 8.8 / 2259 3.2	**19** M	0346 9.2 / 1026 2.8 / 1620 9.3 / 2300 2.7
5 M	0449 9.1 / 1125 3.0 / 1715 9.1 / 2343 2.9	**20** TU	0452 9.8 / 1133 2.2 / 1724 9.9
6 TU	0530 9.5 / 1208 2.7 / 1756 9.5	**21** W	0003 2.2 / 0549 10.4 / 1234 1.7 / ● 1820 10.4
7 W	0024 2.6 / 0608 9.8 / 1248 2.4 / ○ 1834 9.7	**22** TH	0100 1.7 / 0641 10.9 / 1328 1.3 / 1909 10.7
8 TH	0104 2.4 / 0644 10.0 / 1327 2.2 / 1910 9.9	**23** F	0150 1.4 / 0728 11.1 / 1417 1.1 / 1954 10.9
9 F	0140 2.3 / 0720 10.2 / 1403 2.1 / 1946 9.9	**24** SA	0235 1.4 / 0811 11.2 / 1501 1.1 / 2036 10.7
10 SA	0216 2.2 / 0756 10.3 / 1439 2.1 / 2022 9.9	**25** SU	0316 1.5 / 0851 11.0 / 1541 1.4 / 2113 10.4
11 SU	0251 2.3 / 0832 10.3 / 1514 2.2 / 2059 9.9	**26** M	0353 1.9 / 0927 10.5 / 1615 1.8 / 2147 9.9
12 M	0327 2.4 / 0910 10.1 / 1551 2.3 / 2137 9.7	**27** TU	0425 2.4 / 1002 9.9 / 1646 2.4 / 2221 9.4
13 TU	0405 2.6 / 0949 9.9 / 1630 2.6 / 2218 9.4	**28** W	0456 2.9 / 1037 9.3 / 1717 3.0 / 2256 8.8
14 W	0447 2.9 / 1033 9.5 / 1714 2.9 / 2304 9.0	**29** TH	0529 3.5 / 1116 8.6 / 1753 3.6 / ◗ 2339 8.3
15 TH	0536 3.2 / 1124 9.1 / 1806 3.2 / ◗	**30** F	0613 4.0 / 1207 8.0 / 1843 4.1
		31 SA	0040 7.8 / 0717 4.4 / 1324 7.6 / 1957 4.4

FEBRUARY

Time	m	Time	m
1 SU	0205 7.7 / 0844 4.4 / 1453 7.6 / 2121 4.3	**16** M	0203 8.2 / 0849 3.7 / 1452 8.2 / 2136 3.7
2 M	0324 8.0 / 1002 4.0 / 1604 8.1 / 2229 3.8	**17** TU	0338 8.6 / 1019 3.2 / 1620 8.8 / 2258 3.0
3 TU	0424 8.5 / 1102 3.5 / 1657 8.6 / 2323 3.3	**18** W	0449 9.4 / 1131 2.4 / 1723 9.6
4 W	0512 9.1 / 1151 2.9 / 1741 9.2	**19** TH	0000 2.3 / 0544 10.2 / 1230 1.6 / 1814 10.3
5 TH	0009 2.7 / 0553 9.6 / 1235 2.4 / 1821 9.6	**20** F	0053 1.6 / 0632 10.9 / 1320 1.1 / ● 1858 10.8
6 F	0051 2.3 / 0632 10.1 / 1316 2.0 / ○ 1858 10.0	**21** SA	0139 1.2 / 0714 11.2 / 1403 0.8 / 1937 11.0
7 SA	0130 2.0 / 0709 10.4 / 1354 1.7 / 1934 10.3	**22** SU	0219 1.1 / 0752 11.3 / 1441 0.8 / 2013 11.0
8 SU	0207 1.7 / 0745 10.7 / 1430 1.5 / 2010 10.5	**23** M	0254 1.2 / 0827 11.2 / 1513 1.1 / 2045 10.7
9 M	0242 1.6 / 0821 10.9 / 1505 1.4 / 2045 10.6	**24** TU	0324 1.5 / 0859 10.8 / 1541 1.5 / 2114 10.3
10 TU	0317 1.6 / 0857 10.8 / 1539 1.5 / 2121 10.4	**25** W	0350 1.9 / 0928 10.2 / 1605 2.1 / 2141 9.8
11 W	0352 1.8 / 0934 10.5 / 1614 1.9 / 2157 10.0	**26** TH	0414 2.5 / 0955 9.5 / 1629 2.7 / 2208 9.2
12 TH	0429 2.2 / 1011 10.0 / 1650 2.4 / 2235 9.5	**27** F	0439 3.1 / 1023 8.8 / 1655 3.4 / 2238 8.5
13 F	0509 2.7 / 1054 9.4 / 1732 3.0 / ◗ 2322 8.9	**28** SA	0511 3.8 / 1059 8.0 / 1733 4.1 / 2321 7.8
14 SA	0600 3.3 / 1149 8.7 / 1830 3.6	**29** SU	0602 4.4 / 1159 7.3 / 1838 4.7
15 SU	0029 8.4 / 0713 3.8 / 1309 8.2 / 1957 4.0		

MARCH

Time	m	Time	m
1 M	0043 7.3 / 0733 4.8 / 1405 7.1 / 2026 4.8	**16** TU	0156 7.9 / 0845 3.9 / 1458 8.0 / 2136 3.9
2 TU	0245 7.4 / 0923 4.5 / 1540 7.6 / 2200 4.3	**17** W	0336 8.5 / 1018 3.2 / 1618 8.8 / 2253 3.0
3 W	0359 8.1 / 1036 3.6 / 1636 8.3 / 2300 3.5	**18** TH	0441 9.4 / 1124 2.3 / 1713 9.7 / 2350 2.1
4 TH	0450 8.8 / 1129 2.9 / 1720 9.1 / 2348 2.7	**19** F	0531 10.2 / 1215 1.5 / 1758 10.3
5 F	0532 9.6 / 1214 2.2 / 1800 9.8	**20** SA	0037 1.5 / 0614 10.8 / 1300 1.1 / ● 1837 10.8
6 SA	0032 2.1 / 0611 10.2 / 1257 1.7 / ○ 1837 10.3	**21** SU	0118 1.2 / 0652 11.1 / 1339 0.9 / 1912 11.0
7 SU	0113 1.6 / 0649 10.8 / 1336 1.2 / 1914 10.8	**22** M	0154 1.1 / 0727 11.2 / 1411 0.9 / 1944 11.0
8 M	0151 1.2 / 0726 11.2 / 1413 1.0 / 1949 11.1	**23** TU	0224 1.1 / 0759 11.1 / 1439 1.1 / 2013 10.8
9 TU	0226 1.0 / 0803 11.4 / 1448 0.9 / 2025 11.1	**24** W	0251 1.4 / 0827 10.7 / 1504 1.5 / 2039 10.5
10 W	0301 1.0 / 0839 11.3 / 1521 1.1 / 2100 10.9	**25** TH	0315 1.8 / 0854 10.2 / 1527 2.0 / 2103 10.0
11 TH	0336 1.3 / 0914 10.9 / 1554 1.5 / 2134 10.4	**26** F	0338 2.3 / 0918 9.6 / 1550 2.6 / 2127 9.4
12 F	0411 1.8 / 0951 10.2 / 1628 2.2 / 2211 9.7	**27** SA	0402 3.0 / 0942 8.9 / 1615 3.4 / 2152 8.7
13 SA	0449 2.5 / 1032 9.4 / 1701 3.1 / ◗ 2256 8.9	**28** SU	0431 3.6 / 1011 8.1 / 1647 4.1 / 2226 8.0
14 SU	0539 3.3 / 1127 8.5 / 1806 3.8	**29** M	0515 4.3 / 1059 7.4 / 1743 4.7 / 2332 7.3
15 M	0004 8.2 / 0655 3.9 / 1257 7.8 / 1944 3.4	**30** TU	0636 4.7 / 1302 6.9 / 1927 5.0
		31 W	0152 7.2 / 0831 4.6 / 1502 7.4 / 2117 4.5

APRIL

Time	m	Time	m
1 TH	0322 7.9 / 0958 3.8 / 1602 8.2 / 2225 3.6	**16** F	0418 9.4 / 1100 2.2 / 1648 9.6 / 2325 2.2
2 F	0416 8.7 / 1054 3.0 / 1647 9.1 / 2316 2.7	**17** SA	0506 10.1 / 1148 1.7 / 1730 10.2
3 SA	0500 9.6 / 1142 2.2 / 1729 9.9	**18** SU	0009 1.7 / 0547 10.5 / 1230 1.4 / 1807 10.5
4 SU	0001 2.0 / 0542 10.4 / 1227 1.5 / 1808 10.6	**19** M	0048 1.5 / 0623 10.7 / 1305 1.3 / ● 1841 10.7
5 M	0045 1.4 / 0622 11.0 / 1309 1.0 / ○ 1846 11.0	**20** TU	0121 1.4 / 0657 10.8 / 1336 1.3 / 1911 10.7
6 TU	0126 1.0 / 0701 11.4 / 1348 0.8 / 1924 11.3	**21** W	0150 1.5 / 0728 10.7 / 1403 1.5 / 1940 10.6
7 W	0204 0.8 / 0740 11.5 / 1425 0.7 / 2001 11.4	**22** TH	0217 1.6 / 0757 10.4 / 1429 1.7 / 2006 10.4
8 TH	0242 0.8 / 0818 11.4 / 1501 1.0 / 2038 11.1	**23** F	0243 1.9 / 0823 10.0 / 1455 2.2 / 2031 10.0
9 F	0318 1.1 / 0857 10.9 / 1536 1.6 / 2115 10.5	**24** SA	0310 2.3 / 0849 9.5 / 1521 2.7 / 2056 9.4
10 SA	0356 1.7 / 0936 10.1 / 1613 2.3 / 2155 9.7	**25** SU	0337 2.9 / 0915 8.8 / 1548 3.3 / 2123 8.9
11 SU	0438 2.5 / 1022 9.2 / 1657 3.2 / 2245 8.9	**26** M	0408 3.5 / 0946 8.2 / 1623 4.0 / 2159 8.2
12 M	0533 3.3 / 1124 8.3 / 1802 4.0 / ◗	**27** TU	0451 4.1 / 1035 7.6 / 1716 4.5 / ◗ 2259 7.6
13 TU	0001 8.2 / 0656 3.8 / 1304 7.8 / 1944 4.2	**28** W	0600 4.4 / 1210 7.2 / 1840 4.7
14 W	0153 8.1 / 0840 3.7 / 1449 8.1 / 2124 3.7	**29** TH	0048 7.4 / 0735 4.4 / 1404 7.5 / 2019 4.4
15 TH	0319 8.7 / 1001 3.0 / 1558 8.9 / 2232 2.9	**30** F	0226 7.9 / 0903 3.8 / 1512 8.2 / 2135 3.6

Chapter 5

Chart Datum: 5·88 metres below Ordnance Datum (Local)

CHANNEL ISLES – ST HELIER

TIME ZONE (UT)
For Summer Time add ONE
hour in **non-shaded areas**

YEAR 2004

LAT 49°11′N   LONG 2°07′W

TIMES AND HEIGHTS OF HIGH AND LOW WATERS

MAY

Time m	Time m
1 SA 0328 8.7 / 1007 3.0 / 1604 9.1 / 2232 2.8	**16 SU** 0431 9.6 / 1110 2.2 / 1655 9.8 / 2333 2.2
2 SU 0419 9.5 / 1100 2.2 / 1650 9.9 / 2323 2.0	**17 M** 0514 9.9 / 1151 2.0 / 1733 10.0
3 M 0506 10.3 / 1149 1.6 / 1734 10.6	**18 TU** 0012 2.0 / 0551 10.1 / 1228 1.9 / 1807 10.2
4 TU 0010 1.4 / 0550 10.9 / 1236 1.1 / ○ 1816 11.0	**19 W** 0046 1.9 / 0626 10.2 / 1300 1.9 / ● 1840 10.3
5 W 0057 1.0 / 0634 11.2 / 1320 0.9 / 1858 11.3	**20 TH** 0118 1.9 / 0659 10.1 / 1331 2.0 / 1910 10.3
6 TH 0140 0.8 / 0718 11.3 / 1402 0.9 / 1939 11.3	**21 F** 0149 2.0 / 0731 10.0 / 1401 2.1 / 1940 10.1
7 F 0223 0.9 / 0801 11.1 / 1443 1.2 / 2021 11.0	**22 SA** 0219 2.1 / 0801 9.7 / 1431 2.4 / 2009 9.8
8 SA 0305 1.2 / 0845 10.6 / 1524 1.7 / 2103 10.5	**23 SU** 0250 2.4 / 0831 9.3 / 1501 2.8 / 2038 9.5
9 SU 0349 1.8 / 0931 9.9 / 1607 2.4 / 2150 9.8	**24 M** 0321 2.8 / 0903 8.9 / 1534 3.2 / 2111 9.0
10 M 0438 2.4 / 1023 9.1 / 1658 3.2 / 2246 9.0	**25 TU** 0356 3.2 / 0940 8.5 / 1611 3.6 / 2151 8.6
11 TU 0537 3.1 / 1128 8.4 / 1805 3.7 / ○ 2359 8.5	**26 W** 0440 3.6 / 1029 8.1 / 1701 4.0 / 2247 8.2
12 W 0653 3.5 / 1252 8.2 / 1931 3.9	**27 TH** 0537 3.9 / 1137 7.8 / 1806 4.2 ●
13 TH 0127 8.4 / 0815 3.4 / 1415 8.4 / 2051 3.6	**28 F** 0002 8.0 / 0647 3.9 / 1259 7.9 / 1923 4.0
14 F 0243 8.7 / 0925 3.0 / 1520 8.8 / 2155 3.0	**29 SA** 0123 8.2 / 0804 3.6 / 1413 8.4 / 2039 3.6
15 SA 0342 9.2 / 1022 2.5 / 1611 9.4 / 2248 2.5	**30 SU** 0234 8.7 / 0914 3.1 / 1514 9.0 / 2144 2.9
	31 M 0334 9.4 / 1015 2.5 / 1608 9.7 / 2242 2.3

JUNE

Time m	Time m
1 TU 0429 10.0 / 1110 1.9 / 1659 10.3 / 2337 1.7	**16 W** 0522 9.4 / 1152 2.6 / 1737 9.7
2 W 0521 10.5 / 1203 1.5 / 1748 10.8	**17 TH** 0015 2.5 / 0601 9.5 / 1230 2.4 / ● 1814 9.8
3 TH 0029 1.3 / 0611 10.9 / 1255 1.3 / ○ 1836 11.1	**18 F** 0053 2.3 / 0638 9.6 / 1307 2.4 / 1848 9.9
4 F 0120 1.1 / 0701 11.0 / 1344 1.3 / 1923 11.1	**19 SA** 0129 2.3 / 0713 9.6 / 1342 2.4 / 1922 9.9
5 SA 0210 1.0 / 0751 10.9 / 1431 1.4 / 2011 11.0	**20 SU** 0203 2.3 / 0748 9.6 / 1416 2.5 / 1956 9.8
6 SU 0259 1.2 / 0840 10.5 / 1519 1.8 / 2058 10.6	**21 M** 0238 2.4 / 0822 9.4 / 1450 2.6 / 2030 9.7
7 M 0348 1.6 / 0929 10.0 / 1607 2.3 / 2148 10.1	**22 TU** 0312 2.6 / 0857 9.2 / 1525 2.8 / 2106 9.5
8 TU 0439 2.1 / 1020 9.4 / 1658 2.8 / 2240 9.5	**23 W** 0349 2.8 / 0935 9.0 / 1603 3.0 / 2146 9.2
9 W 0533 2.6 / 1115 8.9 / 1754 3.2 / ○ 2339 9.0	**24 TH** 0429 3.0 / 1017 8.7 / 1646 3.3 / 2231 8.9
10 TH 0631 3.0 / 1216 8.6 / 1857 3.5	**25 F** 0515 3.2 / 1105 8.5 / 1737 3.5 / ● 2325 8.7
11 F 0044 8.7 / 0733 3.2 / 1323 8.5 / 2003 3.5	**26 SA** 0609 3.4 / 1206 8.4 / 1838 3.6
12 SA 0152 8.6 / 0835 3.2 / 1427 8.6 / 2105 3.4 ●	**27 SU** 0030 8.6 / 0712 3.4 / 1315 8.5 / 1947 3.5
13 SU 0255 8.7 / 0933 3.1 / 1524 8.8 / 2202 3.1	**28 M** 0141 8.7 / 0823 3.2 / 1425 8.8 / 2059 3.2
14 M 0350 9.0 / 1025 2.9 / 1614 9.1 / 2252 2.9	**29 TU** 0251 9.1 / 0933 2.9 / 1530 9.3 / 2207 2.7
15 TU 0438 9.2 / 1111 2.7 / 1658 9.4 / 2336 2.7	**30 W** 0357 9.5 / 1039 2.4 / 1631 9.9 / 2310 2.1

JULY

Time m	Time m
1 TH 0500 10.0 / 1140 2.0 / 1729 10.4	**16 F** 0544 9.1 / 1210 2.8 / 1756 9.5
2 F 0011 1.7 / 0558 10.4 / 1239 1.7 / ○ 1823 10.8	**17 SA** 0035 2.5 / 0624 9.4 / 1251 2.5 / ● 1834 9.8
3 SA 0109 1.3 / 0653 10.7 / 1334 1.5 / 1915 11.0	**18 SU** 0116 2.3 / 0701 9.6 / 1329 2.4 / 1910 10.0
4 SU 0204 1.1 / 0745 10.8 / 1426 1.4 / 2004 11.1	**19 M** 0153 2.2 / 0736 9.8 / 1405 2.3 / 1945 10.1
5 M 0255 1.1 / 0833 10.7 / 1514 1.5 / 2051 10.9	**20 TU** 0229 2.1 / 0811 9.8 / 1440 2.2 / 2020 10.2
6 TU 0343 1.2 / 0919 10.4 / 1600 1.8 / 2136 10.5	**21 W** 0303 2.1 / 0846 9.8 / 1515 2.2 / 2056 10.1
7 W 0428 1.6 / 1003 9.9 / 1644 2.2 / 2220 10.0	**22 TH** 0338 2.2 / 0921 9.7 / 1550 2.4 / 2132 9.9
8 TH 0511 2.2 / 1046 9.4 / 1726 2.7 / 2304 9.4	**23 F** 0413 2.4 / 0957 9.5 / 1628 2.6 / 2210 9.6
9 F 0554 2.7 / 1130 8.9 / 1811 3.2 / ○ 2353 8.9	**24 SA** 0451 2.7 / 1037 9.2 / 1710 3.0 / 2253 9.2
10 SA 0639 3.2 / 1222 8.5 / 1903 3.7	**25 SU** 0534 3.0 / 1124 8.8 / 1759 3.3 / ● 2347 8.8
11 SU 0051 8.4 / 0732 3.6 / 1324 8.2 / 2004 3.9	**26 M** 0628 3.4 / 1225 8.5 / 1904 3.6
12 M 0159 8.2 / 0834 3.8 / 1431 8.2 / 2111 3.8	**27 TU** 0055 8.6 / 0739 3.6 / 1343 8.5 / 2023 3.5
13 TU 0307 8.2 / 0938 3.7 / 1534 8.5 / 2213 3.6	**28 W** 0219 8.6 / 0904 3.4 / 1505 8.8 / 2145 3.1
14 W 0407 8.5 / 1035 3.4 / 1628 8.8 / 2306 3.2	**29 TH** 0342 8.9 / 1022 3.0 / 1618 9.4 / 2259 2.5
15 TH 0459 8.8 / 1125 3.1 / 1715 9.2 / 2353 2.9	**30 F** 0454 9.5 / 1132 2.4 / 1722 10.1
	31 SA 0005 1.8 / 0554 10.2 / 1233 1.8 / ○ 1817 10.7

AUGUST

Time m	Time m
1 SU 0104 1.3 / 0647 10.7 / 1907 11.2	**16 M** 0101 2.1 / 0644 9.9 / 1315 2.1 / ● 1854 10.3
2 M 0157 0.9 / 0735 11.0 / 1417 1.2 / 1952 11.4	**17 TU** 0139 1.8 / 0719 10.2 / 1351 1.9 / 1929 10.6
3 TU 0244 0.8 / 0818 11.0 / 1501 1.2 / 2035 11.3	**18 W** 0215 1.6 / 0753 10.4 / 1426 1.7 / 2003 10.7
4 W 0326 0.9 / 0858 10.8 / 1541 1.4 / 2113 10.9	**19 TH** 0248 1.6 / 0826 10.5 / 1459 1.7 / 2037 10.7
5 TH 0404 1.3 / 0934 10.4 / 1616 1.9 / 2149 10.4	**20 F** 0320 1.6 / 0859 10.4 / 1533 1.8 / 2111 10.5
6 F 0437 1.9 / 1008 9.8 / 1648 2.5 / 2224 9.7	**21 SA** 0353 1.9 / 0933 10.1 / 1607 2.1 / 2146 10.1
7 SA 0507 2.6 / 1042 9.2 / 1719 3.1 / ○ 2300 8.9	**22 SU** 0426 2.4 / 1008 9.6 / 1644 2.7 / 2224 9.5
8 SU 0539 3.0 / 1120 8.5 / 1757 3.8 / 2345 8.2	**23 M** 0504 3.0 / 1049 9.0 / 1729 3.3 / ○ 2313 8.8
9 M 0622 3.9 / 1213 8.0 / 1853 4.3	**24 TU** 0554 3.6 / 1147 8.4 / 1833 3.8
10 TU 0053 7.7 / 0726 4.4 / 1334 7.7 / 2015 4.5	**25 W** 0024 8.2 / 0711 4.0 / 1316 8.1 / 2005 3.9
11 W 0227 7.5 / 0853 4.4 / 1501 7.9 / 2140 4.2	**26 TH** 0208 8.1 / 0853 4.0 / 1500 8.4 / 2141 3.4
12 TH 0346 7.9 / 1009 4.0 / 1608 8.4 / 2245 3.6	**27 F** 0346 8.6 / 1022 3.9 / 1619 9.3 / 2259 2.6
13 F 0444 8.5 / 1106 3.4 / 1658 8.9 / 2336 3.0	**28 SA** 0455 9.5 / 1130 2.5 / 1718 10.2
14 SA 0529 9.0 / 1153 2.9 / 1740 9.5	**29 SU** 0001 1.8 / 0548 10.3 / 1226 1.7 / 1807 10.9
15 SU 0020 2.5 / 0608 9.5 / 1236 2.5 / 1818 9.9	**30 M** 0054 1.1 / 0635 10.9 / 1315 1.2 / ○ 1852 11.4
	31 TU 0141 0.8 / 0716 11.2 / 1359 1.4 / 1932 11.6

Chart Datum: 5·88 metres below Ordnance Datum (Local)

CHANNEL ISLES – ST HELIER

YEAR **2004**

LAT 49°11'N   LONG 2°07'W

TIMES AND HEIGHTS OF HIGH AND LOW WATERS

SEPTEMBER

Time	m		Time	m
1 0222	0.7	**16** 0152		1.3
0754	11.2	0728		10.9
W 1437	1.0	TH 1404		1.3
2010	11.5	1940		11.2
2 0258	0.9	**17** 0225		1.2
0828	11.0	0801		11.0
TH 1510	1.3	F 1438		1.3
2043	11.1	2014		11.2
3 0329	1.3	**18** 0258		1.4
0859	10.6	0834		10.8
F 1539	1.8	SA 1512		1.6
2114	10.5	2049		10.8
4 0355	2.0	**19** 0330		1.8
0927	10.0	0908		10.4
SA 1605	2.4	SU 1546		2.0
2142	9.7	2123		10.2
5 0419	2.7	**20** 0403		2.4
0954	9.4	0942		9.8
SU 1630	3.1	M 1623		2.7
2210	8.9	2202		9.5
6 0444	3.4	**21** 0441		3.1
1023	8.7	1023		9.0
M 1659	3.8	TU 1710		3.4
2244	8.1	2252		8.6
7 0518	4.2	**22** 0534		3.9
1104	7.9	1125		8.3
TU 1747	4.5	W 1821		4.0
2341	7.4			
8 0620	4.8	**23** 0016		7.9
1224	7.3	0704		4.4
W 1916	4.9	TH 1315		7.9
		2007		4.1
9 0153	7.1	**24** 0222		7.9
0807	4.9	0858		4.1
TH 1434	7.4	F 1505		8.5
2111	4.6	2144		3.4
10 0330	7.6	**25** 0349		8.7
0946	4.4	1020		3.3
F 1549	8.1	SA 1613		9.4
2224	3.9	2252		2.5
11 0425	8.3	**26** 0446		9.7
1045	3.7	1119		2.3
SA 1637	8.8	SU 1705		10.3
2314	3.1	2346		1.7
12 0507	9.1	**27** 0532		10.4
1131	2.9	1208		1.6
SU 1718	9.6	M 1749		11.0
2357	2.4			
13 0544	9.7	**28** 0033		1.1
1213	2.3	0613		11.0
M 1755	10.2	TU 1252		1.2
		○ 1829		11.4
14 0037	1.9	**29** 0115		0.9
0619	10.2	0650		11.2
TU 1252	1.8	W 1331		1.1
● 1830	10.7	1906		11.5
15 0116	1.5	**30** 0151		0.9
0654	10.6	0724		11.2
W 1329	1.5	TH 1405		1.2
1905	11.0	1940		11.3

OCTOBER

Time	m		Time	m
1 0222	1.2	**16** 0159		1.2
0755	11.0	0735		11.2
F 1435	1.5	SA 1415		1.2
2010	10.9	1952		11.3
2 0249	1.6	**17** 0234		1.4
0823	10.6	0811		11.0
SA 1501	1.9	SU 1452		1.5
2038	10.4	2029		10.9
3 0313	2.1	**18** 0309		1.8
0848	10.1	0847		10.6
SU 1525	2.5	M 1530		2.0
2104	9.7	2108		10.2
4 0336	2.8	**19** 0347		2.5
0912	9.5	0926		9.9
M 1549	3.1	TU 1612		2.7
2129	8.9	2153		9.3
5 0400	3.5	**20** 0430		3.3
0938	8.8	1014		9.1
TU 1617	3.9	W 1706		3.4
2157	8.1	◐ 2252		8.5
6 0432	4.3	**21** 0532		4.1
1010	8.1	1126		8.3
W 1700	4.5	TH 1825		4.0
◐ 2244	7.4			
7 0528	4.9	**22** 0026		7.9
1115	7.3	0708		4.4
TH 1824	5.0	F 1317		8.2
		2007		3.9
8 0105	7.0	**23** 0217		8.2
0714	5.2	0850		4.0
F 1352	7.2	SA 1450		8.7
2026	4.8	2130		3.2
9 0258	7.5	**24** 0330		8.9
0907	4.7	1001		3.1
SA 1515	7.9	SU 1552		9.5
2148	4.1	2230		2.4
10 0352	8.3	**25** 0422		9.7
1011	3.8	1055		2.4
SU 1604	8.8	M 1641		10.2
2239	3.2	2320		1.8
11 0433	9.1	**26** 0506		10.3
1057	3.0	1142		1.8
M 1644	9.6	TU 1723		10.7
2322	2.5			
12 0511	9.8	**27** 0004		1.5
1140	2.3	0544		10.7
TU 1723	10.3	W 1223		1.6
		1801		10.9
13 0004	1.9	**28** 0042		1.4
0547	10.4	0620		10.9
W 1221	1.8	TH 1259		1.5
1800	10.8	○ 1837		11.0
14 0044	1.4	**29** 0116		1.5
0623	10.9	0652		10.9
TH 1301	1.4	F 1331		1.6
● 1837	11.3	1910		10.8
15 0123	1.2	**30** 0145		1.7
0659	11.2	0722		10.8
F 1339	1.2	SA 1400		1.8
1914	11.4	1940		10.6
		31 0212		2.0
		0750		10.5
		SU 1427		2.1
		2008		10.1

NOVEMBER

Time	m		Time	m
1 0238	2.4	**16** 0257		1.9
0816	10.1	0837		10.7
M 1453	2.6	TU 1523		1.9
2035	9.6	2104		10.1
2 0305	2.9	**17** 0341		2.5
0842	9.6	0923		10.0
TU 1521	3.1	W 1612		2.5
2103	8.9	2155		9.4
3 0332	3.5	**18** 0432		3.2
0910	9.0	1017		9.4
W 1552	3.7	TH 1710		3.1
2134	8.3	2257		8.8
4 0406	4.2	**19** 0536		3.7
0944	8.3	1126		8.8
TH 1635	4.3	F 1823		3.5
2220	7.6	◐		
5 0458	4.7	**20** 0015		8.4
1041	7.7	0656		4.0
F 1744	4.7	SA 1251		8.6
◐ 2353	7.2	1943		3.5
6 0622	5.0	**21** 0140		8.4
1231	7.4	0817		3.7
SA 1921	4.7	SU 1411		8.8
		2055		3.2
7 0152	7.5	**22** 0250		8.8
0802	4.7	0925		3.3
SU 1413	7.8	M 1515		9.3
2049	4.2	2154		2.7
8 0258	8.1	**23** 0346		9.4
0918	4.0	1021		2.8
M 1513	8.6	TU 1608		9.7
2149	3.4	2245		2.4
9 0347	8.9	**24** 0432		9.8
1012	3.2	1109		2.4
TU 1600	9.3	W 1653		10.0
2239	2.7	2329		2.2
10 0430	9.7	**25** 0513		10.1
1100	2.5	1151		2.2
W 1644	10.1	TH 1733		10.2
2325	2.1			
11 0511	10.3	**26** 0008		2.1
1145	1.9	0549		10.3
TH 1727	10.7	F 1228		2.1
		○ 1810		10.3
12 0009	1.6	**27** 0043		2.1
0551	10.8	0623		10.4
F 1230	1.5	SA 1302		2.1
● 1809	11.1	1844		10.2
13 0053	1.4	**28** 0114		2.1
0632	11.2	0656		10.4
SA 1313	1.3	SU 1333		2.2
1851	11.2	1917		10.1
14 0134	1.3	**29** 0145		2.3
0712	11.3	0726		10.3
SU 1355	1.3	M 1404		2.3
1934	11.1	1949		9.8
15 0215	1.5	**30** 0216		2.5
0754	11.1	0757		10.0
M 1438	1.5	TU 1435		2.6
2018	10.7	2020		9.5

DECEMBER

Time	m		Time	m
1 0246	2.9	**16** 0342		2.1
0827	9.6	0923		10.5
W 1506	3.0	TH 1614		2.0
2052	9.1	2154		9.9
2 0318	3.3	**17** 0432		2.6
0859	9.2	1013		10.0
TH 1540	3.4	F 1706		2.4
2127	8.6	2245		9.4
3 0354	3.7	**18** 0525		3.0
0936	8.8	1107		9.5
F 1621	3.8	SA 1801		2.9
2210	8.2	◑ 2342		8.9
4 0439	4.1	**19** 0624		3.4
1024	8.3	1208		9.0
SA 1713	4.1	SU 1901		3.2
2308	7.9			
5 0538	4.4	**20** 0045		8.6
1130	8.0	0728		3.6
SU 1820	4.2	M 1316		8.7
◑		2003		3.4
6 0025	7.8	**21** 0153		8.5
0652	4.4	0834		3.6
M 1250	8.0	TU 1424		8.7
1936	4.1	2105		3.3
7 0144	8.1	**22** 0257		8.7
0810	4.1	0937		3.4
TU 1405	8.4	W 1526		8.8
2048	3.7	2203		3.2
8 0248	8.6	**23** 0354		9.0
0918	3.5	1033		3.2
W 1507	9.0	TH 1621		9.1
2150	3.1	2254		3.0
9 0343	9.3	**24** 0442		9.3
1017	2.9	1122		2.9
TH 1603	9.6	F 1708		9.3
2245	2.5	2339		2.8
10 0434	9.9	**25** 0525		9.6
1111	2.3	1204		2.7
F 1655	10.2	SA 1750		9.5
2337	2.0			
11 0523	10.5	**26** 0018		2.6
1203	1.8	0603		9.9
SA 1746	10.6	SU 1242		2.5
		○ 1828		9.7
12 0028	1.7	**27** 0056		2.6
0611	10.9	0639		10.0
SU 1254	1.4	M 1318		2.4
● 1836	10.9	1905		9.8
13 0117	1.5	**28** 0130		2.5
0658	11.1	0713		10.0
M 1344	1.3	TU 1352		2.4
1926	10.9	1939		9.7
14 0206	1.6	**29** 0204		2.5
0746	11.1	0747		10.0
TU 1433	1.3	W 1426		2.4
2015	10.8	2012		9.6
15 0254	1.8	**30** 0237		2.6
0834	10.9	0819		9.9
W 1523	1.6	TH 1459		2.6
2104	10.4	2045		9.5
		31 0309		2.8
		0853		9.7
		F 1532		2.8
		2118		9.2

Chart Datum: 5·88 metres below Ordnance Datum (Local)

Chapter 5

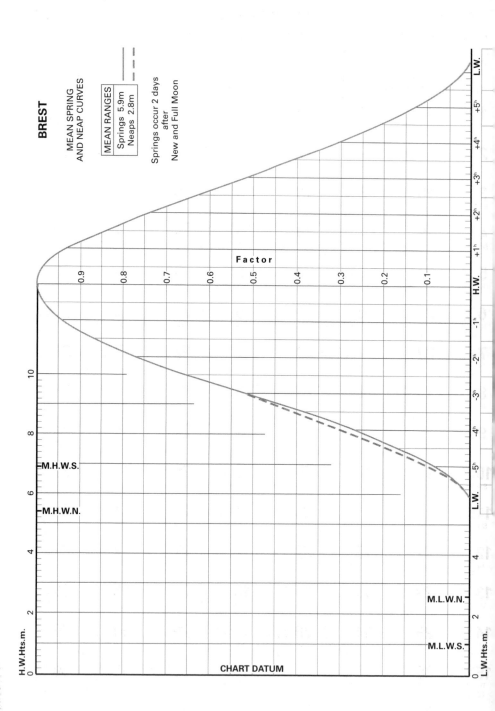

BREST

MEAN SPRING
AND NEAP CURVES

MEAN RANGES
Springs 5.9m
Neaps 2.8m

Springs occur 2 days
after
New and Full Moon

Factor

| TIME ZONE -0100
(French Standard Time)
Subtract 1 hour for UT
For French Summer Time add
ONE hour in **non-shaded areas** | **FRANCE – BREST**
LAT 48°23′N   LONG 4°30′W
TIMES AND HEIGHTS OF HIGH AND LOW WATERS | YEAR **2004** |

JANUARY

Day	Time m		Day	Time m	
1 TH	0610 2.7 / 1214 5.4 / 1839 2.7		**16**	0508 2.4 / 1113 5.7 / F 1745 2.3 / 2355 5.6	
2 F	0053 5.3 / 0716 2.7 / 1319 5.4 / 1942 2.6		**17**	0619 2.4 / 1228 5.7 / SA 1857 2.3	
3 SA	0154 5.4 / 0816 2.6 / 1418 5.5 / 2037 2.5		**18**	0114 5.7 / 0734 2.2 / SU 1345 5.8 / 2009 2.1	
4 SU	0245 5.6 / 0908 2.4 / 1507 5.7 / 2124 2.3		**19**	0224 6.1 / 0844 1.9 / M 1455 6.1 / 2114 1.8	
5 M	0329 5.5 / 0952 2.2 / 1550 5.9 / 2205 2.1		**20**	0326 6.4 / 0947 1.5 / TU 1555 6.4 / 2212 1.5	
6 TU	0408 6.1 / 1032 2.0 / 1629 6.0 / 2243 2.0		**21**	0421 6.8 / 1043 1.2 / W 1648 6.7 / ● 2304 1.2	
7 W	0445 6.3 / 1109 1.8 / 1706 6.2 / ○ 2320 1.8		**22**	0512 7.0 / 1133 0.9 / TH 1736 6.8 / 2352 1.1	
8 TH	0520 6.4 / 1145 1.7 / 1741 6.4 / 2355 1.7		**23**	0558 7.2 / 1220 0.8 / F 1821 6.8	
9 F	0556 6.5 / 1221 1.6 / 1817 6.3		**24**	0041 1.1 / 0642 7.2 / SA 1305 0.9 / 1903 6.7	
10 SA	0032 1.7 / 0631 6.5 / 1257 1.6 / 1853 6.3		**25**	0123 1.2 / 0723 7.0 / SU 1346 1.1 / 1942 6.5	
11 SU	0109 1.7 / 0708 6.5 / 1334 1.6 / 1931 6.2		**26**	0204 1.4 / 0801 6.7 / M 1426 1.4 / 2019 6.2	
12 M	0148 1.8 / 0747 6.4 / 1413 1.7 / 2011 6.1		**27**	0243 1.7 / 0839 6.3 / TU 1504 1.8 / 2056 5.9	
13 TU	0229 1.9 / 0828 6.2 / 1456 1.9 / 2055 5.9		**28**	0323 2.1 / 0918 5.9 / W 1545 2.2 / 2137 5.5	
14 W	0315 2.1 / 0914 6.0 / 1543 2.1 / 2145 5.7		**29**	0408 2.5 / 1003 5.5 / TH 1631 2.6 / ◑ 2227 5.2	
15 TH	0407 2.2 / 1008 5.8 / 1639 2.2 / ◑ 2245 5.5		**30**	0501 2.8 / 1100 5.2 / F 1728 2.9 / 2335 5.0	
			31	0608 3.0 / 1215 5.0 / SA 1840 3.0	

FEBRUARY

Day	Time m		Day	Time m	
1 SU	0059 5.0 / 0728 3.0 / 1337 5.0 / 1957 2.9		**16**	0053 5.5 / 0717 2.4 / M 1336 5.5 / 1957 2.4	
2 M	0213 5.2 / 0839 2.7 / 1444 5.3 / 2058 2.6		**17**	0218 5.8 / 0839 2.1 / TU 1454 5.8 / 2110 2.0	
3 TU	0307 5.5 / 0931 2.4 / 1533 5.6 / 2145 2.3		**18**	0323 6.2 / 0944 1.6 / W 1553 6.2 / 2208 1.6	
4 W	0351 5.9 / 1014 2.1 / 1614 5.9 / 2226 2.0		**19**	0416 6.7 / 1037 1.2 / TH 1641 6.6 / 2256 1.2	
5 TH	0429 6.2 / 1053 1.7 / 1651 6.2 / 2304 1.7		**20**	0502 7.0 / 1123 0.9 / F 1724 6.8 / ● 2340 1.0	
6 F	0506 6.5 / 1129 1.5 / 1727 6.4 / ○ 2340 1.5		**21**	0543 7.2 / 1205 0.8 / SA 1803 6.9	
7 SA	0542 6.7 / 1205 1.3 / 1802 6.6		**22**	0022 0.9 / 0621 7.2 / SU 1243 0.8 / 1838 6.9	
8 SU	0018 1.3 / 0617 6.9 / 1241 1.1 / 1837 6.7		**23**	0059 1.0 / 0656 7.1 / M 1318 1.0 / 1911 6.7	
9 M	0053 1.2 / 0652 6.9 / 1316 1.1 / 1912 6.7		**24**	0134 1.2 / 0728 6.8 / TU 1351 1.3 / 1941 6.4	
10 TU	0130 1.2 / 0728 6.8 / 1353 1.2 / 1949 6.5		**25**	0207 1.5 / 0759 6.5 / W 1423 1.7 / 2012 6.1	
11 W	0209 1.4 / 0806 6.7 / 1432 1.4 / 2028 6.3		**26**	0240 1.9 / 0831 6.0 / TH 1457 2.1 / 2044 5.7	
12 TH	0251 1.6 / 0847 6.4 / 1515 1.8 / 2112 6.0		**27**	0317 2.4 / 0907 5.6 / F 1534 2.6 / 2123 5.3	
13 F	0338 1.9 / 0935 6.0 / 1606 2.1 / ◑ 2207 5.7		**28**	0401 2.8 / 0953 5.1 / SA 1623 3.0 / ○ 2220 5.0	
14 SA	0436 2.3 / 1038 5.6 / 1710 2.5 / 2318 5.5		**29**	0503 3.1 / 1107 4.8 / SU 1734 3.2 / 2350 4.8	
15 SU	0550 2.5 / 1201 5.4 / 1830 2.6				

MARCH

Day	Time m		Day	Time m	
1 M	0632 3.2 / 1253 4.7 / 1911 3.2		**16**	0049 5.4 / 0715 2.5 / TU 1341 5.3 / 1956 2.6	
2 TU	0137 5.0 / 0807 3.0 / 1420 5.0 / 2031 2.9		**17**	0215 5.7 / 0838 2.1 / W 1452 5.8 / 2106 2.1	
3 W	0243 5.4 / 0907 2.5 / 1512 5.5 / 2122 2.4		**18**	0315 6.2 / 0936 1.6 / TH 1543 6.2 / 2157 1.6	
4 TH	0328 5.8 / 0951 2.1 / 1552 5.9 / 2203 2.0		**19**	0403 6.7 / 1023 1.2 / F 1626 6.6 / 2241 1.2	
5 F	0407 6.2 / 1029 1.6 / 1629 6.3 / 2241 1.6		**20**	0444 7.0 / 1105 0.9 / SA 1704 6.8 / ● 2321 1.0	
6 SA	0444 6.6 / 1106 1.2 / 1705 6.6 / ○ 2318 1.2		**21**	0521 7.1 / 1142 0.9 / SU 1738 6.9 / 2357 0.9	
7 SU	0520 6.9 / 1142 1.0 / 1740 6.9 / 2354 1.0		**22**	0554 7.1 / 1215 0.9 / M 1809 6.9	
8 M	0555 7.1 / 1218 0.8 / 1814 7.0		**23**	0031 1.0 / 0625 7.0 / TU 1246 1.1 / 1838 6.8	
9 TU	0032 0.8 / 0630 7.2 / 1254 0.8 / 1849 7.0		**24**	0103 1.2 / 0655 6.8 / W 1316 1.3 / 1906 6.5	
10 W	0109 0.9 / 0706 7.1 / 1331 0.9 / 1925 6.9		**25**	0133 1.5 / 0724 6.4 / TH 1346 1.7 / 1934 6.2	
11 TH	0148 1.0 / 0744 6.9 / 1410 1.2 / 2004 6.6		**26**	0204 1.9 / 0754 6.0 / F 1416 2.1 / 2004 5.9	
12 F	0230 1.4 / 0825 6.5 / 1453 1.7 / 2048 6.2		**27**	0238 2.3 / 0826 5.6 / SA 1451 2.5 / 2039 5.5	
13 SA	0318 1.8 / 0914 5.9 / 1544 2.2 / ◑ 2143 5.7		**28**	0318 2.7 / 0908 5.1 / SU 1536 2.9 / ◐ 2128 5.1	
14 SU	0418 2.3 / 1020 5.4 / 1651 2.6 / 2301 5.4		**29**	0415 3.0 / 1016 4.8 / M 1642 3.2 / 2253 4.8	
15 M	0538 2.6 / 1156 5.1 / 1820 2.8		**30**	0539 3.2 / 1204 4.7 / TU 1818 3.3	
			31	0048 4.9 / 0723 3.0 / W 1342 5.0 / 1951 2.9	

APRIL

Day	Time m		Day	Time m	
1 TH	0204 5.3 / 0830 2.5 / 1438 5.4 / 2047 2.4		**16**	0254 6.2 / 0915 1.6 / F 1521 6.2 / 2135 1.6	
2 F	0254 5.8 / 0917 2.0 / 1520 5.9 / 2131 1.9		**17**	0339 6.5 / 1000 1.3 / SA 1601 6.5 / 2218 1.3	
3 SA	0336 6.3 / 0957 1.5 / 1559 6.4 / 2211 1.5		**18**	0418 6.7 / 1039 1.2 / SU 1637 6.7 / 2255 1.2	
4 SU	0415 6.7 / 1036 1.1 / 1636 6.8 / 2250 1.1		**19**	0453 6.8 / 1113 1.1 / M 1709 6.7 / ● 2330 1.2	
5 M	0452 7.0 / 1114 0.8 / 1712 7.1 / ○ 2328 0.8		**20**	0525 6.8 / 1145 1.2 / TU 1739 6.7	
6 TU	0529 7.3 / 1152 0.6 / 1748 7.2		**21**	0002 1.2 / 0555 6.7 / W 1215 1.3 / 1808 6.6	
7 W	0007 0.6 / 0607 7.3 / 1230 0.7 / 1825 7.2		**22**	0034 1.4 / 0626 6.5 / TH 1245 1.5 / 1836 6.5	
8 TH	0049 0.7 / 0645 7.2 / 1309 0.9 / 1904 7.0		**23**	0104 1.6 / 0656 6.3 / F 1315 1.8 / 1906 6.2	
9 F	0131 0.9 / 0727 6.9 / 1351 1.3 / 1946 6.7		**24**	0136 1.9 / 0727 5.9 / SA 1346 2.1 / 1937 5.9	
10 SA	0216 1.3 / 0812 6.4 / 1438 1.8 / 2035 6.3		**25**	0211 2.2 / 0801 5.6 / SU 1422 2.5 / 2013 5.5	
11 SU	0309 1.8 / 0907 5.8 / 1534 2.3 / 2136 5.7		**26**	0252 2.6 / 0844 5.2 / M 1507 2.8 / 2103 5.2	
12 M	0413 2.3 / 1021 5.3 / 1646 2.7 / ◐ 2300 5.4		**27**	0346 2.9 / 0948 4.9 / TU 1608 3.1 / ◐ 2217 5.0	
13 TU	0536 2.5 / 1159 5.1 / 1817 2.9		**28**	0459 3.0 / 1119 4.8 / W 1730 3.1 / 2350 5.0	
14 W	0042 5.5 / 0708 2.4 / 1331 5.4 / 1944 2.5		**29**	0627 2.9 / 1248 5.0 / TH 1856 2.9	
15 TH	0158 5.8 / 0821 2.0 / 1434 5.8 / 2047 2.0		**30**	0112 5.3 / 0739 2.5 / F 1350 5.4 / 2000 2.4	

Chapter 5

Chart Datum: 3·64 metres below IGN Datum

FRANCE – BREST

TIME ZONE -0100
(French Standard Time)
Subtract 1 hour for UT
For French Summer Time add
ONE hour in **non-shaded areas**

LAT 48°23′N   LONG 4°30′W

TIMES AND HEIGHTS OF HIGH AND LOW WATERS

YEAR 200◄

Time m Time m   Time m Time m   Time m Time m   Time m Time m

MAY

Day	Times / m	Day	Times / m
1 SA	0209 5.7 / 0833 2.0 / 1438 5.9 / 2050 1.9	**16** SU	0307 6.2 / 0928 1.7 / 1530 6.2 / 2148 1.6
2 SU	0256 6.2 / 0918 1.6 / 1521 6.4 / 2135 1.5	**17** M	0347 6.3 / 1008 1.6 / 1606 6.4 / 2227 1.5
3 M	0340 6.6 / 1001 1.1 / 1602 6.8 / 2218 1.1	**18** TU	0424 6.4 / 1043 1.5 / 1640 6.4 / 2302 1.5
4 TU	0422 7.0 / 1043 0.9 / 1643 7.1 / ○2301 0.8	**19** W	0457 6.4 / 1116 1.5 / 1711 6.5 / ●2336 1.5
5 W	0503 7.2 / 1125 0.7 / 1723 7.2 / 2344 0.7	**20** TH	0530 6.4 / 1148 1.6 / 1742 6.4
6 TH	0546 7.2 / 1208 0.8 / 1805 7.2	**21** F	0009 1.6 / 0602 6.3 / 1220 1.7 / 1814 6.3
7 F	0031 0.7 / 0630 7.0 / 1252 1.0 / 1849 7.0	**22** SA	0043 1.7 / 0635 6.1 / 1252 1.9 / 1846 6.2
8 SA	0118 1.0 / 0716 6.7 / 1339 1.3 / 1937 6.7	**23** SU	0117 1.9 / 0709 5.9 / 1326 2.1 / 1921 5.9
9 SU	0209 1.3 / 0808 6.2 / 1431 1.8 / 2032 6.3	**24** M	0153 2.1 / 0746 5.6 / 1404 2.4 / 2000 5.7
10 M	0305 1.7 / 0908 5.8 / 1530 2.2 / 2136 5.9	**25** TU	0235 2.4 / 0831 5.3 / 1448 2.6 / 2048 5.5
11 TU	0410 2.1 / 1020 5.4 / 1640 2.5 / ◐2252 5.6	**26** W	0324 2.6 / 0927 5.1 / 1543 2.7 / 2148 5.3
12 W	0525 2.3 / 1142 5.3 / 1758 2.6	**27** TH	0424 2.7 / 1036 5.1 / 1648 2.8 / ◐2259 5.2
13 TH	0014 5.6 / 0641 2.3 / 1258 5.4 / 1913 2.4	**28** F	0534 2.6 / 1149 5.2 / 1800 2.7
14 F	0125 5.8 / 0748 2.1 / 1359 5.7 / 2014 2.1	**29** SA	0013 5.4 / 0643 2.4 / 1255 5.5 / 1907 2.4
15 SA	0221 6.0 / 0843 1.8 / 1448 6.0 / 2104 1.8	**30** SU	0117 5.7 / 0744 2.1 / 1351 5.8 / 2004 2.0
		31 M	0213 6.1 / 0837 1.7 / 1442 6.2 / 2057 1.6

JUNE

Day	Times / m	Day	Times / m
1 TU	0304 6.4 / 0927 1.3 / 1530 6.6 / 2147 1.2	**16** W	0357 6.0 / 1015 1.9 / 1615 6.1 / 2238 1.8
2 W	0354 6.7 / 1015 1.1 / 1617 6.9 / 2236 1.0	**17** TH	0435 6.0 / 1052 1.9 / 1650 6.2 / ●2315 1.8
3 TH	0442 6.9 / 1103 1.0 / 1704 7.1 / ○2326 0.8	**18** F	0511 6.1 / 1127 1.8 / 1724 6.2 / 2350 1.7
4 F	0531 7.0 / 1151 0.9 / 1752 7.1	**19** SA	0546 6.1 / 1201 1.9 / 1759 6.2
5 SA	0019 0.8 / 0621 6.8 / 1240 1.1 / 1841 7.0	**20** SU	0027 1.8 / 0621 6.0 / 1236 1.9 / 1834 6.2
6 SU	0110 0.9 / 0712 6.6 / 1331 1.3 / 1933 6.8	**21** M	0102 1.8 / 0657 5.9 / 1311 2.0 / 1910 6.1
7 M	0203 1.2 / 0805 6.3 / 1424 1.6 / 2027 6.5	**22** TU	0139 1.9 / 0735 5.8 / 1349 2.1 / 1948 6.0
8 TU	0258 1.5 / 0901 5.9 / 1520 2.0 / 2125 6.1	**23** W	0218 2.0 / 0816 5.7 / 1430 2.2 / 2031 5.8
9 W	0355 1.8 / 1001 5.6 / 1620 2.2 / ◐2226 5.9	**24** TH	0301 2.1 / 0902 5.5 / 1517 2.3 / 2119 5.7
10 TH	0456 2.1 / 1105 5.4 / 1724 2.4 / 2330 5.7	**25** F	0350 2.3 / 0955 5.4 / 1610 2.4 / ◐2214 5.6
11 F	0600 2.2 / 1210 5.4 / 1829 2.4	**26** SA	0447 2.3 / 1055 5.4 / 1710 2.4 / 2317 5.6
12 SA	0037 5.6 / 0703 2.3 / 1313 5.5 / 1931 2.3	**27** SU	0550 2.3 / 1200 5.5 / 1816 2.4
13 SU	0137 5.7 / 0801 2.2 / 1408 5.6 / 2027 2.2	**28** M	0026 5.7 / 0656 2.2 / 1305 5.7 / 1921 2.1
14 M	0230 5.8 / 0851 2.1 / 1455 5.8 / 2116 2.0	**29** TU	0132 5.9 / 0759 1.9 / 1406 6.0 / 2024 1.9
15 TU	0316 5.9 / 0936 2.0 / 1537 6.0 / 2159 1.9	**30** W	0235 6.1 / 0858 1.7 / 1504 6.3 / 2123 1.5

JULY

Day	Times / m	Day	Times / m
1 TH	0334 6.4 / 0954 1.4 / 1559 6.7 / 2220 1.2	**16** F	0419 5.8 / 1033 2.0 / 1634 6.1 / 2258 1.9
2 F	0430 6.6 / 1048 1.2 / 1652 6.9 / ○2314 0.9	**17** SA	0457 6.0 / 1110 1.9 / 1710 6.2 / ●2335 1.7
3 SA	0523 6.8 / 1140 1.1 / 1744 7.0	**18** SU	0532 6.1 / 1145 1.8 / 1745 6.3
4 SU	0008 0.8 / 0614 6.8 / 1231 1.1 / 1834 7.1	**19** M	0011 1.6 / 0607 6.1 / 1220 1.7 / 1820 6.4
5 M	0101 0.8 / 0703 6.7 / 1320 1.2 / 1923 6.9	**20** TU	0046 1.6 / 0642 6.2 / 1255 1.7 / 1854 6.4
6 TU	0151 1.0 / 0751 6.5 / 1409 1.4 / 2011 6.7	**21** W	0121 1.6 / 0717 6.2 / 1331 1.7 / 1930 6.3
7 W	0239 1.3 / 0838 6.2 / 1458 1.6 / 2059 6.4	**22** TH	0157 1.6 / 0753 6.1 / 1408 1.8 / 2007 6.2
8 TH	0327 1.6 / 0926 5.9 / 1548 2.0 / 2148 6.0	**23** F	0235 1.8 / 0832 5.9 / 1449 1.9 / 2048 6.1
9 F	0416 2.0 / 1016 5.6 / 1640 2.3 / ◐2241 5.7	**24** SA	0318 1.9 / 0917 5.8 / 1535 2.1 / 2134 5.9
10 SA	0509 2.3 / 1112 5.3 / 1737 2.5 / 2339 5.4	**25** SU	0407 2.1 / 1009 5.6 / 1629 2.3 / ◐2231 5.7
11 SU	0608 2.5 / 1215 5.2 / 1841 2.6	**26** M	0506 2.3 / 1113 5.5 / 1734 2.4 / 2340 5.5
12 M	0046 5.3 / 0711 2.6 / 1322 5.3 / 1946 2.6	**27** TU	0615 2.4 / 1227 5.5 / 1848 2.3
13 TU	0152 5.3 / 0813 2.5 / 1422 5.4 / 2046 2.4	**28** W	0104 5.6 / 0730 2.3 / 1342 5.8 / 2003 2.1
14 W	0249 5.5 / 0907 2.4 / 1513 5.7 / 2136 2.2	**29** TH	0221 5.8 / 0841 2.0 / 1451 6.1 / 2112 1.7
15 TH	0337 5.6 / 0953 2.2 / 1556 5.9 / 2220 2.0	**30** F	0327 6.2 / 0944 1.6 / 1551 6.5 / 2212 1.3
		31 SA	0425 6.5 / 1040 1.3 / 1645 6.9 / ○2307 0.9

AUGUST

Day	Times / m	Day	Times / m
1 SU	0516 6.7 / 1131 1.1 / 1734 7.1 / 2356 0.7	**16** M	0514 6.3 / 1126 1.6 / 1726 6.6 / ●2350 1.4
2 M	0603 6.9 / 1218 0.9 / 1821 7.2	**17** TU	0547 6.4 / 1200 1.4 / 1759 6.7
3 TU	0046 0.7 / 0646 6.8 / 1303 1.0 / 1904 7.2	**18** W	0024 1.2 / 0620 6.6 / 1234 1.3 / 1832 6.8
4 W	0129 0.8 / 0726 6.7 / 1346 1.1 / 1945 6.9	**19** TH	0058 1.2 / 0653 6.6 / 1308 1.3 / 1906 6.7
5 TH	0210 1.1 / 0805 6.4 / 1427 1.4 / 2024 6.5	**20** F	0132 1.3 / 0727 6.5 / 1344 1.4 / 1941 6.6
6 F	0250 1.5 / 0842 6.1 / 1508 1.8 / 2103 6.1	**21** SA	0208 1.5 / 0803 6.3 / 1423 1.6 / 2018 6.3
7 SA	0330 2.0 / 0922 5.7 / 1552 2.3 / ◑2146 5.7	**22** SU	0248 1.7 / 0844 6.1 / 1507 1.9 / 2102 6.0
8 SU	0415 2.4 / 1010 5.3 / 1643 2.6 / 2240 5.2	**23** M	0335 2.1 / 0933 5.7 / 1559 2.2 / ◐2157 5.6
9 M	0509 2.8 / 1113 5.1 / 1747 2.9 / 2350 5.0	**24** TU	0433 2.4 / 1039 5.5 / 1706 2.5 / 2314 5.3
10 TU	0618 3.0 / 1234 5.0 / 1906 2.9	**25** W	0550 2.7 / 1206 5.4 / 1831 2.5
11 W	0118 5.0 / 0738 2.9 / 1355 5.2 / 2022 2.8	**26** TH	0056 5.3 / 0719 2.6 / 1336 5.6 / 1959 2.3
12 TH	0230 5.2 / 0844 2.7 / 1454 5.5 / 2118 2.4	**27** F	0223 5.7 / 0838 2.2 / 1448 6.1 / 2110 1.8
13 F	0322 5.5 / 0933 2.4 / 1539 5.8 / 2202 2.1	**28** SA	0326 6.1 / 0940 1.7 / 1545 6.5 / 2207 1.3
14 SA	0403 5.8 / 1014 2.1 / 1617 6.1 / 2240 1.8	**29** SU	0417 6.6 / 1031 1.3 / 1634 7.0 / 2256 0.9
15 SU	0439 6.1 / 1051 1.8 / 1652 6.4 / 2316 1.6	**30** M	0502 6.9 / 1117 1.0 / 1719 7.3 / ○2340 0.7
		31 TU	0543 7.0 / 1200 0.8 / 1800 7.3

Chart Datum: 3·64 metres below IGN Datum

TIME ZONE -0100
(French Standard Time)
Subtract 1 hour for UT
For French Summer Time add
ONE hour in **non-shaded areas**

FRANCE – BREST

LAT 48°23′N   LONG 4°30′W

TIMES AND HEIGHTS OF HIGH AND LOW WATERS

YEAR **2004**

SEPTEMBER

Day		Event 1	Event 2	Event 3	Event 4
1	W	0023 0.7	0620 7.0	1239 0.9	1837 7.2
2	TH	0101 0.9	0654 6.8	1316 1.1	1912 7.0
3	F	0136 1.2	0727 6.6	1352 1.4	1945 6.6
4	SA	0209 1.6	0758 6.2	1427 1.8	2018 6.1
5	SU	0244 2.1	0831 5.8	1506 2.3	2054 5.6
6	M	0322 2.5	0911 5.4	1552 2.8	☾ 2142 5.1
7	TU	0412 3.0	1010 5.0	1654 3.1	2256 4.8
8	W	0524 3.2	1144 4.8	1824 3.2	
9	TH	0047 4.7	0702 3.2	1328 5.0	1959 3.0
10	F	0211 5.0	0820 2.9	1432 5.4	2056 2.5
11	SA	0300 5.5	0909 2.4	1515 5.8	2137 2.1
12	SU	0339 5.9	0949 2.0	1552 6.2	2214 1.7
13	M	0414 6.2	1025 1.7	1627 6.5	2249 1.4
14	TU	0448 6.5	1100 1.4	1700 6.8	2323 1.1
15	W	0521 6.8	1135 1.2	1733 7.0	2356 1.0
16	TH	0553 6.9	1209 1.1	1806 7.1	
17	F	0031 1.0	0626 6.9	1244 1.1	1840 7.0
18	SA	0106 1.1	0700 6.8	1320 1.2	1916 6.8
19	SU	0143 1.4	0737 6.6	1400 1.5	1954 6.5
20	M	0224 1.8	0819 6.2	1446 1.9	2040 6.0
21	TU	0312 2.2	0911 5.8	1542 2.3	☾ 2140 5.5
22	W	0415 2.7	1025 5.4	1656 2.6	2310 5.2
23	TH	0543 2.9	1206 5.4	1831 2.6	
24	F	0106 5.3	0721 2.7	1337 5.7	2000 2.2
25	SA	0223 5.7	0835 2.2	1442 6.2	2104 1.7
26	SU	0316 6.2	0929 1.6	1532 6.7	2154 1.2
27	M	0401 6.6	1016 1.2	1617 7.1	2237 0.9
28	TU	0441 6.9	1058 0.8	1657 7.3	○ 2317 0.8
29	W	0517 7.0	1136 0.9	1733 7.3	2354 0.8
30	TH	0550 7.0	1211 1.0	1807 7.1	

OCTOBER

Day		Event 1	Event 2	Event 3	Event 4
1	F	0029 1.1	0621 6.9	1245 1.2	1838 6.9
2	SA	0100 1.4	0650 6.6	1318 1.5	1909 6.5
3	SU	0132 1.7	0720 6.3	1351 1.9	1940 6.1
4	M	0204 2.2	0751 5.9	1427 2.4	2014 5.6
5	TU	0239 2.6	0827 5.5	1510 2.8	2057 5.1
6	W	0325 3.0	0919 5.1	1608 3.2	☾ 2209 4.7
7	TH	0435 3.3	1051 4.8	1736 3.3	
8	F	0003 4.7	0615 3.3	1243 4.9	1919 3.1
9	SA	0135 5.0	0741 3.0	1353 5.3	2019 2.6
10	SU	0225 5.5	0833 2.5	1439 5.8	2102 2.2
11	M	0305 5.9	0915 2.1	1517 6.2	2139 1.7
12	TU	0341 6.4	0953 1.6	1554 6.6	2216 1.3
13	W	0416 6.7	1030 1.3	1630 6.9	2251 1.1
14	TH	0450 7.0	1106 1.1	1705 7.1	● 2327 0.9
15	F	0525 7.1	1143 0.9	1740 7.2	
16	SA	0004 0.9	0600 7.1	1221 1.0	1817 7.1
17	SU	0043 1.1	0638 7.0	1301 1.1	1857 6.9
18	M	0124 1.4	0719 6.7	1346 1.5	1940 6.4
19	TU	0209 1.8	0806 6.3	1436 1.9	2032 5.9
20	W	0303 2.3	0905 5.8	1538 2.3	☾ 2142 5.4
21	TH	0413 2.7	1027 5.5	1656 2.6	2317 5.2
22	F	0543 2.8	1203 5.5	1828 2.5	
23	SA	0059 5.4	0711 2.6	1323 5.9	1946 2.1
24	SU	0205 5.8	0817 2.1	1422 6.3	2044 1.7
25	M	0255 6.3	0909 1.7	1510 6.6	2131 1.4
26	TU	0337 6.6	0953 1.4	1553 6.9	2213 1.2
27	W	0415 6.8	1033 1.2	1631 7.0	2250 1.1
28	TH	0449 6.9	1110 1.2	1705 7.0	○ 2325 1.2
29	F	0521 6.9	1144 1.3	1738 6.9	2358 1.4
30	SA	0551 6.8	1217 1.4	1809 6.6	
31	SU	0030 1.6	0622 6.6	1250 1.7	1841 6.3

NOVEMBER

Day		Event 1	Event 2	Event 3	Event 4
1	M	0101 1.9	0652 6.3	1324 2.0	1913 6.0
2	TU	0134 2.3	0725 6.0	1359 2.4	1948 5.6
3	W	0210 2.6	0801 5.6	1441 2.7	2031 5.2
4	TH	0255 2.9	0850 5.3	1533 3.0	2134 4.9
5	F	0355 3.2	1004 5.0	1645 3.2	☾ 2304 4.8
6	SA	0516 3.3	1137 5.0	1813 3.0	
7	SU	0035 5.0	0641 3.0	1254 5.3	1924 2.7
8	M	0135 5.4	0743 2.6	1350 5.7	2015 2.3
9	TU	0221 5.9	0832 2.2	1436 6.1	2058 1.8
10	W	0303 6.3	0915 1.7	1517 6.5	2139 1.5
11	TH	0342 6.7	0957 1.4	1558 6.8	2219 1.2
12	F	0420 7.0	1038 1.1	1638 7.1	● 2259 1.0
13	SA	0500 7.1	1120 0.9	1719 7.1	2340 1.0
14	SU	0540 7.2	1203 0.9	1801 7.0	
15	M	0026 1.1	0624 7.1	1249 1.1	1847 6.8
16	TU	0113 1.4	0711 6.8	1339 1.4	1937 6.4
17	W	0203 1.8	0804 6.4	1433 1.7	2034 6.0
18	TH	0301 2.2	0907 6.1	1536 2.1	2143 5.6
19	F	0409 2.5	1020 5.8	1647 2.3	☽ 2302 5.4
20	SA	0526 2.6	1138 5.7	1803 2.3	
21	SU	0026 5.5	0641 2.5	1250 5.9	1914 2.2
22	M	0131 5.8	0746 2.2	1351 6.1	2012 1.9
23	TU	0224 6.0	0840 1.9	1441 6.3	2102 1.7
24	W	0308 6.3	0927 1.7	1526 6.5	2145 1.6
25	TH	0347 6.5	1008 1.6	1605 6.5	2224 1.6
26	F	0423 6.6	1046 1.6	1641 6.5	○ 2259 1.6
27	SA	0457 6.6	1122 1.6	1716 6.5	2333 1.7
28	SU	0529 6.6	1156 1.7	1749 6.4	
29	M	0007 1.8	0602 6.4	1230 1.8	1823 6.2
30	TU	0040 2.0	0635 6.3	1305 2.0	1857 6.0

DECEMBER

Day		Event 1	Event 2	Event 3	Event 4
1	W	0114 2.2	0710 6.1	1341 2.2	1934 5.7
2	TH	0151 2.4	0747 5.8	1420 2.4	2015 5.4
3	F	0233 2.6	0831 5.6	1505 2.6	2104 5.2
4	SA	0322 2.8	0925 5.4	1559 2.8	2207 5.1
5	SU	0423 2.9	1031 5.3	1704 2.8	☽ 2319 5.1
6	M	0532 2.9	1143 5.3	1814 2.7	
7	TU	0030 5.3	0641 2.7	1249 5.6	1917 2.4
8	W	0129 5.7	0741 2.4	1347 5.9	2012 2.1
9	TH	0220 6.1	0835 2.0	1439 6.2	2102 1.7
10	F	0308 6.4	0925 1.6	1528 6.6	2149 1.4
11	SA	0355 6.8	1014 1.3	1616 6.8	2237 1.2
12	SU	0441 7.0	1103 1.0	1705 6.9	● 2324 1.1
13	M	0529 7.1	1152 0.9	1753 6.8	
14	TU	0016 1.2	0618 7.1	1242 1.0	1843 6.8
15	W	0106 1.3	0708 7.0	1334 1.1	1935 6.5
16	TH	0158 1.5	0801 6.7	1427 1.4	2029 6.2
17	F	0252 1.8	0857 6.4	1522 1.7	2126 5.9
18	SA	0350 2.1	0955 6.1	1621 2.0	☽ 2227 5.6
19	SU	0452 2.3	1058 5.9	1723 2.2	2332 5.5
20	M	0557 2.4	1203 5.7	1828 2.3	
21	TU	0043 5.5	0703 2.4	1308 5.7	1931 2.3
22	W	0144 5.6	0805 2.3	1407 5.8	2028 2.2
23	TH	0237 5.8	0859 2.2	1459 5.9	2118 2.1
24	F	0323 6.0	0946 2.0	1544 6.0	2201 2.0
25	SA	0404 6.2	1028 1.9	1624 6.1	2240 1.9
26	SU	0441 6.3	1106 1.8	1701 6.2	○ 2316 1.9
27	M	0516 6.4	1142 1.8	1736 6.2	2351 1.9
28	TU	0550 6.4	1216 1.8	1811 6.2	
29	W	0026 1.9	0624 6.4	1251 1.8	1845 6.1
30	TH	0100 1.9	0658 6.3	1325 1.9	1919 6.0
31	F	0135 2.0	0733 6.1	1400 2.0	1955 5.8

Chart Datum: 3·64 metres below IGN Datum

Chapter 5

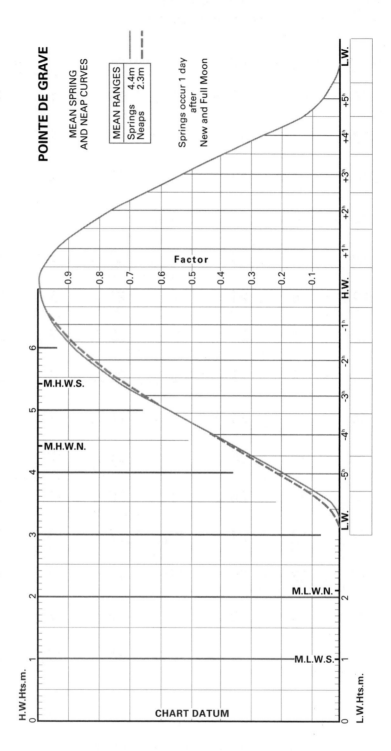

POINTE DE GRAVE

MEAN SPRING
AND NEAP CURVES

MEAN RANGES	
Springs	4.4m
Neaps	2.3m

Springs occur 1 day
after
New and Full Moon

Factor

CHART DATUM

FRANCE – POINTE DE GRAVE

YEAR 2004

TIME ZONE -0100
(French Standard Time)
Subtract 1 hour for UT
For French Summer Time add
ONE hour in **non-shaded areas**

LAT 45°34'N   LONG 1°04'W

TIMES AND HEIGHTS OF HIGH AND LOW WATERS

JANUARY

Day	Time	m	Time	m	Time	m	Time	m
1 TH	0020	4.3	0603	2.2	1237	4.5	1833	2.2
2 F	0122	4.4	0707	2.2	1339	4.5	1935	2.2
3 SA	0214	4.5	0805	2.1	1433	4.6	2027	2.0
4 SU	0259	4.7	0855	2.0	1519	4.7	2113	1.9
5 M	0338	4.8	0939	1.8	1600	4.8	2153	1.8
6 TU	0415	4.9	1019	1.7	1638	4.9	2230	1.7
7 W	0450	5.1	1058	1.6	1714	5.0	2307	1.6
8 TH	0524	5.1	1135	1.5	1748	5.0	2343	1.5
9 F	0558	5.2	1212	1.5	1823	5.0		
10 SA	0021	1.5	0633	5.2	1249	1.4	1858	5.0
11 SU	0057	1.5	0710	5.2	1326	1.5	1936	4.9
12 M	0136	1.5	0749	5.1	1404	1.5	2018	4.8
13 TU	0217	1.6	0833	5.0	1446	1.6	2106	4.7
14 W	0303	1.7	0924	4.9	1533	1.7	2203	4.6
15 TH	0356	1.8	1025	4.8	1629	1.8	2310	4.5
16 F	0458	1.9	1138	4.7	1736	1.9		
17 SA	0026	4.6	0608	1.9	1256	4.7	1847	1.9
18 SU	0136	4.7	0721	1.8	1410	4.8	1957	1.8
19 M	0240	5.0	0831	1.6	1515	5.0	2102	1.6
20 TU	0338	5.2	0935	1.4	1613	5.2	2200	1.4
21 W	0431	5.4	1033	1.2	1705	5.4	2253	1.2
22 TH	0521	5.6	1124	1.0	1752	5.4	2341	1.1
23 F	0608	5.7	1212	1.0	1836	5.4		
24 SA	0029	1.1	0651	5.7	1255	1.0	1917	5.3
25 SU	0111	1.2	0731	5.5	1336	1.1	1954	5.1
26 M	0152	1.3	0809	5.3	1415	1.3	2029	4.9
27 TU	0232	1.5	0845	5.1	1454	1.6	2104	4.6
28 W	0315	1.8	0925	4.8	1537	1.8	2147	4.4
29 TH	0403	2.0	1015	4.5	1626	2.1	2249	4.2
30 F	0501	2.3	1123	4.3	1729	2.3		
31 SA	0014	4.1	0612	2.4	1246	4.2	1843	2.4

FEBRUARY

Day	Time	m	Time	m	Time	m	Time	m
1 SU	0132	4.2	0724	2.4	1401	4.3	1952	2.3
2 M	0232	4.4	0827	2.2	1459	4.4	2047	2.2
3 TU	0320	4.6	0918	2.0	1545	4.6	2133	1.9
4 W	0400	4.8	1002	1.8	1625	4.8	2214	1.7
5 TH	0437	5.0	1042	1.5	1701	5.0	2252	1.5
6 F	0511	5.2	1121	1.4	1735	5.1	2329	1.4
7 SA	0545	5.3	1158	1.2	1808	5.2		
8 SU	0007	1.3	0619	5.4	1234	1.2	1842	5.2
9 M	0044	1.2	0654	5.4	1310	1.2	1917	5.2
10 TU	0120	1.2	0731	5.4	1345	1.2	1955	5.1
11 W	0158	1.2	0811	5.2	1422	1.3	2036	5.0
12 TH	0239	1.4	0856	5.0	1504	1.5	2125	4.8
13 F	0327	1.6	0951	4.8	1555	1.7	2229	4.6
14 SA	0426	1.8	1107	4.5	1701	2.0	2352	4.5
15 SU	0541	2.0	1240	4.5	1822	2.1		
16 M	0121	4.6	0707	1.9	1405	4.6	1947	2.0
17 TU	0234	4.8	0828	1.7	1515	4.8	2059	1.8
18 W	0334	5.1	0933	1.4	1611	5.1	2156	1.5
19 TH	0426	5.4	1027	1.2	1657	5.3	2245	1.2
20 F	0510	5.6	1113	1.0	1738	5.4	2329	1.1
21 SA	0550	5.7	1155	0.9	1815	5.4		
22 SU	0011	1.0	0627	5.7	1234	0.9	1848	5.3
23 M	0049	1.0	0700	5.6	1309	1.1	1917	5.2
24 TU	0124	1.2	0731	5.4	1342	1.2	1944	5.0
25 W	0158	1.3	0801	5.1	1414	1.5	2011	4.8
26 TH	0233	1.6	0835	4.8	1449	1.7	2046	4.5
27 F	0312	1.9	0916	4.5	1529	2.1	2132	4.3
28 SA	0400	2.2	1014	4.2	1622	2.4	2249	4.0
29 SU	0510	2.5	1148	4.0	1743	2.6		

MARCH

Day	Time	m	Time	m	Time	m	Time	m
1 M	0041	4.0	0640	2.5	1328	4.0	1912	2.5
2 TU	0201	4.2	0757	2.3	1435	4.3	2019	2.3
3 W	0256	4.5	0854	2.0	1524	4.6	2110	2.0
4 TH	0338	4.8	0939	1.7	1603	4.8	2152	1.7
5 F	0415	5.1	1020	1.5	1638	5.1	2231	1.4
6 SA	0450	5.3	1058	1.2	1712	5.3	2309	1.2
7 SU	0524	5.5	1136	1.0	1746	5.4	2346	1.0
8 M	0558	5.6	1212	0.9	1820	5.5		
9 TU	0024	0.9	0634	5.6	1247	0.9	1855	5.5
10 W	0100	0.9	0711	5.6	1322	1.0	1931	5.3
11 TH	0137	1.0	0750	5.4	1359	1.2	2011	5.1
12 F	0218	1.2	0834	5.1	1440	1.5	2058	4.9
13 SA	0305	1.5	0930	4.7	1531	1.8	2203	4.6
14 SU	0406	1.8	1054	4.4	1639	2.1	2336	4.0
15 M	0528	2.0	1241	4.3	1811	2.3		
16 TU	0114	4.5	0706	2.0	1406	4.5	1944	2.1
17 W	0228	4.8	0826	1.7	1511	4.8	2052	1.8
18 TH	0326	5.1	0924	1.4	1600	5.1	2144	1.5
19 F	0412	5.4	1012	1.2	1641	5.3	2229	1.2
20 SA	0451	5.5	1053	1.0	1715	5.3	2309	1.1
21 SU	0526	5.6	1131	1.0	1746	5.4	2346	1.0
22 M	0558	5.6	1206	1.0	1814	5.3		
23 TU	0022	1.0	0627	5.5	1237	1.1	1840	5.2
24 W	0053	1.1	0655	5.3	1307	1.3	1906	5.1
25 TH	0124	1.3	0724	5.1	1336	1.5	1934	4.9
26 F	0155	1.5	0756	4.8	1407	1.7	2005	4.7
27 SA	0229	1.8	0833	4.5	1443	2.0	2045	4.4
28 SU	0311	2.1	0923	4.2	1528	2.4	2145	4.1
29 M	0411	2.4	1050	3.9	1641	2.6	2332	4.0
30 TU	0549	2.5	1247	4.0	1823	2.6		
31 W	0115	4.1	0612	2.4	1359	4.2	1939	2.4

APRIL

Day	Time	m	Time	m	Time	m	Time	m
1 TH	0218	4.4	0818	2.1	1450	4.5	2033	2.1
2 F	0304	4.8	0906	1.7	1530	4.9	2118	1.7
3 SA	0344	5.1	0948	1.4	1607	5.2	2200	1.4
4 SU	0421	5.4	1027	1.1	1642	5.4	2240	1.1
5 M	0457	5.6	1106	0.9	1718	5.5	2319	0.9
6 TU	0534	5.7	1144	0.8	1755	5.6	2358	0.8
7 W	0613	5.7	1222	0.8	1832	5.6		
8 TH	0040	0.8	0653	5.6	1300	1.0	1912	5.4
9 F	0119	0.9	0735	5.3	1339	1.2	1956	5.2
10 SA	0203	1.2	0824	5.0	1423	1.5	2047	4.9
11 SU	0253	1.5	0927	4.6	1518	1.9	2157	4.6
12 M	0358	1.8	1100	4.3	1631	2.2	2331	4.5
13 TU	0524	2.0	1240	4.3	1804	2.3		
14 W	0103	4.6	0657	2.0	1356	4.6	1929	2.1
15 TH	0213	4.8	0809	1.7	1454	4.8	2031	1.8
16 F	0307	5.1	0902	1.5	1539	5.0	2121	1.5
17 SA	0350	5.2	0947	1.3	1616	5.1	2204	1.3
18 SU	0425	5.3	1026	1.2	1647	5.2	2243	1.2
19 M	0457	5.4	1102	1.1	1715	5.3	2319	1.1
20 TU	0527	5.4	1134	1.2	1742	5.2	2352	1.2
21 W	0557	5.3	1204	1.2	1809	5.2		
22 TH	0024	1.2	0627	5.2	1233	1.4	1837	5.1
23 F	0054	1.4	0657	5.0	1303	1.5	1907	4.9
24 SA	0125	1.5	0729	4.7	1335	1.7	1940	4.7
25 SU	0159	1.8	0807	4.5	1410	2.0	2019	4.5
26 M	0240	2.0	0856	4.2	1455	2.2	2114	4.3
27 TU	0334	2.3	1010	4.0	1559	2.5	2234	4.1
28 W	0456	2.4	1150	4.0	1727	2.5		
29 TH	0010	4.2	0623	2.3	1308	4.2	1844	2.3
30 F	0123	4.4	0729	2.0	1403	4.5	1944	2.0

Chart Datum: 2·83 metres below IGN Datum

FRANCE – POINTE DE GRAVE

LAT 45°34'N LONG 1°04'W

TIMES AND HEIGHTS OF HIGH AND LOW WATERS

YEAR **2004**

TIME ZONE -0100
(French Standard Time)
Subtract 1 hour for UT
For French Summer Time add
ONE hour in **non-shaded areas**

MAY

Day	Time	m	Time	m	Time	m	Time	m
1 SA	0218	4.7	0822	1.7	1448	4.8	2035	1.7
2 SU	0304	5.0	0908	1.4	1530	5.1	2122	1.4
3 M	0347	5.3	0952	1.1	1610	5.4	2207	1.1
4 TU ○	0429	5.5	1034	1.0	1650	5.5	2251	0.9
5 W	0512	5.6	1116	0.9	1732	5.6	2335	0.8
6 TH	0556	5.6	1158	0.9	1815	5.6		
7 F	0021	0.8	0641	5.5	1241	1.0	1901	5.5
8 SA	0106	1.0	0730	5.2	1325	1.3	1951	5.3
9 SU	0154	1.2	0825	4.9	1414	1.6	2048	5.0
10 M	0248	1.5	0932	4.6	1512	1.9	2157	4.8
11 TU ◑	0353	1.7	1057	4.4	1623	2.1	2318	4.7
12 W	0510	1.9	1220	4.4	1742	2.1		
13 TH	0037	4.7	0629	1.9	1304	4.5	1857	2.0
14 F	0143	4.8	0736	1.7	1425	4.7	1959	1.8
15 SA	0236	4.9	0830	1.6	1509	4.8	2050	1.6
16 SU	0319	5.0	0915	1.5	1545	4.9	2134	1.5
17 M	0355	5.1	0955	1.4	1615	5.0	2215	1.4
18 TU	0429	5.1	1031	1.4	1645	5.1	2251	1.3
19 W ●	0501	5.1	1104	1.4	1715	5.1	2325	1.4
20 TH	0534	5.1	1135	1.4	1746	5.1	2358	1.4
21 F	0607	5.0	1206	1.5	1818	5.0		
22 SA	0031	1.5	0639	4.8	1238	1.6	1850	4.9
23 SU	0104	1.6	0714	4.7	1312	1.7	1925	4.7
24 M	0140	1.7	0753	4.5	1350	1.9	2006	4.6
25 TU	0221	1.9	0840	4.3	1434	2.1	2056	4.4
26 W	0311	2.0	0941	4.2	1530	2.2	2158	4.3
27 TH ◑	0414	2.1	1054	4.2	1638	2.2	2310	4.3
28 F	0525	2.1	1207	4.3	1748	2.1		
29 SA	0023	4.5	0632	1.9	1310	4.5	1851	1.9
30 SU	0127	4.7	0732	1.7	1404	4.8	1948	1.7
31 M	0223	4.9	0825	1.4	1453	5.0	2043	1.4

JUNE

Day	Time	m	Time	m	Time	m	Time	m
1 TU	0315	5.2	0916	1.2	1540	5.2	2135	1.2
2 W	0405	5.3	1005	1.1	1626	5.4	2226	1.0
3 TH ○	0455	5.4	1053	1.0	1714	5.5	2316	0.9
4 F	0545	5.4	1140	1.0	1804	5.5		
5 SA	0006	0.9	0636	5.4	1228	1.1	1855	5.5
6 SU	0058	1.0	0729	5.2	1317	1.3	1948	5.3
7 M	0149	1.1	0824	4.9	1408	1.6	2044	5.2
8 TU	0242	1.3	0924	4.7	1502	1.7	2144	4.9
9 W ◑	0339	1.6	1030	4.5	1603	1.9	2248	4.8
10 TH	0440	1.8	1140	4.4	1708	1.9	2354	4.7
11 F	0546	1.9	1247	4.4	1816	2.0		
12 SA	0057	4.6	0652	1.9	1345	4.5	1919	1.9
13 SU	0154	4.6	0750	1.8	1432	4.6	2015	1.8
14 M	0243	4.7	0840	1.7	1512	4.7	2103	1.7
15 TU	0326	4.7	0924	1.6	1547	4.8	2147	1.6
16 W	0405	4.8	1003	1.6	1622	4.9	2227	1.6
17 TH ●	0442	4.8	1039	1.6	1656	4.9	2304	1.5
18 F	0519	4.8	1113	1.5	1731	5.0	2339	1.5
19 SA	0554	4.8	1147	1.5	1804	4.9		
20 SU	0015	1.5	0628	4.8	1222	1.6	1838	4.9
21 M	0050	1.5	0703	4.7	1257	1.6	1913	4.8
22 TU	0127	1.6	0740	4.6	1335	1.7	1952	4.7
23 W	0206	1.6	0822	4.5	1417	1.8	2036	4.6
24 TH	0249	1.7	0911	4.4	1503	1.9	2127	4.6
25 F ◑	0339	1.8	1009	4.4	1557	1.9	2225	4.5
26 SA	0436	1.8	1113	4.4	1658	1.9	2330	4.5
27 SU	0540	1.8	1219	4.5	1803	1.8		
28 M	0041	4.6	0644	1.7	1323	4.6	1907	1.7
29 TU	0148	4.7	0747	1.6	1418	4.8	2010	1.5
30 W	0251	4.9	0846	1.4	1518	5.1	2110	1.3

JULY

Day	Time	m	Time	m	Time	m	Time	m
1 TH	0350	5.1	0943	1.3	1611	5.3	2208	1.1
2 F ○	0446	5.2	1037	1.1	1704	5.4	2304	1.0
3 SA	0539	5.3	1129	1.1	1756	5.5	2357	0.9
4 SU	0631	5.3	1219	1.1	1847	5.6		
5 M	0051	0.9	0721	5.2	1308	1.2	1937	5.5
6 TU	0139	1.0	0809	5.0	1355	1.3	2026	5.3
7 W	0225	1.2	0856	4.8	1443	1.4	2115	5.1
8 TH	0312	1.4	0945	4.6	1532	1.6	2204	4.8
9 F ◑	0402	1.6	1038	4.4	1627	1.7	2259	4.6
10 SA	0457	1.9	1141	4.4	1728	2.0		
11 SU	0001	4.4	0600	2.0	1249	4.2	1834	2.0
12 M	0105	4.3	0705	2.1	1351	4.3	1938	2.0
13 TU	0208	4.3	0805	2.0	1442	4.4	2035	1.9
14 W	0302	4.4	0857	1.9	1526	4.6	2124	1.8
15 TH	0348	4.5	0941	1.8	1605	4.7	2208	1.7
16 F	0429	4.6	1020	1.7	1642	4.9	2247	1.6
17 SA ●	0506	4.7	1057	1.6	1717	4.9	2324	1.5
18 SU	0541	4.8	1133	1.5	1751	5.0		
19 M	0001	1.4	0614	4.8	1209	1.5	1823	5.0
20 TU	0037	1.4	0647	4.8	1244	1.4	1857	5.0
21 W	0112	1.4	0721	4.8	1319	1.4	1932	4.9
22 TH	0147	1.4	0758	4.7	1356	1.5	2011	4.9
23 F	0224	1.5	0839	4.6	1436	1.6	2055	4.8
24 SA	0306	1.5	0928	4.6	1522	1.7	2147	4.6
25 SU ◑	0355	1.7	1027	4.4	1617	1.8	2250	4.5
26 M	0455	1.8	1137	4.4	1723	1.8		
27 TU	0005	4.5	0605	1.8	1252	4.5	1836	1.8
28 W	0127	4.6	0719	1.8	1403	4.7	1949	1.7
29 TH	0241	4.8	0829	1.6	1506	4.9	2059	1.4
30 F	0345	4.9	0933	1.4	1603	5.2	2202	1.2
31 SA ○	0441	5.1	1029	1.2	1656	5.5	2258	1.0

AUGUST

Day	Time	m	Time	m	Time	m	Time	m
1 SU	0532	5.3	1121	1.1	1745	5.6	2348	0.8
2 M	0618	5.3	1208	1.0	1831	5.6		
3 TU	0037	0.8	0701	5.2	1252	1.0	1915	5.5
4 W	0119	0.9	0740	5.1	1334	1.1	1956	5.3
5 TH	0159	1.1	0816	4.9	1414	1.3	2034	5.1
6 F	0238	1.3	0850	4.6	1456	1.5	2113	4.8
7 SA	0319	1.6	0929	4.4	1543	1.8	2158	4.5
8 SU	0406	1.9	1023	4.2	1638	2.1	2258	4.2
9 M	0504	2.2	1143	4.1	1747	2.3		
10 TU	0018	4.1	0618	2.3	1310	4.1	1904	2.3
11 W	0139	4.1	0732	2.3	1417	4.3	2011	2.2
12 TH	0244	4.2	0833	2.1	1508	4.5	2105	2.0
13 F	0333	4.4	0922	1.9	1549	4.7	2150	1.7
14 SA	0414	4.6	1002	1.7	1625	4.9	2229	1.5
15 SU	0449	4.8	1040	1.5	1659	5.0	2306	1.4
16 M ●	0521	4.9	1116	1.4	1731	5.1	2341	1.3
17 TU	0552	5.0	1151	1.3	1802	5.2		
18 W	0018	1.2	0624	5.0	1225	1.2	1834	5.2
19 TH	0051	1.2	0656	5.0	1258	1.2	1907	5.2
20 F	0123	1.2	0730	5.0	1333	1.2	1944	5.1
21 SA	0158	1.3	0807	4.9	1410	1.4	2024	4.9
22 SU	0236	1.4	0851	4.7	1452	1.5	2114	4.7
23 M ◑	0321	1.6	0948	4.6	1545	1.7	2220	4.4
24 TU	0420	1.9	1107	4.3	1654	1.9	2349	4.3
25 W	0538	2.1	1237	4.4	1820	2.0		
26 TH	0125	4.4	0707	2.0	1356	4.5	1947	1.8
27 F	0240	4.6	0826	1.8	1502	5.0	2100	1.5
28 SA	0341	4.9	0928	1.5	1557	5.3	2157	1.2
29 SU	0432	5.1	1020	1.2	1644	5.5	2246	0.9
30 M ○	0516	5.3	1107	1.0	1727	5.7	2331	0.8
31 TU	0555	5.3	1150	0.9	1807	5.7		

Chart Datum: 2·83 metres below IGN Datum

TIME ZONE -0100
(French Standard Time)
Subtract 1 hour for UT
For French Summer Time add
ONE hour in **non-shaded areas**

FRANCE – POINTE DE GRAVE

LAT 45°34′N   LONG 1°04′W

TIMES AND HEIGHTS OF HIGH AND LOW WATERS

YEAR 2004

SEPTEMBER

Day	Time m	Time m	Time m	Time m
1 W	0014 0.9	0631 5.3	1844 5.6	
2 TH	0051 1.0	0703 5.2	1306 1.1	1918 5.3
3 F	0126 1.2	0731 5.0	1342 1.3	1950 5.1
4 SA	0200 1.4	0759 4.8	1418 1.5	2022 4.8
5 SU	0235 1.7	0832 4.5	1457 1.8	2102 4.4
6 M	0315 2.0	0918 4.2	1545 2.2	◗ 2200 4.1
7 TU	0407 2.3	1037 4.0	1655 2.5	2333 3.9
8 W	0526 2.6	1228 4.0	1828 2.5	
9 TH	0113 3.9	0658 2.6	1349 4.2	1947 2.3
10 F	0221 4.2	0806 2.3	1443 4.4	2042 2.1
11 SA	0309 4.4	0856 2.0	1525 4.7	2125 1.8
12 SU	0347 4.7	0937 1.7	1600 5.0	2203 1.5
13 M	0421 4.9	1014 1.5	1632 5.0	2239 1.3
14 TU	0452 5.1	1050 1.3	1704 5.3	2314 1.2
15 W	0523 5.2	1126 1.2	1735 5.4	2349 1.1
16 TH	0555 5.3	1200 1.1	1808 5.4	
17 F	0024 1.1	0628 5.3	1235 1.1	1842 5.4
18 SA	0057 1.1	0703 5.2	1310 1.1	1919 5.2
19 SU	0132 1.3	0740 5.0	1347 1.3	2001 5.0
20 M	0211 1.5	0825 4.8	1431 1.5	2054 4.6
21 TU	0257 1.8	0926 4.5	1525 1.8	● 2211 4.3
22 W	0400 2.1	1056 4.4	1642 2.1	2354 4.2
23 TH	0529 2.3	1235 4.5	1822 2.1	
24 F	0129 4.4	0707 2.2	1353 4.7	1951 1.8
25 SA	0237 4.7	0821 1.8	1454 5.1	2053 1.5
26 SU	0331 5.0	0916 1.5	1544 5.4	2142 1.2
27 M	0414 5.2	1003 1.2	1626 5.6	2226 1.0
28 TU	0451 5.3	1046 1.0	1703 5.6	O 2306 1.0
29 W	0525 5.3	1126 1.0	1738 5.6	2343 1.0
30 TH	0555 5.3	1202 1.0	1810 5.5	

OCTOBER

Day	Time m	Time m	Time m	Time m
1 F	0019 1.1	0623 5.2	1236 1.2	1840 5.3
2 SA	0051 1.3	0650 5.1	1308 1.4	1910 5.0
3 SU	0122 1.5	0718 4.9	1341 1.6	1941 4.7
4 M	0154 1.8	0751 4.6	1417 1.9	2019 4.4
5 TU	0230 2.1	0832 4.4	1459 2.2	2113 4.1
6 W	0317 2.4	0939 4.1	1602 2.5	◗ 2250 3.9
7 TH	0431 2.7	1135 4.0	1741 2.6	
8 F	0038 3.9	0611 2.7	1307 4.1	1909 2.4
9 SA	0145 4.2	0725 2.4	1406 4.4	2006 2.1
10 SU	0233 4.5	0817 2.1	1449 4.7	2050 1.8
11 M	0311 4.8	0900 1.8	1526 5.0	2128 1.5
12 TU	0345 5.0	0940 1.5	1559 5.3	2205 1.3
13 W	0418 5.3	1018 1.3	1633 5.5	2242 1.1
14 TH	0452 5.4	1056 1.1	1739 5.6	● 2318 1.1
15 F	0527 5.5	1134 1.0	1744 5.6	2354 1.0
16 SA	0603 5.5	1212 1.0	1822 5.5	
17 SU	0033 1.1	0641 5.4	1251 1.1	1904 5.3
18 M	0112 1.3	0718 5.1	1332 1.3	1951 5.0
19 TU	0154 1.6	0815 4.9	1420 1.6	2053 4.6
20 W	0246 1.9	0924 4.7	1520 1.9	◗ 2219 4.4
21 TH	0356 2.2	1057 4.5	1642 2.1	2359 4.3
22 F	0527 2.3	1228 4.6	1818 2.1	
23 SA	0121 4.5	0655 2.2	1339 4.9	1936 1.8
24 SU	0222 4.8	0801 1.8	1437 5.1	2032 1.5
25 M	0310 5.0	0854 1.6	1523 5.3	2118 1.3
26 TU	0349 5.2	0940 1.3	1602 5.4	2200 1.2
27 W	0423 5.3	1021 1.2	1637 5.5	2238 1.2
28 TH	0453 5.3	1059 1.2	1709 5.4	O 2313 1.2
29 F	0522 5.3	1135 1.2	1740 5.3	2346 1.3
30 SA	0551 5.2	1207 1.3	1811 5.2	
31 SU	0018 1.5	0621 5.1	1239 1.5	1842 5.0

NOVEMBER

Day	Time m	Time m	Time m	Time m
1 M	0049 1.6	0651 4.9	1312 1.7	1915 4.7
2 TU	0122 1.9	0725 4.7	1347 1.9	1953 4.5
3 W	0158 2.1	0806 4.5	1428 2.2	2044 4.2
4 TH	0243 2.4	0903 4.3	1522 2.4	2203 4.0
5 F	0346 2.6	1028 4.2	1642 2.6	◗ 2340 4.0
6 SA	0510 2.6	1202 4.2	1808 2.5	
7 SU	0053 4.2	0626 2.5	1310 4.4	1913 2.2
8 M	0144 4.5	0725 2.2	1401 4.7	2003 1.9
9 TU	0227 4.8	0814 1.9	1444 5.0	2046 1.6
10 W	0306 5.1	0900 1.6	1524 5.2	2127 1.4
11 TH	0344 5.3	0944 1.4	1603 5.4	2208 1.2
12 F	0423 5.5	1027 1.2	1644 5.6	● 2249 1.1
13 SA	0503 5.6	1110 1.1	1726 5.6	2330 1.1
14 SU	0545 5.6	1154 1.0	1811 5.5	
15 M	0015 1.2	0631 5.5	1238 1.1	1900 5.3
16 TU	0059 1.4	0721 5.3	1326 1.3	1954 5.0
17 W	0148 1.6	0818 5.1	1418 1.6	2059 4.7
18 TH	0244 1.9	0927 4.9	1520 1.8	2219 4.5
19 F	0352 2.1	1047 4.8	1632 2.0	◗ 2342 4.5
20 SA	0509 2.2	1204 4.8	1751 2.0	
21 SU	0056 4.6	0624 2.1	1312 4.9	1902 1.9
22 M	0155 4.8	0730 1.9	1410 5.0	2000 1.7
23 TU	0242 4.9	0825 1.7	1457 5.1	2049 1.6
24 W	0321 5.0	0913 1.6	1537 5.2	2131 1.5
25 TH	0355 5.1	0956 1.5	1612 5.2	2210 1.5
26 F	0427 5.2	1035 1.4	1646 5.2	O 2246 1.5
27 SA	0459 5.2	1111 1.5	1719 5.1	2320 1.5
28 SU	0531 5.2	1145 1.5	1750 5.0	2352 1.6
29 M	0604 5.1	1218 1.6	1826 4.9	
30 TU	0026 1.7	0637 5.0	1252 1.7	1901 4.7

DECEMBER

Day	Time m	Time m	Time m	Time m
1 W	0101 1.8	0712 4.9	1328 1.8	1939 4.6
2 TH	0138 2.0	0751 4.7	1408 2.0	2023 4.4
3 F	0221 2.2	0838 4.5	1455 2.2	2120 4.2
4 SA	0312 2.3	0936 4.4	1552 2.3	2231 4.2
5 SU	0414 2.4	1047 4.4	1659 2.3	2343 4.3
6 M	0521 2.3	1159 4.5	1806 2.2	
7 TU	0046 4.4	0626 2.2	1303 4.6	1906 2.0
8 W	0140 4.7	0724 2.0	1359 4.8	1959 1.8
9 TH	0228 4.9	0819 1.7	1450 5.1	2049 1.6
10 F	0315 5.2	0911 1.5	1539 5.3	2137 1.4
11 SA	0401 5.4	1002 1.3	1628 5.4	2225 1.2
12 SU	0448 5.5	1052 1.1	1717 5.5	● 2313 1.2
13 M	0537 5.6	1142 1.0	1807 5.5	
14 TU	0001 1.2	0627 5.6	1232 1.1	1859 5.3
15 W	0053 1.3	0720 5.5	1323 1.2	1954 5.2
16 TH	0144 1.5	0816 5.4	1414 1.3	2052 4.9
17 F	0237 1.7	0914 5.2	1508 1.6	2155 4.7
18 SA	0334 1.8	1017 5.0	1606 1.8	◗ 2302 4.6
19 SU	0436 2.0	1123 4.8	1709 1.9	
20 M	0012 4.5	0543 2.0	1230 4.8	1816 2.0
21 TU	0115 4.6	0650 2.0	1333 4.7	1920 2.0
22 W	0209 4.6	0751 2.0	1428 4.8	2016 1.9
23 TH	0254 4.8	0846 1.9	1514 4.8	2105 1.8
24 F	0333 4.9	0933 1.8	1555 4.9	2148 1.7
25 SA	0410 5.0	1016 1.7	1632 4.9	2227 1.7
26 SU	0445 5.1	1054 1.6	1708 5.0	O 2302 1.6
27 M	0520 5.1	1130 1.6	1743 5.0	2337 1.6
28 TU	0553 5.1	1205 1.6	1817 4.9	
29 W	0012 1.7	0626 5.1	1240 1.6	1850 4.8
30 TH	0047 1.7	0659 5.0	1315 1.6	1924 4.8
31 F	0122 1.7	0735 4.9	1351 1.7	2001 4.6

Chapter 5

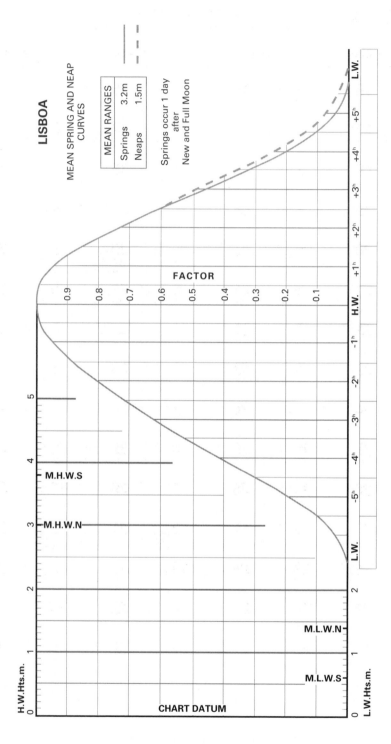

LISBOA

MEAN SPRING AND NEAP CURVES

MEAN RANGES	
Springs	3.2m
Neaps	1.5m

Springs occur 1 day after New and Full Moon

FACTOR

PORTUGAL – LISBOA

LAT 38°42′N   LONG 9°08′W

YEAR **2004**

TIMES AND HEIGHTS OF HIGH AND LOW WATERS

JANUARY

Time m — Time m

Day	Time m	Day	Time m
1 TH	0404 1.4 / 1039 2.9 / 1640 1.3 / 2319 2.9	**16** F	0300 1.2 / 0942 3.1 / 1544 1.1 / 2225 3.0
2 F	0511 1.4 / 1140 2.9 / 1739 1.3	**17** SA	0416 1.1 / 1056 3.1 / 1656 1.1 / 2336 3.2
3 SA	0014 3.0 / 0610 1.3 / 1233 3.0 / 1830 1.2	**18** SU	0531 1.0 / 1209 3.2 / 1805 0.9
4 SU	0101 3.1 / 0659 1.2 / 1320 3.1 / 1913 1.1	**19** M	0041 3.3 / 0640 0.9 / 1315 3.3 / 1906 0.8
5 M	0143 3.2 / 0742 1.1 / 1402 3.1 / 1952 1.0	**20** TU	0141 3.5 / 0741 0.6 / 1414 3.5 / 2001 0.7
6 TU	0221 3.3 / 0820 0.9 / 1441 3.2 / 2027 0.9	**21** W	0236 3.7 / 0835 0.5 / 1508 3.6 / ● 2052 0.6
7 W	0257 3.4 / 0856 0.9 / 1519 3.2 / ○ 2102 0.9	**22** TH	0326 3.9 / 0924 0.4 / 1557 3.6 / 2138 0.5
8 TH	0333 3.5 / 0931 0.8 / 1555 3.3 / 2136 0.8	**23** F	0413 3.9 / 1009 0.3 / 1642 3.6 / 2221 0.6
9 F	0409 3.5 / 1006 0.8 / 1632 3.3 / 2212 0.8	**24** SA	0457 3.9 / 1052 0.4 / 1724 3.5 / 2302 0.6
10 SA	0446 3.5 / 1042 0.7 / 1710 3.3 / 2248 0.8	**25** SU	0538 3.8 / 1131 0.5 / 1803 3.4 / 2341 0.7
11 SU	0525 3.5 / 1119 0.8 / 1749 3.3 / 2327 0.9	**26** M	0617 3.6 / 1210 0.7 / 1840 3.3
12 M	0605 3.5 / 1159 0.8 / 1830 3.2	**27** TU	0021 0.9 / 0655 3.4 / 1249 0.9 / 1919 3.1
13 TU	0009 0.9 / 0648 3.4 / 1244 0.9 / 1916 3.0	**28** W	0103 1.1 / 0735 3.1 / 1332 1.1 / 2002 2.9
14 W	0057 1.0 / 0736 3.3 / 1334 1.0 / 2010 3.0	**29** TH	0152 1.3 / 0823 2.9 / 1424 1.3 / 2059 2.8
15 TH	0153 1.1 / 0833 3.2 / 1434 1.1 / 2114 3.0	**30** F	0255 1.4 / 0925 2.8 / 1531 1.4 / 2211 2.7
		31 SA	0414 1.5 / 1043 2.7 / 1648 1.5 / 2327 2.8

FEBRUARY

Time m — Time m

Day	Time m	Day	Time m
1 SU	0535 1.5 / 1158 2.7 / 1758 1.4	**16** SU	0522 1.2 / 1203 3.0 / 1756 1.2
2 M	0030 2.9 / 0638 1.3 / 1258 2.8 / 1851 1.3	**17** TU	0033 3.3 / 0640 0.9 / 1314 3.2 / 1903 1.0
3 TU	0120 3.1 / 0726 1.1 / 1345 3.0 / 1934 1.1	**18** W	0136 3.5 / 0740 0.7 / 1411 3.4 / 1957 0.8
4 W	0202 3.2 / 0805 1.0 / 1426 3.1 / 2012 1.0	**19** TH	0229 3.7 / 0829 0.5 / 1459 3.6 / 2043 0.6
5 TH	0241 3.4 / 0841 0.8 / 1504 3.3 / 2047 0.8	**20** F	0315 3.9 / 0912 0.4 / 1542 3.7 / ● 2124 0.5
6 F	0318 3.6 / 0916 0.7 / 1541 3.4 / ○ 2123 0.7	**21** SA	0357 4.0 / 0951 0.4 / 1621 3.7 / 2202 0.5
7 SA	0355 3.7 / 0950 0.6 / 1617 3.5 / 2158 0.6	**22** SU	0436 3.9 / 1026 0.4 / 1656 3.7 / 2237 0.5
8 SU	0432 3.8 / 1025 0.5 / 1654 3.5 / 2234 0.6	**23** M	0511 3.8 / 1100 0.5 / 1729 3.6 / 2311 0.6
9 M	0510 3.8 / 1101 0.5 / 1731 3.5 / 2310 0.6	**24** TU	0544 3.7 / 1132 0.7 / 1800 3.4 / 2344 0.8
10 TU	0547 3.7 / 1137 0.6 / 1809 3.5 / 2349 0.7	**25** W	0615 3.5 / 1204 0.9 / 1831 3.3
11 W	0627 3.6 / 1217 0.7 / 1850 3.3	**26** TH	0020 1.0 / 0647 3.2 / 1239 1.1 / 1906 3.1
12 TH	0032 0.8 / 0710 3.4 / 1301 0.9 / 1937 3.2	**27** F	0100 1.2 / 0725 3.0 / 1321 1.3 / 1950 2.9
13 F	0122 1.0 / 0802 3.2 / 1356 1.1 / 2036 3.1	**28** SA	0152 1.5 / 0816 2.7 / 1420 1.5 / 2054 2.7
14 SA	0226 1.1 / 0909 3.0 / 1506 1.2 / 2152 3.0	**29** SU	0313 1.6 / 0936 2.6 / 1548 1.7 / 2226 2.7
15 SU	0350 1.2 / 1035 2.9 / 1633 1.3 / 2316 3.1		

MARCH

Time m — Time m

Day	Time m	Day	Time m
1 M	0455 1.6 / 1120 2.6 / 1722 1.6 / 2354 2.8	**16** TU	0526 1.3 / 1205 3.0 / 1755 1.3
2 TU	0613 1.5 / 1235 2.8 / 1826 1.4	**17** W	0028 3.3 / 0639 1.0 / 1310 3.3 / 1858 1.1
3 W	0053 3.0 / 0703 1.2 / 1324 3.0 / 1912 1.2	**18** TH	0126 3.6 / 0731 0.8 / 1359 3.5 / 1945 0.9
4 TH	0138 3.3 / 0742 1.0 / 1405 3.2 / 1950 1.0	**19** F	0214 3.8 / 0813 0.6 / 1441 3.7 / 2026 0.7
5 F	0218 3.5 / 0818 0.8 / 1442 3.4 / 2027 0.8	**20** SA	0256 3.9 / 0850 0.5 / 1519 3.8 / ● 2103 0.6
6 SA	0257 3.7 / 0853 0.6 / 1519 3.6 / ○ 2102 0.6	**21** SU	0334 4.0 / 0924 0.5 / 1554 3.8 / 2137 0.6
7 SU	0334 3.9 / 0927 0.5 / 1555 3.7 / 2138 0.5	**22** M	0409 3.9 / 0956 0.5 / 1626 3.8 / 2209 0.6
8 M	0412 4.0 / 1002 0.4 / 1632 3.8 / 2213 0.4	**23** TU	0441 3.8 / 1027 0.6 / 1656 3.7 / 2241 0.7
9 TU	0449 4.0 / 1037 0.4 / 1708 3.8 / 2250 0.4	**24** W	0511 3.7 / 1056 0.8 / 1725 3.6 / 2312 0.8
10 W	0527 3.9 / 1114 0.5 / 1746 3.7 / 2329 0.6	**25** TH	0539 3.5 / 1126 0.9 / 1753 3.4 / 2344 1.0
11 TH	0606 3.7 / 1152 0.7 / 1827 3.6	**26** F	0610 3.3 / 1158 1.2 / 1825 3.2
12 F	0011 0.7 / 0650 3.5 / 1236 0.9 / 1913 3.4	**27** SA	0021 1.3 / 0644 3.0 / 1234 1.4 / 1903 3.0
13 SA	0102 1.0 / 0742 3.2 / 1330 1.2 / 2013 3.2	**28** SU	0107 1.5 / 0731 2.8 / 1323 1.6 / 1958 2.8
14 SU	0210 1.2 / 0855 3.0 / 1446 1.4 / 2135 3.0	**29** M	0220 1.7 / 0842 2.6 / 1448 1.8 / 2122 2.8
15 M	0345 1.4 / 1034 2.9 / 1627 1.5 / 2310 3.1	**30** TU	0408 1.7 / 1034 2.6 / 1636 1.8 / 2306 2.8
		31 W	0533 1.5 / 1200 2.8 / 1749 1.6

APRIL

Time m — Time m

Day	Time m	Day	Time m
1 TH	0016 3.1 / 0627 1.3 / 1252 3.1 / 1839 1.3	**16** F	0106 3.6 / 0709 0.9 / 1336 3.5 / 1923 1.0
2 F	0105 3.3 / 0709 1.0 / 1334 3.3 / 1920 1.0	**17** SA	0151 3.8 / 0748 0.8 / 1415 3.7 / 2002 0.8
3 SA	0148 3.6 / 0747 0.8 / 1413 3.6 / 1958 0.8	**18** SU	0230 3.8 / 0822 0.7 / 1451 3.8 / 2037 0.7
4 SU	0228 3.8 / 0823 0.6 / 1451 3.8 / 2035 0.6	**19** M	0306 3.8 / 0854 0.7 / 1524 3.8 / ● 2110 0.7
5 M	0307 4.0 / 0859 0.5 / 1528 3.9 / ○ 2113 0.5	**20** TU	0340 3.8 / 0925 0.7 / 1556 3.8 / 2142 0.7
6 TU	0347 4.1 / 0936 0.4 / 1606 4.0 / 2151 0.4	**21** W	0411 3.7 / 0955 0.8 / 1626 3.7 / 2213 0.8
7 W	0426 4.1 / 1013 0.4 / 1645 4.0 / 2230 0.4	**22** TH	0441 3.6 / 1025 0.9 / 1654 3.6 / 2245 0.9
8 TH	0506 4.0 / 1051 0.5 / 1726 3.9 / 2312 0.6	**23** F	0510 3.4 / 1055 1.0 / 1724 3.5 / 2318 1.1
9 F	0549 3.8 / 1133 0.8 / 1809 3.7 / 2358 0.8	**24** SA	0542 3.2 / 1126 1.2 / 1756 3.3 / 2354 1.3
10 SA	0637 3.5 / 1219 1.0 / 1859 3.5	**25** SU	0618 3.0 / 1201 1.4 / 1834 3.1
11 SU	0055 1.0 / 0736 3.2 / 1318 1.3 / 2003 3.3	**26** M	0040 1.5 / 0704 2.9 / 1249 1.6 / 1925 3.0
12 M	0210 1.3 / 0856 3.0 / 1442 1.6 / ◑ 2129 3.2	**27** TU	0145 1.6 / 0810 2.7 / 1403 1.8 / 2038 2.9
13 TU	0349 1.4 / 1035 3.0 / 1623 1.6 / ◑ 2300 3.0	**28** W	0316 1.6 / 0944 2.7 / 1541 1.8 / 2211 2.9
14 W	0519 1.3 / 1154 3.1 / 1743 1.4	**29** TH	0439 1.5 / 1110 2.9 / 1659 1.6 / 2328 3.1
15 TH	0012 3.4 / 0622 1.1 / 1251 3.3 / 1839 1.2	**30** F	0540 1.3 / 1209 3.1 / 1756 1.4

Chapter 5

PORTUGAL – LISBOA

TIME ZONE (UT)
For Summer Time add ONE hour in **non-shaded areas**

LAT 38°42′N   LONG 9°08′W

TIMES AND HEIGHTS OF HIGH AND LOW WATERS

YEAR 200◄

MAY

Day	Time	m	Day	Time	m
1 SA	0024 / 0627 / SA 1255 / 1842	3.4 / 1.1 / 3.4 / 1.1	**16** SU	0120 / 0715 / SU 1345 / 1933	3.5 / 0.9 / 3.6 / 1.0
2 SU	0111 / 0709 / SU 1338 / 1925	3.6 / 0.8 / 3.6 / 0.8	**17** M	0200 / 0751 / M 1421 / 2010	3.6 / 0.9 / 3.6 / 0.9
3 M	0155 / 0750 / M 1419 / 2006	3.8 / 0.6 / 3.8 / 0.6	**18** TU	0237 / 0824 / TU 1456 / 2045	3.6 / 0.9 / 3.7 / 0.9
4 TU	0238 / 0829 / TU 1500 / O 2047	4.0 / 0.5 / 4.0 / 0.5	**19** W	0312 / 0857 / W 1529 / ● 2119	3.6 / 0.9 / 3.6 / 0.9
5 W	0321 / 0909 / W 1542 / 2130	4.0 / 0.4 / 4.0 / 0.4	**20** TH	0345 / 0928 / TH 1600 / 2152	3.5 / 0.9 / 3.6 / 0.9
6 TH	0405 / 0951 / TH 1625 / 2214	4.0 / 0.5 / 4.0 / 0.5	**21** F	0417 / 0959 / F 1631 / 2225	3.4 / 1.0 / 3.5 / 1.0
7 F	0450 / 1034 / F 1710 / 2301	3.9 / 0.6 / 4.0 / 0.6	**22** SA	0449 / 1031 / SA 1702 / 2300	3.3 / 1.1 / 3.5 / 1.1
8 SA	0539 / 1120 / SA 1758 / 2353	3.7 / 0.8 / 3.8 / 0.8	**23** SU	0524 / 1104 / SU 1737 / 2338	3.2 / 1.2 / 3.3 / 1.2
9 SU	0632 / 1211 / SU 1853	3.5 / 1.1 / 3.6	**24** M	0602 / 1142 / M 1816	3.1 / 1.4 / 3.2
10 M	0054 / 0735 / M 1315 / 1958	1.0 / 3.2 / 1.4 / 3.4	**25** TU	0022 / 0648 / TU 1229 / 1905	1.3 / 2.9 / 1.5 / 3.1
11 TU	0209 / 0852 / TU 1435 / ◑ 2116	1.2 / 3.0 / 1.5 / 3.3	**26** W	0119 / 0746 / W 1331 / 2007	1.4 / 2.8 / 1.6 / 3.0
12 W	0334 / 1015 / W 1600 / 2235	1.3 / 3.0 / 1.5 / 3.3	**27** TH	0228 / 0859 / TH 1448 / ◑ 2121	1.5 / 2.8 / 1.6 / 3.0
13 TH	0450 / 1125 / TH 1712 / 2342	1.2 / 3.1 / 1.4 / 3.4	**28** F	0341 / 1014 / F 1602 / 2234	1.4 / 2.9 / 1.5 / 3.1
14 F	0549 / 1220 / F 1808	1.1 / 3.3 / 1.2	**29** SA	0445 / 1119 / SA 1705 / 2337	1.2 / 3.1 / 1.3 / 3.2
15 SA	0035 / 0636 / SA 1305 / 1853	3.5 / 1.0 / 3.4 / 1.1	**30** SU	0540 / 1212 / SU 1800	1.0 / 3.3 / 1.1
			31 M	0031 / 0630 / M 1301 / 1850	3.5 / 0.9 / 3.5 / 0.9

JUNE

Day	Time	m	Day	Time	m
1 TU	0121 / 0716 / TU 1348 / 1938	3.7 / 0.7 / 3.7 / 0.7	**16** W	0211 / 0758 / W 1431 / 2025	3.3 / 1.0 / 3.5 / 1.0
2 W	0210 / 0802 / W 1435 / 2026	3.8 / 0.6 / 3.9 / 0.5	**17** TH	0249 / 0834 / TH 1506 / ● 2101	3.3 / 1.0 / 3.5 / 1.0
3 TH	0300 / 0847 / TH 1522 / O 2114	3.8 / 0.5 / 4.0 / 0.4	**18** F	0325 / 0907 / F 1540 / 2136	3.3 / 1.0 / 3.5 / 0.9
4 F	0350 / 0934 / F 1610 / 2204	3.8 / 0.6 / 4.0 / 0.4	**19** SA	0400 / 0941 / SA 1614 / 2211	3.3 / 1.0 / 3.5 / 0.9
5 SA	0440 / 1022 / SA 1700 / 2256	3.8 / 0.7 / 3.9 / 0.5	**20** SU	0435 / 1014 / SU 1648 / 2246	3.2 / 1.0 / 3.5 / 1.0
6 SU	0533 / 1112 / SU 1751 / 2350	3.6 / 0.8 / 3.8 / 0.7	**21** M	0511 / 1050 / M 1724 / 2324	3.2 / 1.1 / 3.4 / 1.0
7 M	0627 / 1205 / M 1845	3.4 / 1.0 / 3.7	**22** TU	0550 / 1128 / TU 1804	3.1 / 1.1 / 3.4
8 TU	0048 / 0725 / TU 1303 / 1944	0.9 / 3.3 / 1.2 / 3.4	**23** W	0005 / 0632 / W 1212 / 1848	1.1 / 3.1 / 1.2 / 3.3
9 W	0150 / 0828 / W 1409 / ◑ 2048	1.0 / 3.1 / 1.3 / 3.3	**24** TH	0052 / 0721 / TH 1302 / 1939	1.1 / 3.0 / 1.3 / 3.2
10 TH	0257 / 0935 / TH 1518 / 2155	1.2 / 3.0 / 1.4 / 3.2	**25** F	0145 / 0817 / F 1401 / ◑ 2038	1.2 / 3.0 / 1.3 / 3.1
11 F	0403 / 1040 / F 1626 / 2300	1.2 / 3.0 / 1.4 / 3.2	**26** SA	0246 / 0922 / SA 1507 / 2143	1.2 / 3.0 / 1.3 / 3.2
12 SA	0503 / 1138 / SA 1727 / 2356	1.2 / 3.1 / 1.3 / 3.2	**27** SU	0350 / 1027 / SU 1615 / 2250	1.2 / 3.1 / 1.3 / 3.2
13 SU	0555 / 1228 / SU 1819	1.2 / 3.2 / 1.2	**28** M	0453 / 1129 / M 1719 / 2353	1.1 / 3.2 / 1.1 / 3.3
14 M	0046 / 0640 / M 1312 / 1905	3.3 / 1.1 / 3.3 / 1.1	**29** TU	0552 / 1227 / TU 1820	0.9 / 3.4 / 0.9
15 TU	0130 / 0721 / TU 1353 / 1947	3.5 / 1.0 / 3.4 / 1.0	**30** W	0053 / 0648 / W 1322 / 1918	3.5 / 0.8 / 3.6 / 0.7

JULY

Day	Time	m	Day	Time	m
1 TH	0151 / 0741 / TH 1416 / 2013	3.6 / 0.7 / 3.8 / 0.6	**16** F	0232 / 0816 / F 1448 / 2047	3.2 / 1.0 / 3.4 / 1.0
2 F	0247 / 0833 / F 1509 / O 2106	3.7 / 0.6 / 3.9 / 0.4	**17** SA	0309 / 0851 / SA 1524 / ● 2122	3.2 / 1.0 / 3.5 / 0.9
3 SA	0341 / 0923 / SA 1601 / 2157	3.7 / 0.6 / 4.0 / 0.4	**18** SU	0346 / 0926 / SU 1559 / 2156	3.3 / 0.9 / 3.5 / 0.8
4 SU	0433 / 1013 / SU 1651 / 2248	3.7 / 0.6 / 4.0 / 0.4	**19** M	0421 / 1000 / M 1634 / 2230	3.3 / 0.9 / 3.6 / 0.8
5 M	0523 / 1101 / M 1740 / 2337	3.6 / 0.7 / 3.9 / 0.6	**20** TU	0457 / 1035 / TU 1711 / 2306	3.3 / 0.9 / 3.6 / 0.8
6 TU	0611 / 1149 / TU 1828	3.5 / 0.8 / 3.8	**21** W	0533 / 1112 / W 1748 / 2343	3.3 / 0.9 / 3.5 / 0.9
7 W	0025 / 0659 / W 1238 / 1916	0.7 / 3.3 / 1.0 / 3.5	**22** TH	0612 / 1150 / TH 1828	3.3 / 0.9 / 3.5
8 TH	0115 / 0749 / TH 1329 / 2007	0.9 / 3.2 / 1.1 / 3.3	**23** F	0022 / 0653 / F 1233 / 1911	0.9 / 3.2 / 1.0 / 3.4
9 F	0207 / 0844 / F 1427 / ◑ 2104	1.1 / 3.0 / 1.3 / 3.1	**24** SA	0107 / 0740 / SA 1322 / 2000	1.0 / 3.1 / 1.1 / 3.2
10 SA	0305 / 0944 / SA 1531 / 2207	1.2 / 3.0 / 1.4 / 3.0	**25** SU	0159 / 0836 / SU 1422 / ◑ 2100	1.1 / 3.1 / 1.2 / 3.2
11 SU	0407 / 1048 / SU 1640 / 2312	1.3 / 3.0 / 1.4 / 3.0	**26** M	0302 / 0942 / M 1533 / 2211	1.2 / 3.1 / 1.2 / 3.1
12 M	0510 / 1149 / M 1746	1.3 / 3.0 / 1.4	**27** TU	0414 / 1054 / TU 1650 / 2327	1.2 / 3.1 / 1.2 / 3.2
13 TU	0011 / 0607 / TU 1242 / 1842	3.0 / 1.3 / 3.1 / 1.3	**28** W	0526 / 1203 / W 1804	1.1 / 3.3 / 1.0
14 W	0104 / 0656 / W 1329 / 1929	3.0 / 1.2 / 3.2 / 1.2	**29** TH	0039 / 0632 / TH 1308 / 1909	3.3 / 1.0 / 3.5 / 0.8
15 TH	0150 / 0738 / TH 1410 / 2010	3.1 / 1.1 / 3.3 / 1.1	**30** F	0143 / 0732 / F 1407 / 2007	3.4 / 0.8 / 3.7 / 0.6
			31 SA	0241 / 0825 / SA 1501 / O 2059	3.6 / 0.7 / 3.9 / 0.4

AUGUST

Day	Time	m	Day	Time	m
1 SU	0332 / 0914 / SU 1550 / 2147	3.7 / 0.6 / 4.0 / 0.4	**16** M	0326 / 0908 / M 1540 / ● 2135	3.4 / 0.8 / 3.7 / 0.7
2 M	0420 / 1000 / M 1636 / 2231	3.7 / 0.6 / 4.1 / 0.4	**17** TU	0401 / 0942 / TU 1615 / 2208	3.5 / 0.8 / 3.8 / 0.7
3 TU	0503 / 1043 / TU 1719 / 2313	3.7 / 0.6 / 4.0 / 0.5	**18** W	0436 / 1016 / W 1651 / 2242	3.6 / 0.7 / 3.8 / 0.7
4 W	0545 / 1124 / W 1801 / 2353	3.6 / 0.7 / 3.8 / 0.7	**19** TH	0511 / 1050 / TH 1727 / 2316	3.6 / 0.7 / 3.8 / 0.7
5 TH	0624 / 1204 / TH 1841	3.5 / 0.8 / 3.6	**20** F	0547 / 1126 / F 1804 / 2353	3.5 / 0.8 / 3.7 / 0.8
6 F	0032 / 0704 / F 1247 / 1922	0.9 / 3.3 / 1.0 / 3.3	**21** SA	0625 / 1206 / SA 1844	3.4 / 0.9 / 3.5
7 SA	0115 / 0748 / SA 1334 / ◐ 2008	1.1 / 3.1 / 1.3 / 3.1	**22** SU	0033 / 0709 / SU 1252 / 1930	0.9 / 3.3 / 1.0 / 3.3
8 SU	0204 / 0841 / SU 1434 / 2106	1.3 / 2.9 / 1.5 / 2.9	**23** M	0122 / 0802 / M 1350 / ◑ 2030	1.1 / 3.2 / 1.2 / 3.2
9 M	0307 / 0949 / M 1551 / 2221	1.5 / 2.8 / 1.6 / 2.8	**24** TU	0226 / 0910 / TU 1507 / 2150	1.3 / 3.1 / 1.3 / 3.0
10 TU	0424 / 1106 / TU 1716 / 2340	1.5 / 2.8 / 1.5 / 2.8	**25** W	0349 / 1033 / W 1639 / 2320	1.4 / 3.1 / 1.3 / 3.1
11 W	0539 / 1214 / W 1824	1.5 / 3.0 / 1.4	**26** TH	0516 / 1155 / TH 1803	1.3 / 3.3 / 1.1
12 TH	0044 / 0636 / TH 1307 / 1914	2.9 / 1.4 / 3.1 / 1.3	**27** F	0038 / 0629 / F 1303 / 1908	3.2 / 1.1 / 3.5 / 0.9
13 F	0134 / 0721 / F 1350 / 1954	3.0 / 1.2 / 3.3 / 1.1	**28** SA	0140 / 0727 / SA 1359 / 2001	3.5 / 0.9 / 3.8 / 0.7
14 SA	0214 / 0759 / SA 1428 / 2029	3.2 / 1.0 / 3.5 / 0.9	**29** SU	0232 / 0816 / SU 1449 / 2046	3.7 / 0.7 / 4.0 / 0.5
15 SU	0251 / 0834 / SU 1504 / 2102	3.3 / 1.0 / 3.6 / 0.8	**30** M	0317 / 0900 / M 1533 / O 2127	3.8 / 0.6 / 4.1 / 0.4
			31 TU	0358 / 0940 / TU 1614 / 2206	3.9 / 0.6 / 4.1 / 0.4

PORTUGAL – LISBOA

YEAR **2004**

LAT 38°42′N   LONG 9°08′W

TIMES AND HEIGHTS OF HIGH AND LOW WATERS

SEPTEMBER

Day	Time m	Time m	Time m	Time m	Day	Time m	Time m	Time m	Time m
1 W	0437 3.8	1017 0.6	1653 4.0	2241 0.5	16 TH	0410 3.8	0952 0.6	1626 4.0	2215 0.6
2 TH	0513 3.8	1054 0.6	1729 3.9	2316 0.7	17 F	0445 3.8	1027 0.6	1703 3.9	2249 0.6
3 F	0547 3.6	1129 0.8	1803 3.6	2350 0.9	18 SA	0522 3.8	1103 0.7	1741 3.8	2326 0.8
4 SA	0620 3.4	1206 1.0	1837 3.4		19 SU	0600 3.6	1144 0.8	1822 3.6	
5 SU	0026 1.2	0656 3.2	1247 1.3	1916 3.1	20 M	0007 1.0	0644 3.5	1231 1.0	1911 3.4
6 M	0108 1.4	0740 3.0	1340 1.5	◑ 2006 2.8	21 TU	0057 1.2	0739 3.3	1333 1.3	2017 3.1
7 TU	0206 1.6	0843 2.8	1502 1.7	2126 2.7	22 W	0206 1.5	0854 3.2	1501 1.4	2149 3.0
8 W	0335 1.8	1017 2.8	1647 1.7	2311 2.7	23 TH	0343 1.6	1028 3.2	1644 1.4	2325 3.1
9 TH	0511 1.7	1144 2.9	1803 1.5		24 F	0517 1.5	1151 3.4	1803 1.1	
10 F	0024 2.9	0614 1.6	1241 3.1	1851 1.3	25 SA	0036 3.3	0625 1.2	1254 3.7	1900 0.9
11 SA	0111 3.1	0659 1.6	1324 3.4	1929 1.1	26 SU	0129 3.6	0716 1.0	1345 3.9	1946 0.7
12 SU	0150 3.3	0736 1.1	1403 3.6	2003 0.9	27 M	0214 3.8	0800 0.8	1430 4.1	2026 0.6
13 M	0225 3.5	0810 0.9	1439 3.8	2036 0.8	28 TU	0255 3.9	0839 0.6	1511 4.1	○ 2102 0.5
14 TU	0300 3.7	0844 0.8	1515 3.9	● 2108 0.6	29 W	0332 4.0	0915 0.6	1548 4.1	2136 0.6
15 W	0335 3.8	0918 0.6	1551 4.0	2141 0.6	30 TH	0407 3.9	0950 0.6	1623 4.0	2209 0.7

OCTOBER

Day	Time m	Time m	Time m	Time m	Day	Time m	Time m	Time m	Time m
1 F	0440 3.8	1024 0.7	1656 3.8	2240 0.8	16 SA	0420 4.0	1005 0.6	1640 4.0	2225 0.6
2 SA	0511 3.7	1057 0.9	1727 3.6	2312 1.0	17 SU	0459 3.9	1045 0.7	1722 3.8	2305 0.8
3 SU	0542 3.5	1131 1.1	1759 3.3	2344 1.3	18 M	0542 3.8	1129 0.8	1808 3.6	2349 1.0
4 M	0614 3.3	1209 1.4	1834 3.1		19 TU	0630 3.6	1222 1.1	1903 3.3	
5 TU	0021 1.5	0652 3.1	1257 1.6	1920 2.9	20 W	0044 1.3	0730 3.4	1331 1.3	◐ 2017 3.1
6 W	0111 1.7	0747 2.9	1412 1.8	◑ 2034 2.7	21 TH	0201 1.6	0850 3.2	1505 1.4	2152 3.0
7 TH	0239 1.9	0915 2.8	1603 1.8	2229 2.7	22 F	0341 1.6	1021 3.3	1640 1.3	2317 3.2
8 F	0429 1.9	1058 2.9	1724 1.6	2349 2.9	23 SA	0507 1.5	1137 3.5	1749 1.1	
9 SA	0538 1.7	1203 3.2	1815 1.4		24 SU	0020 3.4	0609 1.3	1236 3.7	1841 0.9
10 SU	0038 3.2	0625 1.4	1250 3.4	1854 1.1	25 M	0108 3.6	0656 1.0	1324 3.8	1923 0.8
11 M	0117 3.4	0704 1.2	1330 3.7	1930 0.9	26 TU	0150 3.8	0737 0.9	1406 3.9	2000 0.7
12 TU	0153 3.6	0740 0.9	1408 3.8	2004 0.8	27 W	0228 3.9	0815 0.8	1445 4.0	2034 0.7
13 W	0229 3.8	0815 0.8	1445 4.0	2038 0.6	28 TH	0304 3.9	0851 0.7	1521 3.9	○ 2107 0.7
14 TH	0305 3.9	0851 0.6	1523 4.1	● 2113 0.6	29 F	0338 3.9	0925 0.8	1555 3.8	2139 0.8
15 F	0342 4.0	0927 0.6	1601 4.1	2148 0.6	30 SA	0410 3.8	0958 0.8	1627 3.6	2210 0.9
					31 SU	0441 3.7	1031 1.0	1658 3.5	2240 1.1

NOVEMBER

Day	Time m	Time m	Time m	Time m	Day	Time m	Time m	Time m	Time m
1 M	0511 3.5	1105 1.1	1729 3.3	2312 1.3	16 TU	0531 3.8	1124 0.7	1803 3.5	2342 1.0
2 TU	0543 3.3	1142 1.3	1805 3.1	2348 1.5	17 W	0623 3.7	1221 0.9	1902 3.3	
3 W	0620 3.2	1227 1.5	1850 2.9		18 TH	0040 1.3	0725 3.5	1330 1.1	2013 3.1
4 TH	0035 1.7	0710 3.0	1331 1.7	1954 2.8	19 F	0154 1.5	0838 3.3	1452 1.3	◐ 2134 3.1
5 F	0147 1.8	0822 2.9	1502 1.7	◑ 2128 2.7	20 SA	0319 1.5	0958 3.3	1612 1.2	2249 3.1
6 SA	0325 1.8	0955 2.9	1625 1.6	2254 2.9	21 SU	0437 1.4	1109 3.4	1718 1.1	2350 3.3
7 SU	0444 1.7	1111 3.1	1725 1.4	2351 3.1	22 M	0539 1.3	1208 3.5	1810 1.0	
8 M	0539 1.4	1206 3.3	1811 1.2		23 TU	0039 3.4	0629 1.1	1257 3.6	1854 0.9
9 TU	0036 3.3	0624 1.2	1256 3.6	1851 0.9	24 W	0123 3.6	0713 1.0	1340 3.6	1932 0.9
10 W	0117 3.6	0705 0.9	1333 3.8	1929 0.8	25 TH	0202 3.7	0752 0.9	1420 3.6	2008 0.8
11 TH	0156 3.8	0744 0.8	1414 3.9	2007 0.6	26 F	0239 3.7	0830 0.8	1457 3.6	○ 2042 0.8
12 F	0236 3.9	0824 0.6	1456 4.0	● 2046 0.6	27 SA	0314 3.7	0905 0.9	1532 3.5	2115 0.9
13 SA	0317 4.0	0905 0.5	1539 4.0	2125 0.6	28 SU	0348 3.6	0940 0.9	1606 3.4	2147 1.0
14 SU	0359 4.0	0948 0.5	1625 3.9	2207 0.6	29 M	0419 3.5	1013 1.0	1638 3.3	2219 1.1
15 M	0443 4.0	1034 0.6	1711 3.7	2252 0.8	30 TU	0450 3.5	1048 1.1	1711 3.2	2252 1.2

DECEMBER

Day	Time m	Time m	Time m	Time m	Day	Time m	Time m	Time m	Time m
1 W	0523 3.4	1125 1.2	1747 3.1	2329 1.3	16 TH	0617 3.7	1215 0.7	1853 3.3	
2 TH	0601 3.3	1207 1.3	1830 3.0		17 F	0031 1.0	0712 3.6	1314 0.9	1952 3.2
3 F	0012 1.4	0646 3.1	1258 1.4	1923 2.8	18 SA	0132 1.2	0813 3.4	1417 1.1	◐ 2057 3.0
4 SA	0108 1.5	0743 3.0	1402 1.5	2030 2.8	19 SU	0239 1.3	0920 3.2	1525 1.2	2204 3.0
5 SU	0220 1.6	0854 3.0	1515 1.4	◑ 2146 2.8	20 M	0350 1.3	1028 3.2	1631 1.2	2309 3.1
6 M	0335 1.5	1008 3.0	1622 1.3	2253 3.0	21 TU	0458 1.3	1131 3.2	1731 1.2	
7 TU	0442 1.4	1113 3.2	1719 1.2	2349 3.2	22 W	0005 3.2	0558 1.2	1227 3.2	1823 1.1
8 W	0538 1.2	1208 3.3	1808 1.0		23 TH	0055 3.3	0650 1.1	1316 3.2	1907 1.0
9 TH	0038 3.4	0628 1.0	1258 3.5	1854 0.8	24 F	0139 3.4	0735 1.0	1400 3.3	1947 1.0
10 F	0124 3.6	0715 0.8	1346 3.7	1939 0.6	25 SA	0220 3.4	0816 0.9	1440 3.3	2024 0.9
11 SA	0210 3.8	0802 0.6	1435 3.8	2024 0.6	26 SU	0257 3.5	0853 0.9	1517 3.3	2059 0.9
12 SU	0257 3.9	0850 0.5	1524 3.8	● 2110 0.5	27 M	0332 3.5	0928 0.9	1552 3.3	2132 0.9
13 M	0345 4.0	0939 0.4	1614 3.8	2157 0.6	28 TU	0405 3.5	1001 0.9	1625 3.2	2205 0.9
14 TU	0434 4.0	1029 0.4	1705 3.7	2245 0.7	29 W	0437 3.5	1035 0.9	1659 3.2	2239 1.0
15 W	0524 3.9	1121 0.6	1758 3.5	2336 0.8	30 TH	0511 3.4	1110 0.9	1734 3.1	2314 1.0
					31 F	0547 3.4	1147 1.0	1812 3.1	2353 1.1

Chapter 5

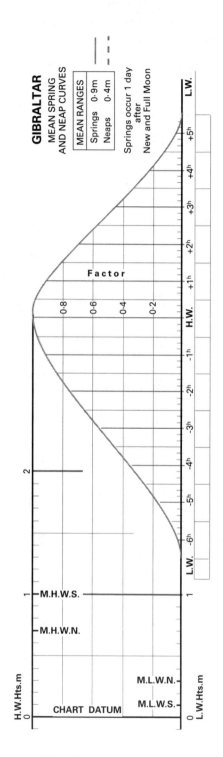

GIBRALTAR
MEAN SPRING
AND NEAP CURVES

MEAN RANGES	
Springs	0·9m
Neaps	0·4m

Springs occur 1 day
after
New and Full Moon

Factor

0·8 0·6 0·4 0·2

H.W.Hts.m
M.H.W.S.
M.H.W.N.
CHART DATUM

L.W.Hts.m
M.L.W.N.
M.L.W.S.

L.W. +5ʰ +4ʰ +3ʰ +2ʰ +1ʰ H.W. -1ʰ -2ʰ -3ʰ -4ʰ -5ʰ -6ʰ L.W.

Register for your **FREE** weekly weather email service from Reeds Almanacs
at www.nauticaldata.com – **NOW!**
weekend weather reports sent to your email address, every Thursday

410

TIME ZONE -0100
(Gibraltar Standard Time)
Subtract 1 hour for UT
For Gibraltar Summer Time add ONE hour in **non-shaded areas**

GIBRALTAR

LAT 36°08'N   LONG 5°21'W

TIMES AND HEIGHTS OF HIGH AND LOW WATERS

YEAR 2004

JANUARY

Day	Time m	Time m	Time m	Time m
1 TH	0400 0.3	1036 0.8	2321 0.7	
2 F	0507 0.3	1135 0.8	1742 0.3	
3 SA	0021 0.7	0602 0.3	1226 0.8	1830 0.2
4 SU	0110 0.8	0646 0.3	1310 0.8	1911 0.2
5 M	0151 0.8	0725 0.2	1350 0.8	1949 0.2
6 TU	0228 0.8	0802 0.2	1429 0.8	2025 0.2
7 W	0303 0.8	0837 0.2	1507 0.9	○ 2100 0.1
8 TH	0337 0.9	0912 0.2	1545 0.9	2134 0.1
9 F	0411 0.9	0947 0.2	1621 0.9	2207 0.1
10 SA	0445 0.9	1023 0.2	1658 0.9	2240 0.1
11 SU	0521 0.9	1100 0.2	1736 0.9	2315 0.1
12 M	0600 0.9	1142 0.2	1818 0.8	2355 0.2
13 TU	0645 0.8	1230 0.2	1906 0.8	
14 W	0041 0.2	0736 0.8	1329 0.2	2000 0.8
15 TH	0140 0.2	0836 0.8	1437 0.2	☽ 2103 0.7
16 F	0253 0.2	0944 0.8	1554 0.2	2218 0.7
17 SA	0417 0.2	1058 0.8	1715 0.2	2338 0.7
18 SU	0536 0.2	1207 0.8	1822 0.1	
19 M	0045 0.8	0636 0.2	1308 0.9	1917 0.1
20 TU	0143 0.8	0728 0.1	1403 0.9	2007 0.0
21 W	0236 0.9	0817 0.1	1455 0.9	● 2054 0.0
22 TH	0325 0.9	0904 0.0	1544 0.9	2138 0.0
23 F	0411 0.9	0949 0.0	1631 0.9	2218 0.0
24 SA	0454 0.9	1032 0.0	1716 0.9	2257 0.0
25 SU	0537 0.9	1113 0.1	1800 0.9	2335 0.1
26 M	0619 0.9	1154 0.1	1844 0.8	
27 TU	0013 0.1	0703 0.8	1237 0.2	1929 0.8
28 W	0055 0.2	0748 0.8	1325 0.2	2017 0.7
29 TH	0143 0.2	0837 0.7	1420 0.3	☽ 2110 0.6
30 F	0246 0.3	0932 0.7	1533 0.3	2216 0.6
31 SA	0414 0.3	1041 0.7	1709 0.3	2341 0.6

FEBRUARY

Day	Time m	Time m	Time m	Time m
1 SU	0538 0.3	1153 0.7	1817 0.3	
2 M	0049 0.7	0632 0.3	1251 0.7	1903 0.2
3 TU	0138 0.7	0714 0.2	1337 0.7	1941 0.2
4 W	0216 0.8	0751 0.2	1418 0.8	2016 0.1
5 TH	0251 0.8	0826 0.1	1456 0.8	2050 0.1
6 F	0324 0.9	0901 0.1	1533 0.9	○ 2122 0.1
7 SA	0357 0.9	0935 0.1	1610 0.9	2154 0.0
8 SU	0430 0.9	1010 0.1	1646 0.9	2227 0.0
9 M	0505 0.9	1047 0.1	1723 0.9	2300 0.1
10 TU	0542 0.9	1125 0.1	1803 0.9	2336 0.1
11 W	0623 0.9	1207 0.1	1847 0.8	
12 TH	0016 0.1	0710 0.8	1257 0.1	1937 0.8
13 F	0105 0.2	0805 0.8	1400 0.2	☽ 2037 0.7
14 SA	0211 0.2	0913 0.7	1526 0.2	2152 0.7
15 SU	0352 0.3	1037 0.7	1712 0.2	2325 0.7
16 M	0538 0.2	1202 0.7	1827 0.1	
17 TU	0044 0.7	0643 0.2	1308 0.8	1921 0.1
18 W	0144 0.8	0734 0.1	1403 0.8	2007 0.0
19 TH	0233 0.9	0818 0.0	1452 0.9	2049 0.0
20 F	0317 0.9	0900 0.0	1536 0.9	● 2127 0.0
21 SA	0358 0.9	0939 0.0	1618 0.9	2202 0.0
22 SU	0436 0.9	1015 0.0	1657 0.9	2235 0.0
23 M	0512 0.9	1050 0.0	1735 0.9	2307 0.0
24 TU	0548 0.9	1123 0.1	1813 0.8	2338 0.1
25 W	0623 0.8	1157 0.1	1851 0.8	
26 TH	0011 0.1	0700 0.8	1233 0.2	1931 0.7
27 F	0047 0.2	0742 0.7	1315 0.2	2017 0.6
28 SA	0135 0.3	0832 0.6	1417 0.3	☽ 2115 0.6
29 SU	0302 0.4	0938 0.6	1622 0.3	2242 0.6

MARCH

Day	Time m	Time m	Time m	Time m
1 M	0512 0.3	1112 0.6	1759 0.3	
2 TU	0020 0.6	0616 0.3	1229 0.6	1846 0.2
3 W	0114 0.7	0657 0.2	1319 0.7	1922 0.2
4 TH	0152 0.7	0733 0.2	1359 0.8	1955 0.1
5 F	0226 0.8	0807 0.1	1437 0.9	2027 0.1
6 SA	0300 0.9	0841 0.1	1514 0.9	○ 2059 0.0
7 SU	0334 0.9	0916 0.0	1551 0.9	2132 0.0
8 M	0409 1.0	0952 0.0	1628 1.0	2206 0.0
9 TU	0445 1.0	1028 0.0	1706 1.0	2240 0.0
10 W	0523 1.0	1106 0.0	1747 0.9	2316 0.1
11 TH	0604 0.9	1146 0.1	1831 0.9	2355 0.1
12 F	0650 0.9	1233 0.1	1922 0.8	
13 SA	0042 0.2	0745 0.8	1335 0.2	2022 0.7
14 SU	0150 0.3	0855 0.7	1515 0.3	2140 0.7
15 M	0353 0.3	1029 0.7	1715 0.2	2321 0.7
16 TU	0546 0.3	1204 0.7	1825 0.2	
17 W	0041 0.7	0645 0.2	1308 0.8	1913 0.1
18 TH	0136 0.8	0729 0.1	1357 0.8	1954 0.1
19 F	0219 0.9	0808 0.0	1440 0.9	2030 0.0
20 SA	0258 0.9	0844 0.0	1519 0.9	● 2104 0.0
21 SU	0335 0.9	0918 0.0	1556 0.9	2136 0.0
22 M	0409 0.9	0951 0.0	1632 0.9	2206 0.0
23 TU	0442 0.9	1022 0.0	1706 0.9	2236 0.0
24 W	0513 0.9	1052 0.1	1740 0.8	2305 0.1
25 TH	0545 0.8	1121 0.1	1815 0.8	2335 0.2
26 F	0617 0.8	1152 0.2	1852 0.7	
27 SA	0007 0.2	0655 0.7	1227 0.2	1936 0.7
28 SU	0048 0.3	0744 0.6	1318 0.3	☽ 2032 0.6
29 M	0201 0.4	0849 0.6	1520 0.3	2148 0.6
30 TU	0428 0.4	1020 0.6	1719 0.3	2327 0.6
31 W	0544 0.3	1152 0.6	1810 0.3	

APRIL

Day	Time m	Time m	Time m	Time m
1 TH	0031 0.7	0627 0.2	1248 0.7	1847 0.2
2 F	0113 0.8	0703 0.2	1329 0.8	1920 0.1
3 SA	0150 0.8	0738 0.1	1408 0.9	1953 0.1
4 SU	0227 0.9	0813 0.0	1447 0.9	2027 0.1
5 M	0305 1.0	0851 0.0	1527 1.0	○ 2103 0.0
6 TU	0343 1.0	0929 0.0	1607 1.0	2140 0.0
7 W	0423 1.0	1007 0.0	1647 1.0	2217 0.0
8 TH	0503 1.0	1047 0.0	1730 1.0	2256 0.1
9 F	0546 0.9	1129 0.1	1817 0.9	2339 0.2
10 SA	0635 0.9	1217 0.2	1911 0.8	
11 SU	0030 0.2	0733 0.8	1324 0.2	2014 0.8
12 M	0146 0.3	0847 0.7	1512 0.3	☽ 2133 0.7
13 TU	0355 0.3	1023 0.7	1657 0.3	2308 0.7
14 W	0535 0.3	1153 0.7	1802 0.2	
15 TH	0020 0.8	0628 0.2	1252 0.8	1846 0.2
16 F	0111 0.8	0709 0.1	1337 0.8	1924 0.1
17 SA	0152 0.9	0744 0.1	1416 0.9	1958 0.1
18 SU	0229 0.9	0818 0.1	1453 0.9	2031 0.1
19 M	0304 0.9	0850 0.0	1529 0.9	● 2103 0.1
20 TU	0337 0.9	0922 0.0	1603 0.9	2134 0.1
21 W	0409 0.9	0953 0.0	1637 0.9	2205 0.1
22 TH	0440 0.9	1023 0.1	1710 0.8	2236 0.1
23 F	0511 0.8	1052 0.1	1744 0.8	2307 0.2
24 SA	0544 0.8	1123 0.2	1822 0.7	2340 0.3
25 SU	0623 0.7	1158 0.2	1907 0.7	
26 M	0022 0.3	0711 0.7	1248 0.3	2002 0.7
27 TU	0130 0.4	0815 0.6	1428 0.3	☽ 2108 0.6
28 W	0323 0.4	0932 0.6	1615 0.3	2225 0.7
29 TH	0449 0.3	1058 0.7	1717 0.3	2335 0.7
30 F	0542 0.2	1202 0.7	1800 0.2	

Chapter 5

Chart Datum: 0·25 metres below Alicante Datum (Mean Sea Level, Alicante)

TIDES

TIME ZONE −0100
(Gibraltar Standard Time)
Subtract 1 hour for UT
For Gibraltar Summer Time add
ONE hour in **non-shaded areas**

GIBRALTAR

LAT 36°08′N LONG 5°21′W

TIMES AND HEIGHTS OF HIGH AND LOW WATERS

YEAR **2004**

MAY

Day	Wk	Time m	Time m	Time m	Time m
1	SA	0025 0.8	0624 0.2	1251 0.8	1837 0.2
2	SU	0109 0.9	0703 0.1	1334 0.9	1914 0.1
3	M	0150 0.9	0742 0.1	1416 0.9	1952 0.1
4	TU	0232 1.0	0823 0.0	1459 1.0	○ 2032 0.1
5	W	0316 1.0	0905 0.0	1543 1.0	2114 0.1
6	TH	0400 1.0	0947 0.0	1628 1.0	2156 0.1
7	F	0445 1.0	1030 0.0	1715 1.0	2241 0.1
8	SA	0532 0.9	1116 0.1	1806 0.9	2328 0.2
9	SU	0625 0.9	1208 0.2	1903 0.8	
10	M	0026 0.3	0726 0.8	1318 0.3	2007 0.8
11	TU	0145 0.3	0839 0.7	1449 0.3	◑ 2118 0.8
12	W	0326 0.3	1000 0.7	1613 0.3	2235 0.8
13	TH	0455 0.3	1120 0.7	1718 0.2	2342 0.8
14	F	0554 0.2	1219 0.8	1807 0.2	
15	SA	0033 0.8	0636 0.2	1306 0.8	1846 0.2
16	SU	0116 0.9	0713 0.1		1922 0.2
17	M	0153 0.9	0748 0.1	1424 0.9	1957 0.1
18	TU	0229 0.9	0822 0.1	1500 0.9	2031 0.1
19	W	0304 0.9	0856 0.1	1536 0.9	● 2106 0.1
20	TH	0338 0.9	0928 0.1	1611 0.9	2140 0.2
21	F	0412 0.9	1001 0.1	1645 0.8	2213 0.2
22	SA	0446 0.8	1032 0.2	1720 0.8	2247 0.2
23	SU	0521 0.8	1105 0.2	1758 0.8	2323 0.3
24	M	0600 0.7	1141 0.2	1841 0.7	
25	TU	0006 0.3	0647 0.7	1259 0.3	1932 0.7
26	W	0105 0.3	0743 0.7	1338 0.3	2029 0.7
27	TH	0222 0.3	0847 0.7	1459 0.3	◐ 2131 0.7
28	F	0338 0.3	0958 0.7	1607 0.3	2236 0.7
29	SA	0443 0.3	1109 0.7	1703 0.3	2336 0.8
30	SU	0539 0.2	1208 0.8	1752 0.2	
31	M	0027 0.9	0627 0.1	1258 0.8	1837 0.1

JUNE

Day	Wk	Time m	Time m	Time m	Time m
1	TU	0115 0.9	0713 0.1	1346 0.9	1921 0.1
2	W	0203 1.0	0759 0.0	1434 0.9	2007 0.1
3	TH	0251 1.0	0845 0.0	1523 1.0	○ 2054 0.1
4	F	0340 1.0	0933 0.0	1613 1.0	2142 0.1
5	SA	0430 1.0	1020 0.1	1703 1.0	2231 0.1
6	SU	0522 0.9	1108 0.1	1754 0.9	2322 0.2
7	M	0616 0.9	1200 0.2	1850 0.9	
8	TU	0019 0.2	0715 0.8	1300 0.2	1949 0.9
9	W	0126 0.3	0818 0.8	1408 0.3	◑ 2050 0.8
10	TH	0239 0.3	0924 0.8	1515 0.3	2152 0.8
11	F	0354 0.3	1033 0.7	1620 0.3	2254 0.8
12	SA	0503 0.3	1137 0.8	1719 0.3	2350 0.8
13	SU	0559 0.2	1230 0.8	1808 0.2	
14	M	0037 0.8	0643 0.2	1316 0.8	1850 0.2
15	TU	0120 0.8	0722 0.2	1358 0.8	1929 0.2
16	W	0159 0.8	0759 0.2	1437 0.8	2007 0.2
17	TH	0237 0.8	0835 0.2	1515 0.8	● 2044 0.2
18	F	0314 0.8	0910 0.2	1551 0.8	2121 0.2
19	SA	0351 0.8	0944 0.2	1625 0.8	2156 0.2
20	SU	0427 0.8	1017 0.2	1659 0.8	2231 0.2
21	M	0503 0.8	1050 0.2	1735 0.8	2308 0.2
22	TU	0541 0.8	1125 0.2	1813 0.8	2348 0.3
23	W	0623 0.8	1204 0.2	1857 0.8	
24	TH	0035 0.3	0711 0.7	1253 0.3	1946 0.8
25	F	0132 0.3	0806 0.7	1352 0.3	◐ 2041 0.8
26	SA	0236 0.3	0908 0.7	1458 0.3	2142 0.8
27	SU	0345 0.2	1018 0.7	1606 0.2	2247 0.8
28	M	0455 0.2	1128 0.8	1713 0.2	2350 0.9
29	TU	0559 0.2	1229 0.8	1811 0.2	
30	W	0047 0.9	0654 0.1	1325 0.9	1903 0.2

JULY

Day	Wk	Time m	Time m	Time m	Time m
1	TH	0141 0.9	0745 0.1	1418 0.9	1954 0.1
2	F	0235 1.0	0835 0.0	1510 0.9	○ 2045 0.1
3	SA	0328 1.0	0924 0.0	1601 1.0	2135 0.1
4	SU	0420 1.0	1011 0.0	1650 1.0	2224 0.1
5	M	0510 1.0	1056 0.1	1739 1.0	2312 0.1
6	TU	0601 0.9	1141 0.1	1829 0.9	
7	W	0001 0.2	0653 0.9	1229 0.2	1919 0.9
8	TH	0053 0.2	0747 0.8	1320 0.2	2011 0.9
9	F	0149 0.2	0843 0.8	1415 0.3	◑ 2104 0.8
10	SA	0249 0.3	0943 0.7	1517 0.3	2200 0.8
11	SU	0359 0.3	1049 0.7	1627 0.3	2301 0.8
12	M	0518 0.3	1155 0.7	1734 0.3	
13	TU	0000 0.8	0618 0.3	1252 0.8	1827 0.3
14	W	0052 0.8	0703 0.2	1339 0.8	1911 0.3
15	TH	0137 0.8	0742 0.2	1421 0.8	1950 0.2
16	F	0218 0.8	0819 0.2	1458 0.8	2028 0.2
17	SA	0257 0.8	0854 0.2	1533 0.9	● 2104 0.2
18	SU	0334 0.9	0927 0.2	1605 0.9	2139 0.2
19	M	0410 0.9	1000 0.2	1637 0.9	2214 0.2
20	TU	0444 0.9	1030 0.2	1709 0.9	2248 0.2
21	W	0520 0.9	1102 0.2	1744 0.9	2325 0.2
22	TH	0558 0.9	1136 0.2	1823 0.9	
23	F	0005 0.2	0641 0.8	1216 0.2	1907 0.9
24	SA	0053 0.2	0731 0.8	1304 0.2	1958 0.8
25	SU	0150 0.2	0830 0.8	1404 0.2	◐ 2057 0.8
26	M	0259 0.3	0939 0.7	1520 0.3	2207 0.8
27	TU	0425 0.2	1058 0.7	1648 0.3	2323 0.8
28	W	0548 0.2	1213 0.8	1803 0.2	
29	TH	0032 0.9	0649 0.1	1315 0.9	1900 0.2
30	F	0132 0.9	0741 0.1	1410 0.9	1952 0.1
31	SA	0228 1.0	0829 0.0	1501 1.0	○ 2041 0.1

AUGUST

Day	Wk	Time m	Time m	Time m	Time m
1	SU	0319 1.0	0914 0.0	1548 1.0	2127 0.1
2	M	0408 1.0	0956 0.0	1633 1.0	2211 0.1
3	TU	0454 1.0	1036 0.0	1716 1.0	2253 0.1
4	W	0538 1.0	1114 0.1	1759 1.0	2333 0.1
5	TH	0623 0.9	1151 0.1	1842 0.9	
6	F	0014 0.2	0709 0.9	1231 0.2	1925 0.9
7	SA	0058 0.2	0758 0.8	1316 0.3	◑ 2011 0.8
8	SU	0146 0.3	0851 0.7	1411 0.4	2101 0.8
9	M	0250 0.4	0955 0.7	1528 0.4	2203 0.7
10	TU	0429 0.4	1117 0.7	1703 0.4	2320 0.7
11	W	0558 0.3	1231 0.7	1809 0.4	
12	TH	0029 0.7	0647 0.3	1323 0.8	1854 0.3
13	F	0120 0.8	0724 0.3	1402 0.8	1933 0.3
14	SA	0201 0.8	0758 0.2	1436 0.9	2008 0.2
15	SU	0238 0.9	0830 0.2	1508 0.9	2043 0.2
16	M	0313 0.9	0902 0.1	1539 1.0	● 2117 0.2
17	TU	0348 1.0	0932 0.1	1610 1.0	2151 0.1
18	W	0422 1.0	1007 0.1	1642 1.0	2225 0.1
19	TH	0457 1.0	1035 0.1	1717 1.0	2300 0.1
20	F	0534 1.0	1109 0.2	1753 1.0	2338 0.2
21	SA	0615 0.9	1145 0.2	1835 0.9	
22	SU	0020 0.2	0703 0.9	1229 0.3	1924 0.9
23	M	0114 0.3	0802 0.8	1326 0.3	◐ 2024 0.8
24	TU	0227 0.4	0913 0.8	1453 0.4	2139 0.7
25	W	0417 0.5	1042 0.8	1647 0.4	2312 0.8
26	TH	0550 0.3	1208 0.8	1806 0.3	
27	F	0031 0.8	0648 0.2	1311 0.9	1900 0.2
28	SA	0131 0.9	0735 0.1	1402 0.9	1947 0.1
29	SU	0221 1.0	0817 0.1	1447 1.0	2030 0.1
30	M	0307 1.0	0856 0.0	1529 1.1	○ 2111 0.1
31	TU	0349 1.0	0933 0.0	1609 1.1	2149 0.1

TIME ZONE -0100
(Gibraltar Standard Time)
Subtract 1 hour for UT
For Gibraltar Summer Time add
ONE hour in **non-shaded areas**

GIBRALTAR

YEAR **2004**

LAT 36°08′N   LONG 5°21′W

TIMES AND HEIGHTS OF HIGH AND LOW WATERS

SEPTEMBER

Day	Time m	Time m	Time m	Time m
1 W	0430 1.0	1007 0.1	1638 1.0	2225 0.1
2 TH	0509 1.0	1040 0.1	1723 1.0	2300 0.1
3 F	0547 0.9	1113 0.2	1759 1.0	2333 0.2
4 SA	0626 0.9	1146 0.2	1835 0.9	
5 SU	0008 0.2	0708 0.8	1223 0.3	1914 0.8
6 M ☾	0047 0.3	0757 0.7	1309 0.4	2001 0.8
7 TU	0141 0.4	0858 0.7	1427 0.5	2102 0.7
8 W	0331 0.4	1025 0.7	1632 0.5	2231 0.7
9 TH	0532 0.4	1202 0.7	1747 0.4	
10 F	0005 0.7	0622 0.3	1255 0.8	1831 0.3
11 SA	0058 0.8	0658 0.3	1332 0.9	1908 0.3
12 SU	0137 0.9	0729 0.2	1404 0.9	1941 0.2
13 M	0212 0.9	0800 0.2	1435 1.0	2015 0.2
14 TU ●	0247 1.0	0830 0.1	1508 1.0	2049 0.1
15 W	0322 1.0	0902 0.1	1541 1.1	2124 0.1
16 TH	0357 1.1	0934 0.1	1615 1.1	2159 0.1
17 F	0433 1.1	1008 0.1	1651 1.1	2235 0.1
18 SA	0512 1.0	1042 0.2	1729 1.1	2312 0.2
19 SU	0553 1.0	1120 0.2	1811 1.0	2354 0.2
20 M	0642 0.9	1203 0.3	1900 0.9	
21 TU ☾	0046 0.3	0742 0.8	1303 0.4	2003 0.8
22 W	0211 0.4	0858 0.8	1450 0.4	2127 0.8
23 TH	0424 0.4	1036 0.8	1654 0.4	2315 0.8
24 F	0546 0.3	1204 0.8	1804 0.3	
25 SA	0031 0.9	0637 0.2	1301 0.9	1851 0.2
26 SU	0123 0.9	0718 0.2	1345 1.0	1931 0.2
27 M	0207 1.0	0754 0.1	1425 1.0	2009 0.1
28 TU ○	0246 1.0	0829 0.1	1503 1.1	2045 0.1
29 W	0324 1.0	0902 0.1	1539 1.1	2120 0.1
30 TH	0401 1.0	0934 0.1	1613 1.1	2153 0.1

OCTOBER

Day	Time m	Time m	Time m	Time m
1 F	0435 1.0	1005 0.1	1646 1.0	2225 0.1
2 SA	0509 1.0	1036 0.2	1718 1.0	2255 0.2
3 SU	0543 0.9	1108 0.3	1750 0.9	2326 0.3
4 M	0621 0.8	1141 0.3	1825 0.8	
5 TU	0000 0.3	0706 0.8	1223 0.4	1911 0.8
6 W ☾	0046 0.4	0808 0.7	1338 0.5	2015 0.7
7 TH	0238 0.5	0929 0.7	1552 0.5	2141 0.7
8 F	0450 0.4	1109 0.7	1712 0.4	2324 0.7
9 SA	0546 0.4	1211 0.8	1758 0.4	
10 SU	0024 0.8	0622 0.3	1251 0.8	1835 0.3
11 M	0105 0.9	0654 0.2	1325 1.0	1909 0.2
12 TU	0141 1.0	0725 0.2	1359 1.0	1943 0.2
13 W	0217 1.0	0757 0.2	1435 1.1	2018 0.1
14 TH ●	0253 1.1	0830 0.1	1511 1.1	2055 0.1
15 F	0331 1.1	0905 0.1	1549 1.1	2133 0.1
16 SA	0411 1.1	0942 0.2	1628 1.1	2211 0.1
17 SU	0451 1.1	1020 0.2	1709 1.1	2251 0.2
18 M	0536 1.0	1101 0.3	1754 1.0	2334 0.2
19 TU	0627 0.9	1149 0.3	1847 0.9	
20 W ☾	0030 0.3	0729 0.8	1258 0.4	1955 0.8
21 TH	0209 0.4	0848 0.8	1456 0.4	2124 0.8
22 F	0410 0.4	1023 0.8	1642 0.4	2307 0.8
23 SA	0523 0.3	1143 0.9	1745 0.3	
24 SU	0017 0.9	0612 0.3	1237 0.9	1829 0.2
25 M	0105 0.9	0651 0.2	1319 1.0	1907 0.2
26 TU	0144 1.0	0725 0.2	1357 1.0	1942 0.1
27 W	0221 1.0	0758 0.1	1432 1.0	2017 0.1
28 TH	0256 1.0	0831 0.1	1506 1.0	2050 0.1
29 F	0331 1.0	0903 0.1	1540 1.0	2123 0.1
30 SA	0404 1.0	0935 0.2	1612 1.0	2154 0.2
31 SU	0437 0.9	1008 0.2	1644 0.9	2225 0.2

NOVEMBER

Day	Time m	Time m	Time m	Time m
1 M	0510 0.9	1040 0.3	1717 0.9	2257 0.3
2 TU	0546 0.8	1115 0.3	1754 0.8	2331 0.3
3 W	0630 0.8	1158 0.4	1841 0.8	
4 TH	0016 0.4	0729 0.7	1308 0.4	1942 0.7
5 F ☾	0147 0.4	0841 0.7	1500 0.5	2056 0.7
6 SA	0350 0.4	1001 0.7	1620 0.4	2222 0.7
7 SU	0455 0.4	1112 0.8	1714 0.3	2335 0.8
8 M	0539 0.4	1202 0.9	1756 0.3	
9 TU	0024 0.9	0615 0.3	1244 0.9	1834 0.2
10 W	0106 0.9	0649 0.2	1323 1.0	1911 0.1
11 TH	0146 1.0	0724 0.2	1403 1.1	1950 0.1
12 F ●	0226 1.0	0801 0.2	1444 1.1	2030 0.1
13 SA	0308 1.1	0840 0.2	1526 1.1	2111 0.1
14 SU	0352 1.1	0921 0.2	1611 1.1	2154 0.1
15 M	0437 1.0	1005 0.2	1656 1.0	2238 0.2
16 TU	0524 1.0	1052 0.2	1746 1.0	2326 0.2
17 W	0618 0.9	1146 0.3	1843 0.9	
18 TH	0026 0.3	0720 0.9	1300 0.4	1950 0.8
19 F ☾	0154 0.4	0833 0.8	1438 0.4	2109 0.8
20 SA	0328 0.4	0953 0.8	1605 0.4	2235 0.8
21 SU	0441 0.3	1106 0.9	1711 0.3	2345 0.8
22 M	0536 0.3	1203 0.9	1800 0.2	
23 TU	0036 0.9	0619 0.2	1248 0.9	1840 0.2
24 W	0119 0.9	0656 0.2	1327 1.0	1917 0.1
25 TH	0157 0.9	0732 0.2	1403 1.0	1953 0.1
26 F ○	0233 0.9	0806 0.2	1439 1.0	2028 0.1
27 SA	0308 0.9	0841 0.2	1514 0.9	2102 0.2
28 SU	0343 0.9	0915 0.2	1549 0.9	2136 0.2
29 M	0416 0.9	0950 0.2	1624 0.9	2209 0.2
30 TU	0450 0.9	1025 0.3	1700 0.9	2242 0.2

DECEMBER

Day	Time m	Time m	Time m	Time m
1 W	0526 0.8	1102 0.3	1738 0.8	2318 0.3
2 TH	0608 0.8	1144 0.3	1822 0.8	2359 0.3
3 F	0657 0.8	1239 0.4	1913 0.7	
4 SA	0058 0.4	0755 0.7	1356 0.4	2012 0.7
5 SU ☾	0224 0.4	0858 0.7	1512 0.4	2119 0.7
6 M	0341 0.4	1005 0.8	1617 0.3	2231 0.7
7 TU	0442 0.4	1108 0.8	1712 0.3	2337 0.8
8 W	0532 0.3	1202 0.9	1800 0.2	
9 TH	0030 0.8	0616 0.2	1250 0.9	1845 0.1
10 F	0118 0.9	0658 0.2	1336 1.0	1929 0.1
11 SA	0205 1.0	0740 0.1	1423 1.0	2014 0.1
12 SU	0252 1.0	0825 0.1	1511 1.0	2100 0.1
13 M	0340 1.0	0912 0.1	1601 1.0	2147 0.1
14 TU	0428 1.0	1000 0.1	1650 1.0	2234 0.1
15 W	0518 1.0	1051 0.2	1742 0.9	2324 0.1
16 TH	0610 0.9	1146 0.2	1837 0.9	
17 F	0019 0.2	0707 0.9	1250 0.3	1936 0.8
18 SA ☽	0123 0.2	0809 0.9	1402 0.3	2040 0.8
19 SU	0234 0.3	0914 0.8	1514 0.3	2149 0.8
20 M	0345 0.3	1020 0.8	1625 0.3	2301 0.8
21 TU	0452 0.3	1123 0.9	1728 0.3	
22 W	0004 0.8	0548 0.3	1216 0.8	1819 0.2
23 TH	0056 0.8	0634 0.2	1302 0.9	1901 0.2
24 F	0140 0.8	0714 0.2	1344 0.9	1940 0.2
25 SA	0220 0.8	0752 0.2	1423 0.9	2018 0.2
26 SU ○	0258 0.9	0830 0.2	1502 0.9	2054 0.1
27 M	0334 0.9	0906 0.2	1539 0.9	2129 0.1
28 TU	0407 0.9	0941 0.2	1615 0.9	2202 0.1
29 W	0440 0.8	1016 0.2	1650 0.8	2235 0.2
30 TH	0513 0.8	1051 0.2	1725 0.8	2307 0.2
31 F	0548 0.8	1128 0.2	1802 0.8	2341 0.2

Chart Datum: 0·25 metres below Alicante Datum (Mean Sea Level, Alicante)

ABBREVIATIONS

AC, ACA	Admiralty Chart, Admiralty Chart Agent	Lt F	Light float
ALL	Admiralty List of Lights	Lt Ho	Lighthouse
ALRS	Admiralty List of Radio Signals	Lt V	Light vessel
Bcst	Broadcast	LW	Low Water
BST	British Summer Time	M	Sea mile(s)
By(s)	Buoy(s)	m	Metre(s)
CD	Chart Datum	Météo	Météorologie/Weather
CG	Coastguard	MF	Medium Frequency
Ch	Channel (VHF)	MHWN	Mean High Water Neaps
chan.	Channel (navigational)	MHWS	Mean High Water Springs
cm	Centimetre(s)	MHz	Megahertz
CROSS	Centre Régional Opérationnel de Surveillance et Sauvetage (MRCC)	MLWN	Mean Low Water Neaps
		MLWS	Mean Low Water Springs
		MMSI	Maritime Mobile Service Identity
CRS	Coast Radio Station(s)	MRCC	Maritime Rescue Co-ordination Centre
DF	Direction Finding		
Dir Lt	Directional light	MRSC	Maritime Rescue Sub-Centre
DSC	Digital Selective Calling	MSI	Maritime Safety Information
DST	Daylight Saving Time	N	North
E	East	NCM	North Cardinal Mark (buoy/beacon)
ECM	East Cardinal Mark (buoy/beacon)		
		Oc	Occulting light
ED	European Datum	PHM	Port-hand Mark (buoy/beacon)
EPIRB	Emergency Position Indicating Radio Beacon		
		Pt(e)	Point(e)
F	Fixed light	R	Red
F	Force	R	River
Fl	Flashing light	Ra	Coast Radar Station
FM	Frequency Modulation	Racon	Radar Transponder Beacon
G	Green	RCC	Rescue Coordination Centre
GMDSS	Global Maritime Distress and Safety System	RG	Emergency RDF Station
		R/T	Radiotelephony
H, Hrs, h	Hour(s)	S	South
H24	Continuous	s	second(s) of time
Hbr	Harbour	SAR	Search and Rescue
Hd	Head, headland	SCM	South Cardinal Mark (buoy/beacon)
HF	High Frequency		
HJ	Day service only, Sunrise to Sunset	SHM	Starboard-hand Mark (buoy/beacon)
ht	Height	Sig	Signal
HW	High Water	Sig Stn	Signal Station
HX	No fixed hours	SMS	Short Message Service
Hz	Hertz	SOG	Speed over the ground
IDM	Isolated Danger Mark (buoy/beacon)	SOLAS	Safety of Life at Sea (IMO Convention)
IMO	International Maritime Organisation	SSB	Single Sideband (Radio)
		SRR	Search & Rescue Region
Inmarsat	International Maritime Satellite System	Stn	Station
		Tfc	Traffic
Is, I	Island, Islet	TSS	Traffic Separation Scheme
Iso	Isophase light	UT	Universal Time
K/Kn	Knot(s)	VHF	Very High Frequency
kHz	Kilohertz	VTS	Vessel Traffic Service
km	Kilometre(s)	W	West
Lat	Latitude	W	White
Ldg	Leading	WCM	West Cardinal Mark (buoy/beacon)
LMT	Local Mean Time		
Long	Longitude	WGS	World Geodetic System (datum)
LT	Local Time		
Lt(s)	Light(s)	WPT	Waypoint
Lt by	Light buoy	Y	Yellow, Amber, Orange

414

INDEX

Admiralty chart symbols .... *back cover*
Area Planners
    Planner key 7
    1 SW England 8
    2 S Central England 10
    3 SE England 12
    4 East England 14
    5 East Scotland 16
    6 NW Scotland 18
    7 SW Scotland 20
    8 Wales, NW England and E Ireland 22
    9 SW England, S Wales and S Ireland 24
    10 Ireland 26
    11 Denmark and NW Germany 28
    12 Germany and N Holland 30
    13 Holland and Belgium 32
    14 N France 34
    15 N Central France and Channel Isles 36
    16 NW France and Biscay 38
    17 W France and NE Spain 40
    18 NW Spain 42
    19 Portugal 44
    20 S Portugal and SW Spain 46
BBC Radio 4 Shipping Forecast 67
Beaufort Scale 66
Belgium CRS weather forecasts 83
Brest tidal coefficients 143
Channel Is weather forecasts 78
Coast Radio Stations, VHF 109
Communications chapter 91
Contents 4
Conversion Tables 6
Danish CRS weather forecasts 80
Danish Shipping Forecast Areas 80
Distance from Dipping Lights Table 62
Distress .... *front cover*
Dover tidal ranges 142
First Aid 117
    Essential information 117
    General medical information 118
    First Aid Kit 120
Flags - International Code ...... *inside front cover*
Foreign Language Glossary 138
French Shipping Forecast Areas 85
French weather forecasts 83
German CRS weather forecasts 81
Gibraltar weather forecasts 89
GMDSS 136
Helicopter rescue 116
IALA Buoyage .... *inside front cover*
Irish CRS weather forecasts 79
Light Recognition .... *inside back cover*
Lights for small craft .... *inside front cover*
Marinas 48
Marinecall 74

MAYDAY 115
Medical help 116
Morse Code .... *inside front cover*
Moonrise & moonset 55, 57
Military exercise areas 132
Navigation chapter 5
Navtex 72
Netherlands CG weather forecasts 82
Netherlands local radio weather forecasts 83
Port Radio Stations
    South coast of England 96
    East coast of England 97
    Scotland 98
    West coast of England and Wales 99
    Ireland 99
    Denmark 100
    Germany 100
    Netherlands 101
    Belgium 102
    North France 103
    Channel Islands 103
    West France 103
    Spain 104
    Portugal 104
    Gibraltar 104
Portuguese weather forecasts 88
Portuguese Shipping Forecast Areas 88
Radar beacons 58
Radio data 94
    Short, medium & long range radio comms .. 94
    The marine VHF band 94
    Medium range MF/RT 95
    Traffic lists 95
    Silence periods 95
    Long range HF radio 95
Radio operation 92
    Phonetic alphabet 92
    Phonetic numerals 92
    Prowords 93
    Punctuation 93
Safety chapter 113
Safety, Think about 114
Secondary Ports & Tidal Differences 150
Shipping forecast record 65
Sounds & Shapes Signals 112
SMS (Short Message Service) 76
Spanish CG MRCC/MRSC weather fcsts 86
Spanish & Portuguese CRS map 87
Spanish Shipping Forecast Areas 86
Special tidal calculation instructions for places
    between Christchurch & Selsey Bill 146
Speed, Time & Distance Table 61
Sunrise & sunset 54, 56
Telephone & Fax Weather Forecasts 74
Tides chapter 141
Tidal calculations 144

Index

Tidal curves - Christchurch to Selsey Bill 240
Tidal gates
Southern England 169
Scotland 172
Irish Sea 175
Menai Strait 176
Tidal streams
English Channel & S Brittany 178
Portland 184
Isle of Wight 186
Channel Islands 192
North Sea 198
Scotland 204
West UK & Ireland 210
Tide Tables - Standard Ports
Aberdeen curves & predictions 286
Aberdeen secondary port data 154
Avonmouth curves & predictions 326
Avonmouth secondary port data 159
Belfast curves & predictions 334
Belfast secondary port data 160
Brest curves & predictions 398
Brest secondary port data 165
Burnham-on-Crouch curves & predictions 262
Cherbourg curves & predictions 382
Cherbourg secondary port data 165
Cobh curves & predictions 342
Cobh secondary port data 161
Cuxhaven curves & predictions 354
Cuxhaven secondary port data 162
Dartmouth curves & predictions 224
Dieppe curves & predictions 374
Dieppe secondary port data 164
Dover curves & predictions 250
Dover secondary port data 151
Dublin curves & predictions 330
Dublin secondary port data 160
Dunkerque curves & predictions 370
Dunkerque secondary port data 164
Esbjerg curves & predictions 346
Esbjerg secondary port data 162
Falmouth curves & predictions 216
Galway curves & predictions 338
Galway secondary port data 161
Gibraltar curves & predictions 410
Gibraltar secondary port data 168
Greenock curves & predictions 310
Greenock secondary port data 157
Helgoland curves & predictions 350
Helgoland secondary port data 162
Holyhead curves & predictions 318
Holyhead secondary port data 158
Hoek van Holland curves & predictions 362
Immingham curves & predictions 274
Immingham secondary port data 153
Le Havre curves & predictions 378
Le Havre secondary port data 164
Leith curves & predictions 282

Leith secondary port data 153
Lerwick curves & predictions 294
Lerwick secondary port data 155
Lisboa curves & predictions 406
Lisboa secondary port data 167
Liverpool curves & predictions 314
Liverpool secondary port data 157
London Bridge curves & predictions 258
London Bridge secondary port data 152
Lowestoft curves & predictions 270
Lowestoft secondary port data 153
Milford Haven curves & predictions 322
Milford Haven secondary port data 158
Oban curves & predictions 306
Oban secondary port data 156
Plymouth curves & predictions 220
Plymouth secondary port data 150
Pointe de Grave curves & predictions 402
Pointe de Grave secondary port data 166
Poole curves & predictions 232
Portland curves & predictions 228
Portland secondary port data 150
Portsmouth curves & predictions 242
Portsmouth secondary port data 150
River Tyne curves & predictions 278
River Tyne secondary port data 153
St Helier curves & predictions 394
St Helier secondary port data 165
St Malo curves & predictions 386
St Malo secondary port data 165
St Peter Port curves & predictions 390
Sheerness curves & predictions 254
Sheerness secondary port data 151
Shoreham curves & predictions 246
Shoreham secondary port data 151
Southampton curves & predictions 236
Southampton secondary port data 151
Stornoway curves & predictions 298
Stornoway secondary port data 155
Ullapool curves & predictions 302
Ullapool secondary port data 155
Vlissingen curves & predictions 366
Vlissingen secondary port data 163
Walton-on-the-Naze curves & predictions . 266
Walton-on-the-Naze secondary port data 152
Wick curves & predictions 290
Wick secondary port data 154
Wilhelmshaven curves & predictions 358
Wilhelmshaven secondary port data 163
UK Shipping Forecast Areas 64
Vessel Traffic Service Charts 105
VHF Direction Finding Services 129
Weather chapter 63
Weather forecasts from HMCG 70
Weather forecasts - Local Radio Stations 68
Weather information, sources 77
Weather terms defined 66
Weather terms in five languages 89